Collins

CONTEMPORARY ITALIAN DICTIONARY

Companion Volumes

Collins Contemporary German Dictionary
Collins Contemporary French Dictionary
Collins Contemporary Spanish Dictionary

Collins

Contemporary Italian Dictionary

Italian—English

Inglese—Italiano

Isopel May, B.A., Ph.D.

Revised by
Antonia Sansica Stott, Dott. Lett.
Lecturer in Italian, University of Edinburgh

Collins: London and Glasgow

General Editor: J. B. Foreman, M.A.
Executive Editor: Iseabail C. Macleod, M.A.
First published 1970
Latest reprint 1972

ISBN 0 00 433424 8
PRINTED IN GREAT BRITAIN
COLLINS CLEAR TYPE PRESS

Contents

Contenuto

Introduction

It is opportune to remind the user of the Dictionary that, although a standard pronunciation exists both in English and in Italian—and this we have used here—pronunciation both in Italy and in the English-speaking world varies from one region to another.

Italian Consonants

The consonants *s* and *z* may be voiced or unvoiced. When they are voiced this sound is indicated in the Dictionary by a dot under the letters *s* and *z*.

Accents used in the Italian-English section of the Dictionary

In this Dictionary, to help the student, the accent has been inserted in all words, marking the open sounds with the 'grave' accent, and the close ones with the 'acute.'

Genders

Rules concerning masculine and feminine forms are indicated in the Supplement. However, to help the student, the feminine form in *-trice* and exceptions to the rules have been indicated in the Dictionary.

Irregularities and Peculiarities in Italian Plurals

All exceptions in plurals of nouns and adjectives ending in the singular in *-cia* and *-gia* and in *-io*, and the plural of all the words, regular or exceptions, nouns or adjectives, of *two* or *more* syllables ending in the singular in *-co* and *-go* have been indicated in the Dictionary.

Some nouns in Italian change their gender in the plural. Some nouns have two plurals with different meanings. Some compounds, as well as certain single nouns, have the same form both for the singular and for the plural; some compounds form their plural either changing both parts of the word, or only one. All these plurals are duly indicated in their place in the Dictionary.

English Pronunciation

In the English-Italian section of the Dictionary the letters and symbols of the International Phonetic Association have been used.

English Irregular Plurals

All irregular plurals have been indicated.

Proper Names and Geographical Names

The most important proper names and geographical names have been incorporated in the main part of the Dictionary.

American Usage

A number of Americanisms have been included and are clearly marked by the abbreviation (*US*) in front of the word.

Abbreviations used in the Dictionary—
Abbreviazioni usate nel Dizionario

aggettivo	a	adjective
abbreviazione	abbr	abbreviation
accusativo	acc	accusative
avverbio	ad	adverb
agricoltura	agr	agriculture
anatomia	anat	anatomy
aggettivo e nome femminile	a nf	adjective and noun feminine
aggettivo e nome maschile	a nm	adjective and noun masculine
aggettivo e nome maschile o femminile	a nmf	adjective and noun masculine or feminine
arcaico	arc	archaic
architettura	arch	architecture
astronomia	astr	astronomy
automobile	aut	automobile
ausiliare	aux	auxiliary
aviazione	av	aviation
biblico	Bibl	Biblical
botanico	bot	botanical
chimica	chem	chemistry
cinema	cin	cinema
congiunzione	cj	conjunction
collettivo	coll	collective
commerciale	com	commercial
cucina	cook	cooking
cosmetici	cosm	cosmetics
articolo definito	def art	definite article
dimostrativo	dem	demonstrative
ecclesiastico	eccl	ecclesiastical
economia	econ	economics
elettricità	el	electricity
femminile	f	feminine
familiare	fam	familiar
figurato	fig	figuratively
finanziario	fin	financial
femminile plurale	fpl	feminine plural
geografico	geogr	geographical
geologia	geol	geology
geometria	geom	geometry
grammatica	gram	grammar
storico	hist	historical
impersonale	impers	impersonal
industria	ind	industry
articolo indefinito	indef art	indefinite article
interiezione	interj	interjection
interrogativo	interrog	interrogative
legale	leg	legal
letterario	liter	literary
maschile	m	masculine
matematica	math	mathematics
meccanica	mech	mechanics
medicina	med	medicine
metallurgia	metal	metallurgy
militare	mil	military
minerale	min	mineral
maschile plurale	mpl	masculine plural
musica	mus	music
nome	n	noun

nautico	naut	nautical
nome femminile	nf	noun feminine
nome maschile	nm	noun masculine
nome maschile o femminile	nmf	noun masculine or feminine
nominativo	nom	nominative
nome proprio	n pr	proper noun
nome femminile plurale	nf pl	noun feminine plural
nome maschile plurale	nm pl	noun masculine plural
nome femminile proprio	nf pr	proper noun feminine
nome maschile proprio	nm pr	proper noun masculine
ornitologia	ornit	ornithology
filosofia	phil	philosophy
fotografia	phot	photography
fisica	phys	physics
plurale	pl	plural
poesia	poet	poetry
politico	pol	political
possessivo	poss	possessive
participio passato	pp	past participle
proprio	pr	proper
predicativo	pred	predicative
preposizione	prep	preposition
pronome	pron	pronoun
qualcosa	qc	something
qualcuno	qlcu	someone
radio	rad	radio
reciproco	recip	reciprocal
riflessivo	refl	reflexive
relativo	rel	relative
religione	reiig	religion
ferrovia	rly	railway
singolare	sing	singular
gergo	sl	slang
qualcuno	s.o.	someone
qualcosa	sth	something
tecnico	tec	technical
telefono	tel	telephone
teatro	theat	theatre
televisione	tv	television
tipografica	typ	typography
Stati Uniti, americano	US	United States, American
generalmente	usu	usually
vedere	v	see
veterinario	vet	veterinary
verbo intransitivo	vi	verb intransitive
verbo passivo	vp	verb passive
verbo riflessivo	vr	verb reflexive
verbo transitivo	vt	verb transitive
verbo transitivo e intransitivo	vti	verb transitive and intransitive
volgare	vulg	vulgar
zoologia	zool	zoology

Italian Pronunciation—Pronuncia Italiana

The Italian alphabet

The Italian alphabet consists of twenty-one letters, of which five are vowels (vocali) a, e, i, o, u; the others are consonants (consonanti).

A	a	G	gi	O	o	U	u
B	bi	H	acca	P	pi	V	vi
C	ci	I	i	Q	qu	Z	zeta
D	di	L	elle	R	erre		
E	e	M	emme	S	esse		
F	effe	N	enne	T	ti		

The letters k, w, x, y (kappa, vi doppio, ics, ipsilon) are used only in words of foreign origin. The letter j (i lungo) is no longer in use.

The Vowels (Le Vocali)

Every vowel in Italian, stressed or unstressed, has a single, distinct sound.

a [ɑ]   as *a* in father

e { open [ɛ] as *e* in seven   unaccented e is always close
{ close [e] as *a* in hate   (without the short 'i' sound)

i [i]   as *i* in ravine

o { open [ɔ] as *o* in cot   unaccented o is always close
{ close [o] as *o* in note   (without the short 'u' sound)

u [u]   as *oo* in moon

Stress in Pronunciation

Most words have the stress on the vowel in the last but one syllable; some on the final vowel, others on the vowels in the third last or fourth last syllable. No written (or printed) accent, however, is used except where the final vowel is stressed, and to avoid ambiguity. (See *Written Accents*)

Diphthongs

Diphthongs are made (1) of the combination of a, e, or o with unaccented i or u; (2) when i and u are combined with each other. In (1) the stress falls on a, e, or o; in (2) sometimes on i, sometimes on u; e.g. fiàba, manièra, fióre; lúi, guída.

Hiatus

Hiatus occurs when two vowels are pronounced separately: pa-úra, le-àle.

The Consonants (Le Consonanti)

The consonants b, d, f, l, m, n, p, t, v are pronounced as in English. In double consonants each consonant is distinctly sounded in order to give a double effect within the same sound, as in: bèllo, birra, còccola, fàccia.

c   is soft, or palatal [tʃ] before e and i (as in cheese): cénere, bàcio, cíbo, fàccia.

c   is hard or guttural [k] before a, o, u and consonants (like k): calamàio, còsa, cuòre, chièsa, clorúro.

ch   (only found before e, i) is hard, or guttural (as in chemist): chílo, che.

g   is soft or palatal [dʒ] before e and i (as in general): generàle, gelóso, ginnàsio.

g is hard or guttural [g] before a, o, u, : (as in god, gruesome): gàra, godiménto, gústo, grído.

gh (only found before e, i) is hard, or guttural (as in ghetto, guinea): ghétto, ghinèa.

gl is hard or guttural [gl] before a, o, u, e (as in gland): glàndola, glèba, glòbo, glucòsio.

gli a single, palatal sound [ʎ] (as in brilliant): gli, fíglio, móglie, màglia.
Exceptions: **Anglia, glicerína, negligènte, geroglífico, gànglio,** where the sound is guttural.

gn a single, palatal sound [ɲ] (similar to opinion, companion): campàgna, agnèllo, bàgno, magnífico, sógno.

h is never pronounced.

qu [kw] (as in question): quàdro, questióne, quínto, quòta. If preceded by c this sound is kept separate from qu giving the effect of a slightly double sound; àcqua, acquirènte, acquísto, nàcque.

r [r] must be distinctly pronounced: ràro, rósso, àrte, tortúra.

s { unvoiced (s aspra, s sorda) [s] (as in silk): sèrvo, séta.
voiced (s dolce, s sonora) [z] (as in rose): ròsa, úso, spòsa. This sound is shown in the Dictionary by a dot under the letter s.

sc before e, i has a single, palatal sound [ʃ] (as in shell): scèna, scéndere. Before a, o, u it has a guttural sound [sk] (as in scholar): scàtola, scolàro, scuòla.

z { unvoiced (z aspra, z sorda) [ts]: zàmpa, zòccolo.
voiced (z dolce, z sonora) [dz]: zàino, zèro, zínco, zòtico. This sound is shown in the Dictionary by a dot under the letter z.

Written Accents

Three written accents are in use in Italy, the acute (ʹ), the grave (ˋ) and the circumflex (ᐱ). The circumflex accent is employed only to indicate that the word has been abbreviated by the omission of part of it. As for the other two accents, there is considerable variation concerning their use. They are invariably indicated as follows: (a) on words in which the accent falls on the last syllable: città, virtù, caffè (See *Stress in Pronunciation*); (b) on monosyllables ending with a diphthong: già, giú, piú; (c) on monosyllables which, if accented, change meaning; dà (part of the verb dare), da (from, by, to); sé (himself), se (if) *etc*; (d) on words which change meaning depending on the position of the accent; àncora (anchor), ancora (still, yet), príncipi (princes), princípi (principles). The acute and grave accents are stress marks, the acute over i and u, the grave over a. With e and o they are pronunciation as well as stress marks, the acute being used for the close sounds, the grave for the open. In many texts, however, only the grave accent is indicated, irrespective of whether the sound may be open or close. In the Italian-English part of this we have inserted the accent in *all* words, marking the open sounds with the 'grave' accent, and the close ones with the 'acute'.

Apostrophe

This indicates the omission of the last vowel of a word and it occurs when the next word begins with a vowel: *eg* la amíca, l'amíca, the girl friend; un bèllo àlbero, un bell'àlbero, a beautiful tree. The apostrophe is not to be used between plural feminine articles and nouns: *eg* le èrbe.

Syllable Division

Italian words are divided into syllables, each syllable normally starting with a consonant.

Double consonants are always separated: ex. **màm-ma; pàl-la; sàs-so.**

When **s** is followed by one or more consonants it belongs to the subsequent syllable: *eg* **ví-schio; pò-sta; à-sma.**

Vowels in diphthongs are not separated: *eg* **fià-ba; fió-re** except when hiatus occurs: *eg* **pa-ú-ra; le-à-le.**

When a word is carried from one line to another, if the word is apostrophized the apostrophe cannot be left at the end of the line. The apostrophe must either be accompanied by the first part of the following word, or it must not be used at all and the full, unapostrophized form should be used instead: *eg* **un's-/míca** or **una/amíca;** *not* **un'/amíca.**

Pronuncia inglese—English Pronunciation

Vocali e Dittonghi inglesi

Simbolo	Esempio inglese	Esempio italiano o Spiegazione
[ɑː]	father ['fɑːðə]	padre
[ʌ]	but [bʌt]	quasi *a*
	come [kʌm]	
	blood [blʌd]	
[æ]	man [mæn]	*e* molto aperta
	cat [kæt]	
[ɛə]	there [ðɛə]	*e* aperta seguita da un suono di
	bear [bɛə]	*a* e da una brevissima *r*
[ai]	fly [flai]	mai
	high [hai]	
	nine [nain]	
[au]	how [hau]	fauna
	house [haus]	
[ei]	day [dei]	é¹ *e* chiusa seguita da un
	name [neim]	leggero suono di *i*
	obey [ə'bei]	
[e]	get [get]	petto *e* breve e stretta
	bed [bed]	
[əː]	bird [bəːd]	*eu* francese
	heard [həːd]	
	word [wəːd]	
[ə]	ago [ə'gou]	*a* brevissima, quàsi priva di
	concern [kən'səːn]	suono
[iː]	tea [tiː]	pino, vino
	see [siː]	
	ceiling ['siːliŋ]	
[i]	it, [it]	*i* breve e stretta, quasi come in
	big [big]	fitto, ritto
[iə]	here [hiə]	*i* + *a* come in zia, mia + un
	hear [hiə]	brevissimo suono di *r*
[ou]	go [gou]	óᵘ *o* chiusa seguita da un lieve
	note [nout]	suono di *u*
	slow [slou]	
[ɔː]	saw [sɔː]	*o* aperta e prolungata come in
	all [ɔːl]	mole
	before [bi'fɔː]	
[ɔ]	hot [hɔt]	*o* aperta e breve come in
	wash [wɔʃ]	notte
	long [lɔŋ]	
[ɔi]	boy [bɔi]	poi
	oil [ɔil]	
[uː]	too [tuː]	*u* prolungata, come in fune,
	you [juː]	luna
	shoe [ʃuː]	
	true [truː]	

Simbolo	Esempio inglese	Esempio italiano
[u]	p*u*t [put] b*oo*k [buk]	*u* breve, come in t*u*tto, p*u*lpito
[uə]	p*oo*r [puə] s*u*re [ʃuə]	*u* prolungata +un breve suono di *a* + un brevissimo suono di *r*

Consonanti inglesi

Simbolo	Esempio inglese	Esempio italiano Spiegazione
[b]	*b*een [biːn] gra*b* [græb]	*b* italiana
[d]	*d*ay [dei] ha*d* [hæd]	*d* italiana
[f]	*f*ather ['fɑːðə]	*f* italiana
[g]	*g*o [gou] bi*g* [big]	*g* dura, come in *g*occia, *gh*iaccio
[ŋ]	lo*ng* [lɔŋ] si*ng* [siŋ]	la *n* è prolungata. La *g* non si pronuncia
[h]	*h*ouse [haus]	*h* aspirata
[j]	*y*oung [jʌŋ] *y*es [jes] mill*i*on ['miljən]	*i* italiana
[k]	*c*ome [kʌm] mo*ck* [mɔk] s*ch*ool [skuːl] *k*ey [kiː]	*c* dura, come in *c*osa, s*c*uola, *ch*iosco
[l]	*l*ook [luk]	*l* italiana
[m]	*m*uch [mʌtʃ] la*mb* [læm] colu*mn* ['kɔləm]	*m* italiana
[n]	*n*oo*n* [nuːn]	*n* italiana
[ŋk]	i*nk* [iŋk] fra*nk* [fræŋk]	*n* +*c* dura
[p]	*p*ush [puʃ] ho*p*e [houp]	*p* italiana
[r]	*r*ed [red] b*r*ead [bred]	*r* non fortemente marcato
[s]	*s*tand [stænd] *s*and [sænd] ye*s* [jes] de*c*ide [di'said]	*s* aspra, come in *s*orte
[z]	(*s* between vowels or at the end of a word) ro*s*e [rouz] hi*s* [hiz] ba*s*es ['beisiz] *z*eal [ziːl]	*s* dolce e *z* dolce, come in ro*s*a e *z*aino
[ʃ]	*sh*all [ʃæl] ma*ch*ine [mə'ʃiːn] mo*ti*on ['mouʃən] spe*ci*al ['speʃəl] mi*ssi*on ['miʃən]	*sc* come in *sc*ene, *sc*ia, *sc*ialle, *sc*iogliere

[tʃ]	chin [tʃin] rich [ritʃ] picture ['piktʃə]	c palatale, come in cento
[t]	tennis ['tenis] sweet [swiːt]	t italiana
[v]	very ['veri] live [liv]	v italiana
[w]	water ['wɔːtə] which [witʃ]	u italiana
[ʒ]	vision ['viʒən] pleasure ['pleʒə] garage ['gærɑːʒ]	j francese, come in journal
[dʒ]	germ [dʒəːm] just [dʒʌst] bridge [bridʒ]	g dolce italiana, come in genio, giusto
[ð]	the [ðə] father ['fɑːðə]	Questo suono non esiste in italiano. È un suono dolce che si ottiene mettendo la lingua tra i denti. Potrebbe, approssimativamente, rappresentarsi con dh
[θ]	think [θiŋk] method ['meθəd]	Questo suono non esiste in italiano. È un suono forte, come l'emissione di un soffio tra i denti. Si avvicina alla c spagnola, come nella parola ceceo
[x]	(Scottish) loch [lɔx]	suono aspirato duro, come nella parola tedesca nach

ː indica che la vocale precedente è lunga.
L'accento principale è indicato dal simbolo ['] che è posto prima della sillaba accentata. L'accento secondario è indicato dal simbolo [ˌ]
Il simbolo fonetico è indicato entro parentesi quadra.

Italian-English

A

a *prep* at, in, to, by, for, on.

abàte *nm* abbot, abbé.

abbacinàre *vt* to blind, dazzle; deceive.

àbbaco *pl* **-chi** *nm* elementary arithmetic book; (*arc*) abacus.

abbadéssa *nf* abbess.

abbagliaménto *nm* dazzling, dimness of sight.

abbagliànte *a* dazzling; *nm* (*aut*) driving beam, (*US*) high beam.

abbagliàre *vt* to dazzle, fascinate, deceive, astonish.

abbaiàre *vi* to bark.

abbaíno *nm* skylight, garret window, garret.

abbandonàre *vt* to leave, quit, abandon; **-rsi** *vr* to give oneself up to, despair.

abbandonataménte *ad* freely, passionately.

abbandonàto *a* abandoned, forsaken, deserted, desolate.

abbandóno *nm* abandonment, desertion.

abbarbicàre *vi* to take root; **-rsi** *vr* to cling (as ivy).

abbaruffàre *vt* to ruffle; **-rsi** *vr* to come to blows.

abbassaménto *nm* lowering, humiliation.

abbassàre *vti* to lower, lessen, abase, humble; **-rsi** *vr* to humble oneself, fall.

abbàsso *ad* below; *interj* down! down with!

abbastànza *ad* enough, fairly, rather.

abbàttere *vt* to throw down, depress, slaughter; to shoot down (a plane); **-rsi** *vr* to lose heart, fall.

abbattiménto *nm* knocking down, felling, overthrow, depression.

abbattùto *a* depressed, cast-down.

abbazía *nf* abbey.

abbecedàrio *nm* first spelling book.

abbelliménto *nm* embellishment, ornament.

abbellíre *vt* to adorn, embellish.

abbeveràre *vt* to water (animals).

abbeveratóio *nm* watering place, drinking trough.

abbiccí *nm* alphabet, rudiments.

abbiènte *a* well-to-do.

abbigliaménto *nm* clothes, clothing, finery.

abbigliàre *vt* to deck, dress.

abbinàre *vt* to pair, link together.

abbindolàre *vt* to wind (skeins); cheat, trick.

abbisognàre *vi and impers* to need, want.

abboccaménto *nm* interview, conversation, talk.

abboccàre *vti* to seize with the mouth; (*fig*) to be deceived; **-rsi** *vr* to have an interview, confer.

abboccàto *a* brimful; (*in speech*) nice; (*of wine*) sweet.

abbonacciàre *vt* to calm, pacify; **-rsi** *vr* (*sea*) to grow calm.

abbonaménto *nm* subscription, discount, season ticket.

abbonàre *vt* to accept as subscriber; (*com*) to deduct, pass (a doubtful account); **-rsi** *vr* to subscribe.

abbonàto *nm* subscriber, season-ticket holder, commuter; (*gas, el*) consumer.

abbondànte *a* abundant, plentiful.

abbondànza *nf* abundance, plenty.

abbondàre *vi* to abound.

abbordàbile *a* accessible, approachable.

abbordàggio *nm* (*naut*) boarding.

abbordàre *vt* to board (a ship), accost; **-rsi** *vr* (*naut*) to collide.

abbórdo *nm* access, approach; (*naut*) boarding.

abbottonàre *vt* to button (up); **-rsi** *vr* to button up, become secretive.

abbozzàre *vt* to outline, sketch, rough-hew.

abbòzzo *nm* rough draught, sketch; *a*. d'uomo manikin.

abbracciaménto, abbràccio *nm* embrace.

abbracciàre *vt* to embrace, contain, include.

abbrancàre *vt* to grasp, seize; **-rsi** *vr* to cling to, grasp.

abbreviàre *vt* to abridge, shorten.

abbreviazióne *nf* abbreviation, abridg(e)ment.

abbronzàre *vt* to tan, bronze, make brown.

abbronzatúra *nf* sunburn, tan, bronzing.

abbruciacchiàre *vt* to scorch, burn slightly.

abbrunàre *vt* to brown, darken; **-rsi** *vr* to go into mourning.

abbruníre *vti* to darken, grow dark, become tanned.

abbrustolíre *vt* to toast, crisp; **-rsi** *vr* to turn brown.

abbrutíre *vt* to brutalize.

abbuiàre *vt* to obscure; **-rsi** *vr* to grow dark, cloud over.

abbuòno nm discount, deduction.
abburattàre vt to sift.
abdicàre vi to abdicate.
abdicazióne nf abdication.
aberrazióne nf abberration, deviation.
abetàia nf fir-wood.
abéte nm fir-tree.
abiètto a abject, base.
abieziόne nf abjectness, baseness.
àbile a able, capable, clever, skilful.
abilità nf ability, dexterity, skill.
abilitàre vt to enable, qualify.
abilitazióne nf qualification.
Abissínia nf Abyssinia.
abissíno a nm Abyssinian.
abísso nm abyss, chasm; (fig) ruin.
abitàbile a habitable.
abitànte nmf inhabitant.
abitàre vti to inhabit, live in, live.
abitàto a inhabited; nm inhabited place.
abitazióne nf dwelling, house.
àbito nm dress, clothes, suit, habit, custom; a. **borghése** civilian clothes.
abituàle a habitual, customary.
abituàre vt to accustom; **-rsi** vr to get accustomed.
abitúdine nf habit, custom.
abitúro nm hovel.
abiúra nf abjuration, recantation.
abiuràre vt to abjure, recant.
ablatívo nm ablative case.
abluzióne nf ablution, purification.
abnegazióne nf self-denial, abnegation.
abolíre vt to abolish, repeal.
abolizióne nf abolition, repeal.
abomináre vt to abominate, detest.
abominazióne nf abomination, detestation.
abominévole a abominable.
abomínio nm abomination, shame.
aborígeno a aboriginal.
aborríre vt to abhor.
abortíre vi to miscarry, abort, fail.
abòrto nm miscarriage, abortion, still-born child; failure.
Abràmo nm pr Abraham.
abrasióne nf abrasion, graze.
abrasívo a nm abrasive.
abrogàre vt to abrogate, repeal.
abrogazióne nf abrogation, repeal.
abruzzése a of the Abruzzi; nm native of the A.
Abrúzzi e Molíse nm pl (geogr) Abruzzi e Molise.
àbside nf apse.
abusàre vt to abuse, misuse, trespass on.
abusívo a abusive, improper.
abúso nm abuse, misuse, infringement (of the law).
A.C. Avànti Crísto ad B.C.
acàcia pl **-cie** nf acacia-tree.
accadèmia nf academy.
accadèmico pl **-ìci** a academic; nm academician.
accadére vi to happen, occur.
accadúto nm event.

accagliàre vt **-rsi** vr to curdle.
accalappiàre vt to catch, ensnare, deceive.
accalcàre vi to crowd up; **-rsi** vr to crowd.
accaldàrsi vr to get heated, excited.
accaldàto a heated (with running etc).
accaloràre vt to heat; **-rsi** vr to get heated.
accampaménto nm encampment, camp.
accampàre vi to camp; vt (reasons etc) to adduce; **-rsi** vr to pitch camp.
accaniménto nm fury, ardour.
accanírsi vr to rage, to concentrate doggedly.
accaníto a pitiless, fierce, obstinate.
accànto ad beside, near.
accantonàre vt to billet.
accaparraménto nm earnest money, deposit; buying up, cornering.
accaparràre vt to conclude (a bargain) by paying earnest money; to buy up, corner.
accapigliàrsi vr to scuffle, to quarrel.
accappatóio nm bathrobe, wrap.
accapponàre vi **fàre** a. **la pèlle** to make the flesh creep; **la pèlle mi si accappona** I've got gooseflesh.
accarezzaménto nm caress.
accarezzàre vt to caress.
accartocciàre vt to wrap up, to crumple up.
accasàre vt to marry; **-rsi** vr to marry, set up house.
accasciaménto nm dejection.
accasciàre vt to depress; **-rsi** vr to fall to the ground, lose heart.
accatastàre vt to heap up, stack.
accattabríghe nm quarrelsome fellow.
accattàre vi to beg.
accattonàggio nm begging.
accattóne nm beggar.
accavalcióne, a cavalcióni ad astride.
accecaménto nm blinding, confusion, obstruction.
accecànte a blinding, dazzling.
accecàre vt to blind: **-rsi** vr to become blind.
accèdere vi to approach, enter.
acceleràre vt to accelerate, quicken, speed up.
acceleràto a accelerated; (of a train) slow.
acceleratóre nm accelerator.
accelerazióne nf acceleration.
accèndere vt to light, kindle; **-rsi** vr to catch fire, grow angry.
accendíno nm (cigarette) lighter.
accendisígaro nm cigarette-lighter.
accennàre vti to indicate, hint, nod.
accénno nm sign, hint.
accensióne nf lighting; (aut) ignition.
accènto nm accent.
accentuàre vt to accentuate.
accerchiàre vt to encircle, surround.
accertaménto nm ascertainment,

assurance, check; (of account) settlement.

accertàre vt to ascertain, (com) to settle, to assess; -rsi vr to make sure.

accéso a alight, flushed, bright.

accessíbile a accessible, approachable.

accèsso nm access, fit, paroxysm.

accessòrio a nm accessory.

accétta nf hatchet, axe.

accettàbile a acceptable.

accettàre vt to accept, agree to; accettànte nm (com) accepter.

accettazióne nf acceptance.

accètto a received with pleasure, welcome, (com) honoured.

acchiappàre vt to catch, trap.

acciaccàre vt to bruise, enfeeble.

acciàcco pl -àcchi nm infirmity, ailment.

acciaiería nf steelworks.

acciàio nm steel.

accidentàle a accidental, casual.

accidentalménte ad accidentally.

accidentàto a (of ground) broken.

accidènte nm accident, misfortune.

accidènti! interj (annoyance) dash it!; (surprise) Good Heavens!

accídia nf idleness, sloth.

accidióso a idle, slothful.

accigliaménto nm frown, sullen air.

accigliàrsi vr to frown, look sullen.

accigliàto a frowning, sullen.

accíngersi vr to set about, prepare oneself.

acciocché cj in order that, so that.

acciuffàre vt to seize by the hair, grasp.

acciúga nf anchovy.

acclamàre vt to acclaim; vi to clap hands, cheer.

acclimàre, acclimatàre vt to acclimatize.

acclimatàrsi vr to grow acclimatized.

acclúdere vt to enclose.

acclúso a enclosed.

accoccolàrsi vr to crouch, squat.

accogliènte a welcoming, cosy.

accogliènza nf reception, welcome.

accògliere vt to receive, welcome.

accollàre vt to put round the neck, yoke; (fig) burden, saddle with; -rsi vr to undertake.

accollàto a high-necked.

accoltellàre vt to stab, knife.

accomandànte nm (com) sleeping partner.

accomandatàrio nm (com) acting partner.

accomàndita nf (com) limited partnership.

accomiatàre vt to dismiss; -rsi vr to take leave of.

accomodaménto nm adjustment, agreement, compromise.

accomodàre vt to repair, mend, arrange, adjust, (com) settle; -rsi vr to sit down, make oneself comfortable, come to terms; s'accòmodi take a seat, please.

accompagnaménto nm accompaniment, retinue.

accompagnàre vt to accompany, escort; -rsi vr to keep company, join, match; (mus) accompany oneself.

acconciàre vt to dress (the hair), adorn, arrange; -rsi vr to deck oneself.

acconciatúra nf hair style.

accóncio a fit, suitable.

accondiscéndere vi to consent, condescend.

acconsentíre vi to consent.

accontentàre vt to content; -rsi vr to be satisfied, be content with.

accónto nm (com) part payment.

accoppiàre vt to couple, pair, yoke; -rsi vr to join together, couple.

accoraménto nm grief, affliction.

accoràre vt to grieve deeply; -rsi vr to be grieved to the heart.

accorciàre vt to shorten; -rsi vr to grow shorter.

accordàre vt to grant; (mus) tune, harmonize, (gram) make agree; conciliate; -rsi vr to agree, be in harmony with.

accòrdo nm agreement, arrangement, (mus) chord, (fig) harmony, accord; èssere d'a. to agree.

accòrgersi vr to perceive, notice, realize, be aware of.

accorgimènto nm circumspection, prudence, device.

accórrere vi to run up, to go to help.

accortézza nf prudence, sagacity, cunning.

accòrto a wary, shrewd, prudent.

accostàre vt to approach, bring near(er); leave ajar; -rsi vr to approach, draw near.

accòsto ad beside, hard by.

accostumàre vt to train, accustom; -rsi vr to get accustomed.

accovacciàrsi vr to cower, crouch.

accozzàglia nf medley, disorderly mass; un'a. di gènte motley crowd.

accreditàre vt to give credit to, to accredit; -rsi vr to gain credit.

accréscere vt to increase.

accrescimènto nm increase, growth.

accudíre vi (of household duties) to attend to.

accumulàre vt to accumulate, heap up; -rsi vr to accumulate.

accumulatóre nm (el) accumulator.

accumulazióne nf accumulation.

accuratézza nf accuracy, care.

accuràto a accurate, neat.

accúsa nf accusation, charge.

accusàre vt to accuse, charge, blame, show, complain of, (com) acknowledge; -rsi vr to accuse oneself, confess.

accusativo a nm accusative.

accusàto nm accused, defendant.

accusatóre nm accuser, prosecutor; pùbblico a. public prosecutor.

acerbità nf acerbity, asperity.

acèrbo *a* unripe, sour, (*fig*) sharp.
àcero *nm* maple-tree.
acetilène *nm* acetylene.
acéto *nm* vinegar.
acetóne *nm* acetone.
acetóso *a* vinegary, sourish.
acidità *nf* acidity, sourness.
àcido *a nm* acid.
àcino *nm* grape, grape-stone.
àcne *nm* acne.
àcqua *nf* water; **a. corrènte** running water; **a. dólce** fresh water; **a. mineràle** mineral water; **a. potàbile** drinking water; **a. di sèltz** soda-water.
acquafòrte *nf* etching.
acquàio *nm* sink.
acquaplàno *nm* aquaplane.
acquaràgia *nf* turpentine.
acquartieràre *vt* (*troops*) to quarter; **-rsi** *vr* to take up quarters.
acquasantièra *nf* holy water stoup.
acquàta *nf* heavy shower.
acquàtico *pl* **-ici** *a* aquatic.
acquattàrsi *vr* to crouch, squat.
acquavìte *nf* rough brandy.
acquazzóne *nm* sudden and heavy shower, downpour.
acquedótto *nm* aqueduct.
acquerellìsta *nmf* painter in water-colours.
acquerèllo *nm* water colour, water-colour painting.
acquerùgiola *nf* drizzle.
acquiescènza *nf* acquiescence.
acquietàre *vt* to appease, pacify.
acquirènte *nmf* purchaser, buyer.
acquisìre *vt* to acquire, obtain.
acquistàre *vt* to acquire, buy; (*fig*) gain, improve.
acquìsto *nm* acquisition, purchase, gain.
acquitrìno *nm* marsh, swamp.
acquitrinóso *a* marshy, boggy.
acquolìna *nf* far venìre l'a. in bócca to make somebody's mouth water.
acquóso *a* watery.
àcre *a* sharp, sour, harsh.
acrèdine *nf* bitterness, sourness; (*fig*) acrimony.
acrimònia *nf* acrimony.
acrimonióso *a* acrimonious.
acròbata *nmf* acrobat.
acrobazìa *nmf* acrobatics *pl*.
acuìre *vt* to sharpen, whet.
acùme *nm* quickness of wit, acumen.
acuminàre *vt* to point, sharpen.
acùstica *nf* acoustics *pl*.
acutézza *nf* acuteness, wit, penetration.
acùto *a* acute, pointed, sharp.
adacquàre *vt* to water, irrigate.
adagiàre *vt* to lay down, make comfortable; **-rsi** *vr* to arrange oneself comfortably; *nm* proverb, saying.
adàgio *ad* slowly, softly, at leisure.
Adàmo *nm pr* Adam.
adattàbile *a* adaptable, applicable.
adattabilità *nf* adaptability.

adattàre *vt* to fit, adapt, adjust; **-rsi** *vr* to adapt oneself.
adàtto *a* fit, proper, right, suitable.
addebitàre *vt* to debit.
addensàre *vt* to make thick; **-rsi** *vr* to grow dense, thicken.
addentàre *vt* to bite.
addentràrsi *vr* to penetrate, probe.
addéntro *ad* within, inside.
addestràre *vt* to train, drill, instruct; (*horse*) break in; **-rsi** *vr* to train oneself, practise.
addétto *a* belonging to, attached; **a. ad un'ambasciàta** attaché at an embassy.
addì *ad* on the (day) of.
addiètro *ad* behind, back(wards), ago.
addìo *ad nm* good-bye.
addirittùra *ad* downright, immediately, outright.
addìrsi *vr and impers* to suit, become.
additàre *vt* to point out, show, indicate.
addizionàre *vt* to add (up).
addizióne *nf* addition, supplement.
addobbàre *vt* to furnish, decorate.
addòbbo *nm* decorative furnishing, hangings.
addolcìre *vt* to sweeten, soften, alleviate.
addoloràre *vt* to afflict, grieve; **-rsi** *vr* to be grieved, grieve.
Addoloràta (l') *nf* Our Lady of Sorrows.
addòme *nm* abdomen.
addomesticàre *vt* to tame; **-rsi** to become tame, become more sociable, grow familiar.
addormentàre *vt* to put to sleep; (*fig*) calm; **-rsi** to fall asleep.
addossàre *vt* to lay upon, place on the back of, place against, charge, load, burden; **-rsi** *vr* to undertake, charge oneself with.
addòsso *ad* on, upon, close by, above; avére **a.** to have on, wear; tiràrsi **a.** to bring upon oneself.
addùrre *vt* to adduce, cite.
adeguàre *vt* to equalize, balance, conform.
adeguàto *a* sufficient.
Adèle *nf pr* Adela.
adèmpiere, adempìre *vt* to fulfil, perform; **-rsi** *vr* to come true.
adempiménto *nm* fulfilment, accomplishment, execution.
aderènte *a* adherent, close-fitting; *nmf* supporter.
aderènza *nf* adherence, adhesion; (*fig pl*) high connections.
aderìre *vt* to adhere, agree.
adescàre *vt* to lure, entice.
adesióne *nf* adhesion, adherence, consent.
adesìvo *a* adhesive.
adèsso *ad* now, at present.
adiacènte *a* adjacent, adjoining, next.

adiacènza *nf* adjacency, vicinity.

adibìre *vt* to destine for use.

àdipe *nm* fat, grease.

adiposità *nf* fatness, plumpness.

adipóso *a* fat, plump.

adiràre *vt* to make angry, provoke; -rsi *vr* to get angry.

àdito *nm* entry, access; dàre a. a give rise to.

adocchiàre *vt* to eye, ogle.

adolescènte *a nmf* adolescent.

adolescènza *nf* adolescence, youth.

Adòlfo *nm pr* Adolph.

adombràre *vt* to shade, conceal; suggest, symbolize; -rsi *vr* to take umbrage.

adoperàre *vt* to use, employ; -rsi *vr* to exert oneself, endeavour.

adoràbile *a* adorable, charming.

adoràre *vt* to adore, worship.

adorazióne *nf* adoration, worship.

adornàre *vt* to adorn, deck; -rsi *vr* to adorn oneself.

adórno *a* adorned, trimmed.

adottàre *vt* to adopt.

adottìvo *a* adoptive, adopted.

adozióne *nf* adoption.

Adriàno *nm pr* Adrian, Hadrian.

Adriàtico *a nm* Adriatic.

adulàre *vt* to flatter.

adulatóre *nm* -trìce *nf* flatterer.

adulatòrio *a* adulatory, flattering.

adulazióne *nf* adulation, flattery.

adulteràre *vt* to adulterate, taint, falsify.

adultèrio *nm* adultery.

adùltero *nm* adulterer.

adùlto *a nm* adult, grown-up.

adunànza *nf* assembly, meeting.

adunàre *vt* to assemble, bring together, convoke; -rsi *vr* to come together, assemble, (mil) fall-in.

adunàta *nf* (mil) fall-in; assembly; a. popolàre mass meeting.

adùnco *pl* -chi a hooked, curved.

aeràre *vt* to air, aerate.

aèro *a* of the air, aerial, airy, unsubstantial; *nm v* aeroplàno.

aerocèntro *nm* air centre.

aerodinàmica *nf* aerodynamics *pl*; aerodinàmico *pl* -ici a aerodynamic, streamlined.

aeròdromo *nm* aerodrome, (US) airdrome.

aeronàutica *nf* aeronautics *pl*, aviation, air force.

aeroplàno *nm* aeroplane, (US) airplane; a. da càccia fighter plane; a. da bombardaménto bomber; a. a reazióne jet plane; a. di lìnea airliner.

aeropòrto *nm* airport.

aerosòl *nm* (chem) aerosol.

àfa *nf* sultry heat.

affàbile *a* affable, friendly.

affabilità *nf* affability.

affaccendàrsi *vr* to occupy oneself, be very busy.

affaccendàto *a* busy.

affacciàre *vt* to bring forward, show ;

-rsi *vr* to show oneself, occur; -rsi su to face (a place).

affamàre *vt* to starve.

affamàto *a* hungry, famished, starving.

affannàre *vt* to trouble, vex; -rsi *vr* to toil, strive, fret, be anxious.

affannàto *a* breathless, panting, distressed.

affànno *nm* shortness of breath, asthma; trouble, anxiety.

affannóso *a* suffocating, troublesome, wearisome, troubled.

affàre *nm* affair, matter, business; uòmo d'affàri businessman.

affarìsta *nm* unscrupulous businessman.

affaróne *nm* good bargain.

affascinànte *a* fascinating.

affascinàre *vt* to fascinate, enchant.

affastellàre *vt* to tie up in bundles, jumble up.

affaticàre *vt* to tire, harass; -rsi *vr* to get tired, toil, strive.

affàtto *ad* entirely; niènte a. not at all.

affermàre *vt* to affirm; -rsi *vr* to assert oneself, make a name for oneself.

affermatìva *nf* affirmative.

affermatìvo *a* affirmative.

affermazióne *nf* statement, assertion, achievement.

afferràre *vt* to seize, grasp, comprehend.

affettàre *vt* to cut in slices; affect, pretend.

affettàto *a* sliced; affected, prim; *nm* sliced ham, salami.

affettazióne *nf* affectation.

affètto *a* affected, afflicted; *nm* affection, love.

affettuosaménte *ad* lovingly, affectionately.

affettuóso *a* affectionate.

affezionàre *vt* to make fond; -rsi *vr* to become fond of, attached to.

affezióne *nf* affection, attachment.

affiancàre *vt* to flank, place side by side.

affiatàre *vt* to bring together; -rsi *vr* to get on well together.

affibbiàre *vt* to buckle, clasp; (fig) give.

affibbiatùra *nf* buckle, clasp.

affidàre *vt* to entrust, confide; -rsi *vr* to trust, rely on.

affievolìre *vt* to weaken; *vi* and -rsi *vr* to grow weak.

affìggere *vt* to affix, stick (up), attach.

affilàre *vt* to whet, grind; -rsi *vr* to become thin.

affiliàre *vt* to affiliate; -rsi *vr* to become a member, join.

affiliazióne *nf* affiliation.

affinàre *vt* to refine, improve, sharpen, make thin; -rsi *vr* to become refined, improve, become sharper, become thinner.

affinatóio *nm* refining furnace.

affinché *cj* so that, in order that.

affíne *a* akin, kindred; *nm* kinsman, relative; **a. di** *cj* in order to, so as to.

affinità *nf* affinity, attraction.

affiocàre, affiochíre *vt* weaken, dim, render hoarse, *vi* become hoarse.

affiochiménto *nm* hoarseness.

affioràre *vi* to come to the surface.

affissàre *vt* to affix, gaze at.

affissióne *nf* bill-posting; **vietàta l'a.** stick no bills.

affísso *a* fixed, posted up; *nm* bill, placard, poster.

affittacàmere *nm* landlord; *nf* landlady.

affittàre *vt* to let, rent, hire, lease.

affítto *nm* rent, hire; **dàre in a.** to let; **prèndere in a.** to rent.

affliggere *vt* to afflict, torment; **-rsi** *vr* to be grieved.

afflítto *a* afflicted, sad.

afflizióne *nf* affliction.

affluènza *nf* crowd, large audience; abundance.

affluíre *vi* to flow, flock.

affogàre *vt* to drown, (fig) smother; *vi* to be drowned; **-rsi** *vr* to drown oneself; **uòvo affogàto** poached egg.

affollàre *vt* to crowd, throng; **-rsi** *vr* to crowd together.

affondàre *vti* to sink, founder, ruin; **-rsi** *vr* to sink, founder, go to the bottom.

affossaménto *nm* trench, entrenchment, sinking.

affrancàre *vt* to free, exempt; (letter) stamp; **-rsi** *vr* to be freed; grow strong.

affrancatúra *nf* postage.

affrànto *a* broken, crushed, overcome.

affratellàre *vt* to make as brothers; **-rsi** *vr* to fraternize.

affrésco *pl* **-chi** *nm* fresco.

affrettàre *vt* to hasten, speed; **-rsi** *vr* to hurry, make haste.

affrontàre *vt* to confront, face, attack; **-rsi** to meet face to face, fight.

affrónto *nm* affront, insult.

affumicàre *vt* to fumigate, smoke-dry, blacken; **-rsi** *vr* to be smoked, grow black.

affústo *nm* (mil) gun-carriage.

afóso *a* sultry, heavy.

Àfrica *nf* Africa.

africàno *a nm* African.

Àgata *nf pr* Agatha.

agènda *nf* notebook, agenda.

agènte *nm* agent, factor, manager; **a. di polizía** policeman.

agenzía *nf* agency; **a. di turísmo** travel agency.

agevolàre *vt* to facilitate, make easy, help.

agévole *a* easy, manageable.

agganciàre *vt* to hook (up).

aggéggio *nm* gadget, device; trifle.

agghiacciàre *vt* to freeze, turn to ice; **-rsi** *vr* to freeze, grow cold.

aggiogàre *vt* to yoke.

aggiornàre *vt* to postpone; bring up to date; *vi* to dawn.

aggiornàto *a* up-to-date.

aggiotàggio *nm* stock-jobbing.

aggiràre *vt* to go round; deceive; **-rsi** *vr* to wander; deal with.

aggiúngere *vt* to add; **-rsi** *vr* to join, be added.

aggiúnta *nf* addition.

aggiúnto *a* added, additional; *nm* adjunct, assistant.

aggiustàre *vt* to adjust, regulate, set to rights, tidy, settle; **-rsi** *vr* to adjust oneself, tidy oneself, come to an agreement.

agglomeràre *vt* **-rsi** *vr* to agglomerate.

agglomeràto *a* agglomerate; *nm* agglomerate, agglomeration.

aggomitolàre *vt* to wind into a ball; **-rsi** *vr* to curl up.

aggranchíre *vt* to benumb.

aggrappàre *vt* to grapple, grasp; **-rsi** *vr* to cling to, lay hold (of).

aggravànte *a* aggravating; *nm* (leg) aggravating circumstance.

aggravàre *vt* to aggravate, weigh upon, oppress; **-rsi** *vr* (illness) to grow worse.

aggràvio *nm* heavy burden, expense, charge; **a. fiscàle** tax.

aggredíre *vt* to attack, assault.

aggregàre *vt* to aggregate.

aggregàto *a* joint, united; *nm* aggregate; block of houses; temporary clerk.

aggregazióne *nf* aggregation.

aggressióne *nf* aggression, attack.

aggressività *nf* aggressiveness.

aggressívo *a* aggressive; *nm* chemical agent used in warfare.

aggressóre *nm* aggressor, assailant.

aggrinzàre *vt* to wrinkle; **-rsi** *vr* to wrinkle, shrivel (up).

aggrottàre *vt* to frown; **a. le cíglia** to frown, knit one's brows.

aggrumàre *vt* to curdle, clot.

aggruppàre *vt* to group, collect, gather; **-rsi** *vr* to form a group.

agguàglio *nm* comparison.

agguantàre *vt* to seize.

agguàto *nm* ambush.

agguerríre *vt* to inure to war, train to arms.

agiatézza *nf* ease, comfort, easy circumstances *pl*.

agiàto *a* in easy circumstances, well-off, comfortable.

àgile *a* agile, nimble.

agilità *nf* agility, nimbleness.

àgio *nm* ease, comfort, leisure.

agíre *vi* to act, operate, behave; (leg) proceed.

agitàre *vt* to agitate, upset, excite; **-rsi** *vr* to get agitated.

agitazióne nf agitation, excitement.
àglio nm garlic.
agnèllo nm lamb.
Agnèse nf pr Agnes.
àgo pl **àghi** nm needle.
agognàre vt to yearn for, covet.
agonía nf agony, anguish.
agonizzàre vi to be in agony, be at the point of death.
agoràio nm needle-case.
Agostíno nm pr Augustine.
agósto nm August.
agràrio a agrarian.
agrèste a rustic, rural.
agrézza nf sourness, tartness.
agrícolo a agricultural.
agricoltóre nm farmer.
agricoltúra nf agriculture.
agrifòglio nm holly.
agrimensóre nm land surveyor.
àgro a sour, sharp; nm sourness; field; country surrounding a town.
agrodólce a bittersweet; nm sweet-and-sour sauce.
agrúmi nm pl citrus fruits pl.
aguzzàre vt to whet, sharpen, point; (fig) stimulate, sharpen.
agúzzo a sharp-pointed.
ahi interj oh!, ouch!
ahimè interj alas!
àia nf threshing floor.
aitànte a strong, sturdy; brave.
aiuòla nf flowerbed.
aiutànte nmf helper, assistant; (mil) a. di càmpo aide-de-camp.
aiutàre vt to help, assist, lend a hand; -rsi vr to make use of.
aiúto nm help, assistance; helper, assistant.
aizzàre vt to instigate, enrage, incite, set on (dogs).
àla nf wing; a. a dèlta (av) delta-wing.
alabàstro nm alabaster.
àlacre a willing, quick.
alacrità nf alacrity, quickness.
alàno nm mastiff.
alàre nm andiron, firedog.
Alàsca nf (geogr) Alaska.
alàto a winged.
àlba nf dawn.
albagía nf haughtiness, conceit.
albanése a nmf Albanian.
Albanía nf (geogr) Albania.
àlbatro nm albatross; (tree) arbutus.
albeggiàre vi to dawn.
albergàre vt to lodge, to harbour.
albergatóre nm hotel-owner.
albèrgo pl **-ghi** nm hotel.
àlbero nm tree; ship's mast.
Albèrto nm pr Albert.
albicòcca nf apricot.
àlbo nm roll, list; èssere iscrítto all'a. degli avvocàti to be called (US admitted) to the bar.
albóre nm dawn.
àlbum nm album.
albúme nm albumen, white of egg.
alcalíno a alkaline.
alcalizzàre vt to alkalize.

àlce nm elk.
alchímia nf alchemy.
alcióne nm kingfisher.
àlcool nm alcohol; **alcoòlico** pl **-ici**, **alcoolizzàto** a nm alcoholic.
alcoolísmo nm alcoholism.
alcúno pron somebody, anybody, (preceded by non) nobody; a any (preceded by non) no; **alcuni** a and pron pl some, a few pl.
Àldo nm pr Aldous.
àlea nf chance, risk; **córrere l'a.** to run the risk.
aleggiàre vi to flutter, try to fly.
Alessàndria nf (geogr) Alexandria (in Egypt).
Alessàndro nm pr Alexander.
alétta nf fin; (av) tab.
alettóne nm (av) aileron.
alfabètico pl **-ici** a alphabetical.
alfabèto nm alphabet.
alfière nm (mil) ensign, standard bearer; (chess) bishop.
alfíne ad at last.
Alfrèdo nm pr Alfred.
àlga nf seaweed.
àlgebra nf algebra.
Algería nf Algeria.
Algèri nf Algiers.
algeríno a nm Algerian.
aliànte nm glider.
àlibi nm (leg) alibi.
alíce nf anchovy.
Alíce nf pr Alice.
alienàre vt to alienate, estrange; -rsi vr to be estranged.
alienàto a estranged, crazy; nm lunatic, mentally deranged person.
alienazióne nf alienation, estrangement, mental derangement.
alièno a alien, adverse.
alimentàre a alimentary; vt to feed, nourish.
alimentàrio a alimentary.
alimentatóre nm nourisher; (mech) feeder.
alimentazióne nf nourishment, food, diet; (mech) feeding.
aliménto nm food, nourishment.
alisèi, vènti nm pl trade winds pl.
aliscàfo nm hydrofoil.
àlito nm breath, breathing; breeze.
allacciàre vt to lace, connect, entangle.
allagaménto nm inundation.
allagàre vt to inundate, overflow, submerge.
allampanàto a emaciated.
allargàre vt to enlarge, extend, widen.
allarmàre vt to alarm, disturb; -rsi vr to be alarmed.
allàrme nm alarm, alert.
allàto ad beside.
allattàre vt to suckle, breast-feed.
alleànza nf alliance, league.
alleàrsi vr to make an alliance.
alleàto a allied; nm ally.
allegàre vt to allege, enclose; (teeth) to set on edge.

allegazióne *nf* allegation.

alleggeríre *vt* to lighten, relieve; **-rsi** *vr* to put on lighter clothing, relieve oneself of.

allegoría *nf* allegory.

allegraménte *ad* cheerfully, merrily.

allegrézza *nf* gaiety, cheerfulness.

allegría *nf* mirth, gladness.

allégro *a* gay, cheerful, merry; (*mus*) allegro.

allenaménto *nm* training.

allenàre *vt* to train, strengthen, invigorate.

allenatóre *nm* trainer, coach.

allentàre *vt* to slacken, relax, diminish; **-rsi** *vr* to get slack; unlace or undo one's clothing.

allergía *nf* allergy.

allèrgico *pl* **-ici** *a* allergic.

allestíre *vt* to prepare, make ready.

allettaménto *nm* allurement.

allettànte *a* alluring.

allettàre *vt* to allure, entice; **-rsi** *vr* (*in illness*) to take to one's bed.

allevaménto *nm* bringing-up, breeding.

allevàre *vt* to bring up, breed.

allevatóre *nm* **-trice** *nf* breeder.

alleviàre *vt* to relieve.

allibíre *vi* to be amazed.

allietàre *vt* to gladden.

alliévo *nm* pupil, student, cadet.

allignàre *vi* to take root, grow.

allineàre *vt* to align, set in rows.

allocuzióne *nf* address, allocution.

allòdola *nf* skylark.

alloggiàre *vti* to lodge, stay, billet.

allòggio *nm* lodgings *pl*, billet, inn.

allontanaménto *nm* removal, distance, estrangement.

allontanàre *vt* to remove, send away; **-rsi** *vr* to go away, withdraw.

allóra *ad* then, at that time.

allorché *cj* when.

allòro *nm* laurel.

allucinàre *vt* to hallucinate; **-rsi** *vr* to suffer from hallucination, deceive oneself.

allucinazióne *nf* hallucination.

allúdere *vi* to allude, refer, hint.

allumínio *nm* aluminium.

allungàre *vt* to lengthen, prolong; (*wine etc*) water; hand; **-rsi** *vr* to grow longer, stretch oneself.

allusióne *nf* allusion.

almanaccàre *vi* to fancy, build castles in the air, puzzle one's brain.

almanàcco *pl* **-àcchi** *nm* almanac, calendar.

alméno *ad* at least.

àlno *nm* alder-tree.

alóne *nm* halo.

alpèstre *a* mountainous, wild.

Àlpi (le) *nf pl* the Alps *pl*.

alpigiàno *nm* inhabitant of a hilly district, mountaineer.

alpinismo *nm* mountaineering.

alpíno *a* alpine; **A.** *nm* soldier of a special Italian alpine division.

alquànto *a* some, a good deal; *ad* somewhat, rather.

Alsàzia *nf* (*geogr*) Alsace.

alsaziàno *a nm* Alsatian.

alt *interj* halt, stop.

altaléna *nf* swing, seesaw.

altaménte *ad* highly, greatly.

altàre *nm* altar; **a. maggióre** high altar.

alteràre *vt* to alter, change; **-rsi** *vr* to get angry, go bad.

alterazióne *nf* change, deterioration, falsification.

altercàre *vi* to quarrel.

alterézza, alterigia *nf* haughtiness, pride, insolence.

alternàre *vt* to alternate.

alternatíva *nf* alternative, alternation.

alternativaménte *ad* alternately, alternatively.

alternatívo *a* alternate, alternative.

altèro *a* dignified, proud, haughty.

altézza *nf* height; (*of cloth*) width; depth; highness; **A. Reàle** Royal Highness.

altezzóso *a* haughty, arrogant.

altíccio *a* tipsy.

altipiàno *nm* plateau, tableland.

altitúdine *nf* altitude, height.

àlto *a* high, tall, loud, deep; (*of cloth*) wide; (*geogr*) upper, northern; *ad* **àlta vóce** aloud.

Àlto Àdige *nm* (*geogr*) South Tyrol.

àlto-atesíno *a nm* South-Tyrolese.

altofórno *nm* blast furnace.

altolocàto *a* high-ranking, important.

altoparlànte *nm* loudspeaker.

altresí *cj* likewise, too.

altrettànto *ad* equally, as much (again); *interj* the same to you!

àltri *pron sing and pl* someone, another, some *pl*.

altrièri, l' *ad* the day before yesterday.

altriménti *ad* otherwise.

àltro *pron and a* (an)other, different, next; (something) else; *interj* not at all!; **per a.** anyhow.

altrónde, d' *ad* besides, on the other hand.

altróve *ad* elsewhere, somewhere else.

altrúi *pron* others, other people *pl*; *a* of other people; **l'a.** *nm* other people's property.

altúra *nf* height, elevation.

alúnno *nm* pupil, schoolboy.

alveàre *nm* beehive.

àlveo *nm* channel, bed of a river.

alzàre *vt* to raise, lift, build; **a. le càrte** to cut the cards; **a. le spàlle** to shrug one's shoulders; **-rsi** *vr* to get up, rise.

alzàta *nf* rise, elevation, shrug.

amàbile *a* amiable, kind, agreeable.

amabilità *nf* amiability, kindness.

amalgamàre *vt* to amalgamate.

amànte *a* loving, fond; *nmf* lover, sweetheart.

amàre *vt* to love, like, be fond of.

amareggiáre *vt* to embitter; -**rsi** *vr* to grow bitter.

amarèna *nf* sour black cherry.

amarézza *nf* bitterness, grief.

amàro *a* bitter, grievous, cruel.

amarràre *vt* to moor.

amatóre *nm* -**tríce** *nf* lover; amateur.

amàzzone *nf* Amazon, horsewoman.

ambascería *nf* embassy, deputation, diplomatic mission.

ambàscia *nf* shortness of breath, anxiety.

ambasciàta *nf* embassy, message.

ambasciatóre *nm* -**tríce** *nf* ambassador.

ambedúe *pron and a pl* both (of).

ambiènte *nm* atmosphere, circle, environment, room.

ambiguità *nf* ambiguity, doubt.

ambíguo *a* ambiguous, doubtful.

àmbio *nm* amble.

ambíre *vt* to long for, covet.

ambizióne *nf* ambition, love of finery, vanity.

ambizióso *a* ambitious, vain, fond of finery.

àmbra *nf* amber.

Ambrógio *nm pr* Ambrose; **ambrosiàno** *a* Ambrosian.

ambulànte *a* walking, itinerant.

ambulànza *nf* ambulance.

ambulatòrio *nm* out-patients' department, first-aid post.

Ambúrgo *nf* (*geogr*) Hamburg.

àmen *nm* amen.

amenità *nf* amenity, agreeableness.

améno *a* pleasant, agreeable.

Amèrica *nf* America.

americàna *nf* cycle relay race.

americàno *a nm* American.

ametísta *nf* amethyst.

amíca *nf* (woman) friend.

amichévole *a* friendly, amiable.

amicízia *nf* friendship.

amíco *pl* -**íci** *a* friendly; *nm* friend, boy-friend.

àmido *nm* starch.

Amlèto *nm pr* Hamlet.

ammaccàre *vt* to bruise, crush; -**rsi** *vr* to get bruised.

ammaestraménto *nm* teaching, instruction, training of animals.

ammaestràre *vt* to teach, instruct; (*animals*) train, tame.

ammainàre *vt* (*sails*) to strike; (*flag*) haul down, lower.

ammalàre *vi* -**rsi** *vr* to fall sick, sicken.

ammalàto *a* sick, ill; *nm* patient.

ammaliàre *vt* to bewitch.

ammànco *pl* -**chi** *nm* shortage, deficit.

ammanettàre *vt* to handcuff.

ammansàre, ammansíre *vt* to make tame, gentle; -**rsi** *vr* to grow tame, gentle.

ammantàre *vt* to mantle, cover, hide, disguise.

ammararáre *vi* (*av*) to alight (on water).

ammassàre *vt* to amass, heap up; -**rsi** *vr* to come together, crowd.

ammàsso *nm* heap, accumulation, (*com*) pool.

ammattíre *vi* to go mad.

ammazzàre *vt* to kill, murder; -**rsi** *vr* to kill oneself; (*fig*) toil hard.

ammazzasètte *nm* braggart, bully.

ammazzatóio *nm* slaughter-house.

ammènda *nf* amends *pl*, fine.

ammendàre *vt* to amend, reform; -**rsi** *vr* to improve, get better.

ammennícolo *nm* gadget, trinket, trifle, pretext, cavil.

amméttere *vt* to admit, allow, receive.

ammezzàre *vt* to halve.

ammezzàto *nm* mezzanine.

ammiccàre *vt* to wink, beckon, (*with the eyes*) make a signal.

amministràre *vt* to administer, rule.

amministratívo *a* administrative.

amministrazióne *nf* administration, government, trusteeship.

ammiràbile *a* admirable, wonderful.

ammiragliàto *nm* admiralty.

ammiràglio *nm* admiral.

ammiràre *vt* to admire.

ammirazióne *nf* admiration, wonder.

ammissíbile *a* admissible.

ammissióne *nf* admission; **tàssa d'a.** entrance fee.

ammobiliàre *vt* to furnish.

ammòdo *a* nice-mannered, respectable; *ad* nicely, carefully.

ammogliàre *vt* to give a wife to; -**rsi** *vr* to take a wife.

ammollàre *vt* to steep, soften; -**rsi** *vr* to be soaked, get wet.

ammollíre *vt* to soften, move (to compassion); -**rsi** *vr* to get soft.

ammoníaca *nf* ammonia.

ammoniménto *nm* admonition, warning.

ammoníre *vt* to admonish, warn, advise.

ammonizióne *nf* admonition, reproof, warning.

ammontàre *nm* (*com*) amount; *vt* to heap; *vi* to amount; -**rsi** *vr* to accumulate.

ammorbidíre *vt* to soften; -**rsi** *vr* to grow soft.

ammortíre *vt* to weaken, deaden.

ammortizzare *vt* to deaden; (*debt*) redeem.

ammorzàre *vt* to extinguish, put out.

ammostàre *vt* (*grapes*) to press.

ammostatóio *nm* wine-press.

ammucchiàre *vt* to heap up.

ammuffíre *vi* to grow stale.

ammutinaménto *nm* mutiny, revolt.

ammutinàrsi *vr* to mutiny, revolt.

amnesía *nf* amnesia.

amnistía nf amnesty.

àmo nm fish-hook; **abboccàre all'a** to take the bait; (fig) to swallow the bait.

amóre nm love, affection; a. **pròprio** self-esteem; **per a. di** for the sake of; **fàre all'a.** to make love.

amoreggiàre vt to flirt.

amorétto nm flirtation, love affair.

amorévole a loving, kind.

amoríno nm Cupid, little darling; (bot) mignonette.

amorosaménte ad lovingly.

amoróso a loving; nm lover, gallant.

ampiézza nf ampleness.

àmpio a ample, wide, spacious.

amplèsso nm embrace.

ampliàre vt to enlarge, extend; **-rsi** vr to become larger, extend.

amplificàre vt to amplify, exaggerate.

amplificatóre nm amplifier.

amplitúdine nf amplitude.

ampólla nf phial, ampoule.

ampollosità nf bombast.

ampollóso a bombastic.

amputàre vt to amputate.

amputazióne nf amputation.

amuléto nm amulet, talisman.

anabbagliànte a anti-dazzle.

anacorèta nm anchorite, hermit.

anacronísmo nm anachronism.

anàgrafe nf registry office.

analfabèta a nmf illiterate.

analfabetísmo nm illiteracy.

anàlisi nf analysis.

analizzàre vt to analyse.

analogía nf analogy.

ananàsso nm pineapple.

anarchía nf anarchy.

anàrchico pl **-ici** a nm anarchic, anarchist.

anatomía nf anatomy.

anatòmico pl **-ici** a anatomic(al); nm anatomist.

anatomizzàre vt to anatomize, dissect.

ànatra nf duck.

ànca nf hip, haunch.

ànche ad also, too, even.

àncora nf anchor.

ancóra ad yet, still, again, even, more, longer.

ancoràggio nm anchorage.

ancoràre vi to anchor.

andaménto nm gait, carriage, trend.

andànte a current, common, cheap, plain; (style) flowing; **artícolo a.** cheap article.

andàre vi to go, call on, proceed; please, suit, happen; **a. a pièdi** to go on foot; nm going, gait; **a lúngo a.** in the long run; **andàrsene** to go away.

andàta nf going; **a. e ritórno** (going) there and back; **bigliétto di a.** single ticket.

andatúra nf gait.

andàzzo nm trend, passing fashion.

Ànde (le) nf pl (geogr) the Andes pl.

andirivièni nm pl coming and going of people, digressions, windings pl.

àndito nm passage, entrance.

Andrèa nm pr Andrew.

andróne nm portal, entrance (hall).

anèddoto nm anecdote.

anelàre vi to long for, pant, be breathless.

anèllo nm ring, ringlet, thimble; (o a chain) link.

anemía nf anaemia.

anèmico pl **-ici** a anaemic.

anestètico pl **-ici** a nm anaesthetic.

anfíbio a amphibious; nm amphibian.

anfiteàtro nm amphitheatre.

anfràtto nm ravine, gorge.

angariàre vt to vex, harass, ill-treat.

Àngela nf pr Angela.

angèlico pl **-ici** a angelic.

àngelo nm angel.

anghería nf vexation, oppression, ill-treatment.

angína nf angina, quinsy.

angipòrto nm blind alley.

anglicàno a nm Anglican.

anglosàssone a nmf Anglo-Saxon; British and American.

angolàre a angular.

àngolo nm angle, corner.

angòscia nf anguish, affliction.

angoscióso a afflicted, grievous.

anguilla nf eel; elusive, nimble person.

angúria nf water-melon.

angústia nf narrowness; want, distress.

angustiàre vt to grieve, vex, harass; **-rsi** vr to be distressed, be afflicted.

angústo a narrow.

ànice nm aniseed.

ànima nf soul, spirit, person.

animàle a nm animal.

animàre vt to animate, enliven; **-rsi** vr to grow animated, take courage, get excited.

animàto a living, lively, animated; **cartóne a.** animated cartoon.

animèlla nf sweetbread.

ànimo nm mind, heart, courage; **fàrsi a.** to pluck up courage; **pèrdersi d'a.** to lose heart.

animosità nf animosity.

animóso a courageous, valiant.

ànitra nf duck.

anitròccolo nm duckling.

Ànna nf pr Anna, Anne, Ann.

annacquàre vt to water, dilute; (fig) moderate.

annaffiàre vt to water, sprinkle.

annaffiatóio nm watering-can.

annàli nm pl annals pl.

annàta nf year; year's profits pl, produce etc.

annebbiàre vt to cloud, dim, darken; **-rsi** vr to grow dim, be overcast.

annegàre vt to drown; vi to be drowned; **-rsi** vr to drown oneself.

annerire vt to blacken, tarnish.
annessióne nf annexation.
annèsso a attached, annexed; nm annex.
annèttere vt to annex.
annichilire vt to annihilate; (fig) dismay.
annidàrsi vr to nestle, nest, hide.
annientaménto nm annihilation, destruction.
annientàre vt to annihilate, destroy; -rsi vr to come to nothing; (fig) abase oneself.
anniversàrio a nm anniversary.
ànno nm year; capo d'a. New Year ('s Day).
annodàre vt to knot; a. amicízie to make friends.
annoiàre vt to bore, vex, tire; -rsi vr to get tired, be bored.
annòna nf victuals pl, provisions pl.
annonàrio a connected with provisions.
annóso a old, ancient.
annotàre vt to note, annotate.
annotazióne nf annotation, note.
annottàre vi -rsi vr to grow dark.
annoveràre vt to number, count.
annuàle a annual, yearly.
annualità nf annuity.
annuàrio nm annual, trade directory; (of members) list.
annuíre vi to nod.
annuità nf yearly instalment.
annullaménto nm annulment, repeal.
annullàre vt to repeal, annul.
annunciàre, annunziàre vt to announce, predict.
annunciazióne nf annunciation; fèsta dell'A. Lady Day.
annúncio, annúnzio nm announcement, advertisement.
Annunziàta nf Our Lady of the Annunciation.
ànnuo a annual, yearly.
annusàre vi to sniff, smell.
anodíno a nm anodyne.
ànodo nm (el) anode.
anomalìa nf anomaly.
anòmalo a anomalous.
anònimo a anonymous.
anormàle a abnormal.
anormalità nf abnormality.
ànsa nf handle.
ansàre vi to pant.
ànsia nf anxiety.
ansietà nf anxiety, anxiousness.
ansimàre vi to pant.
ansióso a anxious, eager.
antagonìsmo nm antagonism.
antagonìsta nmf antagonist, opponent.
antàrtico pl -ici a antarctic.
antecedènte a nm antecedent.
antecedènza nf precedence, priority.
antecessóre nm predecessor.
antefàtto nm preceding event.
anteguèrra a pre-war; nm pre-war times pl.

antemuràle nm rampart, bulwark.
antenàto nm ancestor.
anténna nf feeler, aerial, antenna; a. d'emissióne transmitting aerial; a. di ricezióne receiving aerial.
antepórre vt to put before, prefer.
anteprìma nf preview.
anterióre a prior, former, fore(most).
antiabbagliànte a anti-dazzle.
antiaèreo a (mil) anti-aircraft.
antibiòtico pl -ici a nm antibiotic.
anticàglia nf old rubbish, old curiosity.
anticàmera nf anteroom, hall.
anticàrro a (mil) anti-tank.
antichità nf antiquity.
anticipàre vt to anticipate, pay in advance, forestall; vi arrive earlier.
anticipazióne nf anticipation, advance payment.
anticipo nm advance, earnest; (aut) spark advance.
anticlericàle a nmf anti-clerical.
antico pl -íchi a ancient, antique, obsolete.
anticomunìsta a nmf anti-communist.
antidiluviàno a antediluvian.
antídoto nm antidote.
antifascìsta a nmf antifascist.
antifúrto a nm antitheft.
antìlope nm antelope.
antimeridiàno a antemeridian.
antimilitarìsmo nm antimilitarism.
antipàsto nm hors d'œuvres pl.
antipatìa nf antipathy, dislike.
antipàtico pl -ici a unpleasant, disagreeable.
antìpodi nm pl Antipodes.
antipòrta nf outer door.
antiquàrio nm antiquarian.
antiquàto a antiquated, old-fashioned, out-of-date.
antirúggine a antirust.
antisemìta nmf anti-Semite.
antisemìtico pl -ici a anti-Semitic.
antisemitìsmo nm anti-Semitism.
antisèttico pl -ici a nm antiseptic.
antistànte a before, in front of.
antivigília nf the day before the eve.
antología nf anthology.
Antònia nf pr Antonia.
Antònio nm pr Ant(h)ony.
antracìte nf anthracite.
àntro nm cave, den.
antropòfago pl -gi, -ghi a nm man-eater, cannibal.
antropología nf anthropology.
anulàre nm ring finger.
Ànversa nf (geogr) Antwerp.
ànzi prep before; cj rather, on the contrary.
anzianità nf seniority.
anziàno a elderly, old, senior; nm elder.
anziché cj instead of, rather than.
apatìa nf apathy.
apàtico pl -ici a apathetic.
àpe nf bee.
aperitìvo nm aperitif.

apèrto a open, frank; **all'a.** in the open air; ad frankly.

apertúra nf aperture, opening, hole, span.

apiàrio nm beehive.

ápice nm apex, top, summit.

apocalìsse nf Apocalypse.

apòcrifo a apocryphal.

apogèo nm apogee, acme.

apòlide a nmf stateless (person).

apolítico pl -ici a non-political.

apología nf apology.

apòlogo pl -ghi nm apologue.

apoplessia nf apoplexy.

apoplèttico pl -ici a apoplectic.

apòstata nmf apostate.

apostolàto nm apostleship.

apostòlico pl -ici a apostolic.

apòstolo nm apostle.

appagàre vt to satisfy, content; **-rsi** vr to be satisfied.

appaiàre vt to pair, match, couple; **-rsi** vr to pair, unite.

appallottolàre vt to roll into a ball; **-rsi** vr to coil up.

appaltàre vt to let out or lease out, farm.

appàlto nm undertaking, contract.

appannàggio nm appanage, inheritance.

appannàre vt to tarnish, dim; **-rsi** vr to grow dim, tarnish.

apparàto nm apparatus, adornment, pomp; (theat) scenery.

apparecchiàre vt to prepare, furnish, lay the cloth; **-rsi** vr to get ready.

apparécchio nm apparatus, set; aeroplane; **a. cinematogràfico** (film) projector; **a. fotogràfico** camera; **a. trasmittènte** transmitting set; **a. televisívo** television set.

apparènte a obvious, visible.

apparènza nf appearance; **in a.** apparently.

apparíre vi to appear, show oneself.

appariscènte a gorgeous.

appariscènza nf appearance, showiness.

apparizióne nf apparition, vision.

appartaménto nm flat, (US) apartment; **a. ammobiliàto** furnished flat.

appartàre vt to set apart, separate; **-rsi** vr to withdraw, retire.

appartàto a secluded, remote, solitary.

appartenére vi to belong, concern.

appassionàre vt to move, excite; **-rsi** vr to be excited, eager (about).

appassionàto a eager, enthusiastic.

appassíre vi to fade, wither.

appellàre vt to call, name; **-rsi** to appeal.

appèllo nm appeal, roll-call; **fare l'a.** to call the roll.

appéna ad hardly, scarcely.

appèndere vt to hang up.

appendíce nf appendix, addition.

appendicíte nf appendicitis.

Appenníni nm pl (geogr) the Apennines.

appesantíre vt to make heavy, weigh down; **-rsi** vr to become heavier, stouter.

appetíre vt to long for, desire.

appetíto nm appetite, strong desire; **avére a.** to be hungry.

appetitóso a appetizing, tempting.

appianaménto nm levelling.

appianàre vt to level, smooth.

appiattàre vt to flatten, conceal; **-rsi** vr to squat down, hide oneself.

appiccàre vt to join, hang (up), start; infect; **-rsi** vr to cling.

appiccicàre vt to stick; **-rsi** vr to stick together, hang on.

appiccicaticcio a sticky.

appiccicóso a sticky.

appiè ad at the foot, at the bottom.

appièno ad fully, completely.

appigionàre vt to let, rent, (house) lease.

appigliàrsi vt to cling to, hold on to; (advice etc) follow.

appiglio nm pretext.

appiómbo ad perpendicularly; nm perpendicularity; self assurance.

appisolàrsi vr to doze off.

applaudíre vt to applaud.

applàuso nm applause.

applicàre vt to apply, enforce, appoint; **-rsi** vr to apply oneself, study.

appoggiàre vt to lean, prop, support; **-rsi** vr to lean against, depend upon, trust.

appoggiàto a leaning, supported.

appòggio nm prop, support, favour.

appollaiàrsi vr to roost, perch.

appórre vt to affix, insert; (fig) impute.

apportàre vt to bring, cause.

appòsito a special, suitable.

appòsta ad on purpose.

appostaménto nm ambush, (mil) emplacement.

appostàre vt to waylay; **-rsi** vr to lurk.

apprèndere vt to learn, get to know.

apprendísta nmf apprentice.

apprendistàto nm apprenticeship.

apprensióne nf apprehension.

apprensívo a apprehensive, fearful, quick to perceive.

apprèsso prep near, by, after, behind; ad close by, shortly after.

apprestàre vt to prepare; **-rsi** vr to get ready.

apprezzaménto nm appreciation, estimate, appraisement.

apprezzàre vt to value, rate, appreciate.

appròccio nm approach.

approdàre vi to come to shore, land.

appròdo nm landing place.

approfittàre vi to profit; **-rsi** vr to avail oneself, take advantage.

approfondàre, **-díre** vt to dig, deepen, search out, go into thoroughly.

appropriàre vt to use properly,

adapt; **-rsi** *vr* to appropriate to oneself.

approssimàre *vt* to place near; **-rsi** *vr* to approach, draw near.

approssimativo *a* approximate, rough.

approvàre *vt* to approve, pass.

approvazióne *nf* approval.

approvvigionàre *vt* to victual, provision.

appuntaménto *nm* appointment.

appuntàre *vt* to point, sharpen, pin, tack, blame.

appuntino *ad* just in time, exactly, neatly.

appúnto *nm* note; *ad* precisely, exactly.

appuràre *vt* to verify, ascertain; (*com*) clear.

apribottíglie *nm* bottle-opener.

aprile *nm* April.

apríre *vt* to open, unlock, split, disclose, begin; **-rsi** *vr* to open, expand; (*weather*) clear.

apriscàtole *nm* tin-opener, can-opener.

aquàrio *nm* aquarium.

àquila *nf* eagle; (*fig*) genius.

aquilóne *nm* north wind; (*toy*) kite.

Aquisgràna *nf* (*geogr*) Aachen.

Aràbia *nf* Arabia.

aràbico *pl* **-ici** *a* Arabic, Arabian.

àrabo *a* Arab, Arabian; *nm* Arabic, Arab.

aragósta *nf* lobster.

aràldica *nf* heraldry.

aràldo *nm* herald, harbinger.

arància *nf* orange.

aranciàta *nf* orangeade.

aràncio *a nm* orange, orange (tree).

arancióne *a nm* (*colour*) orange.

aràre *vt* to plough, cultivate.

aratóre *nm* ploughman.

aràtro *nm* plough.

aràzzo *nm* tapestry.

arbitràggio *nm* speculation on the exchange; umpiring.

arbitràre *vi* to arbitrate, umpire, referee; **-rsi** *vr* to take the liberty (to do).

arbitràrio *a* arbitrary.

arbitràto *nm* arbitration.

arbítrio *nm* will, absolute power.

àrbitro *nm* arbiter, umpire, referee.

arbòreo *a* arboreal.

arboréto *nm* grove.

arboscèllo *nm* small tree, shrub.

arbústo *nm* shrub.

àrca *nf* chest, coffer, tomb; **a. di Noè** Noah's Ark.

arcàico *pl* **-ici** *a* archaic.

arcaismo *nm* archaism.

arcàngelo *nm* archangel.

arcàno *a* secret, mysterious; *nm* mystery.

arcàta *nf* archway, arcade.

archeología *nf* archaeology.

archeològico *pl* **-ici** *a* archaeological.

archeòlogo *pl* **-gi, -ghi** *nm* archaeologist.

archétto *nm* small arch; (violin) bow.

architettàre *vt* to draw the plan of; (*fig*) plot, contrive.

architétto *nm* architect.

architettúra *nf* architecture.

archìvio *nm* archives *pl*, record office.

archivísta *nmf* archivist.

Arcibàldo *nm pr* Archibald.

arcidúca *nm* archduke.

arciduchéssa *nf* archduchess.

arcière *nm* archer.

arcígno *a* gruff, surly.

arcipèlago *pl* **-ghi** *nm* archipelago.

arciprète *nm* (*eccl*) dean.

arcivescovàdo *nm* archbishopric.

arcivèscovo *nm* archbishop.

àrco *pl* **-chi** *nm* bow, arch.

arcobaléno *nm* rainbow.

arcuàto *a* arched, bent.

ardènte *a* burning, ardent, eager, spirited.

àrdere *vi* to burn, glow, be on fire, shine.

ardèsia *nf* slate.

ardiménto *nm* boldness, daring.

ardíre *vi* to dare, be bold; *nm* daring, valour.

arditézza *nf* daring, hardihood.

ardíto *a* daring, hardy, bold.

ardóre *nm* ardour, enthusiasm, passion.

àrduo *a* arduous, difficult, dangerous.

àrea *nf* area, surface.

aréna *nf* sand, amphitheatre.

arenàre *vi* to run aground; **-rsi** *vr* to stick fast, be in difficulties.

argentàre *vt* to silver, silver plate.

argentàto *a* silvery, silver, silver-plated.

argentatúra *nf* silver-plating; **a. galvànica** electroplating.

argenteria *nf* silverware.

argentiére *nm* silversmith.

Argentína *nf* Argentina.

argentino *a nm* Argentine.

argentino *a* silvery.

argènto *nm* silver; **a. vívo** mercury, quicksilver.

argentóne *nm* German silver, nickel silver.

argílla *nf* argil, potter's clay.

argillóso *a* clayey.

arginàre *vt* to dam, dike, embank; (*fig*) stem.

àrgine *nm* bank, embankment, dam (*also fig*).

argomentàre *vt* to argue, reason.

argoménto *nm* argument, subject, topic, occasion, synopsis.

arguíre *vi* to infer.

argutézza *nf* finesse, quibble, witticism.

argúto *a* subtle, witty, ingenious.

argúzia *nf* subtlety, piquancy, joke.

ària *nf* air, wind, appearance, song; **all'a. apèrta** out-of-doors.

aridità *nf* aridity, barrenness.

àrido *a* arid, barren, dry.

arieggiàre vt to air; vi to resemble.
aringa nf herring; **a. affumicàta kipper**, (US) smoked herring.
arióso a airy.
aristocràtico pl -**ici** a aristocratic; nm aristocrat.
aristocrazía nf aristocracy.
aritmètica nf arithmetic.
aritmètico pl -**ici** a arithmetical; nm arithmetician.
arlecchíno nm harlequin, buffoon.
àrma nf weapon; (mil) branch, service; coat of arms.
armacòllo, ad ad in a sling.
armàdio nm cupboard, wardrobe.
armaiuòlo nm gunsmith, armourer.
armaménto nm armament, arming, weapons pl.
armàre vt to arm, equip, provide; -**rsi** vr to arm oneself, take up arms.
armàta nf army, navy; **corpo d'a.** army corps.
armàto a armed, equipped; (el) armoured; (building) reinforced; **a màno armàta** by force of arms.
armatúra nf armour, armouring, framework; (el) armature.
Armènia nf (geogr) Armenia.
armèno a nm Armenian.
arménto nm herd of cattle.
armistízio nm armistice.
armonía nf harmony, concord.
armonizzàre vt to harmonize.
Arnàldo nm pr Arnold.
arnése nm tool, utensil.
àrnia nf beehive.
aròma nf aroma, fragrance.
àrpa nf harp.
arpeggiàre vi to play the harp, play in arpeggios.
arpía nf harpy.
arpióne nm hook, hinge.
àrra nf earnest money, pledge.
arrabbiàre vt to make angry; -**rsi** to get angry.
arrabbiàto a furious; rabid.
arrampicàrsi vr to climb.
arrecàre vt to bring, cause.
arredaménto nm furnishings.
arredàre vt to fit out, furnish.
arrèdo nm furniture, furnishings.
arrèndersi vr to surrender, yield, submit.
arrestàre vt to stop, seize, arrest; -**rsi** vr to stop.
arrèsto nm arrest, stop, pause; **in a.** under arrest.
arretràre vt to pull back, withdraw; -**rsi** vr to draw back, recoil.
arretràto a backward; (com) outstanding, in arrears; nm (also pl) arrears pl.
arricchíre vt to enrich, embellish; vi -**rsi** vr to grow rich, thrive.
arricchíto nm profiteer, nouveau riche.
arricciàre vt to curl; **a. il nàso to** frown, show disgust.
arrídere vi to smile upon.
Arrígo nm pr Henry.

arrínga nf harangue, speech.
arringàre vi to harangue.
arrischiàre vt to risk, hazard; -**rsi** vr to venture, dare.
arrischiàto a risky, venturesome, rash.
arrivàre vi to arrive; (fig) to achieve, succeed, happen, understand, fit, be reduced to.
arrivàto a successful; nm a successful man.
arrivedérci(-la) interj goodbye.
arrivísmo nm social climbing.
arrivista nmf social climber, gogetter.
arrívo nm arrival.
arrochíre vt to make hoarse; -**rsi** vr become hoarse.
arrogànte a arrogant, overbearing.
arrogànza nf arrogance.
arrolàre vt to enrol, register; -**rsi** vr to enrol oneself, enlist.
arrossíre vi to blush, be ashamed.
arrostíre vt to roast, toast.
arròsto nm roast meat.
arrotàre vt to whet, grind, wear smooth.
arrotíno nm knife-grinder.
arrotolàre vt to roll up.
arrotondàre vt to round; -**rsi** vr to become round, plump.
arrovellàrsi vr to get angry, worry.
arroventàre vt to make red-hot.
arrovesciàre vt to turn inside out, overthrow; -**rsi** vr to capsize, turn over.
arrovèscio, a rovèscio ad against the grain, on the wrong side, the reverse way.
arruffàre vt to ruffle, tousle, confuse; -**rsi** vr to get ruffled, confused.
arruginíre vi -**rsi** vr to rust, grow rusty.
arsèlla nf mussel.
arsenàle nm arsenal.
arsènico nm arsenic.
àrso a burnt, dried up.
arsúra nf burning heat, drought, thirst.
àrte nf art, skill, profession, artifice.
artéfice nm artificer, artisan, creator.
artèria nf artery; thoroughfare.
àrtico pl -**ici** a arctic, northern.
articolàre vt to articulate, pronounce; a articular.
articolàto a articulate; jointed, hinged.
artícolo nm article; **a. di fóndo** (in newspapers) leading article, leader, (US) editorial; **articoli sportívi** pl sports goods, (US) sporting goods.
artificiàle a artificial.
artifício nm artifice, contrivance, cunning.
artificióso a artful, crafty, sly.
artigianàto nm artisans pl, handicraft, small industry.
artigiàno a (of an) artisan; nm artisan, craftsman.
artiglière nm gunner, artilleryman.

artiglieria nf (mil) artillery.
artiglio nm claw, talon, clutch.
artista nmf artist, artiste, actor, actress, singer.
artistico pl **-ici** a artistic.
àrto nm (anat) limb.
Artúro nm pr Arthur.
arzigogolàre vt to cavil, follow a fantastic argument.
arzigògolo nm cavil, whim.
arzillo a sprightly, nimble.
ascèlla nf armpit.
ascendènte a ascending, ascendant, -ent; nm ascendency, ascendant, ancestor.
ascendènza nf ancestors pl; ascendancy.
ascéndere vi to ascend, rise; amount to.
ascensióne nf ascent, ascension, Ascension Day.
ascensóre nm lift, (US) elevator.
ascésa nf ascent, accession.
ascèsso nm abscess.
ascèta nm ascetic, recluse.
ascètico pl **-ici** a ascetic.
ascetismo nm asceticism.
àscia nf axe, hatchet.
asciugacapélli nm hair-drier.
asciugamàno nm towel.
asciugàre vt to dry, wipe.
asciugatríce (automàtica) nf spin-drier.
asciútto a dry, thin, penniless; **all'a.** in a dry place; **restàre all'a.** to be without money, news etc.
ascoltàre vt to listen, hear, attend; (med) sound.
ascoltatóre nm **-tríce** nf listener, hearer.
ascoltazióne nf, **ascólto** nm listening, hearing; (med) auscultation; **stàre in ascólto** to listen; **dàre ascólto** to lend an ear.
asfàlto nm asphalt.
asfissía nf asphyxia.
asfissiàre vt to asphyxiate.
Àsia nf Asia.
asiàtico pl **-ici** a nm Asiatic, Asian.
asilo nm refuge.
asinàta nf foolish action, foolish remark.
asinería nf stupidity, foolish action, foolish remark.
àsino nm ass.
àsma nf asthma.
asmàtico pl **-ici** a asthmatic.
àsola nf buttonhole.
asparago pl **-gi** nm asparagus.
aspèrgere vt to sprinkle.
asperità nf asperity, harshness.
aspettàre vt to wait for, await; **-rsi** vr to expect, look for.
aspettativa nf expectation, hope; temporary discharge; **in a.** ad on the reserve list.
aspettazióne nf expectation.
aspètto nm aspect, appearance, look; **sàla d'a.** nf waiting room.

aspirànte a aspiring to, sucking up; nmf candidate, competitor.
aspirapólvere nm vacuum cleaner.
aspiràre vt to inhale, suck up; vi aspire to, be a candidate for.
aspirina nf aspirin.
asportàbile a removable.
asportàre vi to remove, extirpate.
asportazióne nf removal.
asprézza nf bitterness, harshness, roughness, sharpness.
asprigno a sourish.
àspro a bitter, rough, sharp, severe, hard.
assaggiàre vt to sample, taste, try.
assàggio nm trial, testing, sampling.
assài nm plenty; ad much, very, enough.
assalire vt to assail, attack.
assaltàre vt to assault, attack.
assàlto nm assault, attack, onset.
assaporàre vt to savour, taste; (fig) to relish.
assassinàre vt to assassinate, murder.
assassínio nm assassination, murder.
assassíno nm assassin, murderer.
àsse nm axis; nf board, plank.
assecondàre vt to favour, support.
assediàre vt to besiege, crowd round.
assèdio nm siege; (fig) pestering.
assegnaménto nm assignment, allotment; reliance.
assegnàre vt to allow, assign, award, fix.
assegnazióne nf assignment, allotment.
assègno nm allowance, cheque; **a. bancàrio** (com) draft; **a. postàle** money order.
assemblèa nf assembly, meeting.
assembraménto nm throng, concourse, assembling.
assembràre vt to assemble; **-rsi** vr to assemble.
assennatézza nf commonsense, wisdom, prudence.
assennàto a sensible, wise, prudent.
assènso nm assent, consent.
assènte a absent; nmf absentee.
assentíre vi to assent, consent, approve.
assènza nf absence.
assènzio nm absinthe.
asserire vt to assert, affirm.
asserragliàre vt to barricade; **-rsi** vr to barricade oneself.
asserzióne nf assertion, declaration.
assessóre nm assessor, magistrate.
assestaménto, assèsto nm arrangement, settlement.
assestàre vt to arrange, settle, set in order, adjust; deliver (a blow).
assetàto a thirsty, dry, eager.
assettàre vt to arrange, trim, put in order; **-rsi** vr to adorn oneself, tidy oneself up.
assètto nm good order, trim; **méttere in a.** to put in order, trim.
asseveràre vi to assert, affirm, declare.

assicuràre vt to secure, assure, declare, insure; (post) register; -rsi vr to fasten oneself, secure for oneself, make sure, insure oneself.

assicurazióne nf assurance, insurance, pledge.

assideraménto nm **assiderazióne** nf frostbite.

assideràre vt to chill, benumb; vi be benumbed, freeze.

assiduità nf assiduity, diligence.

assìduo a assiduous, diligent.

assième ad together.

assillàre vt to urge; harass.

assimilàre vt to assimilate, absorb.

assimilazióne nf assimilation.

assise nf assizes pl.

assistènte nmf attendant, assistant; a. di vólo air hostess.

assistènza nf assistance, aid, help.

assìstere vti to assist, help; be present.

àsso nm ace; **piantàre in a.** to leave in the lurch.

associàre vt to associate, join, take into partnership; -rsi vr to join, become a partner, subscribe.

associazióne nf association.

assodàre vt to consolidate, harden; make sure.

assoggettàre vt to subject, subdue; -rsi vr to subject oneself, submit.

assolàto a exposed to the sun, sunny.

assoldàre vt to recruit; -rsi vr to enlist.

assòlto a acquitted, absolved, released.

assolutaménte ad absolutely.

assolùto a absolute, positive.

assoluzióne nf absolution, acquittal.

assòlvere vt to acquit, absolve, release.

assomigliàre vt to compare; vi to resemble; -rsi vr to be alike, resemble each other.

assonnàto a sleepy, drowsy.

assopìre vt to make sleepy, appease; -rsi vr to doze off.

assorbènte a absorbent; càrta a. blotting paper; a. igiènico nm sanitary towel, (US) sanitary napkin.

assorbìre vt to absorb.

assordaménto, nm deafening.

assordànte a deafening.

assordàre vt to stun, deafen.

assordiménto nm deafening.

assordìre vt to deafen; vi to become deaf.

assortiménto nm assortment, stock.

assortìre vt to stock; (fig) to match.

assortìto a assorted, stocked, matched.

assòrto a absorbed.

assottigliàre vt to thin, sharpen, diminish; -rsi vr to grow thin, diminish.

assuefàre vt to accustom, inure; -rsi vr to grow accustomed, inured.

assúmere vt to assume, take on, engage, raise (to a dignity), undertake, take up.

assúnto nm undertaking, charge, assumption.

assunzióne nf assumption, accession, Assumption.

assurdità nf absurdity.

assúrdo a absurd; nm absurdity.

àsta nf pole, staff, rod, lance; (of writing) stroke; auction.

astànte a present, standing by; nmf bystander, spectator; **mèdico a.** doctor on duty.

astanterìa nf first-aid post.

astèmio a abstemious; nm abstainer.

astenérsi vr to abstain.

astensióne nf abstention.

astinènte a abstinent.

astinènza nf abstinence.

àstio nm hatred, envy, grudge, spite.

astióso a rancorous, spiteful.

astràrre vt to abstract; -rsi vr to turn one's mind from.

astràtto a abstract, abstracted; nm abstract.

astrazióne nf abstraction, absent-mindedness.

astringènte a astringent.

àstro nm star.

astrologìa nf astrology.

astrològico pl -ici a astrological.

astròlogo pl -gì, -ghì nm astrologer.

astronàuta nm astronaut.

astronàutica nf astronautics.

astronomìa nf astronomy.

astronòmico pl -ici a astronomical.

astrònomo nm astronomer.

astrúso a abstruse, obscure.

astúccio nm box, case, sheath.

astutézza nf astuteness, cunning.

astúto a crafty, cunning, deceitful.

astúzia nf astuteness, artfulness, trick.

ateìsmo nm atheism.

Atène nf Athens; **atenièse** a nmf Athenian.

atenèo nm athenaeum, university.

àteo a atheistic; nm atheist.

atlànte nm atlas.

atlàntico pl -ici a gigantic, Atlantic; nm (geogr) the Atlantic.

atlèta nmf athlete.

atlètica nf athletics.

atlètico a athletic.

atmosfèra nf atmosphere.

atòmico pl -ici a atomic.

àtomo nm atom.

atonìa nf atony.

àtono a unstressed.

àtrio nm porch, vestibule.

atróce a atrocious, terrible, cruel.

atrocità nf atrocity.

atrofìa nf atrophy.

atrofizzàre vt to atrophy; -rsi vr to atrophy, waste away.

attaccabottóne nm bore, talker.

attaccabrighe nm wrangler.

attaccaménto nm attachment.

attaccapànni nm hatstand, coat-hanger.

attaccàre vt to tie, fasten, stick, sew on, attack; (horses) harness; hang up; vi take root; be contagious; **a. un bottóne** (fig) to buttonhole someone; **-rsi** vr to stick, to become attached to; quarrel.

attaccatíccio a sticky; (med) contagious; nm burnt taste.

attàcco pl **-àcchi** nm attack, assault; (el) connection, plug.

attecchíre vi to take root, thrive.

atteggiaménto nm attitude.

atteggiàre vt to express in gesture; **-rsi** vr to assume an attitude, expression, pose as.

attempàto a elderly.

attendàrsi vr to camp, pitch tents.

attendènte nm (mil) orderly, batman.

attèndere vt to await, expect; vi to wait for, attend to.

attendíbile a reliable.

attenérsi vr to conform (to).

attentàre vt to attempt; **-rsi** vr to dare.

attentàto nm attempt, outrage.

attènti! interj (mil) attention!

attènto a attentive, careful.

attenuànte a extenuating; nf extenuating circumstance.

attenuàre vt to attenuate, lessen, extenuate.

attenzióne nf care, application.

atterràggio nm (av) landing.

atterràre vti to knock down; (av) to land; (fig) humiliate.

atterríre vt to frighten, terrify; **-rsi** vr to become terrified.

attésa nf waiting, expectation, suspense.

attéso a awaited, expected, longed for.

attestàre vt to attest, testify.

attestàto nm attestation, certificate, proof, token.

attestazióne nf attestation, testimony, token.

attiguità nf contiguity.

attíguo a contiguous, adjacent, next.

attillàrsi vr to dress smartly, dress so as to show off one's figure.

attillàto a close-fitting, smartly dressed.

àttimo nm moment, instant.

attinènte a pertaining, belonging to, relating.

attinènza nf affinity, relation.

attíngere vt (water etc) to draw; (information etc) to get.

attiràre vt to attract, draw, entice; **-rsi** vr to draw upon oneself.

attitúdine nf aptitude, skill; attitude.

attivaménte ad actively, busily.

attivàre vt to activate, set in motion.

attivísmo nm activism.

attivísta nmf activist.

attività nf activity, assets pl.

attívo a active; (com) receivable; nm (com) assets pl, credit account.

attizzàre vt to stir up, incite.

attizzatóio nm poker.

àtto a fit, apt; nm act, action, deed, gesture, certificate, (com) bill; pl proceedings, minutes.

attònito a astonished, amazed.

attòrcere, attorcigliàre vt to twist, wring.

attorcigliaménto nm twisting.

attóre nm actor.

attorniàre vt to enclose, surround.

attórno prep about, round; ad roundabout.

attossicaménto nm poisoning.

attossicàre vt to poison.

attraènte a attractive.

attràrre vt to attract, allure.

attrattíva nf attraction, charm.

attraversàre vt to cross, pass through; thwart.

attravèrso prep across, through.

attrazióne nf attraction.

attrezzàre vt to equip, fit out, supply with, rig.

attrezzatúra nf equipment, plant, organization, rigging.

attrézzo nm tool, implement.

attribuíre vt to ascribe, attribute, assign; **-rsi** vr to claim.

attribúto nm attribute.

attríce nf actress.

attristàre vt to sadden.

attríto nm friction, (fig) dissension.

attruppàrsi vr to gather in crowds, flock together.

attuàbile a practicable, feasible.

attuàle a present, real, actual.

attualità nf actuality, present, reality.

attuàre vt to effect, execute, perform, realize.

attuazióne nf carrying out, realization.

attuffàre vt to immerse, plunge, dip; **-rsi** vr to dive, plunge into the water.

attutíre vt to calm, ease, deaden.

audàce a audacious, bold.

àudio nm (tv) sound; a. **visivo** a audio-visual.

auditóre nm hearer, junior judge.

auditòrio nm auditorium.

audizióne nf audition.

àuge nm apogee; **èssere in a.** vi to be at the zenith of one's fortune.

auguràre vt to wish, augur, foretell; **-rsi** vr to hope.

augúrio nm good wish, augury, omen.

augústo a august, royal.

àula nf hall, classroom.

aumentàre vti to augment, increase, enlarge, grow.

auménto nm growth, increase; (in pay) rise, (US) raise.

àureo a golden, gold.

aurèola nf halo, glory.

auròra nf dawn.

ausiliàre a nmf **-àrio** a auxiliary.

auspício nm auspice; protection, patronage.

austerità nf austerity.

austèro a austere, severe.

Austràlia nf Australia.

australiàna nf pursuit cycle race on a track.

australiàno a nm Australian.

Àustria nf Austria.

austríaco pl **-aci** a nm Austrian.

aut-aut nm dilemma.

autarchía nf autarchy, economic self-sufficiency.

autèntica nf authentication, authoritative approval.

autenticàre vt to authenticate, prove; **còpia autenticàta** certified copy.

autenticità nf authenticity.

autèntico pl **-ici** a authentic.

autísta nm driver, chauffeur.

àuto nf motor car.

autobiografía nf autobiography.

autoblinda inv, **autoblindàta** nf, **autoblindo** inv armoured car.

àutobus nm bus, omnibus.

autocarovàna nf motor convoy.

autocàrro nm lorry, (US) truck.

autocorrièra nf long-distance bus.

autocrazía nf autocracy.

autodidàtta nmf self-taught person.

autodifésa nf self-defence.

autòdromo nm autodrome, circuit.

autògrafo a autographic; nm autograph.

autòma nm automaton.

automàtico pl **-ici** a automatic.

automazióne nf automation.

automèzzo nm motor vehicle.

automòbile nf motor car, (US) automobile; a. **di piàzza** taxi.

automobilísmo nm motoring.

automobilísta nmf motorist.

automobilístico pl **-ici** a motor; **còrsa a.** motor race.

autonomía nf autonomy, self-government; (av, aut) range.

autònomo a autonomous, self-governing.

autoparchéggio, autopàrco pl **-chi** nm car park, parking, (US) parking lot.

autopómpa nf fire-engine.

autopsía nf autopsy.

autóre nm author.

autorespiratóre nm aqualung.

autorévole a authoritative, competent.

autoriméssa nf garage.

autorità nf authority.

autorizzàre vt to authorize.

autorizzazióne nf authorization, permit.

autoscàtto nm (phot) automatic release.

autoscuòla nf driving school.

autostòp nm hitch-hiking; **autostoppísta** nmf hitch-hiker; **fàre l'a.** to thumb a lift, hitch-hike.

autostràda nf motorway.

autotrèno nm motor lorry with trailer, (US) truck.

autríce nf authoress.

autunnàle a autumnal.

autúnno nm autumn, (US) fall.

avallàre vt to guarantee (also fig).

avàllo nm (com) guarantee (also fig).

avambràccio nm forearm.

avàna nm Havana (cigar); a light brown.

avanguàrdia nf vanguard.

avànti ad and prep before, forward, in front of, rather (than); interj forward!

avantièri ad the day before yesterday.

avanzaménto nm advancement, progress, promotion.

avanzàre vt to put forward, advance, promote, surpass, improve, save, put by, be creditor for; vi to advance, be left; **-rsi** vr get on, advance.

avanzàta nf advance.

avànzo nm remainder, remnant, residue, ancient ruin; **d'a.** ad over and above.

avaría nf damage.

avariàre vt to damage.

avarízia nf avarice, niggardliness.

avàro a avaricious, miserly; nm miser.

Àve interj Hail!

avéna nf oats.

avére vt and aux to have, obtain, have on, have to, possess; nm property, wealth, credit.

aviatóre nm airman, **-trice** nf airwoman.

aviazióne nf aviation.

avidaménte ad avidly, greedily, eagerly.

avidità nf avidity, greed, eagerness.

àvido a avid, greedy.

aviolínea nf airline.

avioriméssa nf hangar.

avòrio nm ivory.

avvallaménto nm cavity, subsidence.

avvallàre vt to lower; guarantee; **-rsi** vr to fall in, subside.

avvaloràre vt to strengthen; give value to; **-rsi** to become stronger.

avvampàre vi to burn, be on fire, be inflamed.

avvantaggiàre vt to advantage; **-rsi** vr to better oneself, derive advantage.

avvedérsi vr to perceive, notice.

avvedutézza nf foresight, sagacity.

avvedúto a cautious, provident, sagacious.

avvelenaménto nm poisoning.

avvelenàre vt to poison.

avvenènte a charming, agreeable.

avvenènza nf attractiveness, grace.

avveniménto nm event, incident; (to the throne) accession.

avveníre vi and impers to happen, nm future.

avventàre vt to hurl; vi to be gaudy; **-rsi** vr to throw oneself.

avventàto a imprudent, rash.

avventízio *a* temporary, adventitious.

avvènto *nm* advent, arrival; accession.

avventóre *nm* customer, purchaser.

avventúra *nf* adventure, chance.

avventuràre *vt* -rsi *vr* to venture.

avventurière *nm* adventurer.

avventuróso *a* adventurous, fortunate.

avveràre *vt* to fulfil, prove; -rsi *vr* to come true.

avvèrbio *nm* adverb.

avversàre *vt* to oppose, resist, thwart.

avversàrio *a* contrary, opposing, hostile; *nm* opponent, enemy.

avversióne *nf* aversion, dislike.

avversità *nf* adversity.

avvèrso *a* adverse, contrary.

avvertènza *nf* notice, introduction, care, attention.

avvertimento *nm* notice, warning.

avvertíre *vt* to inform, advise, warn, perceive; *vi* to take care.

avvezzàre *vt* to accustom.

avvèzzo *a* accustomed, used.

avviaménto *nm* setting out, beginning, start.

avviàre *vt* to set going, prepare, begin, start; -rsi *vr* to get going, succeed.

avviàto *a* prosperous.

avvicendàre *vi* to alternate; -rsi *vr* to take turns.

avvicinàre *vt* to put near; -rsi *vr* to approach, draw near.

avvilimento *nm* humiliation, dejection.

avvilíre *vt* to dishearten, abase, humiliate; -rsi *vr* to lose heart, humiliate oneself.

avviluppàre *vt* to entangle, wrap up; -rsi *vr* to wrap oneself up, get entangled.

avvisàglia *nf* skirmish; foreshadowing.

avvisàre *vt* to advise, inform, warn; *vi* to judge, think; -rsi *vr* to think, consider.

avvisàto *a* cautious, prudent.

avvíso *nm* advice, news, bill, advertisement, announcement, warning; **a mio a.** in my opinion.

avvistàre *vt* to sight.

avvitàre *vt* to screw.

avviticchiàre *vt* to twine, twist; -rsi *vr* to be entwined.

avvivàre *vt* to enliven, brighten; -rsi *vr* to become lively, (of fire and fig) rekindle.

avvizzíre *vi* to wither, fade.

avvocatéssa *nf* lady lawyer.

avvocàto *nm* lawyer, advocate, solicitor, defender.

avvocatúra *nf* legal profession.

avvòlgere *vt* to wrap round, entwine; -rsi *vr* to wrap oneself, wind round something.

avvoltóio *nm* vulture.

avvoltolàre *vt* to roll up; -rsi *vr* to roll oneself up, wallow.

aziènda *nf* business, firm, management.

azionàre *vt* to set in action, set going.

azióne *nf* action, deed, battle, movement; (com) share; **a. ordinària** ordinary share, (US) common stock; **a. preferenziàle** preference share, (US) preferred stock.

azionísta *nmf* shareholder, (US) stockholder.

azzannàre *vt* to seize with the teeth.

azzardàre *vt* to hazard, risk; -rsi *vr* to venture.

azzàrdo *nm* hazard, risk; **giuòco d'a.** game of chance.

azzardóso *a* hazardous, risky.

azzeccàre *vt* to hit the mark, guess, chance on.

àzzima *nf* unleavened bread.

azzimàre *vt* to dress smartly; -rsi *vr* to dress oneself up.

azzimàto *a* dressed up.

àzzimo *a* unleavened.

azzittíre *vt* to silence.

azzuffàrsi *vr* to come to blows, scuffle.

azzúrro *a* blue, azure.

B

babbèo *a* silly, foolish; *nm* blockhead.

bàbbo *nm* (fam) daddy.

babbúccia *nf* slipper.

babbuíno *nm* baboon; (fig) fool.

babórdo *nm* (naut) larboard.

bacàre *vi* -rsi *vr* to be worm-eaten, rot.

bàcca *nf* berry.

baccalà *nm* stockfish, cod dried and salted; (fig) tall thin person; fool.

baccàno *nm* great noise, tumult.

baccellieràto *nm* bachelor's degree.

baccellière *nm* (academic) bachelor.

baccèllo *nm* pod; (fig) fool.

bacchétta *nf* rod, staff, stick, wand, maulstick.

bacchettàta *nf* stroke of the cane.

bacchiàre *vt* (fruit) to beat down.

Bàcco *nm* *pr* Bacchus; **per B. by Jove!**

bachèca *nf* show-case.

bacheròzzo *nm* grub, worm.

baciàre *vt* to kiss; -rsi *vr* to (exchange a) kiss.

bacíle *nm* basin.

bacíllo *nm* bacillus.

bacinèlla *nf* small basin.

bacíno *nm* basin, wash-hand basin; (anat) pelvis; (naut) dock; **b. carbonífero** coalfield.

bàcio *nm* kiss.

bàco *pl* **bàchi** *nm* worm, silkworm.

bàda, tenere a *vt* to hold at bay.

badàre *vi* to mind, pay attention to, take care of.

badéssa *nf* abbess.

badía nf abbey.
badíle nm shovel.
bàffo nm moustache, whisker.
baffúto a moustached.
bagagliàio nm luggage van, guard's van, (US) baggage car.
bagàglio nm luggage.
bagattèlla nf trifle, small matter.
baggianàta nf foolery.
baggiàno nm fool.
baglióre nm flash of light, gleam.
bagnànte nmf bather.
bagnàre vt to moisten, wet, bath; -rsi vr to get wet; bathe.
bagnatúra nf bathing, bathing season.
bagníno nm bathing attendant.
bàgno nm bath; bathe, (US) bath; fàre un b. vi to have a bath, to bathe; stànza da b. bathroom.
bagórdo nm orgy, revelling.
Bahàma (le) nf pl the Bahamas pl.
bàia nf bay; joke, banter.
bàio a nm (colour and horse) bay.
baionétta nf bayonet.
bàita nf (alpine) hut.
balaústra, balaustràta nf balustrade.
balbettàre vi to stammer, stutter.
balbettío nm **balbúzia** nf stammer, stammering.
balbuziènte a stammering; nmf stammerer.
Balcàni nm pl the Balkans pl.
balcànico a -**ici** a Balkan.
balconàta nf balcony, (theat) balcony.
balcóne nm balcony.
baldacchíno nm canopy.
baldànza nf boldness, assurance.
baldanzóso a bold, confident.
bàldo a bold, fearless.
baldòria nf bonfire; revel; fàre b. vi to feast, make merry.
Baldovíno nm pr Baldwin.
baléna nf whale.
balenàre vi to lighten, flash.
balenièra nf whaler (ship).
balenío nm (continual) lightning.
baléno nm lightning; in un b. ad immediately, in a flash.
baléstra nf crossbow.
bàlia nf (wet) nurse.
balía nf power, mercy.
balística nf ballistics.
bàlla nf bale, pack; (sl) fib.
ballàbile a suitable for dancing; nm (mus) dance.
ballàre vi to dance.
ballàta nf ballad, ballade.
ballatóio nm gallery, platform.
ballerína nf dancer, dancing girl, ballet-dancer.
balleríno nm dancer, dancing partner.
ballétto nm ballet, interlude.
bàllo nm ball, dance.
ballonzolàre vi to hop about.
ballòtta nf boiled chestnut; ballot.
ballottàggio nm (second) ballot, ballotage

balneàre, balneàrio a bathing.
baloccàre vt to amuse; -rsi vr to amuse oneself, dally, toy with.
balòcco pl -**òcchi** nm plaything, toy.
balordàggine nf stupidity.
balórdo a stupid; nm fool, numskull.
balsàmico pl -**ici** a balmy.
bàlsamo nm balm, balsam.
Bàltico a nm (geogr) Baltic.
baluàrdo nm bastion, bulwark.
bàlza nf cliff, rock; flounce.
balzàre vi to bounce, jump, spring.
bàlzo nm jump, spring.
bambàgia nf cotton wool.
bambína nf little girl.
bambinàia nf nursery governess.
bambinésco pl -**chi** a childish.
bambíno nm baby, child, little boy.
bàmbola nf doll.
bambù nm bamboo.
banàle a common, trivial.
banalità nf banality, triviality.
banàna nf banana; **banàno** banana (-tree).
banca nf bank.
bancarèlla nf street stall.
bancàrio a bank, banking.
bancarótta nf bankruptcy; fàre b. to go bankrupt.
bancarottière nm bankrupt.
banchétto nm banquet.
banchière nm banker.
banchína nf small bench; quay, wharf, waterfront; platform.
banchísa nf ice-pack.
bànco pl -**chi** nm bench, counter, desk, bank, stall, (of jury) box; b. di sàbbia sand bank; b. di ghiàccio ice floe; b. di ròcce reef; b. del lòtto lottery office.
bancogíro nm (com) clearing.
banconòta nf banknote, note, (US) bill.
bànda nf band, side, stripe, gang; da b. ad aside.
banderuòla nf pennon; vane, weathercock.
bandièra nf banner, flag.
bandíre vt to proclaim, announce; banish.
bandíta n. preserve; b. di càccia game preserve.
banditismo nm banditry.
bandíto a outlawed, exiled; nm bandit, outlaw.
banditóre nm public crier, auctioneer.
bàndo nm ban, banishment; announcement.
bandolièra nf shoulder belt.
bàndolo nm head of a skein.
bar nm bar.
bàra nf bier, coffin.
baràcca nf booth, stall; barrack, hut.
baraónda nf confusion, disorder, tumult.
baràre vi (at play) to cheat.
bàratro nm abyss, gulf.
barattàre vt to barter, chaffer, exchange.

barattería *nf* embezzlement, swindling.

barattière *nm* barterer; embezzler, swindler.

baràttolo *nm* small tin or jar.

bàrba *nf* beard; rootlets *pl*; **fàre la b.** *vi* to shave; **fàrsi la b.** to shave (oneself).

barbabiétola *nf* beetroot, (US) beet.

barbagiànni *nm* owl; simpleton.

barbàglio *nm* dazzle.

Bàrbara *nf pr* Barbara.

barbàrico *pl* **-ici**, **bàrbaro** *a* barbarous, cruel.

barbàrie, **barbarità** *nf* barbarity.

barbicàre *vi* to take root.

barbière *nm* barber.

barbóne *nm* long beard, long-bearded man, tramp; poodle.

barbóso *a* boring.

barbugliaménto *nm* stammering, stuttering.

barbugliàre *vi* to stammer, stutter.

barbúto *a* bearded.

bàrca *nf* boat; (*fig*) business.

barcàccia *nf* old boat; (*theat*) stage box.

barcaiuòlo *nm* boatman.

barcamenàrsi *vr* to manage cleverly, steer a middle course.

barcaròla *nf* (*mus*) barcarolle.

Barcellóna *nf* Barcelona.

barchétta *nf* **-o** *nm* small boat.

barcollàre *vi* to rock, sway, totter, waver.

barcollío *nm* rocking.

barcóne *nm* barge, large boat.

bardàre *vt* to harness.

bàrdo *nm* bard.

barèlla *nf* stretcher, handcart.

bargíglio *nm* wattle.

barile *nm* barrel, cask.

barísta *nmf* barman, barmaid.

barítono *nm* baritone.

barlúme *nm* gleam, glimmer.

bàro *nm* cheat, cardsharper.

barocciàio *nm* carter.

baroccíno *nm* small cart, handcart.

baròccio *nm* cart.

baròcco *pl* **-chi** *a* baroque, bizarre; *nm* baroque.

baròmetro *nm* barometer.

baróne *nm* baron.

baronéssa *nf* baroness.

baronétto *nm* baronet.

bàrra *nf* bar, rod, (*naut*) tiller.

barricàre *vt* to barricade.

barricàta *nf* barricade.

barrièra *nf* barrier, palisade.

Bartolomèo *nm pr* Bartholomew.

barúffa *nf* quarrel, brawl.

barzellétta *nf* joke, funny story.

basàre *vt* to base, ground; **-rsi** *vr* to base oneself.

bàse *nf* base, basis, ground; **b. aèrea** air base.

baseball *nm* baseball.

basétta *nf* side whisker.

Basiléa *nf* (*geogr*) Basle.

basílica *nf* basilica.

basílico *pl* **-ichi** *nm* basil.

bassézza *nf* baseness, meanness.

bàsso *a* low, short, mean, (*price*) cheap, (*of material*) narrow, (*mus*) bass.

bassofóndo *nm* (*naut*) shallow; the underworld.

bassorilièvo *nm* bas-relief.

bassòtto *a* stout and short; *nm* tubby man; basset, dachshund.

bassúra *nf* low ground.

bàsta! *interj* enough, stop, that will do.

bastàrdo *a nm* bastard, illegitimate.

bastàre *v impers* to be enough, suffice.

bastiménto *nm* ship, vessel.

bastióne *nm* bastion, rampart.

bàsto *nm* pack saddle.

bastonàre *vt* to beat, cudgel.

bastonàta, **bastonatúra** *nf* beating, thrashing.

bastóne *nm* stick, (US) cane; cudgel, truncheon; (*cards*) clubs.

batòsta *nf* blow, misfortune.

battàglia *nf* battle.

battagliàre *vi* to fight, struggle.

battaglièro *a* fighting, warlike.

battàglio *nm* bell-clapper.

battaglióne *nm* battalion.

battàna *nf* punt.

battellière *nm* boatman.

battèllo *nm* boat; **b. a vapóre** steamer.

battènte *nm* (*of a door*) leaf; shutter; doorknocker.

bàttere *vt* to beat, knock, thrash, throb; (*of waves*) wash; (*of clocks*) strike; **b. bandièra** to sail under colours; **b. càssa** to ask for money; **b. i dènti** to chatter (with cold); **b. le màni** to clap; **b. monéta** to mint money; *vi* to knock against, insist; **-rsi** *vr* to fight, duel; **bàttersela** *vr* to run away.

battería *nf* battery; set of kitchen utensils.

battesimàle *a* baptismal.

battésimo *nm* baptism, christening.

battezzàre *vt* to baptize, christen.

battibaléno *nm* **in un b.** in the twinkling of an eye.

battibécco *pl* **-cchi** *nm* quarrel.

batticuòre *nm* palpitation, fear.

battipànni *nm* carpet-beater.

battistèro *nm* baptistery.

battistràda *nm* outrider, guide; (*of tyres*) tread.

bàttito *nm* heartbeat, palpitation, throbbing, ticking.

battitóre *nm* beater, thresher; (*sport*) server, batsman, striker.

battúta *nf* beating, remark, cue, (*mus*) bar.

battúto *a* beaten, trodden; (*of iron*) wrought; *nm* (*of meat*) hash, stuffing.

batúffolo *nm* small wad.

baúle *nm* trunk, travelling chest.

bàva *nf* slaver, foam; floss silk.

bavaglíno *nm* child's bib.

bavàglio nm gag.
bavarése a nmf Bavarian.
Bavièra nf Bavaria.
bàvero nm coat collar.
bavóso a slavering.
bazàr nm bazaar.
bàzza nf jutting chin; good luck.
bazzècola nf nonsense, trifle.
bazzicàre vt to frequent, haunt.
beàre vt (poet) to make happy; -rsi vr to delight in.
beatificàre vt to beatify.
beatificazióne nf beatification.
beatitúdine nf beatitude, bliss.
beàto a happy, blissful, blessed.
Beatríce nf pr Beatrice, Beatrix.
beccàccia nf woodcock.
beccaccíno nm snipe.
beccàio nm butcher.
beccamòrti nm grave-digger.
beccàre vt to peck; -rsi vr to win, get; (fig) to quarrel.
beccheggiàre vi (naut) to pitch.
becchéggio nm (naut) pitching.
becchíme nm birds' food.
becchíno nm sexton.
bécco pl bécchi nm beak; (of gas) burner; he-goat; cuckold.
beccúccio nm spout.
bécero nm (fam) low fellow, rascal.
becerúme nm cads pl.
beduíno a nm Bedouin.
Befàna nf Epiphany; old woman taking the place of Father Christmas in Italian tales; ugly deformed woman.
bèffa nf jest, mockery, trick.
beffàrdo a mocking; nm mocker.
beffàre vt to mock, ridicule; -rsi vr to deride, make game of.
beffeggiàre vt to deride, mock.
bèga nf dispute; troublesome business.
beghína nf bigot, pietist.
belàre vi to bleat.
belàto nm bleating.
bèlga pl m bèlgi f bèlghe a nmf Belgian.
Bèlgio (il) nm Belgium.
Belgràdo nf Belgrade.
bèlla nf belle, sweetheart, girlfriend; (sport) final.
bellétto nm paint, rouge.
bellézza nf beauty; la b. di as much as.
bèllico pl -ici, bellicóso a warlike, bellicose.
bellimbústo nm dandy, fop.
bellíno a nice, pretty.
bèllo a beautiful, fine, handsome, nice; nm beautiful; lover, boyfriend, beau; beauty; ad finely, nicely; il b. è the best of it is that.
beltà nf beauty.
bélva nf wild beast.
belvedére nm belvedere; vettúra b. observation car.
bemòlle nm (mus) flat.
benché cj although.
bènda nf band, bandage.

bendàre vt to bandage, bind, blindfold.
bène nm good, love, happiness, affection; property, wealth; bèni mòbili nm pl movable property; bèni stàbili real estate; ad well, quite, right; per b. a decent, respectable; star b. to be well; volér b. a vt to like, be fond of.
benedettíno a nm Benedictine.
benedétto a blessed, holy.
benedíre vt to bless, consecrate.
benedizióne nf benediction, consecration.
beneducàto a well-bred.
benefattóre nm benefactor.
benefattríce nf benefactress.
beneficàre vt to benefit, do good to.
beneficènza nf beneficence, charity.
beneficiàre vi to benefit.
benefício, benefízio nm benefit profit; benefice.
benèfico p' -ici a beneficent, beneficial.
benemerènza nf merit.
benemèrito a deserving, meritorious.
beneplàcito nm approval, consent, convenience, option.
benèssere nm well-being.
benestànte a wealthy, well-to-do.
benestàre nm approval, endorsement.
benevolènza nf benevolence, favour.
benèvolo a benevolent, kind.
Bengàla (il) nm Bengal.
bengalése a nmf Bengali.
Beniamíno nm pr Benjamin.
benignità nf benignity, kindness.
benígno a benignant, benign.
beníno ad pretty well, fairly well.
benintéso ad agreed, understood, of course.
beníssimo ad very well, all right.
benóne ad splendidly, very well.
benpensànte a sensible; nmf orthodox, right-minded person.
benportànte a in good health.
benservíto nm testimonial, dismissal.
bensí cj but, rather.
bentornàto a nm welcome back.
benvenúto a nm welcome.
benvolére vt to like; fàrsi b. vr to make oneself liked, win popularity; nm benevolence, affection.
benzína nf petrol, (US) gasoline, benzine.
bére vt to drink, absorb; -rs. una còsa vr to believe implicitly in something; nm drinking, drink.
bergamòtto nm bergamot.
berlína nf pillory; (aut) saloon.
Berlíno nf Berlin.
Bèrna n, Berne.
Bernàrdo nm pr Bernard.
bernòccolo nm bump, swelling.
bernoccolúto a bumpy, knotty.
berrétta nf cap, biretta.
berrétto nm cap, beret; b. bàsco beret.

bersagliàre vt to shoot at, harass.
bersaglière nm sharpshooter, bersagliere.
bersàglio nm aim, butt, mark, target.
bèrta nf raillery, mockery; ram; magpie; **dar la b.** to mock.
Bèrta nf pr Bertha.
bertúccia nf monkey; ugly woman.
bestémmia nf blasphemy, oath.
bestemmiàre vi to curse, swear; vt to blaspheme.
béstia nf animal, beast, brute; idiot.
bestiàle a bestial, brutal.
bestialità nf bestiality, stupidity.
bestiàme nm cattle.
béttola nf tavern.
betúlla nf birch-tree.
bevànda nf drink, beverage.
beveràggio nm beverage, potion.
bevíbile a drinkable, nice to drink.
bevitóre nm, **-tríce** nf drinker.
bevúta nf draught, drinking.
biàcca nf white lead.
biàda nf corn, oats.
biancàstro a whitish.
biancheggiàre vi to grow white, show white.
biancheria nf linen; **b. personàle** underwear.
bianchétto nm white lead, whitewash, bleaching powder.
bianchézza nm whiteness.
biànco pl **-chi** a white, hoary, fair, pale; nm white, whitewash; blank; **lasciàre in b.** to leave blank; **di púnto in b.** ad point-blank.
biancospino pl **-ini** nm hawthorn.
biancúme nm mass of white.
biascicàre vt to mumble.
biasimàbile, biasimèvole a blameworthy, reprehensible.
biasimàre vt to blame, reprove.
biàsimo nm blame, reproof.
Bìbbia nf Bible.
biberon (French) nm inv feeding-bottle.
bíbita nf drink, refreshments pl.
bíblico a biblical.
bibliografía nf bibliography.
bibliogràfico pl **-ici** a bibliographical.
bibliògrafo nm bibliographer.
bibliotèca nf library.
bibliotecàrio nm librarian.
bicarbonàto nm bicarbonate.
bicchière nm drinking glass, tumbler.
bicchierino nm small glass.
biciclétta nf bicycle.
bicòcca nf small hill fort; hovel.
bidè nm bidet.
bidèllo nm beadle, janitor, porter, usher.
bidóne nm (large metal) receptacle.
bièco pl **-chi** a grim, squinting; ad askance.
biennàle a biennial.
biènnio nm space of two years.
biètola nf beet.
bietolóne nm simpleton, fool.

bifólco pl **-chi** nm ploughman, farm labourer, boor.
biforcàrsi vr to divide, fork.
bigamía nf bigamy.
bígamo nm bigamist.
bighellonàre vi to idle, loaf, lounge.
bighellóne nm idler, loafer.
bígio a grey.
bigiottería nf trinkets shop.
bigliettàio v **bigliettàrio**.
bigliettería nf booking office, (US) ticket office; box office.
bigliettàrio nm (of buses etc) conductor; ticket collector, booking clerk, (US railroad) ticket agent; box-office attendant.
bigliétto nm card, letter, note; ticket; **b. di andàta e ritórno** return ticket, (US) round-trip ticket; **b. d'abbonaménto** season ticket; **b. circolàre** tourist ticket.
bigodíno nm (hair-)curler.
bigottería nf **bigottísmo** nm bigotry.
bigòtto a bigoted; nm bigot.
bikini nm bikini.
bilància nf balance, pair of scales.
bilanciàre vt to balance, ponder.
bilancière nm pendulum, balance wheel, fly press, coining press.
bilàncio nm (com) balance sheet, budget.
bilateràle a bilateral.
bíle nf bile, anger.
biliàrdo nm billiards, billiard room, billiard table.
bílico pl **-chi** nm equipoise, balance, pivot.
bilíngue a bilingual; deceitful.
bilióso a bilious, irascible.
bìmba nf **bímbo** nm child, baby.
bimensíle a fortnightly.
bimestràle a bimonthly.
bimèstre nm period of two months.
bimetallísmo nm bimetallism.
bimotóre nm two-engined plane.
binàrio nm rails, railway track; único b. single track; dóppio b. double track; a binary.
bíndolo nm reel, winder, waterwheel; cheat
binòc(c)olo nm field-glass, operaglass, binocular(s).
biòccolo nm (of wool) flock; (of cotton) lump; candle drip; snowflake.
biochìmica nf biochemistry.
biografía nf biography.
biògrafo nm biographer.
biología nf biology.
biòlogo pl **-ogi** nm biologist.
biondeggiàre vi (of corn) to grow yellow, turn golden.
biondèzza nf fairness, flaxen colour.
biòndo a blond, fair, flaxen.
biòssido nm (chem) dioxide.
bipartíre vt to halve; **-rsi** vr to diverge, branch off.
bipartizióne nf division into two parts.
bípede a nm biped.
biplàno nm biplane.

bírba nm hare-brained youngster, rogue.

birbànte nm rogue, dishonest fellow.

birbonàta nf roguish act.

birbóne nm bad fellow, rascal; **fréddo b.** bitter cold.

birbonería nf knavery, roguery.

birichinàta nf mischievous trick.

birichíno a mischievous, cheeky; nm little scamp, urchin.

biríllo nm skittle, ninepin.

Birmània nf Burma.

birmàno a nm Burmese, Burman.

biro nf biro, ball(point) pen.

biroccíno nm small cart.

biròccio nm cart.

birra nf beer.

birràio nm brewer, publican.

birrería nf alehouse, pub, brewery.

bís interj encore.

bisàccia nf knapsack.

bisàvo, bisàvolo nm great-grandfather.

bisbètico pl -ici a crabbed, shrewish.

bisbigliàre vi to whisper.

bisbíglio nm whisper.

bisca nf gambling-house, gaming-den.

Biscàglia nf Biscay.

biscaiuòlo nm gambler.

biscazzière nm gambling-house keeper; (at billiards) marker; gambler.

biscia nf adder, snake.

biscottíno, biscòtto nm biscuit, (US) cookie.

bisestíle a bissextile; **ànno b.** nm leap year.

bisettimanàle a bi-weekly.

bislàcco pl -àcchi a queer, odd.

bislúngo pl -ghi a oblong.

bismúto nm bismuth.

bisnònno nm great-grandfather.

bisógna nf business, need.

bisognàre vi to need, want, be obliged.

bisognévole a needy, necessary; nm requisite.

bisógno nm need, necessity, poverty.

bisognóso a indigent, needy.

bistècca nf beefsteak.

bisticciàre vi -rsi vr to dispute, quarrel.

bistíccio nm quarrel; pun.

bistrattàre vt to ill-treat, offend, wrong.

bisúnto a very greasy.

bitòrzolo nm knob, pimple, wart.

bitorzolúto a pimply.

bítter nm inv bitters.

bitúme nm bitumen.

bivaccàre vi to bivouac.

bivàcco nm bivouac.

bivàlve a nm bivalve.

bívio nm crossroads pl.

bizantino a Byzantine.

bizza nf freak, whim.

bizzàrro a bizarre, odd, queer.

bizzèffe a ad galore, in quantity.

bizzóso a irascible, wayward.

blandízie nf blandishments pl wheedling.

blàndo a affable, bland, wheedling.

blasóne nm blazonry.

blèso a lisping.

blindaménto nm **blindatúra** nf armour-plating.

blindàre vt to armour-plate.

bloccàre vt to block, blockade.

blòcco pl **blòcchi** nm block, block-ade; (com) bulk.

bloc-nòtes nm scribbling pad, (US) scratch pad.

blù a blue.

bluàstro a bluish.

bluffàre vti to bluff.

blúsa nf blouse.

bòa nf (serpent, wrap) boa; (naut) buoy.

boàro nm cowherd.

boàto nm bellowing, thundering.

bobína nf reel of cotton, spool, (el) bobbin.

bócca nf mouth; aperture, opening; **a b. apèrta** ad open-mouthed.

boccàle nm decanter, jug, mug.

boccapòrto nm (naut) hatch(way).

boccàta nf mouthful.

boccheggiàre vi to gasp for air.

bocchíno nm pretty mouth; cigarette-holder, mouthpiece.

bòccia nf water bottle; bud; (game) bowl; **bócce** nf pl (game) bowls pl.

bocciàre vt to fail (in an exam).

bocciatúra nf failure (in an exam).

bòccio nm bud.

bocciòlo nm bud.

bocconcíno nm titbit.

boccóne nm mouthful, bite.

boccóni ad prone, face downwards.

Boèmia nf Bohemia.

boèmo a nm Bohemian.

bofonchiàre vi to grumble, mutter.

bòia nm executioner, hangman.

boicottàggio nm boycotting.

boicottàre vt to boycott.

bòlgia nf dark hole, pit.

bòlide nm meteor, thunderbolt, car driven at great speed.

Bolívia nf Bolivia.

boliviàno a nm Bolivian.

bólla nf blister, bubble; papal bull, seal.

bollàre vt to confirm, mark, seal, stamp.

bollatúra nf sealing, stamping.

bollènte a boiling, fiery.

bollétta nf bill, certificate, note, receipt.

bollettíno nm bulletin, schedule; **b. meteorològico** weather forecast, weather report.

bollicína nf small bubble, pimple.

bollíre vti to boil, bubble up.

bollitúra nf boiling, bubbling.

bóllo nm seal, stamp.

bollóre nm boiling, excessive heat.

bolscevíco pl -íchi a nm Bolshevik.

bólso a asthmatic.

bómba nf bomb, shell; **b. a màno**

hand-grenade; **b. a scòppio ritardàto** delayed action bomb; **b. chímica** gas bomb; **b. esplosíva** high-explosive bomb; **b. fumògena** smoke bomb; **b. incendiària** incendiary bomb.

bombardaménto nm bombardment, bombing.

bombardàre vt to bombard, bomb.

bómbola nf cylinder, bottle; **b. d'ossígeno** oxygen bottle.

bombolóne nm doughnut.

bombonièra nf bonbonniere, (US) candy box.

bonàccia nf (at sea) calm, tranquillity.

bonaccióne nm good-humoured fellow.

bonarietà nf good humour, good nature.

bonàrio a good-humoured.

bongustàio nm gourmet.

bonifica nf land reclamation.

bonificàre vt to reclaim land, put under cultivation; (com) to grant an allowance.

bonomía nf good nature.

bontà nf goodness, kindness.

bontempóne nm jolly person.

borbogliàre vi to rumble, mutter.

borboglío nm rumbling, grumbling.

borbottaménto, **borbottío** nm grumbling, muttering.

borbottàre vi to grumble, mutter.

bòrchia nf boss, stud.

bordèllo nm uproar; brothel.

bórdo nm edge, verge, (US of road) shoulder; border; rim; (naut) board; **a b.** ad on board.

bòrea nm north wind.

borgàta nf village, hamlet.

borghése a bourgeois; nmf middle-class person.

borghesía nf middle class.

bórgo nm village.

Borgógna nf (geogr) Burgundy.

bòria nf haughtiness, arrogance.

borióso a arrogant, vainglorious.

borotàlco pl -chi nm talcum powder.

borràccia nf leather bottle, canteen, water bottle.

borraccína nf kind of moss.

bórro nm ravine.

bórsa nf bag, purse, brief-case, Exchange; **b. di stúdio** bursary, scholarship.

borsaiuòlo nm pickpocket.

borsanéra nf black market.

borseggiàre vt to rob, pick someone's pocket.

borséggio nm bag-snatching, robbery.

borsellíno nm small purse.

borsétta nf handbag.

borsísta nm stockbroker, scholarship holder.

boscàglia nf underwood, wood.

boscaiuòlo nm woodcutter.

boscheréccio a woody, sylvan.

boschétto nm grove, small wood.

boschívo a woody.

bòsco pl -chi nm wood, forest.

boscóso a wooded.

bòsso, **bòssolo** nm box-plant, box-wood.

botànica nf botany.

botànico pl -ici a botanic(al); nm botanist.

bòtola nf trapdoor.

bòtta nf blow; toad.

bottàio nm cooper.

bótte nf barrel, cask.

bottéga nf shop.

bottegàio nm shopkeeper.

botteghíno nm small shop, box-office, lottery, betting shop.

bottíglia nf bottle.

bottiglieria nf bar, wine shop.

bottíno nm booty.

bòtto nm loud bang; blow; (of bell) toll; **di b.** ad suddenly, directly.

bottóne nm button, cufflink; bud; **b. del collétto** collar stud, (US) collar button.

bòve v **búe**.

bovíle nm ox-stall, byre.

bovíno a bovine.

bòzza nf bump, swelling; rough draft, proof sheet, sketch.

bozzétto nm outline, sketch.

bòzzolo nm cocoon.

bràca nf sling, tackle; trouser leg; pl **bràche** breeches, trousers pl.

braccétto, **a** ad arm in arm.

bracciàle nm armlet, bracelet, armband.

braccialétto nm bracelet.

bracciànte nm labourer.

bracciàta nf armful.

bràccio pl **bràccia** (f), (fig) **bràcci** (m) nm arm; branch, inlet, fathom.

bracciuòlo nm elbow-rest, hand-rail; **sèdia a bracciuòli** armchair.

bràcco pl **bràcchi** nm hound.

bràce nf embers pl, charcoal.

bracière nm brazier.

braciòla nf chop, cutlet, steak.

bràma nf desire, longing.

bramàre vt to desire, long for.

bramosía nf longing.

bramóso a eager, longing.

brànchie nf pl gills of fishes pl.

brànco pl -chi nm flock, herd, band.

brancolàre vi to grope.

brancolóni ad gropingly.

brànda nf folding bed, camp bed, hammock.

brandèllo nm rag, tatter, shred.

brandíre vt to brandish.

bràno nm piece, extract, passage.

Brasíle nm Brazil.

brasiliàno a nm Brazilian.

bravàre vt to defy; vi to boast.

bravàta nf bravado, boasting.

bràvo a clever, good (at something), honest, brave; nm cut-throat; interj bravo!

bravúra nf skill, bravery.

bréccia nf breach.

brefotrófio nm orphanage.
Bretàgna nf Brittany, Britain; **Gran B.** Great Britain.
bretèlle nf pl braces pl, (US) suspenders pl.
brètone a nm Breton.
brève a brief, concise, short; nm brief; **in b.** ad in short.
brevettàre vt to patent.
brevétto nm patent; (mil) commission.
breviàrio nm breviary.
brevità nf brevity, conciseness.
brézza nf breeze.
brícco pl **brícchi** nm kettle, pot, jug.
bricconàta, bricconería nf roguery, trick.
briccóne nm rascal, rogue.
bríciola nf crumb.
bríciolo nm bit, morsel.
briga nf quarrel, trouble; **attaccàre b.** to quarrel; **dàrsi b.** to take pains.
brigadière nm brigadier; (US) brigadier general; (carabinieri) sergeant.
brigantàggio nm brigandage.
brigànte nm brigand.
brigantésco p -éschi a of a brigand.
brigàre vt to solicit; vt to intrigue, strive.
brigàta nf brigade, company, party.
Brígida nf pr Bridget, Brigid.
bríglia nf bridle, reins pl.
brillaménto nm glitter; (of mine) explosion.
brillànte a bright, brilliant; nm brilliant.
brillantína nf brilliantine.
brillàre vi to glitter, shine, sparkle.
bríllo a merry, tipsy.
brína, brinàta nf hoar frost.
brinàre vi impers to be white with frost.
brindàre vi to drink a health, toast. toast.
brindèllo nm rag, tatter.
bríndisi nm toast.
brío nm spirit, vivacity.
brióso a lively, spirited, vivacious.
Britànnia nf Britain.
britànnico pl -ici a British.
britànno nm Briton.
brívido nm shiver, shudder.
brizzolàto a speckled, growing grey.
bròcca nf jug, jar, pitcher.
broccàto nm brocade.
bròccolo nm broccoli.
brodàglia nf weak broth, tasteless soup.
bròdo nm broth, soup.
brogliàre vt to intrigue.
bròglio nm intrigue.
bròmo, bromúro nm bromide.
bronchiàle a bronchial.
bronchíte nf bronchitis.
bróncio nm pout, sulkiness; **tenére il b.** vi to sulk.
brónco nm stem, trunk; **brónchi** pl bronchi pl.

brontolàre vi to grumble.
brónzo nm bronze.
brucàre vt to browse, nibble at, (leaves) strip off.
bruciacchiàre vt to scorch, singe.
bruciapélo, a ad point-blank, suddenly.
bruciàre vt to burn.
bruciàta nf roast chestnut.
bruciàto a burnt; nm burning; **gioventù bruciàta** (sl) beat generation; **uómo b.** broken man.
brucióre nm smart, burning.
brúco pl -chi nm caterpillar, grub.
brughièra nf heath, moor.
brulicàme nm swarm.
brulicàre vi to swarm, be crawling with.
brulichío nm swarming.
brúllo a bare, sterile.
brúma nf winter mist; ship-worm.
brúno a brown, dark; nm mourning.
Brúno nm pr Bruno.
bruschézza nf brusqueness, rudeness.
brúsco pl -chi a brusque, rude, tart.
brúscolo nm mote, speck.
brusío nm hubbub, buzz, whispering.
brutàle a brutal.
brutalità nf brutality.
brúto a brutal, unreasoning; nm brute, wild animal, violent person.
bruttàre vt to dirty, soil, stain.
bruttézza nf ugliness.
brútto a ugly, nasty.
búbbola nf hoopoe; idle tale.
búbbolo nm harness bell.
bubbóne nm (med) bubo.
bubbònico pl -ici a bubonic.
búca nf hole, cave, cavity; **b. délle lèttere** letter-box.
bucanéve nf snowdrop.
bucàre vt to bore, pierce, puncture.
bucàto a pierced, riddled; nm wash(ing), clean linen.
búccia nf peel, rind, skin, bark.
búccola nf earring, pendant.
bucherellàre vt to riddle with holes.
búco pl **búchi** nm hole, round opening.
budellàme nm bowels pl, entrails pl.
budèllo pl -a (f), (fig) -i (m) nm bowel, gut, intestine.
budíno nm pudding.
búe pl **buòi** nm ox; (fig) dunce.
búfalo nm buffalo.
bufèra nf storm, hurricane, whirlwind; **b. di néve** blizzard.
buffet nm sideboard, buffet.
buffétto nm fillip, chuck.
búffo a comical, comic, droll, funny, queer; nm gust, puff.
buffonàta nf buffoonery.
buffóne nm buffoon, untrustworthy person.
bugía nf lie; flat candlestick.
bugiàrdo a lying; nm liar.
bugigàttolo nm very small room, cubby-hole.

búio *a* dark; *nm* dark, darkness; **èssere al b.** *vi* (*fig*) to be in the dark.
búlbo *nm* bulb.
Bulgaría (la) *nf* Bulgaria.
búlgaro *a nm* Bulgarian, Bulgar.
bulíno *nm* (*tec*) graver.
bullóne *nm* bolt.
b(u)ongústo *nm* good taste.
buòno *a* good, sound, kind, right, safe; *nm* good; bond, coupon, permit; **a b. mercàto** *ad* cheap; **di buon'óra** *ad* early; **b. del tesòro** Treasury bill.
burattíno *nm* puppet; flighty person.
burbànza *nf* arrogance, insolent bearing.
búrbero *a* crabbed, morose.
burchièllo, búrchio *nm* small canal boat.
búrla *nf* trick, joke; **per b.** *ad* in fun.
burlàre *vt* to play a trick on, make a fool of; *vi* to joke; **-rsi** *vr* to laugh at, make fun of.
burlésco *pl* **-chi** *a* burlesque, ludicrous.
burlétta *nf* jest, joke.
burlévole *a* laughable, comical, humorous.
burlóne *nm* jester, joker.
buròcrate *nm* bureaucrat.
burocràtico *pl* **-ici** *a* bureaucratic.
burocrazía *nf* bureaucracy.
burràsca *nf* storm, tempest.
burrascóso *a* stormy, tempestuous.
búrro *nm* butter.
burróne *nm* ravine.
búsca *nf* quest, search.
buscàre *vt* to earn, gain; **-rsi** *vr* to bring upon oneself.
busíllis *nm* difficulty; **qui sta il b.** here lies the difficulty.
bussàre *vi* to knock.
bússe *nf pl* beating, blows *pl*.
bússola *nf* mariner's compass; sedan chair; inner door, screen; **pèrdere la b.** to be at one's wits' end.
bussolòtto *nm* dice-box.
bústa *nf* envelope, case.
bustàia *nf* corset-maker.
bústo *nm* bust; corset, stays *pl*.
buttàre *vt* to throw; **b. all'ària** to throw up, upset; **-rsi** *vr* to throw oneself.
butteràto *a* pock-marked.
búttero *nm* pock-mark; mounted herdsman.

C

cabína *nf* cabin; **c. telefònica** call box.
cablogràmma *nm* cablegram.
cabotàggio *nm* coasting trade.
cabotièro *a* coasting; *nm* coaster.
cacào *nm* cacao(-tree), cocoa.
càccia *nf* chase, hunt, pursuit, shooting; **andàre a c.** *vi* to go shooting, go hunting.
cacciagióne *nf* game.

cacciàre *vt* to chase, hunt, go hunting, pursue; thrust; **c. un grído** to utter a cry; **-rsi** *vr* to intrude, thrust one's way into.
cacciatóre *nm* **-tríce** *nf* hunter, trapper.
cacciatorpedinière *nf* (torpedo-boat) destroyer.
cacciavíte *nm* screwdriver.
càchi *a* khaki; *nm* persimmon (tree).
càcio *nm* cheese.
cadaúno *pron* (*com*) each.
cadàvere *nm* corpse.
cadavèrico *pl* **-ici** *a* cadaverous, corpselike.
cadènte *a* falling, (*of the sun*) setting.
cadènza *nf* cadence, rhythm, time, step, (*mus*) cadenza.
cadenzàto *a* measured, rhythmical.
cadére *vi* to fall.
cadétto *a* younger, cadet; *nm* cadet.
Càdice *nf* (*geogr*) Cadiz.
caducità *nf* frailty, transiency.
cadúco *pl* **-úchi** *a* frail, transient.
cadúta *nf* fall, ruin.
caffè *nm* coffee, café, **c. concèrto** café-chantant.
caffellàtte *nm* white coffee.
caffettièra *nf* coffee-pot.
caffettière *nm* cafe proprietor.
cafóne *nm* (*south Italy*) peasant; (*fig*) boor.
cagionàre *vt* to cause, occasion.
cagióne *nf* cause, reason, motive; **a c. di** on account of.
cagionévole *a* sickly, weak.
càglio *nm* rennet.
càgna *nf* bitch.
cagnàra *nf* barking, uproar.
cagnésco *pl* **-chi** *a* currish, surly.
cagnolíno *nm* pretty little dog, puppy.
Calàbria *nf* (*geogr*) Calabria.
calabrése *a nmf* Calabrian.
calabróne *nm* hornet.
calamàio *nm* inkstand; cuttlefish.
calamità *nf* calamity, misfortune.
calamíta *nf* magnet, loadstone.
calamitàre *vt* to magnetize.
calamitóso *a* calamitous, disastrous.
càlamo *nm* reed, quill.
calànte *a* sinking, declining, setting, decreasing; **lúna c.** waning moon.
calaprànzi *nm* service lift.
calàre *vt* to let down, lower; (*sail etc*) strike; *vi* to decrease, descend, sink, set.
càlca *nf* crowd, throng.
calcàgno *nm* heel.
calcàre *vt* to tread on, lay stress on, (*drawing*) trace.
calcàre *nm* limestone.
càlce *nf* lime; *nm* bottom, foot; **in c.** *ad* at the foot of the page.
calcestrúzzo *nm* concrete.
calciàre *vt* to kick; **c. in pòrta** (*sport*) to kick at goal.
calciatóre *nm* footballer.
calcína *nf* lime, mortar.
calcinàccio *nm* flake of dry plaster.

calcinàio nm lime-pit.

calcinàre vt to calcine.

càlcio nm kick; (sport) football; butt-end, rifle stock; (chem) calcium; **c. d'àngolo** (sport) corner; **c. d'inízio** (sport) kick-off; **c. di rigóre** (sport) penalty; **c. di punizióne** (sport) free kick.

calcístico pl -ici a football.

càlco pl càlchi nm cast, imprint, tracing.

calcògrafo nm copperplate engraver.

calcolàbile a calculable, computable.

calcolàre vt to calculate, compute, reckon.

calcolatóre m -tríce f a calculating; nm reckoner, computer; (fig) shrewd fellow.

calcolatríce nf reckoner, computer, calculating machine; (fig) shrewd woman.

càlcolo nm calculation, reckoning; (med) stone, calculus; (math) calculus.

caldàia nf boiler.

caldalléssa nf boiled chestnut.

caldarròsta nf roast chestnut.

caldeggiàre vt to favour, foster, protect.

calderàio nm coppersmith.

calderóne nm cauldron; (fig) mixture of things.

càldo a warm, hot; nm heat.

caleidoscòpio nm kaleidoscope.

calendàrio nm calendar, almanac.

calèsse nm gig, carriage.

calettàre vt (mech) to couple, key on; vi to tally, fit.

calía nf gold filing; (fig) old stuff.

càlibro nm calibre.

càlice nm goblet, chalice; (bot) calyx.

calígine nf thick fog, smog, dimness.

caliginóso a foggy, dark.

càlle nf (poet) path; narrow street in Venice.

callífugo pl -ghi nm corn-plaster.

calligrafía nf handwriting.

callista nm chiropodist.

càllo nm corn.

callosità nf callosity.

callóso a callous, hard.

càlma nf calm, quiet, tranquillity, quietness.

calmànte a soothing; nm sedative.

calmàre vt to calm, appease, soften; **-rsi** vr to calm down, become smooth.

càlmo a calm, tranquil, still, cool, (sea) smooth.

càlo nm loss of weight, fall in price, shrinkage.

calóre nm heat, warmth, feverishness.

caloría nf calorie.

calorífero nm radiator; **impiànto centràle di caloríferi** central heating.

caloróso a warm, hearty.

calòscia nf galosh.

calòtta nf skull-cap, calotte; (mech) cap.

calpestàre vt to trample on, oppress.

calpestío nm trampling.

calúnnia nf calumny.

calunniàre vt to calumniate, slander.

calunniatóre nm -tríce nf calumniator, slanderer.

calunnióso a calumnious, slanderous.

Calvàrio nm Calvary, wayside shrine; **calvàrio** nm long suffering.

calvízie nf baldness.

càlvo a bald; nm bald-headed person.

càlza nf stocking; **fàre la c.** vi to knit.

calzamàglia nf tights pl.

calzànte a suitable, appropriate.

calzàre vt (shoes) to put on, wear; vi to fit.

calzatóio nm shoehorn.

calzatúra nf footwear.

calzíno nm sock.

calzolàio nm bootmaker, shoemaker.

calzolería nf shoemaker's shop.

calzóni nm trousers pl, slacks pl; **c. córti, calzoncíni** shorts pl.

camaleónte nm chameleon.

cambiàle nf (com) bill of exchange, draft; **eméttere una c.** to draw a bill.

cambiaménto nm change.

cambiamonéte, cambiavalúte nm money changer.

cambiàre vti to change, alter, turn, exchange; **-rsi** vr to change.

càmbio nm change, exchange; (tec) change gear, (aut) gear, gearbox.

càmera nf chamber, room; **c. da lètto** bedroom; **C. dei Deputàti** House of Commons, (US) House of Representatives; **C. dei Pàri** House of Lords.

cameràta nm comrade; nf dormitory.

camerièra nf maid, servant, waitress; **-re** nm waiter, manservant.

cameríno nm (theat) dressing room.

càmice nm surplice, overall.

camicétta nf blouse.

camícia pl -ície nf shirt, wrapper; (tec) jacket; **c. da nòtte** nightgown, nightdress; **c. di fòrza** strait-jacket.

caminétto nm fireplace.

camíno nm fireplace, chimney.

càmion nm lorry, (US) truck.

camionétta nf (mil) jeep.

camioncíno nm small van, tradesman's delivery van.

camionísta nm lorry driver; (US) truck driver.

cammèllo nm camel.

cammèo nm cameo.

camminaménto nm (mil) communication trench.

camminàre vi to walk, march; (of mechanism) go, work; proceed.

cammíno nm way, road, journey; **cammín facèndo** ad on the way.

camomilla nf camomile.

camòrra *nf* camorra, secret (criminal) society.

camóscio *nm* chamois, shammy.

campàgna *nf* country, estate; campaign.

campagn(u)òlo *a* rustic, country; *nm* peasant, countryman.

campàle *a* (of the) field; battàglia c. *nf* pitched battle.

campàna *nf* bell, bell glass.

campanèlla *nf* small bell; (*bot*) harebell.

campanèllo *nm* (*in the house*) bell.

Campània *nf* (*geogr*) Campania.

campanìle *nm* bell-tower, belfry.

campanilìsmo *nm* local patriotism.

campàno *a nm* (inhabitant) of Campania.

campàre *vt* to save, rescue; (*art*) put into relief; *vi* to live.

campeggiàre *vi* to stand out; camp, encamp.

campéggio *nm* camping, camping place.

campèstre *a* rural, rustic.

Campidòglio (il) *nm* the Capitol (in Rome).

campionàrio *a* sample, trade; *nm* pattern book, sample case.

campionàto *nm* championship.

campióne *nm* champion; (*com*) sample.

càmpo *nm* field, camp; c. d'aviazióne airfield; c. di fortúna emergency landing-ground; méttere in c. *vt* to bring forward, propose.

camposànto *nm* burial ground, cemetery.

camuffàre *vt* to disguise, mask.

Canadà *nm* (*geogr*) Canada.

canadése *a nm* Canadian.

canàglia *nf* mob, rabble, riffraff, rogue.

canàle *nm* canal, channel, pipe; c. navigàbile waterway.

canalizzàre *vt* to canalize.

cànapa *nf* hemp.

canapè *nm* couch, sofa.

Cz.nàrie (le) *nf pl* (*geogr*) the Canary Islands, the Canaries *pl*.

canarìno *a* canary-coloured; *nm* canary.

canàsta *nf* canasta.

cancellàre *vt* to cancel, erase, obliterate.

cancellàta *nf* railing.

cancellatúra *nf* erasure.

cancellería *nf* chancellor's office, chancery; artìcoli di c. articles of stationery.

cancellière *nm* chancellor, registrar.

cancèllo *nm* gate, railing.

cancrèna *nf* gangrene.

càncro *nm* cancer.

candeggiàre *vt* to bleach.

candeggìna *nf* bleach; candéggio *nm* bleaching.

candéla *nf* candle, (*aut*) sparking plug, (*US*) spark plug.

candelàbro *nm* candelabrum.

candelière *nm* candlestick, (*naut*) stanchion.

candelòra *nf* Candlemas.

candidàto *nm* candidate.

candidatúra *nf* candidature.

càndido *a* white; candid, sincere.

candìre *vt* to candy.

candìto *a* candied; *nm* sugar candy.

candóre *nm* whiteness; candour.

càne *nm* dog, (of a gun) cock, (*mech*) catch; c. da càccia hound, sporting dog; c. da guàrdia watchdog; c. barbóne poodle; c. bastàrdo mongrel.

canèstro *nm* basket, hamper; basketful.

cànfora *nf* camphor.

cangiàbile *a* changeable, fickle.

cangiànte *a* changing, (of colour) iridescent; séta c. shot silk.

cangùro *nm* kangaroo.

canìcola *nf* dog-star; dog-days *pl*.

canìle *nm* kennel.

canìno *a* canine; tósse canìna whooping-cough.

canìzie *nf* white hair, old age.

cànna *nf* cane, reed, tube, (gun) barrel, (fishing-)rod, stick, (measure) rod.

cannèlla *nf* spout, spigot, tap; cinnamon.

cannéto *nm* reed thicket, cane field.

cannìbale *nm* cannibal.

cannocchiàle *nm* binoculars *pl*, opera glass, telescope.

cannonàta *nf* cannon-shot.

cannóne *nm* gun, cannon; c. antacàrro anti-tank gun; c. antiaèreo anti-aircraft gun.

cannoneggiaménto *nm* cannonade, cannonading.

cannoneggiàre *vti* to cannonade.

cannonièra *nf* gunboat.

cannonière *nm* gunner.

cannúccia *nf* thin cane, (for drinks) straw, pen-holder, small tube.

canòa *nf* canoe.

cànone *nm* canon, rule; fee, rent.

canònica *nf* vicarage, rectory.

canònico *pl* -ici *a* canonical, regular; drítto di c. canon law; *nm* canon.

canonizzàre *vt* to canonize.

canonizzazióne *nf* canonization.

canottàggio *nm* rowing, canoeing.

canottièra *nf* vest, singlet, (US) undershirt; straw hat.

canòtto *nm* canoe.

cànova *nf* retail shop for wine *etc*.

canovàccio *nm* dishcloth, canvas; plot.

cantànte *a* singing; *nmf* singer.

cantàre *vti* to sing.

cantatóre *a* singing; *nm* singer.

cantatríce *nf* singer.

canterellàre, canticchiàre *vti* to hum, sing softly.

canterìno *a* singing, warbling, chirping.

càntica *nf* poem, song; càntico *nm* canticle, hymn.

cantière *nm* dockyard, ship-building yard.

cantilèna *nf* monotonous song, singsong.

cantina *nf* cellar, wine shop.

cànto *nm* singing, song, poem, canto; corner, side, angle.

cantonàta *nf* corner; blunder.

cantóne *nm* corner; canton.

cantonière *nm* maintenance man on roads, railways *etc*; càsa cantonièra roadman's house.

cantóre *nm* singer, chorister.

cantoria *nf* choir, chancel.

cantúccio *nm* corner, bit.

canúto *a* grey-headed, hoary.

canzonàre *vt* to make fun of, tease; *vi* to joke.

canzonatòrio *a* mocking, teasing.

canzonatúra *nf* mockery, teasing.

canzóne *nf* song, ode, ballad.

canzonière *nm* collection of lyrical poems, song book.

càos *nm* chaos, confusion.

caòtico *pl* -ici *a* chaotic.

capàce *a* able, capable, capacious.

capacità *nf* ability, capacity.

capacitàrsi *vr* to make out, understand.

capànna *nf* -no *nm* hut, cabin.

capannèllo *nm* group of persons, small crowd.

caparbietà *nf* obstinacy, stubbornness.

capàrbio *a* obstinate, stubborn.

capàrra *nf* advance payment, earnest money.

capéllo *nm* hair; capellóne *nm* (*sl*) beatnik.

capellúto *a* hairy.

capelvènere *nm* (*bot*) maidenhair.

capèstro *nm* halter, rope.

capezzàle *nm* bolster.

capézzolo *nm* nipple.

capigliatúra *nf* hair, head of hair.

capinèra *nf* (*bird*) blackcap.

capire *vt* to understand, realize; *vi* to be contained.

capitàle *a* capital, principal, main; deadly; *nm* capital, wealth, assets *pl*; *nf* capital (city).

capitalismo *nm* capitalism.

capitalista *nm* capitalist.

capitanàre *vt* to captain, head.

capitaneria *nf* c. di pòrto harbourmaster's office.

capitàno *nm* captain, commander.

capitàre *vi* to happen, occur, turn up.

capitèllo *nm* (*arch*) capital.

capitolàre *vi* to capitulate; *a* capitular; *nm* capitulary.

capitolino *a* Capitoline.

capitolo *nm* chapter, (*of pact or convention*) article.

capitombolàre *vi* to tumble.

capitómbolo *nm* somersault, tumble.

càpo *nm* head; chief, beginning, end, article, item, cape, promontory; da c. again; in c. a at the end of;

venire a c. di to make out, reason out.

capobànda *pl* capibànda *nm* bandmaster, gang leader.

capòcchia *nf* head of a nail, pin *etc*.

capocòmico *pl* -ici, capicòmici *nm* (*theat*) head of a dramatic company, showman.

capocuòco *pl* capicuòchi *nm* head cook, chef.

capofàbbrica *pl* capifàbbrica *nm* foreman.

capofitto *ad* head downwards, head foremost.

capogíro *pl* -íri *nm* dizziness, giddiness.

capolavóro *pl* -óri *nm* masterpiece.

capolínea *pl* capilínea *nm* terminus.

capolino *nm* small head; fàre c. to peep in.

capoluògo *pl* -ghi, capiluòghi *nm* chief town in a district.

capomàstro *pl* -tri, capimàstri *nm* master builder.

caponàggine *nf* obstinacy.

caporàle *nm* corporal.

caporepàrto *pl* capirepàrto *nm* head of a department, shopwalker, (US) floorwalker, foreman.

caporióne *pl* capirióne *nm* ringleader.

caposàldo *pl* capisàldi *nm* essential point of a speech *etc*; (*mil*) stronghold.

caposquàdra *pl* capisquàdra *nm* foreman; (*mil*) squad leader.

capostazióne *pl* capistazióne *nm* station-master.

capotàvola *pl* capitàvola *nm* head of a table.

capotréno *pl* capitréno *nm* guard, (US) conductor.

capovèrso *pl* -rsi *nm* beginning of a line or paragraph.

capovòlgere *vt* to overturn, upset; -rsi *vr* to capsize, be upset.

càppa *nf* cape, cloak, cope; the letter K.

cappèlla *nf* chapel.

cappellàno *nm* chaplain.

cappellièra *nf* hat-box.

cappèllo *nm* hat.

càpperi! *interj* goodness!

càppero *nm* caper, caper-bush.

càppio *nm* slip-knot, noose.

cappóne *nm* capon.

cappòtto *nm* cloak, overcoat.

cappuccino *nm* capuchin friar; coffee with a little cream.

cappúccio *nm* cowl, hood.

càpra *nf* she-goat.

caprétto *nm* kid, young goat.

capríccio *nm* caprice, whim.

capriccióso *a* capricious, whimsical.

caprifòglio *nm* honeysuckle.

capriòla *nf* doe, roe; caper, capriole.

capriòlo *nm* roebuck.

càpro *nm* he-goat; c. espiatório scapegoat.

càpsula *nf* capsule, percussion cap.

capufficio nm head clerk.
carabina nf carbine.
carabinière nm carabineer, gendarme.
caràffa nf decanter, carafe.
caramèlla nf sweet, (US) candy, toffee, (US) taffy, caramel; monocle.
caràto nm carat; (com) share.
caràttere nm character, quality, style, (typ) type.
caratterística nf characteristic.
caratterístico a characteristic.
caratterizzàre vt to characterize.
carbonàia nf charcoal pit, coalcellar, bunker.
carbonàio nm coalman.
carbònchio nm carbuncle.
carbóne nm coal; c. fòssile pit coal.
carbonèlla nf charcoal, coal cinders.
carbònio nm carbon.
carbonizzàre vt to carbonize.
carburànte nm fuel, petrol, (US) gas, gasoline.
carburatóre nm carburettor.
carcàme nm -àssa nf carcass.
carceràre vt to imprison.
carceràto nm prisoner.
carcerazióne nf imprisonment.
càrcere nm jail, prison.
carcerière nm jailer.
carciòfo nm artichoke.
cardàre vt to card.
cardellíno nm goldfinch.
cardíaco pl -íaci a cardiac.
cardinàle a cardinal, principal; nm cardinal.
càrdine nm hinge; (fig) foundation.
càrdo nm thistle, teasel.
carèna nf (of a ship) keel.
carenàre vt (naut) to careen.
carènza nf lack, scarcity.
carestía nf dearth, famine.
carézza nf caress; high price.
carezzàre vt to caress, fondle, cherish.
carezzévole a caressing, coaxing.
cariàre vt to decay, rot.
càrica nf position, post; (mil) charge; (el) charging; winding.
caricaménto nm loading, charging, winding up.
caricàre vt to charge, load, overburden, exaggerate; c. un orològio to wind up a clock.
caricatóre nm loader, shipper; (of firearms) magazine.
caricatúra nf caricature.
càrico pl -chi a charged, loaded, wound up; nm load, cargo, burden, charge.
càrie nf caries, (of teeth) decay.
caríno a pretty, nice, dear, sweet.
carità nf charity, alms; per c. interj for heaven's sake.
caritatévole a charitable.
carlínga nf (av) cockpit.
Càrlo nm pr Charles.
Carlomàgno nm pr Charlemagne.
carlóna, alla ad in a slovenly manner.

carmelitàno nm Carmelite friar.
carnagióne nf complexion.
carnàle a bodily, physical, carnal, sensual.
carnalità nf carnality, sensuality.
càrne nf flesh, meat.
carnéfice nm executioner, (fig) brutal person.
carneficína nf carnage, slaughter.
carnevàle nm carnival.
Càrniche (Àlpi) nf pl (geogr) Carnic Alps.
carnívoro a carnivorous.
carnóso a fleshy.
càro a dear, expensive; ad dearly, dear; nm high cost; il carovíta the high cost of living; tenér c. to esteem, value.
carógna nf carrion (also fig).
Carolína nf pr Caroline.
caròta nf carrot.
carovàna nf caravan, convoy.
càrpa nf carp.
carpentière nm carpenter.
carpíre vt to seize, snatch; cheat.
carpóne, carpóni ad on all fours.
carradóre nm cartwright.
carràia nf cart road.
carreggiàbile a practicable for carts.
carreggiàta nf track, cart road; gauge; uscíre di c. (fig) to go astray.
carrèllo nm (tec) undercarriage, trolley.
carrétta nf cart.
carrettàta nf cartload.
carrettière nm carrier, carter.
carrétto nm hand-cart.
carrièra nf career, course, speed.
carriòla nf wheelbarrow.
càrro nm cart, wagon, truck; (astr) Great Bear; c. armàto (mil) tank; c. leggèro (mil) light tank; c. fúnebre hearse.
carròzza nf carriage, coach, (US) railway car; c. belvedére observation car; c. ristorànte restaurant car, (US) dining car; c. lètto sleeping car, sleeper.
carrozzàbile a practicable for carriages.
carrozzería nf body of a car, carmaking firm.
carrozzína nf perambulator, (fam) pram, (US) baby carriage.
carrozzíno nm light carriage; (motor cycle) sidecar.
carrúcola nf pulley, sheave.
càrsico pl -ici a Karst.
Càrso nm (geogr) Karst.
càrta nf paper, document, writing, charter, playing card, map; c. d'identità identity card; c. igiènica toilet paper; c. da lèttere writing paper, notepaper.
cartacarbóne pl **cartecarbóne** nf carbon paper.
cartàccia, cartastràccia pl **cartestràcce** nf waste paper.

cartàio *nm* papermaker; (*at cards*) dealer.

cartapècora *pl* **-ore** *nf* parchment.

cartapésta *pl* **cartapéste, cartepéste** *nf* papier-mâché.

cartavetràta *pl* **cartevetràte** *nf* glass paper, sandpaper.

cartéggio *nm* correspondence, collection of letters.

cartèlla *nf* folder, portfolio, writing pad; schoolbag; (*of a manuscript*) sheet; share, bond, score-card, (lottery) ticket.

cartellièra *nf* filing cabinet.

cartèllo *nm* bill, label, signboard, poster.

cartellóne *nm* placard, playbill.

cartièra *nf* paper mill.

cartilàgine *nf* cartilage, gristle.

cartòccio *nm* cornet, paper bag.

cartolàio *nm* stationer.

cartolería *nf* stationer's shop.

cartolína *nf* card; **c. illustràta** picture postcard; **c. postàle** postcard.

cartóne *nm* cardboard; cartoon.

cartúccia *nf* cartridge.

cartuccièra *nf* cartridge belt.

càsa *nf* house, home, family, household; religious community; business firm; **c. di salúte** nursing home.

casàccio, a *ad* at random, haphazard.

casàle *nm* hamlet.

casalíngo *pl* **-ghi** *a* domestic, homely, homemade.

casaménto *nm* tenement house.

casàta *nf* lineage, family.

casàto *nm* surname.

cascàggine *nf* drowsiness, weariness.

cascàre *vi* to fall.

cascàta *nf* fall, waterfall, cascade.

cascemír *nm* cashmere.

cascína *nf* dairy farm, dairy.

caseggiàto *nm* block of houses.

caseifício *nm* dairy.

casèlla *nf* pigeonhole, small compartment; (*beehive*) cell.

casellànte *nm* level-crossing keeper, signalman.

casellàrio *nm* set of pigeonholes.

casèrma *nf* barracks *pl*.

casétta, casettína *nf* cottage, small house.

casíno *nm* little cottage; club, gaming-house.

càso *nm* case; chance, possibility; **a c.** *ad* at random.

casolàre *nm* poor country house.

Càspio, (Mar) *nm* (*geogr*) Caspian (Sea).

càssa *nf* case, chest, coffer, coffin, drum; (*of a gun*) stock; cash, fund; **c. di rispàrmio** savings bank.

cassafòrte *nf* safe.

cassapànca *nf* wooden chest in the form of a bench.

cassàre *vt* to cancel, annul, quash.

cassazióne *nf* annulling, cassation; **corte di c.** (*leg*) court of cassation.

casseruòla *nf* saucepan.

cassétta *nf* box, coach-box, collection box, letter-box.

cassétto *nm* drawer.

cassettóne *nm* chest of drawers.

cassière *nm* cashier, teller.

càsta *nf* caste, rank.

castàgna *nf* chestnut; **castàgno** *nm* chestnut tree; **c. d'India** horsechestnut(tree).

castagnéto *nm* chestnut grove.

castàno *a* chestnut-coloured, brown; **c. scúro** dark brown; **c. chiàro** light brown.

castellàno *nm* lord of a manor.

castèllo *nm* castle, fortress, (*naut*) castle.

castigàre *vt* to punish, chastise, chasten; spoil.

castigàto *a* chaste, pure; (*edition*) expurgated.

castígo *pl* **-ghi** *nm* punishment.

castità *nf* chastity, purity.

càsto *a* chaste, pure.

castòro *nm* beaver.

castràre *vt* to castrate, (*fig*) bowdlerize.

castràto *a* castrated; *nm* mutton.

casuàle *a* casual; accidental.

casualità *nf* chance.

casúpola *nf* hovel.

cataclìsma *nm* cataclysm.

catacómba *nf* catacomb.

catalessi *nf* catalepsy.

catalizzatóre *nm* (*chem*) catalyst.

catalogàre *vt* to catalogue.

catàlogo *pl* **-ghi** *nm* catalogue, list.

catapécchia *nf* hovel.

cataplàsma *nm* poultice.

catapulta *nf* catapult.

catarifrangènte *nm* reflector, reflex reflector.

catàrro *nm* catarrh.

catàsta *nf* pile, heap, stack.

catàsto *nm* register of lands, land office, land tax.

catàstrofe *nf* catastrophe.

catechìsmo *nm* catechism.

categoría *nf* category, class.

categòrico *pl* **-ici** *a* categorical.

caténa *nf* chain, fetter; (*of hills*) range; **c. cingolàta** (*mil*) caterpillar track.

catenàccio *nm* (*door*) bolt.

catenèlla *nf* small chain.

cateràtta *nf* cataract, sluice.

Caterína *nf pr* Catherine, Katherine.

catinèlla *nf* wash-hand basin; **piòvere a catinèlle** *vi* to rain cats and dogs.

catíno *nm* basin.

catràme *nm* tar.

càttedra *nf* desk, teaching post, chair, professorship, pulpit.

cattedràle *nf* cathedral.

cattivàre *vt* to captivate; **-rsi** *vr* to win (*love, favour etc*).

cattivèria *nf* naughtiness, wickedness.

cattività *nf* captivity.

cattìvo *a* bad, naughty, wicked.

Cattolicésimo, Cattolicísmo nm (Roman) Catholicism.

cattolicità nf Catholicism, Catholic countries pl.

cattòlico pl -ici a nm Catholic.

cattúra nf capture, arrest; **mandàto di c.** warrant of arrest.

catturàre vt to arrest, capture.

Càucaso (il) nm (geogr) Caucasus.

caucciù nm indiarubber.

càusa nf cause, origin, reason; (leg) law-suit.

causàle a causal.

causalità nf causality.

causàre vt to cause, occasion.

causticità nf causticity.

càustico pl -ici a nm caustic.

cautaménte ad cautiously.

cautèla nf caution, wariness.

càuto a cautious, wary.

cauzióne nf security, bail, caution money.

càva nf quarry, mine.

cavalcàre vt to mount (a horse etc); vi to ride.

cavalcàta nf ride, cavalcade.

cavalcatúra nf mount.

cavalcavía nm fly-over.

cavalcióni ad astride; **a c. di** astride.

cavalière nm horseman, knight; escort, dancing partner.

cavàlla nf mare.

cavallànte nm stable-man, horse-rider.

cavalerésco pl -chi a chivalrous, knightly, noble.

cavalería nf cavalry, horse pl, chivalry.

cavallerízza nf riding school, horse-woman; **cavallerízzo** nm rider, riding master, ringmaster.

cavallétta nf grasshopper.

cavallétto nm small horse; easel, trestle; (torture) rack.

cavallína nf filly; **córrere la c.** to sow one's wild oats.

cavàllo nm horse; (chess) knight; **c. vapóre** horse-power.

cavàre vt to extract, take out, remove, obtain; **-rsi** vr to get out of.

cavatàppi nm corkscrew.

cavèrna nf cave, cavern.

cavézza nf halter.

càvia nf guinea-pig.

caviàle nm caviar.

caviglia nf ankle (bone).

cavillàre vi to carp, cavil, split hairs.

cavíllo nm cavil, quibble.

cavillóso a cavilling, quibbling.

cavità nf cavity, hole.

càvo a hollow, empty; nm cable, rope; **c. di orméggio** mooring cable.

cavolfióre nm cauliflower.

càvolo nm cabbage; **cavolíni di Bruxelles** brussels sprouts.

cazzòtto nm punch, blow.

céce nm chick-pea.

Cecília nf pr Cecily; **Cecílio** nm pr Cecil.

cecità nf blindness, ignorance.

cèco pl -chi a nm Czech.

Cecoslovàcchia nf Czechoslovakia.

cecoslovàcco pl -chi a nm Czecho-slovak.

cèdere vi to give in, yield; cave in; vt to give up, cede, surrender, transfer.

cedévole a yielding; (of ground) sinking.

cedíbile a transferable.

cèdola nf (com) coupon.

cédro nm cedar, citron.

céfalo nm mullet.

cèffo nm muzzle, snout.

celàre vt to disguise, hide; **-rsi** vr to hide (oneself).

celebrànte nm officiating priest.

celebràre vt to celebrate, praise.

celebrazióne nf celebration.

cèlebre a celebrated, famous.

celebrità nf celebrity.

cèlere a nimble, rapid, swift.

celerità nf celerity, swiftness.

celèste a celestial, divine, heavenly; sky-blue.

cèlia nf jest, joke.

celibàto nm celibacy.

cèlibe a unmarried; nm bachelor.

cèlla nf (of prison, monastery) cell.

cellofàne nm cellophane.

cèllula nf (anat, el) cell.

cellulàre a cellular, honey-combed; nm jail, prison.

cémbalo nm tambourine; harpsi-chord, spinet.

cementàre vt to cement.

ceménto nm cement.

céna nf supper.

cenàcolo nm supper-room, picture of the Last Supper; artistic circle.

cenàre vi to sup.

cenciàia nf -io nm rag-picker.

céncio nm dishclout, rag.

cencióso a ragged, in tatters.

cénere nf ashes pl, cinders pl; **giórno delle céneri** nm Ash Wednesday.

Cenerèntola nf Cinderella.

Cenísio, (Monte) nm (geogr) Cenis.

cénno nm nod, sign, signal, gesture, hint; notice, outline; **far c.** to beckon, nod.

censiménto nm census.

censíre vt to take the census.

cènso nm income, wealth, life annuity; census.

censóre nm censor.

censòrio a censorious.

censúra nf censure, censorship.

censuràre vt to censor, censure.

centellinàre vt to sip.

centenàrio a nm centenarian; nm centenary.

centennàle a centennial.

centèsimo a nm hundredth; nm centesimo, centime, cent.

centígrado a centigrade.

centigràmmo nm centigramme.

centimetro nm centimetre.

centinàio nm hundred; **a centinàia** in hundreds.

cènto *a* hundred.

centràle *a* central, midland; *nf* c. elèttrica power station; c. telefònica telephone exchange; c. atòmica atomic power station.

centralino *nm* telephone exchange.

centralizzàre *vt* to centralize.

centràre *vt* to centre.

cèntro *nm* centre, heart, middle.

centuplicàre *vt* centuplicate, multiply.

cèntuplo *a* centuple, hundredfold.

ceppàia *nf* rooty stump.

céppo *nm* (tree) stump, log, (chopping) block; céppi *pl* shackles *pl* (*also fig*).

céra *nf* wax, polish; aspect, face; c. da scarpe shoé polish.

ceralàcca *nf* sealing wax.

ceràmica *nf* ceramics *pl*.

cérca *nf* quest, search.

cercàre *vt* to look for, seek, strive, try.

cérchia *nf* circle; encircling walls *pl*.

cerchiàre *vt* to hoop.

cerchiàto *a* (*of eyes*) black-ringed.

cérchio *nm* circle, ring, hoop, tyre.

cereàle *a nm* cereal.

cerebràle *a* cerebral.

cèreo *a* waxen, wan.

cerimònia *nf* ceremony.

cerimoniàle *a nm* ceremonial.

cerimonióso *a* ceremonious.

cerìno *nm* wax match, taper.

cernièra *nf* hinge (*of a bag, purse etc*), mount; c. làmpo zip-fastener, (*US*) zipper.

cèrnita *nf* choice, selection, grading.

céro *nm* church candle.

ceròtto *nm* sticking plaster; tedious person.

cèrro *nm* Turkey oak.

certaménte *ad* certainly.

certézza *nf* assurance, certainty.

certificàre *vt* to certify, confirm.

certificàto *nm* certificate, testimonial.

cèrto *a* certain, positive, sure; *ad* certainly, of course.

certósa *nf* Carthusian monastery.

certosìno *nm* Carthusian monk.

certùni *pron pl* a few, some *pl*.

cèrva *nf* hind, doe.

cervellìno *nm* hare-brained person.

cervèllo *nm* brain; brains *pl*, judgment, sense.

cervellòtico *pl* -ici *a* fantastic, queer.

Cervìno, (il) *nm* (*geogr*) the Matterhorn.

cèrvo *nm* deer, stag; càrne di c. venison; c. volànte stag-beetle.

Césare *nm pr* Caesar.

cesellàre *vt* to chisel (*also fig*).

cesèllo *nm* chisel.

cesóie *nf pl* shears *pl*.

cespùglio *nm* bush, thicket.

cessàre *vti* to cease, end, stop.

cessazióne *nf* cessation, end, (*com*) discontinuance.

cessióne *nf* transfer, assignment.

cèsso *nm* water-closet.

césta *nf* basket, hamper.

cestinàre *vt* to throw into the waste-paper basket.

cestino *nm* small basket, waste-paper basket.

césto *nm* (*bot*) head; (*basketball*) basket.

cèto *nm* class, rank.

cetriòlo *nm* cucumber.

che *cj and ad* than, that, whether, but, as soon as, lest; *pron and a* that, what, which, who; che c'è? what is the matter?

che *interj* what! no! never!

checchessìa *pron* whatever.

chèrmisi *nm* crimson.

chetàre *vt* to quiet, silence; -rsi *vr* to grow quiet, silent.

chetichèlla, àlla *ad* quietly, secretly.

chéto *a* quiet, silent.

chi *pron interrog* who, whom, which; *pron rel* he who, whom *etc*; whoever; some . . . others.

chiàcchiera *nf* gossip, prattle, tittle-tattle.

chiacchieràre *vi* to chat, gossip.

chiacchieràta *nf* chat.

chiacchierìo *nm* chattering.

chiacchieróna *nf* -óne *nm* babbler, chatterbox, prattler.

chiàma *nf* rollcall.

chiamàre *vt* to call, name; -rsi *vr* to be called; cóme si chiàma? what is your name?

chiamàta *nf* call, summons.

chiappàre *vt* to catch, seize.

Chiàra *nf pr* Clara, Clare, Claire.

chiaraménte *ad* clearly, frankly.

chiarézza *nf* clearness, fame.

chiarificàre *vt* to clarify.

chiarìre *vt* to clarify, explain; -rsi *vr* to become clear, (*of the weather*) clear up.

chiàro *a* clear, bright, illustrious, *nm* brightness, light, light colour; con quésti chiàri di lúna (*fig*) in these difficult times; *ad* clearly.

chiaróre *nm* brightness, light.

chiaroveggènte *a* clear-sighted, clairvoyant.

chiaroveggènza *nf* clairvoyance.

chiàsso *nm* noise, uproar.

chiassóso *a* noisy.

chiàtta *nf* lighter, barge.

chiavàrda *nf* bolt.

chiàve *nf* key, spanner, (*mus*) clef.

chiavistèllo *nm* bolt.

chiàzza *nf* spot, stain.

chìcchera *nf* cup.

chìcco *pl* -chi *nm* coffee-bean, grain; hailstone; c. d'úva grape.

chièdere *vt* to ask, beg, inquire.

chiérico *pl* -ici *nm* priest in minor orders; chierichétto *nm* altar-boy, choirboy.

chièsa *nf* church.

chìglia *nf* (*naut*) keel.

chílo nm chyle; **fàre il c.** to rest after a meal.

chilo(gràmmo) nm kilo(gramme).

chilòmetro nm kilometre.

chimèra nf chimera, illusion.

chímica nf chemistry.

chímico pl **-ici** a chemical; nm chemist.

chína nf declivity, slope; Peruvian bark.

chinàre vt to bend, bow; **-rsi** vr to bend down, stoop, submit.

chincàglie nf pl **chincaglierìa** nf fancy goods pl, knick-knacks pl.

chincaglière nm fancy-goods merchant.

chiníno nm quinine.

chíno a bent.

chiòccia nf broody hen.

chiòcciola nf snail, sea-shell; screw-nut; **scàla a c.** spiral stair.

chiòdo nm nail; **ròba da chiòdi** dishonest thing or person, badly done (or made) thing; **piantàre chiòdi** to run up debts.

chiòma nf hair, foliage; (of a comet) tail.

chiòsa nf explanatory note, gloss.

chiosàre vt to comment, gloss.

chiòsco pl **-òschi** nm kiosk, (US) newsstand.

chiòstra nf enclosure; (of teeth) set; (of mountains) range.

chiòstro nm cloister; (fig) monastic life.

chiòtto a silent.

chirurgìa nf surgery.

chirúrgico pl **-ici** a surgical.

chirúrgo pl **-úrgi, -úrghi** nm surgeon.

chissà interj who knows!

chitàrra nf guitar.

chitarrísta nmf guitarist.

chiúdere vt to close, enclose, fence; conclude; turn off; **-rsi** vr close, close over, close in, shut oneself up, withdraw.

chiúnque pron rel indef anyone who, whoever, anyone.

chiúsa nf fence, dam, lock, weir; conclusion, close.

chiúso a closed, enclosed; (sky) overcast; (com) settled; nm enclosure, pen.

chiusúra nf closing, close, fastening, fastener, lock.

ci pron us, to us, each other, one another, this, that, it; ad here, there.

ciabàtta nf slipper.

ciabattíno nm cobbler.

ciàlda nf **cialdóne** nm biscuit, wafer.

cialtróna nf slut.

cialtróne nm blackguard, rascal.

cialtronerìa nf slatternliness, rascality.

ciambèlla nf ring-shaped cake; name given to many objects similarly shaped, as an air cushion, lifebelt etc.

ciambellàno nm chamberlain.

ciància nf idle talk, gossip; **ciànce!** nonsense!

cianciàre vi to prate, tattle, gossip.

cianfrusàglia nf trash, odds and ends.

cíano nm cornflower.

cianúro nm cyanide; **c. di potàssio** potassium cyanide.

ciào interj hello!, (US) hi!, (leaving) bye-bye.

ciàrla nf talkativeness, gossip.

ciarlàre vi to talk a lot.

ciarlatanerìa nf quackery.

ciarlatàno nm quack, charlatan.

ciascúno a and pron each, every, each one, every one.

cibàre vt to feed; **-rsi** vr to eat, feed upon.

cibària nf food, victuals pl.

cíbo nm food.

cicàla nf cicada, chatterbox.

cicatrice nf scar.

cicatrizzàre vti **-rsi** vr to cicatrize, heal, skin over.

cícca nf cigar-butt, cigarette-end, quid; (fig) worthless thing.

ciceróne nm cicerone, guide.

cicisbèo nm gallant, lady's man.

ciclamíno nm cyclamen.

ciclísmo nm cycling.

ciclísta nmf cyclist.

ciclóne nm cyclone, hurricane.

ciclostilàre vt to cyclostyle.

ciclostíle nm cyclostyle.

cicógna nf stork.

cicòria nf chicory.

cicúta nf hemlock.

cièco pl **-chi** a blind; nm blind man.

cièlo nm sky, heaven; atmosphere, climate; ceiling.

cífra nf figure, number, cypher.

cifràre vt to write in cypher; (linen) mark.

cíglio pl **ciglia** (f), (fig) **cigli** (m) nm eyelash, eyebrow, edge; **c. della stràda** roadside.

ciglióne nm bank, edge.

cígno nm swan.

cigolàre vi to creak, squeak.

cigolío nm creaking, squeaking.

Cíle nm (geogr) Chile.

cilècca nf disappointment, failure.

cilèno a nm Chilean.

cilício nm hair-shirt, sackcloth.

ciliègia nf cherry; **ciliègio** nm cherry-tree.

cilíndrico pl **-ici** a cylindrical.

cilíndro nm cylinder, roller.

címa nf top, summit, eminence.

cimèlio nm relic, antique.

cimentàre vt to put to the test, try, risk; **-rsi** vr to enter into contest with, strive.

ciménto nm test, risk.

címice nf bug, bed-bug; drawing pin, (US) thumbtack.

ciminièra nf smokestack, chimney, funnel.

cimitèro nm cemetery, burial ground.

cimúrro nm glanders pl; distemper.
Cína nf (geogr) China.
cinciallégra nf tit.
cinedràmma nm screenplay.
cinegiornàle nm newsreel.
cínema nm inv v cinematògrafo.
cinematografàre vt to film.
cinematografía nf cinematography, cinema.
cinematògrafo nm cinema(tograph), picture house, pictures, (US) movies.
cinése a nmf Chinese.
cingallègra nf great tit(mouse).
cíngere vt to gird, encircle, surround.
cínghia nf belt, strap.
cinghiàle nm wild boar.
cíngolo nm girdle, (tec) caterpillar.
cinguettàre vi to chirp, twitter.
cínico pl cínici a cynical; nm cynic.
cinísmo nm cynicism.
cinquànta a fifty.
cinquantèsimo a fiftieth.
cinquantína nf some fifty, about fifty.
cínque a five.
cinquecentísta nmf artist or writer of the 16th century.
cinquecènto a five hundred; nm 16th century.
cinquènnio nm period of 5 years.
cínta nf city walls pl, fence, barrier.
cínto a surrounded, girded; nm belt; c. erniàrio truss.
cintúra nf belt, waistband; c. di salvatàggio lifebelt.
cinturíno nm strap.
ciò pron that, this.
ciòcca nf (of hair) lock, tuft; cluster.
ciòcco pl ciòcchi nm billet of wood, block, log.
cioccolàta nf chocolate (esp. drink).
cioccolatíno nm chocolate (sweet); pl chocolates.
cioccolàto nm chocolate.
cioè ad i.e., namely, that is.
ciondolàre vi to dangle; (fig) idle about; vt to swing, roll (head etc).
ciòndolo nm pendant, trinket.
ciondolóni ad dangling.
ciòtola nf bowl.
ciòttolo nm pebble.
cipíglio nm frown, scowl.
cipólla nm onion, bulb.
cipollína nf spring onion; cipollíne sótto acéto pickled onions.
cíppo nm half column, boundary stone.
ciprèsso nm cypress.
cípria nf face powder.
cipriòta a nmf Cyprian.
Cípro nf (geogr) Cyprus.
círca ad about, nearly; prep as to, concerning, with regard to.
círco pl -chi nm circus.
circolàre vi to circulate, go round; a nf circular.
circolazióne nf circulation, traffic.
círcolo nm circle, club.
circoncisióne nf circumcision.
circondàre vt to surround, enclose.

circondàrio nm district, neighbourhood.
circonferènza nf circumference.
circonlocuzióne nf circumlocution.
circonvallazióne nf ring-road.
circonveníre vt to circumvent, entrap.
circoscrívere vt to circumscribe, limit.
circoscrizióne nf circumscription; area.
circospètto a circumspect.
circospezióne nf circumspection.
circostànte a surrounding.
circostànza nf circumstance.
circuíre vt to surround, circumvent.
circúito nm circuit, compass; córto c. (el) short circuit.
Cirenàica nf (geogr) Cirenaica, Cyrenaica.
cisalpíno a (geogr) cisalpine.
cispadàno a (geogr) cispadane.
cisposità nf bleariness.
cispóso a blear-eyed.
císte nf cyst.
cistèrna nf cistern, tank; tanker.
cistifèllea nf gall-bladder.
citàre vt to cite, quote, mention; summon.
citazióne nf citation, quotation; summons, subpoena.
citòfono nm internal telephone.
citràto nm citrate.
città nf city.
cittadèlla nf citadel.
cittadína nf small town.
cittadinànza nf citizenship; citizens pl.
cittadíno a of a town; nm citizen, townsman.
ciúco pl ciúchi nm donkey.
ciúffo nm forelock, topknot, tuft.
ciúrma nf (naut) ship's crew.
ciurmàglia nf mob, rabble.
ciurmatóre nm scoundrel, swindler.
civétta nf owl; flirt, coquette.
civettàre vi to coquet, flirt.
civettería nf coquetry.
cívico pl -ici a civic.
civíle a civil, civilian.
civilizzàre vt to civilize.
civiltà nf civilization, civility.
civísmo nm civic virtues pl.
clàcson nm (aut) horn.
clamóre nm clamour, outcry.
clamoróso a clamorous, noisy.
clandestíno a clandestine.
Clàra nf pr Clara, Clare, Claire.
clarinétto, claríno nm clarinet.
clàsse nf class, form, rank, (US) grade; schoolroom; c. operàia working class.
clàssico pl -ici a classic(al); nm classic.
classífica nf classification; (sport) position, result.
classificàre vt to classify.
classificazióne nf classification.
Clàudio nm pr Claud.
clàusola nf clause.

claustràle *a* cloistral, claustral.

clausúra *nf* seclusion.

clàva *nf* club, bludgeon.

clavicémbalo *nm* (*mus*) harpsichord.

clavícola *nf* collarbone.

clemènte *a* clement, merciful.

clemènza *nf* clemency, mercy.

clericàle *a* clerical.

clericàto *nm* holy orders *pl*, priesthood.

clèro *nm* clergy.

cliènte *nmf* client, customer.

clientèla *nf* clients *pl*, customers *pl*, patronage, practice.

clíma *nm* climate.

climatèrico *pl* -ici *a* climacteric.

climàtico *pl* -ici *a* climatic; stazióne climàtica *nf* health resort.

clínica *nf* clinical medicine; clinic, nursing home.

clínico *pl* clínici *a* clinical; *nm* clinical doctor.

clistère *nm* (*med*) enema.

cloàca *nf* sewer, drain.

coabitàre *vi* to live together.

coabitazióne *nf* living together.

coadiuvàre *vt* to assist, help.

coagulàre *vt* to coagulate; -rsi *vr* to coagulate, curdle.

coalizióne *nf* coalition.

coàtto *a* forced, compulsory.

coazióne *nf* compulsion.

cobàlto *nm* cobalt.

còc *nm* coke.

cocaína *nf* cocaine.

cócca *nf* (*arrow*) notch; (*of an apron etc*) corner; pet daughter.

coccàrda *nf* cockade.

cocchière *nm* coachman, driver.

còcchio *nm* carriage, coach.

coccinèlla *nf* ladybird.

cocciníglia *nf* cochineal.

còccio *nm* earthenware pot; potsherd.

cocciutàggine *nf* obstinacy.

cocciúto *a* obstinate.

còcco *pl* còcchi *nm* coconut, coconut palm; pet, darling.

coccodríllo *nm* crocodile.

còccola *nf* berry.

coccolàre *vt* to fondle; -rsi *vr* to make oneself snug, nestle.

cocènte *a* hot, burning.

cocómero *nm* watermelon; blockhead.

cocúzzolo *nm* crown of the head; summit, top.

códa *nf* tail, queue; fàre la c. to queue, (*US*) to line up.

codardía *nf* cowardice.

codàrdo *a* cowardly; *nm* coward.

codésto *a and pron* that, that one.

còdice *nm* code, codex.

codicíllo *nm* codicil.

codificàre *vt* to codify.

codíno *nm* small tail, pigtail; reactionary.

coefficiènte *nm* coefficient.

coeguàle *a* co-equal.

coerède *nmf* co-heir(ess).

coerènte *a* coherent, consistent.

coerènza *nf* coherence, consistency.

coesióne *nf* cohesion.

coesístere *vi* to coexist.

coetàneo *a* contemporary.

coèvo *a* coeval.

còfano *nm* coffer, casket; (*aut*) bonnet, (*US aut*) hood.

cogitàre *vi* to cogitate, *v* ponderàre.

cògliere *vt* to pick, gather, catch, hit, seize, grasp.

cognàta *nf* sister-in-law; cognàto *nm* brother-in-law.

cògnito *a* known.

cognizióne *nf* knowledge.

cognóme *nm* surname.

coincidènza *nf* coincidence; (*of trains*) connection.

coincídere *vi* to coincide.

coinvòlgere *vt* to involve.

colà *ad* there.

colaggiù *ad* below, down there, *v* laggiù.

colàre *vt* to strain, sieve, colander; (*metals*) cast; drip; *vi* to drip, trickle, drop, leak.

colassú *ad* up there, *v* lassù.

colàta *nf* casting, flow.

colatóio *nm* colander, strainer; crucible.

colazióne *nf* lunch; príma c. breakfast.

colèi *pron* she, that woman.

colèra *nf* cholera.

coleróso *nm* cholera patient.

colibrí *nm* humming bird.

còlica *nf* colic.

colíno *nm* strainer.

còlla *nf* glue.

collaboràre *vi* to collaborate.

collaborazióne *nf* collaboration.

collàna *nf* necklace; (*of literary works*) series.

collàre *nm* collar.

collàsso *nm* collapse; c. cardíaco heart failure.

collaudàre *vt* to test, try out; approve.

collàudo *nm* test; approval.

collazionàre *vt* to collate, compare.

còlle *nm* hill.

collèga *nmf* colleague.

collegaménto *nm* connection.

collegàre *vt* to connect, join; -rsi *vr* to league, unite.

collègio *nm* boarding school, college; cconstituency.

còllera *nf* anger, wrath.

collèrico *pl* -ici *a* choleric, irascible.

collètta *nf* (*money*) collection, collect.

collettività *nf* collectivity.

collettívo *a nm* collective.

collétto *nm* collar.

collezionàre *vt* to collect.

collezióne *nf* collection.

collezionista *nmf* collector.

collimàre *vi* to agree, tally.

collína *nf* hill.

collinóso *a* hilly.

collírio *nm* collyrium, eyewash.

collisióne *nf* clash, collision.

còllo *nm* neck, collar; piece of luggage; c. del piède instep.

collocaménto *nm* placing, employment, situation; agenzìa di c. employment bureau.

collocàre *vt* to place; give in marriage; invest, employ; -rsi *vr* to get a position; get married.

collocazióne *nf* placing, arrangement; (*of library books*) press-mark, (*US*) call number.

collòquio *nm* conversation, interview.

colluttàre *vi* to scuffle, grapple.

colluttazióne *nf* scuffle, grapple.

colmàre *vt* to fill to overflowing, load, overwhelm.

cólmo *a* full, brimful; *nm* summit, limit.

cólo *nm* sieve, strainer.

colómba *nf* dove; **colómbo** *nm* pigeon; colómbo viaggiatóre carrier pigeon.

colombàia *nf* dovecot.

Colómbia *nf* (*geogr*) Columbia.

colombiàno *a* Columbian.

colònia *nf* colony, settlement.

Colònia *nf* (*geogr*) Cologne; àcqua di C. eau-de-Cologne.

colonizzàre *vt* to colonize.

colónna *nf* column, pillar.

colonnello *nm* colonel.

colòno *nm* farmer, colonist, settler.

coloràne *a* colouring; *nm* dye.

coloràre, colorìre *vt* to colour, dye.

coloràto *pp* a coloured.

colòre *nm* colour, dye; complexion, appearance; pretext; (*cards*) suit.

colorìto *a* coloured, rosy; *nm* colouring, complexion.

colóro *pron* they, those people.

colossàle *a* colossal.

colossèo *nm* Coliseum, Colosseum.

colòsso *nm* colossus.

cólpa *nf* crime, fault, offence, guilt, blame.

colpabilità *nf* culpability.

colpévole *a* culpable, guilty.

colpìre *vt* to hit, strike.

cólpo *nm* blow, stroke, wound, knock, shot; ad un c., di c. *ad* suddenly, unexpectedly.

colpóso *a* (*leg*) culpable, unpremeditated; omicìdio c. manslaughter.

coltellàta *nf* stab, knife wound.

coltellinàio *nm* cutler.

coltellìno *nm* small knife.

coltèllo *nm* knife.

coltivàre *vt* to cultivate, till.

coltivatóre *nm* -trìce *nf* cultivator, farmer.

coltivazióne *nf* cultivation.

cólto *a* cultivated, cultured, educated.

cóltre *nf* coverlet, blanket.

coltróne *nm* quilt.

coltúra *nf* cultivation; breeding, culture.

colúi *pron* he, that man.

comandaménto *nm* command, commandment.

comandànte *nm* commander; c. in secónda second-in-command.

comandàre *vt* to order, command.

comàndo *nm* order, command, leadership; (*mil*) H.Q.; (*av*) control.

combaciàre *vi* to fit together, tally.

combattènte *nm* combatant, soldier; ex c. ex-serviceman, (*US*) veteran.

combàttere *vti* to fight, oppose.

combattiménto *nm* fight, fighting, battle, action.

combinàre *vt* to combine; conclude, settle; plan; *vi* to agree; -rsi *vr* agree, match; happen.

combinazióne *nf* combination, arrangement; chance, coincidence; (*underwear*) combinations *pl*, (*US underwear*) union suit.

combrìccola *nf* band, gang.

combustìbile *a* combustible; *nm* fuel.

combustióne *nf* combustion.

cóme *ad* like, as, how, that, when, why; *interj* what!; c. sta? how do you do?

comèta *nf* comet.

comicità *nf* comicality.

còmico *pl* -ìci *a* comic, comical, funny; *nm* comicality; comedian.

cominciàre *vti* to begin.

comitàto *nm* committee.

comitìva *nf* company, party.

comìzio *nm* assembly, meeting.

commèdia *nf* comedy, play.

commediànte *nmf* player, comedian; (*fig*) hypocrite.

commediògrafo *nm* playwright.

commemoràre *vt* to commemorate.

commemorazióne *nf* commemoration.

commènda *nf* allowance, living; civic honour given in Italy.

commendàbile, -dévole *a* commendable, praiseworthy.

commendàre *vt* to commend, praise.

commendatìzia *nf* (*com*) letter of recommendation.

commendatóre *nm* special title given in Italy for civic merit.

commensàle *nm* table companion, guest, fellow-boarder.

commentàre *vt* to comment.

comménto *nm* comment.

commerciàle *a* commercial.

commerciànte *nm* dealer, merchant, trader.

commerciàre *vi* to deal, trade; *vt* to deal in.

commèrcio *nm* commerce, trade, business.

commésso *a* committed, entrusted; *nm* shop assistant, (*US*) store-clerk; c. viaggiatóre commercial traveller, representative.

commestìbile *a* eatable, edible; -ìli *nm* *pl* eatables *pl*.

comméttere *vt* to commit, entrust, order.

commiàto *nm* dismissal, leave.

commiseràre vt to pity, commiserate.

commiserazióne nf pity, commiseration.

commissariàto nm (mil) commissariat, commissary's office, police station.

commissàrio nm commissary, commissioner, superintendent.

commissionàrio nm commission agent.

commissióne nf errand, commission, order, committee; **fare delle commissióni** vi to do errands, go shopping.

commòsso a moved, touched, affected.

commovènte a moving, touching, affecting.

commozióne nf emotion; (med) concussion.

commuòvere vt to move, touch, affect; **-rsi** vr to be moved, touched.

commutàre vt to commute.

commutatóre a commutating; nm commutator, switch; **c. lùci anabbagliànti** (aut) dimmer switch.

commutatrice nf commutator.

comò nm chest of drawers.

comodìno nm bedside table.

comodità nf comfort, convenience, opportunity.

còmodo a comfortable, convenient, useful; well-to-do; nm comfort, convenience, ease, leisure; **a sùo c.** at your convenience.

compaesàno nm belonging to the same district or village.

compaginàre vt to join firmly together.

compàgine nf connection, joining of parts, structure.

compàgna nf female companion, wife.

compagnìa nf company, society.

compàgno a like, similar; nm companion, comrade, mate, partner; **c. di giuòchi** playmate.

companàtico pl **-ici** nm food eaten with bread.

comparàre vt to compare.

comparatìvo a comparative.

comparàto a comparative; **anatomìa c.** comparative anatomy.

comparazióne nf comparison, simile.

comparìre vi to appear.

compàrsa nf appearance; (theat) supernumerary.

compartecipàre vi to share (in).

compartimènto nm compartment, division.

compartìre vt to divide, share.

compassàto a stiff, formal.

compassionàre vt to pity.

compassióne nf compassion, pity.

compassionévole a exciting or feeling pity, pitiful.

compàsso nm compasses pl.

compatìbile a compatible, excusable.

compatiménto nm compassion, forbearance.

compatìre vt to pity, excuse.

compatriòta nmf compatriot.

compàtto a compact, solid.

compendiàre vt to abridge.

compèndio nm abridgement, compendium.

compensàre vt to compensate, indemnify.

compensàto nm plywood.

compènso nm compensation, reward, indemnity; **in c.** in return.

comperàre v **compràre.**

competènte a competent, qualified.

competènza nf competence, authority; **competènze** pl fees pl.

compètere vi to compete; be due to.

competizióne nf competition, contest.

compiacènte a obliging, complaisant.

compiacènza nf kindness, complaisance; satisfaction.

compiacére vt to please, comply with; **-rsi** vr to be pleased to, condescend.

compiaciménto nm satisfaction, pleasure; congratulation.

compiàngere vt to be sorry for, lament, pity.

compiànto a lamented, regretted; nm regret, pity, lament.

cómpiere vt to accomplish, complete, fulfil, finish.

compilàre vt to compile.

compilazióne nf compilation.

compiménto nm accomplishment, completion, fulfilment.

compìre v **compiere.**

compitàre vt to spell.

compitézza nf courtesy, politeness.

cómpito nm homework, task.

compìto a courteous, polite.

compiùto a accomplished, ended, complete.

compleànno nm birthday.

complementàre a complementary, supplementary.

compleménto nm complement; (mil) reserve.

complessióne nf constitution.

complessità nf complexity.

complessìvo a comprehensive, total.

complèsso a complex, compound; nm whole, set; (mus) band; **in c.** in general, on the whole.

completaménte ad completely, entirely.

completàre vt to complete.

complèto a complete, whole, full; nm (of clothes) suit.

complicàre vt to complicate, make intricate; **-rsi** vr to become complicated, difficult.

complicazióne nf complication.

còmplice nm accomplice.

complimentàre vt to compliment.

compliménto nm compliment; **compliménti** pl congratulations pl;

sènza compliménti frankly, without ceremony.

complimentóso *a* obsequious, ceremonious.

complottàre *vti* to plot, conspire.

complòtto *nm* conspiracy, plot.

componènte *a nmf* component, ingredient, member.

componiménto *nm* arrangement, composition.

compórre *vt* to arrange, compose; conciliate; (*type*) set up; **-rsi** *vr* to consist of.

comportàbile *a* bearable, tolerable; convenient.

comportaménto *nm* behaviour.

comportàre *vt* to bear, tolerate; allow, involve; **-rsi** *vr* to act, behave.

compòrto *nm* delay, respite.

compositóre *nm* composer; (*typ*) compositor.

composizióne *nf* composition, agreement, arrangement.

compostézza *nf* composure, self-possession.

compósto *a* cómpound, composed, sedate, self-possessed; *nm* compound, mixture.

cómpra *nf* purchase.

compràre *vt* to buy, purchase.

compratóre *nm* **-tríce** *nf* buyer.

compravéndita *nf* buying and selling.

comprèndere *vt* to understand, comprehend; comprise, include.

comprendònio *nm* (*fam*) understanding.

comprensíbile *a* comprehensible, intelligible.

comprensibilità *nf* comprehensibility, intelligibility.

comprensióne *nf* comprehension, understanding, sympathy.

comprensívo *a* comprehensive, sympathetic.

compréso *a* included, inclusive.

comprèssa *nf* compress, lozenge.

comprèsso *a* compressed, oppressed.

comprímere *vt* to compress, restrain.

compromésso *nm* compromise; **mettere in c.** to risk.

compromettènte *a* compromising.

compromèttere *vt* to compromise, involve.

comprovàre *vt* to prove, give evidence of.

compúnto *a* contrite, sorry.

compunzióne *nf* compunction, contrition.

computàre *vt* to compute, reckon.

computísta *nmf* accountant, book-keeper.

computistería *nf* accountant's office; book-keeping.

còmputo *nm* account, reckoning.

comunàle *a* communal, municipal.

comúne *a* common, ordinary; *nm* commune, municipality; town hall.

comunicàre *vt* to communicate, announce; administer the Sacrament; **-rsi** *vr* to take the Sacrament.

comunicatíva *nf* facility in explaining and instructing.

comunicàto *nm* bulletin, communiqué.

comunicazióne *nf* communication, connection, message.

comunióne *nf* communion, Communion.

comuníșmo *nm* Communism.

comuníșta *a nmf* Communist.

comunità *nf* community.

comúnque *ad* anyhow, however.

con *prep* with, by, at, from, on, against.

conàto *nm* effort, attempt.

cónca *nf* basin, tub; valley; conch.

concatenàre *vt* to link together.

còncavo *a nm* concave, hollow.

concèdere *vt* to grant, concede, allow.

concedíbile *a* allowable, grantable.

concentraménto *nm* **concentrazióne** *nf* concentration; **càmpo di concentraménto** concentration camp.

concentràre *vt* to concentrate.

concentràto *a* concentrated; *nm* extract, concentrated food.

concepíbile *a* conceivable.

concepiménto *vt* conception.

concepíre *vt* to conceive, imagine.

concèrnere *vt* to concern, relate.

concertàre *vt* to conduct, arrange, concert, plan; **-rsi** *vr* to agree, be agreed.

concertatóre *nm* **-tríce** *nf* **maéstro c. e direttóre d'orchèstra** conductor.

concertísta *nmf* concert artist.

concèrto *nm* concert, concerto; agreement; **di c.** unanimously.

concessionàrio *nm* (*com*) concessionaire, agent.

concessióne *nf* concession, permission.

concètto *nm* concept, conception, idea, (*lit*) conceit.

concettóso *a* pithy, sententious.

concezióne *nf* conception, idea.

conchíglia *nf* sea-shell, conch.

cóncia *nf* tanning, curing.

conciàre *vt* to dress (*skins*), tan; (*fig*) ill-treat.

conciatóre *nm* **-tríce** *nf* tanner.

conciatúra *nf* tanning, dressing.

conciliàbile *a* compatible, reconcilable.

conciliàbolo *nm* conventicle, secret meeting.

conciliàre *vt* to conciliate, reconcile; **-rsi** *vr* to agree; win (*affection etc*).

conciliazióne *nf* conciliation, reconciliation.

concílio *nm* council.

concimàre *vt* to manure.

concíme *nm* compost, dung, manure.

cóncio *a* tanned; knocked about; *nm* dung.

concisióne *nf* concision, conciseness.

conciso *a* concise, brief.
concitamento *nm* excitement tumult.
concitazióne *nf* excitement, agitation, emotion.
concittadíno *nm* fellow citizen.
concludènte *a* conclusive, decisive, energetic.
conclúdere *vt* to conclude, infer; do; *vi* be conclusive.
conclusióne *nf* conclusion, issue; in c. finally.
conclusívo *a* conclusive.
concordàre *vt* to arrange, reconcile; *vi* to agree.
concordàto *a* agreed upon, fixed; *nm* agreement, concordat.
concòrde *a* in agreement, consistent.
concòrdia *nf* harmony, unanimity.
concorrènte *a* concurrent; *nmf* competitor, rival.
concorrènza *nf* concurrence; competition, rivalry.
concórrere *vi* to concur; rival, compete.
concórso *nm* concourse; competition.
concretàre *vt* to make concrete; put into action.
concrèto *a* nm concrete, positive.
concubína *nf* concubine.
concubinàto *nm* concubinage.
concupiscènte *a* covetous.
concupiscènza *nf* concupiscence, lust.
concussióne *nf* concussion; extortion.
condànna *nf* condemnation, conviction.
condannàre *vt* to sentence, condemn.
condensàre *vt* to condense, thicken; -rsi *vr* to condense, grow thick.
condensàto *a* condensed.
condensatóre *nm* -trice *nf* condenser.
condensazióne *nf* condensation.
condiménto *nm* seasoning, condiment, dressing, sauce.
condíre *vt* to season, dress.
condiscendènte *a* condescending, compliant.
condiscendènza *nf* compliance, condescension.
condiscéndere *vi* to condescend, yield.
condiscépolo *nm* fellow-disciple, schoolfellow.
condíto *a* seasoned; (*of salad*) dressed.
condivídere *vt* to share.
condizionàle *a* conditional; *nm* (*gram*) conditional; *nf* (*leg*) conditional sentence.
condizionàre *vt* to condition; qualify.
condizionatóre *nm* air conditioner.
condizióne *nf* condition, rank, situation, qualification; a c. upon condition.
condoglianza *nf* condolence.
condolérsi *vr* to condole, grieve.
condomínio *nm* joint ownership.
condonàre *vt* to remit, condone.

condótta *nf* conduct, behaviour; management; piping system.
condótto *a* mèdico c. panel doctor; *nm* duct, conduit, pipe.
conducènte *nmf* driver; leaseholder.
condúrre *vti* to conduct, lead; -rsi *vr* to act, behave.
conduttóre *nm* -trice *nf* conductor, driver, guide, leader; (*el*) wire.
conduttúra *nf* conduit, main; c. d'àcqua water-pipe.
confabulàre *vi* to confabulate, chat.
confacènte *a* convenient, suitable.
confàrsi *vr* to agree, become, fit, suit.
confederàrsi *vr* to confederate.
confederazióne *nf* confederation.
conferènza *nf* lecture, conference.
conferenzière *nm* lecturer.
conferiménto *nm* bestowal, conferment.
conferíre *vt* to bestow, confer, contribute; *vi* confer (with), agree.
confèrma *nf* confirmation.
confermàre *vt* to confirm, strengthen.
confessàre *vt* to confess, acknowledge; -rsi *vr* to go to confession.
confessióne *nf* confession, faith.
confessóre *nm* confessor.
confètto *nm* bonbon, sweet.
confettúra *nf* jam.
confezionàre *vt* to manufacture, prepare, make up; confezionàto su misúra made to measure; artícolo confezionàto ready-made article.
confezióne *nf* manufacture, preparation; clothes; packing.
conficcàre *vt* to drive in, thrust.
confidàre *vt* to confide, trust; -rsi *vr* to confide in.
confidènte *a* confiding, trusting; *nmf* confidant, bosom friend.
confidènza *nf* confidence, secret, intimacy.
confidenziàle *a* confidential, private.
confidenzialménte *ad* confidentially, privately.
confíggere *vt* to nail, thrust.
configuràre *vt* to shape; (*fig*) symbolize.
confinànte *a* bordering, contiguous.
confinàre *vt* to banish, confine; *vi* to border on; -rsi *vr* to confine oneself; retire.
confíne *nm* border, frontier, limit.
confíno *nm* political confinement.
confísca *nf* confiscation, forfeiture.
confiscàre *vt* to confiscate, forfeit.
conflagrazióne *nf* conflagration.
conflítto *nm* conflict.
confluíre *vi* to flow together.
confóndere *vt* to confuse, confound; -rsi *vr* to get confused; worry.
conformàre *vt* to conform; -rsi *vr* to comply (with).
conformazióne *nf* conformation.
confórme *a* conforming, in agreement.
conformísmo *nm* conformism.
conformísta *nmf* conformist.

conformità *nf* conformity, accordance.

confortàre *vt* to comfort, console, encourage, fortify; **-rsi** *vr* to console oneself, take courage.

confortévole *a* comforting, comfortable.

confòrto *nm* comfort, consolation, support.

confratèllo *nm* (*relig*) fellow-member.

confratèrnita *nf* brotherhood, confraternity.

confrontàre *vt* to compare, confront; *vi* to agree.

confrónto *nm* comparison.

confusióne *nf* confusion, shame.

confúso *a* confused, embarrassed, ashamed; indistinct.

confutàre *vt* to confute, disprove.

confutazióne *nf* confutation.

congedàre *vt* to dismiss; **-rsi** *vr* to resign, take leave.

congèdo *nm* discharge, leave; **in c.** *ad* on leave.

congegnàre *vt* to put together, contrive.

congégno *nm* appliance, gear.

congelaménto *nm* congealment, freezing.

congelàre *vi* to congeal, freeze.

congènere *a* similar.

congènito *a* congenital.

congèrie *nf* heap, mass.

congestionàre *vt* to congest, crowd.

congettúra *nf* conjecture, guess.

congetturàre *vt* to conjecture.

congiúngere *vt* to connect, join; **-rsi** *vr* to join, meet.

congiuntivo *a* conjunctive, (*gram*) subjunctive; *nm* (*gram*) subjunctive.

congiúnto *a* joined, connected, combined; *nm* kinsman, relative.

congiuntúra *nf* conjuncture, circumstance; predicament.

congiúra *nf* conspiracy, plot.

congiuràre *vi* to conspire.

conglomeràre *vt* to conglomerate.

conglomeràto *nm* grouping, conglomerate.

conglutinàre *vt* to conglutinate.

Còngo *nm* (*geogr*) Congo.

congolése *a nmf* Congolese.

congratulàrsi *vr* to congratulate.

congratulazióne *nf* congratulation.

congrèga *nf* gang, set; congregation.

congregàre *vt* to assemble, call together; **-rsi** *vr* to congregate.

congressista *nmf* member of a congress.

congrèsso *nm* congress, conference.

còngruo *a* congruous, suitable.

conguagliàre *vt* to balance, equalize.

conguàglio *nm* adjustment, balancing, levelling.

coniàre *vt* to coin, (*a medal*) strike.

coniglièra *nf* rabbit-hutch.

coníglio *nm* rabbit.

cònio *nm* coinage; die, brand.

coniugàre *vt* to conjugate; **-rsi** *vr* to marry.

coniugazióne *nf* conjugation.

còniuge *nm* husband; *nf* wife; **còniugi** *pl* married couple.

connazionàle *nmf* compatriot.

connèttere *vt* to connect, join, (*fig*) associate; **non c.** to have confused ideas.

convivènte *a* conniving.

convivènza *nf* connivance.

connotàto *nm* distinctive mark; **connotàti** *pl* description (of a person).

connúbio *nm* marriage, union.

còno *nm* cone.

conòcchia *nf* distaff.

conoscènte *nmf* acquaintance.

conoscènza *nf* knowledge, acquaintance; consciousness, cognition.

conóscere *vt* to know, experience, take cognizance of; **farsi c.** to make oneself known; **-rsi** *vr* to know oneself, know each other.

conoscíbile *a* knowable, recognizable; non known.

conosciménto *nm* knowing, knowledge.

conoscitóre *nm* **-trice** *nf* connoisseur, good judge.

conosciúto *a* well-known, famous.

conquista *nf* conquest.

conquistàre *vt* to conquer.

consacràre *vt* to consecrate, dedicate, devote, ordain.

consacrazióne *nf* consecration, ordination.

consanguíneo *a* consanguineous, closely related; *nm* kinsman.

consapévole *a* aware, conscious, acquainted.

consapevolézza *nf* consciousness, knowledge.

cònscio *v* **consapévole**.

consègna *nf* consignment, delivery; **lasciàre in c.** *vt* to deposit.

consegnàre *vt* to consign, deliver.

conseguènte *a* consequent, consistent.

conseguènza *nf* consequence; **in c.** accordingly.

conseguiménto *nm* attainment.

conseguire *vt* to attain, obtain, reach; *vi* to follow, result.

consènso *nm* consent, assent.

consensuàle *a* (*leg*) by mutual consent.

consentire *vi* to consent, agree, yield; *vt* to permit.

consenzìènte *a* approving, consenting.

consèrva *nf* jam, preserve, preservation, reservoir.

conservàre *vt* to keep, preserve; **-rsi** *vr* to last, keep in good health.

conservatóre, *f* **-trice** *a* preserving, preservative, conservative; *nm* preserver, keeper; (*pol*) Conservative.

conservatòrio *nm* academy of music.

conservazióne *nf* preservation, care, maintenance.

consèsso *nm* assembly, meeting.

consideràbile *a* considerable.

consideràre *vt* to consider, regard.

consideràto *a* considerate, thoughtful, careful; esteemed.

considerazióne *nf* consideration, esteem.

considerévole *a* considerable, pretty large.

consigliàre *vt* to advise, counsel; **-rsi** *vr* to ask advice, consult.

consiglière *nm* counsellor, councillor.

consiglio *nm* advice, counsel, council.

consìmile *a* like, similar.

consistènte *a* consistent; firm, substantial.

consistènza *nf* consistence, consistency.

consìstere *vi* to consist.

consòcio *nm* associate, partner.

consolàre *vt* to comfort, console; **-rsi** *vr* to take comfort.

consolàre *a* consular.

consolàto *nm* consulate.

consolazióne *nf* consolation, comfort, delight.

cònsole *nm* consul.

consolidàre *vt* to consolidate, strengthen; **-rsi** *vr* to grow firm.

consolidazióne *nf* **consolidaménto** *nm* consolidation, strengthening.

consonànte *a* consonant, agreeing; *nf* consonant.

consonànza *nf* consonance, agreement.

cònsono *a* consonant, agreeing.

consòrte *nmf* consort, husband, wife.

consortería *nf* clique, set.

consòrzio *nm* society, syndicate.

constàre *vi* to consist, be known, be proved.

constatàre *vt* to ascertain, verify, certify.

constatazióne *nf* ascertainment.

consuèto *a* habitual, usual.

consuetúdine *nf* custom, habit, practice.

consulènte *a* consulting, consultant; *nm* consultant, adviser.

consulènza *nf* advice; **c. legàle** legal advice.

consùlta *nf* council.

consultàre *vt* to consult, examine; **-rsi** *vr* to seek advice, consult.

consultazióne *nf* consultation; **gabinétto di c.** *(med)* consulting room; **libro di c.** reference book.

consùlto *nm* consultation, (medical or legal) opinion.

consumàre *vt* to consume, waste, consummate; **-rsi** *vr* to wear out, consume, pine away, waste away.

consumatóre *nm* consumer.

consumazióne *nf* consumption, consummation; drink or food (in a café etc).

consúmo *nm* consumption, waste; **úso e c.** wear and tear.

consúnto *a* consumed, worn out; consumptive.

consunzióne *nf* *(med)* consumption.

contàbile *a* book-keeping, calculating; *nm* book-keeper, accountant.

contabilità *nf* book-keeping.

contadína *nf* **-no** *nm* peasant.

contadinésco *pl* **-éschi** *a* rustic.

contàdo *nm* country (round a town).

contagiàre *vt* to infect, contaminate.

contàgio *nm* contagion.

contagióso *a* contagious, infectious.

contagócce *nm* dropper.

contaminàre *vt* to contaminate.

contaminazióne *nf* contamination, pollution.

contànte *a* counting, ready; **denàro c.** cash, ready money; *nm* cash.

contàre *vt* to count; relate; consider; *vi* to count, have authority, rely on; **ciò che cónta** what matters.

contatóre *nm* meter, reckoner; **c. a monéta** slot meter; **c. del gas** gasmeter; **c. per parchéggio** parking meter.

contàtto *nm* contact, touch, connection; **spína di c.** contact plug.

cónte *nm* count, earl.

contèa *nf* earldom, county, shire.

conteggiàre *vt* to count, charge.

contéggio *nm* computation, calculation; **c. all'indiètro** countdown.

contégno *nm* behaviour, dignity, gravity.

contegnóso *a* dignified, grave, staid.

contemperàre *vt* to proportion, temper.

contemplàre *vt* to contemplate.

contemplatìvo *a* contemplative.

contemplazióne *nf* contemplation.

contemporaneità *nf* contemporaneousness.

contemporàneo *a nm* contemporary.

contendènte *a* contending, opposing; *nm* rival, opponent, competitor.

contèndere *vt* to contest; *vi* to contend, quarrel; **-rsi** *vr* to contend, be rivals for.

contenére *vt* to contain, hold, restrain; **-rsi** *vr* to behave, control oneself.

contentàre *vt* to content, gratify; **-rsi** *vr* to be pleased, satisfied.

contentatúra *nf* contentment; **di fàcile c.** *ad* easy to please.

contentézza *nf* contentment, satisfaction.

contènto *a* content, glad, satisfied; *nm* contentment, happiness.

contenúto *a* contained; *nm* contents *pl*, subject.

contenzióso *a* contentious.

conterràneo *a* of the same country; *nm* countryman.

contésa *nf* contest, dispute, contention.

contéssa *nf* countess.

contestàre *vt* to contest, deny.

contestazióne *nf* contest, dispute; notification.

contèsto *a* interwoven; *nm* context.

contézza *nf* knowledge.

contiguità *nf* contiguity.
contìguo *a* contiguous, adjoining.
continentàle *a* continental.
continènte *a* temperate, continent; *nm* continent.
continènza *nf* continence, self-restraint.
contingènte *a* contingent; *nm* contingency, contingent; (*com*) quota.
contingènza *nf* contingency, emergency, circumstance.
continuaménte *ad* continuously, continually, constantly.
continuàre *vti* to continue, pursue, go on, last.
continuazióne, continuità *nf* continuation, continuity, duration.
contìnuo *a* continuous, non-stop, lasting; **di c.** *ad* non-stop, continuously.
cónto *nm* account, bill; computation, reckoning; worth.
contòrcere *vt* to contort; **-rsi** *vr* to twist, wring, writhe.
contornàre *vt* to surround, trim.
contórno *nm* contour, outline; vegetables served with a dish of meat.
contorsióne *nf* contortion.
contrabbandière *nm* smuggler.
contrabbàndo *nm* contraband goods *pl*, smuggling.
contrabbàsso *nm* (*mus*) double bass.
contraccambiàre *vt* to return, reciprocate.
contraccàmbio *nm* exchange, return; **rèndere il c.** to give like for like.
contraccólpo *nm* counter-stroke, rebound.
contràda *nf* countryside, district, wide street.
contraddìre *vt* to contradict.
contraddistìnguere *vt* to distinguish, mark.
contraddittòrio *a* contradictory; *nm* debate, cross-examination.
contrad(d)izióne *nf* contradiction.
contraèrea *nf* anti-aircraft artillery; **contraèreo** *a* anti-aircraft.
contraffàre *vt* to counterfeit, forge, imitate; **-rsi** *vr* to disguise oneself.
contraffàtto *a* counterfeit, disguised; deformed.
contraffazióne *nf* counterfeit, forgery.
contrammiràglio *nm* rear-admiral.
contrappélo *nm* the wrong way; **a, di c.** (*fig*) against the grain.
contrappéso *nm* counter-balance, counterpoise.
contrappórre *vt* to contrast, oppose; **-rsi** *vr* to cross, oppose.
contrappùnto *nm* (*mus*) counterpoint.
contrariàre *vt* to thwart, oppose, annoy.
contràrio *a* contrary, opposite, unfavourable, adverse; *nm* contrary, opposite; **al c.** on the contrary.

contràrre *vt* to contract; **-rsi** *vr* to shrink.
contrasségno *nm* countersign, badge, mark.
contrastànte *a* contrasting.
contrastàre *vt* to contest, oppose, resist; *vi* to contrast, clash; **-rsi** *vr* to fight.
contràsto *nm* contrast, opposition, strife, clash.
contrattàcco *nm* counter-attack.
contrattàre *vti* to negotiate, bargain.
contrattèmpo *nm* mishap, hitch; (*mus*) syncopation.
contràtto *a* contracted; *nm* contract, agreement.
contravveléno *nm* antidote.
contravvenìre *vi* to contravene, infringe.
contravvenzióne *nf* contravention, infringement; fine; **fàre una c.** impose a fine.
contrazióne *nf* contraction.
contribuènte *nmf* taxpayer.
contribuìre *vi* to contribute, help, share.
contribùto *nm* contribution, share.
contristàre *vt* to afflict, sadden; **-rsi** *vr* to be afflicted, grieve.
contrìto *a* contrite, penitent.
contrizióne *nf* contrition, penitence.
cóntro *prep* against, opposite.
controfirmàre *vt* to countersign.
controllàre *vt* to check, control, verify, inspect.
contròllo *nm* check, control.
controllóre *nm* controller, ticket-collector, ticket-inspector.
controlùce *ad* against the light.
contropòrta *nf* double door.
controproducènte *a* having the opposite effect.
contropròva *nf* counter-check, counter-vote, evidence.
contrórdine *nm* counter-order.
Controrifórma *nf* Counter-reformation.
controsènso *nm* misinterpretation, nonsense.
controstòmaco *ad* unwillingly.
controvèrsia *nf* controversy, dispute.
controvèrso *a* controversial, doubtful.
controvèrtere *vt* to controvert, dispute.
contumàce *a* contumacious, guilty of default.
contumàcia *pl* **-àcie** *nf* default, contumacy; quarantine.
contumèlia *nf* contumely, abuse.
contundènte *a* bruising; **àrma c.** blunt weapon.
conturbàre *vt* to disturb, trouble; **-rsi** *vr* to be agitated, fret.
contusióne *nf* bruise, contusion.
contuttochè *cj* although.
contuttociò *ad* however, nevertheless.
convalescènte *a nmf* convalescent.
convalescènza *nf* convalescence.

convalidàre *vt* to confirm, corroborate.

convégno *nm* meeting (place).

convenévole *a* convenient, proper, suitable; **convenévoli** *nm pl* compliments, regards, ceremony.

conveniènte *a* convenient, profitable.

conveniènza *nf* convenience, advantage, propriety, proportion.

conveníre *vi* to suit; meet, assemble; agree; *vt* to summon.

convènto *nm* convent, monastery.

convenúto *a* agreed (on), fixed; *nm* agreement; defendant.

convenzionàle *a* conventional.

convenzióne *nf* convention, covenant.

convergènza *nf* convergence.

convèrgere *vi* to converge.

convèrsa *nf* lay sister.

conversàre *vi* to converse, talk.

conversazióne *nf* conversation, talk.

conversióne *nf* conversion.

convèrso *a* converse, opposite; *nm* lay brother.

convertíre *vt* to convert; **-rsi** *vr* to be converted.

convertíto *nm* convert.

convessità *nf* convexity.

convèsso *a* convex.

convettóre *nm* convector.

convincènte *a* convincing.

convíncere *vt* to convince, persuade.

convincimento *nm* **convinzióne** *nf* conviction, persuasion.

convitàto *nm* guest.

convíto *nm* banquet, feast.

convítto *nm* boarding-school.

convivènte *a* living together.

convivènza *nf* cohabitation, living together.

convívere *vi* to cohabit, live together.

convocàre *vt* to convoke, summon.

convogliàre *vt* to convoy, direct.

convòglio *nm* convoy, train.

convulsióne *nf* convulsion, spasm.

convulsívo *a* convulsive, spasmodic.

convùlso *a* convulsive, jerky; *nm* convulsion.

cooperàre *vi* to co-operate.

cooperatíva *nf* (*com*) co-operative society.

cooperazióne *nf* co-operation.

coordinàre *vt* to co-ordinate.

coordinàta *nf* co-ordinate.

copèrchio *nm* cover, lid.

copèrta *nf* blanket, coverlet, rug, cover; (*naut*) deck.

copertína *nf* cover, book-cover, dust-jacket.

copèrto *a* covered, (*of the sky*) overcast; clothed, hidden; *nm* (*at table*) cover, place.

copertóne *nm* (*tyre*) cover; tarpaulin.

copertúra *nf* covering.

còpia *nf* copy, print; plenty, quantity; **c. fotostàtica** (**fotocòpia**) photostat (photocopy); **c. carbóne**

carbon copy; **bèlla c.** fair copy; **brútta c.** rough copy.

copialèttere *nm* letter-book, letter-press.

copiàre *vt* to copy, imitate, transcribe.

copiatívo *a* copying.

copiatúra *nf* copying, transcription.

copióne *nm* (*theat*) script.

copióso *a* abundant, copious.

copísta *nmf* copyist.

copistería *nf* copying office, typing office.

cóppa *nf* cup, goblet; (*aut*) sump, (*US aut*) oil pan.

coppellàre *vt* (*metals*) to assay, test.

còppia *nf* couple, pair.

copricàpo *nm* headgear, hat.

coprifuòco *pl* **-fuòchi** *nm* curfew.

copríre *vt* to cover, hide, protect, shelter, hold (a post); **-rsi** *vr* to put on one's hat, wrap oneself up.

copriteièra *nm* tea-cosy, cap.

coprivivànde *nm* dishcover.

còpto *a* Coptic; *nm* Copt, (*language*) Coptic.

coràggio *nm* courage, valour.

coraggiosaménte *ad* bravely.

coraggióso *a* courageous, valiant.

coràle *a* choral; *nm* chorale.

coràllo *nm* coral.

Coràno *nm* Koran.

coràzza *nf* cuirass, armour-plating.

corazzàre *vt* to armour.

corazzière *nm* cuirassier.

còrba *nf* basket.

corbellàre *vt* to make a fool of, make fun of.

corbellería *nf* foolish act.

corbèllo *nm* (small) basket.

corbézzola *nf* arbutus-berry; **corbézzolo** *nm* arbutus-tree.

còrda *nf* cord, rope, (*of a musical instrument*) string; (*mus*) chord.

cordàme *nm* (*naut*) cordage, ropes *pl*.

cordiàle *a* cordial, hearty, warm; *nm* cordial.

cordicèlla *nf* **cordoncíno** *nm* fine cord, string.

cordòglio *nm* grief, mourning, sorrow.

cordóne *nm* cord; cordon.

Corèa *nf* (*geogr*) Korea.

coreàno *a nm* Korean.

coriàndolo *nm* paper streamer; **coriàndoli** *pl* confetti.

coricàre *vt* to lay down; **-rsi** *vr* to go to bed, lie down.

corísta *nm* chorister, chorus singer.

cornàcchia *nf* crow; (*fig*) croaker.

cornamúsa *nf* (*mus*) bagpipes *pl*.

cornétta *nf* (*mus*) cornet, horn.

cornétto *nm* ear-trumpet, small horn; *pl* French beans *pl*.

corníce *nf* frame, framework.

cornicióne *nm* cornice.

corniòla *nf* (*min*) cornelian.

còrno *pl* **còrna** (*f*), (*instruments*) **còrni** (*m*) *nm* horn.

Cornovàglia nf (geogr) Cornwall.
cornúto a horned; nm cuckold.
còro nm chorus, choir.
coróna nf crown, wreath, garland; (mus) corona.
coronàre vt to crown.
coronàrio a coronary.
coronazióne nf coronation.
corpacciúto a burly, corpulent.
corpétto nm bodice, waistcoat.
còrpo nm body, corpse; mass.
corporàle a bodily, corporal, corporeal.
corporatúra nf size.
corporazióne nf corporation.
corpòreo a corporeal.
corpulènto a corpulent.
corpulènza nf corpulence.
Corràdo nm pr Conrad, Konrad.
corredàre vt to equip, fit up, outfit.
corredíno nm baby's layette.
corrèdo nm equipment, furniture, kit, outfit, trousseau.
corrèggere vt to correct, revise, upbraid; **-rsi** vr to improve, mend one's ways.
correlazióne nf correlation.
corrènte a running, flowing, current, common; nf stream, current; **tenére al c.** to keep informed.
córrere vi to run, flow, (of time) elapse, circulate, (of distance) intervene.
correttaménte ad correctly, properly.
correttézza nf correctness, propriety, honesty.
corrètto a correct, exact, upright, well-bred.
correttóre nm **-trice** nf corrector, (typ) proof-reader.
correzióne nf correction, reform.
corrída nf bullfight.
corridóio nm corridor, passage.
corridóre nm racer, runner.
corrièra nf coach, bus, mail-bus, mail-coach.
corrière nm courier, messenger, carrier, mail, (US) express company; **a vòlta di c.** ad by return of post.
corrispettivo a corresponding; nm equivalent, compensation.
corrispondènte a corresponding, correspondent; nmf correspondent.
corrispondènza nf correspondence, harmony, connection.
corrispóndere vi to correspond, return; vt to pay.
corrivo a easy-going, lenient, rash.
corroboràre vt to corroborate; strengthen.
corroborazióne nf corroboration, support.
corródere vt to corrode, eat away, wear away; **-rsi** vr to corrode, waste away.
corrómpere vt to corrupt, pollute, bribe; **-rsi** vr to rot, become corrupt.
corrosívo a nm corrosive.

corrótto a corrupt(ed).
corrucciàre vi **-rsi** vr to get angry; grieve.
corrúccio nm anger, wrath.
corrugàre vt to corrugate, frown, knit (one's brows); **-rsi** vr wrinkle.
corruscàre vi to scintillate, flash.
corruttèla nf corruption.
corruttibilità nf corruptibility.
corruzióne nf corruption, decay.
córsa nf race, run, running, trip.
corsàro nm corsair, pirate.
corsía nf passage; (of hospital) ward; dormitory; track.
Còrsica nf (geogr) Corsica.
corsívo a nm cursive, italic, italics pl.
córso a passed, plundered; nm course, main street, flow.
còrso a nm Corsican.
córte nf court, hall, tribunal, yard.
cortéccia nf bark, crust.
corteggiaménto nm courtship, wooing.
corteggiàre vt to court, woo.
corteggiatóre nm suitor, wooer, lover.
cortéggio nm attendants pl, retinue.
cortèo nm procession, train.
cortése a courteous, kind, polite.
cortesía nf courtesy, politeness.
cortézza nf shortness, dullness.
cortigiàna nf courtesan.
cortigiàno nm courtier.
cortíle nm court, courtyard, playground.
cortína nf curtain.
córto a short, brief, deficient; **èssere a c. di** to be short of, lack.
corvétta nf curvet; (naut) corvette.
còrvo nm raven, crow, rook.
còsa nf thing, matter, work; **che còsa?** what?; **tànte còse** regards.
cosàcco a nm Cossack.
còscia nf thigh, haunch.
cosciènte a aware, conscious.
cosciènza nf conscience, consciousness, conscientiousness.
coscienzióso a conscientious.
sciòtto nm (of meat) leg.
coscrítto a nm conscript.
coscrizióne nf conscription.
cosí ad as, so, thus, therefore; **c. c. so-so**; **per c. díre** so to speak.
cosicché cj so that.
cosiddétto a so-called.
cosmètico pl **-ici** a nm cosmetic.
còsmico pl **-ici** a cosmic.
còsmo nm cosmos, universe.
cosmòdromo nm cosmodrome, rocket-station.
cosmonàuta nm cosmonaut.
cosmopòlita a nm cosmopolitan, cosmopolite.
còso nm thing, thingummy (word used instead of the real name of something).
cospàrgere vt to sprinkle, strew.
cospètto nm presence.
cospícuo a conspicuous; considerable.
cospiràre vi to conspire, plot.
cospirazióne nf conspiracy.

còsta nf coast, declivity; rib; (of knife, book) back.

costà ad there, in your town.

costaggiù ad down there.

costànte a nf constant, steady, firm, uniform.

Costantinòpoli nf (geogr) Constantinople.

costànza nf constancy, firmness, perseverance.

Costànza nf pr Constance.

Costànza nf (geogr) **lago di C.** Lake of Constance.

costàre vt to cost.

costatàre v **constatàre**.

costatazióne v **constatazióne**.

costàto nm flank, ribs pl, side.

costeggiàre vti to coast, lie along, run along by.

costèi pron she, this woman, that woman.

costernàre vt to appal, dismay; **-rsi** vr to be dismayed.

costì ad there, in your town.

costièra nf coast, shore.

costipàre vt to constipate, give a cold to; **-rsi** vr to become costive, catch a cold.

costipàto a having a cold; constipated.

costipazióne nf (med) cold; constipation.

costituíre vt to constitute, elect; **-rsi** vr to constitute oneself; give oneself up, surrender.

costituzióne nf establishment, constitution.

còsto nm cost.

còstola nf rib; (of knife, book) back.

costolétta nf chop, cutlet.

costóro pron pl they, these (those) people.

costóso a costly, expensive.

costríngere vt to compel, constrain, compress.

costrizióne nf constraint, compulsion, constriction.

costruíre vt to build, construct.

costruttívo a constructive.

costrútto nm construction, profit, meaning.

costruzióne nf construction, building.

costúi pron he, this man, that man.

costumàre vi and impers to be usual, be the fashion, be in the habit of.

costumatézza nf decency, good manners pl, politeness.

costumàto a civil, polite.

costúme nm custom, morals pl; costume.

costúra nf seam.

coténna nf pigskin, scalp; turf.

cotésto a and pron that, pl those.

cotidiàno a nm daily.

cotógna nf quince; **cotógno** nm quince-tree.

cotognàta nf quince jam, jelly.

cotolétta v **costolétta**.

cotonàto nm cotton; silk and cotton fabric.

cotóne nm cotton; **c. idròfilo** cottonwool, (US) absorbent cotton.

cotonièro a cotton.

cotoníficio nm cotton-mill.

còtta nf baking; surplice; **prèndere una c. per** (sl) to have a crush on; get tipsy.

còttimo nm job-work, piecework; **lavoràre a c.** to do piecework.

còtto a cooked; (sl) madly in love; tipsy.

cottúra nf cooking.

covàre vt to brood, brood over cherish secretly, smoulder, hatch.

covàta nf brood, hatch.

covíle nm den, hole.

cóvo nm den.

covóne nm (of corn) sheaf.

Còzie, (Àlpi) nf pl (geogr) Cottian Alps.

còzza nf mussel.

cozzàre vti to butt, collide.

còzzo nm butting, collision, shock.

cràc nm crash, (financial) failure.

Cracòvia nf (geogr) Cracow.

cràmpo nm cramp.

crànio nm skull.

cràpula nf excess guzzling, debauch.

cràsso a crass, gross.

cratère nm crater.

cravàtta nf (neck)tie.

creànza nf breeding, manners pl.

creàre vt to create, cause, appoint.

creatívo a creative.

creàto a created; nm creation universe.

creatóre nm **-tríce** nf creator.

creatúra nf creature, child.

creazióne nf creation, appointment.

credènte a believing; nmf believer.

credènza nf belief, credit; sideboard, pantry.

crédere vti to believe, think, trust; **-rsi** vr to believe oneself.

credíbile a believable, credible.

credibilità nf credibility.

crédito nm credit, esteem.

creditóre nm **-tríce** nf creditor.

crèdo nm creed, credo.

credulità nf credulity.

crèdulo a credulous.

crèma nf cream, custard; (of society) élite; **c. emolliènte** cold cream; **c. evanescènte** vanishing cream; **c. antivàmpa** barrier cream.

cremàre vt to cremate.

crematóio, fórno cremnatório nm crematorium.

cremazióne nf cremation.

crèmiṣi a nm crimson.

crèpa nf chink, (in a wall etc) crack.

crepàccio nm crevasse, large crack.

crepacuòre nm grief, heartbreak.

crepàre vi to burst, crack, split; (fig) die.

crepitàre vi to crackle.

crepitío nm crackling.

crepuscolàre *a* crepuscular, of twilight.

crepúscolo *nm* dusk, gloaming, twilight.

crescènza *nf* growth, increase.

créscere *vi* to grow, increase, (*of prices or water-level*) rise; *vt* to raise, bring up.

crescióne *nm* watercress.

créscita *nf* growth, rise.

crèṣima *nf* chrism, confirmation.

creṣimàre *vt* to confirm; **-rsi** *vr* to be confirmed.

crèspa *nf* wrinkle, ripple, crease.

créspo *a* crisp, frizzy, wrinkled, pleated; *nm* crêpe.

crèsta *nf* crest.

crestomaẓía *nf* anthology.

crèta *nf* chalk, clay.

Crèta *nf* (*geogr*) Crete.

cretinería *nf* foolish act, nonsense.

cretiníṣmo *nm* cretinism, idiocy.

cretíno *nm* cretin, idiot.

crícca *nf* gang.

crícco *pl* **crícchi** *nm* (*tec*) jack.

Crimèa, (la) *nf* (*geogr*) Crimea.

criminàle *a nmf* criminal, offender.

crímine *nm* crime, offence.

criminología *nf* criminology.

crinàle *nm* (*of mountains*) ridge.

crine, críno *nm* horse-hair.

crinièra *nf* mane.

crípta *nf* crypt.

criṣantèmo *nm* chrysanthemum.

críṣi *nf* crisis.

críṣma *nm* chrism, consecrated oil.

cristallàme *nm* crystalware, glass-ware.

cristallería *nf* crystalware, crystal manufactory.

cristallièra *nf* glass case, china cabinet.

cristallíno *a* crystal; crystal-clear; *nm* (*anat*) crystalline lens.

cristallizzàre *vt* **-rsi** *vr* to crystallize.

cristàllo *nm* crystal, glass.

cristianéṣimo *nm* Christianity.

cristianità *nf* Christendom.

cristiàno *a nm* Christian.

Cristína *nf* *pr* Christine, Christina.

Cristo *nm* *pr* Christ.

Cristòforo *nm* *pr* Christopher.

critèrio *nm* criterion, judgement.

crítica *nf* criticism, critique, censure.

criticàre *vt* to criticize, censure.

crítico *pl* **-ici** *a* critical, censorious; *nm* critic.

crivellàre *vt* to riddle, sift.

crivèllo *nm* sieve.

cròcchio *nm* gathering, group.

cróce *nf* cross.

crocerossína *nf* Red Cross nurse.

crocevía *nf* crossroads.

crociàta *nf* crusade.

crociàto *nm* crusader.

crocícchio *nm* crossroads.

crocièra *nf* cruise.

crocifíggere *vt* to crucify.

crocifissióne *nf* crucifixion.

crosifísso *a* crucified; *nm* crucifix.

cròco *pl* **cròchi** *nm* crocus.

crogiuòlo *nm* crucible.

crollàre *vi* to collapse, fall down, slump; *vt* to shake.

cròllo *nm* collapse, fall, ruin, shake.

cròma *nf* (*mus*) quaver.

cromàre *vt* to chromium plate.

cromàtico *pl* **-ici** *a* chromatic.

cromàto *a* chromium-plated.

crònaca *nf* chronicle, news.

crònico *pl* **-ici** *a* (*med*) chronic.

cronísta *nm* chronicler, reporter .

cronología *nf* chronology.

cronològico *pl* **-ici** *a* chronological.

cronometràre *vt* to time.

cronòmetro *nm* chronometer, stop watch.

cròsta *nf* crust, scab.

crostàceo *nm* crustacean, shellfish.

crostíno *nm* piece of toast, crouton.

crostóso *a* crusty.

cròtalo *nm* rattlesnake.

crucciàre *vt* to irritate, worry; **-rsi** *vr* to be troubled, worry.

crúccio *nm* grief, trouble, worry.

cruciàle *a* crucial.

crucivèrba *nm* crossword puzzle.

crudèle *a* cruel.

crudelménte *ad* cruelly.

crudeltà *nf* cruelty.

crudézza *nf* crudeness, rawness.

crúdo *a* raw, crude, harsh.

cruènto *a* bloody, dreadful.

crumíro *nm* blackleg, (*US*) scab, fink.

crúsca *nf* bran; freckles *pl*.

cruscòtto *nm* (*aut*) dashboard, (*av*) instrument panel.

Cúba *nf* (*geogr*) Cuba.

cubàno *a nm* Cuban.

cúbito *nm* cubit, elbow, forearm.

cúbo *nm* cube.

cuccàgna *nf* abundance, plenty; **paéṣe di C.** land of Cockaigne.

cuccétta *nf* berth, bunk.

cucchiaiàta *nf* spoonful.

cucchiaíno *nm* teaspoon.

cucchiàio *nm* spoon.

cúccia *nf* dog's bed.

cúcciolo *nm* puppy.

cúcco *pl* **cúcchi** *nm* darling, pet; **vècchio c.** childish old man.

cúccuma *nf* coffee pot.

cucína *nf* cooking, kitchen, stove.

cucinàre *vt* to cook.

cuciníno *nm* kitchenette, small kitchen.

cucíre *vt* to sew, stitch.

cucitríce *nf* seamstress; sewing machine.

cucitúra *nf* seam, sewing.

cucù *nm* cuckoo; **orológio a c.** cuckoo clock.

cúculo *nm* cuckoo.

cúffia *nf* bonnet, cap; (*rad*) earphone.

cugína *nf* **-o** *nm* cousin.

cúi *pron* which, whom, whose.

culinària *nf* cookery.

cúlla *nf* cradle.

cullàre *vt* to rock (a cradle), lull.

culminànte a culminating, highest.

culminàre vi to culminate.

cúlmine nm apex, top.

cúlo nm buttocks pl, rump.

cúlto nm cult, worship.

cultúra nf culture, cultivation.

cumulàre vt to accumulate.

cúmulo nm accumulation, heap, pile.

cúneo nm wedge.

cuòca nf -o nm cook.

cuòcere vt to cook; vi to vex, hurt.

cuoiàio nm tanner, dealer in leather

cuòio nm leather, skin.

cuòre nm heart, centre, courage.

cupidìgia, cupidità nf cupidity, covetousness, greed.

cúpido a eager, covetous, greedy.

Cupído nm pr Cupid.

cúpo a dark; deep, hollow.

cúpola nf cupola, dome.

cúra nf care, cure; parish; (med) treatment.

curànte, mèdico nm doctor in charge of a case.

curàre vt to care, take care of, (med) treat; -rsi vr to take care of oneself, mind.

curàto nm curate, parish priest.

curatóre nm trustee.

cúria nf senate house, court of justice, the bar.

curiàle a curial; nm lawyer.

curiosàre vi to be curious about, pry into.

curiosità nf curiosity, inquisitiveness.

curióso a curious, inquisitive.

cúrva nf bend, curve.

curvàre vt -rsi vr to bend, curve.

curvatúra nf bending, (tec) camber, curvature.

cúrvo a bent, crooked, curved.

cuscinétto nm small cushion; (tec) bearing.

cuscíno nm cushion, pillow; (tec) buffer.

custòde nm attendant, custodian, janitor, door-keeper.

custòdia nf custody, keeping, care; case.

custodíre vt to guard, keep; -rsi vr to take care of oneself.

cúte nf (human) skin.

cutìcola nf cuticle.

cutréttola nf wagtail.

czar nm tzar, tsar, czar.

czèco pl -èchi a nm Czech.

D

da prep from, to, at, through, for since, by, in, like, as, when.

dabbàsso, da bàsso ad below, down there, downstairs.

dabbenàggine nf ingenuousness, simplicity, stupidity.

dabbène a good, honest, upright.

daccànto, da cànto ad and prep by, close, near.

daccàpo, da càpo ad again, once more, over again.

dacché, da che cj since, as.

dàdo nm die; (mech) nut; (of soup) cube.

daffàre, da fàre nm occupation, work; **un gràn d.** a great to-do.

dàino nm fallow deer; buck.

dàma nf lady, (dance) partner, (chess, cards) queen, (game of) draughts, (US) checkers.

dameríno nm dandy, beau.

damigèlla nf maid of honour; young lady.

damigiàna nf demijohn.

danàro v **denàro.**

danaróso a wealthy.

danése a Danish; nmf Dane.

Danimàrca nf (geogr) Denmark.

dannàre vt to damn; -rsi vr to be damned, strive hard.

dannazióne nf damnation.

danneggiàre vt to damage, harm, impair, injure, spoil.

danneggiàto a damaged, injured; nm (leg) the injured party.

dànno nm damage, injury, loss.

dannóso a harmful, hurtful, detrimental.

dantésco pl -chì a relating to Dante.

dantìsta nmf Dante scholar.

Danúbio nm the Danube.

dànza nf dance, dancing.

danzànte a dancing; **tratteniménto d.** dance, ball.

danzàre vi to dance.

danzatóre nm -trìce nf dancer.

dappertútto ad everywhere.

dappocàggine nf worthlessness, ineptitude.

dappòco a inept, worthless.

dappòi ad afterwards, then.

dapprèsso ad by, close by, near.

dapprìma, da prìma ad at first.

dàre vt to give, produce, yield; vi to hit, stumble, look on to, burst out; -rsi vr to devote oneself, give oneself.

dàre nm (com) debit, liability.

dàrsena nf basin, wet-dock.

dàta nf date; **di vècchia d.** longstanding.

datàre vi to date.

dàto a given; nm datum; **d. che** cj since, as.

datóre nm -trìce nf giver; **d. di lavóro** employer.

dàttero nm date, date-palm.

dattilografàre vt to type.

dattilògrafo nm -fa nf typist.

dattórno, da tórno ad around.

davànti ad and prep before, in front of; a nm front; **il d. della càsa** the front of the house.

davanzàle nm window-sill.

davànzo, d'avànzo ad more than enough, over.

Dàvide nm pr David.

davvéro ad indeed, really, truly; **per d.** in earnest.

dazière nm exciseman, customs officer.

dàzio nm customs duty, excise, toll; **d. doganàle** customs duty.

dèa nf goddess.

debilitàre vt to debilitate, weaken.

debitaménte ad duly, regularly.

débito a due; nm debt, duty.

debitóre nm **-tríce** nf debtor.

débole a feeble, weak; nm weakness.

debolézza nf weakness, debility.

debuttànte nmf novice, debutante.

debuttàre vi to make one's debut.

debútto nm debut.

dècade nf ten days; decade.

decadènte a nm decadent.

decadentísmo nm school of decadent poets.

decadènza nf decline, decay.

decadére vi to decay, decline.

decàno nm dean.

decantàre vt to extol, praise; decant.

decapitàre vt to behead, decapitate.

decapitazióne nf beheading.

decarburàre vt to decarbonize.

deceduto a dead, deceased.

decènne a ten years old.

decènnio nm decade, period of ten years.

decènte a decent, seemly.

decentràre vt to decentralize.

decènza nf decency, seemliness.

decèsso nm death, decease; **àtto di d.** death certificate.

decídere vt to decide, settle; **-rsi** vr to decide, make up one's mind.

decifràre vt to decipher, decode.

dècima nf tenth part, tithe.

decimàle a nm decimal.

decimàre vt to decimate.

dècimo a tenth.

decína nf about ten.

decisaménte ad decidedly, definitely.

decisióne nf decision, resolution.

decisívo a decisive; critical; **voto d.** casting vote.

decíso a decided, determined, resolute.

declamàre vti to declaim.

declamatóre nm declaimer.

declamazióne nf declamation.

declinàre vt to decline; vi to set, wane, deviate; **d. le pròprie generalità** to give one's particulars.

declíno nm decline.

declívio nm declivity, slope.

decollàre vt to behead; vi (av) to take off.

decollazióne nf decapitation.

decòllo nm (av) take-off.

decompórre vt to decompose; **-rsi** vr to decompose, putrefy.

decomposizióne nf decomposition.

decoràre vt to decorate, adorn.

decoratívo a decorative.

decoratóre nm **-tríce** nf decorator.

decorazióne nf decoration, ornament.

decòro nm decorum, dignity.

decoróso a decorous, seemly.

decorrènza nf (com) expiration; **con d. dal** beginning from.

decórrere vi to have effect, count from.

decórso a expired, passed; nm passing, period, course.

decrepitézza nf decrepitude.

decrèpito a decrepit.

decrescènza nf decrease, diminution, wane.

decréscere vi to decrease, wane.

decretàre vt to decree, award.

decréto nm decree.

dècuplo a nm ten times, tenfold.

dèdica nf dedication.

dedicàre vt to dedicate, consecrate, devote; **-rsi** vr to devote oneself.

dèdito a devoted, addicted.

dedizióne nf dedication, devotion.

dedúrre vi to deduce, infer.

deduzióne nf deduction, inference.

defalcàre vt to deduct, subtract.

defenestràre vt to throw out of the window; (fig) drive out of office.

deferènte a deferent, respectful.

deferènza nf deference, respect.

deferíre vi to defer; vt to submit.

defezióne nf defection, desertion.

deficiènte a insufficient, deficient; nmf weak-minded.

deficiènza nf deficiency, weak-mindedness.

definíre vt to define, settle.

definitíva, in ad after all.

definíto a definite.

definizióne nf definition, settlement.

deflagrazióne nf deflagration.

deflèttere vi to deflect; yield.

deformàre vt to deform, deface; **-rsi** vr to get deformed, lose one's shape.

defórme a deformed, ugly.

deformità nf deformity.

defraudàre vt to defraud, deprive.

defúnto a deceased, late.

degeneràre vi to degenerate, get worse.

degenerazióne nf degeneration, deterioration.

degènere a degenerate.

degènte a bedridden; nmf in-patient.

degènza nf period in bed, stay in hospital.

degnàre vt to hold worthy; **-rsi** vr to deign.

degnazióne nf condescension.

dégno a deserving, worthy.

degradàre vt to degrade, debase; **-rsi** vr to degrade oneself.

degustàre vt to taste.

degustazióne nf tasting, sipping.

deificàre vt to deify.

deità nf deity, god, goddess, God.

delatóre nm **-tríce** nf informer.

delazióne nf secret accusation.

dèlega nf (of authority etc) delegation, proxy.

delegàre vt to delegate, depute.

delegàto a delegate(d); nm delegate, deputy.

delegazióne *nf* delegation, committee.

deletèrio *a* deleterious, harmful.

delfíno *nm* dolphin; Dauphin.

deliberàre *vt* to deliberate, pass (a resolution).

deliberazióne *nf* deliberation, resolution.

delicataménte *ad* delicately, gently.

delicatézza *nf* delicacy, sensibility, tact; luxury.

delicàto *a* delicate, fastidious, discreet.

delimitàre *v.* to fix the boundaries.

delineàre *vt* to delineate, outline, sketch.

delinquènte *a nmf* delinquent, criminal.

delinquènza *nf* delinquency.

delinquere *vi* to commit a crime.

delíquio *nm* swoon, fainting fit.

deliràre *vi* to be delirious, rave.

delírio *nm* delirium, raving.

delítto *nm* crime.

delittuóso *a* criminal.

delízia *nf* delight.

deliziàre *vt* to charm, delight; **-rsi** *vr* to delight in, take pleasure in.

delizióso *a* charming, delightful.

dèlta *nm* delta; **àla a d.** (*av*) delta wing.

delucidàre *vt* to explain.

delucidazióne *nf* elucidation, explanation; (*textiles*) decatizing.

delúdere *vt* to disappoint, frustrate; escape.

delusióne *nf* disappointment; deception.

demànio *nm* State property.

demarcazióne *nf* demarcation.

demènte *a nmf* insane, lunatic.

demènza *nf* insanity, lunacy.

demeritàre *vti* to forfeit (one's good opinion), be unworthy of.

democràtico *a* democratic.

democrazía *nf* democracy.

demolíre *vt* to demolish, pull down.

demolizióne *nf* demolition.

dèmone, demònio *nm* demon.

demoníaco *a* demoniac(al).

demoralizzàre *vt* to demoralize.

denàro *nm* money; penny.

denaróso *v* **danaróso.**

denaturàto *a* methylated; **àlcool d.** methylated spirit.

denigràre *vt* to defame, disparage.

denigrazióne *nf* disparagement.

denominàre *vt* to denominate, name.

denominazióne *nf* denomination, name.

denotàre *vt* to denote, signify.

densità *nf* density, thickness.

dènso *a* dense, thick.

dentàta *nf* bite, mark of bite.

dentàto *a* toothed, cogged, dentate, serrated.

dentatúra *nf* (set of) teeth.

dènte *nm* tooth, fang; prong.

dentellàre *vt* to indent, notch.

dentièra *nf* denture, dental plate, false teeth *pl.*

dentifrício *nm* toothpaste.

dentísta *nm* dentist.

dentizióne *nf* dentition, teething.

déntro *ad* and *prep* inside, within; *nm* inside.

denudàre *vt* to denude, strip.

denúncia *nf* report, notification; **d. di matrimònio** marriage banns.

denunciàre *vt* to declare, announce report.

denutríto *a* underfed.

deodorànte *a* deodorizing; *nm* deodorant.

depauperàre *vt* impoverish.

deperiménto *nm* wasting, pining away, decline, deterioration.

deperíre *vi* to waste, pine away, wither, decay.

depilàre *vt* to depilate, remove hairs.

depilatóre *nm* hair remover, depilatory.

depilatòrio *a* depilatory.

depilazióne *nf* hair-removing, depilation.

deploràre *vt* to deplore, lament, blame.

deplorévole *a* deplorable, lamentable, blamable.

depórre *vt* to depose, lay aside, lay down; *vi* to bear witness.

deportàre *vt* to deport, transport.

deportàto *a* deported; *nm* convict.

deportazióne *nf* deportation.

depositàre *vti* to deposit, lodge.

depositàrio *nm* depository.

depòsito *nm* (*mil*) depot; warehouse; deposit; **d. bagàgli** left luggage office, (US) checkroom.

deposizióne *nf* deposition.

depravàre *vt* to corrupt, deprave.

deprecàre *vt* to deprecate; entreat.

depredaménto *nm* **depredazióne** *nf* depredation, pillage.

depredàre *vt* to pillage, plunder.

depressióne *nf* depression.

deprèsso *a* depressed, low-spirited.

deprezzaménto *nm* depreciation.

deprezzàre *vt* to depreciate, disparage, undervalue.

deprimènte *a* depressing; (*med*) sedative.

deprimere *vt* to depress.

depuràre *vt* to purify, purge.

deputàre *vt* to depute, appoint, fix.

deputàto *a* delegated, deputed; *nm* delegate, deputy.

deputazióne *nf* committee, deputation.

deragliaménto *nm* derailment.

deragliàre *vi* to derail, leave the rails.

derelítto *a* abandoned, derelict.

derídere *vt* to deride, laugh at, ridicule.

derisióne *nf* derision, ridicule.

derisòrio *a* derisive, mocking.

deríva *nf* (*naut*) drift, leeway; **alla d.** *ad* adrift, astray.

derivàre *vi* to derive, spring, result, follow; *vt* to divert, derive.

derivàto *a* derived; *nm* derivative, by-product.

derivazióne *nf* derivation.

dèroga *nf* derogation.

derogàre *vi* to derogate, deviate from, contravene.

derogazióne *nf* derogation.

derràta *nf* foodstuffs, commodity.

derubàre *vt* to rob.

désco *pl* **déschi** *nm* dinner table, butcher's block, bench, stool.

descrittìvo *a* descriptive.

descrìvere *vt* to describe, relate.

descrizióne *nf* description.

deşèrto *a* deserted, desolate, lonely; *nm* desert.

desideràre *vt* to desire, long for, wish, want.

desidèrio *nm* wish, desire.

desideróso *a* eager, longing for.

designàre *vt* to appoint, designate, name.

designazióne *nf* designation.

deşinàre *vi* to dine; *nm* dinner, meal.

deşinènza *nf* ending, termination.

desìstere *vi* to desist, give up.

deşolàre *vt* to devastate, distress.

deşolàto *a* desolate, devastated, sorry.

deşolazióne *nf* desolation, devastation, grief.

dèspota *pl* **-ti** *nm* despot.

destàre *vt* to (a)wake, excite, rouse, stir up; **-rsi** *vr* to (a)wake, be roused.

destinàre *vt* to destine, assign, appoint, address, decide.

destinatàrio *nm* addressee, receiver.

destinazióne *nf* destination.

destìno *nm* destiny, fate.

destituìre *vt* to dismiss, remove (from office).

destituìto *a* deprived of, removed from, destitute.

destituzióne *nf* dismissal, removal.

dèsto *a* awake, alert.

dèstra *nf* right hand, right side, (*in politics*) Right.

destreggiàre *vi* to act skilfully, be skilful; **-rsi** *vr* to manage, manœuvre, steer one's course.

destrézza *nf* dexterity, skill.

dèstro *a* right; clever, dexterous; *nm* opportunity, right moment; **cògliere il d.** to seize the chance.

desùmere *vt* to deduce, infer.

detenére *vt* to hold, keep, detain.

detenùto *a* kept back, imprisoned; *nm* prisoner.

detenzióne *nf* detention, unlawful possession.

detergènte *a nm* detergent.

deterioràre *vt* to deteriorate, damage; **-rsi** *vr* to deteriorate, get worse.

determinàre *vt* to determine, define, cause.

detersìvo *a* cleansing; *nm* detergent, detersive, cleansing agent.

detestàre *vt* to detest, hate, loathe.

detonàre *vi* to detonate.

detonazióne *nf* detonation, explosion.

detràrre *vt* to deduct.

detrattóre *nm* **-trìce** *nf* detractor, slanderer.

detrazióne *nf* deduction, detraction, slander.

detriménto *nm* detriment, damage.

detrìto *nm* rubbish, sweepings *pl.*

detroniżżàre *vt* to dethrone.

détta *nf* **a d. di** according to.

dettàfono *nm* dictaphone.

dettagliàre *vt* to detail.

dettàglio *nm* detail, particular; **commèrcio al d.** (*com*) retail trade.

dettàre *vt* to dictate.

dettàto *nm* **dettatùra** *nf* dictation.

détto *a* called, named; *nm* saying, word, joke.

deturpàre *vt* to deface, disfigure.

devastaménto *nm* devastation, ravage.

devastàre *vt* to devastate, ravage.

devastazióne *nf* devastation.

deviaménto *nm* deviation, derailment; (*of traffic etc*) diversion.

deviàre *vt* to deviate, be diverted, swerve, divert.

deviatóio *nm* (*tec*) points *pl*, switch.

deviazióne *nf* deviation, (*road*) diversion, (*US road*) detour; (*mech*) deflection.

devoluzióne *nf* devolution, transfer.

devòlvere *vt* to devolve, assign, transfer.

devóto *a* devout; *nm* devotee.

devozióne *nf* devotion, piety.

di *prep* of, from, for, with, at, in, some, any, than.

dì *nm* day.

diabète *nm* diabetes.

diabètico *pl* **-ici** *a nm* diabetic.

diabòlico *pl* **-ici** *a* diabolic(al).

diàcono *nm* deacon.

diadèma *nm* diadem, tiara.

diàfano *a* diaphanous.

diafràmma *nm* diaphragm; screen.

diàgnosi *nf* diagnosis.

diagnòstica *nf* diagnostics *pl.*

diagnòstico *a* diagnostic; *nm* diagnostician.

diagonàle *a* diagonal; *nf* (*geom*) diagonal; *nm* (*fabric*) twill.

diagràmma *pl* **-ammi** *nm* diagram, chart; (*mus*) scale.

dialettàle *a* dialectal.

dialètto *nm* dialect.

diàlogo *pl* **-ghi** *nm* dialogue.

diamànte *nm* diamond.

diàmetro *nm* diameter.

diàmine! *interj* the deuce! of course!

diàna *nf* morning star, reveille.

Diàna *nf pr* Diana.

diànzi *ad* just now, not long ago.

diàpason *nm* tuning fork, diapason, pitch.

diaposítiva *nf* (*phot*) transparency, slide; (*typ*) direct reversal.
diàrio *a* daily; *nm* diary.
diarrèa *nf* diarrhoea.
diatríba *nf* diatribe, quarrel.
diàvolo *nm* devil.
dibàttere *vt* to debate, discuss; -rsi *vr* to struggle.
dibàttito *nm* debate, discussion, controversy.
dicastèro *nm* (higher) government office, ministry, (*US*) department.
dicèmbre *nm* December.
dicería *nf* hearsay, rumour.
dichiaràre *vt* to declare, state; -rsi *vr* to declare oneself.
dichiarazióne *nf* declaration.
diciannòve *a* nineteen; diciannovè-simo *a* nineteenth.
diciassètte *a* seventeen; diciassettè-simo *a* seventeenth.
diciòtto *a* eighteen; diciottèsimo *a* eighteenth.
dicitóre *nm* -tríce *nf* announcer, speaker, teller.
dicitúra *nf* wording, words.
didascalía *nf* captions, directions, subtitles.
didàttico *pl* -ici *a* didactic.
didéntro *ad* *nm* inside.
dièci *a* ten.
diecína *nf* about ten.
dièta *nf* assembly, diet.
diètro *nm* back; *ad* *and* *prep* after, behind.
difàtti, difàtto *ad* as a matter of fact, in fact.
difèndere *vt* to defend, guard, protect; -rsi *vr* to defend oneself.
difensíva *nf* defensive.
difensívo *a* defensive.
difensóre *nm* defender.
difésa *nf* defence.
difettàre *vi* to be deficient in, lack.
difettívo, difettóso *a* defective, lacking.
difètto *nm* defect, flaw, fault.
diffàlco *pl* -chi *nm* deduction.
diffamàre *vt* to defame, libel.
diffamazióne *nf* defamation.
differènte *a* different; unlike (s.o., sth.).
differènza *nf* difference.
differenziàre *vt* to differentiate, distinguish (between); -rsi *vr* to differ (from), be different.
differiménto *nm* adjournment, deferment.
differíre *vt* to adjourn, defer, postpone; *vi* to be different, differ, disagree.
difficile *a* difficult, hard; hard to please.
difficoltà *nf* difficulty, objection.
difficoltóso *a* full of difficulties, fastidious.
diffída *nf* intimation, notice.
diffidàre *vt* to serve a notice; *vi* to distrust, suspect.
diffidènte *a* diffident, distrustful.

diffidènza *nf* diffidence, distrust, suspicion.
diffóndere *vt* to diffuse, pour, spread; -rsi *vr* to be diffused, spread.
diffusaménte *ad* diffusely, abundantly.
diffusióne *nf* diffusion.
diffúso *a* diffuse,' diffused; long-winded.
difilàto *ad* at once, forthwith.
difteríte *nf* diphtheria.
diga *nf* breakwater, dyke.
digerènte *a* digestive.
digeríbile *a* digestible.
digeríre *vt* to digest, assimilate.
digestióne *nf* digestion.
digestívo *a* *nm* digestive.
digèsto *nm* digest.
digitàle *a* digital; *nf* foxglove; digitalis; imprónte digitàli finger-prints.
digiunàre *vi* to fast.
digiúno *a* fasting, devoid of; *nm* fast.
dignità *nf* dignity.
dignitóso *a* dignified.
digradàre *vi* to slope down, decline; diminish, (*of colours*) shade off.
digrassàre *vi* to remove the fat, skim.
digressióne *nf* digression.
digrignàre *vt* to gnash, grind (one's teeth).
digrossàre *vt* to whittle down, rough-hew; teach the first elements.
diguazzàre *vi* to splash about, paddle; *vi* to shake, stir.
dilaceràre, dilaniàre *vt* to tear (to pieces).
dilagàre *vi* to overflow, spread.
dilapidàre *vt* to dilapidate, squander.
dilatàbile *a* dilatable, extensible.
dilatàre *vt* -rsi *vr* to dilate, expand.
dilatàto *a* dilated, enlarged.
dilatazióne *nf* dilation, expansion.
dilatòrio *a* delaying, dilatory.
dilazionàre *vt* to adjourn, postpone.
dilazióne *nf* delay, respite.
dileggiàre *vt* to mock, ridicule.
diléggio *nm* derision, mockery.
dileguaménto *nm* disappearance.
dileguàre *vt* to disperse, dissipate; -rsi *vr* to dissolve, fade away, vanish.
dilèmma *nm* dilemma.
dilettànte *nmf* amateur, dilettante.
dilettàre *vt* to charm, delight; -rsi *vr* to delight, take pleasure in.
dilettévole *a* charming, delightful.
dilètto *a* beloved, darling; *nm* delight, pleasure.
diligènte *a* diligent.
diligènza *nf* diligence; stagecoach.
dilucidàre *vt* to elucidate.
diluíre *vt* to dilute, water.
dilungàre *vt* to lengthen, prolong; -rsi *vr* to dwell (on).
dilúngo *ad* straight on.
diluviàre *vi* to pour, deluge, rain in torrents.

dilúvio nm deluge, flood.

dimagraménto nm growing thin, slimming; (of ground) impoverishing.

dimagràre, dimagríre vt to make thin; vi to grow thin, lose weight.

dimenàre vt to shake, (tail) wag; -rsi vr to fidget, toss.

dimensióne nf dimension, size.

dimenticànza nf forgetfulness, oblivion.

dimenticàre vt -rsi vr to forget.

diméntico pl -chi a forgetful.

dimésso a humble, modest.

dimestichézza nf familiarity.

diméttere vt to dismiss, remove; forgive; -rsi vr to resign.

dimezzàre vt to halve.

diminuíre vt to abate, diminish, lessen, reduce; vi to decrease.

diminutívo a nm diminutive.

diminuzióne nf diminution, reduction.

dimissióne nf resignation; dàre le dimissióni vi to resign.

dimòra nf abode, dwelling, stay; sènza físsa d. a homeless, vagabond.

dimoràre vi to live, reside; stay; delay.

dimostràre vt to demonstrate, prove, show; -rsi vr to appear, show oneself.

dimostrazióne nf demonstration.

dinàmica nf dynamics.

dinàmico pl -ici a dynamic, energetic.

dinamíte nf dynamite.

dínamo nf (el) dynamo, (US) generator.

dinànzi ad and prep before, opposite, in front.

dinastía nf dynasty.

diniègo pl -ghi nm denial, refusal.

dinoccolàto a disjointed, loose-limbed, shambling.

dintòrno ad and prep about, (a)round; dintórni nm pl neighbourhood.

Dío nm God.

diòcesi nf diocese.

Dionígi nm pr Denis, Dennis.

dipanàre vt to wind into a ball; unravel, disentangle.

dipartiménto nm department.

dipartírsi vr to depart, go away.

dipartíta nf (poet) departure, death.

dipendènte a depending, dependent; nmf subordinate, dependant.

dipendènza nf dependence, dependency.

dipèndere vi to depend (on), derive.

dipíngere vt to paint, depict; -rsi vr to paint oneself.

dipínto a painted; nm painting.

diplóma nm diploma, certificate.

diplomàre vt to confer a diploma; -rsi vr to get a diploma, to graduate.

diplomàtico pl -ici a diplomatic; nm diplomat.

diplomazía nf diplomacy.

dipòrto nm amusement, recreation.

diradaménto nm thinning (out), rarefaction.

diradàre vt to thin out; -rsi vr (of hair etc) to get thin.

diramàre vt to lop, prune; send out; -rsi vr to branch out, ramify, spread.

diramazióne nf branching out, branching off, branch, diffusion.

díre vt to say, tell, speak; nm speech, words, statement, saying.

direttaménte ad directly, direct.

direttíssimo nm express train.

direttíva nf direction, instruction.

dirètto a direct, straight; nm fast train; carròzza dirètta nf through coach (on a train).

direttóre nm -tríce nf director, directress, headmaster, headmistress, manager(ess), (newspaper) editor.

direzióne nf direction, course; management, leadership, office; (tec) steering-gear.

dirigènte a directing, managing; nm manager, (pol) leader.

dirígere vt to direct, address, manage, regulate; -rsi vr to go towards.

dirigíbile nm airship.

dirimpètto ad opposite; d. a prep opposite, in comparison with.

dirítta nf right, right hand, right side.

dirítto a straight, upright, erect, plumb, right; nm right, claim, due, law; ad directly, straight (on); dirítti d'autóre royalties.

dirittúra nf straightness, uprightness.

dirizzàre vi to straighten, prick up (one's ears); -rsi vr to draw oneself up.

diroccàre vt to demolish, dismantle; -rsi vr to fall in ruins.

dirótto a heavy; piànto d. nm flood of tears; piòggia dirótta heavy rain.

dirozzàre vt to rough-hew, civilize, polish; -rsi vr to become civilized, refined.

dirúpo nm rocky precipice.

disabitàto a uninhabited.

disabituàre vt to disaccustom; -rsi vr to lose the habit.

disaccòrdo nm disagreement, discord.

disadàtto a unfit, unsuitable, unbecoming.

disadórno a bare, simple, unadorned.

disaffezióne nf estrangement, disaffection.

disagévole a difficult, uncomfortable.

disagevolézza nf difficulty, discomfort.

disaggradévole a disagreeable.

disagiàto a uncomfortable; poor, needy.

disàgio nm discomfort, uneasiness; sentírsi a d. to feel uncomfortable.

disàmina nf examination, investigation.

disaminàre vt examine.

disappetènza nf lack of appetite.

disapprèndere vt to unlearn, forget.

disapprovàre vt to disapprove of, blame.

disappúnto nm disappointment.

disarmàre vt to disarm; dismantle, (naut) lay up (a ship).

disàrmo nm disarmament.

disàstro nm disaster, accident.

disastróso a disastrous, ruinous.

disattènto a inattentive.

disattenzióne nf inattention, inattentiveness.

disattrezzàre vt (naut) to dismantle.

disavànzo nm deficiency, deficit.

disavvedutézza, disavvertènza nf inadvertency.

disavventúra nf misfortune, mishap.

disavvezzàre vt to disaccustom.

disbórso nm disbursement, outlay.

disbrigàre vt to clear off, dispatch; -rsi vr to extricate oneself, get out (of sth), make haste.

disbrigo pl. -ghi nm dispatch, settlement.

discàpito nm disadvantage, detriment.

discendènte a descending; nmf descendant.

discendènza nf descent; offspring.

discéndere vi to descend, go down; spring from; (of prices, temperature) fall.

discentràto a decentralized; off centre.

discépolo nm disciple, pupil.

discèrnere vt to discern, distinguish.

discerniménto nm discernment, judgement.

discésa nf descent, fall; (rad) lead-in.

dischiúdere vt to disclose, reveal.

disciògliere vt to dissolve, melt; release, untie; -rsi vr to dissolve, melt, get loose.

disciplina nf discipline.

disciplinàre vt to discipline; a disciplinary.

disco pl dischi nm disk, disc; (mus) record; (sport) discus.

díscolo a undisciplined, unruly, wild; nm rogue, scamp.

discolpàre vt to clear from blame, excuse, defend; -rsi vr to clear oneself, justify oneself.

disconoscènza nf ingratitude.

disconóscere vt to disavow, slight, be ungrateful for.

discordànte a discordant, clashing; dissonant; disagreeing.

discordànza nf discordance, dissonance; disagreement.

discordàre vi to disagree; (mus) be out of tune.

discòrde a discordant, dissonant.

discòrdia nf discord, dissension.

discórrere vi to discourse, talk.

discórso nm discourse, speech, talk.

discòsto a distant, far; ad at some distance.

discotéca nf discotheque.

discreditàre vt to discredit; -rsi vr to damage one's reputation.

discrepànza nf discrepancy.

discretaménte ad discreetly, fairly.

discretézza nf discretion, moderation.

discretíva nf power of discernment.

discréto a discreet; moderate, passable, reasonable.

discrezióne nf discretion; a d. according to one's judgement.

discriminàre vt to discriminate.

discriminazióne nf discrimination.

discussióne nf debate, discussion, dispute.

discútere vt to discuss, argue.

discutíbile a debatable, questionable.

disdegnàre v sdegnàre.

disdégno nm contempt, scorn, haughtiness.

disdegnóso a contemptuous, scornful.

disdétta nf notice to leave; bad luck.

disdíre vt to annul, cancel, revoke, unsay; vi to be unbecoming; -rsi vr to be unbecoming; go back on one's word.

disdòro nm dishonour, shame.

disegnàre vt to draw, plan.

diségno nm design, drawing, plan, purpose.

diseredàre vt to disinherit.

disertàre vt to desert; lay waste, ruin.

disertóre a deserter.

diserzióne nf desertion.

disfaciménto nm destruction, ruin, decay.

disfàre vt to undo, break up, take to pieces, untie; -rsi vr to dispose of, get rid of.

disfàtta nf defeat.

disfattísta a nmf defeatist.

disfàtto a undone, defeated, worn-out.

disfída nf challenge, duel.

disfunzióne nf (med) disorder, irregularity.

disgelàre vi to thaw; vt to defrost.

disgràzia nf misfortune, ill luck, accident.

disgraziàto a unfortunate, unlucky; nm wretch.

disgregàre vt -rsi vr to disintegrate, break up.

disguído nm (of post & fig) going astray.

disgustàre vt to disgust, sicken, vex; -rsi vr to take a disgust, dislike for.

disgústo nm disgust, dislike, loathing.

disgustóso a disgusting.

disillúdere vt to disillusion, disenchant.

disillusióne nf disillusion, disenchantment.

disimparàre vt to unlearn, forget.

disimpegnàre vt to redeem, release, fulfil; (naut) clear; **-rsi** vr to free oneself, manage one's own affairs.

disimpégno nm disengagement, release.

disincagliàre vt (naut) to float (a stranded ship).

disinfettànte a nm disinfectant.

disinfettàre vt to disinfect.

disinfezióne nf disinfection.

disingannàre vt to disillusion, undeceive.

disingànno nm disillusionment, undeceiving.

disintegràre vt **-rsi** vr to disintegrate.

disintegrazióne nf disintegration.

disinteressàre vt (com) buy out; to make one lose interest; **-rsi** vr to disinterest oneself.

disinteressàto a disinterested; unselfish; impartial.

disinterèsse nm disinterestedness, unselfishness.

disinvòlto a easy, free, sure of oneself, unconstrained, impudent.

disinvoltúra nf ease, nonchalance, self-possession, impudence.

disistimàre vt not to esteem, to despise.

dislivèllo nm difference of level.

dislocàre vt to displace.

dismisúra nf excess; **a d.** immoderately.

disobbligàre vt to free from obligation.

disoccupàto a out of work, unemployed; nm unemployed person.

disoccupazióne nf unemployment.

disonestà nf dishonesty.

disonèsto a dishonest, indecent.

disonoràre vt to disgrace, dishonour.

disonóre nm disgrace, dishonour, shame.

disópra nm top, upper side; ad and pron above, on, over, upstairs; **al d. di** prep beyond.

disordinàre vt to disorder, disarrange; (in eating, drinking) to exceed.

disordinàto a disorderly, untidy.

disórdine nm disorder, confusion, disorderliness, disturbance.

disorganizzàre vt to disorganize.

disorganizzazióne nf disorganization.

disorientaménto nm disorientation, confusion.

disorientàre vt to confuse, disconcert, lead astray, mislead; **-rsi** vr to be at a loss, not to know where one is.

disòtto a nm lower, bottom, lower side; ad and prep below, under (neath); **al d. di** inferior to; below.

dispàccio nm dispatch; **d. telegràfico** telegram.

disparàto a different, disparate, incongruous, unequal.

dispari a (number) odd; different, unequal.

dispàrte, in ad apart, aside, aloof.

dispèndio nm expense, outlay.

dispendióso a expensive.

dispènsa nf distribution; (of a publication) number; sideboard, pantry; dispensation, exemption; **dispènse universitàrie** duplicated lecture notes.

dispensàre vt to dispense, distribute; exempt.

dispensàrio nm dispensary.

dispepsía nf dyspepsia.

disperàre vi to despair; **-rsi** vr to give oneself up to despair.

disperàto a despairing, desperate, hopeless, wretched; nm destitute creature, desperate creature.

disperazióne nf despair, desperation.

disperdere vt to dispel, disperse, scatter, waste; **-rsi** vr to be scattered, disperse.

dispersióne nf dispersion, loss; (el) leak.

dispèrso a missing, dispersed, lost, scattered; nm (mil) missing soldier.

dispètto nm spite, grudge, pique, vexation.

dispettóso a spiteful.

dispiacénte a sorry; disagreeable.

dispiacére vi to dislike, regret; be disagreeable, displease; **mi dispiàce** I am sorry; nm displeasure, dissatisfaction, grief, regret.

disponíbile a available, free; nm (com) liquid assets pl.

dispórre vti to arrange, direct, dispose, order, regulate; **-rsi** vr to get ready.

dispositívo nm (mech) contrivance, appliance; (phot) adapter; **d. di sicurezza** safety catch.

disposizióne nf arrangement, disposition, disposal, inclination, order; **avére d. per** to have a talent for; **a súa d.** at your disposal.

dispósto a willing, inclined, disposed; arranged; **ben d.** in good order, vigorous.

dispregiàre etc v **disprezzàre**.

disprezzàbile a contemptible, despicable, negligible.

disprezzàre vt to despise, scorn.

disprèzzo nm contempt, sorrow.

disputa nf debate, dispute, quarrel.

disputàre vti to argue, contend, debate, dispute, quarrel; **-rsi** vr to contend (for).

dissanguàre vt to bleed; (fig) impoverish.

dissanguàto a drained of blood; (fig) impoverished.

dissapóre nm disagreement, misunderstanding.

disseminàre vt to disseminate, propagate, scatter, sow.

dissennatézza nf craziness, foolishness, rashness.

dissènso *nm* difference of opinion, dissent.

dissenterìa *nf* dysentery.

dissentìre *vi* to disagree (with).

disseppelliménto *nm* disinterment, exhumation.

disseppellìre *vt* to disinter.

dissertàre *vi* to discourse, expatiate.

dissertazióne *nf* dissertation, thesis.

dissestàre *vt* to ruin, disarrange, derange; **-rsi** *vr* (*financially*) to ruin oneself.

dissestàto *a* in financial straits, badly off.

dissèsto *nm* disorder; financial trouble.

dissetànte *a* refreshing.

dissetàre *vt* to quench (thirst).

dissezióne *nf* dissection.

dissidènte *a* *nmf* dissentient, dissenter.

dissìdio *nm* dissension, discord.

dissigillàre *vt* to unseal.

dissìmile *a* unlike.

dissimulàre *vt* to dissimulate, conceal.

dissipàre *vt* to clear up, dissipate, remove; **-rsi** *vr* to disappear, vanish.

dissipazióne *nf* dissipation.

dissociàre *vt* to dissociate.

dissodàre *vt* (*land*) to clear, till.

dissolùbile *a* dissoluble.

dissolubilità *nf* dissolubility.

dissolutézza *nf* dissoluteness, licentiousness.

dissolùto *a* dissolute, licentious.

dissoluzióne *nf* disintegration, dissolution; dissoluteness.

dissolvènza *nf* (*cin*) fade-out.

dissòlvere *vt* **-rsi** *vr* to dissolve, melt.

dissomigliànza *nf* unlikeness, difference.

dissonànte *a* dissonant, discordant.

dissonànza *nf* dissonance, difference.

dissotterràre *vt* to disinter.

dissuadére *vt* to dissuade, deter.

dissuetùdine *nf* disuse.

distaccaménto *nm* (*mil*) detachment.

distaccàre *vt* to cut off, detach, separate, sever; **-rsi** *vr* to become detached, break off.

distàcco *pl* **-chi** *nm* separation, parting, detachment; (*fig*) indifference.

distànte *a* distant, far, remote; *ad* far away.

distànza *nf* distance; difference.

distanziàre *vt* to space (out), leave behind.

distàre *vi* to be distant.

distèndere *vt* to extend, lay (out), spread, relax; **-rsi** *vr* to stretch out.

distendiménto *nm* **distensióne** *nf* spreading, stretching, relaxing.

distésa *nf* expanse, extent.

distillàre *vti* to distil; trickle.

distillatóio *nm* still.

distillerìa *nf* distillery.

distìnguere *vt* to distinguish; **-rsi** *vr* to become famous, distinguish oneself.

distinguìbile *a* distinguishable.

distìnta *nf* list, note, schedule; **d. dei prèzzi** price list.

distintaménte *ad* distinctly; (*in letters*) faithfully.

distintìvo *a* distinctive; *nm* badge, distinguishing mark.

distìnto *a* distinct; clear; distinguished; **distìnti salùti** (*in a letter*) yours faithfully.

distinzióne *nf* distinction, regard.

distògliere *vt* to deter, dissuade, distract.

distorsióne *nf* distorsion, sprain.

distràrre *vi* to amuse, distract, divert; **-rsi** *vr* to amuse oneself, let one's attention wander.

distràtto *a* absent-minded, inattentive.

distrazióne *nf* absent-mindedness, inattention; recreation.

distrétto *nm* district.

distribuìre *vt* to distribute, arrange, assign, deliver.

distributìvo *a* distributive.

distributóre *a* distributing; *nm* distributor; **d. di benzìna** (*aut*) petrol pump, (US) gasoline pump.

distribuzióne *nf* distribution, layout.

districàre, distrigàre *vt* to disentangle, unravel; **-rsi** *vr* to extricate oneself, free oneself.

distrùggere *vt* to destroy, ruin; **-rsi** *vr* to destroy oneself (each other).

distruzióne *nf* destruction.

disturbàre *vt* to disturb, interrupt, trouble; **-rsi** *vr* to put oneself out, take trouble.

distùrbo *nm* disturbance, trouble, inconvenience, disorder.

disubbidiènte *a* disobedient.

disubbidiènza *nf* disobedience.

disubbidìre *vi* to disobey.

disuguagliànza *nf* disparity, inequality.

disuguàle *a* unequal, dissimilar.

disumàno *a* inhuman.

disunióne *nf* discord, disunion.

disunìre *vt* to disjoin, disunite.

disusàre *vt* to cease using.

disusàto *a* disused; out-of-date; unaccustomed.

disùso *nm* disuse; **cadére in d.** to become obsolete.

ditàle *nm* thimble, finger-stall.

dìto *pl* **dìti, dìta** (*f*) *nm* finger, toe; inch.

dìtta *nf* firm, (commercial) house.

dittàfono *nm* dictaphone.

dittatóre *nm* dictator.

dittatùra *nf* dictatorship.

diùrno *a* day, diurnal; **albèrgo d.** *nm* public baths and lavatories *pl*.

dìva *nf* goddess; great actress or singer.

divagàre *vt* to amuse, divert; *vi* to

digress, wander; **-rsi** *vr* to amuse oneself, relax.

divagazióne *nf* wandering; digression; recreation.

divampàre *vi* to blaze, flare up.

divàno *nm* couch, divan.

divàrio *nm* difference, diversity.

diveníre, diventàre *vi* to become, get, grow, turn.

divèrbio *nm* altercation, dispute.

divergènte *a* divergent, diverging.

divergènza *nf* divergence, divergency.

divèrgere *vi* to diverge, wander from.

diversaménte *ad* differently, otherwise.

diversificàre *vt* to diversify; *vi*, **-rsi** *vr* to differ.

diversióne *nf* deviation, digression, diversion.

diversità *nf* diversity.

diversívo *a* deviating, diverting; *nm* distraction, amusement.

divèrso *a* different, sundry; **divèrsi** *pl* several; **generi diversi** *nm pl* (com) sundries *pl*.

divertènte *a* amusing, entertaining.

divertiménto *nm* amusement, entertainment, recreation.

divertíre *vt* to divert, amuse, entertain; **-rsi** *vr* to amuse oneself, have a good time.

divezzàre *vt* to disaccustom, wean; **-rsi** *vr* to disaccustom oneself.

dividèndo *nm* dividend.

divídere *vt* to divide, share; **-rsi** *vr* to divide, separate.

divièto *nm* prohibition; **d. d'affissióne** 'stick no bills'; **d. di sòsta** 'no parking'.

divinaménte *ad* divinely, beautifully.

divinàre *vt* to divine, foretell.

divincolaménto *nm* wriggle, wriggling, writhing, struggling.

divincolàre *vt* to wriggle; **divincolàrsi** *vr* to writhe, wriggle, struggle free.

divinità *nf* divinity.

divíno *a* divine.

divísa *nf* uniform, livery; (com) currency; hair parting; motto, device; **d. èstera** foreign currency.

divisàre *vti* to devise, plan, resolve.

divisióne *nf* division, department, discord.

divisòrio *a* dividing, separating; **múro d.** *nm* partition wall.

dívo *nm* (film)star.

divoràre *vt* to devour, eat up.

divorziàre *vti* **-rsi** *vr* divorce, get a divorce.

divòrzio *nm* divorce.

divulgàre *vt* to divulge, spread; **-rsi** *vr* to spread.

dizionàrio *nm* dictionary.

dizióne *nf* diction.

do *nm* (mus) C, do.

dóccia *nf* shower(bath), douche;

water-pipe; **fàre la d.** *vi* to take a shower.

docènte *nmf* teacher, university lecturer.

docènza *nf* teaching.

dòcile *a* docile; (of *material*) easily worked.

docilità *nf* docility, meekness.

documentàre *vt* to bring documentary evidence, document.

documentàrio *a* documentary; *nm* documentary film, newsreel.

documénto *nm* document, evidence.

dodicènne *a* twelve years old; *nmf* twelve-year-old.

dodicèsimo *a* twelfth.

dódici *a* twelve.

dogàna *nf* customs, customs office, custom-house.

doganàle *a* customs.

doganière *nm* customs officer.

dòglia *nf* ache, pain; **dòglie** *pl* labour pains.

dògma *nm* dogma, principle.

dogmàtico *pl* **-ici** *a* dogmatic.

dólce *a* sweet, mild, soft; *nm* sweetness; pudding, cake.

dolcézza *nf* sweetness, softness.

dolciúmi *nm pl* sweets *pl*, sweetmeats *pl*.

dolènte *a* grieved, sorry; aching.

dolére *vi* to ache; regret; **-rsi** *vr* to be sorry, complain, grieve, lament, regret.

dòllaro *nm* dollar.

dòlo *nm* fraud.

Dolomíti (le) *nf pl* (geogr) the Dolomites *pl*.

dolorànte *a* aching, painful.

dolóre *nm* ache, grief, pain, regret.

doloróso *a* painful, grievous, sorrowful.

dolóso *a* fraudulent.

domànda *nf* question, request, demand, application; **fàre d.** apply; **fàre una d.** to ask a question, make a request.

domandàre *vt* to ask, demand, request; **-rsi** *vr* to ask oneself, wonder.

domàni *nm and ad* tomorrow; **d. l'àltro** *ad* the day after tomorrow.

domàre *vt* to break in, tame, conquer, extinguish, subdue, overcome.

domatóre *nm* **-trice** *nf* tamer.

domatúra *nf* (of *horses*) breaking, taming.

doménica *nf* Sunday.

domenicàle *a* (of) Sunday.

domenicàno *a nm* Dominican.

domèstica *nf* maid, servant.

domestichézza *nf* domesticity, familiarity, intimacy.

domèstico *pl* **-ici** *a* domestic, familiar; *nm* servant.

domiciliàre *vt* to domiciliate, house; **-rsi** *vr* to live, settle, take up one's abode.

domicílio *nm* abode, domicile.

dominànte a dominant; prevailing.

dominàre vt to command, dominate, govern, overlook, rule; **-rsi** vr to control oneself, master oneself.

dominazióne nf domination, rule.

domínio nm dominion, authority, power, territory, domain.

donàre vt to bestow, confer, grant; vi to be becoming, suit; **-rsi** vr to devote oneself.

donatóre nm **donatríce** nf donor, giver; **d. di sàngue** blood donor.

donazióne nf donation.

dónde ad from where, whence, wherefore.

dondolaménto, dóndolo nm rocking, swaying, swinging.

dondolàre vt **-rsi** vr to rock, sway, swing.

dondolóni ad dangling.

dònna nf woman.

donnaiuòlo nm philanderer, ladies' man.

donnésco pl **-chi** a womanly, feminine, womanish.

dònnola nf weasel.

dóno nm gift, present; talent.

dópo ad and prep after, afterwards, next, later; **e d.?** what next?

dopochè cj after, when, since.

dopodomàni nm the day after tomorrow.

dopoguèrra nm the post-war period.

dopoprànzo nm afternoon.

doppiàggio nm dubbing.

doppiàre vt to double; (cin) dub.

doppière nm two-branched candlestick.

doppiétta nf double-barrelled gun.

doppièzza nf double-dealing, duplicity.

dóppio a double, deceitful, dual; nm double, twice as much.

doppióne nm duplicate, (typ) double.

doràre vt to gild; (cook) glaze, brown, brown.

doratúra nf gilding.

dormicchiàre vi to doze.

dormiglióne nm sleepy fellow, lie-a-bed.

dormíre vti to sleep; nm sleep.

dormitòrio nm dormitory; **d. púbblico** doss house, (US) flophouse.

dormivéglia nf (state) between sleeping and waking.

Dorotèa nf pr Dorothy, Dorothea.

dórso nm back; (of mountain) crest.

dosàre vt to dose.

dòse nf dose.

dòsso nm back.

dotàre vt to endow, give a dowry.

dotàto a gifted, endowed, furnished.

dòte nf dowry, gift, talent.

dòtto a learned; nm scholar.

dottoràto nm doctor's degree.

dottóre nm doctor, physician.

dottoréssa nf (female) graduate, lady doctor.

dottrína nf doctrine, learning, catechism.

dóve ad where, in the case that, whereas; nm where.

dovére vi to be obliged, have to, must, ought, should, be indebted, owe; nm duty, respects.

doveróso a right, dutiful.

dovízia nf abundance, plenty, wealth.

dovúnque ad anywhere, everywhere, wherever.

dozzína nf dozen; board and lodgings.

dozzinàle a common, ordinary.

dozzinànte nmf boarder.

dràga nf (naut) dredge.

dragamíne nf (naut) minesweeper.

dragàre vt (naut) to dredge.

dràgo pl **-ghi** nm dragon.

dràmma nf drachm(a); nm drama.

drammàtica nf dramatic art.

drammàtico pl **-ici** a dramatic.

drammatúrgo pl **-ghi** nm playwright.

drappèllo nm squad.

drappería nf drapery, draper's shop.

dràppo nm silk material.

dràstico pl **-ici** a drastic.

drenàggio nm drainage.

drenàre vt to drain.

drítta nf right; (naut) starboard.

dritto v **diritto**.

drizzàre vt to straighten, prick up, erect, turn, (fig) right; **-rsi** vr stand up, straighten up.

dròga nf drug, spice.

drogàre vt to drug, spice.

droghería nf grocer's shop, (US) grocery.

droghière nm grocer.

dromedàrio nm dromedary.

dubbièzza nf doubt, uncertainty.

dúbbio a doubtful, dubious; nm doubt, suspense; **èssere in d.** to be doubtful; **méttere in d.** vt to question.

dubbióso a doubtful, vague.

dubitàre vi to doubt, question, mistrust.

Dublíno nf (geogr) Dublin.

dublinése a of Dublin; nmf Dubliner.

dúca nm duke.

ducàle a ducal.

ducàto nm ducat; duchy, dukedom.

dúce nm chief, leader.

ducentísta nm writer of the thirteenth century.

duchéssa nf duchess.

dúe a two.

duecènto a two hundred; nm the thirteenth century.

duellàre vi to fight a duel.

duèllo nm duel.

duemíla a nm two thousand.

duétto nm (mus) duet.

dúna nf dune, sand-hill.

dúnque cj so, then, well! what! what about it?

duodècimo a twelfth.

duodenàle a duodenal; **úlcera d.** duodenal ulcer.

duòmo *nm* cathedral.

dúplex *a* teléfono d. two-party line telephone.

duplicàre *vt* to double, duplicate.

duplicatóre *nm* duplicator, multi-graph, (*rad*) doubler.

dúplice *a* double, twofold.

duplicità *nf* duplicity, double-dealing.

duràbile *a* durable, lasting.

durànte *prep* during.

duràre *vi* to last, continue, remain; *vt* to stand, endure.

duràta *nf* duration, period, wear, endurance.

duratúro, durévole *a* durable, lasting.

durézza *nf* hardness, harshness.

dúro *a* hard, harsh, severe, insensible, stupid; *nm* hard, hardship.

dúttile *a* ductile.

E

e, ed *cj* and; **e . . . e** *cj* both . . . and.

ebanista *nm* cabinet-maker.

ebanisteria *nf* cabinet-maker's shop, cabinet-making.

èbano *nm* ebony.

ebbène *cj* well, well then, what about it?

ebrézza *nf* drunkenness, intoxication, rapture.

èbbro *a* drunk, intoxicated, excited, mad.

èbete *a* dull, stupid; *nm* feeble-minded person.

ebetismo *nm* feeble-mindedness.

ebollizióne *nf* boiling, ebullition.

ebrèa -o *a* Hebrew, Jewish; *nm* Hebrew, Jew; *nf* Hebrew, Jewess.

ebúrneo *a* of ivory; ivory-white.

eccedènte *a* exceeding, excessive.

eccedènza *nf* excess, surplus.

eccèdere *vti* to exceed, go too far.

eccellènte *a* excellent.

eccellènza *nf* excellence; (*title*) Excellency.

eccèllere *vi* to excel.

eccèlso *a* lofty, sublime.

eccentricità *nf* eccentricity, strangeness.

eccèntrico *pl* **-ici** *a* eccentric; *nm* eccentric person; (*mech*) cam.

eccepíre *vt* to object, except.

eccessivo *a* excessive, immoderate.

eccèsso *nm* excess, overspill.

eccètera *nf* etcetera.

eccètto *prep* except(ing), save, unless.

eccettuàre *vt* to except.

eccezionàle *a* exceptional.

eccezionalménte *ad* exceptionally, extraordinarily.

eccezióne *nf* exception.

eccídio *nm* massacre, slaughter.

eccitàbile *a* excitable.

eccitaménto *nm* **eccitazióne** *nf* excitement.

eccitànte *a* exciting, stimulating; *nm* stimulant.

eccitàre *vt* to excite, rouse, stimulate; **-rsi** *vr* to get excited.

ecclesiàstico *pl* **-ici** *a* ecclesiastic(al), *nm* clergyman, ecclesiastic.

e(c)clissàre *vt* to eclipse, obscure, outdo; **-rsi** *vr* to be eclipsed, disappear, slip away.

ècco *ad* here is, here are, there is (*etc*); *interj* see! look!

echeggiàre *vi* to echo, resound.

eclissi *nf* eclipse.

èco *pl* **èchi** (m) *nf* echo.

economàto *nm* stewardship, steward's office, treasureship, treasurer's office.

economia *nf* economy, saving, thrift; **fàre delle economie** *vi* to save money.

econòmico *pl* **-ici**; *a* economic(al).

economizzàre *vt* to economize, save.

econòmo *a* economical, thrifty; *nm* bursar, steward, treasurer.

édera *nf* ivy.

Edgàrdo *nm* *pr* Edgar.

edícola *nf* news-stand; small chapel; niche.

edificànte *a* edifying.

edificàre *vt* to build; edify.

edifício *nm* building, edifice.

edíle *a* building; **ingegnère e.** building engineer.

edilizia *nf* building, building industry; **edilízio** *a* building.

Edimbúrgo *nf* (*geogr*) Edinburgh.

èdito *a* published.

editóre *nm* publisher, editor.

editríce *af* **càsa e.** publishing house.

editto *nm* edict.

edizióne *nf* edition.

Edmóndo *nm* *pr* Edmund, Edmond.

Edoàrdo *nm* *pr* Edward.

edòtto *a* acquainted (with), aware (of), informed (of).

educandàto *nm* girls' boarding school, convent boarding school.

educàre *vt* to bring up, train, educate.

educativo *a* educational, instructive.

educàto *a* well-bred, polite, educated.

educazióne *nf* education, training, upbringing, good breeding.

èffe the letter f.

effeminatézza *nf* effeminacy.

effeminàto *a* effeminate, unmanly.

efferatézza *nf* brutality, ferocity.

efferàto *a* brutal, savage.

effervescènte *a* effervescent.

effettívo *a* actual, effective; **effettívi** *nm* *pl* (*mil*) effectives *pl*.

effètto *nm* effect, result, impression.

effettuàbile *a* practicable, feasible.

effettuàre *vt* to carry out, effect, execute, make, produce; **-rsi** *vr* to take place, happen.

effettuazióne *nf* execution, fulfilment.

efficàce *a* effective, effectual, efficacious.

efficàcia *nf* efficacy, efficaciousness, effectiveness.

efficiènte *a* efficient.

efficiènza *nf* effectiveness, efficiency.

effigiàre *vt* to image, make an effigy of, portray, represent.

effìgie *nf* effigy.

effìmero *a* ephemeral, fleeting.

efflorescènte *a* efflorescent.

efflùsso *a* efflux, outflow.

efflùvio *nm* effluvium.

effóndere *vt* to pour forth, exhale; -**rsi** *vr* to break out into, burst, flow, spread.

effusióne *nf* effusion, outpouring.

ègida *nf* protection, shelter, shield.

Egìdio *nm pr* Giles.

Egìtto *nm* (*geogr*) Egypt.

egiziàno *a nm* Egyptian.

égli *pron* he.

egoìsmo *nm* selfishness, egoism.

egoìsta *a* egoistic(al); *nm* egoist.

egrègio *a* egregious, exceptional, remarkable, distinguished.

eguagliànza *nf* equality.

eguagliàre *vt* to (make) equal, level.

eguàle *a* equal, even, like, uniform.

egualménte *ad* equally, alike.

elaboràre *vt* to elaborate, plan, work out.

elargìre *vt* to give liberally, grant, lavish.

elargizióne *nf* donation, generous contribution, gift, grant.

elasticità *nf* elasticity, spring(iness), resilience.

elàstico *pl* -**ici** *a* elastic; *nm* rubber band.

élce *nm* evergreen oak, holm oak.

elefànte *nm* elephant.

elegànte *a* elegant, graceful, (*of speech*) polished.

elegànza *nf* elegance, polish.

elèggere *vt* to choose, elect.

eleggìbile *a* eligible.

elegìa *nf* elegy.

elementàre *a* elementary.

eleménto *nm* element, component; -**ivi** *pl* rudiments *pl*.

elemòsina *nf* alms *pl*, charity.

elemosinàre *vt* to beg.

elemosinièra *nf* -**re** *nm* almoner, alms-giver.

Èlena *nf pr* Helen, Helena.

elencàre *vt* to list, catalogue.

elènco *pl* -**chi** *nm* list, catalogue, inventory; **e. telefònico** telephone directory.

Eleonòra *nf pr* Eleanor, Elinor.

elètto *a* chosen, elect, elected.

elettoràle *a* electoral.

elettoràto *nm* electorate, constituency, franchise.

elettóre *nm* **elettrìce** *nf* elector.

elettràuto *nm* (*aut*) electrical repair shop.

elettricìsta *nm* electrician.

elettricità *nf* electricity.

elèttrico *pl* -**ici** *a* electric(al).

elettrificàre *vt* to electrify.

elettrizzàre *vt* to electrify, (*fig*) thrill.

elèttrodo *nm* electrode.

elettrodomèstici *nm pl* electrical household appliances *pl*.

elettróne *nm* electron.

elettrotècnica *nf* electrical technology.

elettrotréno *nm* electric train.

elevàre *vt* to elevate, erect, lift, raise; -**rsi** *vr* to make one's way, raise oneself.

elevatézza *nf* elevation, loftiness, nobility.

elevatóre *nm* (*tec*) elevator.

elevazióne *nf* elevation, raising, rise.

elezióne *nf* election, appointment.

èlica *nf* propeller, screw.

elicòttero *nm* helicopter.

elìdere *vt* to elide, suppress.

eliminàre *vt* to eliminate.

eliminatòria *nf* (*sport*) preliminary heat.

eliminazióne *nf* elimination, removal.

elioterapìa *nf* heliotherapy, sun treatment.

eliotròpio *nm* heliotrope.

Elìsa *nf pr* Eliza.

Elisabètta *nf pr* Elizabeth, Elisabeth.

elìso *nm* Elysium; *a* Elysian; elided, suppressed.

elisìr *nm* elixir.

élla *pron* she.

èlle the letter l.

èllèboro *nm* Christmas rose, hellebore.

ellìsse *nf* ellipse.

ellìssi *nf* ellipsis.

ellìttico *pl* -**ici** *a* elliptic(al).

élmo *nm* helmet.

elocuzióne *nf* elocution.

elogiàre *vt* to praise, commend, eulogize.

elògio *nm* commendation, eulogy.

eloquènte *a* eloquent, fluent.

eloquènza *nf* eloquence.

elòquio *nm* speech.

èlsa *nf* (*of a sword*) hilt.

elucubràre *vt* to meditate on.

elùdere *vt* to avoid, elude, escape.

elusìvo *a* elusive, evasive.

elvètico *pl* -**ici** *a nm* Helvetic, Helvetian, Swiss.

elzevìro *a nm* (*typ*) Elzevir; leading literary article in a newspaper.

emaciàrsi *vr* to become emaciated.

emaciàto *a* emaciated.

emanàre *vt* to issue, exhale; *vi* emanate, proceed.

emanazióne *nf* emanation, efflux, issuing.

emancipàre *vt* to emancipate, free; -**rsi** *vr* to get emancipated, free oneself.

emancipazióne *nf* emancipation.

Emanuèle nm pr Emmanuel, Immanuel.

embàrgo nm (naut) embargo.

emblèma nm emblem, symbol.

embolìa nf (med) embolism.

embolìsmo nm (astr) embolism.

embrióne nm embryo.

emendaménto nm **emendazióne** nf amendment, amendation, correction.

emendàre vt to amend, emend; -rsi vr to amend.

emergènza nf emergency, exigency.

emèrgere vi to emerge, stand out.

emèrito a emeritus.

emètico pl -ici a nm emetic.

eméttere vt to emit, express, give out, issue.

emicrània nf headache.

emigrànte a nmf emigrant.

emigràre vi to emigrate.

emigràto nm emigrant, exile, refugee.

emigrazióne nf emigration; migration.

Emìlia nf pr Emily, Emilia; **Emìlio** nm pr Emil.

eminènte a eminent, high.

eminènza nf eminence.

emisfèro nm hemisphere.

emissàrio nm emissary.

emissióne nf emission, issue.

emittènte a issuing; nm issuer; **bànca e.** bank of issue; **stazióne e.** (rad etc) sending station.

èmme the letter m.

emofilìa nf haemophilia.

emorragìa nf haemorrhage.

emorròidi nm pl (med) haemorrhoids pl, piles pl.

emotìvo a emotional, sensitive.

emozionànte a exciting, thrilling.

emozionàre vt to move, excite.

emozióne nf emotion.

émpiere v **empìre.**

empietà nf impiety, cruelty.

émpio a impious, cruel.

empìre vt to cram, fill (up).

empìrico pl -ici a empiric(al); nm empiric, empiricist; quack.

empirìsmo nm empiricism.

empòrio nm emporium, department store, vast collection.

emulàre vt to emulate, vie (with).

emulazióne nf emulation, rivalry.

èmulo a nm rival, competitor.

emulsióne nf emulsion.

encìclica nf encyclic(al).

enciclopedìa nf encyclopedia.

encomiàbile a commendable, praiseworthy.

encòmio nm encomium, praise; (mil) mention in dispatches, citation.

endèmico pl -ici a endemic.

endovenóso a intravenous.

Enèa nm pr Aeneas.

energìa nf energy.

enèrgico pl -ici a energetic, powerful.

energùmeno nm madman, one possessed.

ènfasi nf emphasis, stress.

enfiagióne nf swelling.

enfiàre vi -rsi vr to swell.

enigma nm enigma, riddle.

enigmìstica nf libro di e. book of riddles and puzzles.

ennèsimo a (math) nth.

enòrme a enormous, huge, incredible.

enormità nf hugeness, enormity, nonsense.

Enrichétta nf pr Henrietta.

Enrìco nm pr Henry, Harry.

ènte nm being, organization.

entèrico pl -ici a enteric.

enterìte nf (med) enteritis.

entità nf entity, existence, importance.

entomologìa nf entomology.

entràmbi pron and a pl both pl.

entrànte a next, coming.

entràre vi to come in, enter, go in, have to do with.

entràta nf entrance, entry, admission; income, (com) receipts pl, revenue.

entratùra nf entrance; familiar terms.

èntro prep within.

entusiasmàre vt to enrapture; -rsi vr to become enthusiastic.

entusiàsmo nm enthusiasm, rapture.

entusiàsta nmf enthusiast.

entusiàstico pl -ici a enthusiastic.

enumeràre vt to enumerate.

enunciàre vt to enunciate, state, utter.

epàtico pl -ici a (med) hepatic, of the liver.

èpico pl èpici a epic, heroic.

epicureìsmo nm epicureanism.

epicurèo a epicurean; nm epicure.

epidemìa nf epidemic.

epidèrmide nf (med) epidermis, (outer) skin.

Epifanìa nf Epiphany.

epìgono nm imitator, follower; descendant.

epìgrafe nf epigraph, inscription.

epigràmma nm epigram.

epilatòrio a depilatory.

epilessìa nf (med) epilepsy.

epilèttico pl -ici a nm epileptic.

epilogàre v **riepilogàre.**

epìlogo pl -ghi nm epilogue.

episcopàle a episcopal.

episcopàto nm episcopacy; episcopate.

episòdio nm episode.

epìstola nf epistle.

epìteto nm epithet.

època nf epoch, time.

eppùre cj and yet, however, nevertheless.

epuràre vt to purify, refine, remove, purge.

epurazióne nf purge, removal (from office), purification.

equànime a calm, tranquil, well-balanced.

equanimità *nf* equanimity, composure.

equatóre *nm* equator.

equazióne *nf* equation.

equèstre *a* equestrian.

equilibràre *vt* to balance, poise.

equilíbrio *nm* balance, equilibrium.

equilibrísta *nmf* tightrope-walker.

equinòzio *nm* equinox.

equipaggiaménto *nm* equipment, rigging.

equipaggiàre *vt* to equip, fit out; (*naut*) man.

equipàggio *nm* (*naut*) crew, equipage.

equiparàre *vt* to make equal, compare.

equipollènte *a* equivalent.

equità *nf* equity, fairness, impartiality, justice.

equitazióne *nf* riding, horsemanship.

equivalènte *a nm* equivalent.

equivalènza *nf* equivalence.

equivalére *vi* to be equivalent.

equivocàre *vi* to equivocate, make a mistake, misunderstand.

equívoco *pl* **-oci** *a* equivocal, ambiguous; *nm* misunderstanding.

èquo *a* equitable, fair, impartial, just.

èra *nf* era, epoch, age.

eràrio *nm* exchequer, public treasury.

èrba *nf* grass, herb; **in e.** *a* green, immature.

erbàccia *nf* weed.

erbàggio *nm pl* pot herbs *pl*, vegetables *pl*.

erbaiòlo *nm* costermonger, greengrocer.

erbàrio *nm* herbarium.

erbivèndolo *nm* greengrocer.

erborísta *nm* herborist.

erbóso *a* grassy.

erède *nm* heir.

eredità *nf* heritage, inheritance, heredity.

creditàre *vt* to inherit.

ereditàrio *a* hereditary; **príncipe e.** crown prince.

ereditièra *nf* heiress.

eremíta *nm* hermit.

eremitàggio, èremo *nm* hermitage.

eresía *nf* heresy.

erètico *pl* **-ici** *a* heretical; *nm* heretic.

erètto *a* erect; built; founded.

erezióne *nf* erection.

ergàstolo *nm* galleys *pl*, life sentence.

èrica *nf* heath, heather.

erígere *vt* to erect, raise, institute; **-rsi** *vr* to raise oneself, set up for.

Eritrèa *nf* (*geogr*) Eritrea.

eritrèo *a nm* Eritrean.

ermellíno *nm* ermine.

ermètico *pl* **-ici** *a* hermetic, airtight; (*fig*) secret.

ermetísmo *nm* obscurity; (*liter*) a modern Italian school of poetry.

èrmo *a* (*poet*) lonely, solitary; *v* **solitàrio**.

Ernèsto *nm pr* Ernest.

èrnia *nf* (*med*) hernia, rupture; **e. del dísco** slipped disc.

Eròde *nm pr* Herod.

eròe *nm* hero.

erogàre *vt* to bestow, lay out.

eròico *pl* **-ici** *a* heroic.

eroína *nf* heroine; (*drug*) heroin.

eroísmo *nm* heroism.

erómpere *vi* to break out, burst out, flow, rush out.

erosióne *nf* erosion.

eròtico *pl* **-ici** *a* erotic.

erotísmo *nm* eroticism.

érpice *nm* harrow.

errànte *a* errant, wandering.

erràre *vi* to wander, rove, roam, err.

erràto *a* wrong.

èrre the letter r.

erròneo *a* erroneous, faulty, incorrect.

erròre *nm* blunder, error, mistake.

èrta *nf* slope, steep ascent.

èrto *a* steep.

erudíre *vt* to instruct, teach; **-rsi** *vr* to acquire knowledge, become learned.

erudíto *a* learned, scholarly; *nm* scholar.

erudizióne *nf* erudition.

eruttàre *vti* (*of volcano*) erupt, eject, belch.

eruzióne *nf* eruption.

esacerbàre *vt* to embitter, exacerbate.

esageràre *vti* to exaggerate.

esagerazióne *nf* exaggeration.

esalàre *vti* to exhale, give out.

esalazióne *nf* exhalation.

esaltàre *vt* to exalt, praise; **-rsi** *vr* to get excited, become elated.

esaltàto *a* excited, elated, hotheaded; *nm* hot-head, fanatic.

esàme *nm* examination, investigation; **commissióne di e.** board of examiners.

esaminàre *vt* to examine, inspect, investigate, survey, test.

esaminatóre, f -tríce *a* examining; *nm* examiner.

esàngue *a* bloodless.

esànime *a* lifeless, dead.

esasperàre *vt* to exasperate; **-rsi** *vr* to get exasperated.

esasperazióne *nf* exasperation.

esattézza *nf* accuracy, exactness, exactitude, punctuality.

esàtto *a* accurate, exact, precise, punctual.

esattóre *nm* **-tríce** *nf* (*of taxes etc*) collector.

esattoría *nf* Revenue Office.

esaudiménto *nm* satisfaction, fulfilment.

esaudíre *vt* to consent, grant, fulfil, satisfy.

esauriènte *a* exhaustive.

esauriménto *nm* exhaustion, depletion; **e. nervóso** nervous breakdown.

esauríre *vt* to exhaust, use up, wear

out; **-rsi** *vr* to exhaust oneself, run out, run dry.

esaurìto *a* exhausted, worn out, sold out, out of print.

esàusto *a* exhausted.

esautoràre *vt* to deprive of authority.

esazióne *nf* collection, exaction.

èsca *nf* bait, decoy, enticement; tinder (for a lighter).

escandescènte *a* choleric, hottempered.

escandescènza *nf* outburst, sudden burst of rage.

escavazióne *nf* excavation.

eschimése *a nmf* Eskimo.

esclamàre *vi* to cry out, exclaim.

esclamazióne *nf* exclamation.

esclúdere *vt* to except, exclude, leave out, bar.

esclusióne *nf* exclusion, omission.

esclusìva *nf* patent, exclusive right.

esclusività *nf* exclusiveness.

esclusìvo *a* exclusive, sole.

esclúso *a* excluded, excepted.

escogitàre *vt* to contrive, devise, excogitate.

escoriàre *vt* to graze, excoriate.

escoriazióne *nf* abrasion, graze.

escursióne *nf* excursion, trip.

escursionìsta *nmf* excursionist.

esecràre *vt* to execrate.

esecrazióne *nf* execration.

esecutìvo *a* executive, executory; *nm* executive.

esecutóre *a* executory; *nm* **-trìce** *nf* executor, performer, executioner.

esecuzióne *nf* **eseguimento** *nm* execution, performance.

eseguìre *vt* to accomplish, carry out, execute, fulfil, perform.

esémpio *nm* example, instance, pattern, precedent.

esemplàre *a* exemplary, model; *nm* specimen, (of a book) copy; model.

esemplificàre *vt* to exemplify.

esentàre *vt* to excuse, exempt, exonerate, free; **-rsi** *vr* to free oneself.

esènte *a* exempt, free.

esenzióne *nf* exemption (*eccl*) dispensation.

esèquie *nf pl* burial, funeral, obsequies *pl*.

esercènte *nm* dealer, shopkeeper, trader.

esercìre *vt* to carry on, keep, practise; **non e. piú** *vi* to have given up (business or practice).

esercitàre *vt* to exercise, practise, train; **-rsi** *vr* to practise.

esèrcito *nm* army.

esercìzio *nm* exercise, practice, management, drill; (financial) year.

esibìre *vt* to display, exhibit, show; **-rsi** *vr* to offer oneself, show oneself.

esibizióne *nf* exhibition, show.

esibizionìsta *nmf* exhibitionist.

esigènte *a* exacting, exigent, hard to please.

esigènza *nf* exigence, exigency, demand, requirement.

esìgere *vt* to exact, require, demand.

esiguità *nf* exiguity, scantiness.

esìguo *a* exiguous, slender, scanty.

esilarànte *a* exhilarating; cheering.

esilaràre *vt* to cheer up, exhilarate.

èsile *a* slender, slim.

esiliàre *vt* to banish, exile; **-rsi** *vr* to exile oneself, withdraw from.

esiliàto *a* exiled; *nm* exile.

esìlio *nm* exile (state).

esilità *nf* slenderness, weakness.

esìmere *vt* to exempt, excuse; **-rsi** *vr* to excuse oneself, evade.

esìmio *a* excellent, eminent, distinguished.

esistènte *a* existing, existent, extant.

esistènza *nf* existence, life; (*com*) stock.

esìstere *vi* to exist, be, be extant.

esitàre *vi* to hesitate, waver; *vt* (*com*) to sell, dispose of.

èsito *nm* result, outcome, issue, denouement; sale.

esiziàle *a* baneful, fatal.

èsodo *nm* exodus, flight.

esòfago *nm* oesophagus, gullet.

esoneràre *vt* to exempt, exonerate, free, release, relieve.

esònero *nm* dispensation, exemption, exoneration.

esorbitànte *a* exorbitant, excessive.

esorcizzàre *vt* to exorcize.

esordiènte *a* beginning; *nmf* beginner, novice.

esòrdio *nm* beginning, exordium.

esordìre *vi* to begin, start.

esortàre *vt* to admonish, exhort.

esortazióne *nf* exhortation.

esòso *a* greedy, hateful.

esòtico *pl* **-ici** *a* exotic, foreign.

espàndere *vt* to spread; **-rsi** *vr* to expand, open one's heart.

espansióne *nf* expansion, demonstration of affection.

espansività *nf* effusiveness.

espansìvo *a* expansive, unreserved.

espatriàre *vt* to banish, exile; *vi* to emigrate.

espàtrio *nm* expatriation.

espediènte *a nm* expedient.

espèllere *vt* to expel.

esperiènza *nf* experience; experiment.

esperimentàre *vt* to experience; experiment, test.

esperiménto *nm* experiment, test.

esperìre *vt* to carry out; (*leg*) try.

espèrto *a* experienced; *nm* expert.

espettoràre *vt* to cough up, expectorate.

espiàre *vt* to atone, expiate, make amends for.

espiazióne *nf* amends *pl*, atonement, expiation.

espletàre *vt* to fulfil, accomplish, dispatch.

esplicàre *vt* to develop; explain; **e. un'attività** to carry on an activity.

esplícito *a* clear, explicit, express.

esplòdere *vi* to blow up, burst out, explode.

esploràre *vt* to examine, explore, search, (*mil*) reconnoitre.

esploratóre *nm* explorer, (*mil*) scout; **gióvane e.** (Boy) Scout; **esploratríce** *nf* explorer; **gióvane e.** Girl Guide, (US) Girl Scout.

esplorazióne *nf* exploration, (*mil*) reconnaissance.

esplosióne *nf* blowing up, discharge, explosion.

esplosívo *a nm* explosive.

esponènte *nm* exponent.

espórre *vt* to show, exhibit, explain, expose, risk; **-rsi** *vr* to expose oneself, run the risk.

esportàre *vt* to export.

esportàre *a* exporting; *nm* **esportatríce** *nf* exporter.

esportazióne *nf* export, exportation.

esposímetro *nm* (*phot*) exposure meter.

esposizióne *nf* exposure, exhibition, exposition, statement.

espósto *nm* statement, petition; foundling.

espressióne *nf* expression.

espressívo *a* expressive, meaningful.

esprèsso *a* express, expressed, precise; *nm* (*letter, parcel, train*) express, (US, *letter*) fast.

esprimere *vt* to declare, express, signify, utter.

espropriàre *vt* to expropriate, dispossess.

espropriazióne *nf* expropriation.

espugnàre *vt* to (take by) storm.

espulsióne *nf* banishment, expulsion.

espúngere *vt* to expunge, delete.

espurgàre *vt* to expurgate.

espurgazióne *nf* expurgation.

éssa *pron* she.

èsse *nm* the letter s.

essènza *nf* essence.

essenziàle *a* essential, main, principal.

èssere *vi* to be, exist, happen, occur; **e. di** to belong to; **e. per** to be on the point of; *nm* being, state, condition.

essiccàre *vt* to dry; **-rsi** *vr* to dry up.

ésso *pron* he.

èst *nm* east.

èstasi *nf* ecstasy, rapture.

estasiàre *vt* to enrapture, delight; **-rsi** *vr* to be enraptured.

estàte *nf* summer.

estàtico *pl* -**ici** *a* ecstatic.

estemporàneo *a* extemporaneous, extempore, unscripted; **estemporaneamènte** *ad* impromptu, ad lib.

estèndere *vt* to extend, expand; **-rsi** *vr* to extend, stretch.

estensióne *nf* extension, expanse, extent, range.

estenuàre *vt* exhaust; **-rsi** *vr* to become exhausted, weak.

estenuazióne *nf* exhaustion.

Èster *nf pr* Esther.

esterióre *a* exterior, external, outward; *nm* exterior.

esterminàre *vt* to exterminate.

esternàre *vt* to disclose, express, open.

estèrno *a* external, outer; *nm* outside.

èstero *a* foreign; *nm* foreign countries *pl*; **all'e.** abroad.

esterrefàtto *a* terrified, amazed.

estesamènte *ad* extensively.

estéso *a* large, wide, extensive.

estètica *nf* aesthetics *pl*.

estètico *pl* -**ici** *a* aesthetic(al).

èstimo *nm* estimate, valuation, land tax.

estínguere *vt* to extinguish, put out; pay off; **-rsi** *vr* to go out, come to an end, die.

estínto *a* extinguished, deceased; *nm* deceased (person).

estintóre *nm* extinguisher.

estinzióne *nf* extinction, putting out; paying off.

estirpàre *vt* to extirpate, pull out, uproot.

estirpazióne *nf* extirpation, uprooting.

èstone *a nmf* Esthonian.

Estònia *nf* (*geogr*) Esthonia.

estòrcere *vt* to extort.

estorsióne *nf* extortion.

estradizióne *nf* extradition.

estràneo *a* extraneous, not related, alien, foreign; *nm* stranger, foreigner.

estràrre *vt* to dig out, draw out, extract.

estràtto *nm* extract, excerpt, certificate; **e. cónto** (*com*) statement of account.

estrazióne *nf* extraction, digging out; **e. a sòrte** drawing lots.

estremamènte *ad* extremely.

estremità *nf* extremity, end.

estrèmo *a* extreme, farthest; intense, severe; *nm* extremity extreme.

estrinsecàre *vt* to express, manifest.

estrínseco *pl* -**sechi**, **-seci** *a* extrinsic.

èstro *nm* inspiration, fancy, freak.

estróso *a* capricious, freakish, whimsical.

estrovèrso *a* extroverted; *nm* extrovert.

estuàrio *nm* estuary, firth.

esuberànte *a* exuberant, overflowing.

esulàre *vi* to go into exile.

esulceràre *vt* to produce sores.

èsule *nmf* exile (person).

esultànte *a* exultant, rejoicing.

esultàre *vi* to exult, rejoice.

esumazióne *nf* exhumation.

età *nf* age.

ètere *nm* ether.

etèreo *a* airy, ethereal, impalpable.

eternàre *vt* to eternalize, make

endless; **-rsi** *vr* to become eternal, last for ever.
eternità *nf* eternity.
etèrno *a* eternal, everlasting.
ètica *nf* ethics *pl.*
etichétta *nf* etiquette; label.
ètico *pl* **ètici** *a* ethical; (*med*) consumptive.
etimología *nf* etymology.
etimològico *pl* **-ici** *a* etymological.
Etiòpia *nf* (*geogr*) Ethiopia.
etiòpico *pl* **-ici** *a nm* Ethiopian.
etişía *nf* (*med*) consumption.
ètnico *pl* **-ici** *a* ethnic(al).
etrúsco *pl* **-chi** *a nm* Etruscan.
èttaro *nm* hectare.
Èttore *nm pr* Hector.
Eucaristía *nf* Eucharist.
eufemía *nf* euphemism.
eufemíşmo *nm* euphemism.
eufonía *nf* euphony.
euforía *nf* euphoria, light-heartedness.
eufòrico *pl* **-ici** *a* euphoric, elated.
eugàneo *a* (*geogr*) Euganean.
Eugènio *nm pr* Eugene.
eunúco *pl* **-chi** *nm* eunuch.
Euròpa *nf* (*geogr*) Europe.
europèo *a nm* European.
Èva *nf pr* Eve, Eva.
evacuàre *vt* to clear out, evacuate.
evàdere *vt* to dispatch; evade; *vi* to escape.
evanescènte *a* fading, evanescent.
evanescènza *nf* evanescence; (*rad, tv*) fading.
evangelizzàre *vt* to evangelize.
evangèlo *nm* gospel.
evaporàre *vi* to evaporate.
evaporazióne *nf* evaporation.
evaşióne *nf* escape, evasion.
evaşívo *a* evasive.
eveniènza *nf* contingency, eventuality.
evènto *nm* event, result, outcome; in ógni e. at all events.
eventuàle *a* eventual, possible.
evidènte *a* clear, evident, obvious, plain.
evidènza *nf* clearness, evidence, obviousness.
evitàbile *a* avoidable, preventable.
evitàre *vt* to avoid, escape, spare.
evizióne *nf* eviction; recovery of possession.
èvo *nm* age, period, time.
evocàre *vt* to evoke, recall, conjure up.
evoluzióne *nf* evolution.
evvíva *interj* hurrah! long live!
extraconiugàle *a* extramarital.
extraterritorialità *nf* extraterritoriality.

F

fa *ad* ago; *nm* (*mus*) fa, F.
fabbişógno *nm* needs *pl*, requirement; (*com*) estimate of expenditure.
fàbbrica *nf* factory, manufactory, works *pl*, plant; manufacture; building.
fabbricànte *nm* manufacturer; builder.
fabbricàre *vt* to build, manufacture, fabricate.
fabbricàto *nm* building.
fabbricazióne *nf* manufacture, building; invention, forgery.
fàbbro *nm* blacksmith, smith.
fabbroferràio *nm* blacksmith.
faccènda *nf* affair, business, matter.
facchinàggio *nm* porterage.
facchíno *nm* porter.
fàccia *nf* face; f. tòsta impudence.
facciàta *nf* façade, front, (*of a page*) side.
facèto *a* facetious.
facèzia *nf* jest, joke, witticism.
fàcile *a* easy.
facilità *nf* facility, ease, easiness.
facilitàre *vt* to facilitate, make easy.
facilménte *ad* easily.
facoltà *nf* faculty, authority, power.
facoltatívo *a* optional.
facoltóso *a* wealthy, well-to-do.
facóndia *nf* eloquence, fluency.
facóndo *a* eloquent, fluent, talkative.
fàggio *nm* beech-tree.
fagiàno *nm* pheasant.
fagiolíno *nm* French bean, string bean.
fagiòlo *nm* kidney-bean; (*fig*) blockhead.
fàglia *nf* (*silk material*) faille.
fagòtto *nm* bundle; (*mus*) bassoon; fàre f. *vi* to pack up.
faína *nf* beech marten.
fàlce *nf* scythe, sickle.
falciàre *vt* to cut down, mow.
falciatóre *nm* mower; **-trice** *nf* mower, mowing machine; f. da pràto lawn-mower.
fàlco *pl* **-chi**, **falcóne** *nm* falcon, hawk.
falconàra *nf* falcon-house; loophole.
fàlda *nf* (snow)flake, layer, slice, slope, (*of hat*) brim, (*of coat*) tail, (*of mountain*) base, foot.
falegnàme *nm* carpenter, joiner.
falèna *nf* moth; flake of ashes.
fàlla *nf* (*naut*) leak.
fallàce *a* deceptive, fallacious.
falliménto *nm* bankruptcy, failure, insolvency.
fallíre *vi* to fail, go bankrupt; *vt* to miss.
fallíto *a* insolvent, unsuccessful; *nm* bankrupt, failure.
fàllo *nm* fault, defect.
falò *nm* bonfire.

falsàre vt to alter, distort, falsify.
falsarìga pl **-righe** nf a guide to writing straight; (fig) model, example.
falsàrio nm forger.
falsificàre vt to falsify, forge, misrepresent.
falsificazióne nf falsification, forgery.
falsità nf falsity, falsehood.
fàlso a false, wrong, forged, fictitious, deceitful; (of door etc) blind; nm falsehood, forgery, error.
fàma nf fame, renown, reputation.
fàme nf hunger; **avére f.** to be hungry.
famèlico pl **-ici** a famishing, starving.
famigeràto a notorious.
famìglia nf family, household.
familiàre a domestic, familiar, informal; nm relative, intimate, friend, manservant.
familiarità nf familiarity, intimacy.
familiarizzàre vt to familiarize; **-rsi** vr to become familiar.
famóso a famous, renowned, wellknown.
fanàle nm lamp, lantern; (aut) light, lamp; **fanàli di posizione** parking lights.
fanalíno nm **f. di códa** (av) taillamp; (aut) rear lamp.
fanàtico pl **-ici** a nm fanatic.
fanatìsmo nm fanaticism.
fanciúlla nf young girl; **fanciúllo** nm young boy.
fanciullàggine nf childishness.
fanciullésco pl **-chi** a childish.
fanciullézza nf childhood.
fandònia nf lie, idle story, tall tale.
fanfàra nf brass band, fanfare.
fanghìglia nf slush, sludge.
fàngo nm mud, mire.
fangóso a muddy, miry.
fannullóne nm idler, lazybones.
fantasciènza nf science fiction.
fantasìa nf imagination, fancy, fantasy; **gioièlli f.** costume jewellery.
fantàsma nm ghost, phantom, phantasm.
fantasticàre vi to build castles in the air, daydream.
fantàstico pl **-ici** a fantastic; fanciful; wonderful.
fànte nm foot-soldier; (at cards) jack.
fanterìa nf infantry.
fantìno nm jockey.
fantòccio nm puppet (also fig).
farabútto nm rascal, scoundrel.
faraóne nm Pharaoh; (game of) faro.
farcíre vi to stuff.
fardèllo nm bundle, burden.
fàre vti to do, make; have, take, take on, appoint, deem, perform, play, bear, cause; **f. attenzióne** to pay attention; **f. bel tèmpo** to be fine; **f. il bàgno** to take a bath; **f. il mèdico** to be a doctor; **f. fàre una còsa** to have a thing done;

f. lavoràre una persóna to make a person work; **-rsi** vr to become, grow, make oneself, turn; **f. fràte** to turn monk; **f. capìre** to make oneself understood; **f. vedére** to show oneself; nm behaviour, manner.
farfàlla nf butterfly.
farìna nf flour, meal.
farinàceo a farinaceous.
farìnge nf pharynx.
farinóso a floury, mealy.
farisèo nm Pharisee.
farmacèutica nf pharmaceutics pl.
farmacìa nf chemist's shop, (US) drugstore, pharmacy.
farmacìsta nm chemist.
farneticàre vi to be delirious, rave; (fig) talk nonsense.
fàro nm lighthouse.
farràgine nf farrago, medley.
fàrsa nf farce.
farsésco a farcical.
fàscia nf band, bandage, cover, swaddling band.
fasciàme nm (tec) plating, planking.
fasciàre vt to bandage, swaddle, wrap.
fasciatúra nf bandaging, swaddling; (wound) dressing.
fascìcolo nm (of a publication) number; dossier.
fascìna nf fagot, (mil) fascine.
fàscino nm charm, fascination.
fàscio nm bundle, pile; (of light) beam; fasces pl.
fascìsmo nm Fascism.
fascìsta a nmf Fascist.
fàse nf phase, stage, (aut) stroke.
fastèllo nm bundle of wood, faggot.
fastìdio nm annoyance, trouble, vexation.
fastidióso a annoying, troublesome, intolerant.
fàsto nm pomp, splendour, display.
fastóso a gorgeous, splendid, ostentatious.
fasúllo a false.
fàta nf fairy; **paése delle fàte** fairyland.
fatàle a fatal; fated, inevitable.
fatalità nf fatality; destiny, fate.
fatìca nf fatigue, weariness, hard work, difficulty; **a f.** with difficulty.
faticàre vi to toil, work hard.
faticóso a exhausting, fatiguing.
fàto nm destiny, doom, fate, lot.
fàtta nf kind, sort; deed.
fattézze nf pl features pl.
fattìbile a feasible, practicable.
fattìvo a effective, active, efficient.
fàtto a done, made; ripe, fullgrown, fit; nm fact, deed, action, event, matter.
fattóre nm, **-tóra**, **-torèssa** nf factor, bailiff, land agent; (in this sense **-trìce** f) maker.
fattorìa nf farm, land agency, ranch.
fattorìno nm message-boy, messenger, page, (US) bellboy (bellhop).

fattúra nf make, work, making, workmanship; bill, invoice.

fàtuo a conceited, fatuous; **fuòco f.** will-o'-the-wisp.

fàuna nf fauna.

fàuno nm faun.

fàusto a propitious, happy, lucky.

Fàusto nm pr Faust, Faustus.

fautóre nm **-tríce** nf supporter, favourer, protector.

fàva nf bean, broad bean.

favèlla nf language, speech, tongue.

favellàre vi to speak, talk.

favílla nf spark.

fàvo nm honeycomb.

fàvola nf fable, tale, story; laughing stock.

favolóso a fabulous.

favóre nm favour, kindness, approval; **cambiàle di f.** accommodation bill.

favoreggiàre vt to back, favour, support.

favorévole a favourable, propitious, well-disposed.

favorevolménte ad favourably.

favoríre vt to favour, foster, oblige, promote.

favoríto a favourite; nm favourite; **favoríti** pl side whiskers pl.

fazióne nf faction, party; (mil) guard.

fazióso a factious, seditious.

fazzolétto nm handkerchief.

febbràio nm February.

fébbre nf fever, temperature; **avére la f.** to have (run) a temperature.

febbríle a feverish (also fig).

féccia nf dregs pl, scum, sediment.

féci nf pl (med) stool.

fecondàre vt to fecundate, fertilize.

fecondazióne nf fecundation; **f. artificiàle** artificial insemination.

fecóndo a fecund, fertile, fruitful.

féde nf faith, creed, trust, belief, honesty; wedding ring, certificate; **f. di nàscita** birth certificate.

fedéle a faithful, loyal, true; nmf believer, follower.

fedeltà nf faithfulness, fidelity, loyalty.

fèdera nf pillow-case.

federàto a federate.

federazióne nf confederacy, federation.

Federíco nm pr Frederic(k).

fedína nf police record; whisker.

fégato nm liver; (fig) courage.

félce nf fern.

feld-maresciàllo nm (mil) field-marshal.

felíce a happy, lucky.

feliceménte ad happily.

felicità nf happiness, felicity.

felicitàrsi vr to congratulate.

felicitazióne nf congratulation.

felíno a feline.

féltro nm felt.

fémmina nf female, (contemptuous) woman.

femmíneo a womanly, womanish, effeminate.

femminíle a feminine, womanly.

fèndere vt to cleave, cut open, split; **-rsi** vr to burst, crack, split.

fendinébbia nm (aut) fog light.

fenditúra nf cleft, crack, split.

feníce nf (myth) phoenix (also fig).

fènico pl **-ici** a carbolic, phenic.

fenicòttero nm flamingo.

fenòmeno nm phenomenon.

feràce a fertile, fruitful, rich (also fig).

feràle a of death, tragic.

Ferdinàndo nm pr Ferdinand.

fèretro nm bier, coffin.

fèria nf holiday, vacation.

feriàle a working; **giórno f.** working day, weekday.

feriménto nm wounding.

feríre vt to hurt, wound.

feríta nf wound, injury, hurt.

feritóia nf loophole, embrasure; (mech) vent.

fèrma nf (mil) service, term of service; (hunting) pointing.

fermàglio nm brooch, clip, fastener.

fermaménte ad firmly, decidedly, positively.

fermàre vti to stop, fasten, fix, hold; **-rsi** vr to stay, stop, dwell on.

fermàta nf halt, stop, pause.

fermentàre vi to ferment, leaven.

fermentazióne nf fermentation.

ferménto nm ferment, leaven.

fermézza nf firmness, steadiness.

férmo a firm, steady, still; nm firmness; (mech) catch, stop; (leg) provisional arrest; **f. pòsta** poste restante, (US) general delivery.

feróce a ferocious, fierce.

feròcia pl **-cie** nf ferocity, fierceness, savagery.

ferragósto nm August holiday (Aug 15th).

ferraménta nf hardware, ironmongery, iron fittings.

ferraménto nm iron tool.

ferràre vt to add iron fittings, shoe (a horse).

ferràto a iron-plated, shod; **stràda ferràta** railway.

fèrreo a (of) iron; hard, inflexible.

ferrièra nf ironworks pl, iron foundry, iron mine.

fèrro nm iron; pl irons, chains; **f. di cavàllo** horseshoe; **f. da càlza** knitting needle; **f. da stíro** (flat) iron; **età del f.** iron age; **lavóro in f.** ironwork.

ferrovía nf railway, (US) railroad; **f. sotterrànea** underground, (US) subway.

ferroviàrio a (of the) railway; **oràrio f.** nm timetable.

ferrovière nm railwayman, (US) railroader.

fèrtile a fertile, fruitful, prolific.

fertilità nf fertility, fruitfulness (also fig).

fertilizzànte a fertilizing; nm fertilizer.

fertilizzàre vt to fertilize.

fervènte a burning, ardent, fervent.

fèrvere vi to be hot.

fèrvido a fervent, ardent, fervid.

fervóre nm ardour, fervour, zeal.

fesseria nf stupidity (in actions or words).

fésso a cleft, cracked; nm fool.

fessúra nf crack, crevice, fissure, split.

fèsta nf feast, festivity, holiday, merry-making, saint's day, birthday.

festeggiàre vt to celebrate, feast, give a feast for, solemnize, welcome.

festévole a festive, joyous.

festino nm entertainment, party.

festivàl nm festival.

festività nf festivity, gaiety.

festivo a festive.

festóso a gay, merry.

feticcio nm fetish.

fèto nm foetus.

fétta nf slice.

fettúccia nf tape, ribbon.

fettuccìne nf pl noodles.

feudàle a feudal.

fèudo nm feud, fief.

fiàba nf fairy tale, story.

fiàcca nf weariness; laziness.

fiaccàre vt to exhaust, fatigue, wear out; -rsi vr to become tired, weak.

fiaccheràio nm cabman.

fiacchézza nf fatigue, lassitude, weakness, weariness.

fiàcco pl -cchi a exhausted, feeble, tired, weary.

fiàccola nf torch.

fiaccolàta nf torchlight procession.

fiàla nf phial, vial.

fiàmma nf flame, blaze; (naut) pennant.

fiammànte a flaming, glowing, bright; nuòvo f. brand new.

fiammàta nf blaze, fire.

fiammeggiàre vi to blaze, flame, shine.

fiammifero nm match.

fiammìngo pl -ghi a Flemish; nm Fleming; (the) Flemish (language).

fiancheggiàre vt to flank, help, support, border.

fiànco pl -chi nm hip, side, flank.

Fiàndre nf pl Flanders.

fiàsca nf flask.

fiaschetterìa nf wine shop, tavern.

fiàsco pl -chi nm flask; (fig) failure, fiasco; fàre f. to fail.

fiatàre vi to breathe, speak.

fiàto nm breath.

fíbbia nf buckle.

fíbra nf fibre, constitution.

ficcàre vt to drive in, thrust in; -rsi vr to force one's way in, intrude, meddle.

fíco pl -chi nm fig, fig-tree; f. d'India, ficodíndia prickly pear.

fidanzaménto nm betrothal, engagement.

fidanzàre vt to betroth; -rsi vr to become engaged.

fidanzàto a engaged; nm fiancé.

fidàre vt to entrust; -rsi vr to trust, confide, rely on; dare.

fidatézza nf reliability.

fidàto, fído a faithful, trusty.

fído a faithful, loyal; nm devoted follower; (com) credit.

fidúcia nf trust, confidence, reliance.

fiducióso a trusting, confident.

fièle nm gall, bile; (fig) rancour, bitterness.

fienìle nm hayloft; (fig) shabby place.

fièno nm hay.

fièra nf fair, exhibition; wild beast.

fieraménte ad fiercely, proudly, boldly.

fierézza nf fierceness, pride, boldness.

fièro a fierce, proud, bold, stern.

fiévole a feeble, weak, dim.

fífa nf plover, lapwing; (fam) funk.

fíggere vt to fix, fasten; f. gli òcchi su qualcúno to stare hard at somebody.

fíglia nf daughter; (com) counterfoil.

figliàstra nf stepdaughter; **figliàstro** nm stepson.

fíglio nm son, child.

figliòccia nf goddaughter; **figliòccio** nm godson.

figúra nf figure, illustration; (of a novel etc) character; symbol; fàre una bèlla f. to cut a good figure.

figuràccia nf poor figure, sorry figure.

figuràre vti to figure, represent, symbolize; look smart, appear, pretend; -rsi vr to fancy, imagine, picture to oneself.

figuràto a figurative; illustrated.

figurinìsta nmf dress designer.

figuríno nm fashion plate, pattern.

fíla nf line, queue, row.

filànda nf spinning mill.

filantropìa nf philanthropy.

filàntropo nm philanthrope, philanthropist.

filàre vt to spin; vi to run away, take oneself off; nm (of trees etc) row.

filarmònico pl -ici a nm philharmonic, music-lover.

filastròcca nf nonsense rhyme, rigmarole.

filatelìa nf philately, stamp collecting.

filatèlico pl -ici a philatelic; nm philatelist.

filàto a spun; consequent; nm yarn.

filatóio nm jenny, spinning-wheel.

filatóre nm -trice nf spinner.

filétto nm thin thread, border, (mil) stripe; (typ) rule; fillet.

filiàle a filial; nf branch, branch-house or office.

filiazióne nf filiation.

filibustière *nm* freebooter; (*fig*) adventurer, cad.

filigràna *nf* filigree; (*paper*) watermark.

Filippíne (le) *nf pl* the Philippines.

Filíppo *nm pr* Philip.

film *nm* film, (*US*) movie.

filmàre *vt* to film.

filo *nm* thread, flex, wire; trickle; **f. spinàto** barbed wire; **f. flessìbile** flex, (*US*) extension wire; **f. di tèrra** (*rad*) earth wire, (*US*) ground wire; *pl* **fíla** *nf* (*fig*) strings.

filobus *nm* trolley-bus.

filología *nf* philology; study of literary texts.

filóne *nm* (*of mineral*) vein; stream; (*of bread*) long loaf.

filosofía *nf* philosophy.

filosòfico *pl* **-ici** *a* philosophic(al).

filòsofo *nm* philosopher.

filovía *nf* trolley-bus line.

filtràre *vti* to filter, percolate.

filtro *nm* filter, philtre, strainer.

filugèllo *nm* silkworm.

fílza *nf* string, series; **púnto a f.** running stitch.

finàle *a* final, last; *nm* conclusion, finale; *nf* (*sport*) final.

finalménte *ad* finally, at last, lastly.

finalità *nf* finality, aim.

finànche *ad* also, even.

finànza *nf* finance, means.

finanziàrio *a* financial.

finanzière *nm* financier, customs officer.

finchè *cj* as long as; **f. non** till, until.

fine *a* thin, fine, delicate, refined; *nm* aim; *nf* conclusion, end.

finèstra *nf* window.

finestríno *nm* (*of train, car*) window.

finézza *nf* fineness, finesse, politeness, shrewdness.

fíngere *vi* **-rsi** *vr* to pretend, dissemble, feign.

finiménto *nm* finishing; ornament, harness.

finimóndo *nm* end of the world, great uproar, utter ruin.

finíre *vt* to bring to an end, conclude, finish; *vi* to be over, end, finish, give up.

finítimo *a* bordering, neighbouring.

finlandése *a nmf* Finnish, Finn.

Finlàndia *nf* Finland.

fíno *a* fine, thin, sharp; *prep* as far as, to, till, until, from, since; *ad* even.

finòcchio *nm* fennel.

finóra *ad* hitherto, so far, up to now.

fínta *nf* pretence, feint; **fàre f.** *vi* to pretend.

fínto *a* false, sham, artificial; *nm* hypocrite.

finzióne *nf* sham, pretence, fiction.

fío *nm* penalty.

fiocàggine *nf* hoarseness.

fioccàre *vi* to snow in large flakes; (*fig*) shower, abound.

fiòcco *pl* **-chi** *nm* (*of snow*) flake; (*of wool*) knot, tassel; **coi fiòcchi** excellent, first rate.

fiòcina *nf* harpoon.

fiòco *pl* **-chi** *a* hoarse; weak, (*of light*) dim, (*of sound*) faint.

fiónda *nf* catapult, (*US*) slingshot.

fioràia *nf* **-o** *nm* flower-seller.

fiordalíso *nm* cornflower, fleur-de-lis.

fiòrdo *nm* fiord.

fióre *nm* flower, bloom, blossom; (*at cards*) club; **f. di làtte** cream; **f. di quattríni** a lot of money; **a f. d'àcqua** on the surface of the water.

fiorènte *a* blooming, flourishing.

fiorentíno *a nm* Florentine.

fioríre *vi* to flower, thrive.

fiorísta *nmf* florist, flower painter, maker of artificial flowers.

fioríto *a* flowery, full of flowers.

fioritúra *nf* bloom, blossoming; (*fig*) flourishing.

fiòtto *nm* surge, wave.

Firènze *nf* (*geogr*) Florence.

fírma *nf* signature.

firmaménto *nm* firmament.

firmàre *vt* to sign.

fisarmònica *nf* accordion.

fischiàre *vt* to hiss, whistle.

físchio *nm* whistle, hiss; (*in the ears*) buzzing.

fisco *nm* Exchequer, Inland Revenue, (*US*) internal revenue; fisc.

física *nf* physics *pl*.

físico *pl* **-ici** *a* physical; *nm* physique; physicist.

fisiología *nf* physiology.

fisiològico *pl* **-ici** *a* physiological.

fisionomía *nf* countenance, physiognomy.

fisioterapía *nf* physiotherapy.

físo *a* fixed; *ad* fixedly.

fissàre *vt* to fix, fasten; gaze at, appoint, arrange, engage, book; **-rsi** *vr* to be fixed, settle, set one's heart on.

fissazióne *nf* fixed idea, obsession, fixation.

físso *a* fixed, settled; *nm* fixed salary; *ad* fixedly.

fítta *nf* sharp pain, pang.

fittízio *a* fictitious.

fítto *a* driven in, dense, thick; *nm* thick; rent; **a càpo f.** headlong.

fiumàna *nf* flood, swollen river, torrent; (*of people*) stream.

fiúme *nm* river.

fiutàre *vt* to smell, sniff, scent; (*fig*) suspect, guess.

fiúto *nm* scent, (sense of) smell.

flagellàre *vt* to flagellate, scourge.

flagèllo *nm* scourge, whip; calamity.

flagrànte *a* flagrant.

flagrànza *nf* flagrancy.

flanèlla *nf* flannel.

flèbile *a* plaintive, feeble.

flèmma *nf* phlegm; calm.

flessìbile *a* flexible, pliable, pliant.

flessióne *nf* flexion, bending.

flessuóso *a* flexuous, supple.

flèttere *vt* to bend, flex.

flirtàre *vi* to flirt.
floreàle *a* floral.
floridézza *nf* floridness, prosperity.
flòrido *a* florid, flourishing, prosperous.
flòscio *a* flabby, flaccid.
flòtta *nf* fleet, navy.
flottíglia *nf* flotilla.
fluidità *nf* fluidity, fluency.
flúido *a nm* fluid.
fluíre *vi* to flow.
fluorescènte *a* fluorescent.
flússo *nm* flood tide, flux, dysentery.
flútto *nm* breaker, surge, wave.
fluttuànte *a* fluctuating, floating.
fluttuàre *vi* to fluctuate, waver.
fluviàle *a* fluvial, river.
fobía *nf* phobia.
fòca *nf* seal.
focàccia *nf* kind of cake.
fóce *nf* river mouth.
focolàio *nm* centre of infection.
focolàre *nm* fireplace, hearth.
focóso *a* fiery.
fòdera *nf* lining, sheathing.
foderàre *vt* to line, sheathe.
fòdero *nm* scabbard, sheath.
fòga *nf* impetuosity.
fòggia *nf* fashion, form, manner, way.
foggiàre *vt* to fashion, form, shape.
fòglia *nf* leaf, foil.
fogliàme *nm* foliage, leafage.
fòglio *nm* sheet of paper, bank-note, newspaper, (*of metals*) sheet.
fógna *nf* drain, sewer.
fognatúra *nf* sewage, sewerage.
folclòre *nm* folklore.
folclorísta *nmf* folklorist.
folclorístico *pl* -ici *a* pertaining to folklore, folkloristic; (*fam*) folk.
folgoràre *vi* to flash, strike with lightning.
fólgore *nm* thunderbolt.
fòlio *nm* folio.
fòlla *nf* crowd, multitude, throng.
fòlle *a nmf* insane, mad, lunatic; in f. (*aut*) in neutral (gear).
follétto *nm* elf, goblin.
follía *nf* folly, insanity, madness.
fólto *a* thick, dense, bushy; *nm* thickness.
fomentàre *vt* to foment, incite, stir up.
fòmite *nm* tinder; (*fig*) cause, source.
fónda *nf* anchorage.
fóndaco *pl* -achi *nm* store, warehouse.
fondàle *nm* (*theat*) background.
fondamentàle *a* fundamental, basic, essential.
fondaménto *nm* base, foundation, ground.
fondàre *vt* to build, found, ground, rest; -rsi *vr* to be built, founded; rely on.
fondazióne *nf* foundation, institution.
fondènte *a* melting, fusing; *nm* fondant.

fóndere *vt* to melt, fuse, cast, smelt, blend.
fondería *nf* foundry.
fondiària *nf* ground tax.
fonditóre *nm* caster, founder, smelter.
fonditúra *nf* melting, casting.
fóndo *a* deep; *nm* bottom, background, end; fund; artícolo di f. leading article.
fonètica *nf* phonetics *pl*.
fonètico *pl* -ici *a* phonetic.
fonògrafo *nm* gramophone, (US) phonograph; f. automàtico a gettóne jukebox.
fonología *nf* phonology.
fontàna *nf* fountain, source, spring.
fónte *nf* spring, source; *nm* font.
foràggio *nm* fodder, forage.
foràre *vt* to bore, pierce; *vi* to puncture; (*ticket*) to punch.
foratúra *nf* piercing; (*aut*) puncture; hole.
fòrbici *nf pl* scissors, pincers, claws.
forbíre *vt* to furbish, polish.
forbitézza *nf* (*of style*) elegance, polish.
fòrca *nf* pitchfork, gallows *pl*.
forcèlla *nf* forked stick; hairpin; (*of chicken*) wishbone; (*of telephone*) rest; alpine pass.
forchétta *nf* (table) fork.
forcína *nf* hairpin.
forcúto *a* forked.
forènse *a* forensic.
forèsta *nf* forest.
forestàle *a* forestal; guàrdia f. forester.
forestière, forestièro *a* foreign, strange; *nm* foreigner, stranger.
fórfora *nf* dandruff, scurf.
fòrgia *nf* forge.
forgiàre *vt* to forge, shape, form.
forièro *a* portending.
fórma *nf* form, shape, figure; formality.
formàggio *nm* cheese; f. parmigiano Parmesan cheese.
formàle *a* formal, solemn.
formalità *nf* formality.
formalménte *ad* formally.
formàre *vt* to make, create, fashion, form; -rsi *vr* to form, develop.
formàto *a* formed, shaped; *nm* form, size.
formazióne *nf* formation, forming; training.
formíca *nf* ant.
fòrmica *nf* Formica (Registered Trade Name).
formicolàre *vi* to swarm with, tingle.
formidàbile *a* formidable, dreadful.
formóso *a* buxom, shapely.
fórmula *nf* formula.
formulàre *vt* to formulate, express.
fornàce *nf* furnace, kiln.
fornàio *nm* baker.
fornèllo *nm* (kitchen) stove.
forniménto *nm* supply, equipment.

fornire *vt* to furnish, provide, supply; **-rsi** *vr* to provide oneself.

fornitóre *nm* **-trice** *nf* contractor, purveyor, supplier.

fornitúra *nf* stock, supplies *pl.*

fórno *nm* oven, bakery, kiln, furnace.

fóro *nm* hole.

fòro *nm* forum.

fórra *nf* gorge, ravine.

fórse *ad* perhaps.

forsennàto *a* crazy, mad; *nm* madman.

fòrte *a* strong, large, heavy, loud; (*of colour*) fast; *nm* fort, forte, sourness; *ad* strongly, loudly, powerfully.

forteménte *ad* strongly, greatly, loudly, bravely.

fortézza *nf* fortress, fortitude.

fortificàre *vt* to fortify, strengthen; **-rsi** *vr* to acquire strength, grow stronger.

fortúito *a* casual, fortuitous.

fortúna *nf* fortune, luck, chance; **atterràggio di f.** forced landing.

fortunàle *nm* storm at sea.

fortunàto *a* fortunate, lucky.

fortunóso *a* eventful, stormy.

forúncolo *nm* (*med*) boil.

forviàre *vt* to lead astray, mislead, misguide.

fòrza *nf* force, power, strength.

forzàre *vt* to compel, force.

forzàto *a* forced; *nm* convict.

forzière *nm* safe, strong-box.

fóschia *nf* haze, mist.

fósco *pl* **-chi** *a* dark, dull, gloomy, sombre.

fosfàto *nm* (*chem*) phosphate.

fosforescènte *a* phosphorescent.

fosforescènza *nf* phosphorescence.

fòsforo *nm* phosphorus.

fòssa *nf* hole, pit, grave, den, ditch.

fossàto *nm* ditch, moat.

fossétta *nf* dimple.

fòssile *a nm* fossil.

fossilizzàre *vt* **-rsi** *vr* to fossilize.

fòsso *nm* ditch.

fotocèllula *nf* photoelectric cell.

fotocòpia *nf* photocopy.

fotocrònaca *nf* photo reportage.

fotocronista *nmf* press photographer.

fotografàre *vt* to photograph.

fotografìa *nf* photograph, photography; **f. istantànea** snapshot.

fotogràfico *pl* **-ici** *a* photographic; **màcchina fotogràfica** camera.

fotògrafo *nm* photographer.

fotorepòrter *mnf* news photographer.

fotoromànzo *nm* photo strip.

fotostàtico *pl* **-ici** *a* photostatic; **còpia fotostàtica** photostat.

foulard (*French*) *nm* silk scarf.

fra *prep* among, amid, between (two); (*time*) in; *nm* Brother.

frac *nm* evening dress; (*fam*) tails.

fracassàre *vt* **-rsi** *vr* to break in pieces, smash.

fracàsso *nm* crash, fracas, uproar.

fràdicio *a* rotten; wet, wet through.

fradiciúme *nm* mass of wet (or rotten) things.

fràgile *a* brittle, fragile, frail.

fragilità *nf* fragility, brittleness, frailty.

fràgola *nf* strawberry(-plant).

fragóre *nm* crash, loud noise.

fragoróso *a* roaring, very noisy.

fragrànte *a* fragrant, sweet-smelling.

fragrànza *nf* fragrance, aroma.

fraintèndere *vt* to misunderstand.

framassóne *nm* Freemason.

framassonerìa *nf* Freemasonry.

framménto *nm* fragment.

framméttere *vt* to insert, interpose; **-rsi** *vr* to interfere, interpose, intrude, meddle.

fràna *nf* **framaménto** *nm* fall of earth or rock, landslide, subsidence.

franàre *vi* to fall, sink, (*earth etc*) slide down.

Francésca *nf pr* Frances; **Francésco** *nm pr* Francis.

francescàno *a nm* Franciscan.

francése *a* French; *nm* Frenchman; *nf* Frenchwoman.

franchézza *nf* candidness, frankness, openness.

franchìgia *nf* exemption; franchise; (*mil*) time off duty.

Frància *nf* France.

frànco *pl* **-chi** *a* candid, frank; *nm* franc.

francobòllo *nm* (postage) stamp.

Francofòrte *nf* (*geogr*) Frankfort, Frankfurt.

frangènte *nm* breaker, shoal, reef; (*fig*) difficulty.

fràngere *vt* to break to pieces, crush; **-rsi** *vr* to break.

frangétta, fràngia *nf* fringe.

frangiflútti *nm* breakwater.

frangitúra *nf* extraction of oil from olives.

frantóio *nm* (*for olives*) oil-press, stone-crusher.

frantumàre *vt* to break, smash.

frantúmi *nm pl* fragments *pl*, pieces *pl.*

frappé *nm* shake; **agitatóre per f.** milk shake.

frappórre *vt* to interpose, insert; **-rsi** *vr* to interfere.

frasàrio *nm* jargon; phrasing; collection of phrases.

fràsca *nf* spray, twig; inn sign.

fràse *nf* phrase, sentence.

fraseologìa *nf* phraseology.

fràssino *nm* ash, ash-tree.

frastagliàto *a* indented, irregular, uneven.

frastornàre *vt* to disturb, trouble, distract.

frastuòno *nm* din, hubbub.

fràte *nm* friar, monk, brother.

fratellànza *nf* brotherhood.

fratellàstro *nm* half-brother.

fratèllo *nm* brother.

fratèrno *a* brotherly, fraternal.

fratricída *a* fratricidal; *nmf* fratricide.

fratricídio *nm* fratricide.

fràtta *nf* briar patch, thicket.

frattànto *ad* in the meantime, meanwhile.

frattèmpo *nm* meantime, interval; nel f. meanwhile.

frattúra *nf* fracture, break.

fratturàre *vt* to break, fracture.

fraudolènto *a* fraudulent.

frazióne *nf* fraction; group of houses.

fréccia *nf* arrow; **frecciatína** *nf* pungent remark.

freddaménte *ad* coldly, coolly, calmly.

freddàre *vt* to cool; kill; **-rsi** *vr* to grow cold, cool.

freddézza *nf* coldness, coolness, indifference.

fréddo *a* cold, chilly, cool, indifferent; *nm* coldness, cold; **avére f.** *vi* to be cold.

freddolóso *a* chilly, sensitive to cold.

freddúra *nf* cold; nonsense, silly story, pun.

fregàre *vt* to rub, scrub, cross out; (*vulg*) cheat, swindle; **-rsi** *vr* to rub oneself; (*vulg*) **fregàrsene** not to care.

fregàta *nf* rubbing, scrubbing; (*naut*) frigate.

fregiàre *vt* to decorate, adorn; **-rsi** *vr* to adorn oneself.

frégio *nm* frieze, ornament.

frégola *nf* (*of animals*) heat, (*fig*) mania, immoderate desire.

frèmere *vi* to quiver, thrill, tremble, throb, fume, shudder, rustle.

frèmito *nm* quiver, thrill, throb, roaring.

frenàre *vt* to brake, curb; hinder, repress, restrain; **-rsi** *vr* to keep one's temper; refrain from, restrain oneself.

frenesía *nf* frenzy.

frenètico *pl* **-ici** *a* frantic, raving.

fréno *nm* brake, bridle, curb, restraint; **potènza del f.** brake horsepower.

frenologia *nf* phrenology.

frequentàre *vt* to attend, frequent, haunt, consort with.

frequentàto *a* frequented, attended, patronized.

frequènte *a* frequent, quick.

frequenteménte *ad* frequently.

frequènza *nf* frequency, attendance.

frèsa *nf* (milling) cutter.

fresatríce *nf* milling machine.

freschézza *nf* freshness, coolness.

frésco *pl* **-chi** *a* fresh, cool; *nm* coolness, cool; fresco.

frescúra *nf* coolness.

frétta *nf* haste, hurry; **avére f.** *vi* to be in a hurry; **di f., in f.** hastily.

frettolóso *a* hasty, hurried.

frìggere *vt* to fry.

frigidézza, frigidità *nf* frigidness, frigidity.

frígido *a* frigid.

frigorífero *nm* refrigerator.

fringuèllo *nm* finch.

frittàta *nf* omelet.

frittèlla *nf* fritter, pancake.

frítto *a* fried; (*fig*) lost, ruined; *nm* fry, fried food.

frittúra *nf* fry, fried food.

frivolézza *nf* frivolity, frivolousness.

frívolo *a* frivolous, trifling.

frizióne *nf* rubbing, massage, friction.

frizzànte *a* sparkling; (*of air*) biting, pungent.

frizzàre *vi* to tingle, sparkle, sting.

frizzo *nm* witticism, gibe.

frodàre *vt* to defraud, swindle.

fròde *nf* fraud, swindle.

fròdo *nm* poaching, smuggling.

fròllo *a* (*of meat*) tender, (*of game*) high; exhausted; **pàsta fròlla** pastry.

frónda *nf* leafy bough, (the) Fronde.

frondóso *a* leafy.

frontàle *a* frontal; *nm* frontal, mantelpiece.

frónte *nf* forehead; *nm* front; **far f. a** to cope with, face, meet.

fronteggiàre *vt* to face, confront.

frontespízio *nm* frontispiece, title page.

frontièra *nf* border, frontier.

frontóne *nm* (*arch*) fronton, gable.

frónzolo *nm* tassel, frill, trinket.

fronzúto *a* leafy.

fròtta *nf* crowd, throng.

fròttola *nf* fib, lie, nonsense; popular song.

frugàle *a* frugal.

frugàre *vt* to rummage; **-rsi** *vr* to search one's pockets.

frúgolo *nm* little, lively child.

fruíre *vi* to make use of, enjoy.

frullàre *vt* to whip, whisk; *vi* to whir, whirl.

frullíno *nm* (*cook*) whisk.

fruménto *nm* wheat.

fruscío *nm* rustle, rustling.

frústa *nf* lash, scourge, whip.

frustàre *vt* to whip, lash, scourge.

frútta *nf* (*coll*) fruit.

fruttàre *vti* to produce, fructify, pay.

fruttéto *nm* orchard.

frutticultóre *nm* fruit-grower.

fruttífero *a* fruit-bearing; fruitful, profitable.

fruttificàre *vi* to fructify.

fruttivéndolo *nm* fruiterer.

frútto *pl* **-i** (*m*), (*table*) **-a** (*f*) *nm* fruit; profit, result, revenue.

fruttuóso *a* fruitful, profitable.

fu *a* late, deceased.

fucilàre *vt* to shoot.

fucilazióne *nf* shooting, execution.

fucíle *nm* gun, rifle.

fucína *nf* forge, smithy.

fucinàre *vt* to forge.

fúga *nf* flight, escape, avoidance; (*mus*) fugue.

fugàce *a* fleeting, transient.

fugàre *vt* to put to flight, rout.

fuggévole a fleeting, flying.
fuggiàsco pl -schi a nm fugitive, runaway.
fúggi-fúggi nm headlong flight, panic, stampede.
fuggíre vi to flee, run away, take to flight; vt to avoid, shun.
fulgènte a shining, refulgent.
fúlgido a shining, bright, refulgent.
fulgóre nm brightness, splendour, refulgence.
fulíggine nf soot.
fulminànte a fulminating; nm lucifer match, percussion cap.
fulminàre vt to strike with lightning, strike dumb; vi to flash, lighten.
fúlmine nm lightning, thunderbolt.
fulmíneo a quick as lightning, sudden.
fúlvo a reddish, tawny.
fumai(u)òlo nm chimney-pot.
fumànte a smoking, steaming.
fumàre vt to smoke; vietàto f. 'no smoking'.
fumàta nf smoke, smoking, puff of smoke, smoke signal.
fumatóre nm -tríce nf smoker.
fumétto nm usu pl comic strip, cartoon; romànzo a fumétti strip cartoon.
fúmo nm smoke, fume, steam.
fumògeno a smoke-producing.
fumosità nf smokiness.
fumóso a smoky.
funàmbolo nm tight-rope walker.
fúne nf cable, rope.
fúnebre a funeral, funereal.
funeràle nm funeral.
funèreo a funereal, gloomy.
funestàre vt to desolate, distress, sadden, ruin.
funèsto a baneful, disastrous, sorrowful, fatal.
fúngere vi to act as, officiate as.
fúngo pl -ghi nm fungus, mushroom, toadstool.
funicolàre nf funicular.
funivía nf air cable way.
funzionàre vi to act, function, run, work.
funzionàrio nm functionary, official.
funzióne nf function, office, service (in church).
fuochísta nm fireman, stoker.
fuòco pl -chi nm fire; (phot) focus; méttere a f. (phot) to focus; fuochi d'artifízio firework; f. di sbarraménto (mil) barrage fire.
fuorché cj prep except, but, apart from.
fuòri ad prep out, outside, except; al di f. ad outwards.
fuoribórdo nm (naut) outboard motor.
fuorilégge nm outlaw.
fuorisèrie nf inv (aut) custom-built.
fuoruscíto nm exile, outlaw.
fuorviàre vt to mislead; vi go astray, stray.
furbería nf cunning, slyness.

furbésco pl -schi, furbo a artful, cunning, sly, wily.
furènte v furibóndo.
furétto nm ferret.
furfànte nm rascal, scamp.
furfantería nf roguery, piece of roguery.
furgoncíno nm small van.
furgóne nm van, (US railroad) caboose, (rly) brake van.
fúria nf fury, rage, hurry; avére f. to be in a hurry.
furibóndo, furióso a furious, raging.
furóre nm frenzy, fury, rage; fàre f. to be much admired.
furoreggiàre vi to be (all) the rage, make a hit.
furtívo a furtive, sly, stealthy.
fúrto nm theft, robbery.
fúsa nf pl fare le f. to purr.
fuscèllo nm twig, straw; (fig) thin person.
fusièra nf spindle-holder.
fusióne nf fusion, melting, smelting, casting, merging.
fúso a fused, melted.
fúso nm spindle.
fusolièra nf fuselage.
fustàgno nm fustian; corduroy.
fustigàre vt to flog.
fústo nm stock, stem, trunk; barrel, cask; frame; (fam) he-man.
fútile a futile, trifling.
futilità nf futility, pl trifles.
futúro a nm future.

G

gabardína nf gabardine, overcoat.
gabbàre vt to deceive, mock, swindle.
gabbatóre nm -tríce nf deceiver, impostor, swindler.
gàbbia nf cage, coop, jail; topsail.
gabbiàno nm seagull.
gàbbo nm jeering, mockery; prèndere a g. to mock.
gabèlla nf duty, tax (on goods entering a town).
gabellàre vt to tax; (fig) g. per to pass off as.
gabellière nm customs officer.
gabinétto nm cabinet; toilet, closet; (of dentist or doctor) consulting room, surgery, (US) office; g. púbblico public convenience, (US) public comfort station.
Gabrièle nm pr Gabriel.
gaèlico pl -ici a nm Gaelic.
gaffe (French) nf gaffe, blunder.
gaggia nf acacia.
gagliardétto nm pennon.
gagliàrdo a strong, vigorous.
gagliòffo a loutish, rascally; nm lout, rascal.
gaiaménte ad gaily, brightly.
gaièzza nf gaiety, brightness.
gàio a gay, (colour) bright.
gàla nf finery, gala; tenúta di g. (mil) full-dress uniform.

galànte a courteous, gallant (towards women); nm gallant, ladies' man.

galanteggiàre vi to play the gallant.

galantería nf courtesy, gallantry; delicacy, dainty.

galantína nf galantine.

galantuòmo nm honest man, man of honour.

galatèo nm code of manners pl, manners.

galèa nf galley.

galeòtto nm convict, galley slave.

galèra nf galley, jail, hard labour.

Galilèa nf (geogr) Galilee.

galilèo a nm Galilean.

gàlla nf gall, blister; **a g.** afloat.

galleggiànte a floating; nm float, buoy, raft.

galleggiàre vi to float.

galleria nf gallery, tunnel; arcade; (theat) gallery, balcony.

Gàlles nm (geogr) Wales.

gallése a Welsh; nm the Welsh language, Welshman; nf Welshwoman.

gallétta nf ship's biscuit, cracker.

gallína nf hen.

gallinàccio nm turkey-cock: chanterelle.

gàllo nm cock, weathercock, Gaul; **g. domèstico** rooster.

gallonàre vt to braid.

gallóne nm braid, (mil) stripe; (measure) gallon.

galoppàre vi to gallop.

galoppàta nf gallop, galloping.

galoppíno nm errand boy, messenger; **g. elettoràle** canvasser.

galòppo nm gallop.

galòscia nf galosh, golosh.

galvànico pl -ici a galvanic.

galvanizzàre vt to galvanize.

gàmba nf leg; **èsser e in g.** vi to be fit active, clever.

gambacórta nm lame man.

gambàle nm legging.

gambàta nf kick.

gàmbero nm crayfish.

gàmbo nm stalk, stem.

gàmma nf gamut, range, scale.

ganàscia nf jaw.

gàncio nm hook, clasp.

gànghero nm hinge; **fuòri dei gàngheri** furious.

gànglio nm ganglion (also fig).

gàra nf competition, contest, match.

garage (Fr) nm garage.

garagista nm motor mechanic, garage owner.

garànte nm guarantor, surety.

garantíre vt to guarantee, stand surety for, warrant.

garanzía nf guarantee, surety, warrant.

garbàre vi to be agreeable, to be to one's liking, please, suit.

garbatézza nf politeness, kindness.

garbàto a civil, polite.

gàrbo nm courtesy, grace, manner, politeness; **a g.** gracefully, politely.

garbúglio nm entanglement, confusion, disorder.

gareggiàre vi to compete, vie.

garganèlla, bere a vt to gulp down, toss off.

gargaríṣmo nm gargle.

gargarizzàre vt to gargle.

garibaldíno a nm (one who) fought under Garibaldi.

garítta nf sentry box, look-out turret.

garòfano nm carnation, clove.

garrése nm (of horse) withers pl.

garrétto nm back of the heel, (horse) hock.

garríre vi to chirp, warble, screech; (flag) flap.

garrulità nf garrulity.

gàrrulo a garrulous.

gàrza nf heron; gauze.

garzóne nm apprentice, farm servant, shop-boy.

gas nm inv gas; **fornèllo a g.** gas cooker.

gaṣàto, gassàto a aerated.

gassista nm gas-fitter, gasman.

gassómetro nm gasometer.

gassósa nf aerated drink.

gassóso a effervescent, aerated.

gàstrico pl -ici a gastric; **súcco g.** nm gastric juice.

gastrite nf (med) gastritis.

gastronomía nf gastronomy.

gastronòmico pl -ici a gastronomic.

gàtta nf she-cat; **dàre una g. a pelàre** to give a lot of trouble.

gattabúia nf jail, prison.

gattèsco pl -chi a catlike.

gattíno nm kitten.

gàtto nm cat; **èssere quàttro gàtti** to be very few people.

gattóni ad on all fours.

gattopàrdo nm leopard.

gaudènte a jolly, merry; nmf reveller.

gàudio nm joy, bliss, happiness; a joyful, joyous.

gavazzàre vi to revel.

gavétta nf mess tin.

gazósa nf aerated lemonade.

gàzza nf magpie; (fig) babbler, chatterer.

gazzàrra nf uproar.

gazzèlla nf gazelle.

gazzétta nf gazette, newspaper.

gelàre vti to freeze.

gelateria nf ice-cream shop.

gelatière nm ice-cream man.

gelatína nf gelatine, jelly.

gelàto a frozen; nm ice(-cream).

gelidaménte ad icily, coldly.

gèlido a icy, chilly.

gèlo nm freezing weather, frost, ice.

gelóne nm chilblain.

gelosaménte ad jealously.

gelosía nf jealousy, great care; shutter.

gelóso a jealous.

gèlso nm mulberry(-tree).

gelsomíno nm jasmine, jessamine.

Geltrúde nf pr Gertrude.

gemebóndo *a* moaning, plaintive.
gemèllo *a* nm twin; *pl* **gemèlli** twins *pl*; cufflinks *pl*.
gèmere *vi* to groan, moan, trickle, coo.
geminatúra, geminazióne *nf* gemination.
gèmito *nm* groan, moan.
gèmma *nf* gem, jewel; bud.
gemmàre *vt* to bud.
gemmàto *a* full of buds, studded with gems.
gendàrme *nm* gendarme, policeman.
gendarmería *nf* gendarmerie, police.
genealogía *nf* genealogy.
genealògico *pl* -**ici** *a* genealogical.
generàle *a* nm general.
generalità *nf* generality; (*pl*) particulars *pl*.
generalizzàre *vt* to generalize.
generalizzazióne *nf* generalization.
generalmènte *ad* generally, in general.
generàre *vt* to generate, beget, breed, cause, engender, produce.
generatóre *nm* generator; (*aut*) dynamo, (US) generator.
generazióne *nf* generation.
gènere *nm* kind, sort, type; gender; **in g.** *ad* in general; **gèneri** *pl* articles, goods *pl*; **g. di príma necessità** necessaries.
genèrico *pl* -**ici** *a* generic, general.
gènero *nm* son-in-law.
generosamènte *ad* generously.
generosità *nf* generosity.
generóso *a* generous.
gènesi *nf* genesis; **la G.** Book of Genesis.
gengíva *nf* (*in mouth*) gum.
genía *nf* low breed, low set.
geniàle *a* ingenious, clever; genial.
genialità *nf* ingeniousness, talent, genius; geniality.
gènio *nm* genius, talent; **àrma del g.** *nf* (*mil*) engineers *pl*; **andàre a g.** to be to one's liking.
genitàle *a* genital.
gènito *a* born, generated.
genitóre *nm* parent, father; -**trice** *nf* mother; -**tóri** *pl* parents *pl*.
gennàio *nm* January.
Gènova *nf* (*geogr*) Genoa; **genovése** *a* nmf Genoese.
Genovèffa *nf* *pr* Genevieve.
gentàccia, gentàglia *nf* mob, rabble.
gènte *nf* people, folk.
gentildònna *nf* gentlewoman, lady of quality.
gentíle *a* courteous, kind, polite; *a* nm Gentile; pagan, heathen.
gentilézza *nf* kindness, politeness, civility.
gentilízio *a* aristocratic, noble; **stèmma gentilízia** nm coat of arms.
gentilmènte *ad* kindly, politely.
gentiluòmo *nm* gentleman, nobleman.
genuflessióne *nf* genuflection.
genuflèttersi *vr* to genuflect.

genuinità *nf* genuineness.
genuíno *a* genuine, authentic.
genziàna *nf* gentian.
geografía *nf* geography.
geogràfico *pl* -**ici** *a* geographic(al).
geología *nf* geology.
geòmetra *nm* geometer, surveyor.
geometría *nf* geometry.
geomètrico *pl* -**ici** *a* geometric(al).
gerànio *nm* geranium.
geràrca *nm* hierarch; leader.
gerarchía *nf* hierarchy.
gerènte *nm* manager, director.
gerènza *nf* management.
gèrgo *pl* **gèrghi** nm jargon, slang.
gèrla *nf* pannier.
Germània *nf* (*geogr*) Germany.
germànico *pl* -**ici** *a* Germanic; nm (*language*) Germanic.
germàno *a* nm German; *a* germane; **cugíno g.** first cousin; nm blood brother; wild duck.
gèrme *nm* germ, shoot, sprout.
germinàre *vi* to germinate.
germogliàre *vi* to bud, sprout.
germóglio *nm* bud, shoot.
geroglífico *pl* -**ici** *a* hieroglyphic; nm hieroglyph(ic).
Geròlamo, Gerònimo *nm* *pr* Jerome.
Gertrúde *nf* *pr* Gertrude.
Gerusalèmme *nf* (*geogr*) Jerusalem.
gèsso *nm* chalk, plaster of Paris, gypsum.
gèsta *nf* *pl* deeds, exploits, feats *pl*.
gestànte *a* nf expectant mother.
gestazióne *nf* gestation, pregnancy.
gesticolàre *vi* to gesticulate.
gesticolazióne *nf* gesticulation.
gestióne *nf* management.
gestíre *vt* to gesticulate; manage.
gèsto *nm* gesture, act, action.
gestóre *nm* manager, (*rly*) goods superintendent.
Gesù *nm* Jesus.
gesuíta *nm* Jesuit.
gettàre *vt* to throw, cast, fling; -**rsi** *vr* to jump, throw oneself.
gèttito *nm* (*tax*) yield; (*naut*) jettison.
gètto *nm* throw, throwing, jet, sprout, casting; **a g. contínuo** without a break.
gettóne *nm* counter, token.
ghermíre *vt* to claw, collar, seize.
ghétta *nf* gaiter.
ghétto *nm* ghetto.
ghiacciàia *nf* icebox, refrigerator.
ghiacciàio *nm* glacier.
ghiacciàre *vti* -**rsi** *vr* to freeze.
ghiacciàta *nf* iced drink.
ghiàccio *nm* ice.
ghiacci(u)òlo *nm* icicle.
ghiàia *nf* gravel.
ghiànda *nf* acorn.
ghiandàia *nf* jackdaw, jay.
ghiàndola *nf* gland.
ghibellíno *a* nm Ghibelline.
ghigliottína *nf* guillotine.
ghígna *nf* ugly face, grimace.
ghignàre *vi* to sneer.

ghígno nm sneer, grin.

ghinèa nf guinea.

ghíngeri, in ad finely dressed.

ghiótto a gluttonous, greedy.

ghiottóne nm glutton.

ghiottonería nf gluttony; titbit, dainty, rarity.

ghiribízzo nm freak, whim.

ghiribizzóso a freakish, whimsical.

ghirlànda nf garland, wreath.

ghíro nm dormouse.

ghísa nf cast-iron, pig-iron.

già ad already, formerly, once; interj of course, yes.

Giacàrta nf (geogr) Djakarta, Jakarta.

giàcca nf jacket; g. a vènto windcheater, anorak.

giacchè cj as, seeing that, since.

giacènte a lying, lying down, placed; (of capital) unproductive.

giacènza nf stay, demurrage; stock, (of books) unsold copies.

giacére vi to lie, be situated.

giacíglio nm bed, place for lying.

giaciménto nm (geol) layer; (min) deposit.

giacínto nm hyacinth.

Giacòbbe nm pr Jacob.

Giàcomo nm pr James.

giaggi(u)òlo nm Florentine lily, iris.

giaguàro nm jaguar.

giallàstro a yellowish.

giallézza nf yellowness.

giallíno a light yellow.

giàllo a nm yellow; nm thriller; g. d'uòvo (egg) yolk.

Giamàica nf Jamaica.

giàmbo nm iambus.

giammài ad never.

Giappóne nm Japan.

giapponése a nmf Japanese.

giàra, giàrra nf jar.

giardinàggio nm gardening.

giardinétta nf (aut) estate car.

giardinièra nf woman gardener; estate car; flower stand; pickled vegetables.

giardinière nm gardener.

giard no nm garden.

giarrettièra nf garter; (men's) sock suspender, (US) garter.

giavellòtto nm javelin.

gibbóso a humped, hump-backed.

gibèrna nf cartridge box, pouch.

Gibiltèrra nf Gibraltar.

gigànte nm giant; a gigantic.

giganteggiàre vi to tower, rise like a giant.

gigantésco pl -schi a gigantic.

gigantéssa nf giantess.

gíglio nm lily.

gilè nm waistcoat.

gincàna nf (sport) gymkhana.

ginecología nf gynaecology.

ginecòlogo pl -ogi nm gynaecologist.

ginepràio nm thicket of junipers; difficult situation.

ginépro nm juniper.

ginèstra nf broom.

Ginévra nf (geogr) Geneva.

gingillàre vi -rsi vr to dawdle, play, trifle.

gingillíno nm dawdler, loiterer.

gingíllo nm knick-knack, trifle.

gingillóne nm dawdler.

ginnasiàle a of a grammar school, secondary school, (US) high school.

ginnàsio nm grammar school, secondary school, (US) high school.

ginnàsta nmf gymnast, athlete.

ginnàstica nf gymnastics pl.

ginocchièra nf knee-pad.

ginòcchio nm pl ginòcchi, ginòcchia f knee.

ginocchióni ad on one's knees.

Gioacchíno nm pr Joachim.

giocàre, giuocàre vti to play, stake, work, make a fool of; -rsi vr to make a fool of.

giocàta nf game stake.

giocatóre nm -tríce nf player.

giocàttolo nm toy, plaything.

giocherellàre vi to play, toy, trifle.

giòco pl giòchi nm play, game, sport, gambling, pastime, speculation; (mech) clearance.

giocofòrza, èssere v impers to be necessary.

giocolière nm juggler.

giocondità nf gaiety, cheerfulness.

giocóndo a gay, joyous.

giocosità nf mirth, facetiousness.

giocóso a jocose, facetious.

giogàia nf chain of mountains, (of oxen) dewlap.

giógo pl gioghi nm yoke (also fig); mountain ridge, peak.

gióia nf joy, delight; jewel.

gioiellería nf jewellery, jeweller's shop.

gioiellière nm jeweller.

gioièllo nm jewel.

gioiosaménte ad joyfully, joyously.

gioióso a joyful, merry.

gioíre vi to be glad, rejoice.

Giordània nf (geogr) Jordania.

Giordàno nm (geogr) Jordan.

Giórgio nm pr George.

giornalàio nm newsagent, newsboy.

giornàle nm (news)paper, journal, diary; cíne g. newsreel; g. ràdio news bulletin.

giornalièro a daily; nm day labourer.

giornalísmo nm journalism.

giornalísta nmf journalist, reporter.

giornalístico pl -ici a journalistic.

giornalménte ad daily, every day.

giornànte nf charwoman.

giornàta nf day, day's work; vívere alla g. to live from hand to mouth.

giórno nm day; èssere a g. di to be informed of; di g. in the daytime.

giòstra nf joust, tournament, merrygo-round, roundabout.

giostràre vi to joust, tilt.

Giosuè nm pr Joshua.

giovaménto nm advantage, benefit.

gióvane, gióvine a young; nm

young man, youth; *nf* young woman.
giovaníle *a* juvenile, youthful.
Giovànna *nf pr* Jane, Jean, Joan.
Giovànni *nm pr* John.
giovanòtto *nm* young man, bachelor.
giovàre *vi* to be of use, be beneficial; **-rsi** *vr* to avail oneself of, benefit by.
giovedì *nm* Thursday.
giovènca *nf* heifer; **giovènco** *pl* **-chi** *nm* bullock, steer.
gioventù *nf* youth, young people.
giovévole *a* beneficial, profitable.
gioviàle *a* jolly, jovial.
giovialità *nf* joviality.
giovinàstro *nm* hooligan, hoodlum.
giovinétta *nf* young girl; **giovinétto** *nm* lad, young fellow.
giovinézza *v* gioventù.
giradíschi *nm* record player.
giràffa *nf* giraffe.
giramén to *nm* turning; **g. di tèsta** dizziness.
giramóndo *nm* wanderer, globetrotter.
giràndola *nf* Catherine wheel; (*fig*) fickle person.
girànte *a* revolving; *nm* endorser.
giràre *vt* to turn, avoid; (*cin*) shoot, act, tour, endorse; *vi* turn, wind, wander; **-rsi** *vr* to turn round.
girarròsto *nm* roasting jack, spit, turnspit.
girasóle *nm* sunflower.
giràta *nf* turn, walk; endorsement.
giratàrio *nm* (*com*) endorsee.
giravòlta *nf* change of front, turning, twirl.
girèlla *nf* pulley, small wheel; (*draughts etc*) piece; (*fig*) political weathercock.
girellàre *vi* to saunter, stroll.
girèllo *nm* small circle; (*children*) go-cart; (*cut of meat*) rump.
girétto *nm* stroll; **fàre un g.** to go for a stroll.
girévole *a* revolving, turning.
giríno *nm* tadpole.
gíro *nm* turn, round, circle, tour, circulation; endorsement; period of time, stroll; **prèndere in g.** to tease.
giróne *nm* (*in Dante's Inferno*) circle; (*football*) series (of games).
gironzolàre *vi* to stroll.
giropilòta *nm* automatic pilot, (*US*) gyropilot.
girotóndo *nm* dance in a ring; 'ring-a-ring-a-roses'.
girovagàre *vi* to roam, wander.
giròvago *pl* **-ghi** *a* roving, wandering; *nm* wanderer, tramp.
gíta *nf* trip, excursion.
gitànte *nmf* tripper, excursionist.
giú *ad* down; **su per g.** approximately, roughly.
giúbba *nf* jacket, coat.
giubilàre *vi* to exult, jubilate.
giubilèo *nm* jubilee.
giúbilo *nm* jubilation, rejoicing.
Giúda *nm pr* Judas.
giudàico *pl* **-ici** *a* Judaic; Jewish.

giudaísmo *nm* Judaism.
Giudèa *nf* (*geogr*) Judea, Judaea.
giudèo *a nm* Jewish, Jew, Judean.
giudicàre *vti* to judge, think, consider.
giudicàto *a* judged, sentenced; *nm* sentence; **passàre in g.** to be beyond recall.
giúdice *nm* judge, (*title*) Justice.
Giudítta *nf pr* Judith.
giudiziàle, giudizàrio *a* judicial.
giudízio *nm* judgement, opinion, verdict, sentence, prudence; **avére g.** to be sensible; **dènte del g.** wisdom tooth.
giudizióso *a* judicious, sensible.
giudò *nm* judo.
giúgno *nm* June.
Giuliàno *nm pr* Julian.
Giúlie, (Àlpi) *nf pl* (*geogr*) Julian Alps.
Giuliétta *nf pr* Juliet.
Giúlio *nm pr* Julius.
giulívo *a* gay, joyful.
giullàre *nm* jester, minstrel.
giuménta *nf* mare.
giuménto *nm* ass, mule, beast of burden.
giuncàia *nf* **giunchéto** *nm* reed bed.
giuncàta *nf* junket.
giunchíglia *nf* jonquil.
giúnco *pl* **giunchi** *nm* reed, rush.
giúngere *vti* to arrive, reach, go as far as, succeed, join, get at.
giúngla *nf* jungle.
giúnta *nf* addition, increase, makeweight; committee, council; **per g.** in addition, moreover.
giuntàre *vt* to join, sew together.
giuntúra *nf* joint, articulation.
giunzióne *nf* junction, connection.
giuocàre *v* giocàre.
giuòco *v* giòco.
giuraménto *nm* oath.
giuràre *vti* to swear, take an oath.
giuràto *a* sworn; *nm* juryman.
giureconsúlto *nm* jurisconsult.
giurí *nm* giuría *nf* jury.
giurídico *pl* **-ici** *a* juridical.
giurisdizióne *nf* jurisdiction.
giurisprudènza *nf* jurisprudence.
giurísta *nm* jurist.
Giusèppe *nm pr* Joseph.
Giuseppína *nf pr* Josephine.
giústa *prep* according to.
giustaménte *ad* justly, rightly.
giustézza *nf* exactness, propriety.
giustificàre *vt* to justify; **-rsi** *vr* to excuse oneself, justify oneself.
giustificazióne *nf* justification, excuse; (*at school*) absence note.
Giustiniàno *nm pr* Justinian.
Giustíno *nm pr* Justin.
giustízia *nf* justice.
giustiziàre *vt* to execute, put to death.
giustiziàto *a* executed; *nm* executed man.
giustizière *nm* executioner, avenger.

giústo _a_ fair, just, lawful, proper, right; _nm_ just man; **i giústi** _pl_ the just, the right; _ad_ just, precisely.
glàbro _a_ hairless, smooth.
glaciàle _a_ glacial, icy.
gladiatóre _nm_ gladiator.
gladíolo _nm_ gladiolus.
glàndola _nf_ gland.
glandulàre _a_ glandular.
glassàre _vt_ to ice, glaze.
glàuco _pl_ **-chi** _a_ glaucous, greyish blue or green.
glèba _nf_ glebe, soil, earth; **sèrvo della g.** _nm_ serf.
gli _art m pl_ the; _pron m (dat)_ to him, _(idiom)_ to them.
glicerína _nf_ glycerin(e).
glícine _nf_ wistaria.
globàle _a_ global, total, inclusive.
glòbo _nm_ globe; **g. dell'òcchio** eyeball.
glòbulo _nm_ globule.
glòria _nf_ glory.
gloriàrsi _vr_ to boast of, be proud of, pride oneself on.
glorificaménto _nm_ **glorificazióne** _nf_ glorification.
glorificàre _vt_ to glorify.
glorióso _a_ glorious, proud.
glòssa _nf_ gloss, explanation, annotation.
glossàre _vt_ to gloss.
glossàrio _nm_ glossary.
glucòsio _nm_ glucose.
glúteo _a_ gluteal; _nm (anat)_ glutaeus, gluteus.
glutinàto _a_ gluten.
gnaulàre _vi_ to mew.
gnòmo _nm_ gnome, goblin.
gnòstico _pl_ **-ici** _a_ gnostic.
gòbba _nf_ hump.
gòbbo _a_ hump-backed.
góccia, gócciola _nf_ drop.
góccio _nm_ drop.
gocciolaménto _nm_ **gocciolatúra** _nf_ dripping, trickling.
gocciolàre _vti_ to drip, drop, trickle.
gocciolío _nm_ dripping, trickling.
gócciolo _nm_ drop.
godè _nm_ flare; **gónna a g.** flared skirt.
godére _vti_ to enjoy, be glad; **-rsi** _vr_ **-rsela** _vr_ to enjoy oneself.
goderéccio _a_ enjoyable.
godiménto _nm_ enjoyment, pleasure; possession, use.
goffàggine _nf_ awkwardness, clumsiness.
goffaménte _ad_ awkwardly, clumsily.
gòffo _a_ awkward, clumsy.
Goffrèdo _nm pr_ Geoffrey, Godfrey.
gógna _nf_ pillory; **méttere alla g.** to pillory.
góla _nf_ throat; gorge; gluttony; **far g.** to be a temptation.
golétta _nf_ schooner; narrow gorge; collar.
golf _nm_ cardigan, jumper, sweater; golf.
gólfo _nm_ gulf.
goliàrdo _nm_ university student.

golosaménte _ad_ greedily.
golosità _nf_ greed, gluttony.
golóso _a_ greedy, gluttonous.
gólpe _nf_ blight, mildew.
gómena _nf (naut)_ cable, hawser.
gomitàta _nf_ shove with the elbow.
gómito _nm_ elbow.
gomítolo _nm (of thread etc)_ ball.
gómma _nf_ rubber, gum, resin; tyre.
gommapiúma _nf_ foam rubber.
gommàto _a_ gummed.
gommóso _a_ gummy.
góndola _nf_ gondola.
gondolière _nm_ gondolier.
gonfalóne _nm_ flag, standard.
gonfalonière _nm_ standard-bearer.
gonfiàre _vt_ to inflate, swell; **-rsi** _vr_ to swell (up).
gonfiatóio _nm_ inflator, tyre pump.
gonfiatúra _nf_ swelling, inflation, exaggeration, stunt, adulation.
gonfiézza _nf_ swelling.
gónfio _a_ swollen, inflated.
gonfióre _nm_ swelling.
gongolàre _vi_ to rejoice, exult.
goniòmetro _nm_ protractor.
gónna _nf_ skirt; **gonnellíno** _nm_ short skirt; **g. scozzése** kilt.
gónzo _nm_ blockhead, fool.
gòra _nf_ millrace, millpond, pond.
gorgheggiàre _vi_ to trill, warble.
gorghéggio _nm_ trilling, warbling.
gorgièra _nf_ ruff.
górgo _pl_ **-ghi** _nm_ whirlpool, abyss.
gorgogliàre _vi_ to gurgle, bubble.
gorgoglío _nm_ gurgling.
gorilla _nm_ gorilla.
gòta _nf_ cheek.
gòtico _pl_ **-ici** _a_ Gothic.
gòto _nm_ Goth.
gótta _nf_ gout.
gottóso _a_ gouty.
governànte _nm_ ruler, statesman; _nf_ governess, housekeeper.
governàre _vt_ to govern, rule, _(naut)_ steer, _(av)_ control; groom, tend.
governatívo _a_ government(al).
governatóre _nm_ governor, ruler.
govèrno _nm_ government, rule; **g. della càsa** housekeeping.
gózzo _nm_ goitre; bird's crop.
gozzovíglia _nf_ debauch, revelry.
gozzovigliàre _vi_ to revel.
gozzúto _a_ goitrous, goitred.
gracchiàre _vi_ to caw.
gracidaménto _nm_ croaking.
gracidàre _vi_ to croak.
gràcile _a_ weak, delicate, frail.
gracilità _nf_ weakness, thinness.
gradàsso _nm_ blusterer, braggart.
gradazióne _nf_ gradation, shade.
gradévole _a_ agreeable, pleasant.
gradiènte _nm_ gradient.
gradiménto _nm_ liking, pleasure, satisfaction, approval.
gradinàta _nf_ flight of steps.
gradíno _nm_ step.
gradíre _vt_ to like, wish; accept.
gradíto _a_ agreeable, pleasant, welcome.

gràdo nm degree, pleasure, rank, will; **èssere in g. di** to be able to.

graduàle a gradual.

gradualménte ad gradually.

graduàre vt to confer (a degree or rank), graduate, grade.

graduàto a graded, progressive, graduated; nm (mil) non-commissioned officer (N.C.O.).

graduatòria nf classification, pass list.

graduazióne nf graduation; scale.

graffiàre vt to scratch.

graffiatúra nf scratch.

gràffio nm scratch; (naut) grapnel.

grafía nf writing, spelling.

gràfico pl -ici a graphic; nm graph.

grafología nf graphology.

gragnuòla nf (fig) hail, shower.

Gràie, (Àlpi) nf pl (geogr) Graian Alps.

gramàglie nf pl deep mourning.

gramígna nf couch-grass, weed.

grammàtica nf grammar.

grammaticàle a grammatical.

gràmmo nm gramme.

gràmo a miserable, poor, wretched.

gràna nf (tec) grain; (fam) trouble; Parmesan cheese.

granàglie nf pl corn, grain.

granàio nm barn, granary.

granàta nf broom, brush; grenade.

granatière nm grenadier.

granàto a garnet red; nm garnet.

grancàssa nf bass drum.

grànchio nm crab; **prèndere un g.** to make a mistake.

grànde a great, big, high, tall, grown up, wide; nm great man, grandee; **i gràndi** pl grown-ups pl.

grandeggiàre vi to rise to a great height, tower above.

grandézza nf greatness, height, size, grandeur; highness.

grandígia nf pomp, arrogance.

grandinàre vti to hail, shower.

grandinàta nf hailstorm (also fig).

gràndine nf hail.

grandiosità nf grandiosity, grandeur.

grandióso a grand, grandiose.

grandúca nm grand duke; **granduchéssa** nf grand duchess.

granducàto nm grand duchy.

granèllo nm grain, seed.

grànfia nf claw, clutch.

granífero a grain-producing.

graníre vt to grain; (teeth) cut; vi to seed.

granìta nf grated-ice drink, often fruit-flavoured.

granìto nm granite.

gràno nm wheat, corn, grain; (necklace) bead; **g. saracèno** buckwheat.

grantúrco pl -chi nm maize, (US) corn.

granulazióne nf granulation.

granulóso a granulous.

gràppa nf clamp, cramp iron, stalk,

(typ) bracket; brandy.

gràppolo nm bunch, cluster.

grassatóre nm highwayman.

grassazióne nf robbery.

grassétto a nm (typ) heavy-faced, heavy type.

grassézza nf fatness, stoutness; greasiness, abundance.

gràsso a fat, abundant, fertile; **martedí g.** Shrove Tuesday.

grassòccio a plump.

grassúme nm fat substance.

gràta nf grating.

graticciàta nf trellis-work, fence.

graticcio nm hurdle, trellis-work.

graticola nf grill, grate, grating.

gratìfica nf bonus.

gratificàre vt to gratify.

gratificazióne nf bonus, gratuity.

gràtis ad free, gratis.

gratitúdine nf gratitude.

gràto a grateful, obliged; welcome.

grattacàpo nm problem, trouble.

grattacièlo nm skyscraper.

grattàre vt to scrape, scratch.

grattúgia nf grater.

grattugiàre vt to grate.

gratuitaménte ad free of charge, gratuitously.

gratúito a free, gratuitous.

gravàme nm burden, duty, tax.

gravàre vti to burden, load, weigh on.

gràve a heavy, great, serious, stern, grave; nm (phys) body; seriousness; **èssere g.** to be seriously ill.

graveménte ad gravely, heavily, deeply.

gravézza nf heaviness, gravity, weight; tax.

gravidànza nf pregnancy.

gràvido a pregnant, (fig) full, loaded.

gravità nf gravity, seriousness, weight.

gravitàre vi to gravitate.

gravitazióne nf gravitation.

gravosità nf heaviness, oppressiveness.

gravóso a heavy, oppressive.

gràzia nf grace, favour, mercy.

Gràzia nf pr Grace.

graziàre vt to pardon, grant.

gràzie interj thanks, thank you.

graziosità nf prettiness, graciousness.

grazióso a dainty, pretty, gracious.

Grècia nf (geogr) Greece.

grecìsta nmf Hellenist.

grèco pl grèci a nm Greek.

gregàrio a gregarious; nm (mil) private, follower.

grégge nm flock, herd.

gréggio a (of materials) coarse; (fig) crude.

Gregòrio nm pr Gregory.

grembiúle nm apron.

grèmbo nm lap, (fig) bosom.

gremìre vt to crowd, fill; **-rsi** vr to fill up, get crowded.

gremíto a crowded, packed.

gréppia nf crib, manger, rack.

gréppo nm cliff, rock; (of a ditch) edge.

gréto nm pebbly bank.

grettézza nf meanness, stinginess.

grétto a mean, niggardly, stingy.

grève a heavy.

grézzo v **gréggio**.

gridàre vti to shout, cry, scream, call, proclaim.

grído nm cry, shout, scream; **di g.** famous.

grifàgno a predatory, fierce.

grifo nm snout; griffin, griffon.

grifóne nm griffin, griffon.

grigiàstro a greyish.

grígio a nm grey.

grigiovérde a grey-green; nm (mil) grey-green (Italian) uniform.

gríglia nf grate, grating, grill, grid; **alla g.** grilled, (US) broiled.

grillétto nm trigger.

grillo nm cricket; (fig) whim.

grínfia nf claw, clutch.

grínta nf forbidding face.

grínza nf crease, wrinkle.

grinzóso a creased, wrinkled.

grippàre vi (mech) to seize.

grissíno nm breadstick.

grisú nm firedamp.

groenlandése a (of) Greenland; nmf Greenlander.

Groenlàndia nf (geogr) Greenland.

grónda nf eaves pl.

grondàia nf gutter.

grondàre vi to stream, drip; vt to pour.

gròppa nf back, rump.

gròssa nf gross (12 dozen).

grossézza nf bigness, size, thickness, dullness, coarseness.

grossísta nm wholesale dealer, stockist, (US) distributor.

gròsso a big, thick; nm main body, chief part; **pèzzo g.** bigwig.

grossolanità nf coarseness, grossness.

grossolàno a coarse, gross, rude.

gròtta nf cave, grotto.

grottésco pl **-schi** a grotesque; nm grotesqueness.

gand grovíglio nm tangle, confusion.

gru nf crane.

grúccia nf crutch, coathanger; (for birds) perch, (door) handle.

grugníre vi to grunt.

grúgno nm muzzle, snout.

grúllo a foolish, silly, foul.

grúmo nm clot.

grumóso a clotted.

grúppo nm group, knot.

grúzzolo nm hoard, savings pl.

guadàbile a fordable.

guadagnàre vt **-rsi** vr to earn, gain, acquire, win, reach.

guadàgno nm gain, profit.

guadàre vi to ford, wade.

guàdo nm ford.

guài interj woe!

guaína nf sheath, case.

guàio nm trouble, difficulty, accident, misfortune.

guaíre vi to whine, yelp.

guaíto nm yelp, whine.

gualcíre vt to rumple, crease.

Gualtièro nm pr Walter.

guància nf cheek.

guanciàle nm pillow.

guantàio nm glover.

guantièra nf glove box, tray.

guànto nm glove.

guardabòschi nm forester.

guardacàccia, guardiacàccia nm gamekeeper.

guardacòste nm coastguard.

guardàre vt to look at, gaze at, watch, consider, protect, guard; **-rsi** vr to look at oneself, abstain from, beware of, forbear, look at each other.

guardaròba nf cloakroom, wardrobe.

guardarobièra nf cloakroom attendant, linen maid.

guardasigílli nm Lord Privy Seal.

guardàta nf look, glance.

guardatúra nf way of looking.

guàrdia nf guard, watch, look out; **g. del còrpo** bodyguard.

guardiàno nm keeper, watchman.

guardína nf guardroom.

guardíngo pl **-inghi** a cautious.

guarentígia nf guarantee.

guaríbile a curable.

guarigióne nf recovery.

guaríre vt to cure, heal; vi to recover.

guarnigióne nf garrison.

guarníre vt to garnish, trim, furnish.

guarnizióne nf garnishing, trimming.

Guascógna nf (geogr) Gascony.

guascóne a nm Gascon, (fig) gascon, braggart.

guastafèste nm spoilsport, wet blanket.

guastamestièri nm bungler.

guastàre vt to spoil, ruin; **-rsi** vr to spoil, be spoilt, quarrel.

guàsto a spoilt, damaged, decayed, corrupt; nm damage.

guatàre vt to gaze, stare.

guàzza nf heavy dew.

guazzàre vi to paddle, wallow.

guazzétto nm stew.

guèlfo a nm Guelf, Guelph.

guèrcio a squint-eyed.

guèrra nf war.

guerrafondàio nm warmonger.

guerreggiàre vi to (wage) war, fight.

guerrésco pl **-chi** a (of) war, warlike.

guerrièro a warlike; nm warrior.

guerríglia nf guerrilla war.

gúfo nm owl; misanthrope.

gúglia nf spire.

Guglièlmo nm pr William.

guída nf guide, guidance, leadership; (aut) drive, steering, driving; **g. telefònica** telephone directory;

patènte di g. driving licence; scuòla g. driving school.

guidàre vt to guide, lead, manage; drive (a car etc); -rsi vr to conduct oneself, behave.

guiderdóne nm recompense.

Guído nm pr Guy.

guidoslìtta nf bobsleigh.

guinzàglio nm lead, (for dogs) leash.

guìṣa nf manner, way; a g. di like.

guizzàre vi to dart, flash. wriggle out.

guizzo nm flash, wriggle.

gúscio nm shell, pod, cover.

gustàre vti to enjoy, taste, like.

gústo nm taste, fancy, liking, relish.

gustosità nf savouriness, delightfulness.

gustóso a tasty, savoury, delightful, amusing.

gutturàle a guttural.

I

i art m pl the.

iàrda nf yard.

iàto nm hiatus.

iattànza nf boasting, bragging.

iattúra nf misfortune.

ibèri nm pl Iberians.

Ibèria nf (geogr) Iberia.

ibèrico pl -ici a Iberian.

ibridíṣmo nm hybridism.

íbrido a hybrid.

icàstico pl -ici a figurative, graphic.

icòna, icòne nf icon.

iconoclàsta, iconoclàste nm iconoclast.

Iddío nm God.

idèa nf idea, notion, opinion, ideal, intention.

ideàle a nm ideal.

idealíṣmo nm idealism.

idealísta nmf idealist.

idealizzàre vt to idealize.

ideàre vt to imagine, plan.

idèntico pl -ici a identical.

identificàre vt to identify.

identificazióne nf identification.

identità nf identity.

ideología nf ideology.

idillíaco, idíllico a idyllic.

idíllio nm idyll.

idiòma nm language.

idiomàtico pl -ici a idiomatic.

idiosincraṣía nf idiosyncrasy.

idiòta a idiotic; nmf idiot.

idiotíṣmo nm idiom, idiomatic expression.

idiozía nf idiocy.

idolatràre vt to worship, idolize.

idolatría nf idolatry.

idoleggiàre vt to idolize.

ídolo nm idol.

idoneità nf fitness, ability.

idòneo a fit, suitable.

ídra nf hydra.

idrànte nm hydrant, fire-plug, water-plug.

idràulico pl -ici a hydraulic; nm plumber.

ídro nm water snake; (short for) idrovolànte seaplane.

idroelèttrico pl -ici a hydroelectric; centràle idroelèttrica hydroelectric power station.

idròfilo a absorbent; cotóne i. cotton wool, (US) absorbent cotton.

idròfobo a hydrophobic, rabid.

idrògeno nm hydrogen.

idrope nm idropiṣía nf (med) dropsy.

idròpico pl -ici a nm dropsical, dropsical person.

idroplàno nm seaplane.

idropòrto, idroscàlo nm flying-boat station.

ièna nf hyena.

Ièova nm pr Jehovah.

ièri ad yesterday; i. l'àltro the day before yesterday.

iettatóre nm -tríce nf bringer of ill-luck.

iettatúra nf evil eye, misfortune.

igiène nf hygiene.

igiènico pl -ici a hygienic.

ignàro a ignorant, unaware.

ignàvia nf sloth.

ignàvo a slothful.

ígneo a igneous.

ignizióne nf ignition.

ignòbile a ignoble.

ignomínia nf ignominy.

ignominióso a ignominious.

ignorànte a ignorant.

ignorànza nf ignorance.

ignoràre vt to be ignorant of, ignore.

ignòto a unknown; nm unknown person.

ignúdo a naked, unclothed.

igròmetro nm (phys) hygrometer.

il art m the.

ilàre a gay, cheerful.

ilarità nf gaiety, hilarity.

Ílda nf pr Hilda.

ilíaco pl -aci a (anat) iliac; Trojan.

illanguidíre vt to weaken; vi to grow feeble, languish.

illécito a illicit, unlawful.

illegàle a illegal, unlawful.

illegalità nf illegality.

illeggíbile a illegible.

illegittimità nf illegitimacy, unlawfulness.

illegíttimo a illegitimate, unlawful.

illéṣo a unhurt, uninjured.

illetteràto a illiterate, unlettered.

illibatézza nf chastity, purity.

illibàto a chaste, pure.

illiberàle a illiberal.

illimitàto a boundless, unlimited.

illividíre vt to make livid; vi to grow livid.

illògico pl -ici a illogical.

illúdere vt to deceive, delude.

illuminànte a illuminating, (fig) enlightening.

illuminàre vt to enlighten, illuminate, light; -rsi vr to light up.

illuminazióne nf illumination, lighting.

illuminiṣmo nm illuminism.

illuṣióne nf illusion, dream.

illuṣòrio a deceptive, illusory.

illustràre vt to illustrate, explain, make illustrious.

illustratívo a illustrative.

illustrazióne nf illustration.

illústre a famous, illustrious.

imaginífico pl -ici a with a rich imagination.

Imalàia nf (geogr) Himalaya.

imbacuccàre vt to muffle up, wrap.

imbaldanzíre vt to embolden; -rsi vr to grow bold.

imballàggio nm packing, wrapping.

imballàre vt to pack, wrap.

imbàllo nm (aut) racing; packing, wrapping.

imbalsamàre vt to embalm, (animals) stuff.

imbambolàto a bewildered, stunned, dull, drowsy, confused.

imbandieràre vt to beflag.

imbandigióne nf preparation of a banquet, dish, table.

imbandíre vt to prepare a gala meal, lay (the table).

imbarazzànte a embarrassing, awkward.

imbarazzàre vt to embarrass, perplex, hamper.

imbaràzzo nm embarrassment, difficulty; i. di stòmaco indigestion.

imbarcadèro nm landing-place, pier.

imbarcàre vt to put (take) on board, ship; -rsi vr to embark, take ship.

imbarcatóio nm pier.

imbarcazióne nf boat.

imbàrco pl -chi nm embarkation, loading.

imbastíre vt (in sewing) to tack; (fig) to improvise, sketch.

imbàttersi vr to fall in with.

imbattíbile a unbeatable.

imbavagliàre vt to gag.

imbeccàre vt to feed; (fig) prompt.

imbecílle a nmf imbecile.

imbèlle a cowardly, weak.

imbellettàrsi vr to paint one's face.

imbèrbe a beardless.

imbestialíre vi to grow furious.

imbévere vt to imbue, steep; -rsi vr to become imbued with.

imbiancaménto nm whitewashing, bleaching, whitening; (of hair) greying.

imbiancàre, imbianchíre vti to bleach, whiten, whitewash, turn white, grow grey.

imbianchíno nm house-painter.

imbizzarríre -rsi vr (of horses) to rear, grow furious, spirited.

imboccàre vti to feed, prompt, enter, fit, flow into.

imboccatúra nf **imbócco** pl -chi nm mouth, opening, entrance, mouthpiece.

imboscaménto nm hiding, shirking military service.

imboscàre vt -rsi vr to hide, lie in wait, help evade military service, evade military service.

imboscàta nf ambush.

imbottigliàre vt to bottle.

imbottíre vt to pad, stuff.

imbottitúra nf stuffing, wadding, quilting.

imbrattàre vt to daub, dirty.

imbrigliàre vt to bridle, curb.

imbroccàre vt to guess right, hit the mark.

imbrogliàre vt to cheat, swindle, muddle, entangle; -rsi vr to get confused.

imbróglio nm tangle, confused situation, trick, fraud.

imbroglióne nm cheat, swindler.

imbronciàre vi -rsi vr to take offence, sulk.

imbrunàre, imbruníre vi to darken, grow dark.

imbruttíre vt to disfigure, make ugly; vi to grow ugly.

imbucàre vt to post, put into a hole; -rsi vr to creep into a hole.

imburràre vt to butter.

imbúto nm funnel.

imitàre vt to imitate, copy, mimic.

imitatívo a imitative.

imitazióne nf imitation.

immacolàto a immaculate, spotless.

immagazzinàre vi to store.

immaginàre vt to imagine, fancy; -rsi vr to fancy, imagine, picture.

immaginazióne nf imagination, fancy.

immàgine nf image, picture.

immancabilménte ad unfailingly, certainly.

immàne a enormous, huge, frightful.

immangiàbile a uneatable.

immantinénte ad at once, immediately.

immateriàle a immaterial.

immatricolàre vt -rsi vr to matriculate.

immaturità nf immaturity, unripeness.

immatúro a unripe, immature.

immedeṣimàrsi vr to identify oneself with.

immediataménte ad immediately, directly, forthwith.

immediàto a immediate.

immemoràbile a immemorial.

immémore a forgetful, unmindful.

immensità nf immensity.

immènso a immense, vast.

immensuràbile a immeasurable.

immèrgere vt to immerse, dip, plunge; -rsi vr to immerse oneself.

immeritàto a undeserved, unmerited.

immeritévole a undeserving, unworthy.

immersióne nf immersion.

immérso a immersed (also fig).

immigrànte *a nmf* immigrant.
immigràre *vi* to immigrate.
immigrazióne *nf* immigration.
imminènte *a* imminent, impending.
imminènza *nf* imminence.
immischiàre *vt* to bring into, involve; **-rsi** *vr* to interfere, meddle.
immiseríre *vt* to impoverish; *vi* to grow poor.
immissàrio *nm* affluent, tributary.
immòbile *a* immovable, motionless; *nm pl* **gli immòbili** immovables, immovable property, real estate.
immobilità *nf* immobility.
immobilizzàre *vt* to immobilize.
immobilizzazióne *nf* immobilization.
immodèstia *nf* immodesty.
immodèsto *a* immodest.
immolàre *vt* to immolate, sacrifice.
immolazióne *nf* immolation.
immollàre *vt* to wet; **-rsi** *vr* to get wet.
immondézza *nf* uncleanness, filth, garbage.
immondezzàio *nm* garbage heap.
immondízia *nf* garbage, filth.
immóndo *a* unclean, dirty.
immoràle *a* immoral.
immoralità *nf* immorality.
immortalàre *vt* to immortalize.
immortàle *a* immortal.
immortalità *nf* immortality.
immòto *a* motionless.
immúne *a* immune, free, exempt.
immunità *nf* immunity, freedom.
immunizzàre *vt* to immunize; **-rsi** *vr* to become immune.
impaccàre *vt* to pack.
impacchettàre *vt* to make up packets, pack.
impacciàre *vt* to hinder, embarrass, encumber; **-rsi** *vr* to meddle.
impacciàto *a* awkward, embarrassed, self-conscious.
impàccio *nm* encumbrance, obstacle, bother, embarrassment.
impadronírsi *vr* to take possession of, seize, master.
impagàbile *a* priceless, invaluable.
impaginàre *vt* (*typ*) to make up (a book), page.
impagliàre *vt* to cover with straw.
impalàto *a* rigid, stiff.
impalcàre *vt* to board, plank.
impalcatúra *nf* scaffolding.
impallidíre *vi* to turn pale.
impalpàbile *a* impalpable.
impaludàre *vi* **-rsi** *vr* to grow marshy.
impanàto *a* covered with bread crumbs.
impancàrsi *vr* to presume, act like.
impantanàrsi *vr* to sink in the mud, be bogged.
impappinàrsi *vr* to become confused.
imparàre *vt* to learn.
imparatíccio *nm* thing badly learned, beginner's work.

impareggiàbile *a* incomparable.
imparentàrsi *vr* to become related, marry into.
impari *a* odd, uneven, unequal.
impartíre *vt* to impart, bestow, give.
imparziàle *a* impartial, unbiassed.
impassíbile *a* impassible, impassive.
impastàre *vt* to knead, mix.
impàsto *nm* mixture.
impastoiàre *vt* to shackle, hinder, impede.
impauríre *vt* to frighten; **-rsi** *vr* to get frightened.
impaziènte *a* impatient.
impazientíre *vi* **-rsi** *vr* to lose one's patience.
impazientíto *a* irritated, annoyed.
impaziènza *nf* impatience.
impazzàre, impazzíre *vi* to be crazy about, go mad.
impeccàbile *a* impeccable.
impeciàre *vt* to pitch, tar.
impedimènto *nm* impediment, hindrance, obstacle.
impedíre *vt* to prevent, obstruct, hinder.
impegnàre *vt* to bind, engage, pledge, pawn; **-rsi** *vr* to bind, engage oneself, get involved.
impegnatívo *a* binding, exacting.
impègno *nm* engagement, obligation, care.
impenetràbile *a* impenetrable, inscrutable.
impenitènte *a* impenitent.
impenitènza *nf* impenitence.
impensàbile *a* inconceivable, unthinkable.
impensataménte *ad* unexpectedly.
impensàto *a* unthought of, unforeseen, unexpected.
impensieríre *vt* to make uneasy; **-rsi** *vr* to worry.
imperànte *a* ruling, reigning, prevailing.
imperàre *vt* to rule (over).
imperatívo *a nm* imperative.
imperatóre *nm* emperor; **-tríce** *nf* empress.
impercettíbile *a* imperceptible.
imperdonàbile *a* unpardonable.
imperfètto *a nm* imperfect.
imperfezióne *nf* fault, flaw, imperfection.
imperiàle *a* imperial.
imperialísmo *nm* imperialism.
imperiosità *nf* imperiousness.
imperióso *a* domineering, imperious.
imperízia *nf* lack of experience, lack of skill.
impermalírsi *vr* to get cross.
impermeàbile *a nm* waterproof.
impermeabilità *nf* impermeability.
imperniàre *vt* **-rsi** *vr* to pivot, hinge.
impèro *nm* empire, command.
impersonàle *a* impersonal.
impersonàre *vt* to impersonate.
impertèrrito *a* undaunted, fearless.
impertinènte *a* impertinent, saucy.

impertinènza nf impertinence.
imperturbàbile a imperturbable.
imperversàre vi (of diseases, weather etc) to rage.
impèrvio a hard to reach, inaccessible.
ímpeto nm impetus, vehemence, impulse, outburst, transport.
impetràre vt to ask for, obtain.
impetuosità nf impetuosity, impulsiveness.
impetuóso a impetuous, vehement.
impiantàre vt to establish, set up.
impiantìto nm floor.
impiànto nm installation, plant, establishment.
impiastràre vt to daub, plaster, smear.
impiàstro nm plaster; (fig) bore.
impiccagióne nf hanging (on the gallows).
impiccàre vt to hang; **-rsi** vr to hang oneself.
impicciàre etc v **impacciare** etc.
impiccolire vt to make smaller, diminish, lessen.
impiegàre vt to employ, spend, invest; **-rsi** vr to get a post.
impiegàto nm clerk, employee.
impiègo pl **-ghi** nm employment, job, position, use.
impietosíre vt to move to pity; **-rsi** vr to be touched.
impietràre, impietríre vt to petrify.
impigliàre vt to entangle.
impigríre vt to make lazy; **-rsi** vr to grow lazy.
impinguàre vt to fatten, enrich; **-rsi** vr to grow fat, get rich.
impiombàre vt to seal with lead, splice (a cable), stop (a tooth), lead.
impiombatúra nf sealing with lead, stopping (a tooth), splicing (a cable), leading.
implacàbile a implacable, relentless.
implicàre vt to implicate, involve, imply.
implicazióne nf implication.
implìcito a implicit.
implorànte a imploring.
imploràre vt to entreat, implore.
implorazióne nf entreaty.
impolìtico pl **-ici** a impolitic.
impoltroníre vt to make lazy; **-rsi** vr to become lazy.
impolveràre vt to cover with dust.
imponderàbile a nm imponderable.
imponènte a imposing, impressive.
imponènza nf grandeur.
imponíbile a chargeable, taxable.
impopolàre a unpopular.
impopolarità nf unpopularity.
impórre vt to impose; **-rsi** vr to impose oneself, make oneself respected, have success.
importànte a important, weighty; nm important thing.
importànza nf importance.
importàbile a importable.

importàre vt to import, imply, involve, cost; v impers to matter, be of importance.
importazióne nf importation, import.
impòrto nm amount.
importunaménte ad importunately, troublesomely.
importunàre vt to importune, bother.
importunità nf importunity.
importúno a troublesome, importunate, untimely; nm intruder.
imposizióne nf imposition.
impossessàrsi vr to take possession of.
impossíbile a impossible.
impossibilità nf impossibility.
impossibilitàto a unable.
impòsta nf tax, duty; shutter.
impostàre vt to post, (US) mail; set up, lay down.
impostazióne nf posting, formulation, general lines.
impostóre nm impostor, swindler.
impostúra nf imposture, fraud.
impotènte a impotent, powerless.
impotènza nf impotence, powerlessness.
impoveriménto nm impoverishment.
impoveríre vt to impoverish; **-rsi** vr to grow poor.
impraticàbile a impracticable, (road) impassable.
impratichíre vt to train, exercise; **-rsi** vr to practise, exercise oneself.
imprecàre vt to curse, swear.
imprecazióne nf curse, imprecation.
imprecisióne nf inaccuracy, lack of precision.
imprecíso a inaccurate, vague.
impregnàre vt to impregnate.
impremeditàto a unpremeditated.
imprèndere vt to begin, undertake.
imprenditóre nm contractor; **i. di pómpe fúnebri** funeral undertaker.
impreparàto a unprepared.
imprésa nf undertaking, enterprise, deed, contract, firm; **i. autotraspòrti** road haulage firm, (US) truck line.
impresàrio nm contractor, impresario, undertaker.
imprescindíbile a that cannot be ignored, indispensable, absolute.
impressionàbile a impressionable.
impressionànte a striking, impressive.
impressionàre vt to impress, frighten; **-rsi** vr to be frightened.
impressióne nf impression, sensation, imprint.
impressionìsmo nm impressionism.
imprestàre etc v **prestare** etc.
imprevedíbile a unforeseeable.
imprevidènte a improvident.
imprevidènza nf improvidence.
imprevìsto a unexpected, unforeseen; nm unexpected event.

imprigionàre vt to imprison.
imprimé nm printed cloth, print dress.
imprímere vt to impress, imprint, print, engrave.
improbàbile a improbable, unlikely.
improbabilità nf unlikelihood, improbability.
improbità nf dishonesty, wickedness.
ímprobo a dishonest, wicked, hard.
improduttività nf unproductiveness.
improduttívo a unproductive.
imprónta nf impression, mark, print, stamp.
improntàto a stamped, marked with.
impropèrio nm abuse, abusive word.
impropriaménte ad incorrectly, improperly.
improprietà nf impropriety, inaccuracy.
impròprio a improper, unsuitable.
improrogàbile a that cannot be postponed.
impròv(v)ido a improvident, rash.
improvvisaménte ad suddenly, unexpectedly.
improvvisàre vti to extemporize, improvise.
improvvisàta nf surprise.
improvvisàto a improvised, extempore, unscripted.
improvvisatóre nm -**trice** nf extemporizer, improviser.
improvvisazióne nf improvisation.
improvvíso a sudden, unexpected, unforeseen; **all'i.** suddenly.
imprudènte a imprudent, rash.
imprudènza nf imprudence, rashness.
impudènte a impudent, shameless.
impudènza nf impudence, shamelessness.
impudicízia nf immodesty.
impudíco pl -**chi** a immodest, shameless.
impugnàre vt to impugn; grip, take up (arms).
impugnatúra nf grip, hilt.
impulsività nf impulsiveness, rashness.
impulsívo a impulsive.
impúlso nm impulse, impetus.
impunità nf impunity.
impuníto a unpunished.
impuntàrsi vr to be stubborn.
impurità nf impurity.
impúro a impure, unclean.
imputàbile a imputable.
imputàre vt to impute, charge, accuse.
imputàto nm accused, defendant.
imputazióne nf imputation, charge.
imputridíre vt to putrefy, rot.
in prep in, into, on, to, by, at.
inàbile a incapable, unable, unfit.
inabilità nf inability, unfitness.

inabilitazióne nf disability, disqualification.
inabissàrsi vr to sink.
inabitàbile a uninhabitable.
inabitàto a uninhabited.
inaccessíbile a inaccessible.
inaccettàbile a unacceptable.
inaccordàbile a ungrantable; (mus) untunable.
inacerbíre vt to embitter, exacerbate.
inacidíre vt to sour; vi to turn sour.
inadattàbile a unadaptable.
inadàtto a unfit, unsuitable, improper.
inadeguatézza nf inadequacy.
inadeguàto a inadequate, insufficient.
inadempiménto nm non-fulfilment.
inafferràbile a unseizable, elusive.
inalberàre vt to hoist, raise; -**rsi** vr to get angry.
inalienàbile a inalienable.
inalteràbile a unalterable.
inamidàre vt to starch.
inammissíbile a inadmissible.
inamovíbile a irremovable.
inàne a inane, vain.
inanimàto a inanimate.
inanità nf inanity, vanity.
inappagàto a unsatisfied.
inappellàbile a inappellable.
inappetènza nf lack of appetite.
inaridíre vt to parch, dry up; -**rsi** vr to dry up.
inarrivàbile a unattainable, incomparable.
inarticolàto a inarticulate.
inaspettàto a sudden, unexpected.
inaspriménto nm embitterment, exacerbation.
inaspríre vt to embitter, exacerbate; -**rsi** vr to become enbittered.
inastàre vt to hoist.
inattaccàbile a unassailable.
inattendíbile a unreliable, unfounded.
inattéso a unexpected.
inattitúdine nf inaptitude.
inattività nf inactivity.
inattívo a inactive.
inàtto a unapt, unfit; v **disadàtto.**
inattuàbile a impracticable, unfeasible.
inaudíto a unheard-of.
inauguràle a inaugural.
inauguràre vt to inaugurate, open.
inaugurazióne nf inauguration, opening.
inavvertènza nf inadvertence.
inavvertíto a unobserved, careless.
inazióne nf inaction.
incagliàrsi vr (naut) to run aground.
incalcolàbile a incalculable.
incallíre vi to grow callous, harden.
incaloríre vt to heat.
incalvíre vi to grow bald.
incalzàre vt to chase, press, pursue.
incamminàre vt to set going, start; -**rsi** vr to set out.
incanalàre vt to canalize, direct.

incancellàbile *a* indelible.

incandescènte *a* ncandescent, white-hot.

incandescènza *nf* incandescence.

incannàggio *nm* (*of thread etc*) reeling, winding.

incannàta *nf* spindleful.

incantaménto *nm* enchantment, spell.

incantàre *vt* to charm, enchant; **-rsi** *vr* to be enraptured, stop.

incantésimo *nm* charm, enchantment, spell.

incantévole *a* enchanting, charming.

incantevolménte *ad* enchantingly.

incànto *nm* charm, enchantment; (*com*) public sale; **all'i.** by auction.

incanutire *vi* to grow grey.

incapàce *a* incapable, unable.

incapacità *nf* incapacity.

incappàre *vi* to get into, fall in (with).

incapricciàrsi *vr* to take a fancy, become infatuated.

incarceràre *vt* to imprison.

incaricàre *vt* to charge, entrust; **-rsi** *vr* to take upon oneself.

incaricàto *a* charged with, entrusted with; *nm* deputy, chargé d'affaires.

incàrico *pl* **-chi** *nm* task, appointment, commission.

incarnàre *vt* to incarnate, embody.

incarnàto *a* incarnate; (*of nail*) ingrowing; *nm* rosiness.

incarnazióne *nf* incarnation, embodiment.

incartaménto *nm* dossier, documents *pl*.

incartàre *vt* to wrap in paper.

incàrto *v* **incartaménto**.

incassàre *vt* to box, cash, set, encase.

incàsso *nm* takings *pl*.

incastonàre *vt* to set (jewels).

incastràre *vt* to embed, drive in; **-rsi** *vr* to fit, get stuck.

incatenàre *vt* to chain, fetter, enthral.

incàuto *a* incautious, rash.

incavàre *vt* to hollow out, excavate.

incàvo *nm* cavity, hollow, groove, notch, socket.

incendiàre *vt* to set on fire; **-rsi** *vr* to catch fire.

incendiàrio *a nm* incendiary.

incèndio *nm* fire.

inceneriménto *nm* incineration, cremation.

incenerire *vt* to reduce (burn) to ashes.

incensaménto *nm* incensation.

incensàre *vt* to cense; praise.

incènso *nm* incense.

incensuràbile *a* irreproachable.

incentivo *nm* incentive.

inceppàre *vt* to clog, obstruct.

inceràre *vt* to (coat with) wax.

inceràta *nf* oil cloth, tarpaulin.

incertézza *nf* uncertainty, irresolution.

incèrto *a* uncertain, doubtful, irresolute; *nm* uncertainty; **incèrti** *pl* incidental profits *pl*, uncertainties.

incespicàre *vi* to stumble, trip.

incessànte *a* incessant, unceasing.

incèsto *nm* incest.

incestuóso *a* incestuous.

incètta *nf* buying up, cornering.

incettàre *vt* (*com*) to buy up, corner.

incettatóre *nm* **-trice** *nf* buyer up.

inchièsta *nf* inquest, inquiry.

inchinàre *vt* to incline, bow down; **-rsi** *vr* to bow, stoop.

inchino *nm* bow, curtsey.

inchiodàre *vt* to nail, rivet, (*also fig*).

inchiòstro *nm* ink.

inciampàre *vi* to stumble, stumble across.

inciàmpo *nm* stumbling block, difficulty.

incidentàle *a* accidental, casual; incidental; parenthetical.

incidènte *nm* accident, incident, dispute.

incidènza *nf* incidence.

incidere *vt* to engrave, etch, record, incise; *vi* to weigh heavily.

incinta *a f* pregnant.

incipiènte *a* incipient.

incipriàre *vt* to powder.

incisióne *nf* incision, engraving, recording.

incisivo *a* incisive.

inciso *a* incised, engraved; *nm* digression, parenthesis.

incisóre *nm* engraver, etcher.

incitaménto *nm* incitement, instigation, urge.

incitàre *vt* to incite, spur, urge.

incivile *a* uncivilized, uncivil.

inciviliménto *nm* civilization, refining.

incivilire *vt* to civilize, refine; **-rsi** *vr* to become civilized, polite.

inciviltà *nf* incivility, barbarousness.

inclemènte *a* inclement.

inclemènza *nf* inclemency.

inclinàre *vt* to incline, bend; **-rsi** *vr* to incline, lean, slope.

inclinazióne *nf* inclination, slope, propensity.

incline *a* inclined, disposed, prone.

inclito *a* famous, illustrious.

inclúdere *vt* to include, enclose, imply.

inclusióne *nf* inclusion.

inclusivo *a* inclusive.

inclúso *a* included, enclosed.

incoerènte *a* incoherent.

incoerènza *nf* incoherence.

incògnita *nf* (*math*) unknown quantity, unknown factor.

incògnito *a nm* unknown, incognito.

incollàre *vt* to stick, paste, glue.

incollerire *vi* **-rsi** *vr* to get angry.

incollerito *a* angry, enraged.

incolóre *a* colourless.

incolpàre *vt* to accuse, inculpate.

incolpévole *a* blameless, innocent.

incólto *a* uncultivated, unkempt.

incòlume a unharmed, uninjured, safe.

incolumità nf safety.

incombènte a impending.

incombènza nf errand, charge, task, commission.

incómbere vi to impend, hang, fall on.

incominciàre vt to begin, commence.

incomodàre vt to inconvenience, disturb.

incomodàto a indisposed.

incomodità nf discomfort, inconvenience.

incòmodo a inconvenient, uncomfortable; nm inconvenience, trouble.

incomparàbile a incomparable, matchless.

incompatíbile a incompatible.

incompetènte a incompetent, unqualified.

incompetènza nf incompetence.

incompiúto a unfinished, undone.

incomplèto a incomplete.

incompósto a disorderly, uncomely, indecent.

incomprensíbile a incomprehensible.

incomprensióne nf incomprehension.

incompréso a not understood.

incomunicabilità nf incommunicability.

inconcepíbile a inconceivable.

inconciliàbile a irreconcilable, incompatible.

inconcludènte a inconclusive.

inconclúso a unfinished.

incondizionatamènte ad unconditionally.

incondizionàto a unconditional.

incongruènte a incongruous.

incongruènza nf incongruency.

incòngruo a incongruous.

inconsapévole a unconscious, unaware, ignorant.

inconsapevolézza nf unconsciousness, ignorance, unawareness.

incònscio a unconscious; nm the unconscious.

inconseguènte a inconsequent.

inconseguènza nf inconsequence.

inconsideratézza nf inconsiderateness.

inconsideràto a inconsiderate, rash.

inconsistènte a inconsistent; unsubstantial; unfounded.

inconsolàbile a inconsolable.

inconsuèto a unusual.

inconsúlto a unadvised, rash.

incontentàbile a insatiable, exacting.

incontentabilità nf insatiability, inability to be satisfied.

incontestàbile a indisputable, unquestionable.

incontinènte a incontinent.

incontinènza nf incontinence.

incontràre vt to meet, meet with;

vi to be a success; -rsi vr to meet, agree, coincide.

incontrastàto a uncontested.

incóntro nm meeting; match; ad towards, opposite; **i. a** prep towards, opposite, against.

incontrollàbile a uncontrollable.

inconveniènte a inconvenient, unseemly; nm inconvenience, disadvantage.

inconveniènza nf inconvenience.

inconvertíbile a inconvertible.

incoraggiaménto nm encouragement.

incoraggiàre vt to encourage.

incorniciàre vt to frame.

incoronàre vt to crown.

incoronazióne nf coronation.

incorporàre vt to incorporate.

incorpòreo a incorporeal, immaterial.

incoraggiànte a encouraging.

incorreggíbile a incorrigible.

incórrere vt to incur, fall (into); **i. in débiti** to incur debts.

incorrótto a incorrupt.

incorruttíbile a incorruptible.

incorruttibilità nf incorruptibility.

incosciènte a unconscious; lacking conscience, reckless.

incosciènza nf unconsciousness; rashness; lack of conscience.

incostànte a inconstant, fickle, changeable.

incostànza nf inconstancy.

incostituzionàle a unconstitutional.

incredíbile a incredible, unbelievable.

incredibilménte ad incredibly, extraordinarily.

incredulità nf incredulity, unbelief.

incrèdulo a incredulous, unbelieving.

incrementàre vt to increase, promote, encourage.

increménto nm increase, increment.

increscióso a unpleasant.

increspaménto nm **increspatúra** nf rippling, ruffling, curling, wrinkling.

increspàre vt -rsi vr to ruffle, ripple, wrinkle, (of hair) curl.

incriminàre vt to incriminate.

incrinàre vt -rsi vr to crack.

incrociàre vti to cross, cruise; -rsi vr to cross, meet.

incrociatóre nm (naut) cruiser.

incrócio nm crossing, intersection; (of breeds) cross.

incrollàbile a unshakable.

incrostàre vt to encrust; -rsi vr to crust.

incrudelíre vi to be pitiless, commit cruelties.

incrudíre vi to grow harsh, rough.

incruènto a bloodless.

incubatríce af incubating; nf incubator.

incubazióne nf incubation.

íncubo nm nightmare, incubus.

incúdine nf anvil.

inculcàre *vt* to inculcate.
incuràbile *a nmf* incurable.
incurànte *a* careless, indifferent, neglectful.
incùria *nf* carelessness, neglect.
incuriosíre *vt* to make curious, rouse one's curiosity.
incursióne *nf* incursion, inroad; i. aèrea air raid.
incurvàre *vt* to bend, curve.
incustodíto *a* unguarded.
incùtere *vt* to inspire, rouse.
índaco *pl* -chi *nm* indigo.
indaffaràto *a* busy.
indagàre *vt* to inquire, investigate.
indàgine *nf* inquiry, investigation, research.
indebitàrsi *vr* to get into debt.
indébito *a* undue, improper, undeserved, illegal.
indebolíre *vt* to weaken; -rsi *vr* to flag, grow weak(er).
indecènte *a* indecent.
indecènza *nf* indecency.
indecifràbile *a* indecipherable.
indecisióne *nf* indecision, hesitation.
indecíso *a* undecided, hesitant.
indecoróso *a* indecorous, unseemly.
indefèsso *a* indefatigable.
indefettíbile *a* unfailing.
indefiníbile *a* indefinable.
indefiníto *a* indefinite.
indegnità *nf* shame, worthlessness.
indégno *a* undeserving, unworthy, worthless, contemptible.
indelèbile *a* indelible.
indelicatézza *nf* indelicacy.
indelicàto *a* indelicate, tactless.
indemoniàto *a* possessed; *nm* demoniac.
indènne *a* undamaged, unharmed.
indennità *nf* indennízzo *nm* indemnity.
indennizzàre *vt* to indemnify.
indéntro *ad* inwards.
inderogàbile *a* that cannot be transgressed.
indescrivíbile *a* indiscribable.
indeterminàto *a* indeterminate, vague, indefinite.
índi *ad* afterwards, thence, then.
Índia *nf* (*geogr*) India.
indiàno *a nm* Indian; fàre l'i. to feign ignorance.
indiavolàto *a* demoniac, devilish; (*fig*) furious, violent.
indicàre *vt* to indicate, point out, show.
indicatívo *a nm* indicative.
indicàto *a* suitable.
indicatóre *nm* gauge, indicator, guide; i. stradàle traffic sign; i. di velocità (*aut*) speedometer.
indicazióne *nf* indication.
índice *nm* forefinger, index, pointer, sign.
indicíbile *a* unspeakable, indescribable.
indietreggiaménto *nm* withdrawal.

indietreggiàre *vi* to fall back, recoil.
indiètro *ad* behind, back, backwards.
indiféso *a* defenceless.
indifferènte *a* indifferent, unimportant.
indifferènza *nf* indifference, unconcern.
indígeno *a* indigenous; *nm* native.
indigènte *a* indigent, needy.
indigènza *nf* indigence, need.
indigeríbile *a* indigestible.
indigestióne *nf* fàre un' i. di to eat too much of.
indigèsto *a* indigestible, tiresome.
indignàre *vt* to make indignant; -rsi *vr* to grow indignant.
indignazióne *nf* indignation.
indimenticàbile *a* unforgettable.
indimostràbile *a* indemonstrable.
indipendènte *a* independent, self-reliant; (*of flat etc*) self-contained.
indipendenteménte *ad* independently.
indipendènza *nf* independence.
indíre *vt* to announce, call, fix.
indirètto *a* indirect.
indirizzàre *vt* to address, direct; -rsi *vr* to address oneself, have recourse to.
indirízzo *nm* address.
indiscerníbile *a* indiscernible.
indisciplína *nf* indiscipline, unruliness.
indisciplinàto *a* undisciplined, unruly.
indiscréto *a* indiscreet, intrusive, prying.
indiscrezióne *nf* indiscretion, impertinence.
indiscutíbile *a* unquestionable.
indispensàbile *a* indispensable, essential.
indispensabilità *nf* indispensability.
indispensabilménte *ad* indispensably, most necessarily.
indispettíre *vt* to vex; -rsi *vr* to be angry, vexed.
indispórre *vt* to indispose, irritate, upset.
indisposizióne *nf* indisposition.
indispósto *a* indisposed, unwell.
indisputàbile *a* indisputable.
indissolúbile *a* indissoluble.
indistínto *a* faint, indistinct, vague.
indistruttíbile *a* indestructible.
indisturbàto *a* undisturbed.
individuàle *a* individual.
individualísmo *nm* individualism.
individualista *nmf* individualist.
individualità *nf* individuality.
individuàre *vt* to identify, pick out, specify, characterize.
indivíduo *nm* individual, fellow.
indivisíbile *a* indivisible.
indivíso *a* undivided, whole.
indízio *nm* indication, sign.
indòcile *a* unruly, intractable.

índole *nf* nature, disposition, temperament, character.
indolènte *a* indolent, lazy.
indolènza *nf* indolence, laziness.
indolenzíre *vt* to benumb, cramp; **-rsi** *vr* to get numb, get stiff.
indolóre *a* painless.
indomàni, l' *nm* (the) next day.
indòmito *a* indomitable, unconquered, untamed.
Indonèsia *nf* (*geogr*) Indonesia.
indonesiàno *a nm* Indonesian.
indoràre *vt* to gild.
indossàre *vt* to put on, wear.
indossatrice *nf* model, mannequin.
indòsso *ad* on.
indovinàre *vt* to divine, guess, foretell.
indovinàto *a* successful, well-done.
indovinèllo *nm* conundrum, riddle.
indovíno *a* prophetic, foreseeing; *nm* fortune-teller.
indú *a nmf* Hindu, Hindoo.
indubbiaménte *ad* undoubtedly.
indúbbio, indubitàbile *a* undoubted.
indugiàre *vti* to postpone, delay, linger.
indúgio *nm* delay.
indulgènte *a* indulgent.
indulgènza *nf* indulgence, leniency.
indúlgere *vt* to indulge.
induménto *nm* garment.
induríre *vt* to harden; *vi* **-rsi** *vr* to harden, get hard.
indúrre *vt* to inspire, induce; **-rsi** *vr* to decide, resolve.
indústria *nf* industry, skill.
industriàle *a* industrial; *nm* industrialist.
industriàrsi *vr* to do one's best.
industrióso *a* industrious.
induzióne *nf* induction, conjecture.
inebriànte *a* inebriating, intoxicating.
inebriàre *vt* to intoxicate, make drunk; **-rsi** *vr* to get drunk, be enraptured.
ineccepíbile *a* unobjectionable.
inèdia *nf* inanition, starvation, boredom.
inèdito *a* unpublished.
ineducàto *a* ill-bred, impolite.
ineffàbile *a* ineffable.
ineffettuàbile *a* unrealizable.
inefficàce *a* ineffective, ineffectual.
inefficàcia *nf* inefficacy.
inefficiènte *a* inefficient.
ineguagliànza, inegualità *nf* inequality.
ineguàle *a* unlike, unequal, irregular.
inelegànte *a* inelegant.
ineleggíbile *a* ineligable.
ineluttàbile *a* inevitable, inescapable.
inenarràbile *a* unspeakable.
inequivocàbile *a* unequivocal, unmistakable.
inerènte *a* inherent, concerning.
inèrme *a* unarmed, defenceless.

inèrte *a* inert, motionless, limp, lifeless, sluggish.
inèrzia *nf* inertness, idleness, inertia.
inesattézza *nf* inexactness, inaccuracy, mistake.
inesàtto *a* inaccurate, inexact, (*com*) uncollected.
inesaudíto *a* ungranted.
inesauríbile *a* inexhaustible.
inesàusto *a* unexhausted.
inescusàbile *a* inexcusable, unjustifiable.
ineseguíto *a* unperformed, unfulfilled.
inesistènte *a* non-existent.
inesoràbile *a* inexorable, relentless.
inesorabilità *nf* inexorability.
inesperiènza *nf* inexperience.
inespèrto *a* inexperienced, unskilled.
inesplicàbile *a* inexplicable.
inesploràto *a* unexplored.
inesplóso *a* unexploded.
inesprimíbile *a* inexpressible.
inestimàbile *a* inestimable, invaluable.
inettitúdine *nf* ineptitude.
inètto *a* inept, unfit.
inevàso *a* (*com*) outstanding.
inevitàbile *a* inevitable, unavoidable.
inevitabilménte *ad* unavoidably.
inèzia *nf* trifle.
infagottàre *vt* to wrap up, muffle.
infallíbile *a* infallible, unfailing.
infallibilità *nf* infallibility.
infamànte *a* disgraceful, shameful.
infamàre *vt* to disgrace, bring shame upon; **-rsi** *vr* to disgrace oneself.
infàme *a* abominable, infamous.
infàmia *nf* infamy, disgrace, shame.
infangàre *vt* to cover with mud.
infànte *nm* infant, child.
infantíle *a* childlike, childish, infantile.
infànzia *nf* infancy.
infarcíre *vt* to stuff, cram.
infarinatúra *nf* covering with flour, (*fig*) smattering.
infàrto *nm* i. (**cardíaco**) heart attack.
infastidíre *vt* to annoy, vex.
infaticàbile *a* indefatigable, untiring.
infàtti *ad* in fact, really.
infatuàre *vt* to infatuate; **-rsi** *vr* to become infatuated.
infatuazióne *nf* infatuation.
infàusto *a* unlucky.
infecóndo *a* barren, unfruitful.
infedèle *a* unfaithful, faithless, false; *nmf* infidel.
infedeltà *nf* unfaithfulness, infidelity.
infelíce *a* unhappy, unlucky, unsuccessful, inappropriate.
infelicità *nf* unhappiness.
inferióre *a* inferior, lower, below, subordinate; *nmf* inferior, subordinate.
inferiorità *nf* inferiority.
inferíre *vt* to infer, deduce, inflict, (*naut*) hoist, bend (a sail).

infermàrsi *vr* to become an invalid.
infermería *nf* infirmary, sick-room.
infermièra *nf* nurse; **infermière** *nm* hospital attendant, male nurse.
infermità *nf* illness, infirmity.
inférmo *a nm* ill, sick, invalid.
infernàle *a* infernal, hellish.
infèrno *nm* hell.
inferocíre *vti* **-rsi** *vr* to make ferocious, become ferocious.
inferriàta *nf* grating, railing.
infervoràre *vt* to fill with fervour; **-rsi** *vr* to get excited.
infestàre *vt* to infest.
infèsto *a* detrimental, harmful.
infettàre *vt* to infect, pollute.
infettívo *a* infectious, contagious.
infètto *a* infected.
infezióne *nf* infection.
infiacchiménto *nm* enervation, weakening.
infiacchíre *vt* to enervate, weaken; **-rsi** *vr* to grow weak.
infiammàbile *a* inflammable.
infiammabilità *nf* inflammability.
infiammàre *vt* to set on fire, inflame; **-rsi** *vr* to catch fire, become inflamed.
infiammazióne *nf* inflammation.
infído *a* untrustworthy, unfaithful.
infieríre *vi* to be pitiless, rage.
infievolíre *vt* to weaken; **-rsi** *vr* to grow weak.
infilàre *vt* to thread, string, run through, insert, enter; **-rsi** *vr* to thread one's way, slip, put on.
infiltràrsi *vr* to infiltrate, penetrate, seep.
infiltrazióne *nf* infiltration.
infilzàre *vt* to pierce, run through, string, stick.
ínfimo *a* lowest, very low.
infíne *ad* at last, after all, finally.
infingardàggine *nf* laziness, slothfulness.
infingàrdo *a* lazy, slothful.
infíngersi *vr* to feign, simulate.
infinità *nf* infinity, large crowd, lot.
infinitèsimo *a* infinitesimal.
infiníto *a nm* infinite, boundless, endless, infinity.
infioràre *vt* to adorn (strew) with flowers.
infirmàre *vt* to invalidate.
infischiàrsi *vr* not to care for, make light of.
infittíre *vti* to make thick, thicken.
inflazióne *nf* inflation.
inflessíbile *a* inflexible, unmoved.
inflessióne *nf* inflexion.
inflíggere *vt* to inflict.
influènte *a* influential.
influènza *nf* influence, influenza.
influenzàre *vt* to influence, affect, bias.
influenzàto *a* influenced; suffering from influenza.
influíre *vi* to influence.
influsso *nm* influx, influence.

infocàre *vt* to make hot, inflamed.
infondatézza *nf* groundlessness.
infondàto *a* groundless.
infóndere *vt* to infuse, instil.
inforcàre *vt* to pitchfork, bestride; **i. gli occhiàli** to put on one's spectacles.
informàre *vt* to acquaint, let (someone) know, inform; **-rsi** *vr* to find out, inquire.
informatívo *a* informative.
informatóre *a* informing; *nm* **-trice** *nf* informer.
informazióne *nf* (piece of) information; **úfficio i.** enquiry office.
informe *a* shapeless.
informicolíre *vt* to cause a tickling sensation, cause pins and needles.
informità *nf* shapelessness.
infornàta *nf* batch, ovenful.
infortunàto *a* injured.
infortúnio *nm* accident, misfortune.
infossatúra *nf* hollow, cavity.
infradiciàre *vt* to drench, soak; **-rsi** *vr* to get drenched.
inframmettènza *nf* interference, intrusiveness.
infra(m)méttersi *vr* to meddle.
infràngere *vt* to break, shatter; **-rsi** *vr* to break, smash.
infrangíbile *a* unbreakable.
infrànto *a* shattered, crushed (*also fig*).
infrarósso *a* infra-red.
infrazióne *nf* infraction, infringement.
infreddàrsi *vr* to catch a cold.
infreddatúra *nf* cold.
infreddolíto *a* cold.
infrequènte *a* infrequent.
infrequènza *nf* infrequency.
infrigidíre *vt* to chill, become cold.
infruttífero *a* unfruitful, unprofitable.
infruttuóso *a* fruitless, unsuccessful.
infuòri *ad* out; **all'i. di** *prep* except, but, apart from.
infuriàre *vt* to enrage; *vi* rage; **-rsi** *vr* to fly into a passion, lose one's temper.
infusióne *nf* infusion.
infúso *a* infused; *nm* infusion.
ingaggiàre *vt* to engage, enlist.
ingàggio *nm* enlistment, engagement.
ingagliardíre *vt* to invigorate, strengthen; **-rsi** *vr* to grow strong, strengthen.
ingannàre *vt* to deceive, beguile, cheat; **-rsi** *vr* to be mistaken.
ingannatóre *a* deceiving; *nm* **-trice** *nf* deceiver.
ingannévole *a* deceitful, deceptive.
ingànno *nm* deceit, fraud.
ingarbugliàre *vt* to entangle, muddle.
ingegnàrsi *vr* to do one's best, manage.
ingegnère *nm* engineer.
ingegnería *nf* engineering.
ingégno *nm* talent, genius, intelligence; device.

ingegnosità *nf* ingeniousness, ingenuity.

ingegnóso *a* ingenious, clever.

ingelosíre *vt* to make jealous; **-rsi** *vr* to become jealous.

ingeneràre *vt* to engender, cause.

ingènte *a* enormous, huge.

ingentilíre *vt* to refine; **-rsi** *vr* to become refined.

ingenuità *nf* ingenuousness, naïvety, simple-mindedness.

ingènuo *a* ingenuous, naïve.

ingerènza *nf* interference.

ingeríre *vt* to swallow; **-rsi** *vr* to interfere, meddle.

ingessàre *vt* to (set in) plaster.

ingessatúra *nf* plaster, plastering.

Inghiltèrra *nf* (*geogr*) England.

inghiottíre *vt* to swallow (up).

inghirlandàre *vt* to wreathe, garland.

ingiallíre *vi* to make yellow; *vi* to become yellow.

ingigantíre *vt* to magnify, exaggerate.

inginocchiàrsi *vr* to go on one's knees, kneel down.

inginocchiatóio *nm* kneeling-stool.

ingioiellàrsi *vr* to adorn oneself with jewels.

ingiúngere *vt* to order, command.

ingiunzióne *nf* injunction, order.

ingiúria *nf* insult, affront, damage.

ingiuriàre *vt* to abuse, insult.

ingiurióso *a* insulting, offensive.

ingiustaménte *ad* unjustly, wrong.

ingiustificàbile *a* unjustifiable.

ingiustízia *nf* injustice, unfairness.

ingiústo *a* unjust, unfair.

inglése *a nmf* English, the English language, Englishman, Englishwoman.

ingoiàre *vt* to swallow (up).

ingolfàrsi *vr* to form a gulf, plunge into.

ingombrànte *a* cumbersome.

ingombràre *vt* to encumber, obstruct.

ingómbro *a nm* encumbered, obstructed, encumbrance, obstruction.

ingommàre *vt* to gum, stick.

ingordígia *nf* greed(iness).

ingórdo *a nm* greedy, covetous, glutton.

ingórgo *nm* obstruction; **i. stradàle** traffic jam.

ingranàggio *nm* (*tec*) gear, working.

ingranàre *vti* (*tec*) to put into gear, be in gear; get along.

ingranchíre *vt* to benumb.

ingrandiménto *nm* enlargement.

ingrandíre *vt* to amplify, enlarge, exaggerate, increase; **-rsi** *vr* to grow larger, increase.

ingrassàre *vt* to make fat, lubricate, manure, enrich; *vi* **-rsi** *vr* to grow fat.

ingratitúdine *nf* ingratitude.

ingràto *a* ungrateful, thankless, unpleasant, unprofitable.

ingravidàre *vt* to make pregnant; **-rsi** *vr* to become pregnant.

ingraziàrsi *vr* to ingratiate oneself.

ingrediènte *nm* ingredient.

ingrèsso *nm* entry, entrance, admittance; **ingrèssi** (*theat*) standing tickets.

ingrossaménto *nm* enlargement, increase, swelling.

ingrossàre *vt* to make big(ger), increase, swell; **-rsi** *vr* to grow big(ger), rise, swell.

ingròsso, all' *ad* wholesale.

ingualcíbile *a* crease-resistant.

inguantàto *a* wearing gloves.

inguaríbile *a* incurable.

ínguine *nm* groin.

inibíre *vt* to inhibit, forbid, restrain.

inibizióne *nf* inhibition, prohibition.

inidòneo *a* unfit, unsuited.

iniettàre *vt* to inject.

iniezióne *nf* injection.

inimicàre *vt* to estrange, alienate; **-rsi** *vr* to become estranged from.

inimicízia *nf* enmity, hostility.

inimitàbile *a* inimitable.

inintelligíbile *a* unintelligible.

ininterrótto *a* uninterrupted, unbroken, non-stop.

iniquaménte *ad* wickedly, unjustly.

iniquità *nf* iniquity, wickedness.

iníquo *a* iniquitous, wicked.

iniziàle *a nf* initial.

iniziàre *vt* to begin, initiate.

iniziatíva *nf* initiative, enterprise.

iniziàto *a nm* initiated, initiate.

iniziazióne *nf* initiation.

inízio *nm* beginning, commencement.

innacquàre *vt* to water, dilute.

innaffiaménto *nm* watering.

innaffiàre *vt* to water.

innaffiatóio *nm* watering-can.

innalzàre *vt* to raise, heighten; **-rsi** *vr* to rise.

innamoràre *vt* to charm; **-rsi** *vr* to fall in love.

innamoràto *a* in love, loving; *nm* lover, sweetheart.

innànzi *ad and prep* before, on, towards, further.

innàto *a* innate.

innegàbile *a* undeniable.

inneggiàre *vt* to celebrate, exalt.

innervosíre *vt* to get on people's nerves.

innestàre *vt* to graft, inoculate, insert, join.

innèsto *nm* graft, insertion, inoculation.

ínno *nm* anthem, hymn.

innocènte *a nm* innocent.

innocènza *nf* innocence.

inoculazióne *nf* inoculation.

innòcuo *a* harmless, inoffensive.

innominàbile *a* unnamable, unmentionable.

innominàto *a* unnamed, nameless.

innovàre *vt* to innovate, change.

innovazióne *nf* innovation, change.

innumerévole *a* innumerable, numberless.

inoculàre *vt* to inoculate.

inodóro *a* odourless.

inoffensìvo *a* inoffensive, harmless.

inoltràre *vt* to forward, send on; **-rsi** *vr* to advance, penetrate.

inóltre *ad* besides, moreover, furthermore.

inondàre *vt* to flood, inundate.

inondazióne *nf* flood, inundation.

inoperosità *nf* inactivity, idleness.

inoperóso *a* inactive, idle.

inòpia *nf* indigence, poverty, want.

inopinàto *a* unexpected, unforeseen, sudden.

inopportúno *a* inopportune, untimely.

inoppugnàbile *a* unquestionable.

inorgànico *pl* **-ici** *a* inorganic.

inorgoglíre *vt* to make proud; **-rsi** *vr* to become proud.

inorridíre *vt* to horrify; *vi* be horrified.

inosservànte *a* unobservant.

inospitàle, inòspite *a* inhospitable.

inosservànza *nf* non-observance.

inosservàto *a* unobserved.

inossidàbile *a* rustless; **acciàio i.** stainless steel.

inquadràre *vt* to frame; arrange; set.

inquietànte *a* disquieting.

inquietàre *vt* to worry, alarm; **-rsi** *vr* to get angry.

inquietézza *nf* uneasiness.

inquièto *a* restless, uneasy, anxious.

inquietúdine *nf* restlessness, uneasiness, apprehension.

inquilíno *nm* tenant, lodger.

inquinaménto *nm* pollution.

inquinàre *vt* to pollute.

inquirènte *a* inquiring, investigating.

inquisíre *vt* to inquire, investigate.

inquisitóre *nm* **-trice** *nf* inquisitor; *a* inquiring.

inquisizióne *nf* inquisition.

insaccàre *vt* to put in sacks, stuff.

insaccàto *nm* sausages, salame *etc.*

insalàta *nf* salad.

insalatièra *nf* salad-bowl.

insalúbre *a* unhealthy.

insalubrità *nf* unhealthiness.

insanàbile *a* incurable.

insanguinàre *vt* to cover with blood.

insanguinàto *a* blood-stained.

insània *nf* insanity.

insàno *a* insane, crazy.

insaponàre *vt* to lather, soap.

insapúta, all' (di) *ad* unknown (to).

insaziàbile *a* insatiable.

inscatolàre *vt* to tin, can.

inscenàre *vt* to stage (*also fig*).

inscindíbile *a* inseparable.

inscrutàbile *a* inscrutable.

insediàre *vt* to install; **-rsi** *vr* to take up office, take possession.

inségna *nf* insignia *pl*, badge; colours *pl*, flag; signboard.

insegnaménto *nm* teaching, tuition.

insegnànte *a* teaching; *nmf* teacher; **còrpo i.** teaching staff.

insegnàre *vt* to teach.

inseguiménto *nm* chase, pursuit.

inseguíre *vt* to pursue, run after.

inselvatichíre *vt* to make wild; *vi* to grow wild.

insenatúra *nf* inlet.

insensatézza *nf* senselessness, foolishness.

insensàto *a* senseless, foolish.

insensíbile *a* insensible, unfeeling.

insensibilménte *ad* imperceptibly, unfeelingly.

insensibilità *nf* hard-heartedness, insensibility.

inseparàbile *a* inseparable.

inseriménto *nm* insertion.

inseríre *vt* to insert.

inservíbile *a* useless.

inserzióne *nf* inserting, insertion, advertisement.

inserzionísta *nmf* advertiser.

insetticída *a* insecticidal; *nm* insecticide.

insètto *nm* insect, (US) bug.

insídia *nf* ambush, snare.

insidiàre *vti* to lay snares for, make an attempt on.

insidióso *a* insidious.

insième *nm* whole; *ad* together, at the same time.

insígne *a* famous, notorious.

insignificànte *a* insignificant.

insigníre *vt* to decorate, confer (on).

insincerità *nf* insincerity.

insincèro *a* insincere.

insindacàbile *a* that cannot be criticized.

insinuàre *vt* to insinuate, suggest; **-rsi** *vr* to creep into, penetrate.

insinuazióne *nf* insinuation, suggestion.

insípido *a* insipid, tasteless.

insipiènza *nf* foolishness, ignorance.

insistènte *a* insistent, pressing, urgent.

insistènza *nf* insistence.

insistere *vi* to insist.

ínsito *a* inherent.

insoddisfàtto *a* dissatisfied.

insoddisfazióne *nf* dissatisfaction.

insofferènte *a* intolerant, impatient.

insofferènza *nf* intolerance, impatience.

insolazióne *nf* sunstroke.

insolènte *a* insolent, pert.

insolentíre *vti* to abuse, speak insolently.

insolènza *nf* insolence, pertness.

insòlito *a* unusual.

insolúbile *a* insoluble.

insolúto *a* unsolved, outstanding.

insolvènte *a* insolvent.

insolvènza *nf* insolvency.

insolvíbile *a* unpayable; insolvent.

insómma *ad* in conclusion, in short; *interj* well!

insondàbile *a* unfathomable.

insònne *a* sleepless.

insònnia *nf* insomnia, sleeplessness.
insonnolíto *a* sleepy, drowsy.
insopportàbile *a* insupportable, unbearable.
insórgere *vi* to rebel, rise, arise.
insorgiménto *nm* uprising.
insormontàbile *a* insurmountable.
insórto *nm* rebel, rioter.
insospettàbile *a* beyond suspicion.
insospettàto *a* unsuspected, unexpected.
insospettíre *vt* to make suspicious; **-rsi** *vr* to grow suspicious.
insostenìbile *a* untenable.
insozzàre *vt* to soil, sully.
insperàbile *a* beyond hope.
insperataménte *ad* unexpectedly.
insperàto *a* unhoped-for.
inspiegàbile *a* inexplicable.
inspiràre *vt* to inhale; inspire.
instàbile *a* unstable, variable.
instabilità *nf* instability, variability.
installàre *vt* to install; **-rsi** *vr* to install oneself, settle.
installazióne *nf* installation.
instancàbile *a* untiring, indefatigable, tireless.
instauràre *vt* to set up, establish.
instaurazióne *nf* establishment, foundation.
instillàre *vt* to instil.
instradàre *vt* to set on the right road.
insù *ad* up(wards).
insubordinàto *a* insubordinate.
insubordinazióne *nf* insubordination.
insuccèsso *nm* failure.
insudiciàre *vt* to soil, dirty.
insufficiènte *a* insufficient, inadequate.
insufficiènza *nf* insufficiency.
insulàre *a* insular.
insulína *nf* insulin.
insulsàggine *nf* dullness, foolishness.
insúlso *a* dull, foolish.
insultàre *vt* to abuse, insult.
insúlto *nm* insult, affront; (*med*) attack, stroke.
insuperàbile *a* insuperable.
insuperbíre *vt* to make proud; **-rsi** *vr* to grow proud.
insurrezionàle *a* insurrectionary.
insurrezióne *nf* insurrection, rising.
insussistènte *a* non-existent.
insussistènza *nf* non-existence.
intaccàre *vt* to notch; corrode; injure; begin spending.
intagliàre *vt* to engrave, carve.
intagliatóre *nm* engraver, carver.
intàglio *nm* intaglio, carving.
intangíbile *a* intangible.
intànto *ad* meanwhile; **i. che** *cj* while.
intarsiàre *vt* to inlay.
intàrsio *nm* inlay.
intasàre *vt* to choke, obstruct, stop up; **-rsi** *vr* to get stopped up.
intascàre *vt* to pocket.
intàtto *a* intact, uninjured, unsullied.

intavolàre *vt* to board up; put on a board; begin.
integèrrimo *a* honest, upright.
integràle *a* integral; **pàne i.** wholemeal bread.
integràre *vt* to complete, integrate.
integrazióne *nf* integration.
integrità *nf* integrity, uprightness.
íntegro *a* honest, upright, integral.
intelaiatúra *nf* framework, framing.
intellètto *nm* intellect, mind.
intellettuàle *a* intellectual.
intelligènte *a* intelligent, clever.
intelligènza *nf* intelligence, cleverness, knowledge, understanding.
intelligìbile *a* intelligible, comprehensible.
intemeràta *nf* reproof, tirade.
intemeràto *a* irreproachable.
intemperànte *a* intemperate.
intemperànza *nf* intemperance.
intempèrie *nf pl* inclement weather.
intempestívo *a* unseasonable, untimely.
intèndere *vt* to hear; intend, mean; understand; **-rsi** *vr* to be a good judge of; come to an agreement with; understand (each other).
intendiménto *nm* understanding; intention, purpose.
intenditóre *nm* connoisseur, judge.
inteneríre *vt* to soften, move; **-rsi** *vr* to be moved, feel compassion.
intensaménte *ad* intensely.
intensificàre *vt* to intensify, make more frequent.
intensità *nf* intensity.
intensívo *a* intensive.
intènso *a* intense, violent.
intentàre *vt* (*leg*) to bring (an action).
intènto *a* intent; *nm* aim, intent(ion), purpose.
intenzionàle *a* intentional.
intenzióne *nf* intention, wish.
interaménte *ad* entirely, completely.
intercalàre *vt* to insert; *nm* refrain; pet phrase.
intercèdere *vi* to intercede; (*of distance etc*) exist, intervene.
intercessióne *nf* intercession.
intercettàre *vt* to intercept.
intercettazióne *nf* interception.
intercomunàle *nf* (*tel*) trunk call, long-distance call.
intercomunicànte *a* intercommunicating, communicating.
intercórrere *vi* to elapse, pass, happen.
interdétto *a* interdicted, prohibited, disqualified; disconcerted; *nm* interdict.
interdíre *vt* to forbid, interdict, disqualify.
interdizióne *nf* interdiction, disqualification.
interessaménto *nm* interest, concern.
interessànte *a* interesting.
interessàre *vti* to interest, matter; **-rsi** *vr* to take an interest, care.

interessàto *a* interested; *nm* interested party.

interèsse *nm* interest.

interessènza *nf* (*com*) co-interest.

interézza *nf* entirety, integrity.

interferènza *nf* interference.

interferíre *vi* to interfere.

interinàle *a* interim, temporary.

interino *a* provisional.

interióra *nf pl* entrails *pl*, intestines *pl*.

interióre *a* inner; *nm* interior, inside.

interlineàre *vt* to interline; *a* interlinear.

interlocutóre *nm* **-tríce** *nf* interlocutor.

interloquíre *vi* to put in a word, speak.

interlúdio *nm* interlude.

intermediàrio *a* intermediary; *nm* mediator, (*com*) middleman, go-between.

intermèzzo *nm* interval, intermezzo.

interminàbile *a* interminable, endless.

intermissióne *nf* intermission.

intermittènte *a* intermittent.

intermittènza *nf* intermittence.

internaménte *ad* internally, inwardly.

internàre *vt* to intern; **-rsi** *vr* to enter into, penetrate.

internàto *a* interned; *nm* internee; boarding-school.

internazionàle *a* international.

intèrno *a* internal, interior, inner, inside; *nm* interior, inside; **Ministéro degli Intèrni** Home Office.

intéro *a* entire, whole; honest; *nm* whole.

interpellànza *nf* interpellation.

interpellàre *vt* to interpellate, ask.

interpolàre *vt* to interpolate, insert.

interpórre *vt* **-rsi** *vr* to interpose, intervene.

interposizióne *nf* interposition, intervention.

interpretàre *vt* to interpret, construe.

interpretazióne *nf* interpretation.

intèrprete *nmf* interpreter.

interpunzióne *nf* punctuation.

interraménto *nm* interment, burial.

interràre *vt* to bury, inter; fill with earth.

interrogàre *vt* to interrogate, question, consult, examine; **i. con contradittòrio** cross-examine.

interrogatívo *a* interrogative, questioning; *nm* question.

interrogatòrio *nm* interrogation, (cross-)examination.

interrogazióne *nf* interrogation, question.

interrómpere *vt* to interrupt, break (off); **-rsi** *vr* to stop.

interrótto *a* interrupted, cut off; (*of road*) blocked.

interruttóre *nm* interrupter, (*el*) switch.

interruzióne *nf* interruption.

intersecàre *vt* to intersect.

interurbàno *a* telefonàta interurbàna trunk-call.

intervàllo *nm* interval, space.

interveníre *vi* to intervene, interfere; be present; happen.

intervènto *nm* intervention, interference; presence; (*surgical*) operation.

intervenúto *a* present; *nm* person present.

intervísta *nf* interview.

intervistàre *vt* to interview.

intésa *nf* agreement, understanding.

intéso *a* understood, agreed upon; aiming at.

intèssere *vt* to weave.

intestàre *vt* to enter; head; register; **-rsi** *vr* to be obstinate.

intestàto *a* headed; (*com*) registered; stubborn; intestate.

intestazióne *nf* heading, title, headline.

intestinàle *a* intestinal.

intestíno *a* domestic, internal, civil; *nm* intestine.

intiepidíre *vt* to make lukewarm, warm (up); cool, abate; **-rsi** *vr* to cool down; warm up.

intiéro *v* **intéro.**

intimaménte *ad* intimately, deeply.

intimàre *vt* to intimate, order, notify, enjoin.

intimazióne *nf* order, summons, notification.

intimidazióne *nf* intimidation.

intimidíre *vt* to intimidate; **-rsi** *vr* to become shy, get frightened.

intimità *nf* intimacy, familiarity.

íntimo *a* intimate; inner, deep; private; *nm* intimate friend; heart, depth.

intimoríre *vt* to frighten.

intíngere *vt* to dip.

intíngolo *nm* tasty dish, sauce, gravy.

intirizzíre *vt* to (be)numb, stiffen; **-rsi** *vr* to get benumbed.

intisichíre *vi* to grow consumptive.

intitolàre *vt* to entitle; dedicate.

intitolazióne *nf* entitling, title; dedication.

intolleràbile *a* intolerable.

intollerànte *a* intolerant.

intollerànza *nf* intolerance.

intonacàre *vt* to plaster, whitewash, distemper.

intònaco *pl* **-chi** *nm* plaster, whitewash, distemper.

intonàre *vt* to intone; strike up; **-rsi** *vr* to be in tune (harmony) with, tone with.

intonàto *a* in tune, matching.

intonazióne *nf* intonation, tone.

intònso *a* uncut, unshaven, unshorn.

intontiménto *nm* stupor, daze.

intontíre *vt* to stun, daze; **-rsi** *vr* to be stunned, become dazed.

intòppo *nm* hindrance, obstacle,

hitch; **i. stradàle** (traffic) hold up, (US) tie-up.

intorbidàre vt to make turbid, confuse, trouble; **-rsi** vr to become turbid, troubled, grow dim.

intórno ad **i. a** prep around, round, about.

intorpidíre vt to benumb; **vi -rsi** vr to grow numb.

intossicàre vt to poison.

intossicazióne nf poisoning.

intraducíbile a untranslatable.

intralciàre vt to hinder, interfere with, obstruct.

intràlcio nm hindrance, obstruction.

intrallàzzo nm plotting, swindle; black market.

intraméttere v **introméttere.**

intramezzàre vt to interpose, alternate.

intramuscolàre a intermuscular.

intransigènte a intransigent, uncompromising, unmoved.

intransigènza nf intransigence.

intransitívo a nm intransitive.

intraprendènte a enterprising.

intraprendènza nf enterprise.

intraprèndere vt to undertake, venture on.

intrattàbile a intractable.

intrattenére vt to entertain; **-rsi** vr to linger, stop, dwell upon.

intratteniménto nm entertainment.

intrav(v)edére vt to catch a glimpse; have a hazy notion; foresee.

intrecciàre vt to entwine, interlace, plait.

intréccio nm interlacing; (of a play) plot.

intrepidézza, **intrepidità** nf intrepidity, bravery.

intrèpido a fearless, intrepid.

intricàto a intricate, tangled, complicated.

intrigànte a intriguing; nmf intriguer.

intrigàre vi to intrigue; vt to entangle; **-rsi** vr to meddle.

intrígo nm intrigue.

intrínseco pl **-ci** a intrinsic.

intríso a soaked; nm mash, mixture.

intristíre vt to decay, pine away, wilt; grow wicked.

introdúrre vt to introduce, show in; import; **-rsi** vr to get in, introduce oneself.

introduzióne nf introduction.

introitàre vt (com) to cash, get in.

intròito nm (eccl) introit, (com) returns pl, revenue.

intromésso a interposed, introduced, inserted.

introméttere vt to interpose, introduce, insert; **-rsi** vr to intervene, intrude, meddle.

intromissióne nf intervention, intrusion.

intronàre vt to deafen, stun.

introspettívo a introspective.

introspezióne a introspection.

introvàbile a not to be found.

introvèrso a introverted; nm introvert.

intrúglio nm hotch-potch, bad concoction, mess.

intrusióne nf intrusion.

intrúso nm intruder.

intuíre vt to perceive by intuition.

intúito nm **intuizióne** nf intuition.

inuguàle etc v **ineguàle** etc.

inumanità nf inhumanity.

inumàno a inhuman, cruel.

inumàre vt to inhume, inter.

inumidíre vt to moisten, damp.

inurbanità nf incivility.

inurbàno a uncivil, rude.

inusàto a unusual, obsolete.

inusitàto a unusual, obsolete.

inútile a useless, unnecessary.

inutilità nf uselessness.

inutilmènte ad uselessly, in vain.

invadènte a intrusive; nmf intruder.

invadènza nf meddlesomeness.

invàdere vt to invade, break into.

invaghírsi vr to fall in love with, take a liking to.

invalidàre vt to invalidate.

invalidità nf invalidity.

invàlido a invalid, disabled; nm invalid.

invàno ad in vain, vainly.

invariàbile a invariable, unchangeable.

invariàto a unvaried, unchanged.

invasaménto nm obsession, excitement, infatuation.

invasàre vt to obsess, haunt; put in vases.

invasióne nf invasion.

invasóre, f **invaditríce** a invading; nm invader.

invecchiàre vti to make old, grow old; **-rsi** vr to make oneself look old, claim to be older than one is.

invéce ad instead, on the contrary; **i. di** prep instead of.

inveíre vi to inveigh, rail.

inventàre vt to invent.

inventàrio nm inventory.

inventíva nf inventiveness.

inventóre nm **-tríce** nf inventor.

invenzióne nf invention.

inverdíre vi to grow green.

inverecóndia nf immodesty.

inverecóndo a immodest.

invernàle a winter, wintry.

inverniciàre vt to varnish.

inverniciatúra nf varnishing.

invèrno nm winter.

invéro ad really, truly.

inverosimiglianza nf unlikelihood.

inverosímile a unlikely, improbable.

inversióne nf inversion.

invèrso a inverse, opposite, contrary.

invertebràto a invertebrate.

invertíre vt to invert, reverse.

invertíto a inverted; nm invert.

investigàre vt to inquire into, investigate.

investigazióne nf inquiry, investigation.

investiménto *nm* investment; collision.

investíre *vt* to collide with; attack; invest, appoint; -rsi *vr* to take a deep interest in; collide.

invetriàta *nf* pane of glass.

invettíva *nf* invective.

inviàre *vt* to send.

inviàto *nm* messenger, representative, envoy, correspondent.

invídia *nf* envy.

invidiàre *vt* to envy.

invidióso *a* envious.

invigilàre *vt* to watch (over).

invigoríre *vt* to invigorate, strengthen; -rsi *vr* to grow stronger.

inviluppàre *vt* to envelop, hide; -rsi *vr* to wrap oneself up.

invincíbile *a* invincible.

invío *nm* sending, dispatch.

inviolàbile *a* inviolable.

invisíbile *a* invisible.

invíso *a* disliked, hated.

invitànte *a* inviting, attractive, tempting.

invitàre *vt* to invite, ask; (*at cards*) call.

invitàto *nm* guest.

invíto *nm* call, invitation.

invítto *a* undefeated, unconquered, invincible.

invocàre *vt* to invoke, appeal to.

invocazióne *nf* invocation.

invogliàre *vt* to allure, induce, tempt.

involàre *vt* to steal; -rsi *vr* to elope, run away.

invòlgere *vt* to wrap up, envelop, involve.

involontàrio *a* involuntary.

involtàre *vt* to wrap up, pack up.

invòlto *pp of* invòlgere; *nm* bundle, parcel.

invòlucro *nm* covering, envelope.

invulneràbile *a* invulnerable.

inzuccheràre *vt* to sugar.

inzuppàre *vt* to dip, drench, soak.

ío *pron* I.

iòdio *nm* iodine.

iònico *pl* -ici *a* Ionic.

iònio *a* Ionian; l'Iònio *nm* (*geogr*) the Ionian Sea.

iòsa, a *ad* galore.

ipèrbole *nf* hyperbole.

ipersensíbile *a* hypersensitive.

ipertensióne *nf* (*med*) hypertension.

ipnòtico *pl* -ici *a* hypnotic.

ipnotísmo *nm* hypnotism.

ipnotizzàre *vt* to hypnotize.

ipocondría *nf* hypochondria, spleen.

ipocrisía *nf* hypocrisy, cant.

ipòcrita *nmf* hypocrite.

ipotèca *nf* mortgage.

ipotecàre *vt* to mortgage.

ipòtesi *nf* hypothesis.

ippica *nf* horse-racing.

ippico *pl* -ici *a* horse; còrse ippiche horse races.

ippocastàno *nm* horse-chestnut.

ippòdromo *nm* racecourse.

ippopòtamo *nm* hippopotamus.

íra, iracóndia *nf* anger, rage, wrath.

iracóndo *a* irascible, choleric.

Iràk *nm* (*geogr*) Irak, Iraq.

Iràn *nm* (*geogr*) Iran, Persia.

iraniàno *a nm* Iranian, Persian.

irascíbile *a* irascible, irritable, hot-tempered.

irascibilità *nf* irascibility.

iràto *a* angry, in a rage.

Irène *nf pr* Irene, Eirene.

íride *nf* iris; rainbow.

iridescènte *a* iridescent.

Irlànda *nf* (*geogr*) Ireland.

irlandése *a* Irish; *nm* Irishman, (*language*) Irish; *nf* Irishwoman.

Irma *nf pr* Irma.

ironía *nf* irony.

irònico *pl* -ici *a* ironic(al).

iróso *a* angry.

irradiàre *vti* to (ir)radiate.

irradiazióne *nf* irradiation, fall-out.

irragionévole *a* irrational, unreasonable, absurd.

irragionevolézza *nf* unreasonableness, unfairness.

irrazionàle *a* irrational.

irrazionalità *nf* irrationality.

irreàle *a* unreal.

irrealtà *nf* unreality.

irreconciliàbile *a* irreconcilable.

irrecuperàbile *a* irrecoverable.

irredènto *a* unredeemed.

irredimíbile *a* irredeemable.

irrefutàbile *a* irrefutable.

irregolàre *a* abnormal, irregular.

irregolarità *nf* irregularity.

irreligióso *a* irreligious.

irremissíbile *a* impossible to remit.

irremovíbile *a* irremovable, inflexible.

irreparàbile *a* irreparable.

irreperíbile *a* that cannot be found.

irreprensíbile *a* faultless, irreproachable.

irrequietézza *nf* restlessness.

irrequièto *a* restless.

irresistíbile *a* irresistible.

irresolutézza *nf* irresolution, indecision.

irresolúto *a* hesitant, irresolute.

irresponsàbile *a* irresponsible.

irreversíbile *a* irreversible; direzióne i. (*aut*) irreversible steering.

irrevocàbile *a* irrevocable.

irriconoscíbile *a* unrecognisable.

irrídere *vt* to deride, laugh at.

irriducíbile *a* irreducible.

irriflessivo *a* thoughtless.

irrigàbile *a* irrigable.

irrigàre *vt* to irrigate.

irrigazióne *nf* irrigation.

irrigidiménto *nm* stiffening.

irrigidíre *vt* to make stiff; -rsi *vr* to grow (stand) stiff.

irríguo *a* well-watered.

irrilevànte *a* insignificant.

irrimediàbile *a* irremediable.

irrisióne *nf* derision, mockery.

irrisòrio *a* derisory; paltry.

irrispettóso *a* disrespectful.

irritàbile *a* irritable; *(of skin)* sensitive.

irritabilità *nf* irritability; *(of skin)* sensitiveness.

irritànte *a* irritating.

irritàre *vt* to irritate, inflame; **-rsi** *vr* to become angry, inflamed.

irritazióne *nf* irritation, inflammation.

irriverènte *a* irreverent.

irriverènza *nf* irreverence.

irrobustíre *vt* to strengthen; **-rsi** *vr* to grow strong(er).

irrómpere *vi* to break into; swarm; overflow.

irruènte *a* impetuous.

irruènza *nf* impetuosity.

irrugginíre *vti* to make (grow) rusty.

irruzióne *nf* irruption.

irsúto *a* hairy, shaggy.

irto *a* bristling, bushy, shaggy.

Isabèlla *nf pr* Isabella, Isabel.

Isàcco *nm pr* Isaac.

iscrìtto *a* enrolled, entered, registered, inscribed.

iscrívere *vt* to enrol, register, inscribe; **-rsi** *vr* to enter (for).

iscrizióne *nf* inscription, enrolment, matriculation, entry, membership.

Islàm *nm* Islam.

islàmico *pl* **-ici** *a* Islamic.

islamísmo *nm* Islamism.

Islànda *nf (geogr)* Iceland.

islandése *a* Icelandic; *nm* Icelander, Icelandic (language).

ìsola *nf* island, isle.

isolaménto *nm* isolation; *(el)* insulation.

isolàno *a* insular; *nm* islander.

isolànte *a (el)* insulating; *nm* insulator.

isolàre *vt* to isolate; insulate; **-rsi** *vr* to shun society.

isolatóre *nm (el)* insulator.

Isòtta *nf pr* Isolde.

ispanísmo *nm* Hispanicism.

ispettoràto *nm* inspector's office, inspectorate.

ispettóre *nm* **-trice** *nf* inspector.

ispezionàre *vt* to inspect.

ispezióne *nf* inspection.

íspido *a* bristling, rough, shaggy.

ispiràre *vt* to inspire, instil, infuse into; **-rsi** *vr* to draw inspiration.

ispirazióne *nf* inspiration.

Isràèle *nm (geogr)* Israel.

israeliàno *a nm* Israeli.

israelíta *a nmf* Israelite, Jew, Jewess.

israelítico *pl* **-ici** *a* Israelite, Jewish.

issàre *vt* to hoist.

istantànea *nf* snapshot.

istantàneo *a* instantaneous, instant.

istànte *a* instant, pressing; *nm* moment; petitioner.

istànza *nf* request, application, petition.

istèrico *pl* **-ici** *a* hysteric(al).

isterísmo *nm* hysteria, hysterics *pl*.

istésso *v* stesso.

istigàre *vt* to instigate.

istigazióne *nf* instigation.

istintívo *a* instinctive.

istínto *nm* instinct.

istituíre *vt* to institute, found, appoint.

istitúto *nm* institute, school, bank.

istitutóre *nm* **-trice** *nf* founder; tutor, governess.

istituzióne *nf* institution, establishment.

ístmo *nm* isthmus.

istoriàre *vt* to adorn with figures, illustrate.

Ístria *nf (geogr)* Istria; istriàno *a nm* Istrian.

ístrice *nf* porcupine.

istrióne *nm* bad actor, charlatan.

istriònico *pl* **-ici** *a* histrionic.

istruíre *vt* to instruct, teach, inform; **-rsi** *vr* to acquire knowledge, learn.

istruíto *a* educated, well-read.

istrumentàle *a* instrumental.

istruménto *nm* instrument.

istruttívo *a* instructive.

istruttóre *nm* **-trice** *nf* instructor, teacher; **giúdice i.** examining magistrate.

istruttòria *nf* examination, investigation.

istruttòrio *a* preliminary.

istruzióne *nf* education, instruction, learning, order, teaching; **ministèro della Púbblica I.** *nm* Ministry of Education.

istupidíre *vt* to make stupid; *vi* to become stupid.

Itàlia *nf (geogr)* Italy.

italianaménte *ad* after the Italian fashion, in the Italian way.

italianità *nf* Italian feelings, Italian nationality.

Italiàno *a nm* Italian.

itàlico *pl* **-ici** *a nm* Italic, Italian; *(typ)* italics.

iteràre *vt* to iterate, repeat.

iterazióne *nf* iteration, repetition.

itineràrio *nm* itinerary, route.

itterízia *nf (med)* jaundice.

Iugoslàvia *nf (geogr)* Jugoslavia.

iugoslàvo *a nm* Jugoslav.

iunior, iunióre *a* junior.

iúngla *nf* jungle.

iúta *nf* jute.

Iútland *nm (geogr)* Jutland.

ivì *ad* there, therein.

L

la *def art f* the; *pron f (acc)* her, it, *(mus)* la.

là *ad* there; **al di là (di)** *ad and prep* beyond.

làbbro *nm*, *pl m* làbbri, *f* làbbra

lip; i **làbbri di una ferita** the lips of a wound; **mòrdersi le làbbra** to bite one's lips.

làbile *a* fleeting, ephemeral, weak.

labirínto *nm* labyrinth, maze.

laboratòrio *nm* laboratory, workroom.

laboriosità *nf* laboriousness, industry.

laborióso *a* laborious, industrious, hard-working; difficult.

laburísmo *nm* Labourism.

laburísta *a* Labour; *nmf* Labour Party member.

làcca *nf* lacquer.

laccàre *vt* to lacquer, enamel.

lacchè *nm* lackey.

làccio *nm* shoelace, string, snare, noose.

lacerànte *a* tearing, rendin

laceràre *v* to lacerate, rend, tear (up); **-rsi** *vr* to tear, get torn.

lacerazióne *nf* laceration, rent.

làcero *a* in rags, rent, torn.

lacònico *pl* **-ici** *a* laconic.

laconísmo *nm* laconism.

làcrima, làgrima *nf* tear; **scoppiàre in làcrime** *vi* to burst into tears.

lacrimàre *vi* to cry, weep, shed tears; water.

lacrimàto *a* lamented, regretted.

lacrimévole *a* tearful.

lacrimògeno *a* lachrymatory.

lacrimóso *a* lachrymose, tearful, weeping.

lacúna *nf* lacuna, blank, gap.

làdro *a* bewitching, thieving; *nm* thief.

ladróne *nm* robber, highwayman.

ladronería *nf* robbery.

laggiú *ad* down there, there below, over there.

lagnànza *nf* complaint.

lagnàrsi *vr* to complain.

làgo *pl* **-ghi** *nm* lake, pool.

làgrima *v* **làcrima**.

lagúna *nf* lagoon.

laicàto *nm* laity.

làico *pl* **-ici** *a* lay; *nm* layman.

laidézza *nf* foulness, obscenity.

làido *a* dirty, foul, obscene.

làma *nf* blade; *nm* (*priest*) Lama; (*zool*) llama.

lambiccàre *vt* to distil; **-rsi il cervèllo** *vr* to cudgel one's brains.

lambícco *pl* **-chi** *nm* still, alembic.

lambíre *vt* to lap, touch lightly.

lamentàre *vt* to lament, mourn, regret; **-rsi** *vr* to complain, mourn.

lamentazióne *nf* lamentation.

laménto *nm* lament, mourning, complaint.

lamentóso *a* mournful, plaintive.

lamièra *nf* plate, sheet iron.

làmina *nf* blade, thin plate (of metal).

laminàto *a* (*metal*) rolled.

laminatóio *nm* rolling-mill.

làmpada *nf* lamp; **l. ad àrco** arc-lamp.

lampadàrio *nm* chandelier, electric-light pendant.

lampadína *nf* (electric) bulb, small lamp; **l. elèttrica (tascàbile)** torch; (*US*) flashlight.

lampànte *a* clear, obvious.

lampeggiaménto *nm* lightning; flashing.

lampeggiànte *a* flashing.

lampeggiàre *vi* to lighten; flash.

lampionàio *nm* lamp-lighter.

lampioncíno *nm* Chinese lantern, fairylight.

lampióne *nm* street-lamp.

làmpo *nm* lightning, flash; **chiusúra l.** zip fastener, (*US*) zipper.

lampóne *nm* raspberry.

lamprèda *nf* lamprey.

làna *nf* wool; **l. di vétro** (*ind*) fibre glass; **di l.** wool(len).

lanaiuòlo *nm* wool-comber, wool-worker.

lancétta *nf* (*of watch or clock*) hand; lancet.

lància *nf* lance; (*naut*) launch.

lanciabómbe *nm* trench-mortar.

lanciafiàmme *nm* flamethrower.

lanciàre *vt* to throw, launch; **-rsi** *vr* to fling (launch) oneself.

lanciasilúri *nm* torpedo-tube.

lancière *nm* lancer.

làncio *nm* throwing, launching.

lànda *nf* heath, moor.

lanería *nf* woollens *pl*, woollen goods *pl*.

languènte *a* languishing, pining, drooping.

languidaménte *ad* languidly, languorously.

languidézza *nf* languidness.

lànguido *a* languid, weak; (*of light*) faint.

languíre *vi* to languish, pine; (*of light*) fade.

languóre *nm* languor, weakness, faintness.

lanièro *a* woollen, wool; **commèrcio l.** wool trade.

lanifício *nm* wool factory.

lanóso *a* woolly.

lantèrna *nf* lantern, skylight; **l. di sicurézza** safety-lamp.

lanúgine *nf* down (on the skin).

lapidàre *vt* to stone.

lapidàrio *a nm* lapidary.

lapidazióne *nf* stoning.

làpide *nf* memorial tablet, tomb-stone.

làpin *French nm* cony, cony (skin).

làpis *nm* pencil.

lapislàzzuli *nm* lapis-lazuli.

lappóne *a* Lapp; *nm* (*language*) Lapp(ish); *nmf* Lapp, Laplander.

Lappònia *nf* (*geogr*) Lapland.

làrdo *nm* bacon.

largaménte *ad* largely, abundantly, at length, extensively.

largheggiàre *vi* to be generous, lavish.

larghèzza *nf* breadth, width; **l. di**

mèzzi wealth; **l. di vedúte** broad-mindedness.

largíre vt to give liberally.

largizióne nf donation, gift.

làrgo pl **làrghi** a broad, wide, large, generous; nm breadth, width; **fàrsi l.** to make a way for oneself.

làrice nm larch.

larínge nf larynx.

laringíte nf (med) laryngitis.

làrva nf larva, phantom, sham.

larvataménte ad by innuendo.

larvàto a hidden, latent.

làsca pl **-che** nf roach.

lasciapassàre nm pass, permit.

lasciàre vt to abandon, desert, leave (out), let, permit, quit; **l. cadére** to drop; **l. stàre** to let alone; **-rsi** vr to allow (let) oneself.

làscito nm bequest, legacy.

lascivaménte ad lasciviously, lustfully.

lascívia nf lasciviousness, wantonness.

lascívo a lascivious, wanton.

lassatívo a nm laxative.

làsso a (poet) unhappy, weary; nm (of time) lapse, period.

lassú ad up there.

làstra nf (of glass) pane, plate, slab.

lastricàre vt to pave.

làstrico pl **-chi** nm pavement; **lasciàre sul l.** to leave penniless.

latèbra nf (poet) recess, secret place.

latènte a concealed.

lateràle a side, lateral.

lateranénse a Lateran.

Lateràno a nm pr Lateran.

laterízi nm pl bricks pl.

latifondísta nm owner of large landed estate.

latifóndo nm large landed estate.

latinísta nmf Latinist, Latin scholar.

latíno a nm Latin.

latitànte a absconding; **rèndersi l.** to abscond.

latitúdine nf latitude.

làto nm side; **a l. di** beside; **dal l. mío** for my part.

latóre nm **-tríce** nf bearer.

latraménto nm barking.

latràre vi to bark.

latràto nm bark, barking.

latrína nf latrine, lavatory, w.c.

làtta nf tin, can; tin plate.

lattàio nm milkman.

lattànte a breast-fed; nm child at the breast, suckling.

làtte nm milk.

lattemièle nm whipped cream.

làtteo a milky.

latterìa nf (farm or shop) dairy.

latticínio nm dairy product.

lattièra nf milk-jug, milk-pot, cream-jug, (US) creamer.

lattivéndola nf milk-woman; **lattivéndolo** nm milkman.

lattonière nm tinsmith.

lattòsio nm (chem) lactose.

lattúga nf lettuce.

làuda, làude nf laud, hymn of praise, early religious lyric.

làudano nm laudanum.

Làura nf pr Laura.

làurea nf (university) degree.

laureàndo a nm final-year undergraduate.

laureàre vt to confer a degree on; **-rsi** vr to take one's degree.

laureàto a nm graduate.

làuro nm laurel.

lautaménte ad sumptuously, magnificently.

lautézza nf magnificence, sumptuousness.

làuto a magnificent, sumptuous, abundant.

làva nf lava.

lavabiancherìa nf washing machine.

lavàbile a washable.

lavàbo nm wash-basin, (eccl) lavabo.

lavàcro nm (liter) bath, font.

lavàggio nm washing; **l. a sècco** dry cleaning.

lavàgna nf slate, blackboard.

lavamàno nm wash-hand basin.

lavànda nf lavender; washing.

lavandàia nf laundress, washerwoman; **lavandàio** nm laundryman.

lavanderìa nf laundry; **l. automàtica** launderette.

lavandíno nm sink.

lavapiàtti a dish-washing; nmf dishwasher, scullery-boy, scullery-maid.

lavàre vt **-rsi** vr to wash; **l. a sècco** to dry-clean.

lavàta nf wash; (fig) dressing-down, reprimand.

lavatívo nm enema; (vulg) tiresome person, bore.

lavatóio nm wash-house, washboard.

lavatríce nf washerwoman; washing machine.

lavatúra nf washing; **l. a sècco** dry cleaning.

lavorànte nm workman; nf workwoman.

lavoràre vti to work, labour, till.

lavoratívo a working; **giórno l.** working day, weekday.

lavoràto a worked, processed, manufactured, tilled.

lavoratóre nm **-tríce** nf worker; a working.

lavorazióne nf manufacture, working, workmanship, tilling.

lavorìo nm intense activity, intrigue.

lavóro nm work, labour, toil, job; (theat) play.

Làzio nm (geogr) Latium.

Làzzaro nm pr Lazarus.

lazzaróne nm (Neapolitan) beggar; rogue, idler.

le def art f pl the; pron acc f pl them; pron dat f to her.

leàle a loyal, faithful, true, fair.

lealmènte ad loyally, faithfully, fairly.

lealtà nf loyalty, faithfulness, fairness.

lèbbra nf leprosy.

lebbróso a leprous; nm leper.

leccàrda nf dripping-pan.

leccàre vt to lick.

leccàto a affected; **stile l.** affected style.

léccio nm holm-oak.

leccornìa nf dainty, titbit.

lécito a lawful, allowed, right.

lèdere vt to offend, harm, injure.

léga nf league, union, alloy.

legàccio nm string, (of shoes, boots) lace.

legàle a legal, lawful; nm lawyer.

legalità nf legality, lawfulness.

legalizzàre vt to legalize, authenticate.

legalizzazióne nf legalization, authentication.

legalménte ad legally, lawfully.

legàme nm bond, connection, link, tie.

legaménto nm (anat) ligament; binding, linking, connecting.

legàre vt to bind, fasten, alloy, bequeath.

legatàrio nm legatee.

legàto nm ambassador, legate; legacy.

legatóre nm **-trice** nf (book)binder; (leg) testator.

legatorìa nf (book)binder's.

legatùra nf binding, fastening, ligature.

legazióne nf legation.

légge nf law, (of parliament) act.

leggènda nf legend.

leggendàrio a legendary.

lèggere vt to read.

leggerézza nf lightness, nimbleness; levity, thoughtlessness.

leggerménte ad lightly; thoughtlessly.

leggéro, leggièro a light, slight, nimble, thoughtless, frivolous; **péso l.** (boxing) lightweight; **alla leggèra** ad lightly, thoughtlessly; **prèndere alla leggéra** vt to make light of.

leggiadrìa nf prettiness, grace, gracefulness.

leggiàdro a graceful, charming.

leggìbile a legible, readable.

leggìo nm reading-desk, music-stand, lectern.

legióne nf legion.

legislatùra nf legislature.

legislazióne nf legislation.

legittimaménte ad legitimately, lawfully.

legittimità nf lawfulness, legitimacy.

legìttimo a lawful, legitimate.

légna pl **légna** nf wood, firewood; **portàre l. alla sélva** vi to carry coals to Newcastle.

legnai(u)òlo nm woodcutter, joiner, carpenter.

legnàme nm timber, (US) lumber.

legnàta nf blow with a cudgel.

légno nm wood, stick; **di l.** wooden;

l. ricostituìto chipboard; **lavóro in l.** woodwork.

legnóso a woody.

legùme nm vegetable.

lèi pron nom and acc f she, her; you (polite form m and f).

Lèida nf (geogr) Leyden.

lémbo nm edge, hem, strip.

léna nf breath, energy; **di buòna l.** willingly.

Leningràdo nf (geogr) Leningrad.

lenìre vt to soften, soothe.

lenitìvo a lenitive, palliative.

lenocìnio nm pandering; (fig) artifice.

lenóne nm pander, procurer.

lentaménte ad slowly.

lènte nf lentil; lens.

lentézza nf slowness, sluggishness.

lentìcchia nf lentil.

lentìggine nf freckle.

lentigginóso a freckled.

lènto a slow, sluggish; loose.

lènza nf fishing-line, line.

lenzuòlo nm pl **-òla** f (bed)sheet.

Leonàrdo nm pr Leonard.

Leóne nm pr Leo, Leon.

leóne nm lion; **leonéssa** nf lioness.

leopàrdo nm leopard.

Leopòldo nm pr Leopold.

lepidézza nf witticism.

lèpido a witty.

Lepontìne, Àlpi nf pl (geogr) Lepontine Alps.

lèpre nf hare.

lércio a dirty, filthy, foul.

lésina nf awl.

lesinàre vi to be stingy; **l. sul prèzzo** to haggle over the price.

lesióne nf lesion, wound, injury.

léso a hurt, injured, offended.

lessàre vt to boil.

lèssico pl **-ici** nm lexicon.

lessicògrafo nm lexicographer.

lésso a boiled; nm boiled meat.

lestaménte ad quickly, hastily.

lestézza nf agility, quickness, swiftness.

lèsto a agile, quick, swift; ad quickly.

lestofànte nm swindler.

letàle a deadly, lethal.

letamàio nm dung-heap, hovel.

letàme nm dung.

letargìa nf **letàrgo** nm pl **-ghi** lethargy.

letàrgico pl **-ici** a lethargic.

letìzia nf gladness, joy.

léttera nf letter; **alla l.** literally; **bèlle léttere** pl Arts pl.

letteràle a literal.

letteralménte ad literally.

letteràrio a literary.

letteràto a well-read; nm man of letters.

letteratùra nf literature.

lettièra nf bedstead.

lettìga nf stretcher.

lètto nm bed.

lettóne a nmf Latvian; nm Lettish.

Lettònia nf (geogr) Latvia.

lettoràto nm lectureship.

lettóre nm **-tríce** nf reader, lecturer.
lettúra nf reading; **sàla di l.** reading-room.
leucemìa nf leukaemia.
lèva nf (mech) lever; (mil) conscription, draft; **èssere di l.** to be liable to call-up; **la l. del 1960** those called up in 1960.
levànte nm East; **vénto di l.** east wind; **il l.** the Levant.
levantíno a nm Levantine.
levàre vt to lift, raise, remove; **-rsi** vr to get out of the way, rise, take off.
levàta nf rising; (postal) collection.
levatóio a **pónte l.** drawbridge.
levatríce nf midwife.
levigàre vt to smooth.
levrière, levrièro nm greyhound.
lèzio nm **leziosàggine** nf affectation, mannerism.
lezióne nf lesson.
lezióso a affected, mincing.
lézzo nm stink, filth.
li pron m acc pl them.
lì ad there; **giù di l.** thereabouts; **l. per l.** immediately; **èssere l. l. per** to be within an ace of.
libanése a nmf Lebanese.
Líbano nm (geogr) Lebanon.
líbbra nf pound (weight).
libéccio nm southwest wind.
libèllo nm libel.
libèllula nf dragonfly.
liberàle a liberal; nm Liberal.
liberalìsmo nm liberalism.
liberalità nf liberality.
liberaménte ad freely, frankly.
liberàre vt to free, clear, exempt, release; **-rsi** vr to free oneself, get rid of.
liberazióne nf liberation.
Libèria nf (geogr) Liberia.
liberiàno a nm Liberian.
líbero a free.
libertà nf freedom, liberty.
libertinàggio nm libertinage.
libertíno a nm libertine.
Líbia nf (geogr) Libya.
líbico pl **-ici** a nm Libyan.
libìdine nf lust.
libidinóso a lustful.
líbra nf scales.
libràio nm bookseller.
libràre vt to weigh, balance.
librerìa nf bookshop, (US) book store; library; bookcase.
librétto nm (mus) libretto; small book; **l. di bànca** bank-book; **l. di circolazióne** (aut) log-book.
líbro nm book; **l. di càssa** cash-book; **l. giàllo** thriller; **l. maèstro** ledger; **l. di preghière** prayer-book.
liceàle a of a 'liceo'.
licènza nf lease, certificate, licence; dismissal.
licenziaménto nm discharge, dismissal.
licenziàre vt to discharge, dismiss; **-rsi** vr to resign; get one's diploma.

licenzióso a licentious.
licèo nm 'Liceo', secondary school.
lído nm shore, beach.
Liègi nf (geogr) Liège.
lietaménte ad happily, merrily.
lièto a glad, happy, cheerful.
lìéve a light, slight, easy.
lieveménte ad lightly, gently.
lievitàre vt to leaven; vi (of bread etc) rise.
lièvito nm yeast, leaven; **l. di bírra** yeast.
lígio a faithful, observant.
lignàggio nm lineage.
lígure a nm Ligurian.
Ligúria nf (geogr) Liguria.
lílla nf lilac; nm (colour) lilac.
Lílla nf (geogr) Lille.
lillipuziàno a nm Lilliputian.
líma nf (mech) file.
limaccióso a miry, muddy.
limàre vt to file, polish.
límbo nm Limbo.
limitàre vt to limit; nm threshold.
limitazióne nf limitation; **l. dèlle nàscite** birth-control.
límite nm boundary, limit.
limítrofo a adjacent, neighbouring.
límo nm mire, mud.
limonàta nf lemonade.
limóne nm lemon (tree).
limpidézza nf clearness, limpidness.
límpido a limpid, clear.
línce nf lynx.
linciàggio nm lynching.
linciàre vt to lynch.
líndo a clean.
línea nf line.
lineaménti nm pl features pl, lineaments pl.
lineétta nf dash, hyphen.
línfa nf lymph, sap.
linfàtico pl **-ici** a lymphatic.
lingòtto nm ingot.
língua nf tongue, language.
linguàggio nm language.
linguìsta nmf linguist.
linguìstica nf linguistics.
linguìstico pl **-ici** a linguistic.
líno nm flax, linen; **séme di l.** linseed.
linòleum nm linoleum.
Lióne nf (geogr) Lyon; **lionése** anmf (person from) Lyons.
Lípsia nf (geogr) Leipzig.
liquefàre vt **-rsi** vr to liquefy.
liquidàre vt to liquidate.
liquidàto a liquidated, paid off, ruined.
liquidazióne nf liquidation, winding-up.
líquido a liquid; (money) ready; nm liquid.
liquirìzia nf liquorice.
liquóre nm liqueur, liquor.
líra nf (Italian coin) lira; (mus) lyre.
lírica nf lyric, lyrical poem or poetry.
lírico pl **-ici** a lyric, lyrical; nm lyric poet.

lirísmo nm lyricism.
Lisbóna nf (geogr) Lisbon.
lísca nf fishbone.
lisciaménto nm lisciatúra nf smoothing, polishing.
lisciàre vt to smooth, polish; (fig) flatter.
líscio a smooth, plain, (of drink) neat, (US of drink) straight; mèssa líscia low mass; ad smoothly.
liscíva nf lye.
lísta nf strip; list, menu.
listàre vt to line, border.
listíno nm list, price-list.
litanía nf litany.
líte nf lawsuit, quarrel.
litigànte nmf disputant, litigant.
litigàre vi to dispute, quarrel.
litígio nm dispute, quarrel.
litigióso a quarrelsome.
litografàre vt to lithograph.
litografía nf lithography, lithograph.
litoràle a coastal, coast; nm littoral, coastline.
lítro nm litre.
littorànea nf coast road.
littorína nf diesel rail-car.
Lituània nf (geogr) Lithuania.
lituàno a nm Lithuanian.
liturgía nf liturgy.
litúrgico pl -ici a liturgic(al).
liúto nm (mus) lute.
livellàre vt to level.
livèllo nm level; passàggio a l. level-crossing, (US) grade crossing; l. del màre sea-level.
lívido a livid; nm bruise.
Lívio nm pr Livy.
livóre nm envy, hatred.
Livórno nf (geogr) Leghorn.
livrèa nf livery.
lízza nf lists pl.
lo def art m the; pron acc m him, it.
lòbo nm lobe.
locàle a local; nm room, premises pl.
località nf locality.
localizzàre vt to locate, localize.
localménte ad locally.
locànda nf inn.
locandièra nf -re nm innkeeper.
locatàrio nm lessee, tenant.
locatóre nm -trice nf lessor.
locazióne nf lease.
locomotíva nf locomotive.
locomozióne nf locomotion.
locústa nf locust.
locuzióne nf expression, phrase, idiom.
lodàre vt to praise.
lòde nf praise.
lodévole a praiseworthy, laudable, commendable.
lòdola nf lark, skylark.
Lodovíco nm pr Ludovic(k).
logarítmo nm logarithm.
lòggia nf loggia; (masonic) lodge.
loggióne nm (theat) gallery.
lògica nf logic.
lògico pl -ici a logical; nm logician.
lòglio nm darnel.

logoraménto nm wearing out, wearing down, wasting away.
logoràre vt to wear down, wear out; -rsi vr to be worn out.
logorío nm wear and tear.
lógoro a worn down, worn out.
lombàggine nf lumbago.
Lombardía nf (geogr) Lombardy.
lombàrdo a nm Lombard.
lombàta nf (of meat) loin, sirloin.
lómbo nm (human) loin.
lombríco nm earthworm.
Lóndra nf (geogr) London.
londinése a (of) London; nmf Londoner.
longànime a forbearing, patient.
longanimità nf forbearance, patience.
longevità nf longevity.
longèvo a long-lived.
longitudinàle a longitudinal.
longitúdine nf longitude.
lontanaménte ad vaguely, slightly.
lontanànza nf distance; in l. at a distance.
lontàno a distant, far; ad far, far away, far off; da l. from a distance; àlla lontàna at a distance, slightly.
lóntra nf otter.
lónza nf panther; (of meat) loin.
loquàce a loquacious, talkative.
loquacità nf loquacity.
loquèla nf language, way of speaking.
lordàre vt to dirty, soil.
lórdo a dirty; péso l. nm (com) gross weight.
lordúra nf dirt, filth.
Lorèna nf (geogr) Lorraine.
lorenése a of Lorraine; nm Lorrainer.
Lorènzo nm pr Laurence, Lawrence.
lóro pron nom pl they, you; acc pl you, them; dat pl to you, to them; poss a pl your, their.
Losànna nf (geogr) Lausanne.
lósco pl -schi a dubious; one-eyed, squint-eyed; figúra lósca scoundrel.
lòtta nf fight, struggle.
lottàre vi to fight, struggle, wrestle.
lottería nf lottery.
lòtto nm lot, lottery.
lozióne nf lotion.
lubricità nf lubricity.
lúbrico pl -ici a slippery; indecent.
lubrificànte a lubricating; nm lubricant.
lubrificàre vt to lubricate, oil, grease.
lubrificazióne nf lubrication.
Lúca nm pr Luke.
lucchétto nm padlock.
luccicàre vi to glitter, shine.
luccichío nm glitter, sparkle.
lúccio nm (fish) pike.
lúcciola nf firefly, glowworm.
lúce nf light; l. abbagliànte (aut) headlight; l. anabbagliànte (aut) anti-dazzle light; lúci della ribàlta pl (theat) footlights; dare alla l. to give birth to.
lucènte a shiny, shining, bright.

lucentézza *nf* brightness, shine, sheen.
Lucèrna *nf* (*geogr*) Lucerne.
lucèrna *nf* oil-lamp.
lucernàrio *nm* skylight.
lucèrtola *nf* lizard.
Lucía *nf* pr Lucy.
Luciàno *nm* pr Lucian.
lucidaménto, lucidatúra *nf* polishing.
lucidàre *vt* to polish.
lucidatóre *nm* polisher.
lucidatríce *nf* polisher, polishing machine.
lucidézza *nf* brightness, sheen.
lucidità *nf* lucidity, clearness.
lúcido *a* bright, shiny, lucid.
lucígnolo *nm* wick.
lúcro *nm* profit, gain.
lucróso *a* lucrative, profitable.
ludíbrio *nm* mockery, scorn.
lúe *nf* (*med*) contagion, syphilis.
lúglio *nm* July.
lúgubre *a* lugubrious, dismal.
lúi *pron m* (*nom*) he; (*acc*) him.
Luigi *nm* pr Louis, Lewis.
Luísa *nf* pr Louise, Louisa.
Luisiàna *nf* (*geogr*) Louisana.
lumàca *nf* snail; slow person.
lúme *nm* light, lamp; **a quésti lúmi di lúna** in these hard times.
luminàre *nm* great man, luminary.
luminària *nf* public illumination.
lumíno *nm* night-light.
luminosaménte *ad* brightly, luminously.
luminosità *nf* brightness, luminosity.
luminóso *a* luminous, shining, bright.
lúna *nf* moon; **l. di mièle** honeymoon; **chiàro di l.** moonlight.
lunàre *a* lunar.
lunàrio *nm* almanac; **sbarcàre il l.** to make both ends meet.
lunàtico *pl* -**ici** *a* moody.
lunedí *nm* Monday.
lungaménte *ad* for a long time.
lunghézza *nf* length.
lungimirànte *a* far-seeing.
lúngo *pl* -**ghi** *a* long, tall; slow; weak; *prep* along; **a l. for a long time;** **di gran lúnga** by far; **a l. andàre in the long run.**
lungomàre *nm* sea-front.
lungometràggio *nm* feature film.
luògo *pl* -**ghi** *nm* place; **sul l. on the spot; l. comúne** commonplace.
luogotenènte *nm* lieutenant.
lúpa *nf* she-wolf; **lúpo** *nm* wolf.
lupacchiòtto *nm* wolf-cub.
lupanàre *nm* brothel.
lupíno *nm* lupin.
lúppolo *nm* hop (plant).
lúrido *a* dirty, filthy.
luridúme *nm* filth, dirt.
lusínga *nf* allurement, illusion, flattery.
lusingàre *vt* to allure, flatter.
lusinghièro *a* alluring, flattering.
lussàre *vt* (*med*) to dislocate.
lussazióne *nf* dislocation.

Lussembúrgo *nm* (*geogr*) Luxembourg.
lússo *nm* luxury.
lussuóso *a* luxurious.
lussureggiànte *a* luxuriant.
lussureggiàre *vt* to be luxuriant, flourish.
lussúria *nf* lust.
lussurióso *a* lustful.
lustràre *vt* to polish.
lustrascàrpe *nm* shoeblack, (US) shoeshine.
lustríno *nm* sequin.
lústro *a* polished, shining; *nm* lustre.
luteràno *a nm* Lutheran.
Lutèro *nm* pr Luther.
lútto *nm* mourning; **a l. in mourning.**
luttuóso *a* mournful, sad.

M

ma *cj* but; **macchè** *interj* not at all.
màcabro *a* macabre.
maccheróni *nm pl* macaroni.
màcchia *nf* spot, stain, blot; bush, woodland; **alla m.** clandestinely.
macchiàre *vt* to soil, spot, stain; **-rsi** *vr* to get dirty, disgrace oneself.
macchiétta *nf* speck; caricature; eccentric person, (*theat*) character study.
màcchina *nf* machine, engine; car; **m. a vapóre** steam engine; **m. da scrivere** typewriter; **m. fuòri série** (US) custom-built car; **m. decapotàbile** convertible; **m. lavapiàtti** dish-washing machine (dishwasher).
macchinalménte *ad* mechanically, automatically.
macchinàre *vt* to plot.
macchinàrio *nm* machinery.
macchinazióne *nf* machination, plot.
macchinísta *nm* engine driver, (US) engineer.
macedònia *nf* fruit salad, macedoine.
macellàio *nm* butcher.
macellàre *vt* to slaughter, butcher.
macellazióne *nf* slaughter(ing).
macellería *nf* butcher's (shop).
macèllo *nm* slaughter-house, slaughtering, slaughter.
maceràre *vt* to soak, macerate; **-rsi** *vr* to wear oneself out.
maceratóio, màcero *nm* macerating vat.
macerazióne *nf* maceration; (*fig*) mortification (of the flesh).
macèrie *nf pl* debris, remains.
macigno *nm* hard stone; boulder.
macilènto *a* emaciated.
màcina *nf* millstone, grindstone.
macinacaffè (*inv*) *nm* coffee-mill.
macinàre *vt* to grind, mill, crush.
macinatóio *nm* mill, press.
macinazióne *nf* grinding, milling.
maciníno *nm* coffee-mill.
maciullàre *vt* to crush, chew.
Maddaléna *nf* pr Magdalene.

Madèra nf (geogr) Madeira.

màdia nf kneading trough, kitchen cupboard.

màdido a wet, soaked.

madònna nf (arc) lady, madonna; **Madònna** the Virgin Mary, (the) Madonna.

madornàle a enormous, gross, huge.

màdre nf mother; **m. lingua** mother tongue; **càsa m.** (com) head office.

madrepàtria nf mother-country, fatherland.

madrepèrla nf mother-of-pearl.

madresélva nf honeysuckle.

Madríd nf (geogr) Madrid; **madrilèno** a nm of Madrid.

madrigàle nm madrigal.

madrína nf godmother.

maestà nf majesty.

maestóso a majestic, stately, magnificent.

maèstra nf (school)mistress, teacher.

maestràle nm mistral.

maestrànza nf skilled workmen pl, skilled hands pl.

maestría nf mastery, skill.

maèstro a main, principal, masterly; nm schoolmaster, teacher, maestro; **àlbero m.** mainmast; **stràda maèstra** highroad.

màfia nf Mafia.

mafióso a nm (member) of the Mafia.

magàgna nf defect, fault, ailment.

magàri interj if only . . . ! ad maybe, perhaps, even.

magazzinàggio nm storage.

magazzinière nm warehouse-man.

magazzíno nm store, warehouse, store-house.

maggése nm fallow land.

màggio nm (month) May.

maggioràna nf marjoram.

maggiorànza nf majority.

maggioràre vt (com) to increase, put up.

maggiorazióne nf (com) increase, additional charge.

maggiordòmo nm butler.

maggióre a bigger, elder, greater, high(er), larger, older, biggest, eldest; nm superior, elder; (mil) major; pl ancestors.

maggiorènne a of age; nm adult.

maggiorménte ad more, much more, all the more.

magía nf magic.

màgico pl -ici a magic(al).

magistèro nm mastery, teaching.

magistràle a magistral, masterly.

magistràto nm magistrate.

magistratúra nf magistracy.

màglia nf stitch; mesh; vest, jersey, (mech) link; mail; **lavoràre a m.** to knit.

magliería nf hosiery, knitted goods pl.

maglifício nm knitwear factory.

màglio nm mallet; (mech) hammer.

maglióne nm jersey, pullover.

magnanimità nf magnanimity.

magnànimo a magnanimous.

magnàno nm locksmith.

magnàte nm magnate, tycoon.

magnèsia nf magnesia.

magnèsio nm magnesium.

magnète nm magnet, magneto.

magnètico pl -ici a magnetic.

magnetísmo nm magnetism.

magnetizzàre vt to magnetize.

magnetòfono nm tape-recorder.

magnificàre vt to extol, magnify.

magnificènza nf grandeur, splendour.

magnífico pl -ici a magnificent, splendid.

magniloquènza nf grandiloquence.

màgno a great.

magnòlia nf magnolia(-tree).

màgo pl -ghi nm sorcerer, wizard; **i Ré Màgi** the Three Kings.

màgra nf shallow water, shortage; **tèmpi di m.** hard times.

magrézza nf thinness, (of soil) poorness.

màgro a thin, poor; **giòrno di m.** day of abstinence.

mài ad ever, never; **cóme m.?** how is that?; **se m.** in case; if anything.

maiàle nm pig, pork.

maiòlica nf majolica.

maionése nf mayonnaise.

Maiòrca nf (geogr) Majorca.

màis nm maize, Indian corn.

maiúscolo a capital; nm capitals pl.

malaccòrto a imprudent, rash.

malacreànza nf ill-breeding.

malaféde nf bad faith.

malaffàre nm **dònna di m.** whore; **gènte di m.** crooks pl, scum.

malagévole a difficult, hard, unmanageable.

malagiàto a uncomfortable, short of money.

malagràzia nf bad grace, rudeness.

malaménte ad badly.

malandàto a in bad repair, in poor health.

malandríno a roguish; nm robber, rogue.

malànimo nm ill will.

malànno nm infirmity, misfortune.

malapéna, a ad hardly, scarcely.

malària nf malaria.

malàrico pl -ici a malarial.

malatíccio a sickly.

malàto a ill, sick, diseased; nm sick person, patient.

malattía nf disease, illness.

malauguràto a unfortunate, illomened.

malaugúrio nm bad omen.

malavíta nf (criminal) underworld.

malavòglia nf unwillingness, ill-will.

malavventuràto a ill-fated, unlucky.

malazzàto a sickly.

malcapitàto a unfortunate, unlucky.

malcóncio a in a poor way, in tatters.

malcontènto a discontented, dissatisfied; *nm* dissatisfaction discontent.

malcostúme *nm* immorality, corruption, bad habit.

maldèstro *a* awkward, clumsy.

maldicènza *nf* backbiting, slander.

màle *nm* evil, illness, harm; *ad* badly; **mal di dénti** toothache; **mal di góia** sore throat; **mal di tésta** headache; **méno m.** thank Heavens!; **non c'è m.** pretty good; **restàre m.** to be disappointed; **stàre m.** to be ill.

maledètto *a* cursed, damned.

maledíre *vt* to curse.

maledizióne *nf* curse.

maleducàto *a* rude; *nm* ill-bred person.

maleducazióne *nf* bad manners *pl*, rudeness.

malefàtta *nf* mischief.

malefício *nm* witchcraft, spell, misdeed.

malèfico *pl* **-ici** *a* evil, mischievous.

malèrba *nf* weed.

malése *a nmf* Malay.

Malèsia *nf* (*geogr*) Malaya, Malaysia.

malèssere *nm* indisposition, malaise.

malevolènza *nf* ill will, malevolence.

malèvolo *a* malevolent.

malfamàto *a* ill-famed.

malfattóre *nm* **-tríce** *nf* evil-doer, criminal.

malfèrmo *a* unsteady, shaky; (*of health*) poor.

malfído *a* unreliable, uncertain.

malgàrbo *nm* bad grace, rudeness.

malgovèrno *nm* misgovernment, mismanagement.

malgradíto *a* unwelcome.

malgràdo *prep* in spite of, notwithstanding; **mío m.** against my will; **m. (che)** *cj* although.

malía *nf* witchcraft, charm.

malignità *nf* malignity, wickedness.

malígno *a* evil, malicious, malignant.

malinconía *nf* melancholy, sadness.

malincònico *pl* **-ici** *a* melancholy, sad.

malincuòre, a *ad* unwillingly.

malintenzionàto *a* ill-disposed, malicious.

malintéso *a* mistaken; *nm* misunderstanding.

malízia *nf* malice, cunning, trick.

malizióso *a* mischievous, artful.

mallevadóre *nm* bail, surety.

malleverìa, mallevadorìa *nf* bail, suretyship.

malmenàre *vt* to ill-treat, ill-use.

malmésso *a* badly dressed, poorly dressed.

malnutríto *a* underfed.

màlo *a* bad, ill, wicked.

malòcchio *nm* evil eye; **vedére di m.** to dislike.

malóra *nf* ruin.

malóre *nm* sudden illness, indisposition.

malsàno *a* unhealthy, unwholesome.

malsicúro *a* unsafe, uncertain, unreliable.

Màlta *nf* (*geogr*) Malta; **maltése** *a nmf* Maltese.

maltalènto *nm* ill-will.

maltèmpo *nm* bad weather.

maltenúto *a* untidy, badly kept.

màlto *nm* malt.

maltòlto *a* ill-gotten; *nm* ill-gotten goods *pl*.

maltrattaménto *nm* ill-treatment.

maltrattàre *vt* to ill-treat, ill-use.

malumóre *nm* ill-humour, spleen.

malvagiaménte *ad* wickedly.

malvàgio *a* wicked.

malvagità *nf* wickedness.

malvísto *a* unpopular.

malvivènte *nm* gangster, criminal.

malvivènza *nf* delinquency, criminality.

malvolentièri *ad* unwillingly.

malvolére *nm* ill-will, dislike, wickedness.

màmma *nf* mama, mum(my), mother.

mammèlla *nf* breast.

mammífero *nm* mammal.

màmmola *nf* violet.

manàta *nf* handful, slap.

mànca *nf* left-hand, left-hand side.

mancànte *a* lacking, missing, deficient; failing, defective.

mancànza *nf* deficiency, lack, shortness, want; **sentíre la m. di** to miss.

mancàre *vi* to lack, be missing, err; **màncano cínque minúti alle dúe** it is five to two; *vt* to miss; **m. il bersàglio** to miss the mark.

mancàto *a* manqué, unsuccessful.

mància *nf* tip, reward.

manciàta *nf* handful.

mancíno *a* left-handed; treacherous.

Manciúria *nf* (*geogr*) Manchuria.

mànco *pl* **-chi** *a* left; *ad* not even.

mandaménto *nm* borough, district.

mandànte *nm* instigator.

mandàre *vt* to send, emit; **m. vía** to send away; **m. all'ària** to ruin.

mandaríno *nm* mandarin; tangerine.

mandàta *nf* batch; (of key) turn.

mandàto *nm* commission, mandate, order, warrant.

mandíbola *nf* jaw.

mandolíno *nm* mandolin.

màndorla *nf* almond; **màndorlo** *nm* almond-tree.

màndra, màndria *nf* flock, herd.

maneggévole *a* easy to handle, manageable.

maneggiàre *vt* to handle, manage, use; **-rsi** *vr* to conduct oneself, manage.

manéggio *nm* handling, use, management; horsemanship, riding-school; intrigue.

manésco *pl* **-chi** *a* ready with one's fists.

manétte *nf pl* handcuffs *pl*.

manganèllo *nm* cudgel.

manganése *nm* manganese.

mangeréccio *a* edible, eatable.

mangiàre *vti* to eat; *nm* eating.

mangiàta *nf* meal, hearty meal.

mangiatóia *nf* crib, manger.

mangiucchiàre *vti* to nibble, pick at one's food.

mania *nf* mania, fixation.

maníaco *pl* **-aci** *a nm* maniac.

mànica *nf* sleeve; **èssere di m. làrga** to be broad minded; **un àltro pàio di màniche** another kettle of fish; **la M.** the (English) Channel.

mànico *pl* **-chi** *nm* handle.

manicòmio *nm* (lunatic-)asylum.

manicòtto *nm* muff; (*mech*) coupling.

manicure (Fr) *nmf* manicurist, manicure.

manièra *nf* manner, way; **in qualúnque m.** anyhow.

manieràto *a* affected, mannered.

manifattúra *nf* manufacture, workmanship.

manifestàre *vt* to manifest, show; **-rsi** *vr* to reveal oneself.

manifestazióne *nf* display; demonstration.

manifèsto *a* clear, obvious; *nm* manifesto, bill, placard, leaflet.

maníglia *nf* handle.

manigóldo *nm* rascal, villain.

manipolàre *vt* to handle, manipulate, adulterate.

manipolazióne *nf* handling, preparation, manipulation, adulteration.

maniscàlco *pl* **-chi** *nm* farrier.

mànna *nf* manna, godsend.

mannàia *nf* axe.

màno *nf* hand; (*of paint*) coat; **a portàta di m.** within reach; **fuòri di m.** out of reach, out of the way; **strétta di m.** handshake; **di secónda m.** second-hand.

manodòpera *nf* labour, workmanship.

manòmetro *nm* manometer, pressure-gauge.

manométtere *vt* to tamper with, violate.

manomissióne *nf* tampering, violation.

manomòrta *nf* (*leg*) mortmain.

manòpola *nf* handle bar grip, knob, fencing glove, cuff.

manoscrítto *a* handwritten; *nm* manuscript.

manovàle *nm* labourer.

manovèlla *nf* crank, handle, winder.

manòvra *nf* manœuvre, (*rly*) shunting.

manovràre *vt* to manœuvre, shunt, work.

manrovèscio *pl* **manrovèsci** *nm* backhanded blow.

mansàlva *a ad* with impunity.

mansióne *nf* function, duty, office.

mansuefàre *vt* to subdue, tame.

mansuèto *a* meek, mild, docile.

mantèllo *nm* cloak, mantle.

mantenére *vt* to keep (up), maintain; **-rsi** *vr* to keep (oneself).

manteniménto *nm* maintenance, preservation.

màntice *nm* bellows *pl*, (*of a car*) hood.

mànto *nm* cloak, mantle.

Màntova *nf* (*geogr*) Mantua.

mantovàno *a nm* Mantuan.

manuàle *a* manual; *nm* handbook, manual.

manúbrio *nm* handle(-bar), dumbbell.

manufàtto *a* hand-made, manufactured; *nm* hand-made article.

manutenzióne *nf* upkeep, maintenance.

mànzo *nm* steer, beef.

maomettàno *a nm* Mahommedan.

Maométto *nm pr* Mohammed, Mahomet.

màppa *nf* map.

mappamóndo *nm* globe of the world.

marachèlla *nf* trick, prank.

maratóna *nf* marathon (race).

màrca *nf* (*com*) brand, mark, make; **m. da bòllo** revenue stamp; **m. di fàbbrica** trade-mark.

marcàre *vt* to mark.

marchésa *nf* marchioness; **marchése** *nm* marquis.

màrchio *nm* brand, mark; **m. di fàbbrica** trade-mark.

màrcia *nf* (*aut*) gear; march; pus.

marciapiède *nm* pavement, (*US*) sidewalk; platform.

marciàre *vi* to march.

màrcio *a* bad, rotten, tainted; *nm* rottenness, pus.

marcíre *vi* to decay, go bad, rot, waste.

marciúme *nm* rottenness, rotten things *pl*.

màrco *pl* **-chi** *nm* (*coin*) mark.

Màrco *nm pr* Mark.

marconísta *nm* wireless operator.

màre *nm* sea; **in àlto m.** on the high seas; **màl di m.** seasickness.

marèa *nf* tide.

mareggiàta *nf* rough sea.

maresciàllo *nm* marshal; warrant-office·.

marétta *nf* choppy sea.

margarína *nf* margarine.

margherìta *nf* daisy.

Margherìta *nf pr* Margaret.

marginàle *a* marginal.

màrgine *nm* margin, border, edge.

María *nf pr* Mary.

Mariànna *nf pr* Marian(ne).

marína *nf* navy; coast, seaside; **régia m.** Royal Navy; **m. mercantíle** merchant navy.

marinàio *nm* sailor, seaman.

marinàra *nf* duffle coat.

marinàre *vt* to pickle, marinate; **m. la scuòla** to play truant.

marinàto *a* pickled, soused.

maríno *a* marine, (of the) sea.

Màrio *nm pr* Marius.

marionétta *nf* marionette, puppet.

maritàre *vt* to marry; **-rsi** *vr* to get married, marry.

marito *nm* husband.

maríttimo *a* maritime, marine.

marmàglia *nf* rabble.

marmellàta *nf* jam; **m. d'arànce** marmalade.

marmítta *nf* saucepan.

màrmo *nm* marble.

marmòcchio *nm* brat.

marmòreo *a* marble, marmoreal.

marmòtta *nf* marmot; (*fig*) lazybones.

Màrna *nf* (*geogr*) Marne.

marocchíno *a* Moroccan; *nm* Moroccan, Morocco (leather).

Maròcco *nm* (*geogr*) Morocco.

maróso *nm* billow, wave.

marróne *a* brown; *nm* chestnut; blunder.

Marsíglia *nf* (*geogr*) Marseilles; **marsigliése** *a nmf* of Marseilles, Marseillaise.

Màrta *nf pr* Martha.

martedí *nm* Tuesday; **m. gràsso** Shrove Tuesday.

martellàre *vti* to hammer, throb.

martèllo *nm* hammer.

martinèllo, martinétto *nm* (*mech*) jack.

Martíno *nm pr* Martin.

martín pescatóre *nm* kingfisher.

màrtire *nm* martyr.

martírio *nm* martyrdom.

martirizzàre *vt* to martyrize, torture.

màrtora *nf* marten; (*fur*) sable.

martoriàre *vt* to torment, torture.

marxísmo *nm* Marxism.

marxísta *a nm* Marxist, Marxian.

marzapàne *nm* marzipan.

marziàle *a* martial.

marziàno *a* Martian.

màrzo *nm* March.

mascalzóne *nm* rascal, scoundrel.

mascèlla *nf* jaw.

màschera *nf* mask; (*theat*) usher.

mascheràre *vt* to mask; **-rsi** *vr* to disguise oneself.

mascheràta *nf* masquerade.

mascheróne *nm* mask, grotesque face.

maschiètta, alla *ad* **capélli a. m.** shingled hair.

maschíle *a* male, manly, masculine.

màschio *a* male, manly; *nm* male child; inner keep, tower.

maṣnàda *nf* gang, set.

maṣnadière *nm* brigand, robber.

màssa *nf* mass, heap.

massacràre *vt* to massacre, slaughter.

massàcro *nm* massacre, slaughter.

massaggiàre *vt* to massage.

massàggio *nm* massage.

massàia *nf* housewife.

masseria *nf* farm.

masserízie *nf pl* household goods *pl*, household utensils *pl*.

massíccio *a* massy, massive, solid; *nm* massif.

màssima *nf* maxim, rule, saying.

massimaménte *ad* chiefly, especially.

màssimo *a* greatest, highest, utmost, best; *nm* maximum.

màsso *nm* big stone, block, boulder.

massóne *nm* Freemason, mason.

massoneria *nf* Freemasonry.

massònico *pl* **-ici** *a* masonic.

masticàre *vt* to chew, masticate; stammer; **m. una língua** to have a smattering of a language.

masticazióne *nf* chewing, mastication.

màstice *nm* mastic, putty.

mastíno *nm* mastiff.

màstio *nm* donjon, keep.

mastodòntico *pl* **-ici** *a* huge, colossal.

màstro *nm* ledger, master.

matàssa *nf* skein.

matemàtica *nf* mathematics.

matemàtico *pl* **-ici** *a* mathematical.

materàsso *nm* mattress.

matèria *nf* matter, material, subject; **m. príma** raw material.

materiàle *a* material, rough; *nm* material.

materialísmo *nm* materialism.

materialísta *a* materialistic; *nmf* materialist.

materialménte *ad* materially, physically.

maternità *nf* maternity, motherhood.

matèrno *a* motherly, mother's, materna

Matílde *nf pr* Mat(h)ilda.

matíta *nf* pencil.

matríce *nf* matrix, womb, mould; **registro a m.** (*com*) counterfoil register.

matrícola *nf* register, roll; freshman.

matricolàre *vt* **-rsi** *vr* to matriculate.

matricolíno *nm* (*student*) freshman, beginner.

matrígna *nf* stepmother.

matrimoniàle *a* matrimonial, wedding; **anèllo m.** wedding ring; **caméra m.** double room; **letto m.** double bed.

matrimònio *nm* marriage, wedding.

mattacchióne *nm* joker, wag.

mattànza *nf* (*naut*) slaughter of tunny fish.

Mattèo *nm pr* Matthew.

matterèllo *nm* (*cook*) rolling-pin.

mattína *nf* **mattíno** *nm* morning.

mattinàta *nf* forenoon, morning, (*theat*) matinée.

mattinièro *a* early rising.

màtto *a* mad; *nm* madman; **scàcco m.** (*at chess*) checkmate.

mattonàto *nm* brick floor.

mattóne *nm* brick; (*fig*) bore, nuisance.

mattonèlla *nf* tile, briquette.

mattutíno *a* morning; *nm* matins.

maturàre *vti* to ripen, mature.

maturazióne *nf* maturity, ripening, maturation.

maturità nf ripeness, maturity; certificàto di m. leaving certificate.
matúro a ripe, mature, (com) fallen due.
Maurízio nm pr Maurice; ísola M. nf (geogr) Mauritius.
mausolèo nm mausoleum.
màzza nf mallet, sledge-hammer.
mazzàta nf heavy blow (also fig).
màzzo nm bunch; (of cards) pack.
mazzolíno nm posy, small bunch, bouquet.
me pron (oblique case) me, myself.
meccànica nf mechanics.
meccànico pl -ici a mechanical; nm mechanic, mechanician.
meccanísmo nm gear, mechanism, works; m. di stèrzo (aut) steering-gear.
mecenàte nm Maecenas, patron.
medàglia nf medal.
medaglióne nm medallion, locket.
medésimo a and pron same, -self.
mèdia nf average; in m. on the average.
mediàno a median, mean middle; nm (sport) halfback.
mediànte prep by means of.
mediatóre nm mediator, (com) broker.
mediazióne nf mediation, (com) brokerage.
medicàbile a curable, medicable.
medicaménto nm medicament, medicine.
medicàre vt to dress, medicate, treat.
medicàstro nm quack.
medicazióne nm (wounds) dressing, treatment; pòsto di m. first-aid post.
medicína nf medicine, remedy, (US) drug.
medicinàle a medicinal; nm medicine, (US) drug.
mèdico pl mèdici a medical; nm doctor, physician.
mèdio a middle, average, medium; nm mean, middle finger; scuòla mèdia secondary school, (US) junior high school.
mediòcre a mediocre, second-rate.
mediocrità nf mediocrity.
medioevàle a medieval.
medioèvo nm Middle Ages pl.
meditabóndo a pensive, meditative, thoughtful.
meditàre vti to meditate, meditate on.
meditàto a deliberate.
meditazióne nf meditation.
mediterràneo a Mediterranean; nm (geogr) the Mediterranean.
medúsa nf jellyfish, Medusa.
megàfono nm megaphone.
mèglio ad and a better; nm best.
méla nf apple; mèlo nm apple-tree.
melacotógna nf quince.
melagràna nf pomegranate.
melanzàna nf eggplant, aubergine.

melarància nf orange.
melàssa nf molasses, treacle.
melènso a sheepish, silly.
mellífluo a honeyed, mellifluous.
mélma nf mire, mud.
melmóso a miry, muddy.
melodía nf melody.
melòdico pl -ici a melodic.
melodióso a melodious.
melodràmma nm opera.
melodrammàtico a operatic; (fig) melodramatic.
melogràno nm pomegranate (tree).
melóne nm melon.
membràna nf membrane.
membranóso a membranous.
mèmbro nm, pl -bra nf limb; pl -bri m member.
memoràbile a memorable.
memoràndum nm memorandum; notebook.
mèmore a mindful, grateful.
memòria nf memory, remembrance, souvenir, record; a m. by heart; imparàre a m. to memorize; memòrie pl memoirs pl.
menàre vt to lead, take, bring; m. càlci to kick; m. un cólpo to deal a blow; m. le màni to fight; m. il càne per l'àia to beat about the bush; m. gràmo to bring bad luck; m. buòno to bring good luck.
mènda nf blemish, slight defect.
mendicànte a begging, mendicant; nmf beggar.
mendicàre vti to beg.
mendicità nf begging; beggars pl.
mendíco a begging; nm beggar.
meningite nf meningitis.
méno a ad prep less, minus; least; fàre a m. di to do without; le dúe m. cinque 5 minutes to 2; a m. che non unless.
menomaménte ad at all, in the least.
menomàre vt to lessen, detract from; disable, impair.
menomazióne nf reduction, impairment, disablement.
menopàusa nf menopause.
mènsa nf table; (mil) mess; refectory; (eccl) altar.
mensíle a monthly; nm month's pay.
mensilità nf monthly instalment, monthly payment, monthly occurrence.
mensilménte ad monthly.
mènsola nf bracket, console.
ménta nf mint.
mentàle a mental.
mentalità nf mentality.
mènte nf mind, intellect, intention, memory; a m. ad by heart.
mentíre vi to lie; vt to falsify, misrepresent.
ménto nm chin.
mèntre ad and cj while; in quél m. at that moment.
menù nm menu, bill of fare.
menzionàre vt to mention.

menzióne *nf* mention.

menzógna *nf* falsehood, lie.

menzognèro *a* lying, untrue.

meraviglia *nf* wonder, surprise; a m. *ad* wonderfully well.

meravigliàre *vt* to amaze, surprise; -rsi *vr* to be amazed, wonder.

meravigliosaménte *ad* wonderfully, beautifully.

meraviglióso *a* wonderful; *nm* wonder, the supernatural.

mercànte *nm* merchant, trader; fàre orécchio da m. to turn a deaf ear.

mercanteggiàre *vi* to trade, haggle.

mercantile *a* mercantile, merchant; plain; *nm* cargo boat.

mercanzía *nf* merchandise, goods *pl*, wares *pl*.

mercàto *nm* market; bargain, price; a buòn m. cheap, cheaply; per sópra m. besides, moreover; M. Comúne Common Market.

mercatúra *nf* trade, commerce.

mèrce *nf* goods *pl*, merchandise; tréno mèrci goods train.

mercè *nf* mercy; súa m. thanks to him.

mercéde *nf* pay, reward.

mercenàrio *a nm* mercenary.

merceria *nf* haberdasher's shop; mercerie *pl* haberdashery.

merciàio *nm* merciàia *nf* draper, haberdasher.

mercoledì *nm* Wednesday; m. delle cèneri Ash Wednesday.

mercúrio *nm* mercury, quicksilver.

mèrda *nf* (*vulg*) shit.

merènda *nf* afternoon tea, snack.

meridiàna *nf* sun-dial.

meridiàno *a nm* meridian.

meridionàle *a* south, southern; *nmf* southerner.

meridióne *nm* south.

meríggio *nm* midday, noon.

merínga *nf* meringue.

meritaménte, meritataménte *ad* deservedly, justly.

meritàre *vt* to deserve, earn, be worthwhile, require; -rsi *vr* to deserve.

meritévole *a* deserving, worthy.

mèrito *nm* merit; in m. a as regards, as to.

meritòrio *a* deserving, meritorious.

merlatúra *nf* battlement; lace trimming.

merlétto *nm* lace.

mèrlo *nm* blackbird; (*arch*) merlon; simpleton.

merlúzzo *nm* cod(fish).

mèro *a* mere, pure, simple.

mesàta *nf* month's salary.

méscere *vt* to pour, mix.

meschineria, meschinità *nf* meanness, stinginess.

meschíno *a* poor, mean, wretched.

méscita *nf* wine shop.

mescolànza *nf* mixing, mixture.

mescolàre *vt* to mix, stir, (*cards*) shuffle; -rsi *vr* to mix; interfere.

mése *nm* month, month's pay.

mèssa *nf* (*eccl*) Mass; m. in scéna (*theat*) staging; m. in màrcia (*aut*) starter.

messaggeria *nf* haulage trade, mailcoach.

messaggèro *nm* -ra *nf* messenger, (*fig*) forerunner.

messàggio *nm* message.

messàle *nm* missal.

mèsse *nf* crop, harvest.

Messía *nm pr* Messiah.

messicàno *a nm* Mexican.

Mèssico *nm* (*geogr*) Mexico.

mésso *a* arranged, disposed, dressed; *nm* messenger, legate.

mestière *nm* trade, occupation, profession, job, craft.

mestízia *nf* sadness.

mèsto *a* sad, sorrowful.

méstola *nf* -lo *nm* ladle, trowel.

mestruazióne *nf* menstruation.

mèta *nf* destination, aim; (*of straw etc*) pile.

metà *nf* half, middle; a m. prèzzo half-price; a m. stràda half-way.

metabolísmo *nm* metabolism.

metafísica *nf* metaphysics *pl*.

metàfora *nf* metaphor.

metafòrico *pl* -ici *a* metaphoric(al).

metàllico *pl* -ici *a* metallic, metal.

metàllo *nm* metal; fatica del m. metal fatigue.

metallurgia *nf* metallurgy.

metamòrfosi *nf* metamorphosis.

metàno *nm* methane.

metapsíchico *pl* -ici *a* extrasensory.

metèora *nf* meteor.

meteorologia *nf* meteorology.

meteorològico *pl* -ici *a* meteorologic(al); bollettíno m. weather report; previsióni meteorologiche weather forecast; ufficio m. meteorological office, (*US*) weather bureau.

meticcio *a nm* half-breed.

meticolóso *a* meticulous.

metile *nm* methyl.

metòdico *pl* -ici *a* methodical, business-like.

mètodo *nm* method.

metràggio *nm* length (in metres); (*cin*) córto m. short film; lúngo m. feature film.

mètrica *nf* prosody.

mètro *nm* (*measure*) metre.

metronòtte *nm* night watchman.

metròpoli *nf* metropolis.

metropolitàna *nf* underground (railway), (*US*) subway.

metropolitàno *a* metropolitan; *nm* policeman.

méttere *vt* to put, place, set, cause, put forth; *vi* to lead; -rsi *vr* to put oneself, get into, begin, put on, turn.

mezzadria *nf* metayage, (*US*) sharecropping.

mezzàdro *nm* métayer, (*US*) sharecropper.

mezzalàna *nf* mixed wool and cotton cloth; shady person.

Mitto. Mitto

mezzalúna nf half-moon, crescent; mincing knife.
mezzanino nm entresol, mezzanine.
mezzàno a nm middle, medium; mediator, pimp.
mezzanòtte pl **mezzenotti** nf midnight, north.
mèzzo a half; ad half; nm middle; in m. a prep in the middle of; **mèzza età** middle-age.
mezzodì, mezzogiórno nm midday, noonday, south.
mezzómbra nf half-tone.
mezzotèrmine nm compromise.
mezzúccio nm mean expedient.
mi pron acc and dat (to) me; refl myself; nm (mus) E, mi.
miagolàre vi to mew.
mìca nf crumb, grain; ad (fam) not at all.
mìccia nf (for explosives etc) fuse.
Michèle nm pr Michael.
micidiàle a deadly, killing.
mìcio nm tom-cat, (fam) pussy.
micròbo nm microbe.
micròfono nm microphone.
micromotóre nm small motor; motor-scooter.
microscòpico pl **-ici** a microscopic (al).
microscòpio nm microscope.
microsólco pl **-chi** nm long-playing record, microgroove.
midólla nf (bread)crumb, (fruit) pulp.
midóllo nm marrow, pith.
mièle nm honey.
mìetere vt to reap, mow down.
mietitóre nm **-trice** nf reaper, mower.
mietitúra nf reaping.
migliàio nm about a thousand; a **migliàia** by thousands.
mìglio nm millet; nm pl **mìglia** mile; **distànza in mìglia** mileage; pl **mìgli** milestone.
miglioraménto nm improvement.
miglioràre vt to improve.
miglióre a better, best.
migliorìa nf improvement, amelioration.
mignàtta nf leech (also fig).
mignolo nm little finger or toe; olive blossom.
migràre vi to migrate.
migratòrio a migratory.
migrazióne nf migration.
Milàno nf (geogr) Milan; **milanése** a nmf Milanese.
miliardàrio nm multimillionaire, (US) billionaire.
miliàrdo nm milliard, (US) billion.
miliàre a milestone; (med) miliary.
milionàrio nm millionaire.
milióne nm million; **milionèsimo** a millionth.
militànte a militant.
militàre vi to serve in the army, militate; a military; nm soldier.
militarménte ad militarily.

mìlite nm militiaman, soldier, warrior; **M. Ignòto** Unknown Soldier.
milìzia nf army, militia.
millantàre vt **-rsi** vr to boast (of).
millantatóre nm boaster, braggart.
millanterìa nf boast(ing).
mìlle pl **mìla** a thousand; **millèsimo** a thousandth.
millènnio nm millennium.
millepièdi nm millepede.
mìlza nf spleen, milt.
mimetismo nm (mil) camouflage.
mimetizzàre vt **-rsi** vr to camouflage.
mìmica nf gestures pl; mimicry.
mìmo nm mine; mimer.
mìna nf mine; (of pencil) lead.
minàccia nf threat, menace.
minacciàre vt to threaten, menace.
minaccióso a threatening, menacing.
minàre vt to mine, undermine.
minatóre nm miner, collier.
minatòrio a threatening.
mineràle a mineral; nm mineral, ore.
mineralogìa nf mineralogy.
mineràrio a mining.
minèstra nf soup.
mingherlíno a thin, delicate, slender.
miniàre vt to paint in miniature, illuminate (MSS etc).
miniatúra nf miniature.
minièra nf mine; **m. di carbóne** coal-mine.
minimaménte ad at all.
mìnimo a least, lowest, smallest; nm minimum.
ministèro nm office, function, ministry; board, (US) department; cabinet; **pùbblico m.** public prosecutor, (US) district attorney.
minìstro nm minister, secretary of state.
minorànza nf minority.
minoràto a disabled, maimed; nm disabled person, mental deficient.
minorazióne nf diminution, disablement, mental deficiency.
minóre a less(er), smaller, younger, least, minor etc.
minorènne a under age; nm minor; **tribunàle déi minorènni** juvenile court.
minoríle a juvenile; **delinquènza m.** juvenile delinquency; **età m.** minority.
minúscolo a small, minute; **léttera minúscola** small letter; nm (typ) lower-case letter.
minúta nf rough copy, minute.
minúto a minute, small, detailed, petty; nm minute; **al m.** (by) retail.
minúzia nf trifle.
minuzióso a in detail, minute.
minúzzolo nm shred, small bit.
mìo a my; pron mine; **i mièi** pl my family, my people.
mìope a short-sighted; nm short-sighted person.
miopìa nf short-sightedness (also fig).

míra nf aim, target, purpose.
mirábile a admirable, wonderful.
miracoláto a miraculously healed;
nm miraculously healed person.
miràcolo nm miracle; wonder.
miracolóso a miraculous, wonderful.
miràggio nm mirage (also fig).
miràre vt to look at, admire, aim.
miríade nf myriad.
miríno nm (of gun etc) (fore)sight,
(of camera) view-finder.
mírra nf myrrh.
mirtíllo nm bilberry.
mírto nm myrtle.
misantropía nf misanthropy.
misàntropo nm misanthrope.
miscéla nf mixture, blend; **m.**
anticongelànte (aut) antifreeze.
miscellànea nf miscellany.
míschia nf fight, fray.
mischiàre vt to mix, shuffle; -rsi vr
to mix (with).
miscredènte a unbelieving; nmf
unbeliever.
miscredènza nf unbelief, disbelief.
miscúglio nm mixture, medley.
miseràbile a miserable, poor, despicable; nm poor wretch.
miseràndo, miserévole a pitiable.
misèria nf misery, destitution,
distress; shortage; trifle; trouble.
misericòrdia nf mercy, pity.
misericordióso a merciful.
mísero a poor, wretched, mean.
misfàtto nm misdeed, crime.
misògino nm misogynist.
missàggio nm (cin) mixing; **tècnico**
del m. mixer.
missíle a nm missile; **m. radiocomandàto** radio-controlled missile.
missilística nf rocketry.
missionàrio nm missionary.
missióne nf mission.
misterióso a mysterious.
mistèro nm mystery.
misticísmo nm mysticism.
místico pl -ici a nm mystic.
mistificàre vt to mystify, deceive.
místo a mixed; nm mixture; **tréno
m.** train for passengers and goods.
mistúra nf mixture.
misúra nf measure(ment), size;
moderation.
misuràbile a measurable.
misuràre vt to measure, estimate;
limit; try on; pace; -rsi vr to
compete; try on.
misuràto a measured; moderate,
cautious.
míte a gentle, mild, moderate.
mitézza nf gentleness, meekness,
mildness, moderation.
mítico a mythical.
mitigàre vt to allay, appease, relieve.
mitigazióne nf mitigation, allevia-
tion.
míto nm myth.
mitologia nf mythology.
mítra nf mitre, submachine gun.
mitràglia nf (mil) grapeshot.

mitragliàre vt to machine gun.
mitragliatríce nf machine gun.
mitraglière nm machine gunner.
mittènte nmf sender.
mòbile a mobile, moving, movable,
changeable, fickle; nm piece of
furniture.
mobília nf furniture.
mobilière nm cabinet-maker.
mobilità nf mobility.
mobilitazióne nf mobilization.
moccióso nm snotty-nosed child;
brat.
mòccolo nm candle end, small
candle; (fam) swear word.
mòda nf fashion; di m. ad fashionable.
modalità nf modality, formality.
modèlla nf model; **modèllo** nm
model, pattern.
modellàre vt to model, mould,
fashion.
modenése a nmf (native) of Modena.
moderàre vt to moderate, curb,
reduce; -rsi vr to restrain oneself.
moderàto a moderate.
moderazióne nf moderation.
modernità nf modernity.
modernizzàre vt to modernize.
modèrno a modern.
modestaménte ad modestly.
modèstia nf modesty.
modèsto a modest, moderate.
modicità nf moderateness, cheapness.
mòdico pl -ici a moderate, cheap.
modífica nf alteration, change.
modificàre vt to modify, mitigate.
modísta nf milliner.
modisteria nf milliner's shop.
mòdo nm manner, way; ad ógni m.
anyhow, anyway; a m. carefully,
properly; **persóna a m.** well-bred
person; per m. di dire so to speak.
modulàre vt to modulate, formulate.
modulazióne nf modulation.
mòdulo nm (printed) form, (US)
blank.
mògano nm mahogany.
mòggio nm bushel.
mòggio a abashed, quiet, crestfallen.
móglie pl mógli nf wife.
moína nf blandishment, wheedling.
mòla nf grindstone, millstone.
molàre a nm molar; vt to grind, whet.
mòle nf mass, bulk, size.
molècola nf molecule.
molestàre vt to molest, bother, vex,
tease.
molèstia nf trouble, bother.
molèsto a troublesome.
mòlla nf (tec) spring; pl tongs pl.
mollàre vti to loose(n), leave off,
yield.
mòlle a soft, wet, pliable, flabby,
weak, loose; nm soft part; **méttere
in m.** vt to soak, steep.
molléggio nm suspension, springing.
molleménte ad softly, weakly,
languidly.

mollétta *nf* hair-grip, clothespeg, (US) clothespin; *pl* tongs *pl*.

mollézza *nf* softness, feebleness, effeminacy, looseness; *pl* luxury.

mollíca *nf* crumb.

mollúsco *pl* -chi *nm* mollusc.

mòlo *nm* pier, quay.

molòsso *nm* mastiff.

moltéplice *a* manifold, multiple.

moltiplicàre *vt* -rsi *vr* to multiply.

moltiplicazióne *nf* multiplication.

moltiplicità *nf* multiplicity.

moltitúdine *nf* multitude.

mólto *a* much, (*time*) long; *ad* very, much, greatly; *nm* much, a lot.

momentàneo *a* temporary, passing.

moménto *nm* moment, time, chance; **un m.** *ad* a while.

mònaca *nf* nun.

mònaco *pl* -aci *nm* monk.

Mònaco *nf* (*geogr*) Munich; *nm* (*geogr*) Monaco.

monàrca *nm* monarch.

monarchía *nf* monarchy.

monàrchico *pl* -ici *a* monarchic(al).

monastèro *nm* monastery.

monàstico *pl* -ici *a* monastic.

moncheríno *nm* stump.

mónco *pl* -chi *a* maimed, mutilated; *nm* maimed person.

moncóne *nm* stump.

mondanità *nf* worldliness, society life.

mondàno *a* mundane, worldly, society; **víta mondàna** society life; **mondàna** *nf* prostitute.

mondàre *vt* to clean, peel, winnow, (*fig*) cleanse.

mondaríso *nf* rice-picker.

mondiàle *a* worldwide, world, universal.

móndo *a* clean, pure; *nm* world, life, everybody; **un m. di** a world of.

monèlla *nf* tomboy.

monelleria *nf* prank.

monèllo *nm* little rogue, street boy, urchin.

monéta *nf* money, coin, small change.

mòngolo *a* Mongolian; *nm* Mongol.

mongolòide *a nm* mongoloid.

monile *nm* jewel; necklace.

mònito *nm* admonition, warning.

monitóre *nm* monitor, warner.

monòcolo *nm* monocle; one-eyed person.

monogamía *nf* monogamy.

monografía *nf* monograph.

monogràmma *nm* monogram.

monòlogo *pl* -ghi *nm* monologue, soliloquy.

monopàttino *nm* scooter.

monoplàno *nm* monoplane.

monopòlio *nm* monopoly.

monopolizzàre *vt* to monopolize.

monopósto *a nm* (*aut av*) single-seater.

monosíllabo *nm* monosyllable.

monotonía *nf* monotony.

monòtono *a* monotonous.

monsignóre *nm* monsignor.

montacàrichi *nm* goods lift, elevator hoist.

montàggio *nm* (*mech*) assembling, glazing; (*cin*) montage, cutting.

montàgna *nf* mountain.

montagnóso *a* mountainous.

montanàro *a* mountain, of the mountain; *nm* mountaineer, highlander.

montàno *a* mountain; **paése m.** mountain village.

montàre *vti* to mount, set, furnish; climb, rise; (*impers*) to matter; -rsi *vr* to get excited; get swollenheaded.

montatóio *nm* footboard, running board, stirrup.

montatúra *nf* fitting, (*of spectacles*) frame.

montavivànde *nm* service lift, (US) dumbwaiter.

mónte *nm* mount, heap; **m. di pietà** pawnbroker's; **andàre a m.** to come to nothing.

montóne *nm* ram, mutton.

montuosità *nf* hilliness, hill.

montuóso *a* hilly.

monumentàle *a* monumental.

monuménto *nm* monument.

mòra *nf* blackberry, mulberry; delay, respite; game of mor(r)a.

moràle *a* moral; *nf* morals *pl*, ethics, moral; *nm* morale.

moralísta *nmf* moralist.

moralità *nf* morality, morals *pl*.

moralizzàre *vti* to moralize.

morbidaménte *ad* softly, tenderly.

morbidézza *nf* softness, leniency.

mòrbido *a* soft, tender.

morbíllo *nm* (*med*) measles.

mòrbo *nm* disease, plague.

morbosità *nf* morbidness.

morbóso *a* morbid.

mordàce *a* biting, pungent, sarcastic.

mordènte *a* biting, caustic; *nm* (*chem*) mordant; (*mus*) mordent.

mòrdere *vt* to bite, sting.

morèllo *a* jet-black; *nm* black horse.

morènte *a* dying, fading; *nmf* dying man, woman.

morésco *pl* -chi *a* Moorish.

morétta *nf* brunette, Negro girl; **morétto** Negro boy.

morfína *nf* morphia, morphine.

moría *nf* plague, high mortality.

moribóndo *a* dying, moribund.

morigeràto *a* temperate, moderate, of good morals.

moríre *vi* to die; *nm* death.

mormoràre *vti* to murmur, whisper, grumble.

mormorío *nm* murmur, rustling, whisper, complaining, gossip.

mòro *a* black, dark-skinned; *nm* mulberry tree, Moor, Negro.

moróso *a* defaulting, insolvent; *nm* (*fam*) sweetheart, boy-friend.

mòrsa *nf* (*mech*) vice.

morsicàre *vt* to bite.

morsicatúra nf bite.
mòrso nm bite; pang; morsel, bit.
mortàio nm mortar.
mortàle a nm mortal.
mortalità nf mortality.
mortarétto nm cracker.
mòrte nf death.
mortèlla nf myrtle.
mortificàre vt to humiliate, mortify, deaden; **-rsi** vr to mortify oneself, be mortified.
mortificazióne nf humiliation, mortification.
mòrto a dead, deceased.
mortòrio nm funeral, burial.
mortuàrio a mortuary.
mosàico pl **-ici** nm mosaic.
mósca nf fly.
Mósca nf (geogr) Moscow; **moscovíta** a nm Muscovite.
moscatèllo nm muscatel grape.
moscàto nm muscat(el); **nóce moscàta** nutmeg.
mosceríno nm gnat, midge.
moschèa nf mosque.
moschettière nm musketeer.
moschétto nm musket.
móscio a flabby, soft; (fig) dispirited.
moscóne nm big fly, bluebottle.
Mosè nm pr Moses.
Mosèlla nf pr (geogr) Moselle.
mòssa nf move(ment).
mostàrda nf Italian sweet fruit pickles; mustard.
mósto nm must.
mostóso a full of must.
móstra nf exhibition, show, display; pretence.
mostràre vt to show, display, point out, prove; pretend; **-rsi** vr to show oneself, appear.
mostrína nf (mil) collar badge.
móstro nm monster, prodigy.
mostruosità nf monstrosity.
mostruóso a monstrous, enormous.
mòta nf mire, mud.
motivàre vt to give reason for, justify, motivate.
motivazióne nf motivation.
motívo nm motive, motif; **a m. di** on account of, owing to.
mòto nm motion, exercise; revolt; impulse; nf motor-cycle.
motocarrozzétta nf side-car.
motociclétta nf **-cíclo** nm motor-cycle.
motofurgóne nm motorcycle delivery van.
motonàve nf motorship.
motopescheréccio nm motor trawler.
motóre nm motor, engine.
motoríno nm m. **d'avviaménto** (aut) starter-motor.
motorizzàre vt to motorize.
motoscàfo nm motor-boat.
motteggiàre vti to banter, joke, make fun of.
mòtto nm word, saying, motto.
movènte nm motive, reason.

movimentàto a lively, busy, eventful; **stràda movimentàta** busy street.
moviménto nm movement, traffic.
mozióne nf motion.
mozzàre vt to cut off.
mozzicóne nm butt, stub; **m. di sigarétta** cigarette-end.
mózzo nm cabin-boy, stable-boy; (tec) a cut off, docked.
mòzzo nm wheel hub.
múcca nf cow.
múcchio nm heap, pile.
múco pl **-chi** nm mucus.
múda nf moult, moulting season.
múffa nf mould.
muffíre vi to become mouldy.
muffíto a mouldy.
mugghiàre, muggíre vi to bellow, howl, roar.
múgghio, muggíto nm bellow, roar, howling.
mughétto nm lily-of-the-valley.
mugnàio nm miller.
mugolàre vi to whine, yelp.
mulattièra nf mule-track.
mulattière nm muleteer.
mulàtto nm mulatto.
mulièbre a feminine, womanly.
mulinèllo nm whirlpool, whirlwind, (tec) windlass.
mulíno nm mill.
múlo nm mule.
múlta nf fine.
multàre vt to fine.
multicolóre a many-coloured.
multifórme a multiform.
múltiplo a multiple.
múmmia nf (Egyptian) mummy.
mummificàre vt to mummify.
múngere vt to milk, (fig) exploit.
municipàle a municipal, of the town.
município nm municipality, town hall.
munificènza nf generosity, munificence.
munífico pl **-ici** a generous, munificent.
muníre vt to fortify, furnish; **-rsi** vr to equip oneself, fortify oneself.
munizióne nf (mil) ammunition, munitions pl.
muòvere vt **-rsi** vr to move, stir.
muràglia nf wall.
muràle a mural, wall.
muràre vti to build, wall up; **-rsi** vr to shut oneself up.
muratóre nm bricklayer, mason.
muratúra nf masonry, brickwork.
murèna nf moray eel.
múro nm wall; m pl **múri** walls; f pl **múra** (town) walls.
Músa nf Muse.
muschiàto a musky; **ròsa muschiàta** musk-rose.
múschio nm musk, moss.
muscolàre a muscular.
múscolo nm muscle.
muscolóso a muscular.
muscóso a mossy.

musèo *nm* museum.
museruòla *nf* muzzle.
música *nf* music, band.
musicàle *a* musical, music.
musicànte *nm* musician, bandsman.
musicista *nmf* musician, composer.
múso *nm* muzzle, snout; (*fam*) face; **fàre il m.** to pull a long face; **avere il m.** to sulk.
mussàre *vi* to foam, froth.
mussolina *nf* muslin.
mussulmàno *a nm* Mussulman.
mustàcchi *nm pl* moustache.
múta *nf* change, moult, set; (*of hounds*) pack.
mutàbile *a* changeable.
mutabilità *nf* changeability.
mutaménto *nm* change, alteration, variation.
mutànde *nf pl* drawers *pl*, pants *pl*, (US) underpants; **mutandíne** *nf pl* panties; **m. da bàgno** swimming trunks; **m. da ginnàstica** gym shorts.
mutàre *vt* **-rsi** *vr* to change.
mutévole *a* changeable.
mutilàre *vt* to maim, mutilate.
mutilàto *a* maimed, mutilated; *nm* ripple; **m. di guèrra** war cripple.
mutilazióne *nf* mutilation.
mútismo *nm* dumbness, muteness, taciturnity.
múto *a* dumb, mute.
mútua *nf* (**càssa**) **m.** medical insurance.
mutualménte *a* mutually.
mutuànte *a* lending, loan; *nmf* lender.
mutuàre *vt* to borrow, lend.
mútuo *a* mutual, reciprocal; *nm* loan, mortgage.

N

nàcchere *nf pl* castanets *pl*.
nàfta *nf* naphtha, diesel oil; **a n.** oil-fired.
naftalína *nf* naphthalene; moth-balls *pl*.
nàiade *nf* naiad, water nymph.
nàilon *nm* nylon.
nàno *nm* dwarf; *a* dwarf(ish).
Nàpoli *nf* (*geogr*) Naples; **napoletàno** *a nm* Neapolitan.
nàppa *nf* tassel, tuft.
narcíso *nm* daffodil, narcissus.
narcòtico *pl* **-ici** *a nm* narcotic.
narice *nf* nostril.
narràre *vt* to narrate, relate, tell.
narrativa *nf* narrative, fiction.
narratóre *nm* **-tríce** *nf* narrator, story-teller.
narrazióne *nf* narration, tale.
nasàle *a* nasal.
nascènte *a* dawning, rising.
nàscere *vi* to be born, originate, rise.
nàscita *nf* birth; extraction, descent.
nascitúro *a nm* unborn (child).
nascóndere *vt* to conceal, hide; **-rsi** *vr* to hide oneself.

nascondíglio *nm* hiding place.
nascostaménte *ad* secretly; stealthily.
nascósto *a* hidden, secret, underhand; **di n.** secretly, stealthily.
nasèllo *nm* (*fish*) hake, whiting.
nàso *nm* nose; **a lúme di n.** by guesswork.
nàspo *nm* (*tec*) reel, winder.
nàstro *nm* band, ribbon, tape.
nastúrzio *nm* (*bot*) nasturtium, water-cress.
natàle *a* native; **Natàle** *nm* Christmas; **natàli** *nm pl* birth.
natalità *nf* birth-rate.
natalízio *a* (of) Christmas; birthday; *nm* birthday.
natànte *a* floating; *nm* craft.
nàtica *nf* buttock.
natío *a* native.
nativà *nf* nativity.
nativo *a* native, natural; *nm* native.
nàto *a* born, risen, sprung up; **nàta** née.
nàtta *nf* wen.
natúra *nf* nature, kind; **pagàre in n.** to pay in kind.
naturàle *a* genuine, natural.
naturalézza *nf* naturalness.
naturalizzàre *vt* to naturalize.
naturalizzazióne *nf* naturalization.
naturalménte *ad* naturally, of course.
naufragàre *vi* to be (ship)wrecked.
naufràgio *nm* (ship)wreck, failure.
nàufrago *pl* **-ghi** *a nm* shipwrecked (man).
nàusea *nf* nausea, sickness, loathing.
nauseabóndo, nauseànte *a* loathsome, nauseous.
nauseàre *vt* to disgust, nauseate.
nàutica *nf* nautical science.
nàutico *pl* **-ici** *a* nautical.
navàle *a* naval.
nàve *nf* ship, vessel.
navétta *nf* shuttle.
navicèlla *nf* bark, small ship.
navigàbile *a* navigable; **canàle n.** waterway.
navigànte *nm* sailor.
navigàre *vti* to navigate, sail; **n. in cattive àcque** to be badly off.
navigàto *a* experienced.
navigatóre *nm* navigator.
navigazióne *nf* navigation.
naviglio *nm* canal; fleet.
nazionàle *a* national; home-grown.
nazionalismo *nm* nationalism.
nazionalità *nf* nationality.
nazionalizzazióne *nf* nationalization.
nazióne *nf* nation.
nazista *a nmf* Nazi.
nazzarèno *a nm* Nazarene.
ne *pron and ad* of him, his, of her, hers; of it, its; of them, theirs; from there; any, some.
né *cj* neither, nor; **né . . . né** neither . . . nor.
neànche *ad* not even; *cj* neither.

nébbia nf fog, mist.
nebbióso a foggy, hazy.
nebulizzàre vt to atomize, vaporize.
nebulizzatóre nm atomizer, vaporizer.
nebulósa nf nebula.
nebulóso a nebulous, hazy.
nécessaire (Fr) nm beauty case; **n. per únghie** manicure set.
necessariaménte ad necessarily.
necessàrio a necessary, needful; nm what is necessary.
necessità nf necessity, need, poverty.
necessitàre vt to necessitate; vi to be necessary.
necróforo nm gravedigger.
necrològio nm obituary, register of deaths.
nefandézza nf infamy.
nefàndo a abominable, execrable.
nefàsto a ill-omened, unlucky.
nefríte nf nephritis.
negàbile a deniable.
negàre vt to deny.
negatíva nf denial, negative.
negatívo a negative, unfavourable.
negàto a denied, unfit; **èssere n. a qc** to be unsuited for sth.
negazióne nf denial, negative, negation.
neghittóso a slothful.
neglètto a neglected, untidy.
negligènte a careless, negligent.
negligènza nf carelessness, negligence.
negoziàbile a negotiable.
negoziànte nmf dealer, shopkeeper, tradesman.
negoziàre vti to negotiate, deal, trade.
negoziàti nm pl negotiation(s).
negózio nm shop, (US) store; trade, transaction.
negrièro nm slave-trader; (fig) slave-driver.
négro a nm negro.
negromànte nmf necromancer.
negromanzía nf necromancy.
némbo nm (storm)cloud.
nemíco pl -ici a hostile, harmful; nm enemy.
nemméno ad not even.
nènia nf dirge, plaintive song.
nèo nm blemish, (on the skin) mole.
neologísmo nm neologism.
neomicína nf neomycin.
nèon nm neon; **inségna al n.** neon sign.
neonàto a nm newborn (child).
neppúre ad not even.
neràstro a blackish.
nerbàta nf blow with a whip.
nèrbo nm nerve; whip; strength.
néro a black, dark; nm black.
nervatúra nf nervous system, nervation; ribbing.
nèrvo nm nerve, vigour; **avére i nèrvi** to be in a bad temper.
nervosità nf **nervosísmo** nm nerves, nervousness.

nervóso a nervous, excitable; nm irritability.
nèsci: fare il n. to pretend ignorance.
nèspola nf medlar; **nèspolo** nm medlar-tree.
nèsso nm connection, link.
nessúno pron nobody, no one; a no.
nettaménte ad cleanly, clearly.
nettapípe inv nm pipe-cleaner.
nettàre vt to clean, cleanse.
nèttare nm nectar.
nettézza nf cleanliness; **n. urbàna** dustmen pl.
nétto a clean; distinct; exact; net.
neuròlogo pl -ogi nm neurologist.
neutràle a nm neutral.
neutralità nf neutrality.
neutralizzàre vt to neutralize.
nèutro a neutral; nm neuter.
nevàio nm snowfield, glacier.
néve nf snow; **fiòcco di n.** snowflake.
nevicàre vi to snow.
nevicàta nf snowfall, snowstorm.
nevíschio nm sleet.
nevóso a snowy.
nevralgía nf neuralgia.
nevrastenía nf neurasthenia.
nevrastènico pl -ici a nm neurasthenic.
nevròsi nf (med) neurosis.
nevròtico pl -ici a nm neurotic.
nevvéro? interj isn't it (so)?
níbbio nm (bird) kite.
nícchia nf niche.
nicchiàre vi to hesitate.
Niccolò, Nicòla nm pr Nicholas.
níchel nm nickel.
nicotína nf nicotine.
nidiàta nf brood, nestful.
nidificàre vi to build a nest.
nído nm nest, haunt.
niènte pron and nm nothing.
nientediméno ad no less.
Nigèria nf (geogr) Nigeria.
Nílo nm (geogr) Nile.
nínfa nf nymph.
ninfèa nf water-lily.
ninnanànna nf lullaby.
ninnàre vt to lull, sing to sleep.
nínnolo nm trifle, trinket.
nipóte nmf grandson, granddaughter; nephew, niece.
nippònico pl -ici a Japanese.
nitidézza nf clearness.
nítido a clear, distinct.
nitóre nm neatness, brightness.
nitràto nm nitrate.
nitríre vi to neigh.
nitríto nm neigh.
nítro nm nitre, saltpetre.
nitrògeno nm nitrogen.
níveo a snowy, snow-white.
Nízza nf (geogr) Nice; **nizzàrdo** a nm (native) of Nice.
no ad no.
nòbile a nm noble.
nobiliàre a aristocratic.
nobilitàre vt to ennoble.
nobilménte ad nobly.
nobiltà nf nobility, nobleness.

nòcca nf knuckle.

nocchièro nm pilot, steersman.

nòcciolo nm kernel, stone; (fig) point, gist.

nocci(u)òla nf hazel-nut; **nocci(u)òla** nm hazel tree; **nocciolína americàna** peanut.

nóce nf walnut; nm walnut tree.

nocívo a harmful, hurtful.

nòdo nm knot.

nodóso a gnarled, knotty.

Noè nm pr Noah.

nói pron we, us.

nòia nf boredom, vexation.

noiosità nf boredom, bother.

noióso a tiresome, boring.

noleggiaménto nm hiring, chartering.

noleggiàre vt to hire, charter.

noléggio, nòlo nm hire, rental; **a n.** for (on) hire.

nolènte a unwilling; **volènte o n.** willy-nilly.

nòmade a nomadic; nmf nomad.

nóme nm name, noun; **n. pròprio** first name, Christian name.

nomèa nf reputation, notoriety.

nomenclatúra nf nomenclature.

nomígnolo nm nickname.

nòmina nf appointment.

nominàle a nominal.

nominàre vt to name, appoint.

nominatívo a nominative; nm nominative, name.

non ad not; **non . . . che** ad but, only.

nonagenàrio a nm nonagenarian.

nonagèsimo a nm ninetieth.

noncurànte a careless, heedless.

noncurànza nf carelessness, heedlessness.

nondiméno ad nevertheless, still, yet.

nònna nf grandmother; **nònno** nm grandfather.

nonnúlla nm nothing, trifle.

nòno a ninth.

nonostànte prep in spite of, notwithstanding; ad nevertheless.

nonpertànto ad nevertheless, still.

nonsènso nm nonsense.

nontiscordardimé nm forget-me-not.

nòrd nm north; **a n.** to the north; **n. est** north-east; **n. òvest** north-west.

nòrdico pl **-ici** a northern; nm northerner.

Norimbèrga nf (geogr) Nuremberg.

nòrma nf rule, standard, directions; **a n. di légge** according to law.

normàle a nm normal.

normalità nf normality.

normalizzàre vt to normalize.

normalménte ad normally.

Normandía nf (geogr) Normandy.

norvegése a nmf Norwegian.

Norvègia nf (geogr) Norway.

nostalgía nf homesickness.

nostàlgico pl **-ici** a nostalgic.

nostràle, nostràno a domestic, home, of one's own country; **prodòtti nostràli** home produce.

nòstro poss a and pron our, ours.

nostròmo nm boatswain.

nòta nf note, mark, list; **n. a piè di pàgina** footnote; **blòcco per nòte** scribbling block, (US) scratch pad.

notàbile a nm notable.

notàio nm notary.

notàre vt to note, notice; **fàrsi n.** vr to attract attention.

notaríle a notarial.

nòtes nm notebook, agenda.

notévole a noticeable, remarkable.

notevolménte ad considerably, greatly.

notificàre vt to notify.

notífica, notificazióne nf communication, notification.

notízia nf (piece of) news.

notiziàrio nm news bulletin; (cín) newsreel.

nòto a famous, notorious, (well-) known.

notorietà nf notoriety.

notòrio a notorious.

nottàmbulo a night-walking; nm night-walker; somnambulist.

nottàta nf (duration of a) night.

nòtte nf night; **di n.** by night.

nòttola nf bat.

nottúrno a night(ly), nocturnal; nm (mus) nocturne.

novànta a ninety; **novantènne** 90-year-old; **novantèsimo** ninetieth.

nòve a nine.

novecènto a nm nine hundred; twentieth century.

novèlla nf short story, tale.

novellière nm short-story writer.

novellíno a inexperienced; nm beginner, inexperienced person.

novellística nf short-story writing, fiction.

novèllo a new.

novèmbre nm November.

nòvero nm number, class, category.

novilúnio nm new moon.

novità nf newness, novelty, news.

noviziàto nm apprenticeship, novitiate.

novízio nm novice, beginner, apprentice.

nozióne nf idea, notion.

nòzze nf pl wedding, marriage.

núbe nf cloud.

nubifràgio nm cloudburst, downpour.

núbile a (of women) unmarried, marriageable; nf spinster.

núca nf nape (of the neck).

nucleàre a nuclear.

núcleo nm nucleus.

nudaménte ad nakedly, barely, simply, plainly.

nudità nf nakedness, nudity.

núdo a naked, bare; nm nude.

núlla nm and pron nothing.

nullaòsta nm (eccl) nihil obstat; permit; permission.

nullatenènte nm f person who owns nothing.

nullità nf nonentity, nullity, worthlessness.

núllo a null and void.

núme nm deity.

numeràle a nm numeral.

numeràre vt to number.

numerazióne nf numbering.

numèrico pl -ici a numerical.

número nm number.

numeróso a numerous.

numismàtica nf numismatics pl.

núnzio nm nuncio.

nuòcere vt to harm, hurt, damage.

nuòra nf daughter-in-law.

nuotàre vi to swim.

nuotàta nf swim.

nuotatóre nm swimmer; **n. subàcqueo** skin-diver.

nuòto nm swimming; **passàre a n.** to swim across; **n. subàcqueo** skindiving.

nuòva nf (piece of) news.

Nuòva York nf (geogr) New York.

Nuòva Zelànda nf (geogr) New Zealand.

nuòvo a new; **di n.** again.

nutrice nf wet nurse.

nutriènte a nourishing, nutritious.

nutriménto nm nourishment.

nutrire vt to feed, nourish, foster; **-rsi (di)** vr to feed (on).

nutritivo a nourishing, nutritious.

nutrizióne nf feeding, nourishment, nutrition.

nùvola nf -lo nm cloud.

nùvolo, nuvolóso a overcast, cloudy.

nuziàle a wedding.

O

o cj or, or else; **o . . . o** either . . . or, whether . . . or; **o l'úno o l'àltro** pron either; interj oh!

òasi nf oasis.

obbediènte etc v **ubbidiènte** etc.

obbligàre (a) vt to compel, force, oblige; **-rsi** vr to bind oneself, undertake.

obbligazióne nf obligation; (com) bond, debenture.

òbbligo pl -ghi nm duty, obligation.

obbròbrio nm disgrace.

obesità nf obesity.

obèso a corpulent, obese.

òbice nm (mil) howitzer.

obiettàre vt to object.

obiettività nf objectivity, impartiality.

obiettívo a objective, impartial; nm objective; lens.

obiezióne nf objection.

obitòrio nm mortuary, morgue.

oblazióne nf donation, oblation.

oblìo nm forgetfulness, oblivion.

obliquità nf obliquity.

oblìquo a oblique, underhand.

obliteràre vt to obliterate.

oblò nm porthole.

òboe nm (mus) oboe.

òbolo nm donation.

òca nf goose; **pèlle d'o.** gooseflesh.

occasionàle a casual, chance.

occasióne nf occasion, opportunity; **d'o.** second-hand.

occhiàia nf eye-socket, dark circle under eye.

occhialàio nm optician.

occhiàli nm pl spectacles pl, glasses pl.

occhialíno nm lorgnette.

occhialúto a bespectacled.

occhiàta nf glance.

occhieggiàre vt to eye, ogle; vi to peep, peer.

occhièllo nm buttonhole, eyelet.

occhiétto nm **fàre l'o. a qlcu** to wink at s.o.

òcchio nm eye; **a còlpo d'o.** at first sight; **in un bàtter d'o.** in a twinkling of an eye; **a quàttro òcchi** ad privately.

occidentàle a west(ern).

occidènte nm west.

occorrènte a nm necessary, requisite.

occorrènza nf circumstance, necessity, need; **all'o.** in case of need.

occórrere vi impers to be necessary, need, happen; **occórre mólto tèmpo** much time is required; **mi occórrono sòldi** I need money.

occúlto a hidden, occult.

occupànte a occupying; nmf occupant, occupier.

occupàre vt to occupy; **-rsi (di)** vr to attend (to), be busy (with), mind.

occupàto a engaged, busy.

occupazióne nf occupation.

oceànico pl -ici a oceanic.

ocèano nm ocean.

oculàre a eye, ocular; nm eye-piece; **testimòne o.** eye-witness.

oculatézza nf cautiousness, circumspection, wariness.

oculàto a wary, prudent.

oculísta nm eye specialist, oculist.

òde nf ode.

odiàre vt to hate, detest.

odièrno a of today, today's, modern.

òdio pl **òdii** nm hatred, hate.

odióso a hateful, odious.

odissèa nf odyssey.

odontoiàtra nm odontologist, dentist.

odontoiatría nf odontology, dentistry.

odoràre vti to smell, scent.

odoràto nm (sense of) smell.

odóre nm smell, odour, scent.

odoróso a fragrant, odorous.

Ofèlia nf pr Ophelia.

offèndere vt to offend, injure; **-rsi** vr to be offended, take offence.

offensíva nf (mil) offensive.

offensívo a offensive, insulting.

offerènte nmf bidder, offerer.

offèrta nf offer(ing); (com) tender, bid.

offertòrio nm offertory.
offésa nf offence, wrong.
offéso a offended, injured.
officìna nf works, workshop.
offìcio v ufficio.
officióso a obliging; unofficial.
offrìre vt to bid, offer.
offuscaménto nm dimming, darkening, obscuring.
oggettivaménte ad objectively.
oggettìvo a objective, impartial.
oggètto nm article, object, subject.
òggi ad today; o. a òtto today week.
oggidì, oggigiórno ad nowadays.
ógni a each, every; in o. luògo ad everywhere; in o. mòdo ad anyhow; o. tànto ad every now and then.
Ognissànti nm All Saints' Day.
ognóra ad always.
ognúno pron each, everybody, everyone.
ohibò interj come now!
ohimè interj alas!
olà interj hallo!
Olànda nf (geogr) Holland.
olandése a Dutch; nm Dutchman, (the) Dutch (language); nf Dutchwoman.
oleàndro nm oleander.
oleàto a oiled; càrta oleàta greaseproof paper.
oleifìcio nm oil mill.
oleodótto nm (oil) pipeline.
oleóso a greasy, oily.
olfàtto nm (sense of) smell.
oliatóre nm (mech) oil-can, oiler.
olièra nf (oil) cruet.
oligarchìa nf oligarchy.
Olìmpia nf pr Olympia.
olimpìade nf (usually pl) (sport) Olympic games pl, Olympiad.
olìmpico pl -ici a Olympic, Olympian; càlma olìmpica imperturbability.
olimpiónico pl -ici a (sport) Olympic; nm (sport) Olympian.
òlio nm oil.
olìva nf olive; olìvo nm olive tree.
olivàstro a olive(-coloured).
olivéto nm olive grove.
Olìvia nf pr Olive, Olivia.
ólmo nm elm.
olocàusto nm holocaust, sacrifice.
ològrafo nm holograph.
oltraggiàre vt to outrage, insult.
oltràggio nm outrage, insult.
oltraggióso a outrageous.
oltrànza, ad ad to the bitter end.
óltre ad and prep further, beyond, over; o. a, che besides.
oltremàre ad beyond the sea(s), oversea(s).
oltremòdo ad exceedingly.
oltrepassàre vt to go beyond, surpass, outrun, exceed.
oltretómba nm beyond, hereafter.
omàggio nm homage; còpia in o. presentation copy; omàggi pl respects pl; in o. free.
ombelicàle a umbilical.

ombelìco pl -ichi nm navel.
ómbra nf shade, shadow; all'o. in the shade.
ombreggiàre vt to shade.
ombrellàio nm umbrella maker.
ombrèllo nm umbrella; ombrellìno parasol; ombrellóne (beach) umbrella.
ombrétto nm (cosm) eye shadow.
ombróso a (places) shady; (people) touchy.
òmero nm shoulder.
Oméro nm pr Homer.
omertà nf (conspiracy of) silence.
ométtere vt to leave out, omit.
omicìda a homicidal; nmf homicide, murderer.
omicìdio nm homicide, murder.
omissióne nf omission.
òmnibus nm omnibus, bus.
omogèneo a homogeneous.
omòlogo pl -ghi a homologous.
omònimo a homonymous; nm homonym, namesake.
omosessuàle a homosexual.
óncia nf ounce.
ónda nf wave; ondàta nf big wave (also fig).
ónde ad whence; pron whereby; cj so that, in order that; wherefore.
ondeggiaménto nm rocking, swaying; fluttering, wavering.
ondeggiàre vi to rock, wave; hesitate.
ondóso a undulatory, waving.
ondulàre vt to wave; vi to undulate; -rsi i capèlli to wave one's hair.
ondulàto a wavy, undulating, corrugated.
ondulazióne nf undulation; (hair) wave.
ónere nm burden.
oneróso a burdensome, onerous.
onestà nf honesty, uprightness, fairness.
onestaménte ad honestly, modestly, decently.
onèsto a fair, honest, upright.
ònice nf onyx.
onnipossènte, onnipotènte a almighty, omnipotent.
onnisciènza nf omniscience.
onnìvoro a omnivorous.
onomàstico pl -ici a nm name-day.
onomatopéa nf onomatopoeia.
onorànza nf honour, solemnity.
onoràre vt to honour, do credit to; -rsi (di) vr to be proud (of).
onoràrio a honorary; nm fee, honorarium; cittadìno o. freeman.
onoratamènte ad honourably.
onoràto a honoured; honourable.
onóre nm honour.
onorévole a honourable, (also title of parliamentary deputies).
onorevolménte ad honourably.
onorificènza nf honour, title, decoration.
onorìfico pl -ici a honorific.
ónta nf disgrace, shame; ad o. di in spite of.

ontàno nm alder.
opacità nf opacity, opaqueness.
opàco pl -chi a opaque, dull, matt.
opàle nm opal.
òpera nf work, action; opera; institution.
operàbile a operable, workable.
operàio a working; nm workman.
operàre vti to work, act, operate; o. qlcu operate on s.o.
operàto a (cloth) fancy; nm conduct, action; one who has been operated upon.
operatóre nm operator; (cin) cameraman.
operatòrio a operative; surgical; sàla operatòria operating theatre.
operazióne nf operation.
operosità nf activity, industry.
operóso a active, industrious.
opifício nm factory, works.
opinàre vi to be of the opinion.
opinióne nf opinion, contention.
òppio nm opium.
opponènte a opposing, opponent; nmf opponent.
oppórre vt -rsi vr to oppose, object.
opportunaménte ad opportunely, appropriately.
opportunista nmf opportunist.
opportunità nf opportuneness; opportunity.
opportúno a opportune.
opposizióne nf opposition.
opposto a nm opposite.
oppressióne nf oppression.
oppressivo a oppressive.
opprèsso a oppressed.
oppressóre nm oppressor.
opprimènte a oppressive.
opprimere vt to oppress, overwhelm.
oppugnàre vt to attack; (fig) impugn.
oppúre cj or (else).
optàre vi to opt.
opulènto a opulent, rich.
opulènza nf opulence, wealth.
opúscolo nm pamphlet.
óra nf hour, time; che óre sóno? what time is it?; ad now; presently; or óra just now; óra che cj now that.
oràcolo nm oracle.
òrafo nm goldsmith.
oràle a nm oral.
oralménte ad orally, verbally.
oramài ad by this time, now; from now on.
oràrio a per hour; nm timetable; o. d'ufficio office hours; segnàle o. time signal.
oratóre nm -tríce nf orator, speaker.
oratòria nf eloquence, oratory.
oratòrio a oratorial; nm oratory, Sunday school; (mus) oratorio.
Oràzio nm pr Horace.
orazióne nf oration, prayer.
òrbita nf eye-socket, orbit.
òrbo a blind.
Òrcadi (le) nf pl (geogr) the Orkney Islands.

orchèstra nf orchestra.
orchidèa nf orchid.
órcio nm pitcher.
órco pl órchi nm ogre.
òrda nf horde.
ordígno nm tool, device.
ordinàle a ordinal.
ordinaménto nm arrangement, disposition.
ordinànza nf order; (mil) orderly, batman; o. municipàle by-law.
ordinàre vt to order, arrange, ordain; gli ordinài di andàre I ordered him to go.
ordinariaménte ad ordinarily, usually.
ordinàrio a ordinary, normal; coarse; nm professor.
ordinàto a orderly, tidy.
ordinazióne nf order; (eccl) ordination; fàtto su o. a made to order.
órdine nm order; o. del giòrno agenda.
ordíre vt to weave; plot.
ordíto nm warp, web; plot.
orecchíno nm earring.
orécchio nm ear; a o. by ear; dúro d'o. hard of hearing.
orecchióni nm pl (med) mumps.
oréfice nm goldsmith.
oreficería nf goldsmith's shop; things made of gold.
òrfano a nm orphan.
orfanotròfio nm orphanage.
Orfèo nm pr Orpheus.
òrfico pl òrfici a Orphic.
organétto, organíno nm barrel-organ.
orgànico pl -ici a organic.
organismo nm organism.
organista nmf organist.
organizzàre vt to organize.
organizzatóre a organizing; nm -tríce nf organizer.
organizzazióne nf organization.
òrgano nm organ.
orgàsmo nm orgasm, excitement.
òrgia nf orgy.
orgóglio nm pride.
orgogliosaménte ad proudly.
orgoglióso a proud.
orientàle a east(ern), oriental.
orientaménto nm orientation, bearings; o. mediànte ràdio radio bearing.
orientàre vt to set, turn; -rsi vr to find one's bearings or way.
oriènte nm east, orient.
orígano nm origan.
originàle a nm original, eccentric (person).
originalità nf originality, strangeness.
originalménte ad originally, ingeniously.
originàre vti to give rise to; originate.
originariaménte ad originally.
originàrio a original, primary.
orígine nm origin, beginning, cause.

origliàre *vi* to eavesdrop.
orína *nf* urine.
orinatóio *nm* urinal.
oriúndo *a* native; **èssere o. di Róma** to be of Roman origin.
orizzontàle *a* horizontal.
orizzónte *nm* horizon.
Orlàndo *nm pr* Roland.
orlàre *vt* to edge, hem.
orlatúra *nf* edging, hemming.
órlo *nm* edge, hem.
órma *nf* footprint, mark.
ormài *ad* by now.
ormeggiàre *vt* -rsi *vr* to moor.
orméggio *nm* mooring.
ormóne *nm* hormone.
ornamentàle *a* ornamental.
ornaménto *nm* ornament.
ornàre *vt* to adorn, decorate.
ornàto *a* ornate; *nm* decoration.
ornitología *nf* ornithology.
ornitòlogo *pl* -oghi *nm* ornithologist.
óro *nm* gold.
orologería *nf* watchmaking, watchmaker's shop, mechanism of a watch (clock).
orologiàio *nm* watchmaker.
orològio *nm* clock, watch.
oròscopo *nm* horoscope.
orrèndo, orríbile *a* horrible, dreadful.
òrrido *a* horrid; *nm* ravine.
orripilànte *a* terrifying; hideous.
orróre *nm* horror, loathing.
orsacchiòtto *nm* bear cub; (*toy*) teddybear.
órso *nm* bear; (*fig*) unsociable person; **Órsa Maggióre** (*astr*) Great Bear; **Órsa Minóre** Little Bear, **o. grígio** grizzly (bear).
Órsola *nf pr* Ursula.
orsù *interj* come on!
ortàggio *nm* vegetable.
ortènsia *nf* hydrangea.
ortíca *nf* nettle.
orticària *nf* nettlerash.
orticultóre *nm* market gardener, (*US*) truck farmer.
òrto *nm* kitchen garden.
ortodòsso *a* orthodox.
ortografía *nf* orthography, spelling.
ortolàno *nm* greengrocer, market gardener, (*US*) truck farmer.
ortopedía *nf* orthopaedics.
orzaiòlo *nm* stye (on the eyelid).
orzàta *nf* barley water.
òrzo *nm* barley.
osàre *vti* to dare, risk.
Óscar *nm pr* Oscar; **prémio O.** Oscar (prize), (*US*) Academy Award.
oscenità *nf* indecency, obscenity.
oscèno *a* obscene, horrible.
oscillàre *vi* to swing, hesitate, oscillate.
oscillatóre *nm* oscillator.
oscillatòrio *a* oscillatory, oscillating.
oscillazióne *nf* oscillation, swing (ing), fluctuation.
oscuraménto *nm* darkening.

oscuràre *vt* to darken, obscure; -rsi *vr* to grow dark, dim.
oscurità *nf* darkness, obscurity.
oscúro *a* dark, obscure, difficult; **èssere all'o. di** to be ignorant of.
ospedàle *nm* hospital.
ospitàle *a* hospitable.
ospitalità *nf* hospitality.
ospitàre *vt* to give hospitality to.
òspite *nmf* host(ess); guest.
ospízio *nm* asylum, home.
ossatúra *nf* (bone) structure, framework.
òsseo *a* bony, osseous.
ossequiàre *vt* to pay one's respects to.
ossèquio *nm* homage, obedience; ossèqui *pl* regards, respects *pl*.
ossequióso *a* respectful, obsequious.
osservànza *nf* obedience, observance.
osservàre *vt* to observe, watch, examine.
osservatóre *nm* -tríce *nf* observer.
osservatòrio *nm* observatory; (*mil*) observation post, look-out.
osservazióne *nf* observation, remark.
ossessionàre *vt* to obsess, haunt.
ossessióne *nf* obsession.
ossèsso *nm* person possessed.
ossía *cj* or, or rather.
òssido *nm* oxide.
ossídrico *pl* -ici *a* oxyhydrogen.
ossigenàto *a* oxygenized; (*of hair*) peroxided.
ossígeno *nm* oxygen.
òsso *nm*; *m pl* òssi (*meat*) bone ; (*fruit*) stone; *f pl* òssa (human) bone; **di càrne ed òssa** of flesh and blood.
ossúto *a* big-boned, bony.
ostacolàre *vt* to hinder, interfere with.
ostàcolo *nm* hindrance, obstacle; **córsa ad ostàcoli** hurdle-race, steeplechase.
ostàggio *nm* hostage.
òste *nm* innkeeper, publican, (*US*) saloon keeper, landlord.
osteggiàre *vt* to be hostile to, oppose.
ostèllo *nm* mansion; inn; hostel.
Ostènda *nf pr* (*geogr*) Ostend.
ostentàre *vt* to show off; feign.
ostentazióne *nf* ostentation; pretence.
ostería *nf* inn, tavern.
ostéssa *nf* innkeeper's wife.
ostètrica *nf* midwife.
òstia *nf* (*eccl*) Host, wafer.
òstico *pl* -ici *a* difficult, unpleasant.
ostíle *a* hostile.
ostilità *nf* hostility, enmity.
ostilménte *ad* in a hostile manner, with hostility.
ostinàrsi *vr* to insist, persist.
ostinàto *a* obstinate, stubborn.
ostinazióne *nf* obstinacy, persistence.
ostracísmo *nm* ostracism.
òstrica *nf* oyster.
ostruíre *vt* to obstruct, stop (up).

ostruzióne nf obstruction.
Otèllo nm pr Othello.
otorinolaringoiàtra nm ear, nose and throat specialist.
ótre nm (goat)-skin bottle.
ottàgono nm octagon.
ottàno nm (chem) octane.
ottànta a nm eighty; **ottanténne** a eighty-year-old; **ottantésimo** a eightieth; **ottantina** nf about eighty.
ottàva nf octave; **ottàvo** a nm eighth; octavo.
ottemperàre (a) vi to comply (with), obey.
ottenebràre vt to darken, cloud.
ottenére vt to obtain, gain, get.
otteníbile a obtainable.
òttica nf optics.
òttico pl -ici a optic(al); nm optician.
ottimìsmo nm optimism.
ottimìsta nmf optimist.
ottimìstico pl -ici a optimistic.
òttimo a very good, excellent.
òtto a nm eight.
ottòbre nm October.
ottocènto a nm eight hundred; nineteenth century.
ottomàno a nm Ottoman.
ottóne nm brass, brass instrument.
ottuagenàrio a nm octogenarian.
otturàre vt to stop (up).
otturazióne nf plugging; (of tooth) filling, stopping.
ottusità nf obtuseness, bluntness.
ottùso a obtuse, blunt, dull.
ovàia nf ovary.
ovàle a nm oval.
ovàtta nf wadding, cotton wool, (US) absorbent cotton.
ovazióne nf ovation.
óve ad where; cj if, in case.
òvest nm west; a o. in, to the west.
Ovídio nm pr Ovid.
ovíle nm fold, sheep-fold.
ovíno a ovine; nm sheep.
òvolo nm a kind of mushroom.
ovúnque ad anywhere, everywhere, wherever.
ovvéro cj or.
ovviaménte ad obviously, evidently.
ovviàre vt to obviate, avoid.
òvvio a obvious, evident.
oziàre vi to idle, loaf.
òzio nm idleness, leisure.
oziosità nf idleness, laziness.
ozióso a idle.
ozòno nm ozone.

P

pacataménte ad calmly, quietly.
pacatézza nf calmness, quietness.
pacàto a calm, quiet.
pacchétto nm packet, small parcel.
pàcco pl **pàcchi** nm parcel, package.
pàce nf peace.
pachistàno a nm Pakistani.
pacière nm **pacièra** nf peacemaker.

pacificaménte ad peacefully, peaceably.
pacificàre vt to pacify, reconcile.
pacificazióne nf pacification, reconciliation.
pacífico pl -ici a peaceful; **Pacífico** a nm (geogr) Pacific (Ocean).
padàno a (geogr) Po; **la Val Padàna** the Po Valley.
padèlla nf frying-pan; bed-pan; **dàlla p. nèlla bràge** out of the frying-pan into the fire.
padiglióne nm pavilion, tent.
Pàdova nf (geogr) Padua; **padovàno** a nm Paduan.
pàdre nm father.
padríno nm godfather; (in a duel) second.
padróna nf landlady, mistress.
padróne nm landlord, master, owner, proprietor.
padronànza nf command, mastery; **p. di sè** self control.
padronàto nm ownership, possession.
padroneggiàre vt to command, master; vi to play the master.
paeșàggio nm landscape.
paeșàno a country, rustic; nm peasant; fellow-townsman.
paéșe nm country; district; village; town.
paeșìsta nmf landscape painter.
paffùto a chubby, plump.
pàga nf pay, wages pl.
pagàbile a payable.
pagaménto nm payment.
paganèșimo nm paganism.
pagàno a nm pagan, heathen.
pagàre vt to pay, pay for.
pagèlla nf (school-)report.
pàggio nm pageboy.
pagherò nm (com) promissory note, I.O.U.
pàgina nf leaf, page (of a book).
pàglia nf straw; **p. di fèrro** steel wool; **pagliétta** straw-hat.
pagliàccio nm buffoon, clown.
pagliàio nm straw-rick.
pagliericcio nm paillasse.
pagnòtta nf loaf.
pàgo pl **pàghi** a content, satisfied.
pàio pl f **pàia** nm pair.
Pàkistan nm (geogr) Pakistan.
pàla nf shovel; **ruòta a pàle** paddle-wheel.
palàta nf shovelful; blow with a shovel; stroke with an oar.
palatíno a Palatine.
palàto nm palate.
palàzzo nm palace, mansion, building.
pàlco pl **pàlchi** nm platform, stand; (theat) box.
palcoscènico pl -ici nm (theat) stage.
paleșàre vt to disclose, reveal.
paléșe a evident, clear, obvious.
Palestína nf (geogr) Palestine.
palestinése a nmf Palestinian.

palèstra *nf* gymnasium.
palétta *nm* small shovel.
palétto *nm (of the door)* bolt; small pole.
pàlio *nm* horse-race at Siena; silk banner given to winner.
palizzàta *nf* fence, paling, palisade.
pàlla *nf* ball; p. a bàsi baseball; p. a vólo volleyball; pallacanèstro *nf* basketball; pallacòrda *nf* lawn tennis; pallamàglio *nf* croquet; pallanuòto *nf* water polo; p. da cannóne shell; p. da fucíle bullet.
palleggiaménto, palléggio *nm (football)* dribbling; *(tennis)* knock-up.
palliatívo *a nm* palliative.
pallidézza *nf* paleness, pallor.
pàllido *a* pale, pallid.
pallína *nf* little ball, small shot; pallíno *nm* little ball, small shot, pellet; *(bowls)* jack; avére il p. di to have a craze for.
palloncíno *nm* balloon, Chinese lantern.
pallóne *nm* ball, balloon, football.
pallóre *nm* paleness, pallor.
pallòttola *nf* bullet, pellet.
pàlma *nf* palm(tree); *(of the hand)* palm.
palméto *nm* palm-grove.
pàlmo *nm (of the hand, or measure)* palm.
pàlo *nm* pole, post, pile, pylon.
palombàro *nm* diver.
palómbo *nm* dogfish; wood-pigeon.
palpàbile *a* palpable, obvious.
palpàre *vt* to feel, handle, touch; *(med)* palpate.
pàlpebra *nf* eyelid.
palpitànte *a* palpitating, throbbing.
palpitàre *vi* to palpitate, tremble, throb.
pàlpito *nm* beat, throb.
paltò *nm* overcoat.
palúde *nf* marsh.
paludóso, palústre *a* marshy.
Pamèla *nf pr* Pamela.
pàmpino *nm* vine leaf.
Pànama *nf (geogr)* Panama.
panàre *vt* to cover with bread-crumbs.
pànca *nf* bench, form.
pancétta *nf* bacon.
panchétto *nf* footstool, small bench.
pància *nf* stomach, belly.
panciòlle, in *ad* stàre in p. to lounge about.
panciòtto *nm* waistcoat, (US) vest.
Pancràzio *nm pr* Pancras.
pàne *nm* bread, loaf; buòno cóme il p. as good as gold.
panegírico *pl* -ici *nm* panegyric.
panèllo *nm* oilcake.
panettería *nf* baker's shop.
panettière *nm* baker.
panfrútto *nm* fruitcake.
pània *nf* bird-lime; *(fig)* snare.
pànico *pl* -ici *nm* panic.
paníco *pl* -chi *nm* millet.

panière *nm* basket.
panifício *nm* bakehouse, bakery.
pànna *nf* cream; *(aut)* breakdown; p. montàta whipped cream.
pannéggio *nm* drapery.
pannèllo *nm (arch)* panel; p. di finèstra window-pane.
pànno *nm* cloth; pànni *pl* clothes; sè ío fóssi néi tuòi pànni if I were in your place (shoes).
pannolíno *nm* (baby's) napkin, nappy, (US) diaper; sanitary towel.
panoràmico *pl* -ici *a* panoramic.
panpepàto *nm* gingerbread.
pantalóni *nm pl* trousers.
pantàno *nm* bog, swamp.
panteísmo *nm* pantheism.
pantèra *nf* panther.
pantòfola *nf* slipper.
pantomíma *nf (theat)* mime, dumb-show.
Pàola *nf pr* Paula, Pauline.
Pàolo *nm pr* Paul.
papà *nm* daddy, papa.
Pàpa *nm pr* Pope.
papàle *a* papal.
papàto *nm* papacy.
papàvero *nm* poppy.
pàpero *nm* gosling; Paperíno *nm* Donald Duck.
papíro *nm* papyrus.
pàppa *nf* pap.
pappagàllo *nm* parrot; pappagallíno budgerigar, parakeet.
paràbola *nf* parable; parabola.
parabrézza *nm (aut)* windscreen, (US) windshield.
paracadúte *nm* parachute.
paracadutísta *nm* parachutist, para-trooper.
paracénere *nm* fireguard.
paradisíaco *pl* -íaci *a* heavenly, paradisiacal.
paradíso *nm* heaven, paradise.
paradòsso *nm* paradox.
parafàngo *nm (aut)* mudguard, (US) fender.
paraffína *nf* oil, paraffin, (US) kerosene (coal-oil).
paràfrasi *nf* paraphrase.
parafúlmine *nm* lightning con-ductor.
parafuòco *pl* -chi *nm* fireguard.
paràggi *nm pl* neighbourhood.
paragonàre *vt* to compare.
paragóne *nm* comparison; a p. di in comparison with.
paràgrafo *nm* paragraph.
paràlisi *nf* paralysis.
paralítico *pl* -ici *a nm* paralytic.
paralizzàre *vt* to paralyse.
parallelaménte *ad* parallelly.
parallèlo *a nm* parallel *(also fig)*.
paralúme *nm* lampshade.
paraòcchi *nm pl* blinkers *pl*.
parapètto *nm* parapet.
parapíglia *nm* turmoil.
parapiòggia *nm* umbrella.
paràre *vt* to parry, avert; decorate, lead up to.

parasóle nm parasol, (aut) sun-shield.

parassíta nm parasite.

parastatàle a state-controlled.

paràta nf parade; parry, save; màla p. unlucky moment.

paratía nf (naut) bulkhead.

paratífo nm paratyphoid.

paraúrti nm (aut) bumper.

paravènto nm (wind)screen.

parcheggiàre vt to park; **parchèggio** nm parking (place), parking station, carpark, (US) parking lot.

pàrco pl **pàrchi** a frugal, moderate; nm park.

parécchio a a good deal of; ad a lot, much; **parècchi** a and pron m pl **parècchie** a and pron f pl several.

pareggiàre vt to balance, level; vi (sport) to draw; **una scuòla pareggiàta** an officially recognized school.

paréggio nm balance; (sport) draw.

parentàdo nm **parentèla** nf kin pl, kindred, relations pl, relationship.

parènte nmf relation, relative; p. più strétto next-of-kin.

parèntesi nf brackets pl, parenthesis.

parére vi to seem, look like; nm opinion.

paréte nf (internal) wall; (mountain) face.

pàri a equal, (number) even; nm (sing and pl) equal, peer; càmera déi p. House of Lords; nf par; àlla p. au pair; (com) at par.

parificàre v **pareggiàre**.

Parìgi nf (geogr) Paris; **parigíno** a nm Parisian.

parìglia nf (horses) pair; tit for tat.

pariménti ad likewise.

parità nf equality, parity.

parlamentàre vi to parley; a parliamentary; nm Member of Parliament.

parlaménto nm parley; parliament.

parlàre vi to speak, talk; p. chiàro to be plain, speak one's mind.

parmigiàno a nm Parmesan (cheese).

parodìa nf parody.

paròla nf word; p. d'òrdine (mil) password.

parossìsmo nm paroxysm.

parricìda a patricidal; nm parricide (criminal); **parricìdio** nm parricide (crime).

parròcchia nf parish, parish church; **parrocchiàle** a parish; **parrocchiàno** parishioner.

pàrroco pl -oci nm parish priest; (Protestant) parson, minister.

parrúcca nf wig.

parrucchière nm **parrucchièra** nf hairdresser.

parsimònia nf parsimony, sparingness.

pàrte nf part, place, share, side; la màggior p. the majority; da p. aside; in p. partly.

partecipàre vt to announce; vi to share, participate; p. àgli útili to share in the profits.

partecipazióne nf participation; announcement.

partécipe a informed; participating, sharing.

parteggiàre vi to side with, take sides.

Partenóne nm pr Parthenon.

partenopèo a Neapolitan.

partènza nf departure, start(ing).

particélla nf particle.

particìpio nm participle.

particolàre a particular, special; nm particular, detail.

particolareggiàto a detailed.

particolarménte ad particularly, especially, in particular.

partigiàno a partisan; nm partisan, supporter.

partíre vi to depart, leave, set out, start; a p. da domàni starting from tomorrow.

partíta nf match; (US) game; party, (com) lot, entry.

partíto nm (pol) party; (marriage) match; resolution; a p. préso with mind made up.

partitúra nf (mus) score.

partizióne nf division, partition.

pàrto nm (child)birth, delivery.

partorìre vti to bear, give birth to; nm childbearing.

parziàle a partial.

parzialità nf partiality.

pàscere vti -rsi vr to graze, pasture, feed.

pascolàre vti to graze, pasture.

pàscolo nm pasture; (fig) food.

Pàsqua nf Easter; **pasquàle** a Easter.

passàbile a passable.

passàggio nm passage, crossing; (sport) pass; diritto di p. right of way; p. a livèllo level crossing, (US) grade crossing; p. pedonàle pedestrian crossing; èssere di p. to be passing through.

passamanerìa nf **passamàno** nm trimming.

passamontàgna nm Balaclava helmet.

passànte nmf passer-by.

passapòrto nm passport.

passàre vti to pass, spend; p. da to call on; -rsela vr to get on.

passatèmpo nm pastime.

passàto a nm past.

passeggèro a passing, transient; nm passenger, traveller.

passeggiàre vi to (go for a) walk.

passeggiàta nf walk, ride, drive.

passéggio nm promenade, walk.

passerèlla nf foot-bridge; (naut) gangway.

pàssero nm sparrow.

passionàle a passionate, of passion.

passióne nf passion.

passività nf passiveness; (com) liabilities pl.

passívo *a* passive; *nm* passive; (*com*) liabilities *pl.*

pàsso *nm* step, pace; passage; (*geogr*) pass; a p. d'uòmo at a walking pace; di pàri p. at the same rate.

pàsta *nf* dough, pastry; cake; paste, pulp; p. dentifrícia toothpaste; pastína da tè teacake, (*US*) biscuit.

pastèllo *nm* pastel.

pastétta *nf* batter.

pastícca *nf* lozenge, tablet.

pasticcería *nf* confectioner's, confectionary; pasticcière *nm* confectioner.

pasticcíno *nm* small cake, tartlet, (*US*) cookie.

pasticcio *nm* pie; (*fig*) mess; nèi pastícci in a fix.

pastíglia *nf* lozenge, pastille.

pàsto *nm* meal.

pastóia *nf* hobble, pastern; (*fig*) fetters.

pastoràle *a* pastoral; *nm* crozier; *nf* pastoral (letter).

pastóre *nm* shepherd, pastor; pastorèlla *nf* shepherdess.

pastorizzàre *vt* to pasteurize.

pastóso *a* doughy, soft, mellow.

pastràno *nm* (man's) overcoat.

pastúra *nf* pasture.

patàta *nf* potato; patàte frítte chips, (*US*) French fries; patatíne frítte crisps, (*US*) potato chips.

patènte *a* open, obvious; *nf* licence; patentàto *a* trained.

paternàle *nf* scolding.

paternaménte *ad* in a fatherly way, paternally.

paternità *nf* paternity; father's name.

patèrno *a* paternal.

patètico *pl* -ici *a* moving, pathetic.

patíbolo *nm* gallows, gibbet.

patiménto *nm* pain, suffering.

patíre *vti* to endure, suffer.

patología *nf* pathology; patològico *pl* -ici *a* pathological(al).

pàtria *nf* (one's own) country, fatherland.

patriàrca *nm* patriarch; patriarcàle *a* patriarchal.

patrígno *nm* stepfather.

patrimònio *nm* heritage, estate.

pàtrio *a* of one's own country or home.

patriòt(t)a *nmf* patriot.

patriòttico *pl* -ici *a* patriotic.

Patrízia *nf pr* Patricia; Patrízio *nm pr* Patrick.

patrízio *a nm* patrician.

patrocinàre *vt* to defend, support.

patrocinatóre *nm* defender, sponsor, patron.

patrocínio *nm* defence; p. gratúito legal aid.

patróno *nm* patron, defending counsel; patronàto *nm* patronage.

patteggiàre *vti* come to terms, negotiate.

pattinàggio *nm* skating.

pattinàre *vi* to skate.

pàttino *nm* (ice)skate; p. a rotèlle roller skate.

pàtto *nm* pact, condition.

pattúglia *nf* (*mil*) patrol.

pattuíre *vt* to agree (upon), fix.

pattumièra *nf* dustbin, (*US*) garbage can.

paùra *nf* fear, fright; avére p. to be afraid; far p. (a) to frighten; per p. che lest.

paurosaménte *ad* fearfully, frighteningly.

pauróso *a* fearful, frightful.

pàusa *nf* pause.

pavesàre *vt* to adorn, beflag.

pavése *a nm* (inhabitant) of Pavia; *nm* shield.

paviménto *nm* floor.

pavóne *nm* peacock; pavoneggiàrsi *vr* to strut.

pazientàre *vi* to be patient, have patience.

paziènte *a nmf* patient.

paziènza *nf* patience; pèrdere la p. to lose one's temper; *interj* never mind!

pazzésco *a* mad; foolish.

pazzía *nf* madness, foolish action.

pàzzo *a nm* mad(man), lunatic.

pècca *nf* blemish, defect, flaw.

peccaminóso *a* sinful, culpable.

peccàre *vi* to sin, err.

peccàto *nm* sin; che p.! *interj* what a pity!

peccatóre *nm* -tríce *nf* sinner.

pécchia *nf* bee; pecchióne *nm* drone.

péce *nf* pitch.

pechinése *a nmf* Pekin(g)ese.

pècora *nf* sheep, ewe.

pecoríno *nm* sheep's-milk cheese.

peculàto *nm* peculation.

peculiàre *a* peculiar, special.

peculiarità *nf* peculiarity, characteristic.

pedàggio *nm* toll.

pedagógo *nm* pedagogue.

pedàle *nm* pedal, treadle.

pedàna *nf* dais.

pedànte *a nm* pedant(ic).

pedantería *nf* pedantry.

pedàta *nf* kick; footprint.

pedèstre *a* pedestrian; dull.

pediàtra *nmf* paediatrician.

pedicure (*Fr*) *nm* chiropodist.

pedilúvio *nm* foot-bath.

pedína *nf* piece; (*chess*) pawn.

pedinàre *vt* to follow, shadow.

pedóne *nm* pedonàle *a* pedestrian.

pèggio *a nm ad* worse, worst; àlla p. if the worst comes to the worst.

peggioraménto *nm* worsening, deterioration.

peggioràre *vt* to make worse; *vi* to worsen.

peggióre *a* worse, worst.

pégno *nm* pawn, pledge, token; dàre in p. *vt* to pawn; giuòco dèi pégni forfeits *pl.*

pelàre vt to skin, peel; (fig) fleece; -**rsi** vr to go bald.

pellàme nm hides pl, skins pl.

pèlle nf skin.

pellegrinàggio nm pilgrimage.

pellegrinàre vi to wander.

pellegríno a rare, strange; nm pilgrim.

pelletteria nf leather goods pl, leather goods shop.

pellicàno nm pelican.

pelliccería nf furs pl; fur trade; furrier's (shop).

pellíccia nf fur (coat).

pellicciàio nm furrier.

pellícola nf film.

pelliróssa nmf redskin.

pélo nm hair, fur; (cloth) pile; **per un p.** by a hair's breadth.

pelóso a hairy, shaggy.

péltro nm pewter.

pelúria nf down, fluff.

pèlvi nf pelvis.

péna nf punishment; pain; trouble; **in p.** anxious; **far p.** to move to pity; **valére la p.** vi to be worthwhile; **a màla p.** scarcely.

penàle a criminal, penal.

penalista nm criminal lawyer.

penàre (a) vi to suffer, find difficulty (in).

pendàglio nm pendant.

pendènte a hanging, leaning; nm earring, pendant.

pendènza nf slope, gradient, (US) grade.

pèndere vi to hang; lean, slope.

pendíce nf **pendío** nm slope, hillside.

pèndolo nm pendulum; **pèndola** nf clock.

pène nm penis.

penetrànte a penetrating, piercing, acute.

penetràre vti to penetrate.

penetrazióne nf penetration.

penicillína nf penicillin.

peninsulàre a peninsular.

penísola nf peninsula.

penitènte a nmf penitent.

penitènza nf penance, penitence.

penitenziàrio a penitentiary; nm prison, (US) penitentiary.

pénna nf feather; pen.

pennàcchio nm plume.

pennellatúra nf brushwork; (med) painting.

pennèllo nm brush, paint-brush; **a p.** perfectly.

Penníne, (Àlpi) nf pl (geogr) Pennine Alps.

penníno nm nib, (US) penpoint.

pennóne nm pennon; (naut) yard.

penóso a painful.

pentàgono nm pentagon.

pensàre vti to think.

pensatóre nm thinker.

pensièro nm thought, idea.

pensieróso a thoughtful.

pènsile a hanging.

pensilína nf (bus etc) shelter; awning.

pensionànte nmf boarder, lodger.

pensionàre vt to pension (off).

pensionàto a retired; nm pensioner; hostel.

pensióne nf pension; board and lodging; boarding house.

pensóso a pensive, thoughtful.

pentàgono nm pentagon.

Pentecòste nf Whitsun(tide), Pentecost.

pentiménto nm repentance.

pentírsi (di) vr to repent.

péntola nf pot, saucepan.

penúltimo a penultimate.

penúria nf lack, shortage.

penzolàre vi to dangle, hang down.

penzolóni, penzolóne ad dangling, hanging.

peònia nf peony.

pepai(u)òla nf pepper-pot.

pépe nm pepper.

peperóne nm chilli, pepper.

per prep for, through, by; **p. lo più** generally; **p. l'appúnto** just so; **p. vía aèrea** by airmail.

péra nf pear; (el) pear-switch.

perbène a respectable, nice.

percàlle nm cotton cambric.

percentuàle nf percentage.

percepíre vt to perceive; receive.

percettíbile a perceptible.

percezióne nf perception.

perché cj why?; because; (with subjunctive) in order that; nm reason.

perciò ad therefore, thereby.

percórrere vt to pass through, travel over.

percórso nm distance, route.

percòssa nf blow, stroke.

percuòtere vt to strike.

percussióne nf percussion.

perdènte a losing; nmf loser.

pèrdere vti to lose, miss; **p. di vista** to lose sight of; -**rsi** vr to get lost, vanish.

pèrdita nf loss, waste; **a p. d'òcchio** as far as the eye can see.

perdizióne nf perdition.

perdonàbile a pardonable.

perdonàre vt to forgive, pardon.

perdóno nm forgiveness, pardon.

perduràre vi to last, persist.

perdutaménte desperately.

perdúto a lost.

peregrinàre v **pellegrinàre**.

peregríno a uncommon.

perènne a everlasting, perennial.

perentòrio a peremptory.

perfètto a perfect.

perfezionaménto nm perfecting; specialization.

perfezionàre vt perfect, improve; -**rsi** vr to perfect oneself; specialize.

perfezióne nf perfection.

perfídia nf perfidy, wickedness.

pèrfido a perfidious.

perfíno ad even.

perforàre vt to perforate, pierce.
perforatríce nf drill, drilling machine.
perforazióne nf perforation, drilling.
pergamèna nf parchment.
pèrgola nf **pergolàto** nm pergola, arbour.
pericolànte a unsafe.
perícolo nm danger, peril.
pericolóso a dangerous.
periferìa nf periphery, outskirts pl.
perìfrasi nf periphrasis.
perímetro nm perimeter.
periòdico pl **-ici** a nm periodical.
perìodo nm period; (gram) sentence.
peripezìa nf vicissitude, adventure.
perìre vi to die, perish.
periscòpio nm periscope.
perìto a nm expert.
peritonìte nf (med) peritonitis.
perìzia nf skill; survey.
pèrla nf pearl.
perlustràre vt to patrol, reconnoitre.
perlustrazióne nf patrol, reconnaissance.
permalóso a touchy.
permanènte a permanent; nf permanent wave, perm.
permanènza nf stay; **in p.** permanently.
permeàre vt to permeate.
permésso a permitted; nm permission, permit; **p.!** excuse me, allow me.
perméttere (a qlcu di) vt to allow (s.o. to); **-rsi** vr to take the liberty.
pèrmuta nf exchange.
pernìce nf partridge.
pernicióso a pernicious.
pèrno, pèrnio nm pivot.
pernottaménto nm overnight stay.
pernottàre vi to spend the night.
però cj but, however.
péro nm pear tree.
peronòspora nf mildew.
peroràre vti to plead.
perorazióne nf peroration; pleading, defence.
peròssido nm peroxide.
perpendicolàre a nf perpendicular.
perpetràre vt to commit, perpetrate.
perpetuàre vt to perpetuate; **-rsi** vr to continue.
perpètuo a eternal, perpetual.
perplessità nf perplexity.
perplèsso a perplexed, puzzled.
perquisíre vt to search.
perquisizióne nf search.
persecutóre nm persecutor.
persecuzióne nf persecution.
perseguíre vt to follow, pursue.
perseguitàre vt to persecute.
perseverànte a persevering.
perseverànza nf perseverance.
perseveràre vi to persevere.
Pèrsia nf (geogr) Persia, Iran.
persiàna nf shutter, (US) shade.
persiàno a nm Persian.
persìno ad even.
persistènte a persistent, persisting.

persìstere vi to persist.
pèrso a lost; **a tèmpo p.** in one's spare time.
persóna nf person, body; **di p.** in person.
personàggio nm (theat) character, personage.
personàle a personal; nm staff, personnel, body; **questióne p.** private, (US) personal, business.
personalità nf personality.
personalménte ad personally.
personificàre vt to personify.
personificàto a personified; **è la bontà personificàta** he is goodness itself.
perspicàce a shrewd.
perspicàcia nf shrewdness.
perspícuo a clear.
persuadére vt to persuade, convince.
persuasióne nf persuasion, conviction.
persuasìvo a persuasive.
pertànto cj therefore.
pèrtica nf rod, pole, perch.
pertinàce a persistent.
pertinàcia nf pertinacity.
pertinènte a relevant.
pertinènza nf pertinence, relevance; **non è di mìa p.** it is not my business.
perturbàre vt to disturb, perturb.
Perù nm (geogr) Peru; **peruviàno** a nm Peruvian.
perugìno a nm (inhabitant) of Perugia.
pervàdere vt to pervade.
perveníre vi to arrive, reach.
perversióne nf perversion.
perversità nf wickedness.
pervèrso a immoral, wicked.
pervertiménto nm perversion.
pervertíre vt to lead astray, pervert; **-rsi** vr to go astray; **pervèrto** a nm pervert(ed).
pervicàce a obstinate.
pesànte a heavy; wearisome; weighty.
pesantézza nf heaviness.
pesàre vti to weigh.
pesàto a pondered, well-considered.
pèsca nf peach.
pésca nf fishery, fishing.
pescàre vt to fish, catch, (fig) fish out.
pescatóre nm fisherman.
pésce nm fish; **p. rósso** goldfish; **non sapére che pésci pigliàre** to be at one's wits' end; **p. d'aprìle** April fool.
pescecàne nm shark; (fig) profiteer.
pescheréccio a fishing; nm fishingboat.
pescherìa nf fish-market, -shop.
pescivéndolo nm fishmonger.
pèsco nm peach tree.
péso nm weight, burden.
pessimísmo nm pessimism.
pessimísta nmf pessimist.
pessimístico pl **-ici** a pessimistic.

pèssimo *a* very bad.

pésta *nf* footprint, track; **trovàrsi nèlle péste** to be in difficulties.

pestàre *vt* to crush, pound, tread on.

pèste *nf* plague.

pestèllo *nm* pestle.

pestífero *a* pestilential.

pestilènza *nf* pestilence.

pestilenziàle *a* pestilential.

pésto *a* pounded; **búio p.** pitch dark; **càrta pésta** papier-mâché; *nm* Genoese sauce.

pètalo *nm* petal.

petàrdo *nm* petard; *(firework)* cracker.

petizióne *nf* petition.

petrificàre *vt* to petrify.

petrolièra *nf* (oil-)tanker.

petrolífero *a* oil, petroliferous; **pòzzo p.** oil-well.

petròlio *nm* oil, paraffin, *(US)* kerosene.

petróso *a* stony.

pettegolàre *vi* to gossip; **pettego-lézzo** *nm* gossiping.

pettégolo *a* gossiping; *nm (person)* gossip.

pettinàre *vt* to comb; **-rsi** *vr* to do one's hair; **pettinatrice** *nf* hairdresser.

pettinatúra *nf* hairstyle.

pèttine *nm* comb.

pettirósso *nm* robin(redbreast).

pètto *nm* breast, chest; **giàcca a ún (dòppio) pètto** single(double)-breasted jacket.

pettorúto *a* proud, haughty; full-breasted.

petulànte *a* cheeky.

petulànza *nf* arrogance, impertinence.

pèzza *nf* patch, cloth, *(material)* bolt.

pezzènte *nm* beggar.

pèzzo *nm* piece; time; **p. gròsso** big-wig.

piacènte *a* pleasant, attractive.

piacére *vi* to please; **quésto mi piàce** I like this; *nm* pleasure, favour; **avére il p.** *(di)* to be glad *(to)*; **per p.** please.

piacévole *a* pleasant, enjoyable.

piacevolménte *ad* pleasantly, agreeably.

piàga *nf* sore, evil.

piagnistèo *nm* whine, moaning.

piagnucolàre *vi* to whimper.

piàlla *nf* *(tec)* plane; **piallàre** *vt* to plane.

piallatrice *nf* planing machine.

piàna *nf* plain.

pianaménte *ad* quietly, slowly.

pianèlla *nf* slipper.

pianeròttolo *nm* landing.

pianéta *nm* planet.

piàngere *vti* to cry, weep, lament.

pianificàre *vt* to plan.

pianìsta *nmf* pianist.

piàno *a* flat, smooth, plain; *ad* quietly, slowly; *nm* plain, plane; floor; plan.

piano(fòrte) *nm* piano(forte); **p. a códa** grand piano.

piànta *nf* plant; plan, map; sole.

piantagióne *nf* plantation.

piantàre *vt* to plant; fix; quit; **p. in àsso** leave in the lurch; **piàntala!** cut it out! **-rsi** *vr* to place oneself.

piantatóre *nm* **-trice** *nf* planter.

pianterréno *nm* ground floor, *(US)* first floor.

piànto *nm* weeping, tears *pl*.

piantonàre *vt* to keep a watch on, keep under guard.

pianúra *nf* plain.

piàstra *nf* slab, *(of metal)* plate; **piastrélla** *nf* tile.

piastrína *nf* plaque, *(mil)* badge; **p. di riconoscimènto** identity disk, *(US)* identification tag.

piattafórma *nf* platform.

piattíno *nm* saucer.

piàtto *a* flat; *nm* dish, plate; **p. grànde** platter.

piàttola *nf* cockroach; crab-louse; *(fig)* a bore.

piàzza *nf* square; **p. del mercàto** market-place; **p. d'àrmi** parade-ground; **automòbile da p. taxi; fàre p. pulíta** to make a clean sweep.

piazzafòrte *nf* stronghold, fort.

piazzàle *nm* large square.

piazzàre *vt* to place, set; **-rsi** *vr (racing)* to be placed.

piazzísta *nm* commercial traveller.

piazzuòla *nf (aut)* lay-by.

pícca *nf* pique; *(mil)* pike; *pl (cards)* spades *pl*.

piccànte *a* spicy, piquant.

piccàrsi *(di)* *vr* to claim (to); pride oneself (on); persist (in).

picchétto *nm* tent peg, stake; *(mil)* picket; *(cards)* piquet.

picchiàre *vti* to beat, hit, knock, strike; *(av)* dive; **-rsi** *vr* come to blows; **picchiàta** *nf* thrashing; *(av)* dive.

picchiettío *nm* drumming, tapping.

pícchio *nm* blow, knock; wood-pecker.

piccíno *a* little; *nm* child.

piccionàia *nf* loft, pigeon-loft; *(theat)* gallery.

piccióne *nm* pigeon; **p. viaggiatóre** carrier pigeon.

pícco *pl* **pícchi** *nm* peak, top; **a p. perpendicularly; andàre a p.** *(naut)* to go to the bottom.

piccolézza *nf* smallness, trifle.

píccolo *a* small, young, petty; *nm* child; **i píccoli** the little ones.

piccóne *nm* pickaxe.

piccòzza *nf* axe; **p. da alpinísta** ice-axe.

pidocchierìa *nf* stinginess, meanness.

pidòcchio *nm* louse.

pidocchióso *a* filthy; stingy.

piède *nm* foot; **a pièdi** on foot; **a pièdi núdi** barefoot; **stàre in pièdi** to stand.

piedistàllo nm pedestal.
pièga nf crease, fold, pleat; **prèndere úna brútta p.** to take a bad turn; **mèssa in p.** nf (hair) set.
piegàre vti to fold (up), bend; subdue; submit; turn; **-rsi** vr to bend, submit.
pieghettàre vt to pleat.
pieghévole a folding, pliable; submissive.
Piemónte nm (geogr) Piedmont; **piemontése** a nmf Piedmontese.
pièna nf flood; crowd.
pienaménte ad fully, completely, entirely.
pienézza nf fullness.
pièno a full; **in p.** completely.
Pièro nm pr Peter.
pietà nf pity, mercy; piety; (art) pietà.
pietànza nf (main) course.
pietóso a merciful; pitiful, wretched.
piètra nf stone.
pietrificàre vt to petrify.
pietrína nf (for lighters) flint.
Piètro nm pr Peter.
pième nf country parish (church).
pìffero nm (mus) fife.
pigiàma nm pyjamas pl.
pigiàre vti to crush, press; **-rsi** vr to crowd.
pigióne nf rent; **pigionàle** nm tenant.
pigliàre vt to seize, take.
pigmèo nm pygmy.
pignoraménto nm distraint.
pignoràre vt to distrain.
pigolàre vi to chirp.
pigolìo nm chirping, chirruping.
pigraménte ad lazily, sluggishly.
pigrízia nf laziness.
pìgro a lazy, sluggish.
pìla nf heap, pile; (el) battery; (holy-water) stoup.
pilàstro nm pillar.
Pilàto nm pr Pilate.
pìllola nf pill.
pilóne nm pillar; (el) pylon.
pilòta nm pilot.
pilotàre vt to pilot.
pinacotèca nf picture-gallery.
pinéta nf pine-wood.
pìngue a fat.
pinguèdine nf corpulence, fatness.
pinguíno nm penguin.
pìnna nf fin; (swimming) flipper.
pinnàcolo nm pinnacle.
pìno nm pine(-tree).
pìnza nf pliers pl, forceps pl; **pinzétta** nf tweezers pl.
Pío nm pr Pius.
pío a pious, charitable.
pioggerèlla nf drizzle, gentle rain.
piòggia nf rain; **p. radioattìva** fallout.
piòlo nm peg; (of ladder) rung.
piombàre vt to seal, cover (with lead); (tooth) stop; vi fall, plunge.
piómbo nm (metal) lead.
pionière nm pioneer.

piòppo nm poplar.
piovàno a **àcqua piovàna** rainwater.
piòvere vti to rain; **p. a dirótto, p. a catinélle** to pour.
piovigginàre vi to drizzle.
piovigginóso, piovóso a drizzling, rainy.
piovosità nf rainfall.
pìpa nf (smoker's) pipe.
pipistrèllo nm bat.
pìra nf pyre.
piràmide nf pyramid.
piràta nm pirate.
piratería nf piracy.
pírica, pólvere nf gunpowder.
piròfila nf fire-resisting glassware.
piròscafo nm steamer, steamship.
pirotècnica nf fireworks pl, pyrotechnics pl.
piscìna nf fish-pond; swimming-pool.
pisèllo nm pea.
pisolìno nm nap, snooze.
pìsta nf race course, track; (av) runway.
pistàcchio nm pistachio.
pistìllo nm pistil.
pistòla nf pistol.
pistóne nm piston.
pitòcco pl **-òcchi** a stingy; nm beggar; miser.
pittóre nm **-trice** nf painter.
pittorésco a picturesque.
pittúra nf painting.
pitturàre vti to paint.
più ad longer, more, most; **non . . . p.** no longer; **mài p.** never again; **sèmpre p.** more and more; **per di p.** moreover; **per lo p.** generally.
piúma nf feather, plume.
piumíno nm eiderdown; powder-puff.
piuttòsto (che, di) ad rather (than).
pìva nf bagpipe.
pivière nm plover.
pizzería nf pizza shop, pizza restaurant.
pizzicàgnolo nm delicatessen seller.
pizzicàre vti to nip; itch.
pizzichería nf delicatessen shop.
pízzico pl **-chi** nm pinch; **pizzicóre** nm itch.
pízzo nm lace; pointed beard; (mountain) peak.
placàre vt to appease, soothe; **-rsi** vr subside.
plàcca nf plate, plaque; (in throat) spot.
plàcido a placid, peaceful.
plafóne nm ceiling.
plagiàrio nm plagiarist.
plàgio nm plagiarism.
planàre vi (av) to glide down.
planetàrio a planetary; nm planetarium.
plasmàre vt to mould.
plàstica nf plastic; modelling; plastic surgery.
plàtano nm plane (tree).

platèa *nf* (*theat*) stalls *pl*, pit.
plàtino *nm* platinum.
plausíbile *a* acceptable, reasonable.
plàuṣo *nm* applause, praise.
plebàglia *nf* mob, rabble.
plèbe *nf* common people.
plebèo *a* plebeian, vulgar; *nm* commoner.
plebiscíto *nm* plebiscite.
plenàrio *a* plenary.
plenilúnio *nm* full moon.
plenipotenziàrio *a nm* plenipotentiary.
pleuríte *nf* (*med*) pleurisy.
plíco *pl* **plíchi** *nm* envelope, packet.
plotóne *nm* (*mil*) platoon, squad.
plúmbeo *a* leaden.
pluràle *a nm* plural.
pneumàtico *pl* **-ici** *a* pneumatic; *nm* tyre.
po' v pòco.
pòco *pl* **pòchi** *a pron* little (*pl* few); *ad* (very) little, a little while; **fra p.** soon; **p. fa** not long ago; **un po' per** what with . . .
podàgra *nf* (*med*) gout.
podére *nm* farm.
poderóso *a* mighty, powerful.
podestà *nm* mayor.
podíṣmo *nm* (*sport*) walking.
poèma *nm* long poem.
poeṣía *nf* poem, poetry.
poèta *nm* poet.
poetéssa *nf* poetess.
poètico *pl* **-ici** *a* poetical.
poggiàre *vi* to rest; (*mil*) move.
pòggio *nm* hillock, knoll.
poggiòlo *nm* balcony.
pòi *ad* afterwards, then; **da óra in p.** from now on; **da allóra in p.** from that time on; **o príma o p.** sooner or later.
poichè *cj* since, as, for, after, when.
polàcco *pl* **-àcchi** *a* Polish; *nm* Pole.
polàre *a* polar.
polèmica *nf* controversy, polemic(s).
polènta *nf* maize meal.
poligamía *nf* polygamy.
polígamo *a* polygamous; *nm* polygamist.
poliglòtta *a nm* polyglot.
polígono *nm* polygon.
polímero *nm* (*chem*) polymer.
poliomielíte *nf* poliomyelitis.
pòlipo *nm* polyp; (*med*) polypus.
politeàma *nm* theatre.
politècnico *pl* **-ici** *a nm* polytechnic.
politène *nm* polythene.
política *nf* politics, policy.
político *pl* **-ici** *a* politic(al); *nm* politician.
poliviníle *nm* (*chem*) polyvinyl.
poliẓía *nf* police.
poliẓiésco *pl* **-chi** *a* police; **film p.** detective film.
poliẓiòtto *nm* policeman, constable, (*US*) patrolman.
pòliẓẓa *nf* (*com*) policy, bill.
pollàio *nm* hen-house, poultry-yard.
pollàme *nm* poultry.

pollàstra *nf* pullet; **pollàstro** *nm* cockerel.
pollería *nf* poulterer's (shop).
pòllice *nm* thumb, big toe; inch.
pòlline *nm* pollen.
póllo *nm* chicken, fowl.
polluẓióne *nf* pollution.
polmonàre *a* pulmonary.
polmóne *nm* lung.
polmoníte *nf* pneumonia.
pòlo *nm* (*el and geogr*) pole.
Polònia *nf* (*geogr*) Poland.
pólpa *nf* (*fruit*) pulp; boned meat.
polpétta *nf* rissole.
pólpo *nm* octopus.
polsíno *nm* cuff.
pólso *nm* pulse; wrist; **di p.** energetic.
poltíglia *nf* mush, mud, slush.
poltríre *vi* to lie lazily in bed, idle.
poltróna *nf* armchair, orchestra stalls, (*US*) orchestra seat; **poltroncína** *nf* pit stall, (*US*) back orchestra seat.
poltróne *nm* idler.
poltronería *nf* laziness.
pólvere *nf* dust, powder; **p. néra da spàro** gunpowder; **caffè in p.** ground coffee.
polveriẓẓàre *vt* to pulverize.
polveróne *nm* cloud of dust.
polveróso *a* dusty.
pomàta *nf* ointment.
pomèllo *nm* knob, grip; cheek-bone.
pomeridiàno *a* (in the) afternoon.
pomeríggio *nm* afternoon.
pómice *nf* pumice(-stone).
pómo *nm* apple(-tree); head; knob.
pomodòro, pomidòro *pl* **pomodòri, pomidòri** *nm* tomato.
pomogranàto *nm* pomegranate.
pómpa *nf* pump; pomp, display; **far p. di** to display, show off.
pompàre *vt* to pump (up).
pompèlmo *nm* grapefruit.
pompière *nm* fireman; **pompièri** (*córpo dèi*) fire brigade, (*US*) fire department.
pompóso *a* pompous.
pònce *nm* (*drink*) punch.
ponderàre *vti* to ponder, consider.
ponderaẓióne *nf* cautious deliberation, reflection.
ponènte *nm* west.
pónte *nm* bridge; (*naut*) deck.
pontéfice *nm* pontiff, pope.
pontifício *a* papal.
pontíle *nm* landing-stage.
pontóne *nm* pontoon.
popolàno *a* of the (common) people; *nm* man of the people.
popolàre *vt* to populate, people; **-rsi** *vr* to become populated; *a* popular, working-class; **cànto p.** folksong.
popolarésco *pl* **-chi** *a* popular.
popolariẓẓàre *vt* to popularize.
popolaẓióne *nf* people, population.
pòpolo *nm* nation, people.
popolóso *a* populous.
popóne *nm* melon.

póppa *nf* (woman's) breast; (*naut*) stern.

poppàre *vti* to suck.

porcellàna *nf* china, porcelain.

porcheria *nf* dirt, dirty trick.

porcíle *nm* (pig)sty.

pòrco *pl* -ci *nm* pig, swine; *a* dirty, horrible.

porcospíno *nm* hedgehog; porcupine.

pòrfido *nm* porphyry.

pòrgere *vt* to give, hand, offer, present, tender.

pòro *nm* pore.

porosità *nf* porousness.

poróso *a* porous.

pórpora *nf* purple.

pórre *vt* to place, put, set.

pòrro *nm* leek; wart.

pòrta *nf* door, gate, gateway, (*football*) goal.

portabagàgli *nm* porter; luggage rack, (US) baggage rack.

portacénere *nm* ashtray.

portacípria *nm* powder-compact.

portaèrei *nf* aircraft carrier.

portafògli *nm* wallet, pocketbook; **portafòglio** *nm* wallet, pocketbook, portfolio.

portafortúna *nm* mascot.

portalèttere *nm* postman.

portaménto *nm* bearing, carriage.

portamonéte *nm* purse.

portaombrèlli *nm* umbrella stand.

portàre *vt* to bear, bring, carry, take; wear.

portaritràtti *nm* photograph frame.

portasapóne *nm* soap-dish.

portasigarétte *nm* cigarette case.

portàta *nf* capacity; course, dish, importance; range; **a p. di màno** (with)in reach; **di gràn p. far** reaching.

portàtile *a* portable.

portatóre *nm* bearer, holder.

portauòvo *nm* eggcup.

portavivànde *nm* dumbwaiter.

portavóce *nm* mouthpiece; megaphone; spokesman.

portènto *nm* marvel, prodigy.

portentóso *a* prodigious, wonderful.

pòrtico *pl* -ici *nm* porch, portico; *pl* arcade.

portièra *nf* door curtain; doorkeeper('s wife); (*aut*) door.

portière *nm* caretaker, (hotel-) porter, (US) doorman, janitor; (*sport*) goal-keeper.

portinàio *v* **portière**.

portinería *nf* porter's lodge.

pòrto *nm* port, harbour; (*com*) carriage; **p. frànco** carriage free.

Portogàllo *nm* (*geogr*) Portugal.

portoghése *a nmf* Portuguese; (*sl*) gatecrasher.

portóne *nm* main door, front door.

porzióne *nf* portion, share.

pòsa *nf* pause; pose; laying; (*phot*) exposure.

posamíne *nm* (*naut*) mine-layer.

posàre *vt* to lay, put (down); *vi* to pose; rest; **-rsi** *vr* to alight, stay.

posàta *nf* article of cutlery.

posàto *a* sedate, calm.

poscrítto *nm* postscript, footnote.

posdomàni *ad* the day after tomorrow.

positíva *nf* (*phot*) positive.

positívo *a* certain, matter-of-fact, positive.

posizióne *nf* position.

pospórre *vt* to place after, postpone.

posposizióne *nf* postponement.

possedére *vt* to possess.

possedimènto *nm* possession, property.

possènte *a* powerful.

possèsso *nm* possession, property.

possessóre *nm* owner, possessor.

possíbile *a* possible; **fàre tútto il p.** to do one's best.

possibilità *nf* possibility, power.

possidènte *nmf* landowner, property owner.

pòsta *nf* mail, post (office); stake, bet; **p. per l'intèrno** inland mails, (US) domestic mails; **a bèlla p.** on purpose.

postàle *a* post, postal; **vagóne p.** mail van, (US) mail car (railway post office).

postàre *vt* to place, station.

postéggio *nm* park, parking; **p. di tassì** cabrank, (US) cabstand.

pòsteri *nm pl* descendants *pl*, posterity.

posterióre *a* back, hind, posterior.

posterità *nf* posterity.

posticcio *a* artificial, false.

posticipazióne *nf* delay, postponement.

postílla *nf* (foot)note.

postíno *nm* postman.

pósto *a* placed, situated; *nm* place, room, seat; job; **c'è p.?** is there any room?

postulànte *nmf* applicant, petitioner.

pòstumo *a* posthumous.

potàbile *a* drinkable, drinking; **àcqua non p.** water unfit for drinking.

potàre *vt* to lop, prune.

potàssio *nm* potassium.

potènte *a* mighty, powerful.

potènza *nf* might, power, strength.

potenziàle *a nm* potential.

potére *vi* to be able (can), be allowed (may); *nm* authority, power; **può dàrsi** it may be.

pòvero *a* poor; *nm* poor man, beggar.

povertà *nf* poverty.

pozióne *nf* draught, potion.

pózza *nf* puddle, pool.

pozzànghera *nf* puddle.

pózzo *nm* well; mine-shaft.

pranzàre *vi* to dine; lunch.

prànzo *nm* lunch, dinner; **sàla da p.** *nf* dining room; **dópo p.** in the afternoon.

Pràga nf (geogr) Prague.
pratería nf grassland, prairie.
pràtica nf practice, training; affair; **pràtiche religióse** nf pl religious observances.
praticàbile a practicable; **stràda p.** passable road.
praticànte a nmf practising, regular church-goer.
praticàre vt to practise; frequent.
pràtico pl **-ici** a practical, experienced; **èssere p. di** vi to be familiar with.
pràto nm meadow, lawn.
pratolína nf daisy.
Preàlpi (le) nf pl (geogr) the Pre-Alps.
preàmbolo nm preamble.
preavvíso nm forewarning, notice.
precàrio a precarious.
precauzióne nf care, precaution.
precedènte a preceding, previous; nm precedent; **buòni precedènti** good record.
precedenteménte ad previously, formerly.
precedènza nf precedence, priority; **in p.** in advance; previously.
precèdere vt to go before, precede; vi to come first, precede.
precètto nm precept, rule, order.
precettóre nm **-trice** nf teacher, tutor.
precipitàre vt to fling down; vi to crash, fall; **-rsi** vr to rush, throw oneself.
precipitazióne nf fall; haste.
precipitóso a hasty, steep.
precipízio nm precipice.
precípuo a principal, main.
precisaménte ad precisely, exactly.
precisàre vt to specify.
precisióne nf accuracy, exactness.
precíso a accurate, precise, punctual.
preclúdere vt to preclude, bar.
precòce a precocious, premature.
precocità nf precociousness, prematureness.
preconcètto a preconceived; nm preconception, prejudice.
precursóre nm forerunner, precursor.
prèda nf prey, plunder.
predatòrio a predatory.
predàre vt to pillage, plunder, sack.
predecessóre nm predecessor.
predestinàre vt to predestine.
predétto a above-mentioned; foretold.
prèdica nf preaching, sermon.
predicàre vti to preach.
predicàto a preached; exalted; nm predicate.
predicatóre nm preacher.
predilètto a nm favourite.
predilezióne nf partiality, fondness.
prediligere vt to like better, prefer.
predíre vt to foretell, predict.
predispórre vt to predispose, arrange.

predizióne nf prediction; **p. dell'avveníre** fortune-telling.
predomináre vti to (pre)dominate.
predomínio nm predominance, supremacy.
predóne nm marauder, plunderer.
preesistènza nf pre-existence.
prefabbricàre vt to prefabricate.
prefazióne nf preface, introduction.
preferènza nf preference; **a p. di** rather than; **di p.** preferably.
preferenziàle a preferential; **azióni preferenziàli** preference shares, (US) preferred stock.
preferíbile a preferable.
preferíre vt to prefer, like better.
preferíto a nm favourite.
prefètto nm prefect.
prefettúra nf prefecture.
prefiggersi (di) vr to intend (to).
prefiggiménto nm determination, resolve.
prefísso a intended; nm prefix.
pregàre vti to pray, ask; **prègo!** interj not at all, don't mention it.
pregévole a valuable.
preghièra nf prayer, request.
pregiàre vt to appreciate, esteem, value; **-rsi** vr to be honoured, have the honour.
pregiàto a esteemed; (com) favour; valuable; **Pregiatíssimo Signóre** (in letters) Dear Sir.
prègio nm good merit, value.
pregiudicàre vt to injure; prejudice.
pregiudicàto a bound to fail; nm previous offender.
pregiudiziévole a prejudicial, detrimental.
pregiudízio nm prejudice; detriment.
pregnànte a (lit and fig) pregnant.
prégno a full, impregnated; pregnant.
pregustàre vt to anticipate, look forward to.
preistòrico pl **-ici** a prehistoric.
prelàto nm prelate.
prelevaménto nm drawing; (com) withdrawal.
prelevàre vt to draw; withdraw.
prelibàto a delicious, excellent.
preliminàre a nm preliminary.
prelúdio nm prelude.
prematúro a premature, untimely.
premeditàre vt to plan, premeditate.
premeditazióne nf premeditation.
prèmere vt to press; vi to press; matter.
preméssa nf premiss, previous statement.
premèttere vt to premise, say first, state in advance.
premiàre vt to award a prize, reward.
premiazióne nf prizegiving.
preminènte a pre-eminent.
prèmio nm prize, reward; (com) premium.
premuníre vt to fortify; **-rsi** vr to take precautions.

premúra *nf* attention, care; haste.
premurosaménte *ad* solicitously, kindly.
premuróso *a* attentive, solicitous, kind.
prèndere *vt* to take, catch, seize.
prendisóle *nm* sun-suit.
prenotàre *vt* to book, engage.
prenotazióne *nf* booking.
preoccupàre *vt* to make anxious, trouble; **-rsi** *vr* to worry.
preoccupàto *a* anxious, worried.
preoccupazióne *nf* anxiety, care, preoccupation.
preordinàre *vt* to predetermine, prearrange.
preparàre *vt* **-rsi** *vr* to get ready, prepare.
preparatívo *nm* preparation.
preparàto *a* prepared; *nm (chemical etc)* preparation.
preparazióne *nf* preparation.
preponderànte *a* predominant, prevailing.
prepórre *vt* to place before, prefer.
preposizióne *nf* preposition.
prepósto *nm (eccl)* rector, vicar.
prepotènte *a* overbearing; *nm* bully.
prepotènza *nf* arrogance, bullying.
prerogatíva *nf* prerogative.
présa *nf* grip, hold; seizure; *(el)* (wall-)plug; **màcchina da p.** *(cin)* camera.
preságio *nm* omen, presage.
presagíre *vt* to foretell, presage.
preságo *pl* **-ghi** *a* foreboding, having a presentiment of.
prèsbite *a* long-sighted.
prescégliere *vt* to choose, select.
prescíndere *vi* to leave out of account.
prescrívere *vt* to prescribe, order.
prescrizióne *nf* prescription; regulation.
presentàre *vt* to present, introduce; **-rsi** *vr* to present oneself, appear; occur.
presentatóre *nm (rad and tv)* announcer, *(theat)* compère, *(US)* master of ceremonies.
presentazióne *nf* presentation, introduction.
presènte *a nm* present; **tenèr p.** to bear in mind; **i presènti** those present.
presentiménto *nm* presentiment.
presentíre *vt* to have a presentiment, foresee.
presènza *nf* presence; **p. di spírito** presence of mind.
presèpio *nm* crib.
preservàre *vt* to preserve.
prèside *nm* headmaster, principal.
presidènte *nm* president, chairman.
presidenziàle *a* presidential.
presidiàre *vt* to garrison.
presídio *nm* garrison, defence.
presièdere (a) *vi* to preside (at), be in charge (of).
prèssa *nf (mech)* press.

pressànte *a* pressing, urgent.
prèssi *nm pl* neighbourhood.
pressióne *nf* pressure.
prèsso *ad* close by, near; *prep* near, beside, with; *(address)* care of; **p. a pòco** *ad* approximately.
pressochè *ad* almost, nearly.
prestabilíre *vt* to pre-arrange.
prestànte *a* good-looking.
prestàre *vt* to lend; pay *(attention etc)*; **fàrsi p.** *vt* to borrow; **-rsi** *vr* to be fit for, lend oneself.
prestazióne *nf* performance; **prestazióni** *pl* services.
prestigiatóre *nm* conjurer, juggler.
prestígio *nm* prestige, conjuring.
prèstito *nm* loan; **avére in p.** to borrow; **dàre in p.** to lend.
prèsto *ad* soon, early, quickly; *interj* (be) quick! **far p.** to make haste; **al più p.** as soon as possible.
presúmere *vt* to presume, suppose.
presumíbile *a* presumable.
presuntuóso *a* conceited, presumptuous.
presunzióne *nf* presumption.
presuppórre *vti* to (pre)suppose.
presuppósto *a* presupposed; *nm* presupposition.
prète *nm* priest.
pretendènte *nmf* claimant, suitor.
pretèndere *vt* to claim, want; *vi* to claim, pretend.
pretensióne *nf* pretention, claim.
pretésa *nf* claim; pretence; pretension; **sènza pretése** unpretentious.
pretèsto *nm* pretext, occasion.
pretóre *nm* magistrate.
prètto *a* pure, real.
pretúra *nf* magistrate's court.
prevalènte *a* prevalent, prevailing.
prevalènza *nf* prevalence, supremacy.
prevalére *vi* to prevail.
prevedére *vt* to foresee.
prevedíbile *a* to be expected.
preveggènza *nf* foresight.
preveníre *vt* to precede, forestall, prevent, warn.
preventivàre *vt (com)* to estimate.
preventívo *a* preventive; *nm (com)* estimate.
prevenzióne *nf* bias, prejudice, prevention.
previdènte *a* provident.
previdènza *nf* foresight; **p. sociàle** social security.
prèvio *a* previous, subject to.
previsióne *nf* forecast, expectation.
preziosísmo *nm (liter)* preciosity.
preziosità *nf* preciousness, preciosity.
prezióso *a* precious, valuable.
prezzémolo *nm* parsley.
prèzzo *nm* price.
prigióne *nf* gaol, jail, prison, *(US)* penitentiary.
prigionía *nf* imprisonment.
prigionièro *nm* prisoner.
prima *ad* before, sooner, first

formerly; **quànto p.** very soon; **p. di** *prep*, **p. che** *cj* before.

primàrio *a* primary, chief; *nm* chief physician.

primatíccio *a* early.

primàto *nm* pre-eminence; *(sport)* record.

primavèra *nf* spring, springtime.

primaveríle *a* (of the) spring.

primeggiàre *vi* to excel.

primièro *a* first, former, previous.

primitívo *a* primitive, original.

primízia *nf* early fruit or vegetable; novelty.

primo *a nm* first, former; **di príma màno** first hand; **di prím'òrdine** first rate.

primogènito *a nm* first-born.

primòrdio *nm* beginning.

prímula *nf* primrose.

principàle *a* principal, main; *nm* principal, employer, manager.

principalménte *ad* mainly, chiefly.

principàto *nm* principality.

prìncipe *nm* prince; **principéssa** *nf* princess.

principiànte *nmf* beginner.

principiàre *vt* to begin, start.

princìpio *nm* beginning; principle.

prióre *nm* prior.

privàre *vt* to deprive, strip.

privataménte *ad* privately.

privatìsta *nmf* external student.

privatíva *nf* monopoly; tobacconist's.

privàto *a* private; *nm* private citizen.

privazióne *nf* (de)privation.

privilegiàto *a* privileged; *(com)* preference.

privilègio *nm* privilege.

privo (di) *a* devoid (of), lacking (in).

prò *nm* advantage, benefit, profit; **a che p.?** what is the use?; **buòn p. gli fàccia!** much good may it do him!

probàbile *a* probable, likely.

probabilità *nf* probability, chance.

probità *nf* honesty, probity.

problèma *nm* problem.

problemàtico *pl* **-ici** *a* difficult, uncertain.

pròbo *a* honest, upright.

probòscide *nf* trunk; proboscis.

procacciàre *vt* **-rsi** *vr* to get, procure, earn.

procàce *a* provocative.

procacità *nf* procacity, sauciness, impudence.

procèdere *vi* to proceed; behave; *nm* process; behaviour.

procediménto *nm* conduct; course; process.

processàre *vt* *(leg)* to try; **far p. to** bring to trial.

processióne *nf* procession.

procèsso *nm* process; *(leg)* trial.

procìnto *nm* **èssere in p. di** to be on the point of.

proclàma *nm* proclamation.

proclamàre *vt* to proclaim.

proclíve *a* inclined; **proclività** *nf* tendency.

procrastinàre *vti* to postpone, put off.

procreàre *vt* to procreate, generate.

procreazióne *nf* procreation.

procúra *nf* power of attorney, proxy.

procuràre *vt* to get; cause; provide; try; **-rsi** *vr* to get, procure.

procuratóre *nm* attorney, solicitor; *(eccl)* procurator; **P. Generàle** Attorney General.

pròde *a* brave, valiant; *nm* hero.

prodézza *nf* gallant deed, gallantry.

prodigalità *nf* lavishness, prodigality.

prodigàre *vt* to lavish, pour out; **-rsi** *vr* to do one's best.

prodigio *nm* marvel, prodigy.

pròdigo *pl* **-ghi** *a* lavish, prodigal; *nm* prodigal.

proditoriaménte *ad* treacherously.

prodòtto *a* produced; *nm* product, produce.

prodúrre *vt* to produce, yield; cause; **-rsi** *vr* to appear in public; happen.

produttività *nf* productiveness, productivity.

produttívo *a* productive, fruitful.

produttóre *a* producing; *nm* **-trice** *nf* producer, maker.

produzióne *nf* production, manufacture; exhibition.

proèmio *nm* introduction, preface.

profanàre *vt* to profane, debase.

profanazióne *nf* profanation.

profàno *a* profane, secular; *nm* profane, layman.

proferíre *vt* to utter.

professàre *vt* to profess.

professióne *nf* profession, trade, occupation; **di p.** by profession.

professionísta *nm* professional man; *(sport)* professional.

professóre *nm* (school)master, teacher, *(university)* professor; **professoréssa** *nf* professor, mistress.

profèta *nm* prophet; **profetéssa** *nf* prophetess.

profetàre, profetizzàre *vt* to prophesy.

profezía *nf* prophecy.

profferíre *vt* to offer; utter.

proffèrta *nf* offer.

profícuo *a* profitable, useful.

profilàssi *nf* *(med)* prophylaxis.

profílo *nm* profile, outline.

profittàre *vi* to profit, make progress.

profítto *nm* profit, benefit.

proflúvio *nm* overflow, abundance.

profondaménte *ad* deeply, profoundly.

profóndere *vt* to lavish, squander; **-rsi** *vr* to be lavish.

profondità *nf* depth, profundity.

profóndo *a* deep, profound; *nm* depth.

pròfugo *pl* -ghi *nm* refugee.

profumàre *vt* to perfume, scent; -rsi *vr* to put on scent.

profumería *nf* perfumer's shop; perfumery.

profumière *nm* perfumer; negòzio di p. perfumer's shop.

profúmo *nm* perfume, scent.

profusióne *nf* abundance, profusion.

progènie *nf* progeny, descendants *pl*, issue.

progenitóre *nm* ancestor, forefather -trice *nf* ancestor.

progettàre *vt* to plan.

progètto *nm* plan, project, scheme; p. di lègge bill.

prognòsi *nf* (*med*) prognosis.

progràmma *nm* program(me), prospectus, syllabus.

progredíre *vi* to advance, (make) progress.

progredíto *a* advanced, civilized.

progrèsso *nm* progress, headway.

proibíre *vi* to forbid, prohibit, prevent.

proibitívo *a* prohibitive.

proibizióne *nf* prohibition.

proiettàre *vti* to project, cast; (*cin*) to screen.

proièttile *nm* projectile, shell.

proiettóre *nm* searchlight, floodlight; projector; (*aut*) headlight.

proiezióne *nf* projection; (*film*) showing, slide.

pròle *nf pl* children, issue.

proletariàto *nm* proletariat.

proletàrio *a nm* proletarian.

prolífico *pl* -ici *a* prolific.

prolísso *a* long-winded, prolix.

pròlogo *pl* -ghi *nm* prologue.

prolungaménto *nm* prolongation, extension, continuation.

prolungàre *vt* to extend, prolong; -rsi *vr* to continue, extend.

prolusióne *nf* inaugural lecture.

proméssa *nf* promise.

promettènte *a* promising.

prométtere *vti* to promise.

prominènte *a* prominent, jutting.

prominènza *nf* prominence.

promíscuo *a* promiscuous, mixed.

promontòrio *nm* headland, promontory.

promòsso *a* promoted, (*of candidate in exam*) successful.

promozióne *nf* promotion; avére la p. to pass (exam).

promulgàre *vt* to promulgate.

promuòvere *vt* to promote, pass; cause.

pròno *a* prone.

pronóme *nm* pronoun.

pronòstico *pl* -ici *nm* forecast.

prontaménte *ad* readily, immediately, promptly.

prontézza *nf* quickness, readiness, promptitude.

prónto *a* ready, prompt; (*on telephone*) hullo! prónta càssa ready cash.

pronúncia *nf* pronunciation.

pronunciàre *vt* to pronounce, utter; -rsi *vr* to express one's opinion.

propagànda *nf* propaganda, advertising.

propagàre *vt* -rsi *vr* to propagate, spread.

propàggine *nf* ramification, lineage; (*agr*) layer.

propalàre *vt* to divulge, spread.

propèndere *vi* to incline.

propensióne *nf* propensity.

propènso *a* inclined, ready.

propiziàre *vt* -rsi *vr* to propitiate.

propízio *a* favourable, propitious.

proponiménto *nm* resolution, resolve.

propórre *vt* to propose, suggest; -rsi *vr* to intend, resolve.

proporzionàle *a* proportional.

proporzionàto *a* proportioned, proportionate; suitable.

proporzióne *nf* proportion.

propòsito *nm* purpose; a p. by the by, by the way; di p. on purpose.

propósta *nf* proposal, proposition.

propriaménte *ad* properly, really, exactly.

proprietàrio *nm* owner, proprietor; (*US*, *newspaper*) publisher.

pròprio *a* (one's) own, characteristic, *nm* one's own; *ad* exactly, just, really.

propugnàre *vt* to plead for, support.

propulsióne *nf* propulsion.

pròra *nf* (*naut*) bow, prow.

pròroga *nf* adjournment, postponement, extension, respite.

prorogàre *vt* to postpone, put off, extend.

prorómpere *vi* to burst (out), gush.

pròsa *nf* prose; (*theat*) drama.

prosàico *pl* -ici *a* prosaic.

prosciògliere *vt* to release; (*leg*) acquit.

prosciugaménto *nm* draining, reclamation; drying up.

prosciugàre *vt* to drain, dry, reclaim; *vi* and -rsi *vr* to dry (up).

prosciútto *nm* ham.

proscrítto *a* outlawed, exile; *nm* outlaw, exile.

proscrizióne *nf* proscription, banishment.

proseguiménto *nm* continuation.

proseguíre *vt* to continue, go on, pursue.

prosèlito *nm* proselyte.

prosodía *nf* prosody.

prosperàre *vi* to prosper, thrive.

prosperità *nf* prosperity, wealth.

pròspero *a* prosperous, fortunate.

prosperóso *a* prosperous; healthy, plump.

prospettíva *nf* perspective; prospect, view, outlook.

prospètto *nm* prospect, view; prospectus.

prospiciènte *a* facing, opposite.

prossimaménte *ad* before long, in

the near future; (*in film programmes*) coming shortly; *nm* trailer.

prossimità *nf* nearness, proximity, vicinity.

pròssimo *a* near, next; *nm* neighbour; **in un p. avveníre** in the near future.

prostituíre *vt* to prostitute; **-rsi** *vr* to prostitute oneself, sell oneself.

prostitúta *nf* prostitute.

prostituzióne *nf* prostitution.

prostràre *vt* to prostrate, overwhelm; exhaust; **-rsi** *vr* to bow down; get exhausted.

prostrazióne *nf* prostration, exhaustion.

protagonísta *nmf* chief character, protagonist.

protèggere *vt* to protect, defend, support.

proteína *nf* protein.

protèndere *vt* to hold out, stretch; **-rsi in avànti** *vr* to lean forward.

protèsta *nf* protest(ation).

protestànte *a nmf* Protestant.

protestàre *vti* to protest.

protestàto *a* protested (*also com*); **protèsto** *nm* (*com*) protest.

protètto *a* protected, sheltered; *nm* favourite, protégé.

protettóre *nm* **-tríce** *nf* patron, protector.

protezióne *nf* protection, patronage.

protocòllo *nm* protocol; record; **formàto p.** foolscap (size).

protòtipo *nm* prototype.

protràrre *vt* to protract, put off.

protrazióne *nf* protraction, deferment.

protruberànza *nf* protruberance.

protuberànte *a* protuberant, bulging.

pròva *nf* proof; evidence; test; rehearsal.

provàre *vt* to prove; show; try (on); feel; rehearse; **-rsi** *vr* to endeavour, try.

proveniènza *nf* origin, source.

proveníre *vi* to come (from); be caused (by).

provènto *nm* income, proceeds *pl.*

Provènza *nf* (*geogr*) Provence.

provenzàle *a nmf* Provençal.

proverbiàle *a* proverbial.

provèrbio *nm* proverb, saying.

provétta *nf* test-tube.

provètto *a* experienced, skilled.

província *nf* province, district.

provinciàle *a* provincial; **stràda p.** *nf* highway, main road.

províno *nm* test-tube; (*cin*) filmtest.

provocànte *a* provocative.

provocàre *vt* to provoke, cause, stir up.

provocazióne *nf* provocation.

provolóne *nm* a kind of cheese.

provvedére (di) *vt* to provide (with); **p. a** *vi* to provide (for); **-rsi** *vr* to provide oneself.

provvediménto *nm* measure, provision.

provvidènza *nf* providence; (*fig*) boon.

provvidenziàle *a* providential.

pròvvido *a* provident, thrifty.

provvigióne *nf* (*com*) commission; provision.

provvisòrio *a* provisional, temporary.

provvísta *nf* supply.

prúa *v* **próra.**

prudènte *a* prudent, careful.

prudènza *nf* prudence, caution.

prúdere *vi* to itch.

prúgna *nf* plum; **prúgno** *nm* plumtree.

prúno *nm* thorn-bush; thorn.

pruríto *nm* itch(ing).

pseudònimo *a* pseudonymous; *nm* pseudonym, pen-name.

psicanàlisi *nm* psychoanalysis.

psicanalísta *nmf* psychoanalyst.

psichiàtra *nf* psychiatrist; **psichiatría** *nf* psychiatry.

psicología *nf* psychology; **psicològico** *pl* **-ici** *a* psychological; **psicòlogo** *pl* **-ogi** *nm* psychologist.

pubblicàre *vt* to publish, issue.

pubblicazióne *nf* publication, issue.

pubblicità *nf* publicity, advertising.

pubblicitàrio *a* advertising.

púbblico *pl* **-ici** *a* public; *nm* audience, public.

pubertà *nf* puberty.

pudicízia *nf* modesty.

pudíco *pl* **-chi** *a* modest, bashful.

pudóre *nm* decency, modesty.

pueríle *a* childish, puerile.

puerízia *nf* childhood.

pugilàto *nm* boxing.

púgile *nm* boxer, pugilist.

Púglia *nf* (*geogr*) Apulia.

pugliése *a nm* (inhabitant) of Apulia.

pugnalàre *vt* to stab.

pugnalàta *nf* stab.

pugnàle *nm* dagger.

púgno *nm* fist; blow; handful; **in p.** in one's hands; **fàre a púgni** fight, clash.

púlce *nf* flea.

puicíno *nm* chick(en).

pulédro *nm* colt, foal.

puléggia *nf* pulley.

pulíre *vt* to clean, polish, wash.

pulíto *a* clean, clear, neat.

pulízia *nf* cleaning; cleanliness, cleanness.

pullman *nm* motor-coach; (*rly*) Pullman car.

pullóver *nm* pullover.

pullulàre di *vi* to be full of, swarm with, pullulate with.

pulvíscolo *nm* fine dust, motes *pl.*

púlpito *nm* pulpit.

pulsànte *a* pulsating, throbbing; *nm* push-button; **p. da campanèllo** bell push.

pulsàre *vi* to beat, pulsate, throb.

pulsazióne nf beat, pulsation, throb.
pungènte a prickly, stinging, pungent.
púngere vt to prick, sting.
pungiglióne nm sting.
púngolo nm goad, spur.
punìre vt to punish.
punizióne nf punishment.
púnta nf point, tip, end; top; headland; a little; **in p. di pièdi** on tiptoe.
puntàre vt to point, aim; push; bet; **p. i pièdi** to dig one's heels in; vi to head for.
puntàta nf instalment; stake; thrust.
punteggiatúra nf punctuation.
puntéggio nm (sport) score.
puntellàre vt to prop, support.
puntèllo nm prop, support.
puntíglio nm punctilio, obstinacy; spite.
puntiglióso a punctilious, obstinate.
puntina nf (of record player) stylus; **p. da disègno** drawing pin, (US) thumbtack.
púnto nm point, dot, mark, full stop; stitch; spot; a any; **non ... p.** no, none; ad at all; **in p.** exactly; **di p. in biànco** point-blank; **p. e virgola** semicolon; **dúe púnti** colon.
puntuàle a punctual.
puntualità nf punctuality.
puntúra nf prick, sting; injection.
punzecchiàre vt to prick, sting; tease.
pupàzzo nm puppet.
pupìlla nf (eye) pupil.
pupíllo nm **pupílla** nf ward.
púpo nm puppet; (fam) baby.
purchè cj on condition that, provided (that).
púre ad also, too; however, yet.
purézza nf purity.
púrga nf purgative.
purgànte a nm purgative, laxative.
purgàre vt to purge, purify, expurgate.
purgatìvo a laxative, purgative.
purgatòrio nm Purgatory.
purificàre vt to purify, cleanse.
purificazióne nf purification.
purità nf purity.
puritàno a nm Puritan (also fig).
púro a pure; **p. sàngue** thoroughbred.
purpúreo a deep red, purple.
purtròppo ad unfortunately.
pusillànime a cowardly, faint-hearted; nm coward.
putifèrio nm uproar, hullabaloo.
putrèdine nf putridity, rottenness.
putrefàre vi **-rsi** vr to go bad, putrefy, rot.
putrefazióne nf decomposition.
pútrido a putrid, rotten.
puttàna nf whore.
pútto nm (art) cherub, child's figure.
puzzàre vi to smell bad, stink.
púzzo nm bad smell, stench, stink.
púzzola nf polecat.
puzzolènte a fetid, stinking.

Q

qua ad here; **da quàndo in q.?** since when?
quadèrno nm exercise book.
quadràngolo nm quadrangle.
quadrànte nm quadrant, dial, clock-face, sun-dial.
quadràre vt to square; vi to suit.
quadràto a square, strong; nm square.
quàdro nm picture; painting, description; (mil) cadre; **quàdri** pl (cards) diamonds; **a quàdri** (cloth etc) checked.
quaggiù ad down here.
quàglia nf quail.
quàlche a some, any; **q. còsa** pron something, anything; **in q. luògo** somewhere, anywhere.
qualcòsa pron something, anything.
qualcúno pron someone, somebody, anyone, anybody; pl some, any.
quàle a pron which?, what?; as; that, who, whom, whose.
qualìfica nf qualification; title.
qualificàre vt to qualify; call; describe.
qualità nf quality, capacity.
qualóra cj if.
qualsíasi, qualúnque a any, whatever, whichever; **un uòmo q.** an ordinary man.
qualvòlta, ògni cj whenever.
quàndo ad cj when, if, since; **di q. in q.** from time to time; **quand'ànche** even if.
quantità nf quantity, amount.
quànto a ad pron how, how much; as, as much as, what; **q. prìma** as soon as possible; **per q.** though; **quànti** pl as (many), how many.
quantúnque cj (al)though.
quarànta a forty; **quarantèna** nf quarantine; **quarantènne** a forty-year-old; **quarantèsimo** a fortieth; **quarantìna** nf some forty.
quarésima nf Lent.
quaresimàle a Lenten.
quartière nm (city) quarter, district; flat, (US) apartment; (mil) quarters pl; **q. generàle** (mil) H.Q.
quartìno nm quarter of a litre, about half a pint.
quàrto a fourth; nm quarter; quarto.
quàsi ad almost, nearly; hardly; cj as if; **quàsi che** as if.
quassù ad up here.
quàtto a cowering, crouching; **q. q.** very quietly.
quattórdici a fourteen; **quattordicènne** a nmf fourteen-year-old; **quattordicèsimo** a fourteenth.
quattrìno nm farthing; **quattrìni** pl money.
quàttro a four.
quattrocènto a four hundred; nm the 15th century.

quél(lo) *dem a pron* that, that one; whoever; he; the former; **q. che** what.

quèrcia *nf* oak(tree).

querèla *nf* complaint.

querelàre *vt* (*leg*) to proceed against, prosecute; **-rsi** *vr* (*leg*) to bring a complaint.

quésti *dem pron* this man, the latter.

questionàre *vi* to dispute, quarrel.

questionàrio *nm* questionnaire.

questióne *nf* question; dispute, lawsuit.

quésto *dem a pron* this, this one, he, the latter.

questóre *nm* superintendent of police.

quèstua *nf* begging, (*for charity*) collection.

questúra *nf* police station.

questurino *nm* policeman.

qui *ad* here; **q. vicino** close by; **fin q.** so far, till now.

quietànza *nf* receipt.

quietàre *vt* to quiet; **-rsi** *vr* to quieten down.

quiète *nf* quiet, calm, peace, silence, rest.

quièto *a* quiet, calm, still, tranquil.

quìndi *ad* hence, therefore, then, thereby.

quìndici *a* fifteen; **quindicènne** *a nmf* fifteen-year-old; **quindicèsimo** *a* fifteenth.

quindicina *nf* some fifteen; **una q. di giórni** a fortnight or so.

quindicinàle *a nm* fortnightly (magazine).

quinquennàle *a* quinquennial.

quìnta *nf* (*theat*) wing; **diétro le quìnte** *ad* behind the scenes.

quintàle *nm* quintal (100 kilos).

quìnto *a* fifth.

Quirinàle *nm* Quirinal.

quòta *nf* share, instalment; (*av*) altitude, (*naut*) depth.

quotàre *vt* (*com*) to quote; **-rsi** *vr* to subscribe (a sum).

quotàto *a* (*com*) quoted; esteemed, well-liked.

quotazióne *nf* (*com*) quotation; **quotazióni di Bórsa** Stock-Exchange quotations.

quotidiàno *a* daily; *nm* daily paper.

quoto, quoziènte *nm* quotient.

R

rabàrbaro *nm* rhubarb.

rabberciàre *vt* to botch; patch (up).

ràbbia *nf* anger, fury; hydrophobia, rabies.

rabbino *nm* Rabbi.

rabbióso *a* furious, angry; rabid.

rabbonire *vt* to calm, pacify; **-rsi** *vr* to calm down.

rabbrividire *vi* to shiver, shudder.

rabbúffo *nm* rebuke, reprimand.

rabbuiàre *vi* **-rsi** *vr* to grow dark.

rabdomànte *nm* dowser, water diviner.

raccapezzàre *vt* to collect, put together; **-rsi** *vr* to find one's way, make out.

raccapricciànte *a* horrifying, terrifying.

raccapricciàre *vt* to horrify; *vi* **-rsi** *vr* to be horrified, shudder.

raccapriccio *nm* horror.

raccattàre *vt* to pick up, collect.

racchétta *nf* racquet; **r. del tergicristàllo** (*aut*) windscreen wiper, (*US aut*) windshield wiper; **r. per la nève** snowshoes.

racchiúdere *vt* to contain, hold.

raccògliere *vt* to pick up; assemble, gather, collect; receive; fold; **-rsi** *vr* to gather, collect one's thoughts.

raccoglimento *nm* concentration, meditation.

raccòlta *nf* collection, gathering; harvest, harvesting.

raccòlto *a* picked, collected; (*fig*) engrossed; cosy, curled up; *nm* crop, harvest.

raccomandàbile *a* reliable, recommendable.

raccomandàre *vt* to recommend; (*mail*) register; **-rsi** *vr* to entreat; commend oneself; **mi raccomàndo** please.

raccomandàta *nf* registered letter; person recommended.

raccomandàto *a* recommended; registered; *nm* protégé.

raccomandazióne *nf* recommendation; registration.

raccomodàre *vt* to mend, repair; arrange; revive.

raccontàre *vt* to narrate, relate, tell.

raccónto *nm* story, tale, report.

raccorciàre *vt* to shorten; **-rsi** *vr* to grow short(er), shrink.

Rachèle *nf pr* Rachel.

rachítico *pl* **-ici** *a* rickety, stunted.

rachitide *nf* **rachitismo** *nm* rickets.

racimolàre *vt* to scrape together, glean.

ràda *nf* (*naut*) roads *pl*, roadstead.

ràdar *nm* radar.

raddolcire *vt* to soften, soothe, sweeten; **-rsi** *vr* to soften; (*of weather*) become milder.

raddoppiàre *vt* to (re)double.

raddrizzàre *vt* to straighten; correct; **-rsi** *vr* to draw oneself up; improve.

radènte *a* shaving, grazing; **vòlo r.** (*av*) hedgehopping.

ràdere *vt* **-rsi** *vr* to shave (oneself).

radiàre *vt* to expel, strike off.

radiatóre *nm* radiator.

radiazióne *nf* radiation; expulsion.

ràdica *nf* briarwood, root.

radicàle *a nm* radical.

radicàre *vt* **-rsi** *vr* to (take) root.

radice *nf* root; horse-radish.

radiestesìa *nf* sensitivity to radiation.

ràdio *nf* radio, wireless; *nm* radium.

radioascoltatóre nm -**trice** nf, **radioauditóre** nm -**trice** nf listener.

radioattívo a radioactive; **pióggia radioattíva** fall-out; **rèndere r.** to activate.

radiocomandàto a remote controlled.

radiocronísta nmf radio commentator.

radiodiffusióne nf broadcasting, broadcast.

radiofònico pl -**ici** a wireless; **apparècchio r.** wireless set.

radiografía nf radiography.

radiología nf X-ray treatment.

radioscòpico pl -**ici** a radioscopic; **esàme r.** X-ray examination.

radióso a beaming, radiant, bright.

radiotelegrafísta nm wireless operator.

radiotrasmissióne nf broadcasting, broadcast.

radiotrasmittènte a broadcasting; nf broadcasting station.

ràdo a rare, thin, infrequent; **di r.** seldom.

radunàre vt -**rsi** vr to assemble, gather.

radúno nm meeting, gathering, rally.

radúra nf glade, clearing.

ràfano nm horse-radish.

Raffaèle nm pr Raphael.

raffermàre vt to confirm, renew.

raffèrmo a stale.

ràffica nf gust of wind, squall.

raffiguràre vt to represent.

raffilàre vt to sharpen, whet; pare.

raffinaménto nm refining.

raffinàre vt to refine, thin.

raffinatézza nf refinement.

raffinería nf refinery.

rafforzàre vt to reinforce, strengthen; -**rsi** vr to get stronger.

raffreddaménto nm cooling, coolness.

raffreddàre vt to chill, cool; -**rsi** vr to cool, get cold; catch a cold.

raffreddóre nm (med) cold.

raffrenàre vt to check, curb, restrain; -**rsi** vr to check oneself.

raffrontàre vt to compare.

raffrónto nm comparison.

raganèlla nf tree-frog; rattle.

ragàzza nf girl.

ragàzzo nm boy; lad.

raggiànte a radiant.

ràggio nm ray, beam; radius; spoke.

raggiràre vt to cheat, swindle, trick.

raggíro nm trick.

raggiúngere vt to reach; join; achieve; hit.

raggiustàre vt to mend; set in order.

raggranellàre vt to scrape together.

raggrinzíre vt to wrinkle (up).

raggruppaménto nm cluster, group (ing).

raggruppàre vt to collect, set in groups; -**rsi** vr to cluster, form groups.

raggruzzolàre vt to put together, save.

ragguagliàre vt to balance, compare; inform.

ragguàglio nm balance; comparison; information.

ragguardévole a considerable, notable.

ràgia nf rosin, resin; **àcqua r.** turpentine.

ragionaménto nm reasoning, argument.

ragionàre vi to reason, argue, discuss.

ragióne nf reason, right; **avèr r.** to be right.

ragionería nf accountancy, bookkeeping.

ragionévole a reasonable.

ragionevolézza nf reasonableness.

ragionière nm (chartered) accountant, book-keeper.

ragliàre vi to bray.

ràglio nm braying.

ragnatéla nf **ragnatélo** nm spider's web.

ràgno nm spider.

ragú nm ragout.

Raimóndo nm pr Raymond.

rallegraménto nm rejoicing; congratulation.

rallegràre vt to cheer, make glad; -**rsi** vr to rejoice; congratulate.

rallentàre vt to slacken, lessen; **r. il pàsso** to slacken down one's pace; vi to slow down.

ramaiòlo nm ladle.

ramanzína nf telling-off, scolding.

ramàrro nm green lizard.

ràme nm copper.

ramificàre vi -**rsi** vr to branch (out), ramify.

ramificazióne nf ramification.

ramíngo pl -**ghi** a roaming, wandering.

ramíno nm copper kettle; (card game) rummy.

rammaricàrsi vr to be sorry, grieve, regret.

rammàrico pl -**chi** nm grief, regret, bitterness.

rammendàre vt to darn, mend.

ramméndo nm darn, mend.

rammentàre vt to recall, remind; -**rsi** vr to recollect, remember.

rammolliménto nm softening.

rammollíre vt to soften (also fig); move to pity.

ràmo nm branch; (com) line; arm; antler.

ramoscèllo nm spray, twig.

ramóso a branchy.

ràmpa nf flight of steps; steep slope; ramp.

rampicànte a climbing, creeping; nm (zool) climber; (plant) creeper.

rampógna nf rebuke, reproof.

rampóllo nm offspring, shoot.

rampóne *nm* harpoon; crampon.
ràna *nf* frog.
rancidézza *nf* rancidness.
ràncido *a* rancid, rank.
ràncio *nm* (*mil*) rations, mess.
rancóre *nm* grudge, rancour.
randàgio *a* stray, wandering.
randèllo *nm* cudgel.
ranèlla *nf* (*mech*) washer.
Randòlfo *nm pr* Randolph.
ràngo *pl* **rànghi** *nm* rank.
rannicchiàrsi *vr* to crouch, curl up.
rannuvolàre *vi* **-rsi** *vr* to cloud over, grow dark.
ranòcchia *nf* **ranòcchio** *nm* frog.
rantolàre *vi* to breathe heavily, have the death-rattle in one's throat.
ràntolo *nm* heavy breathing, (death-) rattle.
ranúncolo *nm* buttercup.
ràpa *nf* turnip.
rapàce *a* greedy, predatory.
rapacità *nf* greed, rapaciousness.
rapàre *vt* to crop the hair of.
rapidaménte *ad* rapidly.
rapidità *nf* rapidity, swiftness.
ràpido *a* quick, speedy, fast; *nm* express train.
rapiménto *nm* kidnapping; (*fig*) rapture.
rapína *nf* robbery, plunder.
rapinàre *vt* to rob, plunder.
rapinatóre *nm* robber.
rapíre *vt* to abduct, steal, carry off; (*fig*) ravish.
rappacificàre *vt* to pacify, reconcile.
rappezzàre *vt* to patch (up).
rappèzzo *nm* patch.
rappòrto *nm* report, relation, connection; **éssere in buòni rappòrti** to be on good terms.
rappresàglia *nf* reprisal, retaliation.
rappresentànte *nm* representative, agent.
rappresentànza *nf* agency; deputation; representation.
rappresentàre *vt* to represent; (*theat*) perform; **-rsi** *vr* to picture to oneself.
rappresentatívo *a* representative.
rappresentazióne *nf* description; performance.
raraménte *ad* seldom.
rarefàre *vt* **-rsi** *vr* to rarefy.
rarità *nf* rarity; scarcity.
ràro *a* rare.
rasàre *vt* to shave; smooth; **-rsi** *vr* to shave.
raschiàre *vt* to scrape, scratch.
ràschio *nm* irritation in the throat.
rasentàre *vt* to graze; border upon.
rasènte (**a**) *prep* close to.
ràso *a* smooth, shaven; **r. a** *prep* close to; *nm* satin.
rasóio *nm* razor.
raspàre *vt* to rasp, scratch; search through.
rasségna *nf* review, parade.
rassegnàre *vt* to resign; pass in

review; **-rsi** *vr* to resign oneself, submit.
rassegnazióne *nf* resignation.
rasserenàre *vt* to brighten, calm; **-rsi** *vr* to clear up, brighten up.
rassettàre *vt* to tidy, mend.
rassicurànte *a* reassuring.
rassicuràre *vt* to (re)assure; **-rsi** *vr* to make sure, be reassured.
rassicurazióne *nf* assurance, reassurance.
rassodaménto *nm* hardening, (*fig*) consolidation.
rassodàre *vti* to harden, strengthen.
rassomigliànza *nf* likeness, resemblance.
rassomigliàre *vi* **-rsi** *vr* to be alike, resemble.
rastrellàre *vt* to rake; ransack; (*mil*) mop up, comb.
rastrellièra *nf* rack; crib.
rastrèllo *nm* (*tool*) rake.
ràta *nf* instalment; **vèndita a ràte** hire-purchase system, (US) instalment plan.
rateàle *a* by instalments, partial.
ratìfica *nf* ratification.
ratificàre *vt* to ratify.
ràtto *nm* abduction, kidnapping, theft; rat; *a* quick, swift.
rattoppàre *vt* to mend, patch (up).
rattòppo *nm* patch.
rattrappíre *vti* to benumb; contract.
rattristàre *vt* to sadden; **-rsi** *vr* to grieve.
raucèdine *nf* hoarseness.
ràuco *pl* **ràuchi** *a* hoarse.
ravanèllo *nm* radish.
ravvedérsi *vr* to reform, repent.
ravvediménto *nm* reformation, repentance.
ravviàre *vt* to (re)arrange, tidy.
ravvicinàre *vt* to bring closer; reconcile; compare.
ravvisàbile *a* recognizable.
ravvisàre *vt* to recognize.
ravvivàre *vt* to revive (*also fig*).
ravvòlgere *etc v* **avvòlgere** *etc*.
raziocínio *nm* reason(ing), common sense.
razionàle *a* rational.
razióne *nf* ration, portion.
ràzza *nf* race, kind.
ràzza *nf* (*fish*) ray.
razzia *nf* raid; insect-powder.
razziàle *a* racial.
razziàre *vti* to raid, plunder.
ràzzo *nm* rocket, missile; spoke.
razzolàre *vi* to scratch about, rummage.
ré *nm* king.
rè *nm* (*mus*) D, re.
reagíre *vi* to react.
reàle *a* real; royal; *nm* the real, reality.
realìsmo *nm* realism.
realista *nmf* realist; royalist.
realístico *pl* **-ici** *a* realistic.
realizzàre *vt* to realize; **-rsi** *vr* to come true.

realizzazióne *nf* fulfilment; realization; (*theat*) production.
realménte *ad* really, in reality.
realtà *nf* reality.
reàme *nm* kingdom.
reàto *nm* crime.
reattivo *a* reactive; *nm* (*chem*) reagent.
reattóre *nm* reactor; (*av*) jet plane; **r. sperimentàle** breeder reactor.
reazionàrio *a nm* reactionary.
reazióne *nf* reaction; **aèreo a r.** (*av*) jet; **motóre a r.** jet engine.
recapitàre *vt* to deliver.
recàpito *nm* address, delivery.
recàre *vt* to bring, carry; cause; **-rsi** *vr* to go.
recensióne *nf* review.
recensíre *vt* to review.
recènte *a* recent, new.
recenteménte *ad* recently.
recèsso *nm* recess.
recídere *vt* to cut off.
recidíva *nf* relapse.
recíngere *vt* to enclose, fence in.
recínto *a* enclosed; *nm* enclosure.
recipiènte *nm* container, vessel.
recíproco *pl* **-oci** *a* mutual, reciprocal.
recíso *a* cut off; resolute; curt.
rècita *nf* performance, recital.
recitàre *vt* to recite, act, play.
recitazióne *nf* recitation; acting.
reclamàre *vt* to claim; *vi* complain.
réclame *nf* (*Fr*) advertising, advertisement.
reclàmo *nm* complaint.
reclusióne *nf* seclusion; imprisonment.
reclusòrio *nm* penitentiary, prison.
rècluta *nf* (*mil*) recruit.
reclutaménto *nm* recruiting.
reclutàre *vt* to recruit.
recòndito *a* hidden, innermost.
recriminàre *vi* to recriminate.
recriminazióne *nf* recrimination.
recrudescénza *nf* recrudescence.
redarguíre *vt* to reproach.
redattóre *nm* **-trice** *nf* compiler; journalist, writer; (*newspaper*) subeditor, (*US*) copyreader.
redazióne *nf* compiling; editing; editorial staff; editor's office.
redditízio *a* paying, profitable.
rèddito *nm* income, revenue.
redènto *a* redeemed.
redentóre *nm* **-trice** *nf* redeemer; *a* redeeming; **il R.** the Redeemer.
redenzióne *nf* redemption.
redígere *vt* to compile, draw up.
redímere *vt* to redeem.
rèdini *nf pl* reins *pl*.
redivívo *a* risen from the dead; new.
rèduce *a* returning; *nm* survivor; ex-serviceman.
réfe *nm* thread.
referènza *nf* reference, testimonial.
refettòrio *nm* refectory.
refezióne *nf* light meal; **r. scolàstica** school meal.

refrattàrio *a* refractory; fireproof.
refrigerànte *a* refrigerating, refrigerant; *nm* refrigerator, (*US*) icebox.
refrigèrio *nm* cool; relief.
refurtíva *nf* stolen goods *pl*.
regàglie *v* **rigàglie**.
regalàre *vt* to make a present of, present.
regàle *a* regal, royal.
regàlo *nm* gift, present.
regàta *nf* regatta.
reggènte *nm* regent.
reggènza *nf* regency.
règgere *vti* to bear, carry; govern; hold; **-rsi** *vr* to stand; be ruled.
règgia *nf* royal palace.
reggicàlze *nm* suspender belt, (*US*) garter belt, girdle.
reggiménto *nm* regiment; government.
reggipètto, reggiséno *nm* brassière.
regìa *nf* state monopoly; (*theat*) production; (*cin*) direction.
regíme *nm* regime; regimen, diet; **stàre a r.** to be on a diet.
regína *nf* queen.
règio *a* royal.
regióne *nf* region, district.
regísta *nmf* (*theat*) producer, (*cin*) director.
registràre *vt* (*com*) to enter; record, register.
registratóre *nm* **-trice** *nf* registrar, recorder; **r. su nàstro** tape-recorder.
registrazióne *nf* (*com*) entry; recording, registration.
registro *nm* register; registry.
regnàre *vi* to reign.
régno *nm* reign; kingdom.
règola *nf* rule; moderation; **di r. as a** rule; **in r.** in order.
regolamentàre *a* regulation.
regolaménto *nm* regulation; (*of accounts*) settlement.
regolàre *a* regular; *vt* to regulate; settle; **-rsi** *vr* to act, behave.
regolarità *nf* regularity.
regolarizzàre *vt* to regularise.
regolatézza *nf* orderliness, moderation.
regolàto *a* orderly, regular, moderate.
regolazióne *nf* regulation; adjustment.
règolo *nm* (*for lines*) ruler; **r. calcolatóre** sliding rule.
reiètto *a* rejected; *nm* castaway, outcast.
reintegràre *vt* to reinstate, restore; compensate.
relativaménte *ad* relatively, comparatively; **r. a** with regard to.
relatívo *a* relative; comparative; **r. a** concerning.
relatóre *nm* reporter.
relazióne *nf* report; relation; acquaintance; affair; **avèr mólte relazióni** to know many people.
relegàre *vt* to confine, relegate.

religióne nf religion.
religióso a religious; nm member of a religious order.
relíquia nf relic.
relítto nm wreckage.
remàre vi to row, paddle.
rematóre nm rower, oarsman.
reminiscènza nf reminiscence.
remissióne nf remission.
remissívo a meek, submissive.
rèmo nm oar.
remòto a distant, remote, secluded.
réna nf sand(s).
rèndere vt to give back, repay; yield, render; make; **-rsi** vr to become, make oneself; **-rsi cónto di** to realize.
rendicónto nm report, statement.
rendiménto nm rendering, returning (thanks); yield; efficiency.
rèndita nf income, revenue.
rène nm kidney.
renitènte a unwilling, recalcitrant; **r. alla lèva** (mil) failing to appear at the call up.
rènna nf reindeer.
Rèno nm (geogr) Rhine.
rèo a guilty.
repàrto nm department; (mil) detachment, party.
repellènte a repellent, repulsive.
repentàglio nm danger, risk.
repènte, repentíno a sudden.
reperíbile a to be found.
repèrto nm report, evidence, exhibit.
repertòrio nm repertory, inventory.
rèplica nf reply, retort; repetition.
replicàre vt to reply, retort; repeat.
repressióne nf repression.
reprímere vt to repress, check.
rèprobo a nm reprobate.
repúbblica nf republic.
repubblicàno a nm republican.
reputàre vt to consider, deem.
reputàto a esteemed, well thought of.
reputazióne nf reputation.
rèquie nf rest, peace.
requisíre vt to requisition.
requisitòria nf charge, indictment.
requisizióne nf requisition.
résa nf surrender; rendering, return, yield.
residènte a residing; nmf resident.
residènza nf residence, residency.
resíduo a residual; nm residue.
rèsina nf resin.
resistènte a resistant, strong; (colour) fast; **r.** a proof against.
resistènza nf resistance, endurance.
resístere vi to resist, hold out, be proof against.
resocónto nm report; account.
respíngere vt to drive back, reject.
respiràre vti to breathe.
respirazióne nf respiration, breathing.
respíro nm breath; respite.
responsàbile a responsible.
responsabilità nf responsibility.
respònso nm response, answer.

rèssa nf crowd, throng.
restàre v **rimanére.**
restauràre vt to restore.
restàuro nm restoration, repair.
restío a restive, reluctant, unmanageable.
restituíre vt to return, restore.
restituzióne nf restitution, reinstatement.
rèsto nm remainder, rest; (money) change; **rèsti** pl remains pl; **del r.** besides.
restríngere vt to narrow, contract, restrict, tighten; **-rsi** vr to contract, narrow, shrink.
restrizióne nf restriction.
resurrezióne nf **risurrezióne.**
retàggio nm heritage, inheritance.
réte nf net, network, share.
reticènza nf reticence.
Rètiche, (Àlpi) nf pl (geogr) Rhaetian Alps.
reticolàto nm barbed wire entanglement; wire-netting.
retòrica nf rhetoric.
retòrico a rhetorical.
retribuíre vt to pay, reward.
retribuzióne nf pay; retribution.
rètro ad behind; nm back; **védi r.** please turn over (P.T.O.).
retrobottéga nf back-shop.
retrocèdere vt to degrade, reduce in rank; vi to retreat.
retrocucína nm scullery.
retrògrado a nm retrograde, reactionary.
retroscèna nm behind the scenes; underhand dealing.
retrotèrra nf hinterland.
rètta nf charge, terms pl; (geom) straight line; **dàr r. a qlcu** to follow s.o.'s advice.
rettàngolo nm rectangle.
rettífica nf amendment; alteration.
rettificàre vt to rectify, correct.
rettificazióne nf rectification, correction.
rèttile nm reptile.
rettitúdine nf honesty, uprightness.
rètto a straight; honest, right.
rettóre nm rector.
reumatísmo nm rheumatism.
reverèndo a reverend; nm padre.
revisióne nf revision; **r. dèi cónti** audit.
rèvoca nf revocation, repeal.
revocàbile a revokable.
revocàre vt to repeal, revoke.
revòlver nm revolver.
revolveràta nf revolver shot.
ri: common prefix to Italian verbs meaning again or back; thus: **richiúdere** to shut again; **ridàre** to give back etc. For verbs with prefix **ri-** not given below, see entries without prefix.
riabilitàre vt to rehabilitate, requalify; **-rsi** vr to regain one's good name.

riabilitazióne nf rehabilitation.

rialzàre vt to lift up again, heighten; vi go up.

riàlzo nm rise.

riàrso a dry, parched.

riassúnto nm summary, summing-up.

riavérsi vr to recover.

ribadíre vt to clinch, fix; rivet.

ribaldería nf foul deed, knavish trick.

ribàldo nm rascal, scoundrel.

ribàlta nf (theat) footlights, front of the stage.

ribaltàre vti to capsize, overturn.

ribassàre vt to lower, reduce.

ribàsso nm fall, decline; reduction.

ribàttere vt to beat again; repel; (fig) confute.

ribellàrsi vr to rebel, rise (against).

ribèlle a nm rebel.

ribellióne nf rebellion.

ríbes nm redcurrant; blackcurrant.

ribrézzo nm horror, loathing.

ributtànte a revolting.

ricadére vi to fall down again; (have a) relapse.

ricadúta nf relapse.

ricamàre vt to embroider.

ricamatríce nf embroiderer.

ricambiàre vt to change again, reciprocate, repay, return.

ricàmbio nm exchange, return; pèzzo di r. (tec) spare (part).

ricàmo nm embroidery.

ricapitolàre vti to recapitulate, sum up.

ricattàre vt to blackmail.

ricattatóre nm blackmailer.

ricàtto nm blackmail(ing).

ricavàre vt to draw, extract; gain.

ricàvo, ricavàto nm proceeds pl, return.

Riccàrdo nm pr Richard.

ricchézza nf riches pl, richness, wealth.

ríccio a curly; nm lock; hedgehog; sea urchin.

ricciúto a curly.

rícco pl rícchi a rich.

ricérca nf search, pursuit, research, inquiry, demand; àlla r. di in search of.

ricercàre vt to look for again, seek, pursue, investigate.

ricercatézza nf affectation.

ricètta nf prescription; recipe.

ricettàcolo nm receptacle.

ricettàre vt to shelter; receive (stolen goods).

ricettazióne nf receiving stolen goods.

ricévere vt to receive, welcome.

ricevimento nm receiving, reception.

ricevitóre nm receiver.

recevúta nf receipt.

richiamàre vt to (re)call; reprimand.

richiàmo nm recall, call; admonition.

richièdere vt to ask again for; require; send for; apply for.

richièsta nf demand, request.

richièsto a in demand, required, sought after.

rícino, òlio di nm castor oil.

ricognizióne nf (mil) reconnaissance.

ricolmàre vt to fill, overload (with).

ricólmo a brimful.

ricompènsa nf recompense, reward.

ricompensàre vt to recompense, reward.

ricompórre vt to reassemble; (re)compose; -rsi vr to recover oneself.

riconciliàre vt to reconcile.

riconfèrma nf confirmation.

riconoscènte a grateful, thankful.

riconoscènza nf gratitude.

riconóscere vt to recognize, acknowledge.

riconosciménto nm recognition, acknowledgement; identification.

ricopríre vt to cover, hide.

ricordànza nf (poet) recollection, remembrance.

ricordàre vti to remember, recall; remind; mention; -rsi vr to remember, recall.

ricòrdo nm memory, record, souvenir; pl memories pl.

ricorrènza nf recurrence; anniversary; occasion.

ricórrere vi to apply, resort; recur; occur.

ricórso nm petition, claim; recurrence.

ricostituènte a nm tonic.

ricostruzióne nf rebuilding, reconstruction.

ricòtta nf buttermilk curd.

ricoveràre vt to shelter, admit (into hospital); -rsi vr to find shelter.

ricóvero nm refuge, shelter.

ricreàre vt to recreate, refresh; -rsi vr to find recreation.

ricreazióne nf pastime, recreation.

ricrédersi vr to change one's mind.

ricuperàre vt to recover; salvage; make up for.

ricúpero nm recovery; rescue.

ricusàre vt to refuse, reject.

rídda nf confusion, turmoil.

ridènte a smiling, pleasant, bright.

rídere vi to laugh; -rsi (di) vr to laugh (at).

ridícolo a ridiculous; nm ridicule.

ridíre, trovàre da vi to find fault.

ridondànte a redundant.

ridòsso, a ad close by, very near.

ridòtta nf (mil) redoubt.

ridúrre vt to reduce.

riduzióne nf reduction; adaptation, (mus) arrangement.

rielezióne nf re-election.

rièmpire, riempíre vt to fill, stuff; -rsi vr to fill (oneself).

rientràre vi to re-enter, return; be part of; r. in sè to come to oneself.

riepilogàre vti to recapitulate.

riepílogo pl -**ghi** nm recapitulation.

rifacimento nm remaking, reconstruction.

rifàre vt to do again, (re)make; -**rsi** vr to make up one's losses.

rifàtto a done again, rebuilt, remade.

riferíre vt to relate, report, attribute; -**rsi** vr to refer, relate.

rifiatàre vi to breathe (also fig); utter a word.

rifiníre vt to finish, give the last touch to; satisfy.

rifiorìre vi to bloom again, (fig) flourish again.

rifiutàre vti -**rsi** vr to refuse, deny.

rifiúto nm refusal; **rifiúti** pl refuse, scum.

riflessióne nf reflection, deliberation.

riflessìvo a thoughtful; (gram) reflexive.

riflèttere vti to reflect.

riflettóre nm searchlight, floodlight, reflector.

rifluíre vi to flow back, ebb.

riflùsso nm ebb(-tide), reflux.

rifocillàre vt to supply (with food and drink); -**rsi** vr to take refreshment.

rifóndere vt to refund; melt again.

rifórma nf reform(ation).

riformàre vt to amend, reform; (mil) to declare unfit for service.

rifornimento nm supplying, supply; (av, aut) refuelling; **stazióne di r.** (aut) filling station, (US) gas station.

riforníre vt to provide, supply; -**rsi** vr to take in a fresh supply.

rifràngere vt to refract.

rifrazióne nf refraction.

rifréddo nm cold dish.

rifugiàrsi vr to hide oneself, take refuge.

rifugiàto nm refugee.

rifùgio nm refuge, shelter.

rifùlgere vi to shine brightly.

rìga nf line; ruler; row, stripe; (hair) parting.

rigàglie nf pl giblets pl.

rigàgnolo nm brook; gutter.

rigàre vt to rule (lines).

rigattière nm second-hand dealer.

rigeneràre vt -**rsi** vr to regenerate.

rigenerazióne nf regeneration.

rigettàre vti to throw again, throw back, reject; vomit; bud again.

rigidézza, rigidità nf rigidity; strictness.

rìgido a rigid; severe, strict; very cold.

rigiràre vt to turn again; surround; trick; -**rsi** vr to turn round.

rigíro nm turning round; trick.

rìgo pl **righi** nm line.

rigóglio nm bloom, luxuriance.

rigoglióso a luxuriant, flourishing.

rigónfio a puffed up, swollen; nm swelling.

rigóre nm rigour, severity, strictness; **a r. di tèrmini** in the strict sense.

rigorosità nf rigorousness, strictness.

rigoróso a rigorous, severe, strict.

rigovernàre vti to clean, wash up.

riguardànte a regarding, concerning.

riguardàre vt to look at again; regard; concern; -**rsi** vr to take care of oneself.

riguàrdo nm care, consideration, regard, respect; **r. a** concerning.

rigurgitànte a overflowing, swarming.

rigurgitàre vi to flow back, overflow; regurgitate; swarm with.

rilasciàre vt to leave again; release, grant, issue; relax.

rilassaménto nm slackening, relaxation.

rilassàre vt -**rsi** vr to loosen, relax, slacken.

rilegàre vt to bind (again).

rilegatóre nm -**trice** nf bookbinder.

rilegatúra nf binding, bookbinding.

rilevànte a considerable, important.

rilevàre vt to take away again; raise; notice, point out; survey; take; call for.

rilièvo nm relief; importance; remark.

rilúcere vi to glitter, shine.

riluttànte a reluctant.

ríma nf rhyme; **rispóndere per le ríme** to give as good as one gets.

rimandàre vt to send again; send back; defer; reject; refer.

rimaneggiàre vt to rearrange, alter, (pol) shuffle.

rimanènte a remaining; nm remainder.

rimanènza nf remainder, remnant.

rimanére vi to remain; be located; be surprised; rest with.

rimasúglio nm remainder; **rimasúgli** pl remains pl.

rimbàlzo nm rebound; **di r. on the rebound**.

rimbambíre vi to grow childish.

rimbeccàre vt to retort.

rimboccàre vt (trousers) to turn up; (sheets) turn down; (sleeves) roll up.

rimbombàre vi to roar, thunder.

rimbómbo nm roar.

rimborsàbile a repayable.

rimborsàre vt to reimburse, repay.

rimbórso nm reimbursement, repayment.

rimbròtto nm rebuke, reproach.

rimediàre vti to remedy; **r. a** find a remedy for.

rimèdio nm cure, remedy.

rimembrànza nf remembrance.

rimeritàre vt to recompense, reward.

rimescolàre vt to mix up, (cards) shuffle; -**rsi** vr to be upset.

rimèssa nf garage, shed; remittance.

rimèsso a fit again; remitted; meek; **r. a nuòvo** done up; **dénte r.** false tooth.

rimestàre vt to stir up.

riméttere vt to put again, put back, return; remit; lose; defer, refer; vomit; **-rsi** vr to recover; resume; improve; rely on.

rimodernàre vt to modernize, remodel.

rimontàre vti to remount; go up; date back, go back.

rimorchiàre vt to tow.

rimorchiatóre nm (naut) tug(boat).

rimòrchio nm tow; trailer.

rimòrso nm remorse.

rimostrànza nf complaint, protest.

rimostràre vt to show again; vi to remonstrate.

rimozióne nf removal.

rimpàsto nm rearrangement, (pol) shuffle.

rimpatriàre vti to repatriate.

rimpàtrio nm repatriation.

rimpètto v **dirimpètto**.

rimpiàngere vt to lament, regret.

rimpiànto nm regret.

rimpicciolire vti to lessen.

rimproveràre vt to reproach, blame; grudge; **-rsi** vr to blame oneself, repent.

rimpròvero nm rebuke, reproach.

rimuneràre vt to remunerate, reward.

rimunerazióne nf remuneration, reward.

rimuòvere vt to remove; deter, dissuade.

Rinàldo nm pr Reginald, Ronald.

Rinascènza nf v **Rinasciménto**.

rinàscere vi to be born again, revive.

rinasciménto nm rebirth; **R.** Renaissance.

rinàscita nf rebirth, revival.

rincalzàre vt (a plant) to earth up; (bedclothes) tuck in.

rincantucciàrsi vr to creep into a corner, hide oneself.

rincaràre vt (prices) to raise; vi to grow dearer.

rincàro nm rise in prices.

rincasàre vi to return home.

rinchiúdere vt to shut up.

rincórrere vt to chase, pursue.

rincórsa nf run-up.

rincréscere v impers to be sorry, regret, mind.

rincresciménto nm regret.

rincrudire vt to aggravate, embitter; vi to get worse.

rinculàre vi to draw back, recoil.

rinfacciàre vt to cast in s.o.'s teeth, taunt.

rinforzàre vt to make stronger, reinforce; vi to strengthen.

rinfòrzo nm reinforcement.

rinfrancàre vt to reanimate; **-rsi** vr to take heart again; improve.

rinfrescànte a refreshing.

rinfrescàre vt to cool; refresh, restore; vi to get cooler; **-rsi** vr to take refreshment.

rinfrésco pl **-éschi** nm refreshments pl.

rinfusa, àlla ad higgledy-piggledy, in confusion.

ringalluzzire vt to elate, make cocky.

ringentilire vt to refine.

ringhiàre vi to growl, snarl.

ringhièra nf banisters pl, railing.

ringhióso a snarling.

ringiovanire vt to make young(er), rejuvenate; vi to grow young again.

ringraziaménti nm pl thanks pl.

ringraziàre vt to thank.

rinnegaménto nm disowning, denial.

rinnegàre vt to disown, deny.

rinnegàto a nm renegade.

rinnovàbile a renewable.

rinnovaménto nm renewal; revival.

rinnovàre vt to renew; revive.

rinnòvo nm renewal.

rinocerónte nm rhinoceros.

rinomànza nf fame, renown.

rinomàto a famous, renowned.

rinsavire vi to return to reason.

rintanàrsi vr to hide, shut oneself up.

rintoccàre vi (of clock) to strike, (of bell) toll.

rintócco pl **-ócchi** nm (clock) stroke, (bell) tolling, knell.

rintracciàre vt to trace, find (out).

rintronàre vt to deafen; vi resound.

rintuzzàre vt to blunt, abate, retort.

rinúncia, rinúnzia nf renunciation, renouncement.

rinunciàre, rinunziàre vti to give up, renounce.

rinveniménto nm discovery; recovery.

rinvenire vt to discover, find (out); vi to recover one's senses.

rinviàre vt to put off, postpone, adjourn; send back.

rinvigorire vt to make strong(er); **-rsi** vr to grow strong(er).

rinvio nm adjournment, postponement; sending back.

Río délle Amàzzoni (il) nm (geogr) the river Amazon.

rióne nm (town) part, quarter, ward.

riordinàre vt to put in order, rearrange, reorganize.

riorganizzàre vt reorganize.

ripa nf bank, escarpment.

riparàbile a (that) can be mended, repairable.

riparàre vt to shelter, protect; repair, make good; repeat (an exam); vi to make up for, remedy; take shelter; **-rsi** vr to protect oneself.

riparazióne nf reparation; repair; esàmi di r. pl (exams) second session.

ripàro nm cover, shelter, defence.

ripartire vt to distribute, divide, share; vi to start again.

ripartizióne nf distribution, division.

ripercussióne nf repercussion.

ripètere vt to repeat.

ripetitóre nm **-trice** nf repeater; coach, private teacher.

ripetizióne nf repetition; coaching, private lesson.

ripiàno nm shelf; (stair) landing; level place.

ripícco pl -**picchi** nm pique.

rípido a steep.

ripiegàre vt to fold (again); vi to bend; give ground, retire; -**rsi** vr become bent.

ripiègo pl -**ghi** nm expedient, remedy.

ripièno a full, stuffed (with); nm stuffing.

ripórre vt to put away, put back, place; conceal.

riportàre vt to bring again, bring back, report; receive; (com) carry forward; -**rsi** vr to go back, refer.

ripórto nm (com) balance forward.

riposàre vt to rest; put down again; vi -**rsi** vr to rest.

ripóso nm rest, quiet, pause.

ripostíglio nm lumber-room; hiding-place.

riprèndere vt to take again, resume, take back; recover; reprove; vi to begin again; revive; -**rsi** vr to recover, collect oneself; correct oneself.

riprésa nf resumption, revival; recapture, recovery; (cin) shot; (aut) acceleration; recording; (boxing) round.

ripristinàre vt to restore.

ripristino nm restoration.

riprodúrre vt to reproduce; -**rsi** vr to reproduce.

riproduttóre, f -**trice** a reproducing; nm r. acústico pick-up.

riproduzióne nf reproduction.

ripromèttersi vr to intend, propose, expect.

ripròva nf new evidence; confirmation.

riprovàre vt to try again; criticize; (in exams) fail.

ripudiàre vt to repudiate, (leg) renounce.

ripugnànte a disgusting, repugnant.

ripugnànza nf aversion, reluctance.

ripugnàre vi to be repugnant, disgust.

ripúlsa nf refusal, repulse.

risàia nf rice-field.

risalíre vti to go up (again), go back.

risaltàre vt to jump again; vi stand out.

risàlto nm prominence, relief; **dàre r. a** to show up.

risanaménto nm healing, recovery, reformation; (of marsh land) reclamation.

risanàre vt to cure, heal; reclaim, reform.

risarciménto nm compensation, indemnity.

risarcíre vt to compensate, indemnify.

risàta nf laugh(ter).

riscaldaménto nm heating.

riscaldàre vt to heat, warm; -**rsi** vr to warm up, get warm.

riscaldatóre nm -**trice** nf heater, radiator.

riscattàre vt to ransom, redeem.

riscàtto nm redemption, ransom.

rischiaràre vt to illuminate, light up, enlighten; -**rsi** vr to brighten, clear up.

rischiàre vt to risk; vi to run the risk.

rischio nm risk.

rischióso a risky, dangerous, daring.

risciacquàre vt to rinse.

riscontràre vt to check, compare; find.

riscóntro nm checking, comparison; reply.

riscòssa nf insurrection, recovery.

riscuòtere vt (money) to draw, get, receive; rouse, shake; -**rsi** vr to start, be startled.

risentiménto nm resentment.

risentíre vt to feel again, hear again; experience, feel, suffer; vi to feel, show traces; -**rsi** vr to take offence; come to oneself, wake up; -**rsi di** vr to resent.

risentíto a angry, resentful; heard again.

risèrbo nm reserve, discretion, self-restraint.

risèrva nf reserve, reservation; stock, preserve.

riservàre vt to reserve, put off; -**rsi** vr to reserve (to) oneself; intend.

riservatézza nf reserve, prudence.

riservàto a reserved; confidential, private.

riservísta nm reservist.

risíbile a laughable, ridiculous.

risièdere vi to reside.

ríso pl f **rísa** nm laughter.

ríso nm rice.

risolúto a determined, resolute, resolved.

risoluzióne nf resolution; solution.

risòlvere vt to resolve, settle, solve; -**rsi** vr to decide, make up one's mind, be resolved.

risonànza nf resonance, sound.

risonàre vi to resound, echo, ring; vt to ring again; play again.

risórgere vi to rise (again), revive.

risorgiménto nm renascence, revival.

risórsa nf resource.

risparmiàre vt to save, spare.

rispàrmio nm saving.

rispecchiàre vt to reflect; (fig) to mirror.

rispettàbile a respectable, considerable.

rispettàre vt to respect.

rispètto nm respect; regard.

rispettóso a respectful.

risplèndere vi to shine, glitter.

rispondènte a answering, in keeping, in conformity.

rispondènza nf correspondence, agreement.

rispóndere *vi* to answer, reply, respond.

rispósta *nf* answer, reply, response.

rissa *nf* brawl, fray.

ristabilíre *vt* to re-establish, restore; -rsi *vr* to recover one's health.

ristàmpa *nf* reprint, new impression; il libro è in r. the book is being reprinted.

ristampàre *vt* to reprint.

ristorànte *a* restorative; *nm* restaurant, refreshment room.

ristoràre *vt* to refresh, restore; -rsi *vr* to refresh oneself.

ristoratóre, *f* -tríce *a* restorative; *nm* restorer, restaurant.

ristòro *nm* relief, refreshment.

ristrettézza *nf* narrowness, meanness, lack; r. di mèzzi lack of means, straitened circumstances.

ristrétto *a* narrow, limited, restricted, condensed.

risúcchio *nm* eddy, swirl.

risultàre *vi* to result, follow; appear, become known.

risultàto *nm* result.

risurrezióne *nf* resurrection.

risuscitàre *vti* to resuscitate, revive.

risvegliàre *vt* to (a)wake, excite, rouse, stir up; -rsi *vr* to wake up, be roused.

risvéglio *nm* awakening, revival.

risvòlto *nm* lapel, cuff; (*pocket*) flap; (*trousers*) turn-up, (US) cuff.

ritàglio *nm* (*of material*) length, remnant; (*newspaper*) clipping, cutting; ritàgli di témpo *pl* spare time.

ritardàre *vt* to delay, put off, retard; *vi* to be late, delay.

ritardatàrio *nm* latecomer.

ritàrdo *nm* delay; èssere in r. to be late.

ritégno *nm* reserve, restraint.

ritempràre *vt* to fortify, restore, retemper.

ritenére *vt* to keep back, hold; consider, think; -rsi *vr* to consider oneself; restrain oneself.

ritenúta *nf* deduction.

ritiràre *vt* to retract, take back, withdraw; -rsi *vr* to retire, retreat, withdraw; subside; shrink.

ritiràta *nf* retreat; lavatory, (US) rest room.

ritíro *nm* retreat, withdrawal.

** rítmo** *nm* rhythm.

ríto *nm* rite, custom.

ritócco *pl* -ócchi *nm* (finishing) touch.

ritornàre *vi* to return, come (go) back, recur; *vt* to return.

ritornèllo *nm* refrain.

ritórno *nm* return, recurrence; bigliétto di andàta e r. return ticket; èssere di r. to be back.

ritorsióne *nf* retort, retaliation.

ritràrre *vt* to withdraw, draw back; get; represent; deduce; *vr* to withdraw; represent oneself.

ritrattàre *vt* to treat again; retract;

portray; -rsi *vr* to recant; draw oneself.

ritràtto *nm* portrait.

ritrosía *nf* reluctance, shyness.

ritróso *a* bashful, reluctant; a r. backwards.

ritrovàre *vt* to find again, recover; -rsi *vr* to find oneself; meet again; see one's way.

ritrovàto *nm* invention; discovery; device, gadget.

ritròvo *nm* meeting-place, haunt.

rítto *a* erect, straight; *nm* (*of material*) right side.

rituàle *a nm* ritual.

riunióne *nf* gathering, meeting.

riuníre *vt* to re-unite, gather, combine, bring together; -rsi *vr* to come together again, unite.

riuscíre *vi* to succeed, manage, be able; be good at; be, arrive; go out again.

riuscíta *nf* result; success; riuscíto *a* successful.

ríva *nf* bank, shore.

rivàle *a nmf* rival.

rivaleggiàre *vi* to rival, compete.

rivalérsi *vr* to make good one's losses.

rivalità *nf* rivalry.

rivàlsa *nf* revenge.

rivedére *vt* to see again, meet again; revise, check; r. bòzze to read proofs.

rivelàre *vt* to reveal, show, display.

rivelazióne *nf* revelation.

rivéndere *vt* to resell, retail.

rivendicàre *vt* to claim, vindicate.

rivéndita *nf* resale; shop.

rivèrbero *nm* reflection; reverberation.

riverènte *a* reverent, respectful.

riverènza *nf* reverence, respect; bow, curtsey.

riveríre *vt* to respect, venerate, pay one's respects to.

riversàre *vt* to pour (again), pour out (again); throw; -rsi *vr* to flow, pour, rush.

riversíbile *a* reversible.

riversióne *nf* reversion.

rivèrso *a* on one's back.

rivestiménto *nm* covering, coating, lining.

rivestíre *vt* to dress again; clothe, cover, line; (*fig*) hold.

rivièra *nf* coast.

rivíncita *nf* return match; revenge.

rivísta *nf* revision; magazine; parade, review.

rívo *nm* (*poet*) brook, stream.

rivòlgere *vt* to turn; r. la paròla *a* to address; -rsi *vr* to apply, turn.

rivolgiménto *nm* upheaval, change.

rivòlta *nf* revolt, insurrection.

rivoltàre *vt* to turn (over) (again), turn inside out; mix, upset; -rsi *vr* to turn; rebel, revolt.

rivoltèlla *nf* revolver.

rivoluzionàrio *a nm* revolutionary.

rivoluzióne *nf* revolution.
ròba *nf* stuff, things *pl*; **r. da chiòdi** (*person*) bad lot, (*things*) rubbish.
Robèrto *nm pr* Robert.
robustézza *nf* robustness, strength.
robústo *a* robust, strong, sturdy.
rócca *nf* distaff.
ròcca *nf* fortress, rock, stronghold.
rocchétto *nm* reel; (*eccl*) surplice.
ròccia *nf* cliff, rock.
roccióso *a* rocky.
ròco *pl* **ròchi** *a* hoarse.
rodàggio *nm* (*aut*) running in.
Ròdano *nm* (*geogr*) Rhone.
ròdere *vt* to gnaw, nibble; corrode; **-rsi** *vr* to worry, be consumed with.
Rodèsia *nf* (*geogr*) Rhodesia.
rodiménto *nm* gnawing; erosion, worry.
rododèndro *nm* rhododendron.
Rodòlfo *nm pr* Rudolph, Rudolf.
Rodrígo *nm pr* Roderick.
rógna *nf* scabies, mange; (*fig*) nuisance.
rognóne *nm* kidney of animals.
rognóso *a* scabby, mangy.
rògo *pl* **ròghi** *nm* stake, pyre, bonfire.
Róma *nf* (*geogr*) Rome; **romàno** *a nm* Roman.
romanésco *a nm* Roman dialect.
Romanía *nf* (*geogr*) Rumania.
romànico *pl* **-ici** *a* (*arch*) Romanesque; (*language*) Romance.
romanticísmo *nm* Romanticism.
romàntico *pl* **-ici** *a* romantic.
romànza *nf* ballad, song.
romanzésco *pl* **-chi** *a* romantic, adventurous.
romanzière *nm* novelist.
romànzo *nm* romance, novel; *a* (*language*) Romance.
rombàre *vi* to roar.
rómbo *nm* roar; thunder.
romitàggio *nm* hermitage.
romíto *a* lonely, solitary; *nm* hermit.
rómpere *vti* to break.
rompicàpo *nm* puzzle; worry.
rompicòllo *nm* thoughtless person; **a r.** headlong.
rompighiàccio *nm* ice-breaker.
rompiscàtole *inv nmf* bore, tiresome person.
róncola *nf* pruning knife.
rónda *nf* (*mil*) patrol, rounds.
róndine *nf* swallow.
rondóne *nm* (*bird*) swift.
ronzàre *vi* to buzz hum.
ronzíno *nm* jade, worn-out horse.
ronzío *nm* buzzing, humming.
ròrido *v* **rugiadóso.**
ròsa *nf* rose; **colór r.** pink.
rosàio *nm* rose-bush.
rosàrio *nm* rosary.
ròseo *a* rosy.
roséto *nm* rose-garden.
rosicchiàre *vt* to gnaw, nibble.
rosmaríno *nm* rosemary.
róso *a* corroded, gnawed.
rosolàccio *nm* field poppy.

rosolàre *vt* to brown.
rosolía *nf* German measles.
rosóne *nm* rose window, rosette.
ròspo *nm* toad.
rossàstro, rossíccio *a* reddish.
rossétto *nm* lipstick, rouge; **r. indelèbile** kiss-proof lipstick.
ròsso *a nm* red.
rossóre *nm* flush, blush, redness; shame.
rosticceria *nf* cook shop.
ròstro *nm* dais, rostrum.
rotàia *nf* rail.
rotàre *vi* to rotate, revolve.
rotazióne *nf* rotation.
rotèlla *nf* small wheel, castor; (*anat*) kneecap; **pàttini a rotèlle** roller skates.
rotocàlco *nm* rotogravure process.
rotolàre *vti* to roll (up); **-rsi** *vr* to roll, wallow.
ròtolo *nm* roll; **andàre a ròtoli** to go to rack and ruin.
rotolóne *nm* tumble.
rotondàre *vt* to make round.
rotondeggiànte *a* roundish.
rotondità *nf* roundness, rotundity.
rotóndo *a* round, plump, rotund.
ròtta *nf* course; breach; rout; **a r. di còllo** at breakneck speed.
rottàme *nm* wreck, fragment; **rottàmi** *pl* scraps *pl*, rubbish.
ròtto *a* broken; addicted to, accustomed; *nm* break; **per il r. della cúffia** by the skin of one's teeth.
rottúra *nf* breakage, break, breaking-off, rupture.
rovènte *a* red-hot, fiery.
róvere *nm* oak.
rovesciàre *vt* to overthrow, overturn; pour; upset; **-rsi** *vr* to be overturned, capsize; fall (down).
rovèscio *a* inside out; upside down; supine; *nm* reverse, opposite; set back; (*tennis*) backhand; **a r.** inside out, upside down, the wrong way.
rovina *nf* ruin.
rovinàre *vt* to ruin; *vi* to fall with a crash; **-rsi** *vr* to ruin oneself.
rovinóso *a* ruinous.
rovistàre *vti* to rummage, search.
róvo *nm* blackberry bush, bramble.
rozzaménte *ad* roughly, clumsily, rudely.
rozzézza *nf* roughness, rudeness.
rózzo *nm* rough, rude.
rúba, a *ad* in great quantities.
rubacuòri *inv nm* ladykiller.
rubàre *vt* to steal (from).
rubicóndo *a* rubicund, ruddy.
Rubicóne *nm* (*geogr*) Rubicon.
rubinétto *nm* tap, (*US*) faucet.
rubíno *nm* ruby.
rúblo *nm* rouble.
rubríca *nf* newspaper column; address book; rubric.
rúde *a* rough, harsh, hard.
rúdere *nm* remains, ruin *pl*.
rudimentàle *a* rudimentary.

rudiménto nm first principle, rudiment.

ruffiàno nm pander, procurer.

rúga nf wrinkle.

rúggine nf rust, blight; ill-feeling.

rugginóso a rusty.

ruggíre vi to roar.

ruggíto nm roar(ing).

rugiàda nf dew.

rugiadóso a dewy.

rugóso a wrinkled.

ruína etc v **rovína** etc.

rullàre vi to roll.

rullío nm rolling.

rúllo nm (drum etc) roll; (mech) drum-roller, cylinder.

rumèno a nm R(o)umanian.

ruminànte a nm ruminant.

ruminàre vti to ruminate.

rumóre nm noise, rumour.

rumoreggiàre vi to make a noise, rumble.

rumoróso a noisy, loud.

ruòlo nm list, roll, role; **di r.** regular, on the staff.

ruòta nf wheel.

rúpe nf cliff, rock.

ruràle a rural; nm countryman.

ruscèllo nm brook.

russàre vi to snore.

Rússia nf (geogr) Russia.

rússo a nm Russian.

rústico pl **-ici** a country, rustic; unsociable.

ruttàre vi to belch.

rútto nm belching.

ruvidézza nf roughness, coarseness.

rúvido a rough, coarse.

ruzzàre vi to romp.

ruzzolàre vi to roll, tumble down.

ruzzolóne nm fall, tumble; **ruzzolóni**, (a) ad headlong.

S

sàbato nm Saturday.

sàbbia nf sand.

sabotàggio nm sabotage.

saccarina nf saccharine.

saccheggiàre vt to sack, plunder.

sacchéggio nm plunder, sack.

sàcco pl **sàcchi** nm bag, sack; **un s. di** a lot of; **mèttere nel s.** to outwit; **vuotàre il s.** to speak one's mind.

saccóne nm straw mattress.

sacerdòte nm priest.

sacerdotéssa nf priestess.

sacerdòzio nm priesthood.

sacramentàle a sacramental.

sacramentàre vi to swear.

sacraménto nm sacrament.

sacrificàre vti to sacrifice.

sacrifício, sacrifízio nm sacrifice.

sacrilègio nm sacrilege.

sacrílego pl **-eghi** a impious, sacrilegious.

sàcro a holy, sacred.

sacrosànto a sacrosanct; indisputable; well-merited.

sàdico pl **-ici** a nm sadist(ic).

sadísmo nm sadism.

saétta nf arrow; lightning, thunderbolt.

saettàre vti to dart, shoot.

sagàce a sagacious, shrewd, wise.

sagàcia, sagacità nf sagacity, shrewdness.

saggézza nf wisdom.

saggiàre vt to assay, test.

sàggio a wise, sensible; nm wise man; (liter) essay; test, example, sample.

sàgoma nf shape; outline; pattern; character.

sàgra nf annual festival.

sagràto nm hallowed ground (in front of church).

sagrestàno nm sexton.

sagrestía nf sacristy, vestry.

sàio nm sackcloth; (eccl) monk's habit.

sàla nf hall, room; **s. d'aspètto** waiting room.

salamàndra nf salamander.

salàme nm sausage, salami.

salamòia nf brine, pickle.

salàre vt to salt.

salariàre vt to pay wages to.

salariàto a wage-earning; nm wage-earner.

salàrio nm pay, wages.

salàsso nm blood-letting; extortion.

salàto a salty, salted.

saldàre vt to solder, weld, join; (com) to settle.

saldatúra nf soldering, welding.

saldézza nf firmness, steadiness.

sàldo a firm, steady; nm (com) balance; settlement.

sàle nm salt; common-sense; **s. inglése** Epsom salts.

salgèmma nm rock-salt.

sàlice nm willow.

saliènte a nm salient.

salièra nf salt-cellar.

salína nf salt-mine; salt-pan.

salíno a saline, salt(y).

salíre vi to rise, climb, go up, mount; vt to climb, go up.

Salisbúrgo nf (geogr) Salzburg.

saliscéndi (inv) nm latch.

salíta nf ascent, slope.

salíva nf saliva.

sàlma nf corpse.

salmàstro a brackish.

sàlmo nm psalm.

salmóne nm salmon.

salnítro nm saltpetre.

Salomóne nm pr Solomon.

salóne nm hall, reception room.

salòtto nm drawing room, sitting room.

salpàre vi to (set) sail, weigh anchor.

sàlsa nf sauce.

salsèdine nf salt(iness).

salsíccia nf sausage.

sàlso a salt, salty.

saltàre vt to clear, jump (over), skip, miss out; vi to jump, leap, spring.

salterellàre *vi* to hop (about), skip (about).

saltimbànco *pl* -**chi** *nm* acrobat; mountebank.

sàlto *nm* jump, leap; **s. mortàle** somersault.

saltuàrio *a* desultory.

salùbre *a* healthy, wholesome.

salùme *nm* salt meat.

salumería *nf* pork-butcher's (shop); **salumière** *nm* pork-butcher.

salutàre *vt* to greet, salute, say good-bye to, welcome; *a* healthy, salutary.

salúte *nf* health, safety, salvation; **s.**! bless you! **alla s.**! here's health! **càsa di s.** nursing-home.

salúto *nm* greeting, salute; **salúti** *pl* regards *pl*.

sàlva *nf* salvo, volley.

salvacondótto *nm* safe-conduct.

salvadanàio *nm* money-box.

salvagènte (*inv*) *nm* lifebelt, (*US*) life preserver; traffic island.

salvaguardàre *vt* to safeguard.

salvaguàrdia *nf* protection, safeguard.

salvàre *vt* to rescue, save; -**rsi** *vr* to save oneself, escape.

salvatàggio *nm* rescue, salvage.

salvatóre *a* saving; *nm* rescuer, saver, saviour.

salvazióne *nf* salvation.

salvézza *nf* salvation, safety, escape.

sàlvia *nf* (*plant*) sage.

salviétta *nf* napkin, serviette.

sàlvo *a* safe, secure; **sàno e s.** safe and sound; **in s.** in a safe place; *prep* except, save.

samaritàno *a* *nm* Samaritan.

sambúco *pl* -**chi** *nm* elder-tree.

Samuèle *nm* *pr* Samuel.

san *a* Saint.

sanàre *vt* to heal.

sanatòrio *nm* sanatorium.

sancíre *vt* to sanction; ratify.

sàndalo *nm* sandal; sandalwood.

sàngue *nm* blood; **s. fréddo** composure.

sanguígno *a* (of) blood; blood-red; sanguine.

sanguinàrio *a* bloodthirsty; sanguinary.

sanguinàccio *nm* black-pudding.

sanguinàre *vi* to bleed.

sanguinolènto *a* bleeding; bloodstained.

sanguinóso *a* bloody.

sanguisúga *nf* leech; (fig) extortioner.

sanità *nf* health, sanity, soundness.

sanitàrio *a* medical, sanitary; *nm* physician.

sàno *a* healthy, sane; sound, wholesome.

santificàre *vt* to consecrate, hallow, sanctify.

santità *nf* holiness, sanctity.

sànto *a* holy, hallowed; *nm* saint.

santuàrio *nm* sanctuary, shrine.

sanzionàre *vt* to authorize, sanction.

sanzióne *nf* sanction, approval.

sapére *vt* to be able; be acquainted with, get to know; hear; know (how to); learn; smell (of), taste (of); *nm* knowledge, learning.

sapiènte *a* *nm* learned, wise (man).

sapiènza *nf* learning, wisdom.

saponàta *nf* lather, soapsuds.

sapóne *nm* soap; **saponétta** *nf* cake of soap.

sapóre *nm* taste, flavour.

saporitaménte *ad* tastily; **pagàre s.** to pay a very high price.

saporíto, saporóso *a* delicious, savoury.

Sàra *nf* *pr* Sara(h).

saracinésca *nf* rolling shutter; portcullis.

sarcàsmo *nm* sarcasm.

sarcàstico *pl* -**ici** *a* sarcastic.

sàrchio, sarchièllo *nm* hoe.

sarcòfago *pl* -**gi**, -**ghi** *nm* sarcophagus.

Sardégna *nf* (*geogr*) Sardinia.

sardína *nf* sardine.

sàrdo *a* *nm* Sardinian.

sàrta *nf* dressmaker.

sàrtie *nf* *pl* (*naut*) rigging, shrouds *pl*.

sàrto *nm* tailor.

sartoría *nf* tailor's shop.

sassàta *nf* blow from a stone.

sàsso *nm* stone; **rimanére di s.** to be astonished.

sassòfono *nm* saxophone.

Sàtana *nm* *pr* Satan.

satèllite *a* *nm* satellite.

sàtira *nf* satire, lampoon.

satireggiàre *vt* to satirize.

satírico *pl* -**ici** *a* satiric(al); *nm* satirist.

satollàre *vt* to fill up, satiate.

satòllo *a* full, overfed, satiated.

saturàre *vt* to saturate, glut.

Satúrno *nm* Saturn.

sàturo *a* saturated.

Sàul *nm* *pr* Saul.

Savèrio *nm* *pr* Xavier.

sàvio *a* wise; *nm* sage.

Savòia *nf* (*geogr*) Savoy.

saziàre *vt* to satiate, satisfy; -**rsi** *vr* to get tired of.

sazietà *nf* satiety.

sàzio *a* sated; satiated.

sbadatàggine *nf* carelessness, thoughtlessness.

sbadàto *a* careless, heedless.

sbadigliàre *vi* to yawn.

sbadíglio *nm* yawn.

sbagliàre *vt* to mistake; **s. stràda** to take the wrong turning; *vi* *and* -**rsi** *vr* to be mistaken, make a mistake.

sbàglio *nm* error, mistake.

sbalestràto *a* unbalanced, wild.

sballàre *vt* to unpack; *vi* to tell tall tales.

sbalordiménto *nm* astonishment, bewilderment, daze.

sbalordíre *vt* to amaze, astound.

sbalorditivo *a* amazing.

sbalzàre *vt* to throw, toss, emboss.

sbàlzo nm bound; sudden change; a **sbàlzi** by fits and starts; **lavóro a s.** embossed work.

sbandàre vt to disband; vi to skid; (naut) list.

sbaragliàre vt to rout.

sbaràglio nm rout; risk.

sbarazzàre vt to rid; **-rsi** vr to get rid of.

sbarazzíno nm scamp.

sbarbàre vt **-rsi** vr to shave.

sbarbàto a clean-shaven.

sbarcàre vi to disembark, land; **s. il lunàrio** to make both ends meet.

sbàrco pl **sbàrchi** nm landing, unloading.

sbàrra nf bar.

sbarraménto nm (mil) barrage; obstruction.

sbarràre vt to bar, obstruct; (eyes) open wide; (cheque) cross.

sbassàre vt to lower.

sbatacchiàre vt to slam, bang.

sbàttere vti to knock, bang, shake.

sbiadíre vti to fade.

sbièco pl **-chi** a awry, oblique; **di s.** askance.

sbigottiménto nm dismay, astonishment.

sbigottíre vt to dismay, bewilder.

sbilanciàre vt to unbalance, unsettle; **-rsi** vr to speak freely; spend beyond one's means.

sbilàncio nm lack of balance, disproportion.

sbilènco pl **-chi** a crooked, twisted.

sbirciàre vti to cast a sidelong glance.

sbloccàre vt to unblock, clear; decontrol.

sblòcco nm unblocking; (fig) unfreezing.

sboccàre vi to flow into, open into.

sboccàto a foul-mouthed.

sbocciàre vi to blossom, open.

sbócco pl **sbócchi** nm outlet; (river) mouth; (road) end.

sbòrnia nf drunkenness.

sborsàre vt pay out, spend.

sbórso nm disbursement, outlay, payment.

sbottonàre vt to unbutton; **-rsi** vr to unbutton one's clothes; unbosom oneself.

sbozzàre vt to sketch out; **sbòzzo** nm rough draft, sketch.

sbraitàre vi to bawl, shout.

sbranàre vt to tear to pieces.

sbriciolàre vt **-rsi** vr to crumble.

sbrigàre vt to dispatch, finish; **-rsi** vr to hurry up, make haste.

sbrigatívo a hasty, summary.

sbrigliàto a lively, unbridled, wild.

sbrogliàre vt to disentangle, extricate.

sbucàre vi to come out, spring out.

sbucciàre vt to pare, peel, shell, skin.

sbuffàre vi to pant, puff, snort.

scàbbia nf scabies, mange.

scabróso a difficult, rough, rugged.

scacchièra nf chessboard, draughtboard; **scacchière** nm Exchequer; **Cancellière dello s.** Chancellor of the Exchequer.

scacciàre vt to dispel, drive out.

scàcco pl **scàcchi** nm square, check; **s. (màtto)** check(mate); **scàcchi** chess; **a s.** checked, chequered.

scadènte a inferior, of poor quality.

scadènza nf (com) maturity; **a brève s.** in a short time.

scadére vi (com) to be due; expire; lose value; sink.

scafàndro nm diving suit.

scaffàle nm shelf; bookcase.

scàfo nm hull.

scagionàre vt to exculpate, justify.

scàglia nf flake, chip, scale.

scagliàre vt to fling, hurl, throw; **-rsi** vr to hurl oneself, rush.

scaglióne nm echelon.

scàla nf ladder; staircase, stairs pl; scale.

scalàre vt to climb up, to scale; (com) scale down.

scalàta nf climbing.

scalatóre nm **-tríce** nf climber.

scalcinàto a seedy, shabby.

scaldabàgno nm water-heater.

scaldàre vt to heat, warm; **-rsi** vr to warm oneself; get excited.

scaldavivànde (inv) nm dish-warmer.

scaldíno nm hand-warmer, portable warming-pan.

scalfíre vt to graze, scratch.

scalinàta nf (flight of) steps.

scalíno nm step.

scalmanàrsi vr to get agitated.

scàlmo nm (naut) rowlock, (US) oarlock.

scàlo nm landing-place, stop; (rly) **s. mèrci** goods station.

scaloppína nf veal cutlet.

scalpellíno nm stone-cutter, small chisel.

scalpèllo nm chisel.

scalpóre nm fuss.

scàltro a shrewd, crafty.

scàlzo a barefoot(ed).

scambiàre vt to exchange; mistake.

scambiévole a mutual, reciprocal.

scàmbio nm exchange; (rly) points pl, (US) switch.

scamiciàto a shirt-sleeved; nm revolutionary.

scamosciàto a chamois, suède.

scampagnàta nf country excursion.

scampàre vt to rescue, save; vi to escape; **scampàrela bèlla** to have a narrow escape.

scàmpo nm escape, safety; shrimp.

scàmpolo nm remnant.

scancellàre v **cancellàre**.

scandagliàre vt to sound.

scandàglio nm sounding, sounding-rod.

scandalizzàre vt to scandalize, shock.

scàndalo nm scandal.

scandalóso a scandalous, shocking.

Scandinàvia nf (geogr) Scandinavia.

scandínavo *a nm* Scandinavian.

scandíre *vt* to scan; pronounce clearly.

scannáre *vt* to butcher, cut someone's throat.

scannellatúra *nf* groove, fluting.

scànno *nm* bench, seat.

scansafatíche *inv nmf* loafer.

scansáre *vt* to avoid, shun; **-rsi** *vr* to step aside.

scansía *nf* bookcase, set of shelves.

scansióne *nf* scansion.

scantonáre *vi* to turn the corner; sneak off.

scanzonáto *a* free and easy, unconventional.

scapestráto *a* wild, dissolute; *nm* waster.

scapigliáre *vt* to ruffle; **scapigliáto** *a* dishevelled, disorderly, unconventional.

scapitáre *vi* to lose, suffer loss.

scàpito *nm* detriment, loss.

scàpola *nf* shoulder-blade.

scàpolo *a* single; *nm* bachelor.

scappáre *vi* to escape, run away.

scappáta *nf* escapade; short call; trip.

scappaménto *nm* (*mech*) exhaust.

scappatóia *nf* loophole, way out.

scarabèo *nm* beetle; scarab.

scarabocchiáre *vt* to scrawl, scribble.

scarabòcchio *nm* scribble, scribbling.

scarafàggio *nm* cockroach, (US) roach.

scaramúccia *nf* skirmish.

scaraventáre *vt* to fling, hurl.

scarceráre *vt* to release (from prison).

scardináre *vt* to unhinge.

scàrica *nf* volley, shower; (*el*) discharge.

scaricáre *vt* to discharge, unload.

scàrico *pl* **-chi** *a* unloaded, discharged, (*clock*) run down; light; *nm* discharge, unloading, waste; **túbo di s.** exhaust-pipe, waste-pipe.

scarlattína *nf* scarlet fever.

scarlátto *a nm* scarlet.

scarmigliáre *vt* to ruffle.

scàrno *a* lean, thin.

scàrpa *nf* shoe; **scarpóne** *nm* boot; **s. da sci** ski-boot.

scarseggiáre *vi* to be scarce, lack.

scarsézza, scarsità *nf* scarcity, lack.

scàrso *a* scanty, scarce, short.

scartáre *vt* unwrap, reject, discard.

scàrto *nm* discard(ing), refuse; *nm* swerve; **di s.** of inferior quality.

scassináre *vt* to force open.

scassinatóre *nm* burglar, housebreaker.

scàsso *nm* housebreaking.

scatenáre *vt* to unchain, let loose; cause; **-rsi** *vr* to break out.

scàtola *nf* box, tin, can, case; **in s.** tinned.

scatoláme *nm* tins *pl*, cans *pl*, canned food.

scattáre *vi* to be released, go off, spring (up); get angry; *vt* (*phot*) to shoot.

scàtto *nm* click, jerk; impulse; (*tec*) release.

scaturíre *vi* to gush, spring.

scavalcáre *vt* to climb over; oust; excel.

scaváre *vt* to dig out, excavate.

scavezzacòllo *nm* (*fig*) reckless person.

scàvo *nm* excavation.

scégliere *vt* to choose, pick out, select.

scelleratézza *nf* wickedness, crime.

scelleráto *a nm* wicked (man).

scellíno *nm* shilling.

scélta *nf* choice, selection; **di prima s.** choice, top quality.

scélto *a* choice, picked, select(ed).

scemáre *vti* to diminish, lessen.

scèmo *a* foolish, stupid; *nm* fool.

scémpio *a* silly; single; *nm* slaughter.

scèna *nf* scene, stage; **mèttere in s.** (*theat*) to produce, stage.

scenàta *nf* scene; row.

scenàrio *nm* scenario; scenery.

scéndere *vti* to come (go) down, descend.

sceneggiatúra *nf* staging; (*cin*) scenario.

scènico *pl* **-ici** scenic; stage.

sceriffo *nm* sheriff.

scervellàrsi *vr* to cudgel (rack) one's brains.

scèttico *pl* **-ici** *a* sceptical; *nm* sceptic.

scèttro *nm* sceptre.

scévro *a* exempt, free (from).

schèda *nf* card, file-card; voting paper.

schedáre *vt* to file, catalogue.

schedàrio *nm* card-index.

schéggia *nf* splinter.

scheggiáre *vt* **-rsi** *vr* to splinter.

schèletro *nm* skeleton.

schèma *nm* plan, scheme; diagram.

schérma *nf* fencing.

schermírsi *vr* to defend oneself.

schérmo *nm* protection; (*cin*, *tv*) screen; (*phot*) filter.

scherníre *vt* to despise, flout, scoff at.

schérno *nm* derision, taunt.

scherzáre *vi* to jest, joke, make fun.

schérzo *nm* jest, joke, trick.

scherzóso *a* facetious, joking, playful.

schettináre *vi* to roller-skate.

schettíno *nm* roller skate.

schiaccianóci *nm* nutcrackers *pl*.

schiacciànte *a* crushing, overwhelming.

schiacciáre *vt* to crush, squash.

schiaffeggiáre *vt* to slap, smack.

schiàffo *nm* box on the ear, slap; insult.

schiamazzáre *vi* to make a din.

schiamàzzo *nm* din, uproar.

schiantáre *vt* **-rsi** *vr* to break.

schiànto *nm* crash; pang; **di s.** suddenly.

schiariménto nm clearing up; explanation.

schiaríre vt to clear up; explain; -rsi vr to become clear, light, brighten, light up.

schiaríta nf clearing; (fig) improvement.

schiàtta nf race, stock.

schiavitú nf slavery.

schiàvo a slave; nm slave, bondsman.

schièna nf back.

schièra nf band, group; **mèttersi in s.** to fall in.

schieràre vt -rsi vr to draw up, side with.

schiettézza nf purity, frankness.

schiètto a pure, unadulterated; frank.

schifézza nf disgusting thing, disgust.

schifiltóso a fastidious, hard to please.

schífo nm disgust.

schifosàggine nf disgusting action (thing), loathsomeness.

schifóso a disgusting, loathsome.

schiòppo nm gun.

schiúdere vt -rsi vr to open.

schiúma nf foam, froth; scum.

schivàre vt to avoid.

schívo a shy; averse.

schizzàre vt to splash, squirt; sketch; vi spurt, rush.

schízzo nm splash; sketch.

sci nm ski; s. **nàutico** waterski.

scía nf track, wake.

sciàbola nf sabre.

sciacàllo nm jackal.

sciacquàre vt to rinse; **sciàcquo** nm gargling, mouthwash.

sciagúra nf disaster, misfortune.

sciaguratamènte ad unfortunately, miserably; wickedly.

sciaguràto a unlucky, wretched; nm wretch.

scialacquàre vt to squander, waste.

scialàre vi to be wasteful, dissipate; enjoy oneself.

sciàlbo a pale, wan.

sciàlle nm shawl.

scialúppa nf (naut) launch.

sciàme nm crowd, swarm.

sciancàto a lame.

Sciangai nf (geogr) Shanghai.

sciàre vi to ski.

sciàrpa nf scarf, sash.

sciàtto a slovenly, untidy, careless.

scíbile nm knowledge.

scientemènte ad knowingly.

scientificamènte ad scientifically.

scientífico pl -ici a scientific.

sciènza nf science, knowledge.

scienziàto nm scientist.

scímmia nf ape, monkey.

scimmiottàre vt to ape, mimic.

scimuníto a foolish, silly.

scíndere vt to divide, separate.

scintílla nf spark.

scintillàre vi to sparkle, glitter.

scintillío nm sparkling, twinkling.

sciocchézza nf foolishness, nonsense, trifle.

sciòcco pl **sciòcchi** a foolish, silly; nm fool.

sciògliere vt to dissolve, melt; release, untie; -rsi vr to dissolve, melt; free oneself.

scioglilíngua inv nm tonguetwister.

sciòlto a melted; loose, free; nimble.

scioperànte nm striker.

scioperàre vi to (go on) strike.

scioperàto a lazy; nm loafer.

sciòpero nm strike.

sciorinàre vt (clothes) hang out; display.

scipíto a insipid, tasteless.

sciròcco pl -chi nm south-east wind.

sciròppo nm syrup.

scísma nm schism.

scissióne nf division, split.

sciupàre vt to ruin, spoil, waste.

sciupío nm waste.

sciupóne nm waster, spendthrift.

scivolàre vi to slide, slip, skid; **scívolo** nm chute.

scoccàre vt to dart, to throw; vi to strike.

scocciàre vt (fam) to bore, bother.

scocciatóre nm -**trice** nf (fam) bore.

scodèlla nf bowl, soup plate.

scodellàre vt to dish up, serve out; (fig) pour out.

scodinzolàre vi to wag (the tail).

scoglièra nf cliff.

scòglio nm rock, reef; stumbling-block.

scoiàttolo nm squirrel.

scolàre vti to drain, drip.

scolàstico pl -ici a scholastic.

scolàro nm pupil, schoolboy.

scollàto a (dress) low-necked.

scollatúra nf neckline.

scòllo nm neck-opening.

scólo nm drainage; drain-pipe.

scoloríre vt to discolour; vi to fade.

scolpàre vt to exculpate, justify; -rsi vr to apologize; justify oneself.

scolpíre vt sculpture, carve, engrave.

scombinàre vt to disarrange.

scombussolàre vt to disturb, upset.

scomméssa nf bet, wager.

scomméttere vt to bet, wager.

scomodàre vt -rsi vr to trouble, bother.

scomodità nf inconvenience.

scòmodo a uncomfortable, inconvenient; nm trouble.

scompaginàre vt to upset.

scomparíre vi disappear, be lost.

scompàrsa nf disappearance, death.

scompartiménto nm compartment.

scompigliàre vt to upset, confuse.

scompíglio nm confusion, fuss.

scompórre vt to take to pieces, disarrange; -rsi vr to be upset, lose one's temper.

scompósto a dismantled, disordered; upset.

scomúnica nf excommunication.

scomunicàre vt to excommunicate.

sconcertàre vt to baffle, disconcert, puzzle.
sconcézza nf obscenity, disgusting thing.
scóncio a indecent, nasty.
sconclusionàto a rambling.
sconfessàre vt to disavow, disown.
sconfìggere vt to defeat.
sconfinàto a boundless, unlimited.
sconfìtta nf defeat.
sconfortàto a discouraged, disheartened.
sconfòrto nm discouragement, dejection.
scongiuràre vt to implore; remove.
scongiúro nm exorcism.
sconnèttere vt to disconnect.
sconoscènte a ungrateful.
sconosciúto a nm unknown.
sconquassàre vt to smash.
sconquassàto a rickety, tumbledown.
sconsideràto a thoughtless.
sconsigliàre vt to advise against, dissuade.
sconsolàto a disconsolate, depressed.
scontàre vt (com) to deduct, discount; to expiate, pay for; to take for granted.
scontentézza nf discontent.
scontènto a disappointed, dissatisfied; nm discontent.
scónto nm discount.
scontràrsi vr to clash, crash, collide.
scontríno nm check, receipt, ticket.
scóntro nm collision.
scontrosàggine, scontrosità nf cantankerousness, bad temper, peevishness.
scontróso a sulky, peevish, badtempered.
sconveniènte a unseemly, unprofitable.
sconveniènza nf unseemliness, discourtesy.
sconvòlgere vt to derange, upset.
sconvolgiménto nm upset, confusion.
scópa nf broom.
scopàre vi to sweep.
scopèrta nf discovery.
scopèrto a bare, open, unprotected.
scòpo nm aim, end, object, purpose.
scoppiàre vi to burst (out), explode.
scòppio nm burst(ing), explosion; outburst, outbreak.
scoprìre vt to discover, find out; reveal; -rsi vr to uncover oneself.
scoraggiàre vt to dishearten; -rsi vr to get disheartened.
scorbùtico pl -ici a scorbutic; cantankerous; awkward.
scorciàre vt to shorten; **scorciatóia** nf short-cut.
scórcio nm foreshortening; end.
scordàre vt -rsi vr to forget; untune.
scòrgere vt to discern, perceive.
scornàto a humiliated, ridiculed, disgraced.
scòrno nm disgrace, shame.

scorpacciàta nf bellyful.
scorpióne nm scorpion.
scorrazzàre vi to run about.
scórrere vt to run through; raid; glance over; vi to run, slide, flow.
scorrería nf incursion, raid.
scorrettézza nf mistake; bad manners; dishonesty.
scorrètto a incorrect; improper; dishonest, dissolute.
scorrévole a flowing, fluent, gliding.
scorrevolézza nf fluency, smoothness.
scórsa nf glance.
scórso a last, past.
scorsóio a running; **nódo s.** slip-knot.
scòrta nf escort; supply.
scortàre vt to escort.
scortecciàre vt to strip, peel.
scortése a discourteous, rude, uncivil.
scortesía nf rudeness, rude act.
scorticàre vt to flay, fleece, skin.
scorticatúra nf scratch, graze.
scòrza nf bark, peel, rind, skin.
scoscéso a steep.
scòssa nf shake, shock.
scòsso a shaken, upset.
scostàre vt -rsi vr to move (away), shift (aside).
scostumàto a dissolute; rude.
scottàre vt to burn, scald, scorch.
scottatúra nf burn, scald.
scòtto a (cook) overdone; nm score, reckoning.
scovàre vt to dislodge, rouse, find out.
Scòzia nf (geogr) Scotland.
scozzése a Scottish; nm Scot, Scotsman, (language) Scots.
screditàre vt to discredit.
scrédito nm discredit, disgrace.
scremàre vt to skim.
screpolàre vt -rsi vr to chap, crack.
scrèzio nm dispute, quarrel.
scribacchiàre vi to scribble.
scricchiolàre vi to creak.
scricchiolío nm creaking.
scrígno nm casket, jewel-case.
scriminatúra nf (hair) parting.
scritta nf inscription, notice.
scritto a written; nm writing; document.
scrittóio nm writing desk.
scrittóre nm -trìce nf writer.
scrittúra nf (hand)writing; contract.
scritturàre vt (theat) to engage.
scrivanía nf (writing-)desk.
scrìvere vt to write.
scroccàre vt to scrounge.
scròcco pl scròcchi nm scrounging; swindle.
scròfa nf sow.
scrollàre vt to shake, shrug.
scrosciàre vi (rain) to pelt; (fig) thunder.
scròscio nm roar; downpour; **piòvere a s.** to pour.
scrúpolo nm scruple.
scrupolóso a scrupulous.

scrutàre *vt* to investigate, scan.
scrutinàre *vt* to scrutinize.
scrutínio *nm* list of marks; voting; scrutiny.
scucíre *vt* to unsew.
scudería *nf* stable.
scudíscio *nm* lash, whip.
scúdo *nm* shield, protection.
scultóre *nm* sculptor.
scultúra *nf* carving, sculpture.
scuòla *nf* school, schoolhouse; s. diúrna day-school; s. seràle evening school.
scuòtere *vt* to shake; stir up; -rsi *vr* to rouse oneself, stir.
scúre *nf* axe, hatchet.
scúro *a* dark; grim; *nm* darkness; shutter.
scurríle *a* scurrilous.
scúşa *nf* excuse, pretext.
scuşàre *vt* to excuse, forgive, justify; -rsi *vr* to apologize, justify oneself; scúsi excuse me; I beg your pardon.
şdebitàrsi *vr* to pay one's debts.
şdegnàre *vt* to disdain, scorn; -rsi to get angry.
şdégno *nm* disdain; indignation.
şdegnóso *a* disdainful, haughty.
şdentàto *a* toothless.
şdoganàre *vt* to clear (through the customs).
şdolcinàto *a* maudlin, sugary, affected.
şdraiàre *vt* to stretch at full length; -rsi *vr* to lie down, stretch oneself out; şdràio *nm* deck chair.
şdrucciolàre *vi* to slip, slide.
şdrucíre *vt* to tear, unstitch.
se *cj* if, whether; se no or else, otherwise.
sè *refl pron* oneself, himself, herself, itself, themselves *pl*.
sebbène *cj* although, though.
Sebastiàno *nm pr* Sebastian.
seccaménte *ad* drily, bluntly.
seccànte *a* tiresome, irritating; persóna s. a nuisance.
seccàre *vt* to dry; bother, irritate; -rsi *vr* to dry (up); get tired, get annoyed.
seccatúra *nf* nuisance, bother; desiccation.
sécchia *nf* -o *nm* bucket, pail.
sécco *pl* sécchi *a* dry; thin; lavàre a s. to dry-clean.
secolàre *a* age-old; secular, lay; *nm* layman.
sècolo *nm* century, age.
secondàre *v* assecondàre.
secondàrio *a* secondary.
secóndo *a* second; favourable; *nm* second, main dish; di secónda màno second-hand; *prep* according to; s. me in my opinion.
sèdano *nm* celery.
sedàre *vt* to soothe, calm.
sedatívo *a nm* sedative.
sède *nf* centre, seat; residence; office; see.
sedentàrio *a* sedentary.

sedére *vi* to sit; -rsi *vr* to sit down, take a seat.
sèdia *nf* chair.
sedicènte *a* self-styled.
sédici *a* sixteen; sedicènne sixteen-year-old; sedicèsimo sixteenth.
sedíle *nm* seat, bench.
sedizióne *nf* sedition.
sedizióso *a* seditious.
sedúrre *vt* to seduce; entice, charm.
sedúta *nf* sitting; meeting.
seduttóre *nm* -tríce *nf* seducer.
seduzióne *nf* seduction, enticement; charm.
séga *nf* saw.
ségala. ségale *nf* rye.
segàre *vt* to saw.
segatúra *nf* sawing; sawdust.
sèggio *nm* chair, seat; see.
sèggiola *v* sèdia.
segnalàre *vt* to signal; point out; -rsi *vr* to distinguish oneself.
segnalazióne *nf* signal(ling).
segnàle *nm* signal.
segnalíbro *nm* bookmark.
segnàre *vt* to mark, note; (*sport*) score; -rsi *vr* to cross oneself.
ségno *nm* sign, mark.
ségo *pl* séghi *nm* tallow.
segregaménto *nm* segregazióne *nf* segregation, isolation.
segregàre *vt* to isolate, segregate.
segretàrio *nm* -ria *nf* secretary.
segretería *nf* secretary's office.
segretézza *nf* secrecy.
segréto *a nm* secret.
seguàce *nmf* follower, supporter.
seguènte *a* following; next.
seguíre *vt* to follow; supervise; *vi* to follow; result.
seguitàre *vi* to continue, go on, keep on.
séguito *nm* continuation; followers *pl*, retinue; sequel; series; succession; di s. in succession; in s. later on; in s. a *prep* owing to.
sèi *a* six.
seicènto *a* six hundred; *nm* 17th century.
sèlce *nf* flint(stone).
selciàto *nm* pavement; road surface.
selezionàre *vt* to select, choose.
selezióne *nf* selection; digest.
sèlla *nf* saddle.
sellàre *vt* to saddle.
seltz *nm* soda(-water), (US) seltzer.
sélva *nf* forest, wood.
selvaggína *nf* game.
selvàggio *a* savage; wild; rough; *nm* savage.
selvatichézza *nf* wildness; unsociability; uncouthness.
selvàtico *pl* -ici *a* wild, rough.
semàforo *nm* traffic lights.
sembiànte *nm* sembiànza *nf* appearance.
sembràre *v* parére.
sème *nm* seed; cause; semènza seeds *pl*; (*liter*) progeny.
semestràle *a* half-yearly.

semèstre *nm* half-year.
semi- *prefix* half-, semi-.
semicúpio *nm* hip-bath.
sémina, seminagióne *nf* sowing; sowing season.
seminàre *vt* to sow; scatter.
seminàrio *nm* seminary; seminar.
seminàto *a* sown; strewn; *nm* sown field.
seminterràto *nm* basement.
sémola *nf* bran; fine flour; freckles *pl*.
semovènte *a* self-moving, self-propelled.
Sempióne *nm* (*geogr*) Simplon.
sempitèrno *a* everlasting.
sémplice *a* simple, easy; mere, plain; soldàto s. *nm* private (soldier).
semplicità *nf* simplicity.
semplificàre *vt* to simplify.
sèmpre *ad* always, ever; still; per s. forever; s. méno less and less; s. piú more and more; s. che *cj* provided (that).
sènapa, sènape *nf* mustard.
senàto *nm* senate.
senatóre *nm* senator.
senése *a nmf* Sienese.
seníle *a* senile.
senilità *nf* senility.
senióre *a nm* senior.
Sènna *nf* (*geogr*) Seine.
sénno *nm* judgment, sense, wisdom.
séno *nm* bosom, breast; cove, inlet.
sensále *nm* broker, middleman.
sensàto *a* sensible, judicious.
sensazionàle *a* sensational, thrilling.
sensazióne *nf* sensation, feeling.
senseria *nf* brokerage.
sensìbile *a* sensitive; considerable.
sensibilità *nf* sensitiveness, feeling, sensitivity.
sensitìvo *a* sensory; sensitive.
sènso *nm* sense; feeling; meaning; sensation; s. único one way; privo di sènsi unconscious; sensòrio *a* sensory; *nm* sense organ.
sensuàle *a* sensual.
sensualità *nf* sensuality.
sentènza *nf* decree; judgment; maxim.
sentenziàre *vi* to judge; talk sententiously.
sentièro *nm* footpath, path(way).
sentimentàle *a* sentimental.
sentiménto *nm* sentiment; feeling; *pl* senses *pl*.
sentína *nf* bilge.
sentinèlla *nf* (*mil*) sentinel, sentry.
sentíre *vt* to feel; hear, listen to; -rsi *vr* to feel; *nm* feelings *pl*.
sentíto *a* heart-felt, sincere.
sentóre *nm* vague suspicion, inkling.
sènza *prep* without; sènz'àltro *ad* immediately; of course.
separàre *vt* to separate, divide; -rsi *vr* to part, separate.
separataménte *ad* separately.
separazióne *nf* separation, parting.
sepólcro *nm* sepulchre, grave.

sepoltúra *nf* burial; grave; luògo di s. burial place.
seppelliménto *nm* interment, burial.
seppellíre *vt* to bury.
séppia *nf* cuttlefish.
sequèla *nf* series, sequence.
sequestràre *vt* to sequester, sequestrate, distrain upon.
sequèstro *nm* sequestration, distraint.
séra *nf* evening.
seràle *a* evening.
seràta *nf* evening; evening party; (*theat*) evening performance.
serbàre *vt* to put aside; to keep.
serbatóio *nm* reservoir, tank.
sèrbo *nm* in s. in reserve; aside.
serenàta *nf* serenade.
serenità *nf* serenity, calmness.
seréno *a* serene, clear, calm.
sergènte *nm* sergeant.
seriaménte *ad* seriously, gravely.
sèrie *nf* series; set; succession; in s. mass-produced; fuòri s. special, custom-built.
serietà *nf* seriousness, gravity.
sèrio *a* serious, earnest; grave; reliable; sul s. in earnest.
sermóne *nm* sermon; reproof.
sèrpe *nf* -pènte *nm* serpent, snake.
serpeggiàre *vi* to meander, wind; spread.
sèrra *nf* greenhouse, hothouse.
serràglio *nm* menagerie; seraglio.
serramànico, coltèllo a claspknife.
serrànda *nf* (*of a shop*) shutter.
serràre *vt* to lock (up); shut, close; clench; -rsi *vr* to stand close; close up.
serratúra *nf* lock.
sèrva *nf* maid, (woman)servant.
servíle *a* servile, slavish.
servíre *vti* to serve; -rsi *vr* to (make) use (of); help oneself.
servitóre *nm* servant.
servitú *nf* servitude; servants *pl*, staff.
serviziévole *a* obliging.
servízio *nm* service; favour; kindness; di s. on duty; fuòri s. off duty; dònna di s. *nf* maid; mezzo s. part-time service.
sèrvo *nm* (man)servant.
sessànta *a nm* sixty; sessantènne *a nmf* sixty-year-old (person); sessantèsimo *a* sixtieth; sessantína *nf* about sixty.
sessióne *nf* session.
sèsso *nm* sex.
sessuàle *a* sexual.
sèsto *a* sixth; *nm* order; méttere in s. to put in order, tidy.
séta *nf* silk.
setàccio *nm* sieve.
séte *nf* thirst; avér s. to be thirsty.
setería *nf* silk shop; silk goods.
sétola *nf* bristle.
setolóso *a* bristly.
sètta *nf* sect.
settànta *a nm* seventy; settantènne

a nmf seventy-year-old (person); **settantèsimo** *a* seventieth; **settantína** *nf* about seventy.

sètte *a* seven; **settènne** seven-year-old.

settecènto *a* seven hundred; *nm* 18th century.

settèmbre *nm* September.

settentrionàle *a* north(ern), northerly; *nm* northerner.

settentrióne *nm* north.

sèttico *pl* **-ici** *a* septic.

settimàna *nf* week.

settimanàle *a nm* weekly.

sèttimo *a* seventh.

settóre *nm* sector.

settuagenàrio *a nm* septuagenarian.

severaménte *ad* severely, sternly.

severità *nf* severity, strictness, sternness.

sevèro *a* severe, strict, stern.

sevízie *nf pl* cruelty, ill-treatment.

sezionàre *vt* to cut up, dissect.

sezióne *nf* section; department.

sfaccendàre *vi* to bustle about.

sfaccendàto *nm* idler, loafer.

sfacchinàre *vi* to drudge.

sfacchinàta *nf* heavy piece of work.

sfacciatàggine *nf* impudence, insolence.

sfacciàto *a* impudent, shameless.

sfacèlo *nm* break-up, collapse, ruin.

sfamàre *vt* to appease someone's hunger.

sfàrzo *nm* pomp, splendour.

sfarzóso *a* gorgeous, sumptuous.

sfasàto *a* (el) out of phase; (fig) inconsistent, inconsequent.

sfasciàre *vt* to unbandage; demolish, dismantle.

sfatàre *vt* to disprove, discredit.

sfavillàre *vi* to sparkle, shine.

sfavorévole *a* unfavourable.

sfèra *nf* sphere, circle, globe.

sfèrico *pl* **-ici** *a* spherical.

sferràre *vt* (a horse) to unshoe; (a blow) deliver; (an attack) launch.

sfèrza *nf* lash, whip.

sferzàre *vt* to whip, lash, scourge.

sfiatàrsi *vr* to talk oneself hoarse.

sfída *nf* challenge, defiance.

sfidàre *vt* to challenge, dare, defy; **sfído!** *interj* of course.

sfidúcia *nf* distrust, mistrust, lack of confidence.

sfiduciàto *a* discouraged, disheartened.

sfiguràre *vt* to disfigure; *vi* to cut a poor figure.

sfilàre *vt* to unstring, unthread; *vi* to file (past).

sfilàta *nf* row, parade.

sfínge *nf* sphinx.

sfiniménto *nm* exhaustion.

sfiníto *a* exhausted, worn out.

sfioràre *vt* to graze, skim over, touch lightly, touch on.

sfioríre *vi* to wither, fade.

sfoderàre *vt* to remove the lining; (sword etc) draw, display, show off.

sfogàre *vt* to vent, let out; **-rsi** *vr* to give vent to one's feelings, speak frankly.

sfoggiàre *vti* to show off, flaunt.

sfòggio *nm* show, display.

sfogliàre *vt* to pick off leaves; turn over the pages of, run through (a book).

sfógo *pl* **sfóghi** *nm* vent, outlet; eruption.

sfolgorànte *a* blazing, flaming.

sfolgoràre *vi* to blaze, flash.

sfollàre *vt* to disperse; *vi* to disperse, evacuate.

sfondàre *vt* to break (down), knock the bottom out.

sfóndo *nm* background.

sformàto *a* shapeless; *nm* pie, pudding.

sfornàre *vt* to take out of the oven, bring out.

sfortúna *nf* ill-luck, misfortune.

sfortunàto *a* unlucky.

sforzàre *vt* to force strain; **-rsi** *vr* to strive, try hard.

sfòrzo *nm* effort, strain.

sfracellàre *vt* to shatter, smash.

sfrattàre *vt* to turn out, evict.

sfràtto *nm* notice to quit, eviction.

sfrégio *nm* disfigurement; affront.

sfrenatézza *nf* wildness, licentiousness.

sfrenàto *a* unbridled, unrestrained, wild.

sfrontatézza *nf* effrontery, impudence.

sfrontàto *a* brazen, impudent.

sfruttaménto *nm* exploitation.

sfruttàre *vt* to exploit.

sfuggíre *vi* to escape.

sfumàre *vi* to end in smoke, vanish; *vt* (of colours) to shade.

sfumatúra *nf* nuance; shade, shading.

şgabèllo *nm* stool.

şgabuzzino *nm* closet.

şgambettàre *vi* to kick the legs about; toddle.

şgambétto *nm* caper, jump; **fàre uno s. a** to trip (s.o.) up.

şganciàre *vt* to unhook.

şgangheràto *a* ramshackle, rickety, unhinged.

şgarbatézza *nf* rudeness; clumsiness.

şgarbàto *a* rude, unmannerly.

şgarbería *nf* **şgàrbo** *nm* rudeness, offence.

şgargiànte *a* gaudy, showy.

şgelàre *vti* to melt, thaw.

şghémbo *a* crooked, oblique, slanting.

şghignazzàre *vi* to guffaw.

şgobbàre *vi* to drudge, toil, work hard.

şgobbóne *nm* slogger, swot.

şgocciolàre *vi* to drip, trickle.

şgomb(e)ràre *vt* to clear; (mil) to abandon; *vi* to clear out, move out.

şgómb(e)ro *a* clear, empty, free; *nm* removal.

sgomentàre *vt* to dismay, frighten.

sgoménto *a* dismayed, frightened; *nm* dismay, fright.

sgominàre *vt* to rout.

sgonfiàre *vt* to deflate.

sgòrbio *nm* scrawl; (*fig*) ugly dwarf.

sgorgàre *vi* to gush, spout (out).

sgozzàre *vt* to cut s.o.'s throat.

sgradévole *a* disagreeable, unpleasant.

sgrammaticàto *a* ungrammatical.

sgranàre *vt* to shell, husk; **s. gli òcchi** to open the eyes wide.

sgranchíre *vt* -**rsi** *vr* to stretch.

sgravàre *vt* to lighten, relieve, unload; -**rsi** *vr* to relieve oneself, bring forth.

sgraziàto *a* ungraceful, clumsy.

sgretolàre *vt* to crumble, grind, smash.

sgridàre *vt* to rebuke, scold.

sgridàta *nf* rebuke, scolding.

sguaiàto *a* unbecoming, uncomely, coarse.

sgualcíre *vt* to crumple; -**rsi** *vr* to crease.

sgualdrína *nf* strumpet.

sguàrdo *nm* glance, look.

sguarníre *vt* to untrim; (*mil*) withdraw the garrison.

sguàttera *nf* scullery-maid; **sguàttero** *nm* scullery-boy.

sguazzàre *vi* to wallow (*also fig*).

sgusciàre *vt* to hull, shell; *vi* to slip away, steal away.

sí *ad* yes; **dire di s.** to agree.

sí *refl pron* oneself, himself, herself, itself, themselves *pl*; *indef pron* one, people, they; *pron* each other, one another.

sía . . . sía *cj* whether . . . or; both . . . and.

siamése *a nmf* Siamese.

siberiàno *a nm* Siberian.

sibilàre *vi* to hiss, whizz.

síbilo *nm* hiss, whistle, whizzing.

sicàrio *nm* hired assassin.

sicchè *cj* so that.

siccità *nf* drought, dryness.

siccóme *ad cj* as.

Sicília *nf* (*geogr*) Sicily; **siciliàno** *a nm* Sicilian.

sicomòro *nm* sycamore.

sicuraménte *ad* certainly; safely.

sicurézza *nf* certainty, safety, security; **s. di sè** self-possession.

sicúro *a* sure, certain; safe, secure, trusty; *interj* quite so; **al s. in safety.**

sicurtà *nf* security, guarantee; insurance.

siderúrgico *pl* -**ici** *a* iron; **stabiliménto s.** ironworks.

sièpe *nf* hedge.

sièro *nm* serum; whey.

sifílide *nf* syphilis.

sifóne *nm* siphon.

sigarétta *nf* cigarette.

sígaro *nm* cigar.

Sigfrído *nm pr* Siegfried.

sigillàre *vt* to seal.

sigíllo *nm* seal.

Sigismóndo *nm pr* Siegmund.

sígla *nf* monogram, initials.

significànte, significatívo *a* significant; expressive.

significàre *vt* to mean, signify.

significàto *nm* meaning, significance.

signóra *nf* lady; madam, Mrs; **signóre** *nm* gentleman; Mr; sir; **vívere da s.** to live like a lord.

signoreggiàre *vti* to rule, dominate.

signoría *nf* lordship; dominion, rule.

signoríle *a* gentlemanly; ladylike; high-class.

signorína *nf* miss, young lady; **signoríno** *nm* (young) master.

silenziatóre *nm* silencer, (*US aut*) muffler.

silènzio *nm* silence.

silenzióso *a* silent, quiet.

sílice *nf* silica.

síllaba *nf* syllable.

sillabàre *vt* to spell out.

sílo *nm* silo.

sillogísmo *nm* syllogism.

siluràre *vt* to torpedo; (*fig*) give the sack.

silúro *nm* torpedo.

silvèstre *a* sylvan.

Silvèstro *nm pr* Silvester; **la nòtte di San S.** New Year's Eve.

Sílvia *nf pr* Sylvia, Silvia.

simboleggiàre *vti* to symbolize.

simbòlico *pl* -**ici** *a* symbolical.

símbolo *nm* symbol.

similàre *a* similar.

símile *a* alike, such, like; *nm* fellow-creature, like.

similitúdine *nf* simile; similitude.

similménte *ad* the same, likewise.

simmetría *nf* symmetry.

Simóne *nm pr* Simon.

simpatía *nf* liking, attraction; sympathy.

simpàtico *pl* -**ici** *a* agreeable, congenial, nice, pleasant; sympathetic.

simpatizzànte *a* sympathizing; *nmf* sympathizer.

simpatizzàre *vi* to sympathize; take a liking.

simpòsio *nm* symposium, conference.

simulàcro *nm* image, shadow.

simulàre *vt* to simulate, feign, sham.

simulazióne *nf* simulation, shamming.

simultàneo *a* simultaneous.

sinagòga *nf* synagogue.

sinceraménte *ad* sincerely, honestly.

sinceràrsi *vr* to make sure.

sincerità *nf* sincerity, truthfulness, candour.

sincèro *a* sincere, candid, frank.

sincopàto *a* syncopated.

sincronizzatóre *nm* synchronizer.

sindacàto *nm* syndicate, trade union.

síndaco *pl* -**aci** *nm* mayor, (*Scotland*) provost; (*com*) auditor.

sinfonía *nf* symphony.

sinfònico *pl* **-ici** *a* symphonic, symphony.
singhiozzàre *vi* to sob.
singhiózzo *nm* hiccup; sob.
singolàre *a* singular; peculiar, eccentric; rare; single.
singolarità *nf* singularity, strangeness.
síngolo *a* single, each, individual.
sinistra *nf* left (hand).
sinistràto *a* homeless; injured.
sinístro *a* left; ominous, sinister; *nm* accident, mishap.
síno *v* **fíno**.
sínodo *nm* synod.
sinònimo *a* synonymous; *nm* synonym.
sintàssi *nf* syntax.
sintesi *nf* synthesis.
sintètico *pl* **-ici** *a* synthetic(al); concise.
síntomo *nm* symptom.
sinuosità *nf* sinuosity.
sinuóso *a* sinuous, winding.
sinusíte *nf* sinusitis.
sipàrio *nm* (*theat*) (drop) curtain.
Siracúsa *nf* (*geogr*) Syracuse; **siracusàno** *a nm* Syracusan.
sirèna *nf* mermaid; siren, hooter.
Síria *nf* (*geogr*) Syria.
siriàno *a nm* Syrian.
sirínga *nf* (*med*) syringe.
sistèma *nm* system.
sistemàre *vt* to arrange, settle.
sistemàtico *pl* **-ici** *a* systematic, methodical, businesslike.
sistemazióne *nf* arrangement, settlement; position.
síto *nm* place, site, spot.
situàto *a* placed.
situazióne *nf* situation, set-up, position, state.
slacciàre *vt* to unbind, undo, unlace, untie.
slanciàre *vt* to fling, hurl; **-rsi** *vr* to hurl oneself, rush upon, venture.
slanciàto *a* slim, slender.
slàncio *nm* impetus, enthusiasm, impulse.
slattàre *vt* to wean.
slavàto *a* (*of colour*) washed out, pale; dull, insipid.
slàvo *a nm* Slav.
sleàle *a* disloyal; unfair.
slealtà *nf* disloyalty.
slegàre *vt* to untie.
slegàto *a* untied, unbound; incoherent.
slìtta *nf* sledge, sleigh.
slittaménto *nm* skidding, skid; (*mech*) slipping.
slittàre *vi* to skid; sledge; slip.
slogàre *vt* to dislocate.
slogatúra *nf* dislocation.
sloggiàre *vt* to dislodge, drive out; *vi* to clear out, decamp.
smacchiàre *vt* to clean, remove stains.
smàcco *pl* **smàcchi** *nm* humiliation, let down.

smagliànte *a* dazzling, gaudy.
smagliàrsi *vr* (*stockings*) to ladder; (*knitting, net*) to get undone.
smagliatúra *nf* (*of stocking*) ladder, (*US*) run.
smaltàre *vt* to enamel, glaze.
smaltíre *vt* to digest, work off.
smàlto *nm* enamel.
smània *nf* longing, mania, frenzy.
smaniàre *vi* to long for, fret.
smarriménto *nm* loss; bewilderment.
smarríre *vt* to lose, mislay; **-rsi** *vr* to lose one's way, stray; get confused.
smascheràre *vt* to unmask.
smembràre *vt* to dismember.
smemoràto *a* absent-minded, forgetful.
smentíre *vt* to deny; **-rsi** *vr* to eat one's words; **smentíta** *nf* denial, refutation.
smeràldo *nm* emerald.
smèrcio *nm* sale.
smerigliàto *a* **càrta smerigliàta** emery paper; **vètro s.** frosted glass.
smeríglio *nm* emery.
sméttere *vt* to give up, stop wearing; *vi* to give up, leave off, stop.
smílzo *a* slender, slim.
sminuzzàre *vt* to cut up, chop finely.
smistaménto *nm* clearing; (*rly*) shunting, (*US*) switching; (*letters*) sorting.
smistàre *vt* to clear; (*letters*) sort; (*rly*) shunt; (*US*) switch.
smisuràto *a* enormous, immeasurable.
smobiliàre *vt* to strip of furniture.
smobilitàre *vt* to demobilize.
smodàto, smoderàto *a* excessive, immoderate.
smòking *nm* dinner-jacket, (*US*) tuxedo.
smontàre *vt* to take down, take to pieces; discourage; *vi* to alight, get out of.
smórfia *nf* grimace, wry face.
smorfióso *a* mincing, affected.
smòrto *a* pale, wan.
smorzàre *vt* to dim, tone down; quench.
smúnto *a* pale, emaciated.
smuòvere *vt* to shift, move; affect.
smussàre *vt* to bevel, blunt, smooth.
snaturàre *vt* to alter the nature of, pervert.
snellézza *nf* slimness; agility, nimbleness.
snèllo *a* slim; nimble, agile.
snervàre *vt* to enervate, exhaust.
snobbàre *vt* to look down on, cut.
snobìsmo *nm* snobbery.
snodàre *vt* to loosen, untie; make supple; **-rsi** *vr* to get untied; wind.
snudàre *vt* to bare, unsheathe.
soàve *a* sweet, soft, gentle.
soavità *nf* sweetness, softness, gentleness.
sobbalzàre *vi* to start, jump.

sobbarcàrsi vr to take on oneself.
sobbórgo pl -ghi nm suburb.
sobillàre vt to incite, instigate, stir up.
sobrietà nf sobriety, temperance.
sòbrio a sober, temperate.
socchiúdere vt to leave ajar.
soccómbere vi to give in, succumb, yield.
soccórrere vt to help, relieve, succour.
soccórso nm aid, help, relief.
sociàle a social; (com) of partnership.
socialismo nm socialism.
socialista nm socialist; **socialistico** a socialist.
società nf society, community; (com) company, partnership; **s. a responsabilità limitàta** limited liability company, (US) corporation.
sociévole a companionable, sociable.
sòcio nm member, fellow, associate, partner.
sociologìa nf sociology.
sociòlogo pl -gi, -ghi nm sociologist.
sodalizio nm association, guild, society.
soddisfacènte a satisfactory.
soddisfàre vt to satisfy, fulfil; **make amends**.
soddisfazióne nf satisfaction.
sòdio nm sodium.
sòdo a solid, hard, sound, firm.
sofà nm sofa.
sofferènte a suffering, poorly.
sofferènza nf suffering, endurance.
soffermàrsi vr to linger, pause.
soffiàre vti to blow.
sòffice a soft.
soffiétto nm bellows; pl (of carriage) hood; (in a paper) puff.
sóffio nm puff, whiff, breath.
soffìtta nf attic, garret.
soffìtto nm ceiling.
soffocàre vti to choke, suffocate.
soffocazióne nf choking, suffocation.
soffrìre vti to suffer, bear.
Sòfia nf pr (geogr) Sofia.
Sofìa nf pr Sophia, Sophie, Sophy.
sofìsma nm sophism.
sofisticàre vi to sophisticate, quibble; vt to adulterate.
soggettista nmf (cin) scenario writer.
soggettìvo a subjective.
soggètto a subject, liable; nm subject, topic; **s. agli incidènti** accident-prone.
soggezióne nf awe, timidity; subjection.
sogghignàre vi to sneer, grin.
soggiacére vi to be subjected, be liable; succumb.
soggiogàre vt to subdue, subjugate.
soggiornàre vi to sojourn, stay.
soggiórno nm sojourn, stay; **permèsso di s.** permission to stay.
soggiúngere vti to add, reply.
sòglia nf threshold.
sògliola nf (fish) sole.
sognànte a dreaming, dreamy.

sognàre vt to dream of; -rsi vr to imagine, fancy.
sognatóre nm -trice nf dreamer.
sógno nm dream, fancy.
sol nm (mus) sol, G.
solàio nm loft.
solaménte ad only, solely.
solcàre vt to furrow, plough.
sólco pl -chi nm furrow, track, wrinkle, groove.
soldatésca nf soldiery.
soldatésco pl -chi a soldierly.
soldàto nm soldier.
sòldo nm (old Italian coin) soldo; **sòldi** pl pay, money.
sóle nm sun(shine); **al s.** in the sun.
soleggiàto a sunny.
solènne a solemn.
solennità nf solemnity.
solére vi to use, be in the habit of.
solèrte a active, attentive, zealous.
solèrzia nf diligence, industriousness.
solétto a alone; **sólo s.** all alone.
solfàto nm sulphate.
solidàle a joint; loyal to.
solidarietà nf solidarity.
solidità nf solidity; (of colours) fastness.
sòlido a solid; (of colours) fast; sound, reliable.
solilòquio nm soliloquy.
solìsta nmf soloist.
solitàrio a solitary, lonely; nm hermit; (gem and game) solitaire; (game) patience.
sòlito a nm usual, **di s.** usually.
solitúdine nf solitude.
sollàzzo nm amusement, pastime, laughing-stock.
sollecitàre vt to urge, solicit; hasten.
sollécito a prompt; solicitous; nm soliciting (payment etc).
sollecitúdine nf diligence, speed; attention.
solleóne nm dog-days pl.
solleticàre vt to tickle; stimulate.
sollético pl -ichi nm tickle.
sollevàre vt to lift, raise; relieve; -rsi vr to rise.
sollevàto a relieved, cheered up.
sollièvo nm relief, comfort.
sólo a alone, only, sole; **da s.** by oneself; ad but, only.
solstizio nm solstice.
soltànto ad only, solely.
solúbile a soluble.
solubilità nf solubility.
soluzióne nf solution.
solvènte a nm solvent.
solvènza, solvibilità nf solvency.
sòma nf load, burden.
Somàlia nf (geogr) Somaliland.
somàro nm ass, donkey.
somigliànte a like, resembling.
somigliànza nf likeness, resemblance.
somigliàre vi to be like, look like, resemble.
sómma nf addition, sum, amount.

sommaménte *ad* extremely, highly.

sommàre *vt* to add up; *vi* to amount to.

sommàrio *a nm* summary.

sommèrgere *vt* to submerge, flood; -rsi *vr* to sink, dive.

sommergíbile *a* submergible; *nm* submarine.

sommésso *a* meek, subdued.

somministràre *vt* to administer.

somministrazióne *nf* administration; provision, supply.

sommità *nf* summit, top.

sómmo *a* highest, very great; *nm* summit.

sommòssa *nf* rising, rebellion.

sommozzatóre *nm* frogman, skin-diver.

sommuòvere *vt* to excite, rouse, stir up.

sonàglio *nm* harness-bell; rattle.

sonàre *v* suonàre.

sónda *nf* sounding line; probe, feeler; drill.

sondàggio *nm* sounding.

sondàre *vt* to sound, probe.

soneria *nf* striking mechanism; alarm-bell.

sonétto *nm* sonnet.

sonnàmbulo *nm* sleepwalker, somnambulist.

sonnecchiàre *vi* to doze.

sonnellíno *nm* doze, nap.

sonnífero *nm* soporific, narcotic.

sónno *nm* sleep; avér s. to be sleepy.

sonnolènto *a* drowsy, sleepy.

sonnolènza *nf* drowsiness.

sonorità *nf* sonorousness, sonority.

sonòro *a* resonant, sonorous; sound.

sontuosità *nf* sumptuousness.

sontuóso *a* sumptuous.

sopíre *vt* to make drowsy; calm.

sopóre *nm* drowsiness, light sleep.

soporífero *a nm* soporific.

sopperíre *a vi* to provide for.

soppiantàre *vt* to oust, supplant.

sopportàbile *a* bearable, endurable.

sopportàre *vt* to bear, endure, tolerate.

soppressióne *nf* suppression, abolition.

sopprímere *vt* to suppress, abolish, kill.

sópra *prep* above, on, over; di s. upstairs.

soprabbondàre *etc* *v* **sovrabbondàre** etc.

sopràbito *nm* overcoat.

sopracciglio *nm* eyebrow.

sopraddétto *a* above-mentioned.

sopraffàre *vt* to overcome, overwhelm.

sopraffazióne *nf* act of tyranny, abuse of power.

sopraffíno *a* first-class, superfine, exceptional.

sopraggiúngere *vi* to arrive, come up, happen.

sopr(a)intendènte *nm* superintendent.

sopraluògo *pl* -òghi *nm* investigation on the spot.

soprammòbile *nm* nick-nack.

soprannaturàle *a nm* supernatural.

soprannóme *nm* nickname.

soprannúmero *nm* excess, surplus.

sopràno *nm* (mus) soprano.

soprappassàggio *nm* overpass.

soprappensièro *ad* sunk in thought.

soprappiù *nm* extra.

soprapprèzzo *nm* increase in price, surcharge.

soprascàrpa *nf* overshoe, galosh.

soprascrítta *nf* address; superscription.

soprascrítto *a* above(-written).

soprassàlto *nm* start; di s. with a start.

soprassedére *vi* to wait, postpone.

soprattàssa *nf* surtax.

soprattútto *ad* above all, especially.

sopravanzàre *vt* to surpass, exceed; *vi* to be left over.

sopravveníre *vi* to turn up, happen, occur.

sopravvènto *nm* advantage, superiority.

sopravvívere *vi* to outlive, survive.

soprúso *nm* abuse of power; insult, outrage.

soqquàdro *nm* confusion, disorder; a s. topsy-turvy.

sorbíre *vt* to sip; -rsi *vr* to put up with; swallow.

Sorbóna *nf* pr Sorbonne.

sórcio *nm* mouse.

sordaménte *ad* with a dull sound, with a thud; secretly.

sòrdido *a* dirty, filthy.

sordità *nf* deafness.

sórdo *a* deaf; hollow, dull.

sordomúto *a* deaf-and-dumb; *nm* deaf-mute.

sorèlla *nf* sister.

sorellàstra *nf* half-sister.

sorgènte *nf* spring, source; cause.

sórgere *vi* to (a)rise, rise up.

sormontàre *vt* to overcome, surmount.

sornióne *a* sly.

sorpassàre *vt* to overtake; excel, outdo; sorpàsso *nm* (aut) overtaking.

sorpassàto *a* out of date.

sorprendènte *a* surprising, astonishing.

sorprèndere *vt* to surprise; catch.

sorprésa *nf* surprise.

sorrèggere *vt* to support.

sorridènte *a* smiling.

sorrídere *vi* to smile (at); appeal.

sorríso *nm* smile.

sórso *nm* draught; drop; sip.

sòrta *nf* kind, sort.

sòrte *nf* destiny, fortune; lot.

sorteggiàre *vt* to draw by lot.

sortéggio *nm* draw.

sortilègio *nm* witchcraft.

sortíre *vi* to be drawn (by lot); to go out.

sortíta *nf* sally, witty remark.

sorvegliànza nf surveillance, supervision.

sorvegliàre vt to oversee, watch (over).

sorvolàre vt to fly over, pass over.

sospèndere vt to suspend; hang; adjourn, interrupt.

sospensióne nf suspension.

sospéso a hanging, suspended; in suspense, uncertain.

sospettàre vti to suspect.

sospètto a suspicious; suspect; nm suspicion.

sospettóso a suspicious, distrustful.

sospiràre vt to long for, sigh for; vi to sigh.

sospíro nm sigh.

sossópra ad topsy-turvy, upside-down.

sòsta nf halt, stop; respite.

sostantìvo nm noun, substantive.

sostànza nf substance; **in s.** essentially, in short.

sostanziàle a substantial, fundamental.

sostanzióso a substantial, nourishing.

sostàre vi to pause, stop.

sostégno nm support.

sostenére vt to support, sustain, carry, maintain, keep up, endure, hold; **-rsi** vr to lean on, support oneself.

sostenìbile a sustainable, tenable; bearable.

sostentaménto nm sustenance, support.

sostentàre vt to support.

sostenúto a stiff, reserved, distant.

sostituíre vt to replace, take the place of.

sostitúto nm substitute.

sostituzióne nf replacement, substitution.

sottacéti nm pl pickles pl.

sottàna nf skirt, petticoat; (eccl) cassock.

sottentràre (a) vi to take the place (of).

sotterfúgio nm subterfuge.

sottèrra ad underground.

sotterràneo a subterranean, underground; nm cave, vault, dungeon.

sotterràre vt to bury.

sottigliézza nf thinness, fineness; subtlety, quibble.

sottìle a thin, slender; subtle.

sottintèndere vt to imply, understand.

sottintéso a understood, implied; nm allusion.

sótto ad prep under(neath), below; **al di s. di** below.

sottocchio ad before one's eyes.

sottochiàve ad under lock and key.

sottocommissióne nf sub-commission.

sottolineàre vt to underline; emphasize.

sottomàno, di ad underhand(edly).

sottomaríno a nm-submarine.

sottomésso a subject; submissive, respectful.

sottométtere vt to conquer, subdue, subject; **-rsi** vr to give in, submit, yield.

sottomissióne nf submission, subjection.

sottopassàggio nm subway, underpass.

sottopórre vt to subject; submit; **-rsi** vr to submit.

sottoscrívere vt to sign, underwrite; vi subscribe; **-rsi** vr to sign.

sottoscrizióne nf subscription.

sottosegretàrio nm under-secretary.

sottosópra ad topsy-turvy, upside-down.

sottostànte a below.

sottostàre vi to be subjected; lie below; submit.

sottosuòlo nm subsoil.

sottotenènte nm second lieutenant.

sottovèste nf petticoat, slip.

sottovóce ad in a low voice, in an undertone.

sottràrre vt to subtract; steal; take away, deduct; **-rsi** vr to escape from, evade.

sottrazióne nf subtraction, taking away.

sottufficiàle nm non-commissioned officer.

sovènte ad often.

soverchiàre vt to overflow; overcome; surpass.

soverchieria nf insolence, imposition.

sovèrchio a excessive.

soviètico pl **-ici** a Soviet.

sóvra v **sópra**.

sovrabbondànza nf superabundance.

sovrabbondàre vi to superabound.

sovraccàrico pl **-ichi** a overloaded; nm overload; **per s.** in addition, moreover.

sovranità nf sovereignty.

sovrannaturàle v **soprannaturàle**.

sovràno nm sovereign.

sovrastàre vi to hang over, surpass.

sovrumàno a superhuman.

sovveníre vt to assist, help; **far s.** to remind; **-rsi** vr to remember.

sovvenzióne nf subsidy, subvention.

sovversióne nf overthrow, subversion.

sovversívo a subversive; nm subverter.

sovvertíre vt to overthrow, subvert.

sózzo a filthy, loathsome.

sozzúra nf filth.

spaccalégna (inv) nm wood-cutter.

spaccapiètre (inv) nm stone-breaker.

spaccàre vt to cleave, split, break.

spaccatúra nf crack, split.

spacciàre vt to sell; pass off; dispatch; **-rsi** vr to set up as.

spacciàto a done for.

spàccio nm sale; shop.

spàcco pl **spàcchi** nm cleft, split.

spaccóne nm boaster, braggart.
spàda nf sword; pl (cards) spades pl.
Spàgna nf (geogr) Spain.
spagnolétta nf spool; (fam) peanut.
spagn(u)òlo a Spanish; nm Spaniard.
spàgo pl **spàghi** nm string, twine.
spaiàre vt to uncouple.
spalancàre vt to open wide, throw open.
spàlla nf shoulder, back.
spalleggiàre vt to back, support.
spallièra nf (of chair) back.
spallína nf epaulet, shoulder-strap.
spalmàre vt to spread, smear.
spàlto nm glacis.
spàndere vt to spread, divulge; shed; squander.
spànna nf span.
sparàre vt to shoot, fire, discharge.
sparàto a shot; nm shirt-front.
sparatòria nf shooting, exchange of shots.
sparecchiàre vt to clear (away).
spàrgere vt to scatter, shed, spread.
sparíre vi to disappear.
sparizióne nf disappearance.
sparlàre vi to speak ill.
spàro nm shot.
sparpagliàre vt to scatter, spread.
spàrso a shed, loose.
spartiàcque (inv) nm watershed, (US) divide.
spartíre vt to divide, separate.
spartíto nm (mus) score.
spartitràffico (inv) nm traffic island.
spartizióne nf distribution, division, partition.
sparúto a gaunt, lean, thin.
sparvière, sparvièro nm hawk.
spasimànte nm lover, wooer.
spasimàre vi to suffer terribly; yearn.
spàsimo nm pang, (med) spasm.
spassàrsi vr to amuse oneself, enjoy oneself; **spassàrsela** to have a very good time.
spassionàto a dispassionate, impartial.
spàsso nm amusement, pastime; andàre a s. to go for a walk.
spassóso a amusing.
spatriàre v espatriàre.
spauràcchio nm scarecrow; bugbear.
spauríre vt to frighten.
spavaldería nf boldness, defiance; boast.
spavàldo a bold, defiant; nm bold fellow, braggart.
spaventapàsseri (inv) nm scarecrow.
spaventàre vt to frighten, scare.
spaventévole a dreadful, frightful.
spaziàle a space.
spavènto nm fright, fear.
spaventóso a dreadful, frightful.
spaziàre vi to soar.
spazientírsi vr to lose one's patience.
spàzio nm space, distance; interval; room; period of time.
spazióso a broad, roomy, spacious.

spazzacamíno pl -íni nm chimney-sweep.
spazzamíne inv nm minesweeper.
spazzanéve (inv) nm snowplough.
spazzàre vt to sweep.
spazzatúra nf sweeping; sweepings pl.
spazzaturàio, spazzino nm sweeper; dustman, (US) garbageman.
spàzzola nf brush.
spazzolàre vt to brush.
spazzolíno nm small brush; s. da dènti toothbrush.
specchiàrsi vr to look at oneself in the glass, be reflected.
specchièra nf looking-glass, dressing-table.
spècchio nm mirror, looking-glass.
speciàle a special, particular.
specialista nmf specialist.
specialità nf speciality.
specializzàrsi vr to specialize.
specializzazióne nf specialization.
specialménte ad especially.
spècie (inv) nf kind, species, sort; far s. to amaze; in s. especially.
specífica nf (com) detailed list.
specificàre vt to specify.
specificazióne nf specification.
specífico pl -ici a nm specific.
specióso a specious.
speculàre vti to speculate (upon).
speculazióne nf speculation.
spedíre vt send, mail, dispatch, forward.
speditaménte ad quickly, promptly; fluently.
speditézza nf expedition, quickness; fluency.
spedíto a prompt, quick; fluent.
spedizióne nf dispatch, expedition, forwarding, consignment.
spedizionière nm forwarding agent, shipping agent, carrier, (US) express company.
spègnere vt to extinguish, put out, switch off; stifle; kill; -rsi vr to be extinguished, go out; fade away, pass away.
spelàto a hairless; threadbare, worn.
spelónca nf cave, den.
spèndere vti to spend.
spennàre vt to pluck (poultry).
spensieratézza nf light-heartedness.
spensieràto a light-hearted, care-free.
spènto a extinguished; extinct; (of colours, eyes etc) dull.
speràbile a to be hoped for.
sperànza nf hope, expectation.
speranzóso a hopeful.
speràre vt to hope for, expect.
spèrdersi vr to get lost, go astray.
sperdúto a secluded, wild; lost (also fig); ill at ease.
spergiuràre vi to perjure oneself, swear falsely.
spergiúro a perjured; nm perjurer; perjury.
sperimentàle a experimental.

sperimentàre vt to experiment with.
speróne nm spur.
sperperàre vt to dissipate, squander, waste.
spèrpero nm dissipation, waste.
spésa nf expense, cost; shopping; purchase; **spése generàli** running cost, (US) operating cost.
spèsso a dense; thick; ad frequently, often.
spessóre nm thickness.
spettàcolo nm sight, spectacle; performance.
spettànza nf concern; pl dues pl; **èssere di s. di** to be the duty of, concern.
spettàre vi to be the duty of; be the turn of.
spettatóre nm **-tríce** nf spectator, bystander, onlooker.
spettinàto a dishevelled, unkempt.
spèttro nm ghost, spectre.
spettràle a ghostly, spectral.
spettroscòpio nm spectroscope.
spèzie nf pl spices pl.
spezzàre vt to break.
spezzóne nm incendiary bomb.
spía nf spy; telltale.
spiacènte a sorry.
spiacére v dispiacére.
spiacévole a unpleasant.
spiàggia nf beach, shore.
spianàre vt to level, raze, smooth.
spianàta nf open space, clearing; esplanade.
spiantàre vt to uproot; ruin.
spiantàto nm penniless person.
spiàre vt to spy upon, watch for.
spiccàre vt to pick; vi stand out; **s. un salto** to leap; **s. le paròle** to enunciate clearly.
spícchio nm (of garlic) clove, (of fruit) segment, quarter.
spicciàre vt to dispatch; **-rsi** vr to hurry up, make haste.
spicciolàta, alla ad a few at a time.
spícciolo a small; nm small coin; pl change.
spíder nm (aut) two-seater sports car.
spièdo nm spit.
spiegàbile a explicable, justifiable.
spiegàre vt to explain; spread out, display; **-rsi** vr to make oneself understood; open out.
spiegazióne nf explanation.
spietàto a pitiless, ruthless.
spíffero nm draught (of air).
spíga nf ear of corn.
spighétta nf braid.
spigliatézza nf ease, nimbleness.
spigliàto a easy, nimble.
spígo pl **spíghi** nm lavender.
spigolàre vt to glean.
spígolo nm (of table etc) corner.
spílla nf pin, brooch.
spillàre vt to broach, tap, draw.
spíllo nm pin; **spillóne** brooch, (hat-)pin.
spilòrcio a miserly, niggardly, stingy; nm miser.

spína nf thorn; (fish) bone; (elec) plug; **s. dorsàle** backbone, spine.
spinàci nm pl spinach.
spíngere vt to push; drive, induce.
spíno nm thorn.
spinóso a thorny.
spínta nf push, shove.
spinterògeno nm (aut) coil ignition.
spínto a pushed, driven; excessive; daring.
spionàggio nm espionage, spying.
spiovènte a drooping, sloping.
spiòvere vi to stop raining.
spíra nf coil.
spiràglio nm air-hole; gleam of light; breath of air.
spiràle a nf spiral.
spiràre vi to blow; die, expire; vt to exhale.
spiritàto a possessed.
spiritísmo nm spiritualism.
spírito nm spirit, ghost; wit.
spiritóso a witty; alcoholic.
spirituàle a spiritual.
splendènte a bright, brilliant, shining.
splèndere vt to shine, glitter.
splèndido a gorgeous, magnificent, splendid.
splendóre nm splendour, magnificence.
Splúga, (Pàsso déllo) nm (geogr) Splugen Pass.
spodestàre vt to dispossess, oust.
spòglia nf booty, spoil; **spòglie** pl remains pl.
spogliàre vt to strip, undress; despoil; **-rsi** vr to strip oneself, undress.
spogliarèllo nm striptease.
spogliatóio nm dressing-room, cloakroom.
spòglio a bare, undressed; nm examination; **spògli** pl cast-off clothes pl.
spòla nf shuttle; **fàre la s.** to go to and fro, commute.
spolétta nf reel of cotton, (US) spool; (mil) fuse.
spolpàre vt to remove flesh; bleed white.
spolveràre vt to dust; eat up.
spolveràta nf dust(ing), brush(ing).
spónda nf bank, edge.
sponsàli nm pl (poet) wedding.
spontaneità nf spontaneousness, spontaneity.
spontàneo a spontaneous.
spopolàre vt to depopulate.
sporàdico pl **-ici** a sporadic.
sporcàre vt to dirty, soil.
sporcízia nf dirt, filth.
spòrco pl **spòrchi** a dirty, unclean.
sporgènte a jutting out.
spòrgere vt to put out; vi to jut out; **-rsi** vr to lean out.
spòrta nf (shopping)basket.
sportèllo nm (of carriage etc) door, (of booking office) window; counter.

sportívo *a* sporting, sports, sports-manlike; *nm* sportsman.

spòṣa *nf* bride, young wife; **spòṣo** *nm* bridegroom.

spoṣalízio *nm* wedding.

spoṣàre *vt* to marry, wed; **-rsi** *vr* to get married.

spossànte *a* exhausting, enervating.

spossàre *vt* to exhaust, wear out.

spossatézza *nf* exhaustion, weariness.

spossessàre *vt* to dispossess.

spostaménto *nm* shifting, displacement, change.

spostàre *vt* to shift, displace, change.

spostàto *a* out of its place; ill-adjusted; *nm* misfit.

sprànga *nf* bolt, (cross-)bar.

spràzzo *nm* flash, gleam.

sprecàre *vt* to waste, squander.

spréco *pl* **sprèchi** *nm* waste.

sprecóne *nm* waster, squanderer.

spregévole *a* despicable, mean.

spregiàre *v* **sprezzàre**.

sprègio *nm* disdain, scorn.

spregiudicatézza *nf* open-mindedness.

spregiudicàto *a* unbiased, unprejudiced.

sprèmere *vt* to squeeze (*also fig*).

spremúta *nf* squash.

sprezzànte *a* scornful, contemptuous.

sprigionàre *vt* to give off, release; **-rsi** *vr* to spring out, burst forth.

sprizzàre *vi* to spout, spurt.

sprofondaménto *nm* sinking, subsidence, collapse.

sprofondàre *vi* to founder, sink; **-rsi** *vr* to sink, collapse; be absorbed.

spronàre *vt* to spur, urge.

spróne *nm* spur.

sproporzionàto *a* disproportionate.

sproporzióne *nf* disproportion.

spropòsito *nm* blunder, gaffe.

sprovvedére *vt* to leave unprovided; **-rsi** *vr* to deprive oneself.

sprovvista, alla *ad* unawares, unexpectedly.

sprovvísto *a* lacking, unprovided with, unprepared.

spruzzàre *vt* to spray, sprinkle.

sprúzzo *nm* spray, sprinkling.

spudoràto *a* shameless, impudent.

spúgna *nf* sponge.

spugnosità *nf* sponginess.

spugnóso *a* spongy.

spumànte *a* foaming, frothing; *nm* sparkling wine.

spuntàre *vt* to blunt; cut off the end; *vi* to appear, rise.

spuntíno *nm* snack.

sputàre *vti* to spit.

spúto *nm* spit, spittle.

squàdra *nf* square; squad, team.

squadràre *vt* to look up and down; square.

squadríglia *nf* squadron.

squagliàrsi *vr* to melt, thaw; steal away.

squàllido *a* dismal, dreary.

squallóre *nm* dreariness, gloom.

squàlo *nm* shark.

squàma *nf* (*of fish etc*) scale.

squamóso *a* scaly.

squarciagóla, a *ad* at the top of one's voice.

squarciàre *vt* to rend, tear asunder; dispel.

squàrcio *nm* gash, rent, tear; (*of a book etc*) passage.

squartàre *vt* to quarter, cut up.

squassàre *vt* to shake.

squattrinàto *a* penniless.

squilibràto *a* unbalanced.

squilíbrio *nm* want of balance; **s.** **mentàle** madness.

squilla *nf* (small) bell; ring.

squillànte *a* blaring, shrill.

squillàre *vi* to blare; ring, peal.

squíllo *nm* blare, ring.

squiṣitézza *nf* exquisiteness, deliciousness.

squiṣíto *a* exquisite, delicious.

squittíre *vi* to squeak.

ṣradicàre *vt* to eradicate, uproot.

ṣragionàre *vi* to talk nonsense, reason falsely.

ṣregolatézza *nf* disorder, dissoluteness.

ṣregolàto *a* disorderly, dissolute.

stàbile *a* stable, firm, lasting.

stabiliménto *nm* factory, works, plant, establishment.

stabilíre *vt* to establish, fix; ascertain; decide; set; **-rsi** *vr* to settle.

stabilità *nf* stability, firmness.

stabilizzatóre *nm* (*av naut*) stabilizer.

staccaménto *nm* detachment.

staccàre *vt* to detach, remove, separate; **-rsi** *vr* to be different; become detached, break off; leave.

stacciàre *vt* to sieve, sift.

stàccio *nm* sieve.

stàcco *pl* **stàcchi** *nm* separation.

stadèra *nf* (*tec*) steelyard.

stàdio *nm* stadium, sports-ground; phase.

stàffa *nf* footboard; stirrup; **pèrdere le stàffe** to lose one's temper.

staffière *nm* groom.

staffilàre *vt* to whip, lash.

staffíle *nm* whip, lash.

stagionàle *a* seasonal.

stagionàre *vi* to season.

stagióne *nf* season.

stagnàio, stagníno *nm* tin-smith.

stagnànte *a* stagnant.

stagnàre *vt* to solder, tin; *vi* to stagnate.

stàgno *nm* tin; pond, pool.

stàio *pl m* **stài** *f* **stàia** *nm* bushel.

Stalingràdo *nf* (*geogr*) Stalingrad.

stàlla *nf* stable, cowshed.

stallàggio *nm* stabling.

stallière *nm* groom, stableman.

stallóne *nm* stallion.

stamàne, stamàni, stamattína *ad* this morning.

stambúgio nm cubby-hole, little dark room.

stàmpa nf press, print; **stàmpe** pl printed matter.

stampáre vt to print, publish; coin; **-rsi** vr to impress.

stampatèllo nm block letters.

stampáto a printed; nm printed matter; form.

stampèlla nf crutch.

stamperìa nf printing press, printing works.

stàmpo nm die, stamp, kind, sort.

stancáre vt to tire; bore.

stanchézza nf tiredness, weariness.

stànco pl **-chi** a tired, weary.

stànga nf bar; (of carriage) shaft.

stangáre vt to bar; thrash.

stanòtte ad last night; tonight.

stànte a being; **sedúta s.** during the sitting; at once.

stantío a stale.

stantúffo nm piston.

stànza nf room; (poet) stanza; **èssere di s.** (mil) to be stationed.

stanziáre vt to set apart (funds).

stappáre vt to uncork.

stáre vi to stay, remain; stand; live; be.

stàrna nf partridge.

starnutíre vi to sneeze.

starnúto nm sneeze.

staséra ad this evening, tonight.

statále a (of the) state; nm civil servant.

Stàti Uníti nm pl United States pl.

stàtico pl **-ici** a static.

statísta nm statesman.

statística nf statistics.

statístico pl **-ici** a statistical.

stàto nm state, condition, situation; **s. maggióre** (mil) general staff.

stàtua nf statue.

statuària nf statuary.

statunitènse a nmf United States (citizen).

statúra nf height, size, stature.

statúto nm statute; constitution.

stazionàrio a stationary.

stazióne nf station; **s. climàtica** health resort.

stàzza nf (naut) tonnage.

stazzáre vt to gauge, measure; vi (naut) to have a tonnage of.

stécca nf (billiards) cue; (mus) false note; small stick; (umbrella) rib.

steccáto nm fence, paling, rails pl.

stecchíno nm toothpick.

stecchíto a dried up; skinny; stiff and stark.

Stéfano nm pr Stephen.

stélla nf star.

stellàto a starry.

stellétta nf asterisk; (mil) star.

stèlo nm stalk, stem.

stèmma nm coat of arms.

stemperáre vt to melt; mix.

stempiàrsi vr to lose one's hair at the temples, to go bald.

stendàrdo nm standard.

stèndere vt to spread, lay out, hang out, (out)stretch; draw up.

stenografáre vt to write in shorthand.

stenografía nf shorthand.

stenògrafo nm **stenògrafa** nf shorthand-writer, (US) stenographer.

stentáre vi to find it hard to.

stènto nm difficulty; privation, suffering; **a s.** hardly, with difficulty.

stéppa nf steppe.

stereofònico pl **-ici** a stereophonic.

stèrile a sterile, barren, unproductive.

sterilità nf sterility, barrenness.

sterilizzáre vt to sterilize.

sterlína nf pound (sterling).

stermináre vt to exterminate.

stermináto a exterminated; boundless.

stermínio nm extermination.

sterráre vt to dig up, excavate.

sterzáre vt (aut) to steer; **stèrzo** nm (aut) steering wheel, steering.

stésso a pron same, self; nm same.

stesúra nf drawing up, drafting.

stiláre vt to draw up.

stíle nm style.

stílla nf drop.

stilláre vti to drip, ooze, exude.

stílo nm stylus.

stilogràfica, (pénna) nf fountain pen.

stíma nf estimate, estimation, valuation; esteem.

stimáre vt to estimate, value; esteem; consider; **-rsi** vr to think oneself.

stimolànte a stimulating; nm stimulant.

stimoláre vt to drive, goad, stimulate, urge.

stímolo nm goad, spur, stimulus.

stínco pl **-chi** nm shin, shinbone.

stipáre vt **-rsi** vr to crowd, throng.

stipèndio nm salary, wages pl; **s. ridótto** (mèzzo s.) half-pay.

stípite nm (door-)post; (family) stock.

stipuláre vt to stipulate.

stipulazióne nf stipulation.

stiracchiàre vt to stretch; bargain over.

stiracchiàto a forced, unconvincing.

stiráre vt to iron; stretch (out); **-rsi** vr to stretch (oneself).

stíro, fèrro da nm iron.

stírpe nm birth, descent, race.

stitichézza nf constipation.

stítico pl **-ici** a constipated.

stíva nf (naut) hold.

stivàle nm boot; **stivalétto** nm ankle-boot.

stivàre vt to stow.

stízza nf anger.

stizzírsi vr to get angry, get cross.

stizzóso a irritable, ill-tempered.

stoccafisso nm stockfish.

Stoccólma nf (geogr) Stockholm.

stòffa nf material, stuff.

stòico *pl* **-ici** *a* stoical; *nm* stoic.

stòla *nf* stole.

stolidità, stolidézza *nf* stolidity; stupidity.

stòlido *a* stolid; stupid.

stoltézza *nf* foolishness, folly.

stólto *a* foolish; *nm* fool.

stomacàre *vt* to disgust, sicken; **-rsi** *vr* to be disgusted with, be sick of.

stomachévole *a* disgusting, loathsome.

stòmaco *pl* **-chi** *nm* stomach.

stonàre *vi* to be out of tune; be out of place.

stonatùra *nf* false note (*also fig*).

stóppa *nf* tow, oakum.

stóppia *nf* stubble.

stoppìno *nm* wick.

stòrcere *vt* to twist, distort; **-rsi** *vr* to twist, writhe.

stordiménto *nm* dazed state, dizziness.

stordìre *vt* to daze, stun, stupefy.

storditàggine *nf* absent-mindedness, carelessness, foolishness.

stòria *nf* history, story, tale.

stòrico *pl* **-ici** *a* historical; *nm* historian.

storióne *nm* sturgeon.

stormìre *vi* to rustle.

stórmo *nm* flight, flock; **suonàre a s.** to sound the tocsin.

stornàre *vt* to avert, ward off.

stórno, stornèllo *nm* starling.

storpiàre *vt* to cripple, maim, mangle.

storpiatùra *nf* crippling, maiming, mangling.

stórpio *a* crippled; *nm* cripple.

stòrta *nf* sprain.

stòrto *a* twisted, crooked; wrong.

stovìglie *nf pl* crockery.

stra- *prefix* over.

stràbico *pl* **-ici** *a* squint-eyed.

strabiliàre *vi* to be amazed, be astounded.

strabìsmo *nm* squint, squinting.

straboccàre *vi* to overflow.

stracciàre *vt* to tear.

stràccio *a* ragged, torn; *nm* rag.

straccióne *nm* ragamuffin.

stràda *nf* road, street, way; **s. facèndo** on the way.

stradàle *a* road, of the road; *nm* road.

stradóne *nm* large street, main road.

strafalcióne *nm* blunder.

strafàre *vi* to overdo.

stràge *nf* massacre, slaughter, havoc.

stralunàre *vt* to open wide, roll (one's eyes).

stramazzàre *vi* to fall heavily.

strambería *nf* eccentricity, oddity.

stràmbo *a* odd, eccentric.

stràme *nm* litter, straw.

strampalàto *a* odd, eccentric.

stranézza *nf* oddness, strangeness.

strangolàre *vt* to strangle, throttle, choke.

stranièro *a* foreign; *nm* foreigner.

stràno *a* strange, odd, queer, funny.

straordinariaménte *ad* extraordinarily, unusually, enormously.

straordinàrio *a* extraordinary, astonishing, unusual; **edizióne straordinària** *nf* (*newspaper*) special edition; **lavóro s.** *nm* overtime work.

strapazzàre *vt* to ill-treat, ill-use; **-rsi** *vr* to overwork oneself.

strapazzàta *nf* scolding; overwork.

strapàzzo *nm* overwork, over-exertion.

strappàre *vt* to tear, wrench, snatch; **-rsi** *vr* to get torn; tear oneself away.

stràppo *nm* tear, jerk; infringement; **fàre úno s. àlla règola** to make an exception.

straripàre *vi* to overflow.

Strasbúrgo *nf* (*geogr*) Strasbourg.

strascicàre *vt* to drag, shuffle; drawl.

stràscico *pl* **-ichi** *nm* train; sequel.

stratagèmma *nm* stratagem.

strategìa *nf* strategy.

stratègico *pl* **-ici** *a* strategic.

stràto *nm* layer, stratum.

stravagànte *a* odd, strange; *nm* eccentric.

stravagànza *nf* eccentricity, oddness.

straviziàre *vi* to be intemperate.

stravìzio *nm* excess, intemperance.

stravòlto *a* twisted, convulsed.

straziàre *vt* to rend, torture.

stràzio *nm* torment, torture; heartbreak, trouble.

stréga *nf* witch; **stregóne** *nm* wizard.

stregàre *vt* to bewitch.

stregonerìa *nf* witchcraft.

strégua *nf* standard, way.

stremàre *vt* to exhaust.

strènna *nf* Christmas box; gift.

strènuo *a* brave; strenuous, vigorous.

strepitàre *vi* to make an uproar, shout.

strèpito *nm* din, uproar.

strepitóso *a* uproarious, clamorous.

streptocòcco *pl* **-còcchi** *nm* streptococcus.

streptomicìna *nf* streptomycin.

strétta *nf* clasp, embrace, grasp, hold; **s. di màno** handshake.

strettézza *nf* narrowness; poverty; **in strettézze** hard up.

strétto *a* narrow, tight; strict; *nm* strait.

strettóia *nf* difficult situation.

strettóio *nm* (*mech*) press.

stricnìna *nf* strychnine.

stridènte *a* shrill, sharp, strident; jarring, clashing.

strìdere *vi* to creak, screech, jar.

strìdo *nm* cry, screech.

stridóre *nm* screeching, jarring.

strìdulo *a* piercing, shrill.

strìglia *nf* curry-comb.

strigliàre *vt* to curry; rebuke.

strillàre *vi* to scream, shout.

strillo nm scream, shriek, cry.

strillóne nm (news)paper-boy.

striminzito a thin, stunted.

strimpellàre vt to strum, thrum.

strinàto a singed.

strínga nf (shoe)lace.

stringàto a laced; tight; (of style) concise.

stríngere vt to press, tighten, grasp; **-rsi** vr to press (against); shrug; squeeze.

stríscia nf strip, stripe.

strisciàre vt to drag, shuffle; graze; vi to crawl, creep.

stríscio nm graze; **di s.** grazingly.

stritolàre vt to crush.

strizzàre vt to squeeze, wring; **s. l'òcchio** to wink.

stròfa nf strophe.

strofinàccio nm duster, floor-cloth.

strofinàre vt to rub.

strombazzàre vt to trumpet; boast.

stroncàre vt to break (off); criticize harshly.

stroncatúra nf devastating criticism.

stropicciàre vt to rub, shuffle.

stròzza nf throat.

strozzàre vt to strangle, throttle, suffocate; (fig) fleece.

strozzinàggio nm usury.

strozzino nm usurer.

strúggere vt to melt; consume; **-rsi** vr to be consumed; long (for); melt.

struggiménto nm torment; longing.

struménto nm implement, tool, instrument.

strútto nm lard.

struttúra nf structure.

strúzzo nm ostrich.

stuccàre vt to coat with stucco, plaster; surfeit; **-rsi** vr to grow weary.

stuccatúra nf plastering.

stucchévole a filling; sickening, tedious.

stúcco pl **-chi** nm plaster, stucco; **rimanère di s.** to be dumbfounded; a fed-up, sick.

studènte nm **studentéssa** nf student.

studentésco pl **-chi** a student, student-like.

studiàre vti to study; **-rsi** vr to do one's best, try.

studiataménte ad deliberately; with affectation.

stúdio nm study; plan; office; studio; **a bèllo s.** on purpose.

studióso a studious; nm scholar.

stúfa nf stove; **s. elèttrica** electric fire, (US) electric heater.

stufàto nm stew.

stúfo a bored, sick, tired.

stuòia nf mat, matting.

stuòlo nm band, group, troop.

stupefacènte a stupefying; nm drug, narcotic.

stupefàre vt to astonish, stupefy.

stupefazióne nf astonishment, stupefaction.

stupèndo a splendid, stupendous.

stupidàggine nf foolishness; nonsense.

stupidità nf stupidity.

stúpido a stupid; nm fool.

stupíre vt to amaze, astound.

stupóre nm amazement, stupor, daze.

stupràre vt to rape, violate.

stúpro nm rape.

sturàre vt to uncork.

stuzzicadènti (inv) nm toothpick.

stuzzicànte a appetizing.

stuzzicàre vt to prod, pick; tease; whet.

su prep on, upon, over, above; about; towards; ad up, upstairs; on.

subàcqueo a underwater, subaqueous; **pésca subàcquea** underwater fishing.

subaltèrno a nm subordinate.

subbúglio nm turmoil, upheaval.

subcosciènte a nm subconscious.

súbdolo a shifty, underhand.

subentràre vi to take the place of.

subíre vt to undergo, suffer.

subissàre vt to sink, ruin, overwhelm; vi to sink, fall into ruin.

subitàneo a sudden.

súbito a sudden; ad at once, immediately.

sublimàre vt to sublimate.

sublimàto nm sublimate.

sublíme a sublime.

subodoràre vt to get wind of, suspect.

subordinàre vt to subordinate.

subordinazióne nf subordination.

subornàre vt to suborn, bribe.

subornazióne nf subornation.

suburbàno a suburban.

subúrbio nm suburb(s).

subúrra nf slums pl.

succèdere vi to succeed; follow; happen; **-rsi** nm succession.

successióne nf succession.

successívo a following, subsequent.

successo nm success.

successóre nm successor.

succhiàre vt to suck.

succhièllo nm gimlet.

succínto a scanty, succinct.

súcco pl **súcchi** nm juice, essence.

succóso a juicy.

súccubo a (entirely) dominated; nm succubus.

succulènto a succulent.

succursàle nf branch (office).

sud nm (geogr) south; **s. est** south-east; **s. ovest** south-west.

sudafricàno a nm South African.

sudamericàno a nm South American.

sudàre vti to perspire, sweat.

súddito nm subject.

súdicio a dirty, filthy.

sudiciúme nm dirt, filth.

sudóre nm perspiration, sweat.

sufficiènte a sufficient, enough; nm haughty person.

sufficiènza nf enough, sufficient

quantity; (in exams) pass mark; self-sufficiency.
suffísso nm suffix.
suffragàre vt to support.
suffragétta nf suffragette.
suffràgio nm suffrage; approval; **mèssa in s.** Mass for the repose of a soul.
suggellàre vt to seal (up).
suggèllo nm seal.
suggeriménto nm suggestion.
suggeríre vt to suggest; (theat) prompt.
suggeritóre nm (theat) prompter.
suggestionàre vt to hypnotize; influence.
suggestióne nf suggestion; influence.
suggestívo a evocative, suggestive.
súghero nm cork, cork-tree.
súgo pl **-ghi** nm gravy, juice; (fig) pleasure.
suicída a suicidal; nm suicide (person).
suicidàrsi vr to commit suicide.
suicídio nm suicide (act).
suíno a nm swine.
sulfamídico pl **-ici** a sulphamidic; nm sulphonamide.
sulfúreo a sulphureous.
sultàno nm sultan.
súo nm property; poss a and pron his, hers, its, one's.
suòcero nm father-in-law; **suòcera** nf mother-in-law.
suòla nf (of a shoe) sole.
suòlo nm soil, ground.
suonàre vti to sound, play, strike, ring.
suòno nm sound.
suòra nf nun, sister.
superàre vt to outrun; excel; get over, get through; surpass, exceed; **s. di número** outnumber.
supèrbia nf arrogance, pride.
supèrbo a arrogant, proud; superb; lofty.
superficiàle a superficial.
superficialità nf superficiality.
superfície pl **-ci** nf surface, area.
supèrfluo a superfluous, unnecessary; nm surplus.
superióre a higher; superior; upper; above; senior; nm superior.
superiorità nf superiority.
superlatívo a superlative.
supermercàto nm supermarket.
supersònico pl **-ici** a supersonic.
supèrstite a surviving; nmf survivor.
superstizióne nf superstition.
superstizióso a superstitious.
supíno a supine.
suppellèttili nf pl equipment; fittings pl, furnishings pl.
suppergiú ad approximately, nearly, roughly.
supplementàre a supplementary, additional.
suppleménto nm supplement, addition, extra.

supplènte a nmf substitute, temporary (teacher).
supplènza nf temporary post.
súpplica nf entreaty, petition.
supplicàre vt to entreat, implore.
supplichévole a imploring, entreating.
supplíre vi to make up for, replace, substitute for.
supplízio nm torture, torment.
suppórre vt to suppose.
suppòrto nm support; (of an object) rest, stand, bracket, mount.
supposizióne nf supposition.
suppuràre vi to suppurate.
supremazía nf supremacy.
suprèmo a supreme, extraordinary, greatest, highest, last.
surgelaménto nm deep freeze.
surgelàto a nm deep frozen food.
surrealísmo nm surrealism.
surrealísta a nm surrealist.
surriscaldàre vt to overheat.
surrogàre vt to replace, substitute.
surrogàto nm substitute.
Suṣànna nf pr Susan.
suscettíbile a susceptible, touchy.
suscettibilità nf susceptibility, touchiness.
suscitàre vt to give rise to, provoke, rouse.
suṣína nf plum; **suṣíno** nm plum-tree.
susseguènte a subsequent, successive.
sussidiàre vt to subsidize, support, help.
sussídio nm subsidy, aid.
sussiègo pl **-ghi** nm exaggerated dignity, haughtiness.
sussistènza nf existence, subsistence.
sussístere vi to exist, subsist.
sussultàre vi to start, tremble.
sussúlto nm start, tremor.
sussurràre vti to whisper, murmur.
sussúrro nm whisper, murmur.
ṣvagàre vt to amuse; distract someone's attention.
ṣvagàto a absent-minded.
ṣvàgo pl **-ghi** nm amusement, recreation.
ṣvaligiàre vt to rob, burgle.
ṣvalutàre vt to depreciate, undervalue.
ṣvalutazióne nf depreciation, devaluation.
ṣvaníre vi to disappear, vanish.
ṣvaníto a vanished, faded; feeble-minded.
ṣvantàggio nm disadvantage.
ṣvantaggióso a unfavourable, detrimental.
ṣvaporàre vi to evaporate, vanish, lose strength.
ṣvariàto a varied, various.
ṣvedése a Swedish; nmf Swede.
ṣvéglia nf waking-up; alarm clock; (mil) reveille.
ṣvegliàre vt to (a)rouse, wake (up); **-rsi** vr to wake (up).

şvegliatézza *nf* alertness, readiness of mind.

şvéglio *a* awake; quick-witted, alert.

şvelàre *vt* to reveal, disclose.

şvèllere *vt* to extirpate, eradicate.

şveltézza *nf* quickness, rapidity.

şveltíre *vt* to make lively, nimble, quick, slender.

şvèlto *a* quick, alert; slender; *ad* fast, quickly.

şvéndere *vt* to undersell; sell below cost.

şvéndita *nf* clearance sale.

şvenimento *nm* fainting fit, swoon.

şveníre *vi* to faint, swoon.

şventàre *vt* to baffle, foil, thwart.

şventatézza *nf* thoughtlessness, rashness.

şventàto *a* thwarted; heedless, scatter-brained; *nm* scatter-brain.

şventolàre *vt* to wave, flutter.

şventràre *vt* to disembowel; destroy.

şventúra *nf* bad luck, misfortune, mishap.

şventuràto *a* unfortunate, unlucky.

şvergognàre *vt* to disgrace.

şvergognàto *a* shameless.

şvernàre *vi* to winter.

şvestíre *vt* to undress.

Şvezia *nf* (geogr) Sweden.

şvezzàre *vt* to wean.

şviamento *nm* deviation; leading astray; going astray.

şviàre *vt* to divert; lead astray; -rsi *vr* to diverge; go astray.

şvignàrsela *vr* to slip away.

şviluppàre *vt* to develop, work out; -rsi *vr* to develop, grow; break out.

şvilúppo *nm* development, growth, increase.

şvincolàre *vt* to free, redeem, clear.

şvişàre *vt* to disfigure, misrepresent.

şvisceràre *vt* to disembowel; examine thoroughly.

şvisceràto *a* ardent, passionate.

şvista *nf* oversight.

şvitàre *vt* to unscrew.

Şvízzera *nf* (geogr) Switzerland.

şvízzero *a nm* Swiss.

şvogliatézza *nf* listlessness, laziness.

şvogliàto *a* lazy, listless; *nm* lazybones.

şvolazzàre *vi* to fly about, flit, flutter.

şvòlgere *vt* to unwind, unroll; develop; carry out; -rsi *vr* to unfold, unroll; happen, take place.

şvolgimento *nm* unwinding, unrolling; treatment; development.

şvòlta *nf* turn, turning point; winding, bend.

şvoltàre *vi* to turn, bend.

şvoltolàre *vt* to roll; -rsi *vr* to roll about, wallow.

şv(u)otàre *vt* to empty.

T

tabaccàio *nm* -àia *nf* tobacconist.

tabacchería *nf* tobacconist's shop; (US) cigar store.

tabacchièra *nf* snuff-box.

tabàcco *pl* -chi *nm* tobacco; t. da nàso snuff.

tabèlla *nf* table; list, schedule.

tabellóne *nm* notice board, (US) bulletin board; t. d'affissióne hoarding, (US) billboard.

tabernàcolo *nm* tabernacle, shrine.

tabù *nm* taboo.

tàcca *nf* notch; defect.

taccàgno *a* miserly, stingy.

tacchino *nm* turkey.

tàccia *nf* bad reputation; accusation, charge.

tacciàre *vt* to accuse (of), charge (with).

tàcco *pl* -chi *nm* (of a shoe) heel; t. a spillo stiletto heel.

taccuíno *nm* memorandum book, notebook, pocket-book.

tacére *vi* to be silent, keep silence; *vt* to be silent about, leave out, conceal.

tachímetro *nm* (aut) speedometer.

tàcito *a* tacit; silent.

tacitúrno *a* taciturn, sulky.

tafàno *nm* gadfly.

tafferúglio *nm* brawl, fray.

tàglia *nf* ransom, tribute, price on someone's head; size.

tagliabòschi (inv) *nm* woodcutter, woodman.

tagliacàrte (inv) *nm* paper-cutter, paperknife.

tagliàndo *nm* coupon.

tagliàre *vt* to cut, cut off, cut out.

tagliatèlle *nf pl* noodles.

tagliàto *a* cut; cut out; fit.

tagliènte *a* cutting; sharp.

tàglio *nm* cut; (of notes etc) denomination; dress length, (of knife etc) edge.

tagli(u)òla *nf* trap.

tailleur (Fr) *nm* costume.

tàlamo *nm* nuptial bed.

tàlco *pl* -chi *nm* talc, talcum powder.

tàle *a* such, like, similar; *pron* someone; tal dei tàli so-and-so.

talènto *nm* talent; intelligence; will.

talismàno *nm* talisman.

tallóne *nm* heel.

talménte *ad* so, so much, to such a degree.

talóra *v* talvòlta.

tàlpa *nf* mole.

talúno *a* some, certain; *pron* somebody, someone.

talvòlta *ad* sometimes.

tamarindo *nm* tamarind.

tamburino *nm* drummer.

tambúro *nm* drum; cylinder.

tameríce *nf* tamarisk.

tamponàre *vt* to stop, plug.

tampóne *nm* stopper; (med) tampon.

tàna *nf* den, hole, lair.

tànfo nm bad smell, stench.
Tanganica nm (geogr) Tanganyika.
tangènte a tangent.
Tàngeri nm (geogr) Tangier.
tànghero nm boor, bumpkin.
tangíbile a tangible.
tànto a so much, as much; ad so, so long, so much; t. . . . quànto as . . . as, both . . . and; **tànti** a and pron pl as many.
tapíno a miserable, wretched; nm wretch.
tàppa nf halting place; stage; lap.
tappàre vt to cork, plug, stop (up); -rsi vr to shut oneself up; to stop one's ears.
tapparèlla nf rolling shutter.
tappéto nm carpet, rug.
tappezzàre vt to upholster; paper.
tappezzería nf wallpaper; hangings; upholstery.
tappezzière nm paper-hanger; upholsterer.
tàppo nm cork, plug, stopper.
tàra nf tare; defect
tarchiàto a thickset.
tardàre vi to be late, be long, delay; vt to defer.
tàrdi ad late; **far t.** to be late.
tàrdo a slow; dull; tardy, late.
tàrga nf nameplate, number-plate.
tariffa nf tariff.
tarlàto a worm-eaten.
tàrlo nm woodworm.
tàrma nf moth.
taròcchi nm pl tarot.
tàrsia nf inlaid work, marquetry.
tartagliàre vi to stammer, stutter.
tartagliòne nm stammerer.
tàrtaro nm tartar; a nm Tartar.
tartarúga nf tortoise, turtle.
tartassàre vt to harass, bully.
tartína nf canapé.
tartúfo nm truffle.
tàsca nf pocket.
tascàbile a pocket.
tàssa nf tax; (school etc) fee.
tassàmetro nm (aut) taximeter; **t. di parchéggio** parking meter.
tassàre vt to tax; assess.
tassatívo a definite, compulsory.
tassì nm taxi, taxicab.
tassísta nm taxidriver, taximan.
tàsso nm badger; (com) rate; yew-tree.
tastàre vt to touch; feel; sound.
tastièra nf keyboard.
tàsto nm (of musical instrument, typewriter etc) key; touch; subject.
tastóni, a ad gropingly.
tàttica nm tactics pl.
tàttico pl -ici a tactical; nm tactician.
tàtto nm touch; tact.
tatuàggio nm tattoo, tattooing.
tatuàre vt to tattoo.
taumatúrgo nm miracle-worker.
tavèrna nf public house.
tàvola nf table; board; slab.
tavolétta nf tablet, small board; **t. di cioccolàta** bar of chocolate.

tavolíno nm small table, writing-desk.
tàvolo nm table.
tavolòzza nf palette.
tàzza nf cup.
te pron 2nd pers sing oblique case and object you, yourself.
tè nm tea; **pastína da t.** teacake, scone, (US) biscuit.
teatràle a theatrical.
teàtro nm theatre; **t. di varietà** music-hall, (US) vaudeville theatre.
tècnica nf technique.
tècnico pl -ici a technical; nm technician.
tedésco pl -chi a nm German.
tediàre vt to bore, tire, weary.
tèdio nm boredom, tedium, weariness.
tedióso a tedious, irksome, tiresome.
tegàme nm pan.
téglia nf oven-pan.
tégola nf -olo nm brickbat, tile.
teièra nf teapot.
téla nf cloth; linen; (painter's) canvas; (theat) curtain; painting.
telàio nm loom; frame.
teleàrma pl -i nf guided missile.
telecàmera nf (tv) telecamera.
telefèrica nf cable way.
telefonàre vt to telephone.
telefonàta nf telephone call; **t. urbàna** local call; **t. interurbàna** trunk call, long-distance call.
telefònico pl -ici a telephone.
telèfono nm telephone.
telegiornàle nm television news.
telegrafàre vt to telegraph, cable.
telegràfico pl -ici a telegraph(ic).
telegràmma nm telegram, cable.
telepatía nf telepathy.
telería nf linen and cotton goods pl; **negoziànte di telerie** (linen-)draper.
telescòpio nm telescope.
telescrivènte a nf teletype; teleprinter.
televisióne nf television; **t. a gettóne** coin television, (US) fee television; **trasmèttere per t.** to televise.
televisóre nm television set.
tellína nf cockle.
télo nm (of material) length, width.
telóne nm (theat) drop-curtain.
tèma nm theme; composition.
temeràrio a rash, arrogant, foolhardy.
temére vti to be afraid of, dread, fear.
temerità nf rashness, temerity.
tèmpera nf (painting) tempera; distemper; (metal) temper.
temperaménto nm temperament; mitigation.
temperànza nf temperance, moderation.
temperàre vt to mitigate; (pencil) sharpen; temper.
temperatúra nf temperature.
temperíno nm penknife.
tempèsta nf storm, tempest.

tempestàre *vi* to storm; *vt* to harass, assail (*also fig*); adorn.

tempestívo *a* opportune, timely.

tempestóso *a* stormy.

tèmpia *nf* (*anat*) temple.

tèmpio *pl* **-pii** *nm* temple.

tèmpo *nm* time; weather; (*gram*) tense; stage; **che t. fa?** what kind of weather is it?

temporàle *nm* storm.

temporalésco *pl* **-chi** *a* stormy.

temporàneo *a* temporary.

temporeggiàre *vi* to temporize.

tèmpra *nf* temper; character; timbre.

tempràre *vt* to temper; strengthen; mould.

tenàce *a* tenacious, persevering; obstinate.

tenàcia *nf* tenacity, stubbornness.

tenàglia *nf pl* tongs *pl*; pincers *pl*; pliers *pl*.

tènda *nf* curtain; tent; awning.

tendàggio *nm* curtain, (*US*) drape.

tendènza *nf* tendency, trend.

tèndere *vt* to hold out; stretch (out); *vi* to be inclined to; aim.

tendìna *nf* curtain.

tènebre *nf pl* darkness.

tenebróso *a* dark; obscure; mysterious.

tenènte *nm* lieutenant.

teneraménte *ad* tenderly, gently.

tenére *vt* to hold, keep; **t. a** to be proud of, care for, like; **t. da** to take after; **t. per** to side with; **-rsi** *vr* to consider oneself; keep to.

tenerézza *nf* tenderness, affection.

tènero *a* tender, loving; *nm* tender part; affection.

tènia *nf* tapeworm.

tènnis *nm* tennis; **t. su pràto** lawntennis; **tennìsta** tennis-player.

tenóre *nm* tenor; **t. di vìta** standard of living; way of living.

tensióne *nf* tension, strain.

tentàcolo *nm* tentacle.

tentàre *vt* to try, attempt; tempt; (*med*) probe.

tentatìvo *nm* attempt, endeavour; trial.

tentatóre *f* **-trìce** *a* tempting; *nm* tempter; *nf* temptress.

tentazióne *nf* temptation.

tentennaménto *nm* wavering.

tentennàre *vi* to stagger; waver.

tènue *a* slight, thin, fine; soft.

tenuità *nf* thinness, smallness, slightness; softness.

tenùta *nf* estate; uniform.

teología *nf* theology.

teològico *pl* **-ici** *a* theological.

teòlogo *pl* **-ogi** *nm* theologian.

teorèma *nm* theorem.

teorìa *nf* theory.

teòrico *pl* **-ici** *a* theoretical; *nm* theorist.

tèpido *v* **tièpido**.

tepóre *nm* warmth.

terapèutico *pl* **-ici** *a* therapeutic.

terapìa *nf* therapy.

Terèsa *nf pr* T(h)eresa.

tèrgere *vt* to wipe off, dry.

tergicristàllo *nm* (*aut*) windscreen wiper, (*US*) windshield wiper.

tergiversàre *vi* to beat about the bush, hesitate.

tergiversazióne *nf* hesitation.

tèrgo *nm* back; **a t. overleaf; da t.** from behind.

termàle *a* thermal.

tèrme *nf pl* hot baths *pl*; hot springs *pl*; spa.

termINàre *vti* to finish, end.

tèrmine *nm* boundary; date; term; limit; **a rigór di tèrmini** strictly speaking.

termoconvettóre *nm* convector.

termòforo *nm* warming pad.

termòmetro *nm* thermometer.

tèrmos *nm* thermos.

termosifóne *nm* radiator.

tèrno *nm* treble; jackpot.

tèrra *nf* earth, land, ground.

terracòtta *nf* terracotta; baked clay.

terrafèrma *nf* mainland.

terràglia *nf* earthenware, pottery.

terramicìna *nf* terramycin.

Terranòva *nf* Newfoundland.

terrapièno *nm* bank, earthwork.

terràzza *nf* **-àzzo** *nm* terrace.

terremòto *nm* earthquake.

terréno *a* earthly, worldly; *nm* ground, soil; land; **pian t.** ground floor.

terrèstre *a* earthly, terrestrial.

terrìbile *a* terrible, awful, frightful.

territòrio *nm* territory.

terróre *nm* terror, dread.

tèrso *a* clear, terse.

terziàrio *a nm* tertiary.

tèrzo *a* third; *nm* third party.

tésa *nf* (*of hat*) brim; (*of cap*) visor; (*of nets*) cast.

tèschio *nm* skull.

tèsi *nf* thesis.

téso *a* taut, tight, strained.

tesorerìa *nf* treasury.

tesorière *nm* treasurer.

tesòro *nm* treasure; treasury.

tèssera *nf* card; ticket; (*mosaic*) tessera.

tesseraménto *nm* rationing.

tesseràre *vt* to ration.

tèssere *vt* to weave.

tèssile *a nm* textile.

tessitóre *nm* **-trìce** *nf* weaver.

tessitùra *nf* weaving.

tessúto *nm* cloth, fabric; tissue; web; **negòzio di tessúti** draper's shop, (*US*) dry-goods store.

tèsta *nf* head; **t. càlda** hot-head.

testaménto *nm* testament, will.

testàrdo *a* headstrong, stubborn.

testàta *nf* (*of bed, bridge etc*) head; (*newspaper*) heading; butt.

tèste *nmf* witness; **bànco dei tèsti** witness box, (*US*) witness stand.

testícolo *nm* testicle.

testimòne *nmf* witness; **t. oculàre** eyewitness.

testimoniànza nf evidence, testimony, witness.
testimoniàre vti to testify, witness.
tèsto nm text.
testuàle a exact, precise; textual.
testúggine nf tortoise, turtle.
tètano nm tetanus.
tètro a dismal, gloomy.
tétto nm roof; house; **sénza t.** homeless.
tettóia nf penthouse; (of market, station etc) roof.
teutònico pl -ici a Teutonic.
Tévere nm (geogr) Tiber.
ti pron 2nd pers sing object and oblique you, yourself.
tiàra nf tiara.
Tíbet nm (geogr) Tibet.
tibetàno a nm Tibetan.
tíbia nf (mus) pipe; (anat) shinbone, tibia.
ticchettío nm ticking.
tícchio nm caprice, whim.
tiepidézza nf (fig) lukewarmness.
tièpido a lukewarm (also fig).
tifo nm (med) typhus; **fàre il t. per** to be a fan of.
tifòide nf (med) typhoid.
tifóne nm typhoon.
tifóso a typhous; nm (fig cinema, football etc) fan.
tiglio nm lime(tree); fibre.
tigna nf ringworm.
tignòla nf moth.
tigràto a striped, tabby (cat).
tigre nf tiger, tigress.
timbràre vt to stamp, postmark.
timbro nm stamp; **t. postàle** postmark; timbre.
timidézza nf shyness, timidity.
tímido a bashful, shy, timid.
timo nm thyme.
timóne nm (naut) helm, rudder.
timonière nm helmsman, steersman.
timoràto a respectful; scrupulous; devout.
timóre nm fear, awe.
timoróso a timorous, timid.
Timòteo nm pr Timothy.
tímpano nm eardrum; (mus) kettledrum.
tinca nf tench.
tinèllo nm breakfast room; small vat.
tíngere vt to dye, paint, stain.
tíno nm tub, vat.
tinòzza nf (bath-)tub, wash-tub.
tinta nf colour, dye, hue, tint.
tintarélla nf (fam) sun-tan.
tintinnàre vi to tinkle, jingle.
tintóre nm dyer.
tintoría nf dyer's, dye-works; cleaners' shop.
tintúra nf dyeing; tincture.
típico pl -ici a typical.
tipo nm type; model; specimen; **un bel t.** a queer fellow.
tipografía nf typography; printing works.
tipogràfico pl -ici a typographical.
tipògrafo nm printer, typographer.

tiranneggiàre vt to oppress, tyrannize.
tirànnico pl -ici a tyrannical.
tirànnide, tirannía nf tyranny.
tirànno nm tyrant.
tiràre vt to draw, pull, drag; throw; (typ) print; vi shoot at; blow; **tíra vènto** it is windy; **quèsta màcchina tira béne** this car goes like a bird.
tiràta nf draw, pull; stretch; tirade.
tiratóre nm marksman, shooter.
tiratúra nf drawing, pulling; (typ) circulation; edition.
tirchierìa nf stinginess.
tírchio a miserly, stingy; nm miser.
tíro nm draught; fire; throw; trick; **animàle da t.** draught animal.
tirocínio nm apprenticeship; training.
tiròide nf thyroid.
Tiròlo nm (geogr) Tyrol; **tirolése** a nm Tyrolese.
Tirrèno a nm (geogr) Tyrrhenian.
tísi nf (med) consumption.
tísico pl -ici a nm consumptive.
titillàre vt to titillate, tickle.
titolàre a regular; titular; nm regular holder; owner; (of a chair) professor.
títolo nm title; headline; right; qualification; (com) security; stock.
titubànte a hesitating, undecided.
titubànza nf hesitation.
titubàre vi to hesitate, waver.
tízio nm fellow; **Tízio, Càio e Semprónio** Tom, Dick and Harry.
tízzo, tizzóne nm (fire)brand.
toccàre vt to touch, handle; strike; move; (naut) call at; vi to fall on; be the duty of.
tócco pl -chi nm touch; knock; stroke; piece; **al t.** at one o'clock.
tòga nf toga; gown.
tògliere vt to take (away); take off; free; prevent; **t. di mèzzo** to get rid of; **-rsi** vr to get away, get off, get out.
tolétta, toilette (Fr) dressing table; toilet.
tolleràbile a tolerable.
tollerànte a indulgent, tolerant.
tollerànza nf tolerance, endurance; **càsa di t.** brothel.
tolleràre vt to bear, tolerate.
tómba nf grave, tomb.
tómbola nf bingo.
Tommàso nm pr Thomas.
tòmo nm tome, volume.
tònaca nf (monk's) habit, (priest's) cassock; tunic.
tonàre v **tuonàre**.
tondíno nm saucer, small plate.
tóndo a round; nm round; circle; **chiàro e t.** plainly.
tónfo nm splash; thud.
tònico pl -ici a nm tonic.
tonificànte a tonic, bracing.
tonnellàggio nm tonnage.
tonnellàta nf ton.
tónno nm tunny.

tòno nm tone; èssere fuòri t. to be out of tune.

tonsílla nf tonsil.

tonsillíte nf tonsillitis.

tonsúra nf tonsure.

tónto a nm stupid, simpleton.

topàia nf rats' nest; hovel.

topàzio nm topaz.

tòpica nf blunder, gaffe.

tòpo nm mouse, rat; t. di bibliotèca bookworm.

topografía nf topography.

tòppa nf patch; door-lock.

toràce nm thorax.

tórba nf peat.

tórbido a turbid, muddy; gloomy; nm disorder, trouble.

tòrcere vt to wring, twist.

tòrchio nm press.

tòrcia nf torch, candle.

torcicòllo nm stiff neck.

tórdo nm thrush.

Toríno nf (geogr) Turin; torinése a nm Torinese.

tórma nf crowd; swarm; herd.

torménta nf blizzard, snowstorm.

tormentàre vt to torment, torture, worry; -rsi vr to worry.

torménto nm torment, torture.

tormentóso a tormenting, vexing.

tornacónto nm profit.

tornànte a returning; nm bend, turning.

tornàre vi to return; turn out; be correct; fit.

tornèo nm tournament.

tórnio nm (tec) turning lathe.

torníre vt (tec) to turn.

tornitóre nm turner.

tórno nm period; in quél t. thereabouts; tórno tórno all round.

tòro nm bull.

torpedinàre vt to torpedo.

torpèdine nm torpedo.

torpedinièra nf torpedo boat.

torpedóne nm (motor) coach.

tòrpido a torpid, sluggish, dull.

torpóre nm torpor, sluggishness.

tórre nf tower.

torrefazióne nf coffee roasting; coffee store.

torreggiàre vi to loom, tower.

torrènte nm torrent, stream, flood.

torrenziàle a torrential.

tòrrido a torrid; scorching.

torróne nm nougat.

torsióne nf torsion, twist.

tórso nm torso, trunk.

tórsolo nm (fruit) core, (vegetable) stump.

tórta nf cake, tart, (US) pie.

tortièra nf baking tin.

tòrto nm wrong, fault; avér t. to be wrong; a t. unjustly, wrongly; bent, crooked.

tórtora nf turtle-dove.

tortuóso a tortuous, crooked.

tortúra nf torture.

torturàre vt to torture.

torvaménte ad grimly, surlily.

tórvo a grim, surly.

tosàre vt to clip, cut (s.o.'s) hair, shear.

tosatúra nm (sheep-)shearing.

Toscàna nf Tuscany; toscàno a nm Tuscan.

tósse nf cough.

tòssico pl -ici a poisonous; nm poison.

tossíre vi to cough.

tostapàne nm toaster; pàne tostàto toast.

tostàre vt to roast (coffee); toast.

tòsto a hard; fàccia tòsta impudence; ad immediately; t. che cj as soon as.

totàle a nm total.

totalità nf totality, whole.

totalitàrio a absolute, totalitarian.

totalizzàre vt to totalize, score.

totalménte ad totally, completely.

tòtano nm cuttlefish.

tovàglia nf (table)cloth.

tovagliòlo nm napkin, serviette.

tòzzo a squat, stocky, thickset; nm piece; un t. di pàne a piece of bread.

tra prep among, between; t. pòco in a short time.

traballànte a unsteady, staggering.

traballàre vi to stagger, totter; jolt.

trabiccolo nm bed-warmer; rickety vehicle.

traboccàre vi to brim over, overflow.

trabocchétto nm trap.

tracannàre vt to gulp down.

tràccia nf trail, trace, track; outline.

tracciàre vt to trace, draw, mark out, sketch.

tracòlla nf shoulder-belt.

tracòllo nm breakdown, collapse; ruin.

tracotànte a arrogant, overbearing.

tracotànza nf arrogance.

tradiménto nm treason, betrayal, treachery; a t. treacherously.

tradíre vt to betray, deceive, be unfaithful to.

traditóre nm -tríce nf traitor; a treacherous.

tradizionàle a traditional.

tradizióne nf tradition.

tradúrre vt to translate; bring into effect; take to; turn.

traduttóre nm -tríce nf translator.

traduzióne nf translation.

trafelàto a breathless, panting.

trafficànte nm dealer, trafficker.

trafficàre vi to deal, trade, traffic.

tràffico pl -ichi, -ici nm traffic; trade, trading.

trafíggere vt to transfix, pierce.

trafítta nf pang, stabbing pain.

traforàre vt to bore, perforate, pierce.

trafóro nm boring, piercing; tunnelling; tunnel.

trafugàre vt to steal, purloin.

tragèdia nf tragedy.

traghettàre vt to ferry.

traghétto nm ferry.

tràgico pl -ici a tragic; nm tragedian.

tragitto nm passage, way, journey.

traguàrdo nm winning post; (fig) goal.

trainàre v **trascinàre**.

tràino nm haulage; truck; load.

tralasciàre vt to omit; interrupt.

tràlcio nm vine-shoot.

tralíccio nm trellis; ticking.

tralignàre vi to degenerate.

tram nm tram(car), (US) streetcar.

tràma nf weft; plot.

tramandàre vt to hand down.

tramàre vt to weave; plot.

trambústo nm bustle.

tramestìo nm stir, bustle.

tramezzàre vt to partition off; interpose.

tramèzzo nm partition.

tràmite nm way; **per t. di** through.

tramontàna nf north wind.

tramontàre vi to set, fade, wane.

tramónto nm setting, sunset; end.

tramortíre vt to stun; vi to faint.

trampolíno nm springboard; (fig) stepping stone.

tràmpolo nm stilt.

tramutàre vt to alter, change, transform.

tranèllo nm snare, trap.

trangugiàre vt to bolt, gulp down, swallow.

trànne prep but, except, save.

tranquillànte a tranquillizing; nm tranquillizer.

tranquillizzàre vt to tranquillize.

tranquillità nf calm, tranquillity.

tranquíllo a calm, quiet, tranquil.

transatlàntico pl -ici a transatlantic nm liner.

transazióne nf arrangement; composition; transaction.

transìgere vi to come to terms; yield; (com) compound.

transístor nm transistor.

transitàbile a (of a road etc) practicable.

transitàre vi to pass (through).

trànsito nm transit; **t. interrótto** road closed; **vietàto il t.** no thoroughfare.

transitòrio a transitory, transient.

transizióne nf transition.

tranvài v **tram**.

tranvière nm tram conductor; tram driver; (US) streetcar operator.

trapanàre vt to drill; (med) trepan.

tràpano nm drill; (med) trepanning saw.

trapassàre vt to pierce, run through; vi to pass (away).

trapàsso nm death; passage; transfer.

trapelàre vi to transpire, leak out.

trapèzio nm trapeze.

trapiantàre vt to transplant; **-rsi** vr to emigrate, settle.

trapiànto nm transplantation, grafting.

tràppola nf snare, trap.

trapùnta nf quilt, (US) comforter.

trapùnto a quilted.

tràrre vt to draw; get; lead; **tràrsi** vr to draw; get (out); stand (back).

trasalíre vi to start, startle.

trasandàre vt to neglect.

trasandàto a careless, slatternly.

trasbordàre vt to tranship, transfer; (train etc) change.

trascèndere vti to transcend, go beyond; lose one's control.

trascinàre vt to drag, trail; fascinate.

trascórrere vt to pass, spend; vi to elapse, pass.

trascórso a past; nm fault, slip.

trascrívere vt to transcribe.

trascrizióne nf transcription.

trascuràbile a negligible.

trascurànza nf carelessness, negligence, slovenliness.

trascuràre vt to neglect, disregard.

trascuràto a careless, negligent, indifferent, slovenly.

trasecolàre vi to be amazed, startled.

trasferíbile a transferable.

trasferiménto nm change; removal; transfer.

trasferíre vt **-rsi** vr to transfer, remove.

trasfèrta nf transfer; travelling allowance.

trasfiguràre vt to transfigure.

trasfigurazióne nf transfiguration.

trasfóndere vt to transfuse, instil.

trasformàre vt to transform.

trasformatóre nm (elec) transformer.

trasformazióne nf transformation.

trasfusióne nf transfusion.

trasgredíre vti to infringe, transgress.

trasgressióne nf infringement, transgression.

trasgressóre nm infringer, transgressor, offender.

traslocàre vti to move; change one's address.

traslòco pl -chi nm removal.

trasméttere vt to pass on, send, transmit; **t. per ràdio** to broadcast.

trasmissióne nf transmission; broadcast.

trasmodàre vi to exaggerate; exceed.

trasmodàto a excessive, immoderate.

trasmutàre vt to transmute, transform.

trasognàre vi to (day)dream.

trasognàto a dreamy, lost in reverie.

trasparènte a transparent.

trasparíre vi to appear (through); be evident; **lasciàre t.** to betray, reveal.

traspiràre vi to perspire; transpire, leak out.

traspirazióne nf perspiration.

trasportàbile a transportable.

trasportàre vt to carry, convey, transport; transfer.

traspòrto nm transport (also fig).

trastullàrsi vr to amuse oneself, toy with.

trastùllo nm plaything, amusement; (fig) laughing stock.

trasversàle a transverse, cross; nf transversal line, side street.

trasvolàta nf flight across.

trasvolàre vt to fly across.

tràtta nf (com) draft; trade.

trattaménto nm treatment; reception; salary.

trattàre vti to deal with; treat; deal in; discuss; **-rsi** vr impers to be a question (of).

trattatìva nf negotiation.

trattàto nm treaty; treatise.

tratteggiàre vt to outline, sketch.

trattenére vt to keep (back); restrain; deduct; entertain; **-rsi** vr to stay; stop; restrain oneself; help (doing).

tratteniménto nm entertainment; party.

trattenùta nf deduction.

trattìno nm hyphen; dash.

tràtto nm pull; stroke; line, stretch; trait, feature; way of dealing; **tútt'ad un tràtto** all of a sudden.

trattóre nm tractor.

trattorìa nf eating house, restaurant.

travagliàre vt to torment, trouble; **-rsi** vr to worry, toil.

travàglio nm labour, toil; trouble.

travasàre vt to decant, pour off.

tràve nf beam.

travèrsa nf crossbar; side street; (rly) sleeper, (US rly) tie.

traversàle a transversal.

traversàre vt to cross.

traversàta nf crossing, passage.

traversìa nf misfortune, trouble.

travèrso a oblique, transverse; **di t.** askance, the wrong way.

travertìno nm travertine.

travestiménto nm disguise; travesty.

travestìre vt to disguise, travesty.

traviaménto nm going astray; corruption.

traviàre vt to mislead; pervert; **-rsi** vr to go astray.

travicèllo nm joist.

travisàre vt to distort, misrepresent.

travolgènte a overwhelming, overpowering.

travòlgere vt to carry away; overcome, overwhelm; sweep away.

travolgiménto nm overthrow.

trazióne nf traction.

tre a three.

trebbiàre vt to thrash, thresh.

trebbiatrìce nf thresher, threshing machine.

trebbiatùra nf threshing.

tréccia nf plait, pigtail, tress.

trecentìsta nm painter or writer of the 14th century.

trecènto a three hundred; nm 14th century.

trédici a thirteen; **tredicènne** thirteen-year-old; **tredicèsimo** thirteenth.

trégua nf truce, respite.

tremànte a trembling, quivering, shuddering.

tremàre vi to tremble, quake, shake.

tremèndo a awful, dreadful, tremendous; **tremendaménte** ad awfully, dreadfully.

trementìna nf turpentine.

trèmito nm shaking, tremble, trembling.

tremolàre vi to quiver, flicker.

tremolío nm quivering, flickering.

trèmulo a tremulous, trembling.

trèno nm train; **t. di vìta** way of living.

trénta a thirty; **trentènne** thirty-year-old; **trentèsimo** thirtieth; **trentìna** some thirty.

Trènto nf (geogr) Trent, Trento.

trepidàre vi to be anxious; be in a flutter; tremble.

trepidazióne nf anxiety, trepidation.

trèpido a anxious; fluttering, trembling.

treppièdi (inv) nm trivet, tripod.

trésca nf intrigue.

tréspolo nm trestle; rickety vehicle.

triangolàre a triangular.

triàngolo nm triangle.

tribolàre vi to suffer, toil; **far t.** to vex.

tribolazióne nf suffering, tribulation.

tribolo nm suffering, tribulation.

tribórdo nm (naut) starboard.

tribú nf tribe.

tribúna nf platform; gallery; stand.

tribunàle nm (law) court; tribunal.

tribúno nm tribune.

tributàre vt to give; offer; pay.

tributàrio a fiscal; nm tributary.

tribúto nm tribute; tax.

trichèco pl **-chi** nm walrus.

tricolóre a nm tricolour, (usu) Italian flag.

tricòrno nm three-cornered hat.

tridènte nm hay-fork; trident.

triennàle a triennial.

trifòglio nm clover; shamrock; trefoil.

tríglia nf mullet.

trìllo nm trill.

trimestràle a quarterly.

trimèstre nm quarter; term.

trìna nf lace.

trincèa nf trench.

trinceraménto nm entrenchment.

trinceràre vt to entrench; **-rsi** vr to take refuge.

trinchétto, àlbero di nm (naut) foremast.

trinciànte a nm carving (knife).

trinciàre vt to cut.

trinciàto a cut up; nm cut tobacco.

Trinità nf Trinity.

trionfàle a triumphal.

trionfànte a exultant, triumphal.

trionfàre vi to be triumphant, triumph over.

triónfo nm triumph.

triplice a threefold, treble, triple.

triplo a triple; nm triple the amount.

trìpode nm tripod.

trìppa nf tripe; (vulg) paunch.

tripudiàre vi to exult.

tripùdio nm exultation.

trìste a sad, sorrowful; depressing.

tristézza nf sadness, sorrow; gloominess.

trìsto a wicked, wretched; nm rogue.

tritàre vt to mince; pound.

tritàto a minced; nm minced.

tritatùtto inv nm mincing machine.

trìto a minced; worn out; trite.

trìttico pl -ici nm triptych.

trivèlla nf (tec) borer.

trivellàre vt (tec) to bore.

triviàle a low; vulgar.

trivialità nf coarseness, vulgarity; vulgar expression.

trìvio nm crossroad(s).

trofèo nm trophy.

trògolo nm trough.

tròia nf sow.

trómba nf trumpet; bugle; (anat) tube; (of staircase) well.

trombettière nm trumpeter.

troncaménto nm cutting off; breaking off.

troncàre vt to break off; cut off; cut short; interrupt.

trónco pl -chi a broken; truncated; nm trunk.

trónfio a puffed up; conceited.

tròno nm throne.

tròpico pl -ici nm tropic.

tròppo ad too (much); a and pron too much; tròppi pl too many.

tròta nf trout.

trottàre vi to trot; walk fast.

tròtto nm trot.

tròttola nf (whipping) top.

trovàre vt to find (out); meet (with); andàre a t. to go and see; -rsi vr to be, find oneself, meet.

trovàta nf invention, expedient.

trovatèllo nm foundling.

trovatóre nm troubadour.

truccàre vt to make up; -rsi vr to make up one's face.

trùcco pl -cchi nm trick, deceit, make-up.

trùce a fierce, grim.

trucidàre vt to slay, murder.

trùciolo nm chip, shaving.

truculènto, truculènto a truculent.

trùffa nf cheat, swindle; t. alla americàna confidence trick, (US) confidence game.

truffàre vt to cheat, swindle.

truffatóre nm -trice nf cheat, swindler.

trùppa nf troop, band, troupe.

tu pron thou, you (sing); dàre del t. to be on first name terms.

tubàre vi to coo.

tubercolàre a tubercular.

tubercolòsi nf consumption, tuberculosis.

tubercolóso, tubercolòtico a nm consumptive.

tùbero nm tuber.

tùbo nm pipe, tube.

tubolàre a tubular.

tuffàre vt to plunge; -rsi vr to dive, plunge.

tùffo nm dive, plunge.

tùfo nm tufa; tuff.

tugùrio nm hovel.

tulipàno nm tulip.

tùmido a tumid, swollen; (style) pompous.

tumóre nm tumour.

tumulàre vt to bury, inter.

tùmulo nm grave; tumulus.

tumùlto nm tumult, uproar; riot.

tumultuóso a tumultuous; riotous.

tùnica nf tunic.

Túnisi nf (geogr) Tunis; **tunisìno** a nm Tunisian.

Tunisìa nf (geogr) Tunisia.

tùo poss a thy, your; poss pron thine, yours.

tuonàre vi to thunder.

tuòno nm thunder.

t(u)órlo nm (egg) yolk.

turàcciolo nm cork, stopper.

turàre vt to stop, plug, fill up.

tùrba nf crowd, mob, rabble.

turbaménto nm perturbation; excitement; commotion.

turbànte nm turban.

turbàre vt to upset, trouble, disturb; -rsi vr to get upset.

turbìna nf turbine; t. idràulica waterwheel.

turbinàre vi to eddy; whirl.

tùrbine nm whirl, eddy (also fig); hurricane.

turbinìo nm whirling.

turbolènto a turbulent; riotous, stormy.

turchése nf turquoise.

Turchìa nf (geogr) Turkey.

turchìno nm dark blue.

tùrco pl -chi a Turkish; nm Turk.

tùrgido a turgid; pompous.

turìsmo nm tourism.

turìsta nmf tourist.

turìstico pl -ici a tourist.

tùrno nm turn; di t. on duty.

tùrpe a base, vile; disgraceful.

turpitúdine nf baseness, turpitude.

tùta nf mechanic's overall.

tutèla nf guardianship, tutelage; defence.

tutelàre vt to guard, defend, protect.

tutóre nm -trice nf guardian.

tutòrio a tutelar; tutorial.

tuttavìa ad and cj nevertheless, still, yet.

tùtto a all, whole; pron all, everything; **tùtti** pl all pl, everyone; ad wholly, all; nm whole; del t. quite; t. ad un tràtto all of a sudden.

tuttóra ad still.

U

ubbía *nf* false idea; superstition; nonsense.
ubbidiènte *a* obedient.
ubbidiènza *nf* obedience.
ubbidíre *vti* to obey.
ubertà *nf* fertility.
ubertóso *a* fertile, fruitful.
ubicazióne *nf* position, situation.
ubiquità *nf* ubiquity, omnipresence.
ubriacàre *vt* to intoxicate, make drunk; **-rsi** *vr* to get drunk.
ubriacatúra, **ubriachézza** *nf* drunkenness, intoxication.
ubriàco *pl* **-chi** *a* drunk.
ubriacóne *nm* drunkard.
uccellàre *vi* to go fowling.
uccellatóre *nm* fowler.
uccèllo *nm* bird; **u. di bòsco** fugitive from the law.
uccídere *vt* to kill.
uccisióne *nf* killing, murder.
Ucràina *nf* (geogr) Ukraine.
udiènza *nf* audience; hearing; **dàre u.** to receive.
udíre *vt* to hear, listen to.
udíto *nm* (sense of) hearing.
uditóre *nm* **-trice** *nf* listener, hearer.
uditòrio *nm* audience, hearers *pl*.
ufficiàle *a* official; formal; *nm* officer; official.
ufficialmènte *ad* officially.
ufficiàre *vi* to officiate.
ufficio *nm* office; (US) agency; department; duty; **d'u.** officially.
ufficióso *a* unofficial.
uffízio *nm* (religious) office.
úfo, a *ad* gratis.
úggia *nf* boredom; dislike; **avére in u.** to dislike.
uggióso *a* tiresome; dull; gloomy.
Úgo *nm* *pr* Hugh.
ugonòtto *nm* Huguenot.
uguagliànza *nf* equality.
uguagliàre *vt* to (be) equal (to); equalize; **-rsi** *vr* to claim equality; compare oneself.
uguàle *a* equal; same; like, similar.
ugualmènte *ad* equally.
uh! *interj* ah!
úlcera *nf* ulcer.
ulíva *etc* *v* **olíva** *etc*.
ulterióre *a* further; ulterior.
ultimamènte *ad* lately; recently.
ultimàre *vt* to complete, finish.
ultimátum *nm* ultimatum.
último *a* last, latest; utmost; lowest; ultimate.
últra *prefix* ultra, extremely; **non plus últra** *nm* height, acme.
ultrasònico *pl* **-ici** *a* ultrasonic.
ultraviolétto *a* ultra-violet.
ululàre *vi* to howl.
ululàto, úlulo *nm* howl, howling.
umanamènte *ad* humanly, humane-ly.

umanésimo *nm* humanism.
umanista *nm* humanist.
umanità *nf* humanity; mankind.
umanitàrio *a* humanitarian.
umàno *a* human; humane.
Umbèrto *nm* *pr* Humbert.
umidità *nf* dampness, moisture.
úmido *a* damp, moist; *nm* dampness; stew.
úmile *a* humble; modest.
umiliànte *a* humiliating.
umiliàre *vt* to humble; humiliate; mortify; **-rsi** *vr* to abase oneself, humble oneself.
umiliazióne *nf* humiliation, mortification.
umilmènte *ad* humbly; modestly.
umiltà *nf* humility; humbleness.
umóre *nm* humour; mood; **di buòn u.** in a good humour.
umorismo *nm* humour.
umorista *nm* humorist.
umorístico *pl* **-ici** *a* humorous, funny.
un *v* **úno**.
unànime *a* unanimous.
unanimità *nf* unanimity.
uncinétto *nm* crochet hook.
uncíno *nm* hook.
úndici *a* eleven; **undicènne** eleven-year-old; **undicèsimo** eleventh.
úngere *vt* to grease; smear; anoint.
ungherése *a* *nmf* Hungarian.
Ungheria *nf* (geogr) Hungary.
únghia *nf* nail; claw; hoof.
unguènto *nm* ointment.
único *pl* **-ici** *a* only, single, sole; unique.
unificàre *vt* to unify.
unificazióne *nf* unification.
uniformàre *vt* to conform; make uniform; **-rsi (a)** *vr* to comply (with), conform (to).
unifórme *a* *nf* uniform.
uniformità *nf* uniformity.
unigènito *a* only-begotten.
unióne *nf* union, harmony.
uníre *vt* to unite, join; enclose.
unísono *nm* unison; harmony.
unità *nf* unity; unit.
uníto *a* united; **tínta uníta** plain colour.
universàle *a* universal; **giudízio u.** the Last Judgment.
universalità *nf* universality.
università *nf* university.
universitàrio *a* (of a) university; *nm* university student.
univèrso *nm* universe.
úno *indef* *art* a(n), one; *a* one; *indef* *pron* one, someone; **l'úno e l'àltro** both.
únto *nm* grease; fat; *a* greasy.
untuóso *a* greasy, oily; unctuous.
unzióne *nf* unction.
uòmo *nm* man.
uòpo *nm* necessity, need; **èssere d'u.** *impers* to be necessary; **fàre all'u.** to meet the case.
uòvo *pl* *f* **uòva** *nm* egg.

uragàno nm hurricane.
Uràli (gli) nm pl (the) Urals.
uràngo pl **-ghi** nm orang-outang.
urànio nm uranium.
urbanìstica nf town planning.
urbanità nf civility; courtesy; urbanity.
urbanizzàre vt to urbanize.
urbàno a urban; urbane; civil, courteous.
Úrbe (l') nf the 'city', Rome.
urgènte a urgent, pressing.
urgènza nf urgency.
úrgere vi to be urgent, be pressing.
urìna v **orìna**.
urlàre vt to shout, howl, shriek.
úrlo pl **úrli** or f (of humans) **úrla** nm cry; shout; howl, shriek.
úrna nf urn; ballot-box; **andàre àlle úrne** to go to the polls.
urtànte a irritating, annoying.
urtàre vti to knock against; (fig) annoy; hit.
urticària nf nettle-rash, urticaria.
úrto nm collision; push, shove; **èssere in u.** to be at variance, be on bad terms.
usànza nf usage; custom.
usàre vt to use, make use of; vi to be accustomed; be fashionable.
usàto a second-hand; usual; in use.
uscière nm usher.
úscio nm door.
uscíre vi to go (come) out; go off; get out; retire.
uscíta nf going (coming) out; exit; outlet; witty remark; **vía di u.** escape.
usign(u)òlo nm nightingale.
úso a used; accustomed; nm usage; custom.
ússaro,ússero nm hussar.
ustionàre vt to burn, scorch.
ustióne nf burn.
usuàle a usual.
usualménte ad usually.
usufruíre vi to benefit by; take advantage of.
usufrútto nm usufruct.
usúra nf usury.
usuràio nm usurer.
usurpàre vt to usurp.
usurpazióne nf usurpation.
utensíle nm implement, tool, utensil.
utènte nm user; consumer.
útero nm uterus, womb.
útile a useful; nm profit; interest.
utilità nf utility, usefulness, benefit.
utilitària nf (aut) baby car.
utilitàrio a utilitarian.
utilitarìsmo nm utilitarianism.
utilizzàbile a utilizable, that can be made use of.
utilizzàre vt to make use of, utilize.
utilizzazióne nf utilization, use.
utilménte ad usefully.
utopìa nf utopia; chimerical project.
úva nf grapes pl; **u. spína** gooseberry.
úzzolo nm whim, fancy.

V

vacànte a vacant.
vacànza nf holiday, vacation; vacancy; **v. scolàstica** school holidays, (US) recess.
vàcca nf cow.
vaccàro nm cowherd.
vaccinàre vt to vaccinate.
vaccinazióne nf vaccination.
vaccíno nm vaccine.
vacillaménto nm staggering, wobbling; unsteadiness; (fig) hesitation.
vacillànte a tottering, unsteady; wavering, irresolute.
vacillàre vi to totter; be irresolute.
vàcuo a empty; vacuous; vain.
vagabondàggio nm vagabondage, vagrancy; wandering.
vagabondàre vi to roam, rove, wander.
vagabóndo a wandering; nm vagabond; wanderer.
vagaménte ad vaguely; prettily.
vagànte a wandering, roving.
vagàre vi to wander, ramble.
vagheggiàre vt to cherish; long for; look lovingly at; **-rsi** vr to look at oneself complacently.
vagheggíno nm dandy, beau.
vaghézza nf beauty; longing; delight; vagueness.
vagíre vi to wail, whimper.
vagíto nm wail(ing); whimper(ing).
vàglia nf ability; merit; worth; **v. postàle** nm postal order.
vagliàre vt to sift; (fig) weigh.
vàglio nm sieve.
vàgo pl **-ghi** a vague; pretty.
vagóne nm (rly) coach, truck, wagon, (US) car; **v. mèrci** goods van, goods wagon, (US) freight car.
vainíglia v **vanìglia**.
vaiòlo nm smallpox.
valànga nf avalanche.
valdése a nmf Waldensian.
valènte a skilful, clever; valiant.
valentìa nf skill, ability, worth.
Valentíno nm pr Valentine.
valentuòmo pl **-uòmini** nm worthy man.
Valènza nf (geogr) Valencia.
valére vi to be worth; be valid; **v. la péna** to be worth while; **vàle a díre** that is to say; **-rsi** vr to avail oneself, make use.
Valèria nf pr Valerie.
valetudinàrio a nm valetudinarian.
valévole a valid; efficacious.
valicàre vt to cross, pass.
vàlico pl **-ichi** nm crossing; passage; pass.
validità nf validity.
vàlido a valid, efficacious.
valigería nf leather-goods shop; trunk manufactory.
valigia pl **-ie** nf suitcase.
valigiàio nm trunk-maker; leatherware merchant.

vallàta, vàlle nf valley.

vallétto nm valet.

valligiàno nm dalesman, inhabitant of a valley.

valóre nm value, worth; valour.

valorizzàre vt to employ to advantage, turn to account.

valorosaménte ad bravely.

valoróso a brave, valiant.

valsènte nm value, price.

valúta nf value; money.

valutàre vt to value, appraise.

valutazióne nf estimation, valuation.

vàlva nf valve.

vàlvola nf (el) fuse; valve.

vàlzer nm waltz.

vàmpa nf flame; flush.

vampàta nf blaze; blast; flush.

vampíro nm vampire.

vanaglòria nf vainglory, conceit.

vanaglorióso a vainglorious, conceited.

vanaménte ad in vain, vainly.

vandalísmo nm vandalism.

vàndalo nm vandal.

vaneggiàre vi to be delirious, rave.

vànga nf spade.

vangàre vt to dig.

vangèlo nm Gospel.

vaníglia nf vanilla.

vanità nf vanity.

vanitóso a vain, conceited.

vàno a vain, useless; nm space, room.

vantàggio nm advantage; profit; odds.

vantaggiosaménte ad advantageously, to good profit.

vantaggióso a advantageous, profitable.

vantàre vt to boast of; -rsi vr to be proud, boast.

vantería nf boast(ing), brag(ging).

vànto nm boast.

vànvera, a ad at random, nonsensically.

vapóre nm vapour, steam; fume; bastiménto a v. steamer; màcchina a v. steam-engine.

vaporétto nm steamboat.

vaporizzatóre nm vaporizer, atomizer.

vaporóso a airy, filmy, vaporous.

varàre vt to launch.

varcàre vt to cross, pass.

vàrco pl -chi nm passage, way; aspettàre al v. to lie in wait for.

varechína nf chlorine; àcqua di v. bleach.

variàbile a variable, changeable; unsettled.

variaménte ad variously.

variànte a varying; nf variant.

variàre vti to vary, change.

variazióne nf variation, change.

varicèlla nf chicken-pox.

varicóso a varicose.

variegàto a variegated.

varietà nf variety, (theat US) vaudeville.

vàrio a varied, various.

variopínto a many-coloured.

vàro nm launch(ing).

Varsàvia nf (geogr) Warsaw.

vàsca nf basin; tub; bath; pond.

vascèllo nm vessel, ship.

vascolàre a vascular.

vaselína nf vaseline.

vasellàme nm crockery, china.

vàso nm vase; pot; vessel; v. da nòtte chamber(-pot).

vassàllo a nm vassal, subject.

vassóio nm tray.

vastità nf vastness; expanse, extent.

vàsto a vast, wide.

vàte nm (poet) bard, poet; prophet.

Vaticàno nm Vatican.

vaticínio nm prophecy.

vecchiàia, vecchiézza nf old age.

vècchio a old.

véccia nf tare, vetch.

véce nf stead, place; in mía v. in my stead; in v. di instead of; fàre le véci di to act as.

vedére vt to see; fàrsi v. to appear, show oneself.

vedétta nf look-out, sentinel.

védova nf widow; **védovo** nm widower.

vedovànza nf widowhood.

vedovíle a widower's, widow's.

vedúta nf sight, view.

veemènte a vehement.

veemènza nf vehemence.

vegetàle a nm vegetable.

vegetàre vi to vegetate.

vegetariàno a nm vegetarian.

vegetazióne nf vegetation.

vègeto a strong, thriving, vigorous.

veggènte a seeing; nmf seer, prophet, prophetess.

véglia nf waking; watch; wake.

vegliàrdo nm old man.

vegliàre vi to be awake; watch over; watch by.

veglióne nm masked ball.

veícolo nm vehicle.

véla nf sail; a gónfie véle very well.

velàre vt to veil; cloud; conceal.

velataménte ad covertly, by allusions.

velàto a veiled; (fig) covert; (of voice) husky.

veleggiàre vti to sail.

veléno nm poison, venom.

velenóso a poisonous.

velièro nm sailing-boat.

velína, nf flimsy; càrta v. tissue-paper.

velívolo nm aeroplane.

velleità nf foolish ambition, foolish idea.

vèllo nm fleece.

vellutàto a velvety, velvet-like.

vellúto nm velvet.

vélo nm veil.

velóce a swift, quick, rapid.

veloceménte ad swiftly, quickly, fast.

velocità nf speed, velocity.

velòdromo nm cycle-racing track.

véltro nm greyhound.
véna nf vein; **èssere in v.** to be in form; be in the mood.
venàle a venal; market(able).
venatúra nf vein; (of wood) grain.
vendémmia nf grape-gathering; vintage.
vendemmiàre vi to gather grapes.
vendemmiatóre nm **-trice** nf vine-harvester.
véndere vt to sell.
vendétta nf revenge, vengeance.
vendicàre vt to avenge, revenge.
vendicatívo a revengeful, vindictive.
véndita nf sale.
venditóre nm **-trice** nf seller, vendor; **v. ambulànte** hawker, pedlar.
veneràbile a venerable.
veneràre vt to worship; venerate.
venerazióne nf veneration; worship.
venerdì nm Friday; **gli mànca un v.** he has a screw loose.
venèreo a venereal.
Vèneto nm (geogr) Venetia; a of Venetia.
Venèzia nf (geogr) Venice; **veneziàno** a nm Venetian.
veniàle a venial.
venire vi to come; **v. méno** to faint.
ventàglio nm fan.
ventàta nf gust of wind.
vénti a twenty; **ventènne** twenty-year-old; **ventènnio** nm period of twenty years; **ventèsimo** twentieth; **ventína** nf a score.
ventilàre vt to ventilate.
ventilatóre nm ventilator; (aut) fan.
ventilazióne nf ventilation.
vènto nm wind.
ventósa nf sucker.
ventóso a windy.
vèntre nm abdomen, belly.
ventúra nf chance, luck.
ventúro a next, coming, future.
venúta nf arrival, coming.
veràce a truthful; true.
veracità nf veracity.
veraménte ad really, truly, indeed.
verànda nf veranda(h), (US) porch.
verbàle a verbal; nm minutes pl.
verbalménte ad verbally, orally.
verbèna nf vervain, verbena.
vèrbo nm verb; word.
verbosità nf verbosity, prolixity.
verbóso a verbose, prolix.
verdàstro a greenish.
vérde a nm green; **èssere al v.** to be penniless.
verdeggiànte a verdant.
verdeggiàre vi to be (grow) green.
verdétto nm verdict.
verdúra nf vegetables pl; verdure.
verecóndia nf modesty, bashfulness.
verecóndo a modest, bashful.
vérga nf rod; **v. pastoràle** (eccl) crozier.
verginàle a maidenly, virgin.
vérgine nf virgin.

verginità nf virginity.
vergógna nf shame; shyness.
vergognàrsi vr to be ashamed; be shy.
vergognóso a shameful; shy; ashamed.
verífica nf check; verification; (com) audit.
verificàre vt to check; verify; (com) audit; **-rsi** vr to come to pass; come true.
verisimile etc v **verosimile**.
verismo nm realism.
verità nf truth.
veritièro a truthful.
vèrme nm worm.
vermíglio a vermilion.
vèrmut nm vermouth.
vernàcolo a nm vernacular.
vernice nf paint, varnish; (fig) smattering; patent leather; **úna màno di v.** a coat of paint.
verniciàre vt to paint, varnish; polish.
verniciatúra nf painting, varnishing; polishing.
véro a true nm truth; **dàl v.** from life, from nature.
verosimiglìanza nf likelihood; verisimilitude.
verosimile a likely, probable.
verrúca nf wart.
versaménto nm pouring; spilling; payment.
versànte nm side; slope; (com) depositor; payer.
versàre vt to pour; spill; shed; pay; vi to be, live.
versàtile a versatile.
versàto a poured out; spilt; shed; versed; paid.
verseggiàre vti to versify.
versióne nf version; translation.
vèrso nm line; verse; sound; note; way; **non c'è v.** it is impossible; prep towards.
vertènte a regarding.
vertènza nf dispute.
vèrtere vi to be about, concern, regard.
verticàle a vertical.
vèrtice nm vertex; top; height.
vertígine pl **-ini** nf dizziness, giddiness.
vertiginóso a dizzy.
vescíca nf bladder; blister.
vescovàdo nm bishopric; bishop's palace.
vescovíle a episcopal, of a bishop.
véscovo nm bishop.
vèspa nf wasp; (motor-scooter) 'Vespa'.
vespàio nm wasp's nest; (fig) hornet's nest.
vespasiàno nm (public) urinal.
vèspro nm evening; evensong; vespers.
vessàre vt to vex; oppress.
vessazióne nf vexation.
vessíllo nm flag, standard.

vestàglia nf dressing-gown, (US) bathrobe.

vestàle nf vestal.

vèste nf dress; guise; (fig) capacity; **vèsti** pl clothes pl.

vestiàrio nm clothes pl, clothing.

vestìbolo nm hall, vestibule.

vestìgio pl f -**gia** f footprint, track, vestige, trace.

vestìre vt to dress, clothe; -**rsi** vr to dress.

vestìto nm dress; suit.

veteràno a veteran; nm (mil) ex-serviceman, (US) veteran.

veterinària nf veterinary science.

veterinàrio a veterinary; nm veterinary surgeon.

vèto nm veto.

vetràio nm glass-blower; glazier.

vetràta nf glass door; (stained-)glass window.

vetrerìa nf glass manufactory; glassware.

vetrìna nf shop-window; glass case, showcase.

vetrìòlo nm vitriol.

vétro nm glass; window-pane.

vétta nm summit, top.

vettovàglie nf pl provisions pl, victuals pl.

vettùra nf car; cab; carriage; coach; (rly) v. **ristorànte** restaurant car, (US) diner (dining-car).

vetturìno nm driver, cabby.

vetùsto a ancient, old.

vezzeggiàre vt to fondle.

vézzo nm (bad) habit; charm; necklace.

vezzóso a charming; pretty.

vi pron acc and dat you, to you; ad there.

vìa nf street; road; way; **v. di mézzo** compromise.

viabilità nf condition of a road.

viadòtto nm viaduct.

viaggiàre vt to travel, journey.

viaggiatóre nm -**trice** nf traveller; passenger.

viàggio nm journey; tour; voyage; **viàggi** pl travels pl.

viàle nm avenue.

viandànte nm passer-by; traveller.

viavài nm coming and going.

vibràre vti to vibrate; strike; quiver.

vibrazióne nf vibration; quivering.

vicàrio nm vicar.

vìce prefix vice-, assistant, deputy.

vicènda nf event; vicissitude; **a v.** in turn; reciprocally.

vicendévole a mutual; reciprocal.

vicendevolménte ad mutually, each other, one another.

vichìngo pl -**ghi** nm Viking.

vicinànza nf closeness, nearness; neighbourhood, vicinity.

vicinàto nm neighbourhood; neighbours pl.

vicìno a near, neighbouring; nm neighbour; ad close by, near; **v. a** prep beside, close to, near.

vicissitùdine nf vicissitude.

vìcolo nm alley, lane.

vìdeo inv nm (tv) video.

vidimàre vt to authenticate; visa.

vidimazióne nf authentication; visa.

viennése a nmf Viennese.

vieppiù ad more (and more).

vietàre vt to forbid, prohibit.

vigènte a in force.

vìgere vi to be in force.

vigilànte a vigilant, watchful.

vigilànza nf vigilance, watchfulness; look-out.

vigilàre vt to watch over, to keep an eye on; vi to be on one's guard; keep watch.

vìgile a watchful, vigilant; nm policeman.

vigìlia nf eve; vigil.

vigliaccherìa nf cowardice, cowardly action.

vigliàcco pl -**àcchi** a cowardly; nm coward.

vìgna nf **vignéto** nm vineyard.

vignétta nf vignette; cartoon.

vigóre nm vigour; strength; force.

vigorìa nf vigour; strength.

vigoróso a vigorous; strong.

vìle a cowardly; vile; nm coward.

vilipèndere vt to despise, scorn.

vìlla nf villa, country house.

villàggio nm village.

villanìa nf rudeness, abuse.

villàno a rude, uncivil; nm boor, ill-bred fellow; peasant.

villeggiànte nmf holidaymaker, (US) vacationer.

villeggiàre vi to spend one's summer holidays.

villeggiatùra nf holiday (in the country); **luògo di v.** holiday resort.

villeréccio a rustic, rural.

villìno nm small villa.

vilménte ad cowardly; meanly.

viltà nf cowardice; meanness.

vìmine nm osier, withy; **di vìmini** wicker.

vinàio nm wine merchant.

Vincènzo nm pr Vincent.

vìncere vt to win; defeat, overcome, vanquish; -**rsi** vr to master oneself.

vìncita nf winning(s).

vincitóre nm -**trice** nf winner, conqueror.

vincolàre vt to bind; (com) tie up.

vìncolo nm bond, tie.

vinìcolo a wine.

vinìle nm (chem) vinyl.

vìno nm wine.

vìòla nf (mus) viola, viol; (bot) viola; **v. del pensièro** pansy; a nm (colour) violet.

violacciòcca nf wallflower.

violàre vt to violate.

violazióne nf violation.

violentàre vt to rape; violate.

violènto a violent.

violènza nf violence.

violétta nf violet.

violinìsta nmf violinist.

violíno *nm* violin, fiddle.
violoncèllo *nm* violoncello.
viòttola *nf* -olo *nm* lane.
vípera *nf* viper.
viràre *vi* (*naut*) to tack, turn.
viràta *nf* tacking, turn.
Virgílio *nm pr* Virgil.
vírgola *nf* comma; púnto e vírgola semi-colon; virgolétte *nf pl* inverted commas.
viríle *a* manly, virile.
virilità *nf* manliness, virility; manhood.
virtù *nf* virtue.
virtualménte *ad* virtually.
virtuosísmo *nm* virtuousness; virtuosity.
virtuóso *a* virtuous; virtuoso.
virulènto *a* virulent.
víscere *nm* (*anat*) vital organ; visceri *m pl* viscera *pl*; víscere *f pl* bowels (*fig*).
víschio *nm* mistletoe; bird-lime.
vischióso *a* viscous; slimy.
víscido *a* sticky; slippery.
viscónte *nm* viscount.
visíbile *a* visible.
visíbílio *nm* a lot; andàre in v. to go into raptures.
visibilità *nf* visibility.
visibilménte *ad* visibly; clearly.
visièra *nf* visor; (of cap) peak.
visionàrio *a nm* visionary.
visióne *nf* vision; préndere in v. to examine.
vísita *nf* visit; v. mèdica medical examination.
visitàre *vt* to visit; to call on; (*med*) examine.
visitatóre *nm* -tríce *nf* visitor.
vísivo *a* visual.
víso *nm* face; a v. apèrto frankly, openly.
visóne *nm* mink.
víspo *a* brisk, lively.
vísta *nf* sight; outlook, view; conóscere di v. to know by sight; fàr v. di to pretend.
vistàre *vt* to visa.
vísto *a* seen; *nm* visa; méttere il v. to visa.
vistóso *a* gaudy, showy; large.
visuàle *a* visual; *nf* sight; view.
víta *nf* life; living; waist.
vitàlba *nf* traveller's joy, clematis.
vitàle *a* vital.
vitalità *nf* vitality.
vitalízio *a* lasting for life; *nm* life annuity.
vitamína *nf* vitamin(e).
vitamínico *pl* -ici *a* vitaminic.
víte *nf* vine; (*tec*) screw.
vitèllo *nm* calf; càrne di v. veal.
vitellóne *nm* bullock; (*fig*) representative of contemporary jeunesse dorée.
víttima *nf* victim.
vítto *nm* food; board; living.
vittòria *nf* victory.
Vittòrio *nm pr* Victor.

vittorióso *a* victorious.
vituperàre *vt* to vituperate.
vitupèrio *nm* insult, shame, disgrace.
viùzza *nf* narrow street, lane.
viva *interj* hurrah, hurray.
vivàce *a* lively, (US) live; bright; quick.
vivacità *nf* vivacity; quickness; brightness.
vivàio *nm* (of fish or plants) nursery.
vivaménte *ad* deeply, warmly.
vivànda *nf* food; dish.
vivènte *a* living.
vivere *vti* to live; *nm* life, living; v. àlla giornàta to live from hand to mouth.
víveri *nm pl* provisions *pl*, supplies *pl*, victuals *pl*.
vivèzza *nf* liveliness; brightness; vividness.
vívido *a* vivid.
vivificàre *vt* to enliven; give life to.
vivisezióne *nf* vivisection.
vívo *a* living; alive; lively; bright; deep; a viva vóce orally; toccàre nel v. to pierce to the quick.
viziàre *vt* to spoil, vitiate.
viziàto *a* spoilt, vitiated.
vízio *nm* vice; bad habit; defect.
vizióso *a* vicious, depraved.
vízzo *a* withered.
vocabolàrio *nm* vocabulary; dictionary.
vocàbolo *nm* word; term.
vocàle *a* vocal; *nf* vowel.
vocazióne *nf* calling, vocation.
vóce *nf* voice; rumour; a v. orally; ad àlta v. loudly.
vociferàre *vi* to shout; vociferate; rumour.
vociferazióne *nf* shouting; vociferation.
vóga *nf* fashion, vogue; energy; in v. fashionable.
vogàre *vi* to row.
vòglia *nf* desire, wish; will; birthmark.
vói *pron 2nd pers pl nom and oblique* you.
volàno *nm* badminton; shuttlecock; flywheel.
volànte *a* flying; *nm* (*aut*) steering-wheel; *nf* (*police*) flying-squad.
volantíno *nm* leaflet.
volàre *vi* to fly.
volàta *nf* flight; rush.
volàtile *a* winged; volatile.
volenteróso *v.* volonteróso.
volentièri *ad* willingly; màl v. unwillingly.
volére *vti* to will; want; wish; like; take, require; *nm* wish; will.
volgàre *a* vulgar; *nm* vernacular.
volgarità *nf* vulgarity.
vòlgere *vti* -rsi *vr* to turn.
vólgo *pl* -ghi *nm* common herd; populace.
volitívo *a* strong-willed.
vólo *nm* flight; a v. immediately.
volontà *nf* will.

volontário *a* voluntary; *nm* volunteer.
volonteróso *a* willing.
vólpe *nf* fox.
volpíno *a* foxy; crafty; *nm* Pomeranian dog.
vòlta *nf* time; turn; **úna v.** once; **dúe vòlte** twice; (*arch*) vault.
voltàggio *nm* (*el*) voltage.
voltàre *vti* **-rsi** *vr* to turn.
voltàta *nf* turn(ing), bend.
volteggiàre *vi* to fly about, whirl; vault.
vòlto *nm* face, countenance; *a* turned.
volúbile *a* fickle, inconstant.
volúme *nm* volume, quantity.
voluminóso *a* voluminous, bulky.
volutaménte *ad* intentionally, deliberately.
voluttà *nf* delight, pleasure; voluptuousness.
voluttuóso *a* voluptuous.
vómere *nm* ploughshare.
vomitàre *vt* to vomit.
vòmito *nm* vomiting.
vóngola *nf* clam.
voràce *a* voracious, greedy.
voracità *nf* voracity, greed(iness).
voràgine *nf* gulf, abyss.
vòrtice *nm* vortex; whirl(pool).
vorticóso *a* whirling, swirling.
vòstro *poss a* your; *poss pron* yours.
votànte *a* voting; *nm* voter.
votàre *vi* to vote; *vt* to approve; consecrate; offer; **-rsi** *vr* to devote oneself.
votazióne *nf* voting.
votívo *a* votive.
vóto *nm* vow; votive offering; prayer; (*school*) mark; vote.
vulcànico *pl* **-ici** *a* volcanic.
vulcanizzàre *vt* to vulcanize.
vulcàno *nm* volcano.
vulneràbile *a* vulnerable.
vuotàre *vt* to empty.
vuòto *a* empty; vacant; *nm* empty space; vacuum; void; **andàre a v.** to fail.

Z

zafferàno *nm* saffron.
zàffiro *nm* sapphire.
zàino *nm* knapsack, pack.
zàmpa *nf* paw.
zampillànte *a* gushing.
zampillàre *vi* to spurt; spring.
zampíllo *nm* spurt, jet.
zampíno *nm* little paw; (*fig*) finger.
zampógna *nf* bagpipes *pl*; reedpipe.
zampognàro *nm* piper.
zàna *nf* basket; cradle.
zàngola *nf* churn.
zànna *nf* fang; tusk.
zanzàra *nf* mosquito.
zanzarièra *nf* mosquito net.
zàppa *nf* hoe.
zappàre *vt* to dig; hoe.
zappatóre *nm* hoer; (*mil*) pioneer.
zar *nm* czar, tzar.

zàttera *nf* (*naut*) lighter; raft.
zavòrra *nf* ballast.
zàzzera *nf* shock of hair; mane.
zèbra *nf* zebra.
zécca *nf* mint; **nuòvo di z.** brand-new.
zecchíno *nm* sequin.
zèffiro *nm* zephyr.
Zelànda *nf* (*geogr*) Zealand; **Nuòva Z.** New Zealand.
zelànte *a* zealous.
zèlo *nm* zeal.
zènit *nm* zenith.
zènzero *nm* ginger; **pàn di z.** gingerbread.
zéppo *a* full; **piéno z.** crowded, packed.
zerbíno *nm* doormat; dandy.
zerbinòtto *nm* beau, dandy.
zèro *nm* zero, nought.
zia *nf* aunt.
zibaldóne *nm* miscellany, medley.
zibellíno *nm* sable.
zígomo *nm* cheek-bone.
zigzagàre *vi* to zigzag.
zimbèllo *nm* decoy(-bird); laughing-stock.
zincàto *a* zinc plated.
zínco *pl* **-chi** *nm* zinc.
zíngaro *nm* gypsy.
zío *nm* uncle.
zitèlla *nf* spinster; old maid.
zittíre *vti* to hiss.
zitto *a* silent; **stàre z.** to keep quiet.
zizzània *nf* darnel; **seminàre z.** to sow dissension.
zoccolàio *nm* clog-maker.
zòccolo *nm* clog, wooden shoe; hoof; skirting-board.
zodíaco *pl* **-chi** *nm* zodiac.
zolfanèllo *nm* (sulphur) match.
zólfo *nm* sulphur.
zòlla *nf* clod; lump; **zollétta di** zúcchero lump of sugar.
zóna *nf* zone, area.
zónzo, a *ad* idling; strolling.
zoología *nf* zoology.
zoològico *pl* **-ici** *a* zoological.
zoppicànte *a* limping, lame.
zoppicàre *vi* to limp.
zòppo *a* lame, limping.
zòtico *pl* **-ici** *a* boorish; rough; *nm* boor, uncouth fellow.
zúcca *nf* pumpkin; (*US*) squash; (*fig*) pate.
zuccheràre *vt* to sugar; sweeten (*also fig*).
zuccherièra *nf* sugar-basin.
zuccherifício *nm* sugar-refinery.
zúcchero *nm* sugar.
zucchíno *nm* courgette, (*US*) Italian squash.
zúffa *nf* brawl, scuffle.
zufolàre *vi* to whistle.
zúfolo *nm* whistle.
zulú *nm* Zulu.
zúppa *nf* soup; **z. inglése** trifle.
zuppièra *nf* (soup) tureen.
zúppo *a* drenched, soaked.
Zurigo *nf* (*geogr*) Zurich.

English-Italian

A

a [ə] *indef art* un(o), una.
aback [ə'bæk] *ad* all'indietro; **taken a.** sconcertato.
abandon [ə'bændən] *n* abbandono, trasporto; *vt* abbandonare.
abandonment [ə'bændənmənt] *n* abbandono.
abase [ə'beis] *vt* abbassare, umiliare.
abasement [ə'beismənt] *n* umiliazione.
abash [ə'bæʃ] *vt* confondere.
abate [ə'beit] *vt* diminuire, abbassare; *vi* calmarsi, indebolirsi.
abatement [ə'beitmənt] *n* diminuzione, riduzione.
abbé ['æbei] *n* abate.
abbess ['æbis] *n* badessa.
abbey ['æbi] *n* badia.
abbot ['æbət] *n* abate.
abbreviate [ə'briːvieit] *vt* abbreviare.
abbreviation [ə,briːvi'eiʃən] *n* abbreviazione.
abc ['eibiːˈsiː] *n* abbiccì.
abdicate ['æbdikeit] *vti* abdicare.
abdomen ['æbdəmen] *n* addome.
abdominal [æb'dɔminl] *a* addominale.
abduct [æb'dʌkt] *vt* rapire.
abduction [æb'dʌkʃən] *n* ratto.
Abel ['eibəl] *nm pr* Abele.
aberration [,æbə'reiʃən] *n* aberrazione.
abet [ə'bet] *vt* favoreggiare, incitare.
abeyance [ə'beiəns] *n* sospensione.
abhor [əb'hɔː] *vt* aborrire, detestare.
abhorrence [əb'hɔrəns] *n* odio, ripugnanza.
abhorrent [əb'hɔrənt] *a* ripugnante, contrario a.
abide [ə'baid] *vti* sopportare; **a. by** conformarsi a; tener fede a, attenersi a.
ability [ə'biliti] *n* abilità, talento.
abject ['æbdʒekt] *a* abietto, reietto, vile.
abjuration [,æbdʒuə'reiʃən] *n* abiura.
abjure [əb'dʒuə] *vt* abiurare, ripudiare.
ablative ['æblətiv] *a n* ablativo.
ablaze [ə'bleiz] *a* in fiamme; risplendente.
able ['eibl] *a* abile, capace, in grado di.
ablution [ə'bluːʃən] *n* abluzione.
abnegation [,æbni'geiʃən] *n* abnegazione, rinunzia.
abnormal [æb'nɔːməl] *a* anormale.
abnormality [,æbnɔː'mæliti] *n* anormalità; anomalia.

aboard [ə'bɔːd] *ad prep* (*naut*) a bordo.
abode [ə'boud] *n* dimora, domicilio.
abolish [ə'bɔliʃ] *vt* abolire.
abolition [,æbə'liʃən] *n* abolizione.
abominable [ə'bɔminəbl] *a* abominevole.
abomination [ə,bɔmi'neiʃən] *n* abominazione, disgusto.
aboriginal [,æbə'ridʒənl] *a n* aborigeno, indigeno.
abortion [ə'bɔːʃən] *n* aborto.
abortive [ə'bɔːtiv] *a* abortivo, prematuro; (*fig*) fallito.
abound [ə'baund] *vi* abbondare.
abounding [ə'baundiŋ] *a* abbondante, ricco.
about [ə'baut] *prep* circa, intorno a, per; *ad* intorno, presso, qua e là; **to be about** to stare per.
above [ə'bʌv] *ad prep* in alto, al di sopra di; più (alto) che, lassù, più in alto, sopra.
Abraham ['eibrəhæm] *nm pr* Abramo.
abrasion [ə'breiʒən] *n* abrasione, scalfittura.
abreast [ə'brest] *ad* di fianco.
abridge [ə'bridʒ] *vt* abbreviare, ridurre.
abridg(e)ment [ə'bridʒmənt] *n* abbreviazione, compendio.
abroad [ə'brɔːd] *ad* all'estero, fuori.
abrogate ['æbrougeit] *vt* abrogare.
abrogation [,æbrou'geiʃən] *n* abrogazione.
abrupt [ə'brʌpt] *a* brusco, improvviso; ripido.
abscess ['æbsis] *n* ascesso.
abscond [æb'skɔnd] *vi* rendersi latitante, fuggire.
absence ['æbsəns] *n* assenza, mancanza; **a. of mind** distrazione.
absent ['æbsənt] *a* assente; *vr* [əb'sent] **to absent oneself** assentarsi.
absentee [,æbsən'tiː] *n* persona abitualmente assente dal suo domicilio o dal lavoro, scuola, etc.
absently ['æbsəntli] *ad* distrattamente.
absinthe ['æbsinθ] *n* assenzio.
absolute ['æbsəluːt] *a* assoluto, completo; puro.
absolutely ['æbsəluːtli] *ad* assolutamente.
absoluteness ['æbsəluːtnis] *n* assolutezza.
absolution [,æbsə'luːʃən] *n* assoluzione.

absolutism ['æbsəluːtizəm] *n* assolutismo.

absolve [əb'zɔlv] *vt* assolvere.

absorb [əb'sɔːb] *vt* assorbire.

absorbed [əb'sɔːbd] *a* assorbito, assorto.

absorbent [əb'sɔːbənt] *a n* assorbente; **a. cotton** (*US*) cotone idrofilo.

absorbing [əb'sɔːbiŋ] *a* assorbente, interessante.

absorption [əb'sɔːpʃən] *n* assorbimento.

abstain [əb'stein] *vi* astenersi.

abstemious [æb'stiːmiəs] *a* astemio, frugale, moderato.

abstension [æb'stenʃən] *n* astensione.

abstinence ['æbstinəns] *n* astinenza.

abstinent ['æbstinənt] *a* astinente, sobrio.

abstract ['æbstrækt] *a* astratto; *n* astrazione, astratto; *vt* [æb'strækt] astrarre; sottrarre.

abstraction [æb'strækʃən] *n* astrazione; distrazione; sottrazione.

abstruse [æb'struːs] *a* astruso.

absurd [əb'səːd] *a* assurdo, ridicolo.

absurdity [əb'səːditi] *n* assurdità.

absurdly [əb'səːdli] *ad* assurdamente.

abundance [ə'bʌndəns] *n* abbondanza.

abundant [ə'bʌndənt] *a* abbondante.

abuse [ə'bjuːs] *n* abuso, cattivo uso; insulto; *vt* [ə'bjuːz] abusare di, far cattivo uso; insultare.

abusive [ə'bjuːsiv] *a* abusivo; ingiurioso.

abysmal [ə'bizməl] *a* abissale.

abyss [ə'bis] *n* abisso.

Abyssinia [ˌæbi'siniə] *n* Abissinia.

Abyssinian [æbi'siniən] *a n* abissino.

acacia [ə'keiʃə] *n* acacia.

academic [ˌækə'demik] *a n* accademico.

academician [əˌkædə'miʃən] *n* accademico.

academy [ə'kædəmi] *n* accademia.

accede [æk'siːd] *vi* accedere; aderire.

accelerate [æk'seləreit] *vti* accelerare.

acceleration [ækˌselə'reiʃən] *n* accelerazione.

accelerator [ək'seləreitə] *n* acceleratore.

accent ['æksənt] *n* accento, tono; **accent, accentuate** *vt* accentuare.

accentuation [ækˌsentju'eiʃən] *n* accentuazione.

accept [ək'sept] *vt* accettare, approvare.

acceptable [ək'septəbl] *a* accetto, gradevole.

acceptance [ək'septəns] *n* accettazione, accoglienza.

accepter, acceptor [ək'septə] *n* (*com*) accettante.

access ['ækses] *n* accesso.

accessible [æk'sesəbl] *a* accessibile.

accession [æk'seʃən] *n* accessione; aggiunta.

accessory [æk'sesəri] *a n* accessorio; complice.

accident ['æksidənt] *n* accidente, caso; incidente; **by a.** per caso; **a.-prone** soggetto agli incidenti.

accidental [ˌæksi'dentl] *a* casuale, fortuito; *n* (*mus*) accidente.

accidentally [ˌæksi'dentəli] *ad* accidentalmente, per caso.

acclaim [ə'kleim] *vt* acclamare.

acclamation [ˌæklə'meiʃən] *n* acclamazione.

acclimatization [əˌklaimətai'zeiʃən] *n* acclimatazione.

acclimatize [ə'klaimətaiz] *vt* acclimatare.

accommodate [ə'kɔmədeit] *vt* accomodare, comporre; alloggiare.

accommodating [ə'kɔmədeitiŋ] *a* accomodante; compiacente.

accommodation [əˌkɔmə'deiʃən] *n* accomodamento, adattamento; alloggio; sistemazione.

accompaniment [ə'kʌmpənimənt] *n* accompagnamento.

accompanist [ə'kʌmpənist] *n* accompagnatore, -trice.

accompany [ə'kʌmpəni] *vt* accompagnare.

accomplice [ə'kʌmplis] *n* complice.

accomplish [ə'kʌmpliʃ] *vt* compiere, completare, effettuare.

accomplishment [ə'kʌmpliʃmənt] *n* compimento, realizzazione; dote.

accord [ə'kɔːd] *n* accordo, consenso; *vti* accordare, concedere.

accordance [ə'kɔːdəns] *n* accordo, conformità.

according to [ə'kɔːdiŋtu] *prep* secondo.

accordingly [ə'kɔːdiŋli] *ad* in conseguenza, in conformità.

accordion [ə'kɔːdiən] *n* (*mus*) fisarmonica.

accost [ə'kɔst] *vt* rivolgere la parola a, abbordare.

account [ə'kaunt] *n* conto; acconto; importanza; relazione; **on a. of** a causa, (motivo) di; **on no a.** a nessun patto.

account [ə'kaunt] *vt* considerare, stimare; **a. for** spiegare la ragione di.

accountability [əˌkauntə'biliti] *n* responsabilità.

accountable [ə'kauntəbl] *a* responsabile.

accountant [ə'kauntənt] *n* contabile; **chartered a.** ragioniere.

accredit [ə'kredit] *vt* accreditare, fornire di credenziali.

accretion [æ'kriːʃən] *n* accrescimento.

accrue [ə'kruː] *vi* derivare, provenire; accumularsi.

accumulate [ə'kjuːmjuleit] *vt* accumulare, ammassare; *vi* accumularsi.

accumulation [əˌkjuːmjuˈleiʃən] *n* accumulazione, ammasso.

accumulative [əˈkjuːmjulətiv] *a* accumulativo.

accumulator [əˈkjuːmjuleitə] *n* accumulatore.

accuracy [ˈækjurəsi] *n* esattezza, precisione.

accurate [ˈækjurit] *a* esatto, preciso.

accursed [əˈkəːsid] *a* maledetto.

accusation [ˌækjuˈzeiʃən] *n* accusa.

accusative [əˈkjuːzətiv] *a n* accusativo.

accuse [əˈkjuːz] *vt* accusare.

accustom [əˈkʌstəm] *vt* abituare; **a. oneself** *vr* abituarsi.

ace [eis] *n* asso; **within an a.** lì per lì.

acerbity [əˈsəːbiti] *n* acerbità, asprezza.

acetate [ˈæsitit] *n* acetato.

acetone [ˈæsitoun] *n* acetone.

acetylene [əˈsetiliːn] *n* acetilene.

ache [eik] *n* dolore, male; *vi* dolere.

achieve [əˈtʃiːv] *vt* compiere, condurre a termine; raggiungere.

achievement [əˈtʃiːvmənt] *n* compimento; raggiungimento; successo.

aching [ˈeikiŋ] *a* dolorante.

acid [ˈæsid] *a n* acido.

acidify [əˈsidifai] *vt* acidificare.

acidity [əˈsiditi] *n* acidità.

acknowledge [əkˈnɔlidʒ] *vt* ammettere; riconoscere; accusare (ricezione di).

acknowledg(e)ment [əkˈnɔlidʒmənt] *n* ammissione; riconoscimento; l'accusare ricezione

acme [ˈækmi] *n* acme, culmine.

acne [ˈækni] *n* acne.

acolyte [ˈækəlait] *n* accolito.

acorn [ˈeikɔːn] *n* ghianda.

acoustic [əˈkuːstik] *a* acustico; **acoustics** *n pl* acustica.

acquaint [əˈkweint] *vt* informare, mettere al corrente.

acquaintance [əˈkweintəns] *n* conoscenza; conoscente.

acquiesce [ˌækwiˈes] *vi* accettare, acconsentire tacitamente.

acquiescence [ˌækwiˈesns] *n* acquiescenza.

acquiescent [ˌækwiˈesnt] *a* acquiescente, rassegnato.

acquire [əˈkwaiə] *vt* acquisire, acquistare.

acquisition [ˌækwiˈziʃən] *n* acquisizione; acquisto.

acquit [əˈkwit] *vt* assolvere; **a. oneself** *vr* comportarsi.

acquittal [əˈkwitl] *n* assoluzione.

acre [ˈeikə] *n* acro.

acrid [ˈækrid] *a* acre, aspro.

acrimonious [ˌækriˈmouniəs] *a* aspro, astioso.

acrimony [ˈækriməni] *n* acrimonia.

acrobat [ˈækrəbæt] *n* acrobata.

across [əˈkrɔs] *ad prep* attraverso, da un lato all'altro, dall'altra parte.

acrostic [əˈkrɔstik] *n* acrostico.

act [ækt] *n* atto; azione; *vti* agire,

fare, comportarsi; rappresentare, recitare.

acting [ˈæktiŋ] *a* facente; avente funzione di; *n* rappresentazione; modo di recitare.

action [ˈækʃən] *n* azione; combattimento; gesto; processo.

activate [ˈæktiveit] *vt* attivare; rendere radioattivo.

active [ˈæktiv] *a* attivo, energico.

actively [ˈæktivli] *ad* attivamente.

activity [ækˈtiviti] *n* attività, energia.

actor [ˈæktə] *n* attore; **actress** *n* attrice.

actual [ˈæktjuəl] *a* reale, effettivo.

actuality [ˌæktjuˈæliti] *n* realtà.

actually [ˈæktjuəli] *ad* realmente, effettivamente.

actuate [ˈæktjueit] *vt* mettere in azione; trascinare.

acumen [əˈkjumən] *n* acume.

acute [əˈkjuːt] *a* acuto; perspicace.

acuteness [əˈkjuːtnis] *n* acutezza; perspicacia.

adage [ˈædidʒ] *n* adagio, detto, proverbio.

Adam [ˈædəm] *nm pr* Adamo.

adamant [ˈædəmənt] *a* adamantino, inflessibile.

adapt [əˈdæpt] *vt* adattare, modificare.

adaptability [əˌdæptəˈbiliti] *n* adattabilità.

adaptable [əˈdæptəbl] *a* adattabile.

adaptation [ˌædæpˈteiʃən] *n* adattamento.

adapter [əˈdæptə] *n* (*phot*) adattatore; (*el*) pezzo di raccordo.

add [æd] *vti* aggiungere, soggiungere; addizionare, sommare; **to a. up** fare la somma.

adder [ˈædə] *n* vipera.

addict [ˈædikt] *n* tossicomane; [əˈdikt] *vt* abituare, dedicare.

addiction [əˈdikʃən] *n* dedizione, inclinazione.

addition [əˈdiʃən] *n* addizione, somma; aggiunta; **in a. to** oltre a.

additional [əˈdiʃənl] *a* aggiunto; supplementare.

additionally [əˈdiʃnəli] *ad* in aggiunta; inoltre.

addled [ˈædld] *a* guasto; confuso.

address [əˈdres] *n* indirizzo; discorso; destrezza; *vt* indirizzare; rivolgere la parola o lo scritto a.

addressee [ˌædreˈsiː] *n* destinatario.

adduce [əˈdjuːs] *vt* addurre; citare.

Adela [ˈædilə] *nf pr* Adele.

adenoids [ˈædinɔidz] *n pl* adenoidi.

adept [ˈædept] *a n* esperto.

adequate [ˈædikwit] *a* adeguato.

adhere [ədˈhiə] *vi* aderire, attaccarsi.

adherence [ədˈhiərəns] *n* aderenza.

adherent [ədˈhiərənt] *a* aderente, attaccato; *n* partigiano, seguace.

adhesion [ədˈhiːʒən] *n* adesione.

adhesive [ədˈhiːsiv] *a* adesivo, appiccicaticcio; **a. paper** carta gommata; **a. plaster** cerotto adesivo.

adieu [ə'dju:] *interj* n addio.

adipose ['ædipous] *a* adiposo.

adjacent [ə'dʒeisənt] *a* adiacente, attiguo.

adjective ['ædʒiktiv] n aggettivo.

adjoin [ə'dʒɔin] *vti* essere adiacente.

adjoining [ə'dʒɔiniŋ] *a* adiacente, contiguo.

adjourn [ə'dʒə:n] *vt* aggiornare; rimandare.

adjournment [ə'dʒə:nmənt] n rinvio.

adjudge [ə'dʒʌdʒ] *vt* aggiudicare; assegnare.

adjudicate [ə'dʒu:dikeit] *vt* giudicare; aggiudicare.

adjudication [ə,dʒu:di'keiʃən] n aggiudicazione; sentenza.

adjudicator [ə'dʒu:dikeitə] n giudice; arbitro.

adjunct ['ædʒʌŋkt] n aggiunta; aggiunto.

adjure [ə'dʒuə] *vt* implorare, scongiurare.

adjust [ə'dʒʌst] *vt* aggiustare; adattare; regolare.

adjustable [ə'dʒʌstəbl] *a* aggiustabile; regolabile.

adjustment [ə'dʒʌstmənt] n adattamento; regolamento.

adjutant ['ædʒutənt] n aiutante.

ad lib [æd'lib] *ad* all'improntо, estemporaneamente; *vti* improvvisare; *n.* improvvisazione.

adman ['ædmæn] n agente pubblicitario.

admass ['ædmæs] n 'il grosso pubblico'.

administer [əd'ministə] *vt* amministrare; somministrare.

administration [əd,minis'treiʃən] n amministrazione; somministrazione.

administrative [əd'ministrətiv] *a* amministrativo.

administrator [əd'ministreitə] n amministratore.

admirable ['ædmərəbl] *a* ammirabile, ammirevole.

admiral ['ædmərəl] n ammiraglio.

admiralty ['ædmərəlti] n ammiragliato; Ministero della Marina.

admiration [ædmə'reiʃən] n ammirazione.

admire [əd'maiə] *vt* ammirare.

admirer [əd'maiərə] n ammiratore; corteggiatore.

admiring [əd'maiəriŋ] *a* ammirativo.

admissible [əd'misəbl] *a* ammissibile.

admission [əd'miʃən] n ammissione.

admit [əd'mit] *vt* ammettere; riconoscere; lasciar entrare; **a. of** *vi* permettere.

admittance [əd'mitəns] n ammissione; ingresso.

admittedly [əd'mitidli] *ad* certo, certo che.

admonish [əd'mɔniʃ] *vt* ammonire.

admonishment [əd'mɔniʃmənt] n ammonimento; esortazione.

ado [ə'du:] n confusione, trambusto; difficoltà.

adolescence [,ædou'lesns] n adolescenza.

adolescent [,ædou'lesnt] *a* n adolescente.

adopt [ə'dɔpt] *vt* adottare; **adopted** *a* adottato; **adopted son** figlio adottivo.

adoption [ə'dɔpʃən] n adozione.

adoptive [ə'dɔptiv] *a* adottivo.

adorable [ə'dɔːrəbl] *a* adorabile.

adoration [,ædɔː'reiʃən] n adorazione; venerazione.

adore [ə'dɔː] *vt* adorare, venerare.

adorer [ə'dɔːrə] n adoratore.

adorn [ə'dɔːn] *vt* adornare.

adornment [ə'dɔːnmənt] n ornamento.

Adrian ['eidriən] *nm pr* Adriano.

Adriatic [,eidri'ætik] *a* n Adriatico.

adrift [ə'drift] *ad* alla deriva.

adroit [ə'drɔit] *a* destro, abile.

adroitness [ə'drɔitnis] n destrezza, abilità.

adulation [,ædju'leiʃən] n adulazione.

adult ['ædʌlt] *a* n adulto.

adulterate [ə'dʌltəreit] *vt* adulterare.

adulteration [ə,dʌltə'reiʃən] *a* adulterazione, sofisticazione.

adulterer [ə'dʌltərə] n adultero; **adulteress** n adultera.

adultery [ə'dʌltəri] n adulterio.

advance [əd'vɑːns] n avanzamento, marcia in avanti, progresso; (*com*) rialzo; anticipo; *vt* avanzare; aumentare; anticipare; *vi* avanzare; progredire.

advanced [əd'vɑːnst] *a* avanzato, progredito.

advancement [əd'vɑːnsmənt] n avanzamento, progresso, promozione.

advantage [əd'vɑːntidʒ] n vantaggio.

advantageous [,ædvən'teidʒəs] *a* vantaggioso.

advent ['ædvənt] n avvento.

adventitious [,ædven'tiʃəs] *a* avventizio, casuale.

adventure [əd'ventʃə] n avventura, impresa.

adventurer [əd'ventʃərə] n avventuriero.

adventurous [əd'ventʃərəs] *a* avventuroso.

adverb ['ædvə:b] n avverbio.

adverbial [əd'və:biəl] *a* avverbiale.

adversary ['ædvəsəri] n avversario, antagonista.

adverse ['ædvə:s] *a* avverso, contrario, opposto.

adversity [əd'və:siti] n avversità.

advertise ['ædvətaiz] *vti* fare della pubblicità per; mettere annunci, rendere noto.

advertisement [əd'və:tismənt] n annuncio, avviso; inserzione; reclame.

advertiser ['ædvətaizə] n inserzionista; **advertising** a pubblicitario; n pubblicità.

advice [əd'vais] n consigli(o), avviso.

advisable [əd'vaizəbl] a consigliabile, raccomandabile.

advise [əd'vaiz] vt consigliare; avvisare.

advisedly [əd'vaizidli] ad consideratamente, giudiziosamente.

adviser [əd'vaizə] n consigliere.

advisory [əd'vaizəri] a che consiglia; consultivo.

advocate ['ædvəkit] n avvocato; vt ['ædvəkeit] difendere, patrocinare; sostenere.

Aegean [i'dʒiːən] a n (geogr) Egeo.

aerated ['eiəreitid] a gassoso.

aerial ['eəriəl] a aereo, etereo; n (rad) antenna.

aerobatics ['eərou'bætiks] n pl acrobazie aeree.

aerodrome ['eərədroum] n aerodromo.

aerodynamics ['eəroudai'næmiks] n aerodinamica; **aerodynamic** a aerodinamico.

aeronaut ['eərənɔːt] n aeronauta.

aeronautics [ˌeərə'nɔːtiks] n aeronautica.

aeroplane ['eərəplein] n aeroplano, aereo; **fighter a.** aeroplano da caccia.

aerosol ['eərəsɔl] n aerosol.

aesthetic [iːs'θetik] a estetico; **aesthetics** n estetica.

afar, afar off [ə'faːr, ə'faːr'ɔf] ad lontano, in lontananza; **from a.** da lontano.

affability [ˌæfə'biliti] n affabilità.

affable ['æfəbl] a affabile.

affair [ə'feə] n affare; avventura, relazione.

affect [ə'fekt] vt affettare; riguardare; influire su; commuovere.

affectation [ˌæfek'teiʃən] n affettazione.

affected [ə'fektid] a affettato; affetto; commosso.

affection [ə'fekʃən] n affetto, affezione.

affectionate [ə'fekʃnit] a affettuoso.

affidavit [ˌæfi'deivit] n deposizione scritta e giurata, affidavit.

affiliate [ə'filieit] vt affiliare, associare.

affiliation [əˌfili'eiʃən] n affiliazione.

affinity [ə'finiti] n affinità; parentela.

affirm [ə'fəːm] vt affermare, confermare.

affirmation [ˌæfəː'meiʃən] n affermazione, asserzione.

affirmative [ə'fəːmətiv] a affermativo; n affermativa.

affix [ə'fiks] vt affiggere, apporre, attaccare; ['æfiks] n affisso.

afflict [ə'flikt] vt affliggere.

affliction [ə'flikʃən] n afflizione.

affluence ['æfluəns] n affluenza, abbondanza.

affluent ['æfluənt] a ricco; n affluente.

afford [ə'fɔːd] vt fornire, offrire; permettersi il lusso di.

afforestation [æ'fɔris'teiʃən] n imboschimento.

affranchise [ə'fræntʃaiz] vt affrancare, liberare.

affront [ə'frʌnt] n affronto; insulto; vt affrontare; insultare.

afloat [ə'flout] ad a galla.

afoot [ə'fut] ad (fig) in moto, in ballo.

aforesaid [ə'fɔːsed] a predetto.

afraid [ə'freid] a impaurito, pauroso; **to be a.** aver paura.

afresh [ə'freʃ] ad di nuovo, un'altra volta.

Africa ['æfrikə] n Africa.

African ['æfrikən] a n africano.

Afrikan(d)er [ˌæfri'kæn(d)ə] a n sud-africano, di origine olandese.

aft [aːft] ad (naut) a poppa.

after ['aːftə] ad prep cj dopo, dietro, in seguito a; ad imitazione di; dopo che; **a. all** in fin dei conti.

after-effect ['aːftəri'fekt] n conseguenza.

aftermath ['aːftəmæθ] n secondo taglio del fieno; (fig) conseguenze pl, risultati pl.

afternoon ['aːftə'nuːn] n pomeriggio.

afterthought ['aːftəθɔːt] n riflessione, ripensamento.

afterwards ['aːftəwədz] ad dopo, più tardi.

again [ə'gen] ad ancora, di nuovo; altrettanto; **a. and a.** ripetutamente; **now and a.** di quando in quando.

against [ə'genst] prep contro, in opposizione a; di fronte a; **a. the grain** (fig) contro voglia.

agate ['ægət] n agata.

Agatha ['ægəθə] nf pr Agata.

age ['eidʒ] n età; periodo; **of a.** maggiorenne; **under a.** minorenne.

age ['eidʒ] vti invecchiare.

aged ['eidʒid] a vecchio; ['eidʒd] dell'età di.

ageless ['eidʒlis] a di età invariata, sempre giovane.

agency ['eidʒənsi] n agenzia, rappresentanza.

agenda [ə'dʒendə] n ordine del giorno.

agent ['eidʒənt] n agente, rappresentante.

agglomeration [əˌglɔmə'reiʃən] n agglomerazione.

aggrandizement [ə'grændizmənt] n accrescimento (di potenza).

aggravate ['ægrəveit] vt aggravare; (fam) esasperare.

aggravating ['ægrəveitiŋ] a (fam) irritante, insopportabile.

aggregate ['ægrigit] a n aggregato; **in the a.** nel complesso.

aggregation [ˌægri'geiʃən] n aggregazione.

aggression [ə'greʃən] n aggressione.

aggressive [ə'gresiv] *a* aggressivo.
aggressiveness [ə'gresivnis] *n* aggressività.
aggressor [ə'gresə] *n* aggressore.
aghast [ə'gɑːst] *a* stupefatto; terrorizzato.
agile ['ædʒail] *a* agile.
agility [ə'dʒiliti] *n* agilità.
agitate ['ædʒiteit] *vt* agitare; commuovere; discutere.
agitation [ˌædʒi'teiʃən] *n* agitazione, commozione.
agitator ['ædʒiteitə] *n* agitatore.
Agnes ['ægnis] *nf pr* Agnese.
agnostic [æg'nɔstik] *a n* agnostico.
ago [ə'gou] *ad* fa.
agog [ə'gɔg] *a* ansioso, desideroso; *ad* con ansia.
agonized ['ægənaizd] **agonizing** ['ægənaiziŋ] *a* angoscioso.
agony ['ægəni] *n* agonia; angoscia.
agrarian [ə'grɛəriən] *a* agrario.
agree [ə'griː] *vi* accordarsi, convenire; acconsentire; confarsi.
agreeable [ə'griəbl] *a* piacevole, simpatico; disposto; conveniente.
agreeableness [ə'griəblnis] *n* piacevolezza, conformità.
agreement [ə'griːmənt] *n* accordo, contratto, patto.
agricultural [ˌægri'kʌltʃərəl] *a* agricolo.
agriculture ['ægrikʌltʃə] *n* agricoltura.
aground [ə'graund] *ad a* (*naut*) in secco; **to run a.** incagliarsi.
ahead [ə'hed] *ad* (in) avanti.
aid [eid] *n* aiuto, assistenza, sussidio; **first a.** pronto soccorso; *vt* aiutare.
aide-de-camp ['eiddə'kãːŋ] *n* aiutante di campo.
ail [eil] *vi* sentirsi male; *vt* affliggere.
ailing ['eiliŋ] *a* sofferente.
ailment ['eilmənt] *n* indisposizione, malattia.
aim [eim] *n* mira, scopo, proposito; *vti* puntare; *vi* mirare a; aspirare a.
aimless ['eimlis] *a* senza scopo.
air [ɛə] *n* aria; aspetto; atmosfera; (*mus*) aria; *vt* arieggiare, ventilare; **a.-hostess** assistente di volo, 'hostess'; **a. conditioner** condizionatore dell'aria; **a. station** scalo aereo; **a.-raid** incursione aerea.
aircraft (*inv*) ['ɛəkrɑːft] *n* aereo, aerei; **a. carrier** porta erei.
airdrome ['ɛədroum] *n* (*US*) aerodromo.
air force ['ɛəfɔːs] *n* aeronautica, aviazione.
airily ['ɛərili] *ad* gaiamente; spensieratamente.
airiness ['ɛərinis] *n* leggerezza; spensieratezza.
airing ['ɛəriŋ] *n* ventilazione; giretto all'aria aperta.
airless ['ɛəlis] *a* privo d'aria.
airline ['ɛəlain] *n* aviolinea.
airmail ['ɛəmeil] *n* posta aerea.
airman ['ɛəmən] *n* aviatore.

airplane ['ɛəplein] *n* (*US*) aeroplano.
airport ['ɛəpɔːt] *n* aeroporto.
air-pump ['ɛəpʌmp] *n* pompa pneumatica.
airship ['ɛəʃip] *n* dirigibile.
airtight ['ɛətait] *a* a tenuta d'aria.
airway ['ɛəwei] *n* via aerea.
airy ['ɛəri] *a* arioso; leggero; spensierato: aereo; vano.
aisle [ail] *n* navata.
ajar [ə'dʒɑː] *ad* socchiuso.
akimbo [ə'kimbou] *ad* **le mani su i fianchi e i gomiti in fuori.**
akin [ə'kin] *a* affine, parente.
alabaster ['æləbɑːstə] *a n* (di) alabastro.
alacrity [ə'lækriti] *n* alacrità.
Alan ['ælən] *nm pr* Alano.
alarm [ə'lɑːm] *n* allarme; *vt* allarmare, spaventare.
alarm-clock [ə'lɑːmklɔk] *n* (orologio a) sveglia.
alas! [ə'læs] *interj* ahimè!
Albania [æl'beiniə] *n* (*geogr*) Albania.
Albanian [æl'beiniən] *a n* albanese.
albatross [æl'bætrɔs] *n* albatro.
albeit [ɔːl'biːit] *cj* quantunque.
Albert ['ælbət] *nm pr* Alberto.
albino [æl'biːnou] *pl* **albinos** albino.
album ['ælbəm] *n* album.
albumen ['ælbjumin] *n* albume.
alchemy ['ælkimi] *n* alchimia.
alcohol ['ælkəhɔl] *n* alcool.
alcoholic [ˌælkə'hɔlik] *a* alcoolico; *n* alcoolizzato.
alcoholism ['ælkəhɔlizəm] *n* alcoolismo.
alcove ['ælkouv] *n* alcova, recesso.
alder ['ɔːldə] *n* ontano.
alderman ['ɔːldəmən] *n* assessore comunale.
ale [eil] *n* birra; **a.-house** birreria.
alert [ə'ləːt] *a* vigilante, attento; *n* allarme; **on the a.** all'erta.
alertness [ə'ləːtnis] *n* vigilanza; vivacità.
Alexander [ˌælig'zɑːndə] *nm pr* Alessandro.
Alexandria [ˌælig'zɑːndriə] *n* (*geogr*) Alessandria (d'Egitto).
Alfred ['ælfrid] *nm pr* Alfredo.
algebra ['ældʒibrə] *n* algebra.
Algeria [æl'dʒiəriə] *n* (*geogr*) Algeria.
Algerian [æl'dʒiəriən] *a n* algerino.
alias ['eiliæs] *ad* alias; *n* falso nome.
alibi ['ælibai] *n* alibi.
Alice ['ælis] *nf pr* Alice.
alien ['eiliən] *a* estraneo; *n* straniero.
alienate ['eiliəneit] *vt* alienare.
alienation [ˌeiliə'neiʃən] *n* alienazione.
alight [ə'lait] *a* acceso; illuminato; infiammato; *vi* scendere; atterrare.
alike [ə'laik] *a* simile; *ad* parimenti.
alimentary [ˌæli'mentəri] *a* alimentare; alimentario.
alimentation [ˌælimen'teiʃən] *n* alimentazione.
alimony ['æliməni] *n* alimonia, alimenti.

alive [ə'laiv] *a* vivo, vivente; vivace.
alkaline ['ælkəlain] *a* alcalino.
all [ɔːl] *a* tutto; *n pron* tutto; *ad* completamente, del tutto; **not at all!** niente affatto!
allay [ə'lei] *vt* calmare; alleviare; diminuire.
allegation [ˌæle'geiʃən] *n* allegazione, asserzione.
allege [ə'ledʒ] *vt* allegare, asserire.
allegiance [ə'liːdʒəns] *n* fedeltà, obbedienza (al sovrano *etc*).
allegorical [ˌæle'gɔrikəl] *a* allegorico.
allegory ['æligəri] *n* allegoria.
allergic [ə'ləːdʒik] *a* allergico.
allergy ['ælədʒi] *n* allergia.
alleviate [ə'liːvieit] *vt* alleviare; mitigare.
alley ['æli] *n* vicolo.
alliance [ə'laiəns] *n* alleanza; unione.
allied ['ælaid] *a* alleato.
alligator ['æligeitə] *n* alligatore.
alliteration [əˌlitə'reiʃən] *n* allitterazione.
allocate ['æləkeit] *vt* assegnare; distribuire.
allocation [ˌælə'keiʃən] *n* assegnazione.
allot [ə'lɔt] *vt* distribuire; assegnare.
allotment [ə'lɔtmənt] *n* assegnazione, lotto; piccolo pezzo di terreno da coltivare.
allow [ə'lau] *vt* permettere, accordare; **to a. for** tener conto di.
allowable [ə'lauəbl] **allowed** [ə'laud] *a* lecito.
allowance [ə'lauəns] *n* assegno; indennità; riduzione, sconto.
alloy ['ælɔi] *n* lega (metallica); *vt* fondere, mescolare.
All Saints' Day ['ɔːl'seintsdei] *n* Ognissanti.
All Souls' Day ['ɔːl'soulzdei] *n* giorno dei morti.
allude [ə'luːd] *vi* alludere.
allure [ə'ljuə] *vt* allettare, sedurre.
allurement [ə'ljuəmənt] *n* allettamento.
alluring [ə'ljuəriŋ] *a* allettante, seducente.
allusion [ə'luːʒən] *n* allusione.
ally ['ælai] *n* alleato; *vt* [ə'lai] alleare, collegare, unire.
almanac ['ɔːlmənæk] *n* almanacco.
almighty [ɔːl'maiti] *a* onnipotente; **the A.** Dio.
almond ['ɑːmənd] *n* mandorla; **a.-tree** mandorlo.
almoner ['ɑːmənə] *n* elemosiniere.
almost ['ɔːlmoust] *ad* quasi.
alms [ɑːmz] (*inv*) *n* elemosina; **a.-house** ospizio di mendicità.
aloft [ə'lɔft] *ad* in alto.
alone [ə'loun] *a* solo; **to let a.** lasciar stare.
along [ə'lɔŋ] *ad prep* avanti, lungo, per; **come a.!** su via!; **a. with** con.
aloof [ə'luːf] *ad* a distanza; in disparte; *a* freddo, distante, sostenuto.

aloud [ə'laud] *ad* a voce alta, forte.
alphabet ['ælfəbit] *n* alfabeto.
alpine ['ælpain] *a* alpino.
Alps [ælps] *n pl* (*geogr*) Alpi.
already [ɔːl'redi] *ad* già, di già.
Alsace ['ælzæs] *n* Alsazia.
Alsatian [æl'seiʃən] *a n* alsaziano; **A.** (dog) cane lupo.
also ['ɔːlsou] *ad* anche, inoltre, pure.
altar ['ɔːltə] *n* altare; **high a.** altare maggiore.
alter ['ɔːltə] *vti* cambiare, cambiarsi, alterare.
alterable ['ɔːltərəbl] *a* alterabile.
alteration [ˌɔːltə'reiʃən] *n* modificazione, alterazione.
altercation [ˌɔːltə'keiʃən] *n* alterco.
alternate [ɔːl'təːnit] *a* alternato, alterno; *vti* ['ɔːltəneit] alternar(si), avvicendar(si); **alternately** vicendevolmente.
alternation [ˌɔːltə'neiʃən] *n* alternazione.
alternative [ɔːl'təːnətiv] *a* alternativo; *n* alternativa; **alternatively** *ad* alternativamente.
although [ɔːl'ðou] *cj* sebbene, quantunque, benché.
altitude ['æltitjuːd] *n* altitudine, altezza; (*av*) quota.
altogether [ˌɔːltə'geðə] *ad* completamente, nell'insieme.
altruism ['æltruizəm] *n* altruismo.
altruistic [ˌæltru'istik] *a* altruistico.
alum ['æləm] *n* allume.
aluminium [ˌælju'miniəm], (US) **aluminum** [ə'luːminəm] *n* alluminio.
always ['ɔːlwəz] *ad* sempre.
amalgam [ə'mælgəm] *n* amalgama.
amalgamate [ə'mælgəmeit] *vti* amalgamar(si).
amalgamation [əˌmælgə'meiʃən] *n* amalgamazione, fusione.
amass [ə'mæs] *vt* accumulare, ammassare.
amateur ['æmətə] *a n* dilettante.
amaze [ə'meiz] *vt* meravigliare, stupire.
amazement [ə'meizmənt] *n* meraviglia.
amazing [ə'meiziŋ] *a* sorprendente.
Amazon ['æməzən] *n* (*geogr*) Rio delle Amazzoni.
ambassador [æm'bæsədə] *n* ambasciatore.
ambassadress [æm'bæsədris] *n* ambasciatrice.
amber ['æmbə] *n* ambra.
ambiguity [ˌæmbi'gjuiti] *n* ambiguità.
ambiguous [æm'bigjuəs] *a* ambiguo.
ambition [æm'biʃən] *n* ambizione.
ambitious [æm'biʃəs] *a* ambizioso.
amble ['æmbl] *vi* andare lemme lemme; *n* passo lento.
Ambrose ['æmbrouz] *nm pr* Ambrogio; **Ambrosian** *a* ambrosiano.
ambulance ['æmbjuləns] *n* ambulanza.

ambush ['æmbuʃ] *n* agguato, imboscata.

ameliorate [ə'mi:liəreit] *vti* migliorare.

amelioration [ə,mi:liə'reiʃən] *n* miglioramento.

amen ['ɑ:'men] *interj* amen, così sia.

amenable [ə'mi:nəbl] *a* trattabile.

amend [ə'mend] *vti* emendare, emendarsi.

amendment [ə'mendmənt] *n* emendamento.

amends [ə'mendz] *n pl* compenso, riparazione; **to make a.** fare ammenda.

amenity [ə'mi:niti] *n* amenità; **amenities** *n pl* comodità *pl.*

America [ə'merikə] *n* America.

American [ə'merikən] *a n* americano.

amethyst ['æmiθist] *n* ametista.

amiability [,eimiə'biliti] *n* amabilità.

amiable ['eimiəbl] *a* amabile.

amicable ['æmikəbl] *a* amichevole.

amid(st) [ə'mid(st)] *prep* fra, in mezzo a, tra.

amiss [ə'mis] *a* sbagliato; *ad* inopportunamente, in mala parte.

amity ['æmiti] *n* amicizia.

ammonia [ə'mouniə] *n* ammoniaca.

ammunition [,æmju'niʃən] *n* munizioni *pl.*

amnesia [æm'ni:ziə] *n* amnesia.

amnesty ['æmnesti] *n* amnistia.

amok [ə'mɔk] *v* amuck.

among(st) [ə'mʌŋ(st)] *prep* fra, in mezzo a, tra.

amoral [æ'mɔrəl] *a* amorale.

amorous ['æmərəs] *a* amoroso.

amorphous [ə'mɔ:fəs] *a* amorfo.

amount [ə'maunt] *n* ammontare, quantità, somma; *vi* ammontare.

amphibious [æm'fibiəs] *a* anfibio.

amphitheatre ['æmfi,θiətə] *n* anfiteatro.

ample ['æmpl] *a* ampio; abbondante.

amplification [,æmplifi'keiʃən] *n* amplificazione.

amplifier ['æmplifaiə] *n* amplificatore.

amplify ['æmplifai] *vti* ampliare, amplificare.

amputate ['æmpjuteit] *vt* amputare.

amputation [,æmpju'teiʃən] *n* amputazione.

amuck [ə'mʌk] *ad* in un accesso di pazzia sanguinaria.

amulet ['æmjulit] *n* amuleto.

amuse [ə'mju:z] *vt* divertire, svagare.

amusement [ə'mju:zmənt] *n* divertimento, svago.

amusing [ə'mju:ziŋ] *a* divertente; faceto.

an [æn] *indef art* un(o), una.

anachronism [ə'nækrənizəm] *n* anacronismo.

anaemia [ə'ni:miə] *n* anemia.

anaesthetic [,ænis'θetik] *a n* anestetico.

anagram ['ænəgræm] *n* anagramma.

analogous [ə'næləgəs] *a* analogo.

analogy [ə'nælədʒi] *n* analogia.

analysis [ə'næləsis] *pl* **analyses** *n* analisi.

analyze ['ænəlaiz] *vt* analizzare.

analytic(al) [,ænə'litik(əl)] *a* analitico.

anarchist ['ænəkist] *n* anarchico.

anarchy ['ænəki] *n* anarchia.

anathema [ə'næθimə] *n* anatema.

anatomical [,ænə'tɔmikəl] *a* anatomico.

anatomy [ə'nætəmi] *n* anatomia.

ancestor ['ænsistə] *n* antenato.

ancestral [æn'sestrəl] *a* avito.

ancestry ['ænsistri] *n* lignaggio, stirpe.

anchor ['æŋkə] *n* àncora, (fig) salvezza; **at a.** ancorato; *vti* ancorar(si).

anchorage ['æŋkəridʒ] *n* ancoraggio.

anchovy ['æntʃəvi] *n* acciuga.

ancient ['einʃənt] *a* antico, venerabile.

and [ænd, ənd, ən] *cj* e, ed.

andiron ['ændaiən] *n* alare.

Andrew ['ændru:] *nm pr* Andrea.

anecdote ['ænikdout] *n* aneddoto.

anemone [ə'neməni] *n* anemone; **sea a.** attinia.

anew [ə'nju:] *ad* di nuovo.

angel ['eindʒəl] *n* angelo; **guardian a.** angelo custode.

angelic [æn'dʒelik] *a* angelico.

anger ['æŋgə] *n* ira, rabbia; *vt* adirare, far arrabbiare.

angle ['æŋgl] *n* angolo; punto di vista; *vi* pescare all'amo.

angler ['æŋglə] *n* pescatore.

Anglican ['æŋglikən] *a n* anglicano.

angling ['æŋgliŋ] *n* pesca all'amo.

Anglo-Saxon ['æŋglou'sæksən] *a n* anglo-sassone.

angry ['æŋgri] *a* arrabbiato, irato.

anguish ['æŋgwiʃ] *n* angoscia.

angular ['æŋgjulə] *a* angolare.

aniline ['ænilin] *n* anilina.

animadversion [,ænimæd'və:ʃən] *n* censura, critica.

animal ['æniməl] *a n* animale.

animate ['ænimit] *a* animato; *vt* animare.

animation [,æni'meiʃən] *n* animazione.

animosity [,æni'mɔsiti] *n* animosità.

aniseed ['ænisi:d] *n* seme di anice.

anisette [,æni'zet] *n* anisetta.

ankle ['æŋkl] *n* caviglia.

Ann(e) [æn] *nf pr* Anna.

annals ['ænlz] *n pl* annali.

annex(e) ['æneks] *n* annesso; edificio supplementare.

annex [ə'neks] *vt* annettere.

annexation [,ænek'seiʃən] *n* annessione.

annihilate [ə'naiəleit] *vt* annichilire.

annihilation [ə,naiə'leiʃən] *n* annientamento.

anniversary [,æni'və:səri] *a n* anniversario.

annotate ['ænouteit] *vt* annotare.
announce [ə'nauns] *vt* annunciare.
announcement [ə'naunsmənt] *n* annuncio, avviso.
announcer [ə'naunsə] *n* annunziatore, -trice; (*rad*) annunciatore, -trice, presentatore, -trice.
annoy [ə'nɔi] *vt* disturbare, irritare.
annoyance [ə'nɔiəns] *n* fastidio, irritazione.
annoying [ə'nɔiiŋ] *a* noioso, fastidioso.
annual ['ænjuəl] *a* annuale, annuo; *n* annuario; pianta annuale.
annuity [ə'njuiti] *n* annualità.
annul [ə'nʌl] *vt* annullare, abolire.
annulment [ə'nʌlmənt] *n* annullamento.
annunciation [ə'nʌnsi'eiʃən] *n* annunciazione.
anodyne ['ænoudain] *a* anodino.
anoint [ə'nɔint] *vt* ungere; consacrare.
anomalous [ə'nɔmələs] *a* anomalo, irregolare.
anomaly [ə'nɔməli] *n* anomalia, irregolarità.
anon [ə'nɔn] *ad* subito; **ever and a.** di quando in quando.
anonymous [ə'nɔniməs] *a* anonimo.
anorak ['ænəræk] *n* giacca a vento.
another [ə'nʌðə] *a pron* (un) altro; (un) secondo; **one a.** l'un l'altro.
Anselm ['ænselm] *nm pr* Anselmo.
answer ['ɑːnsə] *n* risposta; *vt* rispondere a; **to answer for** rispondere di.
answerable ['ɑːnsərəbl] *a* responsabile.
answering ['ɑːnsəriŋ] *a* in risposta; corrispondente.
ant [ænt] *n* formica.
antagonism [æn'tægənizəm] *n* antagonismo, opposizione.
antagonist [æn'tægənist] *n* antagonista.
Antarctic [ænt'ɑːktik] *a* antartico; *n* Antartico, Antartide.
antecedent [ˌænti'siːdənt] *a n* antecedente.
antechamber ['ænti.tʃeimbə] *n* anticamera.
antedate ['ænti'deit] *vt* anticipare, antidatare.
antediluvian ['æntidi'luːviən] *a n* antidiluviano.
antelope ['æntiloup] *n* antilope.
antenatal ['ænti'neitl] *a* prenatale.
anteroom ['æntirum] *n* anticamera.
anthem ['ænθəm] *n* antifona; inno.
anthology [æn'θɔlədʒi] *n* antologia.
Anthony ['æntəni] *nm pr* Antonio.
anthracite ['ænθrəsait] *n* antracite.
anthropologist [ˌænθrə'pɔlədʒist] *n* antropologo.
anthropology [ˌænθrə'pɔlədʒi] *n* antropologia.
anti-aircraft ['ænti'ɛəkrɑːft] *a* antiaereo.
antibiotic ['æntibai'ɔtik] *a n* antibiotico.

antics ['æntiks] *n pl* stramberie, eccessi *pl.*
antichrist ['æntikraist] *n* anticristo.
anticipate [æn'tisipeit] *vt* anticipare; aspettarsi; pregustare.
anticipation [æn.tisi'peiʃən] *n* anticipazione, anticipo; previsione.
anticlimax ['ænti'klaimæks] *n* improvviso crollo discesa nel banale.
anti-dazzle ['ænti'dæzl] *a* antiabbagliante; **a. headlights** (*aut*) fari anabbaglianti.
antidote ['æntidout] *n* antidoto.
antifogging ['æntifɔgiŋ] *a n* antiappannante, antinebbia.
antifreeze ['æntifriːz] *n* (*aut*) anticongelante.
antifriction ['ænti'frikʃən] *n* antiattrito.
antihistamine ['ænti'histəmiːn] *n* antistamina.
antimacassar ['æntimə'kæsə] *n* copridivano, copripoltrona.
antimilitarism ['ænti'militərizəm] *n* antimilitarismo.
antimony ['æntiməni] *n* antimonio.
antipathy [æn'tipəθi] *n* antipatia, avversione.
antipodes [æn'tipədiːz] *n pl* antipodi *pl.*
antipope ['æntipoup] *n* antipapa.
antiquarian [ˌænti'kwɛəriən] *a n* antiquario.
antiquated ['æntikweitid] *a* antiquato, fuori uso.
antique [æn'tiːk] *a* antico; *n* oggetto antico.
antiquity [æn'tikwiti] *n* antichità, tempi antichi *pl.*
anti-rust ['ænti'rʌst] *a n* antiruggine.
antiseptic [ˌænti'septik] *a n* antisettico.
antisocial ['ænti'souʃəl] *a* antisociale.
anti-theft ['ænti'θeft] *a n* antifurto.
antithesis [æn'tiθisis] *pl* **antitheses** *n* antitesi.
antler ['æntlə] *n* corno di cervo.
Antwerp ['æntwəːp] *n* (*geogr*) Anversa.
anvil ['ænvil] *n* incudine.
anxiety [æŋ'zaiəti] *n* ansia, ansietà.
anxious ['æŋkʃəs] *a* ansioso, preoccupato; desideroso.
any ['eni] *a* alcuno, -ni, del, dei, nessuno, qualche, un po' di; ogni, qualsiasi, qualunque; *pron* alcuno, nessuno.
anybody ['eni,bɔdi], **anyone** ['eniwʌn] *pron* alcuno, qualcuno; nessuno; chiunque.
anyhow ['enihau] *ad* in ogni caso, ad ogni modo; in qualsiasi modo.
anything ['eniθiŋ] *pron* qualche cosa, alcuna cosa; qualunque cosa.
anyway ['eniwei] *ad* in ogni caso, ad ogni modo.
anywhere ['eniwɛə] *ad* dovunque, in qualsiasi luogo.
apart [ə'pɑːt] *ad* a parte, in disparte.

apartheid [ə'pɑːtheit] *n* segregazione razziale.

apartment [ə'pɑːtmənt] *n* stanza, *(US)* appartamento; **a. hotel** *(US)* appartamento d'affitto con servizio.

apathetic [ˌæpə'θetik] *a* apatico, indifferente.

apathy ['æpəθi] *n* apatia, indifferenza.

ape [eip] *n* scimmia; *vt* imitare, scimmiottare.

Apennines ['æpinainz] *n* *pl* Appennini.

aperient [ə'piəriənt] *a n* lassativo.

aperitif [ə'peritif] *n* aperitivo.

aperture ['æpətjuə] *n* apertura, foro.

apex ['eipeks] *pl* **apexes**, **apices** *n* apice, vertice.

aphorism ['æfərizəm] *n* aforisma.

apiary ['eipjəri] *n* apiario.

apiece [ə'piːs] *ad* per ognuno, a testa.

aplomb ['æplɔm] *n* perpendicolarità; sicurezza di sè.

apocalypse [ə'pɔkəlips] *n* apocalisse.

apocryphal [ə'pɔkrifəl] *a* apocrifo.

apogee ['æpoudʒiː] *n* apogeo.

apologetic [əˌpɔlə'dʒetik] *a* pieno di scuse.

apologize [ə'pɔledʒaiz] *vi* scusarsi.

apology [ə'pɔlədʒi] *n* scusa, giustificazione; apologia.

apoplectic [ˌæpə'plektik] *a* apoplettico.

apoplexy ['æpəpleksi] *n* apoplessia.

apostle [ə'pɔsl] *n* apostolo.

apostolic [ˌæpəs'tɔlik] *a* apostolico.

apostrophe [ə'pɔstrəfi] *n* apostrofe; *(gram)* apostrofo.

apostrophize [ə'pɔstrəfaiz] *vt* apostrofare.

appal [ə'pɔːl] *vt* spaventare, atterrire.

appalling [ə'pɔːliŋ] *a* spaventoso.

apparatus [ˌæpə'reitəs] *n* *(anat)* apparato; *(tec)* apparecchio.

apparent [ə'pærənt] *a* chiaro, manifesto; **heir a.** *n* erede legittimo.

apparition [ˌæpə'riʃən] *n* apparizione, fantasma.

appeal [ə'piːl] *n* appello; attrattiva; *vi* appellarsi; attrarre.

appealing [ə'piːliŋ] *ad* supplichevole; attraente.

appear [ə'piə] *vi* apparire; comparire; sembrare.

appearance [ə'piərəns] *n* apparenza; aspetto; apparizione; comparizione.

appease [ə'piːz] *vt* calmare; pacificare.

appeasement [ə'piːzmənt] *n* pacificazione; appagamento.

append [ə'pend] *vt* apporre, aggiungere.

appendicitis [əˌpendi'saitis] *n* appendicite.

appendix [ə'pendiks] *pl* **appendixes**, **appendices** *n* appendice.

appertain [ˌæpə'tein] *vi* appartenere; riferirsi.

appetite ['æpitait] *n* appetito.

appetizing ['æpitaiziŋ] *a* appetitoso.

applaud [ə'plɔːd] *vti* applaudire.

applause [ə'plɔːz] *n* applauso, -si *pl.*

apple ['æpl] *n* mela; **a.-tree** melo.

appliance [ə'plaiəns] *n* apparecchio; applicazione.

applicable ['æplikəbl] *a* applicabile.

applicant ['æplikənt] *n* candidato.

application [ˌæpli'keiʃən] *n* applicazione; domanda; diligenza.

apply [ə'plai] *vti* applicare; applicarsi; rivolgersi, fare domanda.

appoint [ə'pɔint] *vt* stabilire; nominare.

appointed [ə'pɔintid] *a* fissato; arredato, equipaggiato.

appointment [ə'pɔintmənt] *n* appuntamento; nomina; impiego; decreto.

apportion [ə'pɔːʃən] *vt* distribuire.

apportionment [ə'pɔːʃənmənt] *n* ripartizione.

apposite ['æpəzit] *a* apposito, appropriato.

apposition [ˌæpə'ziʃən] *n* apposizione.

appraisal [ə'preizəl] *n* stima, valutazione.

appraise [ə'preiz] *vt* stimare, valutare.

appreciable [ə'priːʃəbl] *a* apprezzabile; considerevole.

appreciate [ə'priːʃieit] *vt* apprezzare; tenere in giusto conto; *vi* aumentare di valore.

appreciation [əˌpriːʃi'eiʃən] *n* apprezzamento; stima; rivalutazione.

apprehend [ˌæpri'hend] *vt* arrestare; comprendere; temere.

apprehension [ˌæpri'henʃən] *n* comprensione; apprensione; timore; arresto.

apprehensive [ˌæpri'hensiv] *a* timoroso; perspicace.

apprentice [ə'prentis] *n* apprendista.

apprenticeship [ə'prentiʃip] *n* apprendistato, tirocinio.

approach [ə'proutʃ] *n* avvicinamento; approccio; accesso; *vti* avvicinare, avvicinarsi.

approachable [ə'proutʃəbl] *a* avvicinabile, accessibile.

approbation [ˌæprə'beiʃən] *n* approvazione, sanzione.

appropriate [ə'proupriit] *a* appropriato, proprio; [ə'proupreit] *vt* appropriarsi; stanziare denaro.

appropriately [ə'proupriitli] *ad* appropriatamente.

appropriation [əˌproupri'eiʃən] *n* appropriazione; stanziamento.

approval [ə'pruːvəl] *n* approvazione, *(com)* prova.

approve [ə'pruːv] *vt* approvare, sanzionare.

approximate [ə'prɔksimit] *a* approssimativo; *vti* approssimar(si).

approximately [ə'prɔksimitli] *ad* approssimativamente.

apricot ['eiprikɔt] n albicocca; a.- tree albicocco.

April ['eiprəl] n aprile.

apron ['eiprən] n grembiule.

apropos ['æprəpou] ad a proposito.

apse [æps] n abside.

apt [æpt] a adatto, atto; a. at bravo in; a. to avente tendenza a.

aptitude ['æptitju:d] n attitudine.

Apulia [ə'pju:liə] n (geogr) Puglia; Apulian a n pugliese.

aqualung ['ækwəlʌŋ] n autorespiratore.

aquarium [ə'kwɛəriəm] n acquario.

aquatic [ə'kwætik] a acquatico.

aqueduct ['ækwidʌkt] n acquedotto.

aquiline ['ækwilain] a aquilino.

Arab ['ærəb] a n arabo.

arabesque [ˌærə'besk] a arabesco.

Arabia [ə'reibiə] n (geogr) Arabia.

Arabian [ə'reibiən] a n arabo, arabico; **Arabic** a n arabico, la lingua araba.

arable ['ærəbl] a arabile.

arbiter ['a:bitə] n arbitro, giudice.

arbitrary ['a:bitrəri] a arbitrario.

arbitrate ['a:bitreit] vti arbitrare.

arbitration [ˌa:bi'treiʃən] n arbitrato.

arbour ['a:bə] n pergolato.

arc [a:k] n arco; a. lamp lampada ad arco.

arcade [a:'keid] n galleria; porticato; portici pl.

arch [a:tʃ] a birichino, furbetto; n arco, volta; vti arcuar(si).

archaeologist [ˌa:ki'ɔlədʒist] n archeologo.

archaeology [ˌa:ki'ɔlədʒi] n archeologia.

archaic [a:'keiik] a arcaico.

archangel ['a:k͵eindʒəl] n arcangelo.

archbishop ['a:tʃ'biʃəp] n arcivescovo.

archbishopric [a:tʃ'biʃəprik] n arcivescovado.

archdeacon ['a:tʃ'di:kən] n arcidiacono.

archduke ['a:tʃ'dju:k] n arciduca.

arched [a:tʃt] a ad arco, arcuato.

archer ['a:tʃə] n arciere.

archery ['a:tʃəri] n tiro con l'arco.

archetype ['a:kitaip] n archetipo.

Archibald ['a:tʃibəld] nm pr Arcibaldo.

archipelago [ˌa:ki'peligou] pl **archipelagoes** n arcipelago.

architect ['a:kitekt] n architetto.

architecture ['a:kitektʃə] n architettura.

archives ['a:kaivz] n pl archivi.

archway ['a:tʃwei] n arcata.

Arctic ['a:ktik] a n artico.

Ardennes [a:'den] n pl (geogr) Ardenne.

ardent ['a:dənt] a ardente.

ardour ['a:də] n ardore.

arduous ['a:djuəs] a arduo; strenuo.

area ['ɛəriə] n area; zona.

arena [ə'ri:nə] n arena.

Argentina [ˌa:dʒən'ti:nə] n (geogr) Argentina.

Argentine ['a:dʒəntain] n (geogr) Argentina.

Argentinian [ˌa:dʒən'tiniən] a n argentino.

argue ['a:gju:] vti argomentare, discutere.

argument ['a:gjumənt] n discussione, ragionamento.

argumentative [ˌa:gju'mentətiv] a polemico.

arid ['ærid] a arido.

aridity [æ'riditi] n aridità.

aright [ə'rait] ad bene, giustamente.

arise [ə'raiz] vi alzarsi; sorgere.

aristocracy [ˌæris'tɔkrəsi] n aristocrazia.

aristocrat ['æristəkræt] n nobile, aristocratico.

aristocratic [ˌæristə'krætik] a aristocratico.

arithmetic [ə'riθmətik] n aritmetica.

arithmetical [ˌæriθ'metikəl] a aritmetico.

ark [a:k] n arca.

arm [a:m] n braccio; bracciuolo; pl **arms** (mil) armi pl; vti armar(si).

armament ['a:məmənt] n armamento.

armchair ['a:m'tʃɛə] n poltrona.

Armenia [a:'miniə] n (geogr) Armenia.

Armenian [a:'mi:niən] a n armeno.

armful ['a:mful] n bracciata.

armistice ['a:mistis] n armistizio.

armlet ['a:mlit] n bracciale.

armour ['a:mə] n armatura, corazza; blindatura; forze corazzate pl.

armoured ['a:məd] a corazzato, blindato; a. car autoblindo.

armoury ['a:məri] n arsenale; armeria.

armpit ['a:mpit] n ascella.

army ['a:mi] n esercito; armata.

Arnold ['a:nld] nm pr Arnaldo, Arnoldo.

aromatic(al) [ˌærou'mætik(əl)] a aromatico.

around [ə'raund] ad all'intorno, in ogni parte; prep intorno a.

arouse [ə'rauz] vt (ri)svegliare; suscitare.

arraign [ə'rein] vt accusare, chiamare in giudizio.

arrange [ə'reindʒ] vt accomodare; disporre; ordinare; (mus) adattare; vi prendere accordi.

arrangement [ə'reindʒmənt] n accomodamento; accordo.

array [ə'rei] n ordine, schiera; mostra; abbigliamento.

arrears [ə'riəz] n pl arretrati.

arrest [ə'rest] n arresto, fermata; vt arrestare, fermare.

arrival [ə'raivəl] n arrivo.

arrive [ə'raiv] vi arrivare, giungere.

arrogance ['ærəgəns] n arroganza.

arrogant ['ærəgənt] a arrogante.

arrogate ['ærougeit] vt arrogarsi, pretendere.

arrow ['ærou] n freccia.

arsenal ['ɑːsinl] n arsenale.

arsenic ['ɑːsnik] n arsenico.

arson ['ɑːsn] n incendio doloso.

art [ɑːt] n arte; **fine arts** pl belle arti pl; **Arts** pl lettere pl.

artery ['ɑːtəri] n arteria.

artesian [ɑːˈtiːziən] a artesiano.

artful ['ɑːtful] a abile; astuto; ingannevole.

arthritis [ɑːˈθraitis] n artrite.

Arthur ['ɑːθə] nm pr Arturo.

artichoke ['ɑːtitʃouk] n carciofo.

article ['ɑːtikl] n articolo; **leading a.** articolo di fondo; vt mettere come apprendista.

articulate [ɑːˈtikjulit] a articolato; distinto, chiaro; n animale articolato; vti [ɑːˈtikjuleit] articolare; pronunciare distintamente; esprimersi.

articulation [ɑːˌtikjuˈleiʃən] n articolazione; pronuncia distinta.

artifice ['ɑːtifis] n artificio, astuzia.

artificial [ɑːtiˈfiʃəl] a artificiale; artificioso.

artificiality [ˌɑːtifiʃiˈæliti] n artificiosità.

artillery [ɑːˈtiləri] n artiglieria.

artilleryman [ɑːˈtilərimən] a artigliere.

artisan [ˌɑːtiˈzæn] n artigiano.

artist ['ɑːtist] n artista; pittore.

artistic [ɑːˈtistik] a artistico.

artless ['ɑːtlis] a ingenuo, semplice.

artlessness ['ɑːtlisnis] n ingenuità, semplicità.

as [æz] ad cj come, nello stesso modo in cui; siccome, mentre; rel pron che; **as … as** così … come, tanto … quanto; **as for** in quanto a; **as long as** finché, purché.

asbestos [æzˈbestəs] n amianto.

ascend [əˈsend] vti ascendere, salire.

ascendency [əˈsendənsi] n ascendente, influenza.

ascension [əˈsenʃən] n ascensione.

ascent [əˈsent] n ascesa, salita.

ascertain [ˌæsəˈtein] vt accertarsi, scoprire.

ascetic [əˈsetik] a ascetico; n asceta.

ascribe [əsˈkraib] vt ascrivere; attribuire.

ash [æʃ] n cenere.

ash(tree) ['æʃ(triː)] n frassino.

ashamed [əˈʃeimd] a vergognoso; **to be a.** of vergognarsi.

ashen ['æʃn] a cinereo, di color cinerino.

ashore [əˈʃɔː] ad a riva, a terra.

ashtray ['æʃtrei] n portacenere.

Asia ['eiʃə] n (geogr) Asia.

Asian ['eiʃən], **Asiatic** [ˌeiʃiˈætik] a n asiatico.

aside [əˈsaid] n parole pronunziate a parte; ad a parte; in disparte.

ask [ɑːsk] vti chiedere; invitare; informarsi.

askance [əsˈkæns] ad obliquamente.

asleep [əˈsliːp] a addormentato; **to fall a.** addormentarsi.

asparagus [əsˈpærəgəs] n (coll) asparago, asparagi.

aspect ['æspekt] n apparenza, aspetto; (of houses etc) esposizione.

aspen ['æspən] n pioppo tremulo.

asperity [æsˈperiti] n asperità; asprezza; rigore.

asperse [əsˈpəːs] vt aspergere; calunniare, denigrare.

aspersion [əsˈpəːʃən] n aspersione; calunnia.

asphalt ['æsfælt] n asfalto.

asphodel ['æsfədel] n asfodelo.

asphyxiate [æsˈfiksieit] vt asfissiare.

aspirate ['æspəreit] vt aspirare.

aspiration [ˌæspəˈreiʃən] n aspirazione.

aspire [əsˈpaiə] vi aspirare, bramare.

aspirin ['æspərin] n aspirina.

aspiring [əsˈpaiəriŋ] a ambizioso.

ass [æs] n asino; **to make an a.** of **oneself** rendersi ridicolo.

assail [əˈseil] vt assalire, attaccare.

assailant [əˈseilənt] n assalitore.

assassin [əˈsæsin] n assassino.

assassinate [əˈsæsineit] vt assassinare.

assassination [əˌsæsiˈneiʃən] n assassinio.

assault [əˈsɔːlt] vt assalire; n assalto.

assemble [əˈsembl] vti riunir(si); (mech) montare.

assembly [əˈsembli] n assemblea, riunione; (mech) montaggio.

assent [əˈsent] n assenso, consenso; vi acconsentire, approvare.

assert [əˈsəːt] vt asserire; rivendicare (un diritto).

assertion [əˈsəːʃən] n asserzione, rivendicazione.

assess [əˈses] vt valutare, stimare; tassare.

assessable [əˈsesəbl] a tassabile, imponibile.

assessment [əˈsesmənt] n tassa; valutazione.

assessor [əˈsesə] n assessore; agente del fisco.

asset ['æset] n bene, vantaggio; pl (com) attivo.

assiduity [ˌæsiˈdjuiti] n assiduità, diligenza.

assiduous [əˈsidjuəs] a assiduo, diligente.

assign [əˈsain] vt assegnare; fissare.

assignee [ˌæsiˈniː] n (com) mandatario.

assignment [əˈsainmənt] n assegnazione; stanziamento; (US) nomina, incarico.

assimilate [əˈsimileit] vt assimilare.

assimilation [əˌsimiˈleiʃən] n assimilazione.

assist [əˈsist] vt assistere, aiutare.

assistance [əˈsistəns] n assistenza, aiuto.

assistant [əˈsistənt] a n assistente; aiuto, aggiunto.

assizes [ə'saiziz] n pl corte d'assise.
associa e [ə'souʃiit] a associato n; socio; vti [ə'souʃieit] associar(si).
association [ə.sousi'eiʃən] n associazione; A. football giuoco del calcio.
assort [ə'sɔːt] vt assortire.
assortment [ə'sɔːtmənt] n assortimento.
assuage [ə'sweidʒ] vt calmare, mitigare.
assume [ə'sjuːm] vt assumere; arrogarsi; presumere.
assuming [ə'sjuːmiŋ] a presuntuoso.
assumption [ə'sʌmpʃən] n assunto; assunzione; supposizione.
assurance [ə'ʃuərəns] n assicurazione; certezza; fiducia in sè.
assure [ə'ʃuə] vt assicurare; rassicurare.
assuredly [ə'ʃuəridli] ad certamente.
asterisk ['æstərisk] n asterisco.
astern [əs'təːn] ad (naut) a poppa.
asthma ['æsmə] n asma.
asthmatic [æs'mætik] a asmatico.
astigmatism [æs'tigmətizəm] n astigmatismo.
astir [ə'stəː] ad a in moto.
astonish [əs'tɔniʃ] vt sorprendere; stupire.
astonishing [əs'tɔniʃiŋ] a sorprendente, straordinario.
astonishingly [əs'tɔniʃiŋli] ad sorprendentemente.
astonishment [əs'tɔniʃmənt] n sorpresa, stupore.
astound [əs'taund] vt stupefare.
astrakhan [.æstrə'kæn] n astracan.
astral ['æstrəl] a astrale.
astray [əs'trei] ad fuori della giusta via; to go a. sviarsi.
astride [əs'traid] ad a cavalcioni.
astringent [əs'trindʒənt] a n astringente.
astrologer [əs'trɔlədʒə] n astrologo.
astrology [əs'trɔlədʒi] n astrologia.
astronaut ['æstrənɔːt] n astronauta.
astronautics [.æstrə'nɔːtiks] n astronautica.
astronomer [əs'trɔnəmə] n astronomo.
astronomical ['æstrə'nɔmikəl] a astronomico.
astronomy [əs'trɔnəmi] n astronomia.
astute [əs'tjuːt] a astuto, sagace.
astuteness [əs'tjuːtnis] n astuzia, scaltrezza.
asunder [ə'sʌndə] ad a pezzi; separatamente.
asylum [ə'sailəm] n asilo; casa di ricovero; lunatic a. manicomio.
at [æt] prep a, da, di, in.
atheism ['eiθiizəm] n ateismo.
atheist ['eiθiist] n ateo.
Athenian [ə'θiːniən] a n ateniese.
Athens ['æθinz] n (geogr) Atene.
athlete ['æθliːt] n atleta.
athletic [æθ'letik] a atletico.
athletics [æθ'letiks] n atletica.

at-home [ət'houm] n ricevimento (a casa).
Atlantic [ət'læntik] a n atlantico.
atlas ['ætləs] n atlante.
atmosphere ['ætməsfiə] n atmosfera.
atmospherics [.ætməs'feriks] n pl (rad) scariche pl.
atom ['ætəm] n atomo.
atomic [ə'tɔmik] a atomico.
atomize ['ætəmaiz] vt atomizzare.
atomizer ['ætəmaizə] n polverizzatore; spruzzatore.
atone [ə'toun] vi espiare.
atonement [ə'tounmənt] n espiazione, riparazione.
atrocious [ə'trouʃəs] a atroce.
atrocity [ə'trɔsiti] n atrocità.
atrophy ['ætrəfi] n atrofia.
attach [ə'tætʃ] vt attaccare; attribuire; fissare; vi attaccarsi, aderire.
attaché [ə'tæʃei] n diplomatico, addetto ad un'ambasciata; a.-case valigetta.
attached [ə'tætʃt] a addetto, assegnato; affezionato.
attachment [ə'tætʃmənt] n attaccamento; affetto; (mech) accessorio.
attack [ə'tæk] n attacco, offensiva; accesso; vt attaccare, assalire.
attain [ə'tein] vt conseguire, ottenere raggiungere; vi arrivare.
attainable [ə'teinəbl] a conseguibile, raggiungibile.
attainment [ə'teinmənt] n conseguimento; pl cultura.
attempt [ə'tempt] n tentativo; attentato; vt provare, tentare; attentare.
attend [ə'tend] vi attendere a; prestare attenzione; dare assistenza; essere presente; vt accompagnare, frequentare.
attendance [ə'tendəns] n servizio; assistenza; frequenza; persone presenti.
attendant [ə'tendənt] n servitore, custode; (theat) maschera. pl seguito;
attention [ə'tenʃən] n attenzione, premura; to pay a. stare attento.
attentive [ə'tentiv] a attento; premuroso.
attenuate [ə'tenjueit] vt attenuare.
attest [ə'test] vti attestare, testimoniare.
attestation [.ætes'teiʃən] n attestazione, conferma.
attic ['ætik] n soffitta, solaio; attico.
attire [ə'taiə] n abbigliamento.
attitude ['ætitjuːd] n atteggiamento; posa.
attorney [ə'təːni] n procuratore, procura; A. General Procuratore Generale; (US) Ministro della Giustizia; district a. (US) pubblico ministero.
attract [ə'trækt] vt attirare.
attraction [ə'trækʃən] n attrazione, attrattiva.
attractive [ə'træktiv] a attraente, attrattivo.

attribute ['ætribjuːt] *n* attributo, qualità; *vt* [ə'tribju(ː)t] attribuire.

attrition [ə'triʃən] *n* attrito.

attune [ə'tjuːn] *vt* armonizzare.

aubergine ['oubəʒiːn] *n* melanzana.

auburn ['ɔːbən] *a* color rame, ramato.

auction ['ɔːkʃən] *n* asta, vendita all'incanto; *vt* vendere all'asta.

auctioneer [,ɔːkʃə'niə] *n* banditore.

audacious [ɔː'deiʃəs] *a* audace.

audacity [ɔː'dæsiti] *n* audacità.

audibility [,ɔːdi'biliti] *n* udibilità.

audible ['ɔːdəbl] *a* udibile.

audibly ['ɔːdəbli] *ad* distintamente.

audience ['ɔːdiəns] *n* pubblico; udienza.

audio-visual [,ɔːdiou'vizjuəl] *a* audiovisivo.

audit ['ɔːdit] *n* controllo; *vt* rivedere (conti).

audition [ɔː'diʃən] *n* audizione; *vti* ascoltare, esibirsi in audizione.

auditor ['ɔːditə] *n* revisore di conti.

auditorium [,ɔːdi'tɔːriəm] *n* sala, auditorio.

auger ['ɔːgə] *n* succhiello.

augment [ɔːg'ment] *vt* aumentare; *vi* crescere.

augmentation [,ɔːgmen'teiʃən] *n* aumento.

augur ['ɔːgə] *n* augure; *vti* predire, presagire.

augury ['ɔːgjuri] *n* presagio, pronostico.

August ['ɔːgəst] *n* agosto.

august [ɔː'gʌst] *a* augusto, maestoso.

Augustin(e) [ɔː'gʌstin] *nm pr* Agostino.

Augustus [ɔː'gʌstəs] *nm pr* Augusto.

aunt [ɑːnt] *n* zia.

aureomycin [,ɔːriou'maisin] *n* aureomicina.

auspice ['ɔːspis] *n* auspicio, augurio.

auspicious [ɔːs'piʃəs] *a* di buon augurio.

austere [ɔs'tiə] *a* austero.

austerity [ɔs'teriti] *n* austerità.

Australia [ɔs'treiliə] *n* (*geogr*) Australia.

Australian [ɔs'treiliən] *a n* australiano.

Austria ['ɔstriə] *n* (*geogr*) Austria.

Austrian ['ɔstriən] *a n* austriaco.

authentic [ɔː'θentik] *a* autentico.

authenticate [ɔː'θentikeit] *vt* autenticare.

authentication [ɔː,θenti'keiʃən] *n* autenticazione.

authenticity [,ɔːθen'tisiti] *n* autenticità.

author ['ɔːθə] *n* autore.

authoritative [ɔː'θɔritətiv] *a* autorevole, autoritario.

authority [ɔː'θɔriti] *n* autorità.

authorization [,ɔːθərai'zeiʃən] *n* autorizzazione.

authorize ['ɔːθəraiz] *vt* autorizzare.

autobiography [,ɔːtoubai'ɔgræfi] *n* autobiografia.

autobus ['ɔːtoubʌs] *n* (*US*) autobus.

autocamp ['ɔːtoukæmp] *n* (*US*) accampamento per automobilisti.

autocrat ['ɔːtəkræt] *n* autocrate.

autodrome ['ɔːtoudroum] *n* autodromo.

autograph ['ɔːtəgrɑːf] *n* autografo; *vt* firmare; (*typ*) autografare.

automatic [,ɔːtə'mætik] *a* automatico; *n* rivoltella.

automatically [,ɔːtə'mætikəli] *ad* automaticamente.

automation [,ɔːtə'meiʃən] *n* automazione.

automobile ['ɔːtəməbiːl] *n* (*US*) automobile.

autonomy [ɔː'tɔnəmi] *n* autonomia.

autopsy ['ɔːtəpsi] *n* autopsia.

autumn ['ɔːtəm] *n* autunno.

autumnal [ɔː'tʌmnəl] *a* autunnale, d'autunno.

auxiliary [ɔːg'ziljəri] *a* ausiliario, -re; *n* ausiliare; *pl* milizie ausiliarie.

avail [ə'veil] *n* utilità, vantaggio; *vi* giovare (a), essere utile (a); *vt* aiutare, favorire; **to a. oneself of** valersi di.

availability [ə'veilə'biliti] *n* disponibilità.

available [ə'veiləbl] *a* disponibile.

avalanche ['ævəlɑːnʃ] *n* valanga.

avarice ['ævəris] *n* avarizia.

avaricious [,ævə'riʃəs] *a* avaro.

avenge [ə'vendʒ] *vt* vendicare.

avenger [ə'vendʒə] *n* vendicatore.

avenue ['ævinjuː] *n* viale; accesso.

aver [ə'vəː] *vt* affermare, asserire.

average ['ævəridʒ] *a* di media categoria, medio; *n* media; (*naut*) avaria; *vt* fare la media.

averse [ə'vəːs] *a* avverso, contrario.

aversion [ə'vəːʃən] *n* avversione, antipatia.

avert [ə'vəːt] *vt* schivare; distogliere.

aviary ['eivjəri] *n* aviario.

aviation [,eivi'eiʃən] *n* aviazione.

avid ['ævid] *a* avido.

avidity [ə'viditi] *n* avidità.

avoid [ə'vɔid] *vt* evitare, schivare.

avoidance [ə'vɔidəns] *n* l'evitare; fuga, scampo.

avowed [ə'vaud] *a* manifesto, aperto, dichiarato.

await [ə'weit] *vt* aspettare.

awake [ə'weik] *a* sveglio; *vti* svegliar(si).

awaken [ə'weikən] *vti* risvegliare, risvegliarsi.

awakening [ə'weikniŋ] *n* risveglio (*also fig*).

award [ə'wɔːd] *n* giudizio; ricompensa; *vt* aggiudicare, assegnare.

aware [ə'wɛə] *a* conscio.

away [ə'wei] *ad* lontano, via.

awe [ɔː] *n* timore misto a venerazione.

awful ['ɔːful] *a* terribile, spaventevole.

awfully ['ɔːfuli] *ad* terribilmente; straordinariamente, molto.

awhile [ə'wail] *ad* un momento.

awkward ['ɔːkwəd] *a* goffo; imbarazzante; imbarazzato; scomodo.

awkwardly ['ɔːkwədli] *ad* goffamente; in modo imbarazzato.
awkwardness ['ɔːkwədnis] *n* goffaggine; difficoltà.
awl [ɔːl] *n* lesina.
awning ['ɔːniŋ] *n* tenda.
awry [ə'rai] *n* storto.
axe [æks] *n* ascia.
axiom ['æksiəm] *n* assioma.
axis ['æksis] *pl* **axes** ['æksiːz] *n* asse.
axle ['æksl] *n* (*mech*) asse.
ay(e) [ai] *ad* sì.
azalea [ə'zeiliə] *n* azalea.
azure ['eiʒə] *a* azzurro.

B

babble ['bæbl] *vti* balbettare; parlare scioccamente.
babbling ['bæbliŋ] *n* balbettio; discorso senza senso.
Babel ['beibəl] *n* Babele; **babel** *n* confusione.
baboon [bə'buːn] *n* babuino.
baby ['beibi] *n* neonato, bimbo; **b. carriage** (*US*) carrozzina.
babyhood ['beibihud] *n* prima infanzia.
babyish ['beibiiʃ] *a* bambinesco, infantile, puerile.
bachelor ['bætʃələ] *n* celibe, scapolo; baccelliere.
bachelorhood ['bætʃələhud] *n* celibato.
bacillus [bə'siləs] *pl* **bacilli** *n* bacillo.
back [bæk] *n* dorso, parte posteriore, schiena; schienale; spalle *pl*; spalliera; *a* posteriore, di dietro, indietro, di ritorno; **be b.** essere di ritorno; **come b.** ritornare.
back [bæk] *vti* spalleggiare; indietreggiare; (*com*) avallare; **b. a horse** puntare su un cavallo.
backbite ['bækbait] *vti* calunniare.
backbone ['bækboun] *n* spina dorsale.
background ['bækgraund] *n* sfondo; ambiente.
backslider ['bæk'slaidə] *n* recidivo.
backward ['bækwəd] *a* riluttante; tardivo.
backwardness ['bækwədnis] *n* lentezza d'intelligenza, ritardo di sviluppo.
backwards ['bækwəds] *ad* (all') indietro, a ritroso.
bacon ['beikən] *n* lardo affumicato, pancetta.
bacterium [bæk'tiəriəm] *pl* **bacteria** *n* batterio.
bacteriology [bæk,tiəri'ɔlədʒi] *n* batteriologia.
bad [bæd] *a* cattivo, colpevole, dannoso, grave, sfavorevole; *n* male; **to go b.** andare a male; **badly** *ad* male, malamente.
badge [bædʒ] *n* distintivo, emblema.

badger ['bædʒə] *n* (*zool*) tasso; *vt* tormentare, molestare.
badness ['bædnis] *n* cattiveria; (*quality*) inferiorità.
baffle ['bæfl] *vt* impedire, frustrare; sconcertare; rendere vano.
baffling ['bæfliŋ] *a* sconcertante.
bag [bæg] *n* borsa, borsetta, sacco, carniere; pesci o selvaggina presi; *vt* insaccare, prendere, rubare.
baggage ['bægidʒ] *n* bagagli(o); **b. car** (*US*) bagagliaio.
bagpipe(s) ['bægpaip(s)] *n* (*usu pl*) cornamusa.
bagpiper ['bægpaipə] *n* suonatore di cornamusa.
bail [beil] *n* cauzione, garanzia, garante; **to go b. for** essere garante di; *vt* procurare la libertà provvisoria a; aggottare (una barca).
bailiff ['beilif] *n* ufficiale giudiziario; fattore di campagna.
bait [beit] *n* esca; *vt* fornire di esca, adescare; tormentare; alimentare; *vi* prendere cibo.
bake [beik] *vt* cuocere al forno; *vi* indurirsi per effetto del calore.
bake-house ['beikhaus] **bakery** ['beikəri] *n* forno.
baker ['beikə] *n* fornaio; **b.'s (shop)** panetteria.
baking ['beikiŋ] *n* cottura al forno; **b. powder** lievito.
balance ['bæləns] *n* bilancia; equilibrio; armonia; (*com*) bilancio, saldo; **b. sheet** bilancio; **to lose one's b.** perdere l'equilibrio; *vti* pesare, bilanciare, mantener l'equilibrio.
balcony ['bælkəni] *n* balcone.
bald [bɔːld] *a* calvo; (*style*) disadorno.
baldness ['bɔːldnis] *n* calvizie *pl*.
Baldwin ['bɔːldwin] *nm pr* Baldovino.
bale [beil] *n* balla; *vt* imballare.
balk [bɔːk] *n* trave rozzamente digrossata; *vt* evitare, ostacolare.
Balkan ['bɔːlkən] *a* balcanico.
Balkans ['bɔːlkəns] *n* Balcani.
ball [bɔːl] *n* palla, pallone, (*thread*) gomitolo; (*dance*) ballo; **ballpoint** (*pen*) penna a sfera.
ballad ['bæləd] *n* ballata.
ballast ['bæləst] *n* (*naut*) zavorra.
ballet ['bælei] *n* balletto, danza classica.
balloon [bə'luːn] *n* pallone; pallone aerostatico; (*cartoons*) fumetto.
ballot ['bælət] *n* scheda (di votazione), scrutinio; *vi* votare a scrutinio segreto; **b. box** urna.
balm [bɑːm] *n* balsamo.
balmy ['bɑːmi] *a* balsamico, fragrante.
balsam ['bɔːlsəm] *n* balsamo.
Baltic ['bɔːltik] *a n* Baltico.
Baltimore ['bɔːltimɔː] *n* Baltimora.
balustrade [,bæləs'treid] *n* balustrata.
bamboo [bæm'buː] *n* bambù.

bamboozle [bæm'buːzl] vt (sl) ingannare, mistificare.

ban [bæn] n bando; scomunica; vt proibire, mettere all'indice.

banal [bə'nɑːl] a banale.

banality [bə'næliti] n banalità.

banana [bə'nɑːnə] n banana.

band [bænd] n banda; legame; striscia; vt legare insieme; vi unirsi.

bandage ['bændidʒ] n benda, fascia.

bandbox ['bændbɒks] n cappelliera.

bandit ['bændit] n bandito.

bandolier [ˌbændə'liə] n bandoliera.

bandsman ['bændzmən] n bandista.

bandy ['bændi] a curvo, storto; vt ribattere, disputare, scambiare parole.

baneful ['beinful] a dannoso, velenoso.

bang [bæŋ] n colpo rumoroso, esplosione, fracasso; vt colpire rumorosamente, sbatacchiare.

bangle ['bæŋgl] n braccialetto.

banish ['bæniʃ] vt bandire, esiliare.

banishment ['bæniʃmənt] n bando, esilio.

banister ['bænistə] n ringhiera, balaustra.

bank [bæŋk] n argine, riva; banca, banco; vt depositare in una banca; b.-note, (US) b. bill banconota; to b. on contare su.

banker ['bæŋkə] n banchiere.

bank holiday ['bæŋk'hɒlədi] n festa civile.

banking ['bæŋkiŋ] n professione bancaria; a bancario.

bankrupt ['bæŋkrəpt] a n fallito; to go b. fallire.

bankruptcy ['bæŋkrəptsi] n fallimento, bancarotta.

banner ['bænə] n bandiera, stendardo.

banns [bænz] n pl pubblicazioni matrimoniali pl.

banquet ['bæŋkwit] n banchetto; vi banchettare.

banter ['bæntə] n beffa; vti prendere in giro, beffarsi.

baptism ['bæptizəm] n battesimo.

baptismal [bæp'tizməl] a battesimale.

baptist(e)ry ['bæptist(ə)ri] n battistero.

baptize [bæp'taiz] vt battezzare.

bar [bɑː] n (s)barra; ostacolo; bar; the bar ordine degli avvocati; vt (s)barrare; escludere; ostacolare; b. tender barista; to be called to the b. (US) to be admitted to the b. essere iscritto all'albo degli avvocati.

barbarian [bɑː'bɛəriən] n barbaro.

barbaric [bɑː'bærik] a barbarico, primitivo.

barbarism ['bɑːbərizem] n barbarie, barbarismo.

barbarity [bɑː'bæriti] n barbarie, crudeltà.

barbarous ['bɑːbərəs] a barbaro.

barbecue ['bɑːbikjuː] n animale

arrostito intero; festa campestre.

barbed [bɑːbd] a dentellato, spinato; pungente; b. wire filo di ferro spinato.

barber ['bɑːbə] n barbiere, parrucchiere.

barbiturate [bɑː'bitjurit] n barbiturico.

bare [bɛə] a nudo, spoglio, scoperto; vt denudare, scoprire.

barefaced ['bɛəfeist] a sfacciato.

barefoot(ed) ['bɛə'fut(id)] a scalzo; ad a piedi nudi.

bareheaded ['bɛə'hedid] a ad a capo scoperto.

barely ['bɛəli] ad appena.

bareness ['bɛənis] n nudità.

bargain ['bɑːgin] n affare; occasione; into the b. per giunta, in più; vi contrattare; to b. for aspettarsi.

barge [bɑːdʒ] n chiatta; lancia di parata; vi to b. into urtare.

baritone ['bæritoun] a n baritono.

bark [bɑːk] n latrato; corteccia, scorza; vi abbaiare; vt scorticare, scorzare.

barley ['bɑːli] n orzo.

barm [bɑːm] n fermento, lievito di birra.

barmaid ['bɑːmeid] n barista.

barman ['bɑːmən] n barista.

barn [bɑːn] n granaio; barnyard aia, cortile (di fattoria).

barnacle ['bɑːnəkl] n cirripede.

barometer [bə'rɔmitə] n barometro.

baron(ess) ['bærən(is)] n barone(ssa).

baronet ['bærənit] n baronetto.

baroque [bə'rouk] a n barocco.

barrack ['bærək] n usu pl caserma; vt alloggiare in caserma; schernire, fischiare.

barrage ['bærɑːʒ] n (mil) sbarramento.

barrel ['bærəl] n barile, botte; (gun) canna.

barren ['bærən] a sterile.

barrenness ['bærənnis] n sterilità.

barricade [ˌbæri'keid] n barricata.

barrier ['bæriə] n barriera; b. cream crema antivampa; sound b. muro del suono.

barrister ['bæristə] n avvocato.

barrow ['bærou] n carriola, carretto.

barter ['bɑːtə] n baratto; vt barattare, scambiare.

Bartholomew [bɑː'θɔləmjuː] nm pr Bartolomeo.

basalt ['bæsɔːlt] n basalto.

base [beis] n base, fondamento; a basso, indegno, vile; vt basare, fondare.

baseball ['beisbɔːl] n (US) 'baseball', palla a basi.

baseless ['beislis] a infondato, senza base.

basement ['beismənt] n seminterrato.

baseness ['beisnis] n bassezza, viltà.

bash [bæʃ] n colpo forte; vt colpire violentemente.

bashful ['bæʃful] *a* timido.

bashfulness ['bæʃfulnis] *n* timidezza.

basic ['beisik] *a* basilare, fondamentale.

basil ['bæzl] *n* basilico.

basin ['beisn] *n* bacino, bacinella; scodella; lavabo; **sugar b.** zuccheriera.

basis ['beisis] *pl* **bases** *n* base, fondamento.

bask [bɑːsk] *vi* godersi il caldo o il sole.

basket ['bɑːskit] *n* cesta, cesto, paniere; **b.ball** pallacanestro.

Basle [bɑːl] *n* (*geogr*) Basilea.

Basque [bæsk] *a n* basco.

bas-relief ['bæsri,liːf] *n* basso rilievo.

bass [bæs] *n* (*fish*) pesce persico; (*mus*) basso.

bassoon [bə'suːn] *n* (*mus*) fagotto.

bastard ['bæstəd] *a n* bastardo.

baste [beist] *vt* imbastire; spruzzare di grasso l'arrosto; bastonare.

bastion ['bæstiən] *n* bastione.

bat [bæt] *n* (*zool*) pipistrello; (*cricket etc*) mazza, (*ping-pong*) racchetta.

batch [bætʃ] *n* (*bread*) infornata; (*goods*) lotto.

bath [bɑːθ] *n* bagno (*US anche di mare*), tinozza; **to take a b.** fare il bagno; *vt* bagnare; *vi* bagnarsi, fare un bagno; **bathrobe** accappatoio.

bathe [beið] *n* (*di mare etc*) bagno; *vti* bagnar(si), (*nel mare etc*) fare il bagno.

bather ['beiðə] *n* bagnante.

bathing ['beiðiŋ] *n* bagnare, bagno, bagni *pl*; **b. costume, b. suit** costume da bagno; **b. cap** cuffia da bagno.

bathos ['beiθos] *n* discesa dal sublime al ridicolo.

batman ['bætmən] *n* (*mil*) attendente.

baton ['bætən] *n* bacchetta; bastone di comando.

battalion [bə'tæljən] *n* battaglione.

batten ['bætn] *n* assicella, traversa in legno; *vt* rinforzare con legno; **to b. down** (*naut*) chiudere un boccaporto.

batter ['bætə] *n* pastella; *vti* battere violentemente; cannoneggiare.

battering-ram ['bætəriŋræm] *n* ariete.

battery ['bætəri] *n* (*mil, el*) batteria, pila.

battle ['bætl] *n* battaglia, combattimento; *vi* combattere, lottare.

battlement ['bætlmənt] *n* merlo, bastione.

bauble ['bɔːbl] *n* ornamento di poco valore; bastone del buffone.

Bavaria [bə'vɛəriə] *n* (*geogr*) Baviera.

Bavarian [bə'vɛəriən] *a n* bavarese.

bawd [bɔːd] *n* mezzana.

bawdiness ['bɔːdinis] *n* oscenità.

bawdy ['bɔːdi] *a* osceno.

bawl [bɔːl] *vi* gridare ad alta voce, schiamazzare.

bay [bei] *n* baia, insenatura del mare; (*bot*) lauro; (*window*) recesso; latrato di grosso cane; *vi* abbaiare, latrare; **to hold at b.** tenere a bada.

bayonet ['beiənit] *n* baionetta.

bazaar [bə'zɑː] *n* bazar.

be [biː] *vi and aux* essere, esistere, vivere, stare, dovere, costare; **to b. in** essere in casa; **to b. long** tardare; **to be two years old** avere due anni.

beach [biːtʃ] *n* lido, spiaggia.

beacon ['biːkən] *n* faro, segnale.

bead [biːd] *n* (*necklace etc*) grano; (*liquids*) goccia; (*rifle*) mirino; **beads** *pl* rosario.

beadle ['biːdl] *n* bidello, sagrestano.

beagle ['biːgl] *n* piccolo cane da caccia.

beak [biːk] *n* becco, rostro.

beaker ['biːkə] *n* coppa, bicchiere.

beam [biːm] *n* trave; (*light*) raggio; sorriso; *vi* risplendere; sorridere.

beaming ['biːmiŋ] *a* raggiante.

bean [biːn] *n* fagiolo, fava; **full of beans** (*sl*) energico, vivace.

bear [bɛə] *n* orso.

bear [bɛə] *vt* portare, sopportare; produrre; *vi* dirigersi, inclinare; **to b. oneself** comportarsi.

bearable ['bɛərəbl] *a* sopportabile.

beard [biəd] *n* barba *vt* sfidare.

bearded ['biədid] *a* barbuto.

beardless ['biədlis] *a* imberbe.

bearer ['bɛərə] *n* latore, portatore.

bearing ['bɛəriŋ] *n* portamento, contegno; **bearings** *pl* orientamento; (*mech*) cuscinetto.

beast [biːst] *n* bestia, animale.

beastly ['biːstli] *a* bestiale; (*sl*) orribile.

beat [biːt] *n* battito, palpito; (*of policeman etc*) giro; *vti* battere, vincere; palpitare; **to b. about the bush** menare il can per l'aia.

beatification [biːˌætifi'keiʃən] *n* beatificazione.

beatify [biː'ætifai] *vt* beatificare.

beating ['biːtiŋ] *n* azione del battere, busse *pl*; sconfitta.

beatitude [biː'ætitjuːd] *n* beatitudine.

beatnik ['biːtnik] *n* beatnik, capellone.

Beatrice ['biətris] **Beatrix** ['biətriks] *nf pr* Beatrice.

beau [bou] *pl* **beaux** *n* damerino; cicisbeo.

beautician [bjuː'tiʃən] *n* estetista.

beautiful ['bjuːtəful] *a* bello.

beautifully ['bjuːtəfli] *ad* meravigliosamente, perfettamente.

beautify ['bjuːtifai] *vt* abbellire.

beauty ['bjuːti] *n* bellezza.

beaver ['biːvə] *n* castoro, castorino.

becalm [bi'kɑːm] *vt* abbonacciare.

because [bi'kɔz] *cj* perchè; **b. of** a causa di.

beckon ['bekən] *vti* chiamare con un cenno.

become [bi'kʌm] *vi* divenire, accadere; *vt* convenire a, star bene a.

becoming [bi'kʌmiŋ] *a* conveniente, che s'addice a.

bed [bed] *n* letto; **bedding** biancheria da letto; (*of animals*) ¹lettiera.

bedclothes ['bedklouðz] *n pl* coperte e biancheria da letto.

bedlam ['bedləm] *n* grande confusione; manicomio.

bedouin ['beduin] *a n* beduino.

bedraggle [bi'drægl] *vt* inzaccherare.

bedridden ['bed.ridn] *a* allettato.

bedroom ['bedrum] *n* camera (da letto).

bedside ['bedsaid] *n* capezzale.

bedstead ['bedsted] *n* fusto del letto.

bee [biː] *n* ape; **beeline** linea diretta.

beech [biːtʃ] *n* faggio.

beef [biːf] *n* manzo; **beefsteak** bistecca; **b. tea** brodo ristretto.

beehive ['biːhaiv] *n* alveare.

beer [biə] *n* birra; **b.-house** birreria.

beeswax ['biːzwæks] *n* cera vergine.

beet(root) ['biːt(ruːt)] *n* barbabietola.

beetle ['biːtl] *n* scarabeo, scarafaggio.

befall [bi'fɔːl] *vti* accadere a, capitare a, succedere.

befit [bi'fit] *vt* essere adatto a, andar bene per.

befitting [bi'fitiŋ] *a* adatto, conveniente.

before [bi'fɔː] *ad* prima, già, avanti; *prep* prima di, davanti a; *cj* prima che.

beforehand [bi'fɔːhænd] *ad* in anticipo.

befriend [bi'frend] *vt* mostrarsi amico di, aiutare.

beg [beg] *vti* domandare, pregare; elemosinare.

beget [bi'get] *vt* generare.

beggar ['begə] *n* mendicante.

beggarly ['begəli] *a* meschino, gretto.

beggary ['begəri] *n* mendicità.

begin [bi'gin] *vti* cominciare, iniziare, intraprendere, mettersi a.

beginner [bi'ginə] *n* principiante.

beginning [bi'giniŋ] *n* principio.

begonia [bi'gouniə] *n* begonia.

begrudge [bi'grʌdʒ] *vt* invidiare, lesinare.

beguile [bi'gail] *vt* ingannare.

behalf [bi'hɑːf] *n* **on b. of** da parte di.

behave [bi'heiv] *vi* comportarsi; (*machines*) funzionare.

behaviour [bi'heivjə] *n* comportamento, condotta; funzionamento.

behead [bi'hed] *vt* decapitare.

behind [bi'haind] *ad* indietro; *prep* dietro a; **b. time** in ritardo; **b. the times** antiquato.

behindhand [bi'haindhænd] *ad a* in arretrato, in ritardo.

behold [bi'hould] *vt* guardare, vedere, contemplare.

beholder [bi'houldə] *n* osservatore, spettatore.

being ['biːiŋ] **for the time b.** per ora;

n essere vivente, ente, esistenza.

belabour [bi'leibə] *vt* bastonare.

belated [bi'leitid] *a* tardivo, in ritardo.

belch [beltʃ] *vti* (e)ruttare; *n* rutto.

beleaguer [bi'liːgə] *vt* assediare.

belfry ['belfri] *n* campanile.

Belgian ['beldʒən] *a n* belga.

Belgium ['beldʒəm] *n* Belgio.

Belgrade [bel'greid] *n* Belgrado.

belief [bi'liːf] *n* credenza, fede, opinione.

believable [bi'liːvəbl] *a* credibile.

believe [bi'liːv] *vti* aver fede, credere, pensare, supporre.

believer [bi'liːvə] *n* credente.

belittle [bi'litl] *vt* denigrare.

bell [bel] *n* campana, campanello; **bellboy,** (*US*) **bellhop** fattorino d'albergo.

bellicose ['belikous] *a* bellicoso.

belligerent [bi'lidʒərənt] *a n* belligerante.

bellow ['belou] *vi* mugghiare, muggire, ruggire; *n* muggito.

bellows ['belouz] *n pl* mantice, soffietto.

belly ['beli] *n* pancia, ventre.

belong [bi'lɔŋ] *vi* appartenere, spettare.

belongings [bi'lɔŋiŋs] *n pl* effetti *pl.*

beloved [bi'lʌv(i)d] *a n* amato, diletto.

below [bi'lou] *prep* sotto (a); al di sotto di; *ad* (al di) sotto, giù.

belt [belt] *n* cinghia, cintura; zona; regione.

bemoan [bi'moun] *vt* compiangere; *vi* lamentarsi.

bench [bentʃ] *n* banco, panca, seggio; ufficio di giudice.

bend [bend] *n* curva, inclinazione; *vt* curvare, piegare; *vi* chinarsi, piegarsi.

beneath [bi'niːθ] *ad prep* al di sotto (di), in basso, sotto.

Benedictine [.beni'diktin] *a n* benedettino.

benediction [.beni'dikʃən] *n* benedizione.

benefaction [.beni'fækʃən] *n* beneficenza.

benefactor ['benifæktə] *n* benefattore.

beneficence [bi'nefisəns] *n* beneficenza.

beneficent [bi'nefisənt] *a* benefico.

beneficial [.beni'fiʃəl] *a* benefico, utile, vantaggioso.

beneficiary [.beni'fiʃəri] *n* beneficiario.

benefit ['benifit] *n* vantaggio, profitto, (*leg*) beneficio; *vt* beneficare; *vi* trarre profitto.

benevolence [bi'nevələns] *n* benevolenza.

benevolent [bi'nevələnt] *a* benevolo, caritatevole.

benign [bi'nain] **benignant** [bi'nignənt] *a* benevolo, benigno.

Benjamin ['bendʒəmin] *nm pr* Beniamino.

bent [bent] *n* curva, inclinazione naturale, tendenza; *a* curvo, deciso; **to be b. on** essere deciso a.

benumb [bi'nʌm] *vt* intorpidire.

benzine ['benziːn] *n* benzina.

bequeath [bi'kwiːð] *vt* lasciare per testamento.

bequest [bi'kwest] *n* lascito, eredità.

bereave [bi'riːv] *vt* privare, spogliare.

bereavement [bi'riːvmənt] *n* perdita di parente, lutto.

beret ['berei] *n* berretto, basco.

bergamot ['bəːgəmɔt] *n* (*bot*) bergamotto.

Berlin [bəː'lin] *n* (*geogr*) Berlino; **Berliner** berlinese.

Bermuda [bəː'mjuːdə] *n* 1. (le) Bermude 2. *pl.*

Bernard ['bəːnəd] *nm pr* Bernardo.

berry ['beri] *n* bacca.

berserk ['bəːsəːk] **to go b.** abbandonarsi a violenza cieca.

berth [bəːθ] *n* cuccetta; (*fig*) impiego; (*naut*) posto d'ancoraggio d'una nave; *vi* (*naut*) ancoreggiare.

Bertha ['bəːθə] *nf pr* Berta.

beryl ['beril] *n* (*min*) berillo.

beseech [bi'siːtʃ] *vt* implorare, supplicare.

beset [bi'set] *vt* assediare, assalire.

beside [bi'said] *prep* accanto a, vicino a; **b. oneself** fuori di sè.

besides [bi'saidz] *ad prep* inoltre, per di più, oltre a.

besiege [bi'siːdʒ] *vt* assediare.

besom ['bizəm] *n* granata, scopa.

best [best] *a* il migliore; *ad* il meglio, nel miglior modo, nel più alto grado; **it il meglio**.

bestial ['bestiəl] *a* bestiale, brutale.

bestiality [,besti'æliti] *n* bestialità, brutalità.

bestir [bi'stəː] *vi* **b. oneself** muoversi, scuotersi.

bestow [bi'stou] *vt* conferire, dare, depositare.

bestowal [bi'stouəl] *n* donazione, concessione.

bestride [bi'straid] *vt* stare a cavallo (a cavalcioni) di.

bet [bet] *n* scommessa; *vti* scommettere.

Bethlehem ['beθlihem] *n* Betlemme.

betoken [bi'touken] *vt* indicare, presagire.

betray [bi'trei] *vt* tradire, palesare.

betrayal [bi'treiəl] *n* tradimento.

betrothal [bi'trouðəl] *n* fidanzamento.

betrothed [bi'trouðd] *a n* fidanzato.

better ['betə] *a* migliore; *ad* meglio; **our betters** *pl* i nostri superiori; *vti* migliorar(e).

betting ['betiŋ] *n* lo scommettere.

between [bi'twiːn] *prep* fra, tra; **betwixt and b.** mezzo e mezzo.

beverage ['bevəridʒ] *n* bevanda.

bevy ['bevi] *n* compagnia; stormo.

bewail [bi'weil] *vti* lamentar(si), deplorare.

beware [bi'wɛə] *vi* stare in guardia.

bewilder [bi'wildə] *vt* confondere, rendere perplesso.

bewildering [bi'wildəriŋ] *a* sbalorditivo, sconcertante.

bewilderment [bi'wildəmənt] *n* confusione.

bewitch [bi'witʃ] *vt* ammaliare, stregare.

beyond [bi'jɔnd] *prep ad* n al di là (di); **the back of b.** il più remoto angolo della terra.

bias ['baiəs] *n* inclinazione, pregiudizio; **on the b.** per sbieco; *vt* far inclinare; influenzare.

bib [bib] *n* bavaglino.

Bible ['baibl] *n* Bibbia.

biblical ['biblikəl] *a* biblico.

bibliography [,bibli'ɔgrəfi] *n* bibliografia.

bibliophile ['biblioufail] *n* bibliofilo.

bicarbonate [bai'kɑːbənit] *n* bicarbonato.

biceps ['baiseps] *n* bicipite.

bicker ['bikə] *vi* litigare, altercare.

bicycle ['baisikl] *n* bicicletta; *vi* andare in bicicletta.

bid [bid] *n* (*at an auction*) offerta, proposta; *vti* comandare; dire.

bidder ['bidə] *n* (*at an auction*) offerente.

biennial [bai'eniəl] *a* biennale.

bier [biə] *n* bara.

big [big] *a* grosso, grande, importante; **bigwig** (*sl*) pezzo grosso.

bigamist ['bigəmist] *n* bigamo.

bigamous ['bigəməs] *a* bigamo.

bigamy ['bigəmi] *n* bigamia.

bigot ['bigət] *n* **bigoted** ['bigətid] *a* bigotto.

bigotry ['bigətri] *n* bigottismo.

bike [baik] *n* (*fam*) bicicletta.

bilateral [bai'lætərəl] *a* bilaterale.

bilberry ['bilbəri] *n* mirtillo.

bile [bail] *n* bile.

bilge [bildʒ] *n* (*naut*) sentina; (*sl*) sciocchezze.

bilingual [bai'liŋgwəl] *a* bilingue.

bilious ['biljəs] *a* biliare; bilioso.

bill [bil] *n* (*bird*) becco; (*notice etc*) cartellone, cartello; (*account*) conto, fattura; (*US*) biglietto di banca, banconota; (*com*) cambiale; (*leg*) progetto di legge; **billboard** spazio per la pubblicità.

billet ['bilit] *n* (*mil*) accantonamento; *vt* accantonare truppe.

billiards ['biljədz] *n pl* biliardo; **billiard saloon** sala del biliardo.

billion ['biljən] *n* bilione, (*US*) miliardo.

billow ['bilou] *n* flutto, maroso.

billowy ['biloui] *a* pieno di marosi; ondeggiante.

bimetallism [bai'metəlizem] *n* bimetallismo.

bin [bin] *n* recipiente per grano, carbone *etc*.

binary ['bainəri] *a* binario.

bind [baind] *vti* (ri)legare; obbligare; it was bound to happen doveva accadere.

binding ['baindiŋ] *a* obbligatorio, impegnativo; *n* legatura, rilegatura.

bindweed ['baindwi:d] *n* convolvolo.

binoculars [bi'nɔkjuləz] *n pl* binocolo.

biographer [bai'ɔgrəfə] *n* biografo.

biographical [baiou'græfikəl] *a* biografico.

biography [bai'ɔgrəfi] *n* biografia.

biological [ˌbaiə'lɔdʒikəl] *a* biologico.

biology [bai'ɔlədʒi] *n* biologia.

biped ['baiped] *a n* bipede.

birch [bə:tʃ] *n* (*bot*) betulla; sferza.

bird [bə:d] *n* uccello.

bird-lime ['bə:dlaim] *n* vischio.

bird's-eye view ['bə:dzai'vju:] panorama a volo d'uccello.

birth [bə:θ] *n* nascita; origine.

birthday ['bə:θdei] *n* compleanno.

birthplace ['bə:θpleis] *n* luogo di nascita.

birthright ['bə:θrait] *n* diritto ereditario; primogenitura.

Biscay ['biskei] *n* Biscaglia.

biscuit ['biskit] *n* biscotto, (US) pastina da tè; soda b. (US) galletta, 'cracker'.

bisect [bai'sekt] *vt* bisecare.

bishop ['biʃəp] *n* vescovo; (*chess*) alfiere.

bismuth ['bizməθ] *n* bismuto.

bison ['baisn] *n* bisonte.

bit [bit] *n* pezzo, pezzetto; (*bread*) boccone; (*bridle*) morso; (*tec*) morsa; punta.

bitch [bitʃ] *n* cagna; lupa; volpe femmina.

bite [bait] *n* morsicatura, morso; boccone; *vt* mordere; abboccare.

biting ['baitiŋ] *a* pungente; sarcastico.

bitter ['bitə] *a* amaro, aspro.

bitterness ['bitənis] *n* amarezza; rancore; (*of climate*) rigidità.

bitumen ['bitjumin] *n* bitume.

bivouac ['bivuæk] *n* bivacco.

bizarre [bi'za:] *a* bizzarro, eccentrico.

blab [blæb] *vt* rivelàre indiscretamente; *vi* chiacchierare.

black [blæk] *a* nero; minaccioso; oscuro; triste.

blackberry ['blæk.beri] *n* mora.

blackbird ['blækbə:d] *n* merlo.

blackboard ['blækbɔ:d] *n* lavagna.

blacken ['blækən] *vt* annerire; diffamare.

blackguard ['blæga:d] *n* mascalzone.

blacking ['blækiŋ] *n* lucido nero per scarpe.

blackish ['blækiʃ] *a* nerastro.

blackleg ['blækleg] *n* crumiro.

blackmail ['blækmeil] *n* ricatto; *vt* ricattare; blackmailer ricattatore.

blackness ['blæknis] *n* nerezza, oscurità.

blackout ['blækaut] *n* oscuramento; perdita temporanea dei sensi.

blacksmith ['blæksmiθ] *n* fabbroferraio.

bladder ['blædə] *n* vescica.

blade [bleid] *n* filo (d'erba); lama.

blame [bleim] *n* biasimo, censura; colpa; *vt* biasimare, censurare.

blameless ['bleimlis] *a* irreprensibile, innocente.

blameworthy ['bleim.wə:ði] *a* biasimevole.

blanch [bla:ntʃ] *vt* scolorire; *vi* impallidire.

Blanche [bla:ntʃ] *nf pr* Bianca.

blancmange [blə'mɔnʒ] *n* biancomangiare.

bland [blænd] *a* blando.

blandishment ['blændiʃmənt] *n* blandizia.

blank [blæŋk] *a* bianco; vuoto; *n* lacuna; spazio in bianco; (US) modulo; b. cheque assegno in bianco; b. verse verso sciolto.

blanket ['blæŋkit] *n* coperta; copertura.

blankly ['blæŋkli] *ad* senza espressione; recisamente.

blare [blɛə] *n* squillo; *vi* squillare; *vt* annunciare a gran voce.

blaspheme [blæs'fi:m] *vti* bestemmiare.

blasphemous ['blæsfiməs] *a* blasfemo; empio.

blasphemy ['blæsfimi] *n* bestemmia.

blast [bla:st] *n* raffica, colpo di vento; esplosione; squillo; *vt* far esplodere; distruggere; maledire; b. off blast-off; b. furnace altoforno.

blasting ['bla:stiŋ] *n* esplosione.

blatant ['bleitənt] *a* rumoroso; sguaiato; evidente.

blaze [bleiz] *n* fiamma, vampata; *vi* divampare, fiammeggiare.

blazer ['bleizə] *n* giacca sportiva; giacca di uniforme scolastica.

bleach [bli:tʃ] *vt* imbiancare.

bleak [bli:k] *a* esposto al vento; squallido; desolato; triste.

blear [bliə] *a* oscuro, confuso; b.-eyed dagli occhi cisposi.

bleat [bli:t] *vi* belare; bleat(ing) *n* belato.

bleed [bli:d] *vi* sanguinare; *vt* salassare; bleeding *n* emorragia.

blemish ['blemiʃ] *n* macchia; difetto (morale o fisico).

blench [blentʃ] *vi* indietreggiare.

blend [blend] *n* miscela, mistura; *vti* mescolar(si).

bless [bles] *vt* benedire, consacrare.

blessed ['blesid] *a* benedetto; beato, santo.

blessing ['blesiŋ] *n* benedizione.

blight [blait] *n* golpe, carbonchio; (*fig*) influenza maligna; *vt* inaridire.

blind [blaind] *a* cieco; *n* tendina, persiana; finzione; *vt* accecare.

blindfold ['blaindfould] *ad* ad occhi bendati; *vt* bendare gli occhi.

blindly ['blaindli] *ad* ciecamente, alla cieca.

blindness ['blaindnis] *n* cecità; mancanza di discernimento.

blink [bliŋk] *n* occhiata, sguardo rapido; guizzo di luce; *vi* battere le palpebre; ammiccare.

blinker ['bliŋkə] *n* (*aut*) lampeggiatore; paraocchi.

bliss [blis] *n* beatitudine; felicità.

blissful ['blisful] *a* beato; delizioso.

blister ['blistə] *n* bolla, vescica; *vt* far venire vesciche a; *vi* coprirsi di vesciche.

blithe [blaið] *a* giocondo.

blitheness ['blaiðnis] *n* giocondità.

blizzard ['blizəd] *n* bufera di neve, tormenta.

bloat [blout] *vti* gonfiar(si).

bloater ['bloutə] *n* aringa affumicata.

blob [blɔb] *n* goccia; macchia.

block [blɔk] *n* blocco; ceppo; gruppo di case; ostacolo; *vt* bloccare, ostacolare.

blockade [blɔ'keid] *n* blocco, assedio.

blockhead ['blɔkhed] *n* stupido.

blond(e) [blɔnd] *a n* biondo.

blood [blʌd] *n* sangue; discendenza, parentela, bellimbusto; **b.-donor** donatore di sangue; **b.-curdling** raccapricciante; **b.-stained** macchiato di sangue.

bloodhound ['blʌdhaund] *n* segugio.

bloodless ['blʌdlis] *a* esangue, pallido.

bloodshed ['blʌdʃed] *n* spargimento di sangue.

bloodshot ['blʌdʃɔt] *a* iniettato di sangue.

bloody ['blʌdi] *a* sanguinoso; sanguinario; insanguinato; (*vulg*) maledetto; *ad* (*vulg*) maledettamente, molto.

bloom [blu:m] *n* fiore, fioritura; incarnato; *vi* fiorire, sbocciare.

blooming ['blu:miŋ] *a* fiorente.

blossom ['blɔsəm] *n* fiore, fioritura; *vi* fiorire.

blot [blɔt] *n* macchia; cancellatura; difetto, colpa; *vt* macchiare; asciugare con carta assorbente; **b. out** cancellare.

blotch [blɔtʃ] *n* macchia, chiazza; sgorbio; pustola; **blotched, blotchy** chiazzato; bitorzoluto.

blotting-paper ['blɔtiŋ,peipə] *n* carta assorbente.

blouse [blauz] *n* blusa, camicetta.

blow [blou] *n* colpo; raffica, soffio; soffiata; *vti* soffiare; suonare (*a wind instrument*); ansare.

blowy ['bloui] *a* ventoso.

blowzy ['blauzi] *a* scapigliato.

blubber ['blʌbə] *n* grasso di balena; *vi* piangere rumorosamente.

bludgeon ['blʌdʒən] *n* randello.

blue [blu:] *a n* azzurro, blu, celeste, turchino; *a* nervoso, depresso, triste;

to have the blues essere depresso.

bluebell ['blu:bel] *n* giacinto selvatico; campanula.

bluebottle ['blu:,bɔtl] *n* moscone.

blue-stocking ['blu:,stɔkiŋ] *n* donna intellettuale, donna saccente.

bluff [blʌf] *a* brusco, franco; *n* inganno, montatura; *vt* ingannare.

bluish ['blu(:)iʃ] *a* bluastro, azzurrognolo.

blunder ['blʌndə] *n* errore grossolano, sbaglio; *vti* condurre maldestramente (un affare); fare un errore.

blunt [blʌnt] *a* smussato; franco; rude; ottuso; *vt* smussare; ottundere.

bluntly ['blʌntli] *ad* bruscamente, esplicitamente.

bluntness ['blʌntnis] *n* rudezza; franchezza; ottusità.

blur [blə:] *n* macchia; offuscamento; *vt* macchiare; offuscare.

blurb [blə:b] *n* soffietto editoriale.

blurt out ['blə:t'aut] *vt* spifferare, riferire senza discrezione.

blush [blʌʃ] *n* rossore; *vi* arrossire.

bluster ['blʌstə] *n* fanfaronata; millanteria; *vi* tempestare; smargiassare; **blusterer** *n* spaccone.

boar [bɔə] *n* verro, cinghiale.

board [bɔ:d] *n* asse, tavola; comitato, commissione; ministero; (*naut*) bordo; **above b.** a carte scoperte; pensione; *pl* (*theat*) palcoscenico; *vti* coprire di assi; prendere a pensione, tenere a pensione; salire a bordo.

boarder ['bɔ:də] *n* convittore, pensionante.

boarding house ['bɔ:diŋhaus] *n* pensione.

boarding school ['bɔ:diŋsku:l] *n* convitto.

boast [boust] *n* vanteria, vanto; *vti* vantar(si).

boastful ['boustful] *a* millantatore.

boat [bout] *n* barca; battello, vapore; **in the same b.** trovarsi nelle stesse condizioni.

boatman ['boutmən] *n* barcaiuolo.

boatswain ['boutswein, 'bousn] *n* (*naut*) nostromo.

bob [bɔb] *vt* tagliare corti (i capelli); *vi* fare inchini; muoversi in su e in giù; **b. up** tornare a galla.

bobbin ['bɔbin] *n* bobina, rocchetto.

bobsleigh ['bɔbslei] *n* bob, guido-slitta.

bodice ['bɔdis] *n* corpetto.

bodiless ['bɔdilis] *a* incorporeo.

bodily ['bɔdili] *a* corporeo; *ad* corporalmente; di peso, in massa.

bodkin ['bɔdkin] *n* punteruolo, passanastro.

Bodleian [bɔd'li(:)ən] *a* bodleiano.

body ['bɔdi] *n* corpo; torso; cadavere; ente; **in a b.** tutti insieme.

bodyguard ['bɔdiga:d] *n* guardia del corpo.

Boer ['bouə] *a n* boero.

bog [bɔg] *n* palude, pantano.

boggle ['bɔgl] *vi* trasalire; esitare.
boggy ['bɔgi] *a* paludoso.
bogie ['bougi] *n* (*rly*) carrello.
bogus ['bougəs] *a* falso, finto; simulato.
Bohemia [bou'hiːmiə] *n* Boemia.
Bohemian [bou'hiːmiən] *a n* boemo; 'bohemien'.
boil [bɔil] *n* (punto di) ebollizione; foruncolo; *vti* (far) bollire; lessare.
boiler ['bɔilə] *n* bollitore; caldaia.
boisterous ['bɔistərəs] *a* chiassoso; turbolento.
bold [bould] *a* audace, temerario; sfacciato; vigoroso; **boldly** *ad* arditamente; sfacciatamente.
boldness ['bouldnis] *n* audacia; sfacciataggine.
bole [boul] *n* tronco d'albero.
bolshevik ['bɔlʃivik] *a n* bolscevico.
bolshevism ['bɔlʃivizəm] *n* bolscevismo.
bolster ['boulstə] *n* cuscino, traversino; *vt* sostenere.
bolt [boult] *n* bullone, catenaccio; spranga; freccia; fulmine; *vt* chiudere a catenaccio; inghiottire in fretta; *vi* darsela a gambe.
bomb [bɔm] *n* bomba; *vti* bombardare.
bombard [bɔm'baːd] *vt* bombardare.
bombardment [bɔm'baːdmənt] *n* bombardamento.
bombast ['bɔmbæst] *n* linguaggio ampolloso.
bombastic [bɔm'bæstik] *a* ampolloso.
bomber ['bɔmə] *n* bombardiere.
bombshell ['bɔmʃel] *n* obice, granata; notizia, evento sconvolgente.
bond [bɔnd] *n* legame, vincolo; obbligazione; (*com*) deposito doganale.
bondage ['bɔndidʒ] *n* schiavitù, servitù.
bondsman ['bɔndzmən] *n* (*com*) garante.
bone [boun] *n* osso; *vt* disossare.
boneless ['bounlis] *a* senz'osso.
bonfire ['bɔn faiə] *n* falò.
Boniface ['bɔnifeis] *nm pr* Bonifazio.
bonnet ['bɔnit] *n* berretto scozzese, cappellino legato con nastri sotto il mento; (*aut*) cofano.
bonny ['bɔni] *a* bello, grazioso.
bonus ['bounəs] *n* compenso; gratifica; extradividendo.
bony ['bouni] *a* ossuto.
boo [buː] *vti* fischiare.
booby ['buːbi] *n* individuo sciocco.
book [buk] *n* libro; *vt* prendere nota di; prenotare; registrare; *vi* fare un biglietto (ferroviario).
book-binder ['buk baində] *n* rilegatore di libri.
book-binding ['buk baindiŋ] *n* rilegatura di libri.
book case ['bukkeis] *n* libreria, scaffale.
booking ['bukiŋ] *n* prenotazione; **b.**

clerk bigliettario; **b. office** biglietteria.
book-keeper ['buk kiːpə] *n* contabile.
book-keeping ['buk kiːpiŋ] *n* contabilità.
booklet ['buklit] *n* libretto, opuscolo.
bookmaker ['buk meikə] *n* allibratore.
bookmark(er) ['buk maːk(ə)] *n* segnalibro.
bookseller ['buk selə] *n* libraio.
bookshop ['bukʃɔp] *n* libreria.
bookstall ['bukstɔːl] *n* edicola, chiosco; bancarella.
bookworm ['bukwəːm] *n* tignuola; (*fig*) topo di biblioteca.
boom [buːm] *n* rimbombo; palo che tien tesa una rete; barriera galleggiante in un porto; improvviso aumento di attività commerciale; *vi* rimbombare; avere un improvviso aumento di attività.
boon [buːn] *n* dono, favore, vantaggio.
boor [buə] *n* persona zotica, villana.
boorish ['buəriʃ] *a* rozzo, zotico.
boost [buːst] *vt* lanciare un prodotto con gran pubblicità; (*el*) elevare la tensione di.
boot [buːt] *n* stivale; (*aut*) portabagagli.
booth [buːð] *n* baracca; **telephone b.** cabina telefonica.
booty ['buːti] *n* bottino.
booze [buːz] *n* (*fam*) bevande alcooliche *pl*; *vi* bere all'eccesso.
borax ['bɔːræks] *n* borace.
border ['bɔːdə] *n* bordo; confine; *a* di confine; *vti* confinare (con); orlare; rasentare.
borderer ['bɔːdərə] *n* abitante di confine.
bordering ['bɔːdəriŋ] *a* di confine, limitrofo.
bore [bɔː] *n* buco, foro; calibro di fucile; noia, seccatura; seccatore; *vt* (per)forare; seccare, annoiare.
boredom ['bɔːdəm] *n* noia.
boric ['bɔːrik] *a* borico.
boring ['bɔːriŋ] *a* noioso.
born [bɔːn] *a* nato; nativo.
borough ['bʌrə] *n* città avente amministrazione autonoma; collegio elettorale; mandamento.
borrow ['bɔrou] *vt* prendere a prestito.
bosom ['buzəm] *n* petto, seno; (*US*) il davanti di una camicia; **b. friend** amico intimo.
boss [bɔs] *n* borchia, ornamento in rilievo; (*sl*) padrone; capo.
bossy ['bɔsi] *a* prepotente; autoritario.
botanic [bə'tænik] *a* botanico.
botanist ['bɔtənist] *n* botanico.
botany ['bɔtəni] *n* botanica.
botch [bɔtʃ] *vt* rappezzare inabilmente.
both [bouθ] *a pron* ambedue, l'uno e

l'altro; **both . . . and** tanto . . . quanto.

bother ['bɔðə] n fastidio; vt seccare; vi preoccuparsi.

bothersome ['bɔðəsəm] a seccante, noioso.

bottle ['bɔtl] n bottiglia; fascio di fieno; vt imbottigliare.

bottom ['bɔtəm] n fondo, base; sedere; **at b.** in fondo.

bottomless ['bɔtəmlis] a senza fondo.

bough [bau] n ramo d'albero.

boulder ['bouldə] n masso roccioso.

bounce [bauns] n rimbalzo, salto; vi (rim)balzare.

bouncer ['baunsə] n (sl) chi getta fuori da un locale gli intrusi.

bouncing ['baunsiŋ] a vigoroso; vivace.

bound [baund] n confine; limite; salto, rimbalzo; a diretto; connesso con; destinato a; vt limitare; vi saltare, rimbalzare.

boundary ['baundəri] n linea di confine.

boundless ['baundlis] a illimitato.

bounteous ['bauntiəs] a benefico, generoso.

bountiful ['bauntiful] a generoso, liberale.

bounty ['baunti] n generosità; premio d'incoraggiamento.

bouquet ['bukei] n mazzolino; profumo.

bourgeois ['buəʒwɑ:] a n borghese; **bourgeoisie** borghesia.

bout [baut] n assalto; accesso; partita.

bovine ['bouvain] a bovino.

bow [bou] n arco; nodo.

bow [bau] n inchino; (ship) prua; vi inchinarsi; sottomettersi.

bowel ['bauəl] n budello; **bowels** pl budella pl; (fig) viscere.

bowl [boul] n ciotola; vaso; recipiente; boccia; palla di legno; vti rotolare.

bowler ['boulə] n bombetta, cappello duro; giocatore di bocce; (cricket) giocatore che serve la palla.

bowling ['bouliŋ], **bowls** [boulz] n gioco delle bocce.

bowsprit ['bousprit] n (naut) bompresso.

box [bɔks] n scatola; cassetta; (driver's) cassetta; (jury) banco; (theat) palco; schiaffo; **b. car** (US) vagone merci chiuso; vt mettere i scatola; vi fare del pugilato.

boxer ['bɔksə] n pugilatore, pugile.

boxing ['bɔksiŋ] n pugilato; **B. Day** il 26 dicembre.

box number ['bɔks,nʌmbə] n casella postale.

box-office ['bɔks'ɔfis] n botteghino del teatro, biglietteria.

boy [bɔi] n ragazzo.

boycott ['bɔikət] vt boicottare.

boyhood ['bɔihud] n fanciullezza.

boyish ['bɔiiʃ] a fanciullesco.

brace [breis] n qualunque cosa che tiene unito; paio; **braces** pl bretelle pl; vt assicurare strettamente.

bracelet ['breislit] n braccialetto.

bracing ['breisiŋ] a invigorante, salubre.

bracken ['brækən] n felce.

bracket ['brækit] n mensola; parentesi; vt mettere fra parentesi.

brackish ['brækiʃ] a salso, salmastro.

brag [bræg] n millanteria, vanteria; vi vantarsi.

braggart ['brægət] n millantatore, spaccone.

braid [breid] n (of hair) treccia; gallone; vt intrecciare; guarnire.

brain [brein] n cervello; (usu pl) intelligenza; **b. washing** lavaggio del cervello; **b.-drain** emigrazione pesante di studiosi e scienziati.

brain [brein] vt accoppare.

brainy ['breini] a (fam) intelligente.

braise [breiz] vt brasare.

brake [breik] n macchia di cespugli; (mech) freno; vt frenare; **b. horsepower** potenza del freno; **foot b.** (aut) freno a pedale; **hand b.** freno a mano; **b. van** (rly) furgone.

bramble ['bræmbl] n pruno, rovo.

bran [bræn] n crusca.

branch [brɑ:ntʃ] n ramo; diramazione; filiale; vi ramificarsi; **to b. off** biforcarsi; **to b. out** estendersi.

brand [brænd] n marchio; tizzone; vt marchiare; stigmatizzare; imprimere.

brandish ['brændiʃ] vt brandire.

brandy ['brændi] n acquavite, cognac.

brash [bræʃ] a impudente; fragile.

brass [brɑ:s] n ottone; (fig) sfrontatezza.

brassiere ['bræsiə] n reggipetto, reggiseno.

brassy ['brɑ:si] a di ottone; impudente.

brat [bræt] n marmocchio; monello.

bravado [brə'vɑ:dou] n bravata, spavalderia.

brave [breiv] a coraggioso; n prode; vt affrontare, sfidare.

bravely ['breivli] ad coraggiosamente.

bravery ['breivəri] n coraggio.

brawl [brɔ:l] n rissa; vi rissare.

brawn [brɔ:n] n muscolo, forza muscolare; soprassata.

brawny ['brɔ:ni] a forte, muscoloso.

bray [brei] vi ragliare.

brazen ['breizn] a d'ottone; impudente; **b.-faced** sfrontato.

brazenly ['breiznli] ad sfacciatamente.

brazier ['breiziə] n braciere.

Brazil [brə'zil] n Brasile.

Brazilian [brə'ziljən] a n brasiliano.

breach [bri:tʃ] n breccia, rottura; vt far breccia in, rompere.

bread [bred] n pane.

breadth [bredθ] n ampiezza, larghezza; (of material) altezza.

break [breik] n rottura; intervallo; vti rompere, spezzare; rompersi, spezzarsi; venir meno a.

breakable ['breikəbl] a fragile.

breakage ['breikidʒ] n rottura.

breakaway ['breikəwei] n separazione; (rly) sbandamento.

breakdown ['breikdaun] n collasso; crollo; esaurimento nervoso; (aut) panna, guasto.

breaker ['breikə] n rompitore; violatore; (of horses) domatore; maroso.

breakfast ['brekfəst] n (prima) colazione.

breaking ['breikiŋ] n rottura; interruzione; infrazione.

breakneck ['breiknek] a rompicollo.

breakwater ['breik‚wɔːtə] n frangiflutti, diga.

breast [brest] n mammella; petto; seno; vt affrontare, lottare con.

breath [breθ] n respiro; fiato; soffio.

breathalyser ['breθəlaizə] n analizzatore del tasso alcoolico.

breathe [briːð] vti respirare; prender fiato; mormorare; infondere; b. forth esalare.

breathing ['briːðiŋ] n respiro, respirazione.

breathless ['breθlis] a ansimante, senza fiato.

breathlessly ['breθlisli] ad con il fiato sospeso.

breathlessness ['breθlisnis] n mancanza di respiro, affanno.

breeches ['britʃiz] n pl calzoni pl, brache pl.

breed [briːd] n discendenza, razza; vti generare; partorire; (ri)prodursi; allevare.

breeder ['briːdə] n allevatore; b. reactor reattore nucleare autofertilizzante.

breeding ['briːdiŋ] n allevamento; educazione, buone maniere pl.

breeze [briːz] n brezza, vento leggero.

breezy ['briːzi] a battuto dal vento, fresco; gioviale.

brethren ['breðrən] n pl confratelli pl.

breviary ['briːvjəri] n breviario.

brevity ['breviti] n brevità, concisione.

brew [bruː] vt fare (un infuso); fare (la birra); (fig) tramare; vi essere in fermentazione; prepararsi.

brewer ['bruː(ː)ə] n fabbricante di birra.

brewery ['bruəri] n fabbrica di birra.

briar v **brier**

bribe [braib] n dono (per corrompere o influenzare); vt corrompere (per mezzo di doni).

bribery ['braibəri] n corruzione.

brick [brik] n mattone; a di mattoni;

to drop a b. commettere un'indiscrezione.

bridal ['braidl] a nuziale; n sposalizio.

bride [braid] n sposa; **bridegroom** sposo.

bridesmaid ['braidzmeid] n damigella d'onore della sposa.

bridge [bridʒ] n ponte, (naut) ponte di comando; (cards) 'bridge', ponte.

Bridget ['bridʒit] nf pr Brigida.

bridle ['braidl] n briglia, freno.

brief [briːf] a breve, conciso; n (leg) riassunto.

briefness ['briːfnis] n brevità.

brier ['braiə] n rosa di macchia, rovo; (pipa di) radica.

brig [brig] n brigantino.

brigade [bri'geid] n brigata.

brigadier [‚brigə'diə] n comandante di brigata.

brigand ['brigənd] n bandito, brigante.

brigandage ['brigəndidʒ] n brigantaggio, banditismo.

bright [brait] a brillante, luminoso, risplendente; gaio, vivace; sveglio, intelligente.

brighten ['braitn] vt rallegrare, rendere più brillante; vi illuminarsi, rischiararsi.

brightness ['braitnis] n splendore; vivacità.

brilliancy ['briljənsi] n splendore.

brilliant ['briljənt] a brillante, lucente; n brillante.

brim [brim] n orlo; bordo, margine; (of hat) tesa, ala; vti colmar(si); **to b. over** traboccare.

brimless ['brimlis] a senza orlo, senz'ala.

brindled ['brindld] a chiazzato.

brine [brain] n acqua salata.

bring [briŋ] vt portare; procurare; addurre; causare; indurre; **to b. up** educare.

brink [briŋk] n orlo; limite estremo.

brisk [brisk] a vivace, svelto.

briskly ['briskli] ad vivacemente; speditamente.

briskness ['brisknis] n vivacità, sveltezza.

bristle ['brisl] n setola, pelo duro e rado; vi andare in collera.

bristly ['brisli] a setoloso.

Britain ['britn] n Britannia; **Great B.** Gran Bretagna.

Britannic [bri'tænik] a britannico.

British ['britiʃ] a britannico, inglese.

Briton ['britn] n britanno.

brittle ['britl] a fragile, friabile.

brittleness ['britlnis] n fragilità friabilità.

broach [broutʃ] n spiedo; vt spillare; cominciare una discussione.

broad [brɔːd] a ampio, largo; indelicato, volgare, (accent) marcato.

broadcast ['brɔːdkɑːst] n trasmissione radiofonica; vt trasmettere per radio; vi parlare alla radio; **broad-**

caster apparecchio trasmittente; chi parla alla radio; **broadcasting** radiodiffusione.

broaden ['brɔːdn] *vti* allargar(si), estender(si).

broadly ['brɔːdli] *ad* largamente; **b. speaking** generalmente parlando.

broadness ['brɔːdnis] *n* larghezza, ampiezza; grossolanità; accento marcato.

brocade [brə'keid] *n* broccato.

brochure ['brouʃuə] *n* opuscolo.

broil [brɔil] *n* lite, tumulto; *vt* arrostire alla griglia o allo spiedo.

broken ['broukən] *a* rotto; (*of weather*) incerto; (*of ground*) accidentato; scoraggiato; scorretto.

broker ['broukə] *n* mediatore, sensale.

bromide ['broumaid] *n* bromuro.

bronchial ['brɔnkiəl] *a* bronchiale.

bronchitis [brɔn'kaitis] *n* bronchite.

bronze [brɔnz] *n* bronzo; *a* bronzeo, di bronzo; *vti* abbronzar(si).

brooch [broutʃ] *n* spilla.

brood [bruːd] *n* covata; *vti* covare; meditare, preoccuparsi.

brook [bruk] *n* ruscello.

broom [brum] *n* ginestra; scopa.

broomstick ['brumstik] *n* manico di scopa.

broth [brɔθ] *n* brodo.

brothel ['brɔθl] *n* bordello.

brother ['brʌðə] *n* fratello; confratello (*pl* **brethren**); **b. in arms** compagno d'armi; **b. in law** cognato.

brotherhood ['brʌðəhud] *n* fratellanza, fraternità; confratérnita.

brotherly ['brʌðəli] *a* fraterno.

brow [brau] *n* fronte; sopracciglio; (*cliff*) orlo; (*hill*) sommità.

browbeat ['braubiːt] *vt* intimidire.

brown [braun] *a* marrone, scuro, abbronzato; *n* color marrone; *vti* rendere (divenire) marrone, abbronzare; rosolare.

brownie ['brauni] *n* folletto; giovane esploratrice.

browse [brauz] *vti* brucare; scorrere libri.

bruise [bruːz] *n* contusione, ammaccatura, livido; *vt* ammaccare.

brunette [bru'net] *a n* bruna.

brunt [brʌnt] *n* urto; **to bear the b.** sopportare il peso.

brush [brʌʃ] *n* spazzola; spazzolata; pennello; *vt* spazzolare; sfiorare.

brushwood ['brʌʃwud] *n* macchia.

brusque [brusk] *a* brusco, rude.

Brussels ['brʌslz] *n* (*geogr*) Bruxelles; **B. sprouts** cavolini di Bruxelles.

brutal ['bruːtl] *a* brutale.

brutality [bru'tæliti] *n* brutalità.

brutalize ['bruːtəlaiz] *vt* abbrutire.

brute [bruːt] *a* brutale; *n* bruto.

brutish ['bruːtiʃ] *a* brutale, bestiale.

bubble ['bʌbl] *n* bolla; progetto vano; rumore di liquido che bolle; *vi* gorgogliare; far bolle; bollire.

buccaneer [ˌbʌkə'niə] *n* pirata.

Bucharest ['bjuːkərest] *n* (*geogr*) Bucarest.

buck [bʌk] *n* daino; coniglio; leprotto; maschio di molti animali; (*US sl*) dollaro.

bucket ['bʌkit] *n* secchia, secchio.

buckle ['bʌkl] *n* fibbia; *vt* affibbiare, fermare; piegare.

buckler ['bʌklə] *n* scudo rotondo; (*fig*) protettore.

buckwheat ['bʌkwiːt] *n* grano saraceno.

bucolic [bjuː'kɔlik] *a* bucolico, pastorale.

bud [bʌd] *n* bocciolo; gemma; germoglio; *vi* germogliare.

Buddha ['budə] *n* Budda.

Buddhist ['budist] *a* buddistico; *n* buddista.

budge [bʌdʒ] *vi* fare un piccolo movimento, muoversi.

budgerigar ['bʌdʒərigɑː] *n* pappagallino.

budget ['bʌdʒit] *n* bilancio preventivo; *vi* fare un bilancio preventivo.

buff [bʌf] *a* scamosciato, marrone; *n* pelle di bufalo; color camoscio.

buffalo ['bʌfəlou] *a* bufalo.

buffer ['bʌfə] *n* (*mech*) respingente.

buffet ['bʌfit] *n* schiaffo; *vt* schiaffeggiare.

buffet ['bufei] *n* credenza, 'buffet'.

buffoon [bʌ'fuːn] *n* buffone.

buffoonery [bʌ'fuːnəri] *n* buffoneria.

bug [bʌg] *n* cimice; (*US*) virus; (*US*) piccolo insetto; **big bug** (*sl*) persona importante.

bugbear ['bʌgbeə] *n* spauracchio.

buggy ['bʌgi] *n* (*US*) carrozzino scoperto, calesse.

bugle ['bjuːgl] *n* buccina.

bugler ['bjuːglə] *n* sonatore di buccina.

build [bild] *n* costruzione; corporatura; *vt* costruire; edificare, fabbricare; *vi* nidificare.

builder ['bildə] *n* costruttore; impresario di costruzioni.

building ['bildiŋ] *a* edile, edilizio; *n* edificio, costruzione.

built [bilt] *a* costruito, formato; **well-b.** ben messo, ben piantato.

bulb [bʌlb] *n* bulbo; lampadina elettrica.

bulbous ['bʌlbəs] *a* bulboso.

Bulgaria [bʌl'gɛəriə] *n* (*geogr*) Bulgaria.

Bulgarian [bʌl'gɛəriən] *a n* bulgaro.

bulge [bʌldʒ] *n* gonfiore, protuberanza; *vi* gonfiarsi.

bulging ['bʌldʒiŋ] *a* sporgente, protuberante.

bulk [bʌlk] *n* massa; la maggior parte; *vi* ammontare, essere voluminoso.

bulkiness ['bʌlkinis] *n* voluminosità.

bulky ['bʌlki] *a* ingombrante, voluminoso.

bull [bul] *n* toro; bolla papale.

bulldog ['buldɔg] *n* bulldog, mastino.

bulldozer ['bul.douzə] n 'bulldozer', scavatrice.

bullet ['bulit] n pallottola; proiettile.

bulletin ['bulitin] n bollettino, notiziario; **news b.** giornale radio; **b. board** (US) tabellone per affissi.

bullfight ['bulfait] n corrida.

bullfinch ['bulfintʃ] n ciuffolotto.

bullion ['buljən] n oro o argento in verghe.

bullock ['bulək] n bue giovane.

bull's eye ['bulzai] n oblò; lente convessa; centro del bersaglio.

bully ['buli] n prepotente, tiranno; manzo lesso in scatola; vt tiranneggiare, fare il bravaccio con.

bulrush ['bulrʌʃ] n giunco.

bulwark ['bulwək] n baluardo; bastione; (naut) parapetto.

bum-boat ['bʌmbout] n battello di rifornimento viveri.

bump [bʌmp] n collisione, colpo, urto; bernoccolo, gonfiore; vti urtare, collidere.

bumper ['bʌmpə] a pieno, abbondante; n (aut) paraurti; (rly) respingente.

bumpkin ['bʌmpkin] n zotico.

bumptious ['bʌmpʃəs] a presuntuoso.

bumpy ['bʌmpi] a (of road) sassoso, ineguale; bernoccoluto.

bun [bʌn] n panetto, piccola focaccia; crocchia di capelli.

bunch [bʌntʃ] n fascio, mazzo; grappolo; vi raggrupparsi.

bundle ['bʌndl] n fagotto, fastello; vt affastellare; **b. off** mandare via senza cerimonie.

bung [bʌŋ] n tappo, grosso turacciolo; vt tappare, otturare.

bungalow ['bʌŋgəlou] n 'bungalow', casetta di costruzione leggera, a un piano.

bungle ['bʌŋgl] n lavoro malfatto, pasticcio; vti fare o aggiustare malamente, guastare.

bunion ['bʌnjən] n callo, infiammazione ai piedi.

bunk [bʌŋk] n cuccetta; sciocchezze.

bunny ['bʌni] n coniglietto.

buoy [bɔi] n boa, gavitello.

buoyancy ['bɔiənsi] n galleggiabilità; (fig) elasticità, brio.

buoyant ['bɔiənt] a capace di stare a galla; leggero; vivace.

burden ['bə:dn] n peso, carico, fardello, onere; ritornello; (naut) tonnellaggio; vt caricare, gravare.

burdensome ['bə:dnsəm] a gravoso, opprimente.

burdock ['bə:dɔk] n (bot) lappola.

bureau [bjuə'rou] pl **bureaux** n scrittoio; ufficio.

bureaucracy [bjuə'rɔkrəsi] n burocrazia.

bureaucrat ['bjuəroukræt] n burocrate.

bureaucratic [.bjuərou'krætik] a burocratico.

burglar ['bə:glə] n scassinatore; **b. alarm** campanello antifurto.

burglary ['bə:gləri] n furto mediante scasso.

burgle ['bə:gl] vt scassinare.

Burgundy ['bə:gəndi] n (geogr) Borgogna; b. vino di Borgogna.

burial ['beriəl] n sepoltura; **b. ground** cimitero; **b. place** sepoltura, tomba.

burlesque [bə:'lesk] a burlesco; n 'burlesque'; farsa.

burly ['bə:li] a grosso e robusto.

Burma ['bə:mə] n Birmania.

Burmese [bə:'mi:z] a n birmano.

burn [bə:n] n bruciatura, scottatura; (scozzese) ruscello; vti bruciare, ardere.

burner ['bə:nə] n becco di lampada o di fornello a gas.

burning ['bə:niŋ] a bruciante, ardente; n bruciatura.

burnish ['bə:niʃ] vt brunire, lustrare.

burrow ['bʌrou] n tana; vi rintanarsi; investigare.

bursar ['bə:sə] n economo; borsista.

bursary ['bə:səri] n borsa di studio.

burst [bə:st] n esplosione, scoppio; vti (far) esplodere, (far) scoppiare; rompere.

bury ['beri] vt seppellire; (fig) dimenticare, nascondere alla vista.

bus [bʌs] pl **buses** n autobus.

busman ['bʌsmən] pl **busmen** n conducente di autobus.

bush ['buʃ] n cespuglio, macchia; (mech) boccola.

bushel ['buʃel] n staio.

bushy ['buʃi] a folto; cespuglioso.

busily ['bizili] ad attivamente.

business ['bizinis] n affare, affari pl; commercio; occupazione; azienda commerciale; **businesslike** metodico, pratico; **b. suit** (US) abito maschile da passeggio.

bust [bʌst] n busto; petto.

bustard ['bʌstəd] n ottarda.

bustle ['bʌsl] n andirivieni, tramestio; vi agitarsi, affaccendarsi.

busy ['bizi] a occupato, affaccendato.

busybody ['bizi.bɔdi] n ficcanaso.

but [bʌt] cj ma, però, se non che; ad prep eccetto, fuorchè, non . . . che; n ma.

butane ['bju:tein] n (chem) butano.

butcher ['butʃə] n macellaio; vt macellare; massacrare.

butchery ['butʃəri] n macello; strage.

butler ['bʌtlə] n maggiordomo.

butt [bʌt] n barile, botte; calcio di fucile; bersaglio; zimbello; cozzo, cornata; vt cozzare.

butter ['bʌtə] n burro; vt imburrare.

buttercup ['bʌtəkʌp] n ranuncolo.

butterfly ['bʌtəflai] n farfalla.

buttock ['bʌtək] n natica.

button ['bʌtn] n bottone; **collar b.** (US) bottoncino per colletto; **buttons** pl (fam) fattorino d'albergo; vt abbottonare.

buttonhole ['bʌtnhoul] *n* occhiello; fiore portato all'occhiello; *vt* far occhielli; (*fig*) attaccar bottone; **buttonholer** attaccabottoni.

buttress ['bʌtris] *n* contrafforte; sostegno.

buxom ['bʌksəm] *a* grassoccio; formoso.

buy [bai] *vt* acquistare, comp(e)rare.

buyer ['baiə] *n* acquirente, compratore.

buzz [bʌz] *vi* ronzare; *n* ronzio.

buzzing ['bʌziŋ] *a* ronzante; *n* ronzio.

by [bai] *prep* da, di, a fianco di, per, vicino a; non più tardi di; **by the way, by the by** a proposito; *ad* vicino, da parte; **to stand by** stare vicino, parteggiare per, essere spettatore; **to put by** metter via.

bye-bye ['baibai] *interj* addio, arrivederci, ciao; *n* (*fam*) nanna.

bygone ['baigɔn] *a* finito, passato.

bye-law ['bailɔː] *n* regolamento locale.

by-pass ['baipɑːs] *n* strada che evita il passaggio per una città.

byre ['baiə] *n* stalla per buoi.

by-road ['bairoud] **byway** ['baiwei] *n* strada secondaria.

bystander ['bai,stændə] *n* spettatore.

by-word ['baiwɔːd] *n* detto comune; oggetto di rimprovero.

Byzantine [bi'zæntiːn] *a n* bizantino.

Byzantium [bi'zæntiəm] *n* Bisanzio.

C

cab [kæb] *n* vettura pubblica; taxi-c. tassì; **c. rank** (US) **c. stand** posteggio di tassì.

cabbage ['kæbidʒ] *n* cavolo.

cabin ['kæbin] *n* cabina, capanna; **c. boy** mozzo di nave.

cabinet ['kæbinit] *n* gabinetto, armadietto, stipo; **c.-maker** ebanista; **C.** Consiglio dei Ministri.

cable ['keibl] *n* cavo; cablogramma; *vi* spedire un cablogramma; **c. car** funicolare.

caboose [kə'buːs] *n* (*naut*) cucina, cambusa, (US *rly*) furgone.

cacao [kə'kaːou] *n* cacao.

cackle ['kækl] *n* schiamazzo; *vi* schiamazzare.

cactus ['kæktəs] *pl* **cactuses, cacti** *n* cactus, pianta grassa.

cad [kæd] *n* furfante.

caddy ['kædi] *n* scatola per custodire il tè; (*golf*) porta-mazze.

cadence ['keidəns] *n* cadenza.

cadet [kə'det] *n* cadetto.

cadge [kædʒ] *vti* scroccare.

Caesar ['siːzə] *nm pr* Cesare.

café ['kæfei] *n* caffè, ristorante.

cafeteria [,kæfi'tiəriə] *n* ristorante 'self-service'.

cage [keidʒ] *n* gabbia.

Cain [kein] *nm pr* Caino.

caique [kai'iːk] *n* caicco, scialuppa.

cairngorm ['kɛəngɔːm] *n* quarzo giallo.

cajole [kə'dʒoul] *vt* blandire, lusingare.

cajolery [kə'dʒouləri] *n* adulazione, allettamento.

cake [keik] *n* torta, dolce, pasticcino; **c. of soap** saponetta; *vti* incrostar (si).

Calabrian [kə'læbriən] *a n* calabrese.

calamitous [kə'læmitəs] *a* calamitoso, disastroso.

calamity [kə'læmiti] *n* calamità, sventura.

calcium ['kælsiəm] *n* (*chem*) calcio.

calculable ['kælkjuləbl] *a* calcolabile.

calculate ['kælkjuleit] *vti* calcolare; contare (su).

calculation [,kælkju'leiʃən] *n* calcolo; previsione.

calculator ['kælkjuleitə] *n* calcolatore; macchina calcolatrice.

calculus ['kælkjuləs] *pl* **calculi** *n* (*math*, *med*) calcolo.

Caledonia [,kæli'douniə] *n* Caledonia, Scozia; **Caledonian** caledone, scozzese.

calendar ['kælində] *n* calendario; annuario; lista.

calender ['kælində] *n* (*mech*) cilindratoio; calandra; *vt* calandrare.

calf [kɑːf] *pl* **calves** *n* vitello; pelle di vitello; piccolo di elefante e di altri mammiferi.

calibre ['kælibə] *n* calibro.

calipers ['kælipəz] *n pl* compassi.

call [kɔːl] *n* chiamata, richiamo; grido; breve visita; diritto; **within c. a** portata di voce; **c. boy** (*theat*) buttafuori; **c. up** chiamata alle armi; **telephone c.** telefonata; *vti* chiamare; gridare; chiamarsi; invocare; fare una breve visita.

caller ['kɔːlə] *n* visitatore.

calling ['kɔːliŋ] *n* occupazione, professione; vocazione.

callous ['kæləs] *a* calloso; insensibile.

callow ['kælou] *a* implume; inesperto; imberbe.

calm [kɑːm] *a* calmo, sereno; *n* calma, tranquillità; *vt* calmare, tranquillare.

calmly ['kɑːmli] *ad* tranquillamente, con calma.

calmness ['kɑːmnis] *n* calma, tranquillità.

calomel ['kæloumel] *n* calomelano.

calorie ['kæləri] *n* caloria.

calumniate [kə'lʌmnieit] *vt* calunniare.

calumny ['kæləmni] *n* calunnia.

Calvary ['kælvəri] *n* Calvario; **c.** Via Crucis, calvario.

Calvinism ['kælvinizəm] *n* calvinismo.

calypso [kæ'lipso] *n* calipso.

camber ['kæmbə] *n* curvatura, inarcamento; *vt* curvare.

cambric ['keimbrik] n cambrì, batista.

camel ['kæməl] n cammello.

cameo ['kæmiou] n cammeo.

camera ['kæmərə] n macchina fotografica; **cameraman** fotoreporter; operatore cinematografico, televisivo; **in c.** a porte chiuse.

camomile ['kæməmail] n camomilla.

camouflage ['kæmuflɑːʒ] n camuffamento, mimetizzazione.

camp [kæmp] n campeggio; campo; accampamento; vi accamparsi, attendarsi; **camp site** camping.

campaign [kæm'pein] n campagna; vi fare una campagna.

camphor ['kæmfə] n canfora.

campus ['kæmpəs] n (US) insieme di terreni, campi di gioco, edifici universitari.

can [kæn] n bidone; (mainly US) scatola di latta per cibi conservati.

can [kæn] vi (3rd sing) essere in grado di; potere; sapere; vt mettere in scatola.

Canada ['kænədə] n Canadà.

Canadian [kə'neidiən] a n canadese.

canal [kə'næl] n canale.

canary [kə'nɛəri] n canarino.

Canary (Islands) [kə'nɛəri ('ailəndz)] n (Isole) Canarie.

cancel ['kænsəl] vt annullare; cancellare; sopprimere.

cancellation [,kænse'leifən] n annullamento, soppressione.

cancer ['kænsə] n cancro.

candid ['kændid] a franco, sincero.

candidate ['kændidit] n candidato.

candidature ['kændiditʃə] n candidatura.

candidness ['kændidnis] n franchezza.

candied ['kændid] a candito.

candle ['kændl] n candela.

Candlemas ['kændlməs] n Candelora.

candlestick ['kændlstik] n candeliere.

candour ['kændə] n franchezza, sincerità.

candy ['kændi] n candito; (US) dolciumi pl; **c. floss**, (US) **cotton c.** zucchero filato.

cane [kein] n bastone da passeggio; canna; bacchetta; **sugar c.** canna da zucchero; vt bastonare.

canine ['keinain] a canino.

canister ['kænistə] n barattolo.

canker ['kæŋkə] n cancro; brutto difetto; influenza corruttrice; vti corromper(si).

cankerous ['kæŋkərəs] a cancrenoso.

canned [kænd] a conservato in scatola; **c. meat** carne in scatola.

cannibal ['kænibəl] n cannibale.

cannon ['kænən] n cannone, cannoni pl; (billiards) carambola.

cannonade [,kænə'neid] n bombardamento, cannoneggiamento.

canny ['kæni] a astuto, abile.

canoe [kə'nuː] n canoa.

canon ['kænən] n canone; canonico.

canonical [kə'nɔnikəl] a canonico.

canonization [,kænənəl'zeifən] n canonizzazione.

canonize ['kænənaiz] vt canonizzare.

canopy ['kænəpi] n baldacchino.

cant [kænt] n pendenza, inclinazione; gergo; ipocrisia.

cantankerous [kən'tæŋkərəs] a intrattabile, litigioso.

canteen [kæn'tiːn] n borraccia da soldato; cantina militare; cassetta per posateria.

canter ['kæntə] n piccolo galoppo; vi andare a piccolo galoppo.

canticle ['kæntikl] n cantico.

cantilever ['kæntiliːvə] n mensola che regge balconi etc; modiglione; **c. bridge** ponte a mensola.

canton ['kæntən] n cantone.

canvas ['kænvəs] n canovaccio, tela; vele pl.

canvass ['kænvəs] vti sollecitare voti, ordini etc.

canvasser ['kænvəsə] n galoppino elettorale.

canyon ['kænjən] n 'canyon', burrone.

cap [kæp] n berretto, copricapo, cuffietta; vt coprire; superare.

capability [,keipə'biliti] n capacità, abilità.

capable ['keipəbl] a abile, capace.

capacious [kə'peifəs] a spazioso, capace.

capaciousness [kə'peifəsnis] n spaziosità, capacità.

capacity [kə'pæsiti] n capacità; competenza; ufficio.

cape [keip] n capo, promontorio; cappa, mantello.

caper ['keipə] n cappero; capriola; (fig) stramberia.

Capetown ['keiptaun] n pr (geogr) Città del Capo.

capillary [kə'piləri] a capillare.

capital ['kæpitl] a capitale; eccellente; maiuscolo; n capitale; lettera maiuscola; (arch) capitello.

capitalism ['kæpitəlizəm] n capitalismo.

capitalist ['kæpitəlist] n capitalista.

capitalize [kə'pitəlaiz] vt capitalizzare.

Capitol ['kæpitl] (the) n Campidoglio; **Capitoline** a capitolino.

capitulate [kə'pitjuleit] vi capitolare, arrendersi.

capitulation [kə,pitju'leifən] n capitolazione, resa.

capon ['keipən] n cappone.

caprice [kə'priːs] n capriccio.

capricious [kə'prifəs] a capriccioso; volubile.

capriciousness [kə'prifəsnis] n capricciosità.

capsize [kæp'saiz] vti capovolger(si).

capstan ['kæpstən] n (naut) argano.

capsule ['kæpsju:l] n capsula; (US) schema.

captain ['kæptin] n capitano, comandante; capo.

caption ['kæpʃən] n intestazione, titolo; (cin) didascalia.

captious ['kæpʃəs] a capzioso; sofistico.

captiousness ['kæpʃəsnis] n capziosità.

captivate ['kæptiveit] vt attrarre; cattivarsi.

captivating ['kæptiveitiŋ] a seducente, affascinante.

captive ['kæptiv] a n prigioniero.

captor ['kæptə] n chi fa prigioniero, catturatore.

capture ['kæptʃə] n cattura; vt catturare.

Capuchin ['kæpjuʃin] n frate cappuccino.

car [ka:] n automobile; carro; (US rly) vagone, (US rly) carrozza; armoured c. (mil) autoblinda; **baggage c.** (US) bagagliaio; **cable c.** funicolare; **freight c.** (US) vagone merci; **mail c.** (US) vagone postale; **restaurant c.** (US) dining c. vagone ristorante; **sleeping c.** vagone letto; **carpark** parcheggio.

carafe [kə'ra:f] n caraffa.

caramel ['kærəmel] n caramello; caramella.

carat ['kærət] n carato.

caravan ['kærəvæn] n carovana, carrozzone; (aut) roulotte.

caraway ['kærəwei] n (bot) comino.

carbine ['ka:bain] n carabina.

carbohydrate ['ka:bou'haidreit] n (chem) carboidrato.

carbolic [ka:'bɔlik] a fenico.

carbon ['ka:bən] n carbonio; **c. paper** carta carbone.

carbonate ['ka:bənit] n carbonato.

carbonic [ka:'bɔnik] a carbonico.

carboniferous [,ka:bə'nifərəs] a carbonifero.

carbonize ['ka:bənaiz] vt carbonizzare.

carbuncle ['ka:bʌŋkl] n carbonchio.

carburettor ['ka:bjuretə] n carburatore.

carcass ['ka:kəs] n carcassa.

card [ka:d] n biglietto da visita; cartoncino; carta da giuoco; cartolina; tessera; vt cardare.

cardboard ['ka:dbo:d] n cartone.

cardiac ['ka:diæk] a cardiaco.

cardigan ['ka:digən] n giacca a maglia.

cardinal ['ka:dinl] a n cardinale.

care [kɛə] n cura, attenzione; preoccupazione; (in) c. of (in indirizzi) presso; vi importare; interessarsi; **to care for** voler bene a; curare; piacere.

careen [kə'ri:n] vti (naut) carenare.

career [kə'riə] n carriera; corsa.

careful ['kɛəful] a accurato, attento, premuroso.

carefully ['kɛəfuli] ad attentamente; con cura.

carefulness ['kɛəfulnis] n accuratezza; attenzione.

careless ['kɛəlis] a negligente, trascurato.

carelessness ['kɛəlisnis] n negligenza, trascuratezza.

caress [kə'res] n carezza; vt accarezzare.

caretaker ['kɛə,teikə] n custode, guardiano, portiere.

cargo ['ka:gou] pl **cargoes** n (d'una nave) carico.

Caribbean [,kæri'bi:ən] a caraibico.

caricature [,kærikə'tjuə] n caricatura; vt caricaturare.

caricaturist [,kærikə'tjuərist] n caricaturista.

Carmelite ['ka:milait] a n carmelitano.

carnage ['ka:nidʒ] n carneficina, strage.

carnal ['ka:nl] a carnale, sensuale.

carnation [ka:'neiʃən] n garofano.

carnival ['ka:nivəl] n carnevale.

carnivorous [ka:'nivərəs] a carnivoro.

carob ['kærəb] n (bot) carruba; **c.-tree** carrubo.

carol ['kærəl] n carola, inno natalizio.

Caroline ['kærəlain] nf pr Carolina.

carotid [kə'rɔtid] n (anat) carotide.

carouse [kə'rauz] vi far baldoria, gozzovigliare.

carousel [kə'rauzəl] n carosello.

carp [ka:p] n carpa; **c. at** vi trovare sempre da ridire su.

carpenter ['ka:pintə] n carpentiere, falegname.

carpentry ['ka:pintri] n carpenteria.

carpet ['ka:pit] n tappeto.

carping ['ka:piŋ] a cavilloso.

carriage ['kæridʒ] n carrozza, vettura; (com) trasporto, prezzo di trasporto; portamento; (US) baby c. carrozzina per bambini.

carrier ['kæriə] n portatore; corriere, spedizioniere; portapacchi di bicicletta.

carrion ['kæriən] n carogna.

carrot ['kærət] n carota.

carry ['kæri] vti portare; trasportare; riportare; raggiungere; **to carry oneself** comportarsi.

cart [ka:t] n carro, calesse; vt trasportare con carro.

cartage ['ka:tidʒ] n trasporto con carri; prezzo di trasporto.

carter ['ka:tə] n carrettiere.

Carthusian [ka:'θju:ziən] a n certosino.

cartilage ['ka:tilidʒ] n cartilagine.

carton ['ka:tən] n cartone; scatola.

cartoon [ka:'tu:n] n cartone; vignetta; cartone animato; **cartoonist** vignettista; disegnatore di cartoni animati.

cartridge ['ka:tridʒ] n cartuccia.

carve [kɑːv] *vt* intagliare, scolpire; trinciare.

carving ['kɑːviŋ] *n* scultura, intaglio; il trinciare; **c. knife** trinciante.

cascade [kæs'keid] *n* cascata; *vi* scrosciare; sparpagliarsi.

case [keis] *n* caso, avvenimento; causa; cassa; astuccio, fodero; valigia.

casement ['keismənt] *n* finestra a due battenti.

cash [kæʃ] *n* cassa; contanti *pl*; *vt* incassare, prelevare.

cashier [kæ'ʃiə] *n* cassiere; *vt* (*mil*) destituire.

cashmere ['kæʃmiə] *n* cachemire, cashmere.

cask [kɑːsk] *n* barile.

casket ['kɑːskit] *n* cofanetto, scrigno.

casserole ['kæsəroul] *n* casseruola.

cassock ['kæsək] *n* tunica dei clero anglicano.

cast [kɑːst] *n* getto, lancio; stampo; insieme degli attori in una rappresentazione; *vti* gettare, lanciare; dedurre; distribuire parti agli attori.

castanets [ˌkæstə'nets] *n pl* nacchere *pl*.

castaway ['kɑːstəwei] *n* naufrago; reietto.

caste [kɑːst] *n* casta.

castigate ['kæstigeit] *vt* castigare, punire.

Castile [kæs'tiːl] *n* Castiglia; **Castilian** *a n* castigliano.

casting ['kɑːstiŋ] *n* getto; colata; distribuzione di parti ad attori.

cast iron ['kɑːst'aiən] *n* ghisa.

castle ['kɑːsl] *n* castello; (*chess*) torre.

castor ['kɑːstə] *n* rotella da mobili; saliera; ampolla; **c. sugar** zucchero raffinato.

castor oil ['kɑːstər'ɔil] *n* olio di ricino.

castrate [kæs'treit] *vt* castrare.

castration [kæs'treiʃən] *n* castrazione.

casual ['kæʒjuəl] *a* casuale, fortuito; (*clothes*) semplice, sportivo.

casually ['kæʒjuəli] *ad* per caso; con noncuranza.

casualty ['kæʒjuəlti] *n* disgrazia; vittima; **c. list** lista delle vittime.

casuist ['kæzjuist] *n* casista.

casuistry ['kæzjuistri] *n* casistica.

cat [kat] *n* gatto.

cataclysm ['kætəklizəm] *n* cataclisma.

catacomb ['kætəkoum] *n* catacomba.

Catalan ['kætələn] *a n* catalano.

catalepsy ['kætələpsi] *n* catalessi.

catalogue ['kætələg] *n* catalogo; *vt* catalogare.

Catalonia [ˌkætə'louniə] *n* Catalogna.

catapult ['kætəpʌlt] *n* catapulta; fionda; *vti* catapultare.

cataract ['kætərækt] *n* cateratta; (*falls*) cascata.

catarrh [kə'tɑː] *n* catarro.

catastrophe [kə'tæstrəfi] *n* catastrofe.

catch [kætʃ] *n* presa, cattura; preda; guadagno fatto; pesca; trappola; paletto di porta; *vti* acchiappare, afferrare; sorprendere; capire.

catching ['kætʃiŋ] *a* contagioso; orecchiabile.

catchword ['kætʃwəːd] *n* richiamo, slogan.

catechism ['kætikizəm] *n* catechismo.

catechize ['kætikaiz] *vt* catechizzare.

categorical [ˌkæti'gɔrikəl] *a* categorico.

category ['kætigəri] *n* categoria.

cater ['keitə] *vi* provvedere cibo; procurare divertimento.

caterer ['keitərə] *n* provveditore di cibo *etc.*

caterpillar ['kætəpilə] *n* bruco; (*mech*) cingola.

catgut ['kætgʌt] *n* minugia.

cathedral [kə'θiːdrəl] *n* cattedrale, duomo.

Catherine ['kæθərin] *nf pr* Caterina.

cathode ['kæθoud] *n* catodo.

catholic ['kæθəlik] *a n* cattolico.

Catholicism [kə'θɔlisizəm] *n* cattolicismo.

cattle ['kætl] *n pl* bestiame.

catty ['kæti] *a* (*fig*) sarcastico, acido.

Caucasus ['kɔːkəsəs] *n* Caucaso; **Caucasian** *a n* caucasico.

cauldron ['kɔːldrən] *n* caldaia.

cauliflower ['kɔliflauə] *n* cavolfiore.

cause [kɔːz] *n* causa, motivo, ragione; *vt* causare, produrre.

causeway ['kɔːzwei] *n* strada rialzata.

caustic ['kɔːstik] *a n* caustico.

causticity [kɔːs'tisiti] *n* causticità.

cauterize ['kɔːtəraiz] *vt* cauterizzare.

caution ['kɔːʃən] *n* prudenza, cautela; avvertimento; cauzione; *vt* mettere in guardia.

cautious ['kɔːʃəs] *a* cauto, prudente.

cautiously ['kɔːʃəsli] *ad* cautamente, con prudenza.

cautiousness ['kɔːʃəsnis] *n* cautela.

cavalcade [ˌkævəl'keid] *n* cavalcata.

cavalier [ˌkævə'liə] *a* brusco, scortese; *n* cavaliere.

cavalry ['kævəlri] *n* cavalleria.

cave [keiv] *n* cava, caverna; **to cave in** cedere schiacciare.

cavern ['kævən] *n* caverna, grotta.

cavernous ['kævənəs] *a* cavernoso.

caviar(e) ['kæviɑː] *n* caviale.

cavil ['kævil] *n* cavillo; *vi* cavillare.

cavity ['kæviti] *n* cavità.

caw [kɔː] *n* gracchiamento; *vi* gracchiare.

Cayenne [kei'en] *n* Caienna; **c. (pepper)** pepe di Caienna.

cease [siːs] *vti* cessare, fermarsi, finire.

ceaseless ['siːslis] *a* continuo, incessante.

ceaselessly ['siːslisli] *ad* incessantemente, di continuo.

Cecil [sesl] *nm pr* Cecilio.
Cecilia [sə'si:liə] **Cecily** ['sesili] *nf pr* Cecilia.
cedar ['si:də] *n* cedro.
ceiling ['si:liŋ] *n* soffitto.
celebrate ['selibreit] *vti* celebrare.
celebrated ['selibreitid] *a* celebre, famoso.
celebration [.seli'breiʃən] *n* celebrazione.
celebrity [si'lebriti] *n* celebrità.
celerity [si'leriti] *n* celerità, rapidità.
celery ['seləri] *n* sedano.
celestial [si'lestiəl] *a* celeste; celestiale.
celibacy ['selibəsi] *n* celibato.
celibate ['selibit] *a n* celibe.
cell [sel] *n* cella; (*anat*) cellula; (*el*) pila; **fuel c.** pila a combustibile.
cellar ['selə] *n* cantina.
cellarer ['selərə] *n* cantiniere.
'cellist ['tʃelist] *n* violoncellista.
'cello ['tʃelou] *n* violoncello.
cellophane ['seləfein] *n* cellofane.
cellular ['seljulə] *a* cellulare.
celluloid ['seljulɔid] *a n* (di) celluloide.
cellulose ['seljulous] *a* celluloso; *n* cellulosa.
Celtic ['keltik] *a* celtico.
cement [si'ment] *n* cemento; *vt* cementare.
cemetery ['semitri] *n* cimitero.
censer ['sensə] *n* incensiere, turibolo.
censor ['sensə] *n* censore; *vt* censurare; **censorship** censura, censorato.
censorious [sen'sɔ:riəs] *a* ipercritico.
censurable ['senʃərəbl] *a* censurabile.
censure ['senʃə] *n* censura, giudizio avverso; *vt* censurare, criticare.
census ['sensəs] *n* censimento, censo.
cent [sent] *n* centesimo di dollaro; (*fam*) soldo.
centaur ['sentɔ:] *n* centauro.
centenarian [.senti'neəriən] *a n* (*persona*) centenario.
centenary [sen'ti:nəri] *a n* centenario.
centennial [sen'teniəl] *a* centennale.
centigrade ['sentigreid] *a* centigrado.
centimetre ['senti'mi:tə] *n* centimetro (0.393 *inches*).
centipede ['sentipi:d] *n* millepiedi.
central ['sentrəl] *a* centrale.
centralization [.sentrəlai'zeiʃən] *n* accentramento.
centralize ['sentrəlaiz] *vt* accentrare.
centre ['sentə] *n* centro; *vti* concentrar(si); (*sport*) centrare.
centrifugal [sen'trifjugəl] *a* centrifugo.
centuple ['sentjupl] *a n* centuplo.
century ['sentʃuri] *n* secolo.
ceramics [si'ræmiks] *n* ceramica.
cereal ['siəriəl] *a n* cereale.
cerebral ['seribrəl] *a* cerebrale.
ceremonial [.seri'mouniəl] *a da* cerimonia; *n* cerimoniale, etichetta.

ceremonious [.seri'mouniəs] *a* cerimonioso.
ceremony ['seriməni] *n* cerimonia; **to stand on c.** fare complimenti.
certain ['sə:tn] *a* certo, sicuro; **for c.** sicuramente; **to make c.** assicurarsi.
certainly ['sə:tnli] *ad* certamente, sicuramente.
certainty ['sə:tnti] *n* certezza, sicurezza.
certifiable ['sə:tifaiəbl] *a* attestabile; che dovrebbe essere attestato pazzo.
certificate [sə'tifikit] *n* certificato.
certification [.sə:tifi'keiʃən] *n* certificazione.
certify ['sə:tifai] *vt* attestare, certificare; (*leg*) autenticare, legalizzare.
certitude ['sə:titju:d] *n* certezza.
cervical ['sə:vikəl] *a* (*anat*) cervicale.
cessation [se'seiʃən] *n* cessazione.
cession ['seʃən] *n* cessione.
cesspit ['sespit] **cesspool** ['sespu:l] *n* pozzo nero.
cetacean [si'teiʃən] *n* cetaceo.
Ceylonese [si'lɔni:z] *a n* cingalese.
chafe [tʃeif] *n* irritazione; *vti* irritar(si) (la pelle); frizionare; (*fig*) irritare, irritarsi.
chaff [tʃɑ:f] *n* pula; paglia; (*fam*) burla.
chaffer ['tʃæfə] *vi* comprare lesinando sul prezzo.
chaffinch ['tʃæfintʃ] *n* fringuello.
chagrin ['ʃægrin] *n* cruccio, dispetto.
chain [tʃein] *n* catena; *vt* incatenare.
chair [tʃeə] *n* sedia; seggio; cattedra; **chairlift** seggiovia; **to take the c.** assumere la presidenza.
chairman ['tʃeəmən] *n* presidente, presidentessa.
chairmanship ['tʃeəmənʃip] *n* presidenza.
chalice ['tʃælis] *n* calice.
chalk [tʃɔ:k] *n* gesso; (*min*) calcare; **by a long c.** di gran lunga.
chalky ['tʃɔ:ki] *a* gessoso; calcareo; pallido, terreo.
challenge ['tʃælindʒ] *n* sfida; *vt* sfidare; obbiettare; provocare.
chamber ['tʃeimbə] *n* aula, sala; (*tec*) camera; **Chamber** Camera; **c. music** musica da camera.
chamberlain ['tʃeimbəlin] *n* ciambellano.
chambermaid ['tʃeimbəmeid] *n* cameriera d'albergo.
chameleon [kə'mi:liən] *n* camaleonte.
chamois ['ʃæmwɑ:] *n* camoscio.
champagne [ʃæm'pein] *n* sciampagna.
champion ['tʃæmpiən] *n* campione; *vt* sostenere (una causa); **championship** campionato.
chance [tʃɑ:ns] *a* fortuito, casuale; *n* caso, sorte, fortuna; occasione; **by c.** per caso; *vti* accadere; (*fam*) arrischiare.
chancel ['tʃɑ:nsəl] *n* presbiterio, coro.
chancellor ['tʃɑ:nsələ] *n* cancelliere.

chancery ['tʃɑːnsəri] n cancelleria.
chancy ['tʃɑːnsi] a incerto, rischioso.
chandelier [ˌʃændi'liə] n lampadario.
chandler ['tʃɑːndlə] n droghiere, fornitore.
change [tʃeindʒ] n cambio, mutamento; danaro spicciolo; resto; vti cambiar(si).
changeable ['tʃeindʒəbl] a mutabile, incostante.
changeableness ['tʃeindʒəblnis] n inconstanza.
changeless ['tʃeindʒlis] a costante, immutabile.
changeling ['tʃeindʒliŋ] n (poet) bimbo sostituito.
changing ['tʃeindʒiŋ] a cangiante, mutevole; n cambio.
channel ['tʃænl] n canale, stretto; the (English) C. la Manica; (fig) via; vt incanalare, (arch) scanalare.
chant [tʃɑːnt] n canto, recitativo monotono.
chaos ['keiɔs] n caos.
chaotic [kei'ɔtik] a caotico.
chap [tʃæp] n screpolatura; (fam) ragazzo, individuo; vti screpolar(si).
chapel ['tʃæpəl] n cappella.
chaperon ['ʃæpəroun] n 'chaperon', accompagnatrice di signorine; vt scortare.
chaplain ['tʃæplin] n cappellano.
chaplaincy ['tʃæplinsi] n carica di cappellano.
chaplet ['tʃæplit] n corona, ghirlanda.
chapter ['tʃæptə] n capitolo.
char [tʃɑː] vti carbonizzar(si).
char(woman) ['tʃɑː(wumən)] n domestica a ore.
character ['kæriktə] n carattere, caratteristica; scrittura; attestato di servizio; individuo eccentrico; personaggio.
characteristic [ˌkæriktə'ristik] a caratteristico; n caratteristica.
characterize ['kæriktəraiz] vt caratterizzare; definire.
charade [ʃə'rɑːd] n sciarada.
charcoal ['tʃɑːkoul] n carbone di legna; (drawing) carboncino.
charge [tʃɑːdʒ] n prezzo, spesa; carica; incarico, cura; accusa; attacco; vti far pagare; incaricare; accusare; caricare di; attaccare.
chargeable ['tʃɑːdʒəbl] a a carico di, addebitabile.
charger ['tʃɑːdʒə] n destriero; (of gun) caricatore; accumulatore elettrico.
chariot ['tʃæriət] n cocchio.
charitable ['tʃæritəbl] a caritatevole.
charitableness ['tʃæritəblnis] n filantropia.
charity ['tʃæriti] n carità, beneficenza.
charlatan ['ʃɑːlətən] n ciarlatano.
Charles [tʃɑːlz] nm pr Carlo.
Charlotte ['ʃɑːlət] nf pr Carlotta.
charm [tʃɑːm] n attrattiva, fascino;

incantesimo; amuleto, ciondolo; vt affascinare, incantare.
charmer ['tʃɑːmə] n incantatore, incantatrice.
charming ['tʃɑːmiŋ] a incantevole.
chart [tʃɑːt] n carta nautica, quadro statistico; vt fare la carta di.
charter ['tʃɑːtə] n carta, documento; vt concedere statuto; noleggiare.
chary ['tʃɛəri] a cauto, prudente, parco di.
chase [tʃeis] n caccia, inseguimento; vt cacciare, inseguire; cesellare.
chasing ['tʃeisiŋ] n cesellatura.
chasm ['kæzəm] n abisso, baratro.
chassis ['ʃæsi] n inv chassis, telaio, intelaiatura.
chaste [tʃeist] a casto, puro.
chastise [tʃæs'taiz] vt castigare.
chastisement ['tʃæstizmənt] n castigo, punizione.
chastity ['tʃæstiti] n castità, purezza.
chat [tʃæt] n chiacchierata; vi chiacchierare.
chattels ['tʃætls] n pl beni mobili pl.
chatter ['tʃætə] vi chiacchierare; (teeth) battere.
chatterbox ['tʃætəbɔks] n chiacchierone, chiacchierona.
chatty ['tʃæti] a ciarliero, chiacchierone.
chauffeur ['ʃoufə] n autista.
cheap [tʃiːp] a a buon mercato; cheaply ad a buon mercato.
cheapen ['tʃiːpən] vt diminuire il prezzo; screditare, sottovalutare.
cheapness ['tʃiːpnis] n basso prezzo, buon mercato.
cheat [tʃiːt] n inganno; ingannatore, imbroglione; vti ingannare, truffare.
cheating ['tʃiːtiŋ] n inganno, truffa.
check [tʃek] n scacco; arresto; freno; controllo; quadretto su stoffa o carta; scontrino; (US) conto; check room (US) deposito bagagli; vt controllare; far arrestare, fermare; (chess) dare scacco.
checkers ['tʃekəz] n (US) giuoco della dama.
checkmate ['tʃek'meit] n scacco matto; vt dare scacco matto a.
checkpoint ['tʃekpɔint] n posto di controllo.
cheek [tʃiːk] n guancia, gota; sfrontatezza.
cheer [tʃiə] n disposizione d'animo, buon umore; applauso; vivande pl; vti applaudire; incoraggiare rallegrare.
cheerful ['tʃiəful] a allegro, di buon umore.
cheerfully ['tʃiəfuli] ad allegramente.
cheerfulness ['tʃiəfulnis] n allegria, buon umore.
cheering ['tʃiəriŋ] a incoraggiante; n acclamazioni.
cheerio ['tʃiəri'ou] interj (fam) ciao, arrivederci!
cheerless ['tʃiəlis] a triste.
cheery ['tʃiəri] a allegro.

cheese [tʃiːz] n formaggio.

chemical ['kemikəl] a chimico.

chemicals ['kemikəlz] n pl prodotti chimici.

chemist ['kemist] n chimico; farmacista.

chemistry ['kemistri] n chimica.

cheque [tʃek] n assegno bancario.

cherish ['tʃeriʃ] vt nutrire; curare con affetto, tener caro.

cherry ['tʃeri] n ciliegia; **c.-tree** ciliegio.

cherub ['tʃerəb] n cherubino.

chess [tʃes] n (gioco degli) scacchi.

chessboard ['tʃesbɔːd] n scacchiera.

chessman ['tʃesmæn] n scacco.

chest [tʃest] n petto, torace; cassa, cassetta; **c. of drawers** cassettone.

chestnut ['tʃesnʌt] n castagna; **c.-tree** castagno; **horse c.** ippocastano.

chew [tʃuː] vt masticare; **to c. the cud** ruminare; **to c. over** meditare.

chick [tʃik] n pulcino.

chicken ['tʃikin] n pollastro, pollo.

chicken-pox ['tʃikinpɔks] n varicella.

chicory ['tʃikəri] n cicoria.

chide [tʃaid] vt sgridare, biasimare.

chief [tʃiːf] a principale, il più importante; n capo.

chiefly ['tʃiːfli] ad sopratutto, principalmente.

chieftain ['tʃiːftən] n (di tribù, clan) capo.

chilblain ['tʃilblein] n gelone.

child [tʃaild] pl **children** ['tʃildrən] n bambino, figlio; **c.-bearing** gravidanza.

childbirth ['tʃaildbəːθ] n parto.

childhood ['tʃaildhud] n infanzia.

childish ['tʃaildiʃ] a infantile, puerile.

childless ['tʃaildlis] a senza figli.

childlike ['tʃaildlaik] a infantile, da bambino.

Chile ['tʃili] n Cile.

Chilean ['tʃiliən] a n cileno.

chill [tʃil] a freddo; n colpo di freddo; sensazione di freddo; vt raffreddare.

chilli ['tʃili] n pepe di Caienna.

chilly ['tʃili] a freddoloso, piuttosto freddo.

chime [tʃaim] n scampanio armonioso; vti battere, scampanare.

chimney ['tʃimni] n camino, fumaiuolo; **c.-corner** angolo del focolare.

chimneysweep ['tʃimniswiːp] n spazzacamino.

chimpanzee [ˌtʃimpən'ziː] n (zool) scimpanzè.

chin [tʃin] n mento.

China ['tʃainə] n Cina.

china ['tʃainə] n porcellana.

Chinese [tʃai'niːz] a n cinese.

chink [tʃiŋk] n crepa, fessura.

chintz [tʃints] n cotone stampato.

chip [tʃip] n frammento, scheggia, truciolo; patata fritta; vt scheggiare, tagliare a piccoli pezzi.

chipboard ['tʃipbɔːd] n legno ricostituito.

chipmunk ['tʃipmʌŋk] n (zool) tamia orientale.

chiropodist [ki'rɔpədist] n pedicure, callista.

chirp [tʃəːp] n cinguettio; vi cinguettare.

chisel ['tʃizl] n cesello, scalpello; vi cesellare.

chivalrous ['ʃivəlrəs] a cavalleresco.

chivalry ['ʃivəlri] n (fig) cavalleria.

chive [tʃaiv] n aglio di serpe.

chloride ['klɔːraid] n cloruro.

chlorine ['klɔːriːn] n cloro.

chloroform ['klɔrəfɔːm] n cloroformio; vt cloroformizzare.

chlorophyl(l) ['klɔrəfil] n (bot) clorofilla.

chocolate ['tʃɔkəlit] n cioccolata; cioccolato, cioccolatino.

choice [tʃɔis] a prelibato, scelto, squisito; n scelta.

choir ['kwaiə] n coro; **choirmaster** maestro di cappella.

choke [tʃouk] n soffocazione; strozzameeto; (mech) regolatore; vti soffocare, soffocarsi; ingombrare.

cholera ['kɔlərə] n colera.

choleric ['kɔlərik] a collerico, irascibile.

choose [tʃuːz] vti scegliere.

choos(e)y ['tʃuːzi] a (fam) schizzinoso, pignolo.

chop [tʃɔp] n colpo d'ascia; costoletta di maiale o di montone; vt tagliare, tagliuzzare.

chopper ['tʃɔpə] n corta ascia, mannaia.

choppy ['tʃɔpi] a increspato, mosso.

choral ['kɔːrəl] a n corale.

chord [kɔːd] n (mus) corda, (mus) accordo.

choreographer [ˌkɔri'ɔgrəfə] n coreografo.

choreography [ˌkɔri'ɔgrəfi] n coreografia.

chorister ['kɔristə] n corista.

chorus ['kɔːrəs] n coro; ritornello.

Christ [kraist] nm pr Cristo.

christen ['krisn] vt battezzare.

Christendom ['krisndəm] n cristianità.

christening ['krisniŋ] n battesimo.

Christian ['kristjən] a n cristiano; **C. name** nome proprio; nome di battesimo.

Christianity ['kristi'æniti] n cristianesimo.

christianize ['kristjənaiz] vt convertire al cristianesimo.

Christina [kris'tiːnə] **Christine** ['kristiːn] nf pr Cristina.

Christmas ['krisməs] n Natale; **C. box** [bɔks] strenna natalizia.

Christopher ['kristəfə] nm pr Cristoforo.

chromatic [krə'mætik] a cromatico.

chrome [kroum] n cromo; vt cromare.

chromium ['kroumiəm] *n* (*chem*) cromo.

chromosome ['krouməsoum] *n* cromosoma.

chronic ['krɔnik] *a* cronico; (*sl*) terribile.

chronicle ['krɔnikl] *n* cronaca.

chronicler ['krɔniklə] *n* cronista.

chronological [.krɔnə'lɔdʒikəl] *a* cronologico.

chronology [krə'nɔlədʒi] *n* cronologia.

chronometer [krə'nɔmitə] *n* cronometro.

chrysalis ['krisəlis] *n* crisalide.

chrysanthemum [kri'sænθəməm] *n* crisantemo.

chubby ['tʃʌbi] *a* paffuto, pienotto.

chuck [tʃʌk] *vt* dare un buffetto a; (*fam*) gettare; (*fam*) sperperare; c. out (*fam*) mettere alla porta; **chucker-out** chi getta fuori da un locale gli intrusi.

chuckle ['tʃʌkl] *n* riso soffocato; *vi* ridere sotto i baffi.

chum [tʃʌm] *n* (*fam*) amico intimo, compagno; *vi* (*fam*) essere amici.

chunk [tʃʌŋk] *n* grosso pezzo, tozzo.

church [tʃəːtʃ] *n* chiesa.

churchman ['tʃəːtʃmən] *n* ecclesiastico.

churchyard ['tʃəːtʃ'jaːd] *n* campo santo.

churl [tʃəːl] *n* zotico, uomo sgarbato o tirchio.

churlish ['tʃəːliʃ] *a* rozzo, sgarbato, tirchio.

churlishness ['tʃəːliʃnis] *n* sgarbatezza, tirchieria.

churn [tʃəːn] *n* zangola; *vti* battere il latte dentro la zangola per farne burro; agitar(si).

chute [ʃuːt] *n* canale di scolo.

ciborium [si'bɔːriəm] *n* ciborio.

cicada [si'kaːdə] *n* cicala.

cicatrize ['sikətraiz] *vti* cicatrizzar(si).

cider ['saidə] *n* sidro.

cigar [si'gaː] *n* sigaro; c. store (US) tabaccheria.

cigarette [.sigə'ret] *n* sigaretta; c. case portasigarette.

cinder ['sində] *n* brace, cenere.

Cinderella [.sində'relə] *n* Cenerentola.

cine-camera [sini'kæmərə] *n* macchina da presa, cinepresa.

cinema ['sinimə] *n* cinema(tografo).

cinematographic [.sini,mætə'græfik] *a* cinematografico.

cinematography [.sinimə'tɔgrəfi] *n* cinematografia.

cinnamon ['sinəmən] *n* cannella, cinnamomo.

cipher ['saifə] *n* zero; nulla, nullità; cifrario, cifra.

circle ['səːkl] *n* cerchio, circolo; orbita; (*theat*) galleria; *vti* circondare, girare intorno a.

circuit ['səːkit] *n* circuito; giro; circoscrizione.

circuitous [sə'kjuːitəs] *a* tortuoso, indiretto.

circular ['səːkjulə] *a n* circolare.

circularize ['səːkjuləraiz] *vt* inviare circolari a.

circulate ['səːkjuleit] *vti* (far) circolare.

circulation [.səːkju'leiʃən] *n* circolazione.

circulatory ['səːkjuːlətəri] *n* circolatorio.

circumcise ['səːkəmsaiz] *vt* circoncidere.

circumcision [.səːkəm'siʒən] *n* circoncisione.

circumference [sə'kʌmfərəns] *n* circonferenza.

circumflex ['səːkəmfleks] *a* circonflesso.

circumlocution [.səːkəmlə'kjuːʃən] *n* circonlocuzione, perifrasi.

circumscribe ['səːkəmskraib] *vt* circoscrivere.

circumspect ['səːkəmspekt] *a* circospetto, cauto.

circumspection [.səːkəm'spekʃən] *n* circospezione.

circumstance ['səːkəmstəns] *n* circostanza, condizione.

circumstantial [.sə'kəm'stænʃəl] *a* circostanziato; indiziario.

circumvent [.sə:kəm'vent] *vt* ingannare, circuire.

circumvention [.səːkəm'ventʃən] *n* circonvenzione, raggiro.

circus ['səːkəs] *n* circo.

Cistercian [sis'təːʃjən] *a n* cistercense.

cistern ['sistən] *n* cisterna, serbatoio.

citadel ['sitədl] *n* cittadella, fortezza.

cite [sait] *vt* citare.

citizen ['sitizn] *n* cittadino; **citizenship** *n* cittadinanza.

citrate ['sitrit] *n* (*chem*) citrato.

citric ['sitrik] *a* citrico.

citron ['sitrən] *n* cedro.

city ['siti] *n* città, centro d'una grande città.

civet ['sivit] *n* zibetto.

civic ['sivik] *a* civico.

civil ['sivl] *a* civile, educato, gentile.

civilian [si'viljən] *n* civile, borghese.

civility [si'viliti] *n* cortesia, educazione.

civilization [.sivilai'zeiʃən] *n* civilizzazione, civiltà.

civilize ['sivilaiz] *vt* incivilire, civilizzare.

claim [kleim] *n* diritto, pretesa; reclamo, rivendicazione; concessione mineraria; *vt* pretendere; reclamare, rivendicare; asserire.

claimant ['kleimənt] *n* pretendente.

clairvoyance [klɛə'vɔiəns] *n* chiaroveggenza.

clairvoyant [klɛə'vɔiənt] *a n* chiaroveggente.

clam [klæm] *n* mollusco bivalve; (*mech*) grappa, morsa.

clamant ['kleimənt] *a* insistente, rumoroso.

clamber ['klæmbə] *vi* arrampicarsi.

clamminess ['klæminis] *n* viscosità.

clammy ['klæmi] *a* freddo umido; viscoso.

clamorous ['klæmərəs] *a* clamoroso.

clamour ['klæmə] *vi* chiedere clamorosamente, fare molto rumore.

clamp [klæmp] *n* pinza, morsa; *vt* tener fermo, assicurare.

clan [klæn] *n* tribù, 'clan'.

clandestine [klæn'destin] *a* clandestino.

clang [klæŋ] **clangour** ['klæŋgə] *n* fragore.

clang [klæŋ] *vti* far risuonare con fragore.

clank [klæŋk] *n* suono metallico, clangore; *vi* produrre un rumore secco, metallico.

clap [klæp] *n* battimano; colpo; *vti* battere le mani, applaudire.

clapper ['klæpə] *n* applauditore; battente, battaglio.

Clara ['klɛərə] **Clare** [klɛə] *n f pr* Clara, Chiara.

claret ['klærət] *n* bordò.

clarification [ˌklærifi'keiʃən] *n* chiarificazione.

clarify ['klærifai] *vt* chiarire; raffinare.

clarinet [ˌklæri'net] *n* (*mus*) clarinetto.

clarity ['klæriti] *n* chiarezza.

clash [klæʃ] *n* collisione, scontro; conflitto; rumore, strepito; *vti* urtar(si), fare strepito.

clashing ['klæʃiŋ] *a* opposto, contrastante.

clasp [klɑːsp] *n* fermaglio, gancio; stretta di mano, abbraccio; *vt* agganciare; stringere, abbracciare.

class [klɑːs] *n* classe; *vt* classificare.

classic ['klæsik] *a n* classico.

classical ['klæsikəl] *a* classico.

classicism ['klæsisizəm] *n* classicismo.

classification [ˌklæsifi'keiʃən] *n* classifica, classificazione.

classify ['klæsifai] *vt* classificare.

clatter ['klætə] *n* acciottolio, fracasso; *vti* far fracasso.

Claud(e) [klɔːd] *nm pr* Claudio.

clause [klɔːz] *n* clausola.

claustrophobia [ˌklɔːstrə'foubiə] *n* claustrofobia.

claw [klɔː] *n* artiglio; *vti* artigliare.

clay [klei] *n* argilla, creta.

clean [kliːn] *a* pulito, netto; innocente, puro; completo; *vt* pulire.

cleaning ['kliːniŋ] *n* pulitura, pulizia; dry-c. lavaggio a secco; **spring c.** pulizia di Pasqua.

cleanliness ['klenlinis] *n* pulizia.

cleanly ['klenli] *a* pulito; ['kliːnli] *ad* in modo pulito.

cleanness ['kliːnnis] *n* pulizia, chiarezza, purezza.

cleanse [klenz] *vt* purificare; pulire.

cleansing ['klenziŋ] *a* purificante; purificazione; detersione; **c. cream** crema detergente.

clear [kliə] *a* chiaro, evidente; libero da ostacoli; *vti* chiarire, chiarificare, schiarir(si); sdoganare.

clearance ['kliərəns] *n* liquidazione; sdoganamento.

clearing ['kliəriŋ] *n* tratto di terreno disboscato per la coltivazione; **c. house** (*com*) stanza di compensazione.

clearly ['kliəli] *ad* chiaramente, distintamente.

clearness ['kliənis] *n* chiarezza.

cleavage ['kliːvidʒ] *n* sfaldamento.

cleaver ['kliːvə] *n* mannaia del macellaio.

clef [klef] *n* (*mus*) chiave.

cleft [kleft] *n* spaccatura, fessura.

clemency ['klemənsi] *n* clemenza.

clement ['klemənt] *a* clemente, mite.

clench [klentʃ] *vt* stringere; (*tec*) ribadire; (*fig*) definire.

clergy ['kləːdʒi] *n* clero.

clergyman ['kləːdʒimən] *n* pastore evangelico, ecclesiastico.

cleric ['klerik] *n* ecclesiastico.

clerical ['klerikəl] *a* clericale; di impiegato; **c. work** lavoro d'ufficio.

clerk [klɑːk] *n* impiegato d'ufficio; (*US*) commesso.

clever ['klevə] *a* intelligente, abile, ingegnoso.

cleverness ['klevənis] *n* intelligenza, abilità, ingegnosità.

click [klik] *n* suono metallico; scatto.

client ['klaiənt] *n* cliente.

clientele [ˌkliːɑːn'teil] *n* clientela.

cliff [klif] *n* rupe a picco, scarpata.

climate ['klaimit] *n* clima.

climatic [klai'mætik] *a* climatico.

climax ['klaimæks] *n* culmine, punto culminante.

climb [klaim] *vti* arrampicarsi, scalare; *n* salita; scalata.

climber ['klaimə] *n* scalatore, (*bot*) pianta rampicante; (*fig*) arrivista.

clinch [klintʃ] *v* clench.

cling [kliŋ] *vi* avvitticchiarsi, aggrapparsi.

clinic ['klinik] *n* clinica.

clinical ['klinikəl] *a* clinico.

clink [kliŋk] *n* tintinnio; (*sl*) prigione; *vti* (far) tintinnare.

clip [klip] *n* fermaglio, gancio; taglio, tosatura; ritaglio; *vt* tagliare, tosare.

clipper ['klipə] *n* goletta; forbici per tosare.

clipping ['klipiŋ] *n* taglio, tosatura; ritaglio di un giornale.

clique [kliːk] *n* cricca.

cloak [klouk] *n* mantello; (*fig*) pretesto; *vt* (*fig*) mascherare.

clock [klɔk] *n* orologio (da muro), pendola; *vti* cronometrare.

clockwork ['klɔkwəːk] n meccanismo d'orologio.

clod [klɔd] n zolla di terra.

clog [klɔg] n zoccolo; intoppo; vt ingombrare, ostruire.

cloister ['klɔistə] n chiostro, convento.

close [klous] a chiuso, rinchiuso; afoso; fitto, stretto; vicino; ad (da) vicino; prep vicino a; n recinto.

close [klouz] n conclusione, fine; vt chiudere, concludere, finire; **closed-circuit television** n televisione a circuito chiuso.

closely ['klousli] ad strettamente; attentamente.

closeness ['klousnis] n prossimità, vicinanza; pesantezza dell'aria.

closet ['klɔzit] n gabinetto, salotto privato, studio; armadio a muro.

closing ['klouziŋ] a di chiusura, ultimo; n chiusura.

closure ['klouʒə] n chiusura, fine.

clot [klɔt] n coagulo, grumo; vi coagularsi, raggrumarsi.

cloth [klɔθ] n stoffa, tela, tessuto; tovaglia.

clothe [klouð] vt (ri)vestire.

clothes [klouðz] n pl indumenti, vestiti pl; **clothespeg**, (US) **clothespin** molletta ferma-bucato.

clothier ['klouðiə] n commerciante in vestiti e stoffe.

clothing ['klouðiŋ] n vestiario, indumenti.

cloud [klaud] n nube, nuvola; vi rannuvolarsi; vt annuvolare, oscurare.

cloudless ['klaudlis] a senza nubi, sereno.

cloudy ['klaudi] a nuvoloso, oscuro.

clove [klouv] n chiodo di garofano.

clover ['klouvə] n trifoglio.

clown [klaun] n buffone, pagliaccio.

clownish ['klauniʃ] a pagliaccesco; rustico.

cloy [klɔi] vt saziare, nauseare.

club [klʌb] n bastone, randello; circolo; (cards) fiori; vt bastonare; **to c. together** pagare il proprio tributo.

cluck [klʌk] vi chiocciare.

clue [kluː] n bandolo, indizio.

clump [klʌmp] n gruppo d'alberi o di cespugli; vi camminare pesantemente.

clumsiness ['klʌmzinis] n goffaggine, mancanza di tatto.

clumsy ['klʌmzi] a goffo, senza tatto.

cluster ['klʌstə] n grappolo, gruppo, sciame; vi crescere in grappoli; raccogliersi in gruppo.

clutch [klʌtʃ] n presa fortissima, stretta; (mech) innesto; vt afferrare, agguantare; **clutches** pl artigli, grinfie pl.

clutter ['klʌtə] n confusione, massa confusa; vti far confusione, ingombrare.

coach [koutʃ] n carrozza, (rly) carrozza, vagone, vettura; pullman; insegnante privato, ripetitore; allenatore di atleti; vt allenare; dare ripetizioni a; **baby c.** carrozzina per bambini.

coagulate [kou'ægjuleit] vti coagulare, coagularsi.

coagulation [kou.ægju'leiʃən] n coagulazione.

coal [koul] n carbone; **c. field** bacino carbonifero.

coalesce [.kouə'les] vi fondersi, unirsi.

coalition [.kouə'liʃən] n coalizione.

coal-mine ['koulmain] n miniera di carbone.

coarse [kɔːs] a ruvido, rozzo, grossolano, volgare.

coarseness ['kɔːsnis] n ruvidezza, grossolanità.

coast [koust] n costa; vt costeggiare.

coastal ['koustl] a costiero.

coastguard ['koustgɑːd] n guardia-coste.

coat [kout] n giacca; mantello; paltò; mano (di vernice); vt rivestire; verniciare; **c.-of-arms** stemma.

coating ['koutiŋ] n rivestimento, strato.

coax [kouks] vt persuadere con le moine, blandire.

cob [kɔb] n cavallo da tiro; cigno maschio; pannocchia di frumentone.

cobalt ['koubɔːlt] n cobalto.

cobble ['kɔbl] n ciottolo; vt selciare con ciottoli; rattoppare.

cobbler ['kɔblə] n ciabattino.

cobra ['koubrə] n (zool) cobra.

cobweb ['kɔbweb] n ragnatela.

cocaine [kə'kein] n cocaina.

cochineal ['kɔtʃiniːl] n cocciniglia.

cock [kɔk] n gallo, maschio di uccelli; rubinetto, spina; mucchio di fieno; cane di fucile; vti drizzar(si); ammucchiare fieno; **c.-eyed** strabico.

cockade [kɔ'keid] n coccarda.

cockchafer ['kɔk.tʃeifə] n maggiolino.

cockerel ['kɔkərəl] n galletto.

cockle ['kɔkl] n (zool) cardio; (bot) loglio; **c.-shell** conchiglia.

cockney ['kɔkni] a n londinese (spesso con senso spregiativo).

cockpit ['kɔkpit] n arena da combattimento; (av) carlinga.

cockroach ['kɔkroutʃ] n scarafaggio.

cockscomb ['kɔkskoum] n cresta di gallo; (bot) amaranto.

cocksure ['kɔk'ʃuə] a presuntuoso.

cocktail ['kɔkteil] n 'cocktail'; **c. cabinet** mobile bar.

cocky ['kɔki] a impertinente, presuntuoso.

cocoa ['koukou] n cacao.

coconut ['koukənʌt] n noce di cocco.

cocoon [kə'kuːn] n bozzolo.

cod [kɔd] n (inv) merluzzo.

coddle ['kɔdl] *vt* vezzeggiare, coccolare.

code [koud] *n* codice, cifrario.

codeine ['koudiːn] *n* codeina.

codex ['koudeks] *pl* **codices** *n* codice.

codicil ['kɔdisil] *n* codicillo.

codification [ˌkɔdifiˈkeiʃən] *n* codificazione.

codify ['kɔdifai] *vt* codificare.

coeducation ['kouˌedjuːˈkeiʃən] *n* istruzione in scuola mista.

coefficient [ˌkouiˈfiʃənt] *n* coefficiente.

coerce [kouˈəːs] *vt* costringere.

coercion [kouˈəːʃən] *n* coercizione.

coercive [kouˈəːsiv] *a* coercitivo.

coexistence ['kouigˈzistəns] *n* coesistenza.

coffee ['kɔfi] *n* caffè; **c. mill** macinino da caffè; **c. pot** caffettiera; **ground c.** caffè tostato; **white c.** caffellatte.

coffer ['kɔfə] *n* cofano, scrigno.

coffin ['kɔfin] *n* cassa da morto, bara.

cog [kɔg] *n* dente d'una ruota; *vt* dentare una ruota.

cogency ['koudʒənsi] *n* forza di persuasione.

cogent ['koudʒənt] *a* convincente, persuasivo.

cogitate ['kɔdʒiteit] *vti* cogitare, ponderare.

cogitation [ˌkɔdʒiˈteiʃən] *n* cogitazione.

cognate ['kɔgneit] *a n* congiunto, parente.

cognizance ['kɔgnizəns] *n* conoscenza, percezione.

cohabit [kouˈhæbit] *vi* coabitare.

cohabitation [ˌkouhæbiˈteiʃən] *n* coabitazione.

co-heir ['kouˈɛə] (*m*) **co-heiress** ['kouˈɛəris] (*f*) *n* coerede.

cohere [kouˈhiə] *vi* aderire; essere coerente.

coherence [kouˈhiərəns] *n* coerenza.

coherent [kouˈhiərənt] *a* coerente.

cohesion [kouˈhiːʒən] *n* coesione.

cohesive [kouˈhiːsiv] *a* coesivo.

coiffure [kwɑːˈfjuə] *n* pettinatura, acconciatura.

coil [kɔil] *n* rotolo, gomitolo; (*snake*) spira; (*el*) bobina; *vt* arrotolare, avvolgere in spire.

coin [kɔin] *n* moneta; *vt* coniare.

coinage ['kɔinidʒ] *n* conio; sistema monetario.

coincide [ˌkouinˈsaid] *vi* coincidere.

coincidence [ˌkouˈinsidəns] *n* coincidenza; combinazione.

coincidental [kouˌinsiˈdentl] *a* coincidente, di coincidenza.

coke [kouk] *n* carbone coke.

colander ['kʌləndə] *n* colapasta, colatoio.

cold [kould] *a* freddo; *n* freddo; raffreddore; **to be c.** aver freddo; **to catch a c.** infreddarsi.

coldly ['kouldli] *ad* freddamente.

coldness ['kouldnis] *n* freddezza.

colic ['kɔlik] *n* colica.

Coliseum [ˌkɔliˈsiəm] *n* Colosseo.

collaborate [kəˈlæbəreit] *vi* collaborare.

collaboration [kəˌlæbəˈreiʃən] *n* collaborazione.

collaborator [kəˈlæbəreitə] *n* collaboratore.

collapse [kəˈlæps] *n* crollo, caduta; (*med*) collasso; *vi* crollare; avere un collasso.

collar ['kɔlə] *n* colletto; (*dogs*) collare; **c. stud**, (*US*) **c. button** bottone del colletto; *vt* afferrare, prendere per il collo.

collate [kɔˈleit] *vt* collazionare.

collateral [kɔˈlætərəl] *a n* collaterale.

collation [kɔˈleiʃən] *n* collazione.

colleague ['kɔliːg] *n* collega.

collect [kəˈlekt] *n* colletta; [kəˈlekt] *vt* raccogliere, mettere insieme, radunare, fare una collezione; *vi* radunarsi; **to c. oneself** riprendersi.

collected [kəˈlektid] *a* raccolto, riunito; padrone di sé.

collection [kəˈlekʃən] *n* riunione, raccolta, colletta, collezione.

collective [kəˈlektiv] *a* collettivo.

collectivity [kəlekˈtiviti] *n* collettività.

collector [kəˈlektə] *n* collezionista; esattore.

college ['kɔlidʒ] *n* collegio; università.

collide [kəˈlaid] *vi* scontrarsi.

collier ['kɔliə] *n* minatore; nave carboniera.

collision [kəˈliʒən] *n* collisione, scontro.

colloquial [kəˈloukwiəl] *a* usato nella conversazione familiare, d'uso corrente; **colloquialism** espressione familiare.

colloquy ['kɔləkwi] *n* colloquio.

collusion [kəˈluːʒən] *n* collusione.

Colombia [kəˈlʌmbiə] *n* (*geogr*) Colombia.

colon ['koulən] *n* due punti; **semi-c.** punto e virgola.

colonel ['kəːnl] *n* colonnello.

colonial [kəˈlouniəl] *a* coloniale.

colonist ['kɔlənist] *n* abitante di colonia.

colonization [ˌkɔlənaiˈzeiʃən] *n* colonizzazione.

colonize ['kɔlənaiz] *vti* colonizzare.

colonnade [ˌkɔləˈneid] *n* colonnato.

colony ['kɔləni] *n* colonia.

colossal [kəˈlɔsl] *a* colossale.

colour ['kʌlə] *n* colore, colorito, tinta; apparenza; pretesto; **colours** *pl* bandiera; *vti* colorare, colorire, colorirsi, dipingere; arrossire.

coloured ['kʌləd] *a* colorato, colorito, di colore; **c. person** persona di colore.

colourful ['kʌləful] *a* pieno di colore, pittoresco.

colouring ['kʌləriŋ] *n* colorante; colorito; arrossimento.

colourless ['kʌləlis] a incolore, pallido; insipido.

colt [koult] n puledro.

column ['kɔləm] n colonna.

columnist ['kɔləmnist] n giornalista, cronista.

coma ['koumə] n coma, torpore.

comb [koum] n pettine; (crest) cresta; favo; vt pettinare, strigliare; (fig) rastrellare, perlustrare.

combat ['kɔmbət] n combattimento, lotta; vti combattere, lottare.

combatant ['kɔmbətənt] a n combattente.

combination [‚kɔmbi'neiʃən] n combinazione.

combine ['kɔmbain] n associazione, sindacato; [kəm'bain] vti combinar(si).

combined [kɔm'baind] a combinato, congiunto; c. ticket biglietto misto.

combing ['koumiŋ] n pettinata; (fig) rastrellamento, perlustramento.

combustible [kəm'bʌstəbl] a n combustibile.

combustion [kəm'bʌstʃən] n combustione.

come [kʌm] vi venire, arrivare, giungere; accadere; to c. back ritornare; to c. in entrare; to c. round passare da; riprendere i sensi.

comedian [kə'mi:diən] n commediante, (attore) comico.

comedown ['kʌmdaun] n (fig) crollo.

comedy ['kɔmidi] n commedia.

comeliness ['kʌmlinis] n avvenenza.

comely ['kʌmli] a avvenente.

comet ['kɔmit] n cometa.

comfort ['kʌmfət] n conforto, consolazione, comodità, agio; vt confortare, consolare.

comfortable ['kʌmfətəbl] a comodo, confortevole; adeguato.

comfortably ['kʌmfətəbli] ad comodamente, con agio.

comforter ['kʌmfətə] n consolatore; lunga sciarpa di lana; (US) trapunta.

comic(al) [kɔmik(l)] a comico, buffo; n pl giornale a fumetti.

coming ['kʌmiŋ] a venturo, prossimo; n venuta, arrivo.

comma ['kɔmə] n virgola.

command [kə'mɑ:nd] n comando, ordine; dominio; vti comandare, ordinare; controllare, dominare.

commandant [‚kɔmən'dænt] n comandante.

commandeer [‚kɔmən'diə] vt requisire.

commander [kɔ'mɑ:ndə] n comandante.

commanding [kɔ'mɑ:ndiŋ] a che comanda; maestoso, dominante.

commandment [kɔ'mɑ:ndmənt] n comandamento.

commemorate [kə'meməreit] vt commemorare.

commemoration [kə‚memə'reiʃən] n commemorazione.

commence [kə'mens] vti cominciare.

commencement [kə'mensmənt] n principio; (US) cerimonia per il conferimento di lauree.

commend [kə'mend] vt lodare; raccomandare.

commendable [kə'mendəbl] a lodevole.

commendation [‚kɔmen'deiʃən] n elogio, raccomandazione.

commensurable [kə'menʃərəbl] a commensurabile.

commensurate [kə'menʃərit] a adeguato, commisurato.

comment ['kɔment] n commento; vi commentare.

commentary ['kɔməntəri] n commentario, commento.

commentator ['kɔmenteitə] n commentatore, radiocronista.

commerce ['kɔmə:s] n commercio.

commercial [kə'mə:ʃəl] a commerciale; (tv etc) pubblicità.

commercialize [kə'mə:ʃəlaiz] vt rendere commerciabile.

commiserate [kə'mizəreit] vt compiangere.

commiseration [kə‚mizə'reiʃən] n commiserazione, pietà.

commissariat [‚kɔmi'sɛəriət] n (mil) commissariato.

commission [kə'miʃən] n commissione, incarico, mandato; brevetto da ufficiale; vt incaricare, dare una carica a, armare, equipaggiare (una nave).

commissionaire [kə‚miʃə'nɛə] n portiere gallonato.

commissioned [kə'miʃənd] a delegato; non-c. officer sottufficiale.

commissioner [kə'miʃənə] n commissario.

commit [kə'mit] vt affidare. consegnare, mandare in prigione, commettere to c. oneself impegnarsi.

commitment [kə'mitmənt] n impegno.

committal [kə'mitl] n consegna, perpetrazione; il mandare in prigione.

committee [kə'miti] n comitato, commissione.

commode [kə'moud] n cassettone.

commodious [kə'moudiəs] a spazioso.

commodity [kə'mɔditi] n merce, prodotto, genere di prima necessità.

commodore ['kɔmədɔ:] n (naut) commodoro; air c. (av mil) generale di brigata.

common ['kɔmən] a comune, usuale, ordinario; n terreno demaniale; c. market mercato comune; c.-sense buonsenso, senso comune; c. stock (US com) azioni ordinarie.

commoner ['kɔmənə] n borghese o popolano.

commonly ['kɔmənli] ad comunemente.

commonplace ['kɔmənpleis] a banale, trito; n banalità, luogo comune.

commons ['kɔmənz] n pl popolo;

House of C. Camera dei Comuni; (*food*) cibo, razioni *pl*; **short c.** scarse razioni *pl*.

commonwealth ['kɔmənwelθ] *n* comunità indipendente.

commotion [kə'mouʃən] *n* agitazione, trambusto.

communal ['kɔmjunl] *a* della comunità, comunale.

communicant [kə'mjuːnikənt] *n* (*eccl*) comunicando; informatore.

communicate [kə'mjuːnikeit] *vti* comunicar(si).

communication [kə,mjuːni'keiʃən] comunicazione.

communicative [kə'mjuːnikətiv] *a* comunicativo.

communion [kə'mjuːnjən] *n* comunione, comunanza.

communiqué [kə'mjuːnikei] *n* comunicato ufficiale.

communism ['kɔmjunizəm] *n* comunismo.

communist ['kɔmjunist] *n* comunista.

community [kə'mjuːniti] *n* comunità.

commutation [,kɔmjuː'teiʃən] *n* commutazione; **c. passenger** (*US rly*) abbonato; **c. ticket** (*US rly*) biglietto di abbonamento.

commute [kə'mjuːt] *vt* commutare; *vi* fare la spola.

commuter [kə'mjuːtə] *n* (*rly*) abbonato.

compact ['kɔmpækt] *n* patto, contratto; portacipria.

compact [kəm'pækt] *a* compatto, conciso.

compactness [kəm'pæktnis] *n* compattezza, concisione.

companion [kəm'pænjən] *n* compagno, socio; dama di compagnia.

companionable [kəm'pænjənəbl] *a* socievole.

companionship [kəm'pænjənʃip] *n* amicizia, compagnia.

company ['kʌmpəni] *n* compagnia, associazione, società; (*naut*) ciurma; **joint stock c.** società per azioni; **limited liability c.** società a responsabilità limitata.

comparable ['kɔmpərəbl] *a* paragonabile.

comparative [kəm'pærətiv] *a n* comparativo; comparato; relativo; **comparatively** relativamente, comparativamente.

compare [kəm'pɛə] *vti* paragonare, confrontare.

comparison [kəm'pærisn] *n* paragone, confronto.

compartment [kəm'paːtmənt] *n* scompartimento.

compass ['kʌmpəs] *n* circonferenza, spazio, portata; bussola; *vt* circondare; realizzare.

compasses ['kʌmpəsiz] *n pl* compasso.

compassion [kəm'pæʃən] *n* compassione, pietà.

compassionate [kəm'pæʃənit] *a* pieno di compassione; *vt* compassionare.

compatibility [kəm,pætə'biliti] *n* compatibilità.

compatible [kəm'pætəbl] *a* compatibile.

compatriot [kəm'pætriət] *n* compatriota.

compel [kəm'pel] *vt* costringere, forzare.

compelling [kəm'peliŋ] *a* irresistibile.

compendious [kəm'pendiəs] *a* compendioso.

compendium [kəm'pendiəm] *pl* **compendiums, compendia** *n* compendio.

compensate ['kɔmpenseit] *vti* compensare, ricompensare.

compensation [,kɔmpen'seiʃən] *n* compenso, indennità.

compère ['kɔmpɛə] *n* (*theat*) presentatore, gareggiare, concorrere.

compete [kəm'piːt] *vi* competere; *vti* presentare.

competence ['kɔmpitəns] *n* competenza, capacità.

competent ['kɔmpitənt] *a* competente, capace.

competition [,kɔmpi'tiʃən] *n* competizione, concorso, gara; (*com*) concorrenza.

competitive [kəm'petitiv] *a* di competizione, di concorso; (*com*) di concorrenza; **c. prices** prezzi di concorrenza.

competitor [kəm'petitə] *n* competitore, concorrente.

compilation [,kɔmpi'leiʃən] *n* compilazione.

compile [kəm'pail] *vt* compilare.

complacency [kəm'pleisnsi] *n* compiacenza, compiacimento.

complacent [kəm'pleisnt] *a* compiaciuto, compiacente.

complain [kəm'plein] *vi* lamentarsi.

complaint [kəm'pleint] *n* lagnanza, reclamo; malattia.

complaisance [kəm'pleizəns] *n* compiacenza, cortesia.

complement ['kɔmplimənt] *n* complemento.

complementary [,kɔmpli'mentəri] *a* complementare.

complete [kəm'pliːt] *a* completo, intero, perfetto; *vt* completare, finire; riempire.

completely [kəm'pliːtli] *ad* completamente.

completion [kəm'pliːʃən] *n* completamento; compimento.

complex ['kɔmpleks] *a* complesso, complicato; *n* complesso.

complexion [kəm'plekʃən] *n* carnagione, colorito.

complexity [kəm'pleksiti] *n* complessità.

compliance [kəm'plaiəns] n condiscendenza; in c. with d'accordo con.

compliant [kəm'plaiənt] a accondiscendente.

complicate ['kɔmplikeit] vt complicare.

complicated ['kɔmplikeitid] a complicato.

complication [ˌkɔmpli'keiʃən] n complicazione.

complicity [kəm'plisiti] n complicità.

compliment ['kɔmplimənt] n complimento; vt ['kɔmpli'ment] congratularsi con.

complimentary [ˌkɔmpli'mentəri] a di complimento, di omaggio, di favore; c. tickets biglietti di omaggio.

comply [kəm'plai] vi accondiscendere, conformarsi.

component [kəm'pounənt] a n componente.

compose [kəm'pouz] vt comporre; calmare.

composed [kəm'pouzd] a composto, calmo.

composer [kəm'pouzə] n compositore.

composite ['kɔmpəzit] a composto, composito.

composition [ˌkɔmpə'ziʃən] n composizione; concordato; tema.

compositor [kəm'pɔzitə] n (typ) compositore.

compost ['kɔmpɔst] n composto, concime; vt concimare.

composure [kəm'pouʒə] n calma, compostezza.

compound ['kɔmpaund] a composto; n miscela, composto; vt [kɔm'paund] comporre, mescolare; vi accordarsi.

comprehend [ˌkɔmpri'hend] vt comprendere, includere.

comprehensible [ˌkɔmpri'hensəbl] a comprensibile.

comprehension [ˌkɔmpri'henʃən] n comprensione.

comprehensive [ˌkɔmpri'hensiv] a comprensivo.

compress ['kɔmpres] n compressa.

compress [kəm'pres] vt comprimere; condensare.

compression [kəm'preʃən] n compressione; (fig) concentrazione.

comprise [kəm'praiz] vt comprendere, includere.

compromise ['kɔmprəmaiz] n compromesso; vti compromettere, accomodare, sistemare.

comptometer [kɔmp'tɔmitə] n macchina calcolatrice.

compulsion [kəm'pʌlʃən] n costrizione, obbligo.

compulsive [kəm'pʌlsiv] a coercitivo.

compulsory [kəm'pʌlsəri] a obbligatorio, forzato.

compunction [kəm'pʌŋkʃən] n compunzione.

computation [ˌkɔmpju:'teiʃən] n computo, calcolo.

compute [kəm'pju:t] vt computare.

computer [kəm'pju:tə] n calcolatore, (macchina) calcolatrice.

comrade ['kɔmrid] n camerata, compagno.

con [kɔn] vt imparare a memoria.

concave ['kɔn'keiv] a concavo, a volta.

conceal [kən'si:l] vt celare, nascondere.

concealment [kən'si:lmənt] n occultamento, nascondiglio.

concede [kən'si:d] vt ammettere; concedere.

conceit [kən'si:t] n vanità, presunzione; ricercatezza; concettismo.

conceited [kən'si:tid] a presuntuoso, vanesio, affettato.

conceivable [kən'si:vəbl] a concepibile.

conceive [kən'si:v] vt concepire.

concentrate ['kɔnsentreit] vti concentrar(si).

concentration [ˌkɔnsen'treiʃən] n concentramento, concentrazione.

concentric [kɔn'sentrik] a concentrico.

concept ['kɔnsept] n concetto.

conception [kən'sepʃən] n concezione.

concern [kən'sə:n] n ansietà, faccenda, ditta, impresa; vt avere a che fare con, concernere, riguardare.

concerned [kən'sə:nd] a interessato; preoccupato.

concerning [kən'sə:niŋ] prep riguardo a, circa.

concert ['kɔnsət] n concerto; accordo.

concert [kən'sə:t] vt concertare.

concertina [ˌkɔnsə'ti:nə] n piccola fisarmonica.

concerto [kən'tʃə:tou] n (mus) concerto; piano c. concerto per pianoforte.

concession [kən'seʃən] n concessione; concessionary a concessionario.

concession(n)aire [kən,seʃə'nɛə] n concessionario.

conciliate [kən'silieit] vt conciliare, guadagnarsi.

conciliation [kən,sili'eiʃən] n conciliazione.

conciliatory [kən'siliətəri] a conciliante.

concise [kən'sais] a breve, conciso.

conciseness [kən'saisnis] n concisione, brevità.

concision [kən'siʒən] n concisione.

conclave ['kɔnkleiv] n conclave.

conclude [kən'klu:d] vti concludere, finire.

concluding [kən'klu:diŋ] a finale, ultimo.

conclusion [kən'klu:ʒən] n conclusione, fine.

conclusive [kən'klu:ziv] *a* conclusivo.

concoct [kən'kɔkt] *vt* mescolare ingredienti; architettare, tramare.

concoction [kən'kɔkʃən] *n* miscuglio, macchinazione.

concomitance [kən'kɔmitəns] *n* concomitanza.

concomitant [kən'kɔmitənt] *a* concomitante; *n* fatto concomitante.

concord ['kɔnkɔ:d] *n* concordia; (*mus*) accordo.

concordance [kən'kɔ:dəns] *n* accordo; concordanza; indice alfabetico.

concordant [kən'kɔ:dənt] *a* concorde, armonioso.

concourse ['kɔnkɔ:s] *n* affluenza, concorso.

concrete ['kɔnkri:t] *a* concreto; *n* calcestruzzo; **reinforced** c. cemento armato.

concubine ['kɔŋkjubain] *n* concubina.

concur [kən'kə:] *vi* concorrere, accordarsi.

concurrence [kən'kʌrəns] *n* concorso, consenso.

concurrent [kən'kʌrənt] *a* concorrente; concorde.

concussion [kən'kʌʃən] *n* scossa, urto; **c. (of the brain)** commozione cerebrale.

condemn [kən'dem] *vt* condannare, biasimare; confiscare.

condemnation [ˌkɔndem'neiʃən] *n* condanna, biasimo.

condensation [ˌkɔnden'seiʃən] *n* condensazione.

condense [kən'dens] *vti* condensar(si); (*fig*) compendiare.

condescend [ˌkɔndi'send] *vi* (ac)condiscendere, degnarsi.

condescending [ˌkɔndi'sendiŋ] *a* condiscendente.

condescension [ˌkɔndi'senʃən] *n* condiscendenza.

condiment ['kɔndimənt] *n* condimento.

condition [kən'diʃən] *n* condizione, stato, patto; *vt* condizionare, porre condizioni; (*US*) rimandare (uno studente).

conditional [kən'diʃənl] *a* n condizionale.

condole [kən'doul] *vi* fare le condoglianze.

condolence [kən'douləns] *n* condoglianza.

condone [kən'doun] *vt* condonare, perdonare.

conducive [kən'dju:siv] *a* contribuente, tendente.

conduct ['kɔndʌkt] *n* condotta, direzione *vt* [kən'dʌkt] condurre, dirigere.

conductor [kən'dʌktə] *n* conduttore, guida, (*tram etc*) bigliettario, (*US rly*) capotreno; controllore; direttore d'orchestra.

conductress [kən'dʌktris] *n* bigliettaria.

conduit ['kɔndit] *n* condotto.

cone [koun] *n* cono (*bot*) pigna.

confection [kən'fekʃən] *n* confezione, composizione; *vt* preparare, confezionare.

confectioner [kən'fekʃənə] *n* pasticciere.

confectionery [kən'fekʃnəri] *n* dolci *pl*, pasticceria.

confederacy [kən'fedərəsi] *n* confederazione; lega; cospirazione.

confederate [kən'fedərit] *a* n confederato, alleato.

confederation [kənˌfedə'reiʃən] *n* confederazione.

confer [kən'fə:] *vti* conferire.

conference ['kɔnfərəns] *n* conferenza, abboccamento, congresso.

conferment [kən'fə:mənt] *n* conferimento.

confess [kən'fes] *vti* confessar(si).

confession [kən'feʃən] *n* confessione.

confessional [kən'feʃənl] *a* n confessionale.

confessor [kən'fesə] *n* confessore.

confetti [kən'feti] *n pl* coriandoli.

confidant(e) [ˌkɔnfi'dænt] *n* confidente.

confide [kən'faid] *vti* confidare.

confidence ['kɔnfidəns] *n* fiducia, confidenza; **self-c.** sicurezza di sè; **c. trick**, (*US*) **c. game** truffa all'americana.

confident ['kɔnfidənt] *a* fiducioso, presuntuoso.

confidently ['kɔnfidəntli] *ad* con sicurezza, con fiducia.

confidential [ˌkɔnfi'denʃəl] *a* confidenziale, privato.

confidentially [ˌkɔnfi'denʃəli] *ad* confidenzialmente.

configuration [kənˌfigju'reiʃən] *n* configurazione.

confine [kən'fain] *vti* confinare; limitar(si).

confines ['kɔnfainz] *n pl* confini *pl*.

confinement [kən'fainmənt] *n* confino, reclusione; parto.

confirm [kən'fə:m] *vt* confermare, ratificare; cresimare.

confirmation [ˌkɔnfə'meiʃən] *n* conferma, ratifica; cresima.

confirmed [kən'fə:md] *a* inveterato, convinto; cresimato.

confiscate ['kɔnfiskeit] *vt* confiscare.

confiscation [ˌkɔnfis'keiʃən] *n* confisca.

conflagration [ˌkɔnflə'greiʃən] *n* conflagrazione.

conflict ['kɔnflikt] *n* conflitto, lotta, urto; *vi* [kən'flikt] lottare, urtarsi.

conflicting [kən'fliktiŋ] *a* opposto, in conflitto.

confluence ['kɔnfluəns] *n* confluenza.

confluent ['kɔnfluənt] *a* n confluente.

conform [kən'fɔ:m] *vti* conformar(si).

conformation [kɔnˌfɔ:'meiʃən] *n* conformazione, adattamento.

conformist [kən'fɔːmist] *n* conformista.

conformity [kən'fɔːmiti] *n* conformità.

confound [kən'faund] *vt* confondere; mandare al diavolo; **c. it!** accidenti!

confounded [kən'faundid] *a* confuso, sconcertato; (*fam*) maledetto.

confraternity [ˌkɔnfrə'təːniti] *n* confraternita.

confront [kən'frʌnt] *vt* affrontare, mettere a confronto.

confrontation [ˌkɔnfrʌn'teiʃən] *n* confronto.

confuse [kən'fjuːz] *vt* confondere, sconcertare.

confused [kən'fjuːzd] *a* confuso, disorientato.

confusion [kən'fjuːʒən] *n* confusione, disordine; imbarazzo.

confute [kən'fjuːt] *vt* confutare.

congeal [kən'dʒiːl] *vti* congelar(si).

congealment [kən'dʒiːlmənt] *n* congelamento.

congenial [kən'dʒiːniəl] *a* affine; simpatico; adatto.

congenital [kən'dʒenitl] *a* congenito.

congest [kən'dʒest] *vt* congestionare; ingorgare.

congested [kən'dʒestid] *a* congestionato; sovrappopolato.

congestion [kən'dʒestʃən] *n* congestione; ingorgamento.

conglomerate [kən'glɔməreit] *vti* conglomerar(si).

conglomeration [kənˌglɔmə'reiʃən] *n* conglomerazione, conglomerato.

congratulate [kən'grætjuleit] *vt* congratularsi con, rallegrarsi con.

congratulation [kənˌgrætju'leiʃən] *n* congratulazione, rallegramento.

congregate ['kɔŋgrigeit] *vti* congregare, unirsi.

congregation [ˌkɔŋgri'geiʃən] *n* congregazione, riunione.

congress ['kɔŋgres] *n* congresso.

congruous ['kɔŋgruəs] *a* congruo.

conic(al) [ˈkɔnik(əl)] *a* conico.

conjectural [kən'dʒektʃərəl] *a* congetturale.

conjecture [kən'dʒektʃə] *n* congettura; *vti* congetturare.

conjoin [kən'dʒɔin] *vti* congiunger(si).

conjoint [ˈkɔndʒɔint] *a* congiunto, unito.

conjugal [ˈkɔndʒugəl] *a* coniugale.

conjugate [ˈkɔndʒugeit] *vti* coniugar(si).

conjugation [ˌkɔndʒu'geiʃən] *n* coniugazione.

conjunction [kən'dʒʌŋkʃən] *n* congiunzione, unione.

conjunctive [kən'dʒʌŋktiv] *a* *n* congiuntivo.

conjuncture [kən'dʒʌŋktʃə] *n* congiuntura.

conjure [ˈkʌndʒə] *vti* evocare; far giochi di prestigio; **c. up** evocare; [kən'dʒuə] scongiurare.

conjurer [ˈkʌndʒərə] *n* prestigiatore.

connect [kə'nekt] *vti* connetter(si), far coincidenza; associare; **connected** connesso, imparentato.

connectedly [kə'nektidli] *ad* coerentemente, logicamente.

connecting [kə'nektiŋ] *a* che connette; di comunicazione, di collegamento.

connection, connexion [kə'nekʃən] *n* collegamento, connessione; legame, rapporto; parentela; (*rly*) coincidenza.

connective [kə'nektiv] *a* connettivo.

connivance [kə'naivəns] *n* connivenza.

connive [kə'naiv] *vi* essere connivente.

connoisseur [ˌkɔni'səː] *n* conoscitore, intenditore.

connotation [ˌkɔnou'teiʃən] *n* significato implicito.

conquer [ˈkɔŋkə] *vti* conquistare, vincere; **conquering** vincente, vittorioso.

conqueror [ˈkɔŋkərə] *n* conquistatore.

conquest [ˈkɔŋkwest] *n* conquista.

Conrad [ˈkɔnræd] *nm pr* Corrado.

conscience [ˈkɔnʃəns] *n* coscienza.

conscientious [ˌkɔnʃi'enʃəs] *a* coscienzioso.

conscientiousness [ˌkɔnʃi'enʃəsnis] *n* coscienziosità.

conscious [ˈkɔnʃəs] *a* consapevole, conscio, cosciente.

consciousness [ˈkɔnʃəsnis] *n* consapevolezza, coscienza, conoscenza.

conscript [ˈkɔnskript] *a* *n* coscritto.

conscription [kən'skripʃən] *n* coscrizione, leva.

consecrate [ˈkɔnsikreit] *vt* consacrare.

consecration [ˌkɔnsi'kreiʃən] *n* consacrazione.

consecutive [kən'sekjutiv] *a* consecutivo.

consensus [kən'sensəs] *n* consenso unanime.

consent [kən'sent] *n* consenso, accordo; *vi* acconsentire.

consequence [ˈkɔnsikwəns] *n* conseguenza, effetto; importanza.

consequent [ˈkɔnsikwənt] *a* conseguente.

consequently [ˈkɔnsikwəntli] *ad* *cj* di conseguenza, conseguentemente.

conservative [kən'səːvətiv] *a* *n* conservatore.

conservatory [kən'səːvətri] *n* serra, (US) conservatorio.

conserve [kən'səːv] *n* conserva; *vt* conservare.

consider [kən'sidə] *vti* considerare, riflettere.

considerable [kən'sidərəbl] *a* considerevole.

considerate [kən'sidərit] *a* riguardoso; premuroso.

consideration [kənˌsidə'reiʃən] *n*

considerazione; importanza; ricompensa.

considering [kən'sidəriŋ] *prep* tenuto conto di, visto che.

consign [kən'sain] *vt* consegnare, mandare.

consignee [ˌkɔnsai'niː] *n* (com) destinatario.

consignment [kən'sainmənt] *n* consegna; (com) partita di merci.

consignor [kən'sainə] *n* (com) mittente.

consist [kən'sist] *vi* consistere.

consistence [kən'sistəns] **consistency** [kən'sistənsi] *n* consistenza, densità.

consistent [kən'sistənt] *a* coerente; costante.

consolation [ˌkɔnsə'leiʃən] *n* consolazione.

console [kən'soul] *vt* consolare.

consoling [kən'souliŋ] *a* consolante.

consolidate [kən'sɔlideit] *vti* consolidar(si).

consolidation [kənˌsɔli'deiʃən] *n* consolidamento.

consonance ['kɔnsənəns] *n* consonanza, armonia, accordo.

consonant ['kɔnsənənt] *a* consono, armonioso; *n* (gram) consonante.

consort ['kɔnsɔːt] *n* consorte, compagno; [kən'sɔːt] *vi* accompagnar(si).

conspicuous [kən'spikjuəs] *a* cospicuo, eminente.

conspiracy [kən'spirəsi] *n* cospirazione, congiura.

conspirator [kən'spirətə] *n* cospiratore.

conspire [kən'spaiə] *vti* cospirare, tramare.

constable ['kʌnstəbl] *n* conestabile, guardia, poliziotto.

Constance ['kɔnstəns] *nf pr* Costanza.

constancy ['kɔnstənsi] *n* costanza, perseveranza.

constant ['kɔnstənt] *a* costante, fedele.

Constantinople [ˌkɔnstænti'noupl] *n* Costantinopoli.

constantly ['kɔnstəntli] *ad* costantemente, continuamente.

constellation [ˌkɔnstə'leiʃən] *n* costellazione.

consternation [ˌkɔnstə'neiʃən] *n* costernazione.

constipate ['kɔnstipeit] *vt* costipare.

constipated ['kɔnstipeitid] *a* stitico.

constipation [ˌkɔnsti'peiʃən] *n* stitichezza.

constituency [kən'stitjuənsi] *n* circoscrizione elettorale.

constituent [kən'stitjuənt] *a* costituente; *n* elettore.

constitute ['kɔnstitjuːt] *vt* costituire.

constitution [ˌkɔnsti'tjuːʃən] *n* costituzione, legge.

constitutional [ˌkɔnsti'tjuːʃənl] *a* costituzionale; *n* passeggiata igienica.

constrain [kən'strein] *vt* costringere; reprimere.

constraint [kən'streint] *n* costrizione, repressione; imbarazzo.

constrict [kən'strikt] *vt* comprimere, contrarre.

constriction [kən'strikʃən] *n* costrizione, contrazione.

construct [kən'strʌkt] *vt* costruire.

construction [kən'strʌkʃən] *n* costruzione.

constructive [kən'strʌktiv] *a* costruttivo.

construe [kən'struː] *vt* (gram) analizzare; tradurre; interpretare.

consul ['kɔnsəl] *n* console.

consular ['kɔnsjulə] *a* consolare.

consulate ['kɔnsjulit] *n* consolato.

consult [kən'sʌlt] *vti* consultar(si).

consultant [kən'sʌltənt] *n* consulente.

consultation [ˌkɔnsəl'teiʃən] *n* consultazione, consulto.

consulting [kən'sʌltiŋ] *a* di consultazione.

consume [kən'sjuːm] *vti* consumar(si).

consumer [kən'sjuːmə] *n* consumatore, utente.

consummate [kən'sʌmit] *a* consumato, perfetto.

consummate ['kɔnsʌmeit] *vt* compiere, consumare.

consummation [ˌkɔnsʌ'meiʃən] *n* consumazione.

consumption [kən'sʌmpʃən] *n* consumo; (med) consunzione, tisi.

consumptive [kən'sʌmptiv] *a n* tisico.

contact ['kɔntækt] *n* contatto; *vti* [kən'tækt] metter(si) in contatto con; essere in contatto.

contagion [kən'teidʒən] *n* contagio.

contagious [kən'teidʒəs] *a* contagioso.

contain [kən'tein] *vt* contenere, includere; reprimere.

container [kən'teinə] *n* recipiente.

contaminate [kən'tæmineit] *vt* contaminare, infettare.

contamination [kənˌtæmi'neiʃən] *n* contaminazione.

contemplate ['kɔntempleit] *vt* contemplare, meditare; progettare.

contemplation [ˌkɔntem'pleiʃən] *n* contemplazione; progetto.

contemplative [kən'templətiv] *a* contemplativo, meditativo.

contemporary [kən'tempərəri] *a n* contemporaneo; coetaneo.

contempt [kən'tempt] *n* disprezzo.

contemptible [kən'temptəbl] *a* spregevole.

contemptuous [kən'temptjuəs] *a* sprezzante.

contend [kən'tend] *vi* contendere, lottare; contestare; sostenere.

content [kən'tent] *a* contento, soddisfatto; *n* contentezza, soddisfazione; *vt* accontentare, soddisfare.

contented [kən'tentid] *a* contento.

contention [kən'tenʃən] *n* contesa, discordia, opinione.

contentious [kən'tenʃəs] *a* litigioso; controverso; (leg) contenzioso.

contentment [kən'tentmənt] *n* il contentarsi; contentezza.

contents ['kɔntents] *n pl* contenuto.

contest ['kɔntest] *n* competizione; contesa; *vt* [kən'test] contestare, disputare.

contestant [kən'testənt] *n* competitore, concorrente.

context ['kɔntekst] *n* contesto.

contiguous [kən'tigjuəs] *a* contiguo.

continence ['kɔntinəns] *n* continenza.

continent ['kɔntinənt] *a* casto, continente, moderato; *n* continente.

continental [,kɔnti'nentl] *a n* continentale.

contingency [kən'tindʒənsi] *n* contingenza.

contingent [kən'tindʒənt] *a n* contingente.

continual [kən'tinjuəl] *a* continuo.

continuation [kən,tinju'eiʃən] *n* continuazione, seguito.

continue [kən'tinjuː] *vti* continuare, persistere, proseguire.

continuity [,kɔnti'njuːiti] *n* continuità.

continuous [kən'tinjuəs] *a* continuo, ininterrotto.

continuously [kən'tinjuəsli] *ad* continuamente, ininterrottamente.

contort [kən'tɔːt] *vt* contorcere.

contortion [kən'tɔːʃən] *n* contorsione.

contour ['kɔntuə] *n* contorno, profilo.

contraband ['kɔntrəbænd] *a n* (di) contrabbando.

contract ['kɔntrækt] *n* contratto, appalto; *vt* [kən'trækt] contrarre; contrattare, appaltare.

contraction [kən'trækʃən] *n* contrazione.

contractor [kən'træktə] *n* contraente; appaltatore; imprenditore.

contradict [,kɔntrə'dikt] *vt* contraddire.

contradiction [,kɔntrə'dikʃən] *n* contraddizione.

contradictory [,kɔntrə'diktəri] *a* contraddittorio.

contralto [kən'træltou] *n* (mus) contralto.

contrariety [,kɔntrə'raiəti] *n* contrarietà, opposizione.

contrary ['kɔntrəri] *a* contrario; ostinato; *n* contrario; *ad* contrariamente; **on the c.** al contrario.

contrast ['kɔntræst] *n* contrasto; *vt* [kən'træst] mettere in contrasto, confrontare; *vi* contrastare.

contravene [,kɔntrə'viːn] *vt* contravvenire.

contravention [,kɔntrə'venʃən] *n* contravvenzione.

contribute [kən'tribjuːt] *vti* contribuire.

contribution [,kɔntri'bjuːʃən] *n* contributo; collaborazione.

contributor [kən'tribjutə] *n* contributore; collaboratore.

contrite ['kɔntrait] *a* contrito.

contrition [kən'triʃən] *n* contrizione.

contrivance [kən'traivəns] *n* invenzione, congegno.

contrive [kən'traiv] *vt* inventare; escogitare, fare in modo di.

control [kən'troul] *n* controllo, freno, autorità; *vt* controllare, frenare, dirigere.

controversial [,kɔntrə'və:ʃəl] *a* controverso.

controversy ['kɔntrəvə:si] *n* controversia.

contumacious [,kɔntju:'meiʃəs] *a* contumace.

contuse [kən'tju:z] *vt* ammaccare, contundere.

contusion [kən'tju:ʒən] *n* contusione.

conundrum [kə'nʌndrəm] *n* indovinello.

convalesce [,kɔnvə'les] *vi* rimettersi in salute.

convalescence [,kɔnvə'lesns] *n* convalescenza.

convalescent [,kɔnvə'lesnt] *a n* convalescente.

convector [kən'vektə] *n* convettore, termo convettore.

convene [kən'viːn] *vti* convocare; convenire.

convenience [kən'viːniəns] *n* comodità, convenienza, vantaggio; **public c.** gabinetto pubblico.

convenient [kən'viːniənt] *a* comodo, conveniente, adatto.

convent ['kɔnvənt] *n* convento.

conventicle [kən'ventikl] *n* conventicola.

convention [kən'venʃən] *n* convenzione.

conventional [kən'venʃənl] *a* convenzionale.

conventual [kən'ventjuəl] *a* conventuale.

converge [kən'və:dʒ] *vi* convergere.

convergent [kən'və:dʒənt] *a* convergente.

conversant [kən'və:sənt] *a* versato (in), bene informato.

conversation [,kɔnvə'seiʃən] *n* conversazione.

converse ['kɔnvə:s] *a n* converso, contrario; *vi* [kən'və:s] conversare.

conversely ['kɔnvə:sli] *ad* viceversa.

conversion [kən'və:ʃən] *n* conversione.

convert ['kɔnvə:t] *n* convertito; *vt* [kən'və:t] convertire.

convertible [kən'və:təbl] *a* convertibile; **c. car** automobile decappottabile.

convex ['kɔn'veks] *a* convesso.

convey [kən'vei] *vt* portare, trasportare; trasmettere; esprimere.

conveyance [kən'veiəns] n mezzo di trasporto.

conveyor [kən'veiə] n portatore; c.-belt (ind) trasportatore a cinghia.

convict ['kɔnvikt] n ergastolano; vt [kən'vikt] dichiarare colpevole.

conviction [kən'vikʃən] n condanna; convinzione.

convince [kən'vins] vt convincere.

convincing [kən'vinsiŋ] a convincente.

convivial [kən'viviəl] a conviviale.

convocation [ˌkɔnvə'keiʃən] n convocazione, assemblea.

convoke [kən'vouk] vt convocare.

convoy ['kɔnvɔi] n convoglio, scorta; vt convogliare, scortare.

convulse [kən'vʌls] vt sconvolgere, agitare, mettere in convulsioni.

convulsion [kən'vʌlʃən] n convulsione.

convulsive [kən'vʌlsiv] a convulsivo.

coo [ku:] vi tubare.

cook [kuk] n cuoco, cuoca; vti cucinare, cuocere; cookbook (US) libro di cucina.

cooker ['kukə] n fornello, cucina; pentola.

cookery ['kukəri] n arte culinaria; c. book libro di cucina.

cookie ['kuki] n (US) biscotto.

cooking ['kukiŋ] n cottura; arte culinaria; cucina.

cool [ku:l] a fresco; calmo; impudente; n fresco, frescura; vti rinfrescar(si).

cooler ['ku:lə] n refrigerante; (sl) gattabuia; air c. (US) condizionatore dell'aria.

cooling ['ku:liŋ] a rinfrescante.

coolly ['ku:lli] ad freddamente, con calma.

coolness ['ku:lnis] n fresco; sangue freddo; sfacciataggine.

coop [ku:p] n stia; vt mettere nella stia, rinchiudere.

co-operate [kou'ɔpəreit] vi cooperare.

co-operation [kou.ɔpə'reiʃən] n cooperazione.

co-operative [kou'ɔpərətiv] a cooperativo.

co-operator [kou'ɔpəreitə] n cooperatore.

co-ordinate [kou'ɔːdineit] vt coordinare; n coordinata.

co-ordination [kou.ɔːdi'neiʃən] n coordinazione.

co-owner ['kou'ounə] n comproprietario.

copartner ['kou'pɑːtnə] n (com) consocio; copartnership società in nome collettivo.

cope [koup] n cappa di ecclesiastico; c. with vi far fronte a, lottare contro.

Copenhagen [ˌkoupn'heigən] n Copenaghen.

co-pilot ['kou'pailət] n (av) secondo pilota.

copious ['koupiəs] a abbondante, copioso.

copiousness ['koupiəsnis] n abbondanza.

copper ['kɔpə] a di rame, color di rame; n rame, moneta di rame, caldaia; (sl) poliziotto; coppers pl moneta spicciola; copperplate engraving incisione su rame.

coppice ['kɔpis] n bosco ceduo.

copulate ['kɔpjuleit] vi accoppiarsi.

copulation [kɔpju'leiʃən] n copulazione, accoppiamento.

copy ['kɔpi] n copia; trascrizione; (journalism) materiale; c. book quaderno; c. reader (US) revisore di stampa; fair c. bella copia; rough c. brutta copia; vt copiare; imitare; trascrivere.

copyright ['kɔpirait] n diritti d'autore pl, proprietà letteraria.

coquet(te) [kou'ket] vi civettare.

coquette [kou'ket] n (donna) civetta.

coral ['kɔrəl] a n (di) corallo.

cord [kɔːd] n corda, funicella; spinal c. spina dorsale; vt legare con una corda.

cordial ['kɔːdiəl] a n cordiale.

cordiality [ˌkɔːdi'æliti] n cordialità.

cordially ['kɔːdiəli] ad cordialmente.

cordon ['kɔːdn] n cordane; vt cordonare.

corduroy ['kɔːdərɔi] n velluto a coste.

core [kɔː] n torsolo; (fig) centro, cuore.

cork [kɔːk] n sughero; tappo, turacciolo; vt tappare, turare.

corkscrew ['kɔːkskruː] n cavatappi.

corn [kɔːn] n grano, cereali, (US) granturco; callo durone; c.-cob pannocchia; cornflakes fiocchi di granturco; cornflour farina di granturco.

cornelian [kɔː'niːliən] n (min) corniola.

corner ['kɔːnə] n angolo; spigolo; (com) accaparramento; vt (fig) mettere alle strette; svoltare; accaparrare; cornerstone pietra angolare.

cornet ['kɔːnit] n (mus) cornetta; cartoccio conico.

cornflower ['kɔːnflauə] n fiordaliso.

cornice ['kɔːnis] n cornicione.

Cornwall ['kɔːnwəl] n Cornovaglia; Cornish a n della Cornovaglia.

coronary ['kɔrənəri] a (anat) coronario; c. thrombosis trombosi delle coronarie.

coronation [ˌkɔrə'neiʃən] n incoronazione.

coroner ['kɔrənə] n magistrato inquirente nei casi di sospetta morte violenta.

coronet ['kɔrənit] n corona nobiliare, diadema.

corporal ['kɔːpərəl] a n corporale; a corporeo; n caporale.

corporate ['kɔːpərit] a corporativo.
corporation [,kɔːpə'reiʃən] n corporazione, (US com) società a responsabilità limitata, azienda municipale; (fam) pancia.
corporative ['kɔːpərətiv] a corporativo.
corporeal [kɔː'pɔːriəl] a corporeo.
corps [kɔː] pl corps n (mil) corpo.
corpse [kɔːps] n cadavere.
corpulence ['kɔːpjuləns] n corpulenza.
corpulent ['kɔːpjulənt] a corpulento.
corpuscle ['kɔːpʌsl] n corpuscolo.
correct [kə'rekt] a corretto, esatto, giusto; vt correggere.
correction [kə'rekʃən] n correzione; punizione.
correctly [kə'rektli] ad correttamente.
correctness [kə'rektnis] n correttezza.
correlate ['kɔrileit] vti essere, mettere in correlazione.
correlation [,kɔri'leiʃən] n correlazione.
correspond [,kɔris'pɔnd] vi corrispondere.
correspondence [,kɔris'pɔndəns] n corrispondenza.
correspondent [,kɔris'pɔndənt] a n corrispondente.
corresponding [,kɔris'pɔndiŋ] a corrispondente.
corridor ['kɔridɔː] n corridoio.
corroborate [kə'rɔbəreit] vt corroborare.
corroboration [kə,rɔbə'reiʃən] n conferma, corroborazione.
corrode [kə'roud] vti corroder(si).
corrosive [kə'rousiv] a n corrosivo.
corrugate ['kɔrugeit] vti corrugar(si); corrugated iron lamiera ondulata; corrugated paper carta increspata.
corrupt [kə'rʌpt] a corrotto, depravato; vti corromper(si).
corruption [kə'rʌpʃən] n corruzione.
corsair ['kɔːsɛə] n corsaro.
corset ['kɔːsit] n corsetto, busto; c.-maker bustaia.
Corsican ['kɔːsikən] a n corso, corsa.
cosiness ['kouzinis] n agio, tepore confortevole, intimità.
cosmetic [kɔz'metik] a n cosmetico.
cosmic ['kɔzmik] a cosmico.
cosmodrome ['kɔzmədroum] n cosmodromo.
cosmogony [kɔz'mɔgəni] n cosmogonia.
cosmography [kɔz'mɔgrəfi] n cosmografia.
cosmonaut ['kɔzmənɔːt] n cosmonauta.
cosmopolitan [,kɔzmə'pɔlitən] a n cosmopolita.
cosmos ['kɔzmɔs] n cosmo.
Cossack ['kɔsæk] n cosacco.
cost [kɔst] n costo, prezzo; costs pl spese processuali pl; vt costare; (com)

fissare il prezzo; running c. (US) spese generali.
costermonger ['kɔstə,mʌŋgə] n venditore ambulante di frutta etc.
costive ['kɔstiv] a stitico.
costiveness ['kɔstivnis] n stitichezza.
costliness ['kɔstlinis] n costosità.
costly ['kɔstli] a costoso.
costume ['kɔstjuːm] n costume; completo.
cosy ['kouzi] a comodo, intimo; tea c. n copriteiera.
cot [kɔt] n lettino per bambini.
coterie ['koutəri] n circolo.
cottage ['kɔtidʒ] n casetta di campagna, 'cottage'.
Cottian Alps ['kɔtiən ælps] n pl Alpi Cozie.
cotton ['kɔtn] n cotone, tela di cotone; a di cotone; c. wool, (US) absorbent c. cotone idrofilo.
couch [kautʃ] n divano.
cough [kɔf] n tosse; vti tossire.
council ['kaunsl] n consiglio, concilio.
councillor ['kaunsilə] n consigliere.
counsel ['kaunsəl] n consigli(o), parere; consulente legale.
counsellor ['kaunslə] n consigliere, (US) avvocato.
count [kaunt] n conto, conteggio; conte; c. of indictment capo d'accusa; countdown conteggio all'indietro; vti contare, numerare, includere.
countenance ['kauntinəns] n viso, espressione; vt approvare, incoraggiare.
counter ['kauntə] n gettone; (in a shop etc) banco, cassa; ad contro, in opposizione.
counteract [,kauntə'rækt] vt agire in opposizione a, neutralizzare.
counter-attack ['kauntərə,tæk] n (mil) contrattacco.
counterbalance ['kauntə,bæləns] n contrappeso.
counterfeit ['kauntəfit] a contraffatto, falsificato; n contraffazione, falsificazione; vt contraffare, falsificare, fingere.
counterfoil ['kauntəfɔil] n (com) matrice.
countermand [,kauntə'maːnd] vt disdire, revocare.
counterpane ['kauntəpein] n copriletto.
counterpart ['kauntəpaːt] n controparte, doppio, duplicato.
counterpoint ['kauntəpɔint] n (mus) contrappunto.
counterpoise ['kauntəpɔiz] n contrappeso; vt controbilanciare.
countersign ['kauntəsain] n contrassegno; controfirma; parola d'ordine; vt controfirmare.
counterweight ['kauntəweit] n contrappeso.
countess ['kauntis] n contessa.
counting-house ['kauntiŋhaus] n ufficio contabile, amministrazione.

countless ['kauntlis] *a* innumerevole.

country ['kʌntri] *n* paese, nazione, patria; campagna; **countryman** compatriota; contadino.

county ['kaunti] *n* contea.

coup [kuː] *n* colpo.

couple ['kʌpl] *n* coppia, paio; *vti* accoppiar(si); (*rly*) agganciare.

coupling ['kʌpliŋ] *n* accoppiamento, (*tec*) agganciamento.

coupon ['kuːpɔn] *n* cedola, tagliando, buono.

courage ['kʌridʒ] *n* coraggio.

courageous [kə'reidʒəs] *a* coraggioso.

courageously [kə'reidʒəsli] *ad* coraggiosamente.

courier ['kuriə] *n* corriere, messaggero.

course [kɔːs] *n* corso, direzione; pista; (*meal*) portata.

court [kɔːt] *n* corte; tribunale; (*tennis*) campo; *vt* corteggiare.

courteous ['kəːtiəs] *a* cortese.

courteousness ['kəːtiəsnis] *n* cortesia.

courtesan [ˌkɔːti'zæn] *n* cortigiana, prostituta.

courtesy ['kəːtisi] *n* cortesia, gentilezza.

courtier ['kɔːtiə] *n* cortigiano.

courtly ['kɔːtli] *a* cortigianesco, cerimonioso.

courtship ['kɔːtʃip] *n* corte, corteggiamento.

courtyard ['kɔːtjɑːd] *n* corte, cortile.

cousin ['kʌzn] *n* cugino, cugina.

cove [kouv] *n* insenatura, piccola baia.

covenant ['kʌvinənt] *n* convenzione, patto; *vti* stipulare, convenire.

cover ['kʌvə] *n* coperta, copertura; coperchio; copertina; riparo; *vt* coprire, nascondere, ricoprire, proteggere; far la cronaca di.

coverage ['kʌvəridʒ] *n* copertura; (*journalism*) servizio d'informazione.

covering ['kʌvəriŋ] *n* coperta; (*com*) garanzia.

coverlet ['kʌvəlit] *n* copriletto.

covet ['kʌvit] *vt* bramare.

covetous ['kʌvitəs] *a* cupido, avido.

covey ['kʌvi] *n* covata (di uccelli).

cow [kau] *n* vacca, mucca, (*di mammiferi*) femmina; *vt* intimidire.

coward ['kauəd] *n* codardo.

cowardice ['kauədis] *n* codardia.

cowardly ['kauədli] *a* codardo; *ad* vilmente.

cower ['kauə] *vi* acquattarsi, farsi piccolo, tremare.

cowl [kaul] *n* cappuccio.

coxcomb ['kɔkskoum] *n* damerino, zerbinotto.

coxswain ['kɔkswein, 'kɔksn] *n* timoniere.

coy [kɔi] *a* ritroso, timido.

coyness ['kɔinis] *n* timidezza, ritrosia.

crab [kræb] *n* granchio; (*mech*) argano; **c. apple** mela selvatica.

crabbed ['kræbid] *a* ruvido, sgarbato; (*writing*) illeggibile.

crack [kræk] *n* fessura, crepa, spacco; incrinatura; schianto, schiocco; *a* di prim'ordine, ottimo; *vti* spaccar(si); **to c. a joke** dire una spiritosaggine.

cracked ['krækt] *a* fesso, incrinato; scervellato.

cracker ['krækə] *n* petardo; galletta.

crackle ['krækl] *vi* crepitare, scricchiolare.

crackling ['krækliŋ] *n* crepitio, scoppiettio.

cracknel ['kræknl] *n* biscotto croccante.

Cracow ['krækou] *n* Cracovia.

cradle ['kreidl] *n* culla; (*for broken limbs*) gabbia, alzacoperte; *vt* cullare.

craft [krɑːft] *n* abilità; arte; furberia, inganno; piccola imbarcazione.

craftily ['krɑːftili] *ad* abilmente, astutamente.

craftiness ['krɑːftinis] *n* furbizia.

craftsman ['krɑːftsmən] *n* artigiano; **craftsmanship** arte dell'artigiano.

crafty ['krɑːfti] *a* furbo, abile.

crag [kræg] *n* picco, roccia scoscesa.

craggy ['krægi] *a* roccioso, dirupato.

cram [kræm] *vti* rimpinzar(si); (*fam*) imbottirsi di nozioni in vista di un esame.

cramp [kræmp] *n* crampo; *vt* impacciare; cagionare crampi a; impedire nei movimenti.

cranberry ['krænbəri] *n* mirtillo nero.

crane [krein] *n* gru; *vti* allungare il collo, sporgersi.

cranium ['kreiniəm] *pl* **crania** *n* cranio.

crank [kræŋk] *n* manovella; (*fig*) individuo eccentrico.

cranny ['kræni] *n* fessura.

crape [kreip] *n* crespo, gramaglie *pl.*

crash [kræʃ] *n* schianto, crollo; cozzo; scontro; *vi* crollare con fracasso, precipitare; urtare (contro).

crass [kræs] *a* crasso, grossolano.

crate [kreit] *n* cassa da imballaggio.

crater ['kreitə] *n* cratere.

cravat [krə'væt] *n* fazzoletto da collo, cravatta.

crave [kreiv] *vti* bramare, implorare.

craven ['kreivn] *a* codardo.

craving ['kreiviŋ] *a* ardente, insaziabile; *n* brama, voglia.

crawl [krɔːl] *vi* strisciare, andare carponi.

crayfish ['kreifiʃ] *n* gambero d'acqua dolce.

crayon ['kreiən] *n* pastello.

craze [kreiz] *n* mania, pazzia; passione; moda.

craziness ['kreizinis] *n* follia; instabilità d'un edificio.

crazy ['kreizi] *a* folle, pazzo; instabile.

creak [kriːk] *n* cigolio; *vi* cigolare, scricchiolare.

cream [kri:m] n panna, crema; (fig) fior fiore; c. jug lattiera.

creamer ['kri:mə] n (US) lattiera.

creamery ['kri:məri] n caseificio, latteria.

crease [kri:s] n grinza, piega; vt piegare; sgualcir(si).

create [kri:'eit] vt creare.

creation [kri:'eifən] n creazione, creato.

creative [kri:'eitiv] a creativa.

creator [kri'eitə] n creatore.

creature ['kri:tʃə] n creatura.

credentials [kri'denʃəls] n pl credenziali pl.

credibility [,kredi'biliti] n credibilità.

credible ['kredəbl] a credibile.

credit ['kredit] n credito, fiducia, reputazione, onore, merito; vt credere, prestar fede a; attribuire, accreditare a.

creditable ['kreditəbl] a degno di fede, di stima, che torna all'onore di.

creditor ['kreditə] n creditore.

credulity [kri'dju:liti] n credulità.

credulous ['kredjuləs] a credulo.

creed [kri:d] n credo, somma degli articoli di fede.

creek [kri:k] n cala, piccola baia, insenatura.

creep [kri:p] vi (of plants) arrampicarsi; insinuarsi; strisciare; n strisciamento; pl brividi pl, pelle d'oca.

creeper ['kri:pə] n pianta rampicante; (fig) persona strisciante.

creepy ['kri:pi] a strisciante, che dà i brividi.

cremate [kri'meit] vt cremare.

cremation [kri'meifən] n cremazione.

crematorium [,kremə'tɔ:riəm] pl crematoria forno crematorio.

creole ['kri:oul] a n creolo.

creosote ['kriəsout] n (chem) creosoto.

crêpe [kreip] n crespo, tessuto di seta.

crescent ['kresnt] a crescente, a mezzaluna; n fila di case disposte a semicerchio.

cress [kres] n crescione.

crest [krest] n cresta, ciuffetto, criniera.

crestfallen ['krest,fɔ:lən] a abbattuto, mortificato.

crevasse [kri'væs] n crepaccio.

crevice ['krevis] n crepa, fessura.

crew [kru:] n ciurma, equipaggio.

crib [krib] n lettino per bimbo; mangiatoia, presepio; (fam) plagio; (sl) traduttore, bigino; vt copiare, plagiare.

cricket ['krikit] n grillo; (sport) 'cricket'.

crime [kraim] n delitto, misfatto.

criminal ['kriminl] a criminale, penale; n criminale, delinquente.

criminology [,krimi'nɔlədʒi] n criminologia.

crimson ['krimzn] a n cremisi.

cringe [krindʒ] vi essere servile, comportarsi servilmente.

crinkle ['kriŋkl] n grinza, crespa; vti increspar(si), spiegazzare.

crinoline ['krinəlin] n crinolina.

cripple ['kripl] n sciancato, zoppo, invalido; vt azzoppare; (fig) diminuire la capacità di.

crisis ['kraisis] n crisi.

crisp [krisp] a croccante; (hair) crespo; (air) frizzante; (style) incisivo; crisps n pl patatine fritte.

crispness ['krispnis] n friabilità; cresposità; freddo intenso; chiarezza.

criterion [krai'tiəriən] pl criteria n criterio.

critic ['kritik] n critico.

critical ['kritikəl] a critico.

criticism ['kritisizəm] n critica, giudizio critico.

criticize ['kritisaiz] vt criticare, fare la critica a.

croak [krouk] vi gracchiare, gracidare; (fig) predire malanni.

croaky ['krouki] a rauco.

crochet ['krouʃei] n lavoro ad uncinetto.

crockery ['krɔkəri] n terraglie pl, vasellame.

crocodile ['krɔkədail] n coccodrillo.

crocus ['kroukəs] n croco.

croft [krɔft] n piccolo podere, campicello.

crone [kroun] n vecchia rugosa.

crony ['krouni] n (fam) vecchio amico.

crook [kruk] n ricurvatura; gancio; bastone da pastore; (sl) malvivente; vti curvar(si).

crooked ['krukid] a curvo, storto; disonesto.

crookedness ['krukidnis] n tortuosità, disonestà.

croon [kru:n] vi canticchiare sotto voce.

crop [krɔp] n raccolto; gozzo d'uccello; frusta; capelli corti; vt mozzare, tosare; mietere, raccogliere; brucare.

croquet ['kroukei] n (sport) 'croquet', pallamaglio.

crosier ['krouʒə] n pastorale.

cross [krɔs] a obliquo, trasversale; di cattivo umore; n croce; incrocio; vt attraversare; incrociare; segnare con una croce; vi incrociarsi.

cross-examine ['krɔsig'zæmin] vt interrogare a contraddittorio.

crossing ['krɔsiŋ] n traversata; incrocio; level c., (US) grade c. passaggio a livello.

crossroads ['krɔsroudz] n pl crocevia.

crossword ['krɔswə:d] n cruciverba.

crotchet ['krɔtʃit] n (mus) semiminima.

crouch [krautʃ] vi accucciarsi, rannicchiarsi.

croup [kru:p] n groppa; (med) crup, difterite.

crow [krou] *n* cornacchia, corvo; (*cock's*) canto; *vi* cantare; **c. over** vantarsi sopra.

crowd [kraud] *n* folla, massa; *vti* affollar(si); **crowded** affollato, popoloso.

crown [kraun] *n* corona; (*head*) sommità; (*hat*) fondo; coronamento; *vt* (in)coronare; **to c. it all** per colmo (di fortuna, di disgrazia).

crucial ['kru:ʃəl] *a* cruciale, critico.

crucible ['kru:sibl] *n* crogiuolo.

crucifix ['kru:sifiks] *n* crocifisso.

crucifixion [ˌkru:si'fikʃən] *n* crocifissione.

crucify ['kru:sifai] *vt* crocifiggere.

crude [kru:d] *a* crudo, grezzo, immaturo, primitivo.

cruel ['kruəl] *a* crudele.

cruelly ['kruəli] *ad* crudelmente.

cruelty ['kruəlti] *n* crudeltà.

cruet ['kru:it] *n* ampolla, ampollina; **c.-stand** ampolliera.

cruise [kru:z] *n* crociera; *vi* fare una crociera; incrociare.

cruiser ['kru:zə] *n* incrociatore; (*US*) automobile della polizia.

crumb [krʌm] *n* briciola, mollica.

crumble ['krʌmbl] *vti* sbriciolar(si), sgretolar(si).

crumple ['krʌmpl] *vti* raggrinzar(si), sgualcir(si).

crunch [krʌntʃ] *vti* sgranocchiare rumorosamente, scricchiolare.

crusade [kru:'seid] *n* crociata.

crusader [kru:'seidə] *n* crociato.

crush [krʌʃ] *n* compressione, schiacciamento; calca; (*sl*) infatuazione, cotta; *vt* schiacciare, frantumare; sgualcire; annientare.

crushing ['krʌʃiŋ] *a* schiacciante; **c. mill** frantoio; **c. plant** impianto di frantumazione.

crust [krʌst] *n* crosta, incrostazione; *vti* incrostar(si).

crustiness ['krʌstinis] *n* irascibilità.

crusty ['krʌsti] *a* crostoso; irritabile.

crutch [krʌtʃ] *n* gruccia, stampella; forcella; inforcatura.

crux [krʌks] *n* punto, nodo.

cry [krai] *n* grido, richiamo, urlo, pianto; *vti* gridare, piangere.

crying ['kraiiŋ] *a* evidente, patente; *n.* pianto.

crypt [kript] *n* cripta.

cryptic ['kriptik] *a* misterioso, nascosto.

crystal ['kristl] *a* di cristallo; *n* cristallo.

crystalline ['kristəlain] *a n* cristallino.

crystallize ['kristəlaiz] *vti* cristallizzar(si).

cub [kʌb] *n* cucciolo di animali selvatici; **c. scout** lupetto.

Cuba ['kju:bə] *n* Cuba: **Cuban** *a n* cubano, cubana.

cube [kju:b] *n* cubo.

cubic ['kju:bik] *a* cubico.

cubicle ['kju:bikl] *n* stanzetta, piccolo locale, cubicolo.

cuckold ['kʌkəld] *n* becco, cornuto.

cuckoo ['kuku:] *n* cuculo, cucù; (*sl*) mezzo scemo.

cucumber ['kju:kəmbə] *n* cetriolo.

cud [kʌd] *n* bolo alimentare di ruminante.

cuddle ['kʌdl] *vt* abbracciare stretto.

cudgel ['kʌdʒəl] *n* clava, randello; *vt* picchiare con la clava, randellare; **to c. one's brains** scervellarsi.

cue [kju:] *n* (*theat*) battuta d'entrata; suggerimento; stecca da biliardo.

cuff [kʌf] *n* polsino; (*US*) risvolto dei pantaloni; pugno, scapaccione; *vt* percuotere, picchiare.

cuisine [kwi:'zi:n] *n* cucina, modo di cucinare.

cul-de-sac ['kuldə'sæk] *n* vicolo cieco.

culinary ['kʌlinəri] *a* culinario.

culminate ['kʌlmineit] *vi* culminare.

culmination [ˌkʌlmi'neiʃən] *n* culminazione, culmine.

culpable ['kʌlpəbl] *a* colpevole.

culprit ['kʌlprit] *n* colpevole; imputato.

cult [kʌlt] *n* culto, venerazione.

cultivate ['kʌltiveit] *vt* coltivare.

cultivated ['kʌltiveitid] *a* coltivato; colto, educato.

cultivation [ˌkʌlti'veiʃən] *n* coltivazione; cultura.

cultivator ['kʌltiveitə] *n* coltivatore, cultore.

cultural ['kʌltʃərəl] *a* culturale.

culture ['kʌltʃə] *n* coltura, allevamento; (*of the mind*) cultura.

cultured ['kʌltʃəd] *a* colto.

cumber ['kʌmbə] *vt* impacciare, ingombrare.

cumbersome ['kʌmbəsəm] *a* ingombrante, poco maneggevole.

cumulative ['kju:mjulətiv] *a* cumulativo.

cunning ['kʌniŋ] *a* astuto, furbo; *n* astuzia, furberia, accortezza.

cup [kʌp] *n* tazza, calice, coppa.

cupboard ['kʌbəd] *n* armadio.

cupidity [kju:'piditi] *n* cupidigia.

cur [kə:] *n* cane bastardo.

curable ['kjuərəbl] *a* guaribile.

curate ['kjuərit] *n* curato.

curative ['kjuərətiv] *a* curativo.

curator [kjuə'reitə] *n* sovrintendente.

curb [kə:b] *n* costrizione, freno; bordo di marciapiede; *vt* frenare, soggiogare.

curds [kə:dz] *n pl* latte cagliato.

curdle ['kə:dl] *vti* cagliare, coagular(si), (*fig*) agghiacciar(si).

cure [kjuə] *n* cura, guarigione, rimedio; *vt* guarire; (*fish*) affumicare.

curfew ['kə:fju:] *n* coprifuoco.

curio ['kjuəriou] *pl* **curios** *n* oggetti rari.

curiosity [ˌkjuəri,ɔsiti] *n* curiosità.

curious ['kjuəriəs] *a* curioso, raro, singolare.

curiously ['kjuəriəsli] *ad* curiosamente, stranamente; **c. enough** strano a dirsi.

curl [kəːl] *n* ricciolo; curva; *vt* arricciare, arricciarsi, sollevarsi in onde, in spire.

curler ['kəːlə] *n* bigodino, ferro per arricciare i capelli; giocatore di 'curling'.

curly ['kəːli] *a* ricciuto.

currant ['kʌrənt] *n* uva sultanina; ribes.

currency ['kʌrənsi] *n* circolazione monetaria, moneta circolante; corso.

current ['kʌrənt] *a* *n* corrente.

curry ['kʌri] *n* salsa fatta di spezie e di aromi; *vt* stufare con aromi; (*leather*) conciare; (*horse*) strigliare; **to c. favour with** adulare, ingraziarsi.

currycomb ['kʌri,koum] *n* striglia.

curse [kəːs] *n* imprecazione, maledizione; sventura, calamità; *vti* bestemmiare, maledire; (*passive*) essere afflitto.

cursed [kəːst] *a* maledetto.

cursive ['kəːsiv] *a* *n* corsivo.

cursory ['kəːsəri] *a* frettoloso, rapido.

curt [kəːt] *a* asciutto, brusco.

curtail [kəː'teil] *vt* abbreviare, accorciare.

curtain ['kəːtn] *n* cortina, tenda, sipario.

curtsy ['kəːtsi] *n* inchino, riverenza.

curve [kəːv] *n* curva; *vti* curvar(si).

cushion ['kuʃən] *n* cuscino; (*mech*) cuscinetto.

custard ['kʌstəd] *n* crema.

custody ['kʌstədi] *n* custodia, imprigionamento.

custom ['kʌstəm] *n* uso, costume, abitudine, clientela; *pl* dazio, dogana; **customhouse** dogana.

customary ['kʌstəməri] *a* abituale, consueto.

customer ['kʌstəmə] *n* avventore, cliente; (*sl*) tipo, individuo.

cut [kʌt] *n* taglio, ferita; affronto; riduzione; (*meat, material etc*) pezzo; *vt* tagliare, trinciare; togliere il saluto a; (*prices*) ridurre; (*cards*) alzare; **short c.** scorciatoia; **cutoff** (US) scorciatoia; ritaglio di giornale.

cuticle ['kjuːtikl] *n* cuticola.

cutler ['kʌtlə] *n* coltellinaio.

cutlery ['kʌtləri] *n* posateria.

cutlet ['kʌtlit] *n* cotoletta.

cutter ['kʌtə] *n* tagliatore; (*mech*) fresa.

cut-throat ['kʌtθrout] *a* accanito; *n* assassino.

cutting ['kʌtiŋ] *a* tagliente; (*fig*) pungente, mordace; *n* taglio; ritaglio, riduzione.

cuttle ['kʌtl] *n* **cuttlefish** seppia; **c.-bone** osso di seppia.

cyanide ['saiənaid] *n* (*chem*) cianuro.

cycle ['saikl] *n* ciclo, bicicletta; *vi* andare in bicicletta.

cyclist ['saiklist] *n* ciclista.

cyclone ['saikloun] *n* ciclone.

cylinder ['silində] *n* cilindro.

cylindrical [si'lindrikəl] *a* cilindrico.

cynic ['sinik] *n* cinico.

cynical ['sinikəl] *a* cinico.

cynicism ['sinisizəm] *n* cinismo.

cypress ['saipris] *n* cipresso.

Cyprus ['saiprəs] *n* Cipro; **Cyprian**, **Cypriot** *n* cipriota.

cyst [sist] *n* ciste.

czar [zɑː] *n* zar.

Czechoslovakia ['tʃekouslou'vækiə] *n* Cecoslovacchia; **Czech** *a* *n* ceco; **Czechoslovak** *a* *n* cecoslovacco.

D

dab [dæb] *n* pezzettino, spalmatina, tocco, schizzo; *vt* toccare leggermente.

dabble ['dæbl] *vi* sguazzare; **to d. in** fare una cosa da dilettante.

dachshund ['dækshund] *n* cane bassotto.

dad [dæd] **daddy** ['dædi] *n* (*fam*) babbo, papà.

daffodil ['dæfədil] *n* narciso.

daft [dɑːft] *a* pazzerello, sciocco.

dagger ['dægə] *n* daga, pugnale.

dahlia ['deiliə] *n* (*bot*) dalia.

daily ['deili] *a* giornaliero, quotidiano; *n* (*giornale*) quotidiano.

daintiness ['deintinis] *n* delicatezza, raffinatezza, ricercatezza.

dainty ['deinti] *a* squisito, delicato, grazioso; schizzinoso; *n* leccornia.

dairy ['dɛəri] *n* latteria, cascina, caseificio; **dairymaid** lattaia; **dairyman** lattaio.

dais ['deiis] *n* pedana.

daisy ['deizi] *n* margherita, pratolina.

dale [deil] *n* vallata.

dally ['dæli] *vi* perdere tempo, gingillarsi, trastullarsi.

Dalmatia [dæl'meiʃə] *n* Dalmazia.

Dalmatian [dæl'meiʃən] *a* *n* dalmata.

dam [dæm] *n* argine, diga; (*of animals*) madre; *vt* arginare.

damage ['dæmidʒ] *n* danno, danni *pl*; perdita; *vt* danneggiare.

damaged ['dæmidʒd] *a* guastato, avariato.

damaging ['dæmidʒiŋ] *a* dannoso, nocivo.

damask ['dæməsk] *n* damasco.

dame [deim] *n* dama, nobildonna.

damn [dæm] *vt* dannare, maledire.

damnation [dæm'neiʃən] *n* dannazione.

damned [dæmd] *a* dannato, maledetto; *ad* (*sl*) maledettamente; molto.

damning ['dæmiŋ] *a* che condanna, schiacciante; che maledice; *n* condanna; maledizione.

damp [dæmp] *a* umido; *n* umidità; *vt* inumidire; (*fig*) scoraggiare.

dampness ['dæmpnis] *n* umidità.

damsel ['dæmzəl] *n* (*poet*) donzella.

damson ['dæmzən] *n* susina dama-scena.

dance [dɑːns] *n* ballo, danza; *vi* ballare, danzare.

dancer ['dɑːnsə] *n* ballerino, ballerina.

dancing ['dɑːnsiŋ] *a* danzante; *n* il ballo, la danza.

dandelion ['dændilaiən] *n* (*bot*) tarassico, (*fam*) soffione.

dandle ['dændl] *vt* dondolare, far ballare sulle ginocchia, vezzeggiare.

dandruff ['dændrif] *n* forfora.

dandy ['dændi] *n* bellimbusto, dame-rino.

Dane [dein] *n* danese.

danger ['deindʒə] *n* pericolo.

dangerous ['deindʒrəs] *a* pericoloso.

dangle ['dæŋgl] *vti* (far) dondolare.

dangling ['dæŋgliŋ] *a* ciondolante, penzoloni.

Daniel ['dænjəl] *nm pr* Daniele.

Danish ['deiniʃ] *a n* danese.

dank [dæŋk] *a* umido e freddo.

Danube ['dænjuːb] *n* Danubio.

dapper ['dæpə] *a* arzillo, vivace.

dappled ['dæpld] *a* chiazzato, pomel-lato.

dare [dɛə] *vi* osare; *vt* sfidare; **I dare say** forse, probabilmente; **dare-devil** scavezzacollo.

daring ['dɛəriŋ] *a* audace, intrepido; *n* audacia.

dark [dɑːk] *a* buio, (o)scuro, tene-broso; *n* oscurità, tenebre *pl*.

darken ['dɑːkən] *vti* oscurar(si).

darkness ['dɑːknis] *n* oscurità, tenebre *pl*, buio.

darling ['dɑːliŋ] *a* caro, diletto; *n* prediletto.

darn [dɑːn] *n* rammendo; *vt* ram-mendare.

darning ['dɑːniŋ] *n* rammendo; **d. needle** ago da rammendo; **d. wool** lana da rammendo.

dart [dɑːt] *n* dardo; balzo, movimen-to rapido; *vt* dardeggiare, lanciare; *vi* balzare, slanciar(si).

dash [dæʃ] *n* slancio, impeto, attacco, colpo; goccio; lineetta; **dashboard** (*aut*) cruscotto; *vti* pre-cipitarsi, urtare violentemente, fran-tumare, frantumarsi, distruggere; **to d. off** fare qualcosa velocemente, scappar via.

dashing ['dæʃiŋ] *a* impetuoso; sgar-giante.

dastard ['dæstəd] *n* codardo, vile; **dastardly** *a* vile, codardo.

dastardliness ['dæstədlinis] *n* viltà.

data ['deitə] *n pl* dati, elementi.

date [deit] *n* dattero; data, scadenza; appuntamento; **out of d.** antiquato; **up to d.** aggiornato; *vti* datare; avere (fissare) un appuntamento.

dative ['deitiv] *a n* dativo.

daub [dɔːb] *n* imbrattamento, pittura malfatta, intonaco; *vt* imbrattare, impiastrare.

daughter ['dɔːtə] *n* figlia; **d.-in-law** nuora.

daunt [dɔːnt] *vt* scoraggiare, spaven-tare.

dauntless ['dɔːntlis] *a* intrepido.

David ['deivid] *nm pr* Davide.

dawdle ['dɔːdl] *vi* bighellonare.

dawn [dɔːn] *n* alba, aurora; inizio; *vi* albeggiare, cominciare ad appa-rire.

day [dci] *n* giorno, giornata, dì; **d. boy** allievo esterno; **d. school** scuola diurna.

daybreak ['deibreik] *n* alba.

daydream ['deidriːm] *n* sogno ad occhi aperti.

day-labourer ['dei,leibərə] *n* lavora-tore a giornata.

daylight ['deilait] *n* (luce del) giorno.

daytime ['deitaim] *n* il giorno, la giornata.

daze [deiz] *n* intontimento, stupore.

dazzle ['dæzl] *vt* abbagliare.

deacon ['diːkən] *n* diacono.

dead [ded] *a* morto; completo, assoluto; *n* morto, morti, (*fig*) profondità; **at d. of night** nel cuor della notte; *ad* completamente, assolutamente.

deaden ['dedn] *vt* ammortire, smor-zare; *vi* affievolirsi.

deadlock ['dedlɔk] *n* punto morto.

deadly ['dedli] *a* mortale; *ad* mortal-mente.

deadness ['dednis] *n* ammortimento, stato di torpore.

deaf [def] *a* sordo.

deafen ['defn] *vt* assordare, stordire; **deafening** assordante.

deaf-mute ['def'mjuːt] *n* sordomuto.

deafness ['defnis] *n* sordità.

deal [diːl] *n* affare, accordo; (*at cards*) mano; legno d'abete o di pino; quantità; **a good d. (of)** molto; *vi* commerciare, trattare; compor-tarsi; *vt* distribuire; assestare (un colpo).

dealer ['diːlə] *n* commerciante, negoziante.

dealing ['diːliŋ] *n* commercio; distri-buzione; condotta; *pl* rapporti *pl*.

dean [diːn] *n* arciprete, decano; preside di facoltà.

dear [diə] *a* caro, costoso; **dear me!** *interj* Dio mio!

dearly ['diəli] *ad* teneramente; a caro prezzo.

dearness ['diənis] *n* caro prezzo.

dearth [dɔːθ] *n* carestia, scarsità.

death [deθ] *n* morte; **deathbed** letto di morte; **d.-rate** mortalità.

debar [di'bɑː] *vt* escludere.

debase [di'beis] *vt* abbassare, svilire.

debatable [di'beitəbl] *a* discutibile, contestabile.

debate [di'beit] *n* dibattito, discus-sione; *vti* dibattere, discutere.

debauch [di'bɔːtʃ] *n* crapula, orgia; *vt* pervertire.

debauchery [di'bɔːtʃəri] n pervertimento, scostumatezza.

debenture [di'bentʃə] n (com) obbligazione.

debilitate [di'biliteit] vt debilitare.

debility [di'biliti] n debolezza, languore.

debit ['debit] n (com) debito; vt addebitare.

debris ['debri] n macerie, detriti.

debt [det] n debito.

debtor ['detə] n debitore.

debunk [diː'bʌŋk] vt ridurre alle giuste proporzioni.

debut ['deibuː] n debutto.

débutante ['debjuːtaːnt] n debuttante.

decade ['dekeid] n decade, decennio.

decadence ['dekədəns] n decadenza.

decadent ['dekədənt] a n decadente.

decalogue ['dekələg] n decalogo.

decant [di'kænt] vt versare, travasare.

decanter [di'kæntə] n caraffa.

decapitate [di'kæpiteit] vt decapitare.

decasyllable ['dekəsiləbl] a n (poet) decasillabo.

decay [di'kei] n decomposizione, decadenza, rovina; vi decadere, decomporsi, deperire, (teeth) cariarsi.

decease [di'siːs] vi decedere, morire.

deceased [di'siːst] a n deceduto, defunto, fu.

deceit [di'siːt] n inganno, frode, falsità.

deceitful [di'siːtful] a ingannevole, falso.

deceitfulness [di'siːtfulnis] n doppiezza, falsità.

deceive [di'siːv] vt ingannare, deludere.

decelerate [diː'seləreit] vti rallentare.

December [di'sembə] n dicembre.

decency ['diːsnsi] n decenza, decoro.

decent ['diːsnt] a decente, decoroso, onesto, per bene.

decentralize [di'sentrəlaiz] vt decentrare.

deception [di'sepʃən] n inganno; illusione.

deceptive [di'septiv] a ingannevole.

deceptiveness [di'septivnis] n carattere ingannevole, fallacia.

decibel ['desibel] n (phys) decibel.

decide [di'said] vti decidere.

decided [di'saidid] a deciso, risoluto, inconfutabile.

decidedly [di'saididli] ad decisamente, indubbiamente.

decimal ['desiməl] a n decimale.

decimate ['desimeit] vt decimare.

decimation [,desi'meiʃən] n decimazione.

decipher [di'saifə] vt decifrare.

deciphering [di'saifəriŋ] n decifrazione.

decision [di'siʒən] n decisione, giudizio; risolutezza.

decisive [di'saisiv] a decisivo; deciso.

decisiveness [di'saisivnis] n risolutezza.

deck [dek] n (naut) ponte, coperta; (US) mazzo di carte da gioco; vt ornare, coprire, rivestire; d. chair sedia a sdraio.

declaim [di'kleim] vti declamare.

declamation [,deklə'meiʃən] n declamazione.

declamatory [di'klæmətəri] a declamatorio.

declaration [,deklə'reiʃən] n dichiarazione.

declare [di'kleə] vt dichiarare, proclamare; vi dichiararsi.

declension [di'klenʃən] n (gram) declinazione.

decline [di'klain] n declino, decadimento; declivio; (price) ribasso; vti declinare, rifiutare; inclinarsi; diminuire.

declivity [di'kliviti] n declivio.

decode [diː'koud] vt decifrare, tradurre.

décolleté [dei'kɔltei] a n scollato; scollatura.

decompose [,diːkəm'pouz] vti decomporre, decomporsi; scomporre, scomporsi.

decomposition [,diːkɔmpə'ziʃən] n decomposizione.

decontrol ['diːkən'troul] vt togliere i controlli a.

decorate ['dekəreit] vt decorare, ornare, (a room) verniciare.

decoration [,dekə'reiʃən] n decorazione, ornamento.

decorator ['dekəreitə] n (pittore) decoratore; **interior d.** arredatore.

decorous ['dekərəs] a decoroso.

decorum [di'kɔːrəm] n decoro.

decoy [di'kɔi] n esca, richiamo; vt allettare, adescare.

decrease ['diːkriːs] n diminuzione; vti [diː'kriːs] diminuire.

decree [di'kriː] n decreto: vt decretare.

decrepit [di'krepit] a decrepito.

decry [di'krai] vt denigrare, screditare.

dedicate ['dedikeit] vt dedicare.

dedicated ['dedikeitid] a dedicato, votato, consacrato; scrupoloso.

dedication [,dedi'keiʃən] n dedica; dedicazione.

deduce [di'djuːs] vt dedurre, desumere.

deduct [di'dʌkt] vt dedurre, sottrarre.

deduction [di'dʌkʃən] n deduzione.

deed [diːd] n azione, atto, fatto, impresa; titolo, contratto.

deem [diːm] vti giudicare, stimare, pensare.

deep [diːp] a profondo; alto; sprofondato; cupo; ad profondamente; n abisso, alto mare.

deep-freeze [diːp'friːz] n surgelamento.

deepen ['diːpən] vti approfondir(si).

deeply ['diːpli] ad profondamente.

deepness ['di:pnis] n profondità.

deer [diə] n (inv) cervo, daino.

deface [di'feis] vt sfigurare; cancellare.

defacement [di'feismənt] n sfregio, cancellazione.

defamation [,defə'meiʃən] n diffamazione, calunnia.

defamatory [di'fæmətəri] a diffamatorio, calunnioso.

defame [di'feim] vt diffamare, calunniare.

default [di'fɔ:lt] n mancanza; insolvenza contumacia; vti render(si) contumace, mancare di pagare.

defaulter [di'fɔ:ltə] n debitore moroso; imputato contumace.

defeat [di'fi:t] n disfatta, sconfitta; vt sconfiggere.

defeatist [di'fi:tist] n disfattista.

defect [di'fekt] n difetto, imperfezione.

defection [di'fekʃən] n defezione.

defective [di'fektiv] a difettoso, imperfetto; mentally d. infermo di mente.

defence [di'fens] n difesa.

defenceless [di'fenslis] a indifeso.

defend [di'fend] vt difendere.

defendant [di'fendənt] n convenuto, imputato.

defender [di'fendə] n difensore.

defensive [di'fensiv] a difensivo; n difensiva.

defer [di'fə:] vt differire, rimandare; essere deferente.

deference ['defərəns] n deferenza.

deferent ['defərənt] a deferente.

deferentially [,defə'renʃəli] ad con deferenza.

deferment [di'fə:mənt] n differimento, rimando; dilazione.

defiance [di'faiəns] n sfida; spavalderia.

defiant [di'faiənt] a ardito, provocante; spavaldo.

deficiency [di'fiʃənsi] n deficienza; (com) disavanzo.

deficient [di'fiʃənt] a deficiente, difettoso, insufficiente.

deficit ['defisit] n disavanzo, deficit.

defile ['di:fail] n gola di montagna, stretto passaggio; vt [di'fail] insozzare; violare; vi procedere in fila, sfilare.

defilement [di'failmənt] n contaminazione, violazione.

define [di'fain] vt definire, determinare, delimitare.

definite ['definit] a definito, preciso.

definition [,defi'niʃən] n definizione.

definitive [di'finitiv] a definitivo; decisivo.

deflate [di'fleit] vt (tyre) sgonfiare; (fin) deflazionare.

deflect [di'flekt] vt (far) deflettere.

deflection [di'flekʃən] n deviazione.

deforest [di'fɔrist] vt disboscare.

deform [di'fɔ:m] vt deformare.

deformed [di'fɔ:md] a deforme.

deformity [di'fɔ:miti] n deformità.

defraud [di'frɔ:d] vt defraudare.

defray [di'frei] vt pagare, sostenere le spese.

defrost [di'frɔst] vt (also com) sgelare; disgelare; (refrigerator) sbrinare; defroster (aut) riscaldatore.

deft [deft] a lesto; agile; abile.

defunct [di'fʌŋkt] a n defunto, deceduto.

defy [di'fai] vt sfidare.

degenerate [di'dʒenərit] a n degenerato; vi [di'dʒenəreit] degenerare.

degradation [,degrə'deiʃən] n degradazione.

degrade [di'greid] vt degradare.

degrading [di'greidiŋ] a degradante.

degree [di'gri:] n grado, laurea.

deign [dein] vti degnar(si).

deity ['di:iti] n deità, divinità.

deject [di'dʒekt] vt deprimere, scoraggiare.

dejected [di'dʒektid] a abbattuto, scoraggiato.

dejection [di'dʒekʃən] n scoraggiamento.

delay [di'lei] n ritardo, indugio; vt ritardare; vi indugiare.

delegate ['deligit] n delegato; ['deligeit] vt delegare.

delegation [,deli'geiʃən] n delegazione.

delete [di'li:t] vt cancellare.

deleterious [,deli'tiəriəs] a deleterio.

deletion [di'li:ʃən] n cancellatura.

deliberate [di'libərit] a cauto, deliberato, misurato; vti [di'libəreit] deliberare.

deliberately [di'libəritli] ad deliberatamente, apposta.

deliberation [di,libə'reiʃən] n deliberazione; decisione.

delicacy ['delikəsi] n delicatezza; leccornia.

delicate ['delikit] a delicato.

delicately ['delikitli] ad delicatamente.

delicious [di'liʃəs] a delizioso, squisito.

deliciousness [di'liʃəsnis] n squisitezza.

delight [di'lait] n diletto, gioia; vti dilettar(si), divertir(si).

delightful [di'laitful] a delizioso, dilettevole, incantevole, molto piacevole.

delightfully [di'laitfuli] ad deliziosamente.

delineate [di'linieit] vt delineare.

delineation [di,lini'eiʃən] n delineazione.

delinquency [di'liŋkwənsi] n delinquenza.

delinquent [di'liŋkwənt] n delinquente.

delirious [di'liriəs] a delirante.

delirium [di'liriəm] n delirio.

deliver [di'livə] vt liberare, salvare;

(med) partorire; consegnare; (speech) pronunciare; (blow) vibrare.

deliverance [di'livərəns] n liberazione; parto; consegna; pronunziamento.

deliverer [di'livərə] n liberatore, salvatore.

delivery [di'livəri] n consegna, distribuzione di posta; parto; il pronunciare un discorso; **cash on d.** (C.O.D.) contro assegno; **deliveryman** (US) fattorino, ragazzo; **general d.** (US) fermo posta.

dell [del] n valletta, conca.

delphinium [del'finiəm] n (bot) fiorcappuccio.

delta ['deltə] n delta; **d.-wing** (av) ala a delta.

delude [di'lju:d] vt illudere, ingannare.

deluge ['delju:dʒ] n diluvio.

delusion [di'lu:ʒən] n illusione; allucinazione.

delusive [di'lju:siv] a ingannevole, illusorio.

delve [delv] vt zappare; (fig) penetrare, sondare.

demagogue ['deməgɔg] n demagogo.

demand [di:'ma:nd] n domanda, richiesta; vt richiedere; domandare, esigere.

demeanour [di'mi:nə] n comportamento.

demented [di'mentid] a demente, pazzo.

demise [di'maiz] n decesso; cessione.

demobilization ['di:ˌmoubilai'zeiʃən] n smobilitazione.

demobilize [di:'moubilaiz] vt smobilitare.

democracy [di'mɔkrəsi] n democrazia.

democrat ['deməkræt] n democratico.

democratic [ˌdemə'krætik] a democratico.

demolish [di'mɔliʃ] vt demolire.

demolition [ˌdemə'liʃən] n demolizione.

demon ['di:mən] n demonio, spirito maligno.

demoniac [di'mouniæk] a demoniaco; n indemoniato.

demonstrate ['demənstreit] vti dimostrare.

demonstration [ˌdeməns'treiʃən] n dimostrazione.

demonstrative [di'mɔnstrətiv] a dimostrativo; espansivo.

demoralization [diˌmɔrəlai'zeiʃən] n demoralizzazione.

demoralize [di'mɔrəlaiz] vt demoralizzare.

demur [di'mə:] n esitazione, irresolutezza; vi esitare; obiettare.

demure [di'mjuə] a affettatamente modesto.

demureness [di'mjuənis] n modestia, affettato candore.

den [den] n covo, tana; (fam) studiolo.

denationalize [di:'næʃnəlaiz] vt snazionalizzare.

denial [di'naiəl] n diniego, rifiuto.

denigrate ['denigreit] vt denigrare.

denigration [ˌdeni'greiʃən] n denigrazione.

denim ['denim] n tessuto di cotone; pl tuta.

Denis ['denis] nm pr Dionigi.

denizen ['denizn] n abitante; straniero naturalizzato.

Denmark ['denma:k] n Danimarca.

denominate [di'nɔmineit] vt denominare.

denomination [diˌnɔmi'neiʃən] n denominazione; (com) taglio, valore.

denote [di'nout] vt denotare, indicare.

denounce [di'nauns] vt denunciare.

dense [dens] a denso, spesso; ottuso.

density ['densiti] n densità; stupidità.

dent [dent] n incavo, intaccatura; (mech) dente; vt intaccare; vi dentellarsi.

dental ['dentl] a n dentale.

dentifrice ['dentifris] n dentifricio.

dentist ['dentist] n dentista.

denture ['dentʃə] n dentiera.

denude [di'nju:d] vt denudare.

denunciation [diˌnʌnsi'eiʃən] n denuncia, accusa.

deny [di'nai] vt negare; rifiutare.

deodorant [di:'oudərənt] n deodorante.

depart [di'pa:t] vi partire; (fig) derogare da; **departed** a passato; **the departed** il defunto, i defunti.

department [di'pa:tmənt] n dipartimento, reparto; **d. store** emporio.

departure [di'pa:tʃə] n partenza; allontanamento; **new d.** nuovo orientamento.

depend [di'pend] vi dipendere, contare su.

dependability [di'pendəbiliti] n fidatezza; (of machine etc) sicurezza di funzionamento.

dependable [di'pendəbl] a fidato, sicuro, attendibile.

dependant, dependent [di'pendənt] n dipendente.

dependence [di'pendəns] n dipendenza; fiducia.

depict [di'pikt] vt dipingere, descrivere.

depilate ['depileit] vt depilare.

depilatory [di'pilətəri] a n depilatorio.

deplete [di'pli:t] vt esaurire, vuotare.

deplorable [di'plɔ:rəbl] a deplorevole.

deplore [di'plɔ:] vt deplorare.

deploy [di'plɔi] vti (mil) spiegar(si).

depopulate [di'pɔpjuleit] vt spopolare.

depopulation [di:ˌpopju'leiʃən] n spopolamento.

deport [di'pɔːt] *vt* deportare, esiliare.

deportation [ˌdiːpɔː'teiʃən] *n* deportazione.

deportment [di'pɔːtmənt] *n* portamento, contegno.

depose [di'pouz] *vt* deporre, togliere di carica.

deposit [di'pɔzit] *n* deposito; versamento; *vt* depositare; versare.

depositary [di'pɔzitəri] *n* depositario.

deposition [ˌdepə'ziʃən] *n* deposizione.

depositor [di'pɔzitə] *n* depositante.

depository [di'pɔzitəri] *n* deposito.

depot ['depou] *n* deposito, magazzino.

depravation [ˌdeprə'veiʃən] *n* corruzione, depravazione.

deprave [di'preiv] *vt* corrompere, depravare.

depravity [di'præviti] *n* depravazione.

deprecate ['deprikeit] *vt* deprecare.

deprecation [ˌdepri'keiʃən] *n* deprecazione.

depreciate [di'priːʃieit] *vt* deprezzare, screditare; *vi* diminuire di valore.

depreciation [diˌpriːʃi'eiʃən] *n* deprezzamento.

depredation [ˌdepri'deiʃən] *n* depredazione.

depress [di'pres] *vt* deprimere.

depressing [di'presiŋ] *a* deprimente.

depression [di'preʃən] *n* depressione.

deprivation [ˌdepri'veiʃən] *n* privazione.

deprive [di'praiv] *vt* privare.

depth [depθ] *n* profondità, fondo; **d.-charge** bomba di profondità; **d.-finder** scandaglio.

deputation [ˌdepjuː'teiʃən] *n* deputazione.

depute [di'pjuːt] *vt* deputare.

deputize ['depjutaiz] *vi* sostituire, fare le veci di.

deputy ['depjuti] *n* delegato, deputato, rappresentante.

derail [di'reil] *vt* far deragliare; *vi* deragliare.

derailment [di'reilmənt] *n* deragliamento.

derange [di'reindʒ] *vt* disordinare, scombussolare.

derangement [di'reindʒmənt] *n* sconvolgimento, confusione.

derelict ['derilikt] *a* abbandonato, derelitto; *n* relitto.

dereliction [ˌderi'likʃən] *n* abbandono; negligenza.

deride [di'raid] *vt* deridere.

derision [di'riʒən] *n* derisione, sarcasmo.

derisive [di'raisiv] *a* derisorio.

derivation [ˌderi'veiʃən] *n* derivazione.

derivative [di'rivətiv] *a n* derivato.

derive [di'raiv] *vti* derivare.

derogate ['derəgeit] *vi* derogare.

derogation [ˌderə'geiʃən] *n* deroga.

derogatory [di'rɔgətəri] *a* derogatorio.

derrick ['derik] *n* argano, gru.

descend [di'send] *vti* scendere, discendere; trasmettersi.

descendant [di'sendənt] *a n* discendente.

descent [di'sent] *n* discesa, pendio; discendenza, lignaggio.

describe [dis'kraib] *vt* descrivere.

description [dis'kripʃən] *n* descrizione; genere, specie.

descriptive [dis'kriptiv] *a* descrittivo.

descry [dis'krai] *vt* discernere, scorgere.

desecrate ['desikreit] *vt* profanare.

desecration [ˌdesi'kreiʃən] *n* profanazione.

desert [di'zəːt] *vti* disertare.

desert ['dezət] *n* deserto.

desert [di'zəːt] *n* (*usu pl*) merito.

deserted [di'zəːtid] *a* deserto, abbandonato.

deserter [di'zəːtə] *n* disertore.

desertion [di'zəːʃən] *n* diserzione.

deserve [di'zəːv] *vt* meritare.

deserving [di'zəːviŋ] *a* degno, meritevole.

desiccate ['desikeit] *vt* essiccare.

design [di'zain] *n* disegno, proposito; *vt* disegnare, proporsi.

designate ['dezigneit] *vt* designare.

designation [ˌdezig'neiʃən] *n* designazione.

designer [di'zainə] *n* disegnatore, modellista.

designing [di'zainiŋ] *a* astuto, intrigante.

desirable [di'zaiərəbl] *a* desiderabile.

desire [di'zaiə] *n* desiderio, passione, voglia, preghiera; *vt* desiderare, pregare.

desirous [di'zaiərəs] *a* desideroso.

desist [di'zist] *vi* desistere.

desk [desk] *n* tavolo, scrittoio, scrivania; cattedra, banco di scuola.

desolate ['desəlit] *a* desolato; ['desəleit] *vt* desolare, devastare.

desolation [ˌdesə'leiʃən] *n* desolazione, distruzione.

despair [dis'pɛə] *n* disperazione; *vi* disperar(si).

despairing [dis'pɛəriŋ] *a* disperato, che fa disperare.

despatch [dis'pætʃ] *v* **dispatch**.

desperate ['despərit] *a* disperato; furioso.

desperately ['despəritli] *ad* disperatamente; gravemente.

desperation [ˌdespə'reiʃən] *n* disperazione, accanimento.

despicability [ˌdespikə'biliti] *n* spregevolezza.

despicable ['despikəbl] *a* spregevole.

despise [dis'paiz] *vt* disprezzare.

despite [dis'pait] *n* dispetto; *prep* a dispetto di, nonostante, malgrado.

despoil [dis'pɔil] *vt* derubare, spogliare.

despondency [dis'pɔndənsi] *n* abbattimento, scoraggiamento.

despondent [dis'pɔndənt] *a* abbattuto, scoraggiato.

despot ['despɔt] *n* despota.

despotic [des'pɔtik] *a* dispotico.

despotism ['despətizəm] *n* dispotismo.

dessert [di'zə:t] *n* 'dessert', dolci e frutta (alla fine del pasto) *pl*.

destination [,desti'neiʃən] *n* destinazione.

destine ['destin] *vt* destinare.

destiny ['destini] *n* destino, fato.

destitute ['destitju:t] *a* bisognoso, privo di mezzi.

destitution [,desti'tju:ʃən] *n* destituzione, miseria.

destroy [dis'trɔi] *vt* distruggere.

destroyer [dis'trɔiə] *n* distruttore; (*naut*) cacciatorpediniere.

destruction [dis'trʌkʃən] *n* distruzione, rovina.

destructive [dis'trʌktiv] *a* distruttivo.

destructiveness [dis'trʌktivnis] *n* potenza distruttiva, mania distruttiva.

desultory ['desəltəri] *a* saltuario, sconnesso.

detach [di'tætʃ] *vt* (di)staccare, separare.

detached [di'tætʃt] *a* distaccato, isolato, obiettivo.

detachment [di'tætʃmənt] *n* distacco; (*mil*) distaccamento.

detail ['di:teil] *n* dettaglio, particolare; *vt* dettagliare; (*mil*) distaccare.

detain [di'tein] *vt* detenere, trattenere.

detect [di'tekt] *vt* scoprire.

detection [di'tekʃən] *n* scoperta, rivelazione.

detective [di'tektiv] *n* 'detective', agente investigativo.

detention [di'tenʃən] *n* detenzione.

deter [di'tə:] *vt* distogliere, scoraggiare.

detergent [di'tə:dʒənt] *a n* detergente; detersivo.

deteriorate [di'tiəriəreit] *vti* deteriorar(si).

deterioration [di,tiəriə'reiʃən] *n* deterioramento.

determinate [di'tə:minit] *a* determinato, definito, deciso.

determination [di,tə:mi'neiʃən] *n* determinazione, risolutezza.

determine [di'tə:min] *vt* determinare, decidere; *vi* decidersi.

determined [di'tə:mind] *a* deciso, risoluto.

deterrent [di'terənt] *n* azione avente un effetto preventivo, freno.

detest [di'test] *vt* detestare.

detestable [di'testəbl] *a* detestabile.

detestation [,di:test'teiʃən] *n* avversione, odio.

dethrone [di'θroun] *vt* detronizzare.

detonate ['detouneit] *vti* (far) detonare.

detonation [,detou'neiʃən] *n* detonazione.

detonator ['detouneitə] *n* detonatore.

detour ['deituə] *n* deviazione d'itinerario, giro; (*US*) deviazione stradale.

detract [di'trækt] *vti* detrarre, sottrarre.

detraction [di'trækʃən] *n* detrazione; diffamazione.

detractor [di'træktə] *n* detrattore; diffamatore.

detriment ['detrimənt] *n* detrimento, danno.

detrimental [,detri'mentl] *a* dannoso.

deuce [dju:s] *n* diavolo, diamine; (*cards*) due; (*tennis*) quaranta pari.

devaluate [di:'væljueit] *vt* svalutare.

devaluation [,di:vælju'eiʃən] *n* svalutazione.

devalue [di:'vælju:] *v* **devaluate**.

devastate ['devəsteit] *vt* devastare.

devastating ['devəsteitiŋ] *a* rovinoso, devastante.

devastation [,devəs'teiʃən] *n* devastazione.

develop [di'veləp] *vt* sviluppare; *vi* svilupparsi.

development [di'veləpmənt] *n* sviluppo.

deviate ['di:vieit] *vti* (far) deviare.

deviation [,di:vi'eiʃən] *n* deviazione.

device [di'vais] *n* mezzo, espediente, progetto, stratagemma; aggeggio; dispositivo.

devil ['devl] *n* diavolo.

devilish ['deviliʃ] *a* diabolico.

devilry ['devlri] *n* diavoleria.

devious ['di:viəs] *a* indiretto, tortuoso, falso.

devise [di'vaiz] *vt* escogitare, progettare; lasciare per testamento.

devoid [di'void] *a* privo.

devolution [,di:və'lu:ʃən] *n* devoluzione.

devolve [di'vɔlv] *vt* devolvere; *vi* ricadere.

devote [di'vout] *vt* consacrare, dedicare.

devoted [di'voutid] *a* devoto, votato.

devotee [,devou'ti:] *n* devoto.

devotion [di'vouʃən] *n* devozione, dedizione.

devour [di'vauə] *vt* divorare.

devout [di'vaut] *a* devoto, pio.

devoutness [di'vautnis] *n* religiosità.

dew [dju:] *n* rugiada.

dewy ['dju:i] *a* rugiadoso.

dexterity [deks'teriti] *n* destrezza.

dexterous ['dekstərəs] *a* destro, abile.

diabetes [,daiə'bi:ti:z] *n* diabete.

diabetic [,daiə'betik] *a* diabetico.

diabolic(al) [,daiə'bɔlik(əl)] *a* diabolico.

diadem ['daiədem] *n* diadema.

diagnose ['daiəgnouz] *vt* diagnosticare.

diagnosis [‚daiəg'nousis] n diagnosi.

diagonal [dai'ægənl] a n diagonale.

diagram ['daiəgræm] n diagramma.

dial ['daiəl] n meridiana, (clock etc) quadrante; (tel) disco combinatore.

dialect ['daiəlekt] n dialetto.

dialectal [‚daiə'lektəl] a dialettale.

dialogue ['daiələg] n dialogo.

diameter [dai'æmitə] n diametro.

diametrically [‚daiə'metrikəli] ad diametralmente.

diamond ['daiəmənd] n diamante, brillante; (geom) rombo; **diamonds** pl (cards) quadri.

diaper ['daiəpə] n tela operata; (US) pannolino.

diaphanous [dai'æfənəs] a diafano.

diaphragm ['daiəfræm] n diaframma.

diarrhoea [‚daiə'riə] n diarrea.

diatribe ['daiətraib] n diatriba.

diary ['daiəri] n diario; agenda.

dictaphone ['diktəfoun] n dittafono.

dictate ['dikteit] vti dettare.

dictation [dik'teiʃən] n dettatura; comando.

dictator [dik'teitə] n chi detta; dittatore.

dictatorial [‚diktə'tɔːriəl] a dittatorio, dittatoriale.

dictatorship [dik'teitəʃip] n dittatura.

diction ['dikʃən] n dizione.

dictionary ['dikʃənri] n dizionario, vocabolario.

didactic [di'dæktik] a didattico.

die [dai] pl **dice** n dado; pl **dies** n (tec) conio, stampo; vi morire; **to d. out** scomparire.

diesel ['diːzəl] n pr diesel; **d. oil** nafta.

diet ['daiət] n dieta, regime; vt mettere a dieta, a regime; vi seguire una dieta.

differ ['difə] vi differire; dissentire.

difference ['difrəns] n differenza; contesa.

different ['difrənt] a differente, diverso.

differential [‚difə'renʃəl] a differenziale.

differentiate [‚difə'renʃieit] vti differenziar(si).

difficult ['difikəlt] a difficile.

difficulty ['difikəlti] n difficoltà; ostacolo.

diffidence ['difidəns] n diffidenza, sfiducia in sè, timidezza.

diffident ['difidənt] a diffidente, timido.

diffuse [di'fjuːs] a diffuso; vti diffonder(si).

diffusion [di'fjuːʒən] n diffusione.

dig [dig] vti scavare, vangare.

digest [di'daidʒest] n riassunto, digesto; vti [dai'dʒest] digerire, assimilare.

digestible [di'dʒestəbl] a digeribile.

digestion [di'dʒestʃən] n digestione.

digestive [di'dʒestiv] a digestivo.

digger ['digə] n scavatore.

digit ['didʒit] n dito, cifra.

dignified ['dignifaid] a composto, dignitoso.

dignify ['dignifai] vt investire di dignità.

dignitary ['dignitəri] n dignitario.

dignity ['digniti] n dignità.

digress [dai'gres] vi fare delle digressioni.

digression [dai'greʃən] n digressione.

dike [daik] n diga.

dilapidate [di'læpideit] vt dilapidare; **dilapidated** in rovina.

dilate [dai'leit] vti dilatar(si).

dilatory ['dilətəri] a dilatorio.

dilemma [di'lemə] n dilemma.

diligence ['dilidʒəns] n diligenza.

diligent ['dilidʒənt] a diligente.

dilute [dai'ljuːt] vt diluire a diluito.

dilution [dai'ljuːʃən] n diluzione.

dim [dim] a indistinto, oscuro; appannato; debole; (intelligence) ottuso; vti offuscar(si), oscurar(si).

dime [daim] n (US) moneta d'argento equivalente ad un decimo di dollaro.

dimension [di'menʃən] n dimensione.

dimensional [di'menʃənl] a di dimensioni; (phys) dimensionale.

diminish [di'miniʃ] vti diminuire.

diminution [‚dimi'njuːʃən] n diminuzione.

diminutive [di'minjutiv] a n diminutivo.

dimness ['dimnis] n oscurità, offuscamento; imprecisione.

dimple ['dimpl] n fossetta.

din [din] n frastuono, rumore; assordante.

dine [dain] vi pranzare.

diner ['dainə] a commensale; (US rly) vagone ristorante.

dinette [di'net] n saletta da pranzo.

dinginess ['dindʒinis] n squallore; sudiciume.

dingy ['dindʒi] a scuro, sporco.

dining ['dainiŋ] n il pranzare; **d. car** (US) vagone ristorante; **d. room** sala da pranzo.

dinner ['dinə] n desinare, pranzo, cena.

dint [dint] n tacca, ammaccatura; **by d. of** prep a forza di.

diocese ['daiəsis] n diocesi.

dioxide [dai'ɔksaid] n (chem) biossido.

dip [dip] n immersione; inclinazione; candela di sego; (intelligence) vti immerger(si), inclinar(si); abbassarsi.

diphtheria [dif'θiəriə] n difterite.

diphthong ['difθɔŋ] n dittongo.

diplomacy [di'plouməsi] n diplomazia.

diplomat ['dipləmæt] n diplomatico.

diplomatic [‚diplə'mætik] a diplomatico.

dipper ['dipə] n chi (s')immerge; (US) mestolo; **the Great Dipper** (US) l'Orsa Maggiore.

dire ['daiǝ] *a* spaventoso, terribile.

direct [di'rekt] *a* diretto; esplicito; *ad* immediatamente; *vt* avviare, dirigere, indirizzare.

direction [di'rekʃǝn] *n* direzione, indicazione.

directive [di'rektiv] *a* direttivo; *n* direttiva, istruzione.

directly [di'rektli] *ad cj* immediatamente, appena che.

directness [di'rektnis] *n* franchezza.

director [di'rektǝ] *n* direttore.

directory [di'rektǝri] *n* (*tel*) elenco, guida, (*US*) consiglio d'amministrazione.

dirge [dǝːdʒ] *n* canto funebre, nenia.

dirt [dǝːt] **dirtiness** ['dǝːtinis] *n* sporcizia, sudiciume.

dirty ['dǝːti] *a* sporco, sudicio; *vt* insudiciare, sporcare.

disability [ˌdisǝ'biliti] *n* incapacità, invalidità.

disable [dis'eibl] *vt* inabilitare, rendere incapace.

disabled [dis'eibld] *a* incapace, invalido.

disabuse [ˌdisǝ'bjuːz] *vt* disingannare.

disadvantage [ˌdisǝd'vaːntidʒ] *n* svantaggio.

disadvantageous [ˌdisædvaːn'teidʒǝs] *a* svantaggioso.

disagree [ˌdisǝ'griː] *vi* dissentire, non andar d'accordo; nucere.

disagreeable [ˌdisǝ'griǝbl] *a* sgradevole, antipatico.

disagreement [ˌdisǝ'griːmǝnt] *n* disaccordo, dissenso.

disallow ['disǝ'lau] *vt* non permettere, non ammettere.

disappear [ˌdisǝ'piǝ] *vi* scomparire, svanire.

disappearance [ˌdisǝ'piǝrǝns] *n* scomparsa.

disappoint [ˌdisǝ'pɔint] *vt* deludere.

disappointed [ˌdisǝ'pɔintid] *a* deluso, scontento.

disappointing [ˌdisǝ'pɔintiŋ] *a* deludente, spiacevole.

disappointment [ˌdisǝ'pɔintmǝnt] *n* delusione, disappunto.

disapproval [ˌdisǝ'pruːvǝl] *n* disapprovazione.

disapprove [ˌdisǝ'pruːv] *vt* disapprovare.

disapproving [ˌdisǝ'pruːviŋ] *a* di disapprovazione.

disapprovingly [ˌdisǝ'pruːviŋli] *ad* con disapprovazione.

disarm [dis'aːm] *vti* disarmare.

disarmament [dis'aːmǝmǝnt] *n* disarmo.

disarrange ['disǝ'reindʒ] *vt* scompigliare, scomporre, disorganizzare.

disarray ['disǝ'rei] *n* disordine, scompiglio.

disarray ['disǝ'rei] *vt* scompigliare.

disaster [di'zaːstǝ] *n* disastro.

disastrous [di'zaːstrǝs] *a* disastroso.

disavow ['disǝ'vau] *vt* disconoscere, sconfessare, ripudiare.

disavowal ['disǝ'vauǝl] *n* rinnegazione, disconoscimento.

disband [dis'bænd] *vti* sbandar(si).

disbelief ['disbi'liːf] *n* incredulità.

disbelieve ['disbi'liːv] *vt* non credere a; **disbeliever** *n* miscredente.

disburden [dis'bǝːdn] *vt* alleggerire d'un peso.

disburse [dis'bǝːs] *vt* sborsare.

disbursement [dis'bǝːsmǝnt] *n* sborso.

disc [disk] *n* disco; **d.-brake** (*aut*) freno a disco; **identity d.** (*mil*) piastrina d'identità; **slipped d.** (*med*) ernia del disco.

discard [dis'kaːd] *vt* scartare.

discern [di'sǝːn] *vt* discernere.

discerning [di'sǝːniŋ] *a* acuto, penetrante.

discernment [di'sǝːnmǝnt] *n* discernimento, acutezza di giudizio.

discharge [dis'tʃaːdʒ] *n* scarico, scarica; emissione; suppurazione; liberazione; pagamento; adempimento; *vi* scaricarsi; suppurare; *vt* scaricare, emettere; liberare; licenziare.

disciple [di'saipl] *n* discepolo.

disciplinarian [ˌdisipli'nɛǝriǝn] *n* chi mantiene una rigida disciplina.

disciplinary ['disiplinǝri] *a* disciplinare.

discipline ['disiplin] *n* disciplina; *vt* disciplinare, castigare.

disclaim [dis'kleim] *vt* negare, ripudiare, non riconoscere.

disclose [dis'klouz] *vt* dischiudere, rivelare.

disclosure [dis'klouʒǝ] *n* rivelazione.

discoloration [disˌkʌlǝ'reiʃǝn] *n* scoloramento, macchia.

discolour [dis'kʌlǝ] *vt* scolorire, macchiare; *vi* scolorirsi, macchiarsi.

discomfiture [dis'kʌmfitʃǝ] *n* sconfitta scoraggiamento.

discomfort [dis'kʌmfǝt] *n* disagio, incomodo.

disconcert [ˌdiskǝn'sǝːt] *vt* sconcertare.

disconcerting [ˌdiskǝn'sǝːtiŋ] *a* sconcertante.

disconnect ['diskǝ'nekt] *vt* sconnettere, staccare.

disconsolate [dis'kɔnsǝlit] *a* sconsolato, triste.

discontent(ment) ['diskǝn'tent (mǝnt)] *n* scontento.

discontented ['diskǝn'tentid] *a* malcontento.

discontinuance [ˌdiskǝn'tinjuǝns] *n* cessazione, interruzione.

discontinue ['diskǝn'tinjuː] *vt* cessare, interrompere.

discord ['diskɔːd] *n* discordia; (*mus*) dissonanza.

discordance [dis'kɔːdǝns] *n* discordanza.

discordant [dis'kɔːdǝnt] *a* discorde, dissenziente; discordante; dissonante.

discotheque ['diskɔtek] *n* discoteca.

discount ['diskaunt] *n* sconto, tara; *vt* [dis'kaunt] scontare, fare la tara a.

discourage [dis'kʌridʒ] *vt* scoraggiare, dissuadere.

discouragement [dis'kʌridʒmənt] *n* scoraggiamento.

discouraging [dis'kʌridʒiŋ] *a* scoraggiante.

discourse ['diskɔːs] *n* discorso; *vi* [dis'kɔːs] discorrere.

discourteous [dis'kɔːtiəs] *a* scortese.

discover [dis'kʌvə] *vt* scoprire.

discoverer [dis'kʌvərə] *n* scopritore.

discovery [dis'kʌvəri] *n* scoperta.

discredit [dis'kredit] *n* discredito; *vt* screditare.

discreditable [dis'kreditəbl] *a* vergognoso.

discreet [dis'kriːt] *a* discreto, prudente, riservato.

discrepancy [dis'krepənsi] *n* discrepanza.

discretion [dis'kreʃən] *n* discrezione, prudenza.

discriminate [dis'krimineit] *vti* discriminare.

discrimination [dis,krimi'neiʃən] *n* discriminazione.

discursive [dis'kəːsiv] *a* discorsivo, digressivo, saltuario.

discus ['diskəs] *n* (*sport*) disco.

discuss [dis'kʌs] *vt* discutere.

discussion [dis'kʌʃən] *n* discussione.

disdain [dis'dein] *n* sdegno; *vt* sdegnare.

disdainful [dis'deinful] *a* sdegnoso.

disdainfully [dis'deinfuli] *ad* sdegnosamente.

disease [di'ziːz] *n* malattia.

diseased [di'ziːzd] *a* malato.

disembark ['disim'baːk] *vti* sbarcare.

disembarkation [,disembaːˈkeiʃən] *n* sbarco.

disenchant ['disin'tʃaːnt] *vt* disincantare, disilludere.

disengage ['disin'geidʒ] *vt* svincolare, liberare.

disentangle ['disin'tæŋgl] *vt* districare, sbrogliare.

disfavour ['dis'feivə] *n* disistima, sfavore.

disfigure [dis'figə] *vt* deturpare, sfregiare.

disfigurement [dis'figəmənt] *n* deturpazione, sfregio.

disgorge [dis'gɔːdʒ] *vt* buttar fuori.

disgrace [dis'greis] *n* disonore, vergogna, disgrazia; *vt* disonorare, far cadere in disgrazia.

disgraceful [dis'greisful] *a* vergognoso, disonorevole.

disgruntled [dis'grʌntld] *a* malcontento, di cattivo umore, irritato.

disguise [dis'gaiz] *n* travestimento, maschera; *vt* travestire, mascherare.

disgust [dis'gʌst] *n* disgusto; *vt* disgustare.

disgusted [dis'gʌstid] *a* disgustato, indignato.

disgusting [dis'gʌstiŋ] *a* disgustoso.

dish [diʃ] *n* piatto; portata; recipiente; **dishwasher** lavapiatti; *vt* mettere nel piatto, servire.

dishearten [dis'haːtn] *vt* scoraggiare.

dishevel [di'ʃevəl] *vt* scapigliare.

dishevelled [di'ʃevəld] *a* scarmigliato, arruffato; disordinato.

dishonest [dis'ɔnist] *a* disonesto.

dishonesty [dis'ɔnisti] *n* disonestà.

dishonour [dis'ɔnə] *n* disonore; (*com*) mancato pagamento; *vt* disonorare; (*com*) rifiutarsi di pagare.

dishonourable [dis'ɔnərəbl] *a* disonorevole.

disillusion [disi'luːʒən] *n* disillusione; *vt* disilludere.

disinclination [,disinkli'neiʃən] *n* antipatia, avversione.

disincline ['disin'klain] *vt* rendere avverso a.

disinfect [,disin'fekt] *vt* disinfettare.

disinfectant [,disin'fektənt] *n* disinfettante.

disinherit ['disin'herit] *vt* diseredare.

disintegrate [dis'intigreit] *vti* disintegrar(si).

disinterested [dis'intristid] *a* disinteressato, imparziale.

disjointed [dis'dʒɔintid] *a* disarticolato; incoerente; sconnesso.

disk [disk] *v* **disc.**

dislike [dis'laik] *n* antipatia; *vt* sentire antipatia per; **I d.** it non mi piace.

dislocate ['disləkeit] *vt* slogare.

dislocation [,dislə'keiʃən] *n* dislocazione, slogatura.

dislodge [dis'lɔdʒ] *vti* sloggiare.

disloyal ['dis'bɔiəl] *a* sleale, infedele.

disloyalty ['dis'bɔielti] *n* slealtà, infedeltà.

dismal ['dizməl] *a* tetro, triste, squallido.

dismantle [dis'mæntl] *vt* smantellare.

dismay [dis'mei] *n* costernazione, sbigottimento; *vt* costernare, sbigottire.

dismember [dis'membə] *vt* smembrare.

dismiss [dis'mis] *vt* licenziare, bandire, allontanare.

dismissal [dis'misəl] *n* licenziamento, rigetto.

dismount ['dis'maunt] *vi* smontare.

disobedience [,disə'biːdjəns] *n* disobbidienza.

disobedient [,disə'biːdjənt] *a* disubbidiente.

disobey ['disə'bei] *vti* disubbidire (a).

disoblige ['disə'blaidʒ] *vt* rifiutare un favore a.

disorder [dis'ɔːdə] *n* disordine; indisposizione; *vt* disordinare; far ammalare.

disorderly [dis'ɔːdəli] *a* disordinato, sregolato.

disorganization [dis,ɔːgənai'zeiʃən] n disorganizzazione.

disorganize [dis'ɔːgənaiz] vt disorganizzare.

disown [dis'oun] vt rinnegare, disconoscere.

disparage [dis'pæridʒ] vt deprezzare, screditare.

disparagement [dis'pæridʒmənt] n denigrazione.

disparaging [dis'pæridʒiŋ] a sprezzante, spregiativo.

disparagingly [dis'pæridʒiŋli] ad con disprezzo, in modo spregiativo.

disparity [dis'pæriti] n disparità, differenza.

dispassionate [dis'pæʃnit] a spassionato, imparziale.

dispatch [dis'pætʃ] n dispaccio; spedizione; prontezza; vt spedire, sbrigare.

dispel [dis'pel] vt dissipare, scacciare.

dispensary [dis'pensəri] n dispensario.

dispensation [,dispen'seiʃən] n dispensa, dispensazione.

dispense [dis'pens] vt dispensare; distribuire.

disperse [dis'pəːs] vt disperdere; vi disperdersi.

dispersion [dis'pəːʃən] n dispersione.

displace [dis'pleis] vt spostare, sostituire; (naut) dislocare, stazzare; **displaced person** profugo.

displacement [dis'pleismənt] n spostamento, sostituzione; (naut) dislocamento.

display [dis'plei] n mostra, esibizione, ostentazione; vt mettere in mostra, esporre, ostentare.

displease [dis'pliːz] vt dispiacere, offendere.

displeasure [dis'pleʒə] n dispiacere, scontento.

disposal [dis'pouzəl] n disposizione; eliminazione; **at your d.** a sua disposizione.

disposable [dis'pouzəbl] a disponibile.

dispose [dis'pouz] vt disporre; **to d. of** disfarsi di, vendere.

disposition [,dispə'ziʃən] n disposizione, carattere, temperamento.

dispossess ['dispə'zes] vt privare, spossessare.

disproportion ['disprə'pɔːʃən] n sproporzione.

disproportionate [,disprə'pɔːʃnit] a sproporzionato.

disprove ['dis'pruːv] vt confutare.

disputable [dis'pjuːtəbl] a discutibile, disputabile; contestabile.

dispute [dis'pjuːt] n disputa, controversia, vertenza; vti disputare.

disqualification [dis,kwɔlifi'keiʃən] n squalifica.

disqualify [dis'kwɔlifai] vt squalificare.

disquieting [dis'kwaiətiŋ] a inquietante.

disregard [,disri'gaːd] n noncuranza; vt ignorare, trascurare, non curarsi di.

disregardful [,disri'gaːdful] a noncurante.

disrepair ['disri'pɛə] n cattivo stato, rovina.

disreputable [dis'repjutəbl] a disonorevole, losco, malfamato.

disrepute ['disri'pjuːt] n scredito; disistima; cattiva fama.

disrespect ['disris'pekt] n mancanza di rispetto, irriverenza.

disrupt [dis'rʌpt] vt rompere, disorganizzare.

disruption [dis'rʌpʃən] n rottura, scissione.

dissatisfaction ['dis,sætis'fækʃən] n malcontento.

dissatisfied ['dis'sætisfaid] a insoddisfatto, scontento.

dissatisfy ['dis'sætisfai] vt non soddisfare.

dissect [di'sekt] vt sezionare; (fig) criticare.

dissection [di'sekʃən] n dissezione.

dissemble [di'sembl] vti simulare, nascondere.

disseminate [di'semineit] vt disseminare, diffondere.

dissemination [di,semi'neiʃən] n disseminazione; (fig) divulgazione.

dissension [di'senʃən] n discordia, dissenso.

dissent [di'sent] n dissenso, dissentimento; vt dissentire.

dissenter [di'sentə] n dissidente.

disservice ['dis'səːvis] n disservizio.

dissident ['disidənt] a n dissidente.

dissimilar [di'similə] a dissimile.

dissimilarity [,disimi'læriti] n dissomiglianza.

dissipate ['disipeit] vti dissipar(si).

dissipated ['disipeitid] a dissoluto, dissipato.

dissipation [,disi'peiʃən] n dissipazione, dispersione.

dissociate [di'souʃieit] vti dissociar(si).

dissociation [di,sousi'eiʃən] n dissociazione, sdoppiamento.

dissoluble [di'sɔljubl] a dissolubile.

dissolute ['disəluːt] a dissoluto.

dissolution [,disə'luːʃən] n dissoluzione, scioglimento; (cin) dissolvenza.

dissolve [di'zɔlv] vti dissciolgier(si), dissolver(si).

dissolvent [di'zɔlvənt] a n dissolvente.

dissonance ['disənəns] n dissonanza.

dissonant ['disənənt] a dissonante; discordante.

dissuade [di'sweid] vt dissuadere.

dissuasion [di'sweiʒən] n dissuasione.

distaff ['distaːf] n conocchia.

distance ['distəns] n distanza.

distant ['distənt] a distante, remoto; (fig) freddo, riservato.

distaste ['dis'teist] n ripugnanza.
distasteful [dis'teistful] a ripugnante, sgradevole.
distemper ['dis'tempə] n indisposizione; (vet) cimurro.
distemper [dis'tempə] vt dipingere a tempera, intonacare.
distend [dis'tend] vti gonfiar(si), dilatar(si).
distil [dis'til] vt distillare; vi stillare.
distillation [.disti'leiʃən] n distillazione.
distillery [dis'tiləri] n distilleria.
distinct [dis'tiŋkt] a ben definito, distinto, diverso.
distinction [dis'tiŋkʃən] n distinzione.
distinctive [dis'tiŋktiv] a distintivo, caratteristico.
distinguish [dis'tiŋgwiʃ] vti distinguere, differenziare.
distinguished [dis'tiŋgwiʃd] a distinto, insigne.
distinguishing [dis'tiŋgwiʃiŋ] a distintivo, caratteristico.
distort [dis'tɔːt] vt distorcere, deformare; svisare.
distortion [dis'tɔːʃən] n distorsione, deformazione.
distract [dis'trækt] vt distrarre; far impazzire.
distracted [dis'træktid] a sconvolto, pazzo.
distraction [dis'trækʃən] n distrazione, svago; follia; disperazione.
distrain [dis'trein] vi sequestrare, fare un sequestro.
distraught [dis'trɔːt] a sconvolto, disperato.
distress [dis'tres] n dolore; miseria; difficoltà; vt affliggere.
distressed [dis'trest] n angustiato, afflitto, in angustie.
distressing [dis'tresiŋ] a penoso, doloroso.
distribute [dis'tribju(ː)t] vt distribuire.
distribution [.distri'bjuːʃən] n distribuzione.
distributor [dis'tribjutə] n distributore, distributrice; (US merchandise) grossista.
district ['distrikt] n distretto; quartiere.
distrust [dis'trʌst] n diffidenza, sfiducia; vt diffidare di.
distrustful [dis'trʌstful] a diffidente, sospettoso.
disturb [dis'təːb] vt disturbare.
disturbance [dis'təːbəns] n agitazione, tumulto.
disunion [dis'juːnjən] n disunione.
disuse ['dis'juːs] n disuso.
ditch [ditʃ] n fossa, fossato.
ditto ['ditou] n lo stesso; ad come sopra.
ditty ['diti] n canzone popolare, ritornello.
divan [di'væn] n divano.
dive [daiv] n tuffo; d. **bombing**

bombardamento in picchiata; vi immergersi, tuffarsi; (av) scendere in picchiata.
diver ['daivə] n tuffatore; palombaro; **skin d.** nuotatore subacqueo, sommozzatore.
diverge [dai'vəːdʒ] vi divergere.
divergence [dai'vəːdʒəns] **divergency** [dai'vəːdʒənsi] n divergenza.
divergent [dai'vəːdʒənt] a divergente.
diverse ['daivə(ː)z] a diverso.
diversify [dai'vəːsifai] vt diversificare, variare.
diversion [dai'vəːʃən] n diversione; **road d., traffic d.** deviazione stradale.
diversity [dai'vəːsiti] n diversità.
divert [dai'vəːt] vt deviare, divertire.
divest [dai'vest] vt spogliare, svestire.
divide [di'vaid] vti divider(si).
dividend ['dividend] n (com) dividendo.
dividers [di'vaidəz] n pl compasso a punte fisse.
divine [di'vain] a divino; n teologo; vti divinare, predire.
diviner [di'vainə] n indovino; **water d.** rabdomante.
diving ['daiviŋ] n il tuffarsi, immersione; **d. board** trampolino; **d. suit** scafandro.
divinity [di'viniti] n divinità; teologia.
divisible [di'vizəbl] a divisibile.
division [di'viʒən] n divisione.
divorce [di'vɔːs] n divorzio; vt divorziare da.
divorcee [di'vɔːsei] n divorziato, divorziata.
divulge [dai'vʌldʒ] vt divulgare.
dizziness ['dizinis] n capogiro, vertigine.
dizzy ['dizi] a vertiginoso; preso da vertigine; **to feel d.** sentirsi girar la testa.
do [duː] vt fare, compiere, eseguire; cucinare; (sl) ingannare; vi comportarsi; stare di salute; andar bene; bastare.
docile ['dousail] a docile.
docility [dou'siliti] n docilità.
dock [dɔk] n bacino portuario; **dockyard** arsenale; vt mozzare; (fam) ridurre; vi entrare in porto.
docker ['dɔkə] n scaricatore di porto.
doctor ['dɔktə] n dottore, medico.
doctrine ['dɔktrin] n dottrina.
document ['dɔkjumənt] n documento.
documentary [.dɔkju'mentəri] a n documentario.
dodge [dɔdʒ] vti scansare, schivare, eludere.
doe [dou] n (deer) daina, (hare) lepre femmina, (rabbit) coniglia; **doeskin** pelle di daino.
dog [dɔg] n cane; **d. days** pl la canicola; **top d.** (fam) persona autorevole; **dogfish** pescecane; **d.**

rose rosa canina; *vt* seguire, pedinare.

dogged ['dɔgid] *a* ostinato, tenace.

doggedly ['dɔgidli] *ad* ostinatamente, indefessamente.

dogma ['dɔgmə] *n* dogma.

dogmatic [dɔg'mætik] *a* dogmatico.

dogmatize ['dɔgmətaiz] *vi* dogmatizzare.

doings ['du(:)iŋz] *n pl* fatti, azioni, occupazioni.

dole [doul] *n* distribuzione caritatevole; **the d.** sussidio dato ai disoccupati; *vt* distribuire in piccole quantità, dare in elemosina.

doleful ['doulful] *a* malinconico, triste.

doll [dɔl] *n* bambola.

dollar ['dɔlə] *n* dollaro.

Dolomites ['dɔləmaits] *n pl* le Dolomiti.

dolphin ['dɔlfin] *n* delfino.

dolt [doult] *n* individuo ottuso.

domain [də'mein] *n* dominio, proprietà terriera.

dome [doum] *n* cupola.

domestic [də'mestik] *a n* domestico, domestica; **d. mails** (US) posta per l'interno.

domicile ['dɔmisail] *n* domicilio.

dominant ['dɔminənt] *a* dominante.

dominate ['dɔmineit] *vti* dominare.

domination [,dɔmi'neiʃən] *n* dominazione, dominio.

domineer [,dɔmi'niə] *vi* spadroneggiare, tiranneggiare.

domineering [,dɔmi'niəriŋ] *a* dispotico, imperioso, prepotente.

Dominic ['dɔminik] *nm pr* Domenico.

dominican [də'minikən] *a n* domenicano.

dominion [də'minjən] *n* dominio.

domino ['dɔminou] *pl* **dominoes** *n* domino.

don [dɔn] *n* insegnante universitario; *vt* indossare, mettersi.

donate [dou'neit] *vt* donare.

donation [dou'neiʃən] *n* donazione.

donkey ['dɔŋki] *n* asino, somaro; **d.-engine** locomotiva di manovra.

donor ['dounə] *n* donatore; **blood d.** donatore di sangue.

doom [du:m] *n* condanna; destino, sorte; *vt* condannare.

doomsday ['du:mzdei] *n* giorno del giudizio.

door [dɔ:] *n* porta, uscio; **doorway** vano della porta.

dope [doup] *n* lubrificante; stimolante; narcotico.

dormant ['dɔ:mənt] *a* assopito; inattivo; caduto in disuso; **d. partner** (com) socio occulto.

dormitory ['dɔ:mitri] *n* dormitorio.

dormouse ['dɔ:maus] *n* ghiro.

dorsal ['dɔ:səl] *a* dorsale.

dose [dous] *n* dose; *vt* dosare, somministrare a dosi; (*drinks*) adulterare.

dot [dɔt] *n* punto, puntino.

dotage ['doutidʒ] *n* rimbambimento.

dotard ['doutəd] *n* vecchio rimbambito.

dote [dout] *vi* essere rimbambito, essere infatuato.

double ['dʌbl] *a* doppio; finto; *n* doppio; *ad* due volte; *vt* raddoppiare; passar intorno a; *vi* voltare improvvisamente.

doubt [daut] *n* dubbio, incertezza; sospetto; *vti* dubitare; sospettare.

doubtful ['dautful] *a* incerto, dubbio, dubbioso.

doubtless ['dautlis] *ad* indubbiamente, senza dubbio.

dough [dou] *n* pasta.

dove [dʌv] *n* colomba.

dowager ['dauədʒə] *n* vedova (che ha un titolo o un patrimonio ereditato dal marito).

dowdy ['daudi] *a* sciatto, trasandato.

down [daun] *n* duna, collinetta; lanugine, peluria; piumino; *a* depresso; *prep* in basso, giù per; *ad* giù, in basso, in giù; **d. with . . .** *interj* a abbasso; *vt* (*fam*) abbattere, gettare terra.

downcast ['daunkɑ:st] *a* abbattuto.

downfall ['daunfɔ:l] *n* caduta, rovescio di fortuna.

downhearted ['daun'hɑ:tid] *a* scoraggiato, abbattuto.

downhill ['daun'hil] *a* discendente; *n* discesa; *ad* in discesa.

downpour ['daunpɔ:] *n* acquazzone.

downright ['daunrait] *a* netto, chiaro; onesto *ad* categoricamente.

downstairs ['daun'stɛəz] *a* del (al) piano di sotto; *ad* giù.

downward ['daunwəd] *a* verso il basso, discendente; **downwards** *ad* in giù, in basso.

dowry ['dauəri] *n* dote.

doze [douz] *n* sonnellino; *vt* sonnecchiare.

dozen ['dʌzn] *n* dozzina.

drab [dræb] *a* grigio, scialbo.

draft [drɑ:ft] *n* (*outline*) abbozzo; brutta copia; assegno, tratta; (*mil*) distaccamento; *vt* redigere; abbozzare; arruolare

drag [dræg] *n* (*naut*) draga; (*agr*) erpice; carrozza a quattro cavalli; (*fig*) ostacolo, peso; *vt* trascinare, dragare.

dragon ['drægən] *n* drago(ne); **dragonfly** libellula.

dragoon [drə'gu:n] *n* (*mil*) dragone.

drain [drein] *n* canale di scolo, fogna, tubo di scarico, tubo per drenaggio; *vt* prosciugare per drenaggio; scolare, bere fino in fondo.

drainage ['dreinidʒ] *n* fognatura, drenaggio.

drake [dreik] *n* anitra maschio.

drama ['drɑ:mə] *n* dramma.

dramatic [drə'mætik] *a* drammatico.

dramatist ['dræmətist] *n* drammaturgo.

dramatize ['dræmətaiz] *vt* drammatizzare; adattare per il teatro.

drape [dreip] *vt* coprire, drappeggiare.

draper ['dreipə] *n* merciaio, negoziante in tessuti.

drapery ['dreipəri] *n* tessuti, drappeggi, commercio in tessuti.

drastic ['dræstik] *a* drastico, energico.

draught [dra:ft] *n* bevanda, pozione; corrente d'aria, (*naut*) pescaggio; trazione.

draughts [dra:fts] *n pl* (*game*) gioco della dama.

draughtsman ['dra:ftsmən] *n* disegnatore.

draughty ['dra:fti] *a* pieno di correnti d'aria.

draw [drɔ:] *n* trazione; attrazione; sorteggio; (*sport*) pareggio; *vti* tirare, (ri)tirarsi, attirare, trascinare; disegnare; tirare a sorte; (*com*) emettere; riscuotere, (*sport*) pareggiare.

drawback ['drɔ:bæk] *n* inconveniente, svantaggio.

drawbridge ['drɔ:bridʒ] *n* ponte levatoio.

drawer ['drɔ:ə] *n* disegnatore; redattore; (*com*) traente; cassetto; **drawers** *n pl* mutande *pl*.

drawing ['drɔ:iŋ] *n* disegno; sorteggio; tiraggio; **d. room** salotto.

drawl [drɔ:l] *n* pronuncia strascicata; *vi* strascicare le parole.

dray [drei] *n* carro pesante.

dread [dred] *n* terrore; *vt* temere.

dreadful ['dredful] *a* terribile.

dreadnought ['drednɔ:t] *n* (*naut*) supercorazzata.

dream [dri:m] *n* sogno: *vti* sognare.

dreamer ['dri:mə] *n* sognatore.

dreamy ['dri:mi] *a* sognante, vago.

dreary ['driəri] *a* triste, cupo.

dredge [dredʒ] *n* draga; *vt* dragare; (*with flour, sugar etc*) spolverizzare (di).

dregs [dregz] *n pl* feccia, fondo, sedimento.

drench [drentʃ] *vt* bagnare, inzuppare; **drenching rain** pioggia dirotta.

dress [dres] *n* abito, vestito, veste, modo di vestirsi; *vti* vestire, vestirsi; (*mil*) allineare; medicare; (*dish*) guarnire.

dresser ['dresə] *n* assistente chirurgo; (*theat*) vestiarista; credenza, dispensa; toletta.

dressing ['dresiŋ] *a* abbigliamento; medicazione; condimento.

dressing-gown ['dresiŋgaun] *n* vestaglia.

dressmaker ['dres,meikə] *n* sarta.

dribble ['dribl] *n* gocciolamento; bava; (*football*) palleggio; *vi* gocciolare; sbavare; (*football*) palleggiare, dribblare.

drift [drift] *n* spinta, direzione, velocità; deriva; *vti* lasciarsi trasportare, andare alla deriva, ammucchiare.

drifter ['driftə] *n* (*naut*) motopeschereccio con tramaglio.

drill [dril] *n* (*mech*) perforatrice, trapano; (*mil*) esercitazioni *pl*; *vt* trapanare; esercitare; *vi* fare esercitazioni.

driller ['drilə] *n* macchina perforatrice.

drilling ['driliŋ] *n* trapanazione; (*mil*) esercitazione; **d. machine** trapano.

drink [driŋk] *n* bevanda, bibita; intemperanza nel bere; *vti* bere.

drinkable ['driŋkəbl] *a* bevibile, potabile.

drinking ['driŋkiŋ] *a* da bere, potabile; *n* il bere, alcoolismo.

drip [drip] *n* gocciolamento, stillicidio; *vi* gocciolare.

dripping ['dripiŋ] *n* grasso sciolto di carne.

drive [draiv] *n* passeggiata in carrozza o in auto; viale; spinta, propulsione; (*aut*) guida; *vt* condurre, guidare; costringere; trasportare; *vi* andare in carrozza, in auto.

drivel ['drivl] *n* bava, saliva; insulsaggine; *vi* sbavare; parlare da sciocco.

driver ['draivə] *n* autista, conducente, conduttore, guidatore, vetturino.

driving ['draiviŋ] *a* propulsore; dinamico; sferzante; **d. rain** pioggia sferzante; *n* (*aut*) guida; (*mech*) comando; **d. school** scuola guida; **d. wheel** (*aut*) volante.

drizzle ['drizl] *n* pioggerella; *vi* piovigginare.

droll [droul] *a* buffo, divertente.

drollery ['drouləri] *n* buffoneria.

dromedary ['drɔmədəri] *n* dromedario.

drone [droun] *n* (*bee*) fuco; ronzio; fannullone; *vi* ronzare, parlare con tono monotono.

droop [dru:p] *n* portamento curvo; accasciamento; *vi* pendere, curvarsi, abbassare, languire.

drop [drɔp] *n* goccia, goccio; caduta; (*prices*) ribasso; (*temperature*) abbassamento; *vt* lasciar cadere; *vi* cadere, diminuire.

dropper ['drɔpə] *n* contagocce.

dropsy ['drɔpsi] *n* (*med*) idropisia.

dross [drɔs] *n* scoria; (*fig*) rifiuto.

drought [draut] *n* siccità.

drove [drouv] *n* branco, gregge, mandria.

drover ['drouvə] *n* mandriano.

drown [draun] *vti* affogare, annegare; **drowning** annegamento, sommersione.

drowse [drauz] *vi* assopirsi, sonnecchiare.

drowsiness ['drauzinis] *n* sonnolenza.

drowsy ['drauzi] *a* sonnolento.

drudge [drʌdʒ] *n* schiavo; sgobbone.

drudge [drʌdʒ] *vi* sfacchinare.
drudgery ['drʌdʒəri] *n* lavoro faticoso, ingrato.
drug [drʌg] *n* droga, prodotto farmaceutico; stupefacente; **drugstore** (US) farmacia.
druggist ['drʌgist] *n* (US) farmacista.
drum [drʌm] *n* tamburo; (*anat*) timpano; (*mech*) rullo; *vi* suonare il tamburo, tamburellare; *vt* inculcare.
drummer ['drʌmə] *n* tamburino, batterista; (US) viaggiatore di commercio; propagandista.
drunk [drʌŋk] *a* ubriaco.
drunkard ['drʌŋkəd] *n* ubriacone.
drunken ['drʌŋkən] *a* ubriaco.
drunkenness ['drʌŋkənnis] *n* ubriachezza.
dry [drei] *a* asciutto, arido, secco; privo d'interesse; *vt* asciugare, seccare, esaurire; *vi* evaporare completamente, seccarsi; **to d. clean** lavare a secco; **d.-goods store** (US) negozio di tessuti.
dryly ['draili] *ad* seccamente.
dryness ['drainis] *n* aridità, secchezza.
dual ['djuːəl] *a* doppio, duplice; **d. carriageway** strada a doppia carreggiata.
dub [dʌb] *vt* (*cin*) doppiare; **dubbing** *n* doppiaggio.
dubious ['djuːbiəs] *a* dubbio, equivoco, incerto.
Dublin ['dʌblin] *n* Dublino.
duchess ['dʌtʃis] *n* duchessa.
duchy ['dʌtʃi] *n* ducato.
duck [dʌk] *n* anitra, anatra; *vti* immerger(si), tuffar(si); *vi* abbassare il capo improvvisamente.
duckling ['dʌkliŋ] *n* anatroccolo.
duct [dʌkt] *n* canale, tubo, condotto; (*anat*) vaso.
due [djuː] *a* dovuto, debito, adeguato; *n* dovuto, quota, tassa; **to be d.** dover arrivare.
duel ['djuːəl] *n* duello.
duet [djuː'et] *n* duetto.
duke [djuːk] *n* duca.
dukedom ['djuːkdəm] *n* ducato.
dull [dʌl] *a* tardo, lento; (*colour*) smorto; (*sound*) sordo; triste, monotono; *vt* intorpidire, smorzare, istupidire.
dullard ['dʌləd] *n* individuo ottuso.
dullness ['dʌlnis] *n* lentezza, mancanza di vivacità, monotonia, ottusità.
duly ['djuːli] *ad* debitamente, a tempo debito.
dumb [dʌm] *a* muto; **dumbwaiter** (US) montavivande.
dumbfound [dʌm'faund] *vt* stupefare, confondere.
dumbness ['dʌmnis] *n* mutismo.
dummy ['dʌmi] *n* fantoccio, manichino, uomo di paglia; **baby's d.** succhiotto, tettarella.
dump [dʌmp] *n* deposito di rifiuti;

(*mil*) deposito di munizioni; *vt* scaricare.
dumpling ['dʌmpliŋ] *n* grossa polpetta di pasta bollita; (*sl*) individuo, animale piccolo e rotondetto.
dumpy ['dʌmpi] *a* tarchiato, tozzo.
dun [dʌn] *n* grigio scuro; *n* creditore importuno; *vt* domandare insistentemente il pagamento.
dunce [dʌns] *n* ignorante, stupido.
dune [djuːn] *n* duna.
dung [dʌŋ] *n* letame, sterco.
dungarees [,dʌŋgə'riːz] *n pl* tuta.
dungeon ['dʌndʒən] *n* prigione sotterranea, segreta.
dupe [djuːp] *n* credulone, gonzo; *vt* gabbare, ingannare.
duplicate ['djuːplikit] *a n* duplicato; *vt* ['djuːplikeit] duplicare.
duplicator ['djuːplikeitə] *n* copialettere.
duplicity [djuː'plisiti] *n* doppiezza.
durability [,djuərə'biliti] *n* durabilità.
durable ['djuərəbl] *a* durevole.
duration [djuə'reiʃən] *n* durata.
duress [djuə'res] *n* costrizione, violenza, imprigionamento.
during ['djuəriŋ] *prep* durante.
dusk [dʌsk] *n* crepuscolo.
dusky ['dʌski] *a* oscuro, fosco.
dust [dʌst] *n* polvere; *vt* spolverare; impolverare, cospargere di.
duster ['dʌstə] *n* strofinaccio.
dusting ['dʌstiŋ] *n* spolverare, spolveratura; (*fig*) bastonatura.
dustman ['dʌstmən] *pl* **dustmen** *n* spazzino, spazzaturaio.
dusty ['dʌsti] *a* polveroso.
Dutch [dʌtʃ] *a n* olandese.
dutiful ['djuːtiful] *a* ubbidiente, rispettoso.
duty ['djuːti] *n* dovere; rispetto; servizio; imposta, tassa.
dwarf [dwɔːf] *a n* nano; *vt* rimpicciolire.
dwell [dwel] *vi* dimorare, abitare; soffermarsi.
dwelling ['dweliŋ] *n* abitazione, dimora.
dwindle ['dwindl] *vi* consumarsi, rimpicciolirsi.
dye [dai] *n* tintura, tinta; *vt* tingere; *vi* tingersi, prendere il colore di.
dyer ['daiə] *n* tintore.
dying ['daiiŋ] *a* morente, moribondo.
dynamic [dai'næmik] *a* dinamico; **dynamics** *n pl* dinamica.
dynamite ['dainəmait] *n* dinamite.
dynamo ['dainəmou] *pl* **dynamos** *n* dinamo.
dynasty ['dinəsti] *n* dinastia.
dysentery ['disntri] *n* dissenteria.
dyspepsia [dis'pepsiə] *n* dispepsia.

E

each [i:tʃ] *a pron* ciascuno, ogni, ognuno; **e. other** l'un l'altro.

eager ['i:gə] *a* ardente, avido.

eagerly ['i:gəli] *ad* ardentemente, avidamente.

eagerness ['i:gənis] *n* premura, ansia, brama.

eagle ['i:gl] *n* aquila.

ear [iə] *n* orecchio, orecchia; spiga.

earl [ə:l] *n* conte dell'aristocrazia inglese.

earldom ['ə:ldəm] *n* contea.

earliness ['ə:linis] *n* ora mattutina; precocità.

early ['ə:li] *a* primo; mattutino, prossimo, prematuro; *ad* di buon'ora, presto.

earn [ə:n] *vt* guadagnare, meritare.

earnest ['ə:nist] *a* serio, fervido; *n* anticipo, caparra, pegno; **in e.** seriamente, sul serio.

earnestness ['ə:nistnis] *n* serietà.

earnings ['ə:niŋz] *n pl* guadagni *pl.*

ear-ring ['iə:riŋ] *n* orecchino.

earth [ə:θ] *n* terra, suolo; tana; **e. wire** (*el*) filo di terra.

earthen ['ə:θən] *a* di terra, di terracotta.

earthenware ['ə:θənwεə] *n* terraglia.

earthly ['ə:θli] *a* terreno, terrestre.

earthquake ['ə:θkweik] *n* terremoto.

earthworm ['ə:θwə:m] *n* lombrico.

earthy ['ə:θi] *a* di terra, terroso; grossolano.

earwig ['iəwig] *n* forfecchia.

ease [i:z] *n* agio, comodo, riposo; *vt* calmare, dar sollievo a, allentare, alleggerire.

easel ['i:zl] *n* cavalletto.

easily ['i:zili] *ad* facilmente, comodamente.

easiness ['i:zinis] *n* disinvoltura, facilità.

east [i:st] *n* est, oriente; *a* orientale.

Easter ['i:stə] *n* Pasqua.

easterly ['i:stəli] *a* (*vento, direzione*) d'est, dell'est.

eastern ['i:stən] *a* orientale, dell'est.

eastward ['i:stwəd] *a ad* est, verso est.

easy ['i:zi] *a* agevole, comodo, disinvolto, facile.

eat [i:t] *vti* mangiare.

eatable ['i:təbl] *a* mangiabile; *a n* commestibile.

eating ['i:tiŋ] *a* che consuma, (*fig*) che rode; *n* il mangiare.

eaves [i:vz] *n pl* gronda.

eavesdrop ['i:vzdrop] *vi* origliare.

ebb [eb] *n* riflusso; **e.-tide** bassa marea; *vi* rifluire, abbassarsi.

ebony ['ebəni] *a* d'ebano; *n* ebano.

eccentric [ik'sentrik] *a n* eccentrico.

eccentricity [,eksen'trisiti] *n* eccentricità.

ecclesiastic [i,kli:zi'æstik] *a n* ecclesiastico.

echelon ['eʃələn] *n* (*mil*) scaglione.

echo ['ekou] *n* eco; *vt* ripetere; *vi* echeggiare.

eclectic [ek'lektik] *a n* eclettico.

eclipse [i'klips] *n* eclissi; *vt* eclissare.

economic [,i:ke'nɔmik] *a* economico; **economical** economico, economo; **economics** *n pl* economia, scienze economiche.

economist [i:'kɔnəmist] *n* economista.

economize [i:'kɔnəmaiz] *vti* economizzare.

economy [i:'kɔnəmi] *n* economia.

ecstasy ['ekstəsi] *n* estasi.

ecstatic [eks'tætik] *a* estatico.

eczema ['eksimə] *n* eczema.

eddy ['edi] *n* vortice; *vi* girar vorticosamente, turbinare.

Eden ['i:dn] *n* Eden, Paradiso Terrestre.

Edgar ['edgə] *nm pr* Edgardo.

edge [edʒ] *n* bordo, margine, orlo, filo tagliente; *vt* bordare, orlare; *vi* avanzare obliquamente; **to be on e.** avere i nervi tesi.

edgeways ['edʒweiz] **edgewise** ['edʒwaiz] *ad* di taglio; a mala pena.

edgy ['edʒi] *a* affilato, tagliente; (*fig*) nervoso.

edible ['edibl] *a* commestibile, mangereccio.

edict ['i:dikt] *n* editto.

edification [,edifi'keiʃən] *n* edificazione.

edifice ['edifis] *n* edificio.

edify ['edifai] *vt* (*fig*) edificare.

edifying ['edifaiiŋ] *a* edificante.

Edinburgh ['edinbərə] *n* Edimburgo.

edit ['edit] *vt* curare l'edizione di; (*cin*) curare il montaggio.

edition [i'diʃən] *n* edizione.

editor ['editə] *n* editore, direttore, redattore d'un giornale *etc.*

editorial [,edi'tɔ:riəl] *a* editoriale, redazionale; *n* articolo di fondo.

educate ['edju:keit] *vt* istruire, educare.

education [,edju:'keiʃən] *n* istruzione.

educational [,edju:'keiʃənl] *a* educativo.

Edward ['edwəd] *nm pr* Edoardo.

eel [i:l] *n* anguilla.

eerie ['iəri] *a* misterioso, che ispira paura, soprannaturale.

efface [i'feis] *vt* cancellare.

effect [i'fekt] *n* effetto, conseguenza; significato; **effects** *pl* beni, effetti, oggetti personali *pl*; *vt* effettuare, compiere.

effective [i'fektiv] *a* efficace, effettivo.

effectively [i'fektivli] *ad* efficacemente, effettivamente.

effectual [i'fektjuəl] *a* efficace, valido.

effectuate [i'fektjueit] *vt* effettuare.

effeminacy [i'feminəsi] *n* effeminatezza.

effeminate [i'feminit] *a* effeminato.

effervesce [.efə'ves] *vi* essere effervescente, spumare.

effervescence [.efə'vesns] *n* effervescenza.

effervescent [.efə'vesnt] *a* effervescente; vivace, spumeggiante.

effete [e'fi:t] *a* indebolito, esausto.

efficacious [.efi'keiʃəs] *a* efficace.

efficacy ['efikəsi] *n* efficacia.

efficiency [i'fiʃənsi] *n* efficienza.

efficient [i'fiʃənt] *a* efficiente.

efficiently [i'fiʃəntli] *ad* con competenza, efficacemente.

effigy ['efidʒi] *n* effigie.

effort ['efət] *n* sforzo.

effortless ['efətlis] *a* senza sforzo, agevole, piano; passivo.

effrontery [e'frʌntəri] *n* sfrontatezza.

effusion [i'fju:ʒən] *n* effusione.

effusive [i'fju:siv] *a* espansivo, esuberante.

egg [eg] *n* uovo; *vt* incitare, istigare; eggcup porta-uovo.

egoism ['egouizəm] *n* egoismo.

egoist ['egouist] *n* egoista.

egotism ['egoutizəm] *n* egotismo.

egotist ['egoutist] *n* egotista.

Egypt ['i:dʒipt] *n* Egitto.

Egyptian [i'dʒipʃən] *a n* egiziano.

eight [eit] *a n* otto; eighth *a n* ottavo.

eighteen ['ei'ti:n] *a n* diciotto; eighteenth *a n* diciottesimo.

eighty ['eiti] *a n* ottanta; eightieth *a n* ottantesimo.

Eire ['ɛərə] *n* Irlanda.

either ['aiðə] *a pron* l'uno o l'altro, ognuno dei due; *ad* neanche, nemmeno; e. . . . or *cj* o . . . o.

ejaculate [i'dʒækjuleit] *vt* emettere; *vi* esclamare.

ejaculation [i.dʒækju'leiʃən] *n* esclamazione.

eject [i:'dʒekt] *vt* emettere, espellere.

elaborate [i'læbərit] *a* elaborato; *vt* [i'læbəreit] elaborare.

elaboration [i.læbə°'reiʃən] *n* elaborazione.

elapse [i'læps] *vi* passare, trascorrere.

elastic [i'læstik] *a n* elastico.

elasticity [.elæs'tisiti] *n* elasticità.

elate [i'leit] *vt* esaltare, inebriare.

elation [i'leiʃən] *n* esaltazione, esultanza.

elbow ['elbou] *n* gomito; *vt* prendere a gomitate; *vi* farsi largo a gomitate; e. room spazio, agio.

elder ['eldə] *a* più vecchio, maggiore; *n* maggiore; dignitario della chiesa; (*bot*) sambuco.

elderly ['eldəli] *a* anziano.

Eleanor ['elinə] *nf pr* Eleonora.

elect [i'lekt] *a* eletto, scelto; *vti* eleggere, scegliere.

election [i'lekʃən] *n* elezione.

elector [i'lektə] *n* elettore.

electoral [i'lektərəl] *a* elettorale.

electorate [i'lektərit] *n* elettorato, elettori *pl*.

electric [i'lektrik] *a* elettrico; e. fire heater stufa elettrica.

electrical [i'lektrikəl] *a* elettrico.

electrician [ilek'triʃən] *n* elettricista.

electricity [ilek'trisiti] *n* elettricità.

electrification [i.lektrifi'keiʃən] *n* elettrificazione.

electrify [i'lektrifai] *vt* elettrificare; elettrizzare.

electrocardiogram [i'lektrou'kɑːdiogram] *n* elettrocardiogramma.

electrocute [i'lektrəkjuːt] *vt* fulminare; giustiziare sulla sedia elettrica.

electrocution [i.lektrə'kjuːʃən] *n* elettroesecuzione.

electronic [ilek'trɔnik] *a* elettronico.

electronics [ilek'trɔniks] *n* elettronica.

elegance ['eligəns] *n* eleganza.

elegant ['eligənt] *a* elegante.

elegy ['elidʒi] *n* elegia.

element ['elimənt] *n* elemento.

elemental [.eli'mentl] *a* degli elementi; fondamentale.

elementary [.eli'mentəri] *a* elementare, rudimentale.

elephant ['elifənt] *n* elefante.

elevate ['eliveit] *vt* elevare, innalzare.

elevation [.eli'veiʃən] *n* elevazione.

elevator [.eli'veitə] *n* ascensore, montacarichi.

eleven [i'levn] *a n* undici; eleventh *a n* undicesimo.

elf [elf] *n* elfo, folletto.

Elia(h) Elias ['iːliə, i'laiəs] *nm pr* Elia.

elicit [i'licit] *vt* tirar fuori, attirare.

elide [i'laid] *vt* elidere.

eligibility [.elidʒə'biliti] *n* eleggibilità.

eligible ['elidʒəbl] *a* eleggibile, desiderabile.

eliminate [i'limineit] *vt* eliminare.

elimination [i.limi'neiʃən] *n* eliminazione.

elision [i'liʒən] *n* elisione.

Elizabeth [i'lizəbəθ] *nf pr* Elisabetta.

Elizabethan [i.lizə'bi:θən] *a* elisabetiano.

elk [elk] *n* alce.

ellipse [i'lips] *n* ellisse.

ellipsis [i'lipsis] *pl* ellipses *n* ellissi.

elliptic(al) [i'liptik(əl)] *a* ellittico.

elm [elm] *n* olmo.

elocution [.elə'kjuːʃən] *n* elocuzione.

elongate ['iːlɔŋgeit] *vti* allungar(si); prolungare.

elope [i'loup] *vi* fuggire (con un amante).

elopement [i'loupmənt] *n* fuga di amanti.

eloquence ['eləkwəns] *n* eloquenza.

eloquent ['eləkwənt] *a* eloquente.

eloquently ['eləkwəntli] *ad* con eloquenza, con calore.

else [els] *ad* altrimenti; *a* altro.

elsewhere ['els'wɛə] *ad* altrove.

elucidate [i'luːsideit] *vt* delucidare, chiarire.

elucidation [i‚lu:si'deiʃən] n delucidazione, (s)chiarimento.

elude [i'lu:d] vt eludere, sfuggire a.

elusive [i'lu:siv] a evasivo, sfuggevole.

emaciate [i'meiʃieit] vt emaciare, far dimagrire.

emaciation [i‚meisi'eiʃən] n macilenza.

emanate ['eməneit] vti emanare.

emanation [‚emə'neiʃən] n emanazione.

emancipate [i'mænsipeit] vt emancipare.

emancipation [i‚mænsi'peiʃən] n emancipazione.

Emanuel [i'mænjuəl] nm pr Emanuele.

embalm [im'ba:m] vt imbalsamare.

embankment [im'bæŋkmənt] n argine, diga.

embargo [em'ba:gou] n embargo.

embark [im'ba:k] vti imbarcar(si); (fig) intraprendere.

embarkation [emba:'keiʃən] n imbarco.

embarrass [im'bærəs] vt imbarazzare.

embarrassing [im'bærəsiŋ] a imbarazzante.

embarrassment [im'bærəsmənt] n imbarazzo.

embassy ['embəsi] n ambiasciata.

embellish [im'beliʃ] vt abbellire.

embellishment [im'beliʃmənt] n abbellimento.

ember ['embə] n (usu pl) brace, ceneri ardenti pl; e. days i tre giorni di digiuno delle quattro Tempora.

embezzle [im'bezl] vt appropriarsi fraudolentemente.

embezzlement [im'bezlmənt] n appropriazione indebita.

embitter [im'bitə] vt amareggiare, inasprire.

emblem ['embləm] n emblema, simbolo.

embody [im'bodi] vt incarnare, personificare; includere.

embolden [im'bouldən] vt incoraggiare, imbaldanzire.

embolism ['embəlizəm] n (med) embolia.

emboss [im'bos] vt ornare con rilievi.

embrace [im'breis] n abbraccio; vt abbracciare; comprendere.

embrasure [im'breiʒə] n (mil) feritoia; (arch) strombatura di porta (o finestra).

embroider [im'broidə] vt ricamare.

embroidery [im'broidəri] n ricamo.

embroil [im'broil] vt imbrogliare.

embryo ['embriou] pl **embryos** n embrione.

emerald ['emərəld] n smeraldo.

emerge [i'mə:dʒ] vi emergere; sbucare.

emergence [i'mə:dʒəns] n emersione, apparizione improvvisa.

emergency [i'mə:dʒənsi] n emergenza.

emergent [i'mə:dʒənt] a emergente, sorgente.

emery ['eməri] n smeriglio; e. paper carta smerigiata.

emetic [i'metik] a n emetico.

emigrant ['emigrənt] a n emigrante.

emigrate ['emigreit] vi emigrare.

emigration [‚emi'greiʃən] n emigrazione.

Emily ['emili] nf pr Emilia.

eminence ['eminəns] n eminenza; altura.

eminent ['eminənt] a eminente.

emissary ['emisəri] a n emissario.

emission [i'miʃən] n emissione.

emit [i'mit] vt emettere.

Emmanuel [i'mænjuəl] nm pr Emanuele.

emollient [i'moliənt] a n emolliente.

emolument [i'moljumənt] n emolumento.

emotion [i'mouʃən] n commozione, emozione.

emotional [i'mouʃənəl] a emotivo, impressionabile, commovente.

emperor ['empərə] n imperatore.

emphasis ['emfəsis] n enfasi.

emphasize ['emfəsaiz] vt dare enfasi a, mettere in rilievo, sottolineare.

emphatic [im'fætik] a enfatico.

empire ['empaiə] n impero.

empirical [em'pirikəl] a empirico.

employ [im'ploi] n impiego; vt impiegare.

employee [‚emploi'i:] n impiegato.

employer [im'ploiə] n datore di lavoro, padrone.

employment [im'ploimənt] n impiego, occupazione.

emporium [em'po:riəm] n emporio.

empower [im'pauə] vt autorizzare.

empress ['empris] n imperatrice.

emptiness ['emptinis] n vuoto, vacuità.

empty ['empti] a vuoto, vacante; n pl i vuoti; to return the empties restituire i vuoti; vti vuotar(si).

emulate ['emjuleit] vt emulare.

emulation [‚emju'leiʃən] n emulazione.

emulsion [i'mʌlʃən] n emulsione.

enable [i'neibl] vt mettere in grado (di), permettere.

enact [i'nækt] vt mettere in atto; recitare.

enactment [i'næktmənt] n decreto, legge.

enamel [i'næməl] n smalto; vt smaltare.

enamour [i'næmə] vt innamorare.

encamp [in'kæmp] vti accampar(si).

encampment [in'kæmpmənt] n accampamento.

enchant [in'tʃa:nt] vt incantare.

enchanter [in'tʃa:ntə] n incantatore, mago.

enchanting [in'tʃa:ntiŋ] a incantevole, affascinante.

enchantment [in'tʃɑːntmənt] n incantesimo, incanto.

enchantress [in'tʃɑːntris] n incantatrice, maga.

encircle [in'səːkl] vt accerchiare.

enclose [in'klouz] vt accludere; rinchiudere, circondare.

enclosure [in'klouʒə] n recinto; (com) allegato.

encompass [in'kʌmpəs] vt circondare, abbracciare.

encore [ɔŋ'kɔː] interj n bis; vt chiedere il bis (di).

encounter [in'kauntə] n incontro; scontro; vt incontrare, affrontare.

encourage [in'kʌridʒ] vt incoraggiare.

encouragement [in'kʌridʒmənt] n incoraggiamento.

encroach [in'kroutʃ] vi intromettersi illegalmente, usurpare i diritti altrui.

encroachment [in'kroutʃmənt] n usurpazione, abuso.

encumber [in'kʌmbə] vt ingombrare, gravare.

encumbrance [in'kʌmbrəns] n impedimento, ingombro; ipoteca.

encyclical [en'siklikəl] a (eccl) enciclico; n (eccl) enciclica.

encyclopaedia [en,saiklou'piːdiə] n enciclopedia.

end [end] n fine; scopo; morte; estremità; vti finire.

endanger [in'deindʒə] vt mettere in pericolo.

endear [en'diə] vt rendere caro.

endearing [en'diəriŋ] a tenero, affettuoso.

endearment [en'diəmənt] n tenerezza, carezza; term of e. vezzeggiativo.

endeavour [in'devə] n sforzo, tentativo; vi sforzarsi, tentare.

endemic [en'demik] a endemico.

ending ['endiŋ] n conclusione, termine; (gram) desinenza.

endive ['endiv] n indivia.

endless ['endlis] a interminabile.

endorse [in'dɔːs] vt firmare, girare, confermare, sanzionare.

endorsement [in'dɔːsmənt] n (com) girata; approvazione.

endow [in'dau] vt dotare.

endowment [in'daumənt] n dotazione; dote, pregio.

endurance [in'djuərəns] n resistenza, pazienza, sopportazione.

endure [in'djuə] vt sopportare, tollerare; vi durare, continuare.

enduring [in'djuəriŋ] a tollerante, paziente; durevole.

enema ['enimə] n clistere.

enemy ['enimi] a n nemico.

energetic [,enə'dʒetik] a energico.

energy ['enədʒi] n energia.

enervate ['enəːveit] vt snervare.

enfeeble [in'fiːbl] vt indebolire.

enfold [in'fould] vt avvolgere, abbracciare.

enforce [in'fɔːs] vt imporre, far osservare.

enforcement [in'fɔːsmənt] n imposizione; applicazione.

enfranchise [in'fræntʃaiz] vt affrancare, liberare; dare il diritto di voto.

enfranchisement [in'fræntʃizmənt] n affrancamento, liberazione.

engage [in'geidʒ] vt impegnare, prenotare; assumere in servizio; vi entrare in, occuparsi di, impegnarsi.

engaged [in'geidʒd] a impegnato; fidanzato; occupato.

engagement [in'geidʒmənt] n impegno; fidanzamento.

engaging [in'geidʒiŋ] a attraente.

engender [in'dʒendə] vt generare, produrre.

engine ['endʒin] n macchina, motore.

engineer [,endʒi'niə] n ingegnere; (US) macchinista; (mil) soldato del Genio.

engineer [,endʒi'niə] vt (fam) macchinare, architettare.

engineering [,endʒi'niəriŋ] n ingegneria.

England ['iŋglənd] n Inghilterra.

English ['iŋgliʃ] a n inglese; **Englishman** Inglese.

engrave [in'greiv] vt incidere; (fig) imprimere.

engraving [in'greiviŋ] n incisione.

engross [in'grous] vt assorbire (attenzione); to become **engrossed** astrarsi.

engulf [in'gʌlf] vt inghiottire, sommergere.

enhance [in'hɑːns] vt aumentare, intensificare.

enigma [i'nigmə] n enigma.

enigmatic [,enig'mætik] a enigmatico.

enjoin [in'dʒɔin] vt ingiungere, ordinare.

enjoy [in'dʒɔi] vt divertirsi, godere.

enjoyable [in'dʒɔiəbl] a piacevole, divertente.

enjoyment [in'dʒɔimənt] n godimento, piacere.

enlarge [in'lɑːdʒ] vt espandere, estendere, ingrandire; vi allargarsi; dilungarsi.

enlargement [in'lɑːdʒmənt] n allargamento, ingrandimento.

enlighten [in'laitn] vt (fig) illuminare.

enlightenment [in'laitnmənt] n spiegazione, schiarimento.

enlist [in'list] vti arruolar(si).

enlistment [in'listmənt] n arruolamento.

enliven [in'laivn] vt ravvivare.

enmity ['enmiti] n inimicizia, ostilità.

ennoble [i'noubl] vt nobilitare.

ennui [ɑː'nwi] n noia.

enormity [i'nɔːmiti] n enormità.

enormous [i'nɔːməs] a enorme.

enough [i'nʌf] a sufficiente; ad abbastanza, sufficientemente; n il necessario, sufficienza.

enquire [in'kwaiə] v **inquire**.

enrage [in'reidʒ] *vt* far arrabbiare, imbestialire.

enrapture [in'ræptʃə] *vt* estasiare, incantare.

enrich [in'ritʃ] *vt* arricchire.

enrol(l) [in'roul] *vt* iscrivere, registrare; arruolare.

enrolment [in'roulmənt] *n* iscrizione, registrazione; arruolamento.

enshrine [in'ʃrain] *vt* custodire come cosa sacra, rinchiudere.

ensign ['ensain] *n* bandiera, insegna.

enslave [in'sleiv] *vt* asservire, fare schiavo.

enslavement [in'sleivmənt] *n* asservimento, schiavitù.

ensnare [in'snɛə] *vt* irretire, prendere al laccio.

ensue [in'sju:] *vi* risultare, seguire.

ensure [in'ʃuə] *vt* assicurare.

entail [in'teil] *n* assegnazione, eredità inalienabile; *vt* comportare, implicare; intestare a.

entangle [in'tæŋgl] *vt* aggrovigliare, impegolare.

entanglement [in'tæŋglmənt] *n* groviglio, imbroglio.

enter ['entə] *vt* entrare; iscrivere; **to e. into** (*fig*) entrare in, iniziare.

enterprise ['entəpraiz] *n* impresa.

enterprising ['entəpraiziŋ] *a* intraprendente.

entertain [,entə'tein] *vt* divertire, intrattenere, ricevere; nutrire (sospetti).

entertaining [,entə'teiniŋ] *a* divertente, piacevole.

entertainment [,entə'teinmənt] *n* divertimento, trattenimento.

enthralling [in'θrɔ:liŋ] *a* ammaliante, incantevole.

enthusiasm [in'θju:ziæzəm] *n* entusiasmo.

enthusiast [in'θju:ziæst] *n* entusiasta.

enthusiastic [in,θju:zi'æstik] *a* entusiastico.

entice [in'tais] *vi* adescare, allettare.

enticement [in'taismənt] *n* seduzione, allettamento, lusinga.

enticing [in'taisiŋ] *a* seducente, attraente.

entire [in'taiə] *a* completo, intero.

entirely [in'taiəli] *ad* interamente, completamente.

entirety [in'tairəti] *n* interezza; integrità.

entitle [in'taitl] *vt* intitolare, aver diritto a.

entity ['entiti] *n* entità.

entomb [in'tu:m] *vt* inumare.

entombment [in'tu:mmənt] *n* inumazione.

entrails ['entreilz] *n pl* intestini, viscere *pl*.

entrance ['entrəns] *n* entrata, ingresso; **e. fee** tassa d'iscrizione.

entrance [in'tra:ns] *vt* incantare, estasiare.

entrap [in'træp] *vt* intrappolare, raggirare.

entreat [in'tri:t] *vt* implorare, supplicare.

entreaty [in'tri:ti] *n* preghiera, supplica.

entrench [in'trentʃ] *vt* trincerare.

entrenchment [in'trentʃmənt] *n* trinceramento.

entrust [in'trʌst] *vt* affidare, commettere.

entry ['entri] *n* entrata, ingresso, iscrizione, annotazione.

entwine [in'twain] *vt* intrecciare.

enumerate [i'nju:məreit] *vt* enumerare.

enunciate [i'nʌnsieit] *vt* enunciare.

enunciation [i,nʌnsi'eiʃən] *n* enunciazione.

envelop [in'veləp] *vt* avvolgere; (*mil*) accerchiare.

envelope ['enviloup] *n* busta, involucro.

enviable ['enviəbl] *a* invidiabile.

envious ['enviəs] *a* invidioso.

environment [in'vaiərənmənt] *n* ambiente.

environs [in'vaiərənz] *n pl* dintorni *pl*.

envisage [in'vizidʒ] *vt* immaginare, vedere, figurarsi.

envoy ['envɔi] *n* inviato, ministro plenipotenziario.

envy ['envi] *n* invidia; *vt* invidiare.

epaulet(te) ['epoulet] *n* (*mil*) spallina.

ephemeral [i'femərəl] *a* effimero, fuggevole.

epic ['epik] *a* epico; *n* epica.

epicure ['epikjuə] *n* epicureo.

epicurean [,epikjuə'ri:ən] *a* n epicureo.

epidemic [,epi'demik] *a* epidemico; *n* epidemia.

epigram ['epigræm] *n* epigramma.

epigraph ['epigra:f] *n* epigrafe.

epilepsy ['epilepsi] *n* epilessia.

epileptic [,epi'leptik] *a* n epilettico.

epilogue ['epilɔg] *n* epilogo.

Epiphany [i'pifəni] *n* Epifania.

episcopacy [i'piskəpəsi] *n* episcopato.

episcopal [i'piskəpəl] *a* episcopale.

episode ['episoud] *n* episodio.

epistle [i'pisl] *n* epistola.

epitaph ['epita:f] *n* epitaffio.

epithet ['epiθet] *n* epiteto.

epitome [i'pitəmi] *n* epitome, compendio.

epitomize [i'pitəmaiz] *vt* compendiare, riassumere.

epoch ['i:pɔk] *n* epoca.

equable ['ekwəbl] *a* equo.

equal ['i:kwəl] *a n* uguale; *vt* uguagliare.

equality [i:'kwɔliti] *n* uguaglianza.

equalize ['i:kwəlaiz] *vt* uguagliare, pareggiare.

equally ['i:kwəli] *ad* ugualmente.

equanimity [,i:kwə'nimiti] *n* equanimità.

equate [i'kweit] *vt* uguagliare; paragonare.

equation [i'kweiʃən] *n* equazione.

equator [i'kweitə] *n* equatore.

equatorial [ˌekwə'tɔːriəl] *a* equatoriale.

equerry [i'kweri] *n* scudiero.

equestrian [i'kwestriən] *a* equestre.

equilibrium [ˌiːkwi'libriəm] *n* equilibrio.

equinox [ˈiːkwinɔks] *n* equinozio.

equip [i'kwip] *vt* equipaggiare, attrezzare.

equipage [ˈekwipidʒ] *n* attrezzatura; equipaggio.

equipment [i'kwipmənt] *n* equipaggiamento, attrezzatura.

equitable [ˈekwitəbl] *a* equo, giusto.

equity [ˈekwiti] *n* equità.

equivalent [i'kwivələnt] *a n* equivalente.

equivocal [i'kwivəkəl] *a* ambiguo, equivoco, sospetto.

era [ˈiərə] *n* era.

eradicate [i'rædikeit] *vt* sradicare.

erase [i'reiz] *vt* cancellare, raschiare.

eraser [i'reizə] *n* raschietto; gomma per cancellare.

erasure [i'reiʒə] *n* cancellatura.

erect [i'rekt] *a* eretto, ritto; *vt* erigere, innalzare.

erection [i'rekʃən] *n* elevazione, erezione.

ermine [ˈəːmin] *n* ermellino.

Ernest [ˈəːnist] *nm pr* Ernesto.

erode [i'roud] *vt* erodere, consumare.

erosion [i'rouʒən] *n* erosione.

erotic [i'rɔtik] *a* erotico.

err [əː] *vi* errare, sbagliare.

errand [ˈerənd] *n* commissione, incarico.

errant [ˈerənt] *a* errante.

erratic [i'rætik] *a* irregolare; eccentrico; erratico.

erroneous [i'rouniəs] *a* erroneo, scorretto.

error [ˈerə] *n* errore, sbaglio; colpa.

erudite [ˈerjuːdait] *a* erudito.

erudition [ˌerjuː'diʃən] *n* erudizione.

erupt [i'rʌpt] *vi* (*volcano*) eruttare, entrare in eruzione.

eruption [i'rʌpʃən] *n* eruzione, scoppio.

erysipelas [ˌeri'sipiləs] *n* erisipela.

escalator [ˈeskəleitə] *n* scala meccanica; scala mobile.

escapade [ˌeskə'peid] *n* (*fig*) scappata.

escape [is'keip] *n* fuga, scampo, scappamento; *vti* fuggire; evitare; sfuggire.

escapism [is'keipizəm] *n* evasione (dalla realtà).

eschew [is'tʃuː] *vt* astenersi da, evitare.

escort [ˈeskɔːt] *n* scorta; [is'kɔːt] *vt* scortare.

Eskimo [ˈeskimou] *pl* **Eskimoes** *a n* esquimese.

especial [is'peʃəl] *a* speciale.

especially [is'peʃəli] *ad* specialmente, sopratutto.

espionage [ˌespiə'nɑːʒ] *n* spionaggio.

esplanade [ˌesplə'neid] *n* spianata; lungomare.

esquire [is'kwaiə] *n* signore (usato negli indirizzi dopo il cognome); **John Smith Esq.** Egregio Signor John Smith.

essay [ˈesei] *n* saggio; tema; prova; *vt* tentare, provare.

essence [ˈesns] *n* essenza.

essential [i'senʃəl] *a n* essenziale.

essentially [i'senʃəli] *ad* essenzialmente, fondamentalmente.

establish [is'tæbliʃ] *vt* stabilire, fondare, istituire; constatare; **established** stabilito, affermato.

establishment [is'tæbliʃmənt] *a* stabilimento, istituzione; ordine costituito; accertamento.

estate [is'teit] *n* tenuta, proprietà; stato.

esteem [is'tiːm] *n* considerazione, stima; *vt* considerare, stimare.

Esther [ˈestə] *nf pr* Ester.

estimable [ˈestiməbl] *a* stimabile, degno di stima.

estimate [ˈestimit] *n* stima, valutazione, preventivo; [ˈestimeit] *vt* stimare, valutare.

estimation [ˌesti'meiʃən] *n* stima, valutazione.

estrange [is'treindʒ] *vt* alienare, estraniare, inimicarsi.

estrangement [is'treindʒmənt] *n* alienazione, allontanamento.

estuary [ˈestjuəri] *n* estuario.

etch [etʃ] *vt* incidere all'acquaforte.

etching [ˈetʃiŋ] *n* acquaforte, incisione.

eternal [iː'təːnl] *a* eterno.

eternity [iː'təːniti] *n* eternità.

ether [ˈiːθə] *n* etere.

ethereal [iː'θiəriəl] *a* etereo.

ethics [ˈeθiks] *n* etica.

Ethiopia [ˌiːθi'oupiə] *n* Etiopia.

Ethiopian [ˌiːθi'oupiən] *a* etiopico, *n* etiope.

etiquette [ˌeti'ket] *n* etichetta.

Etna [ˈetnə] *n* Etna.

Etruscan [i'trʌskən] *a n* etrusco.

etymology [ˌeti'mɔlədʒi] *n* etimologia.

Eucharist [ˈjuːkərist] *n* Eucarestia.

Eugene [juː'ʒein] *nm pr* Eugenio.

eulogy [ˈjuːlədʒi] *n* elogio.

eunuch [ˈjuːnək] *n* eunuco.

euphemism [ˈjuːfimizəm] *n* eufemismo.

euphony [ˈjuːfəni] *n* eufonia.

Europe [ˈjuərəp] *n* Europa.

European [ˌjuərə'piːən] *a n* europeo.

euthanasia [ˌjuːθə'neiziə] *n* eutanasia.

evacuate [i'vækjueit] *vt* evacuare, sfollare.

evacuation [iˌvækju'eiʃən] *n* evacuazione, sfollamento.

evacuee [i vækjuː'iː] *n* sfollato.

evade [i'veid] *vt* evitare, schivare.

evaluate [i'væljueit] *vt* valutare.

evanescence [.i:və'nesns] *n* evanescenza.

evanescent [.i:və'nesnt] *a* evanescente.

evangelic(al) [.i:væn'dʒelikəl] *a* evangelico; **evangelist** *n* evangelista.

evaporate [i'væpəreit] *vti* (far) evaporare.

evaporation [i.væpə'reiʃən] *n* evaporazione.

evasion [i'veiʒən] *n* evasione, sotterfugio.

evasive [i'veisiv] *a* evasivo.

Eve [i:v] *nf pr* Eva.

eve [i:v] *n* vigilia.

even ['i:vən] *a* pari; uguale; piatto; uniforme; *ad* anche, perfino; *vt* uguagliare, uniformare.

evening ['i:vəniŋ] *n* sera.

evenly ['i:vənli] *ad* uniformemente; in parti uguali; pianamente; con calma.

evenness ['i:vənnis] *n* uguaglianza, uniformità.

event [i'vent] *n* avvenimento, evento.

eventful [i'ventful] *a* pieno di avvenimenti, memorabile.

eventual [i'ventjuəl] *a* finale, eventuale; **eventually** *ad* finalmente.

ever ['evə] *ad* mai, sempre.

evergreen ['evəgri:n] *a n* sempreverde.

everlasting [.evə'lɑ:stiŋ] *a* eterno; *n* eternità.

evermore [.evə'mɔ:] *ad* sempre; **for e.** per sempre.

every ['evri] *a* ogni, ciascuno, tutti; **e. now and then** di quando in quando; **e. other day** un giorno sì, e un giorno no.

everybody ['evribɔdi] **everyone** ['evriwʌn] *pron* ognuno, tutti *pl*.

everyday ['evridei] *a* di ogni giorno, quotidiano.

everything ['evriθiŋ] *pron* ogni cosa, tutto.

everywhere ['evriwɛə] *ad* in ogni luogo, ovunque.

evict [i:'vikt] *vt* espellere, sfrattare.

eviction [i:'vikʃən] *n* espulsione, sfratto.

evidence ['evidəns] *n* evidenza, prova, testimonianza; **to give e.** deporre.

evident ['evidənt] *a* evidente, chiaro.

evil ['i:vl] *a* cattivo, maligno, funesto; *ad* male; *n* male.

evince [i'vins] *vt* manifestare, dimostrare.

evocative [i:'vɔkətiv] *a* evocatore.

evoke [i'vouk] *vt* evocare.

evolution [.i:və'lu:ʃən] *n* evoluzione, sviluppo.

evolve [i'vɔlv] *vti* evolver(si).

ewe [ju:] *n* pecora (femmina).

ewer ['ju:ə] *n* brocca.

exact [ig'zækt] *a* esatto, preciso; *vt* esigere.

exacting [ig'zæktiŋ] *a* esigente, impegnativo.

exactitude [ig'zæktitju:d] **exactness** [ig'zæktnis] *n* esattezza, precisione.

exactly [ig'zæktli] *ad* esattamente; proprio; precisamente.

exaggerate [ig'zædʒəreit] *vt* esagerare.

exaggeration [ig.zædʒə'reiʃən] *n* esagerazione.

exalt [ig'zɔːlt] *vt* esaltare.

exaltation [.egzɔːl'teiʃən] *n* esaltazione.

examination [ig.zæmi'neiʃən] *n* esame; visita (medica).

examine [ig'zæmin] *vt* esaminare; visitare.

examiner [ig'zæminə] *n* esaminatore.

example [ig'zɑːmpl] *n* esempio.

exasperate [ig'zɑːspəreit] *vt* esasperare.

exasperation [ig.zɑːspə'reiʃən] *n* esasperazione.

excavate ['ekskəveit] *vt* scavare.

excavation [.ekskə'veiʃən] *n* scavo.

exceed [ik'si:d] *vti* eccedere, superare.

exceedingly [ik'si:diŋli] *ad* estremamente.

excel [ik'sel] *vi* eccellere, essere superiore a.

excellence ['eksələns] *n* eccellenza, superiorità.

excellency ['eksələnsi] *n* (titolo) eccellenza.

excellent ['eksələnt] *a* eccellente, ottimo.

except [ik'sept] *prep* eccetto, eccettuato, ad eccezione di, tranne; *vt* eccettuare; *vi* obiettare; **excepting** eccetto, tranne.

exception [ik'sepʃən] *n* eccezione, obiezione.

exceptional [ik'sepʃənl] *a* eccezionale.

exceptionally [ik'sepʃənəli] *ad* eccezionalmente, in via eccezionale.

excerpt ['eksəːpt] *n* estratto, citazione.

excess [ik'ses] *n* eccesso; **e. fare** supplemento.

excessive [ik'sesiv] *a* eccessivo, smoderato.

exchange [iks'tʃeindʒ] *n* cambio, scambio; borsa; (tel) centrale telefonica; *vt* (s)cambiare.

exchequer [iks'tʃekə] *n* Scacchiere, Tesoro, Fisco.

excise [ek'saiz] *n* imposta indiretta, dazio sul consumo.

exciseman [ek'saizmæn] *pl* **-men** *n* daziere.

excitable [ik'saitəbl] *a* eccitabile, impressionabile.

excite [ik'sait] *vt* eccitare, provocare, entusiasmare.

excitement [ik'saitmənt] *n* agitazione, eccitazione; trambusto.

exciting [ik'saitiŋ] *a* eccitante, emozionante.

exclaim [iks'kleim] *vi* esclamare.

exclamation [,eksklə'meiʃən] *n* esclamazione.

exclude [iks'klu:d] *vt* escludere.

exclusion [iks'klu:ʒən] *n* esclusione.

exclusive [iks'klu:siv] *a* esclusivo, scelto.

excommunicate [,eksə'mju:nikeit] *vt* scomunicare.

excommunication ['ekskə,mju:ni-'keiʃən] *n* scomunica.

excrement ['ekskrimənt] *n* escremento.

excrete [eks'kri:t] *vt* espellere, secernere.

excruciating [iks'kru:ʃieitiŋ] *a* atroce, lancinante.

excursion [iks'kə:ʃən] *n* escursione, gita.

excusable [iks'kju:zəbl] *a* scusabile, perdonabile.

excuse [iks'kju:z] *n* scusa, pretesto; *vt* scusare, perdonare, dispensare da.

execrable ['eksikrəbl] *a* esecrabile.

execrate ['eksikreit] *vt* esecrare.

execute ['eksikju:t] *vt* eseguire, mettere in esecuzione; giustiziare.

execution [,eksi'kju:ʃən] *n* esecuzione; sequestro.

executioner [,eksi'kju:ʃənə] *n* boia, carnefice.

executive [ig'zekjutiv] *a* esecutivo; *n* direzione, dirigente.

executor [ig'zekjutə] *n* esecutore.

exemplar [ig'zemplə] *n* esemplare, modello.

exemplary [ig'zempləri] *a* esemplare.

exemplify [ig'zemplifai] *vt* illustrare con esempi; fare copia autentica di.

exempt [ig'zempt] *a* esente; *vt* esentare.

exemption [ig'zempʃən] *n* esenzione.

exercise ['eksəsaiz] *n* esercizio, esercitazione; *vti* esercitar(si).

exert [ig'zə:t] *vt* esercitare, fare uso di; to e. oneself sforzarsi.

exertion [ig'zə:ʃən] *n* sforzo; impiego, uso.

exhalation [,ekshə'leiʃən] *n* esalazione.

exhale [eks'heil] *vt* esalare.

exhaust [ig'zɔ:st] *n* (*mech*) scarico, scappamento; *vt* esaurire, vuotare; (*gas etc*), aspirare; *vi* (*gas etc*) scaricarsi.

exhauster [ig'zɔ:stə] *n* aspiratore, ventilatore di scarico.

exhaustion [ig'zɔ:stʃən] *n* esaurimento.

exhaustive [ig'zɔ:stiv] *a* esauriente.

exhibit [ig'zibit] *n* oggetto mandato ad un'esposizione; (*leg*) reperto; *vt* esibire, esporre.

exhibition [,eksi'biʃən] *n* esibizione, esposizione, mostra; borsa di studio.

exhibitioner [,eksi'biʃənə] *n* chi usufruisce di una borsa di studio.

exhibitor [ig'zibitə] *n* espositore.

exhilarate [ig'ziləreit] *vt* esilarare.

exhilaration [ig,zilə'reiʃən] *n* eccitazione, entusiasmo, allegria.

exhort [ig'zɔ:t] *vt* esortare.

exhortation [,egzɔ:'teiʃən] *n* esortazione.

exigency [ek'sidʒənsi] *n* esigenza.

exigent ['eksidʒənt] *a* esigente.

exile ['eksail] *n* esilio; esule; *vt* bandire, esiliare.

exist [ig'zist] *vi* esistere.

existence [ig'zistəns] *n* esistenza.

existentialism [,egzis'tenʃəlizəm] *n* esistenzialismo.

existentialist [,egzis'tenʃəlist] *a n* esistenzialista.

existing [ig'zistiŋ] *a* esistente, attuale.

exit ['eksit] *n* uscita.

exodus ['eksədəs] *n* esodo.

exonerate [ig'zɔnəreit] *vt* esonerare.

exoneration [ig,zɔnə'reiʃən] *n* esonero.

exorbitant [ig'zɔ:bitənt] *a* esorbitante.

exorcism ['eksɔ:sizəm] *n* esorcismo.

exorcize ['eksɔ:saiz] *vt* esorcizzare.

exotic [eg'zɔtik] *a* esotico; *n* pianta esotica.

expand [iks'pænd] *vti* espander(si), sviluppar(si).

expanse [iks'pæns] *n* spazio, distesa.

expansion [iks'pænʃən] *n* espansione, estensione.

expansive [iks'pænsiv] *a* espansivo.

expatiate [eks'peiʃieit] *vi* diffondersi, spaziare.

expatriate [eks'pætrieit] *vt* espatriare.

expect [iks'pekt] *vt* aspettar(si); prevedere; supporre; sperare.

expectancy [iks'pektənsi] *n* aspettativa, attesa; aspettazione.

expectant [iks'pektənt] *a* in attesa; e. mother donna incinta.

expectation [,ekspek'teiʃən] *n* aspettativa, speranza.

expectorate [eks'pektəreit] *vt* espettorare.

expediency [iks'pi:diənsi] *n* convenienza, opportunità.

expedient [iks'pi:diənt] *a* conveniente; *n* espediente, mezzo ingegnoso.

expedite ['ekspidait] *vt* accelerare, sbrigare.

expedition [,ekspi'diʃən] *n* impresa, spedizione; prontezza.

expel [iks'pel] *vt* espellere, cacciare.

expend [iks'pend] *vt* consumare, spendere.

expenditure [iks'penditʃə] *n* spesa.

expense [iks'pens] *n* spesa.

expensive [iks'pensiv] *a* costoso, dispendioso.

experience [iks'piəriəns] *n* esperienza; *vt* provare, sperimentare.

experiment [iks'perimənt] *n* esperimento, prova; *vi* sperimentare.

experimental [eks,peri'mentl] *a* sperimentale.

expert ['ekspə:t] *a* abile, esperto; *n* esperto, perito, specialista.

expertise ['ekspə:ti:z] *n* abilità, pratica (di).

expertly ['ekspə:tli] *ad* espertamente, abilmente.

expiate ['ekspieit] *vt* espiare.

expiation [.ekspi'eifən] *n* espiazione.

expiration [.ekspaiə'reifən] *n* scadenza, termine.

expire [iks'paiə] *vti* scadere, spirare.

expiry [iks'paiəri] *n* termine, scadenza.

explain [iks'plein] *vti* spiegare.

explanation [.eksplə'neifən] *n* spiegazione, chiarimento.

explanatory [iks'plænətəri] *a* esplicativo, chiarificatore.

explicit [iks'plisit] *a* esplicito, chiaro.

explode [iks'ploud] *vti* (far) esplodere; (*fig*) rivelare la falsità di.

exploit ['eksplɔit] *n* gesta, impresa; [iks'plɔit] *vt* sfruttare, utilizzare.

exploitation [.eksplɔi'teifən] *n* sfruttamento, utilizzazione.

exploration [.eksplɔ:'reifən] *n* esplorazione.

explore [iks'plɔ:] *vt* esplorare.

explorer [iks'plɔ:rə] *n* esploratore, esploratrice.

explosion [iks'plouʒən] *n* esplosione, scoppio.

explosive [iks'plousiv] *a n* esplosivo.

exponent [eks'pounənt] *n* esponente, interprete.

export ['ekspɔ:t] *n* esportazione, genere esportabile; *vt* [eks'pɔ:t] esportare.

expose [iks'pouz] *vt* esporre, smascherare.

exposition [.ekspə'zifən] *n* esposizione.

expostulate [iks'pɔstjuleit] *vi* fare rimostranze, protestare.

expostulation [iks'pɔstju'leifən] *n* rimostranza, protesta.

exposure [iks'pouʒə] *n* esposizione, (*phot*) esposizione, posa; smascheramento, scandalo.

expound [iks'paund] *vt* commentare, spiegare.

express [iks'pres] *a* esplicito, espresso; *n* (*letter*) espresso; (*train*) direttissimo; *vt* esprimere; spremere; (*US*) spedire per espresso; **e. company** (*US*) servizio corriere.

expression [iks'prefən] *n* espressione.

expressive [iks'presiv] *a* espressivo.

expropriate [eks'prouprieit] *vt* espropriare.

expulsion [iks'pʌlfən] *n* espulsione.

expurgate ['ekspə:geit] *vt* (es)purgare.

expurgation [.ekspə:'geifən] *n* espurgazione.

exquisite ['ekskwizit] *a* squisito; (*pain*) acuto.

exquisiteness ['ekskwizitnis] *n* squisitezza.

ex-service ['eks'sə:vis] *a* che ha prestato servizio militare; **ex-serviceman** *n* ex-combattente.

extant [eks'tænt] *a* esistente ancora.

extemporary [iks'tempərəri] *a* estemporaneo, improvvisato.

extempore [eks'tempəri] *a* improvvisato, estemporaneo; *ad* estemporaneamente.

extemporize [iks'tempəraiz] *vt* improvvisare.

extend [iks'tend] *vti* estender(si); prolungare; prorogare; porgere.

extension [iks'tenfən] *n* estensione, prolungamento; proroga; **e. wire** (*US el*) filo flessibile.

extensive [iks'tensiv] *a* esteso, largo.

extensively [iks'tensivli] *ad* ampiamente, estensivamente.

extent [iks'tent] *n* estensione; grado; punto; portata.

extenuate [eks'tenjueit] *vt* attenuare, scusare.

extenuating [eks'tenjueitiŋ] *a* attenuante.

extenuation [eks.tenju'eifən] *n* attenuazione.

exterior [eks'tiəriə] *a n* esterno, esteriore.

exterminate [eks'tə:mineit] *vt* sterminare.

extermination [eks.tə:mi'neifən] *n* sterminio.

external [eks'tə:nl] *a n* esterno.

extinct [iks'tiŋkt] *a* estinto, spento.

extinction [iks'tiŋkfən] *n* estinzione.

extinguish [iks'tiŋgwif] *vt* estinguere, spegnere.

extinguisher [iks'tiŋgwifə] *n* spegnitoio, estintore.

extirpate ['ekstə:peit] *vt* estirpare.

extirpation [.ekstə:'peifən] *n* estirpazione.

extol [iks'tɔl] *vt* esaltare, estollere.

extort [iks'tɔ:t] *vt* estorcere.

extortion [iks'tɔ:fən] *n* estorsione.

extortionate [iks'tɔ:fnit] *a* (*price*) eccessivo, esorbitante.

extra ['ekstrə] *a* extra, straordinario; superiore; *ad* extra, in più; straordinariamente *n* extra; supplemento; (*theat*) comparsa; **e.-postage** soprattassa.

extract ['ekstrækt] *n* estratto; *vt* [iks'trækt] estrarre.

extraction [iks'trækfən] *n* estrazione, origine.

extradite ['ekstrədait] *vt* (*leg*) estradare.

extradition [.ekstrə'difən] *n* estradizione.

extraneous [eks'treiniəs] *a* estraneo.

extraordinary [iks'trɔ:dnri] *a* straordinario.

extrasensory ['ekstrə'sensəri] *a* al di là dei sensi.

extraterritorial ['ekstrə.teri'tɔ:riəl] *a* estraterritoriale.

extravagance [iks'trævigəns] *n* prodigalità; stravaganza.

extravagant [iks'trævigənt] *a* prodigo; stravagante.

extreme [iks'tri:m] *a n* estremo.

extremely [iks'tri:mli] *ad* estremamente.

extremism [iks'tri:mizəm] *n* (*pol*) estremismo.

extremity [iks'tremiti] *n* estremità; estremo; eccesso; estremo pericolo; bisogno; dolore.

extricate ['ekstrikeit] *vt* districare.

extrinsic [eks'trinsik] *a* estrinseco.

extrovert ['ekstrouvə:t] *n* estroverso.

exuberance [ig'zju:bərəns] *n* esuberanza.

exuberant [ig'zju:bərənt] *a* esuberante.

exult [ig'zʌlt] *vi* esultare.

exultation [,egzʌl'teiʃən] *n* esultanza.

eye [ai] *n* occhio; sguardo; vista.

eyeball ['aibɔ:l] *n* bulbo oculare.

eyebrow ['aibrau] *n* sopracciglio.

eyelash ['ailæʃ] *n* ciglio.

eyelid ['ailid] *n* palpebra.

eyesight ['aisait] *n* vista, potere visivo.

eyewitness ['æ,witnis] *n* testimonio oculare; *vt* guardare, osservare.

F

fable ['feibl] *n* favola.

fabric ['fæbrik] *n* tessuto; struttura.

fabricate ['fæbrikeit] *vt* inventare, (*fig*) fabbricare.

fabrication [,fæbri'keiʃən] *n* contraffazione, invenzione.

fabulous ['fæbjuləs] *a* favoloso.

façade [fə'sɑːd] *n* facciata.

face [feis] *n* faccia, viso; facciata; faccetta; (*of a watch*) quadrante; *vt* affrontare, fronteggiare; guardare verso.

facet ['fæsit] *n* sfaccettatura, faccetta.

facetious [fə'si:ʃəs] *a* faceto, gioviale.

facial ['feiʃəl] *a* facciale.

facile ['fæsail] *a* facile; scorrevole; superficiale; affrettato.

facilitate [fə'siliteit] *vt* facilitare, agevolare.

facility [fə'siliti] *n* facilità; destrezza; *pl* agevolazioni; attrezzature.

facing ['feisiŋ] *a* che sta di fronte; *n* (*buildings*) rivestimento; (*dress*) risvolto.

facsimile [fæk'simili] *n* facsimile.

fact [fækt] *n* fatto, realtà.

faction ['fækʃən] *n* fazione.

factious ['fækʃəs] *a* fazioso.

factor ['fæktə] *n* fattore.

factory ['fæktəri] *n* fabbrica, manifattura.

factual ['fæktjuəl] *a* effettivo, reale.

faculty ['fækəlti] *n* facoltà.

fad [fæd] *n* mania.

fade [feid] *n* (*cin*) dissolvenza; *vi* appassire; sbiadire; dileguarsi; svanire.

faded ['feidid] *a* appassito; sbiadito.

fag [fæg] *n* lavoro faticoso; (*sl*) sigaretta.

fag(g)ot ['fægət] *n* fascina.

fail [feil] *n* fallo; *vt* abbandonare; mancare a; bocciare; *vi* fallire; mancare, essere insufficiente; (*com*) fallire.

failing ['feiliŋ] *a* debole, scarso; *n* debolezza, difetto, mancanza; *prep* in mancanza di.

faille [feil] *n* faglia, tessuto di seta.

failure ['feiljə] *n* fallimento, fiasco, insuccesso; mancanza.

faint [feint] *a* debole, lieve, (*of colours*) pallido; *n* svenimento; *vi* svenire.

faintness ['feintnis] *n* debolezza, languore.

fair [fɛə] *a* bello; biondo; chiaro; sereno; giusto; leale; onesto; *ad* bene, onestamente; *n* fiera, mercato.

fairly ['fɛəli] *ad* lealmente; abbastanza.

fairness ['fɛənis] *n* bellezza; bianchezza, biondezza; onestà, equità.

fairy ['fɛəri] *a* fatato; *n* fata; **fairy tale** fiaba.

fairyland ['fɛərilænd] *n* paese delle fate.

faith [feiθ] *n* fede, fiducia.

faithful ['feiθful] *a* fedele, leale.

faithfully ['feiθfəli] *ad* fedelmente; **Yours f.** distinti saluti.

faithless ['feiθlis] *a* miscredente; sleale, falso.

fake [feik] *n* contraffazione, falso; *vti* falsificare; fingere.

falcon ['fɔ:lkən] *n* falcone.

fall [fɔ:l] *n* caduta; abbassamento; ribasso; rovina; cascata; (*US*) autunno; *vi* cadere; diminuire; toccare in sorte.

fallacious [fə'leiʃəs] *a* fallace.

fallacy ['fæləsi] *n* errore; sofisma; fallacia.

fallibility [,fæli'biliti] *n* fallibilità.

fallible ['fæləbl] *a* fallibile.

falling ['fɔ:liŋ] *a* cadente; *n* caduta; scadenza.

fall-out ['fɔ:laut] *n* pioggia radioattiva.

fallow ['fælou] *a* incolto; *n* maggese.

false [fɔ:ls] *a* falso, finto, ingannevole.

falsehood ['fɔ:lshud] *n* menzogna.

falsify ['fɔ:lsifai] *vt* falsificare.

falsity ['fɔ:lsiti] *n* falsità.

falter ['fɔ:ltə] *vi* balbettare; esitare; vacillare.

fame [feim] *n* fama.

famed [feimd] *a* rinomato, famoso, celebre.

familiar [fə'miljə] *a n* familiare.

familiarity [fə,mili'æriti] *n* familiarità.

familiarize [fə'miljəraiz] *vt* familiarizzare.

family ['fæmili] *n* famiglia; **f. name** cognome.

famine ['fæmin] *n* carestia.

famish ['fæmiʃ] *vti* affamare; morire di fame.

famous ['feiməs] *a* famoso, celebre.

fan [fæn] *n* ventaglio, ventilatore; (*sl*) tifoso d'uno sport; *vt* sventolare, ventilare; (*fig*) stimolare, alimentare.

fanatic [fə'nætik] *a n* fanatico.

fanaticism [fə'nætisizəm] *n* fanatismo.

fanciful ['fænsiful] *a* capriccioso, fantasioso; immaginario.

fancy ['fænsi] *n* fantasia, capriccio, desiderio; *vt* creare con la fantasia, immaginare, desiderare.

fanfare ['fænfeə] *n* fanfara.

fang [fæŋ] *n* zanna.

fantastic [fæn'tæstik] *a* fantastico.

fantasy ['fæntəsi] *n* fantasia, immaginazione.

far [faː] *a* lontano, remoto; *ad* a grande distanza; di gran lunga, molto; **so f.** fino a, fin qui; **faraway** lontano; **f.-fetched** esagerato, ricercato, stiracchiato; **f. off** molto lontano; **f.-reaching** di lunga portata.

farce [faːs] *n* farsa.

farcical ['faːsikəl] *a* farsesco.

fare [fɛə] *n* cibo, nutrimento; (*train etc*) prezzo di una corsa, passeggero; *vi* stare, trovarsi, vivere, mangiare.

farewell ['fɛə'wel] *n* addio.

farm [faːm] *n* fattoria, podere; **farmyard** aia; *vt* coltivare, prendere, dare in appalto; *vi* fare l'agricoltore.

farmer ['faːmə] *n* agricoltore, fittavolo.

farming ['faːmiŋ] *n* il lavoro dei campi; agricoltura; coltivazione.

farrier ['færiə] *n* maniscalco.

farther ['faːðə] *a* più lontano, ulteriore *ad* anche, inoltre, più a lungo; più lontano.

farthest ['faːðist] *a* il più lontano, estremo; *ad* più lontano.

farthing ['faːðiŋ] *n* quarto di 'penny'; (*fig*) cosa di nessun valore.

fascinate ['fæsineit] *vt* affascinare.

fascination [,fæsi'neiʃən] *n* fascino.

fascism ['fæʃizəm] *n* (*pol*) fascismo.

fascist ['fæʃist] *a n* fascista.

fashion ['fæʃən] *n* moda, modello; modo, stile; *vt* fare, foggiare, creare secondo un modello.

fashionable ['fæʃnəbl] *a* alla moda, di moda; elegante.

fast [faːst] *a* fermo, fisso, saldo; rapido, veloce; (*fig*) dissoluto; *n* astinenza, digiuno; *ad* rapidamente; fermamente, saldamente; *vi* digiunare.

fasten ['faːsn] *vt* assicurare, attaccare, fissare; *vi* attaccarsi.

fastener ['faːsnə] *n* chiusura, fermaglio; **zip f.** chiusura lampo.

fastening ['faːsniŋ] *n* chiusura, fermatura.

fastidious [fæs'tidiəs] *a* di gusti difficili, schizzinoso.

fastidiousness [fæs'tidiəsnis] *n* l'essere di gusti difficili.

fasting ['faːstiŋ] *a* di digiuno; *n* digiuno.

fat [fæt] *a* grasso; corpulento; ricco, fertile; *n* grasso.

fatal ['feitl] *a* fatale, funesto.

fatalism ['feitəlizəm] *n* fatalismo.

fatality [fə'tæliti] *n* fatalità, sventura, morte accidentale.

fate [feit] *n* fato, destino.

fated ['feitid] *a* destinato.

fateful ['feitful] *a* fatale, decisivo.

father ['faːðə] *n* padre; *vt* procreare; **f.-in-law** suocero.

fatherhood ['faːðəhud] *n* paternità.

fatherless ['faːðəlis] *a* orfano di padre.

fatherly ['faːðəli] *a* paterno.

fathom ['fæðəm] *n* misura di profondità (*metri 1,83 circa*); *vt* scandagliare; (*fig*) capire.

fathomless ['fæðəmlis] *a* incommensurabile, impenetrabile.

fatigue [fə'tiːg] *n* fatica; *vt* affaticare, stancare.

fatiguing [fə'tiːgiŋ] *a* faticoso, sfibrante.

fatness ['fætnis] *n* grassezza.

fatten ['fætn] *vti* ingrassare.

fatty ['fæti] *a* adiposo, grasso.

fatuity [fə'tjuːiti] *n* fatuità.

fatuous ['fætjuəs] *a* fatuo.

faucet ['fɔːsit] *n* (*US*) rubinetto.

fault [fɔːlt] *n* difetto, colpa, fallo; **to a f.** all'eccesso.

faultless ['fɔːltlis] *a* irreprensibile, perfetto.

faulty ['fɔːlti] *a* difettoso, imperfetto.

faun [fɔːn] *n* fauno.

favour ['feivə] *n* favore, parzialità; *vt* favorire.

favourable ['feivərəbl] *a* favorevole, propizio.

favourite ['feivərit] *a n* favorito.

fawn [fɔːn] *a n* cerbiatto; color fulvo; *vi* accarezzare, adulare.

fear [fiə] *n* paura, timore; *vti* temere, aver paura.

fearful ['fiəful] *a* spaventoso, timoroso.

fearless ['fiəlis] *a* ardimentoso, impavido.

fearsome ['fiəsəm] *a* spaventoso.

feasible ['fiːzəbl] *a* fattibile, possibile.

feast [fiːst] *n* festa, festino, *vt* festeggiare; *vi* banchettare, far festa.

feat [fiːt] *n* atto eroico, prodezza.

feather ['feðə] *n* penna, piuma.

feature ['fiːtʃə] *n* fattezza, lineamento; configurazione; caratteristica.

February ['februəri] *n* febbraio.

feckless ['feklis] *a* inefficiente.

fecund ['fiːkənd] *a* fecondo.

fecundity [fiˈkʌnditi] *n* fecondità.

federal ['fedərəl] *a* federale.

federate ['fedərit] *a* (con)federato.

federation [,fedə'reiʃən] *n* (con)federazione.

fee [fiː] *n* onorario, emolumento; (*enrolment, examination etc*) tassa; *vt* pagare un onorario a.

feeble ['fiːbl] *a* debole.

feebleness ['fiːblnis] n debolezza.
feed [fiːd] n alimento, (fam) mangiata; (mech) alimentazione, rifornimento; vti nutrir(si).
feeder ['fiːdə] n alimentatore; (bib) bavaglino; (stream) affluente; (rly) linea secondaria; (feeding bottle) biberon, poppatoio.
feeding ['fiːdiŋ] n alimentazione, nutrimento.
feel [fiːl] n sensazione (tattile); vti sentir(si), avere la sensazione di, percepire.
feeler ['fiːlə] n antenna; tentacolo; (fig) sondaggio, approccio; (mech) sonda.
feeling ['fiːliŋ] a sensibile; n sentimento, sensazione, sensibilità.
feign [fein] vti fingere, simulare.
feint [feint] n finta; (mil) finto attacco; vi fare una finta.
felicitate [fi'lisiteit] vt felicitarsi con, congratularsi con.
felicitation [fi,lisi'teiʃən] n felicitazione, congratulazione.
felicitous [fi'lisitəs] a felice, appropriato.
felicity [fi'lisiti] n felicità.
feline ['fiːlain] a n felino.
fell [fel] n collina brulla; pelle, vello; a feroce vt abbattere.
fellow ['felou] n individuo; camerata, compagno, socio; **fellowship** compagnia; amicizia; associazione; borsa di studio.
felon ['felən] n criminale.
felony ['feləni] n crimine.
felt [felt] n feltro.
female ['fiːmeil] a femminile, di sesso femminile; n femmina.
feminine ['feminin] a femminile.
fen [fen] n terreno acquitrinoso.
fence [fens] n recinto, stecconato; ricettatore; vt chiudere con un recinto; ricettare; vi tirar di scherma; (fig) schermirsi.
fencing ['fensiŋ] n scherma; recinto.
fend [fend] vt f. off parare; f. for oneself provvedere a se stesso.
fender ['fendə] n paraurti; parafuoco; (US aut) parafango.
fennel ['fenl] n finocchio.
Ferdinand ['fəːdinənd] nm pr Ferdinando.
ferment ['fəːment] n fermento; [fəːˈment] vti (far) fermentare; (fig) fomentare.
fermentation [,fəːmen'teiʃən] n fermentazione.
fern [fəːn] n felce.
ferocious [fə'rouʃəs] a feroce.
ferocity [fə'rɔsiti] n ferocia.
ferret ['ferit] n furetto; f. out vt scoprire.
ferrule ['feruːl] n ghiera.
ferry ['feri] n traghetto, ferryboàt; vt traghettare.
fertile ['fəːtail] a fertile.
fertility [fəːˈtiliti] n fertilità.
fertilize ['fəːtilaiz] vt fertilizzare.

fervent ['fəːvənt] a fervente.
fervid ['fəːvid] a fervido.
fervour ['fəːvə] n fervore.
fester ['festə] vi suppurare.
festival ['festivəl] n festa, celebrazione; (mus etc) festival.
festive ['festiv] a festivo, gioioso.
festivity [fes'tiviti] n festività, festa.
festoon [fes'tuːn] n festone; vt adornare con festoni.
fetch [fetʃ] vt andare a prendere; valere, fruttare.
fête [feit] n festa; vt festeggiare.
fetid ['fetid] a fetido.
fetish ['fiːtiʃ] n feticcio.
fetter ['fetə] n catena; **fetters** pl ceppi pl; vt mettere in ceppi; intralciare.
fettle ['fetl] n condizione, stato.
feud [fjuːd] n contesa, inimicizia.
feudal ['fjuːdəl] a feudale.
feudalism ['fjuːdəlizəm] n feudalismo.
fever ['fiːvə] n febbre.
feverish ['fiːvəriʃ] a febbricitante, febbrile.
few [fjuː] a pron pl pochi; a f. alcuni, un certo numero; the f. la minoranza.
fiancé [fi'ãːnsei] n fidanzato; **fiancée** fidanzata.
fiasco [fi'æskou] n insuccesso, fiasco.
fib [fib] n (fam) piccola bugia.
fibre ['faibə] n fibra.
fibreglass ['faibəglɑːs] n lana di vetro.
fibrous ['faibrəs] a fibroso.
fickle ['fikl] a incostante, volubile.
fickleness ['fiklnis] n incostanza, volubilità.
fiction ['fikʃən] n prosa narrativa; finzione, invenzione.
fictitious [fik'tiʃəs] a fittizio.
fiddle ['fidl] n (fam) violino; vti (fam) suonare il violino; gingillarsi.
fidelity [fi'deliti] n fedeltà.
fidget ['fidʒit] n irrequietezza; vi essere irrequieto, agitarsi.
fidgety ['fidʒiti] a irrequieto.
field [fiːld] n campo.
fiend [fiːnd] n demonio, spirito maligno.
fiendish ['fiːndiʃ] a demoniaco, diabolico.
fiendishly ['fiːndiʃli] ad diabolicamente.
fierce [fiəs] a feroce, violento; ardente.
fiercely ['fiəsli] ad ferocemente; ardentemente; furiosamente.
fierceness ['fiəsnis] n ferocia; ardore, furia.
fiery ['faiəri] n infiammato, focoso.
fife [faif] n piffero.
fifteen ['fif'tiːn] a n quindici; **fifteenth** a n quindicesimo, decimo quinto.
fifth [fifθ] a n quinto.
fifty ['fifti] a n cinquanta; **fiftieth** a n cinquantesimo.

fig (tree) ['fig(tri:)] n (pianta di) fico.

fight [fait] n battaglia, combattimento; vti combattere, lottare.

fighter ['faitə] n combattente; (av) caccia.

figment ['figmənt] n finzione, invenzione.

figurative ['figjurətiv] a figurativo; figurato; ornato.

figure ['figə] n cifra; figura; vti figurarsi, raffigurare; f. out calcolare; **figurehead** uomo di paglia.

filament ['filəmənt] n filamento.

filch [filtʃ] n refurtiva; vt rubacchiare.

file [fail] n lima; fila; filza, schedario; vti archiviare, ordinare; (far) marciare in fila; limare.

filial ['filiəl] a filiale.

filibuster ['filibʌstə] n (US) ostruzionista; vi ostruzionare.

filigree ['filigri:] n filigrana.

fill [fil] n sazietà; vt riempire; (position) occupare; (tooth) otturare; vi riempirsi.

fillet ['filit] n nastro; filetto.

filling ['filiŋ] n riempitura; ripieno; (tooth) otturazione; f. station (aut) stazione di rifornimento.

fillip ['filip] n lo schioccare delle dita; (fig) stimolo; vti schioccare le dita; (fig) stimolare.

filly ['fili] n puledra.

film [film] n film, pellicola; patina; (fig) velo; vt incendiare.

filmy ['filmi] a velato, vaporoso.

filter ['filtə] n filtro; vti filtrare; f.-tip cigarette sigaretta con filtro.

filth [filθ] **filthiness** ['filθinis] n sudiciume; oscenità.

filthy ['filθi] a sudicio; osceno.

fin [fin] n pinna.

final ['fainl] a finale, ultimo, decisivo; n (sport) gara finale; pl esami finali pl; **finalist** n (sport) finalista.

finale [fi'nɑ:li] n (mus) finale.

finally ['fainəli] ad finalmente, alla fine; definitivamente.

finance [fai'næns] n finanza; vt finanziare.

financial [fai'nænʃəl] a finanziario.

financier [fai'nænsiə] n finanziere.

finch [fintʃ] n fringuello.

find [faind] n scoperta, ritrovamento; vt trovare; f. out scoprire.

fine [fain] a bello; delicato; fine, raffinato; ad bene; n multa; vt multare.

fineness ['fainnis] n bellezza; finezza.

finery ['fainəri] n abiti delle feste pl, fronzoli pl.

finesse [fi'nes] n finezza, sottigliezza.

finger ['fiŋgə] n dito; vt tastare, toccare delicatamente; **fingerprint** impronta digitale.

finical ['finikəl], **finicky** ['finiki] a pignolo, affettato, schizzinoso.

finish ['finiʃ] n rifinitura, ultimo tocco; fine; vti finire, perfezionare.

finite ['fainait] a definito, limitato; (gram) finito.

Finland ['finlənd] n Finlandia.

Finn [fin] n finlandese.

Finnish ['finiʃ] a finlandese.

fiord [fjɔ:d] n fiordo.

fir (tree) ['fə:(tri:)] n abete.

fire ['faiə] n fuoco, incendio; (gun) tiro; vt incendiare; sparare.

firearms ['faiərɑ:mz] n pl armi da fuoco pl.

fire brigade ['faiəbri,geid] n corpo dei pompieri.

fire department ['faiədi:'pɑ:tmənt] n (US) corpo dei pompieri.

fire-escape ['faiəris,keip] n uscita di sicurezza.

fire-extinguisher ['faiəriks,tiŋgwiʃə] n estintore, pompa antincendio.

firefly ['faiəflai] n lucciola.

fireman ['faiəmən] pl **firemen** n pompiere.

fireplace ['faiəpleis] n caminetto, camino.

fireproof ['faiəpru:f] a incombustibile.

fireside ['faiəsaid] n focolare.

firewood ['faiəwud] n legna da ardere.

firework ['faiəwə:k] n fuoco d'artifizio.

firing ['faiəriŋ] n combustione; scarica, sparo; f. party, f. squad (mil) plotone d'esecuzione.

firm [fə:m] a duro; saldo, stabile; deciso; n ditta.

firmament ['fə:məmənt] n firmamento.

firmly ['fə:mli] ad fermamente; saldamente.

firmness ['fə:mnis] n fermezza; stabilità.

first [fə:st] n primo; ad prima, in primo luogo.

firth [fə:θ] n (scozzese) estuario.

fish [fiʃ] pl **fishes**, **fish** n pesce; vti pescare.

fisher(man) ['fiʃə(mən)] pl **fishermen** n pescatore.

fishery ['fiʃəri] n pesca; riserva di pesca; vivaio.

fishing ['fiʃiŋ] a di pesca, per la pesca; n pesca; f. hook amo; f. line lenza; f. rod canna da pesca.

fishmonger ['fiʃ,mʌŋgə] n pescivendolo.

fish-pond ['fiʃpɔnd] n vasca per pesci.

fishy ['fiʃi] a di pesce; (fig) dubbio, equivoco.

fission ['fiʃən] n fissione.

fissure ['fiʃə] n crepa, fessura.

fist [fist] n pugno.

fit [fit] a adatto, appropriato, conveniente, idoneo; in buona salute; n misura; accesso, convulsione; vti adattare; prepararsi a; convenire, star bene.

fitful ['fitful] a spasmodico, irregolare.

fitfully ['fitfuli] *ad* a sbalzi; irregolarmente.

fitness ['fitnis] *n* opportunità; buona salute.

fitting ['fitiŋ] *a* adatto, conveniente; *n (of a dress etc)* prova; *(usu pl)* accessori, arredi, infissi *pl*.

fittingly ['fitiŋli] *ad* convenientemente.

five [faiv] *a n* cinque.

fix [fiks] *n (fam)* dilemma, difficoltà; *vt* fissare, aggiustare; stabilire; **to f. up** accomodare.

fixation [fik'seifən] *n* fissazione.

fixative ['fiksətiv] *a* fissativo; *n* fissativo, fissatore.

fixed [fikst] *a* fisso, fissato.

fixing ['fiksiŋ] *n (phot)* fissaggio.

fixture ['fikstfə] *n* infisso; *(sport)* data fissata; impianto di gas, luce *etc*.

fizz [fiz] *n (sl)* spumante, bevanda effervescente; *vi* frizzare.

fizzle ['fizl] *vi* frizzare, sibilare; **to f. out** far fiasco.

flabbergast ['flæbəgɑːst] *vt (fam)* sbalordire.

flabbiness ['flæbinis] *n* flaccidezza.

flabby ['flæbi] *a* cascante, floscio.

flaccid ['flæksid] *a* flaccido.

flag [flæg] *n* bandiera; *(bot)* iride; *(stone)* pietra da lastrico; *vi* perdere le forze.

flagellate ['flædʒileit] *vt* flagellare.

flagellation [flædʒe'leifən] *n* flagellazione.

flagon ['flægən] *n* bottiglione.

flagrancy ['fleigrənsi] *n* flagranza.

flagrant ['fleigrənt] *a* flagrante.

flair [flɛə] *n* fiuto, intuizione.

flake [fleik] *n* fiocco; lamina, scaglia; *vti* sfaldar(si).

flaky ['fleiki] *a* scaglioso; fioccoso; *(pastry)* sfogliato.

flamboyant [flæm'bɔiənt] *a* sgargiante.

flame [fleim] *n* fiamma; *vi* fiammeggiare.

flaming ['fleimiŋ] *a* infuocato, ardente.

Flanders ['flɑːndəz] *n (geogr)* Fiandre.

flank [flæŋk] *n* fianco; *vt* fiancheggiare.

flannel ['flænl] *a n* (di) flanella.

flap [flæp] *n* falda, lembo, tesa, colpo d'ala; *vt* agitare, sbattere.

flare [flɛə] *n* chiarore intenso, fiammata improvvisa; *(av)* razzo; *vi* brillare di luce viva, avvampare.

flash [flæf] *n* baleno, lampo, vampata; **flashback** *(cin)* scena retrospettiva; **flashbulb** lampada per fotolampo; **flashlight** lampadina elettrica; *(naut)* luce intermittente; **flashpoint** temperatura di infiammabilità; *vti* lanciare, balenare, sfavillare.

flashy ['flæfi] *a (fam)* sgargiante, vistoso, appariscente.

flask [flɑːsk] *n* fiasco.

flat [flæt] *a* piano, piatto; monotono,

uniforme; reciso; *n* appartamento; piano di casa; **service flats** appartamenti di affitto con servizio.

flatly ['flætli] *ad* freddamente, recisamente.

flatness ['flætnis] *n* monotonia, uniformità.

flatten ['flætn] *vt* appiattire.

flatter ['flætə] *vt* adulare, lusingare.

flattering ['flætəriŋ] *a* adulatorio.

flattery ['flætəri] *n* adulazione.

flatulence ['flætjuləns] *n* flatulenza.

flaunt [flɔːnt] *vt* ostentare.

flautist ['flɔːtist] *n* flautista.

flavour ['fleivə] *n* aroma, gusto, sapore; *vt* dare gusto a, aromatizzare.

flaw [flɔː] *n* difetto, pecca.

flax [flæks] *n* lino.

flaxen ['flæksən] *a* di lino; biondo.

flay [flei] *vt* scorticare, pelare.

flea [fliː] *n* pulce.

fleck [flek] *n* lentiggine; macchietta; particella.

fledge [fledʒ] *vi* mettere le ali.

fledged [fledʒd] *a (of bird)* pennuto; piumato.

fledgling ['fledʒliŋ] *n* uccellino appena uscito dal nido.

flee [fliː] *vi* fuggire.

fleece [fliːs] *n* vello; *vt (sl)* pelare, derubare.

fleecy ['fliːsi] *a* lanoso, velloso.

fleet [fliːt] *n* flotta.

fleeting ['fliːtiŋ] *a* fugace, transitorio.

Fleming ['flemiŋ] *n* fiammingo.

Flemish ['flemif] *a n* fiammingo.

flesh [flef] *n* carne.

fleshy ['flefi] *a* polposo, grasso.

flex [fleks] *n (el)* filo flessibile.

flexibility [,fleksə'biliti] *n* flessibilità.

flexible ['fleksəbl] *a* flessibile.

flick [flik] *n* colpetto, schiocco; buffetto; *(sl)* cinema; *vt* colpire; dare un buffetto; **f. knife** coltello a molla.

flicker ['flikə] *n* barlume; tremolio; battito; *vi* tremolare, vacillare, brillare debolmente.

flight [flait] *n* volo; stormo; *(av)* squadriglia; rampa di scale; fuga.

flightily ['flaitili] *ad* capricciosamente, leggermente.

flighty ['flaiti] *a* frivolo, incostante.

flimsiness ['flimzinis] *n* tenuità, inconsistenza; frivolezza.

flimsy ['flimzi] *a* tenue, leggero; frivolo.

flinch [flintf] *vi* indietreggiare, ritirarsi.

fling [fliŋ] *n* getto, lancio; godimento completo, baldoria; *vt* gettare, lanciare.

flint [flint] *n* pietra focaia, selce; *(of cigarette lighter)* pietrina.

flinty ['flinti] *a* petroso; crudele, duro.

flip [flip] *vt* sbattere leggermente; **egg-flip** uova sbattute, zabaione.

flippancy ['flipənsi] *n* leggerezza, mancanza di serietà.

flippant ['flipənt] *a* leggero, irrispettoso.

flipper ['flipə] *n* pinna, ala natatoria.

flirt [flə:t] *n* ragazza civettuola; damerino; amoreggiamento, 'flirt'; *vt* agitare; *vi* civettare, 'flirtare'.

flirtation [flə:'teiʃən] *n* amoreggiamento, 'flirt'.

flit [flit] *vi* volare, svolazzare; sloggiare.

float [flout] *n* galleggiante; carro per processione; *vti* galleggiare, far galleggiare.

floater ['floutə] *n* galleggiante.

floating ['floutiŋ] *a* galleggiante, fluttuante; f. capital (*com*) capitale circolante.

flock [flɔk] *n* branco, gregge; bioccolo, fiocco di lana; *vi* riunirsi a stormi.

floe [flou] *n* banchisa.

flog [flɔg] *vt* frustare.

flogging ['flɔgiŋ] *n* bastonatura, fustigazione.

flood [flʌd] *n* diluvio, inondazione, allagamento; *vt* inondare, sommergere.

floodlight ['flʌdlait] *n* riflettore; *vt* illuminare con riflettori.

floor [flɔ:] *n* pavimento, piano (di casa); *vt* pavimentare, ridurre al silenzio; atterrare.

flop [flɔp] *n* tonfo; fiasco, insuccesso; *vi* camminare (sedersi) goffamente; (*sl*) far fiasco; **flophouse** (US) dormitorio pubblico.

floral ['flɔ:rəl] *a* floreale.

Florence ['flɔ:rəns] *n* (*geog*) Firenze; **Florentine** *a n* fiorentino, fiorentina.

florid ['flɔrid] *a* florido, prosperoso.

florin ['flɔrin] *n* fiorino (*in Inghilterra, moneta da due scellini*).

florist ['flɔrist] *n* fiorista, fioraio, floricultore.

flotilla [flou'tilə] *n* flottiglia.

flotsam ['flɔtsəm] *n* relitti *pl*; merci ritrovate galleggianti sul mare *pl*.

flounce [flauns] *n* falpalà; *vt* ornare di volani; *vi* dimenarsi, muoversi in modo agitato.

flounder ['flaundə] *n* (*fish*) passerino; *vi* agitarsi, dibatersi; condurre una cosa male, fare errori.

flour ['flauə] *n* (fior di) farina.

flourish ['flʌriʃ] *n* fioritura; (*of trumpets*) squillo; (*writing*) svolazzo; *vi* fiorire; (*fig*) prosperare; *vt* (*stick etc*) brandire.

flout [flaut] *vt* insultare, schernire.

flow [flou] *n* flusso, corso, corrente; abbondanza; f. of words facilità; *vi* fluire, scorrere.

flower ['flauə] *n* fiore; **flowerbed** aiuola; fiorire, produrre fiori.

flowery ['flauəri] *a* fiorito.

flowing ['flouiŋ] *a* fluente, corrente, sciolto, fluido; *n* flusso, corso.

flu [flu:] *n* (*fam*) influenza.

fluctuate ['flʌktjueit] *vi* fluttuare.

fluctuation [‚flʌktju'eiʃən] *n* oscillazione, fluttuazione.

flue [flu:] *n* conduttura d'un camino, tubo.

fluency ['fluːənsi] *n* fluidità, scioltezza, facilità (di parola).

fluent ['fluːənt] *a* fluente, scorrevole, dalla parola facile.

fluff [flʌf] *n* lanugine, peluria.

fluid ['fluːid] *a n* fluido.

fluke ['fluːk] *n* (*naut*) marra; (*zool*) distoma epatico; (*fam*) vantaggio inaspettato, colpo di fortuna.

flunkey ['flʌŋki] *n* valletto.

fluorescent [fluə'resnt] *a* fluorescente.

flurry ['flʌri] *n* agitazione; improvviso colpo di vento, o scroscio di pioggia.

flush [flʌʃ] *n* rossore, afflusso di sangue al volto; *vt* sciacquare (con acqua abbondante); *vi* arrossire.

fluster ['flʌstə] *n* agitazione, eccitazione; *vti* agitare, agitarsi.

flute [fluːt] *n* flauto.

flutter ['flʌtə] *n* svolazzamento; agitazione; (*sl*) speculazione; *vt* agitare; *vi* agitarsi, svolazzare.

flux [flʌks] *n* flusso.

fly [flai] *n* mosca; *vti* (far) volare.

flying ['flaiiŋ] *a* volante, sventolante; breve.

foal [foul] *n* puledro.

foam [foum] *n* schiuma, spuma; *vi* schiumare, spumeggiare.

fob (off) [fɔb] *vt* imbrogliare, appioppare *qc a qlcu*.

focus ['foukəs] *n* fuoco; in f. a fuoco; out of f. fuori fuoco, sfocato.

fodder ['fɔdə] *n* foraggio.

foe [fou] *n* avversario, nemico.

fog [fɔg] *n* nebbia.

foggy ['fɔgi] *a* nebbioso.

foible ['fɔibl] *n* lato debole.

foil [fɔil] *n* foglia sottile di metallo; cosa che serve a porre in risalto; *vt* frustrare; far perdere le tracce.

foist [fɔist] *vt* introdurre di nascosto, far accettare con un trucco.

fold [fould] *n* piega, spira; ovile; (*fig*) Chiesa; *vt* piegare; (*arms*) incrociare; *vi* ripiegarsi.

folder ['fouldə] *n* (manifestino) pieghevole; cartella, cartelletta; piegatore; pince-nez.

folding ['fouldiŋ] *a* pieghevole; *n* piega; f. bed branda.

foliage ['fouliidʒ] *n* fogliame.

folk [fouk] *n* gente, popolo; (*fam*) la propria famiglia.

folklore ['fouklɔ:] *n* folclore.

follow ['fɔlou] *vt* seguire; inseguire; *vi* conseguire, derivare.

follower ['fɔlouə] *n* seguace, discepolo, *pl* ammiratori *pl*; **following** *a* seguente; *n* seguito.

folly ['fɔli] *n* follia.

foment [fou'ment] *vt* fomentare.

fond [fɔnd] *a* affezionato, appassionato; **to be f. of** voler bene a, amare.

fondle ['fɔndl] *vt* accarezzare.

fondly ['fɔndli] *ad* appassionatamente, amorevolmente.

fondness ['fɔndnis] *n* affettuosità indulgente, tenerezza, passione.

font [fɔnt] *n* fonte battesimale.

food [fuːd] *n* cibo, alimento, nutrimento.

fool [fuːl] *n* idiota, sciocco; (*court*) buffone; *vt* imbrogliare, ingannare; *vi* fare lo sciocco.

foolery ['fuːləri] *n* buffonata, sciocchezza.

foolhardy ['fuːl,haːdi] *a* temerario.

foolish ['fuːliʃ] *a* sciocco, stolto.

foolishness ['fuːliʃnis] *n* sciocchezza, stoltezza.

foot [fut] *pl* **feet** *n* piede; fanteria; misura lineare corrispondente a 30,5 cm. circa.

football ['futbɔːl] *n* calcio, pallone per il calcio; **association f.** gioco del calcio; **Rugby f.** pallovale, rugby; **footballer** giocatore di calcio.

foot-bridge ['futbridʒ] *n* ponte per soli pedoni, cavalcavia.

foothold ['futhould] *n* punto d'appoggio; (*fig*) piede.

footlights ['futlaits] *n pl* (*theat*) luci della ribalta.

footman ['futmən] *n* servo in livrea.

footnote ['futnout] *n* poscritto, postilla.

footpath ['futpaːθ] *n* sentiero.

footprint ['futprint] *n* orma, impronta.

footstep ['futstep] *n* passo, suono di passi.

footstool ['futstuːl] *n* sgabello.

for [fɔː] *prep* per, a, di, a causa di; *cj* perché.

forage ['fɔridʒ] *n* foraggio.

foray ['fɔrei] *n* incursione, scorreria.

forbear ['fɔːbɛə] *n* antenato.

forbear [fɔː'bɛə] *vi* trattenersi da.

forbearance [fɔː'bɛərəns] *n* pazienza, sopportazione.

forbearing [fɔː'bɛəriŋ] *a* paziente.

forbid [fə'bid] *vt* proibire, vietare.

forbidding [fə'bidiŋ] *a* severo; ripugnante.

force [fɔːs] *n* forza, violenza; (*of law*) vigore; **forces** *pl* truppe *pl*; *vt* costringere, forzare.

forceful ['fɔːsful] *a* energico.

forceps ['fɔːseps] *n pl* pinze chirurgiche *pl*, forcipe.

forcible ['fɔːsəbl] *a* impetuoso, violento.

ford [fɔːd] *n* guado; *vt* passare a guado.

fordable ['fɔːdəbl] *a* guadabile.

fore [fɔː] *a* anteriore; *n* davanti, parte anteriore.

fore-arm ['fɔːraːm] *n* avambraccio.

foreboding [fɔː'boudiŋ] *n* presagio, presentimento.

forecast ['fɔːkaːst] *n* previsione; *vt* pronosticare.

forecastle ['fouksl] *n* (*naut*) castello di prua.

forefather ['fɔː,faːðə] *n* antenato.

forefinger ['fɔː,fiŋgə] *n* indice.

forefront ['fɔːfrʌnt] *n* prima linea; posizione d'importanza.

forego [fɔː'gou] *vt* rinunziare a, privarsi di.

foregoing [fɔː'gouiŋ] *a* precedente; **foregone** *a* previsto.

foreground ['fɔːgraund] *n* primo piano.

forehead ['fɔrid] *n* fronte.

foreign ['fɔrin] *a* estero, straniero, forestiero, estraneo.

foreigner ['fɔrinə] *n* straniero, (*fam*) forestiero.

foreman ['fɔːmən] *pl* **foremen** *n* capo-officina; capomastro; capo dei giurati.

foremost ['fɔːmoust] *a* primo; *ad* in testa, in avanti.

forenoon ['fɔːnuːn] *n* mattino.

forensic [fə'rensik] *a* forense.

forerunner ['fɔːˌrʌnə] *n* precursore.

foresee [fɔː'siː] *vt* prevedere.

foreshadow [fɔː'ʃædou] *vt* adombrare; presagire.

foresight ['fɔːsait] *n* preveggenza; prudenza.

forest ['fɔrist] *a* forestale; *n* foresta; **forestry** silvicultura.

forestall [fɔː'stɔːl] *vt* prevenire, anticipare; (*com*) fare incetta.

forester ['fɔristə] *n* guardia forestale.

foretaste ['fɔːteist] *n* pregustazione.

foretell [fɔː'tel] *vt* predire, pronosticare.

forethought ['fɔːθɔːt] *n* previdenza.

forever [fə'revə] *ad* per sempre, eternamente.

forewarn [fɔː'wɔːn] *vt* (pre)avvertire.

foreword ['fɔːwəːd] *n* prefazione.

forfeit ['fɔːfit] *n* multa, pegno; perdita; *vt* perdere il diritto a, dover pagare, essere privato di.

forfeiture ['fɔːfitʃə] *n* multa, perdita.

for(e)gather [fɔː'gæðə] *vi* adunarsi; incontrarsi, fraternizzare.

forge [fɔːdʒ] *n* fornace, fucina; *vt* forgiare, contraffare, falsificare; **to f. ahead** avanzare.

forger ['fɔːdʒə] *n* falsificatore.

forgery ['fɔːdʒəri] *n* contraffazione, documento falso.

forget [fə'get] *vti* dimenticare.

forgetful [fə'getful] *a* dimentico, distratto, immemore.

forgetfulness [fə'getfulnis] *n* smemorataggine, oblio.

forgivable [fə'givəbl] *a* perdonabile.

forgive [fə'giv] *vt* perdonare.

forgiveness [fə'givnis] *n* perdono, remissione.

forgiving [fə'giviŋ] *a* clemente, indulgente.

fork [fɔːk] *n* forchetta; *vi* biforcarsi.

forlorn [fə'lɔːn] *a* abbandonato,

infelice; **f. hope** vana speranza, impresa disperata.

form [fɔːm] *n* forma; modulo; banco di scuola, classe; covo di lepre; *vti* formar(si).

formal ['fɔːməl] *a* formale, cerimonioso.

formality [fɔː'mæliti] *n* formalità.

formally ['fɔːməli] *ad* formalmente.

formation [fɔː'meiʃən] *n* formazione.

former ['fɔːmə] *a* precedente, primo, antico; *pron* (di due persone) il primo.

formerly ['fɔːməli] *ad* già, un tempo.

formidable ['fɔːmidəbl] *a* formidabile.

formula ['fɔːmjulə] *pl* **formulae, formulas** *n* formula.

formulate ['fɔːmjuleit] *vt* formulare.

forsake [fə'seik] *vt* abbandonare.

fort [fɔːt] *n* forte, fortezza.

forte ['fɔːti] *n* attitudine speciale, forte; (*mus*) forte.

forth [fɔːθ] *ad* (in) avanti, fuori.

forthcoming [fɔːθ'kʌmiŋ] *a* prossimo, presso a venire, vicino alla pubblicazione.

forthright ['fɔːθrait] *a* franco; esplicito; *ad* immediatamente, esplicitamente.

forthwith ['fɔːθ'wiθ] *ad* immediatamente, senz'altro.

fortification [ˌfɔːtifi'keiʃən] *n* fortificazione.

fortify ['fɔːtifai] *vt* fortificare.

fortitude ['fɔːtitjuːd] *n* forza d'animo.

fortnight ['fɔːtnait] *n* due settimane *pl*, quindici giorni, quindicina.

fortnightly ['fɔːtˌnaitli] *a* quindicinale; *ad* ogni quindici giorni.

fortress ['fɔːtris] *n* fortezza, roccaforte.

fortuitous [fɔː'tjuːitəs] *a* fortuito, casuale.

fortunate ['fɔːtʃnit] *a* fortunato, favorevole.

fortune ['fɔːtʃən] *n* fortuna, destino; **f.-telling** predizione dell'avvenire.

forty ['fɔːti] *a n* quaranta; **fortieth** *a n* quarantesimo.

forward ['fɔːwəd] *a* avanzato; precoce; spinto; *ad* (in) avanti, in poi; *vt* far proseguire, spedire, promuovere.

forwarding ['fɔːwədiŋ] *n* spedizione; **f. agent** (*com*) spedizioniere.

forwards ['fɔːwədz] *ad v* **forward.**

fossil ['fɔsl] *n* fossile.

fossilize ['fɔsilaiz] *vti* fossilizzar(si).

foster ['fɔstə] *vt* allevare, nutrire; incoraggiare.

foul [faul] *a* sporco, sudicio, osceno; (*sport*) sleale; **f. play** intrigo, azione disonesta; *n* (*sport*) fallo.

foully ['faulli] *ad* sudiciamente; ignobilmente.

foulness ['faulnis] *n* sporcizia, oscenità.

found [faund] *vt* fondare; fondere; *vi* fondarsi.

foundation [faun'deiʃən] *n* fondazione; fondamenta *pl*; istituzione.

founder ['faundə] *n* fondatore; fonditore.

founder ['faundə] *vt* affondare, (*a horse*) azzoppare; *vi* affondare, sprofondarsi.

foundling ['faundliŋ] *n* trovatello.

foundry ['faundri] *n* fonderia.

fountain ['fauntin] *n* fontana, fonte; **f. pen** penna stilografica.

four [fɔː] *a n* quattro; **fourth** *a n* quarto.

fourfold ['fɔːfould] *a* quadruplo.

fourteen ['fɔː'tiːn] *a n* quattordici; **fourteenth** *a n* quattordicesimo.

fowl [faul] *n* pollo, uccello.

fox [fɔks] *n* volpe.

foxhound ['fɔkshaund] *n* bracco.

foxy ['fɔksi] *a* (*fig*) astuto, scaltro.

fraction ['frækʃən] *n* frazione.

fractious ['frækʃəs] *a* litigioso, permaloso.

fracture ['fræktʃə] *n* frattura; *vti* fratturar(si).

fragile ['frædʒail] *a* fragile.

fragment ['frægmənt] *n* frammento.

fragrance ['freigrəns] *n* fragranza.

fragrant ['freigrənt] *a* fragrante.

frail [freil] *a* fragile, debole.

frailty ['freilti] *n* fragilità.

frame [freim] *n* cornice; struttura, intelaiatura; (*bicycle*) telaio; (*spectacles*) montatura; *vt* incorniciare; dar forma a; inventare.

framework ['freimwəːk] *n* struttura, ossatura.

franc [fræŋk] *n* franco (moneta).

France [frɑːns] *n* Francia.

Frances ['frɑːnsis] *nf pr* Francesca.

franchise ['fræntʃaiz] *n* franchigia, diritti di voto *pl*.

Francis ['frɑːnsis] *nm pr* Francesco.

Franciscan [fræn'siskən] *a n* francescano.

Frank [fræŋk] *nm pr* Franco.

frank [fræŋk] *a* aperto, franco, schietto.

frankness ['fræŋknis] *n* franchezza, schiettezza.

frantic ['fræntik] *a* fuori di sè, frenetico.

frantically ['fræntikəli] *ad* freneticamente; terribilmente.

fraternal [frə'təːnəl] *a* fraterno.

fraternity [frə'təːniti] *n* fraternità, confraternità.

fraternize ['frætənaiz] *vi* fraternizzare.

fratricide ['frætrisaid] *n* fratricida, fratricidio.

fraud [frɔːd] *n* frode, truffa; impostore.

fraudulent ['frɔːdjulənt] *a* fraudolento.

fraught [frɔːt] *a* carico (di).

fray [frei] *n* zuffa, rissa; *vti* logorar(si).

freak [friːk] *n* capriccio, anomalia.

freakish ['friːkiʃ] *a* capriccioso.

freckle ['frekl] *n* lentiggine; *vti* macchiar(si) di lentiggini.

Frederic(k) ['fredrik] *nm pr* Federico.

free [friː] *a* libero; gratis, gratuito; (*com*) franco; *vt* liberare.

freedom ['friːdəm] *n* libertà; disinvoltura; familiarità.

freely ['friːli] *ad* liberamente; gratuitamente.

freeman ['friːmən] *pl* **freemen** *n* cittadino onorario.

freemason ['friːˌmeisn] *n* frammassone.

freemasonry ['friːˌmeisnri] *n* frammassoneria.

freethinker ['friːˈθiŋkə] *n* libero pensatore.

freeze [friːz] *n* (*of prices etc*) congelamento, blocco; *vti* congelar(si), gelare, irrigidir(si).

freezer ['friːzə] *n* congelante; frigorifero; cella frigorifera.

freezing ['friːziŋ] *a* gelido, glaciale; *n* congelamento; **below f. point** sotto zero.

freight [freit] *n* nolo, carico; *vt* (*ship*) caricare, noleggiare; **f. car** (*US*) vagone merci.

French [frentʃ] *a n* francese; **Frenchman** *n* francese; **F. fries** (*US*) patate fritte.

frenzied ['frenzid] *a* frenetico.

frenzy ['frenzi] *n* frenesia.

frequency ['friːkwənsi] *n* frequenza.

frequent ['friːkwənt] *a* frequente; *vt* [friˈkwent] frequentare.

frequently ['friːkwəntli] *ad* frequentemente.

fresco ['freskou] *pl* **frescos, frescoes** *n* affresco.

fresh [freʃ] *a* fresco; nuovo; (*of water*) dolce; inesperto.

freshen ['freʃn] *vti* rinfrescar(si), rinvigorir(si).

freshly ['freʃli] *ad* in modo fresco; di fresco, recentemente.

freshness ['freʃnis] *n* freschezza.

fret [fret] *n* inquietudine, irritazione; (*arch*) fregio, greca; *vt* agitare, irritare; fregare, rodere; *vi* impazientirsi, irritarsi.

fretful ['fretful] *a* irritabile.

fretwork ['fretwəːk] *n* lavoro d'intaglio, lavoro a greca.

friar ['fraiə] *n* frate.

friction ['frikʃən] *n* attrito, frizione.

Friday ['fraidi] *n* venerdì.

friend [frend] *n* amico; **F.** quacchero.

friendless ['frendlis] *a* senza amici.

friendliness ['frendlinis] *n* cordialità.

friendly ['frendli] *a* amichevole, amico; *ad* amichevolmente.

friendship ['frendʃip] *n* amicizia.

frieze [friːz] *n* fregio.

frigate ['frigit] *n* fregata.

fright [frait] *n* spavento, paura.

frighten ['fraitn] *vt* spaventare.

frightful ['fraitful] *a* spaventoso.

frigid ['fridʒid] *a* glaciale, frigido, freddo.

frigidity [friˈdʒiditi] *n* freddezza, frigidità.

frill [fril] *n* frangia, gala increspata.

fringe [frindʒ] *n* frangia, frangetta; bordo, limite; *vt* ornare di frangia.

frisk [frisk] *vi* far salti, salterellare.

frisky ['friski] *a* saltellante, vivace.

fritter ['fritə] *n* frittella; frammento; *vt* suddividere in frammenti; (*time*) sciupare.

frivolity [friˈvɔliti] *n* frivolezza, vanità.

frivolous ['frivələs] *a* frivolo.

frizzle ['frizl] *vti* arricciar(si); sfriggere.

fro [frou] *ad* indietro; **to and f.** avanti e indietro.

frock [frɔk] *n* veste, vestito intero; (*monk's*) tonaca.

frog [frɔg] *n* rana; alamaro.

frolic ['frɔlik] *n* scherzo, spasso; *vi* far salti, scherzare.

frolicsome ['frɔliksəm] *a* allegro, gaio.

from [frɔm] *prep* da, per.

front [frʌnt] *a* di fronte, davanti; *n* parte anteriore, facciata; (*mil*) fronte; *vti* essere di fronte a; affrontare.

frontage ['frʌntidʒ] *n* facciata, prospetto.

frontal ['frʌntl] *a n* frontale.

frontier ['frʌntiə] *a n* (di) frontiera.

frontispiece ['frʌntispiːs] *n* frontespizio.

frost [frɔst] *n* gelo; (*sl*) fiasco; **hoar-f.** brina.

frostbite ['frɔstbait] *n* congelamento.

frosty ['frɔsti] *a* gelato, gelido.

froth [frɔθ] *n* schiuma, spuma; chiacchierata vuota.

frothy ['frɔθi] *a* schiumoso, spumoso; vuoto.

frown [fraun] *n* aggrottamento delle ciglia, cipiglio; *vi* aggrottare le ciglia.

frowsy ['frauzi] *a* sciatto, sporco; di cattivo odore.

fructify ['frʌktifai] *vi* fruttificare.

frugal ['fruːgəl] *a* frugale.

fruit [fruːt] *n* frutto, frutta *pl*.

fruiterer ['fruːtərə] *n* commerciante in frutta, fruttivendolo.

fruitful ['fruːtful] *a* fruttifero, produttivo, fecondo.

fruitfulness ['fruːtfulnis] *n* fertilità, fecondità.

fruition [fruːˈiʃən] *n* fruizione; (*fig*) godimento.

fruitless ['fruːtlis] *a* infruttuoso, sterile.

fruity ['fruːti] *a* che sa di frutta; (*fig*) piccante.

frump [frʌmp] *n* donna vestita di abiti fuori moda.

frustrate [frʌsˈtreit] *vt* frustrare.

frustration [frʌs'treiʃən] n frustrazione, delusione.

fry [frai] n fritto, frittura; (zool) avannotto; (fig) persone di poca importanza; **small f.** vti friggere.

frying pan ['fraiiŋ‚pæn] n padella.

fuddle ['fʌdl] vt confondere, intontire, ubriacare.

fuel [fjuəl] n combustibile, carburante; (fig) esca, alimento.

fuelling ['fjuəliŋ] n approvvigionamento, rifornimento combustibili.

fugitive ['fju:dʒitiv] a n fuggitivo.

fugue [fju:g] n (mus) fuga.

fulfil [ful'fil] vt soddisfare, compiere.

fulfilment [ful'filmənt] n adempimento, realizzazione, compimento.

full [ful] a pieno; ad completamente, perfettamente, in pieno; n pieno, colmo; vt follare, gualcare.

fuller ['fulə] n follatore.

ful(l)ness ['fulnis] n pienezza, abbondanza.

fully ['fuli] ad completamente, interamente.

fulminate ['fʌlmineit] vti fulminare.

fulsome ['fulsəm] a disgustoso, nauseante.

fumble ['fʌmbl] vti frugare, maneggiare senza abilità, annaspare.

fume [fju:m] n fumo, vapore; accesso di rabbia; vi sottoporre a vapori chimici; vi emettere vapori; essere in collera.

fumigate ['fju:migeit] vt fumigare.

fumigation [‚fju:mi'geiʃən] n fumigazione.

fun [fʌn] n allegria, divertimento, svago.

function ['fʌŋkʃən] n funzione; cerimonia; vi funzionare.

functional ['fʌŋkʃənl] a funzionale.

fund [fʌnd] n fondo, capitale.

fundamental [‚fʌndə'mentl] a fondamentale.

funeral ['fju:nərəl] a funebre, funerario; n funerale.

funereal [fju:'niəriəl] a funereo, lugubre, funebre.

fungus ['fʌŋgəs] n fungo.

funicular [fju:'nikjulə] a n funicolare.

funk [fʌŋk] n (sl) panico, timore.

funnel ['fʌnl] n imbuto; ciminiera di nave.

funny ['fʌni] n buffo, comico, strano.

fur [fə:] n pelliccia, pelo; incrostazione.

furbish ['fə:biʃ] vt forbire, lustrare.

furious ['fjuəriəs] a furioso, furibondo.

furl [fə:l] vt ammainare, chiudere.

furlough ['fə:lou] n (mil etc) licenza, permesso.

furnace ['fə:nis] n fornace; caldaia di termosifone.

furnish ['fə:niʃ] vt fornire, rifornire; ammobiliare.

furnishings ['fə:niʃiŋs] n pl arredamento.

furniture ['fə:nitʃə] n mobilia, mobili pl.

furrier ['fʌriə] n pellicciaio.

furrow ['fʌrou] n solco; ruga; traccia; vt solcare.

furry ['fə:ri] a peloso; di pelliccia; coperto di pelliccia; patinoso.

further ['fə:ðə] a altro, ulteriore; ad oltre, più avanti; vt favorire, promuovere.

furthermore ['fə:ðə'mɔ:] ad per di più, inoltre.

furtive ['fə:tiv] a furtivo.

fury ['fjuəri] n furore, furia.

furze [fə:z] n ginestra spinosa.

fuse [fju:z] n spoletta, (el) valvola; vti fonder(si), far esplodere.

fuselage ['fju:zilɑ:ʒ] n (av) fusoliera.

fusillade [‚fju:zi'leid] n scarica di fucili.

fusion ['fju:ʒən] n fusione.

fuss [fʌs] n trambusto, scalpore; vi agitarsi; far confusione.

fussily ['fʌsili] ad con esagerata attenzione; con inutile indaffaramento.

fussy ['fʌsi] a brontolone; di difficile contentatura.

fustian ['fʌstiən] n fustagno.

fusty ['fʌsti] a ammuffito, che sa di muffa.

futile ['fju:tail] a futile.

future ['fju:tʃə] a n futuro, avvenire.

futurity ['fju:tuəriti] n avvenire.

fuzz [fʌz] n lanugine; increspatura di capelli.

fuzzy ['fʌzi] a lanuginoso; dai capelli crespi; confuso; (phot) sfocato.

G

gabardine ['gæbədi:n] n gabardina.

gabble ['gæbl] n barbugliamento; vt pronunciare in modo inarticolato o confuso; vi parlare indistintamente.

gable ['geibl] n (arch) timpano, frontone; **g. roof** tetto a due spioventi.

Gabriel ['geibriəl] nm pr Gabriele.

gad [gæd] vi bighellonare; **g. about** a n vagabondo.

gadfly ['gædflai] n tafano.

gadget ['gædʒit] n (fam) congegno, aggeggio.

Gaelic ['geilik] a gaelico.

gag [gæg] n bavaglio; (sl) battuta improvvisata; vt imbavagliare; vi (sl) improvvisare battute.

gage [geidʒ] n pegno.

gaiety ['geiəti] n gaiezza.

gaily ['geili] ad gaiamente.

gain [gein] n guadagno; vt guadagnare; vi (clock) andare avanti.

gainings ['geiniŋz] n pl utili, profitti.

gainsay [gein'sei] vt contraddire.

gait [geit] n andatura.

gaiter ['geitə] n ghetta.

galaxy ['gæləksi] n galassia; (fig) assemblea brillante.

gale [geil] n bufera di vento.

gall [gɔ:l] n bile, fiele; malignità; vt

irritare; scorticare; **gallstone** calcolo biliare.

gallant ['gælənt] *a* intrepido, valoroso; galante; *n* galante, cavaliere.

gallantry ['gæləntri] *n* valore; galanteria.

galleon ['gæliən] *n* (*naut*) galeone.

gallery ['gæləri] *n* galleria; (*theat*) loggione.

galley ['gæli] *n* galea; (*naut*) cambusa.

gallivant [ˌgæli'vænt] *vi* andare a zonzo.

gallon ['gælən] *n* gallone (*misura inglese di capacità = litri 4,543*).

gallop ['gæləp] *n* galoppo; *vti* (far) galoppare.

gallows ['gælouz] *n pl* forca, patibolo.

galore [gə'lɔː] *n* abbondanza; *ad* a bizzeffe.

galosh [gə'lɔʃ] *n* galoscia; soprascarpa.

galvanic [gæl'vænik] *a* (el) galvanico; (*fig*) galvanizzante.

galvanize ['gælvənaiz] *vt* galvanizzare.

gambit ['gæmbit] *n* (*chess*) gambetto; (*fig*) iniziativa, attacco.

gamble ['gæmbl] *n* gioco d'azzardo; *vti* giocare d'azzardo, speculare rischiosamente.

gambler ['gæmblə] *n* giocatore d'azzardo, speculatore.

gambling ['gæmblin] *n* giochi d'azzardo *pl*, **g. house** bisca.

gambol ['gæmbəl] *n* piroetta, capriola; *vi* piroettare.

game [geim] *n* gioco, partita; caccia, selvaggina.

gamekeeper ['geim,kiːpə] *n* guardacaccia.

gammon ['gæmən] *n* parte più bassa d'un prosciutto, prosciutto affumicato; (*fig*) inganno.

gamut ['gæmət] *n* gamma, serie completa.

gander ['gændə] *n* papero.

gang [gæŋ] *n* banda; squadra; combriccola.

ganglion ['gæŋgliən] *n* ganglio.

gangrene ['gæŋgriːn] *n* cancrena.

gangster ['gæŋstə] *n* 'gangster', bandito.

gangway ['gæŋwei] *n* corridoio, passaggio; passerella.

gaol [dʒeil] *n* prigione.

gaoler ['dʒeilə] *n* carceriere.

gap [gæp] *n* breccia, fenditura; (US) passo di montagna; (*fig*) divergenza; lacuna.

gape [geip] *n* spaccatura; apertura della bocca; sbadiglio; *vi* sbadigliare; spalancare la bocca.

garage ['gærɑːʒ] *n* autorimessa, 'garage'.

garb [gɑːb] *n* abbigliamento

garbage ['gɑːbidʒ] *n* rifiuti *pl*; **g. can** (US) pattumiera.

garble ['gɑːbl] *vt* falsificare (una storia).

garden ['gɑːdn] *n* giardino; *vi* lavorare di giardinaggio.

gardener ['gɑːdnə] *n* giardiniere.

gardening ['gɑːdniŋ] *n* giardinaggio.

gargle ['gɑːgl] *n* gargarismo; *vi* fare gargarismi.

gargoyle ['gɑːgɔil] *n* gargolla; figura grottesca.

garish ['gɛəriʃ] *a* abbagliante, sgargiante.

garland ['gɑːlənd] *n* ghirlanda.

garlic ['gɑːlik] *n* aglio.

garment ['gɑːmənt] *n* articolo di vestiario, indumento.

garnish ['gɑːniʃ] *n* (cook) guarnizione, contorno; *vt* guarnire, ornare.

garret ['gærət] *n* abbaino, soffitta.

garrison ['gærisn] *n* guarnigione; *vt* fornire di guarnigione.

garrulity [gæ'ruːliti] *n* loquacità.

garrulous ['gæruləs] *a* garrulo, loquace.

garter ['gɑːtə] *n* giarrettiera.

gas [gæs] *pl* **gases** *n* gas; **g. cooker** cucina a gas, fornello a gas; **g. meter** contatore del gas; **g. stove** cucina a gas.

gash [gæʃ] *n* squarcio; *vt* fare uno squarcio.

gasoline ['gæsəliːn] (US) benzina.

gasp [gɑːsp] *n* respiro affannoso, rantolo; sussulto; *vti* boccheggiare, ansare; soffocare un'esclamazione.

gassy ['gæsi] *a* gassoso.

gastric ['gæstrik] *a* gastrico.

gastritis [gæs'traitis] *n* gastrite.

gastronomical [ˌgæstrə'nɔmikəl] *n* gastronomico.

gastronomy [gæs'trɔnəmi] *n* gastronomia.

gate [geit] *n* cancello, (*of town*) porta.

gateway ['geitwei] *n* portone, entrata.

gather ['gæðə] *vt* (rac)cogliere, radunare; fare le pieghe; *vi* radunarsi; (med) venire a suppurazione.

gathering ['gæðəriŋ] *n* adunata, assemblea; (med) ascesso.

gaudy ['gɔːdi] *a* sfarzoso e di cattivo gusto.

gauge [geidʒ] *n* apparecchio misuratore, misura base, stima; *vt* misurare con esattezza; (*fig*) formarsi un concetto di.

gauger ['geidʒə] *n* collaudatore.

gaunt [gɔːnt] *a* macilento, sparuto.

gauntlet ['gɔːntlit] *n* grosso guanto che copre il polso, guanto di armatura.

gauntness ['gɔːntnis] *n* macilenza.

gauze [gɔːz] *n* garza, velo.

gawky ['gɔːki] *a* goffo, sguaiato, balordo.

gay [gei] *a* allegro, gaio; vistoso; brillante; (*fig*) dissoluto.

gaze [geiz] *n* sguardo fisso; *vi* guardare fisso.

gazelle [gə'zel] *n* gazzella.

gazette [gə'zet] *n* gazzetta.

gazetteer [ˌgæzi'tiə] n dizionario geografico.

gear [giə] n equipaggiamento, congegno, ingranaggio, meccanismo, (aut) marcia; **in g.** in marcia.

gelatin(e) ['dʒelətiːn] n gelatina.

geld [geld] vt castrare.

gelding ['geldiŋ] n cavallo castrato.

gelignite ['dʒelignait] n (chem) nitroglicerina.

gem [dʒem] n gemma, gioiello.

gender ['dʒendə] n genere; sesso.

genealogical [ˌdʒiːniə'bdʒikəl] a genealogico.

genealogy [ˌdʒiːni'ælədʒi] n genealogia.

general ['dʒenərəl] a n generale.

generality [ˌdʒenə'ræliti] n generalità, maggioranza.

generalization [ˌdʒenərəlai'zeiʃən] n generalizzazione.

generalize ['dʒenərəlaiz] vti generalizzare.

generally ['dʒenərəli] ad generalmente, di solito.

generate ['dʒenəreit] vt generare.

generation [ˌdʒenə'reiʃən] n generazione.

generative ['dʒenərətiv] a generativo, produttivo.

generator ['dʒenəreitə] n generatore, (US aut) dinamo, generatore.

generosity [ˌdʒenə'rɔsiti] n generosità.

generous ['dʒenərəs] a generoso.

generously ['dʒenərəsli] ad generosamente.

genetic [dʒi'netik] a genetico.

Geneva [dʒi'niːvə] n Ginevra.

Genevieve [ˌdʒenə'viːv] nf pr Genoveffa.

genial ['dʒiːniəl] a amabile, piacevole; (climate) mite.

geniality [ˌdʒiːni'æliti] n amabilità, giovialità.

genital ['dʒenitl] a genitale.

genitals ['dʒenitlz] n pl organi genitali.

genitive ['dʒenitiv] a n genitivo.

genius ['dʒiːniəs] n genio, talento.

Genoa ['dʒenouə] n Genova; **Genoese** a n genovese.

genocide ['dʒenousaid] n genocidio.

genteel [dʒen'tiːl] a (ironic) compito, manieroso.

gentle ['dʒentl] a dolce, mite; nobile.

gentlefolk ['dʒentlfouk] n gente che appartiene alle classi elevate.

gentleman ['dʒentlmən] n gentiluomo, signore.

gentlemanly ['dʒentlmənli] a da gentiluomo, signorile.

gentleness ['dʒentlnis] n dolcezza, tenerezza, grazia.

gentlewoman ['dʒentlˌwumən] n gentildonna, signora.

gently ['dʒentli] ad con delicatezza, dolcemente.

gentry ['dʒentri] n piccola nobiltà.

genuine ['dʒenjuin] a genuino.

genuineness ['dʒenjuinis] n genuinità.

geodesy [dʒi:'ɔdisi] n geodesia.

Geoffrey ['dʒefri] nm pr Goffredo.

geographic(al) [dʒiə'græfik(əl)] a geografico.

geography [dʒi'ɔgrəfi] n geografia.

geology [dʒi'ɔlədʒi] n geologia.

geometric [dʒiə'metrik] a geometrico.

geometry [dʒi'ɔmitri] n geometria.

George [dʒɔːdʒ] nm pr Giorgio.

Georgian ['dʒɔːdʒiən] a n georgiano, georgiana.

geranium [dʒi'reiniəm] n geranio.

geriatric [ˌdʒeri'ætrik] a geriatrico.

geriatrics [ˌdʒeri'ætriks] n geriatria.

germ [dʒəːm] n germe.

German ['dʒəːmən] a n tedesco.

Germany ['dʒəːməni] n Germania.

germinate ['dʒəːmineit] vi germinare.

germination [ˌdʒəːmi'neiʃən] n germinazione.

Gertrude ['gəːtruːd] nf pr Gertrude.

gestation [dʒes'teiʃən] n gestazione.

gesticulate [dʒes'tikjuleit] vi gesticolare.

gesticulation [dʒesˌtikju'leiʃən] n il gesticolare.

gesture ['dʒestʃə] n gesto; vi gestire. gesticolare.

get [get] vt ottenere, ricevere, guadagnare, prendere, portare, persuadere; vi arrivare, raggiungere, divenire.

gewgaw ['gjuːgɔː] n ninnolo.

geyser ['giːzə] n sorgente calda; apparecchio scaldabagno.

ghastly ['gaːstli] a spaventoso, spettrale.

gherkin ['gəːkin] n cetriolino.

ghetto ['getou] pl **ghettos** n ghetto.

ghost [goust] n spirito, fantasma; **The Holy G.** lo Spirito Santo.

ghostly ['goustli] a spettrale.

ghoul [guːl] n spirito maligno che divora i cadaveri; (fig) persona orribile e crudele.

ghoulish ['guːliʃ] a demoniaco, macabro.

giant ['dʒaiənt] a n gigante; **giantess** n gigantessa.

gibber ['dʒibə] vi parlare rapidamente e senza senso.

gibberish ['gibəriʃ] n parole senza senso.

gibbet ['dʒibit] n forca, patibolo.

gibe [dʒaib] n beffa, scherno; vti beffar(si), schernire.

giblets ['dʒiblits] n pl rigaglie pl.

Gibraltar [dʒi'brɔːltə] n Gibilterra.

giddiness ['gidinis] n vertigine; incostanza.

giddy ['gidi] a in preda a vertigini; incostante.

gift [gift] n dono, regalo, donazione.

gig [gig] n calessino; (naut) lancia.

gigantic [dʒai'gæntik] a gigantesco.

giggle ['gigl] n risatina sciocca; vi ridere scioccamente.

gigue [ʒiːg] n (mus) giga.

gild [gild] vt (in)dorare.

gilding ['gildiŋ] n doratura.

Giles [dʒailz] nm pr Egidio.

gill [gil] n misura di capacità liquida (litri ,0142).

gilt [gilt] a dorato; n doratura.

gimcrack ['dʒimkræk] a appariscente e di nessun valore; n cianfrusaglia.

gimlet ['gimlit] n succhiello.

gin [dʒin] n gin; trappola.

ginger ['dʒindʒə] n zenzero; **gingerbread** pan di zenzero.

gingerly ['dʒindʒəli] a guardingo; ad con precauzione.

gingham ['giŋəm] n percalle a righe o quadretti, rigatino.

gipsy, gypsy ['dʒipsi] n zingaro, zingara; a zingaresco.

giraffe [dʒi'rɑːf] n giraffa.

gird [gəːd] vt cingere, circondare; vi beffare.

girder ['gəːdə] n (mech) trave maestra, putrella.

girdle ['gəːdl] n cintura; cerchia; busto; vt recingere; chiudere con una cintura.

girl [gəːl] n ragazza, fanciulla.

girlhood ['gəːlhud] n adolescenza (di ragazza).

girlish ['gəːliʃ] a di (da) ragazza.

girth [gəːθ] n circonferenza; sottopancia; vt cingere.

gist [dʒist] n punto essenziale, sostanza.

give [giv] vti dare, cedere; g. and take n compromesso, concessione reciproca.

gizzard ['gizəd] n (of birds) ventriglio.

glacial ['gleisiəl] a glaciale.

glacier ['glæsiə] n ghiacciaio.

glad [glæd] a contento, lieto.

glade [gleid] n radura.

gladiator ['glædieitə] n gladiatore.

gladiolus [,glædi'ouləs] pl **gladioli** n gladiolo.

gladly ['glædli] ad con piacere, volentieri.

gladness ['glædnis] n contentezza.

glamour ['glæmə] n fascino, magia.

glamorous ['glæmərəs] a affascinante.

glance [glɑːns] n occhiata, sguardo; vi dare un'occhiata, gettare uno sguardo.

glancing ['glɑːnsiŋ] a fugace, rapido.

gland [glænd] n glandola.

glanders ['glændəz] n pl cimurro.

glandular ['glændjulə] a glandolare.

glare [glɛə] n bagliore, luce abbagliante; sguardo furibondo; vi risplendere di luce abbagliante; guardare con rabbia.

glaring ['glɛəriŋ] a abbagliante; manifesto.

glass [glɑːs] n vetro, vetri pl; bic-

chiere; cristallo; telescopio; **glasses** pl occhiali pl.

glassy ['glɑːsi] a vitreo.

Glaswegian [glæs'wiːdʒən] a n abitante di Glasgow.

glaze [gleiz] n smalto, vernice; vt fornire di vetri; smaltare, verniciare.

glazier ['gleiziə] n vetraio.

gleam [gliːm] n barlume, debole raggio di luce; vi luccicare, balughinare.

glean [gliːn] vti spigolare, raccogliere.

gleaning ['gliːniŋ] n spigolatura.

glebe [gliːb] n gleba.

glee [gliː] n giubilo; (mus) canone.

glen [glen] n valletta.

glib [glib] a liscio, scorrevole, pronto.

glide [glaid] vi scivolare, trascorrere.

glider ['glaidə] n (av) aliante; (naut) idroplano.

gliding ['glaidiŋ] a scorrevole, (av) che plana; n (av) volo a vela.

glimmer ['glimə] n luce debole e incerta; vi mandare una luce fioca.

glimpse [glimps] n rapida visione; vt intravvedere.

glint [glint] n luccichio; vi luccicare.

glisten ['glisn] n scintillio, luccichio; vi scintillare, luccicare.

glitter ['glitə] n scintillio; vi scintillare.

glittering ['glitəriŋ] a scintillante, brillante; n scintillio.

gloaming ['gloumiŋ] n crepuscolo.

gloat [glout] vi guardare con gioia perversa, gongolare.

globe [gloub] n globo.

gloom [gluːm] n tenebre pl, tristezza.

gloomy ['gluːmi] a fosco, tetro, triste.

glorification [,glɔːrifi'keiʃən] n glorificazione.

glorify ['glɔːrifai] vt glorificare.

glorious ['glɔːriəs] a glorioso, magnifico.

gloriously ['glɔːriəsli] ad gloriosamente, splendidamente.

glory ['glɔːri] n gloria, splendore; vi esultare, gloriarsi.

gloss [glɔs] n chiosa, glossa; lucentezza; (fig) vernice; vt lucidare; chiosare.

glossary ['glɔsəri] n glossario.

glossy ['glɔsi] a lucido, lucente.

glove [glʌv] n guanto.

glow [glou] n incandescenza, calore; ardore; vi rosseggiare; essere incandescente; ardere.

glow-worm ['glouwəːm] n lucciola.

glower ['glauə] vi guardare con cipiglio.

glucose ['gluːkous] n (chem) glucosio.

glue [gluː] n colla; vt incollare.

glum [glʌm] a accigliato, taciturno.

glut [glʌt] n sovrabbondanza, sazietà.

glutinous ['gluːtinəs] a gluttinoso.

glutton ['glʌtn] n ghiottone.

gluttonous ['glʌtənəs] a ghiotto, goloso.

gluttony ['glʌtni] n golosità, ingordigia.

glycerine ['glisəri:n] n glicerina.

gnarled [nɑ:ld] a nodoso, nocchieruto, pieno di nodi.

gnash [næʃ] vt digrignare (i denti).

gnat [næt] n moscerino.

gnaw [nɔ:] vt rodere, rosicchiare.

gnome [noum] n gnomo.

go [gou] vi andare, farsi; **g.-ahead** a (fam) intraprendente; n segnale di passare all'azione; **g.-between** intermediario; **g.-getter** (US fam) arrivista.

goad [goud] n pungolo, stimolo; vt mandar avanti col pungolo, stimolare.

goal [goul] n meta, traguardo; (football) porta, rete; "gol."

goat [gout] n capra; **g.-herd** capraio.

gobble ['gɔbl] vt ingoiare a grossi bocconi.

goblet ['gɔblit] n calice, coppa.

goblin ['gɔblin] n folletto, spirito maligno.

god [gɔd] n dio, divinità; idolo.

godchild ['gɔdtʃaild] n figlioccio.

goddess ['gɔdis] n dea.

godfather ['gɔd,fɑ:ðə] n padrino.

godhead ['gɔdhed] n divinità.

godless ['gɔdlis] a ateo, empio.

godlessness ['gɔdlisnis] n ateismo; empietà.

godliness ['gɔdlinis] n devozione, religiosità.

godly ['gɔdli] a devoto, religioso.

godmother ['gɔd,mʌðə] n madrina.

godsend ['gɔdsend] n dono del cielo, fortuna inaspettata.

godson ['gɔdsʌn] n figlioccio.

goggle ['gɔgl] vi stralunare (gli occhi).

goggles ['gɔglz] n pl occhiali di protezione; (sl) occhialoni.

going ['gouiŋ] n partenza; l'andare; andamento; a ben avviato.

goitre ['gɔitə] n gozzo.

gold [gould] a aureo, d'oro; n oro, danaro.

golden ['gouldən] a aureo, d'oro, dorato.

goldfinch ['gouldfintʃ] n cardellino.

goldfish ['gouldfiʃ] n pesce rosso.

goldsmith ['gouldsmiθ] n orefice.

golosh [gə'lɔʃ] v galosh.

gondolier [,gɔndə'liə] n gondoliere.

gong [gɔŋ] n gong.

good [gud] a buono; n bene; **g. day** buon giorno; **g. night** buona sera, buona notte.

good-bye ['gud'bai] interj addio, arrivederci.

good-for-nothing ['gudfə,nʌθiŋ] a inutile; n buono a nulla.

goodly ['gudli] a bello, buono; considerevole.

good-natured ['gud'neitʃəd] a di buon carattere.

goodness ['gudnis] n bontà, generosità.

goods ['gudz] n pl merci pl; **g.-train** treno merci; **g.-van** vagone merci chiuso.

goodwill ['gud'wil] n buona volontà, benevolenza, favore.

goose [gu:s] pl **geese** n oca.

gooseberry ['guzbəri] n uva spina.

gorge ['gɔ:dʒ] n strozza; vt ingozzare; vi rimpinzarsi; gola di montagna.

gorgeous ['gɔ:dʒəs] a magnifico, sontuoso, sgargiante.

gorilla [gə'rilə] n gorilla.

gorse [gɔ:s] n ginestra spinosa.

gory ['gɔ:ri] a insanguinato.

gosling ['gɔzliŋ] n paperetto.

gospel ['gɔspəl] n vangelo.

gossamer ['gɔsəmə] n sottile filo di ragnatela, velo finissimo.

gossip ['gɔsip] n chiacchiera, pettegolezzo; individuo pettegolo; vi pettegolare.

Gothic ['gɔθik] a gotico.

gouache [gu'ɑ:ʃ] n guazzo.

gourd [guəd] n zucca.

gourmet ['guəmei] n buongustaio, conoscitore.

gout [gaut] n gotta.

gouty ['gauti] a gottoso.

govern ['gʌvən] vti governare.

governable ['gʌvənəbl] a docile.

governess ['gʌvənis] n istitutrice.

governing ['gʌvəniŋ] a governante, dirigente.

government ['gʌvənmənt] n governo.

governor ['gʌvənə] n governatore; (sl) padrone, capo, padre.

gown [gaun] n veste, vestito, toga; **dressing g.** veste da camera, vestaglia.

grab [græb] vt afferrare, impadronirsi con la violenza di.

grabble ['græbl] vi andare a tastoni.

grace [greis] n grazia, favore; vt adornare, favorire.

Grace [greis] nf pr Grazia.

graceful ['greisful] a aggraziato, grazioso.

gracefulness ['greisfulnis] n grazia.

gracious ['greiʃəs] a condiscendente, grazioso.

gradation [grə'deiʃən] n gradazione.

grade [greid] n grado; (US) pendenza; (US) classe; classificazione; vt classificare, graduare; **g. crossing** (US) passaggio a livello.

gradient ['greidiənt] n pendenza, gradiente.

gradual ['grædjuəl] a n graduale.

gradually ['grædjuəli] ad gradualmente, gradatamente; a poco a poco.

graduate ['grædjuit] n laureato; (US) diplomato; ['grædjueit] vt graduare; vi laurearsi.

graduation [,grædju'eiʃən] n laurea, (US) licenza, diploma; graduazione.

graft [grɑ:ft] n innesto; vt innestare.

grain [grein] n grano; grana; venatura.

gram(me) [græm] n grammo.

grammar ['græmə] n grammatica.

grammarian [grə'mɛəriən] n grammatico.

grammatical [grə'mætikəl] a grammaticale.

gramophone ['græməfoun] n gramofono.

granary ['grænəri] n granaio.

grand [grænd] a grande, grandioso, imponente, maestoso, principale.

grandchild ['græntʃaild] pl **grandchildren** n nipote, nipotino, nipotina.

granddaughter ['græn,dɔ:tə] n nipote, nipotina.

grandeur ['grændʒə] n magnificenza, splendore.

grandfather ['grænd,fɑ:ðə] n nonno.

grandiose ['grændious] a grandioso, pomposo.

grandmother ['græn,mʌðə] n nonna.

grandparent ['græn,pɛərənt] n nonno, nonna.

grandson ['grænsʌn] n nipote, nipotino.

grandstand ['grænstænd] n tribuna d'onore.

grange [greindʒ] n fattoria, casa signorile di campagna.

granite ['grænit] n granito.

grant [grɑ:nt] n concessione, borsa di studio, donazione; vt ammettere, concedere.

grape [greip] n (acino d') uva; (mil) carica di mitraglia; **grapefruit** pompelmo.

graph [grɑ:f] n grafico.

graphic ['græfik] a grafico.

graphite ['græfait] n grafite.

grapnel ['græpnəl] n ancoretta, uncino.

grapple ['græpl] n ancoretta, rampone; lotta corpo a corpo; vt assicurare con l'ancoretta; vi venire alle prese; lottare.

grasp [grɑ:sp] n presa, stretta; comprensione; vt afferrare.

grasping ['grɑ:spiŋ] a avaro, avido.

grass [grɑ:s] n erba.

grasshopper ['grɑ:s,hɔpə] n grillo, saltamartino; (av mil) apparecchio di collegamento.

grassy ['grɑ:si] a erboso.

grate [greit] n grata, griglia, inferriata; vt munire di grata; grattugiare; vi stridere; irritare.

grateful ['greitful] a grato, riconoscente.

grater ['greitə] n grattugia.

gratification [,grætifi'keiʃən] n gratificazione, soddisfazione.

gratify ['grætifai] vt gratificare.

grating ['greitiŋ] a irritante; stridente; n grata, inferriata.

gratitude ['grætitju:d] n gratitudine, riconoscenza.

gratuitous [grə'tju:itəs] a gratuito, ingiustificato.

gratuity [grə'tju:iti] n gratifica, mancia.

grave [greiv] a austero, grave, serio; n tomba.

gravel ['grævəl] n ghiaia; vt ricoprire di ghiaia; (fig) imbarazzare.

graveyard ['greivjɑ:d] n camposanto, cimitero.

gravitate ['græviteit] vi gravitare.

gravitation [,grævi'teiʃən] n gravitazione.

gravity ['græviti] n gravità.

gravy ['greivi] n sugo di carne, salsa.

gray [grei] v grey.

graze [greiz] n abrasione; vt escoriare, scalfire, sfiorare; vt pascere, pascolare.

grazing ['greiziŋ] n pascolo, pastura.

grease [gri:s] n grasso, unto; materia lubrificante; vt lubrificare, ungere.

greasy ['gri:zi] a grasso, unto, untuoso.

great [greit] a grande, nobile.

Great Britain ['greit'britn] n Gran Bretagna.

greatly ['greitli] ad grandemente, molto.

greatness ['greitnis] n grandezza.

Greece [gri:s] n Grecia.

greed [gri:d] n bramosia, cupidigia.

greedily ['gri:dili] ad avidamente, golosamente.

greediness ['gri:dinis] n avidità, golosità.

greedy ['gri:di] a ghiotto, goloso, avido.

Greek [gri:k] a n greco.

green [gri:n] a verde; n verde, verzura; **greens** pl erbaggi pl, verdura.

greenery ['gri:nəri] n verdura.

greenfinch ['gri:nfintʃ] n verdone.

greengage ['gri:ngeidʒ] n susina claudia.

greengrocer ['gri:n,grousə] n erbivendolo, ortolano.

greenhouse ['gri:nhaus] n serra.

Greenland ['gri:nlənd] n Groenlandia.

Greenlander ['gri:nləndə] n groenlandese.

greenness ['gri:nnis] n color verde; (fig) immaturità, inesperienza.

greet [gri:t] vt salutare (all'arrivo).

greeting ['gri:tiŋ] n saluto.

Gregory ['gregəri] nm pr Gregorio.

grenade [gre'neid] n (mil) granata.

grenadier [,grenə'diə] n granatiere.

grey, gray [grei] a n grigio.

greyhound ['greihaund] n levriero.

greyness ['greinis] n grigiore.

grid [grid] n grata, griglia; (map) quadrettatura.

grief [gri:f] n afflizione, dolore.

grievance ['gri:vəns] n lagnanza; torto.

grieve [gri:v] vti addolorar(si), affligger(si).

grievous ['gri:vəs] a doloroso, penoso, grave, serio.

grill [gril] *n* (vivanda alla) griglia; *vt* arrostire alla griglia; sottoporre ad un severo interrogatorio; *vi* esser tormentato (dal caldo).

grim [grim] *a* fosco, torvo, severo.

grimace [gri'meis] *n* smorfia.

grime [graim] *n* sudiciume.

grimy ['graimi] *a* sudicio.

grin [grin] *n* sogghigno, largo sorriso; *vi* sogghignare.

grind [graind] *n* lavoro faticoso e ingrato; *vt* arrotare, macinare; (*fig*) opprimere; *vi* sgobbare.

grinder ['graində] *n* arrotino; macina, dente molare.

grindstone ['graindstoun] *n* macina, mola.

grip [grip] *n* presa, stretta; controllo; impugnatura; capacità di fermare l'attenzione; *vi* afferrare, tenere fermo.

gripe [graip] *vt* afferrare; causare dolori al ventre.

grisly ['grizli] *a* orribile, spaventoso.

grist [grist] *n* grano da macinare, malto preparato per la fabbricazione della birra.

gristle ['grisl] *n* cartilagine.

grit [grit] *n* sabbia, grana; (*fam*) forza di carattere.

grizzled ['grizld] *a* brizzolato.

groan [groun] *n* gemito, lamento; *vi* gemere, lamentarsi.

grocer ['grousə] *n* droghiere.

grocery ['grousəri] *n* (generi di) drogheria, (US) (negozio, generi di) drogheria.

grog [grɔg] *n* (*fam*) bevanda alcoolica calda, 'grog'.

groggy ['grɔgi] *a* brillo; barcollante; vacillante; malfermo.

groin [grɔin] *n* inguine.

groom [grum] *n* stalliere; palafreniere; *vt* strigliare.

groove [gruːv] *n* scanalatura, solco; *vt* scanalare, solcare.

grope [group] *vi* andare tentoni, brancolare.

groping(ly) ['groupiŋ(li)] *ad* (a) tentoni.

gross [grous] *a* grossolano, volgare, (*com*) lordo, complessivo; *n* grossa.

grossness ['grousnis] *n* grossolanità, volgarità.

grotesque [grou'tesk] *a n* grottesco; **grotesqueness** *n* bizzarria, grottesco.

grotto ['grɔtou] *pl* **grottos, grottoes** *n* grotta.

ground [graund] *n* terra, terreno, suolo; base; motivo; sfondo; *vt* basare, fondare; istruire bene; *vi* incagliarsi; **grounds** *pl* deposito, fondi *pl*; (*of mansion*) parco, giardini *pl*; **g. floor** pianterreno; **g. wire** (US *rad*) filo di terra.

grounding ['graundiŋ] *n* base, conoscenza.

groundless ['graundlis] *a* infondato.

group [gruːp] *n* gruppo; *vti* raggruppar(si).

grouse [graus] *n* gallo di montagna; *vi* (*fam*) brontolare.

grove [grouv] *n* boschetto.

grovel ['grɔvl] *vi* strisciare a terra, umiliarsi.

grow [grou] *vi* crescere, aumentare, svilupparsi, divenire; *vt* coltivare.

grower ['grouə] *n* coltivatore.

growl [graul] *n* borbottio rabbioso; *vi* brontolare, borbottare irosamente.

grown-up ['grounʌp] *a n* adulto.

growth [grouθ] *n* crescita, sviluppo, progresso; (*med*) escrescenza morbosa, tumore.

grub [grʌb] *n* larva, bruco; (*sl*) cibo; *vt* zappare, sgobbare.

grubby ['grʌbi] *a* sporco, verminoso.

grudge [grʌdʒ] *n* astio, rancore; *vt* lesinare;, invidiare.

grudgingly ['grʌdʒiŋli] *ad* a malincuore, malvolentieri.

gruel ['gruəl] *n* pappa d'avena; **to give s.o. his g.** darne un fracco a qlcu.

gruelling ['gruəliŋ] *a* estenuante.

gruesome ['gruːsəm] *a* orribile, orripilante.

gruff [grʌf] *a* burbero, sgarbato.

gruffness ['grʌfnis] *n* burbanza.

grumble ['grʌmbl] *vi* borbottare, brontolare.

grumpy ['grʌmpi] *a* (*fam*) irritabile, bisbetico.

grunt [grʌnt] *n* grugnito, brontolio; *vti* grugnire, brontolare.

guarantee [ˌgærən'tiː] *n* garanzia, garante; *vt* garantire, essere garante per.

guarantor [ˌgærən'tɔː] *n* garante; (*com*) avallante.

guard [gɑːd] *n* guardia; (*rly*) capotreno; *vt* custodire, proteggere, sorvegliare.

guarded ['gɑːdid] *a* prudente, guardingo, cauto.

guardedly ['gɑːdidli] *ad* in modo guardingo, con circospezione.

guardian ['gɑːdiən] *n* guardiano, tutore; **guardianship** protezione, tutela.

guerrilla [gə'rilə] *pl* **guerrillas** *n* guerriglia; guerrigliere.

guess [ges] *n* congettura, supposizione; *vti* congetturare, indovinare, supporre.

guest [gest] *n* ospite.

guffaw [gʌ'fɔː] *n* risata fragorosa.

guidance ['gaidəns] *n* guida, direzione.

guide [gaid] *n* guida, cicerone; *vt* guidare, dirigere.

guild [gild] *n* corporazione.

guile [gail] *n* artificio, astuzia, inganno.

guileless ['gaillis] *a* semplice, ingenuo.

guillotine [ˌgilə'tiːn] *n* ghigliottina; *vt* ghigliottinare.

guilt [gilt] *n* colpa, colpevolezza.

guiltless ['giltlis] *a* innocente.

guilty ['gilti] *a* colpevole.

Guinea ['gini] *n* Guinea.

guinea ['gini] *n* ghinea (*moneta inglese antica, che valeva ventun scellini*).

guinea-pig ['ginipig] *n* porcellino d'india, cavia.

guise [gaiz] *n* apparenza, foggia, guisa.

guitar [gi'tɑː] *n* chitarra.

gulf [gʌlf] *n* golfo; abisso; vortice.

gull [gʌl] *n* gabbiano; *vt* gabbare, ingannare.

gullet ['gʌlit] *n* gola, esofago.

gully ['gʌli] *n* burrone.

gulp [gʌlp] *n* atto dell'inghiottire, quantità inghiottita in una volta; *vt* inghiottire voracemente, trangugiare.

gum [gʌm] *n* gomma; gengiva; *vt* ingommare.

gun [gʌn] *n* cannone, fucile, arma da sparo; **gunfire** sparatoria, cannoneggiamento; **gunman** (*US sl*) rapinatore.

gunboat ['gʌnbout] *n* (*naut*) cannoniera.

gunner ['gʌnə] *n* artigliere.

gunpowder ['gʌn͵paudə] *n* polvere da sparo.

gunshot ['gʌnʃɔt] *n* colpo di arma da fuoco.

gunsmith ['gʌnsmiθ] *n* armaiolo.

gurgle ['gɜːgl] *n* gorgoglio; *vi* gorgogliare.

gush [gʌʃ] *n* fiotto, zampillo; effusione sentimentale; *vti* sgorgare in gran copia, zampillare; fare esagerate effusioni.

gushing ['gʌʃiŋ] *a* zampillante; espansivo.

gust [gʌst] *n* (*of wind, rain*) raffica, (*of wind*) colpo; (*of rage*) scoppio.

gusto ['gʌstou] *n* entusiasmo, piacere.

gusty ['gʌsti] *a* burrascoso.

gut [gʌt] *n* budello, intestino; *vt* sbudellare, sventrare.

gutter ['gʌtə] *n* grondaia, cunetta.

guttural ['gʌtərəl] *a* gutturale.

Guy [gai] *nm pr* Guido.

guy [gai] *n* (*mech*) cavo; figura grottesca, spauracchio; (*US*) individuo.

guzzle ['gʌzl] *vti* mangiare o bere a crepapelle.

gymnasium [dʒim'neiziəm] *n* palestra.

gymnast ['dʒimnæst] *n* ginnasta.

gymnastics [dʒim'næstiks] *n pl* ginnastica.

gypsy ['dʒipsi] *v* **gipsy**.

gyrate [͵dʒaiə'reit] *vi* girare, turbinare.

H

haberdasher ['hæbədæʃə] *n* merciaio.

haberdashery ['hæbədæʃəri] *n* merceria.

habit ['hæbit] *n* abitudine; abito.

habitable ['hæbitəbl] *a* abitabile.

habitation [͵hæbi'teiʃən] *n* abitazione.

habitual [hə'bitjuəl] *a* abituale.

hack ['hæk] *n* intaccatura, taglio; cavallo da nolo; individuo sfruttato in un lavoro gravoso; *vt* colpire con arma da taglio; tagliuzzare; *vi* tossire a colpi secchi.

hackney ['hækni] *n* **h. cab** vettura da nolo; **hackneyed** *a* banale.

haddock ['hædək] *n* specie di merluzzo.

haemorrhage ['heməridʒ] *n* emorragia.

haft [hɑːft] *n* elsa, manico.

hag [hæg] *n* megera, strega.

haggard ['hægəd] *a* magro, sparuto.

haggle ['hægl] *vi* disputare, lesinare sul prezzo, contrattare.

Hague (the) [ðə'heig] *n* l'Aja.

hail [heil] *n* grandine; saluto; *vi* grandinare; *vt* chiamare a gran voce.

hair [hɛə] *n* capello, capelli *pl*; pelo; **h.'s breadth** spessore di un capello, distanza minima; **haircut** taglio di capelli; **hairline** corda di crine; **hairpin** forcina.

hairdresser ['hɛə͵dresə] *n* parrucchiere, parrucchiera.

hairless ['hɛəlis] *a* calvo, senza peli.

hairy ['hɛəri] *a* peloso, irsuto.

halcyon ['hælsiən] *a* calmo; *n* alcione.

hale [heil] *a* robusto, sano, vigoroso.

half [hɑːf] *pl* **halves** *a* mezzo; *n* metà, mezzo; *ad* a metà, (a) mezzo; **half-brother** fratellastro; **half-hour** mezz'ora; **half-pay** mezzo stipendio; **half-way** a mezza strada; **half-witted** corto d'intelletto; **half-yearly** semestrale, due volte all'anno.

halfpenny ['heipni] *pl* **half-pennies, halfpence** *n* mezzo penny.

halibut ['hælibət] *n* (*fish*) passera.

hall [hɔːl] *n* aula, salone, sala di ricevimento; vestibolo.

hallo(a)! [hə'lou] *interj* salve!; (*tel*) pronto!

hallow ['hælou] *vt* consacrare; **hallowed** *a* santo, benedetto.

hallucination [hə͵luːsi'neiʃən] *a* allucinazione.

halo ['heilou] *pl* **halos, haloes** *n* alone, aureola.

halt [hɔːlt] *n* sosta, fermata; *vi* fare una sosta, fermarsi; esitare; zoppicare.

halter ['hɔːltə] *n* capestro; cavezza.

halve [hɑːv] *vt* dimezzare.

ham [hæm] *n* prosciutto; coscia.

Hamburg ['hæmbəːg] *n* Amburgo.

hamburger ['hæmbəːgə] *n* polpetta di carne e cipolla tritata; panino imbottito di tale polpetta.

hamlet ['hæmlit] *n* piccolo villaggio.

hammer ['hæmə] *n* martello; (*gun*)

cane; *vt* martellare; (*fam*) ficcare in testa; battere.

hammering ['hæməriŋ] *a* martellamento, battuta.

hammock ['hæmək] *n* amaca.

hamper ['hæmpə] *n* cesta; (*naut*) accessori ingombranti; *vt* impedire, ostacolare.

hamster ['hæmstə] *n* criceto.

hand [hænd] *n* mano; (*of clocks etc*) lancetta; calligrafia; (*cards*) mano; (*worker*) operaio; *vt* consegnare, porgere.

handbag ['hændbæg] *n* borsetta.

handbill ['hændbil] *n* volantino.

handbook ['hændbuk] *n* manuale.

handcuff ['hændkʌf] *n usu pl* -manette *pl*; *vt* mettere le manette a.

handful ['hændful] *n* manata, pugno; (*fam*) persona, cosa difficile da trattarsi.

handicap ['hændikæp] *n* ostacolo; (*sport*) 'handicap', corsa pareggiata.

handicraft ['hændikra:ft] *n* arte, lavoro dell'artigiano.

handiwork ['hændiwə:k] *n* lavoro (a mano).

handkerchief ['hæŋkətʃif] *n* fazzoletto.

handle ['hændl] *n* manico; maniglia; (*fig*) occasione; *vt* maneggiare, manipolare.

handlebar ['hændlba:] *n* manubrio di bicicletta.

handshake ['hændʃeik] *n* stretta di mano.

handsome ['hænsəm] *a* bello, ben proporzionato; generoso.

handwriting ['hænd,raitiŋ] *n* calligrafia, scrittura.

handy ['hændi] *a* abile, destro; a portata di mano.

hang [hæŋ] *vt* appendere, attaccare, impiccare; *vi* dipendere, pendere.

hangar ['hæŋə] *a* aviorimessa, 'hangar'.

hangman ['hæŋmən] *pl* -men *n* boia, carnefice.

hank [hæŋk] *n* matassa; (*naut*) anello della randa.

hanker ['hæŋkə] *vi* bramare.

haphazard ['hæp'hæzəd] *n* puro caso; *ad* a caso.

hapless ['hæplis] *a* sfortunato.

happen ['hæpən] *vi* accadere, avvenire, capitare, succedere.

happening ['hæpəniŋ] *n* avvenimento.

happily ['hæpili] *ad* felicemente, fortunatamente.

happiness ['hæpinis] *n* felicità.

happy ['hæpi] *a* felice, propizio.

harangue [hə'ræŋ] *n* arringa; *vt* arringare.

harass ['hærəs] *vt* seccare, tormentare.

harbinger ['ha:bindʒə] *n* messaggero; precursore.

harbour ['ha:bə] *n* porto, rifugio; *vt* ccogliere, albergare; (*fig*) nutrire.

hard [ha:d] *a* duro, difficile; *ad* con insistenza, con difficoltà, molto.

harden ['ha:dn] *vt* indurire, rendere insensibile; *vi* indurirsi, diventare insensibile.

hardihood ['ha:dihud] *n* ardimento, arditezza.

hardiness ['ha:dinis] *n* robustezza, resistenza fisica.

hardly ['ha:dli] *ad* appena, a mala pena, scarsamente.

hardness ['ha:dnis] *n* durezza.

hardship ['ha:dʃip] *n* avversità, disagio, privazione.

hardware ['ha:dwɛə] *n* ferramenta *pl*.

hardy ['ha:di] *a* ardito; resistente.

hare [hɛə] *n* lepre.

harem ['hɛərem] *n* harem.

haricot ['hærikou] *n* fagiolo.

hark! [ha:k] *interj* ascolta(te)!

harlequin ['ha:likwin] *n* arlecchino.

harlot ['ha:lət] *n* prostituta.

harm [ha:m] *n* danno, male; *vt* danneggiare, far male a.

harmful ['ha:mful] *a* dannoso, nocivo.

harmless ['ha:mlis] *a* innocuo.

harmlessly ['ha:mlisli] *ad* in modo innocuo.

harmonica [ha:'mɔnikə] *n* armonica; armonica a bocca.

harmonics [ha:'mɔniks] *n pl* armonia.

harmonious [ha:'mouniəs] *a* armonioso.

harmonium [ha:'mouniəm] *n* armonium.

harmonize ['ha:mənaiz] *vti* armonizzare.

harmony ['ha:məni] *n* armonia.

harness ['ha:nis] *n* bardatura, finimenti *pl*; *vt* bardare; (*fig*) utilizzare.

harp [ha:p] *n* arpa; *vi* insistere fino ad annoiare.

harpoon [ha:'pu:n] *n* fiocina; *vt* fiocinare.

harpsichord ['ha:psikɔ:d] *n* clavicembalo.

harpy ['ha:pi] *n* arpia; (*fig*) megera.

harrow ['hærou] *n* erpice; *vt* erpicare; (*fig*) straziare.

harsh [ha:ʃ] *a* aspro, crudele, severo.

harshness ['ha:ʃnis] *n* asprezza, severità.

hart [ha:t] *n* cervo, daino.

harum-scarum ['hɛərəm'skɛərəm] *a* avventato, irresponsabile.

harvest ['ha:vist] *n* messe, raccolto; *vt* mietere, raccogliere.

harvester ['ha:vistə] *n* mietitore.

hash [hæʃ] *n* specie di ragù; (*fig*) pasticcio; *vt* sminuzzare; (*fig*) fare un pasticcio di.

hasp [ha:sp] *n* fermaglio.

hassock ['hæsək] *n* grosso cuscino usato come inginocchiatoio.

haste [heist] *n* fretta, furia.

hasten ['heisn] *vti* affrettar(si).

hastily ['heistili] *ad* frettolosamente, di furia.

hastiness ['heistinis] *n* fretta, precipitazione; irritabilità.

hasty ['heisti] *a* frettoloso, avventato; irritabile.

hat [hæt] *n* cappello; **hatbox** cappelliera.

hatch [hætʃ] *n* mezza porta; (*naut*) boccaporto; covata; *vt* covare; macchinare; *vi* (*of eggs*) schiudersi; (*of birds*) nascere.

hatchet ['hætʃit] *n* accetta.

hate [heit] *n* odio; *vt* odiare.

hateful ['heitful] *a* odioso.

hatpin ['hætpin] *n* spillone (da cappello).

hatred ['heitrid] *n* odio; astio.

hatter ['hætə] *n* cappellaio.

haughtiness ['hɔːtinis] *n* arroganza, superbia.

haughty ['hɔːti] *a* arrogante, superbo.

haul [hɔːl] *n* retata; tirata; (*fig*) guadagno; refurtiva; *vt* tirare, trascinare, rimorchiare.

haulage ['hɔːlidʒ] *n* trasporto.

haulier ['hɔːliə] *n* imprenditore di trasporti, impresa autotrasporti.

haunch [hɔːntʃ] *n* anca, coscia.

haunt [hɔːnt] *n* ritrovo; *vt* frequentare; ossessionare, perseguitare; **haunted** *a* frequentato, perseguitato, infestato da fantasmi.

Havana [hə'vænə] *n* Avana.

have [hæv] *vt aux* avere, ricevere, fare; **h. to** dovere.

haven ['heivn] *n* porto, rifugio.

haversack ['hævəsæk] *n* zaino, sacco da montagna.

havoc ['hævək] *n* devastazione, distruzione.

hawk [hɔːk] *n* falco; *vt* portare in giro (merci) per la vendita; *vi* cacciare col falco.

hawker ['hɔːkə] *n* venditore ambulante.

hawser ['hɔːzə] *n* (*naut*) gomena, piccolo cavo.

hawthorn ['hɔːθɔːn] *n* biancospino.

hay [hei] *n* fieno.

haycock ['heikɔk] **haystack** ['heistæk] *n* mucchio di fieno.

hazard ['hæzəd] *n* azzardo, rischio; *vt* arrischiare, azzardare.

hazardous ['hæzədəs] *a* rischioso.

haze [heiz] *n* nebbia, nebbiolina; (*fig*) confusione di mente.

hazel ['heizl] *n* nocciolo, nocciola.

hazy ['heizi] *a* nebbioso, indistinto, vago.

he [hiː] *pron* egli, lui; (*prefix with names of animals*) maschio.

head [hed] *n* capo, testa; (*arrow*) punta; (*bed*) capezzale; (*page*) testata; *vt* capeggiare; intestare; *vi* colpire con la testa; dirigersi; **headmaster** *n* direttore di scuola, preside.

headache ['hedeik] *n* male di capo, emicrania.

heading ['hedin] *n* intestazione, titolo, (*av*) rotta.

headland ['hedlənd] *n* capo, promontorio.

headlight ['hedlait] *n* (*aut*) faro (anteriore).

headlong ['hedlɔn] *a* impetuoso, precipitoso; *ad* (a) capofitto.

headmost ['hedmoust] *a* il più avanzato.

headquarters ['hed'kwɔːtəz] *n pl* Quartier Generale.

headstrong ['hedstrɔn] *a* ostinato, testardo.

headway ['hedwei] *n* progresso, cammino.

heady ['hedi] *a* violento; testardo; inebriante.

heal [hiːl] *vt* guarire, sanare.

healing ['hiːlin] *a* salutare; *n* guarigione.

health ['helθ] *n* salute.

healthy ['helθi] *a* sano, salutare, salubre.

heap [hiːp] *n* cumulo, mucchio; *vt* accumulare, ammucchiare.

hear [hiə] *vt* ascoltare; *vti* sentire, udire; apprendere.

hearing ['hiərin] *n* udito; udienza; ascolto; **within h.** a portata di voce.

hearsay ['hiəsei] *n* diceria, voce.

hearse [hɔːs] *n* carro funebre.

heart [hɑːt] *n* cuore; **heartbeat** pulsazione; **heartbreak** crepacuore.

heartache ['hɑːteik] *n* crepacuore.

heartbroken ['hɑːt,broukən] *a* straziato.

heartburn ['hɑːtbəːn] *n* bruciore di stomaco.

hearten ['hɑːtn] *vt* incoraggiare, rincorare.

heartening ['hɑːtnin] *a* incoraggiante.

hearth [hɑːθ] *n* focolare.

heartily ['hɑːtili] *ad* cordialmente; vigorosamente.

heartless ['hɑːtlis] *a* senza cuore, insensibile.

hearty ['hɑːti] *a* cordiale; vigoroso.

heat [hiːt] *n* calore, caldo; *vt* riscaldare, infiammare.

heater ['hiːtə] *n* riscaldatore; **electric h.** stufetta elettrica.

heath [hiːθ] *n* brughiera, erica.

heathen ['hiːðən] *a n* pagano.

heather ['heðə] *n* erica.

heating ['hiːtin] *n* riscaldamento; **h. element** resistenza.

heave [hiːv] *n* spinta; conato di vomito; *vt* alzare con fatica; (far) sollevare; *vi* spingere; ansimare; sollevarsi.

heaven ['hevn] *n* cielo.

heavenly ['hevnli] *a* celeste, celestiale, divino.

heavily ['hevili] *ad* pesantemente; molto.

heaviness ['hevinis] *n* pesantezza; oppressione.

heavy ['hevi] *a* pesante, opprimente;

h. **sea** mare grosso; h.-**hearted** col cuore triste; **heavyweight** (boxing) peso massimo.

Hebrew ['hiːbruː] a n ebraico, ebreo.

Hebrides ['hebridiz] n (isole) Ebridi.

heckle ['hekl] n carda; vt cardare; tempestare di domande.

hectic ['hektik] a (med) etico, tisico; agitato; febbrile.

Hector ['hektə] nm pr Ettore.

hedge [hedʒ] n siepe.

hedgehog ['hedʒhɔg] n porcospino, riccio (also fig).

heed [hiːd] n attenzione; vt fare attenzione a, badare a.

heedful ['hiːdful] a attento, cauto.

heedless ['hiːdlis] a disattento, incurante.

heel [hiːl] a calcagno, tacco, tallone; vt mettere i tacchi a.

hefty ['hefti] a forte, vigoroso; piuttosto pesante.

hegemony [hiː'gemoni] n egemonia.

heifer ['hefə] n giovenca.

height [hait] n altezza, altura; culmine.

heighten ['haitn] vt innalzare, intensificare.

heinous ['heinəs] a atroce, odioso.

heir [ɛə] n erede; **heiress** ereditiera.

heirloom ['ɛəluːm] n cimelio di famiglia.

Helen ['helin] nf pr Elena.

helicopter ['helikɔptə] n elicottero.

hell [hel] n inferno.

hello [he'lou] interj salve!; (tel) pronto!

helm [helm] n (naut) timone.

helm(et) ['helm(it)] n elmetto, casco.

helmsman ['helmzmən] pl -**men** n timoniere.

help [help] n aiuto, assistenza, rimedio; vt aiutare, soccorrere; evitare; servire (cibo a tavola).

helper ['helpə] n aiuto, aiutante, soccorritore, soccorritrice.

helpful ['helpful] a servizievole, utile.

helping ['helpiŋ] n (food) porzione.

helpless ['helplis] a impotente.

helplessness ['helplisnis] n impotenza; mancanza di iniziativa.

helpmate ['helpmeit] n collaboratore, compagno.

helter-skelter ['heltə'skeltə] ad alla rinfusa.

hem [hem] n orlo, bordura; vt orlare; **to h. in** circondare.

hemisphere ['hemisfiə] n emisfero.

hemlock ['hemlɔk] n cicuta.

hemorrhage ['heməridʒ] n emorragia.

hemp [hemp] n canapa.

hemstitch ['hemstitʃ] n orlo a giorno.

hen [hen] n gallina; femmina di vari uccelli.

hence [hens] ad di qui a, perciò, quindi.

henceforth ['hens'fɔːθ] ad d'ora in avanti.

henchman ['hentʃmən] pl **henchmen** n (pol) seguace, accolito.

Henry ['henri] nm pr Enrico.

her [həː] pron a la, lei; di lei, suo (sua, sue, suoi); **to h.** le, a lei; **herself** pron ella medesima, lei stessa.

herald ['herəld] n araldo; vt annunciare, proclamare.

heraldry ['herəldri] n araldica.

herb [həːb] n erba aromatica.

herbalist ['həːbəlist] n erborista.

herd [həːd] n branco, gregge, mandria; vt custodire bestiame; vi formare gregge.

herdsman ['həːdzmən] pl -**men** n mandriano.

here [hiə] ad qui, costì.

hereabout(s) ['hiərə,baut(s)] ad all'intorno, qui vicino.

hereafter [hiər'aːftə] n vita futura; ad d'ora in poi.

hereditary [hi'reditəri] a ereditario.

heredity [hi'rediti] n eredità.

heresy ['herəsi] n eresia.

heretic ['herətik] a n eretico.

herewith ['hiə'wið] ad con questo, qui accluso.

heritage ['heritidʒ] n eredità (also fig).

hermetically [həː'metikəli] ad ermeticamente.

hermit ['həːmit] n eremita.

hermitage ['həːmitidʒ] n eremitaggio.

hernia ['həːniə] n ernia.

hero ['hiərou] n eroe; protagonista.

heroic [hi'rouik] a eroico.

heroine ['herouin] n eroina; protagonista.

heroism ['herouizəm] n eroismo.

heron ['herən] n airone.

herring ['heriŋ] n aringa; **smoked h.** (US) aringa affumicata.

hers [həːz] pron il suo, la sua, i suoi, le sue; di lei.

hesitant ['hezitənt] a esitante, titubante.

hesitate ['heziteit] vi esitare.

hesitation [,hezi'teiʃən] n esitazione.

heterogeneous ['hetərou'dʒiːniəs] a eterogeneo.

hew [hjuː] vt abbattere; spaccare.

heyday ['heidei] n apogeo, apice.

hiatus [hai'eitəs] n iato; lacuna.

hibernate ['haibəneit] vi svernare, essere in ibernazione.

hiccup, hiccough ['hikʌp] vi (avere il) singhiozzo; n singhiozzo.

hide [haid] n cuoio, pelle; vti nasconder(si), celar(si).

hideous ['hidiəs] a mostruoso, ripugnante.

hideousness ['hidiəsnis] n mostruosità.

hideout ['haidaut] n nascondiglio.

hiding ['haidiŋ] n nascondiglio; (fam) fustigazione.

hierarchy ['haiəraːki] n gerarchia.

higgledy-piggledy ['higldi'pigldi] ad alla rinfusa.

high [hai] a alto; importante; (time) avanzato; (colour) acceso; **h. altar** altare maggiore; **h. school** scuola media; **h. water** alta marea.

highbrow ['haibrau] an intellettuale.

highland ['hailənd] a montanaro; n usu pl regione montuosa.

highlander ['hailəndə] n montanaro.

highly ['haili] ad molto, estremamente.

highness ['hainis] n (title) altezza.

highway ['haiwei] n strada maestra; (US) autostrada; **highwayman** bandito.

hike [haik] vi n (fare una) escursione a piedi.

hiker ['haikə] n escursionista (a piedi).

hilarious [hi'lɛəriəs] a ilare, allegro.

hill [hil] n colle, collina.

hilliness ['hilinis] n natura collinosa.

hillock ['hilək] n collinetta, poggio.

hillside ['hilsaid] n pendio.

hilltop ['hiltɔp] n sommità della collina.

hilly ['hili] a collinoso.

hilt [hilt] n elsa, impugnatura.

him [him] pron lui, lo; **to h.** gli, a lui; **himself** egli stesso, proprio lui, si, se stesso, quello.

Himalaya [ˌhiməˈleiə] n Imalaia.

Himalayan [ˌhiməˈleiən] a n imalaiano, imalaiana.

hind [haind] n cerva, daina; a posteriore.

hinder ['haində] a posteriore; vt ['hində] impedire, ostacolare.

hindrance ['hindrəns] n impedimento, ostacolo.

hinge [hindʒ] n cardine; vt munire di cardini; vi dipendere.

hint [hint] n allusione, accenno; vti alludere, accennare.

hinterland ['hintəlænd] n retroterra.

hip [hip] n anca, fianco.

hippopotamus [ˌhipəˈpɔtəməs] n ippopotamo.

hire ['haiə] n nolo, affito; vt affittare, noleggiare; **h.-purchase system** (sistema di) vendita a rate.

hireling ['haiəliŋ] n mercenario.

hirsute ['həːsjuːt] a irsuto, ispido.

his [hiz] a pron (il) suo, di lui.

hiss [his] n fischio, sibilo; vti fischiare, sibilare.

historian [his'tɔːriən] n storico.

historic [his'tɔrik] a importante; (gram) storico.

historical [his'tɔrikəl] a storico.

history ['histəri] n storia.

histrionic [ˌhistri'ɔnik] a istrionico.

hit [hit] n colpo; successo; tentativo fortunato; vt colpire.

hitch [hitʃ] n nodo, impedimento, ostacolo.

hitch-hike ['hitʃhaik] vi fare l'autostop.

hitch-hiker ['hitʃˌhaikə] n chi fa l'autostop.

hitch-hiking ['hitʃˌhaikiŋ] n autostop.

hither ['hiðə] ad qui, qua; **h. and thither** qua e là.

hitherto ['hiðə'tuː] ad finora.

hive [haiv] n alveare.

hoar [hɔː] a canuto, grigio; **h.-frost** brina.

hoard [hɔːd] n ammasso, tesoro; vti ammassare, fare incetta di.

hoarding ['hɔːdiŋ] n assito, impalcatura; **advertisement h.** spazio per la pubblicità, tabellone d'affissione.

hoarse [hɔːs] a rauco.

hoarsely ['hɔːsli] ad raucamente.

hoarseness ['hɔːsnis] n raucedine.

hoary ['hɔːri] a canuto, venerabile.

hoax [houks] n inganno, tiro scherzoso; vt ingannare.

hobble ['hɔbl] n zoppicamento, pastoia; vi zoppicare; vt impastoiare.

hobbledehoy ['hɔbldi'hɔi] n adolescente goffo.

hobby ['hɔbi] n svago preferito, 'hobby'.

hock [hɔk] n garretto (di cavallo).

hockey ['hɔki] n pallamaglio, 'hockey'; **ice h.** hockey sul ghiaccio.

hoe [hou] n zappa; vti zappare.

hog [hɔg] n maiale, porco.

hogmanay [ˌhɔgmə'nei] n (in Scozia) ultimo giorno dell'anno.

hogshead ['hɔgzhed] n grossa botte della capacità di galloni 52½ (= litri 238,5).

hoist [hɔist] n montacarichi; vt innalzare, sollevare.

hold [hould] n presa, stretta; luogo fortificato; (naut) stiva; vt contenere; tenere; trattenere; vi tenere (duro).

holder ['houldə] n detentore, possessore.

holding ['houldiŋ] n possesso, tenuta.

hole [houl] n buca, buco, cavità; tana; (sl) situazione difficile.

holiday ['hɔlidei] n giorno festivo, vacanza; **holidaymaker** villeggiante.

holiness ['houlinis] n santità.

Holland ['hɔlənd] n Olanda.

hollow ['hɔlou] a cavo, vuoto; (fig) falso; n cavità, buca; vt incavare, scavare.

holly ['hɔli] n agrifoglio.

holm [houm] n leccio.

holster ['houlstə] n fondina di pistola.

holy ['houli] n sacro, santo.

homage ['hɔmidʒ] n omaggio.

home [houm] n casa, focolare domestico, patria; a domestico, familiare, nazionale; **homecoming** ritorno al focolare.

homeland ['houmlænd] n patria.

homeless ['houmlis] a senza tetto, senza patria.

homely ['houmli] a casalingo; insignificante; semplice.

home-made ['houm'meid] a fatto in casa.

homesick ['houmsik] a nostalgico.

homesickness ['houmsiknis] *n* nostalgia.

homeward ['houmwəd] *a ad* verso casa, verso il proprio paese.

homework ['houmwə:k] *n* compito per casa.

homicide ['homisaid] *n* omicida; omicidio.

homogeneous [,homə'dʒi:niəs] *a* omogeneo.

homosexual ['houmou'seksjuəl] *a* omosessuale.

hone [houn] *n* cote; *vt* affilare.

honest ['onist] *a* onesto, leale.

honestly ['onistli] *ad* onestamente, sinceramente.

honesty ['onisti] *n* onestà, lealtà.

honey ['hʌni] *n* miele.

honeycomb ['hʌnikoum] *n* favo.

honeymoon ['hʌnimu:n] *n* luna di miele; viaggio di nozze.

honeysuckle ['hʌni,sʌkl] *n* caprifoglio.

honorary ['onərəri] *a* onorario.

honour ['onə] *n* onore, onoranza; (*title*) eccellenza; *vt* onorare.

honourable ['onərəbl] *a* onorevole.

hood [hud] *n* cappuccio; (*US*) cofano di automobile; mantice di carrozza; *vt* incappucciare.

hoodwink ['hudwiŋk] *vt* bendare gli occhi a; (*fig*) ingannare.

hoof [hu:f] *pl* **hoofs, hooves** *n* zoccolo.

hook [huk] *n* uncino, gancio, amo; *vt* agganciare, prendere all'amo.

hooked [hukt] *a* adunco.

hooligan ['hu:ligən] *n* giovinastro.

hoop [hu:p] *n* cerchio.

hoot [hu:t] *n* grido della civetta; schiamazzo; (*train*) fischio; *vi* gridare; suonare il clacson; *vt* deridere.

hooter ['hu:tə] *n* sirena; clacson.

hop [hop] *n* balzo, salto su un piede; luppolo; *vi* saltare su un piede.

hope [houp] *n* speranza; *vti* sperare.

hopeful ['houpful] *a* speranzoso, ottimista.

hopeless ['houplis] *a* disperato, senza rimedio, senza speranza.

hopelessly ['houplisli] *ad* irrimediabilmente, senza speranza.

Horace ['horəs] *nm pr* Orazio.

horde [hɔ:d] *n* orda.

horizon [hə'raizn] *n* orizzonte.

horizontal [,hori'zontl] *a* orizzontale.

hormone ['hɔ:moun] *n* ormone.

horn ['hɔ:n] *n* corno; (*insect*) antenna; (*aut*) clacson.

hornet ['hɔ:nit] *n* calabrone.

horoscope ['horəskoup] *n* oroscopo.

horrible ['horəbl] *a* orribile.

horrid ['horid] *a* orrido, odioso.

horrify ['horifai] *vt* far inorridire.

horror ['horə] *n* orrore.

horse [hɔ:s] *n* cavallo, *pl* cavalleria; **horseshoe** ferro di cavallo.

horseback ['hɔ:sbæk] *n* groppa; **on h.** *ad* a cavallo, in sella.

horseman ['hɔ:smən] *n* cavaliere; **horsewoman** amazzone.

horsemanship ['hɔ:smənʃip] *n* equitazione.

horticultural [,hɔ:ti'kʌltʃərəl] *a* riguardante l'orticultura.

horticulture ['hɔ:tikʌltʃə] *n* orticultura.

hose [houz] *n* tubo flessibile; idrante; calze *pl*.

hosiery ['houʒəri] *n* maglieria.

hospice ['hospis] *n* ospizio.

hospitable ['hospitəbl] *a* ospitale.

hospital ['hospitl] *n* (o)spedale.

hospitality [,hospi'tæliti] *n* ospitalità.

host [houst] *n* ospite (che ospita); albergatore, oste; moltitudine, schiera; ostia.

hostage ['hostidʒ] *n* ostaggio.

hostel ['hostəl] *n* pensionato; ostello.

hostess ['houstis] *n* padrona di casa, ospite; (*av*) "hostess."

hostile ['hostail] *a* ostile.

hostility [hos'tiliti] *n* ostilità.

hot [hot] *a* caldo, ardente, veemente, (*food*) piccante; **hothead** testa calda, persona impulsiva; **h. line** linea diritta; **hotplate** fornello, piastra riscaldante; **h.-water bottle** borsa dell'acqua calda.

hotel [hou'tel] *n* albergo; **hotelier** albergatore.

hound [haund] *n* cane da caccia; *vt* inseguire, perseguitare.

hour ['auə] *n* ora.

hourly ['auəli] *a ad* ogni ora.

house [haus] *n* casa; *vt* alloggiare; (*harvest*) portare dentro il raccolto; **full h.** (*theat*) tutto esaurito.

housebreaker ['haus,breikə] *n* scassinatore.

housecoat ['hauskout] *n* vestaglia.

household ['haushould] *n* famiglia, compresi i domestici; *a* di (da) famiglia, casalingo, domestico.

householder ['haus,houldə] *n* capofamiglia.

housekeeper ['haus,ki:pə] *n* governante, di casa.

housekeeping ['haus,ki:piŋ] *n* governo della casa.

housetop ['haustop] *n* tetto della casa.

housewife ['hauswaif] *n* massaia, casalinga; ['hʌzif] astuccio da lavoro tascabile.

housework ['hauswə:k] *n* lavoro domestico.

housing ['hauziŋ] *n* l'accogliere, l'alloggiare; alloggio, abitazione.

hovel ['hovəl] *n* casupola, tugurio.

hover ['hovə] *vi* librarsi, gravitare; ronzare intorno; sorvolare.

how [hau] *ad* come, quanto.

however [hau'evə] *ad cj* comunque, però, tuttavia.

howitzer ['hauitsə] *n* obice.

howl [haul] *n* ululato, urlo; *vi* ululare, urlare.

hub [hʌb] n (mech) mozzo di ruota; (fig) punto centrale.

hubbub ['hʌbʌb] n suono confuso, tumulto.

huddle ['hʌdl] n folla disordinata; vti ammucchiare confusamente, affollarsi, accalcarsi, stringersi insieme.

hue [hju:] n colore, tinta; clamore.

huff [hʌf] n risentimento, stizza.

hug [hʌg] n (fam) abbraccio, stretta; vt (fam) abbracciare stretto; (fig) restare attaccato a.

huge [hju:dʒ] a enorme.

hugeness ['hju:dʒnis] n grandezza smisurata.

Hugh [hju:] nm pr Ugo.

huguenot ['hju:gənɔt] n ugonotto.

hulk [hʌlk] n (naut) carcassa.

hull [hʌl] n baccello; (naut) scafo.

hullabaloo ['hʌləbə'lu:] n fracasso, baccano, confusione.

hullo [hʌ'lou] interj ciao, salve!; (tel) pronto!

hum [hʌm] n ronzio; vi ronzare; canticchiare a labbra chiuse; (fam) essere in grande attività.

human ['hju:mən] a umano.

humane [hju:'mein] a umano, umanitario.

humanism ['hju:mənizəm] n umanesimo.

humanist ['hju:mənist] n umanista.

humanitarian [hju:.mæni'tɛəriən] a filantropico, umanitario; n filantropo.

humanity [hju:'mæniti] n umanità.

humanly ['hju:mənli] ad umanamente.

humble ['hʌmbl] a umile; vt umiliare; to eat h. pie scusarsi umilmente.

humbly ['hʌmbli] ad umilmente, con sottomissione.

humbug ['hʌmbʌg] n (fam) frottola, inganno, ipocrisia; impostore, ipocrita; interj sciocchezze!

humdrum ['hʌmdrʌm] a noioso, monotono.

humid ['hju:mid] a umido.

humidity [hju:'miditi] n umidità.

humiliate [hju:'milieit] vt umiliare.

humiliation [hju:.mili'eiʃən] n umiliazione.

humility [hju:'militi] n umiltà.

humorist ['hju:mərist] n umorista.

humorous ['hju:mərəs] a umoristico, spiritoso.

humour ['hju:mə] n senso dell'umorismo, vena; vt assecondare.

hump [hʌmp] n gobba, protuberanza; (fig) malumore; **humpbacked** gobbo.

hunch [hʌntʃ] n gobba, protuberanza; (fig) impressione, sospetto; **hunchbacked** gobbo.

hundred ['hʌndrəd] a n cento.

hundredfold ['hʌndrədfould] a n centuplo.

hundredth ['hʌndrədθ] a n centesimo.

hundredweight ['hʌndrədweit] n (cwt) misura di peso di 112 libbre (=chili 50,8).

Hungarian [hʌŋ'gɛəriən] a n ungherese.

Hungary ['hʌŋgəri] n Ungheria.

hunger ['hʌŋgə] n fame; vi bramare; vt affamare.

hungry ['hʌŋgri] a affamato, desideroso; be h. aver fame.

hunk [hʌŋk] n grosso pezzo.

hunt [hʌnt] n caccia, gruppo di cacciatori; vti cacciare.

hunter ['hʌntə] n cacciatore.

hunting ['hʌntiŋ] n caccia.

huntsman ['hʌntsmən] pl -men n cacciatore.

hurdle ['həːdl] n graticcio, ostacolo; h. race corsa ad ostacoli.

hurdy-gurdy ['həːdi.gəːdi] n organetto a manovella.

hurl [həːl] vt scagliare.

hurly-burly ['həːli.bəːli] n mischia, tumulto.

hurrah [hu'rɑː] interj urrah!

hurricane ['hʌrikən] n ciclone, uragano.

hurriedly ['hʌridli] ad in gran fretta, precipitosamente.

hurry ['hʌri] n fretta, premura; vti affrettarsi.

hurt [həːt] n ferita, danno; vti far male a, danneggiare, dolere.

hurtful ['həːtful] a dannoso, nocivo.

hurtle ['həːtl] vti scagliar(si). precipitarsi.

husband ['hʌzbənd] n marito; vt amministrare con parsimonia, risparmiare.

husbandman ['hʌzbəndmən] pl -men n agricoltore.

husbandry ['hʌzbəndri] n agricoltura; amministrazione domestica.

hush [hʌʃ] n silenzio, quiete; vti (far) tacere.

husk [hʌsk] n buccia.

husky ['hʌski] a pieno di bucce; (voice) rauco, velato.

hussar [hu'zɑː] n ussaro.

hussy ['hʌsi] n civetta, donna leggera.

hustle ['hʌsl] n spinta, trambusto; vt spingere.

hut [hʌt] n capanna; (mil) baracca.

hutch [hʌtʃ] n conigliera; gabbia; casotto.

hyacinth ['haiəsinθ] n giacinto.

hybrid ['haibrid] a n ibrido.

hydrant ['haidrənt] n idrante.

hydrate ['haidreit] n idrato.

hydroelectric ['haidroui'lektrik] a idroelettrico.

hydroplane ['haidrouplein] n idroplano, idrovolante.

hydrogen ['haidridʒən] n idrogeno.

hydropsy ['haidrɔpsi] n idropisia.

hyena [hai'iːnə] n iena.

hygiene ['haidʒiːn] n igiene.

hygienic [hai'dʒiːnik] *a* igienico.
hymn [him] *n* inno.
hyperbole [hai'pəːbəli] *n* iperbole.
hypersensitive ['haipəː'sensitiv] *a* ipersensibile, ipersensitivo.
hyphen ['haifən] *n* lineetta, tratto d'unione.
hypnotism ['hipnətizəm] *n* ipnotismo.
hypochondriac [,haipou'kɔndriæk] *a n* ipocondriaco.
hypocrisy [hi'pɔkrəsi] *n* ipocrisia.
hypocrite ['hipəkrit] *n* ipocrita.
hypocritical [,hipə'kritikəl] *a* ipocrita.
hypodermic [,haipə'dəːmik] *a* ipodermico.
hypothesis [hai'pɔθisis] *pl* **hypotheses** *n* ipotesi.
hypothetical [,haipou'θetikəl] *a* ipotetico.
hysteria [his'tiəriə] *n* isterismo.
hysterical [his'terikəl] *a* isterico.
hysterics [his'teriks] *n* attacco isterico.

I

I [ai] *pron* io.
Ia(i)n [iən] *nm pr* (*scozzese*) Giovanni.
ice [ais] *n* ghiaccio, gelato; *vt* ghiacciare; (*cook*) glassare.
iceberg ['aisbəːg] *n* massa di ghiacci galleggianti, 'iceberg'.
ice-cream ['ais'kriːm] *n* gelato.
Iceland ['aislənd] *n* Islanda.
Icelander ['aisləndə] *n* islandese.
Icelandic [ais'lændik] *a n* islandese.
icicle ['aisikil] *n* ghiacciolo.
icing ['aisiŋ] *a* (*sugar*) al velo; *n* (*cook*) glassa.
icy ['aisi] *a* gelato, gelido, ghiacciato.
idea [ai'diə] *n* idea.
ideal [ai'diəl] *a n* ideale.
idealism [ai'diəlizəm] *n* idealismo.
idealist [ai'diəlist] *n* idealista.
identikit [ai'dentikit] *n* identi-kit.
identic(al) [ai'dentik(əl)] *a* identico.
identification [ai,dentifi'keiʃən] *n* identificazione, riconoscimento; **i. tag** (*US mil*) piastrina di riconoscimento.
ideology [,aidi'ɔlədʒi] *n* ideologia.
idiocy ['idiəsi] *n* idiozia.
idiom ['idiəm] *n* idiotismo, espressione idiomatica; idioma.
idiomatic [,idiə'mætik] *a* idiomatico.
idiot ['idiət] *n* idiota.
idiotic [,idi'ɔtik] *a* idiota, stupido.
idle ['aidl] *a* indolente, ozioso, inutile, vano; *vi* oziare; *vt* sprecare (tempo) in ozio.
idleness ['aidlnis] *n* indolenza, ozio.
idly ['aidli] *ad* pigramente, inutilmente.
idol ['aidl] *n* idolo.
idolater [ai'dɔlətə] *n* idolatra.
idolatry [ai'dɔlətri] *n* idolatria.
idolize ['aidəlaiz] *vt* idolatrare.

idyl(l) ['idil] *n* idillio.
if [if] *cj* se; **if anything** se mai; **if so** in tal caso.
ignition [ig'niʃən] *n* ignizione, accensione; **i. key** (*aut*) chiavetta dell'accensione.
ignoble [ig'noubl] *a* ignobile.
ignominious [,ignə'miniəs] *a* ignominioso.
ignominy ['ignəmini] *n* ignominia.
ignoramus [,ignə'reiməs] *n* ignorante.
ignorance ['ignərəns] *n* ignoranza.
ignorant ['ignərənt] *a* ignorante.
ignore [ig'nɔː] *vt* far finta di non sentire, di non vedere, ignorare, trascurare.
ill [il] *a* (am)malato; dannoso, malefico; *ad* male; *n* male, danno.
illegal [i'liːgəl] *a* illegale.
illegality [,ili'gæliti] *n* illegalità.
illegible [i'ledʒəbl] *a* illeggibile.
illegitimacy [,ili'dʒitiməsi] *n* illegittimità.
illegitimate [,ili'dʒitimit] *a* illegittimo.
illiberal [i'libərəl] *a* illiberale, tirchio.
illicit [i'lisit] *a* illecito.
illiterate [i'litərit] *a n* analfabeta.
illness ['ilnis] *n* malattia.
illogical [i'lɔdʒikəl] *a* illogico.
illuminate [i'ljuːmineit] *vt* illuminare; miniare.
illumination [i,ljuːmi'neiʃən] *n* illuminazione; miniatura.
illusion [i'luːʒən] *n* illusione.
illusive [i'luːsiv] *a* illusorio.
illustrate ['iləstreit] *vt* illustrare.
illustration [,iləs'treiʃən] *n* illustrazione.
illustrious [i'lʌstriəs] *a* illustre.
image ['imidʒ] *n* immagine.
imagery ['imidʒəri] *n pl* immagini; linguaggio figurato.
imaginable [i'mædʒinəbl] *a* immaginabile.
imaginary [i'mædʒinəri] *a* immaginario.
imagination [i,mædʒi'neiʃən] *n* immaginazione.
imaginative [i'mædʒinətiv] *a* immaginativo, fantasioso.
imagine [i'mædʒin] *vti* immaginare, figurarsi, farsi un'idea.
imbecile ['imbisiːl] *a n* imbecille.
imbibe [im'baib] *vt* assimilare, assorbire, bere.
imbue [im'bjuː] *vt* imbevere, impregnare.
imitate ['imiteit] *vt* imitare.
imitation [,imi'teiʃən] *n* imitazione.
immaculate [i'mækjulit] *a* immacolato.
immaterial [,imə'tiəriəl] *a* immateriale, di nessuna importanza.
immature [,imə'tjuə] *a* immaturo.
immeasurable [i'meʒərəbl] *a* incommensurabile.

immediacy [i'mi:diəsi] n immedia-
tezza.
immediate [i'mi:diet] a immediato.
immediately [i'mi:diətli] ad immediatamente.
immemorial [,imi'mɔ:riəl] a im-
memorabile.
immense [i'mens] a immenso.
immensity [i'mensiti] n immensità.
immerse [i'mə:s] vt immergere.
immersion [i'mə:ʃən] n immersione.
immigrant ['imigrənt] a n immi-
grante.
immigrate ['imigreit] vi immigrare.
immigration [,imi'greiʃən] n immi-
grazione.
imminent ['iminənt] a imminente.
immobility [,imou'biliti] n immobilità.
immobilize [i'moubilaiz] vt immobilizzare.
immoderate [i'mɔdərit] a smodato.
immodest [i'mɔdist] a immodesto,
impudico.
immolate ['imouleit] vt immolare.
immoral [i'mɔrəl] a immorale.
immorality [,imə'ræliti] a n immoralità.
immortal [i'mɔ:tl] a n immortale.
immortality [,imɔ:'tæliti] n immortalità.
immortalize [i'mɔ:tələaiz] vt im-
mortalare.
immovable [i'mu:vəbl] a immobile,
inamovibile.
immune [i'mju:n] a immune.
immunity [i'mju:niti] n immunità.
immunization [,imju:nai'zeiʃən] n
immunizzazione.
immutability [i,mju:tə'biliti] n im-
mutabilità.
immutable [i'mju:təbl] a immutabile.
imp [imp] n diavoletto.
impact ['impækt] n collisione, urto.
impair [im'pεə] vt danneggiare,
menomare.
impalpable [im'pælpəbl] a impalpa-
bile.
impart [im'pɑ:t] vt impartire, comunicare.
impartial [im'pɑ:ʃəl] a imparziale.
impartiality ['im,pɑ:ʃi'æliti] n im-
parzialità.
impassible [im'pɑ:səbl] a impassibile.
impassioned [im'pæʃənd] a appassionato, eloquente.
impassive [im'pæsiv] a impassibile.
impatience [im'peiʃəns] n impa-
zienza.
impatient [im'peiʃənt] a impaziente.
impeach [im'pi:tʃ] vt accusare,
imputare.
impeccable [im'pekəbl] a impecca-
bile.
impecunious [,impi'kju:niəs] a senza
denaro, povero.
impede [im'pi:d] vt impedire, ostacolare.
impediment [im'pedimənt] n impedimento, ostacolo.

impel [im'pel] vt costringere, spingere.
impend [im'pend] vi sovrastare,
incombere.
impenetrable [im'penitrəbl] a impenetrabile.
impenitent [im'penitənt] a impeni-
tente.
imperative [im'perətiv] a n impera-
tivo.
imperceptible [,impə'septəbl] a impercettibile.
imperfect [im'pə:fikt] a n imperfetto.
imperfection [,impə'fekʃən] n imperfezione.
imperial [im'piəriəl] a imperiale; n
(beard) pizzo; imperiale.
imperialism [im'piəriəlizəm] n im-
perialismo.
imperil [im'peril] vt mettere in
pericolo.
imperious [im'piəriəs] a imperioso.
imperishable [im'periʃəbl] a im-
perituro.
impermeable [im'pə:miəbl] a impermeabile.
impersonal [im'pə:snl] a impersonale.
impersonate [im'pə:səneit] vt interpretare impersonare.
impertinence [im'pə:tinəns] n impertinenza.
impertinent [im'pə:tinənt] a impertinente.
imperturbable [,impə:'tə:bəbl] a
imperturbabile.
impervious ['im'pə:viəs] a impervio,
inaccessibile (also fig).
impetuosity [im,petju'ɔsiti] n impetuosità.
impetuous [im'petjuəs] a impetuoso.
impetus ['impitəs] n impeto.
impiety [im'paiəti] n empietà.
impinge [im'pindʒ] vi venire in urto
(con); interferire (in).
impious ['impiəs] a empio.
implacable [im'plækəbl] a implaca-
bile.
implant [im'plɑ:nt] vt impiantare,
instillare.
implement ['implimənt] n arnese,
utensile; vt ['impliment] effettuare,
completare.
implicate ['implikeit] vt implicare.
implication [,impli'keiʃən] n impli-
cazione; by i. implicitamente, per
induzione.
implicit [im'plisit] a implicito.
implicitly [im'plisitli] ad implicitamente.
implied [im'plaid] a implicito, sottinteso.
imploration [,implɔ:'reiʃən] n im-
plorazione.
implore [im'plɔ:] vt implorare.
imply [im'plai] vt implicare, significare; insinuare.
impolite [,impə'lait] a scortese,
sgarbato.
import ['impɔ:t] n (articolo di)
importazione; importanza; significa-

to; *vt* [im'pɔːt] significare; (*com*) importare.

importance [im'pɔːtəns] *n* importanza.

important [im'pɔːtənt] *a* importante.

importation [,impɔː'teiʃən] *n* importazione.

importer [im'pɔːtə] *n* importatore.

importunate [im'pɔːtjunit] *a* importuno, insistente.

importune [,impɔː'tjuːn] *vt* importunare.

impose [im'pouz] *vt* imporre.

imposing [im'pouziŋ] *a* maestoso, imponente.

imposition [,impə'ziʃən] *n* imposizione, imposta; inganno.

impossibility [im,pɔsə'biliti] *n* impossibilità.

impossible [im'pɔsəbl] *a* impossibile.

impostor [im'pɔstə] *n* impostore.

imposture [im'pɔstʃə] *n* impostura, inganno.

impotence ['impətəns] *n* impotenza.

impotent ['impətənt] *a* impotente.

impound [im'paund] *vt* sequestrare, confiscare.

impoverish [im'pɔvəriʃ] *vt* impoverire.

impracticable [im'præktikəbl] *a* impraticabile.

impregnable [im'pregnəbl] *a* impregnabile.

impregnate [im'pregneit] *vt* impregnare.

impress [im'pres] *vt* imprimere, impressionare.

impression [im'preʃən] *n* impressione, impronta; stampa.

impressionability [im,preʃnə'biliti] *n* impressionabilità, sensibilità.

impressionable [im'preʃnəbl] *a* impressionabile.

impressive [im'presiv] *a* impressionante, solenne.

imprint [im'print] *vt* imprimere, stampare; *n* ['imprint] impressione; impronta; stampa.

imprison [im'prizn] *vt* imprigionare.

imprisonment [im'priznmənt] *n* prigionia, carcere.

improbable [im'prɔbəbl] *a* improbabile.

impromptu [im'prɔmptjuː] *a* improvvisato, estemporaneo; *ad* all'improntu, estemporaneamente.

improper [im'prɔpə] *a* improprio, sconveniente, scorretto.

impropriety [,imprə'praiəti] *n* improprietà, sconvenienza.

improve [im'pruːv] *vti* migliorare.

improvement [im'pruːvmənt] *n* miglioramento, progresso, progressi *pl*.

improvidence [im'prɔvidəns] *n* improvidenza.

improvident [im'prɔvidənt] *a* improvidente.

improvise ['imprəvaiz] *vt* improvvisare.

imprudence [im'pruːdəns] *n* imprudenza.

imprudent [im'pruːdənt] *a* imprudente.

impudence ['impjudəns] *n* impudenza, sfacciataggine.

impudent ['impjudənt] *a* impudente, sfacciato.

impulse ['impʌls] *n* impulso.

impulsive [im'pʌlsiv] *a* impulsivo.

impulsiveness [im'pʌlsivnis] *n* impulsività.

impunity [im'pjuːniti] *n* impunità.

impure [im'pjuə] *a* impuro.

impurity [im'pjuəriti] *n* impurità.

imputation [,impjuː'teiʃən] *n* imputazione.

impute [im'pjuːt] *vt* imputare, attribuire.

in [in] *prep ad* a, in, entro, dentro, durante, secondo.

inability [,inə'biliti] *n* inabilità.

inaccessible [,inæk'sesəbl] *a* inaccessibile.

inaccuracy [in'ækjurəsi] *n* inaccuratezza, imprecisione.

inaccurate [in'ækjurit] *a* inaccurato, impreciso.

inaction [in'ækʃən] *n* inattività.

inactive [in'æktiv] *a* inattivo.

inadequate [in'ædikwit] *a* inadeguato, insufficiente.

inadmissible [,inəd'misəbl] *a* inammissibile.

inadvertent [,inəd'vəːtənt] *a* involontario.

inane [i'nein] *a* inane, sciocco, vacuo.

inanimate [in'ænimit] *a* inanimato.

inanity [i'næniti] *n* inanità, vacuità.

inapplicable [in'æplikəbl] *a* inapplicabile.

inappropriate [,inə'proupriit] *a* non appropriato, improprio.

inapt ['in'æpt] *a* inadatto, inetto.

inarticulate [,inɑː'tikjulit] *a* inarticolato, indistinto.

inasmuch as [inəz'mʌtʃæz] *ad* visto che, poiché, in quanto che.

inattention [,inə'tenʃən] *n* disattenzione, distrazione.

inattentive [,inə'tentiv] *a* disattento, distratto.

inaudible [in'ɔːdəbl] *a* impercettibile, inafferabile.

inaugurate [i'nɔːgjureit] *vt* inaugurare.

inborn ['in'bɔːn] *a* innato.

inbreeding ['in'briːdiŋ] *n* incrocio tra animali affini.

incalculable [in'kælkjuləbl] *a* incalcolabile.

incandescence [,inkæn'desns] *n* incandescenza.

incandescent [,inkæn'desnt] *a* incandescente.

incantation [,inkæn'teiʃən] *n* incantesimo, parole magiche.

incapability [in,keipə'biliti] *n* incapacità, inettitudine.

incapable [in'keipəbl] *a* incapace, inetto.

incapacitate [ˌinkə'pæsiteit] *vt* rendere inabile, incapace.

incapacity [ˌinkə'pæsiti] *n* inabilità, incapacità.

incarcerate [in'kɑːsəreit] *vt* incarcerare.

incarceration [inˌkɑːsə'reiʃən] *n* incarcerazione.

incarnate [in'kɑːnit] *a* incarnato; *vt* ['inkɑːneit] incarnare.

incautious [in'kɔːʃəs] *a* incauto.

incendiary [in'sendjəri] *a n* incendiario.

incense ['insens] *n* incenso; *vt* [in'sens] incensare; *vi* fare arrabbiare.

incentive [in'sentiv] *n* incentivo, motivo.

incessant [in'sesnt] *a* continuo, incessante.

incest ['insest] *n* incesto.

incestuous [in'sestjuəs] *a* incestuoso.

inch [intʃ] *n* pollice (*misura lineare* = cm 2,54); *vt* spostarsi gradatamente.

incidence ['insidəns] *n* incidenza.

incident ['insidənt] *n* avvenimento, episodio, incidente; *a* incidente, inerente.

incidental [ˌinsi'dentl] *a* casuale, fortuito.

incision [in'siʒən] *n* incisione.

incisive [in'saisiv] *a* incisivo, penetrante.

incite [in'sait] *vt* incitare, stimolare.

incitement [in'saitmənt] *n* incitamento, stimolo.

incivility [ˌinsi'viliti] *n* scortesia.

inclemency [in'klemənsi] *n* inclemenza.

inclement ['inklemənt] *a* inclemente.

inclination [ˌinkli'neiʃən] *n* inclinazione, propensità; pendio.

incline [in'klain] *n* pendio, piano inclinato; *vti* inclinare, essere incline.

include [in'kluːd] *vt* includere, comprendere.

inclusion [in'kluːʒən] *n* inclusione.

inclusive [in'kluːsiv] *a* compreso, inclusivo.

incoherence [ˌinkou'hiərəns] *n* incoerenza.

incoherent [ˌinkou'hiərənt] *a* incoerente.

income ['inkəm] *n* reddito, entrata.

incoming ['inˌkʌmiŋ] *a* entrante, che succede ad altri; *n* l'entrare, il flusso; *pl* entrate.

incommunicability [ˌinkə'mjuːnikəbiliti] *n* incomunicabilità.

incomparable [in'kɔmpərəbl] *a* incomparabile.

incompatible [ˌinkəm'pætəbl] *a* incompatibile.

incompetence [in'kɔmpitəns] *n* incompetenza.

incompetent [in'kɔmpitənt] *a* incompetente.

incomplete [ˌinkəm'pliːt] *a* incompleto, incompiuto.

incomprehensible [inˌkɔmpri'hensəbl] *a* incomprensibile.

inconceivable [ˌinkən'siːvəbl] *a* inconcepibile.

inconclusive [ˌinkən'kluːsiv] *a* inconcludente.

incongruous [in'kɔŋgruəs] *a* incongruo.

inconsequent [in'kɔnsikwənt] *a* illogico, inconseguente.

inconsequential [in'kɔnsikwəntʃəl] *a* inconseguente, irrilevante.

inconsiderable [ˌinkən'sidərəbl] *a* trascurabile.

inconsiderate [ˌinkən'sidərit] *a* sconsiderato; senza riguardi.

inconsistent [ˌinkən'sistənt] *a* inconsistente, incompatibile.

inconsolable [ˌinkən'souləbl] *a* inconsolabile.

inconspicuous [ˌinkən'spikjuəs] *a* incospicuo, insignificante.

inconstancy [in'kɔnstənsi] *n* incostanza.

inconstant [in'kɔnstənt] *a* incostante.

incontinent [in'kɔntinənt] *a* incontinente.

inconvenience [ˌinkən'viːniəns] *n* disturbo, inconveniente, disagio; *vt* incomodare, disturbare.

inconvenient [ˌinkən'viːniənt] *a* incomodo, scomodo.

inconvertible [ˌinkən'vəːtəbl] *a* inconvertibile.

incorporate [in'kɔːpəreit] *vt* incorporare; *a* [in'kɔːpərit] unito in corporazione.

incorporeal [ˌinkɔː'pɔːriəl] *a* immateriale, incorporeo.

incorrect [ˌinkə'rekt] *a* inesatto, scorretto, sbagliato..

incorrectness [ˌinkə'rektnis] *n* inesattezza, scorrettezza.

incorrigible [in'kɔridʒəbl] *a* incorreggibile.

incorruptible [ˌinkə'rʌptəbl] *a* incorruttibile.

increase ['inkriːs] *n* aumento, incremento; *vti* [in'kriːs] aumentare, (far) crescere.

incredible [in'kredəbl] *a* incredibile.

incredulity [ˌinkri'djuːliti] *n* incredulità.

incredulous [in'kredjuləs] *a* incredulo.

increment ['inkrimənt] *n* incremento, guadagno.

incriminate [in'krimineit] *vt* incriminare, incolpare.

incubate ['inkjubeit] *vti* covare; essere in incubazione.

incubation [ˌinkju'beiʃən] *n* incubazione.

incubator ['inkjubeitə] *n* incubatrice.

inculcate ['inkʌlkeit] *vt* inculcare.

inculpate ['inkʌlpeit] *vt* incolpare.

incumbent [in'kʌmbənt] *a* incombente, obbligatorio; *n* titolare d'un beneficio ecclesiastico.

incur [in'kə:] *vt* incorrere in.
incurable [in'kjuərəbl] *a* incurabile.
incursion [in'kə:ʃən] *n* incursione.
indebted [in'detid] *a* indebitato, grato.
indecency [in'di:snsi] *n* indecenza.
indecent [in'di:snt] *a* indecente.
indecipherable ['indi'saifərəbl] *a* indecifrabile.
indecision [,indi'siʒən] *n* indecisione.
indecisive [,indi'saisiv] *a* indeciso, non decisivo.
indecorous [in'dekərəs] *a* indecoroso, sconveniente.
indeed [in'di:d] *ad* davvero, infatti, in realtà.
indefatigable [,indi'fætigəbl] *a* instancabile.
indefensible [,indi'fensəbl] *a* indefensibile.
indefinite [in'definit] *a* indefinito.
indelible [in'delibl] *a* indelebile.
indelicacy [in'delikəsi] *n* indelicatezza.
indelicate [in'delikit] *a* indelicato.
indemnify [in'demnifai] *vt* indennizzare, risarcire.
indemnity [in'demniti] *n* indennità, risarcimento.
indent ['indent] *n* dentellatura, tacca; contratto, documento; requisizione; *vti* [in'dent] dentellare, intaccare; stendere un documento in due copie; requisire.
indentation [,inden'teiʃən] *n* dentellatura.
indenture [in'dentʃə] *n* dentellatura; contratto.
independence [,indi'pendəns] *n* indipendenza.
independent [,indi'pendənt] *a* indipendente.
independently [,indi'pendəntli] *ad* indipendentemente, separatamente.
indescribable [,indis'kraibəbl] *a* indescrivibile.
indestructible [,indis'trʌktəbl] *a* indistruttibile.
indeterminate [,indi'tə:minit] *a* indeterminato.
index ['indeks] *n* indice.
India ['indiə] *n* India.
Indian ['indiən] *a n* indiano.
indicate [in'dikətiv] *vt* indicare.
indication [,indi'keiʃən] *n* indicazione, segno, sintomo.
indicative [in'dikətiv] *a* indicativo, che indica.
indicator ['indikeitə] *n* indicatore; **mileage i.** contachilometri.
indict [in'dait] *vt* accusare.
indictment [in'daitmənt] *n* accusa, imputazione.
indifference [in'difrəns] *n* indifferenza.
indifferent [in'difrənt] *a* indifferente, mediocre.
indigence ['indidʒəns] *n* indigenza.
indigenous [in'didʒinəs] *a* indigeno.
indigent ['indidʒənt] *a* indigente.

indigestible [,indi'dʒestəbl] *a* indigeribile, indigesto.
indigestion [,indi'dʒestʃən] *n* imbarazzo di stomaco; dispepsia.
indignant [in'dignənt] *a* indignato, sdegnato.
indignantly [in'dignəntli] *ad* con indignazione, con sdegno.
indignation [,indig'neiʃən] *n* indignazione, sdegno.
indignity [in'digniti] *n* offesa, trattamento indegno.
indigo ['indigou] *n* indaco.
indirect [,indi'rekt] *a* indiretto.
indiscernible [,indi'sə:nəbl] *a* indiscernibile.
indiscreet [,indis'kri:t] *a* indiscreto; sconsiderato.
indiscretion [,indis'kreʃən] *n* indiscrezione; imprudenza.
indiscriminate [,indis'kriminit] *a* indiscriminato.
indispensable [,indis'pensəbl] *a* indispensabile.
indispose [,indis'pouz] *vt* indisporre.
indisposed [,indis'pouzd] *a* indisposto; maldisposto.
indisposition [,indispə'ziʃən] *n* indisposizione.
indisputable ['indis'pju:təbl] *a* indiscutibile, sicuro.
indisputed ['indis'pju:tid] *a* indiscusso.
indissoluble [,indi'sɔljubl] *a* indissolubile.
indistinct [,indis'tiŋkt] *a* indistinto, confuso.
indistinctness [,indis'tiŋktnis] *n* mancanza di chiarezza.
indistinguishable [,indis'tiŋgwiʃəbl] *a* indistinguibile.
indite [in'dait] *vt* comporre, redigere.
individual [,indi'vidjuəl] *a* singolo, individuale; *n* individuo.
individuality [,indi,vidju'æliti] *n* individualità.
indivisible [,indi'vizəbl] *a* indivisibile.
Indo-China ['indou'tʃainə] *n* Indocina.
Indo-Chinese ['indou'tʃai'ni:z] *a n* indocinese.
indolence ['indələns] *n* indolenza.
indolent ['indələnt] *a* indolente.
indomitable [in'dɔmitəbl] *a* indomabile; indomito.
indoor ['indɔ:] *a* che ha luogo in casa, da eseguirsi in casa; **indoors** *ad* dentro, in casa.
indrawn ['in'drɔ:n] *a* chiuso in se stesso, introverso.
indubitable [in'dju:bitəbl] *a* indubitabile.
induce [in'dju:s] *vt* indurre.
inducement [in'dju:smənt] *n* allettamento, incentivo.
induction [in'dʌkʃən] *n* induzione; investitura.
inductive [in'dʌktiv] *a* induttivo.
indulge [in'dʌldʒ] *vti* indulgere,

lasciar libero corso a; abbandonarsi.
indulgence [in'dʌldʒəns] n indulgenza, compiacenza; licenza.
indulgent [in'dʌldʒənt] a indulgente.
industrial [in'dʌstriəl] a industriale.
industrialist [in'dʌstriəlist] n industriale.
industrialization [in'dʌstriəlai'zeiʃən] n industrializzazione.
industrious [in'dʌstriəs] a attivo, operoso.
industry ['indəstri] n industria, attività.
inebriate [i'niːbriit] vt inebriare, ubriacare.
ineffable [in'efəbl] a ineffabile.
ineffective [,ini'fektiv] a inefficace.
ineffectual [,ini'fektjuəl] a inefficace, vano.
inefficacy [in'efikəsi] n inefficacia.
inefficiency [,ini'fiʃənsi] n inefficienza; inefficacia; incapacità.
inefficient [,ini'fiʃənt] a inefficiente, poco capace.
inelegant [in'eligənt] a inelegante.
ineligible [in'elidʒəbl] a ineleggibile.
inept [i'nept] a inetto.
ineptitude [i'neptitjuːd] n inettitudine.
inequality [,iniː'kwɔliti] n ineguaglianza.
inert [i'nəːt] a inerte.
inertia [i'nəːʃjə] n inerzia.
inertness [i'nəːtnis] n inerzia, apatia.
inestimable [in'estiməbl] a inestimabile.
inevitability [in,evitə'biliti] n inevitabilità.
inevitable [in'evitəbl] a inevitabile.
inexact [,inig'zækt] a inesatto.
inexcusable [,iniks'kjuːzəbl] a imperdonabile.
inexhaustible [,inig'zɔːstəbl] a inesauribile.
inexorable [in'eksərəbl] a inesorabile.
inexpensive [,iniks'pensiv] a poco costoso, a buon mercato.
inexperience [,iniks'piəriəns] n inesperienza.
inexperienced [,iniks'piəriənst] a inesperto.
inexplicable [in'eksplikəbl] a inesplicabile, inspiegabile.
inexpressible [,iniks'presəbl] a inesprimibile.
inexpressive [,iniks'presiv] a inespressivo.
infallibility [in,fælə'biliti] n infallibilità.
infallible [in'fæləbl] a infallibile.
infamous ['infəməs] a infame.
infamy ['infəmi] n infamia.
infancy ['infənsi] n infanzia.
infant ['infənt] a infantile, nascente; n neonato, bambino, infante.
infantry ['infəntri] n fanteria.
infatuate [in'fætjueit] vt infatuare.
infatuated [in'fætjueitid] a infatuato; fanatico di.

infatuation [in,fætju'eiʃən] n infatuazione.
infect [in'fekt] vt infettare.
infection [in'fekʃən] n infezione.
infectious [in'fekʃəs] a infettivo, contagioso.
infer [in'fəː] vt inferire, dedurre.
inference ['infərəns] n conclusione, deduzione.
inferior [in'fiəriə] a n inferiore.
inferiority [in,fiəri'ɔriti] n inferiorità.
infernal [in'fəːnl] a infernale.
infertile [in'fəːtail] a improduttivo, non fertile.
infest [in'fest] vt infestare.
infidel ['infidəl] a n infedele, miscredente.
infidelity [,infi'deliti] n infedeltà.
infiltrate ['infiltreit] vti infiltrar(si).
infinite ['infinit] a n infinito.
infinitive [in'finitiv] a n (gram) infinito.
infinity [in'finiti] n infinità.
infirm [in'fəːm] a infermo, debole; irresoluto.
infirmary [in'fəːməri] n infermeria, ospedale.
infirmity [in'fəːmiti] n infermità; irresolutezza.
inflame [in'fleim] vt infiammare.
inflammable [in'flæməbl] a infiammabile.
inflammation [,inflə'meiʃən] n infiammazione.
inflammatory [in'flæmətəri] a infiammatorio.
inflate [in'fleit] vti gonfiare, gonfiarsi.
inflation [in'fleiʃən] n gonfiamento; inflazione.
inflect [in'flekt] vt inflettere.
inflexion [in'flekʃən] n inflessione.
inflexible [in'fleksəbl] a inflessibile rigido.
inflict [in'flikt] vt infliggere.
infliction [in'flikʃən] n inflizione.
influence ['influəns] n ascendente, influenza, influsso; vt influenzare.
influential [,influ'enʃəl] a influente, autorevole.
influenza [,influ'enzə] n (med) influenza.
influx ['inflʌks] n afflusso, flusso.
inform [in'fɔːm] vt informare.
informal [in'fɔːml] a non ufficiale, senza formalità; irregolare.
informality [,infɔː'mæliti] n assenza di formalità; (leg) irregolarità.
informant [in'fɔːmənt] n informatore.
information [,infə'meiʃən] n informazione, informazioni pl; accusa.
informer [in'fɔːmə] n delatore.
infrequent [in'friːkwənt] a infrequente, raro.
infringe [in'frindʒ] vt trasgredire.
infringement [in'frindʒmənt] n infrazione, trasgressione.
infuriate [in'fjuərieit] vt infuriare, rendere furioso.

infuse [in'fju:z] *vt* infondere, instillare, mettere in infusione; stare in infusione.

infusion [in'fju:ʒən] *n* infusione, infuso.

ingenious [in'dʒi:niəs] *a* ingegnoso.

ingenuity [,indʒi'nju:iti] *n* abilità inventiva, ingegnosità.

ingenuous [in'dʒenjuəs] *a* ingenuo; **ingenuousness** *n* ingenuità.

ingle-nook ['iŋglnuk] *n* angolo del focolare.

inglorious [in'glɔ:riəs] *a* inglorioso.

ingot ['iŋgət] *n* lingotto.

ingrained [in'greind] *a* radicato; inveterato.

ingratiate [in'greiʃieit] *vt* ingraziarsi.

ingratitude [in'grætitju:d] *n* ingratitudine.

ingredient [in'gri:diənt] *n* ingrediente.

inhabit [in'hæbit] *vt* abitare, occupare.

inhabitable [in'hæbitəbl] *a* abitabile.

inhabitant [in'hæbitənt] *n* abitante.

inhale [in'heil] *vt* aspirare.

inhaler [in'heilə] *n* inalatore.

inhere [in'hiə] *vi* essere inerente.

inherent [in'hiərənt] *a* inerente, intrinseco.

inherit [in'herit] *vti* ereditare.

inheritance [in'heritəns] *n* eredità.

inhibit [in'hibit] *vt* inibire, impedire.

inhibition [,inhi'biʃən] *n* inibizione.

inhospitable [in'hɔspitəbl] *a* inospitale.

inhuman [in'hju:mən] *a* barbaro, inumano.

inhumanity [,inhu'mæniti] *n* inumanità.

inimical [i'nimikəl] *a* nemico, ostile.

inimitable [i'nimitəbl] *a* inimitabile.

iniquity [i'nikwiti] *n* iniquità.

initial [i'niʃəl] *a n* iniziale; *vt* firmare con le sole iniziali.

initiate [i'niʃiit] *n* iniziato; *vt* [i'niʃieit] iniziare.

initiation [i,niʃi'eiʃən] *n* iniziazione.

initiative [i'niʃiətiv] *n* iniziativa.

inject [in'dʒekt] *vt* iniettare.

injection [in'dʒekʃən] *n* iniezione.

injudicious [,indʒu:'diʃəs] *a* sconsiderato, avventato.

injunction [in'dʒʌŋkʃən] *n* ingiunzione.

injure ['indʒə] *vt* danneggiare, ferire, nuocere a.

injurious [in'dʒuəriəs] *a* nocivo, ingiurioso.

injury ['indʒəri] *n* ferita, torto, danno.

injustice [in'dʒʌstis] *n* ingiustizia.

ink [iŋk] *n* inchiostro; **inkstand** calamaio; **inkwell** calamaio, infisso.

inkling ['iŋkliŋ] *n* indizio, sospetto.

inky ['iŋki] *a* d'inchiostro, nero come l'inchiostro, macchiato d'inchiostro.

inland ['inlənd] *a n* (di un paese) interno, nell'interno, verso l'interno; **i. revenue** fisco.

inlay ['inlei] *n* intarsio; *vt* intarsiare.

inlet ['inlet] *n* insenatura, piccola baia.

inmate ['inmeit] *n* inquilino; persona alloggiata in un istituto.

inmost ['inmoust] *a* il più interno, profondo.

inn [in] *n* albergo, locanda; **innkeeper** locandiere, oste.

innate ['i'neit] *a* innato, istintivo.

inner ['inə] *a* interiore, interno.

innocence ['inəsns] *n* innocenza.

innocent ['inəsnt] *a n* innocente.

innocuous [i'nɔkjuəs] *a* innocuo.

innovate ['inouveit] *vt* innovare.

innovation [,inou'veiʃən] *n* innovazione.

innuendo [,inju:'endou] *n* allusione, insinuazione.

innumerable [i'nju:mərəbl] *a* innumerevole.

inoculate [i'nɔkjuleit] *vt* inoculare; vaccinare; innestare; inculcare.

inoculation [i,nɔkju'leiʃən] *n* inoculazione.

inoffensive [,inə'fensiv] *a* inoffensivo.

inopportune [in'ɔpətju:n] *a* inopportuno, intempestivo.

inordinate [i'nɔ:dinit] *a* eccessivo, smoderato.

in-patient ['in,peiʃənt] *n* ammalato degente in ospedale.

input ['input] *n* (*mech, el*) entrata, alimentazione; **i. energy** energia immessa.

inquest ['inkwest] *n* inchiesta.

inquire [in'kwaiə] *vt* domandare; *vi* indagare, informarsi, fare ricerche *pl*.

inquiringly [in'kwaiəriŋli] *ad* interrogativamente, con aria interrogativa.

inquiry [in'kwaiəri] *n* investigazione, inchiesta.

inquisition [,inkwi'ziʃən] *n* inquisizione.

inquisitive [iŋ'kwizitiv] *a* curioso, indagatore.

inquisitively [in'kwizitivli] *ad* con curiosità; indiscretamente.

inquisitor [in'kwizitə] *n* inquisitore.

inroad ['inroud] *n* incursione; scorreria, sottrazione.

insane [in'sein] *a* folle, pazzo.

insanity [in'sæniti] *n* follia, pazzia.

insatiable [in'seifjəbl] *a* insaziabile.

inscribe [in'skraib] *vt* iscrivere; incidere.

inscription [in'skripʃən] *n* iscrizione.

inscrutable [in'skru:təbl] *a* inscrutabile.

insect ['insekt] *n* insetto.

insecticide [in'sektisaid] *n* insetticida.

insecure [,insi'kjuə] *a* malsicuro.

insecurity [,insi'kjuəriti] *n* mancanza di sicurezza.

insemination [in,semi'neiʃən] *n*

(*med*) fecondazione; **artificial i.** fecondazione artificiale.

insensibility [in‚sensə'biliti] *n* incoscienza, insensibilità.

insensible [in'sensəbl] *a* inconscio; insensibile; privo di sensi.

insensitive [in'sensitiv] *a* insensibile.

inseparable [in'sepərəbl] *a* inseparabile.

insert [in'sə:t] *vt* inserire.

insertion [in'sə:ʃən] *n* inserzione, aggiunta.

inside ['in'said] *a* interno, interiore; *n* interno; *ad* dentro; *prep* dentro; **i. out** rivoltato, a rovescio.

insider ['in'saidə] *n* chi è addentro, iniziato.

insidious [in'sidiəs] *a* insidioso.

insight ['insait] *n* penetrazione, intuito.

insignificant [‚insig'nifikənt] *a* insignificante.

insincere [‚insin'siə] *a* insincero, falso.

insincerity [‚insin'seriti] *n* insincerità, falsità.

insinuate [in'sinjueit] *vt* insinuare; introdurre.

insinuation [in‚sinju'eiʃən] *n* insinuazione.

insipid [in'sipid] *a* insipido, insulso.

insipidity [‚insi'piditi] *n* insipidezza, insulsaggine.

insist [in'sist] *vi* insistere.

insistence [in'sistəns] *n* insistenza.

insistent [in'sistənt] *a* insistente.

insolence ['insələns] *n* insolenza.

insolent ['insələnt] *a* insolente.

insoluble [in'sɔljubl] *a* insolubile.

insolvency [in'sɔlvənsi] *n* insolvenza.

insolvent [in'sɔlvənt] *a* insolvente.

insomnia [in'sɔmniə] *n* insonnia.

inspect [in'spekt] *vt* ispezionare, controllare.

inspection [in'spekʃən] *n* ispezione, controllo.

inspector [in'spektə] *n* ispettore, controllore.

inspiration [‚inspə'reiʃən] *n* ispirazione.

inspire [in'spaiə] *vt* ispirare.

instability [‚instə'biliti] *n* instabilità.

install [in'stɔ:l] *vt* installare, insediare.

installation [‚instə'leiʃən] *n* insediamento; (*el etc*) impianto, installazione.

instalment [in'stɔ:lmənt] *n* rata; puntata; **i. plan** (*US*) (sistema di) vendita a rate.

instance ['instəns] *n* esempio, istanza; **for i.** ad esempio.

instant ['instənt] *a* immediato; (*month*) corrente; *n* istante, momento.

instantaneous [‚instən'teiniəs] *a* istantaneo.

instantly ['instəntli] *ad* immediatamente.

instead [in'sted] *ad* invece (di).

instep ['instep] *n* collo del piede.

instigate ['instigeit] *vt* istigare.

instigation [‚insti'geiʃən] *n* istigazione.

instigator ['instigeitə] *n* istigatore, istigatrice.

instil(l) [in'stil] *vt* instillare.

instinct ['instiŋkt] *n* istinto.

instinctive [in'stiŋktiv] *a* istintivo.

institute ['institju:t] *n* istituto, istituzione; *vt* istituire.

institution [‚insti'tju:ʃən] *n* istituzione, ente; (*eccl*) nomina.

instruct [in'strʌkt] *vt* istruire, informare.

instruction [in'strʌkʃən] *n* istruzione, insegnamento; *pl* istruzione, disposizione.

instructive [in'strʌktiv] *a* istruttivo.

instructor [in'strʌktə] *n* istruttore, maestro, (*US*) lettore universitario; **instructress** maestra, insegnante.

instrument ['instrumənt] *n* strumento; arnese.

instrumental [‚instru'mentl] *a* strumentale.

insubordinate [‚insə'bɔ:dnit] *a* insubordinato, indisciplinato.

insufficiency [‚insə'fiʃənsi] *n* insufficienza.

insufficient [‚insə'fiʃənt] *a* insufficiente.

insular ['insjulə] *a* insulare.

insulate ['insjuleit] *vt* isolare.

insulation [‚insju'leiʃən] *n* isolamento.

insult ['insʌlt] *n* insulto; *vt* [in'sʌlt] insultare.

insuperable [in'sju:pərəbl] *a* insuperabile, insormontabile.

insurance [in'ʃuərəns] *n* (*com*) assicurazione.

insure [in'ʃuə] *vt* assicurare.

insurer [in'ʃuərə] *n* (*com*) assicuratore.

insurgency [in'sə:dʒənsi] *n* sollevarsi; insurrezione.

insurgent [in'sə:dʒənt] *a n* insorto.

insurmountable [‚insə:'mauntəbl] *a* insormontabile.

insurrection [‚insə'rekʃən] *n* insurrezione.

intact [in'tækt] *a* intatto, intero.

intake ['inteik] *n* immissione; presa (*pump*) aspirazione.

intangible [in'tændʒəbl] *a* intangibile.

integer ['intidʒə] *n* numero intero.

integral ['intigrəl] *a n* integrale.

integrate ['intigreit] *a* integrale, intero; *vt* integrare, completare.

integration [‚inti'greiʃən] *n* integrazione.

integrity [in'tegriti] *n* integrità.

intellect ['intilekt] *n* intelletto.

intellectual [‚inti'lektjuəl] *a n* intellettuale.

intelligence [in'telidʒəns] *n* intelligenza; informazioni *pl*, notizie *pl*.

intelligent [in'telidʒənt] *a* intelligente.

intelligentsia [in͵teli'dʒentsiə] *n* intellettuali, classe colta.

intelligibility [in͵telidʒə'biliti] *n* intelligibilità.

intelligible [in'telidʒəbl] *a* intelligibile; comprensibile; chiaro.

intemperance [in'tempərəns] *n* intemperanza.

intemperate [in'tempərit] *a* smoderato, violento; dedito al bere; (*climate*) rigido.

intend [in'tend] *vti* intendere, proporsi.

intended [in'tendid] *a* intenzionale, deliberato.

intense [in'tens] *a* intenso; (*fig*) profondo, ipersensibile.

intensification [in͵tensifi'keiʃən] *n* intensificazione.

intensify [in'tensifai] *vti* intensificar (si).

intensity [in'tensiti] *n* intensità.

intensive [in'tensiv] *a* intensivo, intenso.

intent [in'tent] *a* intento; *n* scopo.

intention [in'tenʃən] *n* intenzione, proposito.

intentional [in'tenʃənl] *a* intenzionale, premeditato.

inter [in'tə:] *vt* interrare, seppellire.

interact [͵intər'ækt] *vt* esercitare azione reciproca.

interaction [͵intər'ækʃən] *n* azione reciproca.

intercede [͵intə:'si:d] *vi* intercedere.

intercept [͵intə:'sept] *vt* intercettare.

interception [͵intə:'sepʃən] *n* intercettamento; interruzione.

interchange [͵intə:'tʃeindʒ] *n* scambio; *vti* scambiar(si).

interchangeable [͵intə:'tʃeindʒəbl] *a* scambievole.

intercourse ['intə:kɔ:s] *n* relazione, rapporto; **sexual i.** rapporti sessuali *pl*.

interdependent [͵intədi'pendənt] *a* interdipendente.

interdict ['intə:dikt] *n* interdetto (papale); *vt* [͵intə:'dikt] interdire, vietare.

interdiction [͵intə:'dikʃən] *n* divieto, interdizione, interdetto.

interest ['intrist] *n* interesse, interessi *pl*, interessamento; *vt* interessare.

interesting ['intristiŋ] *a* interessante.

interfere [͵intə'fiə] *vi* intervenire, intromettersi, ostacolare, interferire.

interference [͵intə'fiərəns] *n* interferenza, ingerenza, intralcio.

interim ['intərim] *n* interim, lasso di tempo; *ad* nel frattempo; *a* provvisorio, temporaneo.

interior [in'tiəriə] *a* interiore, interno; *n* interno.

interject [͵intə:'dʒekt] *vti* interporre.

interjection [͵intə:'dʒekʃən] *n* interiezione; (*fig*) intromissione.

interlace [͵intə:'leis] *vt* intrecciare.

interleave ['intəli:v] *vt* interfogliare.

interlock [͵intə:'lɔk] *n* (*cin*) sincronizzazione; *vti* allacciar(si); (*cin*) sincronizzare.

interlocutor [͵intə:'lɔkjutə] *n* interlocutore.

interloper ['intə:loupə] *n* intruso.

interlude ['intə:lu:d] *n* interludio, intervallo.

intermediate [͵intə:'mi:diət] *a* intermedio.

interment [in'tə:mənt] *n* inumazione, seppellimento.

interminable [in'tə:minəbl] *a* interminabile.

intermingle [͵intə:'miŋgl] *vti* inframmischiar(si).

intermission [͵intə:'miʃən] *n* intervallo, interruzione, pausa.

intermittent [͵intə:'mitənt] *a* intermittente.

intern [in'tə:n] *vt* internare.

internal [in'tə:nl] *a* interno; **i. revenue** (*US*) fisco.

international [͵intə:'næʃənl] *a n* internazionale.

internment [in'tə:nmənt] *n* internamento.

interpellation [in͵tə:pe'leiʃən] *n* interpellanza.

interplay ['intə:'plei] *n* gioco (di colori etc.); azione reciproca.

interpolate [in'tə:pouleit] *vt* interpolare.

interpose [͵intə:'pouz] *vti* interpor (si).

interpret [in'tə:prit] *vti* interpretare; fare da interprete.

interpreter [in'tə:pritə] *n* interprete.

interrogate [in'terəgeit] *vt* interrogare.

interrogation [in͵terə'geiʃən] *n* interrogazione.

interrogative [͵intə'rɔgətiv] *a n* interrogativo.

interrogatory [͵intə'rɔgətəri] *a n* interrogatorio.

interrupt [͵intə'rʌpt] *vt* interrompere.

interruption [͵intə'rʌpʃən] *n* interruzione.

intersect [͵intə:'sekt] *vti* intersecar (si).

intersection [͵intə:'sekʃən] *n* intersecazione.

intersperse [͵intə:'spə:s] *vt* spargere qua e là, disseminare, inframmezzare.

intertwine [͵intə:'twain] *vti* intrecciar(si).

interval ['intəvəl] *n* intervallo.

intervene [͵intə:'vi:n] *vi* intervenire, intromettersi; **intervening** interveniente; **in the intervening time** nel frattempo.

intervention [͵intə:'venʃən] *n* intervento.

interview ['intəvju:] *n* intervista, abboccamento; *vt* intervistare.

intestate [in'testit] *a* intestato, senza disposizioni testamentarie.

intestinal [in'testinl] *a* intestinale.

intestine [in'testin] *a* intestino, interno; *n* intestino; *n pl* intestino.

intimacy ['intiməsi] *n* intimità.

intimate ['intimit] *a* intimo; *vt* ['intimeit] intimare, comunicare, suggerire.

intimation [‚inti'meiʃən] *n* intimazione, avviso.

intimidate [in'timideit] *vt* intimidire.

intimidation [in‚timi'deiʃən] *n* intimidazione.

into ['intu] *prep* in.

intolerable [in'tɔlərəbl] *a* intollerabile.

intolerance [in'tɔlərəns] *n* intolleranza.

intolerant [in'tɔlərənt] *a* intollerante.

intonation [‚intou'neiʃən] *n* intonazione.

intone [in'toun] *vt* intonare.

intoxicate [in'tɔksikeit] *vt* ubriacare, inebriare.

intoxication [in‚tɔksi'keiʃən] *n* ubriachezza, ebbrezza.

intransigent [in'trænsidʒənt] *a* intransigente.

intrepid [in'trepid] *a* intrepido.

intrepidity [‚intri'piditi] *n* intrepidità.

intricacy ['intrikəsi] *n* groviglio, viluppo.

intricate ['intrikit] *a* intricato, involuto.

intrigue [in'tri:g] *n* intrigo, macchinazione; *vi* intrigare, macchinare; *vt* (sl) stuzzicare la curiosità di.

intriguing [in'tri:giŋ] *a* intrigante; interessante.

intrinsic [in'trinsik] *a* intrinseco.

introduce [‚intrə'dju:s] *vt* introdurre, presentare.

introduction [‚intrə'dʌkʃən] *n* introduzione, presentazione.

introductory [‚intrə'dʌktəri] *a* introduttivo, preliminare.

introspection [‚introu'spekʃən] *n* introspezione.

introspective [‚introu'spektiv] *a* introspettivo.

introvert ['introuvə:t] *a n* introvertito, introverso.

intrude [in'tru:d] *vti* intromettersi.

intruder [in'tru:də] *n* intruso.

intrusion [in'tru:ʒən] *n* intrusione.

intuition [‚intju:'iʃən] *n* intuito, intuizione.

intuitive [in'tju:itiv] *a* intuitivo.

inundate ['inʌndeit] *vt* inondare.

inure [i'njuə] *vt* indurire, abituare.

invade [in'veid] *vt* invadere.

invader [in'veidə] *n* invasore.

invalid ['invəli:d] *a n* invalido, infermo; *vt* (mil) riformare; [in'vælid] *a* non valido, nullo.

invalidate [in'vælideit] *vt* infirmare.

invalidity [‚invə'liditi] *n* invalidità.

invaluable [in'væljuəbl] *a* inestimabile.

invariable [in'vɛəriəbl] *a* invariabile.

invasion [in'veiʒən] *n* invasione.

invective [in'vektiv] *n* invettiva.

inveigh [in'vei] *vi* inveire.

inveigle [in'vi:gl] *vt* adescare, sedurre.

invent [in'vent] *vt* inventare.

invention [in'venʃən] *n* invenzione.

inventive [in'ventiv] *a* inventivo.

inventor [in'ventə] *n* inventore.

inventory ['inventri] *n* inventario; *vt* inventariare.

inversion [in'və:ʃən] *n* inversione.

invert [in'və:t] *vt* invertire.

invest [in'vest] *vt* investire.

investigate [in'vestigeit] *vti* investigare.

investigation [in‚vesti'geiʃən] *n* investigazione, indagine.

investigator [in'vestigeitə] *n* investigatore, investigatrice.

investiture [in'vestitʃə] *n* investitura.

investment [in'vestmənt] *n* (com) investimento.

inveterate [in'vetərit] *a* inveterato, ostinato.

invidious [in'vidiəs] *a* sgradevole, odioso.

invigorate [in'vigəreit] *vt* invigorire, rinforzare.

invincible [in'vinsəbl] *a* invincibile.

inviolate [in'vaiəlit] *a* inviolato.

invisible [in'vizəbl] *a* invisibile.

invitation [‚invi'teiʃən] *n* invito.

invite [in'vait] *vt* invitare.

inviting [in'vaitiŋ] *a* invitante, attraente.

invocation [‚invou'keiʃən] *n* invocazione.

invoice ['invɔis] *n* (com) fattura; *vt* (com) fatturare.

invoke [in'vouk] *vt* invocare.

involuntary [in'vɔləntəri] *a* involontario.

involve [in'vɔlv] *vt* implicare, coinvolgere, comportare.

inward ['inwəd] *a* interno, intimo; **inwards** verso l'interno.

inwardly [in'inwədli] *ad* internamente, (fig) intimamente.

iodine ['aiədi:n] *n* iodio.

Ionian [ai'ouniən] *a n* Ionio.

irascible [i'ræsibl] *a* irascibile; irritabile.

irate [ai'reit] *a* irato.

Ireland ['aiələnd] *n* Irlanda.

iris ['aiəris] *n* iride, (bot) iris, giaggiolo.

Irish ['aiəriʃ] *a n* irlandese.

irksome ['ə:ksəm] *a* fastidioso, tedioso.

iron ['aiən] *a* ferreo, di ferro, in ferro; *n* ferro; ferro da stiro; *vt* stirare; ferrare; **i. age** età del ferro; **i. industry** industria siderurgica; **i. foundry** fonderia; **i. ore** minerale di ferro.

ironclad ['aiənklæd] *a* corazzato; *n* corazzata.

ironical [ai'rɔnikəl] *a* ironico.

ironmonger ['aiən‚mʌŋgə] n negoziante in ferramenta.
ironmongery ['aiən‚mʌŋgəri] n ferramenta.
ironwork ['aiənwəːk] n lavoro in ferro, costruzione in ferro.
irony ['aiərəni] n ironia.
irradiate [i'reidieit] vti irradiare.
irrational [i'ræʃənl] a irrazionale.
irreconcilable [i'rekənsailəbl] a irreconciliabile.
irrefutable [i'refjutəbl] a irrefutabile.
irregular [i'regjulə] a irregolare, anormale.
irrelevant [i'relivənt] a non appropriato, non pertinente.
irremovable [‚iri'muːvəbl] a irremovibile.
irreparable [i'repərəbl] a irreparabile.
irreplaceable [‚iri'pleisəbl] a insostituibile.
irrepressible [‚iri'presəbl] a irreprimibile, irrefrenabile.
irreproachable [‚iri'proutʃəbl] a irreprensibile.
irresistible [‚iri'zistəbl] a irresistibile.
irresolute [i'rezəluːt] a irresoluto.
irresolution ['i‚rezə'luːʃən] n irresolutezza.
irrespective [‚iris'pektiv] a senza riguardo a.
irresponsible [‚iris'pɔnsəbl] a irresponsabile.
irreverent [i'revərənt] a irriverente.
irrevocable [i'revəkəbl] a irrevocabile.
irrigate ['irigeit] vt irrigare.
irrigation [‚iri'geiʃən] n irrigazione.
irritable ['iritəbl] n irritabile.
irritably ['iritəbli] ad irritabilmente.
irritant ['iritənt] a n irritante.
irritate ['iriteit] vt irritare.
irritation [‚iri'teiʃən] n irritazione.
irruption [i'rʌpʃən] n irruzione.
Isabel ['izəbel] nf pr Isabella.
Islam ['izlaːm] n pr Islam.
Islamic [iz'læmik] a islamico, maomettano.
island ['ailənd] n isola; (road) salvagente.
islander ['ailəndə] n isolano.
isolate ['aisəleit] vt isolare.
isolation [‚aisə'leiʃən] n isolamento.
Israel ['izreiəl] n Israele.
Israeli [iz'reili] a n israeliano.
Israelite ['izriəlait] n israelita.
issue ['isjuː] n uscita, sbocco; (notes etc) emissione; (publication) tiratura, edizione; (offspring) discendenza; vt pubblicare; rilasciare; vi uscire.
isthmus ['isməs] n istmo.
it [it] pron esso, essa, lo, la; **its** a (il) suo, (la) sua; **itself** pron si, se stesso, se stessa.
Italian [i'tæliən] a n italiano.
italics [i'tæliks] n pl corsivo.
Italy ['itəli] n Italia.
itchy ['itʃi] a che prude.

itch [itʃ] n prurito, scabbia; vi prudere.
item ['aitəm] n articolo, numero; (com) voce.
iterate ['itəreit] vt ripetere.
itinerant [i'tinərənt] a ambulante, girovago.
itinerary [ai'tinərəri] n itinerario.
ivory ['aivəri] a di (in) avorio; n avorio.
ivy ['aivi] n edera.

J

jab [dʒæb] vt colpire con oggetto appuntito.
jabber ['dʒæbə] vti pronunciare rapidamente e indistintamente, mormorare, borbottare.
jack [dʒæk] n (naut) bandiera; (mech) cricco; (spit) girarrosto; (cards) fante; (bowls) boccino; **j. of all trades** factotum.
jackal ['dʒækɔːl] n sciacallo.
jackass ['dʒækæs] n somaro.
jackdaw ['dʒækdɔː] n cornacchia, taccola.
jacket ['dʒækit] n giacca, giacchetta; buccia; rivestimento; copertina di libro.
jackknife ['dʒæknaif] n coltello a serramanico.
jackpot ['dʒækpɔt] n (poker) posta; **to hit the j.** fare una grossa vincita.
Jacob ['dʒeikəb] nm pr Giacobbe.
Jacobite ['dʒækəbait] n giacobita.
jade [dʒeid] n giada; vecchia cavalla; donnaccia.
jag [dʒæg] n punta di roccia, sporgenza appuntita.
jagged ['dʒægid] a dentellato, frastagliato.
jail [dʒeil] n carcere, prigione; vt incarcerare.
jailer ['dʒeilə] n carceriere.
jam [dʒæm] n conserva di frutta, marmellata; blocco; compressione; ingorgo di traffico; vt comprimere, bloccare, bloccarsi.
Jamaica [dʒə'meikə] n Giamaica.
Jamaican [dʒə'meikən] a n giamaicano.
James [dʒeimz] nm pr Giacomo.
Jane [dʒein] nf pr Giovanna, Gianna.
jangle ['dʒæŋgl] n suono aspro e discordante; vti (far) fare rumori discordanti; vociare sgarbatamente, berciare.
janitor ['dʒænitə] n bidello; (US) portiere.
January ['dʒænjuəri] n gennaio.
Japan [dʒə'pæn] n Giappone.
Japanese [‚dʒæpə'niːz] a n giapponese.
jar [dʒaː] n giara, vaso, barattolo; suono aspro; vi vibrare; produrre un'impressione sgradevole; vt scuotere.

jargon ['dʒɑ:gən] n gergo, linguaggio professionale.

jasmine ['dʒæsmin] n gelsomino.

jasper ['dʒæspə] n diaspro.

jaundice ['dʒɔːndis] n itterizia.

jaunt [dʒɔːnt] n gita, scampagnata.

jaunty ['dʒɔːnti] a arzillo, vivace.

javelin ['dʒævlin] n giavellotto.

jaw [dʒɔː] n mascella; **jaws** pl fauci pl, mandibola.

jay [dʒei] n ghiandaia.

jealous ['dʒeləs] a geloso.

jealousy ['dʒeləsi] n gelosia.

Jean [dʒiːn] nf pr Giovanna.

jeans [dʒiːnz] n pl calzoni di tela, tuta.

jeer [dʒiə] n derisione, scherno; vti beffarsi, deridere, schernire.

Jeffrey ['dʒefri] nm pr Goffredo.

jelly ['dʒeli] n gelatina.

jellyfish ['dʒelifiʃ] n medusa.

jeopardize ['dʒepədaiz] vt mettere in pericolo.

jeopardy ['dʒepədi] n repentaglio, pericolo.

Jericho ['dʒerikou] n Gerico.

jerk [dʒəːk] n scatto, strattone; vti dare uno strattone; sobbalzare.

jerkin ['dʒəːkin] n giacca a vento; giustacuore.

Jerome [dʒə'roum] nm pr Gerolamo.

jersey ['dʒəːzi] n camicetta a maglia; maglione; maglia sportiva.

Jerusalem [dʒə'ruːsələm] n Gerusalemme.

jest [dʒest] n scherzo, beffa, zimbello; vi scherzare.

jester ['dʒestə] n burlone, buffone.

jesuit ['dʒezjuit] n gesuita; ipocrita.

Jesus ['dʒiːzəs] nm pr Gesù.

jet [dʒet] n zampillo, getto; (chem) becco; giaietto.

jetsam ['dʒetsəm] n (naut) relitti pl di mare.

jettison ['dʒetisn] vt gettare in mare (un carico); (fig) disfarsi di.

jetty ['dʒeti] n gettata, molo.

Jew [dʒuː] n ebreo, giudeo, israelita.

jewel ['dʒuːəl] n gioiello.

jeweller ['dʒuːələ] n gioielliere.

jewel(le)ry ['dʒuːəlri] n gioielli pl, gioielleria.

Jewess ['dʒuː(:)is] n ebrea, israelita.

Jewish ['dʒuː(:)iʃ] a ebreo, giudaico, israelitico.

jib [dʒib] vi recalcitrare; vt (naut) orientare.

jig [dʒig] n giga.

jigsaw ['dʒigsɔː] n sega da traforo; **j. puzzle** gioco di pazienza.

jilt [dʒilt] n donna capricciosa; vt abbandonare il fidanzato o la fidanzata.

jingle ['dʒiŋgl] n tintinnio; vti far tintinnare.

Joan [dʒoun] nf pr Giovanna.

job [dʒɔb] n lavoro, occupazione, posto, faccenda.

jockey ['dʒɔki] n fantino.

jocose [dʒə'kous] a giocoso.

jocular ['dʒɔkjulə] a allegro, scherzoso.

jocund ['dʒɔkənd] a giocondo.

jog [dʒɔg] n gomitata, spinta; andatura lenta; vti urtare col gomito, spingere; procedere adagio.

joggle ['dʒɔgl] n leggera scossa.

John [dʒɔn] nm pr Giovanni.

join [dʒɔin] n giuntura, congiunzione; vti associarsi a, congiungere, unirsi a; raggiungere.

joiner ['dʒɔinə] n falegname.

joint [dʒɔint] a articolazione, giuntura; parte di bestia macellata.

jointly ['dʒɔintli] ad unitamente, assieme, collettivamente.

joke [dʒouk] n facezia, scherzo, tiro, barzelletta, burla; vi scherzare.

jolly ['dʒɔli] a allegro, festoso, giovanile.

jolt [dʒoult] n scossa, sobbalzo; vti (far) sobbalzare.

Jonathan ['dʒɔnəθən] nm pr Gionata.

Jordan ['dʒɔːdn] n Giordano, Giordania.

Jordanian [dʒɔː'deiniən] a n giordanico, giordano.

Joseph ['dʒouzif] nm pr Giuseppe; **Josephine** nf pr Giuseppina.

Joshua ['dʒɔʃwə] nm pr Giosuè.

jostle ['dʒɔsl] vt spingere, urtare col gomito; vi lottare.

jot [dʒɔt] n iota, particella minima.

journal ['dʒəːnl] n giornale, periodico; diario.

journalism ['dʒəːnəlizəm] n giornalismo.

journalist ['dʒəːnəlist] n giornalista.

journalistic [,dʒəːnə'listik] a giornalistico.

journey ['dʒəːni] n viaggio; vi viaggiare, fare un viaggio.

journeyman ['dʒəːnimən] n meccanico o operaio qualificato che lavora a giornata.

joust [dʒaust] n torneo.

jovial ['dʒouviəl] a allegro, gioviale.

joviality [,dʒouvi'æliti] n giovialità.

joy [dʒɔi] n gioia.

Joy [dʒɔi] nm pr Gioia.

joyful ['dʒɔiful] a gioioso.

joyfully ['dʒɔifuli] ad gioiosamente, allegramente.

joyfulness ['dʒɔifulnis] n allegrezza, gioia.

joyless ['dʒɔilis] a senza gioia, triste.

joyous ['dʒɔiəs] a gioioso, gaio.

jubilant ['dʒuːbilənt] a esultante, giubilante.

jubilation [,dʒuːbi'leiʃən] n esultanza, giubilo.

jubilee ['dʒuːbiliː] n giubileo.

judaic [dʒu(:)'deiik] a giudaico, ebraico.

Judaism ['dʒuːdeiizəm] n giudaismo.

Judas ['dʒuːdəs] nm pr Giuda.

judge [dʒʌdʒ] n giudice; vti giudicare.

judgment ['dʒʌdʒmənt] n giudizio, sentenza, punizione divina.

judicial [dʒu(ː)'diʃəl] *a* giudiziario, imparziale.
judicious [dʒu(ː)'diʃəs] *a* giudizioso.
Judith ['dʒuːdiθ] *nf pr* Giuditta.
jug [dʒʌg] *n* brocca, caraffa, boccale.
juggle ['dʒʌgl] *n* gioco di prestigio; *vi* far giochi di destrezza o di prestigio, raggirare.
juggler ['dʒʌglə] *n* prestigiatore; impostore.
Jugoslav ['juːgouslɑːv] *a n* iugoslavo.
Jugoslavia ['juːgouslɑːviə] *n* Iugoslavia.
jugular ['dʒʌgjulə] *a n* (vena) giugulare.
juice [dʒuːs] *n* succo; (*sl*) benzina.
juicy ['dʒuːsi] *a* succoso; (*sl*) interessante.
jukebox ['dʒuːkbɔks] *n* grammofono a gettone, 'jukbox'.
Juliet ['dʒuːliət] *nf pr* Giulietta.
Julius ['dʒuːliəs] *nm pr* Giulio.
July [dʒu(ː)'lai] *n* luglio.
jumble ['dʒʌmbl] *n* confusione, mescolanza; *vt* mescolare, gettare insieme alla rinfusa.
jump [dʒʌmp] *n* salto; *vti* saltare, fare un salto.
jumper ['dʒʌmpə] *n* saltatore; maglione, golf.
jumpy ['dʒʌmpi] *n* nervoso, irrequieto, teso.
junction ['dʒʌŋkʃən] *n* congiunzione, unione; nodo ferroviario.
juncture ['dʒʌŋktʃə] *n* congiuntura, giuntura, stato di cose.
June [dʒuːn] *n* giugno.
jungle ['dʒʌŋgl] *n* giungla.
junior ['dʒuːniə] *a n* chi è più giovane, chi ha grado o posizione inferiore.
juniper ['dʒuːnipə] *n* ginepro.
junk [dʒʌŋk] *n* articoli marinareschi *pl*, articoli *pl* di scarto.
junket ['dʒʌŋkit] *n* giuncata.
jurisdiction [,dʒuəris'dikʃən] *n* giurisdizione.
jurisprudence ['dʒuəris,pruːdəns] *n* giurisprudenza.
jurist ['dʒuərist] *n* giurista.
juror ['dʒuərə] *n* giurato.
jury ['dʒuəri] *n* giuria.
just [dʒʌst] *a* giusto, retto; *ad* appena; esattamente, proprio; j. now or ora.
justice ['dʒʌstis] *n* giustizia, giudice.
justifiable ['dʒʌstifaiəbl] *a* giustificabile.
justification [,dʒʌstifi'keiʃən] *n* giustificazione.
justify ['dʒʌstifai] *vt* giustificare.
justly ['dʒʌstli] *ad* giustamente, a buon diritto.
justness ['dʒʌstnis] *n* giustizia.
jut [dʒʌt] *n* sporgenza; *vi* sporgere.
juvenile ['dʒuːvenail] *a* giovane, giovanile; *n* giovane, minorenne.
juxtaposition [,dʒʌkstəpə'ziʃən] *n* giustapposizione.

K

kale, kail [keil] *n* cavolo riccio.
kangaroo [,kæŋgə'ruː] *n* canguro.
kapok ['keipɔk] *n* capoc.
Katharine, Katherine ['kæθərin] **Kathleen** ['kæθliːn] *nf pr* Caterina.
kedge [kedʒ] *n* (*naut*) ancorotto.
keel [kiːl] *n* (*naut*) chiglia; chiatta; *vt* (*naut*) carenare.
keen [kiːn] *a* acuminato, acuto; amante, appassionato, forte, intenso; be keen on essere amante di.
keenness ['kiːnnis] *n* acutezza, perspicacia; passione; entusiasmo.
keep [kiːp] *n* mantenimento; (*of castle*) torrione; *vt* tenere, mantenere, conservare, trattenere; festeggiare; *vi* continuare, conservarsi, mantenersi.
keeper ['kiːpə] *n* custode, guardiano.
keeping ['kiːpiŋ] *n* custodia, armonia.
keepsake ['kiːpseik] *n* ricordo, pegno d'affetto.
keg [keg] *n* bariletto.
ken [ken] *n* comprensione, conoscenza.
kennel ['kenl] *n* canile.
Kenya ['kenjə] *n* Kenia.
kerb [kəːb] *n* bordo del marciapiede.
kernel ['kəːnl] *n* mandorla, gheriglio; (*fig*) nocciolo.
kerosene ['kerəsiːn] *n* (*US*) petrolio raffinato.
kestrel ['kestrəl] *n* gheppio.
kettle ['ketl] *n* bollitore, bricco.
key [kiː] *n* chiave; (*mus*) chiave, tasto.
kick [kik] *n* calcio; (*mil*) rinculo; *vti* dare (tirare) calci (a,).
kid [kid] *n* capretto; (*fam*) ragazzino; *vti* (*sl*) prendere in giro, scherzare.
kidnap ['kidnæp] *vt* rapire una persona.
kidney ['kidni] *n* rene, rognone; carattere, tipo.
kill [kil] *vt* ammazzare, uccidere.
killer ['kilə] *n* uccisore, assassino; lady k. dongiovanni.
killing ['kiliŋ] *a* mortale, distruttivo; (*fam*) affascinante; *n* uccisione, carneficina.
kiln [kiln] *n* fornace.
kilogramme ['kiləgræm] *n* chilo (grammo).
kilometre ['kilə,miːtə] *n* chilometro.
kilt [kilt] *n* 'kilt', gonnellino degli scozzesi.
kin [kin] *n* parentela, congiunti, parenti *pl*.
kind [kaind] *a* buono, gentile; *n* genere, sorta, specie, tipo.
kindergarten ['kində,gɑːtn] *n* giardino d'infanzia.
kindle ['kindl] *vt* accendere, destare, infiammare, suscitare.

kindly ['kaindli] *a* benevolo, gentile; *ad* benevolmente, gentilmente.

kindness ['kaindnis] *n* benevolenza, bontà, gentilezza.

kindred ['kindrid] *a* affine; *n* affinità, parentela, parenti *pl*.

king [kiŋ] *n* re.

kingdom ['kiŋdəm] *n* regno, reame.

kingfisher ['kiŋ‚fiʃə] *n* martin pescatore.

kingly ['kiŋli] *a* da re, regale.

kink [kiŋk] *n* nodo; (*fig*) capriccio, ghiribizzo.

kinsfolk ['kinzfouk] *n* congiunti, parenti *pl*.

kinsman ['kinzmən] *n* congiunto, parente.

kiosk ['kiːɔsk] *n* chiosco, edicola.

kipper ['kipə] *n* aringa salata e affumicata.

kiss [kis] *n* bacio; *vt* baciare.

kit [kit] *n* utensili, attrezzi *pl*; borsa utensili; **kitbag** sacco militare.

kitchen ['kitʃin] *n* cucina.

kitchenette [‚kitʃin'et] *n* cucinino.

kite [kait] *n* nibbio; aquilone.

kitten ['kitn] *n* gattino, micino.

knack [næk] *n* abilità, facoltà.

knapsack ['næpsæk] *n* zaino.

knave [neiv] *n* briccone, furfante; (*cards*) fante.

knavery ['neivəri] *n* bricconeria.

knavish ['neiviʃ] *a* da briccone, disonesto.

knead [niːd] *vt* impastare; massaggiare.

knee [niː] *n* ginocchio.

kneel [niːl] *vi* inginocchiarsi.

knell [nel] *n* rintocco funebre.

knickerbockers ['nikəbɔkəz] *n pl* calzoni *pl* alla zuava.

knickers ['nikəz] *n pl* mutande da donna *pl*; *v also* **knickerbockers**.

(k)nick-(k)nack ['niknæk] *n* ninnolo.

knife [naif] *n* coltello; *vt* accoltellare.

knight [nait] *n* cavaliere; (*chess*) cavallo.

knighthood ['naithud] *n* titolo di cavaliere.

knightly ['naitli] *a* cavalleresco.

knit [nit] *vti* lavorare a maglia; saldar(si); corrugare (la fronte); congiunger(si).

knitting ['nitiŋ] *n* lavoro a maglia; **k. needle**, **k. pin** ferro da calza.

knob [nɔb] *n* bernoccolo; pomo.

knock [nɔk] *n* colpo, urto; il bussare (alla porta); *vti* bussare; colpire, urtare, picchiare; **to k. down** abbattere; assegnare all'asta; **to k. out** mettere fuori combattimento.

knocker ['nɔkə] *n* battente.

knoll [noul] *n* collinetta, poggio.

knot [nɔt] *n* nodo, groviglio; *vti* annodar(si).

knotty ['nɔti] *a* nodoso; ingarbugliato.

know [nou] *vti* conoscere, sapere.

knowing ['nouiŋ] *a* abile, accorto.

knowingly ['nouiŋli] *ad* scientemente, a bello studio.

knowledge ['nɔlidʒ] *n* conoscenza, cognizioni *pl*, sapere.

knowledgeable ['nɔlidʒəbl] *a* intelligente, ben informato.

knuckle ['nʌkl] *n* nocca (delle dita), articolazione, giuntura; **k.-duster** pugno di ferro.

L

label ['leibl] *n* cartellino, etichetta; *vt* mettere le etichette a, classificare.

laboratory [lə'bɔrətəri] *n* laboratorio.

laborious [lə'bɔːriəs] *a* faticoso; laborioso.

laboriousness [lə'bɔːriəsnis] *n* laboriosità; fatica.

labour ['leibə] *n* fatica, lavoro faticoso; doglie del parto *pl*; *vi* affaticarsi, lavorare faticosamente; **hard l.** lavori forzati *pl*; **l. party** partito laburista.

labourer ['leibərə] *n* bracciante.

laburnum [lə'bəːnəm] *n* avorno, laburno.

labyrinth ['læbərinθ] *n* labirinto.

lace [leis] *n* merletto, pizzo; laccio da scarpe; *vt* allacciare; guarnire con merletti.

lacerate ['læsəreit] *vt* lacerare.

laceration [‚læsə'reiʃən] *n* lacerazione.

lachrymose ['lækrimous] *a* lacrimoso.

lack [læk] *n* mancanza; *vt* mancare di; *vi* mancare.

lackadaisical [‚lækə'deizikəl] *a* affettato, languido.

lackey ['læki] *n* lacchè.

laconic [lə'kɔnik] *a* laconico.

lacquer ['lækə] *n* lacca.

lad [læd] *n* giovanetto, ragazzo.

ladder ['lædə] *n* scala a piuoli.

lade [leid] *vt* caricare una nave.

lading ['leidiŋ] *n* carico.

ladle ['leidl] *n* mestolo.

lady ['leidi] *n* signora, gentildonna; **L. Day** Festa dell'Annunciazione.

ladybird ['leidibəːd] *n* coccinella.

ladylike ['leidilaik] *a* da signora, distinto, signorile.

ladyship ['leidiʃip] *n* Eccellenza (*titolo delle signore dell'aristocrazia*).

lag [læg] *vi* indugiare; farsi tirare; **to l. behind** restare indietro.

lagoon [lə'guːn] *n* laguna.

lair [lɛə] *n* covo, tana.

laird [lɛəd] *n* (*scozzese*) proprietario terriero.

laity ['leiiti] *n* laicato.

lake [leik] *n* lago.

lamb [læm] *n* agnello.

lame [leim] *a* zoppo; *vt* azzoppare.

lameness ['leimnis] *n* zoppaggine.

lament [lə'ment] *n* lamento, pianto,

elegia funebre; *vt* lamentar(si), rimpiangere.

lamentable ['læməntəbl] *a* lamentevole, deplorevole.

lamentation [ˌlæmen'teiʃən] *n* lamentazione, lamento.

lamented [lə'mentid] *a* deplorato; compianto.

lamp [læmp] *n* lampada, lampione, lucerna, fanale; (*fig*) lume.

lampoon [læm'puːn] *n* satira, pasquinata.

lamprey ['læmpri] *n* lampreda.

lance [lɑːns] *n* lancia; rampone; *vt* tagliare col bisturi.

lancer ['lɑːnsə] *n* lanciere.

lancet ['lɑːnsit] *n* bisturi.

land [lænd] *n* terra, suolo, terreno; paese; *vt* sbarcare, atterrare; porsi (in una situazione).

landed ['lændid] *a* terriero.

landing ['lændiŋ] *n* approdo, sbarco; atterraggio; pianerottolo.

landlord ['lænlɔːd] **landlady** ['lændˌleidi] *n* padrone, padrona di terre o case affittate, locandiere, locandiera.

landmark ['lænmɑːk] *n* punto di riferimento, pietra miliare, pietra di confine.

landowner ['lændˌounə] *n* proprietario di terre.

landscape ['lænskeip] *n* paesaggio.

lane [lein] *n* vicolo, viottolo.

language ['læŋgwidʒ] *n* lingua, linguaggio.

languid ['læŋgwid] *a* languido.

languish ['læŋgwiʃ] *vi* languire.

languor ['læŋgə] *n* languore.

lank [læŋk] **lanky** ['læŋki] *a* alto e magro.

lanolin(e) ['lænəlin] *n* lanolina.

lantern ['læntən] *n* lanterna.

lap [læp] *n* grembo; lembo, falda; (*races*) giro di pista; *vt* lambire; avvolgere, ripiegare; bere rumorosamente; (*of dogs*) lappare; **to l. up** leccare il piatto, mangiar tutto; **lapping waves** maretta.

lapdog ['læpdɔg] *n* cagnolino.

lapel [lə'pel] *n* risvolto.

Lapland ['læplænd] *n* Lapponia.

Lapp [læp] **Laplander** ['læplændə] *a n* lappone.

lapse [læps] *n* decorso, lasso (di tempo), intervallo; errore; perdita di validità; *vi* passare, trascorrere, decadere; (*fig*) cadere.

larboard ['lɑːbəd] *n* (*naut*) babordo.

larceny ['lɑːsni] *n* furto, ladrocinio.

larch [lɑːtʃ] *n* larice.

lard [lɑːd] *n* lardo.

larder ['lɑːdə] *n* dispensa.

large [lɑːdʒ] *a* grande, ampio, spazioso; considerevole; numeroso.

largely ['lɑːdʒli] *ad* largamente, in gran misura.

largeness ['lɑːdʒnis] *n* grandezza, estensione.

lark [lɑːk] *n* allodola; (*fam*) burla, scherzo.

larynx ['læriŋks] *n* laringe.

lascivious [lə'siviəs] *a* lascivo.

lasciviousness [lə'siviəsnis] *n* lascivia.

lash [læʃ] *n* ciglio; frusta(ta); sferza(ta); sarcasmo; *vt* frustare, sferzare, incitare; assicurare con una corda; **to l. its tail** agitare la coda; **to l. out** prorompere (in); (*horse*) sferrare calci.

lashing ['læʃiŋ] *n* frustata; *pl* (*fam*) abbondanza.

lass [læs] *n* fanciulla, ragazza.

last [lɑːst] *n* ultimo, scorso, estremo; *ad* per ultimo; l'ultima volta; finalmente; *n* ultimo; fine; (*shoe*) forma; *vi* durare.

lasting ['lɑːstiŋ] *a* duraturo, durevole.

lastly ['lɑːstli] *a* in conclusione, per ultimo.

latch [lætʃ] *n* saliscendi, serratura a scatto; *vt* chiudere con saliscendi.

late [leit] *a* tardivo; in ritardo; recente; ultimo; fu, defunto; *ad* tardi; **latecomer** ritardatario.

lately ['leitli] *ad* recentemente, ultimamente.

latent ['leitənt] *a* latente.

lateral ['lætərəl] *a* laterale.

latest ['leitist] *a* recentissimo, ultimo.

lathe [leið] *n* tornio.

lather ['lɑːðə] *n* schiuma, saponata; sudore schiumoso; *vt* insaponare, coprir(si) di schiuma.

latin ['lætin] *a n* latino.

latitude ['lætitjuːd] *n* latitudine; (*fig*) larghezza, libertà.

latrine [lə'triːn] *n* latrina.

latter ['lætə] *a pron* (*di due*) quest'ultimo, il secondo.

latterly ['lætəli] *ad* di recente.

lattice ['lætis] *n* grata, traliccio.

laudable ['lɔːdəbl] *a* lodevole.

laugh(ter) ['lɑːf(tə)] *n* risata, riso.

laugh [lɑːf] *vi* ridere.

laughable ['lɑːfəbl] *a* buffo, comico.

launch [lɔːntʃ] *n* (*naut*) lancia, varo; *vt* varare; *vti* lanciar(si) in.

launder ['lɔːndə] *vti* lavare e stirare, fare il bucato.

launderette [lɔːnd'ret] *n* lavanderia automatica (dove il cliente fa il bucato da sè).

laundress ['lɔːndris] *n* lavandaia.

laundry ['lɔːndri] *n* lavanderia, bucato; **laundryman** lavandaio.

Laura ['lɔːrə] *nf pr* Laura.

laurel ['lɔrəl] *n* alloro, lauro.

Laurence ['lɔrəns] *nm pr* Lorenzo.

lavatory ['lævətəri] *n* gabinetto, latrina.

lavender ['lævində] *n* lavanda.

lavish ['læviʃ] *a* generoso, prodigo; *vt* prodigare, profondere.

law [lɔː] *n* diritto, legge.

lawful ['lɔːful] *a* legale, legittimo.

lawfully ['lɔːfuli] *ad* legittimamente, legalmente.

lawfulness ['lɔ:fulnis] *n* legalità, legittimità.

lawgiver ['lɔ:,givə] *n* legislatore.

lawless ['lɔ:lis] *a* illegale, illegittimo.

lawn [lɔ:n] *n* prato; batista; **lawn-mower** falciatrice per prati; **l. tennis** tennis su prato.

Lawrence ['lɔrəns] *nm pr* Lorenzo.

lawsuit ['lɔ:su:t] *n* causa, procedimento legale.

lawyer ['lɔ:jə] *n* avvocato.

lax [læks] *a* negligente, rilassato.

laxative ['læksətiv] *n* lassativo.

lay [lei] *a* laico, secolare; *n* (*of ground*) configurazione; *vti* collocare, (de)porre, stendere, adagiare; coricarsi; scommettere; **to l. down** deporre; (*law*) dettare; (*project*) tracciare; (*life*) fare sacrifizio di; **to l. out** spendere; spiegare; **to l. up** ammassare; **laid up** allettato.

lay-by ['leibai] *n* piazzuola.

layer [leiə] *n* strato; (*agr*) propaggine.

layette [lei'et] *n* corredino da neonato.

layman ['leimən] *n* laico, secolare.

laze [leiz] *vi* passare (il tempo) in ozio, oziare.

laziness ['leizinis] *n* indolenza, pigrizia.

lazy ['leizi] *a* indolente, pigro.

lead [li:d] *n* direzione, guida; (*dog*) guinzaglio; *vt* condurre, dirigere, guidare; *vi* fare da guida.

lead [led] *n* piombo, scandaglio; *vt* impiombare, saldare col piombo.

leaden ['ledn] *a* di piombo, plumbeo.

leader ['li:də] *n* capo, duce; articolo di fondo d'un giornale.

leadership ['li:dəʃip] *n* direzione, comando.

leading ['li:diŋ] *a* dominante, eminente, principale; **l. article** articolo di fondo.

leaf [li:f] *pl* **leaves** *n* foglia; foglio, pagina; (*door*) battente; (*table*) asse.

leafless ['li:flis] *a* senza foglie, sfrondato.

leaflet ['li:flit] *n* manifestino, volantino.

leafy ['li:fi] *a* coperto di foglie, fronzuto.

league [li:g] *n* lega, società; *vt* unir(si) in lega.

leak [li:k] *n* falla; *vi* far acqua, perdere; **to l. out** trapelare.

leakage ['li:kidʒ] *n* perdita, indiscrezione.

leaky ['li:ki] *a* che perde, che cola.

lean [li:n] *a* magro, scarno; *vti* appoggiare, appoggiarsi, inclinarsi.

leaning ['li:niŋ] *a* pendente, inclinato; *n* inclinazione; **the Leaning Tower of Pisa** la Torre pendente di Pisa.

leanness ['li:nnis] *n* magrezza.

leap [li:p] *n* balzo, salto; *vi* balzare, saltare; **l. year** anno bisestile.

learn [lə:n] *vt* imparare.

learned ['lə:nid] *a* dotto, erudito.

learning ['lə:niŋ] *n* erudizione, sapere.

lease [li:s] *n* contratto d'affitto; *vt* affittare; **leasehold** *a* in affitto; *n* durata di un contratto d'affitto; **leaseholder** *n* affittuario.

leash [li:ʃ] *n* guinzaglio.

least [li:st] *a* il più piccolo, il minimo; *n* il meno; *ad* meno, minimamente; **at l.** almeno.

leather ['leðə] *n* cuoio, pelle; *a* di cuoio, di pelle.

leave [li:v] *n* licenza, permesso; congedo, commiato; *vt* abbandonare, lasciare; *vi* partire.

leaven ['levn] *n* lievito; *vt* far lievitare.

leaving ['li:viŋ] *n* partenza; *pl* avanzi, rifiuti.

Lebanese [,lebə'ni:z] *a n* libanese.

Lebanon ['lebənən] *n* Libano.

lecherous ['letʃərəs] *a* lascivo, vizioso.

lechery ['letʃəri] *n* lascivia; libertinaggio.

lecture ['lektʃə] *n* conferenza; lezione universitaria; ramanzina; *vti* tenere una conferenza, o lezione; ammonire.

lecturer ['lektʃərə] *n* conferenziere; libero docente.

lectureship ['lektʃəʃip] *n* carica di libero docente.

ledge [ledʒ] *n* ripiano, sporgenza.

ledger ['ledʒə] *n* (*com*) libro mastro.

lee [li:] *n* (*naut*) sottovento.

leech [li:tʃ] *n* sanguisuga.

leek [li:k] *n* porro.

leer [liə] *n* occhiata bieca, occhiata maliziosa; *vi* guardar di traverso.

leeward ['li:wəd] *a* di sottovento; *ad* in direzione di sottovento.

left [left] *a* sinistro, manco, mancino; *n* sinistra; *ad* a sinistra; **l.-handed** mancino.

leftovers ['left,ouvəz] *n pl* rimasugli, resti *pl*.

leg [leg] *n* gamba; (*fowl*) coscia; (*birds etc*) zampa; (*table etc*) piede.

legacy ['legəsi] *n* legato, lascito.

legal ['li:gəl] *a* legale.

legality [li(:)'gæliti] *n* legalità.

legalization [,li:gəlai'zeiʃən] *n* legalizzazione.

legalize ['li:gəlaiz] *vt* legalizzare.

legate ['legit] *n* legato.

legatee [,legə'ti:] *n* legatario.

legation [li'geiʃən] *n* legazione.

legend ['ledʒənd] *n* leggenda.

legendary ['ledʒəndəri] *a* leggendario.

legging ['legiŋ] *n* gambale; *pl* ghette *pl*.

Leghorn ['leghɔ:n] *n* Livorno.

legible ['ledʒəbl] *a* leggibile.

legion ['li:dʒən] *n* legione.

legionary ['li:dʒənəri] *a* legionario.

legislation [,ledʒis'leiʃən] *n* legislazione.

legislative ['ledʒislətiv] *a* legislativo.

legislator ['ledʒisleitə] n legislatore.
legislature ['ledʒisleitʃə] n legislatura, corpo legislativo.
legitimacy [li'dʒitiməsi] n legittimità.
legitimate [li'dʒitimit] a legittimo.
leisure ['leʒə] n agio, ozio, comodo, ritagli di tempo.
leisurely ['leʒəli] a fatto con comodo, a proprio agio; ad senza fretta.
lemon ['lemən] n limone.
lemonade ['lemə'neid] n limonata.
lend [lend] vt prestare; vi fare un prestito.
lending ['lendiŋ] n prestito.
length [leŋθ] n lunghezza; taglio di stoffa.
lengthen ['leŋθən] vti allungar(si).
lengthy ['leŋθi] a lungo, prolisso.
lenient ['li:niənt] a indulgente.
lens [lenz] n lente.
Lent [lent] n quaresima.
lenten ['lentən] a quaresimale, da quaresima.
lentil ['lentl] n lenticchia.
Leo ['li:(:)ou] nm pr Leone.
Leonard ['lenəd] nm pr Leonardo.
leopard ['lepəd] n leopardo.
Leopold ['liəpould] nm pr Leopoldo.
leper ['lepə] n lebbroso.
leprosy ['leprəsi] n lebbra.
lesbian ['lezbiən] a lesbico; n lesbica.
lesion ['li:ʒən] n lesione.
less [les] a meno, minore; n meno; ad prep meno.
lessee [le'si:] n locatario.
lessen ['lesn] vti diminuire, rimpicciolir(si).
lessening ['lesniŋ] n diminuzione, attenuazione.
lesser ['lesə] a minore.
lesson ['lesn] n lezione.
lest [lest] cj per paura che.
let [let] vt lasciare, permettere; dare in affitto; l. **down** abbassare; allungare; sciogliere; deludere; l. **off** lasciar andare; perdonare, (a shot etc) far partire.
lethal ['li:θəl] a letale, mortale.
lethargic [le'θɑ:dʒik] a letargico.
lethargy ['leθədʒi] n letargo.
letter ['letə] n lettera.
lettuce ['letis] n lattuga.
leukaemia [lju'ki:miə] n leucemia.
Levantine ['levəntain] a levantino.
level ['levl] a livellato, orizzontale, pari; n spianata, livello; l. **crossing** passaggio a livello; vt livellare, spianare, pareggiare; (fig) dirigere.
lever ['li:və] n (mech) leva.
leverage ['li:vəridʒ] n (mech) azione d'una leva, sistema di leve.
levity ['leviti] n frivolezza, leggerezza.
levy ['levi] n leva; imposta, tributo; vt arruolare; (tax etc) imporre.
lewd [lju:d] a impudico, lascivo.
lewdness ['lju:dnis] n lascivia.
Lewis ['lu:(:)is] nm pr Luigi.

lexicographer [,leksi'kɔgrəfə] n lessicografo.
lexicon ['leksikən] n lessico.
liability [,laiə'biliti] n obbligo; disposizione a; responsabilità; pl (com) passività.
liable ['laiəbl] a soggetto, responsabile.
liar ['laiə] n bugiardo.
libation [lai'beifən] n libagione.
libel ['laibəl] n libello, calunnia, diffamazione; vt diffamare a mezzo di libello.
libellous ['laibləs] a diffamatorio.
liberal ['libərəl] a n liberale.
liberality [,libə'ræliti] n liberalità.
liberate ['libəreit] vt liberare.
liberation [,libə'reifən] n liberazione.
Liberia [lai'biəriə] n Liberia.
libertine ['libə(:)ti:n] a n libertino.
liberty ['libəti] n libertà; licenza.
librarian [lai'brɛəriən] n bibliotecario.
library ['laibrəri] n biblioteca.
libretto [li'bretou] ol **librettos** n libretto (d'opera).
Libya ['libiə] n Libia.
Libyan ['libiən] a libico.
licence ['laisəns] n licenza, patente, permesso.
license ['laisəns] vt autorizzare, dar permesso a.
licentious [lai'senfəs] a licenzioso.
lichen ['laikən] n lichene.
lick [lik] n leccata; vt leccare, lambire.
lid [lid] n coperchio.
lie [lai] n bugia, menzogna; (of ground) configurazione; vi mentire; giacere, stare, trovarsi; l. **down** sdraiarsi.
lieutenant [lef'tenənt] n luogotenente, tenente.
life [laif] n vita; l. **insurance** assicurazione sulla vita; l. **preserver** (US) salvagente; bastone sfollagente.
lifebelt ['laifbelt] n cintura di salvataggio, salvagente.
lifeboat ['laifbout] n scialuppa di salvataggio.
life-giving ['laif,giviŋ] a vivificante.
lifeguard ['laifgɑ:d] n (US) bagnino.
lifeless ['laiflis] a inanimato, senza vita.
lifelike ['laiflaik] a realistico, vivido.
life-long ['laiflɔŋ] a che dura tutta la vita.
lifetime ['laiftaim] n durata della vita.
lift [lift] n ascensore, montacarichi; passaggio; vt alzare, elevare, sollevare; vi (of weather) schiarire.
ligament ['ligəmənt] n legamento.
ligature ['ligətʃuə] n legatura.
light [lait] a chiaro, biondo, luminoso; leggero; n luce, lampada, lume; finestra; vt accendere; vi illuminar(si).
lighten ['laitn] vti alleggerir(si), accender(si), rischiararsi.

lighter ['laitə] *n* accendisigaro, accendino; (*naut*) chiatta.

light-hearted ['lait'hɑːtid] *a* allegro, ottimista.

lighthouse ['laithaus] *n* faro.

lighting ['laitiŋ] *n* illuminazione.

lightless ['laitlis] *a* privo di luce.

lightly ['laitli] *ad* leggermente; agilmente; un poco.

light-minded ['lait'maindid] *a* frivolo, sconsiderato.

lightning ['laitniŋ] *n* lampi *pl*; (flash of) l. lampo.

lightsome ['laitsəm] *a* allegro, gaio.

lightweight ['laitweit] *n* peso leggero.

Ligurian [li'gjuəriən] *a n* ligure.

like [laik] *a* simile, uguale, somigliante; *prep* come, a somiglianza di; *n* altrettanto, la stessa cosa, *pl* simpatia; *vti* amare, piacere, volere; I l. that ciò mi piace; as you l. come vuoi.

likelihood ['laiklihud] *n* verosimiglianza, probabilità.

likely ['laikli] *a* probabile, verosimile; *ad* probabilmente.

liken ['laikən] *vt* paragonare.

likeness ['laiknis] *n* somiglianza, aspetto, ritratto.

likewise ['laikwaiz] *ad* parimenti, inoltre, altrettanto.

liking ['laikiŋ] *n* gùsto, inclinazione, simpatia.

lilac ['lailək] *a* (di) color lilla; *n* lilla.

lilt [lilt] *n* cadenza, ritmo.

lily ['lili] *n* giglio.

limb [lim] *n* arto, membro; ramo; (*sl*) ragazzo sventato.

limber ['limbə] *vt* l. up (*sport*) scaldarsi i muscoli, mettersi\ in forma.

lime [laim] *n* calce; vischio; tiglio; cedro.

limelight ['laimlait] *n* (*theat*) luce della ribalta.

limit ['limit] *n* limite; (*sl*) il colmo; *vt* limitare.

limitation [.limi'teiʃən] *n* limitazione.

limited ['limitid] *a* limitato; l. liability company (*com*) società a responsabilità limitata.

limp [limp] *a* debole, floscio, inerte; *n* andatura zoppicante; *vi* zoppicare.

limpet ['limpit] *n* patella.

limpid ['limpid] *a* limpido.

linden ['lindən] *n* tiglio.

line [lain] *n* linea; equatore; limite; lenza; ruga; (*com*) ramo; *pl* (*of an actor*) parte.

line [lain] *vt* rigare, segnare; foderare; riempire; to l. up allinear(si), (*US*) fare la coda.

lineage ['liniidʒ] *n* lignaggio.

lineal ['liniəl] *n* diretto, in linea diretta.

lineament ['liniəmənt] *n* lineamento, tratto.

linear ['liniə] *a* lineare.

linen ['linin] *n* biancheria, tela di lino; *a* di lino.

liner ['lainə] *n* (*naut*) transatlantico.

linger ['liŋgə] *vi* indugiare, andare lentamente, attardarsi.

linguist ['liŋgwist] *n* linguista, poliglotta.

linguistics [liŋ'gwistiks] *n* linguistica.

lining ['lainiŋ] *n* fodera.

link [liŋk] *n* anello (di catena), legame, vincolo; *vt* congiungere, vincolare; *vi* collegarsi; **cufflinks** gemelli per polsini.

links [liŋks] *n* *pl* (*costruzione sing.*) campo da golf.

linnet ['linit] *n* fanello.

linoleum [li'nouliəm] *n* linoleum.

linseed ['linsiːd] *n* seme di lino.

lint [lint] *n* filaccia, garza.

lintel ['lintl] *n* architrave, mensola di caminetto.

lion ['laiən] *n* leone; (*fig*) celebrità.

lioness ['laiənis] *n* leonessa.

lip [lip] *n* labbro; (*sl*) discorso impudente; l. service fedeltà a parole, ipocrisia.

lipstick ['lipstik] *n* rossetto, matita per labbra.

liquefy ['likwifai] *vti* liquefar(si).

liqueur [li'kjuə] *n* liquore.

liquid ['likwid] *a n* liquido.

liquidate ['likwideit] *vti* liquidare.

liquidation [.likwi'deiʃən] *n* liquidazione.

liquor ['likə] *n* bevanda alcoolica.

liquorice ['likəris] *n* liquiriza.

Lisbon ['lizbən] *n* Lisbona.

lisp [lisp] *n* pronuncia blesa; *vi* parlare bleso.

lissom(e) ['lisəm] *a* flessibile, pieghevole.

list [list] *n* elenco, lista, ruolo; (*prices etc*) bollettino; (*naut*) sbandamento; *vt* elencare.

listen ['lisn] *vi* ascoltare.

listener ['lisnə] *n* ascoltatore.

listless ['listlis] *a* indifferente, svogliato.

listlessness ['listlisnis] *n* svogliatezza.

litany ['litəni] *n* litania.

literacy ['litərəsi] *n* grado di istruzione.

literal ['litərəl] *a* letterale.

literary ['litərəri] *a* letterario.

literate ['litərit] *a* non analfabeta; letterato.

literature ['litəritʃə] *n* letteratura.

lithe [laið] *a* flessibile, flessuoso.

lithograph ['liθəgrɑːf] *n* litografia.

lithography [li'θɔgrəfi] *n* litografia.

Lithuania [.liθju(ː)'einiə] *n* Lituania.

Lithuanian [.liθju(ː)'einiən] *a n* lituano.

litigant ['litigənt] *n* litigante, parte in causa.

litigate ['litigeit] *vti* essere in causa, contestare.

litigation [.liti'geiʃən] *n* lite, causa.

litre ['liːtə] *n* litro.

litter ['litə] *n* lettiera, lettiga; (*of animals*) figliata; scarti e rifiuti *pl*; confusione; *vt* spargere disordinatamente; apprestare la lettiera per; *vt* (*of animals*) figliare.

little ['litl] *a* piccolo, breve, poco, un po' di; *ad* poco; *n* poco.

live [laiv] *a* vivente, vivo; [liv] *vi* vivere, abitare.

livelihood ['laivlihud] *n* mezzi di sussistenza *pl*, mantenimento.

liveliness ['laivlinis] *n* vivacità, animazione.

lively ['laivli] *a* vivo, vivace.

liven ['laivn] *vt* ravvivare.

liver ['livə] *n* fegato.

livery ['livəri] *n* livrea; **l.-stable** stallaggio.

livid ['livid] *a* livido; (*fam*) furioso.

living ['liviŋ] *a* vivente; *n* (*mezzi per vivere*) vita; beneficio ecclesiastico.

lizard ['lizəd] *n* lucertola.

llama ['lɑːmə] *n* (*zool*) lama.

load [loud] *n* carico, peso; *vt* caricare, colmare.

loaf [louf] *pl* **loaves** *n* pane in cassetta; pagnotta; (*sl*) testa; *vi* oziare.

loafer ['loufə] *n* fannullone.

loam [loum] *n* argilla sabbiosa.

loan [loun] *n* prestito.

loath [louθ] *a* restio, riluttante.

loathe [louð] *vt* detestare, sentire ripugnanza per.

loathing ['louðiŋ] *n* ripugnanza.

loathsome ['louðsəm] *a* nauseante, ripugnante.

lobby ['lɔbi] *n* corridoio (in un pubblico edificio).

lobster ['lɔbstə] *n* aragosta.

local ['loukəl] *a* locale, del luogo.

locality [lou'kæliti] *n* località.

localize ['loukəlaiz] *vt* localizzare.

locally ['loukəli] *ad* localmente.

locate [lou'keit] *vt* individuare, situare.

location [lou'keiʃən] *n* posizione, (*com*) locazione.

lock [lɔk] *n* serratura; (*canal*) chiusa; (*hair*) ciocca, ciuffo; *vt* chiudere a chiave, serrare.

locker ['lɔkə] *n* armadietto.

locket ['lɔkit] *n* medaglione.

locksmith ['lɔksmiθ] *n* fabbro.

locomotion [,loukə'mouʃən] *n* locomozione.

locomotive ['loukə,moutiv] *a* locomotivo, locomotore; *n* locomotiva.

locust ['loukəst] *n* locusta.

lode [loud] *n* filone metallifero.

lodge [lɔdʒ] *n* casetta (*spesso al cancello d'un parco*); (*freemasons*) loggia; *vti* alloggiare; collocare; (*appeal*) presentare, sporgere.

lodger ['lɔdʒə] *n* inquilino.

lodging ['lɔdʒiŋ] *n* alloggio, *usu pl* stanze prese in affitto.

loft [lɔft] *n* abbaino, solaio.

loftiness ['lɔftinis] *n* altezza, elevatezza, nobiltà; superbia.

lofty ['lɔfti] *a* alto; altero; elevato, nobile.

log [lɔg] *n* ceppo, tronco; (*naut*) diario di bordo.

logarithm ['lɔgəriθəm] *n* logaritmo.

loggerhead ['lɔgəhed] **at loggerheads with** *ad* in urto con.

logic ['lɔdʒik] *n* logica.

logical ['lɔdʒikəl] *a* logico.

logician [lou'dʒiʃən] *n* logico.

loin [lɔin] *n* lombo, lombata; *pl* (*poet*) fianchi, lombi *pl*.

loiter ['lɔitə] *vi* bighellonare, indugiare.

loiterer ['lɔitərə] *n* bighellone, perdigiorno.

loll [lɔl] *vi* adagiarsi; pigramente; (*tongue*) penzolare.

lollipop ['lɔlipɔp] *n* lecca-lecca.

Lombard ['lɔmbəd] *a n* lombardo.

Lombardy ['lɔmbədi] *n* Lombardia.

London ['lʌndən] *n* Londra; **Londoner** *n* Londinese.

lone [loun] *a* solitario, solo, isolato.

loneliness ['lounlinis] *n* solitudine.

lonely ['lounli] *a* solo, solitario; desolato.

lonesome ['lounsəm] *a* solitario, malinconico.

long [lɔŋ] *a* lungo; *ad* a lungo, lungamente, per molto tempo; *n* molto tempo; *vi* bramare, desiderare ardentemente; **l.-sighted** presbite; preveggente; **l.-suffering** paziente, tollerante; **l.-standing** di lunga data.

longing ['lɔŋiŋ] *n* brama, desiderio ardente.

longitude ['lɔŋitjuːd] *n* longitudine.

longwinded ['lɔŋ'windid] *a* prolisso, noioso.

look [luk] *n* sguardo, occhiata, espressione; aspetto; bellezza; *vi* guardare, sembrare; **to l. for** cercare; **to l. like** somigliare a.

looking-glass ['lukiŋglɑːs] *n* specchio.

lookout ['luk'aut] *n* guardia; vigilanza; vista; (*fig*) prospettiva.

loom [luːm] *n* telaio; *vi* apparire all'orizzonte.

loop [luːp] *n* cappio, laccio, nodo scorsoio; gancio; punto a maglia; *vti* far cappio, annodare.

loophole ['luːphoul] *n* feritoia; (*fig*) scappatoia.

loose [luːs] *a* sciolto, libero, slegato, rilassato; scorretto; sfrenato; *vt* sciogliere, slegare, liberare.

loosen ['luːsn] *vti* allentar(si).

looseness ['luːsnis] *n* scioltezza; (*fig*) rilassatezza; libertinaggio; (*style etc*) imprecisione.

loot [luːt] *n* bottino; *vt* saccheggiare.

lop [lɔp] *vt* potare, tagliare.

lopsided ['lɔp'saidid] *a* asimmetrico, sbilenco.

loquacious [lou'kweiʃəs] *a* loquace.

loquacity [lou'kwæsiti] *n* loquacità.

lord [lɔːd] *n* signore.
lordly ['lɔːdli] *a* signorile; altero; sontuoso.
lordship ['lɔːdʃip] *n* signoria.
lore [lɔː] *n* tradizioni *pl*.
lorry ['lɔri] *n* autocarro, camion.
lose [luːz] *vti* perdere, perdersi; sciupare.
loser ['luːzə] *n* chi perde, perdente; **to be a good l.** saper perdere.
loss [lɔs] *n* perdita.
lot [lɔt] *n* destino, sorte; lotto, quantità, quota.
lotion ['louʃən] *n* lozione.
lottery ['lɔtəri] *n* lotteria.
lotus ['loutəs] *n* loto.
loud [laud] *a* rumoroso, sonoro, alto, forte; (*colours*) vistoso; *ad* ad alta voce, forte.
loudness ['laudnis] *n* frastuono, rumorosità, vistosità.
Louis ['lu(ː)i] *nm pr* Luigi.
Louisa [lu(ː)'iːzə] **Louise** [lu(ː)'iːz] *nf pr* Luisa, Luigia.
lounge [laundʒ] *n* (*theat*) ridotto; (*hotel*) salone, vestibolo; salotto; **l. suit** abito maschile da passeggio; *vi* andare a zonzo, bighellonare, poltrire.
lour ['lauə] *vi* corrugare le sopracciglia; (*weather*) minacciare, oscurarsi.
louse [laus] *pl* **lice** *n* pidocchio.
lousy ['lauzi] *a* pidocchioso; (*fig*) sporco, vile, schifoso.
lout [laut] *n* zoticone.
lovable ['lʌvəbl] *a* amabile.
love [lʌv] *n* amore; saluti affettuosi *pl*; *vti* amare.
loveliness ['lʌvlinis] *n* leggiadria.
lovely ['lʌvli] *a* bello, attraente.
lover ['lʌvə] *n* amante; innamorato, innamorata.
loving ['lʌviŋ] *a* affettuoso, tenero; d'amore.
lovingly ['lʌviŋli] *ad* amorosamente, affettuosamente, teneramente.
low [lou] *a* basso, abbattuto, depresso; *ad* in basso, a voce bassa; *vi* muggire.
lower ['louə] *vti* abbassar(si).
lowering ['louəriŋ] *n* abbassamento, ribasso.
lowland ['loulənd] *n* bassopiano, pianura.
Lowlands ['louləndz] *n pl* Scozia meridionale.
lowly ['louli] *a* basso, umile; *ad* umilmente.
loyal ['lɔiəl] *a* leale, fedele.
loyalty ['lɔiəlti] *n* lealtà, fedeltà.
lozenge ['lɔzindʒ] *n* pasticca, losanga.
lubricant ['luːbrikənt] *n* lubrificante.
lubricate ['luːbrikeit] *vt* lubrificare.
lubrication [,luːbri'keiʃən] *n* lubrificazione.
lucid ['luːsid] *a* chiaro, lucido.
lucidity [luːsiditi] *n* lucidità.
Lucie, Lucy ['luːsi] *nf pr* Lucia.
luck [lʌk] *n* fortuna, sorte.
luckless ['lʌklis] *a* sfortunato.

lucky ['lʌki] *a* fortunato, propizio.
lucrative ['luːkrətiv] *a* lucrativo.
lucre ['luːkə] *n* lucro.
ludicrous ['luːdikrəs] *a* ridicolo, comico.
luff [lʌf] *n* (*naut*) orzata; *vi* (*naut*) orzare.
lug [lʌg] *vti* trascinare, tirare.
luggage ['lʌgidʒ] *n* bagaglio(o); **l. van** bagagliaio; **left-l. office (room)** deposito bagagli.
lugubrious [luː'guːbriəs] *a* lugubre.
Luke [luːk] *nm pr* Luca.
lukewarm ['luːkwɔːm] *a* tiepido; indifferente.
lull [lʌl] *n* calma, tregua; *vti* acquietar(si); cullare.
lullaby ['lʌləbai] *n* ninna-nanna.
lumbago [lʌm'beigou] *n* lombaggine.
lumber ['lʌmbə] *n* legname da costruzione; mobili *pl*; di scarto; cianfrusaglie.
luminary ['luːminəri] *n* luminare.
luminous ['luːminəs] *a* luminoso.
lump [lʌmp] *n* massa, pezzo, pezzetto, blocco; gonfiore; *vt* ammassare, riunire in blocco.
lumpy ['lʌmpi] *a* grumoso, bernoccoluto.
lunacy ['luːnəsi] *n* demenza, pazzia.
lunar ['luːnə] *a* lunare.
lunatic ['luːnətik] *a n* demente, pazzo.
lunch [lʌntʃ] *n* (seconda) colazione; (US) spuntino; *vi* fare (la seconda) colazione; (US) fare uno spuntino.
luncheon ['lʌntʃən] *n* seconda colazione, pasto del mezzogiorno; (US) spuntino.
lung [lʌŋ] *n* polmone.
lupin(e) ['luːpin] *n* (*bot*) lupino.
lurch [ləːtʃ] *n* traballamento; *vi* traballare; **to leave in the l.** lasciare nelle peste.
lure [ljuə] *n* adescamento; *vt* adescare.
lurid ['ljuərid] *a* livido, spettrale, terribile.
lurk [ləːk] *vi* appiattarsi, stare in agguato.
luscious ['lʌʃəs] *a* dolce, succolento, delizioso.
lush [lʌʃ] *a* lussureggiante; succoso.
lust [lʌst] *n* lussuria, concupiscenza, brama; *vi* desiderare ardentemente, bramare.
lustful ['lʌstful] *a* lussurioso, bramoso.
lustre ['lʌstə] *n* lucentezza, lustro; lampadario a gocce.
lustrous ['lʌstrəs] *a* lustro, rilucente.
lusty ['lʌsti] *a* sano e robusto, vigoroso.
lute [luːt] *n* (*mus*) liuto.
Lutheran ['luːθərən] *a n* luterano.
Luxemburg ['lʌksəmbəːg] *n* Lussemburgo.
luxuriance [lʌg'zjuəriəns] *n* esuberanza, rigoglio.

luxuriant [lʌg'zjuəriənt] *a* lussureg-giante, rigoglioso.
luxurious [lʌg'zjuəriəs] *a* lussuoso.
luxury ['lʌkʃəri] *n* lusso.
lyceum [lai'siəm] *n* liceo.
lye [lai] *n* lisciva.
lying ['laiiŋ] *a* bugiardo, menzogne-ro; *n* menzogna.
lying-in ['laiiŋ'in] *n* parto.
lymph [limf] *n* linfa, vaccino.
lynch [lintʃ] *vt* linciare.
lynx [liŋks] *n* lince.
Lyons ['laiənz] *n* Lione.
lyre ['laiə] *n* (*mus*) lira.
lyric ['lirik] *n* lirica, poesia lirica.
lyrical ['lirikəl] *a* lirico.

M

macabre [mə'kɑːbr] *a* macabro.
macadam [mə'kædəm] *n* macadam.
macadamize [mə'kædəmaiz] *vt* ma-cadamizzare.
macaroon [,mækə'ruːn] *n* amaretto, spumiglia.
macaroni [,mækə'rouni] *n* macche-roni *pl*, pasta.
mace [meis] *n* mazza; (*chem*) macis.
macerate ['mæsəreit] *vt* macerare.
machination [,mæki'neiʃən] *n* mac-chinazione, trama.
machine [mə'ʃiːn] *n* macchina.
machinery [mə'ʃinəri] *n* macchina-rio, meccanismo; (*fig*) macchina.
mackerel ['mækrəl] *n* sgombro.
mackintosh ['mækintɔʃ] *n* imper-meabile.
mad [mæd] *a* matto, furioso; (*of dog*) idrofobo.
madam ['mædəm] *n* (*vocative*) signo-ra.
madden ['mædn] *vt* far impazzire.
maddening ['mædniŋ] *a* che fa impazzire; esasperante.
Madeira [mə'diərə] *n* Madera.
madly ['mædli] *ad* pazzamente, alla follia.
madness ['mædnis] *n* pazzia, follia.
madrigal ['mædrigəl] *n* madrigale.
maecenas [mi'siːnæs] *n* mecenate.
magazine [,mægə'ziːn] *n* magazzino; periodico, rivista; caricatore di arma.
Magdalen(e) ['mægdəlin] *nf pr* Maddalena.
maggot ['mægət] *n* baco; (*fig*) capriccio, ubbia.
magic ['mædʒik] *n* magia; **magic(al)** *a* magico.
magician [mə'dʒiʃən] *n* mago.
magistrate ['mædʒistrit] *n* magistra-to.
magnanimous [mæg'næniməs] *a* magnanimo.
magnate ['mægnit] *n* magnate.
magnesia [mæg'niːʃə] *n* magnesia.
magnesium [mæg'niːziəm] *n* ma-gnesio.
magnet ['mægnit] *n* magnete, cala-mita.

magnetic [mæg'netik] *a* magnetico.
magnetism ['mægnitizəm] *n* magne-tismo.
magnetize ['mægnitaiz] *vt* magnetiz-zare.
magnificence [mæg'nifisns] *n* ma-gnificenza.
magnificent [mæg'nifisnt] *a* magni-fico, sontuoso.
magnify ['mægnifai] *vt* ampliare, ingrandire; **magnifying glass** *n* lente d'ingrandimento.
magnitude ['mægnitjuːd] *n* grandez-za, vastità.
magnolia [mæg'nouliə] *n* magnolia.
magpie ['mægpai] *n* gazza.
mahogany [mə'hɔgəni] *n* mogano.
maid [meid] *n* domestica; fanciulla; zitella; **old m.** vecchia zitella.
maiden ['meidn] *a* verginale, nubile; *n* fanciulla, vergine.
maidenhood ['meidnhud] *n* verginità.
maidenly ['meidnli] *a* di fanciulla, delicato, modesto.
mail [meil] *n* posta, corrispondenza; maglia di ferro; **m. car** (*US*) vagone postale; **mailman** (*US*) portalettere; *vt* mandare per posta.
maim [meim] *vt* mutilare, storpiare.
main [mein] *a* principale; *n* condut-tura principale; l'essenziale.
mainland ['meinlənd] *n* continente.
mainly ['meinli] *ad* per lo più, principalmente.
maintain [men'tein] *vt* mantenere, sostenere.
maintenance ['meintinəns] *n* man-tenimento, manutenzione.
maize [meiz] *n* granturco, mais.
majestic [mə'dʒestik] *a* maestoso.
majesty ['mædʒisti] *n* maestà.
major ['meidʒə] *a* maggiore; *n* (*mil*) maggiore.
Majorca [mə'dʒɔːkə] *n* Maiorca.
majority [mə'dʒɔriti] *n* maggioranza; maggiore età.
make [meik] *n* fabbricazione, fattura, marca; *vt* fare, creare, fabbricare; rendere; **m. for** *vi* dirigersi; **m.-believe** finta, finzione.
maker ['meikə] *n* creatore, fabbri-cante.
makeshift ['meikʃift] *a* improvvisa-to; *n* espediente, ripiego.
make-up ['meikʌp] *n* confezione, composizione; comportamento; truc-co, cosmetici.
making ['meikiŋ] *n* creazione, fattu-ra, confezione.
maladjusted ['mælə'dʒʌstid] *a* dis-adatto, incapace di inserirsi (in una società *etc*).
maladjustment ['mælə'dʒʌstmənt] *n* incapacità di adattamento, inadat-tabilità.
malady ['mælədi] *n* malattia.
malaise [mæ'leiz] *n* malessere.
malaria [mə'lɛəriə] *n* malaria.
Malay [mə'lei] *a n* malese.

male [meil] *a* maschile; *n* maschio.
malevolence [mə'levələns] *n* malevolenza.
malevolent [mə'levələnt] *a* malevolo.
malice ['mælis] *n* malizia, malignità.
malicious [mə'liʃəs] *a* maligno, malevolo.
malign [mə'lain] *a* maligno; *vti* calunniare, malignare.
malignant [mə'lignənt] *a* maligno, malevolo.
malinger [mə'liŋgə] *vi* fingersi malato.
malleable ['mæliəbl] *a* malleabile.
mallet ['mælit] *n* mazzuolo, martello di legno.
mallow ['mælou] *n* malva.
malnutrition ['mælnju(ː)'triʃən] *n* malnutrizione; denutrizione.
malt [mɔːlt] *n* malto.
Malta ['mɔːltə] *n* Malta; **Maltese** *a n* maltese.
maltreat [mæl'triːt] *vt* maltrattare.
mamma [mə'maː] *n* (*fam*) mamma.
mammal ['mæməl] *n* mammifero.
man [mæn] *pl* **men** *n* uomo, persona, essere umano; (*draughts*) pedina; (*chess*) pezzo; *vt* presidiare; far funzionare; farsi coraggio.
manacle ['mænəkl] *n usu pl* manetta; restrizione, impedimento; *vt* ammanettare.
manage ['mænidʒ] *vt* amministrare, dirigere, gestire; riuscire.
manageable ['mænidʒəbl] *a* trattabile, maneggevole.
management ['mænidʒmənt] *n* amministrazione, gestione, direzione.
manager ['mænidʒə] *n* amministratore, direttore.
managing ['mænidʒiŋ] *a* dirigente; **m. director** consigliere delegato.
Manchuria [mænt'tʃuəriə] *n* Manciuria.
mandarin ['mændərin] *n* mandarino; (*bot*) mandarino.
mandate ['mændeit] *n* mandato.
mandolin(e) ['mændəlin] *n* mandolino.
mane [mein] *n* criniera.
manful ['mænful] *a* maschio, virile.
mange [meindʒ] *n* rogna, scabbia.
manger ['meindʒə] *n* greppia, mangiatoia.
mangle ['mæŋgl] *n* mangano; *vt* manganare, maciullare, straziare.
mangy ['meindʒi] *a* rognoso.
manhole ['mænhoul] *n* botola.
manhood ['mænhud] *n* età virile, virilità.
mania ['meiniə] *n* mania.
maniac ['meiniæk] *a n* pazzo furioso; maniaco.
manicure ['mænikjuə] *n* manicure.
manifest ['mænifest] *a* manifesto, evidente; *n* (*com*) manifesto, nota di carico; *vti* manifestar(si), rivelare.
manifestation [,mænifes'teiʃən] *n* manifestazione.
manifesto [,mæni'festou] *n* mani-

festo, *pl* **manifesto(e)s** *n* manifesto, proclama.
manifold ['mænifould] *a* molteplice, multiforme.
manikin ['mænikin] *n* nano, omino; manichino.
manipulate [mə'nipjuleit] *vt* manipolare, maneggiare.
manipulation [mə,nipju'leiʃən] *n* manipolazione.
mankind [mæn'kaind] *n* genere umano, umanità.
manliness ['mænlinis] *n* virilità, mascolinità.
manly ['mænli] *a* maschio, virile.
mannequin ['mænikin] *n* indossatore, indossatrice.
manner ['mænə] *n* maniera, modo; **manners** *pl* buone maniere *pl*, educazione.
mannerism ['mænərizəm] *n* manierismo; affettazione; (*fam*) gesto consueto, ticchio.
mannerly ['mænəli] *a* cortese, educato.
mannish ['mæniʃ] *a* mascolino.
manoeuvre [mə'nuːvə] *n* manovra; *vti* manovrare.
manor ['mænə] *n* grande proprietà terriera; maniero.
manse [mæns] *n* (*Scozia*) residenza d'un parroco presbiteriano.
mansion ['mænʃən] *n* palazzo, villa.
manslaughter ['mæn,slɔːtə] *n* omicidio colposo.
mantelpiece ['mæntlpiːs] *n* mensola del camino, caminetto.
mantle ['mæntl] *n* mantello, manto.
Mantua ['mæntjuə] *n* Mantova; **Mantuan** *a n* mantovano.
manual ['mænjuəl] *a n* manuale.
manufactory ['mænju'fæktəri] *n* fabbrica.
manufacture [,mænju'fæktʃə] *n* fabbricazione, manifattura; manufatto; *vt* fabbricare, confezionare.
manufacturer [,mænju'fæktʃərə] *n* fabbricante; industriale.
manure [mə'njuə] *n* concime; *vt* concimare.
manuscript ['mænjuskript] *a n* manoscritto.
many ['meni] *a pl* molti, **-te** *pl*; *n* molti; **a good m.** un buon numero di; **a great m.** moltissimi; **the m.** la folla.
map [mæp] *n* carta geografica, mappa; *vt* rappresentare su una carta; **to m. out** progettare in ogni particolare.
maple ['meipl] *n* acero.
mar [maː] *vt* guastare, sciupare.
marble ['maːbl] *n* marmo, pallina (di vetro).
March [maːtʃ] *n* marzo.
march [maːtʃ] *n* frontiera, confine; (*mil*) marcia; (*mus*) marcia; *vi* confinare, (far) marciare.
marchioness ['maːʃənis] *n* marchesa.
mare [mɛə] *n* cavalla, giumenta;

shank's m. il cavallo di S. Francesco.

Margaret ['mɑːgərit] **Marguerite** [‚mɑːgə'riːt] *nf pr* Margherita.

margarine [‚mɑːdʒə'riːn] *n* margarina.

margin ['mɑːdʒin] *n* bordo, margine.

marginal ['mɑːdʒinəl] *a* marginale; di confine.

marigold ['mærigould] *n* calendula.

marinade ['mærineid] *n* (*cook*) salsa marinata; *vt* marinare.

marine [mə'riːn] *a* marino, marittimo; *n* marina.

mariner ['mærinə] *n* marinaio.

marionette [‚mæriə'net] *n* marionetta.

marital ['mæritl] *a* coniugale.

maritime ['mæritaim] *a* marittimo.

marjoram ['mɑːdʒərəm] *n* maggiorana.

mark [mɑːk] *n* segno, marca, marchio; bersaglio; (*school*) voto, (*German coin*) marco; *vt* marcare, segnare; prestare attenzione a.

Mark [mɑːk] *nm pr* Marco.

market ['mɑːkit] *n* mercato; *vt* esporre o vendere in mercato; **m. gardener** ortolano, orticoltore.

marketable ['mɑːkitəbl] *a* vendibile.

marketing ['mɑːkitiŋ] *n* compravendita.

marking-ink ['mɑːkiŋ'iŋk] *n* inchiostro indelebile.

marksman ['mɑːksmən] *n* tiratore scelto.

marl [mɑːl] *n* marna.

marmalade ['mɑːməleid] *n* marmellata (di agrumi).

marmot ['mɑːmət] *n* marmotta.

maroon [mə'ruːn] *a* marrone rossastro; *n* individuo abbandonato su qualche isola o spiaggia deserta; *vt* abbandonare su un'isola o spiaggia deserta.

marquess, -quis ['mɑːkwis] *n* marchese.

marriage ['mæridʒ] *n* matrimonio, nozze.

marriageable ['mæridʒəbl] *a* ammogliabile, maritabile.

marrow ['mærou] *n* midollo; zucchino.

marry ['mæri] *vti* maritar(si), sposar(si).

Marseilles [mɑː'seilz] *n* Marsiglia.

marsh [mɑːʃ] *n* acquitrino, palude.

marshal ['mɑːʃəl] *n* maresciallo; *vt* ordinare, disporre per ordine.

marshy ['mɑːʃi] *a* paludoso.

marten ['mɑːtin] *n* martora.

Martha ['mɑːθə] *nf pr* Marta.

martial ['mɑːʃəl] *a* marziale.

Martin ['mɑːtin] *nm pr* Martino.

martin ['mɑːtin] *n* rondicchio.

martinet [‚mɑːti'net] *n* zelante della disciplina, castigamatti.

martyr ['mɑːtə] *n* martire.

martyrdom ['mɑːtədəm] *n* martirio.

marvel ['mɑːvəl] *n* meraviglia; *vi* meravigliarsi.

marvellous ['mɑːviləs] *a* meraviglioso.

Marxist ['mɑːksist] *a n* marxista.

Mary ['mɛəri] *nf pr* Maria.

mascot ['mæskət] *n* portafortuna, mascotte.

masculine ['mɑːskjulin] *a* maschile; mascolino; (*fig*) maschio.

mash [mæʃ] *vt* mescolare, schiacciare; **mashed potatoes** purè di patate; **potato masher** schiacciapatate.

mask [mɑːsk] *n* maschera; *vt* mascherare.

masochism ['mæzəkizəm] *n* masochismo.

mason ['meisn] *n* muratore; massone.

masonic [mə'sɔnik] *a* massonico.

masonry ['meisnri] *n* lavoro in muratura; massoneria.

masque [mɑːsk] *n* rappresentazione allegorica.

masquerade [‚mæskə'reid] *n* mascherata; *vi* mascherarsi, travestirsi.

mass [mæs] *n* messa; massa; *vti* ammassar(si); **m. meeting** adunata popolare, comizio.

massacre ['mæsəkə] *n* massacro; *vt* massacrare.

massage ['mæsɑːʒ] *n* massaggio.

massive ['mæsiv] *a* compatto, massiccio.

massy ['mæsi] *a* massiccio, imponente.

mast [mɑːst] *n* (*naut*) albero.

master ['mɑːstə] *n* signore, signorino; professore, maestro; **M. of Arts** laureato in lettere; **m. of ceremonies** (*theat*) presentatore; *vt* dominare, impadronirsi (di).

masterful ['mɑːstəful] *a* imperioso.

masterly ['mɑːstəli] *a* abile.

masterpiece ['mɑːstəpiːs] *n* capolavoro.

mastery ['mɑːstəri] *n* maestria, padronanza, supremazia.

masticate ['mæstikeit] *vt* masticare.

mastiff ['mæstif] *n* mastino.

mat [mæt] *a* opaco; *n* stuoia, sottopiatto, sottovaso *etc*; *vt* coprire con stuoie; **matted hair** capelli arruffati.

match [mætʃ] *n* fiammifero; uguale; gara, partita; matrimonio, partito; avversario; *vti* accoppiare, maritare; armonizzare; opporre; uguagliare.

matchless ['mætʃlis] *a* incomparabile, senza pari.

mate [meit] *n* compagno; (*naut*) secondo; scacco matto; *vti* accoppiar(si); dare scacco matto.

material [mə'tiəriəl] *a* materiale, essenziale; *n* materiale, materia.

materialism [mə'tiəriəlizəm] *n* materialismo.

materialistic [mə‚tiəriə'listik] *a* materialistico.

materialize [mə'tiəriəlaiz] *vti* materializzare, materializzarsi, avverarsi.

materially [mə'tiəriəli] *ad* materialmente, fisicamente.

maternal [mə'tɔːnl] *a* materno.

maternity [mə'tɔːniti] *n* maternità; **m. hospital** casa di maternità.

mathematical [ˌmæθi'mætikəl] *a* matematico.

mathematician [ˌmæθimə'tiʃən] *n* matematico.

mathematics [ˌmæθi'mætiks] *n* matematica.

matin ['mætin] *n* mattutino.

matinée ['mætinei] *n* (*theat*) 'matinée', mattinata.

matriculate [mə'trikjuleit] *vti* immatricolar(si).

matriculation [məˌtrikju'leiʃən] *n* immatricolazione.

matrimonial [ˌmætri'mouniəl] *a* matrimoniale, coniugale.

matrimony ['mætriməni] *n* matrimonio.

matron ['meitrən] *n* matrona, capoinfermiera; vigilatrice.

matter ['mætə] *n* affare, faccenda; materia, questione; *vi* importare; (*med*) emettere pus; **m.-of-fact** *a* positivo, pratico; **what is the m.?** che c'è?

Matterhorn ['mætəhɔːn] *n* Monte Cervino.

Matthew ['mæθjuː] *nm pr* Matteo.

mattress ['mætris] *n* materasso.

mature [mə'tjuə] *a* maturo; (*com*) scaduto; *vti* (far) maturare; (*com*) scadere.

maturation [ˌmætju'reiʃən] *n* maturazione.

maturity [mə'tjuəriti] *n* maturità; (*com*) scadenza.

maudlin ['mɔːdlin] *a* brillo e piagnucoloso.

maul [mɔːl] *n* maglio; *vt* malmenare, percuotere.

Maurice ['mɔris] *nm pr* Maurizio.

mauve [mouv] *a n* (color) ciclamino.

mawkish ['mɔːkiʃ] *a* sdolcinato, sentimentale.

mawkishness ['mɔːkiʃnis] *n* sentimentalità sdolcinata.

maxim ['mæksim] *n* massima.

maximum ['mæksiməm] *a* massimo.

May [mei] *n* maggio; **M. Day** il 1 maggio.

may [mei] *v difettivo* potere, avere il permesso di.

mayflower ['mei'flauə] *n* biancospino.

mayonnaise [ˌmeiə'neiz] *n* (*cook*) maionese.

mayor [mɛə] *n* sindaco.

maze [meiz] *n* labirinto.

me [miː] *pron* mi, me.

meadow ['medou] *n* prato.

meagre ['miːgə] *a* povero, scarso, scarno.

meal [miːl] *n* pasto; farina.

mean [miːn] *a* basso, vile, gretto, mediocre; (*average*) medio; *n* mezzo;

---

media; *vti* significare, proporsi, destinare.

meander [mi'ændə] *n* meandro, tortuosità; *vi* vagare; (*fig*) divagare.

meaning ['miːniŋ] *a* espressivo, significativo; *n* significato, intenzione.

meaningful ['miːniŋful] *a* pieno di significato, significativo, espressivo.

meanness ['miːnnis] *n* bassezza, tirchieria.

meantime, -while [miːn'taim, -wail] *n* frattempo; *ad* nel frattempo, intanto.

measles ['miːzlz] *n* (*med*) morbillo.

measurable ['meʒərəbl] *a* misurabile.

measure ['meʒə] *n* misura; *vti* misurare.

measured ['meʒəd] *a* misurato, cadenzato, ritmico.

measurement ['meʒəmənt] *n* misura.

meat [miːt] *n* carne; cibo.

meaty ['miːti] *a* carnoso, polposo; sostanzioso.

mechanic [mi'kænik] *n* meccanico.

mechanical [mi'kænikəl] *a* meccanico.

mechanics [mi'kæniks] *n pl* meccanica.

mechanism ['mekənizəm] *n* meccanismo.

medal ['medl] *n* medaglia.

medallion [mi'dæliən] *n* medaglione.

meddle ['medl] *vi* immischiarsi, intromettersi.

meddler ['medlə] *n* persona inframettente.

meddlesome ['medlsəm] *a* inframettente.

mediaeval [ˌmedi'iːvəl] *a* medi(o)evale.

mediate ['miːdieit] *vi* far da mediatore, interporsi.

mediation [ˌmiːdi'eiʃən] *n* mediazione, intervento.

medical ['medikəl] *a* medico; *n* (*fam*) studente di medicina.

medicate ['medikeit] *vt* medicare.

medicinal [me'disinl] *a* medicinale.

medicine ['medsin] *n* medicina.

mediocre [ˌmiːdi'oukə] *a* mediocre.

mediocrity [ˌmiːdi'ɔkriti] *n* mediocrità.

meditate ['mediteit] *vti* macchinare; meditare.

meditation [ˌmedi'teiʃən] *n* meditazione.

mediterranean [ˌmeditə'reiniən] *a* mediterraneo; *a n* Mediterraneo.

medium ['miːdjəm] *a* medio; *n* mezzo, strumento; medium

medlar ['medlə] *n* (*bot*) nespola, -o.

medley ['medli] *n* miscellanea, miscuglio.

meek [miːk] *a* mite, remissivo.

meekness ['miːknis] *n* mansuetudine, sottomissione.

meet [miːt] *n* riunione di cacciatori; *vti* incontrar(si), far la conoscenza di.

meeting ['mi:tiŋ] *n* incontro, riunione, duello; **m. place** luogo di ritrovo.

megalomania ['megǝlou'meiniǝ] *n* megalomania.

megaphone ['megǝfoun] *n* megafono.

melancholy ['melǝnkǝli] *a* malinconico; *n* malinconia.

mellifluous [me'lifluǝs] *a* mellifluo.

mellow ['melou] *a* maturo, succoso, tenero; *vti* ammorbidir(si), maturar(si).

mellowness ['melounis] *n* maturità, succosità; (*fig*) comprensione, maturità.

melodious [mi'loudiǝs] *a* melodioso.

melodrama ['melǝ.drɑ:mǝ] *n* dramma a lieto fine.

melodramatic [.melǝdrǝ'mætik] *a* melodrammatico.

melody ['melǝdi] *n* melodia.

melon ['melǝn] *n* melone, popone; **water m.** anguria, cocomero.

melt [melt] *n* fusione; *vt* fondere, sciogliere; *vi* fondersi, sciogliersi, dissolversi; (*fig*) intenerirsi.

member ['membǝ] *n* membro.

membership ['membǝʃip] *n* insieme dei membri di una associazione, funzione di membro.

membrane ['membrein] *n* membrana.

memento [mǝ'mentou] *n* memento; oggetto ricordo.

memoir ['memwɑ:] *n* (*pl* **book**) ricordi *pl*.

memorable ['memǝrǝbl] *a* memorabile.

memorandum [.memǝ'rændǝm] *pl* **memoranda** *n* memorandum, appunto; **m. book** taccuino, agenda.

memorial [mi'mɔ:riǝl] *a* commemorativo; *n* memoriale, monumento (alla memoria).

memorize ['memǝraiz] *vt* imparare a memoria.

memory ['memǝri] *n* memoria, ricordo.

menace ['menǝs] *n* minaccia; *vt* minacciare.

menacing ['menisiŋ] *a* minaccioso, torvo.

mend [mend] *n* rammendo; riparazione; *vt* accomodare, rammendare, riparare, correggere; *vi* correggersi; rimettersi (in salute).

mendacious [men'deiʃǝs] *a* mendace.

mendicant ['mendikǝnt] *a n* mendicante.

menial ['mi:niǝl] *a* servile, umile; *n* servo.

menstruation [.menstru'eiʃǝn] *n* mestruazione.

mental ['mentl] *a* mentale.

mentality [men'tæliti] *n* mentalità.

mention ['menʃǝn] *n* accenno, menzione; *vt* accennare a, menzionare; **don't m. it!** *interj* di niente!

mercantile ['mǝ:kǝntail] *a* mercantile.

mercenary ['mǝ:sinǝri] *a n* mercenario.

merchandise ['mǝ:tʃǝndaiz] *n* mercanzie *pl*, merce.

merchant ['mǝ:tʃǝnt] *n* mercante, commerciante.

merciful ['mǝ:siful] *a* misericordioso, pietoso.

merciless ['mǝ:silis] *a* spietato.

mercurial [mǝ:'kjuǝriǝl] *a* mutevole, eccitabile.

mercury ['mǝ:kjuri] *n* mercurio.

mercy ['mǝ:si] *n* misericordia, pietà, carità.

mere [miǝ] *a* mero, puro, schietto, semplice.

merely ['miǝli] *ad* puramente, semplicemente.

merge [mǝ:dʒ] *vti* immergersi, assorbire, amalgamarsi.

meridian [mǝ'ridiǝn] *a n* meridiano.

meringue [mǝ'ræŋ] *n* meringa.

merit ['merit] *n* merito; *vt* meritare.

meritorious [.meri'tɔ:riǝs] *a* meritorio.

mermaid ['mǝ:meid] *n* sirena.

merriment ['merimǝnt] *a* allegria.

merry ['meri] *a* allegro, brioso.

mesh [meʃ] *n* maglia, rete; *vt* prendere nella rete; (*mech*) ingranare.

mesmerize ['mezmǝraiz] *vt* ipnotizzare.

mess [mes] *n* confusione, pasticcio; mensa, pasto preso da una comunità; *vt* fare confusione in, un pasticcio di; *vi* mangiare alla mensa.

message ['mesidʒ] *n* ambasciata, messaggio.

messenger ['mesindʒǝ] *n* messaggero.

Messiah [me'saiǝ] *n* Messia.

metal ['metl] *n* metallo; **m. fatigue** fatica del metallo.

metallic [mi'tælik] *a* metallico, di metallo.

metallurgy [me'tælǝdʒi] *n* metallurgia.

metamorphosis [.metǝ'mɔ:fǝsis] *n* metamorfosi.

metaphor ['metǝfǝ] *n* metafora.

metaphoric(al) [.metǝ'fɔrik(ǝl)] *a* metaforico.

metaphysical [.metǝ'fizikǝl] *a* metafisico.

metaphysics [.metǝ'fiziks] *n pl* metafisica.

meteor ['mi:tiǝ] *n* meteora.

meteorological [.mi:tiǝrǝ'lɔdʒikǝl] *a* metereologico; **m. office** ufficio metereologico.

meter ['mi:tǝ] *n* contatore, misuratore.

method ['meθǝd] *n* metodo.

methodical [mi'θɔdikǝl] *a* metodico.

methodist ['meθǝdist] *n* metodista.

methyl ['meθil] *n* (*chem*) metile.

meticulous [me'tikjulǝs] *a* meticoloso.

metre ['mi:tǝ] *n* metro; metro poetico; ritmo.

metric ['metrik] *a* metrico.

metrical ['metrikəl] *a* (*linear measure*) metrico.

metropolis [mi'trɔpəlis] *n* metropoli.

metropolitan [,metrə'pɔlitən] *a n* metropolitano.

mettle ['metl] *n* ardore, coraggio, foga.

mew [mju:] *n* miagolìo; gabbia (per falchi); **mews** *pl* scuderie, stalle *pl* (disposte intorno ad un cortile).

mew [mju:] *vi* miagolare.

Mexican ['meksikən] *a n* messicano.

Mexico ['meksikou] *n* Messico.

Michael ['maikl] *nm pr* Michele.

Michaelmas ['miklməs] *n* festa di S. Michele.

microbe ['maikroub] *n* microbo.

microgroove ['maikrou,gru:v] *n* microsolco.

microphone ['maikrəfoun] *n* microfono.

microscope ['maikrəskoup] *n* microscopio.

microscopic(al) [,maikrə'skɔpik(əl)] *a* microscopico.

mid [mid] *a* medio, mezzo.

midday ['middei] *n* mezzogiorno.

middle ['midl] *a* intermedio, medio, di mezzo; *n* mezzo, centro; **M. Ages** Medioevo; **m.-aged** di mezza età; **m. class** borghesia.

middleman ['midlmæn] *pl* **-men** *n* (*com*) intermediario.

middling ['midliŋ] *a* medio, mediocre; *ad* discretamente.

midge [midʒ] *n* moscerino.

midget ['midʒit] *n* omiciattolo, cosa piccolissima.

midland ['midlənd] *a* centrale; **the Midlands** *pl* contee dell'Inghilterra centrale.

midnight ['midnait] *a n* (di) mezzanotte.

midshipman ['midʃipmən] *pl* **-men** *n* (*naut*) cadetto.

midst [midst] *n* mezzo, centro.

midsummer ['mid,sʌmə] *n* periodo del solstizio d'estate.

midway ['mid'wei] *ad* a metà strada.

midwife ['midwaif] *n* levatrice.

midwifery ['midwifəri] *n* ostetricia.

might [mait] *past tense of* **may**; *n* forza, potenza.

mighty ['maiti] *a* possente, potente; *ad* (*fam*) molto.

mignonette [,minjə'net] *n* reseda.

migraine ['mi:grein] *n* emicrania.

migrate [mai'greit] *vi* emigrare, trasmigrare.

migration [mai'greiʃən] *n* migrazione, emigrazione.

migratory ['maigrətəri] *a* migratore, migratorio.

Milan [mi'læn] *n* Milano; **Milanese** *a n* milanese.

mild [maild] *a* dolce, mite, blando.

mildew ['mildju:] *n* muffa.

mildness ['maildnis] *n* dolcezza, mitezza.

mile [mail] *n* miglio (= *metri* 1609).

mileage ['mailidʒ] *n* distanza in miglia; **m. recorder** contachilometri.

milestone ['mailstoun] *n* pietra miliare.

militant ['militənt] *a* militante; *n* attivista.

military ['militəri] *a* militare; **the m.** i militari.

militate ['militeit] *vi* **m. against** opporsi a.

militia [mi'liʃə] *n* milizia.

milk [milk] *n* latte; *vti* mungere.

milkmaid ['milkmeid] *n* mungitrice.

milkman ['milkmən] *n* lattaio.

milky ['milki] *a* latteo, di latte; **the M. Way** la Via Lattea.

mill [mil] *n* mulino, fabbrica; *vt* macinare.

millennium [mi'leniəm] *n* millennio.

millepede ['milipi:d] *n* millepiedi.

miller ['milə] *n* mugnaio.

millet ['milit] *n* miglio.

milliard ['miliɑ:d] *n* miliardo, (*US*) bilione.

milliner ['milinə] *n* modista.

million ['miljən] *a n* milione; **millionaire** milionario.

millpond ['milpɔnd] *n* gora di mulino.

millstone ['milstoun] *n* macina di mulino.

mimic ['mimik] *a* imitativo; *n* mimo; imitatore; contraffazione.

mimicry ['mimikri] *n* mimesi; mimica; mimetismo.

mince [mins] *n* carne tritata; *vt* tritare; abbreviare; (*fig*) mitigare; parlare con affettazione.

mincing ['minsiŋ] *a* affettato.

mind [maind] *n* mente, intelligenza; animo, opinione; memoria; *vt* badare a, occuparsi di, fare attenzione a, importare; spiacere.

mindful ['maindful] *a* attento, memore.

mine [main] *n* mina, miniera; *pron* (il) mio *etc*; *vti* scavare, estrarre; minare.

miner ['mainə] *n* minatore.

mineral ['minərəl] *a n* minerale.

mingle ['miŋgl] *vti* mescolar(si), mischiar(si).

miniature ['minətʃə] *a n* (in) miniatura.

minim ['minim] *n* (*mus*) minima.

minimize ['minimaiz] *vt* minimizzare.

minimum ['miniməm] *a n* minimo.

mining ['mainiŋ] *a* minerario; *n* lavoro nelle miniere.

minion ['minjən] *n* favorito; **m. of the law** (*fam*) poliziotto.

miniskirt ['miniskə:t] *n* minigonna.

minister ['ministə] *n* ministro; *vi* dare aiuto.

ministration [,minis'treiʃən] *n* aiuto, assistenza.

ministry ['ministri] *n* ministero.

mink [miŋk] *n* visone.

minnow ['minou] n pesciolino d'acqua dolce.

minor ['mainə] a minore; n minorenne.

minority [mai'nɔriti] n minoranza; minorità.

minster ['minstə] n chiesa d'un monastero, cattedrale.

minstrel ['minstrəl] n menestrello.

mint [mint] n zecca; (fig) grossa somma; menta; vt coniare.

minuet [,minju'et] n minuetto.

minus ['mainəs] prep meno, privo di; a n meno.

minute [mai'nju:t] a minuto, piccolissimo; ['minit] n minuto; nota, minuta; **minutes** pl verbale.

minuteness [mai'nju:tnis] n minutezza, piccolezza.

minx [miŋks] n ragazza sfacciata.

miracle ['mirəkl] n miracolo.

miraculous [mi'rækjuləs] a miracoloso.

mirage [mi'rɑ:ʒ] n miraggio.

mire ['maiə] n fango, pantano.

mirror ['mirə] n specchio; vt rispecchiare.

mirth [mə:θ] n allegria.

miry ['maiəri] a fangoso.

misadventure ['misəd'ventʃə] n disgrazia.

misanthrope ['mizənθroup] n misantropo.

misanthropy [mi'sænθrəpi] n misantropia.

misapply ['misə'plai] vt applicare erroneamente.

misapprehend ['mis,æpri'hend] vt fraintendere.

misbehave ['misbi'heiv] vi comportarsi male.

misbehaviour ['misbi'heivjə] n cattivo contegno.

miscalculate ['mis'kælkjuleit] vti calcolare male.

miscarriage [mis'kæridʒ] n aborto; disguido postale; insuccesso; errore.

miscarry [mis'kæri] vi abortire; andare smarrito; fallire.

miscellaneous [,misi'leiniəs] a miscellaneo.

miscellany [mi'seləni] n miscellanea.

mischance [mis'tʃɑ:ns] n disgrazia, sventura.

mischief ['mistʃif] n male, danno, malizia, birichinata.

mischievous ['mistʃivəs] a cattivo, dannoso; malizioso, furbo.

misconception ['miskən'sepʃən] n concetto erroneo, malinteso.

misconduct [mis'kɔndəkt] n cattiva condotta; cattiva amministrazione; adulterio.

misconstrue ['miskən'stru:] vt fraintendere.

misdeed ['mis'di:d] n misfatto.

misdemeanour [,misdi'mi:nə] n cattiva condotta, infrazione alla legge.

misdirection ['misdi'rekʃən] n indirizzo sbagliato, informazione sbagliata.

miser ['maizə] n avaro.

miserable ['mizərəbl] a triste, infelice; miserabile.

miserly ['maizəli] a avaro, sordido.

misery ['mizəri] n infelicità; indigenza, pl avversità.

misfire ['mis'faiə] vi far cilecca (also fig).

misfit ['misfit] n indumento mal riuscito; (fam) individuo spostato.

misfortune [mis'fɔ:tʃən] n disgrazia, sfortuna.

misgiving [mis'giviŋ] n apprensione; presentimento.

mishap ['mishæp] n disgrazia, incidente.

misinform ['misin'fɔ:m] vt informar male.

misinterpret ['misin'tə:prit] vt interpretar male.

misjudge ['mis'dʒʌdʒ] vt giudicare male.

mislay [mis'lei] vt smarrire, metter fuori posto.

mislead [mis'li:d] vt sviare, ingannare.

misleading [mis'li:diŋ] a ingannevole, che fa sbagliare.

mismanage ['mis'mænidʒ] vt amministrar male, dirigere male.

mismanagement ['mis'mænidʒmənt] n cattiva amministrazione.

misplace ['mis'pleis] vt collocare male.

misprint ['mis'print] n errore di stampa; [mis'print] vt stampare con errori.

misrepresent ['mis,repri'zent] vt travisare.

misrule ['mis'ru:l] n malgoverno.

miss [mis] n signorina (premesso al nome di donna non sposata); colpo mancato, insuccesso; vti non afferrare, non colpire, perdere, sbagliare; sentire la mancanza di; (fig) far cilecca, mancare; **to m. out** tralasciare, saltare.

missal ['misəl] n messale.

missile ['misail] n proiettile, missile; **guided m.** missile teleguidato.

missing ['misiŋ] a mancante, assente, disperso.

mission ['miʃən] n missione.

missionary ['miʃnəri] a n missionario.

misspell ['mis'spel] vt sbagliar l'ortografia di, scrivere erratamente.

mist [mist] n foschia, caligine; **Scotch m.** pioggia leggera.

mistake [mis'teik] n errore, sbaglio; vti scambiare, fraintendere, sbagliarsi.

mistaken [mis'teikən] a erroneo, sbagliato.

Mister ['mistə] n Mr Signor(e).

mistletoe ['misltou] n vischio.

mistress ['mistris] n padrona; maestra; amante; Mrs ['misiz] Signora.

mistrust ['mis'trʌst] n diffidenza, sfiducia; vt diffidare di.

mistrustful ['mis'trʌstful] a diffidente.

misty ['misti] a nebbioso.

misunderstand ['misʌndə'stænd] vt capir male, fraintendere.

misunderstanding ['misʌndə'stændiŋ] n malinteso; dissapore.

misuse ['mis'juːs] n abuso, uso sbagliato; maltrattamento; vt ['mis'juːz] maltrattare; usar male; abusare di.

mite [mait] n piccola moneta, piccolo contributo; (chil) piccino.

mitigate ['mitigeit] vt mitigare, attenuare.

mitre ['maitə] n mitra.

mitten ['mitn] n mezzo guanto, manopola.

mix [miks] vti mescolare, mescolarsi, armonizzare, associarsi; to m. up confondere.

mixture ['mikstʃə] n miscela, miscuglio, mistura.

mix-up ['miks'ʌp] n confusione, baruffa.

moan [moun] n gemito, lamento; vi gemere, lamentarsi.

moat [mout] n fosso, fossato.

mob [mɔb] n folla tumultuante, plebaglia; vt assalire, accalcarsi.

mobile ['moubail] a mobile.

mobility [mou'biliti] n mobilità.

mobilization [‚moubilai'zeiʃən] n mobilitazione.

mobilize ['moubilaiz] vt mobilitare.

mock [mɔk] a falso, finto, imitato; vti ingannare; deridere, burlarsi di.

mockery ['mɔkəri] n derisione, scherno, beffa.

mode [moud] n modo, maniera, moda.

model ['mɔdl] a modello; n modello, modella; vt modellare.

moderate ['mɔdərit] a moderato, modico; vti ['mɔdəreit] moderare, moderarsi, (weather) calmarsi.

moderation [‚mɔdə:'reiʃən] n moderazione.

modern ['mɔdən] a n moderno.

modernity [mɔ'də:niti] n modernità.

modernization [‚mɔdə:nai'zeiʃən] n rimodernamento.

modernize ['mɔdə:naiz] vt rimodernare.

modest ['mɔdist] a modesto.

modesty ['mɔdisti] n modestia.

modification [‚mɔdifi'keiʃən] n modificazione.

modify ['mɔdifai] vt modificare.

modulation [‚mɔdju'leiʃən] n modulazione.

Mohammed [mou'hæmid] nm pr Maometto.

Mohammedan [mou'hæmidən] a n maomettano.

moist [mɔist] a umido.

moisten ['mɔisn] vti inumidir(si).

moistness ['mɔistnis] moisture ['mɔistʃə] n umidità.

molar ['moulə] a n molare.

mole [moul] n molo, talpa.

molest [mou'lest] vt molestare.

mollify ['mɔlifai] vt addolcire, ammollire.

mollusc ['mɔləsk] n mollusco.

moment ['moumənt] n momento; importanza.

momentary ['mouməntəri] a momentaneo, transitorio.

momentous [mou'mentəs] a grave, importante.

Monaco ['mɔnəkou] n Monaco (Principato di).

monarch ['mɔnək] n monarca.

monarchy ['mɔnəki] n monarchia.

monastery ['mɔnəstəri] n monastero.

monastic [mə'næstik] a monastico.

Monday ['mʌndi] n lunedì.

monetary ['mʌnitəri] a monetario.

money ['mʌni] n denaro, moneta, soldi pl.

Mongol ['mɔŋgəl] a n mongolo.

Mongolian [mɔŋ'gouliən] a mongolo; n lingua mongolica.

mongoloid ['mɔŋ gɔlɔid] a n mongoloide.

mongoose ['mɔŋguːs] n mangosta.

mongrel ['mʌŋgrəl] n meticcio; cane bastardo; a ibrido, misto.

monitor ['mɔnitə] n consigliere; (el) monitore; dispositivo di controllo.

monk [mʌŋk] n monaco.

monkey ['mʌŋki] n scimmia.

monocle ['mɔnəkl] n monocolo.

monogram ['mɔnəgræm] n monogramma.

monograph ['mɔnəgrɑːf] n monografia.

monologue ['mɔnəlɔg] n monologo.

monopolize [mə'nɔpəlaiz] vt monopolizzare.

monopoly [mə'nɔpəli] n monopolio.

monosyllable ['mɔnə‚siləbl] n monosillabo.

monotonous [mə'nɔtənəs] a monotono.

monotony [mə'nɔtəni] n monotonia.

monsoon [‚mɔn'suːn] n monsone.

monster ['mɔnstə] a enorme, mostruoso; n mostro.

monstrance ['mɔnstrəns] n ostensorio.

monstrosity [mɔns'trɔsiti] n mostruosità.

monstrous ['mɔnstrəs] a mostruoso.

Mont Blanc [mɔ̃:m'blɑ̃:ŋ] n Monte Bianco.

Mont Cenis [‚mɔ̃:nsə'niː] n Moncenisio.

month [mʌnθ] n mese.

monthly ['mʌnθli] a mensile; ad mensilmente; n rivista mensile.

monument ['mɔnjumənt] n monumento.

monumental [‚mɔnju'mentl] a monumentale.

mood [mu:d] *n* stato d'animo, umore; (*verb*) modo.

moody ['mu:di] *a* di malumore; lunatico.

moon [mu:n] *n* luna.

moonlight ['mu:nlait] *n* chiaro di luna.

moor [muə] *n* brughiera; *vt* (*naut*) ormeggiare.

Moor [muə] *n* moro, marocchino.

mooring ['muəriŋ] *n* (*naut*) ormeggio.

Moorish ['muəriʃ] *a* moro, moresco.

mop [mɔp] *n* scopa di stracci, strofinaccio; *vt* pulire, asciugare (un pavimento).

mope [moup] *vi* essere abbattuto, depresso.

moral ['mɔrəl] *a n* morale; **morals** *pl* condotta, costumi *pl*.

morale [mɔ'ra:l] *n* il morale, lo stato d'animo.

moralist ['mɔrəlist] *n* moralista.

morality [mə'ræliti] *n* morale, moralità.

moralize ['mɔrəlaiz] *vi* moralizzare.

morass [mə'ræs] *n* palude.

morbid ['mɔ:bid] *a* morboso.

morbidity [mɔ:'biditi] *n* morbosità.

mordant ['mɔ:dənt] *a* pungente, acuto.

more [mɔ:] *a* più; *ad* più, di più.

moreover [mɔ:'rouvə] *ad* inoltre, per di più.

morganatic [,mɔ:gə'nætik] *a* morganatico.

morgue [mɔ:g] *n* 'morgue', obitorio.

moribund ['mɔribʌnd] *a n* morente, moribondo.

Mormon ['mɔ:mən] *a n* mormone.

morning ['mɔ:niŋ] *n* mattina, -no, mattinata.

Moroccan [mə'rɔkən] *a n* marocchino.

Morocco [mə'rɔkou] *n* (*geogr*) Marocco.

morocco [mə'rɔkou] *n* (*leather*) marocchino.

moron ['mɔ:rɔn] *n* deficiente, idiota.

morose [mə'rous] *a* tetro, imbronciato, non socievole.

moroseness [mə'rousnis] *n* tetraggine.

morphia ['mɔ:fiə] **morphine** ['mɔ:fi:n] *n* (*chem*) morfina.

Morris ['mɔris] *nm pr* Maurizio.

morsel ['mɔ:səl] *n* boccone, pezzetto.

mortal ['mɔ:tl] *a n* mortale.

mortality [mɔ:'tæliti] *n* mortalità.

mortar ['mɔ:tə] *n* mortaio, calcina.

mortgage ['mɔ:gidʒ] *n* ipoteca; *vt* ipotecare.

mortify ['mɔ:tifai] *vti* mortificar(si); incancrenire.

mortmain ['mɔ:tmein] *n* (*leg*) manomorta.

mortuary ['mɔ:tjuəri] *a* mortuario; *n* camera mortuaria.

mosaic [mə'zeiik] *a n* (di) mosaico.

Moscow ['mɔskou] *n* Mosca.

Moses ['mouziz] *nm pr* (*Bibl*) Mosè.

Moslem ['mɔzlem] *a n* musulmano.

mosque [mɔsk] *n* moschea.

mosquito [məs'ki:tou] *n* zanzara.

moss [mɔs] *n* muschio; terreno paludoso.

most [moust] *a* il più, la maggior parte; *ad* il più, di più, molto; **mostly** principalmente, per lo più.

mote [mout] *n* bruscolo, pagliuzza.

motel [mou'tel] *n* 'motel', autostello.

moth [mɔθ] *n* falena; tarma, tignola.

mother ['mʌðə] *n* madre; **m.-in-law** suocera; **m.-of-pearl** madreperla; **m. tongue** madre lingua.

motherhood ['mʌðəhud] *n* maternità.

motherly ['mʌðəli] *a* materno.

motif [mou'ti:f] *n* motivo, idea dominante.

motion ['mouʃən] *n* moto, movimento; mozione; *vi* fare cenno a.

motionless ['mouʃənlis] *a* senza moto, immobile.

motivation [,mouti'veiʃən] *n* motivazione; motivo, movente.

motive ['moutiv] *a* motore; *n* motivo, movente; causa.

motley ['mɔtli] *a* multicolore, eterogeneo.

motor ['moutə] *a* motore; *n* motore, macchina; **m. car** automobile; **motorway** autostrada.

motorcade ['moutəkeid] *n* (*US*) sfilata di automobili.

motoring ['moutəriŋ] *a* automobilismo.

motorist ['moutərist] *n* automobilista.

mottle ['mɔtl] *vt* chiazzare, macchiare.

motto ['mɔtou] *pl* **mottoes** *n* motto.

mould [mould] *n* muffa; terriccio; modello, forma, stampo; *vt* formare, modellare, plasmare.

mouldy ['mouldi] *a* ammuffito.

moult [moult] *n* muda; *vi* mudare.

mound [maund] *n* montagnola; tumulo, mucchio.

mount [maunt] *n* colle, monte; cavallo, montatura; *vt* ascendere, salire, montare, far salire su; incorniciare.

mountain ['mauntin] *n* montagna, monte.

mountaineer [,maunti'niə] *n* montanaro, alpinista.

mountainous ['mauntinəs] *a* montuoso.

mountebank ['mauntibæŋk] *n* ciarlatano, saltimbanco.

mourn [mɔ:n] *vti* piangere, lamentarsi, portare il lutto.

mourner ['mɔ:nə] *n* persona in lutto; chi accompagna un funerale; prefica.

mournful ['mɔ:nful] *a* lugubre, triste.

mourning ['mɔːniŋ] n lutto.

mouse [maus] pl **mice** n topo, sorcio.

moustache [məs'tɑːʃ] n baffo, baffi pl.

mousy ['mausi] a grigio topo; scialbo, insignificante, (person) timido, silenzioso.

mouth [mauθ] n bocca; foce; apertura.

mouthful ['mauθful] n boccone.

mouthpiece ['mauθpiːs] n (mus instrument) imboccatura; bocchino; (fig) portavoce.

movable ['muːvəbl] a mobile, (leg) mobiliare; **movables** n pl beni mobili.

move [muːv] n movimento; mossa; vti muovere, muoversi, traslocare; commuovere; spingere; procedere.

movement ['muːvmənt] n movimento, moto.

movies ['muːviz] n pl (US fam) cinematografo.

moving ['muːviŋ] a commovente; mobile.

mow [mou] vt falciare, mietere.

mower ['mouə] n falciatore; (mech) falciatrice.

Mr v Mister.

Mrs v mistress.

much [mʌtʃ] ad molto, pressappoco; a pron molto.

muck [mʌk] n concime, letame; sudiciume.

mud [mʌd] n fango; **m.-bath** (med) fangature pl; **mudguard** (aut) parafango; **m.-pie** formina di terra, di sabbia.

muddle ['mʌdl] n confusione, disordine; vt confondere, guastare; **muddler** n confusionario, pasticcione.

muddy ['mʌdi] a fangoso.

muff [mʌf] n manicotto.

muffin ['mʌfin] n piccola focaccia.

muffle ['mʌfl] vt imbacuccare, avvolgere, bendare, coprire, soffocare; **muffler** ['mʌflə] n sciarpa pesante; (US aut) silenziatore.

mufti ['mʌfti] n abito borghese.

mug [mʌg] n bicchiere, boccale; (sl) faccia.

muggy ['mʌgi] a afoso, umido.

mulberry ['mʌlbəri] n gelso moro, mora.

mule [mjuːl] n mulo; pianella.

mull [mʌl] vt **mulled wine** vino caldo.

mullet ['mʌlit] n triglia; muggine.

mullion ['mʌliən] n (arch) colonnina divisoria d'una finestra bifora.

multiform ['mʌltifɔːm] a multiforme.

multiple ['mʌltipl] a n multiplo.

multiplication [ˌmʌltipli'keiʃən] n moltiplicazione.

multiplicity [ˌmʌlti'plisiti] n molteplicità.

multiply ['mʌltiplai] vti moltiplicar(si).

multiracial ['mʌltiˌreiʃəl] a dalle molte razze, plurirazziale.

multitude ['mʌltitjuːd] n moltitudine.

mumble ['mʌmbl] n borbottio; vi borbottare.

mummy ['mʌmi] n mummia; (fam) mamma.

mumps [mʌmps] n parotite, (fam) orecchioni.

munch [mʌntʃ] vt masticare, sgranocchiare.

mundane ['mʌndein] a mondano, del mondo.

Munich ['mjuːnik] n Monaco (di Baviera).

municipal [mjuː'nisipəl] a municipale.

municipality [mjuːˌnisi'pæliti] n municipalità.

munificent [mjuː'nifisnt] a munifico.

munitions [mjuː'niʃəns] n pl munizioni pl.

mural ['mjuərəl] a murale; n affresco.

murder ['məːdə] n assassinio; vt assassinare.

murderer ['məːdərə] n assassino.

murderous ['məːdərəs] a assassino, micidiale.

murky ['məːki] a fosco, tenebroso.

murmur ['məːmə] n mormorio; vi mormorare.

muscle ['mʌsl] n muscolo.

Muscovite ['mʌskəvait] a n moscovita.

muscular ['mʌskjulə] a muscolare; muscoloso.

muse [mjuːz] n musa; vi meditare, essere assorto in un pensiero.

museum [mjuː'ziəm] n museo.

mushroom ['mʌʃrum] n fungo.

music ['mjuːzik] n musica; **m.-hall** teatro di varietà.

musical ['mjuːzikəl] a musicale.

musician [mjuː'ziʃən] n musicista.

musk [mʌsk] n muschio.

musket ['mʌskit] n moschetto.

musketeer [ˌmʌski'tiə] n moschettiere.

musketry ['mʌskitri] n moschetteria, fucileria.

Muslim ['muslim] a n musulmano.

muslin ['mʌzlin] n mussola.

mussel ['mʌsl] n arsella, cozza, muscolo.

Mussulman ['mʌslmən] a n musulmano.

must [mʌst] n mosto, muffa.

must [mʌst] v dovere.

mustard ['mʌstəd] n senape; difettivo mostarda.

muster ['mʌstə] a adunata, parata; vti raccoglier(si), radunar(si).

mustiness ['mʌstinis] n muffa.

musty ['mʌsti] a ammuffito.

mute [mjuːt] a n muto.

mutilate ['mjuːtileit] vt mutilare.

mutilation [ˌmjuːti'leiʃən] n mutilazione.

mutineer [.mjuːti'niə] n ammutinato.

mutinous ['mjuːtinəs] a ammutinato, rivoltoso; ribelle.

mutiny ['mjuːtini] n ammutinamento; vi ammutinarsi.

mutter ['mʌtə] n borbottio; vi borbottare.

mutton ['mʌtn] n carne di montone o di pecora.

mutual ['mjuːtjuəl] a mutuo, reciproco.

muzzle ['mʌzl] n muso; museruola; (gun etc) bocca; vt mettere la museruola a; (fig) costringere al silenzio.

muzzy ['mʌzi] a confuso, inebetito; instupidito (dall'alcool).

my [mai] a (il) mio, (la) mia etc; **myself** pron io stesso, mi, me stesso.

myriad ['miriəd] a n miriade.

myrrh [məː] n mirra.

myrtle ['məːtl] n mirto.

mysterious [mis'tiəriəs] a misterioso.

mystery ['mistəri] n mistero.

mystic(al) ['mistik(əl)] a n mistico.

mystify ['mistifai] vt mistificare; ingannare; disorientare.

myth [miθ] n mito.

mythological [.miθə'bdʒikəl] a mitologico.

mythology [mi'θɔlədʒi] n mitologia.

N

nag [næg] n (fam) cavallo, -lino; vti (fam) brontolare; tormentare.

nail [neil] n unghia; artiglio; chiodo; vt inchiodare; **on the n.** puntualmente, senz'indugio.

naïve [nai'iːv] a ingenuo, semplice.

naked ['neikid] a nudo, disadorno; evidente; indifeso.

nakedness ['neikidnis] n nudità.

name [neim] n nome; reputazione; vt chiamare, designare, nominare.

nameless ['neimlis] a senza nome, anonimo, innominato; indicibile.

namely ['neimli] ad cioè.

namesake ['neimseik] n omonimo.

nanny ['næni] n bambinaia, balia.

nap [næp] n pisolino, sonnellino; (of material) pelo; vi fare un pisolino, sonnecchiare.

nape [neip] n nuca.

naphtha ['næfθə] n nafta.

napkin ['næpkin] n tovagliolo, pannolino.

Naples ['neiplz] n Napoli.

Napoleon [nə'pouliən] nm pr Napoleone.

narcissus [nɑː'sisəs] n narciso.

narcotic [nɑː'kɔtik] a n narcotico.

narrate [næ'reit] vt narrare.

narration [næ'reifən] n narrazione.

narrative ['nærətiv] a narrativo; n narrazione, racconto.

narrator [næ'reitə] n narratore.

narrow ['nærou] a stretto, ristretto;

minuzioso; n (usu pl) stretto, gola; vt restringere.

narrowly ['nærouli] ad a stento; minuziosamente.

narrowness ['nærounis] n strettezza, ristrettezza.

nasal ['neizəl] a n nasale.

nastiness ['nɑːstinis] n cattiveria; sporcizia; indecenza.

nasturtium [nəs'təːʃəm] n nasturzio.

nasty ['nɑːsti] a disgustoso; cattivo; indecente.

nation ['neiʃən] n nazione.

national ['næʃənl] a nazionale.

nationalism ['næʃnəlizəm] n nazionalismo.

nationality [.næʃə'næliti] n nazionalità.

nationalization [.næʃnəlai'zeiʃən] n nazionalizzazione.

nationalize ['næʃnəlaiz] vt nazionalizzare.

native ['neitiv] a n indigeno, nativo.

nativity [nə'tiviti] n natività, nascita.

natty ['næti] a ben aggiustato, in ghingheri.

natural ['nætʃrəl] a naturale.

naturalist ['nætʃrəlist] n naturalista.

naturalization [.nætʃrəlai'zeiʃən] n naturalizzazione.

naturalize ['nætʃrəlaiz] vt naturalizzare.

naturally ['nætʃrəli] ad naturalmente, per natura.

nature ['neitʃə] n natura.

naught [nɔːt] n nulla, zero.

naughtiness ['nɔːtinis] n cattiveria, disubbidienza, impertinenza.

naughty ['nɔːti] a cattivo, disubbidiente.

nausea ['nɔːsiə] n nausea.

nauseate ['nɔːsieit] vti nauseare.

nauseous ['nɔːsiəs] a disgustoso, nauseante.

nautical ['nɔːtikəl] a nautico.

naval ['neivəl] a navale.

nave [neiv] n navata.

navel ['neivəl] n ombelico.

navigability [.nævigə'biliti] n navigabilità.

navigable ['nævigəbl] a navigabile.

navigate ['nævigeit] vti navigare.

navigation [.nævi'geiʃən] n navigazione.

navigator ['nævigeitə] n navigatore.

navvy ['nævi] n sterratore.

navy ['neivi] n flotta; marina.

Nazarene [.næzə'riːn] a n nazzareno.

Nazareth ['næzəriθ] n Nazaret.

Nazi ['nɑːtsi] a n nazista.

Neapolitan [niə'pɔlitən] a n napoletano.

near [niə] a vicino, intimo; ad presso, vicino; prep vicino a; vti approssimar(si), avvicinar(si).

nearby ['niəbai] a ad prep vicino.

nearly ['niəli] ad quasi; da vicino, strettamente.

nearness ['niənis] *n* prossimità, vicinanza, intimità.

neat [ni:t] *a* lindo, accurato; (*of drinks*) liscio; chiaro e conciso.

neatly ['ni:tli] *ad* accuratamente; abilmente; elegantemente.

neatness ['ni:tnis] *n* pulizia, ordine, accuratezza, proprietà.

necessarily ['nesisərili] *ad* necessariamente.

necessary ['nesisəri] *a n* necessario.

necessitate [ni'sesiteit] *vt* richiedere, necessitare.

necessity [ni'sesiti] *n* necessità.

neck [nek] *n* collo.

neckerchief ['nekətʃif] *n* fazzoletto da collo.

necklace ['neklis] *n* collana.

necktie [nektai] *n* cravatta.

necrology [ne'krɔlədʒi] *n* necrologia; necrologio.

necromancer ['nekroumænsə] *n* negromante.

necromancy ['nekroumænsi] *n* negromanzia.

nectar ['nektə] *n* nettare.

need [ni:d] *n* bisogno; *vti* aver bisogno di; essere necessario, occorrere.

needful ['ni:dful] *a* necessario.

neediness ['ni:dinis] *n* indigenza, miseria.

needle ['ni:dl] *n* ago; **knitting n.** ferro da calza.

needless ['ni:dlis] *a* inutile.

needy ['ni:di] *a* bisognoso, indigente.

nefarious [ni'fɛəriəs] *a* abominevole.

negation [ni'geiʃən] *n* negazione.

negative ['negətiv] *a* negativo; *n* negativa.

neglect [ni'glekt] *n* negligenza, trascuratezza; *vi* negligere, trascurare.

neglectful [ni'glektful] *a* negligente, trascurato.

negligence ['neglidʒəns] *n* negligenza, trascuratezza.

negligent ['neglidʒənt] *a* negligente, trascurato.

negligible ['neglidʒəbl] *a* trascurabile.

negotiate [ni'gouʃieit] *vti* negoziare, trattare.

negotiation [ni,gouʃi'eiʃən] *n* trattativa, negoziati *pl*.

negro ['ni:grou] *n* negro; **negress** negra.

neigh [nei] *vi* nitrire.

neighbour ['neibə] *n* prossimo, vicino.

neighbourhood ['neibəhud] *n* vicinato, dintorni, vicinanze *pl*.

neighbouring ['neibəriŋ] *a* limitrofo, vicino.

neighbourly ['neibərli] *a* amichevole, da buon vicino.

neither ['naiðə] *a pron* nè l'uno nè l'altro; *cj* nè, neppure; **neither . . . nor** nè . . . nè.

neon ['ni:ɔn] *n* (*chem*) neon; **n. lights** luci al neon.

nephew ['nevju] *n* nipote (di zio).

nerve [nə:v] *n* nervo; *pl* nervi *pl*; sangue freddo; (*fam*) sfrontatezza.

nervous ['nə:vəs] *a* eccitabile, nervoso; pauroso, timido.

nervousness ['nə:vəsnis] *n* nervosismo; timidezza.

nervy ['nə:vi] *a* (*fam*) eccitabile, nervoso.

nest [nest] *n* nido; covo; *vi* nidificare.

nestle ['nesl] *vi* annidarsi; accoccolarsi.

nestling ['nesliŋ] *n* uccellino di nido.

net [net] *a* netto; *n* rete; *vt* prendere con la rete, pescare; (*fig*) irretire; *vi* far le reti.

Netherlands ['neðələndz] *n pl* Paesi Bassi.

netting ['netiŋ] *n* rete; reticolato.

nettle ['netl] *n* ortica.

network ['netwə:k] *n* rete, reticolato.

neuralgia [njuə'rældʒə] *n* nevralgia.

neurasthenia [,njuərəs'θiniə] *n* neurastenia, nevrastenia.

neurasthenic [,njuərəs'θenik] *a* nevrastenico.

neurosis [njuə'rousis] *n* neurosi, nevrosi.

neurotic [njuə'rɔtik] *a* nervoso; *n* neurotico, neuropatico.

neuter ['nju:tə] *a* neutrale, neutro; *n* neutro; individuo che si tiene neutrale.

neutral ['nju:trəl] *n* neutrale; *a* neutro.

neutrality [nju'træliti] *n* neutralità.

neutralize ['nju:trəlaiz] *vt* neutralizzare.

never ['nevə] *ad* non . . . mai, mai.

nevertheless [,nevəðə'les] *ad cj* nondimeno, ciò nonostante, tuttavia.

new [nju:] *a* nuovo, fresco, novello; **n.-born child** neonato.

New Guinea [nju'gini] *n* Nuova Guinea.

New Hebrides [nju'hebrədi:z] *n pl* Nuove Ebridi.

newly ['nju:li] *ad* di fresco, di recente.

news [nju:z] *n* (*sing*) notizie *pl*; a piece of n. una notizia; **newsagent** giornalaio; **newsreel** cinegiornale; **newsstand** edicola.

newspaper ['nju:s,peipə] *n* giornale.

newt [nju:t] *n* (*zool*) tritone.

New York ['nju:'jɔ:k] *n* Nuova York.

New Zealand [nju:'zi:lənd] *n* Nuova Zelanda.

New Zealander [nju:'zi:ləndə] *n* neozelandese.

next [nekst] *a* prossimo, seguente, più vicino; *ad* poi, subito, dopo; *prep* accanto a, vicino a.

nib [nib] *n* pennino.

nibble ['nibl] *vti* rosicchiare; abboccare.

Nice [ni:s] *n* Nizza.

nice [nais] *a* buono; amabile, simpatico; grazioso, bello; esatto, scrupoloso; difficile (di gusti); sottile.

nicety ['naisiti] *n* delicatezza; sottigliezza; **to a n.** con estrema esattezza.

niche [nitʃ] *n* nicchia.

Nicholas ['nikələs] *nm pr* Nicola, Niccolò.

nick [nik] *n* tacca; **in the n. of time** appena in tempo.

nickel ['nikl] *n* nichel.

nickname ['nikneim] *n* nomignolo, soprannome.

niece [niːs] *n* nipote (di zio).

Nigeria [nai'dʒiəriə] *n* (geogr) Nigeria.

Nigerian [nai'dʒiəriən] *a n* (abitante) della Nigeria.

niggard ['nigəd] *n* avaro.

niggardliness ['nigədlinis] *n* avarizia.

niggardly ['nigədli] *a* avaro.

nigger ['nigə] *n* negro.

night [nait] *n* notte, sera.

nightfall ['naitfɔːl] *n* tramonto, crepuscolo; **at n.** sull'imbrunire.

nightingale ['naitingeil] *n* usignuolo.

nightly ['naitli] *a* notturno; di ogni notte; *ad* di notte; ogni notte.

nightmare ['naitmɛə] *n* incubo.

nihilist ['naiilist] *n* nichilista.

Nile [nail] *n* Nilo.

nimble ['nimbl] *a* agile; svelto, sveglio.

nimbleness ['nimblnis] *n* agilità, sveltezza.

nine [nain] *a n* nove; **ninth** *a* nono.

nineteen ['nain'tiːn] *a n* diciannove; **nineteenth** *a* diciannovesimo.

ninetieth ['naintiiθ] *a* novantesimo.

ninth [nainθ] *a n* nono.

ninety ['nainti] *a n* novanta.

nip [nip] *n* morso, pizzicotto, detto sarcastico, aria gelida, (of liquor) goccia.

nip [nip] *vt* pizzicare; mordere; stroncare.

nipper ['nipə] *n* pinza, pinzetta; (sl) monello, ragazzo.

nipple ['nipl] *n* capezzolo.

nippy ['nipi] *a* pungente; (sl) svelto.

nitrate ['naitreit] *n* nitrato.

nitre ['naitə] *n* nitrato di potassio.

no [nou] *a* nessuno; *ad* no, non, niente.

nobility [nou'biliti] *n* nobiltà.

noble [noubl] *a n* nobile.

nobleman ['noublmən] *pl* **-men** *n* nobile, nobiluomo.

nobleness ['noublnis] *n* nobiltà.

nobody ['noubədi] *pron* nessuno.

nocturnal [nɔk'təːnl] *a* notturno.

nocturne ['nɔktəːn] *n* (mus) notturno.

nod [nɔd] *n* cenno affermativo del capo; *vti* annuire; chinare il capo; sonnecchiare.

noise [nɔiz] *n* rumore, chiasso, clamore.

noiseless ['nɔizlis] *a* senza rumore, silenzioso.

noisily ['nɔizili] *ad* rumorosamente.

noisiness ['nɔizinis] *n* rumorosità.

noisy ['nɔizi] *a* rumoroso; turbolento.

nomad ['nouməd] *n* nomade.

nomadic [nou'mædik] *a* nomade.

nominal ['nɔminl] *a* nominale.

nominate ['nɔmineit] *vt* designare, proporre, nominare.

nomination [ˌnɔmi'neiʃən] *n* designazione, nomina.

nominative ['nɔminətiv] *a n* nominativo.

nonchalant ['nɔnʃələnt] *a* noncurante, indifferente.

nonconformist ['nɔnkən'fɔːmist] *a n* anticonformista.

nonconformity ['nɔnkən'fɔːmiti] *n* anticonformismo.

nondescript ['nɔndiskript] *a* non classificabile, qualunque.

none [nʌn] *pron* nessuno; *ad* niente, affatto, per nulla; **n. the less** nondimeno.

nonentity [nɔ'nentiti] *n* persona insignificante, nullità.

non-existent ['nɔnig'zistənt] *a* inesistente.

nonsense ['nɔnsəns] *n* assurdità, schiocchezza.

nonsensical [nɔn'sensikəl] *a* assurdo, privo di senso.

non-stop ['nɔn'stɔp] *a* ininterrotto; *ad* ininterrottamente.

noodle ['nuːdl] *n* semplicione; (cook) taglierini.

nook [nuk] *n* angolo, cantuccio, recesso.

noon [nuːn] *n* mezzogiorno; **noonday** *a n* mezzogiorno.

noose [nuːs] *n* nodo scorsoio; (fig) trappola.

nor [nɔː] *cj* nè, neppure, nemmeno.

Nordic ['nɔːdik] *a* nordico.

normal ['nɔːməl] *a* normale; perpendicolare; *n* perpendicolare; norma.

Norman ['nɔːmən] *a n* normanno.

Normandy ['nɔːməndi] *n* Normandia.

Norse [nɔːs] *a n* norvegese, lingua norvegese.

Norseman ['nɔːsmən] *pl* **-men** *n* norvegese.

north [nɔːθ] *a* nordico, settentrionale; *ad* a (verso) nord; *n* nord, settentrione; **n.-east** nord-est; **n.-west** nord-ovest.

northerly ['nɔːðəli] *a* del nord.

northern ['nɔːðən] *a* del nord, nordico.

northward(s) ['nɔːθwəd(s)] *ad* verso nord.

Norway ['nɔːwei] *n* Norvegia.

Norwegian [nɔː'wiːdʒən] *a n* norvegese.

nose [nouz] *n* naso.

nosegay ['nouzgei] *n* mazzolino di fiori.

nostalgia [nɔs'tældʒiə] *n* nostalgia.

nostalgic [nɔs'tældʒik] *n* nostalgico.

nostril ['nɔstril] *n* narice.

not [nɔt] *ad* non.

notable ['noutǝbl] *a* notevole; *n* notabile.

notably ['noutǝbli] *ad* notevolmente; considerevolmente; sensibilmente.

notary ['noutǝri] *n* notaio.

notation [nou'teiʃǝn] *n* notazione.

notch [nɔtʃ] *n* incisione, tacca; *vt* dentellare.

note [nout] *n* (*mus*) nota; segno; appunto, biglietto; *vt* notare, prender nota di; **notepaper** carta da lettere.

notebook ['noutbuk] *n* taccuino, bloc-notes.

noted ['noutid] *a* noto, rinomato.

noteworthy ['nout,wǝːði] *a* degno di nota.

nothing ['nʌθiŋ] *pron* niente, nulla; *ad* per nulla; *n* zero, niente.

nothingness ['nʌθiŋnis] *n* il nulla, inesistenza.

notice ['noutis] *n* avviso; notifica; preavviso; disdetta; recensione; **noticeboard** tabellone per affissi.

noticeable ['noutisǝbl] *a* notevole, visibile.

noticeably ['noutisǝbli] *ad* notevolmente; percettibilmente.

notification [,noutifi'keiʃǝn] *n* notificazione, notifica.

notify ['noutifai] *vt* notificare.

notion ['nouʃǝn] *n* nozione, idea, opinione.

notoriety [,noutǝ'raiǝti] *n* notorietà.

notorious [nou'tɔːriǝs] *a* notorio.

notwithstanding ['nɔtwið'stændiŋ] *ad prep* nonostante, malgrado, tuttavia.

nougat ['nuːgaː] *n* torrone.

nought [nɔːt] *n* niente, zero.

noun [naun] *n* nome, sostantivo.

nourish ['nʌriʃ] *vt* nutrire.

nourishment ['nʌriʃmǝnt] *n* nutrimento, nutrizione.

novel ['nɔvǝl] *a* nuovo, insolito; *n* romanzo.

novelist ['nɔvǝlist] *n* romanziere.

novelty ['nɔvǝlti] *n* novità.

November [nou'vembǝ] *n* novembre.

novice ['nɔvis] *n* novizio.

noviciate, novitiate [nou'viʃiit] *n* noviziato.

now [nau] *ad cj* ora, allora, ora che; *n* questo momento.

nowadays ['nauǝdeiz] *ad* al giorno d'oggi.

nowhere ['nouwɛǝ] *ad* in nessun luogo, da nessuna parte.

noxious ['nɔkʃǝs] *a* dannoso, nocivo.

nozzle ['nɔzl] *n* becco, beccuccio; (*pump*) beccaglio.

nuance [nju'ãːns] *n* sfumatura.

nuclear ['njuːkliǝ] *a* nucleare.

nucleus ['njuːkliǝs] *n* nucleo.

nude [njuːd] *a n* nudo.

nudge [nʌdʒ] *n* gomitata; *vt* toccare col gomito.

nudist ['njuːdist] *n* nudista.

nudity ['njuːditi] *n* nudità.

nugget ['nʌgit] *n* pepita d'oro.

nuisance ['njuːsns] *n* fastidio, seccatura.

null [nʌl] *a* nullo.

nullify ['nʌlifai] *vt* annullare.

nullity ['nʌliti] *n* nullità.

numb [nʌm] *a* intorpidito.

number ['nʌmbǝ] *n* numero.

numbness ['nʌmnis] *n* intorpidimento, torpore.

numeral ['njuːmǝrǝl] *a n* numerale.

numerous ['njuːmǝrǝs] *a* numeroso.

nun [nʌn] *n* monaca, suora.

nunnery ['nʌnǝri] *n* convento (di monache).

nuptial ['nʌpʃǝl] *a* nuziale; *n pl* nozze *pl*.

Nuremberg ['njuǝrǝmbǝːg] *n* Norimberga.

nurse [nǝːs] *n* infermiera; bambinaia, balia, nutrice; *vt* assistere, curare, nutrire; (*fig*) covare (*hatred etc*); coltivare, accarezzare.

nursery ['nǝːsri] *n* stanza dei bambini; (*of plants*) vivaio.

nursing ['nǝːsiŋ] *a* che allatta, nutre; *n* allattamento, nutrire; professione di infermiera.

nurture ['nǝːtʃǝ] *n* allevamento, cura, educazione; *vt* nutrire, allevare, educare.

nut [nʌt] *n* noce, nocciola; (*mech*) dado; a hard n. (*sl*) un osso duro.

nutcracker ['nʌt,krækǝ] *n* (*usu pl*) schiaccianoci.

nutmeg ['nʌtmeg] *n* noce moscata.

nutrition [nju'triʃǝn] *n* nutrizione.

nutritious [nju'triʃǝs] *a* nutriente.

nutshell ['nʌtʃel] *n* guscio di noce; in a n. in poche parole.

nuzzle ['nʌzl] *vti* frugare (col muso); accoccolarsi (vicino a).

nylon ['nailǝn] *n* nailon.

nymph [nimf] *n* ninfa.

O

oaf [ouf] *pl* **oafs, oaves** *n* persona goffa, semplicione.

oak [ouk] *n* quercia.

oakum ['oukǝm] *n* stoppa.

oar [ɔː] *n* remo; **oarlock** (US) scalmo.

oarsman ['ɔːzmǝn] *n* rematore.

oasis [ou'eisis] *pl* **oases** *n* oasi.

oat [out] *n* (*usu pl*) avena.

oath [ouθ] *n* bestemmia, giuramento.

oatmeal ['outmiːl] *n* farina d'avena.

obduracy ['ɔbdjurǝsi] *n* ostinazione.

obdurate ['ɔbdjurit] *a* ostinato.

obedience [ǝ'biːdiǝns] *n* ubbidienza.

obedient [ǝ'biːdiǝnt] *a* ubbidiente.

obeisance [ou'beisǝns] *n* inchino; omaggio.

obelisk ['ɔbilisk] *n* obelisco.

obey [ǝ'bei] *vti* ubbidire a; ubbidire.

obituary [ǝ'bitjuǝri] *n* necrologia.

object ['ɔbdʒikt] *n* oggetto; fine, scopo; persona o cosa di aspetto ridicolo; *vti* [əb'dʒekt] obiettare, opporre, opporsi.

objection [əb'dʒekʃən] *n* obiezione.

objectionable [əb'dʒekʃnəbl] *a* offensivo.

objective [əb'dʒektiv] *a n* obiettivo, oggettivo.

oblation [ou'bleiʃən] *n* oblazione.

obligation [ˌɔbli'geiʃən] *n* obbligo, debito, dovere, impegno.

obligatory [ɔ'bligətəri] *a* obbligatorio.

oblige [ə'blaidʒ] *vt* obbligare; fare un favore a.

obliging [ə'blaidʒiŋ] *a* gentile, compiacente.

oblique [ə'bli:k] *a* obliquo.

obliterate [ə'blitəreit] *vt* cancellare.

obliteration [əˌblitə'reiʃən] *n* obliterazione, cancellatura.

oblivion [ə'bliviən] *n* oblio.

oblivious [ə'bliviəs] *a* dimentico, immemore.

oblong ['ɔblɔŋ] *a* oblungo.

obnoxious [əb'nɔkʃəs] *a* detestabile; nocivo.

oboe ['oubou] *n* (*mus*) oboe.

obscene [ɔb'si:n] *a* osceno.

obscenity [ɔb'seniti] *n* oscenità.

obscure [əb'skjuə] *a* oscuro; *vt* oscurare.

obscurity [əb'skjuəriti] *n* oscurità.

obsequies ['ɔbsikwiz] *n pl* esequie, funerali *pl*.

obsequious [əb'si:kwiəs] *a* ossequioso, servile.

observance [əb'zə:vəns] *n* osservanza; (*religious*) pratica.

observant [əb'zə:vənt] *a n* osservante; *a* attento, rispettoso.

observation [ˌɔbzə'veiʃən] *n* osservazione.

observatory [əb'zə:vətri] *n* osservatorio.

observe [əb'zə:v] *vti* osservare, praticare; rilevare.

observer [əb'zə:və] *n* osservatore.

obsess [əb'ses] *vt* ossessionare.

obsession [əb'seʃən] *n* ossessione.

obsolete ['ɔbsəli:t] *a* caduto in disuso, antiquato.

obstacle ['ɔbstəkl] *n* ostacolo, impedimento.

obstetrics [ɔb'stetriks] *n* ostetricia.

obstinacy ['ɔbstinəsi] *n* ostinazione.

obstinate ['ɔbstinit] *a* ostinato.

obstinately ['ɔbstinitli] *ad* ostinatamente.

obstreperous [əb'strepərəs] *a* indisciplinato, rumoroso.

obstruct [əb'strʌkt] *vt* ostruire; ritardare, impedire.

obstruction [əb'strʌkʃən] *n* ostacolo, ostruzione.

obstructive [ɔb'strʌktiv] *a* ostruente, ostruttivo.

obtain [əb'tein] *vt* ottenere.

obtrude [əb'tru:d] *vti* imporre, imporsi, intromettersi.

obtuse [əb'tju:s] *a* ottuso.

obviate ['ɔbvieit] *vt* ovviare a.

obvious ['ɔbviəs] *a* ovvio, evidente.

occasion [ə'keiʒən] *n* occasione; motivo.

occasional [ə'keiʒənl] *a* occasionale, accidentale, di quando in quando.

occasionally [ə'keiʒnli] *ad* di quando in quando, occasionalmente.

occult [ɔ'kʌlt] *a* occulto.

occupancy ['ɔkjupənsi] *n* occupazione, presa di possesso.

occupant ['ɔkjupənt] *n* occupante, locatario.

occupation [ˌɔkju'peiʃən] *n* occupazione; impiego, professione.

occupy ['ɔkjupai] *vt* occupare, prendere possesso di; impiegare.

occur [ə'kə:] *vi* accadere; venire in mente a; ricorrere.

occurrence [ə'kʌrəns] *n* avvenimento, evento.

ocean ['ouʃən] *n* oceano.

ochre ['oukə] *n* ocra.

o'clock [ə'klɔk] **it is two o.** sono le due.

octave ['ɔktiv] *n* ottava.

October [ɔk'toubə] *n* ottobre.

octopus ['ɔktəpəs] *n* piovra, polipo.

octosyllable ['ɔktou.siləbl] *a* ottosillabico; *n* ottonario.

ocular ['ɔkjulə] *a* oculare.

oculist ['ɔkjulist] *n* oculista.

odd [ɔd] *a* dispari, scompagnato; occasionale; bizzarro, strano.

oddity ['ɔditi] *n* stranezza, singolarità; persona eccentrica.

oddment ['ɔdmənt] *n* (*usu pl*) scampoli, rimanenze.

oddness ['ɔdnis] *n* disparità; bizzarria; stranezza.

odds [ɔdz] *n pl* differenza; disaccordo; probabilità; vantaggio; **o. and ends** *pl* avanzi, resti, cianfrusaglie *pl*.

ode [oud] *n* ode.

odious ['oudiəs] *a* odioso.

odium ['oudiəm] *n* odio, odiosità.

odorous ['oudərəs] *a* fragrante, odoroso.

odour ['oudə] *n* odore; reputazione.

odyssey ['ɔdisi] *n* odissea.

oesophagus [i:'sɔfəgəs] *n* esofago.

of [ɔv] *prep* di; a, in; da.

off [ɔf] *ad* via, lontano, a distanza; *prep* (via) da, distante da; *a* esterno; laterale; remoto; libero; **o.-peak** di consumo ridotto.

offal ['ɔfəl] *n* regaglie; rifiuti *pl*.

offence [ə'fens] *n* offesa; colpa, reato, trasgressione.

offend [ə'fend] *vti* offendere; trasgredire.

offender [ə'fendə] *n* offensore, delinquente, reo.

offensive [ə'fensiv] *n* offensiva; *a* offensivo; aggressivo.

offer ['ɔfə] *n* offerta, proposta; *vti* offrir(si), presentar(si).

offering ['ɔfəriŋ] *n* offerta; sacrificio.

offertory ['ɔfətəri] *n* offertorio; (*collection*) colletta.

offhand ['ɔf'hænd] *a* casuale; improvvisato; alla buona; *ad* lì per lì.

office ['ɔfis] *n* ufficio, carica, ministero; (*US*) gabinetto medico.

officer ['ɔfisə] *n* ufficiale.

official [ə'fiʃəl] *a* ufficiale; *n* funzionario, impiegato, ufficiale.

officiate [ə'fiʃieit] *vi* esercitare le funzioni di; (*eccl*) officiare.

officious [ə'fiʃəs] *a* intromettente; ufficioso.

offing ['ɔfiŋ] *n* largo, mare aperto, distanza dalla costa; **in the o.** al largo; (*fig*) in vista.

offset ['ɔfsət] *n* compenso, equivalente; germoglio; rampollo; *vt* controbilanciare.

offshoot ['ɔfʃuːt] *n* germoglio; derivato.

offside ['ɔf'said] *n* (*football etc*) fuori gioco.

offspring ['ɔfspriŋ] *n* prole, rampollo; prodotto.

often ['ɔfn] *ad* spesso.

ogle ['ougl] *vt* adocchiare, guardare sottecchi.

ogre ['ougə] *n* orco.

oil [ɔil] *n* olio; petrolio; *vt* lubrificare, ungere; **oilcloth** tela cerata; **o. pan** (*US aut*) coppa; **oilskin** tela impermeabile; **fuel o.** nafta.

oily ['ɔili] *a* oleoso, untuoso.

ointment ['ɔintmənt] *n* unguento, pomata.

old [ould] *a* vecchio; antico; usato; **o.-fashioned** antiquato.

olden ['ouldən] *a* antico.

oleander [ˌouli'ændə] *n* oleandro.

oligarchy ['ɔligɑːki] *n* oligarchia.

olive ['ɔliv] *a* d'oliva; d'olivo; olivastro; *n* olivo, oliva.

omelet(te) ['ɔmlit] *n* frittata.

omen ['oumen] *n* augurio, presagio.

ominous ['ɔminəs] *a* sinistro, infausto.

omission [ou'miʃən] *n* omissione.

omit [ou'mit] *vt* omettere.

omnibus ['ɔmnibəs] *pl* **-buses** *n* (*usu* **bus**) autobus, omnibus.

omnipotence [ɔm'nipətəns] *n* onnipotenza.

omnipotent [ɔm'nipətənt] *a* onnipotente.

on [ɔn] *prep* su, sopra; a; di; in; per; *ad* addosso; indosso; avanti; in poi; **off and o.** di quando in quando, intermittentemente.

once [wʌns] *ad* una volta, un tempo; *cj* una volta che.

on-coming ['ɔn,kʌmiŋ] *a* prossimo, che si avvicina.

one [wʌn] *a* uno; unico, uno solo; *pron* uno; si; questo, quello, codesto; **o. another** l'un l'altro; si; **o.-sided** unilaterale; **o.-way ticket** (*US*) biglietto d'andata; **o.-way traffic** circolazione a senso unico.

oneness ['wʌnnis] *n* identità, unione, accordo.

onerous ['ɔnərəs] *a* oneroso.

onion ['ʌnjən] *n* cipolla.

onlooker ['ɔn,lukə] *n* spettatore.

only ['ounli] *a* solo, unico; *ad* solo, solamente, soltanto, unicamente: *cj* eccetto che.

onset ['ɔnset] *n* inizio.

onslaught ['ɔnslɔːt] *n* aggressione, assalto.

onto ['ɔntu] *prep* su, sopra.

onus ['ounəs] *n* peso, onere, responsabilità.

onward ['ɔnwəd] *a* avanzato; progressivo; **onwards** *ad* (in) avanti.

onyx ['ɔniks] *n* onice.

ooze [uːz] *n* melma, fango; *vi* colare, fluire lentamente; **to o. out** trapelare.

oozy ['uːzi] *a* melmoso.

opal ['oupəl] *n* opale.

opaque [ou'peik] *a* opaco.

open ['oupən] *a* aperto; franco; libero; **in the o.** *ad* all'aperto; **o. air** l'aria aperta, l'aperto; *vti* aprir(si).

opener ['oupnə] *n* tin, can o. apriscatole; **bottle o.** apribottiglie.

open-eyed ['oupn'aid] *a ad* ad occhi aperti.

open-handed ['oupn'hændid] *a* generoso.

open-hearted ['oupən,hɑːtid] *a* cordiale, espansivo.

opening ['oupəniŋ] *a* che si apre, inaugurale, iniziale; *n* apertura, inaugurazione, inizio.

openly ['oupənli] *ad* apertamente; pubblicamente.

openness ['oupənnis] *n* (*fig*) franchezza.

opera ['ɔpərə] *pl* **operas** *n* opera.

operate ['ɔpəreit] *vti* operare; **operating room** (*or* **theatre**) *n* sala operatoria.

operation [ˌɔpə'reiʃən] *n* operazione; azione.

operative ['ɔpərətiv] *a* efficace; operativo, operante; operatorio; attivo, *n* lavorante, operaio.

operator ['ɔpəreitə] *n* operatore.

Ophelia [ɔ'fiːliə] *nf pr* Ofelia.

ophthalmic [ɔf'θælmik] *a* oftalmico.

opiate ['oupiit] *a* oppiato; *n* narcotico.

opine [ou'pain] *vi* opinare, essere del parere.

opinion [ə'pinjən] *n* opinione, parere.

opinionated [ə'pinjəneitid] *a* ostinato, dogmatico.

opium ['oupiəm] *n* oppio.

opponent [ə'pounənt] *n* antagonista, rivale; *a* contrario, opposto.

opportune ['ɔpətjuːn] *a* opportuno.

opportunity [ˌɔpə'tjuːniti] *n* occasione, opportunità.

oppose [ɔ'pouz] *vt* opporre, contrapporre, opporsi a.

opposite ['ɔpəzit] *a* contrario, opposto; *prep* dirimpetto a, di faccia a; *n* opposto.

opposition [ˌɔpə'ziʃən] *n* opposizione.

oppress [ə'pres] *vt* opprimere.

oppression [ə'preʃən] n oppressione.
oppressive [ə'presiv] a oppressivo.
opprobrious [ə'proubriəs] a obbrobrioso.
opt [ɔpt] vi optare.
optic ['ɔptik] a ottico.
optical ['ɔptikəl] a ottico.
optician [ɔp'tiʃən] n ottico.
optics ['ɔptiks] n ottica.
optimism ['ɔptimizəm] n ottimismo.
optimist ['ɔptimist] n ottimista.
optimistic [ˌɔpti'mistik] a ottimistico.
option ['ɔpʃən] n opzione, scelta.
optional ['ɔpʃənl] a facoltativo.
opulence ['ɔpjuləns] n opulenza.
opulent ['ɔpjulənt] a opulento.
or [ɔː] cj o, oppure.
oracle ['ɔrəkl] n oracolo.
oral ['ɔːrəl] a orale.
orange ['ɔrindʒ] a di color arancio, arancione; n arancia; (tree, colour) arancio.
oration [ɔː'reiʃən] n orazione; discorso.
orator ['ɔrətə] n oratore.
oratory ['ɔrətəri] n oratorio.
orb [ɔːb] n cerchio; globo; orbita.
orbit ['ɔːbit] n orbita.
Orcadian [ɔː'keidiən] a delle isole Orcadi; n abitante delle isole Orcadi.
orchard ['ɔːtʃəd] n frutteto.
orchestra ['ɔːkistrə] n orchestra; **o. seat** (US theat) poltrona.
orchid ['ɔːkid] n orchidea.
ordain [ɔː'dein] vt ordinare; decretare.
ordeal [ɔː'diːl] n cimento, dura prova.
order ['ɔːdə] n ordine; (com) ordinazione; **in o. that** affinchè; vt ordinare.
orderliness ['ɔːdəlinis] n ordine, disciplina.
orderly ['ɔːdəli] a ordinato, disciplinato; n (mil) ordinanza.
ordinal ['ɔːdinl] a n ordinale.
ordinance ['ɔːdinəns] n decreto, ordinanza.
ordinary ['ɔːdnri] a ordinario, comune, solito.
ordination [ˌɔːdi'neiʃən] n (eccl) ordinazione.
ordnance ['ɔːdnəns] n (mil) artiglieria; sussistenza.
ore [ɔː] n minerale.
organ ['ɔːgən] n organo.
organic [ɔː'gænik] a organico.
organism ['ɔːgənizəm] n organismo.
organist ['ɔːgənist] n organista.
organization [ˌɔːgənai'zeiʃən] n organizzazione.
organize ['ɔːgənaiz] vt organizzare.
organizer ['ɔːgənaizə] n organizzatore.
orgasm ['ɔːgæzəm] n orgasmo, eccitazione.
orgy ['ɔːdʒi] n orgia.

oriel ['ɔːriəl] n (arch) finestra sporgente.
orient ['ɔːriənt] a n (poet) orientale, oriente; vti orientare, orientarsi.
oriental [ˌɔːri'entl] a orientale.
origin ['ɔridʒin] n origine.
original [ə'ridʒənl] a n originale; a originario.
originality [ə.ridʒ'næliti] n originalità.
originate [ə'ridʒineit] vt originare, dare origine a; vi avere origine.
Orkney Islands ['ɔːkni'ailəndz] n Isole Orcadi.
ornament ['ɔːnəmənt] n ornamento; vt adornare, ornare.
ornamental [ˌɔːnə'mentl] a ornamentale.
ornate [ɔː'neit] a adorno, ornato, riccamente decorato.
ornithology [ˌɔːni'θɔlədʒi] n ornitologia.
ornithologist [ˌɔːni'θɔlədʒist] n ornitologo.
orphan ['ɔːfən] a n orfano; vt rendere orfano.
orphanage ['ɔːfənidʒ] n brefotrofio, orfanotrofio.
Orpheus ['ɔːtjuːs] nm pr Orfeo.
orthodox ['ɔːθədɔks] a ortodosso.
orthodoxy ['ɔːθədɔksi] n ortodossia.
orthography [ɔː'θɔgrəfi] n ortografia.
orthopaedic [ˌɔːθou'piːdik] a ortopedico.
Oscar ['ɔskə] nm pr Oscar.
oscillate ['ɔsileit] vi oscillare; vt (far) oscillare.
oscillation [ˌɔsi'leiʃən] n oscillazione.
osier ['ouʒə] n vimine.
osprey ['ɔspri] n ossifraga.
Ostend [ɔs'tend] n Ostenda.
ostensible [ɔs'tensəbl] a apparente; finto.
ostensibly [ɔs'tensibli] ad apparentemente, con il pretesto di.
ostentation [ˌɔsten'teiʃən] n ostentazione; sfarzo.
ostentatious [ˌɔsten'teiʃəs] a ostentato; sfarzoso.
ostler ['ɔslə] n stalliere.
ostracism ['ɔstrəsizəm] n ostracismo.
ostracize ['ɔstrəsaiz] vt dare l'ostracismo a, bandire.
ostrich ['ɔstriʃ] n struzzo.
other ['ʌðə] a pron altro.
Othello [ou'θelou] nm pr Otello.
otherwise ['ʌðəwaiz] ad altrimenti.
otter ['ɔtə] n lontra.
ought [ɔːt] v aux impers (al condizionale) dovere.
ounce [auns] (abbr oz) oncia.
our ['auə] a (il) nostro etc; **ours** pron (il) nostro etc; **ourselves** pron ci, noi stessi.
oust [aust] vt espellere; soppiantare.
out [aut] ad fuori; **o. of** prep fuori da, fuori di; a motivo di, per; **o. of date** fuori moda; arcaico; **o. of door(s)** all'aperto, fuori di casa.

outbid [aut'bid] *vt* offrire un prezzo più alto.

outbreak ['aut'breik] *n* eruzione; scoppio; sommossa.

outburst ['aut'bə:st] *n* esplosione; (*fig*) scoppio, accesso.

outcast ['autka:st] *a n* abbandonato, reietto.

outcome ['autkʌm] *n* esito, risultato.

outcry ['autkrai] *n* clamore, grido; scalpore.

outdo [aut'du:] *vt* superare.

outdoor ['autdɔ:] *a* all'aperto.

outer ['autə] *a* esteriore; esterno.

outermost ['autəmoust] *a* estremo; il più remoto.

outfit ['autfit] *n* corredo, equipaggiamento.

outfitter ['autfitə] *n* fornitore (di articoli di abbigliamento).

outgoing [aut'gouiŋ] *a* uscente; in partenza; *n* uscita; *pl* spese.

outgrow [aut'grou] *vt* sorpassare in crescita, diventare troppo grande per.

outhouse ['authaus] *n* edificio annesso.

outing ['autiŋ] *n* passeggiata; gita, scampagnata.

outlandish [aut'lændiʃ] *a* strano; remoto.

outlaw ['aut'lɔ:] *n* bandito, fuori legge; *vt* bandire.

outlay ['aut'lei] *n* spesa.

outlet ['autlet] *n* sbocco, uscita.

outline ['autlain] *n* contorno, schizzo; *vt* schizzare, tracciare i contorni di.

outlive [aut'liv] *vt* sopravvivere a.

outlook ['autluk] *n* vista, prospettiva, modo di vedere.

outlying ['aut.laiiŋ] *a* fuori mano, periferico.

outnumber [aut'nʌmbə] *vt* superare in numero.

outpatient ['aut.peiʃənt] *n* malato esterno.

outplay [aut'plei] *vt* superare in un gioco, battere.

outpost ['autpoust] *n* (*mil*) avamposto.

outpouring [aut'pɔ:riŋ] *n* sfogo, effusione.

output ['autput] *n* produzione.

outrage ['autreidʒ] *n* oltraggio; *vt* oltraggiare; violare.

outrageous [aut'reidʒəs] *a* oltraggioso; atroce; eccessivo.

outright ['autrait] *ad* immediatamente, completamente, in blocco; *a* completo.

outrun [aut'rʌn] *vt* oltrepassare, superare.

outset ['autset] *n* inizio, principio.

outside [aut'said] *a* esteriore, esterno, superficiale; *prep* fuori di; all'infuori di; *ad* all'esterno, esternamente, fuori, all'aperto; *n* l'esterno, apparenza esteriore; massimo.

outsider ['aut'saidə] *n* estraneo; (*horse*) cavallo non classificato.

outskirts ['autskə:ts] *n pl* periferia.

outspoken [aut'spoukən] *a* esplicito, franco.

outstanding [aut'stændiŋ] *a* prominente; di rilievo, eminente; (*com*) arretrato, in sospeso.

outstretched [aut'stretʃt] *a* disteso, spiegato, aperto.

outstrip [aut'strip] *vt* distanziare, vincere.

outward ['autwəd] *a* esterno; esteriore, o. **bound** (*naut*) diretto a un porto straniero; **outwards** esternamente.

outwear [aut'wɛə] *vt* durare più a lungo di, logorare con continuo uso.

outweigh [aut'wei] *vt* superare di peso; superare in importanza.

outwit [aut'wit] *vt* superare in furberia.

oval ['ouvəl] *a n* ovale.

ovary ['ouvəri] *n* (*anat*) ovaia; ovario.

ovation [ou'veiʃən] *n* ovazione.

oven ['ʌvn] *n* forno.

over ['ouvə] *prep* su, sopra, al di sopra di; attraverso a; *ad* al di sopra; dall'altra parte; in aggiunta; di nuovo, completamente, dal principio alla fine; *a* eccessivo.

overall ['ouvərɔ:l] *a* completo, globale; *n* (*usu pl*) grembiule; tuta.

overbalance [.ouvə'bæləns] *n* eccedenza; *vti* superare di peso; (far) perdere l'equilibrio.

overbearing [.ouvə'bɛəriŋ] *a* imperioso, prepotente.

overboard ['ouvəbɔ:d] *ad* fuori bordo, in mare.

overburden [.ouvə'bə:dn] *vt* sovraccaricare.

overcast ['ouvəka:st] *a* coperto di nubi; *vt* offuscare; cucire a sopraggitto.

overcharge ['ouvə'tʃa:dʒ] *n* sovrapprezzo; *vti* sovraccaricare; chiedere troppo di prezzo.

overcloud [.ouvə'klaud] *vti* coprire di nubi, (r)annuvolarsi.

overcoat ['ouvəkout] *n* soprabito, cappotto.

overcome [.ouvə'kʌm] *vt* vincere, sopraffare.

overconfidence ['ouvə'kɔnfidəns] *n* presunzione; eccessiva sicurezza di sè.

overcrowd [.ouvə'kraud] *vt* affollare all'eccesso.

overdo [.ouvə'du:] *vti* esagerare; cuocere troppo; strafare; affaticare.

overdose ['ouvədous] *n* dose eccessiva.

overdraft ['ouvədra:ft] *n* (*com*) credito allo scoperto.

overdraw ['ouvə'drɔ:] *vt* (*com*) trarre allo scoperto; (*fig*) esagerare.

overdress ['ouvə'dres] *vi* vestire in modo troppo vistoso.

overdrive ['ouvə'draiv] n eccessivo sforzo; eccessivo sfruttamento; (tec) moltiplicatore di velocita; vt affaticare, sfruttare troppo.

overdue ['ouvə'dju:] a (com) in sofferenza, scaduto; in ritardo.

overeat ['ouvər'i:t] vi mangiare troppo.

overestimate ['ouvər'estimeit] vt sopravvalutare.

overexcited ['ouvərik'saitid] a sovraeccitato.

overflow ['ouvə'flou] n traboccamento; [,ouvə'flou] vt inondare; vi stripare, traboccare.

overgrown ['ouvə'groun] a cresciuto troppo; coperto di.

overhang ['ouvəhæŋ] vti incombere su, sovrastare (a).

overhaul ['ouvəho:l] n revisione, verifica, esame accurato; riparazione.

overhead ['ouvəhed] a superiore; ad di sopra, in alto; n pl spese generali pl.

overhear [,ouvə'hiə] vt udire per caso.

overlap [,ouvə'læp] vti sovrapporre, sovrapporsi.

overleaf ['ouvə'li:f] ad sul verso, sul retro (della pagina).

overload ['ouvəloud] n sovraccarico; vt sovraccaricare.

overlook [,ouvə'luk] vt guardare dall'alto, sorvegliare; passar sopra, trascurare, non accorgersi di.

overnight ['ouvə'nait] a ad durante la notte.

overpass ['ouvəpa:s] n soprappassaggio; vt [,ouvə'pa:s] sorpassare; trasgredire; ignorare.

overpay ['ouvə'pei] vt pagare più del dovuto.

overpower [,ouvə'pauə] vt sopraffare, vincere.

overpowering [,ouvə'pauəriŋ] a schiacciante, irresistibile.

overrate ['ouvə'reit] vt sopravvalutare.

overreach [,ouvə'ri:tʃ] vti oltrepassare, spingersi al di là di; to o. oneself fare il passo più lungo della gamba.

override ['ouvə'raid] vti far scorrerie; (fig) infrangere, annullare, non tener conto di.

overrun [,ouvə'rʌn] vt invadere; oltrepassare.

oversea(s) ['ouvə'si:(z)] a d'oltre mare; ad oltremare.

overseer ['ouvəsiə] n capo operaio, sopraintendente.

overshadow [,ouvə'ʃædou] vt ombreggiare; (fig) oscurare, eclissare.

overshoe ['ouvəʃu:] n soprascarpa.

oversight ['ouvəsait] n svista; sorveglianza.

oversleep ['ouvə'sli:p] vi dormire oltre l'ora giusta.

overspill ['ouvəspil] n l'eccesso, l'in più.

overstate ['ouvə'steit] vt esagerare.

overstatement ['ouvə'steitmənt] n esagerazione.

overstrain ['ouvə'strein] vti sforzar(si) eccessivamente.

overt ['ouvə:t] a aperto, pubblico, visibile.

overtake [,ouvə'teik] vt raggiungere; sorpassare.

overtax ['ouvə'tæks] vt abusare di; gravare di imposte.

overthrow ['ouvəθrou] n rovesciamento, disfatta; vt [,ouvə'θrou] rovesciare, abbattere.

overtime ['ouvətaim] n lavoro straordinario.

overtire ['ouvə'taiə] vt stancare troppo, strapazzare.

overtop ['ouvə'tɔp] vt sovrastare, superare di altezza.

overture ['ouvətjuə] n offerta, proposta; (mus) preludio, sinfonia.

overturn ['ouvətə:n] vti capovolgere, rovesciar(si).

overweight ['ouvəweit] a che supera il peso; n eccedenza di peso.

overwhelm [,ouvə'welm] vt sopraffare, opprimere, schiacciare.

overwork ['ouvə'wə:k] vti (far) lavorare troppo.

overwrought ['ouvə'rɔ:t] a esausto; sovreccitato; troppo ornato.

owe [ou] vt dovere, essere in debito di.

owing ['ouiŋ] a dovuto, che resta da pagare; o. to prep a causa di.

owl [aul] n civetta; gufo.

own [oun] a proprio; vti possedere; confessare, riconoscere.

owner ['ounə] n possessore, proprietario.

ownership ['ounəʃip] n proprietà, possesso.

ox [ɔks] pl oxen n bue.

oxide ['ɔksaid] n ossido.

oxygen ['ɔksidʒən] n ossigeno.

oyster ['ɔistə] n ostrica.

P

pace [peis] n andatura, passo; vt misurare a passi; vi andare al passo.

Pacific [pə'sifik] n Pacifico.

pacific [pə'sifik] a pacifico.

pacifism ['pæsifizəm] n pacifismo.

pacifist ['pæsifist] n pacifista.

pacify ['pæsifai] vt pacificare.

pack [pæk] n pacco, involto; peso; (mil) zaino; (hounds) muta; (cards) mazzo; (ice) banchisa; (thieves) banda; vt imballare, impaccare, stipare; (med) fare impacchi a; to p. up fare le valigie.

package ['pækidʒ] n balla, collo, pacco; p. holiday (or tour) villeggiatura o gita turistica spesata in anticipo.

packet ['pækit] n pacchetto; **p.-boat** (*naut*) vapore postale.

packing ['pækiŋ] n imballaggio; fare le valigie; (*of food*) confezione.

pact [pækt] n patto.

pad [pæd] n blocco di carta; cuscinetto; imbottitura; zampa di animale; (*med*) tampone; vt imbottire; tamponare.

padding ['pædiŋ] n imbottitura.

paddle ['pædl] n (*naut*) pagaia; vt remare con la pagaia; sguazzare nell'acqua.

paddock ['pædək] n recinto per i cavalli da corsa; chiuso.

padlock ['pædlɔk] n lucchetto.

Padua ['pædjuə] n Padova; **Paduan** a n padovano.

pagan ['peigən] a n pagano.

page [peidʒ] n pagina; paggio; **pageboy** fattorino d'albergo.

pageant ['pædʒənt] n corteo o spettacolo storico.

pageantry ['pædʒəntri] n sfarzo, spettacolo sfarzoso.

pail [peil] n secchia, secchio.

pain [pein] n dolore, male, sofferenza, pena; vt affliggere, far soffrire.

painful ['peinful] a doloroso, penoso.

painfully ['peinfuli] ad dolorosamente, penosamente.

painless ['peinlis] a indolore.

painstaking ['peinz,teikiŋ] a coscienzioso.

paint [peint] n pittura; vernice; colore; belletto; vt dipinger(si).

painter ['peintə] n pittore; decoratore; imbianchino.

painting ['peintiŋ] n pittura; quadro.

pair [pɛə] n paio, coppia; vt accoppiare, appaiare; vi accoppiarsi.

Pakistan [,pɑːkis'tɑːn] n Pakistan.

Pakistani [,pɑːkis'tɑːni] a n pachistano.

palace ['pælis] n palazzo.

paladin ['pælədin] n paladino.

palatable ['pælətəbl] a gradevole.

palate ['pælit] n palato; gusto.

palaver [pə'lɑːvə] n discussione, chiacchiere.

pale [peil] a pallido, scialbo, chiaro; n palo; palizzata; vi impallidire.

paleness ['peilnis] n pallore.

Palestine ['pælistain] n Palestina.

Palestinian [,pæles'tiniən] a n palestinese.

palette ['pælit] n tavolozza.

palisade [,pæli'seid] n palizzata.

pall [pɔːl] n coltre funebre; vi diventare insipido, non essere più interessante.

pallet ['pælit] n giaciglio, pagliericcio.

palliasse ['pæliæs] n pagliericcio.

palliate ['pælieit] vt mitigare.

palliative ['pæliətiv] a n palliativo.

pallid ['pælid] a pallido.

pallor ['pælə] n pallore.

palm [pɑːm] n (*tree*) palma; (*hand*) palmo.

palpable ['pælpəbl] a palpabile; evidente.

palpitate ['pælpiteit] vi palpitare.

palpitation [,pælpi'teiʃən] n palpitazione.

palsy ['pɔːlzi] n paralisi.

palter ['pɔːltə] vi tergiversare.

paltry ['pɔːltri] a di poco valore, meschino.

pamper ['pæmpə] vt trattare con soverchia indulgenza, viziare.

pamphlet ['pæmflit] n opuscolo.

pan [pæn] n padella, tegame.

pancake ['pænkeik] n frittella.

pandemonium ['pændi'mouniəm] n pandemonio.

pander ['pændə] n mezzano, ruffiano; vi fare il mezzano; (*fig*) accarezzare i gusti.

pane [pein] n vetro di finestra.

panegyric [,pæni'dʒirik] n panegirico.

panel ['pænl] n pannello; commissione; **p. doctor** dottore della mutua.

pang [pæŋ] n dolore acuto, spasimo.

panic ['pænik] n panico.

panorama [,pænə'rɑːmə] n panorama.

pansy ['pænzi] n viola del pensiero.

pant [pænt] n palpitazione, palpito; vi ansimare; desiderare ardentemente.

pantaloons [,pæntə'luːns] n pl pantaloni pl.

pantheism ['pænθiːizəm] n panteismo.

panther ['pænθə] n pantera.

pantomime ['pæntəmaim] n pantomima.

pantry ['pæntri] n dispensa.

pap [pæp] n pappa.

papa [pə'pɑː] n papà, babbo.

papacy ['peipəsi] n papato.

papal ['peipəl] a papale.

paper ['peipə] n carta; documento; giornale; dissertazione, saggio; vt tappezzare; **wrapping p.** carta da imballaggio; **waste p.** carta straccia.

paper-hanger ['peipə,hæŋə] n tappezziere.

paper-mill ['peipəmil] n cartiera.

papist ['peipist] n papista.

papyrus [pə'paiərəs] n papiro.

par [pɑː] n pari, parità.

parable ['pærəbl] n parabola.

parachute ['pærəʃuːt] n paracadute.

parachutist ['pærəʃuːtist] n paracadutista.

parade [pə'reid] n mostra; parata, sfilata, rivista; vt far mostra di; vi sfilare in parata.

paradise ['pærədais] n paradiso.

paradox ['pærədɔks] n paradosso.

paradoxical [pærə'dɔksikəl] a paradossale.

paraffin ['pærəfin] n paraffina, petrolio.

paragon ['pærəgən] n paragone, modello.

paragraph ['pærəgrɑːf] n paragrafo, capoverso.

Paraguay ['pærəgwai] n Paraguai.

Paraguayan [ˌpærəˈgwaiən] a n paraguaiano.

parallel ['pærəlel] a parallelo; n parallela; parallelo; confronto.

paralyse ['pærəlaiz] vt paralizzare.

paralysis [pəˈrælisis] n paralisi.

paralytic [ˌpærəˈlitik] a n paralitico.

paramount ['pærəmaunt] a sovrano, supremo.

parapet ['pærəpit] n parapetto.

paraphernalia [ˌpærəfəˈneiliə] n (fam) armamentario, roba.

paraphrase ['pærəfreiz] n parafrasi.

parapsychology ['pærəsaiˈkɔlədʒi] n metapsichica.

parasite ['pærəsait] n parassita.

parasol ['pærəsol] n ombrellino, parasole.

paratrooper ['pærətruːpə] n paracadutista.

paratyphoid ['pærəˈtaifɔid] n paratifo.

parboil ['pɑːbɔil] vt bollire parzialmente.

parcel ['pɑːsl] n pacco; pezzo di terra; vt to p. up impaccare.

parch [pɑːtʃ] vt disseccare, inaridire; vi diventare riarso.

parchment ['pɑːtʃmənt] n pergamena.

pardon ['pɑːdn] n perdono, amnistia; vt perdonare.

pardonable ['pɑːdnəbl] a perdonabile, scusabile.

pare [pɛə] vt (fruit) sbucciare; (nails) tagliare.

parent ['pɛərənt] n genitore m, genitrice f genitori pl.

parentage ['pɛərəntidʒ] n origini, natali pl.

parental [pəˈrentl] a paterno, materno, di genitori.

parenthesis [pəˈrenθisis] n parentesi.

Paris ['pæris] n Parigi.

parish ['pæriʃ] n parrocchia.

parishioner [pəˈriʃənə] n parrocchiano.

Parisian [pəˈriziən] a n parigino.

park [pɑːk] n parco; (aut) posteggio.

parking ['pɑːkiŋ] n (aut) parcheggio, posteggio; (US) aiuola spartitraffico; p. meter contatore per parcheggio; p. place, (US) p. lot area per parcheggio, posteggio.

parlance ['pɑːləns] n parlata, gergo.

parley ['pɑːli] n discussione, parlamento; vi discutere, parlamentare.

parliament ['pɑːləmənt] n parlamento.

parliamentary [ˌpɑːləˈmentəri] a parlamentare.

parlour ['pɑːlə] n salotto.

Parmesan [ˌpɑːmiˈzæn] a parmigiano.

parochial [pəˈroukiəl] a parrocchiale.

parody ['pærədi] n parodia; vt parodiare.

paroxysm ['pærəksizəm] n parossismo.

parricide ['pærisaid] n parricida, parricidio.

parrot ['pærət] n pappagallo.

parry ['pæri] n parata; vt evitare; parare.

parse [pɑːz] vt fare l'analisi (grammaticale o logica) di.

parsimonious [ˌpɑːsiˈmouniəs] a parsimonioso, economo.

parsimony ['pɑːsiməni] n parsimonia, economia.

parsley ['pɑːsli] n prezzemolo.

parsnip ['pɑːsnip] n pastinaca.

parson ['pɑːsn] n parroco (anglicano); (fam) pastore.

part [pɑːt] n parte; vtl divider(si), separar(si).

partake [pɑːˈteik] vi partecipare.

partial ['pɑːʃəl] a parziale, propenso verso.

partiality [ˌpɑːʃiˈæliti] n parzialità; favoritismo; predilezione.

participant [pɑːˈtisipənt] a partecipe; n partecipante.

participate [pɑːˈtisipeit] vi partecipare; prendere parte a.

participation [pɑːˌtisiˈpeiʃən] n partecipazione.

participle ['pɑːtisipl] n (gram) participio.

particle ['pɑːtikl] n particella; (eccl) particola.

particular [pəˈtikjulə] a particolare, speciale; minuzioso; n particolare, dettaglio; informazione; in p. in particolare.

particularly [pəˈtikjuləli] ad particolarmente, dettagliatamente.

parting ['pɑːtiŋ] n separazione; congedo; (hair) scriminatura, divisa.

partisan [ˌpɑːtiˈzæn] a n partigiano.

partition [pɑːˈtiʃən] n divisione; spartizione; tramezzo.

partly ['pɑːtli] ad in parte.

partner ['pɑːtnə] n compagno, ballerina, -no, marito, moglie; (com) socio; partnership (com) società, associazione.

partridge ['pɑːtridʒ] n pernice.

party ['pɑːti] n partito; brigata; trattenimento, festa, festicciola; (leg) parte in causa.

pass [pɑːs] n passo, valico; situazione; passaggio; (mil) permesso, lasciapassare; vti passare; accadere; vt attraversare; superare; approvare (una legge); to p. away morire; to p. by passare davanti a; passare sotto silenzio.

passable ['pɑːsəbl] a discreto, passabile; attraversabile.

passage ['pæsidʒ] n passaggio; traversata; varco; corridoio; brano.

passenger ['pæsindʒə] n passeggiero, viaggiatore.

passer-by ['pɑːsə'bai] n passante.

passing ['pɑːsiŋ] a passante; passeggiero, casuale; n passaggio; trapasso, morte.

passion ['pæʃən] n passione.

passionate ['pæʃənit] a appassionato; passionale; irascibile.

passive ['pæsiv] a n passivo.

passport ['pɑːspɔːt] n passaporto.

password ['pɑːswəːd] n parola d'ordine.

past [pɑːst] a passato, scorso; finito; prep al di là di; ad oltre; n passato.

paste [peist] n pasta; colla; vt incollare.

pasteboard ['peistbɔːd] n cartone grosso.

pastel ['pæstəl] n pastello.

pastime ['pɑːstaim] n passatempo.

pastor ['pɑːstə] n (eccl) pastore.

pastoral ['pɑːstərəl] a n pastorale.

pastry ['peistri] n pasticceria; **p. board** asse per la pasta.

pasture ['pɑːstʃə] n pascolo, pastura; vti far pascolare.

pat [pæt] n colpetto, tocco leggero; panetto di burro; a pronto, adatto; ad a proposito; vt accarezzare, dare un piccolo colpo su, dare un buffetto a.

patch [pætʃ] n toppa; piccolo pezzo di terreno; macchia; vt rattoppare, mettere insieme alla meglio; **patchwork** rappezzatura, mescolanza, mosaico.

patent ['peitənt] a evidente, ovvio; brevettato, patentato; n brevetto; **p. leather** n cuoio verniciato; vt brevettare.

patentee [.peitən'tiː] n detentore di brevetto.

paternal [pə'təːnl] a paterno.

paternity [pə'təːniti] n paternità.

path [pɑːθ] n sentiero, viottolo.

pathetic [pə'θetik] a commovente, patetico.

pathfinder ['pɑːθ.faində] n esploratore, pioniere.

pathologic(al) [.pæθə'lɔdʒik(əl)] a patologico.

pathology [pə'θɔlədʒi] n patologia.

pathos ['peiθɔs] n pathos, commozione.

pathway ['pɑːθwei] n sentiero.

patience ['peiʃəns] n pazienza.

patient ['peiʃənt] a n paziente.

patriarch ['peitriɑːk] n patriarca.

patriarchal [.peitri'ɑːkəl] a patriarcale.

Patricia [pə'triʃə] nf pr Patrizia.

patrician [pə'triʃən] a n patrizio.

Patrick ['pætrik] nm pr Patrizio.

patrimony ['pætriməni] n patrimonio.

patriot ['peitriət] n patriota.

patriotic [.pætri'ɔtik] a patriottico.

patriotism ['pætriətizəm] n patriottismo.

patrol [pə'troul] n (mil) pattuglia; vt perlustrare; vi pattugliare.

patrolman [pə'troulmæn] pl -men n (US) poliziotto.

patron ['peitrən] n patrono, mecenate.

patronage ['pætrənidʒ] n patronato, patrocinio; (shop) concorso di avventori.

patronize ['pætrənaiz] vt patrocinare; trattare con aria condiscendente; essere cliente abituale di.

patter ['pætə] n picchiettio, scalpitio; (rain) ticchettio; parlata, cicaleccio; vi picchiettare; camminare con passetti rapidi; parlare meccanicamente.

pattern ['pætən] n campione, modello.

Paul [pɔːl] nm pr Paolo.

Pauline ['pɔːliːn] nf pr Paola, Paolina.

paunch ['pɔːntʃ] n pancia, pancione.

pauper ['pɔːpə] n povero, mendicante.

pauperism ['pɔːpərizəm] n indigenza.

pauperize ['pɔːpəraiz] vt impoverire.

pause [pɔːz] n pausa; vi fare una pausa, fermarsi.

pave [peiv] vt pavimentare; (fig) preparare il terreno.

pavement ['peivmənt] n marciapiede, selciato.

pavilion [pə'viljən] n padiglione.

paw [pɔː] n zampa.

pawn [pɔːn] n pegno; (chess) pedina; vt impegnare.

pawnbroker ['pɔːn.broukə] n chi presta denaro su pegno.

pawnshop ['pɔːnʃɔp] n monti di pegni.

pay [pei] n paga, salario, retribuzione; vt pagare, rimunerare; vi dar frutti, rendere.

payable ['peiəbl] a pagabile.

payment ['peimənt] n pagamento, saldo.

pea [piː] n pisello.

peace [piːs] n pace, ordine pubblico; **peacemaker** paciere.

peaceable ['piːsəbl] **peaceful** ['piːsful] a pacifico, tranquillo.

peach [piːtʃ] n pesca.

peacock ['piːkɔk] n pavone.

peak [piːk] n cima, picco; punta; visiera.

peal [piːl] n scampanio; salva d'artiglieria; scroscio; rombo; vi risuonare, scampanare, tuonare.

peanut ['piːnʌt] n arachide, nocciolina americana; **p. butter** pasta di arachidi.

pear [peə] n pera; **p. tree** pero.

pearl [pəːl] n perla.

peasant ['pezənt] n contadino; a contadinesco, rustico.

peasantry ['pezəntri] n contadini pl.

peat [piːt] n torba.

pebble ['pebl] n ciottolo, sassolino.

peck [pek] vti beccare.

peculiar [pi'kju:liə] *a* peculiare, particolare; strano.

peculiarity [pi.kju:li'æriti] *n* caratteristica.

peculiarly [pi'kju:liəli] *ad* particolarmente; stranamente.

pecuniary [pi'kju:niəri] *a* pecuniario.

pedagogue ['pedəgɔg] *n* pedagogo.

pedal ['pedl] *n* pedale.

pedant ['pedənt] *n* pedante.

pedantic [pe'dæntik] *a* pedantesco, pedante.

pedantry ['pedəntri] *n* pedanteria.

peddle ['pedl] *vt* vendere al minuto; *vi* fare il venditore ambulante.

pedestal ['pedistl] *n* piedistallo.

pedestrian [pi'destriən] *a* pedestre; *n* pedone.

pedigree ['pedigri:] *n* albero genealogico; (*animals*) pedigree.

pedlar ['pedlə] *n* venditore ambulante.

peel [pi:l] *n* buccia; *vt* sbucciare.

peep [pi:p] *n* occhiata, sguardo furtivo o timido; *vi* far capolino, guardare furtivamente, lasciarsi intravedere, spuntare.

peer [piə] *n* pari; *vi* spuntare; scrutare.

peerage ['piərid3] *n* la nobiltà; almanacco nobiliare.

peevish ['pi:viʃ] *a* stizzoso, irritabile.

peewit ['pi:wit] *n* pavoncella.

peg [peg] *n* cavicchio, piuolo; molletta; (*fam*) bevanda alcoolica.

Pekinese [,pi:ki'ni:z] *a n* pechinese.

Peking [pi:'kiŋ] *n* Pechino.

pelf [pelf] *n* denaro, lucro.

pelican ['pelikən] *n* pellicano.

pellet ['pelit] *n* pallina; pallottola; pillola.

pell-mell ['pel'mel] *n* confusione, mischia; *ad* confusamente, alla rinfusa.

pelt [pelt] *n* pelle grezza; scroscio di pioggia; velocità; colpo di proiettile; *vt* colpire; *vi* (*of rain*) battere con violenza, correre.

pelvis ['pelvis] *n* (*anat*) pelvi, bacino.

pen [pen] *n* penna; piccolo recinto per animali; *vt* scrivere; chiudere (animali) in un recinto; **penpoint** (*US*) pennino; **ballpoint** p. penna a sfera; **fountain** p. penna stilografica.

penal ['pi:nl] *a* penale.

penalize ['pi:nəlaiz] *vt* penalizzare.

penalty ['penlti] *n* penalità, punizione; **p. kick** (*football*) calcio di rigore; **p. stroke** (*golf*) colpo di ammenda.

penance ['penəns] *n* penitenza.

pencil ['pensl] *n* matita.

pendant ['pendənt] *n* ciondolo, pendente.

pending ['pendiŋ] *a* pendente; in sospeso; *prep* durante, fino a.

pendulum ['pendjuləm] *n* pendolo.

penetrate ['penitreit] *vti* penetrare.

penetration [,peni'treiʃən] *n* penetrazione, acutezza.

penguin ['pengwin] *n* pinguino.

penicillin [,peni'silin] *n* penicillina.

peninsula [pi'ninsjulə] *n* penisola.

peninsular [pi'ninsjulə] *a* peninsulare.

penitence ['penitəns] *n* penitenza.

penitent ['penitənt] *a n* penitente.

penitentiary [,peni'tenʃəri] *a* penitenziale; *n* riformatorio, (*US*) penitenzario.

penknife ['pennaif] *n* temperino.

penniless ['penilis] *a* senza un soldo.

penny ['peni] *n* 'penny', soldo; **penny-farthing** bicicletta antiquata; **penny-worth** un soldo di.

pension ['penʃən] *n* pensione; *vt* pensionare.

pensioner ['penʃənə] *n* pensionato, pensionata.

pensive ['pensiv] *a* malinconico, pensoso.

pensiveness ['pensivnis] *n* malinconia.

Pentecost ['pentikɔst] *n* Pentecoste.

penthouse *n* tettoia; (*US*) appartamento sul tetto di un edificio.

penurious [pi'njuəriəs] *a* bisognoso; avaro.

penury ['penjuri] *n* penuria.

peony ['piəni] *n* peonia.

people ['pi:pl] *n* popolo, nazione; (*costruzione pl*) gente, parenti *pl*; *vt* popolare.

pep [pep] *n* (*sl*) iniziativa, vigore.

pepper ['pepə] *n* pepe.

peppercorn ['pepəkɔ:n] *n* grano di pepe.

peppermint ['pepəmint] *n* menta peperita, caramella di menta.

peppery ['pepəri] *a* pepato; pungente; collerico.

perambulator ['præmbjuleitə] **pram** [præm] *n* carrozzina per bambini.

perceive [pə'si:v] *vt* percepire, accorgersi di, scorgere.

percentage [pə'sentid3] *n* percentuale.

perceptible [pə'septəbl] *a* percettibile.

perceptibly [pə'septəbli] *ad* in modo percettibile.

perception [pə'sepʃən] *n* percezione; intuizione.

perceptiveness [pə'septivnis] *n* percettività.

perch [pə:tʃ] *n* (*bird's*) posatoio, gruccia; (*measure 25,293 sq metres*) pertica; pesce persico; *vi* appollaiarsi, posarsi.

perchance [pə'tʃa:ns] *ad* (*arc*) forse, per caso.

percolate ['pə:kəleit] *vti* filtrare.

percolator ['pə:kəleitə] *n* filtro; macchina per il caffè.

percussion [pə:'kʌʃən] *n* percussione.

perdition [pə:'diʃən] *n* perdizione.

peremptory [pə'remptəri] *a* perentorio.

perennial [pə'reniəl] *a n* (*of plant*) perenne.

perfect ['pə:fikt] *a n* perfetto; *vt* perfezionare.

perfection [pə'fekʃən] *n* perfezione.

perfectionist [pə'fekʃənist] *n* perfezionista.

perfidy ['pə:fidi] *n* perfidia.

perfidious [pə'fidiəs] *a* perfido.

perforate ['pə:fəreit] *vti* forare; penetrare; (*mech*) perforare.

perform [pə'fɔ:m] *vt* adempiere, compiere; eseguire; rappresentare.

performance [pə'fɔ:məns] *a* adempimento; rappresentazione, recita.

performer [pə'fɔ:mə] *n* esecutore, attore.

perfume ['pə:fju:m] *n* profumo; *vt* profumare.

perfunctory [pə'fʌŋktəri] *a* meccanico, superficiale.

perhaps [pə'hæps] *ad* forse.

peril ['peril] *n* pericolo.

perilous ['periləs] *a* pericoloso.

perilously ['periləsli] *ad* pericolosamente.

period ['piəriəd] *n* epoca, periodo.

periodic [,piəri'ɔdik] *a* periodico.

periodical [,piəri'ɔdikəl] *a n* periodico.

periphery [pə'rifəri] *n* periferia.

periscope ['periskoup] *n* periscopio.

perish ['periʃ] *vti* (far) perire.

perishable ['periʃəbl] *a* deperibile, perituro, deteriorabile.

periwinkle ['peri,wiŋkl] *n* pervinca.

perjure ['pə:dʒə] *vr*; **p. oneself** spergiurare.

perjury ['pə:dʒəri] *n* spergiuro.

perk [pə:k] *vti* **to p. up** drizzare; (*fig*) rallegrare.

perky ['pə:ki] *a* birichino; impertinente.

perm [pə:m] *v* **permanent wave.**

permanence ['pə:mənəns] *n* permanenza.

permanent ['pə:mənənt] *a* permanente; **p. wave** (ondulazione) permanente.

permeate ['pə:mieit] *vt* permeare.

permissible [pə'misəbl] *a* lecito.

permission [pə'miʃən] *n* permesso.

permissive [pə'misiv] *a* che permette, tollerante; permissivo.

permit ['pə:mit] *n* permesso, autorizzazione; *vti* [pə'mit] permettere.

pernicious [pə:'niʃəs] *a* pernicioso, nocivo.

peroration [,perə'reiʃən] *n* perorazione.

peroxide [pə'rɔksaid] *n* (*chem*) perossido.

perpendicular [,pə:pən'dikjulə] *a n* perpendicolare.

perpetrate ['pə:pitreit] *vt* perpetrare.

perpetual [pə'petjuəl] *a* perpetuo.

perpetuate [pə'petjueit] *vt* perpetuare.

perplex [pə'pleks] *vt* imbarazzare, rendere perplesso.

perplexity [pə'pleksiti] *n* perplessità.

perquisite ['pə:kwizit] *n* mancia; guadagno occasionale.

perquisition [,pə:kwi'ziʃən] *n* perquisizione.

persecute ['pə:sikju:t] *vt* perseguitare; importunare.

persecution [,pə:si'kju:ʃən] *n* persecuzione.

persecutor ['pə:sikju:tə] *n* persecutore.

perseverance [,pə:si'viərəns] *n* perseveranza.

persevere [,pə:si'viə] *vi* perseverare

Persia ['pə:ʃə] *n* Persia.

Persian ['pə:ʃən] *a n* persiano.

persist [pə'sist] *vi* persistere, durare.

persistence [pə'sistəns] *n* persistenza, perseveranza.

persistent [pə'sistənt] *a* persistente, tenace.

persistently [pə'sistəntli] *ad* persistentemente, tenacemente.

person ['pə:sn] *n* persona.

personage ['pə:snidʒ] *n* personaggio, personalità.

personal ['pə:snl] *a* personale; **p. business** (*US*) questione personale.

personality [,pə:sə'næliti] *n* personalità.

personally ['pə:snəli] *ad* personalmente.

personification [pə:,sɔnifi'keiʃən] *n* personificazione.

personify [pə:'sɔnifai] *vt* personificare.

personnel [,pə:sə'nel] *n* personale.

perspective [pə'spektiv] *n* prospettiva.

perspicacious [,pə:spi'keiʃəs] *a* perspicace.

perspicacity [,pə:spi'kæsiti] *n* perspicacia.

perspiration [,pə:spə'reiʃən] *n* traspirazione, sudore.

perspire [pəs'paiə] *vi* sudare, traspirare.

persuade [pə'sweid] *vt* persuadere.

persuasion [pə'sweiʒən] *n* persuasione, fede.

persuasive [pə'sweisiv] *a* persuasivo; *n* motivo.

pert [pə:t] *a* impertinente; sveglio.

pertain [pə:'tein] *vi* concernere.

pertinacious [,pə:ti'neiʃəs] *a* pertinace.

pertinent ['pə:tinənt] *a* pertinente, proprio.

pertness ['pə:tnis] *n* impertinenza; vivacità.

perturb [pə'tə:b] *vt* perturbare, turbare.

perturbation [,pə:tə:'beiʃən] *n* turbamento.

Peru [pə'ru:] *n* Perù.

perusal [pə'ru:zəl] *n* lettura attenta.

peruse [pə'ru:z] *vt* leggere attentamente; esaminare.

Peruvian [pə'ru:viən] *a n* peruviano.

pervade [pə:'veid] *vt* pervadere, permeare.

pervasive [pə:'veisiv] *a* penetrante; invadente.

perverse [pə'və:s] *a* perverso.

perversion [pə'və:ʃən] *n* perversione, pervertimento.

perversity [pə'və:siti] *n* perversità.

pervert [pə'və:t] *vt* pervertire.

pessimism ['pesimizəm] *n* pessimismo.

pessimist ['pesimist] *n* pessimista.

pessimistic [.pesi'mistik] *a* pessimistico.

pest [pest] *n* peste, individuo noiosissimo.

pester ['pestə] *vt* importunare, infastidire; infestare.

pestilence ['pestiləns] *n* pestilenza.

pestilent ['pestilənt] *a* pestilenziale.

pestle ['pesl] *n* pestello.

pet [pet] *a* favorito; vezzeggiato; *n* animale favorito, beniamino; cattivo umore, collera; *vt* vezzeggiare.

petal ['petl] *n* petalo.

Peter ['pi:tə] *nm pr* Pietro.

petition [pi'tiʃən] *n* petizione, supplica; *vt* presentare una petizione a.

petitioner [pi'tiʃənə] *n* supplicante, postulante.

petrify ['petrifai] *vt* pietrificare.

petrol ['petrəl] *n* benzina.

petroleum [pi'trouliəm] *n* petrolio.

petticoat ['petikout] *n* sottoveste, sottana.

petty ['peti] *a* piccolo, insignificante, meschino; **p. officer** sottufficiale di marina.

petulant ['petjulənt] *a* petulante.

petunia [pi'tju:niə] *n* (*bot*) petunia.

pew [pju:] *n* banco in chiesa.

pewter ['pju:tə] *n* peltro.

phantom ['fæntəm] *n* fantasma.

Pharaoh ['fɛərou] *n* faraone.

Pharisee ['færisi:] *n* fariseo.

pharmacy ['fɑ:məsi] *n* farmacia, scienza farmaceutica.

phase [feiz] *n* fase.

pheasant ['feznt] *n* fagiano.

phenomenon [fi'nɔminən] *n* fenomeno.

phenomenal [fi'nɔminl] *a* fenomenale; (*phil*) fenomenico.

phial ['faiəl] *n* fiala.

Philadelphia [.filə'delfiə] *n* Filadelfia.

philanderer [fi'lændərə] *n* donnaiolo.

philanthropic [.filən'θrɔpik] *a* filantropico.

philanthropist [fi'lænθrəpist] *n* filantropo.

philanthropy [fi'lænθrəpi] *n* filantropia.

philatelist [fi'lætəlist] *n* filatelico.

philately [fi'lætəli] *n* filatelia.

Philip ['filip] *nm pr* Filippo.

philologist [fi'lɔlədʒist] *n* filologo.

philology [fi'lɔlədʒi] *n* filologia.

philosopher [fi'lɔsəfə] *n* filosofo.

philosophic(al) [.filə'sɔfik(l)] *a* filosofico.

philosophy [fi'lɔsəfi] *n* filosofia.

philter, philtre ['filtə] *n* filtro.

phlegm [flem] *n* flemma.

phlegmatic [fleg'mætik] *a* flemmatico.

phobia ['foubiə] *n* fobia.

phoenix ['fi:niks] *n* fenice.

phonetic [fə'netik] *a* fonetico.

phonetics [fou'netiks] *n pl* fonetica.

phonograph ['founəgrɑ:f] *n* fonografo.

phosphate ['fɔsfeit] *n* fosfato.

phosphorous ['fɔsfərəs] *n* fosforo.

photocopy ['foutoukɔpi] *n* fotocopia.

photoflash ['foutouflæʃ] *n* fotografia al lampo di magnesio.

photograph ['foutəgrɑ:f] *n* fotografia; *vt* fotografare.

photographer [fə'tɔgrəfə] *n* fotografo.

photographic [.foutə'græfik] *a* fotografico.

photography [fə'tɔgrəfi] *n* (*arte fotografica*) fotografia.

photostat ['foutoustæt] *n* apparecchio fotostatico; copia fotostatica.

phrase [freiz] *n* frase.

phraseology [.freizi'ɔlədʒi] *n* fraseologia.

physical ['fizikəl] *a* fisico.

physician [fi'ziʃən] *n* medico.

physicist ['fizisist] *n* fisico.

physics ['fiziks] *n pl* fisica.

physiognomy [.fizi'ɔnəmi] *n* fisionomia.

physiotherapy [.fiziə'θerəpi] *n* fisioterapia.

physique [fi'zi:k] *n* fisico, costituzione fisica.

pianist ['piənist] *n* pianista.

piano [pi'ænou] *n* pianoforte.

pick [pik] *n* piccone; scelta; *vt* cogliere; **p. up** raccogliere; (*rad*) captare; scegliere.

picket ['pikit] *n* (*mil*) picchetto.

pickle ['pikl] *n* salamoia; situazione spiacevole.

pickpocket ['pik,pɔkit] *n* borsaiolo.

pick-up ['pikʌp] *n* (*el*) riproduttore acustico, fonorivelatore, 'pick-up'; (*tv*) dispositivo di presa.

picnic ['piknik] *n* 'pic-nic', scampagnata.

pictorial [pik'tɔ:riəl] *a* pittorico, illustrato.

picture ['piktʃə] *n* dipinto, quadro, ritratto; **pictures** *pl* (*fam*) cinematografo.

picture ['piktʃə] *vt* dipingere, descrivere, figurarsi.

picturesque [.piktʃə'resk] *a* pittoresco.

pie [pai] *n* pasticcio di carne, torta di frutta; (*ornit*) gazza.

piece [pi:s] *n* pezzo; (*material*) pezza;

(*mus*) composizione; **piecework** lavoro a cottimo.

piecemeal ['pi:smi:l] *ad* pezzo a pezzo, a pezzi e a bocconi.

Piedmont ['pi:dmənt] *n* Piemonte; **piedmontese** *a n* piemontese.

pier [piə] *n* banchina, molo; pilastro.

pierce [piəs] *vti* penetrare, forare.

piercing ['piəsiŋ] *a* penetrante; *n* perforamento.

piety ['paiəti] *n* religiosità, pietà.

pig [pig] *n* maiale, porco.

pigeon ['pidʒin] *n* piccione, colombo.

pigeonhole ['pidʒinhoul] *n* nicchia di colombaia; casella; **set of pigeonholes** casellario; *vt* incasellare, archiviare.

pigtail ['pigteil] *n* treccina stretta di capelli, codino.

pike [paik] *n* picca; (*fish*) luccio.

pilchard ['piltʃəd] *n* sardella.

pile [pail] *n* ammasso, mucchio; pira; (*el*) pila; palafitta; (*nap*) pelo; **piles** *pl* (*med*) emorroidi.

pile [pail] *vt* accumulare, ammucchiare, esagerare.

pilfer ['pilfə] *vt* rubacchiare.

pilgrim ['pilgrim] *n* pellegrino.

pilgrimage ['pilgrimidʒ] *n* pellegrinaggio.

pill [pil] *n* pillola.

pillage ['pilidʒ] *n* saccheggio; *vt* saccheggiare.

pillar ['pilə] *n* colonna, pilastro.

pillory ['piləri] *n* berlina, gogna; *vt* mettere alla berlina.

pillow ['pilou] *n* guanciale, cuscino; (*mech*) cuscinetto.

pilot ['pailət] *n* pilota; *vt* pilotare.

pimple ['pimpl] *n* foruncolo.

pin [pin] *n* spillo; **pins and needles** (*fig*) formicolio.

pincers ['pinsəz] *n pl* pinze; tanaglie *pl*.

pinch [pintʃ] *n* pizzico; (*snuff*) presa; *vti* pizzicare; stringere; privare del necessario; far soffrire.

pincushion ['pin,kuʃin] *n* portaspilli.

pine [pain] *n* pino; *vi* languire, struggersi.

pink [piŋk] *a* rosa; *n* color rosa; garofano; (*fig*) fiore, modello, perfezione.

pinnacle ['pinəkl] *n* pinnacolo; (*fig*) apogeo.

pinpoint ['pinpoint] *vt* localizzare, determinare con esattezza.

pint [paint] *n* pinta (*circa mezzo litro*).

pioneer [,paiə'niə] *n* pioniere.

pious ['paiəs] *a* pio, devoto.

pip [pip] *n* seme di frutto; (*cards etc*) macchia; (*officer's*) stelletta; (*sl*) malumore.

pipe [paip] *n* tubo; canna; cornamusa, zampogna; pipa; vena di minerale; *vi* suonare (la cornamusa etc).

piper ['paipə] *n* sonatore di cornamusa, pifferaio.

piquant ['pi:kənt] *a* piccante.

pique [pi:k] *n* picca, risentimento; *vt* ferire l'orgoglio di, offendere.

piracy ['paiərəsi] *n* pirateria.

pirate ['paiərit] *n* pirata.

pistol ['pistl] *n* pistola.

piston ['pistən] *n* pistone, stantuffo.

pit [pit] *n* abisso; buca, cava, cavità; miniera, (*theat*) platea.

pitch [pitʃ] *n* pece; (*degree*) grado; intensità; massimo punto; (*mus*) tono; *vt* lanciare, piantare, fissare al suolo; *vi* (*naut*) beccheggiare.

pitcher ['pitʃə] *n* brocca.

piteous ['pitiəs] *a* commovente, pietoso.

pitfall ['pitfɔ:l] *n* trappola; (*fig*) inganno.

pith [piθ] *n* midollo, parte essenziale.

pitiable ['pitiəbl] *a* compassionevole.

pitiful ['pitiful] *a* pietoso, miserando.

pitiless ['pitilis] *a* crudele, spietato.

pittance ['pitəns] *n* elemosina, piccola parte o quantità, piccola somma.

pity ['piti] *n* pietà, compassione; **what a p.!** *interj* che peccato!; *vt* compiangere.

Pius ['paiəs] *nm pr* Pio.

pivot ['pivət] *n* pernio.

placard ['plækɑ:d] *n* affisso, manifesto.

placate [plə'keit] *vt* placare.

place [pleis] *n* luogo, località, posto; *vt* collocare, mettere, posare.

placid ['plæsid] *a* placido.

plagiarize ['pleidʒjəraiz] *vt* plagiare.

plague [pleig] *n* peste, pestilenza; *vt* tormentare, vessare.

plain [plein] *a* piano, liscio; chiaro, evidente, sincero; insignificante; *n* pianura, piano; **p. clothes** abiti borghesi.

plainly ['pleinli] *ad* chiaramente; semplicemente.

plaintiff ['pleintif] *a* querelante.

plaintive ['pleintiv] *a* lamentoso.

plait [plæt] *n* piega; treccia; *vt* pieghettare; intrecciare.

plan [plæn] *n* piano, progetto, disegno; (*building etc*) pianta; *vt* progettare, pianificare.

plane [plein] *a* piano; *n* piano, (*tool*); pialla; (*tree*) platano; aereo.

planet ['plænit] *n* pianeta.

plank [plæŋk] *n* asse, tavola.

plant [plɑ:nt] *n* pianta, impianto; *vt* piantare.

plantation [plæn'teiʃən] *n* piantagione.

planter ['plɑ:ntə] *n* piantatore, colono.

plaque [plɑ:k] *n* placca.

plaster ['plɑ:stə] *n* cerotto; impiastro; gesso, intonaco, stucco; *vt* applicare un cerotto a; intonacare.

plasterer ['plɑ:stərə] *n* imbianchino; gessaio.

plastic ['plæstik] *a* plastico; **plastics** *n sing* plastica.

plasticine ['plæstisi:n] *n* plastilina.

plate [pleit] *n* piatto; lamina; placca,

targa; argenteria; (book) tavola fuori testo; dentiera; vt placcare, rivestire.

plateau ['plætou] pl **plateaux, plateaus** in altipiano.

platform ['plætfɔːm] n piattaforma; pianoro; (rly) marciapiede.

platinum ['plætinəm] n platino.

platitude ['plætitjuːd] n banalità.

platonic [plə'tɔnik] a platonico.

platoon [plə'tuːn] n (mil) plotone.

platter ['plætə] n piatto grande.

plausibility [ˌplɔːzə'biliti] n plausibilità.

plausible ['plɔːzəbl] a plausibile.

play [plei] n gioco, divertimento; commedia, dramma; vti giocare, rappresentare; suonare; **playground** n cortile (di scuola) per la ricreazione; **playmate** compagno di giuochi; **plaything** giocattolo.

player ['pleiə] n giocatore; suonatore; attore.

playful ['pleiful] a giocoso, scherzoso.

plea [pliː] n difesa, scusa.

plead [pliːd] vti addurre come pretesto; dichiararsi; perorare, supplicare.

pleading ['pliːdiŋ] a supplichevole; n discussione d'una causa.

pleasant ['pleznt] a piacevole, simpatico.

please [pliːz] vti piacere (a).

pleasing ['pliːziŋ] a piacente, attraente, ameno, piacevole.

pleasure ['pleʒə] n piacere.

plebeian [pli'biːən] a n plebeo.

plebiscite ['plebisit] n plebiscito.

pledge [pledʒ] n pegno, garanzia; promessa; brindisi; vt impegnare; brindare a.

plenipotentiary [ˌplenipə'tenʃəri] a n plenipotenziario.

plentiful ['plentiful] a abbondante, copioso.

plenty ['plenti] n abbondanza.

pleurisy ['pluərisi] n pleurite.

pliable ['plaiəbl] **pliant** ['plaiənt] a pieghevole, flessibile; docile, influenzabile.

pliers ['plaiəz] n pl pinze pl.

plight [plait] n condizione, situazione.

plimsolls ['plimsəlz] n pl scarpe di tela.

plod [plɔd] vi camminare con passi lenti e pesanti; sgobbare.

plodder ['plɔdə] n sgobbone.

plot [plɔt] n complotto, cospirazione; (novel etc) intreccio, trama; piccolo pezzo di terreno; vt fare la pianta di; vti complottare.

plotter ['plɔtə] n cospiratore.

plough [plau] a aratro; vti arare; vt (sl) bocciare agli esami.

plover ['plʌvə] n piviere, pavoncella.

pluck [plʌk] n (fig) coraggio; frattaglie; vt strappare, pelare, tirare.

plucky ['plʌki] a coraggioso.

plug [plʌg] n tappo; tampone; (el) spina, tabacco compresso.

plum [plʌm] n prugna; susina.

plumage ['pluːmidʒ] n penne pl.

plumb [plʌm] vt misurare la profondità di, scandagliare; ad a piombo; (fig) esattamente; (US) assolutamente.

plumber ['plʌmə] n idraulico.

plumbing ['plʌmiŋ] n impiombatura; impianto idraulico.

plume [pluːm] n piuma; (mil) pennacchio.

plump [plʌmp] a grassoccio, paffuto.

plumpness ['plʌmpnis] n rotondità di forme.

plunder ['plʌndə] n saccheggio, bottino; vt depredare, saccheggiare.

plunge [plʌndʒ] n immersione, tuffo; vti immerger(si), tuffar(si).

plural ['pluərəl] a n plurale.

plus [plʌs] a in più; n più, quantità addizionale, quantità positiva.

plush [plʌʃ] n felpa; a felpato; comodo, elegante.

ply [plai] vt maneggiare; occuparsi di; importunare; vi andare avanti e indietro regolarmente.

plywood ['plaiwud] n legno compensato.

pneumatic [njuːˈmætik] a n pneumatico.

pneumonia [njuːˈmouniə] n polmonite.

poach [poutʃ] vt cuocere (uova) in camicia; vi andare a caccia di frodo.

poacher ['poutʃə] n cacciatore di frodo; bracconiere.

pocket ['pɔkit] n tasca; vt intascare, appropriarsi di; **p.-book** taccuino, libro formato tascabile.

pod [pɔd] n baccello.

poem ['pouim] n poesia, poema.

poet ['pouit] n poeta.

poetic [pou'etik] a poetico.

poetics [pou'etiks] n poetica.

poetry ['pouitri] n poesia.

poignancy ['pɔinənsi] n (of grief) acutezza; commozione; mordacità.

poignant ['pɔinənt] a acuto, vivo, cocente; mordace.

point [pɔint] n punto, punta, promontorio; vt (sharpen) fare la punta a; (emphasize) dar rilievo a; **to p. at** additare; **to p. out** indicare, far osservare.

point-blank ['pɔint'blæŋk] a diretto; orizzontale; ad orizzontalmente; chiaro e tondo; a bruciapelo.

pointed ['pɔintid] a appuntito, aguzzo; (fig) evidente; mordace.

pointer ['pɔintə] n indicatore; lancetta; cane da ferma.

pointless ['pɔintlis] a senza punta; (fig) inutile.

poise [pɔiz] n equilibrio; portamento; vt equilibrare.

poison ['pɔizn] n veleno; vt avvelenare.

poisonous ['pɔiznəs] a velenoso.

poke [pouk] n spinta; vt spingere; (fire) attizzare; frugare; **to buy a pig in a p.** comperare la gatta nel sacco.

poker ['poukə] n attizzatoio.

Poland ['poulənd] n (geogr) Polonia.

polar ['poulə] a polare; (el) magnetico; (fig) opposto.

Pole [poul] n polacco.

pole [poul] n palo; pertica (misura di lunghezza uguale a m. 5 circa); polo.

polemic [pə'lemik] n polemica.

police [pə'liːs] n polizia.

policeman [pə'liːsmən] n poliziotto, agente di polizia, vigile urbano.

policy ['pɔlisi] n politica; linea di condotta; polizza.

poliomyelitis [ˌpoulioumaiə'laitis] n poliomielite.

Polish ['pouliʃ] a polacco.

polish ['pɔliʃ] n lucidatura; lucido, vernice; raffinatezza; vt lucidare, lustrare; raffinare.

polite [pə'lait] a cortese, educato, gentile.

politeness [pə'laitnis] n cortesia, educazione.

political [pə'litikəl] a uomo politico, politicante.

politician [ˌpɔli'tiʃən] n uomo politico, politicante.

politics ['pɔlitiks] n pl politica, scienza politica.

poll [poul] n votazione; scrutinio; lista elettorale; voti; **polling** a votante; n votazione elettorale.

pollen ['pɔlin] n polline.

pollute [pə'luːt] vt contaminare; corrompere.

pollution [pə'luːʃən] n contaminazione.

polygamy [pə'ligəmi] n poligamia.

polyvinyl ['pɔli'vinl] a polivinilico; n polivinile.

poliphony [pə'lifəni] n (mus) polifonia.

polythene ['pɔliθiːn] n politene.

pomade [pə'maːd] n pomata.

pomegranate ['pɔmˌgrænit] n melagrana.

pomp [pɔmp] n pompa, fasto.

Pompeian [pɔm'piːən] a pompeiano.

Pompeii ['pɔmpiai] n Pompei.

pompous ['pɔmpəs] a pomposo.

pompousness ['pɔmpəsnis] n sussiego.

pond [pɔnd] n laghetto, stagno; vivaio.

ponder ['pɔndə] vti meditare, ponderare.

ponderous ['pɔndərəs] a ponderoso, pesante.

pontiff ['pɔntif] n pontefice, papa.

pontoon [pɔn'tuːn] n pontone.

pony ['pouni] n cavallino, "pony".

poodle ['puːdl] n cane barbone, barboncino.

pool [puːl] n stagno, pozzanghera; (com) fondo comune; (com) 'pool'; sindacato; **football p.** totocalcio; **p. room** (US) sala del biliardo.

poop [puːp] n (naut) poppa.

poor [puə] a povero, scarso.

poorly ['puəli] a indisposto; ad poveramente, dimessamente.

pop [pɔp] n scoppio, sparo; vti (far) esplodere; entrare, uscire (di colpo); (cork) saltare.

Pope [poup] n papa; (Russian priest) pope.

popery ['poupəri] n papismo.

poplar ['pɔplə] n pioppo.

poppy ['pɔpi] n papavero.

populace ['pɔpjuləs] n plebaglia, popolaccio.

popular ['pɔpjulə] a popolare.

popularity [ˌpɔpju'læriti] n popolarità.

populate ['pɔpjuleit] vt popolare.

population [ˌpɔpju'leiʃən] n popolazione.

populous ['pɔpjuləs] a popoloso.

porcelain ['pɔːslin] n porcellana.

porch [pɔːtʃ] n portico, porticato.

porcupine ['pɔːkjupain] n porcospino.

pore [pɔː] n poro; vi studiare assiduamente.

pork [pɔːk] n carne di maiale.

pornographic [ˌpɔːnə'græfik] a pornografico.

porous ['pɔːrəs] a poroso.

porphyry ['pɔːfiri] n porfido.

porpoise ['pɔːpəs] n focena.

porridge ['pɔridʒ] n pappa di farina d'avena.

port [pɔːt] n porto; (naut) fianco sinistro della nave; vino d'Oporto.

portable ['pɔːtəbl] a portatile.

portal ['pɔːtl] n portale; **p. vein** vena porta.

portend [pɔː'tend] vt presagire.

portent ['pɔːtent] n portento; presagio.

porter ['pɔːtə] n facchino; portiere, portinaio.

porterage ['pɔːtəridʒ] n facchinaggio.

portfolio [pɔːt'fouliou] n cartella; portafoglio ministeriale.

portion ['pɔːʃən] n porzione, parte; destino.

portly ['pɔːtli] a corpulento; di portamento dignitoso.

portmanteau [pɔːt'mæntou] n baule armadio.

portrait ['pɔːtrit] n ritratto.

portray [pɔː'trei] vt ritrarre; rappresentare.

Portugal ['pɔːtjugəl] n Portogallo.

Portuguese [ˌpɔːtju'giːz] a n portoghese.

pose [pouz] n posa, affettazione.

position [pə'ziʃən] n posizione; condizione; impiego, posto.

positive ['pɔzitiv] a preciso, certo, reale, positivo; n cosa positiva, (il) positivo; (phot) positiva.

posse ['pɔsi] n manipolo di persone incaricate di far rispettare l'ordine pubblico.

possess [pə'zes] *vt* possedere.
possession [pə'zeʃən] *n* possesso, possedimento.
possessive [pə'zesiv] *a* possessivo.
possibility [,pɔsə'biliti] *n* possibilità.
possible ['pɔsəbl] *a* possibile.
possibly ['pɔsəbli] *ad* possibilmente, forse; (*in the negative*) assolutamente.
post [poust] *n* posta; impiego, posto; palo, pilastro; *vt* affiggere; impostare; imbucare;; pubblicare; (*com*) registrare, collocare; **p. office** ufficio postale.
postage ['poustidʒ] *n* affrancatura.
postal ['poustəl] *a* postale; **p. order** vaglia postale.
poster ['poustə] *n* affisso, manifesto pubblicitario, cartellone.
poste-restante ['poust'restɑ̃:nt] *n* fermo posta.
posterior [pɔs'tiəriə] *a* posteriore; *n* deretano, sedere.
posterity [pɔs'teriti] *n* posterità.
posthumous ['pɔstjuməs] *a* postumo.
postman ['poustmən] *n* portalettere, postino.
postpone [poust'poun] *vt* posporre, rimandare.
postponement [poust'pounmənt] *n* rinvio.
postscript ['pousskript] *n* poscritto.
postulate ['pɔstjuleit] *vti* richiedere; supporre.
posture ['pɔstʃə] *n* posizione, atteggiamento.
posy ['pouzi] *n* mazzo di fiori.
pot [pɔt] *n* vaso; pentola.
potash ['pɔtæʃ] *n* potasso.
potassium [pə'tæsiəm] *n* potassio.
potato [pə'teitou] *pl* **potatoes** *n* patata; **p. chips** (*US*) patatine fritte.
potent ['poutənt] *a* potente, forte.
potentate ['poutənteit] *n* potentato.
potential [pə'tenʃəl] *a* potenziale.
pother ['pɔðə] *n* confusione, pandemonio.
potion ['pouʃən] *n* pozione.
potted ['pɔtid] *a* conservato, in conserva.
pottery ['pɔtəri] *n* terraglie, stoviglie *pl*.
pouch [pautʃ] *n* bisaccia, borsa; carniera.
poulterer ['poultərə] *n* pollivendolo.
poultice ['poultis] *n* cataplasma.
poultry ['poultri] *n* pollame, gallinacei domestici *pl*.
pounce [pauns] *n* balzo; *vti* avventarsi, piombare (su).
pound [paund] (*abbr* **lb**) *n* libbra (*uguale a grammi* 453); (*abbr* £) lira sterlina; recinto per bestiame; *vt* pestare, frantumare.
pour [pɔə] *vt* versare; *vi* diluviare.
pout [paut] *vi* fare il broncio.
poverty ['pɔvəti] *n* miseria, povertà.
powder ['paudə] *n* polvere; cipria; *vt* incipriare; polverizzare; spolveriz-

zare; **p.-puff** piumino per la cipria; **powdery** *a* friabile; polveroso.
power ['pauə] *n* potere, potenza, forza, energia; **p. station** centrale elettrica.
powerful ['pauəful] *a* potente, possente.
powerless ['pauəlis] *a* impotente.
practical ['præktikəl] *a* pratico, fattibile.
practically ['præktikəli] *ad* praticamente; quasi, virtualmente.
practice ['præktis] *n* pratica, abitudine; esercizio; clientela; lavoro professionale.
practise ['præktis] *vti* esercitar(si), praticare.
practitioner [præk'tiʃnə] *n* professionista (medico); **general p.** medico generico.
prairie ['prɛəri] *n* prateria.
praise [preiz] *n* elogio, lode; *vt* lodare.
praiseworthy ['preiz,wə:ði] *a* lodevole, degno di lode.
prance [prɑ:ns] *vi* (*of horses*) impennarsi; camminare con spavalderia.
prank [præŋk] *n* scherzo, tiro.
prattle ['prætl] *n* cicaleccio infantile; *vi* cianciare, cinguettare.
prawn [prɔ:n] *n* gambero.
pray [prei] *vti* pregare.
prayer ['preiə] *n* preghiera; **p.-book** libro di preghiere.
preach [pri:tʃ] *vti* predicare.
preacher ['pri:tʃə] *n* predicatore.
precarious [pri'kɛəriəs] *a* precario.
precaution [pri'kɔ:ʃən] *n* precauzione.
precede [pri:'si:d] *vti* precedere.
precedence [pri:'si:dəns] *n* precedenza.
precedent ['presidənt] *n* precedente.
preceding [pri:'si:diŋ] *a* precedente.
precept ['pri:sept] *n* precetto.
precinct ['pri:siŋkt] *n* recinto; **precincts** *pl* confini, limiti *pl*.
preciosity [,preʃi'ɔsiti] *n* preziosità, ricercatezza.
precious ['preʃəs] *a* prezioso, ricercato.
precipice ['presipis] *n* precipizio.
precipitate [pri'sipiteit] *a* precipitoso, avventato; *vti* precipitare.
precipitous [pri'sipitəs] *a* erto, scosceso.
precise [pri'sais] *a* preciso.
precisely [pri'saisli] *ad* precisamente, esattamente, in punto.
precision [pri'siʒən] *n* precisione.
preclude [pri'klu:d] *vt* precludere, escludere.
precocious [pri'kouʃəs] *a* precoce.
preconceived ['pri:kən'si:vd] *a* preconcetto.
precursor [pri:'kə:sə] *n* precursore.
predecessor ['pri:disesə] *n* predecessore.
predicament [pri'dikəmənt] *n* situazione difficile o pericolosa.

predict [pri'dikt] *vt* predire.
predilection [ˌpriːdiˈlekʃən] *n* predilezione.
predispose ['priːdisˈpouz] *vt* predisporre.
predominance [priˈdɔminəns] *n* predominio.
predominant [priˈdɔminənt] *a* predominante.
predominate [priˈdɔmineit] *vi* predominare.
pre-eminent [priːˈeminənt] *a* preminente.
prefab ['priːˈfæb] *n* (*fam*) casa prefabbricata.
prefabricate ['priːˈfæbrikeit] *vt* prefabbricare.
preface ['prefis] *n* prefazione; (*eccl*) prefazio.
prefect ['priːfekt] *n* prefetto.
prefer [priˈfəː] *vt* preferire.
preferable ['prefərəbl] *a* preferibile.
preference ['prefərəns] *n* preferenza; **p. shares** (*com*) azioni privilegiate, (*or* preferenziali).
prefix ['priːfiks] *n* prefisso.
pregnancy ['pregnənsi] *n* gravidanza.
pregnant ['pregnənt] *a* gravida, incinta; pregno, significativo.
prejudice ['predʒudis] *n* pregiudizio; *vt* compromettere, pregiudicare.
prejudicial [ˌpredʒuˈdiʃəl] *a* pregiudizievole, dannoso.
prelate ['prelit] *n* prelato.
preliminary [priˈliminəri] *a n* preliminare.
prelude ['preljuːd] *n* preludio.
premature [ˌpreməˈtjuə] *a* prematuro.
premier ['premiə] *a* primo; *n* primo ministro.
premise, premiss ['premis] *n* premessa.
premise [priˈmaiz] *vt* premettere.
premises ['premisiz] *n pl* edificio, locali *pl*.
premium ['priːmiəm] *n* (*com*) premio, aggio.
premonition [ˌpriːməˈniʃən] *n* premonizione, presentimento.
preparation [ˌprepəˈreiʃən] *n* preparazione, preparativo.
preparatory [priˈpærətəri] *a* preparatorio.
prepare [priˈpɛə] *vti* preparar(si).
prepay ['priːˈpei] *vt* pagare in anticipo.
preponderant [priˈpɔndərənt] *a* preponderante.
preponderate [priˈpɔndəreit] (**over**) *vi* predominare, prevalere.
preposition [ˌprepəˈziʃən] *n* preposizione.
prepossess [ˌpriːpəˈzes] *vt* influenzare.
prepossessing [ˌpriːpəˈzesiŋ] *a* simpatico, attraente.
prepossession [ˌpriːpəˈzeʃən] *n* prevenzione; predisposizione.

preposterous [priˈpɔstərəs] *a* assurdo.
prerogative [priˈrɔgətiv] *n* prerogativa.
presage ['presidʒ] *n* presagio.
presbyterian [ˌprezbiˈtiəriən] *a n* presbiteriano.
prescribe [prisˈkraib] *vti* prescrivere.
prescription [prisˈkripʃən] *n* ricetta medica.
presence ['prezns] *n* presenza.
present ['preznt] *a* presente; attuale; *n* presente, regalo, dono; *vt* presentare; regalare a.
presentation [ˌprezenˈteiʃən] *n* presentazione; dono, omaggio.
presentiment [priˈzentimənt] *n* presentimento.
presently ['prezntli] *ad* tra poco, presto, poco dopo, di lì a poco.
preservation [ˌprezəˈveiʃən] *n* conservazione, preservazione.
preservative [priˈzəːvətiv] *a n* preservativo.
preserve [priˈzəːv] *n* conserva, marmellata; (*game etc*) riserva; *vt* preservare, conservare, mettere in conserva.
preside [priˈzaid] *vi* presiedere.
presidency ['prezidənsi] *n* presidenza.
president ['prezidənt] *n* presidente.
presidential [ˌpreziˈdenʃəl] *a* presidenziale.
press [pres] *n* torchio; pressione; folla; (*mech*) pressa; stampa; armadio; *vti* premere, comprimere, stringere; urgere, affollarsi.
pressing ['presiŋ] *a* pressante, insistente, urgente.
pressure ['preʃə] *n* pressione.
prestige [presˈtiːʒ] *n* prestigio.
presume [priˈzjuːm] *vti* presumere, supporre.
presumption [priˈzʌmpʃən] *n* presunzione; supposizione.
presumptive [priˈzʌmptiv] *a* presuntivo, presunto.
presumptuous [priˈzʌmptjuəs] *a* presuntuoso.
presuppose [ˌpriːsəˈpouz] *vt* presupporre.
pretence [priˈtens] *n* pretesa; pretesto, finzione.
pretend [priˈtend] *vt* fingere, pretendere; *vi* aspirare, vantare diritti su.
pretension [priˈtenʃən] *n* pretensione, pretesa, diritto.
pretentious [priˈtenʃəs] *a* pretenzioso.
pretext ['priːtekst] *n* pretesto.
prettiness ['pritinis] *n* grazia, leggiadria.
pretty ['priti] *a* grazioso, carino; *ad* discretamente, piuttosto, un po'.
prevail [priˈveil] *vi* prevalere; **to p. (up)on** persuadere.
prevalent ['prevələnt] *a* prevalente.

prevaricate [pri'værikeit] *vi* tergiversare; mentire.

prevarication [pri,væri'keiʃən] *n* tergiversazione; menzogna.

prevent [pri'vent] *vt* impedire.

prevention [pri'venʃən] *n* impedimento; misura preventiva.

preventive [pri'ventiv] *a* preventivo; *n* misura preventiva.

preview ['priːvjuː] *n* visione privata, anteprima; 'prossimamente'.

previous ['priːviəs] *a* anteriore, precedente.

previously ['priːviəsli] *ad* precedentemente.

prevision [priː'viʒən] *n* previsione.

prey [prei] *n* preda; **p. upon** *vi* predare; consumare.

price [prais] *n* prezzo.

priceless ['praislis] *a* inestimabile; (*sl*) impagabile.

prick [prik] *n* puntura; (*fig*) pungolo, rimorso; *vt* pungere, punzecchiare; drizzare (gli orecchi).

prickle ['prikl] *n* pungiglione; puntura.

prickly ['prikli] *a* spinoso; **p. pear** fico d'India.

pride [praid] *n* orgoglio, superbia; **p. oneself on** gloriarsi di, vantarsi.

priest [priːst] *n* prete, sacerdote.

priesthood ['priːsthud] *n* sacerdozio.

prig [prig] *n* pedante, saccente.

priggish ['prigiʃ] *a* affettato, pedante.

prim [prim] *a* affettato, cerimonioso.

primacy ['praiməsi] *n* primato, supremazia.

primarily ['praimərili] *ad* in primo luogo, essenzialmente.

primary ['praiməri] *a* primario, originario, fondamentale, principale.

primate ['praimeit] *n* arcivescovo, primate.

prime [praim] *a* primo; di prima qualità; *n* fiore, rigoglio.

primeval [prai'miːvəl] *a* primitivo, primordiale.

primitive ['primitiv] *a* primitivo.

primordial [prai'mɔːdiəl] *a* primordiale.

primrose ['primrouz] *n* primula.

prince [prins] *n* principe.

princely ['prinsli] *a* principesco.

princess [prin'ses] *n* principessa.

principal ['prinsəpəl] *a* principale; *n* principale, capo, direttore, superiore, rettore; (*com*) capitale.

principality [,prinsi'pæliti] *n* principato.

principle ['prinsəpl] *n* principio.

print [print] *n* impronta, orma, stampa; tessuto di cotone stampato; *vt* imprimere; pubblicare, stampare.

printer ['printə] *n* tipografo, stampatore.

printing ['printiŋ] *n* stampa, tiratura.

prior ['praiə] *a* antecedente, precedente; *n* priore; *ad* anteriormente, prima di.

priority [prai'ɔriti] *n* priorità.

prism ['prizəm] *n* prisma.

prison ['prizn] *n* prigione, penitenziario, carcere.

prisoner ['priznə] *n* prigioniero, detenuto.

pristine ['pristain] *a* pristino.

privacy ['praivəsi] *n* intimità, segreto, ritiro, vita privata.

private ['praivit] *n* soldato semplice; *a* privato; **p. business** questione personale.

privateer [,praivə'tiə] *n* nave corsara.

privation [prai'veiʃən] *n* privazione.

privet ['privit] *n* ligustro.

privilege ['privilidʒ] *n* privilegio.

privy ['privi] *a* privato; **p. to** a conoscenza di.

prize [praiz] *n* premio; *vt* apprezzare, valutare.

probability [,prɔbə'biliti] *n* probabilità.

probable ['prɔbəbl] *a* probabile.

probate ['proubit] *n* verifica di testamento.

probation [prə'beiʃən] *n* prova; noviziato; libertà condizionata.

probationer [prə'beiʃnə] *n* apprendista; novizio; chi si trova in libertà condizionata.

probe [proub] *n* (*med*) sonda; *vt* sondare; scandagliare.

probity ['proubiti] *n* probità.

problem ['prɔbləm] *n* problema.

problematic [,prɔbli'mætik] *a* problematico.

procedure [prə'siːdʒə] *n* procedimento; procedura.

proceed [prə'siːd] *vi* procedere, avanzare; derivare.

proceeding [prə'siːdiŋ] *n* atto, azione, condotta, procedimento.

proceeds ['prousiːdz] *n pl* provento, ricavo.

process ['prouses] *n* corso, processo; *vt* sottoporre a procedimento.

procession [prə'seʃən] *n* processione, corteo.

proclaim [prə'kleim] *vt* proclamare.

proclamation [,prɔklə'meiʃən] *n* proclama(zione).

proclivity [prə'kliviti] *n* inclinazione, tendenza.

procrastinate [prou'kræstineit] *vti* procrastinare.

procrastination [prou,kræsti'neiʃən] *n* indugio, procrastinazione.

procreate ['proukrieit] *vt* procreare.

procreation [,proukri'eiʃən] *n* procreazione.

procure [prə'kjuə] *vt* procurar(si).

prod [prɔd] *a* pungolo, stimolo; *vt* stimolare.

prodigal ['prɔdigəl] *a n* prodigo.

prodigious [prə'didʒəs] *a* prodigioso.

prodigy ['prɔdidʒi] *n* prodigio.

produce ['prɔdjuːs] *n* prodotti *pl*; *vti* [prə'djuːs] produrre; presentare.

producer [prə'djuːsə] *n* produttore; (*theat*) regista, impresario.

product ['prɔdəkt] n prodotto.
production [prə'dʌkʃən] n produzione.
productive [prə'dʌktiv] a produttivo.
productivity [‚prɔdʌk'tiviti] n produttività.
profanation [‚prɔfə'neiʃən] n profanazione.
profane [prə'fein] a profano; vt profanare.
profess [prə'fes] vti professare; esercitare; insegnare.
profession [prə'feʃən] n professione.
professional [prə'feʃənl] a di professione, professionale; n professionista.
professor [prə'fesə] n professore; **professorship** professorato.
proffer ['prɔfə] vt offrire.
proficiency [prə'fiʃənsi] n abilità, perizia.
proficient [prə'fiʃənt] a n esperto, competente.
profile ['proufail] n profilo.
profit ['prɔfit] n guadagno, profitto, utile, vantaggio; vt giovare; vi (ap)profittare, trarre vantaggio.
profitable ['prɔfitəbl] a vantaggioso.
profiteer [‚prɔfi'tiə] n profittatore; (fig) pescecane.
profligacy ['prɔfligəsi] n dissolutezza, licenziosità.
profligate ['prɔfligit] a n dissoluto.
profound [prə'faund] a profondo.
profuse [prə'fju:s] a abbondante; prodigo.
profusion [prə'fju:ʒən] n profusione.
progeny ['prɔdʒini] n progenie.
prognosticate [prəg'nɔstikeit] vt pronosticare.
program(me) ['prougræm] n programma.
progress ['prougres] n avanzata; corso; progresso; vi [prə'gres] progredire, fare progressi.
progressive [prə'gresiv] a progressivo.
prohibit [prə'hibit] vt proibire, vietare.
prohibition [‚proui'biʃən] n proibizione, divieto.
prohibitive [prə'hibitiv] a proibitivo.
project ['prɔdʒekt] n progetto; vt [prə'djekt] proiettare; vi sporgere.
projectile ['prɔdʒiktail] n proiettile.
projection [prə'dʒekʃən] n proiezione; sporgenza.
proletariat [‚proule'tɛəriət] n proletariato.
prolific [prə'lifik] a prolifico.
prolix ['prouliks] a prolisso.
prologue ['proulɔg] n prologo.
prolong [prə'lɔŋ] vt prolungare.
promenade [‚prɔmi'nɑːd] n passeggiata; lungomare.
prominence ['prɔminəns] n prominenza, risalto.

prominent ['prɔminənt] a prominente, cospicuo.
promiscuity [‚prɔmis'kju:iti] n promiscuità.
promiscuous [prə'miskjuəs] a promiscuo.
promise ['prɔmis] n promessa; vti promettere.
promising ['prɔmisiŋ] a promettente.
promissory ['prɔmisəri] a che contiene una promessa, promettente.
promontory ['prɔməntri] n promontorio.
promote [prə'mout] vt incoraggiare, promuovere.
promotion [prə'mouʃən] n promozione.
prompt [prɔmpt] a pronto, sollecito; vt incitare; suggerire.
prompter ['prɔmptə] n (theat) suggeritore.
promptitude ['prɔmptitju:d] n prontezza, sollecitudine.
promptness ['prɔmptnis] n prontezza.
promulgate ['prɔməlgeit] vt promulgare.
promulgation [‚prɔməl'geiʃən] n promulgazione.
prone [proun] a incline, propenso; prono, prostrato.
proneness ['prounnis] n inclinazione, propensione.
prong [prɔŋ] n rebbio; punta.
pronoun ['prounaun] n pronome.
pronounce [prə'nauns] vt pronunciare, -ziare; dichiarare.
pronounced [prə'naunst] a pronunziato.
pronunciation [prə‚nʌnsi'eiʃən] n pronuncia, -zia.
proof [pru:f] n prova; (print) bozza di stampa.
prop [prɔp] n appoggio, puntello; (theat) attrezzo scenico; vt puntellare, sostenere.
propaganda [‚prɔpə'gændə] n propaganda.
propagate ['prɔpəgeit] vti propagar(si).
propagation [‚prɔpə'geiʃən] n propagazione.
propel [prə'pel] vt spingere avanti.
propeller [prə'pelə] n (mech) elica; propulsore.
propensity [prə'pensiti] n propensione, tendenza.
proper ['prɔpə] a proprio, appropriato, vero e proprio.
properly ['prɔpəli] ad per bene, come si deve, correttamente.
property ['prɔpəti] n proprietà, beni; qualità.
prophecy ['prɔfisi] n profezia.
prophesy ['prɔfisai] vti profetizzare.
prophet ['prɔfit] n profeta.
prophetic [prə'fetik] a profetico.
propinquity [prə'piŋkwiti] n vicinanza.
propitiate [prə'piʃieit] vt propiziare.

propitious [prə'pi∫əs] *a* propizio.

proportion [prə'pɔ:∫ən] *n* proporzione.

proportional [prə'pɔ:∫ənl] *a* proporzionale.

proportionate [prə'pɔ:∫nit] *a* proporzionato.

proposal [prə'pouzəl] *n* proposta; proposta di matrimonio.

propose [prə'pouz] *vt* proporre; **p. a toast to** fare un brindisi a; *vi* proporre; fare una proposta di matrimonio.

proposition [ˌprɔpə'zi∫ən] *n* asserzione; proposta; proposizione.

propound [prə'paund] *vt* proporre.

proprietor [prə'praiətə] *n* proprietario.

propriety [prə'praiəti] *n* correttezza, proprietà; opportunità.

prorogation [ˌprourə'gei∫ən] *n* proroga, rinvio.

prosaic [prou'zeiik] *a* prosaico.

proscribe [prous'kraib] *vt* proscrivere.

proscription [prous'krip∫ən] *n* proscrizione.

prose [prouz] *n* prosa; **p. writer** prosatore.

prosecute ['prɔsikju:t] *vti* perseguire, proseguire; procedere contro, querelare.

prosecution [ˌprɔsi'kju:∫ən] *n* prosecuzione; (*leg*) processo.

prosecutor ['prɔsikju:tə] *n* prosecutore; querelante; **public p.** pubblico ministero.

proselyte ['prɔsilait] *n* proselito.

proselytize ['prɔsilitaiz] *vi* fare proseliti.

prosody ['prɔsədi] *n* prosodia.

prospect ['prɔspekt] *n* vista; prospettiva, speranza; *vt* [prəs'pekt] esplorare.

prospective [prəs'pektiv] *a* eventuale, probabile.

prospectus [prəs'pektəs] *n* programma, prospetto.

prosper ['prɔspə] *vi* prosperare.

prosperity [prɔs'periti] *n* prosperità.

prosperous ['prɔspərəs] *a* prospero.

prostitute ['prɔstitju:t] *n* prostituta.

prostitution [ˌprɔsti'tju:∫ən] *n* prostituzione.

prostrate ['prɔstreit] *a* prosternato; (*fig*) prostrato; *vt* [prɔs'treit] prosternare; (*fig*) prostrare.

prostration [prɔs'trei∫ən] *n* prostrazione.

protagonist [prə'tægənist] *n* protagonista.

protect [prə'tekt] *vt* proteggere.

protection [prə'tek∫ən] *n* protezione; salvacondotto.

protective [prə'tektiv] *a* protettivo.

protector [prə'tektə] *n* protettore.

protégé ['prouteʒei] *n* protetto.

protein ['prouti:n] *n* proteina.

protest ['proutest] *n* protesta; (*com*) protesto; *vti* [prə'test] protestare.

protestant ['prɔtistənt] *a n* protestante.

Protestantism ['prɔtistəntizəm] *n* protestantesimo.

protocol ['proutəkɔl] *n* protocollo.

protoplasm ['proutəˌplæzəm] *n* protoplasma.

prototype ['proutətaip] *n* prototipo.

protract [prə'trækt] *vt* protrarre.

protraction [prə'træk∫ən] *n* protrazione; disegno su scala.

protrude [prə'tru:d] *vt* sporgere, spingere avanti; *vi* proiettarsi, sporgere.

protuberance [prə'tju:bərəns] *n* protuberanza.

proud [praud] *a* fiero, orgoglioso; superbo.

prove [pru:v] *vt* dimostrare, provare; *vi* mostrarsi, riuscire.

Provençal [ˌprɔvɑ:n'sɑ:l] *a n* provenzale; lingua provenzale.

Provence [prɔ'vɑ̃:s] *n* Provenza.

provender ['prɔvində] *n* foraggio.

proverb ['prɔvəb] *n* proverbio.

proverbial [prə'və:biəl] *a* proverbiale.

provide [prə'vaid] *vti* provvedere, fornire; **to p. against** premunirsi contro.

provided [prə'vaidid] *cj* purchè, a patto che.

providence ['prɔvidəns] *n* provvidenza; previdenza.

provident ['prɔvidənt] *a* provvido; previdente.

providential [ˌprɔvi'den∫əl] *a* provvidenziale.

province ['prɔvins] *n* provincia; (*fig*) competenza, sfera d'azione.

provincial [prə'vin∫əl] *a n* provinciale.

provision [prə'viʒən] *n* preparativo, provvedimento; clausola; *pl* provviste, viveri; *vt* approvvigionare.

provisional [prə'viʒənl] *a* provvisorio.

provocation [ˌprɔvə'kei∫ən] *n* provocazione.

provocative [prə'vɔkətiv] *a* provocante.

provoke [prə'vouk] *vt* provocare.

provoking [prə'voukiŋ] *a* provocante.

prow [prau] *n* (*naut*) prora, prua.

prowess ['prauis] *n* prodezza.

prowl [praul] *vi* vagare in cerca di preda.

proximity [prɔk'simiti] *n* prossimità.

proxy ['prɔksi] *n* procura; procuratore.

prude [pru:d] *n* donna eccessivamente pudica.

prudence ['pru:dəns] *n* prudenza.

prudent ['pru:dənt] *a* prudente, circospetto, giudizioso.

prudery ['pru:dəri] *n* eccessiva pudicizia.

prudish ['pru:di∫] *a* pudibondo; schifiltoso.

prune [pruːn] *n* prugna secca; *vt* potare, sfrondare.
prurient ['pruəriənt] *a* lascivo.
Prussia ['prʌʃə] *n* Prussia.
pry [prai] *vi* curiosare, ficcare il naso.
psalm [sɑːm] *n* salmo.
pseudonym ['sjuːdənim] *n* pseudonimo.
psychedelic [,saikə'delik] *a* psichedelico.
psychiatrist [sai'kaiətrist] *n* psichiatra.
psychiatry [sai'kaiətri] *n* psichiatria.
psychic ['saikik] *a* psichico.
psychologic(al) [,saikə'lɔdʒik(l)] *a* psicologico.
psychology [sai'kɔlədʒi] *n* psicologia.
psychosis [sai'kousis] *n* psicosi.
puberty ['pjuːbəti] *n* pubertà.
public ['pʌblik] *a n* pubblico; p. convenience, (US) p. comfort station gabinetto pubblico; p. house spaccio di birra e bevande alcooliche.
publican ['pʌblikən] *n* oste; proprietario di bar.
publication [,pʌbli'keiʃən] *n* pubblicazione.
publicity [pʌb'lisiti] *n* pubblicità.
publish ['pʌbliʃ] *vt* pubblicare; promulgare.
publisher ['pʌbliʃə] *n* editore; (of newspaper) (US) proprietario.
pucker ['pʌkə] *n* crespa, grinza; *vt* corrugare, increspare; *vi* raggrinzirsi.
pudding ['pudiŋ] *n* budino, dolce.
puddle ['pʌdl] *n* pozzanghera.
puerility [pjuə'riliti] *n* puerilità.
Puerto Rican ['pwəːtou'riːkən] *a n* portoricano.
Puerto Rico ['pwəːtou'riːkou] *n* Portorico.
puff [pʌf] *n* sbuffo; soffio; piumino da cipria, pubblicità con elogi esagerati; *vt* gonfiare soffiando; fare una pubblicità esagerata a; *vi* ansimare; sbuffare; soffiare; p. pastry pasta sfoglia.
pug [pʌg] *n* (clay) argilla; (dog) cagnolino; p. nose naso camuso.
pugilist ['pjuːdʒilist] *n* pugile.
pugnacious [pʌg'neiʃəs] *a* pugnace, battagliero.
pugnacity [pʌg'næsiti] *n* spirito battagliero.
pull [pul] *n* strattone, tirata; (sl) influenza; vantaggio; *vt* strappare, tirare.
pullet ['pulit] *n* pollastrella.
pulley ['puli] *n* (mech) puleggia.
pullover ['pul,ouvə] *n* 'pullover', golf.
pulmonary ['pʌlmənəri] *a* polmonare.
pulp [pʌlp] *n* polpa; (paper making) pasta.
pulpit ['pulpit] *n* pulpito.
pulsate [pʌl'seit] *vti* battere, pulsare.
pulsation [pʌl'seiʃən] *n* pulsazione.
pulse [pʌls] *n* polso, battito.

pulverize ['pʌlvəraiz] *vti* polverizzar(si).
pumice ['pʌmis] *n* pomice.
pump [pʌmp] *n* pompa; *vti* pompare; (fam) cercare di estrarre informazioni.
pumpkin ['pʌmpkin] *n* zucca.
pun [pʌn] *n* gioco di parole.
punch [pʌntʃ] *n* pugno; (fam) vigore; punzone; ponce; *vt* perforare; dare pugni a.
punctual ['pʌŋktjuəl] *a* puntuale.
punctuality [,pʌŋktju'æliti] *n* puntualità.
punctuate ['pʌŋktjueit] *vt* punteggiare.
punctuation [,pʌŋktju'eiʃən] *n* punteggiatura.
puncture ['pʌŋktʃə] *n* puntura; (tyre) foratura.
pungent ['pʌndʒənt] *a* pungente, acuto, mordace.
punish ['pʌniʃ] *vt* punire.
punishable ['pʌniʃəbl] *a* punibile.
punishment ['pʌniʃmənt] *n* punizione.
punt [pʌnt] *n* chiatta, pontone; barchino; *vti* navigare su chiatta.
punter ['pʌntə] *n* puntatore (alle corse etc).
puny ['pjuːni] *a* piccolo e debole.
pup [pʌp] **puppy** ['pʌpi] *n* cucciolo.
pupil ['pjuːpil] *n* alunno, -na; scolaro, -ra, (eye) pupilla.
puppet ['pʌpit] *n* burattino, marionetta.
purchase ['pəːtʃəs] *n* acquisto; *vt* acquistare, comperare.
purchaser ['pəːtʃəsə] *n* acquirente, compratore.
pure [pjuə] *a* puro.
pureness ['pjuənis] *n* purezza.
purgative ['pəːgətiv] *a* purgativo; *n* purgante.
purgatory ['pəːgətəri] *n* purgatorio.
purge [pəːdʒ] *n* purga(nte); epurazione; *vti* purgar(si), purificar(si).
purification [,pjuərifi'keiʃən] *n* purificazione.
purify ['pjuərifai] *vt* purificare.
puritan ['pjuəritən] *a n* puritano.
puritanism ['pjuəritənizəm] *n* puritanismo.
purity ['pjuəriti] *n* purezza, purità.
purl [pəːl] *vi* mormorare, gorgogliare; p. knitting lavoro a punto rovescio.
purloin [pəː'lɔin] *vt* rubare, sottrarre.
purple ['pəːpl] *a* purpureo, violaceo; *n* porpora.
purport ['pəːpət] *n* significato; tenore; *vt* [pəː'pɔːt] significare.
purpose ['pəːpəs] *n* fine, proposito, scopo; *vti* proporsi, avere intenzione di.
purr [pəː] *vi* far le fusa.
purse [pəːs] *n* borsa, portamonete.
purser ['pəːsə] *n* (naut) commissario di bordo.

pursuance [pə'sju:rəns] n continuazione; esecuzione.

pursue [pə'sju:] vti inseguire; continuare; perseguire.

pursuer [pə'sju:ə] n inseguitore; (Scots law) attore.

pursuit [pə'sju:t] n inseguimento; occupazione.

purvey [pə:'vei] vti provvedere, fornire.

purveyor [pə:'veiə] n fornitore.

pus [pʌs] n (med) pus.

push [puʃ] n spinta; (el) pulsante; pressione; energia; momento critico; **p.-button switch** interruttore a pulsante; **p. cart** carretto a mano; passeggino; vt spingere, far pressioni su.

pushing ['puʃiŋ] a energico; intraprendente; invadente.

pusillanimous [,pju:si'læniməs] a pusillanime.

puss [pus] n micio; **pussy** micino.

put [put] vt mettere, porre; **p. off** differire; (fig) scoraggiare; distrarre; **p. on** indossare; **p. out** mettere fuori; spegnere; **p. up** contribuire; costruire; (cards) puntare; alloggiare; **p. up with** sopportare.

putrefaction [,pju:tri'fækʃən] n putrefazione.

putrefy ['pju:trifai] vti putrefar(si).

putrid ['pju:trid] a putrido.

puttee ['pʌti:] n mollettiera.

putty ['pʌti] n stucco; mastice.

puzzle ['pʌzl] n enigma, indovinello, rebus; perplessità; vt rendere perplesso.

puzzling ['pʌzliŋ] a sconcertante, imbarazzante.

pygmy ['pigmi] a n pigmeo.

pyjamas [pi'dʒɑ:məz] n pl pigiama.

pylon ['pailɔn] n pilone.

pyramid ['pirəmid] n piramide.

pyre ['paiə] n pira, rogo.

pyrotechnic ['pairou'teknik] a pirotecnico.

Q

quack [kwæk] n ciarlatano; verso dell'anatra; vi (duck) schiamazzare.

quackery ['kwækəri] n ciarlataneria; empirismo.

quadrangle ['kwɔ,dræŋgl] n quadrangolo; corte quadrangolare interna.

quadrant ['kwɔdrənt] n quadrante.

quadrille [kwə'dril] n quadriglia.

quadruped ['kwɔdruped] a n quadrupede.

quadruple ['kwɔdrupl] a quadruplice, quadruplo; n quadruplo.

quaff [kwɑ:f] vt tracannare.

quagmire ['kwægmaiə] n pantano, palude.

quail [kweil] n quaglia; vi scoraggiarsi.

quaint [kweint] a curioso, strano; caratteristico.

quaintness ['kweintnis] n bizzarria, singolarità.

quake [kweik] n scossa, tremito; vi tremare.

Quaker ['kweikə] a n quacquero.

qualification [,kwɔlifi'keiʃən] n requisito, titolo, qualifica; condizione.

qualify ['kwɔlifai] vt qualificare, abilitare; autorizzare; modificare; restringere; vi rendersi idoneo.

quality ['kwɔliti] n qualità.

qualm [kwɔ:m] n nausea; (fig) scrupolo.

quandary ['kwɔndəri] n imbarazzo, incertezza, situazione difficile.

quantity ['kwɔntiti] n quantità.

quarantine ['kwɔrənti:n] n quarantena.

quarrel ['kwɔrəl] n litigio, lite; vi litigare.

quarrelsome ['kwɔrəlsəm] a litigioso.

quarry ['kwɔri] n cava; preda.

quarryman ['kwɔrimən] n cavatore.

quart [kwɔ:t] n quarto di gallone.

quarter ['kwɔ:tə] n quarto; quartiere; direzione; località; trimestre; vt dividere in quarti; (mil) acquartierare.

quarter-deck ['kwɔ:tədek] n (naut) cassero.

quarterly ['kwɔ:təli] a trimestrale; ad trimestralmente; n pubblicazione trimestrale.

quartermaster ['kwɔ:tə,mɑ:stə] n (mil) furiere.

quartet [kwɔ:'tet] n (mus) quartetto.

quartz [kwɔ:ts] n quarzo.

quash [kwɔʃ] vt schiacciare, annullare.

quatrain ['kwɔtrein] n quartina.

quaver ['kweivə] n trillo, tremolio, vibrazione; (mus) croma; vi tremolare, vibrare.

quay [ki:] n banchina, molo.

queasy ['kwi:zi] a delicato di stomaco; nauseato; scrupoloso.

queen [kwi:n] n regina.

queenly ['kwi:nli] a da (di) regina, regale.

queer [kwiə] a strano, bizzarro, eccentrico; dubbio, sospetto; debole, che ha le vertigini.

quell [kwel] vt reprimere, soffocare.

quench [kwentʃ] vt spegnere, estinguere, calmare.

querulous ['kwerjuləs] a querulo, lamentevole.

query ['kwiəri] n domanda, punto interrogativo; vt mettere in dubbio, interrogare.

quest [kwest] n ricerca, inchiesta.

question ['kwestʃən] n domanda; questione; vt interrogare, mettere in dubbio.

questionable ['kwestʃənəbl] a discutibile, dubbio.

questionnaire [ˌkwestiə'nɛə] n questionario.

queue [kjuː] n coda; vi to q. up fare la coda.

quibble ['kwibl] n gioco di parole, cavillo; vi far giochi di parole, cavillare.

quick [kwik] a rapido, svelto, pronto, vivace, vivo; ad presto, rapidamente; n vivo, parte vitale.

quicken ['kwikən] vt affrettare, stimolare; vi animarsi, affrettarsi..

quickness ['kwiknis] n rapidità, prontezza, acutezza.

quicksand ['kwiksænd] n sabbia mobile.

quicksilver ['kwikˌsilvə] n mercurio, argento vivo.

quiet ['kwaiət] a quieto, tranquillo, dolce, sobrio; n quiete, tranquillità.

quiet(en) ['kwaiət(n)] vti acquietar(si), calmar(si).

quietness ['kwaiətnis] n quiete, riposo, silenzio.

quill [kwil] n penna, penna d'oca.

quilt [kwilt] n trapunta; vt trapuntare.

quince [kwins] n cotogna.

quinine [kwi'niːn] n chinino.

quinsy ['kwinzi] n (med) tonsillite.

quintal ['kwintl] n quintale.

quintet [kwin'tet] n (mus) quintetto.

quip [kwip] n battuta spiritosa, motto pungente.

quire ['kwaiə] n quaderno, insieme di 24 fogli di carta da scrivere.

quirk [kwəːk] n arguzia; svolazzo.

quit [kwit] a sdebitato, libero; vt abbandonare, lasciare; vi andarsene.

quite [kwait] ad completamente, del tutto, proprio.

quits [kwits] a pari.

quiver ['kwivə] n brivido, fremito; faretra; vi fremere, tremare.

quiz [kwiz] n beffa, scherzo, indovinello, 'quiz'; vt burlare, porre quesiti, esaminare.

quizzical ['kwizikəl] a canzonatorio.

quoit [kɔit] n grosso anello piatto di metallo o di gomma.

quorum ['kwɔːrəm] n 'quorum'.

quota ['kwoutə] n quota.

quotation [kwou'teiʃən] n citazione; (com) quotazione; q. marks virgolette.

quote [kwout] vt citare; (com) quotare.

quotidian [kwɔ'tidiən] a quotidiano.

quotient ['kwouʃənt] n quoziente.

R

rabbi ['ræbai] n rabbino.

rabbit ['ræbit] n coniglio; (fam) giocatore scadente; r.-warren conigliera.

rabble ['ræbl] n folla tumultuante, plebaglia.

rabid ['ræbid] a rabbioso, fanatico; r. dog cane idrofobo.

rabies ['reibiːz] n idrofobia.

race [reis] n corsa; razza, stirpe; racecourse (US) racetrack ippodromo; vt far andar a gran velocità, far correre; vi correre, gareggiare in velocità.

racehorse ['reishɔːs] n cavallo da corsa.

Rachel ['reitʃəl] nf pr Rachele.

racial ['reiʃəl] a razziale.

rack [ræk] n (luggage, rly) rete; (fodder) rastrelliera; (plates etc) scolapiatti; tortura della ruota; rovina; vt torturare; to r. one's brains scervellarsi.

racket ['rækit] n racchetta; chiasso.

racy ['reisi] a piccante; vigoroso, vivace.

radar ['reidɑː] n radar.

radiance ['reidiəns] n splendore.

radiant ['reidiənt] a raggiante.

radiate ['reidieit] vi irradiare; brillare.

radiation [ˌreidi'eiʃən] n radiazione, irradiazione.

radiator ['reidieitə] n radiatore, termosifone.

radical ['rædikəl] a n radicale.

radio ['reidiou] pl radios n radio; r. set apparecchio radio(fonico).

radioactive ['reidiou'æktiv] a radioattivo.

radiogram ['reidiougræm] n radiogramma; radiogrammofono.

radiography [ˌreidi'ɔgrəfi] n radiografia.

radish ['rædiʃ] n ravanello.

radius ['reidiəs] n raggio.

raffle ['ræfl] n lotteria; vt estrarre a sorte.

raft ['rɑːft] n chiatta, zattera.

rafter ['rɑːftə] n trave, puntone.

rag [ræg] n cencio, straccio, brandello; (sl) baldoria.

ragamuffin ['rægəˌmʌfin] n piccolo straccione.

rage [reidʒ] n collera, rabbia; (fam) persona o cosa di gran moda; vi essere furibondo, infuriarsi.

ragged ['rægid] a cencioso, stracciato; imperfetto; senza uniformità.

raid [reid] n incursione, scorreria; vt razziare, fare un'incursione.

rail [reil] n inferriata, ringhiera; (rly) rotaia; sbarra; vt chiudere con, cingere di, cancellata o sbarre; to r. at ingiuriare.

railing ['reiliŋ] n ringhiera, parapetto di ferro, inferriata, cancellata.

raillery ['reiləri] n leggera satira.

railway ['reilwei] (US) railroad [reilroud] n ferrovia, strada ferrata.

rain [rein] n pioggia; vi piovere; r. water acqua piovana.

rainbow ['reinbou] n arcobaleno.

raincoat ['reinkout] n impermeabile.

rainfall ['reinfɔːl] n piovosità, caduta di pioggia.

rainy ['reini] *a* piovoso.

raise [reiz] *n* (*US*) (di stipendio) aumento; *vt* alzare, levare, sollevare; allevare, coltivare; elevare, innalzare, aumentare; dare occasione a; raccogliere.

raisin ['reizn] *n* uva passa.

rake [reik] *n* rastrello; (*fig*) libertino; *vt* rastrellare; passare in rassegna; abbracciare con lo sguardo; (*mil*) colpire d'infilata.

rakish ['reikiʃ] *a* dissoluto.

rally ['ræli] *n* adunata; ricupero di forze; *vt* raccogliere; rianimare; *vi* rianimarsi, schierarsi.

ram [ræm] *n* ariete, montone; (*mil*) ariete; (*naut*) sperone; *vt* conficcare; (*naut*) speronare; sbattere contro.

ramble ['ræmbl] *n* passeggiata senza meta precisa; *vi* vagare; divagare.

rambler ['ræmblə] *n* chi passeggia senza meta; divagatore.

rambling ['ræmbliŋ] *a* errante, vagante; incoerente, sconnesso; (*plants*) rampicante.

ramification [,ræmifi'keiʃən] *n* ramificazione.

ramify ['ræmifai] *vi* ramificar(si).

ramp [ræmp] *n* salita, rampa.

rampant ['ræmpənt] *a* aggressivo; violento; esuberante; rampante.

rampart ['ræmpa:t] *n* bastione.

ramrod ['ræmrɔd] *n* bacchetta di fucile.

ramshackle ['ræm,ʃækl] *a* sgangherato.

ranch [ra:ntʃ] *n* 'ranch', grande fattoria con bestiame.

rancid ['rænsid] *a* rancido.

rancidity [ræn'siditi] *n* rancidezza.

rancour ['ræŋkə] *n* rancore.

Randolph ['rændɔlf] *nm pr* Rodolfo.

random ['rændəm] *a* fatto a caso; at r. *ad* a casaccio.

range [reindʒ] *n* serie; fila; (*mountains*) catena; distesa; campo, sfera; gamma; campo da tiro, raggio, gittata; cucina economica; *vt* collocare, disporre; *vi* (e)stendersi, distribuirsi; errare, vagare.

rank [ræŋk] *a* lussureggiante; rancido, puzzolente; indecente; *vt* classificare, assegnare un grado a; *vi* essere nel grado di; *n* rango, grado, fila.

rankle ['ræŋkl] *vi* inasprirsi, bruciare.

rankness ['ræŋknis] *n* esuberanza, rigoglio; rancidezza; indecenza.

ransack ['rænsæk] *vt* frugare, saccheggiare.

ransom ['rænsəm] *n* riscatto; *vt* riscattare.

rant [rænt] *vti* declamare, usare un linguaggio ampolloso.

rap [ræp] *n* colpo, colpetto, picchio; *vt* battere, colpire, picchiare.

rapacious [rə'peiʃəs] *a* rapace.

rape [reip] *n* ratto; stupro; *vt* rapire; stuprare; violentare.

Raphael ['ræfeiəl] *nm pr* Raffaele.

rapid ['ræpid] *a* rapido, veloce; erto; *n* rapida.

rapidity [ræ'piditi] *n* rapidità, velocità.

rapier ['reipiə] *n* stocco, spadino.

rapine ['ræpain] *n* rapina.

rapture ['ræptʃə] *n* estasi, rapimento.

rapturous ['ræptʃərəs] *a* estatico.

rare [rɛə] *a* raro; poco cotto.

rareness ['rɛənis] **rarity** ['rɛəriti] *n* rarità; rarefazione.

rascal ['ra:skəl] *n* briccone, furfante.

rascality [ra:s'kæliti] *n* furfanteria.

rash [ræʃ] *a* avventato, imprudente, sconsiderato; *n* eruzione cutanea.

rasher ['ræʃə] *n* fetta sottile di pancetta o prosciutto.

rashness ['ræʃnis] *n* avventatezza, imprudenza, sconsideratezza.

rasp [ra:sp] *n* raspa, raschietto; *vt* raspare, raschiare; *vi* stridere.

raspberry ['ra:zbəri] *n* lampone.

rat [ræt] *n* topo, ratto; (*pol*) disertore, girella; (*blackleg*) crumiro; *vi* andare alla caccia dei topi; (*pol*) defezionare.

rate [reit] *n* tasso; aliquota, prezzo, tariffa; (con)tributo; passo, velocità; *vt* calcolare, valutare; tassare, considerare; classificare; *vi* classificarsi.

rather ['ra:ðə] *ad* piuttosto, alquanto, un po'; (*fam*) certamente.

ratification [,rætifi'keiʃən] *n* ratifica.

ratify ['rætifai] *vt* ratificare.

rating ['reitiŋ] *n* valutazione, stima; classifica, posizione; classificazione.

ratio ['reiʃiou] *pl* **ratios** *n* rapporto, proporzione, ragione.

ration ['ræʃən] *n* razione; *vt* razionare.

rational ['ræʃənl] *a* razionale, ragionevole.

rattle ['rætl] *n* sonaglio; tintinnio, strepito, rumore; rantolo; chiacchierio vuoto; chiacchierone; *vi* produrre un rumore secco; ciarlare; *vt* (*sl*) innervosire.

raucous ['rɔ:kəs] *a* rauco, aspro.

ravage ['rævidʒ] *n* danno, devastazione; *vt* devastare, saccheggiare.

rave [reiv] *n* delirio; infatuazione; *vi* delirare; (*fam*) andare in estasi; infuriare.

ravel ['rævəl] *vti* ingarbugliar(si), sfilacciarsi.

raven ['reivn] *a* corvino; *n* corvo.

ravenous ['rævinəs] *a* affamato, vorace.

ravine [ræ'vi:n] *n* burrone.

raving ['reiviŋ] *a* delirante; *n* delirio.

ravish ['ræviʃ] *vt* rapire, violentare; (*fig*) estasiare.

ravishing ['ræviʃiŋ] *a* incantevole.

raw [rɔ:] *a* crudo; greggio; (*wound*) scoperto, vivo; (*fig*) inesperto; (*weather*) freddo e umido.

rawness ['rɔ:nis] *n* crudezza; inesperienza; (*weather*) rigore.

ray [rei] n raggio.

rayon [´reiɔn] n raion, seta artificiale.

Raymond [´reimənd] nm pr Raimondo.

raze, rase [reiz] vt radere al suolo, distruggere completamente.

razor [´reizə] n rasoio.

re- [´ri:] prefisso usato davanti a verbi e sostantivi ri- (qualora non si trovasse il vocabolo sotto la forma composta si cerchi la forma senza prefisso).

reach [ri:tʃ] n portata; possibilità; estensione; tiro; out of r. a irraggiungibile; vt arrivare a, (rag)giungere, tendere; vi estendersi.

react [ri:´ækt] vi reagire.

reaction [ri:´ækʃən] n reazione.

reactive [ri:´æktiv] a reattivo, reagente.

reactor [ri:´æktə] n reattore.

read [ri:d] vt leggere; (of instruments) segnare.

readable [´ri:dəbl] a interessante, piacevole.

reader [´ri:də] n lettore, lettrice; libro di lettura.

readily [´redili] ad prontamente; volentieri; facilmente.

readiness [´redinis] n prontezza, facilità.

reading [´ri:diŋ] n lettura, interpretazione; **r. desk** leggio; **r. room** sala di lettura.

ready [´redi] a pronto, preparato; facile, disinvolto; **r.-made** confezionato; **r. money** denaro in contanti.

real [´ri:əl] a n reale; a autentico; vero; (leg) immobile.

realism [´riəlizəm] n realismo.

realist [´riəlist] n realista.

realistic [riə´listik] a realistico.

reality [ri:´æliti] n realtà.

realization [ˌriəlai´zeiʃən] n percezione; realizzazione; compimento.

realize [´riəlaiz] vt accorgersi, capire, rendersi conto; realizzare; convertire in denaro.

really [´riəli] ad davvero, realmente.

realm [relm] n reame, regno.

ream [ri:m] n risma.

reap [ri:p] vt mietere, raccogliere.

reaper [´ri:pə] n mietitore, mietitrice, (mech) mietitrice.

rear [riə] n (mil) retroguardia; coda, parte posteriore, retro; vt allevare, coltivare, educare; costruire, ergere; vi (horse) impennarsi; **r. admiral** (naut) contrammiraglio; **in the r.**, **at the r.** indietro.

reason [´ri:zn] n ragione, ragionevolezza; vi ragionare, persuadere.

reasonable [´ri:znəbl] a ragionevole.

reasonableness [´ri:znəblnis] n ragionevolezza.

reasoning [´ri:zniŋ] n ragionamento, argomentazione.

reassure [ˌri:ə´ʃuə] vt rassicurare.

rebate [´ri:beit] n (com) riduzione, sconto, rimborso.

rebel [´rebl] a n ribelle; vi [ri´bel] ribellarsi.

rebellion [ri´beljən] n ribellione, rivolta.

rebellious [ri´beljəs] a ribelle.

rebound [ri´baund] n reazione, rimbalzo; vi rimbalzare.

rebuff [ri´bʌf] n rifiuto; rabbuffo; vt respingere.

rebuke [ri´bju:k] n rimprovero; vt rimproverare.

recall [ri´kɔ:l] n richiamo; revoca; vt richiamare, ricordare; revocare.

recant [ri´kænt] vti abiurare, ritrattar(si).

recantation [ˌri:kæn´teiʃən] n abiura, ritrattazione.

recapitulate [ˌri:kə´pitjuleit] vt riassumere, ricapitolare.

recapitulation [ˌri:kəpitju´leiʃən] n ricapitolazione.

recede [ri:´si:d] vi recedere; diminuire.

receding [ri:´si:diŋ] a rientrante, sfuggente; **r. chin** mento sfuggente; **r. hair** calvizie incipiente.

receipt [ri´si:t] n ricevimento, ricevuta, quietanza.

receive [ri´si:v] vti ricevere.

receiver [ri´si:və] n ricevitore; (rad) apparecchio radioricevente.

recent [ri´si:nt] a recente.

receptacle [ri´septəkl] n ricettacolo.

reception [ri´sepʃən] n ricevimento, accoglienza.

recess [ri´ses] n luogo appartato, nicchia, recesso; tregua; (US) vacanza scolastica.

recipe [´resipi] n ricetta.

recipient [ri´sipiənt] n ricevente, chi riceve.

reciprocal [ri´siprəkl] a reciproco.

reciprocate [ri´siprəkeit] vt contraccambiare, ricambiare.

reciprocity [ˌresi´prɔsiti] n reciprocità.

recital [ri´saitl] n esposto, racconto, "recital", esibizione di un solista, di un attore.

recitation [ˌresi´teiʃən] n recitazione.

recite [ri´sait] vt recitare; (leg) esporre.

reckless [´reklis] a avventato, temerario.

reckon [´rekən] vti calcolare, contare, considerare, supporre, contare su.

reckoning [´rekəniŋ] n computo, calcolo, resa dei conti.

reclaim [ri´kleim] vt (land) bonificare, rivendicare.

reclamation [ˌreklə´meiʃən] n bonifica, rivendicazione.

recline [ri´klain] vi essere o mettersi in posizione inclinata.

recluse [ri´klu:s] n anacoreta.

recognition [ˌrekəg´niʃən] n riconoscimento.

recognize [´rekəgnaiz] vt riconoscere.

recoil [ri´kɔil] n indietreggiamento, rinculo; vi indietreggiare, rinculare.

recollect [ˌrekə'lekt] *vt* ricordare, ricordarsi.

recollection [ˌrekə'lekʃən] *n* reminiscenza, ricordo.

recommend [ˌrekə'mend] *vt* raccomandare.

recommendation [ˌrekəmen'deiʃən] *n* raccomandazione.

recompense ['rekəmpens] *n* ricompensa; *vt* ricompensare.

reconcile ['rekənsail] *vt* (ri)conciliare.

reconcilement [ˌrekən'sailmənt] **reconciliation** [ˌrekənsili'eiʃən] *n* (ri) conciliazione.

recondite [ri'kɔndait] *a* recondito.

reconstruct ['riːkəns'trʌkt] *vt* ricostruire.

reconstruction ['riːkəns'trʌkʃən] *n* ricostruzione.

record ['rekɔːd] *n* registrazione; documento; verbale, atto; archivio, (*sport*) record, primato; (*gramophone*) disco; **r.-player** giradischi, grammofono; *vt* [ri'kɔːd] mettere a verbale; registrare, riportare, notare; (*disc*) incidere.

recorder [ri'kɔːdə] *n* apparecchio registratore; (*leg*) cancelliere; (*mus*) flauto dolce; **tape r.** magnetofono, registratore a nastro.

recount [ri'kaunt] *vt* raccontare.

recourse [ri'kɔːs] *n* ricorso.

recover [ri'kʌvə] *vt* ricuperare, riprendere; *vi* riaversi, ricuperare la salute.

recovery [riː'kʌvəri] *n* guarigione; ricupero.

re-create ['riːkri'eit] *vt* ricreare.

recreate ['rekrieit] *vt* ricreare, divertire.

recreation [ˌrekri'eiʃən] *n* ricreazione, divertimento.

recruit [ri'kruːt] *n* recluta; (*fig*) novizio; *vt* reclutare; rinvigorire; *vi* ricuperare la salute.

rectangle ['rek.tæŋgl] *n* rettangolo.

rectification [ˌrektifi'keiʃən] *n* rettificazione.

rectify ['rektifai] *vt* rettificare, correggere.

rectitude ['rektitjuːd] *n* rettitudine.

rector ['rektə] *n* parroco; rettore.

rectory ['rektəri] *n* canonica.

recumbent [ri'kʌmbənt] *a* appoggiato, semi-sdraiato.

recuperate [ri'kjuːpəreit] *vti* ricuperare, ristabilirsi.

recur [ri'kəː] *vi* ricorrere, ritornare.

recurrence [ri'kʌrəns] *n* ricorrenza, ritorno.

recurrent [ri'kʌrənt] *a* ricorrente, periodico.

red [red] *a n* rosso; **r.-hot** rovente; (*fig*) ardente.

redden ['redn] *vti* arrossare, arrossire.

reddish ['rediʃ] *a* rossastro, rossiccio.

redeem [ri'diːm] *vt* redimere, riabilitare, riscattare, salvare.

redeemer [ri'diːmə] *n* redentore.

redemption [ri'dempʃən] *n* redenzione, salvezza.

redness ['rednis] *n* rossore.

redolent ['redoulənt] *a* fragrante, profumato.

redouble [ri'dʌbl] *vti* raddoppiar(si), intensificar(si).

redoubt [ri'daut] *n* (*mil*) ridotta.

redoubtable [ri'dautəbl] *a* formidabile.

redound [ri'daund] *vi* ridondare.

redress [ri'dres] *n* atto di giustizia riparatrice, riparazione; *vt* riparare, raddrizzare.

reduce [ri'djuːs] *vt* ridurre.

reduction [ri'dʌkʃən] *n* riduzione.

redundant [ri'dʌndənt] *a* ridondante, sovrabbondante.

re-echo [riː'ekou] *vt* ripetere; *vi* riecheggiare.

reed [riːd] *n* canna; (*poet*) zampogna.

reef [riːf] *n* scoglio, scogliera, banco; (*naut*) terzaruolo.

reek [riːk] *n* fumo, esalazione, fetore; *vi* fumare, puzzare.

reel [riːl] *n* arcolaio, aspo, bobina, spoletta, rocchetto; rotolo, rullo; vacillamento; danza scozzese; *vt* avvolgere su un rocchetto; *vi* girare, vacillare.

re-election ['riːi'lekʃən] *n* rielezione.

refectory [ri'fektəri] *n* refettorio.

refer [ri'fəː] *vt* ascrivere, attribuire, riferire; rimandare a; *vi* alludere, riferire, rivolgersi a.

referee [ˌrefə'riː] *n* arbitro; *vti* fare da arbitro, arbitrare.

reference ['refrəns] *n* riferimento, allusione; referenza; competenza; **r. book** libro di consultazione.

refill ['riː'fil] *n* ricambio; *vti* riempire, riempirsi; ricaricare.

refine [ri'fain] *vt* ingentilire, (r)affinare; *vi* ingentilirsi, raffinarsi; sottilizzare.

refinement [ri'fainmənt] *n* raffinamento; (*fig*) raffinatezza, finezza.

reflect [ri'flekt] *vt* riflettere; *vi* riflettere, meditare; gettare biasimo.

reflection [ri'flekʃən] *n* riflessione; riflesso.

reflective [ri'flektiv] *a* riflessivo.

reflector [ri'flektə] *n* riflettore.

reflex ['riːfleks] *a* riflesso.

reflexive [ri'fleksiv] *a* (*gram*) riflessivo.

reform [ri'fɔːm] *n* riforma; *vti* riformar(si).

reformation [ˌrefə'meiʃən] *n* riforma.

reformer [ri'fɔːmə] *n* riformatore.

refract [ri'frækt] *vt* rifrangere.

refraction [ri'frækʃən] *n* rifrazione.

refractor [ri'fræktə] *n* rifrattore.

refractory [ri'fræktəri] *a* refrattario, ribelle.

refrain [ri'frein] *n* ritornello; *vi* frenarsi, trattenersi.

refresh [ri'freʃ] *vt* ravvivare, rianimare, rinfrescare, rinvigorire; *vi* ristorarsi.

refreshing [ri'freʃiŋ] *a* rinfrescante, ristoratore.

refresher [ri'freʃə] *n* chi, cosa che rinfresca; **r. course** corso di aggiornamento.

refreshment [ri'freʃmənt] *n* rinfresco, ristoro.

refrigerator [ri'fridʒəreitə] *n* frigorifero.

refuel [ri'fjuəl] *vti* (*av, aut*) rifornire, rifornirsi di carburante.

refuge ['refjuːdʒ] *n* rifugio.

refugee [ˌrefjuːˈdʒiː] *n* profugo, rifugiato.

refund ['riːfʌnd] *n* rimborso; [ri'fʌnd] *vt* rifondere, rimborsare.

refusal [ri'fjuːzəl] *n* rifiuto; diritto di opzione.

refuse ['refjuːs] *n* rifiuti, scarti *pl*.

refuse [ri'fjuːz] *vti* rifiutare, negare.

refute [ri'fjuːt] *vt* confutare, ribattere.

regain [ri'gein] *vt* riguadagnare, riacquistare, ricuperare; raggiungere di nuovo.

regal ['riːgəl] *a* regale.

regale [ri'geil] *vt* intrattenere.

regality [ri'gæliti] *n* regalità.

regard [ri'gɑːd] *n* considerazione, stima; *vt* riguardare, considerare, concernere; **regards** *pl* ossequi, saluti; **with r. to.** **regarding** riguardo a, per quanto riguarda.

regardless [ri'gɑːdlis] *a* incurante, senza riguardo; **r. of** a dispetto di, nonostante.

regatta [ri'gætə] *n* regata.

regency ['riːdʒənsi] *n* reggenza.

regenerate [ri'dʒenəreit] *vti* rigenerare, rigenerarsi.

regent ['riːdʒənt] *n* reggente.

regicide ['redʒisaid] *n* regicida, regicidio.

regime [rei'ʒiːm] *n* regime.

regiment ['redʒimənt] *n* reggimento.

regimental [ˌredʒi'mentl] *a* reggimentale.

Reginald ['redʒinld] *nm pr* Reginaldo.

region ['riːdʒən] *n* regione.

regional ['riːdʒənl] *a* regionale.

register ['redʒistə] *n* registro; registratore; (*mech*) valvola di regolazione; (*mus, type*) registro; *vt* registrare; (*post*) raccomandare; (*luggage*) assicurare; *vi* (far) iscrivere il proprio nome su un registro; **r. of voters** lista elettorale.

registrar [ˌredʒis'trɑː] *n* archivista, ufficiale dello stato civile.

registration [ˌredʒis'treiʃən] *n* registrazione; iscrizione; (*post*) raccomandazione; (*luggage*) assicurazione.

registry ['redʒistri] *n* ufficio del registro, ufficio di stato civile; ufficio di collocamento.

regression [ri'greʃən] *n* regresso.

regret [ri'gret] *n* rammarico, rim-

pianto; *vt* rimpiangere, deplorare, rammaricarsi di.

regretful [ri'gretful] *a* dolente.

regrettable [ri'gretəbl] *a* deplorevole, increscioso.

regrettingly [ri'gretiŋli] *ad* con rammarico, con dispiacere.

regular ['regjulə] *a n* regolare.

regularity [ˌregju'læriti] *n* regolarità.

regulate ['regjuleit] *vt* regolare.

regulation [ˌregju'leiʃən] *a* regolamentare; *n* regolamento, regola.

regulator ['regjuleitə] *n* regolatore.

rehabilitation ['riːəˌbili'teiʃən] *n* riabilitazione.

rehearsal [ri'həːsəl] *n* prova.

rehearse [ri'həːs] *vt* provare.

reign [rein] *n* regno; *vi* regnare.

reimburse [ˌriːim'bəːs] *vt* rimborsare, rifondere.

rein [rein] *n* redine.

reindeer ['reindiə] *n* renna.

reinforce [ˌriːin'fɔːs] *vt* rinforzare, rafforzare.

reinforcement [ˌriːin'fɔːsmənt] *n* rinforzo.

reinstate [ˌriːin'steit] *vt* ricollocare, rimettere, reintegrare.

reiterate [riː'itəreit] *vt* reiterare.

reiteration [riːˌitəreiʃən] *n* reiterazione.

reject [ri'dʒekt] *vt* rigettare, respingere; (*mil*) riformare.

rejection [ri'dʒekʃən] *n* rigetto, rifiuto.

rejoice [ri'dʒɔis] *vi* gioire, rallegrarsi; *vt* rallegrare.

rejoicing [ri'dʒɔisiŋ] *n* gioia, letizia; **rejoicings** *pl* festeggiamenti *pl*.

rejoin [ri'dʒɔin] *vt* raggiungere, riunire; *vi* ribattere, rispondere.

rejoinder [ri'dʒɔində] *n* risposta.

rejuvenate [ri'dʒuːvineit] *vti* ringiovanire.

relapse [ri'læps] *n* ricaduta; *vi* ricadere.

relate [ri'leit] *vt* narrare; *vi* aver rapporto, riferirsi.

relation [ri'leiʃən] *n* relazione, rapporto; parente.

relationship [ri'leiʃənʃip] *n* relazione, rapporto; parentela.

relative ['relətiv] *a* relativo; *n* parente.

relativity [ˌrelə'tiviti] *n* relatività.

relax [ri'læks] *vt* allentare, rilassare, diminuire; *vi* allentarsi, rilassarsi.

relaxation [ˌriːlæk'seiʃən] *n* rilassamento, distensione, ricreazione, riposo, diminuzione.

relay ['riːlei] *n* (*horses*) cavalli di ricambio, (*dogs*) muta di ricambio; **r. race** corsa a staffetta; *vt* sostituire; (*rad*) ritrasmettere.

release [ri'liːs] *n* liberazione; (*mech*) scarico; *vt* liberare, sciogliere.

relegate ['religeit] *vt* relegare.

relent [ri'lent] *vi* piegarsi, intenerirsi.

relentless [ri'lentlis] *a* inflessibile, rigido.

relevance ['relivəns] relevancy ['relivānsi] n attinenza, pertinenza.

relevant ['relivənt] a attinente, pertinente.

reliability [ri͵laiə'biliti] n attendibilità; fidatezza.

reliable [ri'laiəbl] a fidato; attendibile.

reliance [ri'laiəns] n fiducia.

reliant [ri'laiənt] a fiducioso; che fa assegnamento.

relic ['relik] n reliquia; relics pl reliquie, avanzi, resti pl.

relief [ri'li:f] n sollievo; aiuto, soccorso; cambio; diversivo; rilievo.

relieve [ri'li:v] vt alleviare, mitigare, soccorrere, sollevare, liberare, dare il cambio a.

religion [ri'lidʒən] n religione.

religious [ri'lidʒəs] a religioso; a devoto, pio.

relinquish [ri'liŋkwiʃ] vt abbandonare, rinunziare a.

relish ['reliʃ] n gusto, sapore, piacere, condimento; vt (far) gustare, trovar piacere.

reluctance [ri'lʌktəns] n riluttanza.

reluctant [ri'lʌktənt] a riluttante.

rely [ri'lai] vi fare assegnamento (su), contare (su), fidarsi (di).

remain [ri'mein] vi restare, rimanere; avanzare.

remainder [ri'meində] n resto, rimanenza.

remaining [ri'meiniŋ] a restante, rimanente.

remains [ri'meins] n pl avanzi, resti, reliquie pl, resti mortali pl, spoglie pl.

remand [ri'mɑːnd] vt rimandare in carcere.

remark [ri'mɑːk] n commento, osservazione; vti notare, osservare.

remarkable [ri'mɑːkəbl] a eccezionale, notevole.

remedy ['remidi] n rimedio, medicina; vt porre rimedio a.

remember [ri'membə] vt ricordare, ricordar(si di), rammentar(si di).

remembrance [ri'membrəns] n ricordo, memoria, rimembranza; remembrances pl saluti, ossequi pl.

remind [ri'maind] vt ricordare a, richiamare alla memoria di, rammentare a.

reminder [ri'maində] n ricordo, promemoria.

reminiscence [͵remi'nisns] n reminiscenza.

reminiscent [͵remi'nisnt] a che richiama alla memoria.

remiss [ri'mis] a negligente, trascurato.

remission [ri'miʃən] n remissione, condono.

remit [ri'mit] vt rimettere, perdonare.

remittance [ri'mitəns] n (com) rimessa.

remnant ['remnənt] n resto, scampolo.

remonstrance [ri'mɔnstrəns] n rimostranza.

remonstrate ['remənstreit] vi protestare, fare rimostranza.

remorse [ri'mɔːs] n rimorso.

remorseful [ri'mɔːsful] a pieno di rimorsi.

remorseless [ri'mɔːslis] a spietato.

remote [ri'mout] a lontano, remoto.

removal [ri'muːvəl] n rimozione, trasferimento, trasloco.

remove [ri'muːv] vti rimuovere; levare; trasferirsi, traslocare.

remunerate [ri'mjuːnəreit] vt rimunerare.

remuneration [ri͵mjuːnə'reiʃən] n rimunerazione.

remunerative [ri'muːnərətiv] a rimunerativo.

renaissance, renascence [rə'neisəns] n rinascimento.

rend [rend] vt lacerare, strappare.

render ['rendə] vt rendere, tradurre; (fats) sciogliere; (oil) raffinare.

rendering ['rendəriŋ] n resa, traduzione, interpretazione.

rendezvous ['rɔndeivuː] n (mil) luogo di raduno; appuntamento; vi riunirsi.

renegade ['renigeid] n rinnegato, traditore.

renew [ri'njuː] vt rinnovare.

renewal [ri'njuːəl] n rinnovamento.

rennet ['renit] n caglio; mela ranetta.

renounce [ri'nauns] vt rinunciare a, ripudiare.

renouncement [ri'naunsmənt] n rinunzia.

renovate ['renouveit] vt rinnovare.

renovation [͵renou'veiʃən] n rinnovamento.

renown [ri'naun] n fama, rinomanza.

renowned [ri'naund] a celebre, famoso.

rent [rent] n affitto, nolo; strappo; vt dare o prendere in affitto; vi venire affittato; rental canone d'affitto; rental library (US) biblioteca circolante.

renunciation [ri͵nʌnsi'eiʃən] n rinuncia.

repair [ri'pɛə] n riparazione, restauro; vt riparare, restaurare, rimediare a; vi recarsi, rifugiarsi; in good r. in buono stato.

reparation [͵repə'reiʃən] n riparazione, risarcimento.

repartee [͵repɑː'tiː] n risposta pronta.

repast [ri'pɑːst] n pasto.

repatriate [riː'pætrieit] n rimpatriato; vti rimpatriare.

repay [ri'pei] vt ripagare; restituire; ricompensare.

repayment [riː'peimənt] n rimborso; ricompensa.

repeal [ri'piːl] vt abrogare, revocare.

repeat [ri'piːt] vt ripetere.

repel [ri'pel] *vt* respingere; ripugnare a.

repent [ri'pent] *vti* pentirsi (di).

repentance [ri'pentəns] *n* pentimento.

repentant [ri'pentənt] *a* pentito.

repertoire ['repətwɑ:] *n* repertorio.

repertory ['repətəri] *n* repertorio.

repetition [ˌrepi'tiʃən] *n* ripetizione.

replace [ri'pleis] *vt* ricollocare, rimettere; sostituire.

replacement [ri'pleismənt] *n* ricollocamento; sostituzione.

replenish [ri'pleniʃ] *vt* riempire.

replete [ri'pli:t] *a* pieno, sazio.

repletion [ri'pli:ʃən] *n* pienezza, sazietà.

replica ['replikə] *n* replica, copia.

reply [ri'plai] *n* risposta; *vi* rispondere.

report [ri'pɔ:t] *n* rapporto, relazione, resoconto; detonazione; *vt* fare un rapporto di, riferire, fare la cronaca di; *vi* fare il cronista.

reporter [ri'pɔ:tə] *n* corrispondente, cronista.

repose [ri'pouz] *n* riposo; *vi* riposarsi, basarsi.

repository [ri'pɔzitəri] *n* deposito, magazzino; (*fig*) confidente.

reprehensible [ˌrepri'hensəbl] *a* biasimevole.

represent [ˌrepri'zent] *vt* rappresentare.

representation [ˌreprizen'teiʃən] *n* rappresentazione.

representative [ˌrepri'zentətiv] *a* rappresentativo; *n* rappresentante.

repress [ri'pres] *vt* reprimere, frenare.

repression [ri'preʃən] *n* repressione.

reprieve [ri'pri:v] *n* dilazione; *vt* accordare una dilazione a.

reprimand ['reprimɑ:nd] *n* rimprovero; *vt* rimproverare.

reprint ['ri:'print] *n* ristampa; *vt* ristampare.

reprisal [ri'praizəl] *n* rappresaglia.

reproach [ri'proutʃ] *n* rimprovero, vergogna; *vt* rimproverare.

reproachful [ri'proutʃful] *a* di rimprovero.

reprobate ['reproubeit] *a n* reprobo; *vt* riprovare.

reproduce [ˌri:prə'dju:s] *vti* riprodur(si).

reproduction [ˌri:prə'dʌkʃən] *n* riproduzione.

reproductive [ˌri:prə'dʌktiv] *a* riproduttivo.

reproof [ri'pru:f] *n* biasimo, rimprovero.

reprove [ri'pru:v] *vt* biasimare, rimproverare.

reptile ['reptail] *n* rettile.

republic [ri'pʌblik] *n* repubblica.

republican [ri'pʌblikən] *a n* repubblicano.

repudiate [ri'pju:dieit] *vt* ripudiare, rinnegare.

repugnance [ri'pʌgnəns] *n* ripugnanza.

repugnant [ri'pʌgnənt] *a* ripugnante.

repulse [ri'pʌls] *n* ripulsa, rifiuto; *vt* respingere.

repulsion [ri'pʌlʃən] *n* repulsione.

repulsive [ri'pʌlsiv] *a* repellente, ripulsivo.

reputable ['repjutəbl] *a* rispettabile.

reputation [ˌrepju:'teiʃən] *n* reputazione; rispettabilità.

repute [ri'pju:t] *n* reputazione, fama; *vt* giudicare, reputare.

request [ri'kwest] *n* domanda, richiesta; *vt* domandare, pregare, richiedere.

require [ri'kwaiə] *vt* richiedere, esigere; aver bisogno di.

requirement [ri'kwaiəmənt] *n* richiesta, esigenza; bisogno; requisito.

requisite ['rekwizit] *a* necessario, richiesto; *n* requisito.

requisition [ˌrekwi'ziʃən] *n* requisizione; *vt* requisire.

requital [ri'kwaitl] *n* contraccambio; ricompensa.

requite [ri'kwait] *vt* ricompensare; contraccambiare.

rescue ['reskju:] *n* liberazione, salvezza, soccorso; *vt* liberare, salvare.

research [ri'sə:tʃ] *n* indagine, ricerca; **r. worker** ricercatore, investigatore.

resemblance [ri'zembləns] *n* (ras) somiglianza.

resemble [ri'zembl] *vt* (as)somigliare a, rassomigliare.

resent [ri'zent] *vt* risentirsi di, risentire.

resentment [ri'zentmənt] *n* risentimento, rancore.

reservation [ˌrezə'veiʃən] *n* riserva; prenotazione.

reserve [ri'zə:v] *n* reticenza, riserbo, riserva; *vt* riservare, prenotare.

reservoir ['rezəvwɑ:] *n* serbatoio.

reside [ri'zaid] *vi* risiedere.

residence ['rezidəns] *n* residenza.

resident ['rezidənt] *a n* residente.

residential [ˌrezi'denʃəl] *a* adatto per case di abitazione, residenziale.

residue ['rezidju:] *n* residuo, resto.

resign [ri'zain] *vt* rinunziare a; *vi* dimettersi, rassegnare le dimissioni.

resignation [ˌrezig'neiʃən] *n* dimissioni *pl*; rassegnazione.

resilience [ri'ziliəns] *n* elasticità, capacità di ricupero.

resilient [ri'ziliənt] *a* elastico, rimbalzante; che ha la capacità di ricupero.

resin ['rezin] *n* resina.

resist [ri'zist] *vt* resistere a; *vi* resistere.

resistance [ri'zistəns] *n* resistenza.

resistant [ri'zistənt] *a* resistente.

resolute ['rezəlu:t] *a* risoluto.

resolution [ˌrezə'lu:ʃən] *n* risolutezza, decisione; soluzione, risoluzione.

resolve [ri'zɔlv] *n* decisione; *vt*

risolvere, sciogliere; *vi* decidere, risolversi.

resonance ['reznəns] *n* risonanza.

resonant ['reznənt] *a* risonante.

resort [ri'zɔːt] *n* ricorso, risorsa; luogo di soggiorno; *vi* ricorrere a; affluire.

resound [ri'zaund] *vi* risuonare, echeggiare.

resource [ri'sɔːs] *n* risorsa, mezzo, espediente, ingegnosità.

resourceful [ri'sɔːsful] *a* pieno di risorse.

respect [ris'pekt] *n* rispetto, stima; riguardo, aspetto; *vt* rispettare, tenere in considerazione; **respects** *pl* ossequi *pl*.

respectability [ri,spektə'biliti] *n* rispettabilità.

respectable [ris'pektəbl] *a* rispettabile, per bene, considerevole.

respectably [ri'spektəbli] *ad* rispettabilmente; decentemente.

respectful [ris'pektful] *a* rispettoso.

respecting [ris'pektiŋ] *prep* riguardo a.

respective [ris'pektiv] *a* rispettivo, relativo.

respiration [,respə'reiʃən] *n* respirazione.

respirator ['respəreitə] *n* (*med*) respiratore; (*mil*) maschera anti-gas.

respite ['respait] *n* tregua, respiro.

resplendent [ris'plendənt] *a* (ri) splendente.

respond [ris'pɔnd] *vi* rispondere.

respondent [ris'pɔndənt] *n* (*leg*) convenuto, imputato.

response [ris'pɔns] *n* risposta, responso; reazione; (*eccl*) responsorio.

responsibility [ris,pɔnsə'biliti] *n* responsabilità.

responsible [ris'pɔnsəbl] *a* responsabile.

responsive [ris'pɔnsiv] *a* sensibile a.

responsiveness [ris'pɔnsivnis] *n* rispondenza, sensibilità.

rest [rest] *n* riposo; resto, rimanente; *pron pl* gli altri, le altre *pl*; *vt* posare, appoggiare; *vi* riposarsi, stare quieto.

restaurant ['restərɔːŋ] *n* ristorante; **r. car** vettura ristorante.

restful ['restful] *a* riposante, tranquillo.

restitution [,resti'tjuːʃən] *n* restituzione, risarcimento.

restive ['restiv] *a* restio, recalcitrante.

restless ['restlis] *a* irrequieto, agitato.

restlessness ['restlisnis] *n* irrequietezza, agitazione.

restoration [,restə'reiʃən] *n* restauro, restaurazione, restituzione, ricupero, ripristino.

restore [ris'tɔː] *vt* rimettere, restaurare, restituire, ricuperare, ripristinare.

restrain [ris'trein] *vt* reprimere, trattenere.

restraint [ris'treint] *n* controllo, freno, ritegno; detenzione.

restrict [ris'trikt] *vt* restringere, limitare.

restriction [ris'trikʃən] *n* restrizione.

restrictive [ris'triktiv] *a* restrittivo.

result [ri'zʌlt] *n* risultato, esito; *vi* risultare, risolversi.

resultant [ri'zʌltənt] *a n* risultante.

resume [ri'zjuːm] *vti* riprendere.

resumption [ri'zʌmpʃən] *n* ripresa.

resurrection [,rezə'rekʃən] *n* risurrezione.

resuscitate [ri'sʌsiteit] *vti* risuscitare.

retail ['riːteil] *n* vendita al minuto; **ad** al minuto; *vt* vendere al minuto; raccontare dettagliatamente.

retailer ['riːteilə] *n* venditore al minuto.

retain [ri'tein] *vt* mantenere; conservare.

retaliate [ri'tælieit] *vt* ricambiare; *vi* rendere la pariglia.

retaliation [ri,tæli'eiʃən] *n* rappresaglia.

retard [ri'taːd] *vt* ritardare.

retch [riːtʃ] *vi* avere conati di vomito.

retention [ri'tenʃən] *n* ritenzione, conservazione; memoria.

retentive [ri'tentiv] *a* ritentivo, tenace.

reticence ['retisəns] *n* reticenza.

reticent ['retisənt] *a* reticente, riservato.

retinue ['retinjuː] *n* seguito.

retire [ri'taiə] *vti* ritirar(si).

retirement [ri'taiəmənt] *n* ritiro, collocamento a riposo.

retort [ri'tɔːt] *n* ritorsione, risposta incisiva; (*chem*) storta; *vti* ritorcere, ribattere.

retrace [ri'treis] *vt* rintracciare, ripercorrere, tornare indietro.

retract [ri'trækt] *vt* ritrattare; *vi* disdirsi.

retreat [ri'triːt] *n* (*mil*) ritirata; ritiro; *vi* ritirarsi.

retrench [ri'trentʃ] *vt* diminuire, ridurre; *vi* economizzare.

retribution [,retri'bjuːʃən] *n* retribuzione, ricompensa.

retrieve [ri'triːv] *vt* ricuperare, riacquistare il possesso di, riparare; (*game*) riportare.

retriever [ri'triːvə] *n* cane da presa.

retrograde ['retrougreid] *a* retrogrado; inverso.

retrospect ['retrouspekt] *n* sguardo retrospettivo.

retrospective [,retrə'spektiv] *a* retrospettivo.

return [ri'təːn] *n* ritorno; restituzione; prospetto statistico; *usu pl* provento, guadagno; *vt* contraccambiare; restituire; rimandare; *vi* (ri)tornare; replicare, rispondere.

reunion ['ri:'ju:njən] *n* riunione.

reveal [ri'vi:l] *vt* rivelare.

revel ['revl] *n* baldoria, gozzoviglia; *vi* fare baldoria, gozzovigliare, dilettarsi.

revelation [.revi'leiʃən] *n* rivelazione.

revenge [ri'vendʒ] *n* vendetta, rivincita; *vti* vendicar(si).

revengeful [ri'vendʒful] *a* vendicativo.

revenue ['revinju:] *n* entrata; reddito; fisco; **r. stamp** marca da bollo; **r. tax** imposta sull'entrata.

reverberate [ri'və:bəreit] *vti* riverberar(si), riecheggiare, rimbombare.

reverberation [ri.və:bə'reiʃən] *n* riverbero; riverberazione.

revere [ri'viə] *vt* riverire, venerare.

reverence ['revərəns] *n* riverenza, venerazione.

reverend ['revərənd] *a n* reverendo.

reverent ['revərənt] *a* riverente.

reverie ['revəri] *n* sogno ad occhi aperti, fantasticheria.

reversal [ri'və:səl] *n* rovesciamento, inversione.

reverse [ri'və:s] *a* contrario, inverso, rovescio, opposto; *n* il rovescio, l'opposto, il contrario; *vt* rovesciare, capovolgere, invertire; *vi* girare in senso inverso.

reversible [ri'və:səbl] *a* reversibile, revocabile; (*mech*) a inversione di marcia.

reversion [ri'və:ʃən] *n* reversione, ritorno.

revert [ri'və:t] *vi* ritornare.

review [ri'vju:] *n* rivista, recensione; revisione; sguardo retrospettivo; *vt* passare in rivista; recensire; rivedere; *vi* scrivere recensioni.

reviewer [ri'vju:ə] *n* recensore, critico d'una rivista.

revile [ri'vail] *vt* ingiuriare, insultare; *vi* inveire.

revise [ri'vaiz] *vt* rivedere, correggere.

revision [ri'viʒən] *n* revisione, correzione.

revival [ri'vaivəl] *n* rinascita, risveglio, riesumazione.

revive [ri'vaiv] *vt* far rivivere, risvegliare, riesumare; *vi* riprendere i sensi, ritornare in uso, in vita.

revoke [ri'vouk] *vt* revocare, ritirare.

revolt [ri'voult] *n* rivolta, insurrezione; senso di disgusto; *vt* rivoltare; *vi* ribellarsi, rivoltarsi; provar disgusto.

revolting [ri'voultiŋ] *a* disgusting.

revolution [.revə'lu:ʃən] *n* rivoluzione; giro.

revolutionary [.revə'lu:ʃnəri] *a n* rivoluzionario.

revolve [ri'vɔlv] *vt* rivolgere; meditare; *vi* girare.

revolver [ri'vɔlvə] *n* rivoltella, "revolver".

revue [ri'vju:] *n* (*theat*) rivista.

revulsion [ri'vʌlʃən] *n* revulsione, ripugnanza.

reward [ri'wɔ:d] *n* compenso, ricompensa; *vt* (ri)compensare.

Reynold ['renld] *nm pr* Rinaldo.

rhapsody ['ræpsədi] *n* rapsodia.

rhetoric ['retərik] *n* retorica.

rhetorical [ri'tɔrikəl] *a* retorico.

rheumatic [ru:'mætik] *a* reumatico; **rheumatics** *n pl* reumatismi *pl*.

rheumatism ['ru:mætizəm] *n* reumatismo.

Rhine [rain] *n* Reno.

rhinoceros [rai'nɔsərəs] *n* rinoceronte.

Rhodes [roudz] *n* Rodi.

Rhodesia [rou'di:ziə] *n* Rodesia.

Rhodesian [rou'di:ziən] *a n* di Rodesia, della Rodesia.

rhododendron [.roudə'dendrən] *n* rododendro.

Rhone [roun] *n* Rodano.

rhubarb ['ru:ba:b] *n* rabarbaro.

rhyme, rime [raim] *n* rima; *vt* mettere in rima; *vi* rimare.

rhythm ['riðəm] *n* ritmo.

rhythmic(al) ['riðmik(əl)] *a* ritmico.

rib [rib] *n* costola; (*umbrella etc*) stecca.

ribald ['ribəld] *a* osceno, sboccato.

ribaldry ['ribəldri] *n* linguaggio osceno.

rib(b)and ['ribənd] **ribbon** ['ribən] *n* nastro.

rice [rais] *n* riso.

rich [ritʃ] *a* ricco.

Richard ['ritʃəd] *nm pr* Riccardo.

riches ['ritʃiz] *n pl* ricchezza, -ze.

richly ['ritʃli] *ad* riccamente; ampiamente.

richness ['ritʃnis] *n* ricchezza, sontuosità.

rick [rik] *n* (*of straw etc*) cumulo, mucchio.

rickets ['rikits] *n* rachitismo.

rickety ['rikiti] *a* rachitico; sgangherato, traballante.

rid [rid] *vt* liberare, sbarazzare.

riddance ['ridəns] *n* liberazione.

riddle ['ridl] *n* enigma, indovinello; crivello; vaglio; *vt* crivellare; vagliare; *vi* proporre indovinelli.

ride [raid] *n* cavalcata, galoppata, corsa; *vt* cavalcare, percorrere a cavallo; *vi* cavalcare, andare a cavallo; in bicicletta *etc*; (*naut*) essere all'ancora; (*fig*) opprimere.

rider ['raidə] *n* cavaliere, cavallerizzo; aggiunta, codicillo.

ridge [ridʒ] *n* (*of mountains*) cresta, spartiacque; (*agr*) porca.

ridicule ['ridikju:l] *n* ridicolo; *vt* mettere in ridicolo.

ridiculous [ri'dikjuləs] *a* ridicolo.

ridiculously [ri'dikjuləsli] *ad* ridicolamente; in modo assurdo.

riding ['raidiŋ] *n* cavalcata; equitazione; **r. school** scuola di equitazione, maneggio.

rife [raif] *a* comune; prevalente; rigoglioso.

riff-raff ['rifræf] *n* plebaglia.

rifle ['raifl] n fucile, carabina; **rifleman** fuciliere; vt derubare, vuotare.

rift [rift] n crepa, spaccatura.

rig [rig] n (naut) attrezzatura; (fam) abbigliamento; vt (naut) attrezzare.

right [rait] a giusto, retto, esatto; destro; corretto; n il giusto, il bene; il diritto; destra; vt correggere; (rad) drizzare; vendicare; vi raddrizzarsi; **to be r.** aver ragione; ad bene, direttamente; a destra; **r. away** immediatamente.

righteous ['raitʃəs] a retto, virtuoso.

rightful ['raitful] a legittimo, giusto.

rightly ['raitli] ad giustamente; esattamente.

rigid ['ridʒid] a rigido, inflessibile.

rigidity [ri'dʒiditi] n rigidezza, inflessibilità.

rigmarole ['rigməroul] n filastrocca.

rigorous ['rigərəs] a rigido, rigoroso.

rigour ['rigə] n rigore; intransigenza.

rill [ril] n ruscelletto.

rim [rim] n orlo, bordo, margine; (wheel) cerchione; (spectacles) montatura.

rind [raind] n buccia, corteccia; (cheese, bread) crosta.

ring [riŋ] n anello; cerchio; scampanellata; colpo di telefono; crocchio; (boxing) 'ring', quadrato; (sport) pista, recinto; vt accerchiare; suonare (il campanello); vi suonare, tintinnare; **to r. up** chiamare per telefono.

ringleader ['riŋ‚li:də] n capo d'una sommossa.

ringlet ['riŋlit] n ricciolo.

rink [riŋk] n recinto per pattinaggio.

rinse [rins] vt risciacquare; n risciucquata.

riot ['raiət] n schiamazzo, tumulto, rivolta; vi tumultuare.

riotous ['raiətəs] a sedizioso, tumultuante; dissoluto.

rip [rip] n squarcio, strappo; persona dissoluta; vt squarciare, strappare; (fam) andare a tutta velocità.

ripe [raip] a maturo.

ripen ['raipən] vti maturare.

ripeness ['raipnis] n maturità.

ripple ['ripl] n increspatura, piccola onda; vi incresparsi.

rise [raiz] n (sun) levata; sorgere, ascesa, salita, aumento; vi alzarsi, levarsi, salire, sorgere, aumentare, insorgere.

risk [risk] n rischio; vt rischiare, mettere in pericolo.

risky ['riski] a arrischiato, rischioso.

rite [rait] n rito.

ritual ['ritjuəl] a n rituale.

rival ['raivəl] a n rivale; vt rivaleggiare.

rivalry ['raivəlri] n rivalità.

river ['rivə] n fiume.

rivet ['rivit] n chiodo, rivetto; vt inchiodare, ribadire, fissare.

rivulet ['rivjulit] n fiumicello.

roach [routʃ] n (fish) carpa; scarafaggio.

road [roud] n strada, via; (naut) rada; **r. diversion** deviazione stradale; **r. haulier(s)** impresa autotrasporti.

roadhouse ['roudhaus] n albergo, locanda, trattoria sulla strada.

roadside ['roudsaid] n bordo della strada.

roam [roum] vt percorrere; vi girovagare, vagare.

roan [roun] a n roano.

roar [rɔ:] n mugghio, muggito; rombo; (laughter, applause) scroscio; vti mugghiare, ruggire; urlare.

roast [roust] a n arrosto; vti arrostir(si), (coffee) tostar(si).

rob [rɔb] vt (de)rubare, spogliare, svaligiare.

robber ['rɔbə] n ladro, rapinatore; ladrone.

robbery ['rɔbəri] n furto, rapina.

robe [roub] n lungo manto da cerimonie, toga; vti vestirsi.

Robert ['rɔbət] nm pr Roberto.

robin (**redbreast**) ['rɔbin('redbrest)] n pettirosso.

robot ['roubɔt] n 'robot', automa.

robust [rə'bʌst] a robusto, vigoroso.

rock [rɔk] n roccia, scoglio; rocca; vti cullar(si), dondolar(si).

rocket ['rɔkit] n razzo, missile; vi elevarsi come un razzo, (of prices) salire vertiginosamente.

rocking ['rɔkiŋ] a a dondolo, barcollante; **r. chair** sedia a dondolo.

rocky ['rɔki] a roccioso.

rod [rɔd] n bacchetta; verga; canna (da pesca), (measure) pertica.

rodent ['roudənt] a n roditore.

Roderick ['rɔdərik] nm pr Rodrigo.

roe [rou] n capriolo; (fish) uova di pesce.

Roger ['rɔdʒə] nm pr Ruggero.

rogue [roug] n briccone, furfante; birichino, bricconcello.

roguery ['rougəri] n furfanteria.

roguish ['rougiʃ] a furbo, malizioso.

roguishness ['rougiʃnis] n bricconeria; furberia, malizia.

roister ['rɔistə] vi far baccano.

Roland ['roulənd] nm pr Orlando.

role [roul] n ruolo.

roll [roul] n rotolo; rullo, elenco; (naut) rullio, (thunder etc) rombo; panino; vt avvolgere, rotolare; vi rotolare, ruzzolare, rullare; (time) scorrere.

roller ['roulə] n rullo, cilindro; (sea) maroso; **r. skates** pattini a rotelle.

rolling stock ['rouliŋstɔk] n (rly) materiale rotabile.

Roman ['roumən] a n romano.

romance [rə'mæns] n romanzo cavalleresco; (mus) romanza; romanticheria, idillio; vi romanzare. **R.** a romanzo.

Romanesque [,roumə'nesk] *a* romanico; *n* (*arch*) stile romanico.

romantic [rə'mæntik] *a* romantico; romanzesco.

romanticism [rə'mæntisizəm] *n* romanticismo.

Rome [roum] *n* Roma.

romp [rɔmp] *n* giuoco rumoroso; ragazza indiavolata; *vi* giocare rumorosamente.

Ronald ['rɔnld] *nm pr* Rinaldo.

roof [ru:f] *n* tetto; *vt* ricoprire con tetto, fare il tetto a.

rook [ruk] *n* cornacchia; (*chess*) torre.

room [rum] *n* camera, stanza; posto, spazio; possibilità.

roomy ['rumi] *a* spazioso, vasto.

roost [ru:st] *n* posatoio di uccelli; pollaio; *vi* appollaiarsi; (*fam*) andare a dormire.

rooster ['ru:stə] *n* gallo domestico.

root [ru:t] *n* radice; *vt* fissare saldamente; **to r. up** sradicare; *vi* radicarsi.

rope [roup] *n* corda, fune; (*pearls*) filo.

Rosalind ['rɔzəlind] *nf pr* Rosalinda.

rosary ['rouzəri] *n* rosario.

rose [rouz] *n* rosa.

rosemary ['rouzməri] *n* rosmarino.

rosy ['rouzi] *a* roseo.

rot [rɔt] *n* marciume, putrefazione; malattia delle pecore; (*sl*) sciocchezze; *vt* far marcire; *vi* imputridire, marcire.

rotate [rou'teit] *vti* (far) rotare; coltivare a rotazione.

rotation [rou'teifən] *n* rotazione, successione.

rote [rout] *n* memoria meccanica.

rotten ['rɔtn] *a* marcio, putrido; (*sl*) disgustoso; (*fig*) corrotto.

rotund [rou'tʌnd] *a* rotondo.

rotundity [rou'tʌnditi] *n* rotondità.

rouble ['ru:bl] *n* rublo.

rouge [ru:ʒ] *n* rossetto; *vt* imbellettare; *vi* mettersi il rossetto.

rough [rʌf] *a* (*ground*) accidentato; grossolano, rozzo, rude, ruvido; approssimativo; violento, (*sea*) agitato, (*weather*) tempestoso.

roughen ['rʌfən] *vti* irruvidir(si), diventare (rendere) rozzo.

roughly ['rʌfli] *ad* approssimativamente; ruvidamente, violentemente.

roughness ['rʌfnis] *n* rozzezza, ruvidezza; grossolanità, violenza.

Roumania [ru:'meiniə] *v* **Rumania**.

round [raund] *a* circolare, rotondo, tondo; *n* cerchio, sfera; (*tour*) giro; (*rung*) piolo; (*applause*) scoppio, ronda; *ad* all'intorno, in giro; *prep* intorno a; *vt* arrotondare; completare; girare; *vi* completarsi.

roundabout ['raundəbaut] *a* indiretto, tortuoso; *n* giostra; (*traffic*) traffico a senso unico.

roundly ['raundli] *ad* vigorosamente; chiaro e tondo.

rouse [rauz] *vt* destare, (ri)svegliare; incitare, provocare; *vi* svegliarsi.

rout [raut] *n* folla tumultuante, sommossa; (*mil*) rotta, sconfitta; *vt* (*mil*) mettere in rotta, sbaragliare; **to r. out** cacciar fuori, snidare.

route [ru:t] *n* via, rotta; (*mil*) (ordini di) marcia; **r. march** marcia d'allenamento.

routine [ru:'ti:n] *n* 'routine', pratica, abitudine meccanica.

rove [rouv] *vi* errare, vagabondare.

rover ['rouvə] *n* giramondo; (*scouts*) 'rover'; pirata.

row [rou] *n* (*fam*) baccano, lite rumorosa.

row [rau] *n* fila, filare; gita in barca a remi; *vt* far andare a forza di remi; *vi* remare, vogare.

rowdy ['raudi] *a* rumoroso, litigioso.

rowel ['rauəl] *n* stella di sperone.

royal ['rɔiəl] *a* reale, regale, regio; eccellente.

royalist ['rɔiəlist] *n* realista, monarchico.

royalty ['rɔiəlti] *n* regalità, sovranità; membro di famiglia reale; diritto d'autore.

rub [rʌb] *n* fregata, frizione; (*fig*) difficoltà, ostacolo; *vt* fregare, strofinare, lucidare; *vi* fregarsi, logorarsi.

rubber ['rʌbə] *n* gomma, caucciù; strofinaccio; (*cards*) partita tripla; *pl* (*US*) soprascarpe di gomma.

rubbish ['rʌbiʃ] *n* rifiuti, scarti *pl*; cosa di nessun valore, sciocchezza.

rubble ['rʌbl] *n* pietrisco, frantumi di pietra.

Rubicon ['ru:bikən] *n pr* Rubicone.

rubric ['ru:brik] *n* rubrica.

ruby ['ru:bi] *n* rubino.

rudder ['rʌdə] *n* (*naut*) timone.

ruddy ['rʌdi] *a* rubicondo, vermiglio; (*sl*) maledetto.

rude [ru:d] *a* rude, offensivo, sgarbato; vigoroso.

rudeness ['ru:dnis] *n* sgarbatezza, grossolanità.

rudiment ['ru:dimənt] *n* rudimento.

rudimental [,ru:di'mentl] *a* rudimentale.

Rudolf, Rudolph ['ru:dɔlf] *n pr* Rodolfo.

rue [ru:] *n* (*bot*) ruta; *vt* pentirsi di.

rueful ['ru:ful] *a* lamentevole, triste.

ruff [rʌf] *n* gorgiera; (*of bird*) collare.

ruffian ['rʌfiən] *n* malfattore, ribaldo.

ruffle ['rʌfl] *n* guarnizione pieghettata; increspatura; *vt* arruffare, increspare; (*fig*) irritare.

rug [rʌg] *n* coperta (da viaggio); tappetino.

rugby ['rʌgbi] *n* (*sport*) 'rugby', pallaovale.

rugged ['rʌgid] *a* ruvido, scabro, irregolare; aspro, austero, inflessibile; (*US*) vigoroso.

ruggedness ['rʌgidnis] *n* ruvidezza,

scabrosità, irregolarità; asprezza inflessibilità.

ruin ['ruin] *n* rovina, macerie, ruderi *pl*; *vt* rovinare.

ruinous ['ruinəs] *a* rovinoso; in rovina.

rule [ru:l] *n* regola, norma; regolo, riga; governo; *vt* dominare, governare, regolare; rigare; *vi* aver dominio.

ruler ['ru:lə] *n* sovrano, governatore; regolo, riga.

ruling ['ru:liŋ] *a* dominante, prevalente; *n* regolamento; governo; rigatura.

rum [rʌm] *n* rum.

Rumania [ru:'meiniə] *n* Romania.

Rumanian [ru:'meiniən] *a n* romeno.

rumble ['rʌmbl] *n* (*thunder etc*) rombo; brontolio; rumoreggiamento; *vi* brontolare; rumoreggiare.

ruminate ['ru:mineit] *vti* ruminare; meditare, rumiginare.

rumination [,ru:mi'neiʃən] *n* ruminazione.

rummage ['rʌmidʒ] *vti* frugare, rovistare.

rumour ['ru:mə] *n* diceria.

rump [rʌmp] *n* groppa, posteriore.

rumple ['rʌmpl] *vt* sgualcire; (*hair*) arruffare.

run [rʌn] *n* corsa, gita, giro; tragitto, corso; periodo, successione, serie; recinto di animali; *vt* far correre; condurre, gestire; *vi* correre; decorrere; scorrere; fuggire; diffondersi.

runaway ['rʌnəwei] *n* fuggiasco.

rung [rʌŋ] *n* piolo.

runner ['rʌnə] *n* corridore; messo; (*mil*) staffetta; passatoia; (*millstone*) macina; **r. bean** fagiolo rampicante; **r.-up** (*sport*) secondo arrivato.

runway ['rʌnwei] *n* pista di decollo, pista di lancio.

rupture ['rʌptʃə] *n* rottura; (*med*) ernia.

rural ['ruərəl] *a* rurale, campestre.

ruse [ru:z] *n* astuzia, stratagemma.

rush [rʌʃ] *n* giunco; afflusso, assalto, impeto; *vt* prendere d'assalto; *vi* affluire, precipitarsi.

rusk [rʌsk] *n* pane biscottato.

russet ['rʌsit] *a* color ruggine.

Russia ['rʌʃə] *n* Russia.

Russian ['rʌʃən] *a n* russo.

rust [rʌst] *n* ruggine; *vt* corrodere; *vi* arrugginire.

rustic ['rʌstik] *a* rustico, grezzo.

rusticate ['rʌstikeit] *vt* sospendere (studenti universitari); *vi* vivere in campagna.

rustle ['rʌsl] *n* fruscio, stormire; *vti* (far) frusciare, (far) stormire.

rusty ['rʌsti] *a* arrugginito, rugginoso.

rut [rʌt] *n* (*groove*) solco; (*fig*) abitudine inveterata; (*of animals*) fregola; *vt* solcare; *vi* essere in fregola, in calore.

ruthless ['ru:θlis] *a* spietato.

rye [rai] *n* segale.

S

Sabbath ['sæbəθ] *n* (*Jewish*) sabato, (*Christian*) domenica.

sable ['seibl] *a* di zibellino; *n* zibellino.

sabotage ['sæbətɑ:ʒ] *n* sabotaggio; *vt* sabotare.

sabre ['seibə] *n* sciabola.

saccharine ['sækərin] *n* saccarina.

sack [sæk] *n* sacco; saccheggio; (*sl*) licenziamento; *vt* insaccare; saccheggiare; (*sl*) licenziare.

sacking ['sækiŋ] *n* tela da sacchi.

sacrament ['sækrəmənt] *n* sacramento.

sacred ['seikrid] *a* sacro, consacrato.

sacrifice ['sækrifais] *n* sacrificio; *vt* sacrificare.

sacrilege ['sækrilidʒ] *n* sacrilegio.

sacristan ['sækristən] *n* sagrestano.

sacristy ['sækristi] *n* sagrestia.

sad [sæd] *a* triste, doloroso, funesto.

sadden ['sædn] *vt* rattristare.

saddle ['sædl] *n* sella; *vt* sellare; (*fig*) addossare, gravare.

sadistic [sə'distik] *a* sadico.

sadness ['sædnis] *n* tristezza.

safe [seif] *a* sano, salvo, sicuro, intatto, al sicuro, cauto; *n* cassaforte; (*arms*) sicura.

safe conduct ['seif'kɔndəkt] *n* salvacondotto.

safeguard ['seifgɑ:d] *n* salvaguardia, difesa.

safety ['seifti] *n* sicurezza, salvezza; **s. belt** cintura di sicurezza; **s. pin** spilla di sicurezza; **s. island** salvagente (stradale).

saffron ['sæfrən] *n* zafferano.

sag [sæg] *vi* curvarsi, piegarsi, (*of prices*) cedere.

saga ['sɑ:gə] *n* saga; romanzo fiume.

sagacious [sə'geiʃəs] *a* sagace.

sagacity [sə'gæsiti] *n* sagacia, perspicacia.

sage [seidʒ] *a n* saggio; *n* salvia.

sageness ['seidʒnis] *n* saggezza.

sail [seil] *n* vela, gita o viaggio su imbarcazione a vela; *vti* navigare, veleggiare, salpare, sorvolare.

sailer ['seilə] *n* veliero.

sailor ['seilə] *n* marinaio.

saint [seint] *a n* santo (*abbr* St).

saintly ['seintli] *a* santo.

sake [seik] *n* amore, causa, motivo.

salacious [sə'leiʃəs] *a* salace.

salad ['sæləd] *n* insalata.

salamander ['sælə,mændə] *n* salamandra.

salary ['sæləri] *n* stipendio.

sale [seil] *n* vendita; svendita.

saleable ['seiləbl] *a* smerciabile, vendibile.

salesman ['seilzmən] *n* venditore, viaggiatore commesso, piazzista.

salient ['seiliənt] *a n* saliente.

saliva [sə'laivə] *n* saliva; **salivary** *a* salivare.

sallow ['sælou] *a* olivastro; *n* salice.

sally ['sæli] *n* sortita; battuta spiritosa; *vi* balzar fuori, fare una sortita.

salmon ['sæmən] *n* salmone.

salon ['sælɔ:ŋ] *n* salone; galleria d'arte.

saloon [sə'lu:n] *n* sala da ricevimenti; (*US*) bar; **s. car** (*aut*) berlina, macchina chiusa; **s. keeper** (*US*) oste, proprietario di bar.

salt [sɔ:lt] *a* amaro, salato, salso; *n* sale; *vt* salare.

saltiness ['sɔ:ltnis] *n* gusto di sale.

saltpetre ['sɔ:lt,pi:tə] *n* salnitro.

salty ['sɔ:lti] *a* salato, salmastro; piccante.

salutary ['sæljutəri] *a* salutare.

salutation [,sælju:'teiʃən] *n* saluto.

salute [sə'lu:t] *n* saluto; (*mil*) salva; *vt* salutare.

salvage ['sælvidʒ] *n* salvataggio, ricupero; *vt* salvare.

salvation [sæl'veiʃən] *n* salvezza.

salver ['sælvə] *n* vassoio.

salvo ['sælvou] *pl* **salvoes** *n* (*mil*) salva.

same [seim] *a pron* medesimo, stesso.

sameness ['seimnis] *n* identità, uniformità.

sample ['sɑ:mpl] *n* campione, modello, esemplare; **samples** *pl* campionario; *vt* assaggiare.

sanatorium [,sænə'tɔ:riəm] *n* sanatorio.

sanctify ['sæŋktifai] *vt* santificare.

sanctimonious [,sæŋkti'mouniəs] *a* santarello, bigotto, ipocrita.

sanction ['sæŋkʃən] *n* sanzione; *vt* autorizzare, ratificare, sanzionare.

sanctity ['sæŋktiti] *n* santità.

sanctuary ['sæŋktjuəri] *n* santuario, asilo.

sand [sænd] *n* sabbia, rena; **sandbank** banco di sabbia; **sandhill** duna; **sandpaper** cartavetrata.

sandal ['sændl] *n* sandalo.

sandwich ['sænwidʒ] *n* 'sandwich', panino ripieno; **open s.** tartina.

sandy ['sændi] *a* sabbioso; (*colour*) giallo-rossastro.

sane [sein] *a* sano di mente, equilibrato.

sanguinary ['sæŋgwinəri] *a* sanguinario.

sanguine ['sæŋgwin] *a* sanguigno, rubicondo; ottimista.

sanitary ['sænitəri] *a* igienico, sanitario.

sanitation [,sæni'teiʃən] *n* igiene.

sanity ['sæniti] *n* sanità di mente.

Santa Claus [,sæntə'klɔ:z] *nm pr* Babbo Natale.

sap [sæp] *n* linfa, succo; (*mil*) scavo d'approccio, trincea; *vt* minare (*also* fig).

sapling ['sæpliŋ] *n* alberello.

sapper ['sæpə] *n* zappatore; (*mil*) geniere, genio.

sapphire ['sæfaiə] *n* zaffiro.

sappy ['sæpi] *a* ricco di linfa, succoso.

Saracen ['særəsn] *a n* saraceno.

Sarah ['sɛərə] *nf pr* Sara.

sarcasm ['sɑ:kæzəm] *n* sarcasmo.

sarcastic [sɑ:'kæstik] *a* sarcastico.

sardine [sɑ:'di:n] *n* sardina.

Sardinia [sɑ:'diniə] *n* Sardegna.

Sardinian [sɑ:'diniən] *a n* sardo.

sardonic [sɑ:'dɔnik] *a* sardonico.

sash [sæʃ] *n* cintura, sciarpa; telaio scorrevole di finestra.

Satan ['seitən] *nm pr* Satana.

satchel ['sætʃəl] *n* cartella di scolaro.

sate [seit] *vt* satollare, saziare.

satellite ['sætəlait] *a n* satellite.

satiate ['seiʃieit] *vt* saziare.

satiation [,seiti'eiʃən] **satiety** [sə-'taiəti] *n* sazietà.

satin ['sætin] *n* raso.

satire ['sætaiə] *n* satira.

satiric(al) [sə'tirik(əl)] *a* satirico.

satirist ['sætərist] *n* scrittore satirico.

satirize ['sætəraiz] *vt* satireggiare.

satisfaction [,sætis'fækʃən] *n* soddisfazione.

satisfactorily [,sætis'fæktərili] *ad* soddisfacentemente.

satisfactory [,sætis'fæktəri] *a* soddisfacente.

satisfy ['sætisfai] *vt* soddisfare; convincere, persuadere.

saturate ['sætʃəreit] *vt* saturare.

saturation [,sætʃə'reiʃən] *n* saturazione.

Saturday ['sætədi] *n* sabato.

saturnine ['sætə:nain] *a* cupo, taciturno, tetro.

sauce [sɔ:s] *n* intingolo, salsa; (*fig*) impertinenza.

saucepan ['sɔ:spən] *n* casseruola.

saucer ['sɔ:sə] *n* piattino, sottocoppa.

sauciness ['sɔ:sinis] *n* impertinenza.

saucy ['sɔ:si] *a* impertinente.

saunter ['sɔ:ntə] *vi* andare a zonzo.

sausage ['sɔsidʒ] *n* salsiccia, salame.

sauté ['soutei] *a* (*cook*) saltato in padella, fritto.

savage ['sævidʒ] *a n* selvaggio; *a* barbaro, brutale.

savageness ['sævidʒnis] **savagery** ['sævidʒəri] *n* brutalità, ferocia.

save [seiv] *prep* ad eccezione di, salvo; *vt* salvare, conservare, economizzare, risparmiare; *vi* fare economie.

saving ['seiviŋ] *a* economico; *n* risparmio, economia.

saviour ['seivjə] *n* salvatore, redentore.

savour ['seivə] *n* gusto, sapore; *vi* sapere di, aver il gusto; *vt* assaporare, gustare; insaporire.

savoury ['seivəri] *a* saporito, piccante; *n* salatino.

Savoy [sə'vɔi] *n* Savoia.

Savoyard [sə'vɔiɑ:d] *a n* savoiardo.

saw [sɔ:] *n* sega; massima, proverbio; *vt* segare.

sawdust ['sɔ:dʌst] *n* segatura.

sawmill ['sɔ:mil] *n* segheria.

sawyer ['sɔːjə] n segatore.
Saxon ['sæksn] a n sassone.
Saxony ['sæksni] n Sassonia.
saxophone ['sæksəfoun] n sassofono.
say [sei] vti dire, affermare, asserire.
saying ['seiiŋ] n massima, proverbio.
scab [skæb] n crosta, scabbia; (US) crumiro.
scabbard ['skæbəd] n fodero, guaina.
scabby ['skæbi] a pieno di croste, scabbioso.
scaffold ['skæfəld] n patibolo.
scaffolding ['skæfəldiŋ] n impalcatura, intelaiatura.
scald [skɔːld] n scottatura; vt scottare, ustionare.
scalding ['skɔːldiŋ] a bollente, scottante; n scottatura.
scale [skeil] n gradazione, scala; scaglia, squama; bilancia; vti scalare, graduare; vi squamarsi.
scalp [skælp] n cuoio capelluto; vt scotennare.
scalpel ['skælpəl] n (med) scalpello.
scaly ['skeili] a squamoso, coperto di incrostazioni.
scamp [skæmp] n birichino, mascalzoncello.
scamper ['skæmpə] vi correre; s. away svignarsela.
scan [skæn] vt scandire; scrutare attentamente; vi (verse) essere corretto.
scandal ['skændl] n scandalo.
scandalize ['skændəlaiz] vt scandalizzare.
scandalous ['skændələs] a scandaloso.
Scandinavia [,skændi'neiviə] n Scandinavia.
Scandinavian [,skændi'neiviən] a n scandinavo.
scansion ['skænʃən] n scansione.
scant [skænt] a esiguo, insufficiente, scarso.
scantiness ['skæntinis] n esiguità, scarsezza.
scanty ['skænti] a limitato, ristretto, scarso.
scapegoat ['skeipgout] n capro espiatorio.
scapegrace ['skeipgreis] n scapestrato.
scapular(y) ['skæpjulər(i)] n scapolare.
scar [skaː] n cicatrice, segno.
scarce [skɛəs] a scarso, raro.
scarcely ['skɛəsli] ad appena, a mala pena, a stento.
scarcity ['skɛəsiti] n scarsezza, penuria.
scare [skɛə] n panico, spavento; vt spaventare.
scarecrow ['skɛəkrou] n spauracchio, spaventapasseri.
scarf [skaːf] n sciarpa.
scarlet ['skaːlit] a n rosso scarlatto.
scathing ['skeiðiŋ] a sarcastico, mordace.
scatter ['skætə] vti sparger(si).

scavenger ['skævindʒə] n spazzino.
scene [siːn] n scena; scenata.
scenery ['siːnəri] n scenario, veduta, panorama, paesaggio.
scenic ['siːnik] a scenico, teatrale.
scent [sent] n odore, profumo; fiuto; vt fiutare; profumare.
sceptic ['skeptik] n scettico.
sceptical ['skeptikəl] a scettico.
scepticism ['skeptisizəm] n scetticismo.
sceptre ['septə] n scettro.
schedule ['ʃedjuːl] n inventario, lista; orario, programma.
scheme [skiːm] n piano, progetto; vt progettare; vi fare progetti, intrigare.
schism ['sizəm] n scisma.
schismatic [siz'mætik] a n scismatico.
schizophrenic [,skitsou'frenik] a n schizofrenico.
scholar ['skɔlə] n erudito, studioso, studente detentore d'una borsa di studio.
scholarly ['skɔləli] a dotto, erudito.
scholarship ['skɔləʃip] n dottrina, erudizione; borsa di studio.
scholastic [skə'læstik] a n scolastico.
school [skuːl] n scuola; vt disciplinare, domare; **schoolhouse** scuola.
schooling ['skuːliŋ] n insegnamento, istruzione.
schoolmaster ['skuːlˌmɑːstə] n insegnante, maestro, professore.
schoolroom ['skuːlrum] n aula scolastica.
schooner ['skuːnə] n (naut) goletta.
sciatica [sai'ætikə] n sciatica.
science ['saiəns] n scienza; **s. fiction** fantascienza.
scientific [,saiən'tifik] a scientifico.
scientist ['saiəntist] n scienziato.
scimitar ['simitə] n scimitarra.
scintillate ['sintileit] vt scintillare, brillare.
scion ['saiən] n (plants) pollone; (fig) erede, rampollo.
scissors ['sizəz] n pl forbici pl.
scoff [skɔf] vti **s. at** beffare, deridere.
scold [skould] n donna bisbetica; vti rimproverare, sgridare.
scone [skɔn] n pastina da tè.
scoop [skuːp] n paletta, ramaiuolo; (fig, press) notizia, servizio in esclusiva; vt vuotare; (press) accapararrsi una notizia; **to s. up** raccogliere con la pala.
scooter ['skuːtə] n monopattino; 'scooter', motoretta.
scope [skoup] n portata, campo d'azione, prospettiva.
scorch [skɔːtʃ] n scottatura; vt scottare.
score [skɔː] n ventina; punto; punteggio; numero di punti; conto; scotto; tacca; (mus) spartito; vt intaccare, marcare, segnare; segnare punti, mettere in conto; (mus) orche-

strare; *vi* assicurarsi un vantaggio, aver fortuna.

scorn [skɔːn] *n* disprezzo, sdegno; *vt* disprezzare.

scornful ['skɔːnful] *a* sdegnoso.

scornfully ['skɔːnfuli] *ad* sprezzantemente, sdegnosamente.

scorpion ['skɔːpiən] *n* scorpione.

Scot [skɔt] *n* scozzese.

Scotch [skɔtʃ] **Scottish** ['skɔtiʃ] *a* scozzese.

Scotland ['skɔtlənd] *n* Scozia.

Scots [skɔts] *a* scozzese.

Scotsman [skɔtsmən] *n* scozzese.

scoundrel ['skaundrəl] *n* farabutto, mascalzone.

scour ['skauə] *vt* pulire fregando; perlustrare.

scourge [skəːdʒ] *n* frusta, sferza; *vt* fustigare, sferzare.

scout [skaut] *n* esploratore, vedetta; *vt* respingere con sdegno; *vi* esplorare.

scowl [skaul] *n* sguardo torvo; *vi* guardare torvo.

scrabble ['skræbl] *vi* frugare affannosamente.

scraggy ['skrægi] *a* ossuto, scarno.

scramble ['skræmbl] *n* parapiglia, lotta, confusione; *vi* affrettarsi, arrampicarsi con mani e piedi; *vt* arraffare, (*eggs*) strapazzare.

scrap [skræp] *n* frammento, pezzetto; rottame; *vt* scartare; **scrapbook** album di ritagli.

scrape [skreip] *n* raschiatura, graffio; (*fam*) impiccio, situazione difficile; *vt* raschiare, scrostare, sfregare; **to s. through** cavarsela.

scraper ['skreipə] *n* raschietto; (*mat*) puliscisuola.

scrapings ['skreipiŋz] *n pl* risparmi.

scrappy ['skræpi] *a* frammentario.

scratch [skrætʃ] *a* male assortito, eterogeneo; *n* graffio; linea di partenza; *vti* graffiare, grattare, raspare; **to start from s.** partire da zero; **to come up to s.** (*fig*) farsi onore; **s. pad** (*US*) blocco per note, nòtes.

scratchy ['skrætʃi] *a* scarabocchiato; scricchiolante.

scrawl [skrɔːl] *n* scarabocchio; *vti* scarabocchiare.

scream [skriːm] *n* strillo, urlo; *vi* strillare, urlare.

screech [skriːtʃ] *n* strillo acuto; *vi* strillare.

screed [skriːd] *n* lunga filastrocca.

screen [skriːn] *n* parafuoco, paravento; difesa, riparo; (*cin*, *TV*) schermo; *vt* proteggere, riparare; proiettare.

screw [skruː] *n* vite; (*sl*) strozzino; (*sl*) ronzino; (*sl*) paga; *vti* avvitare; (*fig*) opprimere.

screwdriver ['skruːˌdraivə] *n* cacciavite.

scribble ['skribl] *n* scarabocchio; *vti*

scarabocchiare; **scribbling block** blocco per note, nòtes.

scribbler ['skriblə] *n* imbrattacarte.

scribe [skraib] *n* copista, scriba.

scrimmage ['skrimidʒ] *n* schermaglia.

script [skript] *n* scrittura; (*typ*) corsivo; (*theat etc*) copione, sceneggiatura.

scripture ['skriptʃə] *n* sacra scrittura.

scroll [skroul] *n* pergamena; rotolo di carta; svolazzo; (*arch*) voluta.

scrub [skrʌb] *n* sottobosco, macchia; *vti* strofinare energicamente.

scruff [skrʌf] *n* (*of the neck*) collottola.

scruple ['skruːpl] *n* scrupolo; *vi* esitare, farsi scrupolo di.

scrupulosity [ˌskruːpjuˈlɔsiti] *n* scrupolosità.

scrupulous ['skruːpjuləs] *a* scrupoloso.

scrutinize ['skruːtinaiz] *vt* scrutinare.

scrutiny ['skruːtini] *n* esame minuzioso, scrutinio.

scud [skʌd] *n* fuga, rapida corsa; *vi* correre velocemente.

scuffle ['skʌfl] *n* baruffa, parapiglia; *vi* azzuffarsi.

scull [skʌl] *n* remo; *vti* vogare con remi corti.

scullery ['skʌləri] *n* retrocucina.

sculptor ['skʌlptə] *n* scultore.

sculptural ['skʌlptʃərəl] *a* di scultura, scultorio.

sculpture ['skʌlptʃə] *n* scultura; *vt* scolpire.

scum [skʌm] *n* schiuma, (*also fig*) feccia, scoria.

scurf [skəːf] *n* forfora.

scurrility [skʌˈriliti] *n* scurrilità.

scurrilous ['skʌriləs] *a* scurrile.

scurry ['skʌri] *n* corsa frettolosa; *vi* correre, affrettarsi.

scurvy ['skəːvi] *a* basso, vile; *n* scorbuto.

scuttle ['skʌtl] *n* recipiente per il carbone; fuga precipitosa; (*naut*) portello; *vt* (*naut*) affondare; *vi* svignarsela.

scythe [saið] *n* falce.

sea [siː] *n* mare; **s. level** livello del mare; **s. power** potenza navale; **s. shell** conchiglia; **s. voyage** viaggio per mare.

seafarer ['siːˌfɛərə] *n* navigatore.

seal [siːl] *n* sigillo, suggello, timbro; (*zool*) foca; *vt* bollare, sigillare, suggellare.

sealing wax ['siːliŋwæks] *n* ceralacca.

seam [siːm] *n* costura, cucitura; cicatrice; (*geol*) giacimento.

seaman ['siːmən] *n* marinaio.

seamstress ['semstris] *n* cucitrice.

seaplane ['siːplein] *n* idrovolante.

seaport ['siːpɔːt] *n* porto di mare.

sear [siə] *vt* bruciare, cauterizzare, disseccare, (*fig*) indurire.

search [səːtʃ] *n* ricerca, indagine, inchiesta; perquisizione; *vt* perquisire; *vi* cercare, fare ricerche, perlustrare.

searching ['səːtʃiŋ] *a* indagatore, penetrante, minuzioso.

searchlight ['səːtʃlait] *n* riflettore.

seaside ['siː'said] *n* spiaggia, mare; **s. resort** stazione balneare.

season ['siːzn] *n* stagione; epoca; tempo; *vt* condire; stagionare; acclimatare; *vi* divenire stagionato.

seasonable ['siːznəbl] *a* di stagione; tempestivo.

seasoning ['siːzniŋ] *n* condimento; stagionatura.

seat [siːt] *n* posto (a sedere), panca, sedia, sedile, seggio; sede; residenza; sedere, deretano; *vt* far sedere, offrire posti a sedere a; **four-seater** (*aut*) automobile a quattro posti.

seaweed ['siːwiːd] *n* alga.

Sebastian [si'bæstiən] *nm pr* Sebastiano.

secede [si'siːd] *vi* separarsi.

secession [si'seʃən] *n* secessione, separazione.

secluded [si'kluːdid] *a* ritirato, appartato.

seclusion [si'kluːʒən] *n* ritiro, solitudine, reclusione.

second ['sekənd] *a n* secondo; *vt* appoggiare, assecondare; **s.-hand** di seconda mano.

secondary ['sekəndəri] *a* secondario, subordinato.

secrecy ['siːkrisi] *n* segretezza.

secret ['siːkrit] *a n* segreto.

secretary ['sekrətri] *n* segretario, -a.

secrete [si'kriːt] *vt* secernere; nascondere.

secretion [si'kriːʃən] *n* secrezione.

secretive ['siːkritiv] *a* riservato, poco comunicativo.

sect [sekt] *n* setta.

sectarian [sek'tɛəriən] *a n* settario.

section ['sekʃən] *n* sezione, paragrafo; parte.

sector ['sektə] *n* settore.

secular ['sekjulə] *a n* secolare.

secularization ['sekjulərai'zeiʃən] *n* secolarizzazione.

secularize ['sekjuləraiz] *vt* secolarizzare.

secure [si'kjuə] *a* sicuro, al sicuro, fiducioso, tranquillo; *vt* assicurare, garantire; procurarsi.

security [si'kjuəriti] *n* sicurezza, garanzia.

sedan [si'dæn] *n* portantina.

sedate [si'deit] *a* calmo, pacato.

sedateness [si'deitnis] *n* calma, pacatezza.

sedative ['sedətiv] *a n* sedativo, calmante.

sedentary ['sedntəri] *a n* sedentario.

sedge [sedʒ] *n* carice.

sediment ['sedimənt] *n* sedimento.

sedition [si'diʃən] *n* sedizione.

seditious [si'diʃəs] *a* sedizioso.

seduce [si'djuːs] *vt* sedurre.

seduction [si'dʌkʃən] *n* seduzione.

sedulous ['sedjuləs] *a* assiduo, diligente.

see [siː] *n* diocesi, sede; *vti* vedere; capire; visitare.

seed [siːd] *n* seme, semenza; *vi* produrre semi.

seedling ['siːdliŋ] *n* pianticella, alberello.

seedy ['siːdi] *a* pieno di semi: (*fig*) male in arnese, indisposto.

seek [siːk] *vti* cercare, perseguire.

seem [siːm] *vi* sembrare, parere.

seeming ['siːmiŋ] *a* apparente.

seemly ['siːmli] *a* di bell'aspetto, decoroso.

seep [siːp] *vi* filtrare, penetrare.

seer ['siːə] *n* veggente, profeta.

seesaw ['siːsɔː] *n* altalena.

seethe [siːð] *vi* bollire; essere in fermento.

segment ['segmənt] *n* segmento.

segregate ['segrigeit] *vti* segregar(si).

segregation [,segri'geiʃən] *n* segregazione.

Seine [sein] *n* Senna.

seize [siːz] *vt* afferrare, impadronirsi di, confiscare, sequestrare.

seizure ['siːʒə] *n* presa, confisca; (*med*) attacco.

seldom ['seldəm] *ad* di rado, raramente.

select [si'lekt] *a* scelto; *vt* scegliere, selezionare.

selection [si'lekʃən] *n* assortimento, scelta, selezione.

self [self] *n* l'io, l'individuo, se stesso.

self-command ['selfkə'maːnd] *n* padronanza di sè.

self-conceit ['selfkən'siːt] *n* presunzione.

self-confidence ['self'kɔnfidəns] *n* sicurezza di sè.

self-conscious ['self'kɔnʃəs] *a* impacciato; (*phil*) autocosciente.

self-contained ['selfkən'teind] *a* riservato; autonomo, indipendente.

self-control ['selfkən'troul] *n* padronanza di sè.

self-defence ['selfdi'fens] *n* autodifesa.

self-denial ['selfdi'naiəl] *n* abnegazione.

self-government ['self'gʌvnmənt] *n* autonomia.

selfish ['selfiʃ] *a* egoista, egoistico.

selfishness ['selfiʃnis] *n* egoismo.

selfless ['selflis] *a* altruistico, disinteressato.

self-made ['self'meid] *a* che deve tutto a se stesso, che si è fatto da sè.

self-reliance ['selfri'laiəns] *n* fiducia in sè.

self-supporting ['selfsə'pɔːtiŋ] *a* indipendente.

self-service ['self'səːvis] *a n* 'self service', (di) locale in cui ci si serve da sè.

self-taught ['self'tɔːt] *a* autodidatta.

sell [sel] *vt* vendere; *vi* trovare smercio, vendersi.

semaphore ['semәfɔ:] n semaforo.

semblance ['semblәns] n aspetto, apparenza; parvenza; somiglianza.

semicircle ['semi.sә:kl] n semicerchio.

seminar ['seminɑ:] n (university) seminario.

seminary ['seminәri] n seminario.

semolina [semә'li:nә] n semolino.

senate ['senit] n senato.

senator ['senәtә] n senatore.

send [send] vt mandare, inviare, spedire; **to s. for** mandare a chiamare; **sender** mittente, speditore.

senile ['si:nail] a senile.

senility [si'niliti] n senilità.

senior ['si:niә] a n maggiore, più anziano, seniore, decano.

seniority [.si:ni'ɔriti] n anzianità.

sensation [sen'seiʃәn] n sensazione, scalpore.

sensational [sen'seiʃәnl] a sensazionale.

sense [sens] n senso; conoscenza; buon senso; significato.

senseless ['senslis] a inanime; assurdo, senza significato.

sensibility [.sensi'biliti] n sensibilità.

sensible ['sensәbl] a sensato, ragionevole, cosciente.

sensitive ['sensitiv] a sensibile, sensitivo, suscettibile.

sensitiveness ['sensitivnis] **sensitivity** [.sensi'tiviti] n sensibilità, suscettibilità.

sensorial [sen'sɔ:riәl] a sensorio.

sensual ['sensjuәl] a sensuale, voluttuoso.

sensuality [.sensju'æliti] n sensualità, voluttà.

sensuous ['sensjuәs] a dei sensi, sensitivo.

sentence ['sentәns] n sentenza, condanna; frase, periodo; massima; vt condannare.

sentiment ['sentimәnt] n sentimento, idea; sentimentalità.

sentimental [.senti'mentl] a sentimentale.

sentinel ['sentinl] **sentry** ['sentri] n (mil) sentinella.

sentry-box ['sentriboks] n garitta.

separate ['separeit] vti divider(si), separar(si); ['separit] a separato, distinto.

separately ['sepәritli] ad separatamente, singolarmente.

separation [.sepә'reiʃәn] n separazione.

sepia ['si:piә] n seppia; color seppia.

September [sәp'tembә] n settembre.

septic ['septik] a settico.

sepulchral [si'pʌlkrәl] a sepolcrale.

sepulchre ['sepәlkә] n sepolcro; **whited s.** sepolcro imbiancato, ipocrita.

sequel ['si:kwәl] n seguito.

sequence ['si:kwәns] n serie, successione.

sequestered [si'kwestәd] a remoto, solitario.

sequestrate [si'kwestreit] vt sequestrare.

sequestration [.si:kwes'treiʃәn] n sequestro.

serenade [.seri'neid] n serenata.

serene [si'ri:n] a calmo, sereno.

serenity [si'reniti] n serenità.

serf [sә:f] n servo della gleba.

serge [sә:dʒ] n 'serge', saia.

sergeant ['sɑ:dʒәnt] n sergente.

serial ['siәriәl] a periodico, a puntate; n romanzo a puntate, pubblicazione periodica.

series ['siәri:z] n serie.

serious ['siәriәs] a serio, grave.

seriously ['siәriәsli] ad seriamente, sul serio; gravemente.

seriousness ['siәriәsnis] n serietà, gravità.

sermon ['sә:mәn] n predica, sermone, (fam) predicozzo.

serpent ['sә:pәnt] n serpente.

serrated [se'reitid] a dentellato, seghettato.

servant ['sә:vәnt] n domestico, -ca, servitore, servo, -va; funzionario.

serve [sә:v] vti servire.

service ['sә:vis] n servizio; ufficio (divino), funzione (religiosa), **s. flats** appartamenti d'affitto con servizio; **s. lift** montavivande.

serviceable ['sә:visәbl] a utile, pratico.

serviette [.sә:vi'et] n tovagliolo.

servile ['sә:vail] a servile, abbietto.

servility [sә:'viliti] n servilità.

servitude ['sә:vitju:d] n servitù, schiavitù.

session ['seʃәn] n sessione.

set [set] a fisso, stabilito, ostinato; n collezione, serie, servizio; cricca, crocchio; partita, gioco; (rad) apparecchio; (teeth) dentiera; vt disporre, mettere; fissare; montare; regolare; (type) comporre; vi applicarsi; disporsi, mettersi; solidificarsi; tramontare; **set up** sistemazione, situazione, stato di cose.

settee [se'ti:] n divano.

setter ['setә] n cane da ferma.

setting ['setiŋ] n montaggio; messa in scena; solidificazione; (gem) montatura; (typ) composizione; **hair s.** messa in piega.

settle ['setl] vt accomodare, fissare, stabilire, sistemare; calmare; pagare, saldare; vi fissarsi, sistemarsi, stabilirsi.

settlement ['setlmәnt] n contratto, accordo, sistemazione; saldo; colonia, colonizzazione.

settler ['setlә] n colonizzatore, colono.

seven ['sevn] a n sette; **seventh** a settimo.

seventeen ['sevn'ti:n] a n diciassette; **seventeenth** a diciassettesimo.

seventy ['sevnti] a n settanta; **seventieth** a settantesimo.

sever ['sevə] *vti* staccar(si), separar (si).

several ['sevrəl] *a* diverso, separato; *a pron pl* parecchi(e) *pl.*

severance ['sevərəns] *n* distacco, separazione.

severe [si'viə] *a* severo, austero; rigido; violento.

severity [si'veriti] *n* severità; rigore.

Seville ['sevil] *n* Siviglia.

sew [sou] *vti* cucire.

sewage ['sju:idʒ] *n* acque di scolo *pl.*

sewer ['sjuə] *n* conduttura, fogna.

sex [seks] *n* sesso.

sexton ['sekstən] *n* sagrestano; becchino.

sexual ['seksjuəl] *a* sessuale.

shabbiness ['ʃæbinis] *n* l'essere male in arnese; grettezza.

shabby ['ʃæbi] *a* male in arnese; gretto.

shackle ['ʃækl] *n* anello di metallo; *vt* mettere in ceppi; (*fig*) ostacolare; **shackles** *pl* ceppi, manette, ferri *pl.*

shade [ʃeid] *n* ombra; paralume; riparo dalla luce; sfumatura; tinta; *vt* adombrare; ombreggiare; proteggere, riparare; sfumare.

shading ['ʃeidiŋ] *n* ombreggiatura, sfumatura.

shadow ['ʃædou] *n* ombra; fantasma; *vt* seguire come un'ombra.

shadowy ['ʃædoui] *a* ombroso; indistinto.

shady ['ʃeidi] *a* fresco, ombreggiato; (*fig*) equivoco, losco.

shaft [ʃɑ:ft] *n* lancia; fusto; freccia, strale; (*light*) raggio; manico; (*mine*) pozzo.

shag [ʃæg] *n* tabacco forte; cormorano crestato.

shaggy ['ʃægi] *a* irsuto, ispido, peloso.

shagreen [ʃæ'gri:n] *n* zigrino.

shake [ʃeik] *n* scossa, urto, tremore; (*mus*) trillo; *vt* scuotere, scrollare; turbare; *vi* tremare, vacillare, agitarsi; (*mus*) trillare; **milk s.** frappè.

shaky ['ʃeiki] *a* tremolante, vacillante; malsicuro; debole; precario.

shale [ʃeil] *n* argilla schistosa; **s. oil** olio minerale, olio di schisto.

shallow ['ʃælou] *a* basso, poco profondo; (*fig*) superficiale; *n* bassofondo, secca.

shallowness ['ʃælounis] *n* poca profondità, superficialità.

sham [ʃæm] *a* finto, simulato; *n* finta, inganno, impostura; *vti* fingere, simulare.

shamble ['ʃæmbl] *vi* avere, camminare con, una andatura goffa o strascicante.

shambles ['ʃæmblz] *n* carneficina, macello, disordine, confusione.

shame [ʃeim] *n* vergogna, obbrobrio, onta; *vt* svergognare, indurre, costringere (per vergogna) a.

shamefaced ['ʃeimfeist] *a* vergognoso; confuso.

shameful ['ʃeimful] *a* vergognoso, disonorevole.

shameless ['ʃeimlis] *a* svergognato, sfacciato, impudente.

shampoo [ʃæm'pu:] *n* lavatura dei capelli, 'shampoo'; *vt* lavare i capelli, fare lo 'shampoo'.

shamrock ['ʃæmrɔk] *n* trifoglio (emblema nazionale dell'Irlanda).

Shanghai [ʃæŋ'hai] *n* Sciangai.

shank [ʃæŋk] *n* gamba, stinco.

shape [ʃeip] *n* forma, figura, stampo; *vt* foggiare, formare, modellare; *vi* assumere forma, presentarsi.

shapeless ['ʃeiplis] *a* informe.

shapely ['ʃeipli] *a* ben fatto, ben proporzionato.

share [ʃɛə] *n* parte, porzione, quota; (*com*) azione; **ordinary s.** azione ordinaria; *vt* (con)dividere, spartire, distribuire; *vi* partecipare.

shareholder ['ʃɛə,houldə] *n* azionista.

shark [ʃɑ:k] *n* pescecane, squalo; furfante, speculatore; *vti* truffare, vivere di truffe.

sharp [ʃɑ:p] *a* acuto, affilato, aguzzo, penetrante; improvviso; piccante; scaltro; vivace; in (*mus*) diesis; *ad* in punto, puntualmente.

sharpen ['ʃɑ:pən] *vt* affilare, aguzzare, eccitare.

sharpness ['ʃɑ:pnis] *n* acutezza, acume; astuzia; prontezza, vivacità.

shatter ['ʃætə] *vti* frantumar(si), fracassar(si).

shave [ʃeiv] *n* rasatura; sfioramento; *vt* radere, tagliare; *vti* rader(si), far(si) la barba; **to have a close s.** salvarsi per miracolo, scamparla bella.

shaving ['ʃeiviŋ] *n* il rader(si); truciolo.

shawl [ʃɔ:l] *n* scialle.

she [ʃi:] *pron* ella, lei, colei; *n* femmina.

sheaf [ʃi:f] *n* covone, fascio.

shear [ʃiə] *vti* tosare, pelare; spogliare.

shears [ʃiəz] *n pl* cesoie *pl.*

sheath [ʃi:θ] *n* astuccio, fodero, guaina.

sheathe [ʃi:ð] *vt* rimettere nel fodero, inguainare.

shed [ʃed] *n* capannone, rimessa; *vt* spargere, spogliarsi di, versare.

sheen [ʃi:n] *n* lustro, splendore.

sheep [ʃi:p] *pl* **sheep** *n* pecora.

sheepish ['ʃi:piʃ] *a* vergognoso, timido, impacciato.

sheer [ʃiə] *a* puro, semplice; a piombo, perpendicolare; *ad* a piombo, verticalmente.

sheet [ʃi:t] *n* lenzuolo; foglio; giornale; lamina; (*of ice*) lastra, (*of water*) specchio.

shelf [ʃelf] *n* scaffale; palchetto, ripiano; scoglio.

shell [ʃel] *n* conchiglia; guscio; involucro; proiettile; *vt* sgusciare;

sbucciare; bombardare; **shellfish** crostaceo.

shelter ['ʃeltə] n riparo, rifugio, difesa; vt mettere al coperto, riparare; vi rifugiarsi; **air-raid s.** rifugio antiaereo.

shelve [ʃelv] vt mettere sugli scaffali; (fig) differire, mettere in disparte.

shepherd ['ʃepəd] n pastore; **shepherdess** pastorella.

sheriff ['ʃerif] n sceriffo.

sherry ['ʃeri] n 'sherry', vino di Xeres.

shield [ʃiːld] n scudo; difesa, protezione; vt difendere, proteggere.

shift [ʃift] n cambiamento; espediente; turno; abito da donna; vt cambiare, spostare, trasferire; vi cambiar di posto, cambiarsi, spostarsi.

shifty ['ʃifti] a volubile, furbo, ambiguo; **s. glance** sguardo sfuggente.

shilling ['ʃiliŋ] n scellino.

shimmer ['ʃimə] n luccichio, scintillio.

shin [ʃin] n stinco, coscia; (beef) garretto; **s.-bone** tibia.

shindy ['ʃindi] n (fam) chiasso, baccano.

shine [ʃain] n lucentezza, splendore; vi brillare, splendere.

shingle ['ʃiŋgl] n ghiaia; tegola di legno; **shingles** pl (med) fuoco di S. Antonio; vt tagliare (capelli) alla garçonne.

shiny ['ʃaini] a rilucente; lucido.

ship [ʃip] n nave, bastimento; vt imbarcare, spedire; vi imbarcarsi.

shipbroker ['ʃip,broukə] n sensale marittimo.

shipbuilding ['ʃip,bildiŋ] n costruzione navale.

ship-chandler ['ʃip'tʃɑːndlə] n fornitore navale.

shipmate ['ʃipmeit] n compagno di bordo.

shipment ['ʃipmənt] n imbarco, spedizione.

shipping ['ʃipiŋ] n imbarco, marina mercantile, forze navali pl.

shipwreck ['ʃiprek] n naufragio.

shipwright ['ʃiprait] n (naut) maestro d'ascia.

shipyard ['ʃipjɑːd] n cantiere navale, arsenale.

shire ['ʃaiə] n contea.

shirk [ʃəːk] vt schivare, sfuggire.

shirt [ʃəːt] n camicia da uomo; **s. front** sparato di camicia.

shiver ['ʃivə] n brivido; frantume, scheggia; vi rabbrividire, tremare; vti rompere (andare) in frantumi.

shoal [ʃoul] n secca, bassofondo; banco di pesci; folla, ressa.

shock [ʃɔk] n colpo, urto, forte emozione, scossa; massa di capelli incolti; vt offendere, scandalizzare, urtare.

shocker ['ʃɔkə] n cosa che colpisce, romanzo scandalistico.

shocking ['ʃɔkiŋ] a scandaloso.

shoddy ['ʃɔdi] a scadente e appariscente; n cascame; (fig) roba scadente e appariscente.

shoe [ʃuː] n scarpa; ferro da cavallo; vt calzare; ferrare.

shoemaker ['ʃuː,meikə] n calzolaio.

shoot [ʃuːt] n germoglio; partita di caccia; vt colpire, fucilare; vi andare a caccia, sparare; germogliare; lanciarsi.

shooting ['ʃuːtiŋ] n sparatoria; caccia; **s. pain** dolore lancinante; **s. star** stella cadente.

shop [ʃɔp] n bottega, negozio, spaccio; vi fare delle compere; **s. assistant** commesso; **to talk s.** parlare di affari; **s. window** vetrina.

shopkeeper ['ʃɔp,kiːpə] n negoziante.

shore [ʃɔː] n spiaggia, riva, sponda; puntello; vt puntellare.

short [ʃɔːt] a breve, corto; (height) basso; brusco, conciso, ristretto; ad di botto; **s.-cut** scorciatoia; **s.sighted** miope.

shortage ['ʃɔːtidʒ] a scarsezza.

shorten ['ʃɔːtn] vti accorciar(si), diminuir(si).

shorthand ['ʃɔːthænd] n stenografia; **s. typist** stenodattilografo; **s. writer** stenografo.

shortly ['ʃɔːtli] ad in breve, tra poco.

shortness ['ʃɔːtnis] n brevità, cortezza; insufficenza.

shot [ʃɔt] n colpo; sparo; scarica; palla, proiettile; tiratore; tiro; portata.

shotgun ['ʃɔtgʌn] n fucile da caccia.

shoulder ['ʃouldə] n spalla; (of road) bordo della strada; vt addossarsi, prendere sulle spalle.

shout [ʃaut] n grido; vti gridare.

shove [ʃʌv] n spinta; vti spingere.

shovel ['ʃʌvl] n pala, palata; vt ammucchiare, spalare; rimpinzarsi la bocca di.

show [ʃou] n mostra, esibizione; esposizione; ostentazione, pompa; spettacolo; vt far vedere, mostrare.

shower ['ʃauə] n acquazzone, rovescio; doccia; vt far piovere; vi diluviare.

showery ['ʃauəri] a temporalesco.

showman ['ʃoumən] n imbonitore; direttore, capocomico.

showy ['ʃoui] a appariscente, vistoso.

shrapnel ['ʃræpnl] n shrapnel.

shred [ʃred] n brandello, pezzetto, ritaglio; vt sminuzzare, tagliuzzare.

shrew [ʃruː] n bisbetica.

shrewd [ʃruːd] a accorto, perspicace, scaltro.

shrewdness ['ʃruːdnis] n accortezza, perspicacia.

shriek [ʃriːk] n grido acuto, strillo; vti strillare, gridare.

shrike [ʃraik] n averla.

shrill [ʃril] *a* stridulo; *vti* stridere.

shrimp [ʃrimp] *n* gamberetto; *(fig)* omiciattolo.

shrine [ʃrain] *n* reliquario, santuario.

shrink [ʃriŋk] *vt* far restringere; *vi* restringersi, ritirarsi; indietreggiare.

shrivel [ˈʃrivl] *vti* raggrinzar(si).

shroud [ʃraud] *n* sudario; velo; *vt* avvolgere, coprire, nascondere.

Shrove Tuesday [ˈʃrouvˈtjuːzdi] *n* martedì grasso.

shrub [ʃrʌb] *n* arbusto, cespuglio; *(US)* bibita di succo di frutta.

shrug [ʃrʌg] *n* alzata di spalle; *vi* stringersi nelle spalle.

shudder [ˈʃʌdə] *n* brivido; *vi* rabbrividire.

shuffle [ˈʃʌfl] *n* andatura strascicata; il mescolare le carte; *vt* *(cards)* mescolare; muovere con fatica, strasciicare; *vi* muoversi con fatica, strascicarsi; ricorrere a sotterfugi.

shun [ʃʌn] *vt* evitare, scansare.

shunt [ʃʌnt] *n* *(rly)* binario di smistamento; *(el)* derivazione; *vt* *(rly)* smistare; *(el)* derivare.

shut [ʃʌt] *vti* chiuder(si).

shutter [ˈʃʌtə] *n* imposta, persiana; *(phot)* otturatore.

shuttle [ˈʃʌtl] *n* navetta, spoletta.

shy [ʃai] *a* timido; diffidente, *(horse)* ombroso; *vt* lanciare; *vi* pigliar ombra.

shyness [ˈʃainis] *n* timidezza.

Siamese [ˌsaiəˈmiːz] *a n* siamese.

Siberia [saiˈbiəriə] *n* Siberia.

Siberian [saiˈbiəriən] *a n* siberiano.

sibilant [ˈsibilənt] *a n* sibilante.

sibyl [ˈsibil] *n* sibilla.

Sicilian [siˈsiliən] *a n* siciliano.

Sicily [ˈsisili] *n* Sicilia.

sick [sik] *a* (am)malato, sofferente; nauseato; stanco.

sicken [ˈsikn] *vt* disgustare; *vi* ammalarsi, disgustarsi.

sickle [ˈsikl] *n* falcetto, falce.

sickly [ˈsikli] *a* di salute cagionevole, malaticcio; nauseante.

sickness [ˈsiknis] *n* malattia; nausea.

sickroom [ˈsikrum] *n* camera per ammalati.

side [said] *n* fianco, lato; riva; parte, partito; *vi* parteggiare.

sideboard [ˈsaidbɔːd] *n* credenza.

side-effect [ˈsaidiˈfekt] *n* effetto secondario.

sidelong [ˈsaidlɔŋ] *a* obliquo; *ad* obliquamente.

sidewalk [ˈsaidwɔːk] *n* *(US)* marciapiede.

sideways [ˈsaidweiz] *ad* lateralmente, a sghembo.

sidle [ˈsaidl] *vi* camminare di sghembo; diportarsi untuosamente.

siding [ˈsaidiŋ] *n* *(rly)* binario morto.

siege [siːdʒ] *n* assedio.

sieve [siv] *n* crivello, staccio; *vt* stacciare.

sift [sift] *vt* setacciare.

sigh [sai] *n* sospiro; *vi* sospirare.

sight [sait] *n* vista, occhi *pl*; *(gun)* mirino; spettacolo, visione; *(fam)* gran quantità; *vt* avvistare; prendere la mira di; **s.-seeing** visita turistica.

sightless [ˈsaitlis] *a* cieco.

sightly [ˈsaitli] *a* avvenente, bello.

Sigismond, Sigismund [ˈsigismənd] *nm pr* Sigismondo.

sign [sain] *n* segno, cenno; insegna; *vti* firmare, segnare.

signal [ˈsignl] *a* cospicuo, notevole; *n* segnale, segnalazione, segno; *vti* segnalare.

signatory [ˈsignətəri] *n* firmatario.

signature [ˈsignitʃə] *n* firma; *(typ)* segnatura; *(mus)* indicazione.

signet [ˈsignit] *n* sigillo.

significance [sigˈnifikəns] *n* significato; espressione; importanza.

significant [sigˈnifikənt] *a* significativo, importante.

signify [ˈsignifai] *vt* significare, far sapere, voler dire; *vi* importare.

silence [ˈsailəns] *n* silenzio.

silencer [ˈsailənsə] *n* *(aut)* silenziatore.

silent [ˈsailənt] *a* silenzioso, muto.

silhouette [ˌsilu(ː)ˈet] *n* profilo; *vti* profilar(si).

silk [silk] *a* di seta; *n* seta.

silken [ˈsilkən] *a* serico, di seta; *(fig)* insinuante.

silkiness [ˈsilkinis] *n* morbidezza, lucentezza.

silkworm [ˈsilkwəːm] *n* baco da seta.

silky [ˈsilki] *a* di seta, serico; morbido.

sill [sil] *n* davanzale; soglia.

silliness [ˈsilinis] *n* stupidità, sciocchezza.

silly [ˈsili] *a* sciocco, stupido.

silt [silt] *n* sedimento di fango o sabbia; *vti* ostruir(si) per fango o sabbia.

silver [ˈsilvə] *a* d'argento; *n* argento.

silversmith [ˈsilvəsmiθ] *n* argentiere.

silvery [ˈsilvəri] *a* argenteo, -tato, -tino.

similar [ˈsimilə] *a n* simile; *a* somigliante, analogo.

similarity [ˌsimiˈlæriti] *n* somiglianza.

simile [ˈsimili] *n* paragone, similitudine.

simmer [ˈsimə] *vti* (far) bollire lentamente; *(fig)* essere sul punto di scoppiare per, ribollire di.

Simon [ˈsaimən] *nm pr* Simone.

simony [ˈsaiməni] *n* simonia.

simper [ˈsimpə] *n* sorriso melenso; *vi* sorridere in modo melenso.

simple [ˈsimpl] *a* semplice; *n* erba medicinale.

simpleton [ˈsimpltən] *n* semplicione.

simplicity [simˈplisiti] *n* semplicità.

simplification [ˌsimplifiˈkeiʃən] *n* semplificazione.

simplify [ˈsimplifai] *vt* semplificare.

simulate [ˈsimjuleit] *vt* simulare.

simulation [ˌsimjuˈleiʃən] *n* simulazione.

simultaneous [ˌsimǝl'teiniǝs] *a* simultaneo.

simultaneously [ˌsimǝl'teiniǝsli] *ad* simultaneamente.

sin [sin] *n* peccato; *vi* peccare.

since [sins] *ad cj prep* d'allora in poi; da quando; poichè; da.

sincere [sin'siǝ] *a* sincero.

sincerity [sin'seriti] *n* sincerità.

sinecure ['sinikjuǝ] *n* sinecura.

sinew ['sinju:] *n* nervo, tendine; nerbo.

sinewy ['sinju:i] *a* nerboruto, gagliardo.

sinful ['sinful] *a* peccaminoso, colpevole.

sing [siŋ] *vti* cantare.

singe [sindʒ] *vt* bruciare, bruciacchiare.

singer ['siŋǝ] *n* cantante, cantore.

singing ['siŋiŋ] *a* cantante, canterino; *n* canto.

single ['siŋgl] *a* solo, unico; semplice; singolo, celibe, nubile; *vt* distinguere; scegliere; **s. ticket** (*rly*) biglietto d'andata.

singular ['siŋgjulǝ] *a n* singolare; *a* caratteristico, particolare.

singularity [ˌsiŋgju'læriti] *n* singolarità; stranezza.

singularly ['siŋgjulǝli] *ad* singolarmente, particolarmente.

sinister ['sinistǝ] *a* sinistro, funesto.

sink [siŋk] *n* acquaio; sentina; *vt* affondare, immergere; nascondere; investire denaro a fondo perduto; *vi* affondare; declinare; sparire, tramontare.

sinless ['sinlis] *a* innocente, puro.

sinner ['sinǝ] *n* peccatore, -trice.

sinuous ['sinjuǝs] *a* sinuoso.

sip [sip] *n* sorso; *vti* centellinare.

siphon ['saifǝn] *n* sifone.

sir [sǝ:] *n* (*vocative*) signore, 'Sir', titolo premesso a nome proprio di cavaliere, baronetto.

sire ['saiǝ] *n* sire.

siren ['saiǝrin] *n* sirena.

sirloin ['sǝ:lɔin] *n* lombo di manzo.

sister ['sistǝ] *n* sorella; suora; **s.-in-law** cognata.

sisterhood ['sistǝhud] *n* comunità religiosa.

sisterly ['sistǝli] *a* da (di) sorella.

sit [sit] *vi* sedere, stare seduto; **to s. down** mettersi a sedere.

site [sait] *n* sito, luogo, posizione.

sitting ['sitiŋ] *a* seduto; in seduta; *n* seduta; posa; riunione; **s. room** salotto, stanza di soggiorno.

situated ['sitjueitid] *a* posto, situato.

situation [ˌsitju'eifǝn] *n* posizione; situazione; condizioni *pl*; impiego, posto.

six [siks] *a n* sei; **sixth** *a* sesto.

sixpence ['sikspǝns] *n* mezzo scellino.

sixteen ['siks'ti:n] *a n* sedici; **sixteenth** *a* sedicesimo.

sixty ['siksti] *a n* sessanta; **sixtieth** *a* sessantesimo.

sizable ['saizǝbl] *a* piuttosto grande.

size [saiz] *n* grandezza, dimensione; formato; misura; **s. up** *vt* valutare, giudicare.

skate [skeit] *n* pattino; (*fish*) razza; *vi* pattinare; schettinare.

skating ['skeitiŋ] *n* pattinaggio.

skein [skein] *n* matassa.

skeleton ['skelitn] *n* scheletro; ossatura.

sketch [sketʃ] *n* abbozzo, bozzetto, schizzo; *vti* abbozzare, schizzare, fare degli schizzi.

skew [skju:] *a* obliquo, sbieco.

skewer ['skjuǝ] *n* spiedo; *vt* infilare sullo spiedo.

ski [ski:] *n* sci; *vi* sciare.

skid [skid] *n* slittamento; (*av*) pattino di coda; **s. chain** (*aut*) catena antisdrucciolevole; **side s.** (*aut*) sbandamento; *vi* sbandare, slittare; scivolare.

skier ['ski:ǝ] *n* sciatore.

skiff [skif] *n* (*naut*) schifo.

skilful ['skilful] *a* abile, destro, esperto.

skill [skil] *n* abilità, destrezza, perizia.

skilled [skild] *a* esperto, specializzato.

skim [skim] *vt* schiumare, scremare; sfiorare, dare un'occhiata a; **skimmed milk** latte scremato.

skimmer ['skimǝ] *n* schiumatoio.

skimp [skimp] *vt* lesinare, tenere a stecchetto.

skimpy ['skimpi] *a* scarso, misero.

skin [skin] *n* pelle; *vt* pelare; sbucciare, scorticare; **s. diver** nuotatore subacqueo, sommozzatore; **s. diving** nuoto subacqueo.

skinny ['skini] *a* magro, macilento.

skip [skip] *n* balzo; *vt* omettere, passare sopra; *vi* balzare, saltare.

skipper ['skipǝ] *n* capitano di nave mercantile o peschereccia.

skirmish ['skǝ:miʃ] *n* scaramuccia; *vi* scaramucciare.

skirt [skǝ:t] *n* sottana, gonna; falda, lembo; *vt* costeggiare, rasentare, confinare con.

skirting ['skǝ:tiŋ] *n* orlo, bordo; zoccolatura; **s. board** zoccolo.

skit [skit] *n* parodia, frizzo.

skittish ['skitiʃ] *a* capriccioso, volubile, vivace.

skittle ['skitl] *n* birillo.

skulk [skʌlk] *vi* celarsi, nascondersi, sottrarsi al proprio dovere.

skull [skʌl] *n* cranio, teschio.

skunk [skʌŋk] *n* moffetta; (*fig*) individuo ignobile.

sky [skai] *n* cielo, volta del cielo.

skylark ['skaila:k] *n* allodola.

skylight ['skailait] *n* lucernario.

skyline ['skailain] *n* orizzonte.

skyscraper ['skaiˌskreipǝ] *n* grattacielo.

slab [slæb] *n* grossa fetta; lastra.

slack [slæk] *a* allentato, fiacco, indolente; fermo, stagnante.

slacken ['slækən] *vti* allentar(si), moderar(si).

slackness ['slæknis] *n* fiacchezza, rilassatezza; (*com*) fermo.

slag [slæg] *n* scoria, -ie.

slake [sleik] *vt* estinguere; soddisfare.

slam [slæm] *n* sbatacchiamento; *vti* sbatacchiar(si), scaraventare.

slander ['slɑːndə] *n* calunnia; *vt* calunniare, diffamare.

slanderer ['slɑːndərə] *n* calunniatore, diffamatore.

slanderous ['slɑːndərəs] *a* calunnioso, diffamatorio.

slang [slæŋ] *n* gergo.

slant [slɑːnt] *n* inclinazione, pendio; posizione obliqua; (*fig*) prospettiva; *vt* disporre obliquamente; *vi* inclinarsi.

slap [slæp] *n* colpo, schiaffo; *vt* colpire, schiaffeggiare; gettare, scaraventare.

slapdash ['slæpdæʃ] *a* impetuoso; affrettato, superficiale.

slapstick ['slæpstik] *n* farsa grossolana.

slash [slæʃ] *n* squarcio, taglio; *vt* squarciare, tagliare; criticare ferocemente.

slate [sleit] *n* ardesia; tegola d'ardesia; lavagna.

slattern ['slætən] *n* donna sciatta.

slaughter ['slɔːtə] *n* carneficina, macello; *vt* macellare, massacrare.

Slav [slɑːv] *a n* slavo.

slave [sleiv] *n* schiavo; *vi* sgobbare.

slaver ['sleivə] *n* negriero; nave negriera.

slaver ['slævə] *n* bava, saliva; *vi* sbavare.

slavery ['sleivəri] *n* schiavitù.

Slavic ['slævik] *a n* slavo, lingua slava.

slavish ['sleiviʃ] *a* abietto, servile.

slavishness ['sleiviʃnis] *n* servilismo.

Slavonic [slə'vɔnik] *a n* slavo, lingua slava.

slay [slei] *vt* ammazzare, trucidare.

sled [sled] *n* (*US*) slitta.

sledge [sledʒ] *n* slitta; **s.-hammer** mazza da fabbro.

sleek [sliːk] *a* liscio; *vt* lisciare.

sleep [sliːp] *n* sonno; *vi* dormire.

sleeper ['sliːpə] *n* dormiente; (*rly*) traversa, -sina; cuccetta; (*av*) poltrona letto; (*US rly*) vagone letto.

sleepiness ['sliːpinis] *n* sonnolenza.

sleepless ['sliːplis] *a* insonne.

sleeplessness ['sliːplisnis] *n* insonnia.

sleepwalker ['sliːp,wɔːkə] *n* sonnambulo.

sleepy ['sliːpi] *a* assonnato, sonnolento.

sleet [sliːt] *n* nevischio; *vi* cadere nevischio.

sleeve [sliːv] *n* manica.

sleigh [slei] *n* slitta.

slender ['slendə] *a* slanciato, snello, sottile; esiguo, piccolo, scarso.

slenderness ['slendənis] *n* snellezza; scarsità.

slice [slais] *n* fetta; parte, porzione; *vt* affettare, dividere.

slide [slaid] *n* scivolata; scivolo; (*phot*) diapositiva, lastra; vetrino per microscopio; *vt* far scorrere; *vi* scivolare, sdrucciolare; **sliding** scorrevole, mobile; **sliding roof** (*aut*) 'capote', soffietto.

slight [slait] *a* magro, esile, esiguo; insufficiente, scarso; superficiale; *n* affronto, mancanza di riguardo; *vt* mancare di rispetto a, non far caso di.

slim [slim] *a* esile, slanciato, sottile; *vi* dimagrire.

slime [slaim] *n* melma, sostanza viscida in genere.

slimness ['slimnis] *n* snellezza, esilità.

slimy ['slaimi] *a* melmoso, viscido.

sling [sliŋ] *n* fionda; striscia di tela per sostenere un braccio ammalato; **s. shot** (*US*) fionda; *vt* scagliare con la fionda; sospendere.

slink [sliŋk] *vi* svignarsela, sgattaiolare.

slip [slip] *n* scivolone, sdrucciolone; errore, svista, passo falso; guinzaglio; federa; sottabito; *vt* far scivolare in; *vi* scivolare, sdrucciolare; andare furtivamente; sbagliare, scappare; **s. on** *vt* (*garment*) infilare.

slipper ['slipə] *n* pantofola, ciabatta.

slippery ['slipəri] *a* sdrucciolevole; viscido; (*fig*) incostante, poco scrupoloso.

slipshod ['slipʃɔd] *a* trasandato, trascurato.

slit [slit] *n* fessura, lunga incisione; *vt* fendere, tagliare a strisce.

sloe [slou] *n* prugnola.

slogan ['slougən] *n* grido di guerra; (*com*) motto pubblicitario, motto, "slogan".

sloop [sluːp] *n* (*naut*) scialuppa, corvetta.

slop [slɔp] *n* (*usu pl*) risciacquatura di piatti; liquidi sporchi.

slope [sloup] *n* pendenza, pendio; *vt* inclinare; *vi* essere in pendenza.

sloppy ['slɔpi] *a* bagnato; (*fig*) sciatto; sdolcinato.

slot [slɔt] *n* buco o foro oblungo; **s.-machine** distributore automatico.

sloth [slouθ] *n* pigrizia, ignavia.

slothful ['slouθful] *a* indolente, pigro.

slouch [slautʃ] *n* andatura dinoccolata; *vi* camminare in modo dinoccolato; **s. hat** cappello a cencio.

slough [slau] *n* palude, pantano; [slʌf] *vti* (*of snakes*) cambiare la pelle; (*fig*) liberarsi di.

sloven ['slʌvn] *n* persona trasandata.

slovenliness ['slʌvnlinis] *n* sudiceria, sciatteria.

slovenly ['slʌvnli] *a* disordinato, trasandato.

slow [slou] *a* lento; tardo; in ritardo; *ad* adagio; *vti* rallentare.

slowness ['slounis] *n* lentezza, indolenza.

slug [slʌg] *n* lumaca.

sluggard ['slʌgəd] *n* poltrone.

sluggish ['slʌgiʃ] *a* indolente, neghittoso, lento.

sluggishness ['slʌgiʃnis] *n* indolenza.

sluice [sluːs] *n* cateratta, chiusa; *vt* bagnare abbondantemente; *vi* scorrere violentemente.

slum [slʌm] *n* quartiere popolare e sudicio.

slumber ['slʌmbə] *n* sonno; *vi* dormire.

slump [slʌmp] *n* tracollo, brusco ribasso di prezzi, improvviso arresto nelle richieste di vendita; *vi* cadere, precipitare.

slur [sləː] *n* calunnia, insulto, macchia, pronuncia indistinta; (*mus*) legatura; *vt* pronunciare indistintamente; (*mus*) legare.

slush [slʌʃ] *n* fanghiglia, neve sciolta.

slut [slʌt] *n* donna trasandata, sudiciona.

sly [slai] *a* astuto, furbo, scaltro.

slyness ['slainis] *n* astuzia, furberia, scaltrezza.

smack [smæk] *n* schiaffo; schiocco; gusto, sapore di; peschereccio; *vt* schiaffeggiare; schioccare; *vi* aver sapore di, sapere di.

small [smɔːl] *a* piccolo; limitato; scarso; umile; meschino.

smallness ['smɔːlnis] *n* piccolezza.

smallpox ['smɔːlpɒks] *n* vaiolo.

smart [smaːt] *a* acuto, intelligente, sveglio; elegante; *n* bruciore, dolore acuto; *vi* dolere, bruciare; soffrire.

smartness ['smaːtnis] *n* vivacità, spirito; eleganza.

smash [smæʃ] *n* scontro, urto, rovina; fallimento; *vt* fracassare, frantumare; *vi* fracassarsi; fallire.

smattering ['smætəriŋ] *n* infarinatura.

smear [smiə] *n* macchia; *vt* imbrattare, macchiare.

smell [smel] *n* fiuto; odorato, olfatto; odore; *vt* fiutare, sentire l'odore di; (*fig*) sospettare; *vi* odorare, aver l'odore di.

smelt [smelt] *vt* fondere.

smelting ['smeltiŋ] *n* fusione.

smile [smail] *n* sorriso; *vi* sorridere.

smirk [sməːk] *n* sorriso affettato; *vi* sorridere affettatamente.

smith [smiθ] *n* fabbro.

smithy ['smiði] *n* fucina.

smock [smɒk] *n* grembiule da bambino; blusa da operaio.

smog [smɔg] *n* 'smog', caligine.

smoke [smouk] *n* fumo; *vt* fumare, affumicare; *vi* emettere fumo; **smoked herring** (*US*) aringa affumicata.

smoker ['smoukə] *n* fumatore; (*rly*) carrozza per fumatori.

smoky ['smouki] *a* fumoso.

smooth [smuːð] *a* levigato, liscio; calmo; blando, mellifluo; *vt* levigare, lisciare, piallare, spianare; *vi* calmarsi, rasserenarsi.

smoothness ['smuːðnis] *n* levigatezza; scorrevolezza; calma.

smother ['smʌðə] *n* nuvola di polvere *etc*; *vt* asfissiare, soffocare; coprire; opprimere; spegnere.

smoulder ['smouldə] *vi* bruciare senza fiamma, covare sotto la cenere.

smudge [smʌdʒ] *n* chiazza; sgorbio; *vt* chiazzare, macchiare.

smug [smʌg] *a* ipocrita, soddisfatto di sè.

smuggle ['smʌgl] *vt* far entrare di contrabbando; *vi* esercitare il contrabbando.

smuggler ['smʌglə] *n* contrabbandiere.

smut [smʌt] *n* macchia di fuliggine.

smutty ['smʌti] *a* fuligginoso, sporco; (*fig*) osceno.

snack [snæk] *n* spuntino.

snag [snæg] *n* nodo; sporgenza; (*fig*) intoppo, difficoltà.

snail [sneil] *n* chiocciola; lumaca.

snake [sneik] *n* serpe, serpente.

snap [snæp] *n* schiocco; rumore secco; (*phot*) istantanea; (*fig*) brio, vivacità; *vt* rompere con rumore secco; schioccare; fare l'istantanea a; *vi* fare un rumore secco, rompersi.

snappish ['snæpiʃ] *a* bisbetico, secco, stizzoso.

snapshot ['snæpʃɔt] *n* (*phot*) istantanea.

snare [snɛə] *n* insidia; laccio; trappola; *vt* prendere al laccio, in trappola.

snarl [snaːl] *n* groviglio; ringhio; *vt* aggrovigliare; *vi* aggrovigliarsi, ringhiare.

snatch [snætʃ] *vt* afferrare, ghermire, strappare.

sneak [sniːk] *n* (*fam*) persona vile; (*school sl*) spia; *vi* strisciare.

sneaking ['sniːkiŋ] *a* basso, servile; nascosto.

sneer [sniə] *n* (sog)ghigno, sarcasmo; *vi* sogghignare, deridere.

sneeze [sniːz] *n* starnuto; *vi* starnutire; *s.* at disprezzare.

sniff [snif] *n* l'annusare, il fiutare; *vti* annusare, fiutare; aspirare.

snigger ['snigə] *n* risolino cinico; *vi* ridere sotto i baffi, ridacchiare.

snip [snip] *n* forbiciata, ritaglio; *vti* tagliuzzare, tagliare.

snipe [snaip] *n* beccaccino.

sniper ['snaipə] *n* chi caccia beccaccini; (*mil*) franco tiratore.

snippet ['snipit] *n* pezzettino, ritaglio.

snivel ['snivəl] *vi* piagnucolare; simulare contrizione, dolore.

snob [snɔb] n 'snob'.

snobbery ['snɔbəri] n snobismo.

snobbish ['snɔbiʃ] a snobistico, snob.

snooze [snu:z] n pisolino, sonnellino; vi fare un pisolino.

snore [snɔ:] n il russare; vi russare.

snorkel ['snɔ:kəl] n 'snorkel', presa d'aria per nuotatori e sommergibili.

snort [snɔ:t] n sbuffo; vi sbuffare.

snout [snaut] n muso, grugno.

snow [snou] n neve; vi nevicare.

snowdrift ['snoudrift] n ammasso di neve, raffica di neve.

snowdrop ['snoudrɔp] n bucaneve.

snowflake ['snoufleik] n fiocco di neve.

snow-plough ['snouplau] n spazzaneve.

snowshoe ['snouʃu:] n racchetta per la neve.

snowstorm ['snoustɔ:m] n tormenta.

snowy ['snoui] n nevoso, niveo, candido.

snub [snʌb] a (nose) camuso; n rimprovero, affronto; vt rimproverare, umiliare.

snuff [snʌf] n tabacco da fiuto; vti fiutare, annusare.

snuffers ['snʌfəz] n pl smoccolatoio.

snuffle ['snʌfl] vi respirare rumorosamente; parlare nel naso; parlare in tono piagnucoloso.

snug [snʌg] a comodo, riparato dalle intemperie.

snuggle ['snʌgl] vi rannicchiarsi.

so [sou] ad così, a questo modo, tanto, perciò, quindi; s. as to tanto . . . da; s. that cj così che, di modo che.

soak [souk] vt bagnare, immergere, inzuppare.

soap [soup] n sapone.

soapy ['soupi] a saponoso.

soar [sɔ:] vi librarsi sulle ali, volare in alto.

sob [sɔb] n singhiozzo; vi singhiozzare.

sober ['soubə] a sobrio, moderato nel bere; equilibrato; sensato; serio.

soberness ['soubənis] sobriety [sou-'braiəti] n moderazione, temperanza.

sociable ['souʃəbl] a socievole.

social ['souʃəl] a sociale.

socialism ['souʃəlizəm] n socialismo.

socialist ['souʃəlist] a n socialista.

socialite ['souʃəlait] n (US) membro dell'alta società.

society [sə'saiəti] n società, associazione, compagnia.

sociology [,sousi'ɔlədʒi] n sociologia.

sock [sɔk] n calzino, soletta; s. suspender giarrettiera.

socket ['sɔkit] n orbita, cavità; (teeth) alveolo.

sod [sɔd] n zolla erbosa.

soda ['soudə] n soda; s.-water (acqua di) seltz; s. biscuit (US) galletta, 'cracker'.

sodden ['sɔdn] a impregnato d'acqua, fradicio; (fig) istupidito dal bere.

sodium ['soudiəm] n sodio.

sofa ['soufə] n sofa.

Sofia ['soufiə] n Sofia.

soft [sɔft] a morbido, molle, soffice; cedevole; delicato; mite, conciliante.

soften ['sɔfn] vti ammollir(si), mitigar(si), intenerir(si).

softly ['sɔftli] ad dolcemente; sommessamente, adagio.

softness ['sɔftnis] n morbidezza; delicatezza; mitezza.

soggy ['sɔgi] a bagnato; (bread) mal cotto.

soil [sɔil] n suolo, terra, terreno; macchia; sporcizia; vt insozzare, sporcare; vi sporcarsi.

sojourn ['sɔdʒə:n] n soggiorno; vi soggiornare.

solace ['sɔləs] n sollievo, consolazione; vt consolare, sollevare.

solar ['soulə] a solare.

solder ['sɔldə] n saldatura; vt saldare.

soldier ['souldʒə] n soldato, militare.

soldierly ['souldʒəli] a marziale, militare.

soldiery ['souldʒəri] n soldati pl, soldatesca.

sole [soul] a solo, unico; n pianta del piede; suola; (fish) sogliola; vt risolare.

solecism ['sɔlisizəm] n solecismo.

solemn ['sɔləm] a solenne.

solemnity [sə'lemniti] n solennità; rito solenne.

solemnize ['sɔləmnaiz] vt solennizzare.

solicit [sə'lisit] vt chiedere con insistenza.

solicitor [sə'lisitə] n avvocato, procuratore legale.

solicitous [sə'lisitəs] a premuroso, sollecito; desideroso.

solicitude [sə'lisitju:d] n sollecitudine, premura.

solid ['sɔlid] a solido; compatto; massiccio; intero; pieno; posato, serio; (com) solvibile; n corpo solido.

solidarity [,sɔli'dæriti] n solidarietà.

solidify [sə'lidifai] vti solidificar(si).

solidity [sə'liditi] n solidità; (com) solvenza.

soliloquy [sə'liləkwi] n soliloquio.

solitary ['sɔlitəri] a solo, solitario.

solitude ['sɔlitju:d] n solitudine.

solo ['soulou] pl solos n (mus) assolo; (av) volo solitario.

solstice ['sɔlstis] n solstizio.

soluble ['sɔljubl] a solubile.

solution [sə'lju:ʃən] n soluzione, risoluzione.

solve [sɔlv] vt risolvere, sciogliere, spiegare.

solvent ['sɔlvənt] a n solvente; a (com) solvibile.

Somali [sou'mɑ:li] n somalo.

Somaliland [sou'mɑ:lilænd] n Somalia.

sombre ['sɔmbə] a fosco, tenebroso; triste.

some [sʌm] *a* pron qualche, alcuni, del; ne; un po' di; *ad* all'incirca, circa.

somebody ['sʌmbədi] *pron* qualcuno.

somehow ['sʌmhau] *ad* in qualche modo, in un modo o nell'altro.

someone ['sʌmwʌn] *pron* qualcuno.

somersault ['sʌməsɔ:lt] *n* capriola, salto mortale.

something ['sʌmθiŋ] *pron* qual(che) cosa; *ad* un po'.

sometime ['sʌmtaim] *a* di un tempo, antico; *ad* un tempo, un giorno o l'altro; **s.** soon uno di questi giorni.

sometimes ['sʌmtaimz] *ad* talvolta.

somewhat ['sʌmwɔt] *ad* piuttosto, un po'.

somewhere ['sʌmwɛə] *ad* in qualche parte.

somnambulism [sɔm'næmbjulizəm] *n* sonnambulismo.

somnambulist [sɔm'næmbjulist] *n* sonnambulo.

somniferous [sɔm'nifərəs] *a* soporifero, sonnifero.

somnolent ['sɔmnələnt] *a* sonnolento.

son [sʌn] *n* figlio; **s.-in-law** genero.

song [sɔŋ] *n* canto, canzone; romanza.

songster ['sɔŋstə] *n* uccello canterino.

sonnet ['sɔnit] *n* sonetto.

sonorous ['sɔnərəs] *a* sonoro.

soon [su:n] *ad* fra poco, presto, tosto; **sooner** piuttosto.

soot [sut] *n* fuliggine.

soothe [su:ð] *vt* calmare, placare; blandire.

soothing ['su:ðiŋ] *a* calmante, lenitivo.

soothsayer ['su:θ,seiə] *n* indovino.

sooty ['suti] *a* fuligginoso, nero.

sop [sɔp] *n* pezzo di pane o altro inzuppato; (*fig*) dono propiziatorio.

sophism ['sɔfizəm] *n* sofisma.

sophist ['sɔfist] *n* sofista.

sophisticate [sə'fistikeit] *vti* sofisticare.

sophisticated [sə'fistikeitid] *a* sofisticato, raffinato.

sophistry ['sɔfistri] *n* sofisticheria, cavilli *pl*.

soporific [,sɔpə'rifik] *a* soporifero; *n* sonnifero, narcotico.

soprano [sə'prɑːnou] *pl* **sopranos** *n* soprano.

sorcerer ['sɔːsərə] *n* mago, stregone.

sorceress ['sɔːsəris] *n* strega, fattucchiera.

sorcery ['sɔːsəri] *n* magia, stregoneria.

sordid ['sɔːdid] *a* sordido, spilorcio, ignobile.

sordidness ['sɔːdidnis] *n* sordidezza, grettezza.

sore [sɔː] *a* dolorante; infiammato; addolorato, irritato; grave; *n* piaga, ulcera.

sorely ['sɔːli] *ad* gravemente, fortemente.

soreness ['sɔːnis] *n* dolore, irritazione.

sorrel ['sɔrəl] *n* acetosa; cavallo sauro; *a* di color sauro.

sorrow ['sɔrou] *n* afflizione, dolore; sventura; *vi* addolorarsi, rattristarsi.

sorrowful ['sɔrəful] *a* addolorato, doloroso.

sorry ['sɔri] *a* dispiacente, dolente; meschino, misero.

sort [sɔːt] *n* sorta, genere, specie, tipo; *vt* selezionare, classificare, smistare.

sortie ['sɔːtiː] *n* (*mil*) sortita.

so-so ['sousou] *a* discreto; *ad* così così.

sot [sɔt] *n* ubriacone inveterato.

sough [sau] *vi* gemere; (*wind*) sussurrare.

soul [soul] *n* anima, spirito; (*fig*) incarnazione.

soulful ['soulful] *a* pieno di sentimento.

sound [saund] *n* rumore, suono; sonda; (*geogr*) stretto; *a* giusto, logico; profondo; sano, solido, ben fondato; *ad* profondamente; *vt* suonare, far risonare; sondare, scandagliare; *vi* sembrare; suonare, risonare.

sounding ['saundiŋ] *n* sonorità; (*med*) auscultazione; (*naut*) scandaglio.

soundness ['saundnis] *n* sanità, solidità.

soup [su:p] *n* minestra, brodo, zuppa.

sour [sauə] *a* acido, agro, aspro, amaro; (*of soil*) sterile; *vt* fare inacidire; (*fig*) esacerbare; *vi* inacidire, inasprirsi.

source [sɔːs] *n* fonte, origine, sorgente.

sourish ['sauəriʃ] *a* acidulo.

sourness ['sauənis] *n* acidità, asprezza; (*fig*) acrimonia.

souse [saus] *n* salamoia; *vt* marinare.

south [sauθ] *n* mezzogiorno, sud; *a* del sud, meridionale; *ad* a sud.

South Africa [,sauθ'æfrikə] *n* Sud Africa.

southerly ['sʌðəli] *a* del sud, meridionale; *ad* a sud.

southern ['sʌðən] *a* del sud.

southerner ['sʌðənə] *n* meridionale.

southward ['sauθwəd] *a* verso sud; **southwards** *ad* verso sud.

south-west [sauθ'west] *a* di sud-ovest; *n* sud-ovest; *ad* verso sud-ovest.

souvenir [,su:və'niə] *n* ricordo.

sovereign ['sɔvrin] *a* sovrano, supremo; *n* sovrano; sterlina d'oro.

sovereignty ['sɔvrənti] *n* sovranità.

sow [sou] *vt* seminare, spargere.

sow [sau] *n* scrofa.

spa [spɑː] *n* stazione termale.

space [speis] *n* spazio, estensione, luogo; periodo di tempo; *a* spaziale; *vt* disporre ad intervalli.

space-craft ['speiskrɑːft] **space-ship** ['speisʃip] *n* astronave.

spacious ['speiʃəs] *a* ampio, spazioso.

spaciousness ['speiʃəsnis] *n* ampiezza, spaziosità.

spade [speid] *n* badile, vanga; (*cards*) picche.

Spain [spein] *N* Spagna.

span [spæn] *n* spanna, palmo; apertura; breve durata, periodo; *vt* abbracciare, misurare, estendersi attraverso.

spangle ['spæŋgl] *n* lustrino.

Spaniard ['spænjəd] *n* spagnolo.

spaniel ['spænjəl] *n* 'spaniel', cane spagnolo; (*fig*) persona servile.

Spanish ['spæniʃ] *a* spagnolo.

spank [spæŋk] *vt* sculacciare.

spanner ['spænə] *n* (*mech*) chiave.

spar [spa:] *n* (*naut*) alberatura; pugilato; *vi* allenarsi nel pugilato; avere un battibecco.

spare [spɛə] *a* magro; parco, frugale; disponibile, libero; di ricambio, di riserva; *n* pezzo di ricambio; *vt* fare a meno di; risparmiare, mettere da parte; *vi* essere risparmiatore.

sparing ['spɛəriŋ] *a* economo, parco.

sparingly ['spɛəriŋli] *ad* in moderazione; limitatamente.

spark [spa:k] *n* favilla, scintilla, barlume; (*fig*) bellimbusto; *vi* emettere scintille; **sparking plug**, (US) **s. plug** (*aut*) candela.

sparkle ['spa:kl] *n* bagliore, scintillio, vivacità; *vi* brillare, scintillare.

sparkling ['spa:kliŋ] *a* scintillante, brillante; (*wine*) spumante.

sparrow ['spærou] *n* passero.

sparse [spa:s] *a* rado, sparso, che si trova ad intervalli irregolari.

sparsely ['spa:sli] *ad* scarsamente, poco; qui e là.

spasm ['spæzəm] *n* contrazione, spasimo.

spasmodic [spæs'mɔdik] *a* spasmodico.

spastic ['spæstik] *a* spastico.

spat [spæt] *n* ghetta.

spate [speit] *n* piena, straripamento.

spatter ['spætə] *vti* impillaccherare, spruzzare.

spawn [spɔ:n] *n* (*of fish etc*) uova *pl*; micelio; *vt* generare, produrre; *vi* deporre le uova.

speak [spi:k] *vi* parlare; *vt* pronunziare.

speaker ['spi:kə] *n* parlatore, oratore; Presidente della Camera dei Comuni; **loud-s.** alto parlante.

spear [spiə] *n* arpione, lancia; *vt* trafiggere con arpione; o lancia.

special ['speʃəl] *a* speciale, particolare; *n* treno speciale; edizione straordinaria di giornale.

specialist ['speʃəlist] *n* specialista.

speciality [,speʃi'æliti] *n* specialità.

specialize ['speʃəlaiz] *vti* specializzar(si).

species ['spi:ʃiz] *pl* **species** *n* specie, genere, sorta.

specific [spi'sifik] *a n* specifico; *a* caratteristico.

specification [,spesifi'keiʃən] *n* specificazione.

specify ['spesifai] *vt* specificare.

specimen ['spesimin] *n* campione, esemplare, saggio.

specious ['spi:ʃəs] *a* specioso.

speck [spek] *n* macchiolina; punto; *vt* chiazzare, macchiare.

speckle ['spekl] *n* macchiolina; *vt* segnare con macchioline, variegare.

spectacle ['spektəkl] *n* spettacolo, vista; **spectacles** *pl* occhiali *pl*.

spectacular [spek'tækjulə] *a* spettacolare, spettacoloso.

spectator [spek'teitə] *n* spettatore.

spectral ['spektrəl] *a* spettrale.

spectre ['spektə] *n* fantasma, spettro.

speculate ['spekjuleit] *vi* speculare.

speculation [,spekju'leiʃən] *n* speculazione, congettura, meditazione.

speculator ['spekjuleitə] *n* speculatore.

speech [spi:tʃ] *n* discorso, orazione; favella, linguaggio.

speechless ['spi:tʃlis] *a* muto, senza parole; sbalordito.

speed [spi:d] *n* velocità, rapidità, sveltezza; *vti* affrettar(si); **to s. up** accelerare.

speedometer [spi'dɔmitə] *n* (*aut*) tachimetro.

speedway ['spi:dwei] *n* pista, circuito; (US) autostrada.

speedy ['spi:di] *a* pronto, rapido, veloce.

spell [spel] *n* incantesimo, magia, fascino; breve periodo; *vti* compitare; significare.

spellbound ['spelbaund] *a* affascinato, incantato.

spelling ['speliŋ] *n* ortografia.

spend [spend] *vt* spendere; impiegare, passare, trascorrere; *vi* consumarsi; spendere.

spendthrift ['spendθrift] *a n* prodigo.

sperm [spə:m] *n* sperma.

spew [spju:] *vt* vomitare.

sphere [sfiə] *n* sfera; ambiente.

spherical ['sferikəl] *a* sferico.

sphinx [sfiŋks] *n* sfinge.

spice [spais] *n* spezie *pl*; aroma, sapore.

spick-and-span ['spikən'spæn] *a* lucido come uno specchio, lindo e ordinato.

spicy ['spaisi] *a* aromatico, piccante.

spider ['spaidə] *n* ragno.

spigot ['spigət] *n* zipolo; (US) rubinetto.

spike [spaik] *n* aculeo, chiodo, punta; spiga.

spiky ['spaiki] *a* munito di aculei, irto; (*fig*) di carattere difficile, spinoso.

spill [spil] *n* atto del versare; (*fam*) caduta, rovesciamento, (*pipe light*) legnetto; *vt* rovesciare, versare, spargere; *vi* cadere, rovesciarsi.

spin [spin] n giro, giretto; rotazione; vt filare, far girare, raccontare (una storia); vi girare, roteare.

spinach ['spinidʒ] n spinaci pl.

spindle ['spindl] n fuso; perno; a s.-shanked dalle gambe lunghe e sottili.

spin-drier ['spin'draiə] n asciugatrice automatica.

spine [spain] n spina (dorsale).

spineless ['spainlis] a senza spina dorsale; molle, senza carattere.

spinet ['spinit] n (mus) spinetta.

spinning ['spiniŋ] n filatura; s. wheel filatoio.

spinster ['spinstə] n zitella.

spiral ['spaiərəl] a spirale.

spire ['spaiə] n spira, spirale; guglia.

spirit ['spirit] n spirito.

spirited ['spiritəd] a brioso, vivace, ardente.

spiritless ['spiritlis] a avvilito, senz'energia.

spiritual ['spiritjuəl] a spirituale; n canto religioso dei negri degli S.U.

spiritualism ['spiritjuəlizəm] n spiritismo.

spiritualist ['spiritjuəlist] n spiritualista; spiritista.

spirt [spə:t] n getto, zampillo improvviso.

spit [spit] n spiedo; lingua di terra che avanza nel mare; sputo; badile, vanga; vt infilzare nello spiedo; sputare; pronunciare con violenza; vi sputare; piovigginare; mandar faville.

spite [spait] n dispetto, rancore; vt contrariare, vessare; in s. of prep a dispetto di, malgrado.

spiteful ['spaitful] a dispettoso, malevolo.

spitefully ['spaitfuli] ad per dispetto; con astio.

spitefulness ['spaitfulnis] n dispetto, malevolenza.

spittle ['spitl] n saliva, sputo.

spittoon [spi'tu:n] n sputacchiera.

splash [splæʃ] n spruzzo, tonfo; pillacchera; vt impillaccherare; spruzzare; vi sollevare spruzzi; cadere nell'acqua con un tonfo.

splashboard ['splæʃbɔ:d] n (aut) parafango anteriore.

splay [splei] a largo e piatto; voltato verso l'esterno; obliquo; vti (arch) svasare; essere in posizione obliqua; slogare.

spleen [spli:n] n milza; bile, ipocondria.

splendid ['splendid] a splendido.

splendour ['splendə] n splendore.

splice [splais] n unione, intrecciatura; (naut) impiombatura; vt congiungere, unire; impiombare.

splint [splint] n scheggia; (med) stecca.

splinter ['splintə] n scheggia.

split [split] a spaccata; n fenditura,

spaccatura; scisma; vti fender(si), spaccar(si), scheggiar(si).

splutter ['splʌtə] vti barbugliare; (in speech) sputacchiare; (of pen) spruzzare.

spoil [spoil] n usu pl bottino; vti deteriorar(si), guastar(si), viziare.

spoke [spouk] n raggio.

spokesman ['spouksmən] n portavoce.

spoliation [.spouli'eiʃən] n spoliazione.

sponge [spʌndʒ] n spugna; spugnatura; s. cake biscotto spugnoso; sponger (fig) parassita, scroccone; vt cancellare, lavare con la spugna; vi vivere a scrocco.

spongy ['spʌndʒi] a spugnoso, poroso.

sponsor ['spɔnsə] n garante, madrina f, padrino m.

spontaneity [.spɔntə'ni:iti] n spontaneità.

spontaneous [spɔn'teiniəs] a spontaneo.

spool [spu:l] n bobina, rocchetto.

spoon [spu:n] n cucchiaio.

spoonful ['spu:nful] n cucchiaiata.

sporadic [spə'rædik] a sporadico.

spore [spɔ:] n spora.

sport [spɔ:t] n gioco, divertimento; sport; (fig) persona di spirito; vi divertirsi, giocare; vt ostentare; sports requisites (or sports goods) articoli sportivi.

sporting ['spɔ:tiŋ] a sportivo; s. goods (US) articoli sportivi.

sportive ['spɔ:tiv] a gioviale, sportivo.

sportsman ['spɔ:tsmən] n sportivo; (US) giocatore d'azzardo.

spot [spɔt] n luogo, posto, punto; macchia, (fam) piccola quantità; vti macchiar(si); vt (fam) individuare, scoprire.

spotless ['spɔtlis] a immacolato, senza macchia.

spotlight ['spɔtlait] n luce della ribalta, riflettore.

spouse [spauz] n coniuge, marito m, moglie f.

spout [spaut] n becco; (of teapot etc) beccuccio; (of liquid) getto; tubo di scarico; vi gettare, spruzzare; vti scaricare, scaturire, zampillare; (fig) declamare.

sprain [sprein] n storta; vt storcere.

sprat [spræt] n spratto; (fam) bimbetto.

sprawl [sprɔ:l] vi sdraiarsi, stare sdraiato, in modo scomposto.

spray [sprei] n schiuma, spruzzo; rametto, ramoscello; vt spruzzare.

spread [spred] n distesa, estensione; (fam) banchetto; vt diffondere, propagare, spargere, spiegare, stendere; vi spargersi, spiegarsi, stendersi.

spree [spri:] n (fam) baldoria.

sprig [sprig] n rametto; (fig) giovincello.

sprightliness ['spraitlinis] n spirito, vivacità.

sprightly ['spraitli] a spiritoso, vivace.

spring [sprɪŋ] n balzo, salto; molla; fonte, sorgente; (season) primavera; vt far scattare; vi balzare; derivare, provenire; sorgere.

springtime ['sprɪŋtaim] n tempo di primavera.

springy ['sprɪŋi] a elastico.

sprinkle ['sprɪŋkl] n aspersione, spruzzatina; vt aspergere, spruzzare.

sprinkling ['sprɪŋklɪŋ] n spruzzamento; spruzzatina; aspersione; (fig) pizzico, infarinatura.

sprint [sprint] n (sport) scatto finale, 'sprint'; vi correre alla massima velocità.

sprite [sprait] n folletto, spiritello.

sprout [spraut] n germoglio; (vegetable) cavolino di Bruxelles; vt germogliare, spuntare.

spruce [spruːs] a azzimato, attillato; n abete rosso.

spry [sprai] a arzillo, vivace.

spur [spəː] n sprone, sperone; (fig) incitamento; vt incitare, spronare, stimolare.

spurious ['spjuəriəs] a falso, spurio.

spuriousness ['spjuəriəsnis] n contraffazione, falsità.

spurn [spəːn] vt respingere a calci; (fig) disprezzare, rifiutare con sdegno.

spurt [spəːt] n breve sforzo violento; vti fare un breve sforzo violento, scattare; schizzare.

sputter ['spʌtə] vi parlare incoerentemente, barbugliare, sputacchiare.

spy [spai] n spia; vti spiare.

squab [skwɔb] n piccioncino; cuscinetto.

squabble ['skwɔbl] n bisticcio; vi bisticciar(si).

squad [skwɔd] n squadra.

squadron ['skwɔdrən] n (mil) squadra, squadrone; (naut, av) squadriglia.

squalid ['skwɔlid] a squallido, sordido.

squall [skwɔːl] n raffica, turbine; (fig) litigio.

squalor ['skwɔlə] n squallore, miseria.

squander ['skwɔndə] vt scialacquare.

square [skwɛə] a quadro, quadrato; robusto; giusto, onesto; preciso; sostanzioso; n quadrato; piazza; (instrument) squadra; ad angolo retto, direttamente; vt quadrare; elevare al quadrato; (fam) corrompere; vi adattarsi, conformarsi.

squash [skwɔʃ] n spremuta; cosa schiacciata; (fam) ressa; (US) melopopone; Italian s. (US) zucchino; vti schiacciar(si), spremere; vt (fam) stroncare, soffocare.

squat [skwɔt] a tarchiato, tozzo; rannicchiato; vi accosciarsi, rannicchiarsi.

squawk [skwɔːk] n grido rauco; vti

emettere un grido rauco; lamentarsi.

squeak [skwiːk] n grido acuto, squittio, stridore; vi squittire, stridere, cigolare; parlare con voce stridula.

squeaky ['skwiːki] a (voice) acuto; che squittisce; cigolante, stridente.

squeal [skwiːl] n strillo, squittio; vi strillare.

squeamish [ˈskwiːmiʃ] a delicato di stomaco; schizzinoso.

squeamishness ['skwiːmiʃnis] n delicatezza di stomaco; schizzinosità.

squeeze [skwiːz] n compressione, spremitura, stretta; ressa; vti spremere, spremersi, stringere, stringersi; estorcere.

squelch [skweltʃ] vti fare il rumore del piede tirato su dal fango molle; diguazzare; (fig) soffocare, sopprimere.

squib [skwib] n petardo, razzo; pasquinata, satira.

squid [skwid] n seppia.

squint [skwint] n strabismo; sguardo furtivo; vi guardare obliquamente; essere strabico; aver tendenza verso.

squire ['skwaiə] n gentiluomo di campagna; (hist) scudiero.

squirm [skwəːm] vi contorcersi; provare imbarazzo, o umiliazione.

squirrel ['skwirəl] n scoiattolo.

squirt [skwəːt] n schizzetto; siringa; vti schizzare.

stab [stæb] n pugnalata; vt pugnalare.

stability [stə'biliti] n stabilità.

stabilize ['steibilaiz] vt stabilizzare.

stable ['steibl] a fermo, stabile; n scuderia, stalla.

stack [stæk] n ammasso, mucchio, catasta; pagliaio, gruppo di camini sul tetto; (fam) grande quantità; vt ammucchiare, accatastare.

stadium ['steidiəm] pl **stadia** n stadio, campo sportivo.

staff [staːf] n appoggio, sostegno; bastone; personale; corpo insegnante, (mil) stato maggiore; vt fornire di personale.

stag [stæg] n cervo, cerbiatto; s. beetle cervo volante.

stage [steidʒ] n palcoscenico, teatro; tappa; fase; periodo; scena; vt (theat) mettere in scena.

stagger ['stægə] n barcollamento, passo incerto; vt far barcollare; (fig) sbalordire; vi barcollare, vacillare.

stagnant ['stægnənt] a stagnante.

stagnate ['stægneit] vi stagnare, subire una stasi ristagnare.

stagnation [stæg'neiʃən] n ristagno; stasi.

staid [steid] a posato, serio.

stain [stein] n macchia; onta; colore, tinta; vt macchiare; dipingere.

stainless ['steinlis] a senza macchia; s. steel acciaio inossidabile.

stair [stɛə] n gradino, scalino; pl scala.

staircase ['stɛəkeis] n scala, tromba delle scale.

stake [steik] n palo; rogo; posta, premio; vt sostenere, delimitare con pali; rischiare; scommettere.

stale [steil] a raffermo, stantio; spossato, trito; vti rendere, diventare stantio.

stalemate ['steil'meit] n (chess) stallo; (fig) punto morto; vt fare stallo a; (fig) portare a un punto morto.

stalk [stɔːk] n gambo, stelo; andatura maestosa; inseguimento di selvaggina; vi camminare maestosamente; inseguire selvaggina.

stall [stɔːl] n stalla; stallo; bancherella; chiosco, edicola; scanno; (theat) poltrona.

stallion ['stæljən] n stallone.

stalwart ['stɔːlwət] a robusto, vigoroso.

stammer ['stæmə] n balbettamento, balbuzie; vi balbettare, tartagliare.

stamp [stæmp] n francobollo; bollo; marchio, timbro; impronta; vt affrancare; bollare, timbrare; imprimere; vi pestare i piedi.

stampede [stæm'piːd] n fuga precipitosa e tumultuante.

stanch [stɑːntʃ] v **staunch**.

stanchion ['stɑːnʃən] n puntello; sbarra.

stand [stænd] n arresto, pausa; posizione; posteggio; posto; banco; edicola; palco, tribuna; leggio, piedistallo; (exhibition) "stand"; vt appoggiare, mettere in piedi; affrontare, resistere a, sopportare; vi stare ritto, stare in piedi; fermarsi.

standard ['stændəd] n bandiera, stendardo; modello, livello; a classico, normale.

standardize ['stændədaiz] vt standardizzare.

standing ['stændiŋ] n posizione, riputazione.

standpoint ['stændpɔint] n punto di vista.

standstill ['stændstil] n punto morto, ristagno.

stanza ['stænzə] n (poet) stanza, strofa.

staple ['steipl] a principale; n (com) prodotto principale.

star [stɑː] n stella, astro; asterisco; (theat etc) divo, -va; vt segnare con l'asterisco; ornare di stelle; vi essere attore di cartello.

starboard ['stɑːbəd] n (naut) tribordo.

starch [stɑːtʃ] n amido; (fig) formalismo; vt inamidare.

stare [stɛə] n sguardo fisso; vi fissare, guardare fisso.

starfish ['stɑːfiʃ] n stella di mare.

stark [stɑːk] a rigido; completo; ad del tutto, completamente.

starling ['stɑːliŋ] n stornello.

starlit ['stɑːlit] a stellato.

starry ['stɑːri] a stellato; scintillante.

start [stɑːt] n partenza, avvio, inizio; sobbalzo, sussulto; vantaggio; vt mettere in moto, iniziare; vi partire; sobbalzare, trasalire.

starter ['stɑːtə] n iniziatore, fondatore, (aut) avviamento.

startle ['stɑːtl] vt far trasalire.

startling ['stɑːtliŋ] a impressionante, sensazionale.

starvation [stɑː'veiʃən] n fame, inedia.

starve [stɑːv] vti (far) morire di fame; vi agognare.

state [steit] n stato, nazione; condizioni pl; grado, qualità, dignità; pompa; vt affermare, asserire, formulare, specificare, stabilire.

stateliness ['steitlinis] n imponenza, maestosità.

stately ['steitli] a imponente, maestoso, solenne.

statement ['steitmənt] n affermazione, dichiarazione; deposizione testimoniale; rendiconto.

statesman ['steitsmən] pl -men n statista, uomo di stato; **statesmanship** arte di governo.

static ['stætik] a statico.

station ['steiʃən] n stazione; grado; posto, posizione sociale; vt assegnare un posto a, collocare.

stationary ['steiʃnəri] a stazionario, fisso.

stationer ['steiʃnə] n cartolaio.

stationery ['steiʃnəri] n cartoleria.

statistic [stə'tistik] a statistico; n pl statistica.

statuary ['stætjuəri] a statuario; n scultura, statuaria.

statue ['stætju:] n statua.

statuesque [,stætju'esk] a statuario.

stature ['stætʃə] n statura.

status ['steitəs] n stato, condizione sociale, situazione; s. **symbol** simbolo di posizione sociale.

statute ['stætju:t] n statuto, legge.

statutory ['stætjutəri] a statutario, fissato dalla legge.

staunch [stɔːntʃ] a fedele, leale; solido; vt (med) tamponare.

stave [steiv] n doga; strofa, stanza; (mus) rigo; vt praticare un foro in; **to s. off** allontanare, stornare.

stay [stei] n permanenza, soggiorno; sostegno; (leg) sospensione; vt trattenere, arrestare, ritardare; vi rimanere, stare, soggiornare; n pl busto, corsetto.

stead [sted] n luogo, vece.

steadfast ['stedfəst] a costante, risoluto.

steadiness ['stedinis] n costanza, fermezza.

steady ['stedi] a costante, fermo, posato, stabile.

steak [steik] n fetta di carne o pesce.

steal [sti:l] vt rubare, sottrarre; vi rubare; muoversi furtivamente.

stealth [stelθ] *n* movimento, o atto, furtivo.

stealthily ['stelθili] *ad* furtivamente, di nascosto.

stealthy ['stelθi] *a* clandestino, furtivo.

steam [sti:m] *n* vapore; *vt* esporre a vapore; cuocere a vapore; *vi* emettere vapore, fumare; **s. roller** rullo compressore.

steamboat ['sti:mbout] *n* battello a vapore.

steamer ['sti:mə] *n* piroscafo, vapore.

steamship ['sti:mʃip] *n* piroscafo, vapore.

steed [sti:d] *n* destriero, corsiero.

steel [sti:l] *n* acciaio; *vt* ricoprire, rivestire di acciaio; (*fig*) fortificare; indurire; **steelwork** lavoro in acciaio, *pl* acciaierie.

steely ['sti:li] *a* di acciaio; (*fig*) duro, inflessibile, di ferro.

steep [sti:p] *a* erto, ripido, scosceso; (*fam*) esorbitante; *n* erta, precipizio.

steeple ['sti:pl] *n* campanile.

steeplechase ['sti:pltʃeis] *n* corsa ad ostacoli.

steepness ['sti:pnis] *n* ripidezza.

steer [stiə] *vti* dirigere, guidare, governare, dirigersi.

steer [stiə] *n* (*zool*) giovenco.

steerage ['stiəridʒ] *n* governo del timone; parte della nave riservata ai passeggeri di 3ª classe.

steersman ['stiəzmən] *pl* -men *n* timoniere.

stem [stem] *n* gambo; stelo; ramo, rampollo, stirpe; (*gram*) tema, radicale; *vt* arginare, arrestare, contenere.

stench [stentʃ] *n* fetore, tanfo.

stencil ['stensl] *n* stampino, decorazione fatta con stampino; **s. copy** copia a ciclostile.

stenographer [ste'nɔgrəfə] *n* stenografo *m*, stenografa *f*.

stenography [ste'nɔgrəfi] *n* stenografia.

step [step] *n* passo; gradino, scalino; piolo, provvedimento, *pl* scalinata; scala a mano; *vt* misurare a passi; *vi* andare, venire, camminare.

stepbrother ['step,brʌðə] *n* fratellastro; **stepdaughter** *n* figliastra; **stepfather** *n* patrigno; **stepmother** *n* matrigna; **stepsister** *n* sorellastra; **stepson** *n* figliastro.

Stephen ['sti:vn] *nm pr* Stefano.

stepping-stone ['stepiŋstoun] *n* pietra per guadare; (*fig*) trampolino.

stereophonic [,steriə'fɔnik] *a* stereofonico.

stereoscope ['stiəriəskoup] *n* stereoscopio.

stereoscopic [,steriə'skɔpik] *a* stereoscopico.

stereotype ['stiəriətaip] *n* stereotipo.

sterile ['sterail] *a* sterile.

sterility [ste'riliti] *n* sterilità.

sterling ['stə:liŋ] *a* genuino, puro, di

buona lega; **pound s.** (lira) sterlina.

stern [stə:n] *a* austero, rigido, severo; *n* (*naut*) poppa; deretano.

sternness ['stə:nnis] *n* austerità, severità.

stertorous ['stɔ:tərəs] *a* affannoso.

stew [stju:] *n* ragù, stufato; vivaio di pesci; *vti* cuocere a fuoco lento.

steward ['stjuəd] *n* amministratore; dispensiere; cameriere di bordo; **stewardess** cameriera di bordo.

stick [stik] *n* bacchetta; bastone; ramo, stecco; *vt* ficcare, conficcare; appiccicare, incollare; *vi* aderire, rimanere attaccato; **s.-in-the-mud** persona priva di iniziativa.

sticker ['stikə] *n* attacchino; scocciatore; etichetta gommata.

stickler ['stiklə] *n* sostenitore accanito; pignolo.

sticky ['stiki] *a* appiccicoso, viscido; (*fig*) poco accomodante.

stiff [stif] *a* duro, inflessibile, rigido; intorpidito; (*price*) caro; difficile; impacciato.

stiffen ['stifn] *vt* indurire, irrigidire; inamidare; indolenzire; *vi* irrigidirsi, rassodarsi.

stiffness ['stifnis] *n* rigidezza; intorpidimento, indolenzimento; difficoltà.

stifle ['staifl] *vti* soffocare; *vt* estinguere.

stifling ['staifliŋ] *s* soffocante.

stigma ['stigmə] *n* marchio, segno (d'infamia).

stigmatize ['stigmətaiz] *vt* stigmatizzare.

stiletto [sti'letou] *pl* -os, -oes *n* stiletto; **s. heels** tacchi a spillo.

still [stil] *a* calmo, fermo, immobile; tranquillo, silenzioso; *ad* ancora, tuttora, tuttavia; *n* silenzio, quiete; alambicco; *vt* calmare, far tacere.

stillness ['stilnis] *n* calma, quiete, tranquillità.

stilt [stilt] *n* trampolo.

stilted ['stiltid] *a* ricercato, affettato, privo di naturalezza.

stimulant ['stimjulənt] *a n* stimolante.

stimulate ['stimjuleit] *vt* stimolare.

stimulating ['stimjuleitiŋ] *a* stimolante, eccitante.

stimulation [,stimju'leiʃən] *n* stimolo.

stimulus ['stimjuləs] *n* stimolo; pungolo.

sting [stiŋ] *n* pungiglione; puntura; (*insect*) pungolo; (*fig*) frecciata, sarcasmo; *vt* pungere; (*fig*) irritare, far arrabbiare.

stinginess ['stindʒinis] *n* spilorceria, tirchieria.

stingy ['stindʒi] *a* spilorcio, tirchio.

stink [stiŋk] *n* fetore, puzzo; *vi* puzzare.

stint [stint] *n* limite, restrizione; compito; *vt* lesinare, limitare, tenere a stecchetto.

stipend ['staipend] n (eccl) stipendio.
stipulate ['stipjuleit] vti pattuire, stipolare.
stipulation [‚stipju'leiʃən] n patto, stipolazione.
stir [stə:] n il rimescolare, l'attizzare; trambusto, movimento; vt agitare, muovere, rimescolare; vi muoversi; to s. up stimolare, eccitare.
stirrup ['stirəp] n staffa.
stitch [stitʃ] n punto (di cucitura); maglia; vt cucire.
stoat [stout] n ermellino.
stock [stɔk] n riserva, scorta; bestiame; famiglia, stirpe; ceppo, tronco; (rifle) calcio; (com) azioni pl; s. market mercato finanziario; common s. (US) azioni ordinarie; stocks and shares valori di borsa, titoli; vt tenere in magazzino; provvedere, rifornire.
stockbroker ['stɔk‚broukə] a agente di cambio.
stockfish ['stɔkfiʃ] n stoccafisso.
Stockholm ['stɔkhoum] n Stoccolma.
stocking ['stɔkiŋ] n calza (lunga).
stockist ['stɔkist] n (com) grossista; fornitore.
stocky ['stɔki] a tarchiato.
stodgy ['stɔdʒi] a indigesto, pesante.
stoic ['stouik] a n stoico; stoically stoicamente.
stoke [stouk] vt attizzare (il fuoco), alimentare (la caldaia); vi fare il fuochista.
stoker ['stoukə] n fuochista.
stole [stoul] n stola.
stolid ['stɔlid] a stolido, imperturbabile.
stolidity [stɔ'liditi] n stolidezza, stolidità.
stomach ['stʌmək] n stomaco; (fig) coraggio; vt ingoiare, subire, tollerare.
stone [stoun] n pietra, sasso; (fruit) nocciolo; misura di peso (= 14 libbre, kg 6,45); (med) calcolo; vt lapidare; togliere il nocciolo a.
stony ['stouni] a pietroso; (fig) duro, freddo.
stool [stu:l] n sgabello; escremento, feci pl.
stoop [stu:p] n curvatura, inclinazione del corpo in avanti; vi curvarsi, chinarsi; umiliarsi; essere curvo.
stop [stɔp] n arresto, fermata; punto d'interpunzione; vt arrestare, sospendere; ostruire; (ot)turare; vi fermarsi, cessare.
stoppage ['stɔpidʒ] n arresto, cessazione: ostruzione; (med) occlusione.
stopper ['stɔpə] n tampone, tappo, turacciolo.
storage ['stɔ:ridʒ] n immagazzinamento, deposito, (com) magazzinaggio.
store [stɔ:] n grande magazzino, emporio, (US) negozio; provvista, pl provvigioni, abbondanza; vt approvvigionare, immagazzinare;

storehouse magazzino deposito; s. clerk (US) commesso.
storey, story ['stɔ:ri] n piano (d'una casa).
stork [stɔ:k] n cicogna.
storm [stɔ:m] n burrasca, tempesta, temporale; scoppio; vi essere violento, infuriare; vt prendere d'assalto.
stormy ['stɔ:mi] a tempestoso; (fig) violento.
story ['stɔ:ri] n storia, novella, racconto, favola, frottola; storyteller narratore; (fam) bugiardo.
stout [staut] a forte, robusto, ben piantato, corpulento; n birra scura.
stout-hearted ['staut'hɑ:tid] a coraggioso, intrepido.
stoutness ['stautnis] n corpulenza.
stove [stouv] n fornello, stufa, cucina.
stow [stou] vt collocare accuratamente, stivare; (sl) smettere.
stowage ['stouidʒ] n (naut) stivaggio.
stowaway ['stouəwei] n passeggero clandestino.
straddle ['strædl] vti stare a cavalcioni di, cavalcare, divaricare, stare a gambe divaricate.
straggle ['strægl] vi disperdersi, sbandarsi, sparpagliarsi.
straggler ['stræglə] n ritardatario; soldato sbandato.
straggling ['strægliŋ] a sparso, isolato; s. beard barba rada.
straight [streit] a diritto; retto; (US drinks) liscio; ad direttamente.
straighten ['streitn] vti raddrizzar (si).
straightforward [streit'fɔ:wəd] a franco, leale, retto; semplice, facile.
straightforwardness [streit'fɔ:wədnis] n franchezza, rettitudine; semplicità, chiarezza.
straightness ['streitnis] n dirittura.
strain [strein] n tensione, sforzo, strappo muscolare; tono; razza, pl melodia; vt sforzare, mettere a dura prova; filtrare; vi sforzarsi; filtrare; procedere faticosamente.
strainer ['streinə] n colino.
strait [streit] n (geogr) stretto; difficoltà, imbarazzo; s.-waistcoat (or -jacket) camicia di forza; in straitened circumstances in difficoltà, in strettezze.
strand [strænd] n filo di corda, fune; riva, spiaggia; vt far arenare; vi arenarsi.
strange [streindʒ] a strano, bizzarro; estraneo; insolito, nuovo; forestiero, sconosciuto.
strangeness ['streindʒnis] n stranezza, singolarità, novità.
stranger ['streindʒə] n estraneo, sconosciuto, forestiero.
strangle ['stræŋgl] vt strangolare, soffocare; (fig) reprimere.
strap [stræp] n cinghia, correggia; vt legare con una cinghia.
strapping ['stræpiŋ] a robusto, ben piantato.

stratagem ['strætidʒəm] n strata-gemma.

strategic [strə'tiːdʒik] a strategico.

strategist ['strætidʒist] n stratega.

strategy ['strætidʒi] n strategia.

stratum ['strɑːtəm] pl **strata** n strato; strato sociale.

straw [strɔː] n paglia; festuca; pagliuzza; (fig) cosa da nulla; **the last s.** il colmo, la goccia che fa traboccare il vaso.

strawberry ['strɔːbəri] n fragola.

stray [strei] a smarrito; casuale, sporadico; vi smarrirsi, sviarsi, errare.

streak ['striːk] n striscia, stria; (fig) vena; vt striare; vi muoversi velocemente.

streaky ['striːki] a striato, a strisce.

stream [striːm] n corrente, corso d'acqua, fiotto, fiume; vt versare a fiotti; vi fluire, scorrere.

streamer ['striːmə] n banderuola; nastro; (newspaper US) testata.

streamline ['striːmlain] n (aut, av) linea aerodinamica; vt dare linea aerodinamica; (fig) ordinare, semplificare.

street [striːt] n via, strada; **streetcar** (US) tram.

strength [strenθ] n forza, forze pl, robustezza, vigore.

strengthen ['strenθən] vt fortificare, rafforzare.

strengthless ['strenθlis] a debole, senza forza.

strenuous ['strenjuəs] a strenuo; vigoroso; arduo.

strenuousness ['strenjuəsnis] n accanimento.

stress [stres] n sforzo, tensione; accento, enfasi; importanza; vt mettere l'accento su, mettere in rilievo, sottolineare.

stretch [stretʃ] n distesa, tratto; stiramento; vt (e)stendere; sgranchire; esagerare; vi (e)stendersi, stirarsi.

stretcher ['stretʃə] n barella.

strew [struː] vt cospargere, disseminare.

strict [strikt] a stretto, esatto; (fig) severo.

strictness ['striktnis] n esattezza, severità.

stricture ['striktʃə] n censura, critica.

stride [straid] n passo lungo; vt scavalcare; vi camminare a gran passi.

strident ['straidənt] a stridente, stridulo.

strife [straif] n conflitto.

strike [straik] n sciopero; scoperta di giacimento minerario; vt battere, colpire; accendere; impressionare; vi colpire; scioperare; (clock) suonare.

striker ['straikə] n scioperante; battitore.

striking ['straikiŋ] a sorprendente, impressionante, rimarchevole.

string [striŋ] n corda, spago, stringa; serie; fila, filza; vt (pearls etc) infilare; **to s. up** (violin etc) accordare.

stringent ['strindʒənt] a rigoroso, severo.

stringy ['striŋi] a filamentoso; fibroso.

strip [strip] n striscia; vt denudare, privare, spogliare; vi spogliarsi, svestirsi.

stripe [straip] n striscia; (mil) gallone.

strive [straiv] vi sforzarsi, lottare.

stroke [strouk] n colpo; battuta; (med) colpo; sferzata; tratto; carezza; vt accarezzare, lisciare.

stroll [stroul] n giretto, passeggiata; vi andare a zonzo, bighellonare.

strong [strɔŋ] a forte, robusto, saldo.

stronghold ['strɔŋhould] n roccaforte, cittadella.

strop [strɔp] n coramella; vt affilare un rasoio.

strophe ['stroufi] n strofa.

structure ['strʌktʃə] n struttura, costruzione.

struggle ['strʌgl] n combattimento, lotta; vi lottare, divincolarsi.

strum [strʌm] n strimpellamento; vti strimpellare.

strut [strʌt] vi pavoneggiarsi, camminare impettito.

stub [stʌb] n troncone; mozzicone; (cheque book etc) matrice; vt sradicare; sbattere; spegnere.

stubble ['stʌbl] n stoppia, stoppie pl; barba ispida.

stubborn ['stʌbən] a ostinato, testardo.

stubbornness ['stʌbənnis] n ostinazione, testardaggine.

stucco ['stʌkou] n stucco.

stud [stʌd] n borchia; bottoncino da colletto; allevamento di cavalli da corsa.

student ['stjudənt] n studente, studentessa.

studio ['stjudiou] n (artist's) studio; (cin) teatro di posa.

studious ['stjudiəs] a studioso.

study ['stʌdi] n studio; applicazione; premura; vt studiare, esaminare attentamente; vi studiare, darsi la pena.

stuff [stʌf] n materia; roba; sostanza; stoffa, tessuto; cosa di nessun valore; vt imbottire, infarcire, rimpinzare; impagliare; vi rimpinzarsi.

stuffing ['stʌfiŋ] n imbottitura; (cook) ripieno.

stuffy ['stʌfi] a chiuso, senz'aria; (of weather) afoso, (fam) di idee antiquate; noioso.

stultify ['stʌltifai] vt infirmare, neutralizzare.

stumble ['stʌmbl] n passo falso; (fig) errore; vi incespicare, inciampare, fare errori.

stump [stʌmp] n ceppo, tronco;

moncherino; mozzicone; vt confondere, mettere nell'imbarazzo; vi camminare goffamente.

stumpy ['stʌmpi] a tarchiato, tozzo.

stun [stʌn] vt assordare, stordire; far perdere i sensi a.

stunning ['stʌniŋ] a stordente, assordante; (sl) meraviglioso.

stunt [stʌnt] n (sl) bravata; trovata pubblicitaria, notizia sensazionale; (av) acrobazia; vt arrestare lo sviluppo di.

stupefy ['stjupifai] vt istupidire.

stupendous [stju'pendəs] a stupendo.

stupid ['stjupid] a stupido.

stupidity [stju'piditi] n stupidità.

stupor ['stjupə] n stupore; (med) torpore.

sturdiness ['stə:dinis] n gagliardia, vigore.

sturdy ['stə:di] a robusto, vigoroso, gagliardo.

sturgeon ['stə:dʒən] n storione.

stutter ['stʌtə] n balbuzie; vi essere balbuziente.

sty [stai] n porcile.

sty(e) [stai] n orzaiolo.

style [stail] n stile; distinzione; titolo; stilo; (com) ragion sociale.

stylish ['stailiʃ] a elegante, distinto, alla moda.

stylus ['stailəs] n stilo, puntina per grammofono.

suave [swɑːv] a mellifluo; garbato.

subaltern ['sʌbltən] a n subalterno.

subdue [səb'dju:] vt domare, soggiogare, vincere.

sub-editor ['sʌb'editə] n redattore aggiunto, revisore di stampa.

subject ['sʌbdʒikt] a soggetto; suscettibile; n argomento; soggetto; materia di studio; suddito; vt [səb'dʒekt] assoggettare, sottoporre.

subjection [səb'dʒekʃən] n soggezione, sottomissione.

subjective [səb'dʒektiv] a n soggettivo.

subjugate ['sʌbdʒugeit] vt soggiogare.

subjunctive [səb'dʒʌŋktiv] n (gram) congiuntivo.

sub-let ['sʌb'let] vt subaffittare.

sublime [sə'blaim] a sublime.

submarine ['sʌbmərin] a sottomarino; n sommergibile.

submerge [səb'mə:dʒ] vti sommerger(si), immerger(si).

submersion [səb'mə:ʃən] n sommersione.

submission [səb'miʃən] n sottomissione.

submissive [səb'misiv] a remissivo, sottomesso.

submit [səb'mit] vt sottomettere, sottoporre; vi cedere, rassegnarsi.

subordinate [sə'bɔ:dnit] a subordinato; n subalterno; vt subordinare.

suborn [sʌ'bɔ:n] vt subornare.

subscribe [səb'skraib] vt sottoscrivere a; vi aderire, sottoscriversi.

subscriber [səb'skraibə] n sottoscritto; (com) contraente; abbonato.

subscription [səb'skripʃən] n abbonamento; quota d'iscrizione.

subsequent ['sʌbsikwənt] a successivo, susseguente.

subservient [səb'səviənt] a ossequiente, servile; subordinato.

subside [səb'said] vi abbassarsi, (waters) decrescere; cedere, (ground) sprofondare; calmarsi, diminuire.

subsidence [səb'saidəns] n abbassamento, cedimento.

subsidiary [səb'sidjəri] a sussidiario, accessorio, supplementare.

subsidize ['sʌbsidaiz] vt sussidiare, sovvenzionare.

subsidy ['sʌbsidi] n sussidio, sovvenzione.

subsist [səb'sist] vi sussistere.

subsistence [səb'sistəns] n sussistenza, sostentamento.

substance ['sʌbstəns] n sostanza.

substantial [səb'stænʃəl] a sostanzioso; sostanziale.

substantiate [səb'stænʃieit] vt provare, dar fondamento a.

substitute ['sʌbstitjuːt] n sostituto, surrogato; vt sostituire.

substitution [ˌsʌbsti'tjuːʃən] n sostituzione.

subterfuge ['sʌbtəfjuːdʒ] n sotterfugio.

subterranean ['sʌbtə'reiniən] a sotterraneo.

subtle ['sʌtl] a sottile, delicato, tenue, indefinibile; astuto, ingegnoso.

subtlety ['sʌtlti] n sottigliezza; astuzia.

subtract [səb'trækt] vt sottrarre.

subtraction [səb'trækʃən] n sottrazione.

suburb ['sʌbə:b] n sobborgo.

suburban [sə'bə:bən] a suburbano, della periferia.

subversive [sʌb'və:siv] a sovversivo, sovvertitore.

subvert [sʌb'və:t] vt sovvertire.

subway ['sʌbwei] n sottopassaggio, (US) metropolitana.

succeed [sək'si:d] vt succedere a; vi riuscire, aver successo, salire a.

success [sək'ses] n successo, fortuna.

successful [sək'sesful] a fortunato.

successfully [sək'sesfuli] ad con successo, felicemente.

succession [sək'seʃən] n successione; serie.

successive [sək'sesiv] a successivo, consecutivo.

successor [sək'sesə] n successore.

succinct [sək'siŋkt] a conciso, succinto.

succour ['sʌkə] n soccorso; vt aiutare, soccorrere.

succulent ['sʌkjulənt] a succulento; squisito.

succumb [sə'kʌm] *vi* soccombere.

such [sʌtʃ] *a pron* tale; questo; simile.

suck [sʌk] *vt* succhiare; poppare; assorbire.

sucker ['sʌkə] *n* (*of insect*) succhiatoio; (*of leech*) ventosa; (*fig*) credulone; parassita.

suckle ['sʌkl] *vt* allattare.

suckling ['sʌkliŋ] *n* lattante, poppante.

suction ['sʌkʃən] *n* succhiamento; aspirazione.

sudden ['sʌdn] *a* improvviso, imprevisto.

suddenly ['sʌdnli] *ad* (tutt')ad un tratto, improvvisamente.

suddenness ['sʌdnnis] *n* subitaneità.

suds [sʌdz] *n* saponata.

sue [sju:] *vt* citare in giudizio.

suède [sweid] *n* pelle scamosciata.

suet ['sjuit] *n* grasso, sugna.

suffer ['sʌfə] *vt* soffrire, subire, tollerare; *vi* soffrire, patire.

sufferance ['sʌfərəns] *n* sopportazione, tolleranza.

suffering ['sʌfəriŋ] *a* sofferente; *n* sofferenza.

suffice [sə'fais] *vt* essere sufficiente per; *vi* bastare.

sufficient [sə'fiʃənt] *a* bastevole, sufficiente; *n* quantità sufficiente.

suffix ['sʌfiks] *n* (*gram*) suffisso.

suffocate ['sʌfəkeit] *vt* soffocare, asfissiare.

suffocation [.sʌfə'keiʃən] *n* soffocazione, asfissia.

suffrage ['sʌfridʒ] *n* suffragio, diritto di voto.

suffragette [.sʌfrə'dʒet] *n* suffragetta.

suffuse [sə'fju:z] *vt* diffondersi su, coprire.

sugar ['ʃugə] *n* zucchero; (*fig*) parole dolci *pl*; **castor s.** zucchero in polvere; **icing s.** zucchero a velo.

suggest [sə'dʒest] *vt* suggerire, proporre.

suggestion [sə'dʒestʃən] *n* suggerimento, proposta.

suggestive [sə'dʒestiv] *a* che richiama alla mente; allusivo; suggestivo.

suicidal [sui'saidl] *a* suicida; (*fig*) disastroso.

suicide ['sjuisaid] *n* suicida; suicidio.

suit [sju:t] *n* abito completo; petizione, supplica; causa; (*cards*) colore, seme; *vt* soddisfare, convenire a, giovare a; donare a; *vi* addirsi, andar bene, convenire.

suitable ['sju:təbl] *a* adatto, conveniente.

suitably ['sju:təbli] *ad* appropriatamente; opportunamente.

suite [swi:t] *n* sèguito; serie.

suitor ['sju:tə] *n* aspirante, corteggiatore; (*leg*) attore in una causa.

sulk [sʌlk] *vi* tenere il broncio.

sulky ['sʌlki] *a* imbronciato, scontroso.

sullen ['sʌlən] *a* cupo, imbronciato.

sullenness ['sʌlənnis] *n* umor nero, intrattabilità.

sully ['sʌli] *vt* macchiare, disonorare.

sulphur ['sʌlfə] *n* zolfo.

sulphuric [sʌl'fjuərik] *a* solforico.

sultan ['sʌltən] *n* sultano.

sultana [səl'tɑ:nə] *n* sultana, uva sultanina.

sultry ['sʌltri] *a* afoso, soffocante.

sum [sʌm] *n* addizione, somma; *vt* addizionare, sommare; **s. up** riassumere.

summary ['sʌməri] *n* riassunto; *a n* sommario.

summer ['sʌmə] *n* estate.

summery ['sʌməri] *a* estivo.

summit ['sʌmit] *n* sommità, vetta, apice.

summon ['sʌmən] *vt* chiamare, mandare a chiamare, convocare; (*leg*) citare.

summons ['sʌmənz] *n* (*leg*) citazione; convocazione; (*mil*) chiamata.

sump [sʌmp] *n* pozzo nero; (*aut*) coppa.

sumptuous ['sʌmptjuəs] *a* sontuoso.

sun [sʌn] *n* sole.

sunbeam ['sʌnbi:m] *n* raggio di sole.

sunburnt ['sʌnbə:nt] *a* abbronzato.

Sunday ['sʌndi] *n* domenica.

sunder ['sʌndə] *vt* scindere, separare.

sundry ['sʌndri] *a* parecchi, diversi; **sundries** *n pl* bagatelle *pl*; spese varie *pl*.

sunlight ['sʌnlait] *n* luce del sole; **s. treatment** elioterapia.

sunny ['sʌni] *a* pieno di sole, solatio, assolato; (*fig*) allegro.

sunrise ['sʌnraiz] *n* alba, levata del sole.

sunset ['sʌnset] *n* tramonto.

sunshine ['sʌnʃain] *n* (luce del) sole; (*fig*) gioia, felicità.

sup [sʌp] *vi* cenare.

superb [sju:'pə:b] *a* superbo, magnifico, splendido.

supercilious [.sju:pə'siliəs] *a* arrogante, sdegnoso.

superficial [.sju:pə'fiʃəl] *a* superficiale.

superfluous [sju'pə:fluəs] *a* superfluo.

superhuman [.sju:pə'hjumən] *a* sovrumano.

superintend [.sju:prin'tend] *vti* sovrintendere (a).

superintendent [.sju:prin'tendənt] *n* sovrintendente.

superior [sju'piəriə] *a n* superiore.

superiority [sju.piəri'oriti] *n* superiorità.

superlative [sju'pə:lətiv] *a* superlativo, eccellente; *n* superlativo.

supermarket ['sju:pə.mɑ:kit] *n* 'supermarket', supermercato.

supernatural [.sju:pə'nætʃrəl] *a* sovrannaturale.

supersede [.sju:pə'si:d] *vt* rimpiazzare, sostituire, sostituirsi(a).

supersonic ['sju:pə'sɔnik] *a* ultra-sonoro; (*av*) supersonico.

superstition [.sju:pə'stiʃən] *n* super-stizione.

superstitious [.sju:pə'stiʃəs] *a* super-stizioso.

superstructure ['sju:pə.strʌktʃə] *n* sovrastruttura.

supervene [.sju:pə'vi:n] *vi* soprav-venire.

supervise ['sju:pəvaiz] *vt* sorve-gliare, sovrintendere a.

supervision [.sju:pə'viʒən] *n* sorve-glianza, sovrintendenza.

supine ['sju:pain] *a* supino; inerte.

supper ['sʌpə] *n* cena.

supplant [sə'plɑ:nt] *vt* soppiantare.

supple ['sʌpl] *a* flessibile, pieghevole, agile; (*fig*) docile.

supplement ['sʌplimənt] *n* supple-mento; ['sʌpliment] *vt* aggiungere a, completare, integrare.

suppleness ['sʌplnis] *n* flessibilità, pieghevolezza.

suppliant ['sʌpliənt] *a* suppliche-vole; *n* supplicante, supplice.

supplicate ['sʌplikeit] *vt* supplicare.

supplication [.sʌpli'keiʃən] *n* suppli-ca(zione).

supplier [sə'plaiə] *n* fornitore, forni-trice.

supply [sə'plai] *n* approvvigiona-mento, fornitura, rifornimento, scor-ta; *vt* approvvigionare, (ri)fornire, provvedere; supplire.

support [sə'pɔ:t] *n* sostegno, appog-gio, aiuto, mantenimento; *vt* soste-nere, mantenere; assecondare.

supportable [sə'pɔ:təbl] *a* sopporta-bile.

supporter [sə'pɔ:tə] *n* fautore, soste-nitore; (*sport*) tifoso.

suppose [sə'pouz] *vt* supporre, ri-tenere.

supposedly [sə'pouzidli] *ad* presumi-bilmente, per ipotesi.

supposition [.sʌpə'ziʃən] *n* supposi-zione, ipotesi.

suppress [sə'pres] *vt* sopprimere; (*fig*) soffocare, nascondere.

suppression [sə'preʃən] *n* soppres-sione.

suppurate ['sʌpjuəreit] *vi* (*med*) suppurare.

supremacy [sju'preməsi] *n* suprema-zia.

supreme [sju'pri:m] *a* supremo.

surcharge ['sə:tʃɑ:dʒ] *n* soprattassa, soprapprezzo.

sure [ʃuə] *a* certo, sicuro; *ad* (*fam*) sicuro.

surely ['ʃuəli] *ad* sicuramente, senza dubbio, certo, certamente.

sureness ['ʃuənis] *n* certezza, sicurez-za.

surety ['ʃuəti] *n* garanzia; garante, mallevadore.

surf [sə:f] *n* frangente, risacca; **s.-boat** barca piatta per navigare tra

i frangenti; **s.-riding** sport dell'ac-quaplano.

surface ['sə:fis] *n* superficie.

surfeit ['sə:fit] *n* sovrabbondanza, sazietà.

surge [sə:dʒ] *n* onda, onde *pl*; *vi* ondeggiare.

surgeon ['sə:dʒən] *n* chirurgo.

surgery ['sə:dʒəri] *n* chirurgia; gabi-netto medico; ambulatorio.

surgical ['sə:dʒikəl] *a* chirurgico.

surliness ['sə:linis] *n* scontrosità, villania.

surly ['sə:li] *a* scontroso, villano.

surmise ['sə:maiz] *n* congettura; *vt* congetturare, sospettare.

surmount [sə:'maunt] *vt* sormontare, sorpassare.

surname ['sə:neim] *n* cognome.

surpass [sə:'pɑ:s] *vt* sorpassare, supe-rare.

surplice ['sə:pləs] *n* (*eccl*) cotta.

surplus ['sə:pləs] *n* eccedenza, so-vrappiù.

surprise [sə'praiz] *n* sorpresa; *vt* sorprendere.

surprisingly [sə'praiziŋli] *ad* sor-prendentemente, tra la sorpresa generale.

surrealism [sə'riəlizəm] *n* surrealis-smo.

surrender [sə'rendə] *n* resa; cessione, consegna; (*com*) riscatto; *vt* cedere; rinunziare a, abbandonare; *vi* arren-dersi, sottomettersi.

surreptitious [.sʌrəp'tiʃəs] *a* clan-destino.

surround [sə'raund] *vt* attorniare, circondare.

surroundings [sə'raundiŋz] *n* *pl* dintorni *pl*, ambiente.

survey ['sə:vei] *n* esame; rilevamento topografico; sguardo generale; in-dagine; [sə'vei] *vt* esaminare, dare uno sguardo generale a, rilevare.

surveyor [sə'veiə] *n* ispettore; agri-mensore, geometra.

survival [sə'vaivəl] *n* sopravvivenza.

survive [sə'vaiv] *vt* sopravvivere (a).

survivor [sə'vaivə] *n* superstite.

Susan ['suzn] *nf pr* Susanna.

susceptibility [sə.septi'biliti] *n* su-scettibilità.

susceptible [sə'septəbl] *a* suscetti-bile, sensibile.

suspect ['sʌspekt] *a* sospetto; *n* persona sospetta; *vt* sospettare, diffidare di.

suspend [səs'pend] *vt* sospendere, differire.

suspender [səs'pendə] *n* giarrettiera; *pl* (*US*) bretelle.

suspense [səs'pens] *n* ansietà, in-decisione, sospensione d'animo, in-certezza; **in s.** nell'incertezza, in sospeso.

suspension [səs'penʃən] *n* sospen-sione.

suspicion [səs'piʃən] *n* sospetto.

suspicious [səs'piʃəs] a sospettoso, diffidente.

sustain [səs'tein] vt sostenere; prolungare; subire; mantenere.

sustenance ['sʌstinəns] n nutrimento, vitto, sostentamento.

swab [swɔb] n strofinaccio; (naut) radazza; (med) tampone.

swaddling clothes ['swɔdliŋklouðz] n fasce pl.

swagger ['swægə] n fanfaronata, spavalderia; vi camminare con sussiego, vantarsi.

swaggerer ['swægərə] n fanfarone.

swain [swein] n (poet) contadino, rustico innamorato.

swallow ['swɔlou] n rondine; vt inghiottire, ingoiare.

swamp ['swɔmp] n palude.

swampy ['swɔmpi] a paludoso.

swan [swɔn] n cigno.

swap [swɔp] n scambio, baratto; vt barattare.

sward [swɔːd] n distesa erbosa.

swarm [swɔːm] n sciame, frotta, gran numero; vi sciamare, brulicare.

swarthy ['swɔːði] a bruno, di carnagione scura.

swastika ['swɔstikə] n svastica, croce uncinata.

swathe [sweið] n benda, fascia; vt fasciare, bendare.

sway [swei] n oscillazione; influenza, dominio; vt far oscillare; influenzare; vi oscillare.

swear [swɛə] vti (far) giurare; vi bestemmiare, imprecare.

sweat [swet] n sudore; vti sudare; (fig) sfruttare.

sweater ['swetə] n chi suda; maglione di lana.

Swede [swiːd] n svedese; **swede** rapa svedese.

Sweden ['swiːdn] n Svezia.

Swedish ['swiːdiʃ] a svedese.

sweep [swiːp] n scopata, spazzata; spazzacamino; distesa; movimento circolare; (mil) rastrellamento; vt scopare, spazzare; (mil) rastrellare; vi muoversi rapidamente.

sweeper ['swiːpə] n chi scopa; spazzino.

sweeping ['swiːpiŋ] a vasto, sconfinato; impetuoso; assoluto.

sweepings ['swiːpiŋz] n pl spazzatura.

sweet [swiːt] a dolce, profumato, tenero, amabile; n dolce, dolciume.

sweetbread ['swiːtbred] n animella.

sweeten ['swiːtn] vt addolcire, inzuccherare.

sweetheart ['swiːthɑːt] n innamorato, -a.

sweetmeat ['swiːtmiːt] n (usu pl) dolciumi, frutta candita.

sweetness ['swiːtnis] n dolcezza, tenerezza, profumo.

swell [swel] n il sollevarsi delle acque; (sl) elegantone; a (fam) elegante; vti gonfiar(si), ingrossar(si).

swelling ['sweliŋ] n gonfiamento, gonfiore.

swelter ['sweltə] vi essere oppresso dal caldo, sudare; n afa, caldo opprimente.

sweltering ['sweltəriŋ] a soffocante; molle di sudore.

swerve [swəːv] vi deviare, fare uno scarto.

swift [swift] a agile, rapido, svelto, veloce; n rondone.

swiftness ['swiftnis] n agilità, rapidità, velocità.

swill [swil] n risciacquatura; n risciacquata; vt risciacquare; vi bere all'eccesso.

swim [swim] n nuotata; (fig) corrente degli affari, della vita sociale; vi nuotare.

swimmer ['swimə] n nuotatore.

swimming ['swimiŋ] n nuoto; s. pool piscina.

swindle ['swindl] n truffa; vti truffare, imbrogliare.

swindler ['swindlə] n imbroglione, truffatore.

swine [swain] n pl maiali pl, suini pl; (fig) porco.

swing [swiŋ] n dondolio; oscillazione; altalena; ritmo; vt dondolare; vi dondolare; oscillare; pendere; (of boat) muoversi sull'ancora.

swipe [swaip] n colpo violento, manata; vt colpire violentemente; (sl) rubacchiare.

swirl [swəːl] n vortice, turbine.

swish [swiʃ] n fruscio; sibilo; sferzata.

Swiss [swis] a n svizzero.

switch [switʃ] n (mech) interruttore; commutatore; (rly) scambio; bastoncino, verga; treccia finta.

Switzerland ['switsələnd] n Svizzera.

swivel ['swivl] n (mech) perno.

swoon [swuːn] n deliquio, svenimento; vi svenire, venir meno.

swoop [swuːp] n calata improvvisa, attacco; vt to s. down piombare su.

swop v swap.

sword [sɔːd] n spada.

swordsman ['sɔːdzmən] pl -men n spadaccino.

swot [swɔt] n (sl) sgobbone, secchia; vi (sl) sgobbare.

sycamore ['sikəmɔː] n sicomoro.

syllable ['siləbl] n sillaba.

syllabus ['siləbəs] n programma scolastico, prospetto.

syllogism ['silədʒizəm] n sillogismo.

sylvan ['silvən] a silvano, silvestre.

Sylvia ['silviə] nf pr Silvia.

symbol ['simbəl] n simbolo.

symbolic [sim'bɔlik] a simbolico.

symbolize ['simbəlaiz] vt simboleggiare.

symmetrical [si'metrikəl] a simmetrico.

symmetry ['simitri] n simmetria.

sympathetic [ˌsimpə'θetik] a sensibile, comprensivo.

sympathetically [͵simpə'θetikli] *ad* con comprensione.

sympathize ['simpəθaiz] *vi* condividere i sentimenti altrui, aver comprensione, compassione.

sympathy ['simpəθi] *n* comprensione, partecipazione ai sentimenti altrui, compassione.

symphony ['simfəni] *n* sinfonia.

symposium [sim'pouziəm] *n* simposio.

symptom ['simptəm] *n* sintomo.

symptomatic [͵simptə'mætik] *a* sintomatico.

synagogue ['sinagɔg] *n* sinagoga.

synchronize ['siŋkrənaiz] *vti* sincronizzare.

syndicate ['sindikit] *n* sindacato.

synod ['sinəd] *n* sinodo.

synonym ['sinənim] *n* sinonimo.

synonymous [si'nɔniməs] *a* sinonimo.

syntax ['sintæks] *n* (*gram*) sintassi.

synthesis ['sinθisis] *n* sintesi.

synthetic [sin'θetik] *a* sintetico.

syphilis ['sifilis] *n* (*med*) sifilide.

Syracuse ['saiərəkjuz] *n* Siracusa.

Syria ['siriə] *n* Siria.

Syriac ['siriæk] *a n* siriaco, lingua siriaca.

Syrian ['siriən] *a n* siriano.

syringe [si'rindʒ] *n* (*med*) siringa; *vt* (*med*) siringare.

syrup ['sirəp] *n* sciroppo, melassa.

system ['sistim] *n* sistema; organizzazione; metodo.

systematic [͵sisti'mætik] *a* sistematico, metodico.

T

tab [tæb] *n* linguetta, (*mil*) mostrina; cartellino; (*av*) aletta compensatrice.

tabernacle ['tæbənækl] *n* tabernacolo.

table ['teibl] *n* tavola, -lo; prospetto, tabella; **t. of contents** *n* indice; **t. d'hôte** pasto a prezzo fisso.

table-cloth ['teiblklɔθ] *n* tovaglia.

tablet ['tæblit] *n* tavoletta; lapide; pastiglia.

taboo [tə'buː] *a* tabù, proibito; *n* tabù, interdizione.

tabulate ['tæbjuleit] *vt* ordinare in tavole sinottiche; catalogare.

tabulator ['tæbjuleitə] *n* (*mech*) tabulatore, incolonnatore.

tacit ['tæsit] *a* implicito, sottinteso, tacito.

taciturn ['tæsitəːn] *a* taciturno.

tack [tæk] *n* bulletta, chiodo; (*fig*) linea di condotta, tattica; *vt* inchiodare; imbastire; *vi* (*naut*) virare.

tackle ['tækl] *n* (*naut*) sartiame; attrezzi; *vt* affrontare, mettere mano a.

tacky ['tæki] *a* appiccicaticcio.

tact [tækt] *n* tatto.

tactful ['tæktful] *a* pieno di tatto.

tactical ['tæktikəl] *a* tattico.

tactics ['tæktiks] *n pl* tattica; espedienti *pl*.

tactless ['tæktlis] *a* senza tatto.

tadpole ['tædpoul] *n* girino.

taffy ['tæfi] *n* (*US*) caramella.

tag [tæg] *n* punta metallica; puntale; cartellino di spedizione, etichetta; frase o luogo comune; ritornello.

tail [teil] *n* coda, estremità; *vt* mettere la coda a; (*sl*) pedinare; *vi* essere in coda a.

tailor ['teilə] *n* sarto.

taint [teint] *n* infezione; marchio; *vti* corromper(si), infettar(si).

take [teik] *vti* prendere, afferrare; acquistare; accettare; condurre, portare; catturare; rubare; considerare, ritenere; attaccare; **t. in** ricevere; capire; ingannare; **t. off** togliere; (*av*) decollare; fare la caricatura a; **t. on** assumere, intraprendere; **t. over** succedere in.

take-off ['teikɔf] *n* (*av*) decollo; (*sport*) linea di partenza; caricatura.

taking ['teikiŋ] *a* attraente, piacevole; contagioso; *n* presa; *pl* (*com*) incasso.

talcum ['tælkʌm] *n* talco.

tale [teil] *n* racconto, novella.

talent ['tælənt] *n* talento, attitudine.

talk [tɔːk] *n* abboccamento, colloquio, conversazione, discorso, chiacchiere *pl*; *vti* parlare, conversare; chiacchierare, discorrere (su, di).

talkative ['tɔːkətiv] *a* loquace.

talkies ['tɔːkiz] *n pl* (*sl*) film sonoro.

tall [tɔːl] *a* alto; grande; incredibile.

tallow ['tælou] *n* sego.

tally ['tæli] *n* tacca; conto; piastrina di contrassegno; *vi* concordare con corrispondere a; *vt* calcolare; spun tare.

talon ['tælən] *n* artiglio.

tamarind ['tæmərind] *n* tamarindo.

tamarisk ['tæmərisk] *n* tamerice, tamarisco.

tame [teim] *a* domestico, addomesticato; docile, mansueto; insipido; *vt* domare, addomesticare.

tameness ['teimnis] *n* docilità.

tamper ['tæmpə] *vi* immischiarsi; (*fig*) corrompere, falsificare.

tan [tæn] *n* concia; abbronzatura; tanè; *vt* conciare (*skins*), abbronzare.

tandem ['tændəm] *n* tandem.

tang [tæŋ] *n* sapore; asprigno piccante; odore penetrante; accento speciale.

tangent ['tændʒənt] *n* tangente.

tangerine [͵tændʒə'riːn] *n* mandarino.

tangible ['tændʒəbl] *a* tangibile.

Tangier [tæn'dʒiə] *n* Tangeri.

tangle ['tæŋgl] *n* complicazione, garbuglio; *vti* complicar(si), ingarbugliar(si).

tank [tæŋk] *n* cisterna, serbatoio, vasca; (*mil*) carro armato.

tankard ['tæŋkəd] *n* grosso boccale.

tanker ['tæŋkə] *n* nave cisterna.

tanner ['tænə] *n* conciatore; (*sl*) mezzo scellino.

tannery ['tænəri] *n* conceria.

tannin ['tænin] *n* tannino.

tantalize ['tæntəlaiz] *vt* tormentare, lusingare.

tantamount ['tæntəmaunt] *a* equivalente.

tantrum ['tæntrəm] *n* furie, nervi *pl.*

tap [tæp] *n* spina; rubinetto; qualità di birra; colpetto, picchio; *vt* spillare; battere, picchiare leggermente; intercettare.

tape [teip] *n* nastro, passamano, fettuccia; **t.-recorder** registratore a nastro.

taper ['teipə] *vt* affusolar(si); *n* candela, stoppino.

tapering ['teipəriŋ] *a* affusolato, a punta.

tapestry ['tæpistri] *n* arazzi *pl*; tappezzeria.

tapeworm ['teipwə:m] *n* tenia.

tar [ta:] *n* catrame; *vt* incatramare.

tardiness ['ta:dinis] *n* lentezza; riluttanza.

tardy ['ta:di] *a* lento, tardo; riluttante.

tare [teə] *n* tara; veccia.

target ['ta:git] *n* bersaglio; (*fig*) obiettivo, mira.

tariff ['tærif] *n* tariffa.

tarmac ['ta:mæk] *n* macadam al catrame; (*av*) pista di decollo, di atterraggio.

tarnish ['ta:niʃ] *vti* appannar(si), offuscar(si), ossidar(si); (*fig*) macchiar(si).

tarpaulin [ta:'pɔ:lin] *n* copertone impermeabile, tessuto incerato.

tarry ['ta:ri] *a* incatramato, bituminoso; ['tæri] *vi* indugiare, ritardare.

tart [ta:t] *a* agro, aspro; *n* torta di frutta; (*sl*) sgualdrina.

tartan ['ta:tən] *n* tessuto di lana scozzese; (*naut*) tartana.

tartar ['ta:tə] *n* tartaro.

tartaric [ta:'tærik] *a* tartarico.

tartness ['ta:tnis] *n* asprezza; (*fig*) mordacità.

task [ta:sk] *n* compito, mansione, lavoro, incarico; *vt* mettere a prova, affaticare.

tassel ['tæsəl] *n* fiocco, nappa.

taste [teist] *n* gusto, sapore, assaggio; *vt* assaggiare; *vi* avere gusto di, sapere di.

tasteful ['teistful] *a* di buon gusto.

tasteless ['teistlis] *a* senza gusto, insipido.

tasty ['teisti] *a* saporito.

tatter ['tætə] *n* brandello, straccio; *vt* ridurre a brandelli, stracciare.

tattle ['tætl] *n* chiacchierio, ciarla; *vi* chiacchierare, ciarlare.

tattler ['tætlə] *n* chiacchierone, pettegolo.

tattoo [tə'tu:] *n* tatuaggio; (*mil*)

ritirata; (*il*) tamburellare; *vt* tatuare.

taunt [tɔ:nt] *n* sarcasmo, scherno, rimprovero; *vt* rinfacciare; ingiuriare, schernire.

taut [tɔ:t] *a* teso, rigido.

tavern ['tævən] *n* osteria, trattoria.

tawdry ['tɔ:dri] *a* vistoso e di cattivo gusto.

tawny ['tɔ:ni] *a* abbronzato, fulvo, tanè.

tax [tæks] *n* imposta, tassa, gravame, onere; *vt* tassare, mettere a dura prova; accusare, tacciare.

taxable ['tæksəbl] *a* tassabile.

taxation [tæk'seiʃən] *n* tassazione, tasse *pl.*

taxi ['tæksi] *n* auto pubblica, tassì; **taximeter** tassametro; **t.-rank** posteggio di tassì.

tea [ti:] *n* tè; **teacup** tazza da tè; **teapot** teiera; **teaspoon** cucchiaino da tè.

teach [ti:tʃ] *vt* insegnare, istruire, ammaestrare; **t.-in** 'teach-in'.

teacher ['ti:tʃə] *n* insegnante.

teaching ['ti:tʃiŋ] *n* insegnamento, dottrina.

teak [ti:k] *n* tek (albero, legno).

team [ti:m] *n* (*horses*) tiro; squadra.

tear [teə] *vti* lacerar(si), strappar(si); *vi* correre precipitosamente.

tear [tiə] *n* lacrima, lagrima.

tearful ['tiəful] *a* lacrimoso, piangente.

tearless ['tiəlis] *a* senza lacrime.

tease [ti:z] *n* importuno, seccatore; *vt* stuzzicare, tormentare; (*textiles*) cardare.

teasel, teazle ['ti:zl] *n* cardo; (*mech*) scardasso.

teat [ti:t] *n* capezzolo.

technical ['teknikəl] *a* tecnico.

technicality [,tekni'kæliti] *n* tecnicismo, particolare tecnico.

technician [tek'niʃən] *n* tecnico.

technique [tek'ni:k] *n* tecnica.

technology [tek'nɔlədʒi] *n* tecnologia.

tedious ['ti:diəs] *a* tedioso, noioso.

tedium ['ti:diəm] *n* tedio, noia.

teem [ti:m] *vi* abbondare, brulicare di.

teenager ['ti:n,eidʒə] *n* chi ha meno di vent'anni, adolescente.

teens [ti:nz] *n pl* età da 13 a 19 anni.

teething ['ti:ðiŋ] *n* dentizione.

teetotal(ler) [ti:'toutl(ə)] *a n* astemio.

telecast ['telika:st] *vt* teletrasmettere; *n* trasmissione televisiva.

telegram ['teligræm] *n* telegramma.

telegraph ['teligra:f] *n* telegrafo; *vti* telegrafare.

telegraphic [teli'græfik] *a* telegrafico.

telepathy [ti'lepəθi] *n* telepatia.

telephone ['telifoun] *n* telefono; *vti* telefonare.

telephonic [,teli'fɔnik] *a* telefonico.

telephonist [ti'lefənist] *n* telefonista.

telescope ['teliskoup] *n* telescopio; cannocchiale.

televiewer ['telivjuə] *n* telespettatore, telespettatrice.

televise ['telivaiz] *vt* teletrasmettere.

television ['teli,viʒən] *n* televisione.

tell [tel] *vt* dire; informare; raccontare; ingiungere, ordinare.

teller ['telə] *n* chi riferisce; (*com*) cassiere.

telltale ['telteil] *a n* pettegolo; *a* indiscreto.

temerity [ti'meriti] *n* temerità.

temper ['tempə] *n* carattere, indole; umore; collera; (*metal*) tempera; *vt* mitigare, modificare, temperare, temprare; *vi* (*metal*) temprarsi.

temperament ['tempərəmənt] *n* temperamento, carattere.

temperance ['tempərəns] *n* temperanza, moderazione, astinenza dall'alcool.

temperate ['tempərit] *a* (*climate*) temperato, moderato, sobrio.

temperature ['tempritʃə] *n* temperatura, febbre.

tempest ['tempist] *n* tempesta.

tempestuous [tem'pestjuəs] *a* tempestoso, violento.

templar ['templə] *n* templare.

temple ['templ] *n* tempia; tempio.

temporal ['tempərəl] *a* temporale.

temporary ['tempərəri] *a* temporaneo, transitorio.

temporize ['tempəraiz] *vi* temporeggiare.

tempt [tempt] *vt* tentare, indurre.

temptation [temp'teiʃən] *n* tentazione.

tempter ['temptə] *n* tentatore; **the t.** il Diavolo.

tempting ['temptiŋ] *a* allettante, seducente.

ten [ten] *a n* dieci; **tenth** *a n* decimo.

tenable ['tenəbl] *a* difendibile, che si può tenere, sostenibile.

tenacious [ti'neiʃəs] *a* tenace, adesivo.

tenacity [ti'næsiti] *n* tenacia.

tenancy ['tenənsi] *n* affitto, locazione.

tenant ['tenənt] *n* affittuario, locatario, inquilino.

tend [tend] *vi* tendere, essere diretto; *vt* curare, sorvegliare.

tendency ['tendənsi] *n* tendenza .

tender ['tendə] *a* tenero, delicato, sensibile; *n* (*com*) offerta; (*rly*) tender; (*naut*) lancia; *vt* offrire, porgere; *vi* (*com*) concorrere ad un appalto.

tenderness ['tendənis] *n* tenerezza.

tendon ['tendən] *n* tendine.

tenement ['tenimənt] *n* abitazione, appartamento; **t. house** casa popolare; casamento.

tennis ['tenis] *n* tennis.

tenor ['tenə] *n* tenore.

tense [tens] *a* teso; *n* (*gram*) tempo.

tension ['tenʃən] *n* tensione.

tent [tent] *n* tenda.

tentacle ['tentəkl] *n* tentacolo.

tentative ['tentətiv] *a* sperimentale, di prova.

tenuous ['tenjuəs] *a* tenue, sottile.

tenure ['tenjuə] *n* possesso, diritto di possesso, durata di possesso.

tepid ['tepid] *a* tiepido.

term [təːm] *n* termine, periodo di tempo; trimestre; (*leg*) sessione; *vt* chiamare, denominare; **terms** *pl* condizioni, patti; rapporti *pl*.

termagant ['təːməgənt] *n* bisbetica, virago.

terminate ['təːmineit] *vti* finire, terminare.

termination [,təːmi'neiʃən] *n* conclusione, fine; (*gram*) desinenza.

terminus ['təːminəs] *n* capolinea.

terminology [,təːmi'nɔlədʒi] *n* terminologia.

termite ['təːmait] *n* termite.

terrace ['terəs] *n* terrazzo, terrapieno; terrazza; fila di case.

terrestrial [ti'restriəl] *a* terrestre.

terrible ['terəbl] *a* terribile.

terrier ['teriə] *n* cane terrier.

terrific [tə'rifik] *a* terrificante; (*fam*) magnifico.

terrify ['terifai] *vt* atterrire, terrificare.

territorial [,teri'tɔːriəl] *a* territoriale; *n* soldato della milizia territoriale.

territory ['teritəri] *n* territorio.

terror ['terə] *n* terrore.

terrorist ['terərist] *n* terrorista.

terse [təːs] *a* conciso, incisivo.

terseness ['təːsnis] *n* concisione.

test [test] *n* prova, esperimento, saggio; (*chem*) reagente; *vt* collaudare, provare; (*chem*) analizzare.

testament ['testəmənt] *n* testamento.

testify ['testifai] *vt* testimoniare.

testimonial [,testi'mouniəl] *a* testimoniale; *n* benservito, certificato di servizio, attestato.

testimony ['testiməni] *n* testimonianza.

testy ['testi] *a* irritabile, risentito.

tetanus ['tetənəs] *n* tetano.

tether ['teðə] *n* pastoia; *vt* impastoiare; **at the end of one's t.** all'estremo delle proprie risorse, al limite della pazienza.

Teutonic [tju'tɔnik] *a* teutonico.

text [tekst] *n* testo, argomento.

textile ['tekstail] *a* tessile; *n* tessuto, fibra tessile.

textual ['tekstjuəl] *a* testuale.

texture ['tekstʃə] *n* tessitura; tessuto; trama.

Thames [temz] *n* Tamigi.

than [ðæn] *cj prep* di, che, di quello che (non), di quanto.

thank [θæŋk] *vt* ringraziare.

thankful ['θæŋkful] *a* grato, riconoscente.

thankfulness ['θæŋkfulnis] *n* gratitudine, riconoscenza.

thankless ['θæŋklis] *a* ingrato.

thanklessness ['θæŋklisnis] n ingratitudine.

thanks [θæŋks] n pl grazie, ringraziamenti pl.

thanksgiving ['θæŋks,giviŋ] n ringraziamento solenne; **T. (Day) (US)** giorno del ringraziamento.

that [ðæt] pl **those** [ðouz] a pron quello etc, ciò; che, il quale, la quale etc; cj che; ad (fam) così, a tal segno, tanto.

thatch [θætʃ] n tetto di paglia; vt coprire di paglia.

thaw [θɔ:] n (di)sgelo; vti disgelar(si), sciogliersi); (fig) commuover(si).

the [ðə, ði] def art il, lo, la, i, gli, le; ad (before comparatives) quanto ... tanto.

theatre ['θiətə] n teatro.

theatrical [θi'ætrikəl] a scenico, teatrale; (fig) affettato, manierato.

theft [θeft] n furto.

their [ðɛə] poss a il loro etc; **theirs** poss pron il loro etc.

them [ðem] pron li, le, loro; **themselves** pron pl se stessi, si etc.

theme [θi:m] n tema, argomento.

then [ðen] ad allora, poi, in séguito; dunque, perciò, quindi; a di allora.

thence [ðens] ad di là; quindi, pertanto.

thenceforth ['ðens'fɔ:θ] ad d'allora in poi

Theodore ['θiədɔ:] nm pr Teodoro.

theologian [θiə'loudʒən] n teologo.

theological [θiə'lɔdʒikəl] a teologico.

theology [θi'ɔlədʒi] n teologia.

theorem ['θiərəm] n teorema.

theoretical [θiə'retikəl] a teorico.

theory ['θiəri] n teoria.

therapeutic [,θerə'pju:tik] a terapeutico.

therapist ['θerəpist] n terapeuta.

therapy ['θerəpi] n terapia.

there [ðɛə] ad là, vi, lì, ci.

thereby ['ðɛə'bai] ad così, perciò.

thereabout(s) ['ðɛərəbaut(s)] ad all'incirca, a un dipresso, nei dintorni pl.

therefore ['ðɛəfɔ:] ad perciò.

Theresa [ti'ri:zə] nf pr Teresa.

thereupon ['ðɛərə'pɔn] ad al che.

thermometer [θə'mɔmitə] n termometro.

thermos ['θə:mɔs] n termos.

thesis ['θi:sis] pl **theses** n tesi.

they [ðei] pron pl essi, esse, loro.

thick [θik] a denso, fitto, folto, grosso, spesso.

thicken ['θikən] vti condensar(si), infittire, infoltire.

thicket ['θikit] n boschetto, macchiá.

thickness ['θiknis] n densità, foltezza; spessore, strato.

thief [θi:f] n ladro.

thieve [θi:v] vi fare il ladro.

thievish ['θi:viʃ] a ladresco.

thigh [θai] n coscia.

thimble ['θimbl] n ditale.

thin [θin] a magro, delicato, fine,

leggero, rado, sparso, sottile; vti assottigliar(si), diradar(si).

thing [θiŋ] n cosa, coso.

think [θiŋk] vti pensare, credere, ritenere.

thinker ['θiŋkə] n pensatore.

thinness ['θinnis] n magrezza, sottigliezza, tenuità.

third [θə:d] a terzo.

thirst [θə:st] n sete; (fig) avidità, brama.

thirsty ['θə:sti] a assetato, avido; be t. aver sete.

thirteen ['θə:'ti:n] a n tredici; **thirteenth** a n tredicesimo.

thirty ['θə:ti] a n trenta; **thirtieth** a n trentesimo.

this [ðis] pl **these** [ði:z] dem a pron questo etc.

thistle ['θisl] n cardo.

thither ['ðiðə] ad là, in quella direzione; **hither and t.** qua e là.

Thomas ['tɔməs] nm pr Tommaso.

thong [θɔŋ] n cinghia, correggia.

thorn [θɔ:n] n spina.

thorny ['θɔ:ni] a spinoso.

thorough ['θʌrə] a completo, intero; perfetto, esauriente.

thoroughbred ['θʌrəbred] a purosangue, che ha stile; n purosangue.

thoroughfare ['θʌrəfɛə] n arteria di gran traffico, strada principale.

thoroughness ['θʌrənis] n perfezione.

thou [ðau] pron tu.

though [ðou] cj benchè, quantunque, sebbene.

thought [θɔ:t] n pensiero.

thoughtful ['θɔ:tful] a pensieroso, pensoso; attento; previdente.

thoughtfully ['θɔ:tfuli] ad pensosamente, pensierosamente; premurosamente.

thoughtfulness ['θɔ:tfulnis] n meditazione; attenzione; previdenza; premura.

thoughtless ['θɔ:tlis] a irriflessivo, sconsiderato.

thoughtlessly ['θɔ:tlisli] ad sventatamente; negligentemente, trascuratamente.

thoughtlessness ['θɔ:tlisnis] n sconsideratezza, mancanza di riguardo.

thousand ['θauzənd] a n mille; **thousandth** a n millesimo.

thrall [θrɔ:l] n schiavo, schiavitù.

thrash [θræʃ] vt bastonare, battere.

thrashing ['θræʃiŋ] n bastonatura, legnate.

thread [θred] n filo; vt infilare, (far) passare attraverso.

threadbare ['θredbɛə] a consumato, logoro; (fig) vieto, trito.

threat [θret] n minaccia.

threaten ['θretn] vt minacciare.

three [θri:] a n tre.

threefold ['θri:fould] a triplice, triplo.

threshold ['θreʃhould] n soglia.

thrice [θrais] ad tre volte.

thrift [θrift] n economia, frugalità.

thrifty ['θrifti] a economico, frugale.

thrill [θril] n fremito, palpito; vt elettrizzare, far rabbrividire; vi fremere, vibrare.

thriller ['θrilə] n dramma, film poliziesco, libro, film giallo.

thrive [θraiv] vi crescere, prosperare, svilupparsi vigorosamente.

throat [θrout] n gola.

throb [θrɔb] n pulsazione, vibrazione; vi battere, pulsare, vibrare.

throes [θrouz] n pl sofferenza acuta.

throne [θroun] n trono.

throng [θrɔŋ] n calca, folla, ressa; vt affollare, ingombrare; vi affollarsi, affluire.

throttle ['θrɔtl] n (mech) valvola; (aut) acceleratore; vt strangolare.

through [θru:] a diretto; prep attraverso, per; per mezzo di; ad da parte a parte.

throughout [θru'aut] prep da un capo all'altro di; per tutta la durata di; ad completamente, dappertutto.

throw [θrou] n getto, lancio, tiro; vt buttare, gettare, lanciare.

thrush [θrʌʃ] n tordo.

thrust [θrʌst] n pressione, spinta; vti cacciar(si), conficcar(si), introdur(si) a viva forza.

thud [θʌd] n rumore sordo, tonfo.

thug [θʌg] n teppista, furfante.

thumb [θʌm] n pollice; vt sfogliare; lasciar ditate su; **thumbtack** (US) puntina da disegno; **to t. a lift** chiedere un passaggio facendo l'autostop.

thump [θʌmp] n rumore sordo, colpo; vt battere, percuotere.

thunder ['θʌndə] n tuono, -ni pl; vt pronunciare con voce tonante; vi tuonare.

thunderbolt ['θʌndəboult] n fulmine.

thunderstruck ['θʌndəstrʌk] a fulminato; sbalordito.

Thursday ['θɔːzdi] n giovedì.

thus [ðʌs] ad così, in tal modo.

thwart [θwɔːt] n (naut) banco di rematore; vt contrariare, frustrare.

thy [ðai] a poss tuo, tua, tuoi, tue.

thyme [taim] n timo.

tiara [ti'ɑːrə] n tiara; diadema.

tick [tik] n battito; ticchettio; (fam) attimo; (insect) zecca; (fam) credito; vi battere, fare tic-tac.

ticket ['tikit] n biglietto, cartellino; **t. agent** (US rly) bigliettario; **t. office** (US rly) biglietteria.

tickle ['tikl] n solletico; vt solleticare; stuzzicare; divertire; vt far solletico.

ticklish ['tikliʃ] a che sente molto il solletico; (fig) delicato, scabroso.

tidal ['taidl] a della marea; **t. wave** onda di marea; (fig) impulso travolgente.

tide [taid] n marea; (fig) corrente.

tidings ['taidiŋz] n pl notizie, nuove.

tidy ['taidi] a ordinato, preciso, lindo; (fam) considerevole; **to t. up** vt rassettare, mettere in ordine.

tie [tai] n cravatta; legame, vincolo; (sport) pareggio; (US rly) traversina; vt legare, unire; vi (sport) pareggiare; **cup-t.** eliminatoria di torneo; **t.-up** ingorgo stradale.

tier [tiə] n fila; ordine graduato (di posti).

tiff [tif] n (fam) bisticcio.

tiger ['taigə] **tigress** (f) n tigre.

tight [tait] a aderente, attillato, stretto; teso; (sl) brillo; n pl calzamaglia.

tighten ['taitn] vti serrar(si), stringer(si), tirare.

tightness ['taitnis] n strettezza; tensione; oppressione di petto.

tile [tail] n mattonella, piastrella, tegola; vt coprire di tegole etc.

till [til] n cassa; prep fino a, sino a; cj finchè (non); vt coltivare (la terra).

tillage ['tilidʒ] n coltivazione.

tilt [tilt] n inclinazione, giostra, torneo; copertone; vti (far) inclinare; giostrare.

timber ['timbə] n alberi pl di alto fusto, legname da costruzione.

time [taim] n tempo; epoca; ora; volta; vt cronometrare, scegliere il momento giusto per.

timeless ['taimlis] a eterno, infinito; senza tempo; fuori del tempo.

timely ['taimli] a opportuno, tempestivo.

timid ['timid] a timido.

timidity [ti'miditi] n timidezza.

timorous ['timərəs] a timoroso.

Timothy ['timəθi] nm pr Timoteo.

tin [tin] n stagno; latta; scatola, barattolo di latta; **tinned** in scatola; **t.-opener** apriscatole.

tincture ['tiŋktʃə] n tintura; tinta; leggero aroma; (fig) infarinatura.

tinder ['tində] n (per fuoco) esca.

tinfoil ['tinfɔil] n lamina di stagno, stagnola.

tinge [tindʒ] n lieve coloritura, sfumatura; vt colorire leggermente, sfumare.

tingle ['tiŋgl] vi sentire un formicolio; fremere.

tinker ['tiŋkə] n stagnino.

tinkle ['tiŋkl] n tintinnio.

tinkle ['tiŋkl] vti (far) tintinnare.

tinsel ['tinsəl] n 'lamè'; orpello.

tint [tint] n tinta; sfumatura; vt colorire; sfumare.

tiny ['taini] a minuscolo.

tip [tip] n punta; cima; puntale; mancia; informazione segreta, suggerimento; vt mettere la punta; (far) inclinare; dare la mancia; avvisare; vi ribaltare.

tipple ['tipl] n (fam) forte bevanda alcoolica; vi bere parecchio.

tippler ['tiplə] n bevitore abituale.

tipsy ['tipsi] a alticcio, brillo.

tiptoe ['tiptou] n punta dei piedi; **on t.** ad in punta di piedi.

tirade [tai'reid] n tirata, filippica.

tire ['taiə] n cerchione di ruota, pneumatico (v. **tyre**); vti stancar(si).
tired ['taiəd] a stanco.
tiredness ['taiədnis] n stanchezza.
tiresome ['taiəsəm] a faticoso, noioso.
tissue ['tisju:] n tessuto; **t. paper** carta velina.
titbit ['titbit] n boccone delicato, leccornia.
tithe [taið] n decima, tassa.
Titian ['tiʃiən] nm pr Tiziano.
title ['taitl] n titolo; appellativo; **t. page** frontespizio.
titter ['titə] vi ridacchiare.
titular ['titjulə] a n titolare; **t. saint** santo patrono.
to [tu:] prep a; per; rispetto a; verso, in; fino a; contro.
toad [toud] n rospo.
toady ['toudi] vt adulare; n parassita.
toast [toust] n pane abbrustolito; brindisi; vt abbrustolire; fare un brindisi a; vi brindare.
toaster ['toustə] n graticola; tostino; tostapane.
tobacco [tə'bækou] n tabacco.
tobacconist [tə'bækənist] n tabaccaio; **t.'s shop** tabaccheria.
toboggan [tə'bɔgən] n toboga; vi andare in toboga; (of prices US) calare.
today [tə'dei] n ad oggi.
toddle ['tɔdl] vi fare i primi passi.
toddler ['tɔdlə] n infante ai primi passi.
toe [tou] n dito del piede.
toffee ['tɔfi] n caramella.
together [tə'geðə] ad insieme, assieme.
toil [tɔil] n fatica, lavoro faticoso; vi faticare.
toilet ['tɔilit] n toeletta; gabinetto
toilsome ['tɔilsəm] a faticoso, laborioso.
token ['toukən] n segno, pegno.
Toledo [tɔ'leidou] n Toledo.
tolerable ['tɔlərəbl] a tollerabile, sopportabile; discreto.
tolerance ['tɔlərəns] n tolleranza, sopportazione, indulgenza.
tolerant ['tɔlərənt] a tollerante, indulgente.
tolerate ['tɔləreit] vt tollerare, sopportare.
toleration [,tɔlə'reiʃən] n tolleranza.
toll [toul] n gabella, pedaggio, tassa; rintocco di campana; vti suonare a rintocco.
tomato [tə'mɑ:tou] n pomodoro.
tomb [tu:m] n tomba.
tombstone ['tu:mstoun] n pietra sepolcrale.
tom-cat ['tɔm'kæt] n gatto (maschio).
tomorrow [tə'mɔrou] n ad domani.
ton [tʌn] n tonnellata.
tone [toun] n tono; vt dare il tono a; vi armonizzare, intonarsi.
tongs [tɔŋz] n pl molle, mollette pl.

tongue [tʌŋ] n lingua; linguaggio; (of bell) battaglio; (strip) linguetta.
tonic ['tɔnik] a n tonico, ricostituente.
tonight [tə'nait] n ad stanotte; stasera.
tonnage ['tʌnidʒ] n tonnellaggio.
tonsil ['tɔnsl] n tonsilla.
tonsure ['tɔnʃə] n tonsura.
too [tu:] ad troppo; anche; inoltre, per di più; pure.
tool [tu:l] n arnese, attrezzo, strumento, utensile.
tooth [tu:θ] n dente.
toothache ['tu:θeik] n mal di dente.
toothless ['tu:θlis] a senza denti, sdentato.
top [tɔp] n cima, culmine; coperchio; (toy) trottola; vt coprire, coronare, raggiungere la sommità di; sorpassare.
topaz ['toupæz] n topazio.
topic ['tɔpik] n argomento, soggetto.
topical ['tɔpikəl] a d'attualità.
topmost ['tɔpmoust] a (il) più alto.
topographic(al) [,tɔpə'græfik(l)] a topografico.
topography [tə'pɔgrəfi] n topografia.
topsyturvy ['tɔpsi'tə:vi] ad sossopra, a soqquadro.
torch [tɔ:tʃ] n torcia, fiaccola; lampadina tascabile.
torment ['tɔ:ment] n tormento; [tɔ:'ment] vt tormentare.
tornado [tɔ:'neidou] n tornado, ciclone.
torpedo [tɔ:'pi:dou] n torpedine, siluro.
torpid ['tɔ:pid] a torpido, apatico, inerte.
torpor ['tɔ:pə] n torpore, apatia.
torrent ['tɔrənt] n torrente.
torrid ['tɔrid] a torrido.
tortoise ['tɔ:təs] n tartaruga, testuggine.
tortuous ['tɔ:tjuəs] a tortuoso.
torture ['tɔ:tʃə] n tortura; vt torturare.
Tory ['tɔ:ri] a n (pol) conservatore.
toss [tɔs] n lancio; moto brusco; beccheggio; vt buttare in aria; sballottare, scuotere; vi dimenarsi; giocare a testa o croce.
tot [tɔt] n piccino; bicchierino.
total ['toutl] a n totale.
totter ['tɔtə] vi barcollare, vacillare.
touch [tʌtʃ] n tatto, tocco, colpetto; contatto; leggero attacco; accenno; un po' di; vt toccare; commuovere; riguardare; vi toccarsi; **to t. at** (naut) far scalo; **to t. up** ritoccare.
touching ['tʌtʃiŋ] a commovente.
touchstone ['tʌtʃstoun] n pietra di paragone.
touchy ['tʌtʃi] a suscettibile, permaloso.
tough [tʌf] a duro, difficile, resistente, tenace; (of meat) tiglioso.
toughen ['tʌfn] vti indurir(si).

toughness ['tʌfnis] *n* durezza, tenacia; difficoltà.

tour [tuə] *n* giro, gita, viaggio; *vi* fare un viaggio, una gita, un giro, visitare.

tourism ['tuərizəm] *n* turismo.

tourist ['tuərist] *n* turista.

tournament ['tuənəmənt] *n* torneo.

tousle ['tauzl] *vt* scarmigliare.

tout [taut] *vi* sollecitare ordini; (*com*) fare la piazza.

tow [tou] *n* stoppa; rimorchio; *vt* rimorchiare.

toward(s) [tə'wɔːd(z)] *prep* verso; *a* favore di.

towel ['tauəl] *n* asciugamano.

tower ['tauə] *n* torre; *vi* torreggiare.

town [taun] *n* città; **town hall** municipio.

toy [tɔi] *n* balocco, giocattolo; *vi* giocherellare, trastullarsi.

trace [treis] *n* traccia, orma, impronta; residuo; *vt* tracciare; rintracciare; seguire le tracce.

track [træk] *n* traccia, cammino, pista; sentiero; binario; rotta; scia; *vt* seguire la traccia di; snidare.

tract [trækt] *n* tratto, distesa; trattato, opuscolo.

tractable ['træktəbl] *a* trattabile, docile.

traction ['trækʃən] *n* trazione.

tractor ['træktə] *n* (*mech*) trattore, trattrice.

trade [treid] *n* commercio, traffico; mestiere, occupazione; *vti* commerciare, trattare; scambiare; **T. Union** sindacato; **t. winds** (venti) alisei *pl*.

trader ['treidə] *n* commerciante; nave mercantile.

tradesman ['treidzmən] *n* commerciante, negoziante.

tradition [trə'diʃən] *n* tradizione.

traditional [trə'diʃənl] *a* tradizionale.

traduce [trə'djuːs] *vt* calunniare, diffamare.

traffic ['træfik] *n* traffico; circolazione; *vti* trafficare, commerciare; **t. lights** semaforo.

tragedian [trə'dʒiːdiən] *n* tragediografo; attore tragico.

tragedy ['trædʒidi] *n* tragedia.

tragic(al) ['trædʒik(əl)] *a* tragico.

trail [treil] *n* traccia, scia, strascico, pista; *vt* seguire la traccia di, strascicare; *vi* strisciare, trascinarsi.

trailer ['treilə] *n* rimorchio, roulotte; (*cin*) 'prossimamente'.

train [trein] *n* treno; sèguito; strascico; serie; *vt* allenare, ammaestrare, allevare; *vi* allenarsi.

trainer ['treinə] *n* allenatore.

training ['treiniŋ] *n* allenamento, ammaestramento, esercitazione.

trait [treit] *n* tratto, caratteristica.

traitor ['treitə] *n* traditore.

tram(car) ['træm(kɑː)] *n* tram.

trammel ['træməl] *n* tramaglio; *pl*

impedimenti, ostacoli *pl*; *vt* impedire, impastoiare.

tramp [træmp] *n* viaggio a piedi; calpestio; vagabondo; *vt* attraversare a piedi; *vi* camminare con passo pesante.

trample ['træmpl] *n* calpestio; *vti* calpestare.

trance [trɑːns] *n* trance, catalessi ipnotica.

tranquil ['træŋkwil] *a* tranquillo.

tranquility [træŋ'kwiliti] *n* tranquillità.

transact [træn'zækt] *vt* eseguire, trattare, negoziare.

transaction [træn'zækʃən] *n* affare, operazione; (*leg*) transazione; *pl* atti, verbali di società.

transatlantic ['trænzət'læntik] *a* transatlantico.

transcend [træn'send] *vti* trascendere.

transcendent [træn'sendənt] *a* trascendente; **transcendental** *a* trascendentale.

transcribe [træns'kraib] *vt* trascrivere.

transcript ['trænskript] *n* copia; riproduzione.

transfer ['trænsfəː] *n* trasferimento; cessione; (*com*) storno; decalcomania.

transfer [træns'fəː] *vt* trasferire; (*com*) stornare; decalcare.

transferable [træns'fəːrəbl] *a* trasferibile.

transfiguration ['trænsfigju'reiʃən] *n* trasfigurazione.

transfigure [træns'figə] *vt* trasfigurare.

transfix [træns'fiks] *vt* trafiggere, trapassare; pietrificare.

transform [træns'fɔːm] *vt* trasformare.

transformation [ˌtrænsfə'meiʃən] *n* trasformazione, metamorfosi.

transformer [træns'fɔːmə] *n* trasformatore.

transfuse [træns'fjuːz] *vt* travasare; (*fig*) trasfondere.

transfusion [træns'fjuːʒən] *n* trasfusione.

transgress [træns'gres] *vt* contravvenire a, trasgredire.

transgression [træns'greʃən] *n* trasgressione.

transgressor [træns'gresə] *n* trasgressore.

transient ['trænziənt] *a* transitorio fugace.

transistor [træn'sistə] *n* transistor.

transit ['trænsit] *n* transito.

transition [træn'siʒən] *n* transizione, passaggio.

transitive ['trænsitiv] *a* transitivo.

transitory ['trænsitəri] *a* transitorio.

translatable [træns'leitəbl] *a* traducibile.

translate [træns'leit] *vt* tradurre.

translation [træns'leiʃən] *n* traduzione.

translator [træns'leitə] n traduttore.

translucent [træns'luːsnt] a traslucido, trasparente, diafano.

transmigration [ˌtrænzmai'greiʃən] n trasmigrazione.

transmission [trænz'miʃən] n trasmissione.

transmit [trænz'mit] vt trasmettere.

transmitter [trænz'mitə] n trasmettitore.

transparency [træns'pɛərənsi] n trasparenza; (phot) diapositiva.

transparent [træns'pɛərənt] a trasparente.

transpire [træns'paiə] vi trasparire, trapelare.

transplant [træns'plɑːnt] vt trapiantare.

transport ['trænspɔːt] n trasporto, mezzo di trasporto; violenta emozione; estasi; [træns'pɔːt] vt trasportare, rapire.

transportation [ˌtrænspɔː'teiʃən] n trasporto, deportazione.

transpose [træns'pouz] vi trasporre, spostare.

trans-ship [træns'ʃip] vt (naut) trasbordare.

transubstantiation ['trænsəbˌstænʃi'eiʃən] n transubstanziazione.

trap [træp] n trappola; botola; calesse; vt prendere in trappola.

trap-door ['træp'dɔː] n botola.

trapeze [trə'piːz] n trapezio.

trapper ['træpə] n cacciatore di pelli.

trappings ['træpiŋz] n pl bardatura, finimenti pl.

trash [træʃ] n robaccia; sciocchezze.

traumatic [trɔː'mætik] a traumatico.

travel ['trævl] n viaggi pl; vi viaggiare.

traveller ['trævlə] n viaggiatore.

traverse ['trævəs] a trasversale; n traversa; vt attraversare; contestare.

travesty ['trævisti] n parodia; vt parodiare.

trawl [trɔːl] n rete a strascico; vti pescare con strascico.

trawler ['trɔːlə] n motopeschereccio a strascico.

tray [trei] n vassoio; (of a trunk) scompartimento.

treacherous ['tretʃərəs] a traditore, sleale.

treachery ['tretʃəri] n tradimento, slealtà.

treacle ['triːkl] n melassa.

tread [tred] n passo; parte di suola che tocca la terra; (of tyre) battistrada; (of stair step) pedata; vt calpestare; vi mettere il piede, camminare.

treadle ['tredl] n pedale.

treason ['triːzn] n tradimento.

treasonable ['triːznəbl] a proditorio.

treasure ['treʒə] n tesoro; vt custodire, tener caro.

treasurer ['treʒərə] n tesoriere.

treasury ['treʒəri] n tesoreria, tesoro.

treat [triːt] n festa, trattenimento; piacere; vt trattare; offrire un trattenimento a; (med) curare; vi negoziare, trattare.

treatise ['triːtiz] n trattato, dissertazione.

treatment ['triːtmənt] n trattamento, cura.

treaty ['triːti] n trattato, patto.

treble ['trebl] a n triplo; (mus) soprano; vti triplicar(si).

tree [triː] n albero.

trefoil ['trefɔil] n trifoglio.

trellis ['trelis] n traliccio; graticcio.

tremble ['trembl] n trèmito, tremore; vi tremare.

tremendous [tri'mendəs] a tremendo, terribile; (fam) straordinario.

tremor ['tremə] n tremore.

tremulous ['tremjuləs] a tremulo.

trench [trentʃ] n trincea, fosso.

trenchant ['trentʃənt] a tagliente, incisivo.

trend [trend] n orientamento, direzione, tendenza; vi tendere a, dirigersi.

Trent [trent] n Trento.

trepidation [ˌtrepi'deiʃən] n trepidazione.

trespass ['trespəs] n trasgressione, infrazione; violazione di proprietà; vi commettere un'infrazione, trasgredire, abusare di.

trespasser ['trespəsə] n trasgressore, contravventore.

tress [tres] n treccia.

trestle ['tresl] n cavalletto, trespolo.

trial ['traiəl] n esperimento, prova; processo; pl tribolazione.

triangle ['traiæŋgl] n triangolo.

triangular [trai'æŋgjulə] a triangolare.

tribe [traib] n tribù.

tribulation [ˌtribju'leiʃən] n tribolazione.

tribunal [trai'bjuːnl] n tribunale.

tribune ['tribjuːn] n tribuno; tribuna.

tributary ['tribjutəri] n affluente; a n tributario.

tribute ['tribjuːt] n tributo.

trice [trais] n istante; in a t. in un batter d'occhio.

trick [trik] n tiro; trucco; abitudine; espediente; vt ingannare; vi giocar tiri.

trickery ['trikəri] n inganno, stratagemma.

trickle ['trikl] n gocciolio; ruscelletto; vi gocciolare.

trickster ['trikstə] n raggiratore.

tricky ['triki] a furbo, ingannevole; difficile.

tricolour ['trikələ] a n tricolore.

tricycle ['traisikl] n triciclo.

trident ['traidənt] n tridente.

triennial [trai'eniəl] a triennale.

trifle ['traifl] n bagatella, bazzecola; (cook) zuppa inglese; vti gingillarsi, scherzare.

trifler ['traiflə] n persona frivola.

trifling ['traiflin] *a* insignificante; frivolo.

trigger ['trigə] *n* grilletto; **to t. off** *vt* dare inizio a.

trigonometry [.trigə'nɔmitri] *n* trigonometria.

trill [tril] *n* trillo; *vti* trillare.

trim [trim] *a* accurato, azzimato; *n* ordine, assetto, stato; *vt* aggiustare, rassettare; guarnire; tagliare.

trimming ['trimin] *n* guarnizione.

Trinity ['triniti] *n* trinità.

trinket ['trinkit] *n* gingillo, ninnolo.

trio ['triou] *pl* **trios** *n* (*mus*) trio, terzetto.

trip [trip] *n* gita, viaggio; incespicamento, passo falso, sgambetto; *vt* far inciampare, far sbagliare; *vi* inciampare, far un passo falso; **to t. along** saltellare.

tripe [traip] *n* trippa; (*sl*) sciocchezze *pl*.

triple ['tripl] *a* triplice; *vti* triplicar(si).

triplet ['triplit] *n* terzina; bimbo nato di parto trigemino.

triplicate ['triplikit] *a* triplicato; triplice; ['triplikeit] *vt* triplicare.

tripod ['traipɔd] *n* treppiedi; tripode.

Tripoli ['tripəli] *n* Tripoli.

trite [trait] *n* trito, banale, comune.

triteness ['traitnis] *n* banalità.

triton ['traitn] *n* tritone.

triumph ['traiəmf] *n* trionfo; *vi* trionfare.

triumphant [trai'ʌmfənt] *a* trionfante.

trivet ['trivit] *n* treppiedi.

trivial ['triviəl] *a* insignificante, banale, senza importanza.

triviality [.trivi'æliti] *n* banalità, cosa di nessuna importanza.

troll [troul] *vi* pescare con esca girante.

trolley ['trɔli] *n* carrello; (*el*) rotella di presa; **t. bus** filobus; **t. car** (*US*) vettura tranviaria.

trombone [trɔm'boun] *n* (*mus*) trombone.

troop [tru:p] *n* (*mil*) truppa; frotta; compagnia teatrale; *vti* radunar(si), sfilare.

trooper ['tru:pə] *n* (*mil*) soldato di cavalleria; cavallo di truppa; (*naut*) nave per il trasporto di truppe.

trophy ['troufi] *n* trofeo.

tropic ['trɔpik] *n* tropico.

tropical ['trɔpikəl] *a* tropicale.

trot [trɔt] *n* trotto, trottata; *vi* trottare.

trotter ['trɔtə] *n* trottatore, zampa, zampino.

troubadour ['trubəduə] *n* trovatore.

trouble ['trʌbl] *n* disturbo, guaio, seccatura, imbroglio, disordine; *vt* disturbare, turbare, importunare, affliggere; *vi* preoccuparsi prendersi la briga di.

troubled ['trʌbld] *a* agitato, inquieto.

troublesome ['trʌblsəm] *a* fastidioso, molesto, noioso.

trough [trɔf] *n* trogolo.

trousers ['trauzəz] *n pl* calzoni pantaloni *pl*.

trout [traut] *n* trota.

trowel ['trauəl] *n* cazzuola; trapiantatoio.

truant ['truənt] *a n* pigro, svogliato, vagabondo; **play t.** marinare la scuola.

truce [tru:s] *n* tregua, armistizio.

truck [trʌk] *n* baratto; (*rly*) vagone merci; (*US*) autocarro; **t. farmer** (*US*) ortolano, orticoltore; **t. line** (*US*) impresa autotrasporti; **t. trailer** (*US*) rimorchio di autocarro.

truckle ['trʌkl] *vi* mostrarsi servile.

truculent ['trʌkjulənt] *a* truculento.

trudge [trʌdʒ] *vt* percorrere faticosamente; *vi* camminare faticosamente.

true [tru:] *a* vero, fedele, leale.

truffle ['trʌfl] *n* tartufo.

truism ['truizəm] *n* truismo, verità lapalissiana.

truly ['tru:li] *ad* veramente, sinceramente; **yours t.** vostro devotissimo.

trump [trʌmp] *n* (*cards*) briscola, atout; (*fam*) persona eccellente; *vti* giocare una briscola, degli atouts.

trumpery ['trʌmpəri] *a* senza valore; *n* chincaglieria, orpello.

trumpet ['trʌmpit] *n* tromba; *vi* strombazzare, suonare la tromba; (*elephant*) barrire.

trumpeter ['trʌmpitə] *n* trombettiere.

truncate ['trʌnkeit] *vt* troncare, mozzare.

truncheon ['trʌntʃən] *n* bastone, randello.

trundle ['trʌndl] *vti* (far) correre, ruzzolare.

trunk [trʌnk] *n* tronco; baule; proboscide; *pl* calzoni corti, calzoncini.

truss [trʌs] *n* fascio, fastello, (*building*) travatura; (*med*) cinto erniario; *vt* (*of chicken etc, before cooking*) legare le ali; immobilizzare.

trust [trʌst] *n* fede, fiducia; custodia; (*com*) credito; *vt* aver fiducia in, fidarsi di; *vi* sperare vivamente.

trustee [trʌs'ti:] *n* fiduciario, amministratore.

trusteeship [trʌs'ti:ʃip] *n* amministrazione fiduciaria.

trustful ['trʌstful] *a* fiducioso.

trustworthy ['trʌst.wəði] *a* fidato, attendibile.

trusty ['trʌsti] *a* fedele, fidato.

truth [tru:θ] *n* verità.

truthful ['tru:θful] *a* veritiero, verace.

truthfully ['tru:θfuli] *ad* sinceramente; fedelmente, esattamente.

truthfulness ['tru:θfulnis] *n* veracità, sincerità.

try [trai] *vt* provare, tentare, mettere alla prova, saggiare; (*leg*) processare; *vi* provare, sforzarsi.

trying ['traiiŋ] *a* difficile, penoso.

tsar [tsɑ:] *n* zar.

tub [tʌb] *n* tino, tinozza, vasca da bagno; (*naut*) barcaccia.

tubby ['tʌbi] *a* tondo e grasso.

tube [tju:b] *n* tubo; (*London*) ferrovia sotterranea; (*US rad*) valvola; **test t.** provetta.

tubercle ['tju:bəkl] *n* tubercolo.

tubercular [tju(:)'bə:kjulə] *a* tubercolare; tubercoloso.

tuberculosis [tju(:),bə:kju'lousis] *n* tubercolosi.

tuberculous [tju'bə:kjuləs] *a* tubercoloso, tubercolotico.

tubular ['tju:bjulə] *a* tubolare.

tuck [tʌk] *n* piega, basta; (*sl*) cibo; *vt* fare pieghe in; **t. in** ripiegare; (*fam*) mangiare avidamente; **t. up** rimboccare.

Tuesday ['tju:zdi] *n* martedì.

tuft [tʌft] *n* ciuffo, fiocco, cespuglio.

tug [tʌg] *n* strappo, sforzo; strazio; (*naut*) rimorchiatore; *vti* tirare con forza, rimorchiare.

tuition [tju'iʃən] *n* insegnamento, istruzione.

tulip ['tju:lip] *n* tulipano.

tumble ['tʌmbl] *n* capitombolo; *vt* buttar giù, rovesciare; *vi* cadere, capitombolare, fare acrobazie.

tumbler ['tʌmblə] *n* acrobata; bicchiere.

tumour ['tju:mə] *n* tumore.

tumult ['tju:mʌlt] *n* tumulto.

tumultuous [tju'mʌltjuəs] *a* tumultuoso.

tun [tʌn] *n* botte, tino.

tuna ['tu:nə] *n* tonno.

tune [tju:n] *n* aria, melodia; accordo; *vt* accordare; **to t. in** (*rad*) sintonizzare.

tuneful ['tju:nful] *a* armonioso, melodioso.

tunic ['tju:nik] *n* tunica.

tunnel ['tʌnl] *n* galleria, traforo, tunnel.

tunny ['tʌni] *n* tonno.

turban ['tə:bən] *n* turbante.

turbid ['tə:bid] *a* torbido.

turbine ['tə:bin] *n* turbina.

turbot ['tə:bət] *n* rombo.

turbulence ['tə:bjuləns] *n* turbolenza, agitazione.

turbulent ['tə:bjulənt] *a* turbolento.

tureen [tə'ri:n] *n* zuppiera.

turf [tə:f] *n* zolla erbosa, tappeto, erboso.

turgid ['tə:dʒid] *a* turgido; (*fig*) ampolloso.

Turin [tju'rin] *n* Torino; **Turinese** *a n* torinese.

Turk [tə:k] *n* turco.

Turkey ['tə:ki] *n* Turchia.

turkey ['tə:ki] *n* tacchino.

Turkish ['tə:kiʃ] *a n* turco.

turmoil ['tə:mɔil] *n* baccano, tumulto.

turn [tə:n] *n* giro, curva, voltata, piega; turno; passeggiata; inclina-zione; *vt* cambiare; girare; trasformare; voltare; tornire; tradurre; *vi* girare; divenire, farsi; rivolgersi, voltarsi; trasformarsi. **turntable** (*rly*) piattaforma girevole, (*of record player*) piatto, giradischi.

turncoat ['tə:nkout] *n* girella.

turncock ['tə:nkɔk] *n* fontaniere.

turner ['tə:nə] *n* tornitore.

turning ['tə:niŋ] *a* girevole; *n* svolta, voltata; **t. point** *n* svolta decisiva.

turnip ['tə:nip] *n* rapa.

turnover ['tə:n,ouvə] *n* rovesciamento; (*com*) giro di affari; torta.

turpentine ['tə:pəntain] *n* trementina, acqua ragia.

turquoise ['tə:kwɑ:z] *n* turchese.

turret ['tʌrit] *n* torre, torretta.

turtle ['tə:tl] *n* tartaruga; **t.-dove** *n* tortora.

Tuscan ['tʌskən] *a n* toscano.

Tuscany ['tʌskəni] *n* Toscana.

tusk [tʌsk] *n* zanna.

tussle ['tʌsl] *n* rissa, zuffa; *vi* azzuffarsi.

tutor ['tju:tə] *n* istitutore, precettore; tutore; *vt* istruire, essere il precettore di.

tutorial [tju'tɔ:riəl] *a* tutorio; *n* lezione a un piccolo gruppo di studenti.

twang [twæŋ] *n* suono acuto, suono nasale; *vt* pronunciare con tono nasale; *vi* fare un suono acuto o nasale.

tweed [twi:d] *n* tessuto di lana cardata, "tweed".

tweezers ['twi:zəz] *n pl* pinze, pinzette *pl*.

twelfth [twelfθ] *a n* dodicesimo.

twelve [twelv] *a n* dodici.

twenty ['twenti] *a n* venti; **twentieth** *a n* ventesimo.

twice [twais] *ad* due volte.

twig [twig] *n* rametto, ramoscello.

twilight ['twailait] *n* crepuscolo.

twin [twin] *a n* gemello.

twine [twain] *n* cordicella, spago; *vti* attorcigliar(si), intrecciar(si), torcer(si).

twinge [twindʒ] *n* dolore lancinante, fitta; (*fig*) rimorso.

twinkle ['twiŋkl] *n* luccichio, scintillio; *vi* luccicare, scintillare; ammiccare, strizzare l'occhio.

twinkling ['twiŋkliŋ] *n* scintillio, balenio; **in the t. of an eye** in un baleno, in un batter d'occhio.

twirl [twə:l] *n* ghirigoro, piroetta.

twist [twist] *n* filo ritorto; rotolo di tabacco; filoncino (di pane); torsione; tendenza; capriccio; (*dance*) "twist"; *vti* contorcer(si), intrecciar(si), torcer(si).

twister ['twistə] *n* torcitore; (*sl*) truffatore; compito difficile, situazione ingarbugliata; **tongue-t.** scioglilingua.

twit [twit] *vt* rinfacciare.

twitch [twitʃ] n contrazione spasmodica; vt dare uno strattone a; vi contorcersi spasmodicamente.

twitter ['twitə] n cinguettio, pigolio; (fam) agitazione; vi cinguettare, pigolare.

two [tu:] a n due.

twofold ['tu:fould] a doppio, duplice.

tycoon [tai'ku:n] n (sl) capitalista, magnate.

type [taip] n tipo, modello, genere; carattere tipografico.

typewrite ['taiprait] vt dattilografare.

typewriter ['taip,raitə] n macchina per scrivere.

typhoid ['taifɔid] a tifoide; n febbre tifoidea.

typhoon [tai'fu:n] n tifone.

typhus ['taifəs] n (med) tifo.

typical ['tipikəl] a tipico.

typify ['tipifai] vt rappresentare, simboleggiare, esemplificare.

typist ['taipist] n dattilografo, -fa.

typographer [tai'pɔgrəfə] n tipografo.

typography [tai'pɔgrəfi] n tipografia.

tyrannical [ti'rænikəl] a tirannico, dispotico.

tyrannize ['tirənaiz] vti tiranneggiare.

tyranny ['tirəni] n tirannia.

tyrant ['taiərənt] n tiranno.

tyre, tire ['taiə] n pneumatico.

Tyrol ['tiroul] n Tirolo.

Tyrolean [ti'rouliən] **Tyrolese** [.tiri'li:z] a n tirolese.

U

ubiquitous [ju'bikwitəs] a onnipresente.

ubiquity [ju'bikwiti] n ubiquità.

udder ['ʌdə] n mammella.

Uganda [ju'gændə] n Uganda.

ugliness ['ʌglinis] n bruttezza.

ugly ['ʌgli] a brutto.

Ukraine [ju'krein] n Ucraina.

ulcer ['ʌlsə] n ulcera.

ulcerate ['ʌlsəreit] vti ulcerare.

ulceration [.ʌlsə'reiʃən] n ulcerazione.

Ulster ['ʌlstə] n Ulster.

ulterior [ʌl'tiəriə] a ulteriore.

ultimate ['ʌltimit] a finale, fondamentale.

ultimatum [.ʌlti'meitəm] n ultimatum.

ultraviolet ['ʌltrə'vaiəlit] a ultravioletto.

umbrage ['ʌmbridʒ] n (fig) ombra, sospetto; offesa.

umbrella [ʌm'brelə] n ombrello.

Umbria ['ʌmbriə] n Umbria; **Umbrian** a n umbro.

umpire ['ʌmpaiə] n arbitro; vti arbitrare.

un- [ʌn] prefisso (avente significato negativo se unito ad aggettivi,

avverbi e sostantivi, indicante il contrario o l'annullamento dell'azione, se unito a verbi; qualora non si trovasse il vocabolo sotto la forma composta, si cerchi la forma senza prefisso).

unable ['ʌn'eibl] a inabile, incapace.

unabridged ['ʌnə'bridʒd] a non abbreviato, intero; u. edition edizione integrale.

unaccountable ['ʌnə'kauntəbl] a inesplicabile; irresponsabile.

unaccustomed ['ʌnə'kʌstəmd] a insolito; non abituato.

unacquainted ['ʌnə'kweintid] a to be u. with non conoscere.

unadulterated [.ʌnə'dʌltəreitid] a non adulterato, genuino.

unaffected ['ʌnə'fektid] a semplice, senz'affettazione, non influenzato.

unanimity [.junə'nimiti] n unanimità.

unanimous [ju'næniməs] a unanime.

unanswerable [ʌn'ɑ:nsərəbl] a irrefutabile.

unassuming ['ʌnə'sju:miŋ] a modesto, senza pretese.

unattended ['ʌnə'tendid] a solo, incustodito.

unaware ['ʌnə'weə] a inconsapevole, inconscio; **unawares** ad all'improvviso, di sorpresa.

unbearable [ʌn'bɛərəbl] a insopportabile.

unbecoming ['ʌnbi'kʌmiŋ] a sconveniente; che non sta bene, che non si addice.

unbelief ['ʌnbi'li:f] n incredulità, scetticismo.

unbeliever [.ʌnbi'li:və] n persona incredula, miscredente.

unbend ['ʌn'bend] vt raddrizzare; vi raddrizzarsi, rilassarsi; (fig) farsi affabile.

unbending ['ʌn'bendiŋ] a inflessibile.

unbidden ['ʌn'bidn] a spontaneo, non invitato.

unblemished [ʌn'blemiʃt] a senza macchia, perfetto.

unborn ['ʌn'bɔ:n] a non ancora nato, futuro.

unbridled [ʌn'braidld] a sfrenato.

unburden [ʌn'bə:dn] vt alleggerire; u. oneself confidarsi con qlcu.

unbutton ['ʌn'bʌtn] vti sbottonare, sbottonarsi.

uncanny [ʌn'kæni] a misterioso, strano; inquietante.

uncertain [ʌn'sə:tn] a incerto, poco sicuro.

uncertainty [ʌn'sə:tnti] n incertezza.

unchangeable [ʌn'tʃeindʒəbl] a immutabile, invariabile.

uncle ['ʌŋkl] n zio.

unclean [ʌn'kli:n] a impuro, sporco.

uncomfortable [ʌn'kʌmfətəbl] a scomodo, spiacevole.

uncommon [ʌn'kɔmən] a raro.

uncompromising [ʌn'kɔmprəmaiziŋ] *a* intransigente, inflessibile, assoluto.

unconcerned ['ʌnkən'sɜːnd] *a* indifferente.

unconditional ['ʌnkən'diʃənl] *a* incondizionato, assoluto.

unconquered ['ʌn'kɔŋkəd] *a* invitto.

unconscious [ʌn'kɔnʃəs] *a* inconscio, inconsapevole, privo di sensi.

uncouth [ʌn'kuθ] *a* goffo, rozzo.

uncouthness [ʌn'kuθnis] *n* goffaggine, rozzezza.

uncover [ʌn'kʌvə] *vt* scoprire, svelare; *vi* scoprirsi.

unction ['ʌnkʃən] *n* unzione, parole melliflue *pl*.

unctuous ['ʌŋktjuəs] *a* untuoso, mellifluo.

undaunted [ʌn'dɔːntid] *a* imperterrito, intrepido.

undecided ['ʌndi'saidid] *a* indeciso, indefinito.

under ['ʌndə] *prep* sotto, al di sotto di; in corso di; *ad* sotto.

underclothes ['ʌndəklouðz] *n pl*, **underclothing** ['ʌndəklouðiŋ] *n* biancheria personale, intima.

undercurrent ['ʌndə,kʌrənt] *n* corrente sottomarina, corrente nascosta.

underdeveloped ['ʌndədi'veləpt] *a* sottosviluppato.

underdone ['ʌndə'dʌn] *a* poco cotto, al sangue.

underfed ['ʌndə'fed] *a* denutrito.

undergo [,ʌndə'gou] *vt* subire, sottoporsi a, sopportare.

undergraduate [,ʌndə'grædjuit] *n* studente universitario.

underground ['ʌndəgraund] *a* sotterraneo; *n* sottosuolo; movimento clandestino; metropolitana, ferrovia sotterranea; *ad* sotto terra.

undergrowth ['ʌndəgrouθ] *n* sottobosco.

underhand ['ʌndəhænd] *a* clandestino, subdolo.

underlie [,ʌndə'lai] *vt* costituire la base di.

underline ['ʌndəlain] *vt* sottolineare.

undermine [,ʌndə'main] *vt* minare.

underneath [,ʌndə'niːθ] *ad prep* sotto, al di sotto (di).

underrate [,ʌndə'reit] *vt* sottovalutare.

undersell [,ʌndə'sel] *vt* vendere sotto prezzo.

undersigned ['ʌndəsaind] *a* sottoscritto.

understand [,ʌndə'stænd] *vti* capire, comprendere; dedurre; sottintendere; apprendere.

understandable [,ʌndə'stændəbl] *a* comprensibile.

understanding [,ʌndə'stændiŋ] *a* comprensivo; intelligente.

understatement ['ʌndə'steitmənt] *n* attenuazione dei fatti.

undertake [,ʌndə'teik] *vti* intraprendere, impegnarsi a.

undertaker ['ʌndə,teikə] *n* imprenditore di pompe funebri.

undertaking [,ʌndə'teikiŋ] *n* impresa.

undervalue ['ʌndə'væljuː] *vt* sottovalutare.

underwrite ['ʌndərait] *vt* sottoscrivere; (com) assicurare.

underwriter ['ʌndə,raitə] *n* firmatario; (com) assicuratore.

undisturbed ['ʌndis'təːbd] *a* indisturbato, imperturbato.

undo ['ʌn'duː] *vt* disfare, sciogliere, annullare, rovinare.

undoing ['ʌn'duiŋ] *n* rovina.

undone ['ʌn'dʌn] *a* slacciato, disfatto, rovinato, incompiuto, intentato.

undress ['ʌn'dres] *vti* svestire, svestirsi, spogliarsi(si).

undue ['ʌn'djuː] *a* indebito, eccessivo.

undulate ['ʌndjuleit] *vi* ondeggiare, fluttuare.

undulation [,ʌndju'leiʃən] *n* ondulazione.

unearth ['ʌn'əːθ] *vt* dissotterrare.

unearthly [ʌn'əːθli] *a* soprannaturale, spettrale; (fam) impossibile.

uneasiness [ʌn'iːzinis] *n* disagio, inquietudine, ansia.

uneasy [ʌn'iːzi] *a* ansioso, inquieto.

unequal ['ʌn'iːkwəl] *a* ineguale, impari, non all'altezza di.

unequalled ['ʌn'iːkwəld] *a* senza pari.

unerring ['ʌn'əːriŋ] *a* infallibile.

uneven ['ʌn'iːvən] *a* ineguale; dispari; irregolare, accidentato.

unevenness ['ʌn'iːvənnis] *n* disuguaglianza; natura accidentata, irregolarità.

unexpected ['ʌniks'pektid] *a* inatteso, imprevisto.

unfair ['ʌn'fɛə] *a* ingiusto.

unfairness ['ʌn'fɛənis] *n* ingiustizia.

unfaithful ['ʌn'feiθful] *a* infedele, sleale; inesatto.

unfavourable ['ʌn'feivərəbl] *a* sfavorevole.

unfeeling [ʌn'fiːliŋ] *a* insensibile, spietato.

unfinished ['ʌn'finiʃt] *a* incompiuto, non rifinito.

unfit ['ʌn'fit] *a* inadatto, inabile; indegno.

unfold ['ʌn'fould] *vt* aprire, spiegare; svelare; svolgere.

unforgettable ['ʌnfə'getəbl] *a* indimenticabile.

unfortunate [ʌn'fɔːtʃnit] *a* sfortunato, infelice; **unfortunately** sfortunamente.

unfrock ['ʌn'frɔk] *vt* spretare.

ungainly ['ʌn'geinli] *a* goffo.

ungrateful [ʌn'greitful] *a* ingrato.

unguent ['ʌŋgwənt] *n* unguento.

unhappiness [ʌn'hæpinis] *n* infelicità.

unhappy [ʌn'hæpi] *a* infelice, poco felice; inopportuno.

unhealthy [ʌn'helθi] *a* malsano; malaticcio.

unheard of [ʌn'həːdɔv] *a* inaudito.

unhurt ['ʌn'həːt] *a* illeso, incolume.

unicorn ['junikɔːn] *n* unicorno.

uniform ['junifɔːm] *a* uniforme; *n* divisa, uniforme.

uniformity [ˌjuni'fɔːmiti] *n* uniformità.

unilateral ['juni'lætərəl] *a* unilaterale.

unimpaired ['ʌnim'pɛəd] *a* non danneggiato, intatto.

unintelligence ['ʌnin'telidʒəns] *n* mancanza di intelligenza.

unintelligent ['ʌnin'telidʒənt] *a* ottuso, stupido.

union ['junjən] *n* unione, accordo, alleanza; **u. suit** (*US*) combinazione.

unique [juː'niːk] *a* unico, solo.

unison ['juːnizn] *a n* unisono.

unit ['juːnit] *n* unità, unità di misura.

unitarian [ˌjuːni'tɛəriən] *a n* unitario.

unite [juː'nait] *vti* congiunger(si), unir(si).

United States [juˌnaitid'steits] *n pl* Stati Uniti (d'America).

unity ['juːniti] *n* unità, uniformità, armonia.

universal ['juːni'vəːsəl] *a n* universale.

universality [ˌjuːnivəː'sæliti] *n* universalità.

universe ['juːnivəːs] *n* universo.

university [ˌjuːni'vəːsiti] *n* università.

unjust ['ʌn'dʒʌst] *a* ingiusto.

unkempt ['ʌn'kempt] *a* spettinato, incolto.

unkind [ʌn'kaind] *a* scortese, cattivo.

unkindness [ʌn'kaindnis] *n* scortesia, cattiveria.

unknown ['ʌn'noun] *a* sconosciuto, ignoto; *n* ignoto.

unless [ən'les] *cj* a meno che non, se non.

unlike ['ʌn'laik] *a* dissimile; *prep* diversamente da.

unlikely [ʌn'laikli] *a* inverosimile, improbabile.

unload ['ʌn'loud] *vt* scaricare, (*fin*) liberarsi di.

unlock ['ʌn'lɔk] *vt* aprire, disserrare.

unlooked-for [ʌn'luktfɔː] *a* inaspettato, inatteso.

unlucky ['ʌn'lʌki] *a* sfortunato; sinistro.

unmake ['ʌn'meik] *vt* disfare.

unman ['ʌn'mæn] *vt* scoraggiare, snervare.

unmannerly [ʌn'mænəli] *a* sgarbato.

unmistakable ['ʌnmis'teikəbl] *a* chiaro, indubbio.

unmoved ['ʌn'muːvd] *a* immobile, impassibile.

unnatural [ʌn'nætʃrəl] *a* contro natura, artificioso.

unnecessary [ʌn'nesisəri] *a* inutile, superfluo.

unnerve ['ʌn'nəːv] *vt* snervare.

unobtrusive ['ʌnəb'truːsiv] *a* discreto, modesto, riservato.

unpleasant [ʌn'pleznt] *a* sgradevole, spiacevole.

unpopular ['ʌn'pɔpjulə] *a* impopolare.

unpretending ['ʌnpri'tendiŋ] **unpretentious** ['ʌnpri'tenʃəs] *a* modesto, senza pretese.

unpublished ['ʌn'pʌbliʃt] *a* inedito.

unquestionable [ʌn'kwestʃənəbl] *a* indiscutibile, indubitabile.

unreadable ['ʌn'riːdəbl] *a* (*of writing, of a book*) illeggibile.

unreasonable [ʌn'riːznəbl] *a* irragionevole.

unreasonableness [ʌn'riːznəblnis] *n* irragionevolezza, assurdità.

unrequited ['ʌnri'kwaitid] *a* non corrisposto, non compensato.

unrest ['ʌn'rest] *n* fermento, agitazione.

unruly [ʌn'ruːli] *a* sregolato, indisciplinato.

unsavoury ['ʌn'seivəri] *a* (*fig*) ripugnante, disgustoso.

unscripted ['ʌn'skriptid] *a* improvvisato, estemporaneo.

unseemly [ʌn'siːmli] *a* indecoroso, sconveniente.

unseen ['ʌn'siːn] *a* non visto; **u. translation** traduzione a prima vista.

unselfish ['ʌn'selfiʃ] *a* disinteressato, altruista.

unsettle ['ʌn'setl] *vt* sconvolgere, turbare.

unsightly [ʌn'saitli] *a* brutto, deforme.

unspeakable [ʌn'spiːkəbl] *a* indicibile, inqualificabile.

unsteady ['ʌn'stedi] *a* vacillante, instabile, variabile.

unsure [ʌn'ʃuə] *a* malsicuro, incerto.

untidy [ʌn'taidi] *a* disordinato, sciatto.

until [ən'til] *prep* fino a, prima di; *cj* finchè (non).

untimely [ʌn'taimli] *a* prematuro, intempestivo.

untiring [ʌn'taiəriŋ] *a* instancabile.

untold ['ʌn'tould] *a* indicibile; innumerevole.

unusual [ʌn'juːʒuəl] *a* insolito.

unwary [ʌn'wɛəri] *a* imprudente, incauto.

unwelcome [ʌn'welkəm] *a* malaccolto, sgradito.

unwell ['ʌn'wel] *a* indisposto, sofferente.

unwilling ['ʌn'wiliŋ] *a* riluttante.

unworthy ['ʌn'wəːði] *a* indegno.

up [ʌp] *prep* su per; *ad* in alto; in piedi; su, in su; **up to** fino a; *a* che va verso l'alto.

upbraid [ʌp'breid] *vt* rimproverare.

upbraiding [ʌp'breidiŋ] *n* rimproveri *pl*.

upbringing ['ʌp.briŋiŋ] n educazione.

upheaval [ʌp'hi:vəl] n sollevamento, subbuglio, scompiglio.

uphill ['up'hil] a erto, faticoso; ad in salita, in su.

uphold [ʌp'hould] vt sostenere, mantenere.

upholsterer [ʌp'houlstərə] n tappezziere.

upholstery [ʌp'houlstəri] n tappezzeria, imbottitura.

upkeep ['ʌpki:p] n mantenimento, manutenzione.

upland ['ʌplənd] a alto, montagnoso; n altipiano.

uplift ['ʌplift] n incoraggiamento; vt [ʌp'lift] alzare, sollevare.

upon [ə'pɔn] prep sopra, su; al momento di.

upper ['ʌpə] a più in alto, più elevato, superiore.

uppermost ['ʌpəmoust] a ad il più alto, il più importante, sopra a tutti.

upright ['ʌp'rait] a diritto, eretto, in piedi; (fig) onesto, retto; ad in posizione verticale.

uprightness ['ʌp'raitnis] n perpendicolarità; rettitudine.

uproar ['ʌp.rɔː] n tumulto, baraonda.

uproarious [ʌp'rɔːriəs] a rumoroso, fragoroso; tumultuoso.

uproariously [ʌp'rɔːriəsli] ad rumorosamente; tumultuosamente.

uproot [ʌp'ruːt] vt estirpare, sradicare, svellere.

upset [ʌp'sɛt] n capovolgimento, rovesciamento; vt capovolgere, rovesciare, sconvolgere.

upshot ['ʌpʃɔt] n esito, risultato finale.

upside-down ['ʌpsaid'daun] ad in disordine, sottosopra; capovolto.

upstairs ['ʌp'stɛəz] a del piano superiore; ad su, al piano di sopra.

upstart ['ʌpstaːt] n villano rifatto, nuovo ricco.

up-to-date ['ʌptu'deit] a aggiornato; alla moda.

upward ['ʌpwəd] a che si muove verso l'alto; **upwards** ad in alto, verso l'alto.

urban ['əːbən] a urbano, di città.

urbane [əː'bein] a urbano, cortese.

urbanity [əː'bæniti] n urbanità, cortesia.

urchin ['əːtʃin] n monello; **sea u.** riccio di mare.

urge [əːdʒ] n stimolo, impulso; sprone; vt incalzare, spingere.

urgency ['əːdʒənsi] n urgenza.

urgent ['əːdʒənt] a urgente.

urine ['juərin] n orina.

urn [əːn] n urna; bricco.

Uruguay ['uːrugwai] n Uruguay.

us [ʌs] pron noi, ci.

usage ['juːzidʒ] n uso, trattamento, usanza.

use [juːs] n uso, impiego; utilità;

abitudine, usanza; [juːz] vt usare, servirsi di, utilizzare, adoperare.

useful ['juːsful] a utile, vantaggioso.

usefulness ['juːsfulnis] n utilità.

useless ['juːslis] a inutile, vano, inefficace.

uselessness ['juːslisnis] n inutilità.

user ['juːzə] n chi usa, utente; (leg) usufruttuario.

usher ['ʌʃə] n usciere; **to u. in** vt introdurre, annunciare.

usual ['juːʒuəl] a usuale, solito; **as u.** ad come al solito.

usurer ['juːʒərə] n usuraio.

usurp [juː'zəːp] vt usurpare.

usurpation [.juːzəː'peiʃən] n usurpazione.

usurper [juː'zəːpə] n usurpatore.

usury ['juːʒuri] n usura.

utensil [ju'tensl] n utensile, arnese, strumento.

uterus ['juːtərəs] n utero.

utilitarian [.juːtili'tɛəriən] a utilitario; n (phil) utilitarista.

utility [juː'tiliti] n utilità, vantaggio.

utilization [.juːtilai'zeiʃən] n utilizzazione.

utilize ['juːtilaiz] vt utilizzare.

utmost ['ʌtmoust] a n massimo, estremo.

utter ['ʌtə] a assoluto, completo; vt emettere, pronunciare.

utterance ['ʌtərəns] n pronuncia, modo di parlare; espressione, sfogo.

V

vacancy ['veikənsi] n posto vacante, vuoto; (fig) vacuità.

vacant ['veikənt] a vacante, vuoto, libero; vacuo.

vacate [və'keit] vt lasciar libero.

vacation [və'keiʃən] n vacanza, -ze pl; **vacationist** (US) villeggiante.

vaccinate ['væksineit] vt vaccinare.

vaccination [.væksi'neiʃən] n vaccinazione.

vaccine ['væksiːn] n vaccino.

vacillate ['væsileit] vi vacillare.

vacillation [.væsi'leiʃən] n vacillamento, irresolutezza.

vacuity [væ'kjuiti] n vacuità.

vacuous ['vækjuəs] a vacuo, vuoto, privo di espressione.

vacuum ['vækjuəm] n vuoto, vuoto pneumatico.

vagabond ['vægəbɔnd] a n vagabondo.

vagary ['veigəri] n capriccio, ghiribizzo.

vagrant ['veigrənt] a ambulante, vagabondo; n vagabondo, accattone.

vague [veig] a vago, impreciso.

vain [vein] a vano, vanitoso.

vainglorious [vein'glɔːriəs] a vanaglorioso.

vainglory [vein'glɔːri] n vanagloria.

vale [veil] n (poet) valle, vallata.

Valentine ['væləntain] *nm pr* Valentino.

valentine ['væləntain] *n* innamorato, fidanzato; biglietto amoroso (che si invia il giorno di S. Valentino).

valet ['vælit] *n* cameriere personale.

valiant ['væliənt] *a* valoroso, prode.

valid ['vælid] *a* valido.

validity [və'liditi] *n* validità.

valley ['væli] *n* valle.

valour ['vælə] *n* valore, coraggio.

valuable ['væljuəbl] *a* costoso, prezioso; *n* oggetto di valore.

valuation [ˌvælju'eifən] *n* valutazione, stima.

value ['vælju:] *n* valore, pregio; *vt* valutare, stimare.

valueless ['væljulis] *a* di nessun valore.

valve [vælv] *n* (*mech*, *anat*) valvola.

vamp [væmp] *n* (*shoe*) tomaia, rimonta; (*mus*) accompagnamento improvvisato; (*sl*) donna fatale; *vt* fare la rimonta; (*mus*) improvvisare; (*sl*) adescare.

vampire ['væmpaiə] *n* vampiro.

van [væn] *n* camioncino, furgoncino; (*rly*) bagagliaio; **brake v.** (*rly*) furgone.

vandal ['vændəl] *a n* vandalo.

vandalism ['vændəlizəm] *n* vandalismo.

vane [vein] *n* banderuola.

vanguard ['vænga:d] *n* avanguardia.

vanilla [və'nilə] *n* vaniglia.

vanish ['vænif] *vi* svanire, sparire, dileguarsi.

vanity ['væniti] *n* vanità.

vanquish ['væŋkwif] *vt* sopraffare, vincere.

vantage ['va:ntidʒ] *n* (*tennis*) vantaggio; **v. ground** posizione elevata.

vaporize ['veipəraiz] *vti* vaporizzar(si).

vaporous ['veipərəs] *a* vaporoso.

vapour ['veipə] *n* vapore.

variable ['vɛəriəbl] *a* variabile; *n* (*math*) quantità variabile.

variance ['vɛəriəns] *n* disaccordo; **at v.** *ad* in disaccordo con.

variation [ˌvɛəri'eifən] *n* variazione.

varicose ['værikous] *a* varicoso.

varied ['vɛərid] *a* vario, variato.

variegate ['vɛərigeit] *vt* screziare, variegare.

variety [və'raiəti] *n* varietà; **v. theatre** teatro di varietà.

various ['vɛəriəs] *a* diverso, vario, parecchi.

varnish ['va:nif] *n* vernice; *vt* verniciare.

vary ['vɛəri] *vt* variare, modificare; *vi* variare, essere diverso.

vase [va:z] *n* vaso.

vaseline ['væsilin] *n* vasellina.

vassal ['væsəl] *n* vassallo.

vast [va:st] *a* vasto, immenso.

vastness ['va:stnis] *n* vastità, immensità.

vat [væt] *n* tino, tinozza.

Vatican ['vætikən] *n* Vaticano.

vaudeville ['voudəvil] *n* 'vaudeville', operetta, (*US*) spettacolo di varietà; **v. theater** (*US*) teatro di varietà.

vault [vɔ:lt] *n* (*arch*) volta; cantina; sotterraneo; tomba; volteggio, salto; *vt* costruire a volta; *vti* saltare.

vaulting ['vɔ:ltiŋ] *n* salto, volteggio; **pole v.** salto con l'asta.

vaunt [vɔ:nt] *n* vanteria, vanto; *vti* vantarsi di.

veal [vi:l] *n* vitello.

veer [viə] *vi* (*wind*) cambiar direzione; (*fig*) cambiar opinione.

vegetable ['vedʒitəbl] *a* vegetale; *n pl* verdura; ortaggio, legume; **v. marrow** zucchino.

vegetarian [ˌvedʒi'tɛəriən] *a n* vegetariano.

vegetate ['vedʒiteit] *vi* vegetare.

vegetation [ˌvedʒi'teifən] *n* vegetazione.

vehemence ['vi:iməns] *n* veemenza.

vehement ['vi:imənt] *a* veemente.

vehicle ['vi:ikl] *n* veicolo.

veil [veil] *n* velo; *vt* velare.

vein [vein] *n* vena; (*fig*) umore.

vellum ['veləm] *n* pergamena.

velocity [vi'lɔsiti] *n* velocità.

velvet ['velvit] *a n* (di) velluto.

venal ['vi:nl] *a* venale.

vendor ['vendɔ:] *n* venditore.

veneer [vi'niə] *n* impiallacciatura; (*fig*) vernice.

venerable ['venərəbl] *a* venerabile.

venerate ['venəreit] *vt* venerare.

veneration [ˌvenə'reifən] *n* venerazione.

venereal [vi'niəriəl] *a* venereo.

Venetian [vi'ni:fən] *a n* veneziano.

Venezuela [ˌvene'zweilə] *n* Venezuela.

vengeance ['vendʒəns] *a* vendetta.

venial ['viniəl] *a* veniale.

Venice ['venis] *n* Venezia.

venison ['venzn] *n* carne di cervo, di daino.

venom ['venəm] *n* veleno.

venomous ['venəməs] *a* velenoso; (*fig*) malevolo.

vent [vent] *n* buco, foro; sbocco; conduttura di camino; (*fig*) sfogo; *vt* dare sfogo a.

ventilate ['ventileit] *vt* ventilare.

ventilation [ˌventi'leifən] *n* ventilazione.

ventilator ['ventileitə] *n* ventilatore.

ventriloquism [ven'triləkwizəm] *n* ventriloquio.

ventriloquist [ven'triləkwist] *n* ventriloquo.

venture ['ventfə] *n* impresa, avventura; rischio; speculazione; *vti* arrischiarsi, avventurarsi, osare.

venturesome ['ventfəsəm] *a* avventuroso, ardito.

Venus ['vi:nəs] *n pr* Venere.

veracious [və'reifəs] *a* verace, veridico.

veracity [və'ræsiti] *n* veracità.

verb [vəːb] *n* (*gram*) verbo.
verbal ['vəːbəl] *a* verbale.
verbatim [vəːˈbeitim] *a* testuale; *ad* testualmente.
verbose [vəːˈbous] *a* verboso.
verbosity [vəˈbɔsiti] *n* verbosità.
verdant ['vəːdənt] *a* verdeggiante.
verdict ['vəːdikt] *n* verdetto.
verdure ['vəːdʒə] *n* vegetazione, verde, verzura.
verge [vəːdʒ] *n* bordo, limite, orlo; punto estremo; *vi* confinare; declinare, tendere verso.
verger ['vəːdʒə] *n* sagrestano.
Vergil ['vəːdʒil] *n* Virgilio.
verification [ˌverifiˈkeiʃən] *n* verifica.
verify ['verifai] *vt* verificare, controllare.
verity ['veriti] *n* verità.
vermilion [vəːˈmiljən] *n* cinabro, vermiglione; (*colour*) vermiglio.
vermin ['vəːmin] *n pl* animali nocivi, insetti parassiti *pl*.
verminous ['vəːminəs] *a* infestato da animali nocivi, da insetti parassiti.
vermouth ['vəːməθ] *n* vermut, vermouth.
vernacular [vəːˈnækjulə] *a n* vernacolo.
vernal ['vəːnl] *a* primaverile.
Verona [viˈrounə] *n* Verona; **Veronese** *a n* veronese.
versatile ['vəːsətail] *a* versatile.
versatility [ˌvəːsəˈtiliti] *n* versatilità.
verse [vəːs] *n* verso, -si *pl*, poesia.
versed [vəːst] *a* versato, abile.
version ['vəːʃən] *n* versione.
vertex ['vəːteks] *pl* **vertices** *n* vertice.
vertical ['vəːtikəl] *a* verticale.
vertigo ['vəːtigou] *n* vertigine, -ni *pl*.
vervain ['vəːvein] *n* verbena.
verve [vəːv] *n* 'verve', brio; energia, vigore.
very ['veri] *a* stesso, proprio; *ad* molto, assai.
Vespers ['vespəz] *n pl* vespri *pl*.
vessel ['vesl] *n* recipiente; nave, vascello; (*anat*) vaso.
vest [vest] *n* maglia; (*US*) panciotto.
vestibule ['vestibjuːl] *n* vestibolo.
vestige ['vestidʒ] *n* vestigio, orma, traccia.
vestment ['vestmənt] *n* (*eccl*) paramento sacerdotale.
vestry ['vestri] *n* sagrestia; consiglio d'amministrazione d'una parrocchia.
veteran ['vetərən] *a n* veterano.
veterinary ['vetərinəri] *a n* veterinario.
veto ['viːtou] *pl* **vetoes** *n* veto; diritto di veto.
vex [veks] *vt* irritare.
vexation [vekˈseiʃən] *n* irritazione.
vexatious [vekˈseiʃəs] *a* irritante, fastidioso.
via [vaiə] *prep* per la via di, via.
viaduct ['vaiədʌkt] *n* viadotto.
vial ['vaiəl] *n* fiala.

viand ['vaiənd] *n* (*usu pl*) cibo, provvista.
vibrant ['vaibrənt] *a* vibrante.
vibrate [vaiˈbreit] *vi* vibrare.
vibration [vaiˈbreiʃən] *n* vibrazione.
vicar ['vikə] *n* parroco, vicario.
vicarage ['vikəridʒ] *n* canonica, dignità di parroco.
vicarious [viˈkɛəriəs] *a* sopportato per un altro, vicario.
vice [vais] *n* vizio; morsa; sostituto, vice; *v.-president* vice presidente.
viceroy ['vaisrɔi] *n* viceré.
vicinity [viˈsiniti] *n* vicinanza.
vicious ['viʃəs] *a* vizioso, cattivo; (*style etc*) scorretto.
vicissitude [viˈsisitjuːd] *n* vicissitudine, vicenda.
victim ['viktim] *n* vittima.
victimize ['viktimaiz] *vt* far vittima di.
victor ['viktə] *n* vincitore.
Victor ['viktə] *nm pr* Vittorio.
Victoria [vikˈtɔːriə] *nf pr* Vittoria.
victorious [vikˈtɔːriəs] *a* vittorioso.
victory ['viktəri] *n* vittoria.
victual ['vitl] *vt* vettovagliare.
victuals ['vitlz] *n pl* vettovaglie *pl*.
video ['vaidiou] *a* (*tv*) video; *n* (*US*) televisione.
vie [vai] *vi* gareggiare, rivaleggiare.
Vienna [viˈenə] *n* Vienna; **Viennese** *a n* viennese.
view [vjuː] *n* vista, veduta, paesaggio; visione; opinione; *vt* guardare attentamente, considerare.
vigil ['vidʒil] *n* veglia; vigilia.
vigilance ['vidʒiləns] *n* vigilanza.
vigilant ['vidʒilənt] *a* vigilante.
vigorous ['vigərəs] *a* vigoroso.
vigour ['vigə] *n* vigore.
viking ['vaikin] *n* vichingo.
vile [vail] *a* vile, abietto.
vileness ['vailnis] *n* viltà, abiezione.
villa ['vilə] *n* villa.
village ['vilidʒ] *n* villaggio, paese.
villager ['vilidʒə] *n* villico, abitante di villaggio.
villain ['vilən] *n* mascalzone, furfante.
villainous ['vilənəs] *a* scellerato, infame.
villainy ['viləni] *n* scelleratezza, infamia.
Vincent ['vinsənt] *nm pr* Vincenzo.
vindicate ['vindikeit] *vt* rivendicare.
vindication [ˌvindiˈkeiʃən] *n* rivendicazione.
vindictive [vinˈdiktiv] *a* vendicativo.
vine [vain] *n* vite.
vinegar ['vinigə] *n* aceto.
vineyard ['vinjəd] *n* vigna, vigneto.
vintage ['vintidʒ] *n* vendemmia, raccolto.
vinyl ['vainil] *n* vinile.
viola [viˈoulə] *n* viola.
violate ['vaiəleit] *vt* violare; trasgredire, infrangere.
violation [ˌvaiəˈleiʃən] *n* violazione, infrazione.

violence ['vaiələns] n violenza.
violent ['vaiələnt] a violento.
violet ['vaiəlit] a violetto, di color viola; n violetta, viola mammola; color viola.
violin [ˌvaiə'lin] n (mus) violino.
violinist ['vaiəlinist] n violinista.
viper ['vaipə] n vipera.
virago [vi'rɑːgou] n virago, donna violenta.
Virgil ['vəːdʒil] nm pr Virgilio.
virgin ['vəːdʒin] a n vergine.
virginity [vəː'dʒiniti] n verginità.
virile ['virail] a virile.
virility [vi'riliti] n virilità.
virtual ['vəːtjuəl] a virtuale, di fatto.
virtue ['vəːtjuː] n virtù.
virtuous ['vəːtjuəs] a virtuoso.
virulence ['viruləns] n virulenza.
virulent ['virulənt] a virulento.
virus ['vaiərəs] n virus.
visa ['vizzə] n visto consolare; vt vistare.
visage ['vizidʒ] n viso.
viscose ['viskouz] n viscosa.
viscount(ess) ['vaikaunt(is)] n visconte(ssa).
viscous ['viskəs] a viscoso.
visibility [ˌvizi'biliti] n visibilità.
visible ['vizəbl] a visibile.
vision ['viʒən] n visione; (sight) vista.
visionary ['viʒnəri] a n visionario; a immaginario, chimerico.
visit ['vizit] n visita; vt visitare, far visita a.
visitation [ˌvizi'teiʃən] n visita ufficiale; (eccl) visitazione.
visitor ['vizitə] n visitatore, ospite.
visor ['vaizə] n visiera.
vista ['vistə] n vista, scorcio panoramico, lunga serie; v. dome car (US rly) carrozza panoramica.
visual ['vizjuəl] a visuale, visivo.
visualize ['vizjuəlaiz] vti immaginare; rendere visibile.
vital ['vaitl] a vitale, (fig) essenziale, importante; v. statistics statistiche anagrafiche; (fam) misure femminili.
vitality [vai'tæliti] n vitalità.
vitamin ['vitəmin] n vitamina.
vitiate ['viʃieit] vt viziare; corrompere; invalidare.
vitreous ['vitriəs] a vitreo.
vitriol ['vitriəl] n vetriolo.
vituperate [vi'tjupəreit] vt vituperare.
vituperation [vi,tjupə'reiʃən] n vituperazione.
vivacious [vi'veiʃəs] a vivace.
vivacity [vi'væsiti] n vivacità.
vivid ['vivid] a vivace, vivo, vivido.
vividness ['vividnis] n vivezza, vivacità.
vivify ['vivifai] vt vivificare.
vivisection [ˌvivi'sekʃən] n vivisezione.
vixen ['viksn] n volpe femmina.
vizier [vi'ziə] n visir.
vocabulary [və'kæbjuləri] n vocabolario.

vocal ['voukəl] a vocale.
vocalist ['voukəlist] n cantante.
vocation [vou'keiʃən] n vocazione.
vocative ['vɔkətiv] n vocativo.
vociferate [vou'sifəreit] vi vociferare, vociare.
vociferous [və'sifərəs] a vociferante, clamoroso.
vogue [voug] n voga, moda.
voice [vɔis] n voce; grido; (of animals) verso; vt esprimere, intonare.
void [vɔid] a n vuoto; a privo, nullo.
volatile ['vɔlətail] a volatile.
volatility [ˌvɔlə'tiliti] n volatilità.
volatilize [vɔ'lætilaiz] vti volatilizzar(si).
volcanic [vɔl'kænik] a vulcanico.
volcano [vɔl'keinou] n vulcano.
volition [vou'liʃən] n volizione.
volley ['vɔli] n raffica, scarica, salva.
volt [voult] n (el) volt.
voltage ['voultidʒ] n (el) voltaggio.
voluble ['vɔljubl] a fluente, loquace.
volume ['vɔljuːm] n volume.
voluminous [və'ljuːminəs] a voluminoso.
voluntary ['vɔləntəri] a volontario.
volunteer [ˌvɔlən'tiə] n soldato volontario; vti offrir(si) volontariamente.
voluptuary [və'lʌptjuəri] n individuo sensuale.
voluptuous [və'lʌptjuəs] a voluttuoso.
voluptuousness [və'lʌptjuəsnis] n voluttà.
vomit ['vɔmit] vti vomitare.
voracious [və'reiʃəs] a vorace.
voracity [vɔ'ræsiti] n voracità.
vortex ['vɔːteks] n vortice.
votary ['voutəri] n devoto, seguace fedele.
vote [vout] n voto, votazione; vti votare.
voter ['voutə] n votante, elettore.
votive ['voutiv] a votivo.
vouch [vautʃ] vt attestare, confermare; to v. for rispondere di, garantire per.
voucher ['vautʃə] n documento giustificativo, pezza d'appoggio; buono, tagliando; (com) ricevuta.
vouchsafe [vautʃ'seif] vt accordare, concedere.
vow [vau] n promesso, voto; vt far voto di, giurare.
vowel ['vauəl] n vocale.
voyage ['vɔidʒ] n viaggio (per mare); vi navigare, fare una traversata.
vulgar ['vʌlgə] a volgare.
vulgarity [vʌl'gæriti] n volgarità.
vulnerable ['vʌlnərəbl] a vulnerabile.
vulture ['vʌltʃə] n avvoltoio.

W

wad [wɔd] n batuffolo; stoppaccio; (sl) denaro.

wadding ['wɔdiŋ] n imbottitura, ovatta.

waddle ['wɔdl] vi camminare dondolandosi (come le anitre).

wade [weid] vti attraversare a guado; procedere faticosamente.

wafer ['weifə] n wafer, cialda, ostia.

waft [wɑːft] n soffio, alito, zaffata; vt diffondere, spandere.

wag [wæg] n burlone; vti scodinzolare.

wage(s) ['weidʒ(iz)] n (usu pl) paga, salario; **to w. war** muover guerra.

wager ['weidʒə] n scommessa; vt scommettere.

waggle ['wægl] n dimenamento, dondolamento; vt dimenare, dondolare.

wag(g)on ['wægən] n carro.

wagtail ['wægteil] n cutrettola.

waif [weif] n trovatello; **waifs and strays** relitti, oggetti smarriti pl.

wail [weil] n lamento, gemito; vi lamentarsi; (of baby) vagire.

wainscot ['weinskət] n rivestimento in legno; zoccolo (di parete).

waist [weist] n vita, cintola.

waistcoat ['weiskout] n panciotto, gilè.

wait [weit] n attesa; vi aspettare, attendere; servire a tavola; **to w. upon** servire.

waiter ['weitə] **waitress** ['weitris] n (d'albergo etc) cameriere, -ra.

waive [weiv] vt rinunziare a, desistere da.

wake [weik] n scia; veglia; vti risvegliar(si), svegliar(si); vegliare.

wakeful ['weikful] a sveglio, insonne, vigile.

wakefulness ['weikfulnis] n insonnia, vigilanza.

waken ['weikən] vti svegliar(si).

Wales [weilz] n Galles.

walk [wɔːk] n passeggiata; percorso; passo; viale; **w. of life** professione, mestiere; ceto; **sidewalk** (US) marciapiede; vt far camminare, percorrere; vi camminare, passeggiare, andare a piedi.

walker ['wɔːkə] n camminatore, pedone.

walking ['wɔːkiŋ] a che cammina, ambulante; n il camminare; **w. stick** bastone da passeggio.

wall [wɔːl] n muro; mura pl; parete; vt cingere di mura.

wallet ['wɔlit] n portafoglio; borsa.

wallow ['wɔlou] vi avvoltolarsi, sguazzare.

wallpaper ['wɔːl,peipə] n tappezzeria, carta da parato.

walnut ['wɔːlnət] n noce.

walrus ['wɔːlrəs] n tricheco.

Walter ['wɔːltə] nm pr Walter, Gualtiero.

waltz [wɔːls] n valzer; vi ballare il valzer.

wan [wɔn] a pallido, smorto.

wand [wɔnd] n bacchetta.

wander ['wɔndə] vi vagabondare, errare, vagare; divagare; vaneggiare.

wanderer ['wɔndərə] n vagabondo.

wane [wein] n declino, decrescenza; vi declinare, decrescere; (moon) calare.

want [wɔnt] n bisogno, deficienza, mancanza, miseria; vt desiderare, volere; aver bisogno di, mancare di; vi occorrere, mancare.

wanton ['wɔntən] a licenzioso, lascivo; capriccioso; senza scopo.

wantonness ['wɔntənnis] n licenziosità; leggerezza.

war [wɔː] n guerra; vi guerreggiare, far guerra.

warble ['wɔːbl] vti gorgheggiare, trillare, cantare.

ward [wɔːd] n custodia, guardia; tutela; pupillo; (of town) quartiere; (hospital) corsia; **to w. off** schivare, evitare, parare, respingere.

warden ['wɔːdn] n custode, guardiano; (of school, prison etc) direttore.

warder ['wɔːdə] n carceriere.

wardrobe ['wɔːdroub] n armadio, guardaroba.

warehouse ['wɛəhaus] n magazzino.

wares [wɛəz] n pl merce, mercanzia, articoli pl.

warfare ['wɔːfɛə] n guerra, stato di guerra.

wariness ['wɛərinis] n cautela, prudenza.

warlike ['wɔːlaik] a bellicoso, marziale.

warm [wɔːm] a caldo; caloroso, cordiale; vti riscaldar(si), scaldar(si); eccitar(si).

warmth [wɔːmθ] n calore.

warn [wɔːn] vt avvertire, ammonire, mettere in guardia, avvisare.

warning ['wɔːniŋ] n ammonimento, avvertimento, preavviso; (leg) diffida.

warp [wɔːp] n ordito; (of wood) curvatura; (fig) pervertimento; vt curvare, pervertire; vi curvarsi, deformarsi.

warrant ['wɔrənt] n autorizzazione, mandato, ordine; garanzia; vt autorizzare, garantire.

warranty ['wɔrənti] n garanzia.

warren ['wɔrin] n conigliera.

warrior ['wɔriə] n guerriero.

wart [wɔːt] n verruca.

wary ['wɛəri] a cauto, guardingo.

wash [wɔʃ] n lavata, lavatura, (linen) bucato; (art) acquerello; (waves) sciabordio; (slops) risciacquatura di piatti; (walls etc) mano di colore; vti lavar(si); vt imbiancare; metallizzare; bagnare; **to w. away** trascinar via, lavar via; **to w. up** lavare i piatti, rigovernare; **w.-out** (fig) un fallimento completo; **washday** (US) giorno di bucato.

washer ['wɔʃə] n lavatore, -trice; **dishwasher** lavastoviglie.

washing ['wɔʃiŋ] n bucato, lavata;

w. day giorno di bucato; **w. machine** lavatrice; **w. powder** detersivo.

wasp [wɔsp] *n* vespa.

wastage ['weistidʒ] *n* consumo, sciupio.

waste [weist] *a* deserto, desolato; *n* rifiuti *pl*; spreco, perdita; consumo; *vt* sprecare, dissipare; *vi* consumarsi, deperire.

wasteful ['weistful] *a* prodigo, spendereccio, dissipatore, rovinoso.

wastefulness ['weistfulnis] *n* prodigalità, sciupio.

wasting ['weistiŋ] *a* che consuma, che indebolisce; *n* sciupio, spreco; devastazione, deperimento.

watch [wɔtʃ] *n* orologio; veglia; guardia, sentinella; osservazione; *vt* osservare, sorvegliare, spiare; *vi* vegliare, vigilare; **watchdog** cane di guardia; **w.-post** posto di guardia; **watchword** parola d'ordine.

watchful ['wɔtʃful] *a* guardingo, vigilante.

watchfulness ['wɔtʃfulnis] *n* vigilanza, cautela.

watchman ['wɔtʃmən] *pl* **-men** *n* guardia (notturna), guardiano.

water ['wɔtə] *n* acqua; *vt* innaffiare; (*horse*) abbeverare; (*drink*) diluire; *vi* (*eyes*) piangere; **w. bottle** bottiglia per acqua, borraccia; **hot-w. bottle** bottiglia dell'acqua calda.

water-closet ['wɔtə,klɔzit] *n* gabinetto.

water-colour ['wɔtə,kʌlə] *n* acquarello.

watercourse ['wɔtəkɔːs] *n* corso d'acqua, canale.

waterfall ['wɔtəfɔːl] *n* cascata.

watering-can ['wɔtəriŋkæn] *a* annaffiatoio.

waterpipe ['wɔtəpaip] *n* conduttura d'acqua.

watering-place ['wɔtəriŋ,pleis] *n* abbeveratoio, luogo di rifornimento d'acqua; stazione balneare, termale.

water-lily ['wɔtə,lili] *n* ninfea.

waterproof ['wɔtəpruːf] *a n* impermeabile.

waterskiing ['wɔtəskiːŋ] *n* sci nautico.

watertight ['wɔtətait] *a* impermeabile, stagno.

waterway ['wɔtəwei] *n* canale navigabile.

water-wheel ['wɔtəwiːl] *n* (*mech*) turbina idraulica.

waterworks ['wɔtəwəːks] *n* impianto idrico.

watery ['wɔtəri] *a* acquoso.

wattle ['wɔtl] *n* canniccio, graticcio; (*birds*) bargiglio; (*fish*) barbetta.

wave [weiv] *n* onda, flutto; (*hand*) cenno; (*wand*) colpo; *vt* agitare; ondulare; *vi* ondeggiare, fluttuare; far segno di.

waver ['weivə] *vi* vacillare.

wavy ['weivi] *a* ondulato; ondoso; ondeggiante.

wax [wæks] *n* cera; ceralacca; cerume; *vt* incerare; dare la cera a.

waxen ['wæksən] *a* di cera, cereo.

way [wei] *n* via, strada; mezzo, modo; abitudine; passaggio; direzione; stato; **by the w.** strada facendo; (*fig*) a proposito.

wayfarer ['wei,fɛərə] *n* viandante.

wayside ['weisaid] *n* margine della strada.

wayward ['weiwəd] *a* ostinato; capriccioso.

waywardness ['weiwədnis] *n* ostinazione; capricciosità.

we [wiː] *pron pl* noi.

weak [wiːk] *a* debole.

weaken ['wiːkən] *vti* indebolir(si).

weakling ['wiːkliŋ] *n* creatura debole; debole, inetto.

weakly ['wiːkli] *a* di debole costituzione; *ad* debolmente.

weakness ['wiːknis] *n* debolezza.

wealth [welθ] *n* ricchezza, -ze *pl*.

wealthy ['welθi] *a* ricco.

wean [wiːn] *vt* svezzare; (*fig*) togliere il vezzo di.

weapon ['wepən] *n* arma.

wear [wɛə] *n* uso, consumo; durata; abbigliamento; *vt* portare, indossare, avere; *vti* consumar(si); durare; **to w. on** passare lentamente.

weariness ['wiərinis] *n* stanchezza, tedio, disgusto.

wearisome ['wiərisəm] *a* stancante, faticoso, tedioso.

weary ['wiəri] *a* stanco; *vti* stancar(si).

weasel ['wiːzl] *n* donnola.

weather ['weðə] *n* (*atmosferico*) tempo; *vt* esporre alle intemperie, resistere a, sopportare; **w. bureau** (*US*) ufficio metereologico.

weathercock ['weðəkɔk] *n* banderuola.

weave [wiːv] *vt* tessere; (*fig*) imbastire, ordire.

weaver ['wiːvə] *n* tessitore.

weaving ['wiːviŋ] *n* tessitura.

web [web] *n* tela, tessuto; (*bird's foot*) membrana; (*spider's*) ragnatela; (*fig*) trama.

wed [wed] *vti* sposar(si).

wedding ['wediŋ] *n* nozze *pl*, sposalizio, matrimonio.

wedge [wedʒ] *n* cuneo, bietta; *vt* incuneare, incastrare; *vi* incunearsi.

wedlock ['wedlɔk] *n* matrimonio, stato coniugale.

Wednesday ['wenzdi] *n* mercoledì.

wee [wiː] *a* (*fam*) piccolo, minuscolo.

weed [wiːd] *n* erbaccia, mala erba; *vt* sarchiare; **to w. out** estirpare; (*fig*) eliminare.

weeds [wiːdz] *n pl* gramaglie *pl*.

weedy ['wiːdi] *a* pieno di erbacce; (*fig*) magro, sparuto.

week [wiːk] *n* settimana.

weekday ['wiːkdei] *n* giorno feriale, giorno lavorativo.

weekend ['wiːk'end] n 'weekend', (vacanza di) fine settimana.

weekly ['wiːkli] a n settimanale; ad ogni settimana.

weep [wiːp] vti piangere; trasudare.

weeping ['wiːpiŋ] a piangente; trasudante; n pianto, lacrime.

weft [weft] n (di tessuto) trama.

weigh [wei] vti pesare; (naut) levare l'ancora.

weight [weit] n peso; importanza; **lightweight** (sport) peso leggero; (US sl) persona di nessuna importanza.

weighty ['weiti] a pesante, gravoso; importante.

weir [wiə] n diga, sbarramento.

weird [wiəd] a misterioso, soprannaturale; (fam) bizzarro.

welcome ['welkəm] a gradito, ben accetto; n benvenuto, buona accoglienza; vt accogliere cordialmente, dare il benvenuto a; gradire; **w.!** benvenuto!

weld [weld] vt saldare.

welding ['weldiŋ] n saldatura.

welfare ['welfeə] n benessere, prosperità.

well [wel] n pozzo, fonte; tromba delle scale; vi scaturire.

well [wel] a bene, buono, in buona salute; ad bene; **w.-off**, **w.-to-do** a agiato, benestante.

Welsh [welʃ] a gallese; n (lingua) gallese; **Welshman** n gallese.

welt [welt] n (shoe) tramezza.

welter ['weltə] n tumulto, confusione; vi avvoltolarsi; essere sballottato; essere immerso; **welterweight** (sport) peso medio-leggero.

wen [wen] n natta, gozzo.

wench [wentʃ] n (arc) ragazza; ragazzotta, popolana, donna di servizio.

west [west] n occidente, ovest, ponente.

westerly ['westəli] a occidentale; ad da (verso) ovest.

western ['westən] a occidentale.

westward ['westwəd] a volto ad ovest; **westwards** ad verso ovest.

wet [wet] a bagnato; umido, piovoso; (of paint) fresco; n umidità, pioggia, tempo piovoso; vt bagnare, inumidire; **w. blanket** guastafeste; **w. nurse** balia.

wether ['weðə] n castrato.

wetness ['wetnis] n umidità.

whack [wæk] n bastonata, colpo; (sl) parte.

whale [weil] n balena.

whaler ['weilə] n baleniere, (naut) baleniera.

wharf [wɔːf] n banchina, molo.

wharfage ['wɔːfidʒ] n diritti di banchina pl.

what [wɔt] a rel interrog che, quale; pron interrog rel indef che cosa, ciò che, quello che.

whatever [wɔt'evə] a qualunque, qualsiasi; pron rel indef qualunque cosa, tutto ciò che.

whatsoever [ˌwɔtsou'evə] a pron (arc) qualunque cosa.

wheat [wiːt] n grano, frumento.

wheedle ['wiːdl] vt ottenere con le moine, persuadere con le moine.

wheel [wiːl] n ruota; (naut) ruota del timone; (aut) volante; vti spingere o tirare (veicolo); (far) girare, turbinare.

wheelbarrow ['wiːl,bærou] n carriola.

wheeze [wiːz] n respiro affannoso; vi ansimare.

whelk [welk] n buccina.

when [wen] ad cj quando.

whence [wens] cj ad da dove, donde, da che cosa; n origine.

whenever [wen'evə] ad tutte le volte che, in qualunque momento.

where [wɛə] ad dove.

whereabouts ['wɛərəbauts] ad dove, in che parte.

whereas [wɛər'æz] cj mentre, (leg) siccome.

whereby [wɛə'bai] ad per la qual cosa.

wherefore ['wɛəfɔː] ad perciò; (interrog) perchè; n causa, motivo.

wherein [wɛər'in] ad nel quale; (interrog) in che cosa.

whereupon [ˌwɛərə'pɔn] ad al che, in conseguenza di che.

wherever [wɛər'evə] ad dovunque, in qualunque luogo.

whet [wet] vt affilare; stimolare.

whether ['weðə] cj se, sia che.

whetstone ['wetstoun] n cote.

which [witʃ] pron rel (riferito ad animali o cose) che, il quale etc; a pron interrog (riferito a persone, animali e cose) quale.

whichever [witʃ'evə] a pron indef qualunque.

whiff [wif] n boccata (d'aria etc).

whig [wig] a n liberale, membro del partito liberale.

while [wail] n momento, tempo; cj mentre; finchè; sebbene.

whilst [wailst] cj mentre.

whim [wim] n capriccio.

whimper ['wimpə] n piagnucolio; vi piagnucolare.

whimsical ['wimzikəl] a capriccioso, stravagante.

whimsy ['wimzi] n capriccio.

whine [wain] n (of dogs) uggiolio, piagnucolio; vi uggiolare, piagnucolare.

whip [wip] n frusta, scudiscio; vt frustare, sferzare; battere; cucire a sopraggitto; (of cream) montare, frullare; **w. hand** vantaggio; **to w. out** cacciar fuori; **to w. round** girarsi bruscamente.

whirl [wəːl] n turbine, vortice; vt roteare; vi girare, roteare, turbinare, susseguirsi vorticosamente.

whirligig ['wəːligig] n giostra; carosello; girandola.

whirlpool ['wə:lpu:l] *n* vortice d'acqua, gorgo.

whirlwind ['wə:lwind] *n* turbine di vento.

whisk [wisk] *n* frullino; movimento rapido; scopetta; *vt* frullare; spazzolare, (*eggs etc*) sbattere; *vti* muover(si) rapidamente, spazzar via.

whisker ['wiskə] *n* basetta; (*cat*) baffo.

whiskey, whisky ['wiski] *n* whisky.

whisper ['wispə] *n* bisbiglio, mormorio; *vti* bisbigliare, mormorare.

whist [wist] *n* 'whist', gioco di carte.

whistle ['wisl] *n* fischio, fischietto; *vti* fischiare.

whit [wit] *n* quantità minima; **W.** Sunday domenica di Pentecoste.

white [wait] *a* bianco; **w.-collar worker** impiegato.

whiten ['waitn] *vti* imbiancare.

whiteness ['waitnis] *n* bianchezza.

whitewash ['waitwɔʃ] *n* calce per imbiancare, intonaco; (*US sport*) vittoria schiacciante; *vt* imbiancare; (*fig*) riabilitare.

whiting ['waitiŋ] *n* merlano.

whittle ['witl] *vt* tagliuzzare; **to w. down** assottigliare.

whiz(z) [wiz] *n* sibilo; *vi* sibilare, passare sibilando.

who [hu:] *pron interrog* chi; *rel* chi, che, il quale *etc.*

whoever [hu'evə] *pron indef* chiunque.

whole [houl] *a* intero, tutto; *n* il tutto, l'intero, il totale; **on the w.** nel complesso, tutto considerato.

whole-hearted ['houl'ha:tid] *a* caloroso, cordiale.

whole-heartedly ['houl'ha:tidli] *ad* calorosamente, cordialmente.

wholesale ['houlseil] *n* vendita all'ingrosso; *a ad* all'ingrosso.

wholesome ['houlsəm] *a* sano, salubre.

wholly ['houlli] *ad* completamente, del tutto.

whom [hu:m] *pron rel interrog* che, chi, il quale, la quale, i quali, le quali.

whooping cough ['hupiŋkɔf] *n* pertosse.

whore [hɔ:] *n* prostituta.

whortleberry ['wə:tl,beri] *n* mirtillo.

whose [hu:z] *pron rel interrog* di cui, il cui, del quale *etc*, di chi? a chi?

whosoever [,husou'evə] *pron indef* chiunque.

why [wai] *ad interrog* perchè; *interj* ma, ma certo, ma via; *n* il perchè, motivo, causa.

wick [wik] *n* lucignolo, stoppino.

wicked ['wikid] *a* maligno, malvagio, perfido, perverso.

wickedness ['wikidnis] *n* malignità, malvagità, perfidia, perversità.

wicker ['wikə] *n* vimine; **wickerwork** lavoro in vimini.

wicket ['wikit] *n* cancellino, porticina; (*cricket*) porta.

wide [waid] *a* largo, vasto; (*of material*) alto; *ad* bene, completamente; **w.-open** spalancato; **w.-awake** completamente sveglio; **widely** *ad* largamente, molto.

widen ['waidn] *vti* allargar(si), ampliar(si).

widespread ['waidspred] *a* esteso, diffuso.

widow ['widou] *n* vedova.

widower ['widouə] *n* vedovo.

width [widθ] *n* larghezza; (*of material*) altezza.

wield [wi:ld] *vt* tenere, maneggiare, reggere.

wieldy ['wi:ldi] *a* maneggevole.

wife [waif] *n* moglie.

wig [wig] *n* parrucca.

wigwam ['wigwæm] *n* 'wigwam', tenda di pellirosse.

wild [waild] *a* selvaggio, selvatico; tempestoso, violento.

wilderness ['wildənis] *n* deserto, landa solitaria, luogo selvaggio.

wildfire ['waild,faiə] *n* fuoco greco; lampo di caldo.

wildness ['waildnis] *n* selvatichezza, ferocia.

wile [wail] *n* astuzia, inganno; *vt* ingannare, adescare.

wilful ['wilful] *a* caparbio, ostinato; (*leg*) premeditato.

wilfulness ['wilfulnis] *n* ostinazione, caparbietà.

Wilhelmina [,wilhel'mi:nə] *nf pr* Guglielmina.

wiliness ['wailinis] *n* astuzia.

will [wil] *n* volontà; (*leg*) testamento; *vti* volere; disporre, lasciare per testamento; costringere.

William ['wiljəm] *nm pr* Guglielmo.

willing ['wiliŋ] *a* disposto (a), volonteroso; volontario.

willingly ['wiliŋli] *ad* volontieri.

willingness ['wiliŋnis] *n* buona volontà.

willow ['wilou] *n* salice.

willy-nilly ['wili'nili] *ad* volente o nolente.

Wilma ['wilmə] *nf pr* Vilma.

wilt [wilt] *vt* far appassire; *vi* appassire, languire.

wily ['waili] *a* astuto, malizioso.

wimple ['wimpl] *n* soggolo.

win [win] *n* successo, vittoria; *vt* vincere, conquistare, ottenere; persuadere; *vi* vincere.

wince [wins] *vi* ritrarsi improvvisamente, trasalire.

winch [wintʃ] *n* (*mech*) argano, manovella.

wind [waind] *vt* avvolgere; (*watch etc*) caricare; *vi* serpeggiare.

wind [wind] *n* vento; fiato; soffio; sentore.

windfall ['windfɔ:l] *n* frutto fatto cadere dal vento; (*fig*) fortuna inaspettata.

windlass ['windləs] n (mech) argano.
windmill ['winmil] n mulino a vento.
window ['windou] n finestra; vetrina.
windpipe ['windpaip] n trachea.
windscreen ['windskri:n] (US) **windshield** ['windʃi:ld] n (aut) parabrezza; **w. wiper** tergicristallo.
windward ['windwəd] n parte da cui spira il vento; a situato dalla parte da cui spira il vento; ad contro vento.
windy ['windi] a ventoso, esposto al vento; (fig) verboso, vuoto.
wine [wain] n vino; **wineglass** bicchiere da vino; **wineshop** osteria, spaccio di vini.
wing [wiŋ] n ala; volo; pl (theat) quinte; (aut) parafango.
winged [wiŋd] a alato.
wink [wiŋk] n batter d'occhio, ammicco, cenno; vi ammiccare, strizzar l'occhio, batter le palpebre; brillare con intermittenza.
winkle ['wiŋkl] n chiocciola di mare.
winner ['winə] n vincitore.
winning ['winiŋ] a vincente, vincitore; avvincente, attraente; n pl vincita.
winnow ['winou] vt vagliare, spulare, ventilare.
winsome ['winsəm] a (poet) pieno di grazia, amabile.
winter ['wintə] n inverno; a d'inverno, invernale; vi passare l'inverno, svernare.
wintry ['wintri] a invernale, freddo.
wipe [waip] n strofinata, asciugatura, spolverata; vt asciugare, pulire, strofinare.
wire ['waiə] n filo metallico; telegrafo, telegramma; vti assicurare con filo metallico; (el) installare fili elettrici; telegrafare.
wireless ['waiəlis] a senza fili; n radio; **w. valve** valvola.
wiry ['waiəri] a magro e nerboruto.
wisdom ['wizdəm] n saggezza, sapienza, prudenza, giudizio.
wise [waiz] a saggio, savio, prudente, avveduto; **none the wiser** senza saperne più di prima.
wish [wiʃ] n desiderio; augurio; cosa desiderata; vti desiderare, volere; augurare.
wishful ['wiʃful] a desideroso, bramoso; **w. thinking** un pio desiderio.
wisp [wisp] n ciuffo, ciuffetto, striscia; **will-o'-the-w.** fuoco fatuo.
wistaria [wis'teəriə] n glicine.
wistful ['wistful] a nostalgico, pensoso, preoccupato.
wit [wit] n spirito, arguzia; intelligenza; pl ingegno, cervello.
witch [witʃ] n strega, ammaliatrice.
witchcraft ['witʃkrɑ:ft] n magia, stregoneria.
witchery ['witʃəri] n incantesimo, fascino.
with [wið] prep con, insieme a; da;

presso; di, per; **to be w. it** essere aggiornato.
withdraw [wið'drɔ:] vti ritirar(si).
wither ['wiðə] vt far avvizzire; vi avvizzire, inaridirsi.
withhold [wið'hould] vt trattenere; rifiutare, negare.
within [wi'ðin] prep entro, dentro; in meno di, fra; ad dentro, all'interno.
without [wi'ðaut] prep senza (di), fuori di; ad fuori; n esterno.
withstand [wið'stænd] vt resistere a, opporsi a, sostenere.
witness ['witnis] n testimone, teste, testimonianza; vti testimoniare, essere presente a, firmare come teste; **w. box**, (US) **w. stand** banco dei testi.
witticism ['witisizəm] n frizzo, motto di spirito.
witty ['witi] a spiritoso.
wizard ['wizad] n mago, stregone.
wizardry ['wizədri] n magia, stregoneria.
wizened ['wiznd] a raggrinzito.
wobble ['wɔbl] vi barcollare, dondolare.
woe [wou] n (poet) dolore, sventura.
woeful ['wouful] a doloroso, triste.
wolf [wulf] n lupo; vt divorare.
wolfish ['wulfiʃ] a da lupo, crudele, vorace.
woman ['wumən] pl **women** ['wimin] n donna, -ne.
womanhood ['wumənhud] n condizione di donna, maturità della donna.
womanish ['wuməniʃ] a effeminato.
womanly ['wumənli] a femminile, di donna.
womb [wu:m] n grembo, utero.
wonder ['wʌndə] n meraviglia, miracolo, prodigio; vi meravigliarsi, domandarsi.
wonderful ['wʌndəful] a meraviglioso, prodigioso.
wonderland ['wʌndəlænd] n paese delle meraviglie.
woo [wu:] vt corteggiare, fare la corte a.
wood [wud] n bosco; legno; botte.
woodcut ['wudkʌt] n incisione su legno, xilografia.
wooded ['wudid] a boschivo, coperto di boschi.
wooden ['wudn] a di legno, legnoso; senz'espressione.
woodland ['wudlənd] n luogo boscoso.
woodman ['wudmən] pl **-men** n guarda boschi, guardia forestale, taglialegna.
woodpecker ['wud,pekə] n picchio.
woodwork ['wudwə:k] n lavoro in legno.
woodworm ['wudwə:m] n tarlo.
woody ['wudi] a boscoso; legnoso.
woof [wu:f] n tessitura, trama.
wool [wul] n lana.

woollen ['wulin] *a* di lana; *n* articolo di lana.

woolly ['wuli] *a* lanoso; *n* indumento di lana.

word [wəːd] *n* parola; *vt* esprimere con parole, mettere in parole.

wordy ['wəːdi] *a* verboso; consistente di parole.

work [wəːk] *n* lavoro; *pl* opere, lavori *pl*; meccanismo; macchinario; fabbrica, officina, stabilimento; *vt* lavorare; azionare; *vi* lavorare; funzionare; **to w. out** esaurire; calcolare; **t. w. up** eccitare.

workable ['wəːkəbl] *a* eseguibile, praticabile, realizzabile.

worker ['wəːkə] *n* lavoratore, operaio.

workhouse ['wəːkhaus] *n* ospizio di mendicità.

workman ['wəːkmən] *pl* **-men** *n* operaio, artigiano.

workmanship ['wəːkmənʃip] *n* abilità, tecnica, fattura.

workshop ['wəːkʃop] *n* laboratorio, officina.

world [wəːld] *n* mondo; **worldwide** mondiale.

worldliness ['wəːldlinis] *n* mondanità.

worldly ['wəːldli] *a* terreno, mondano.

worm [wəːm] *n* verme, baco, lombrico; *vti* muoversi insidiosamente; **w.-eaten** tarlato.

wormwood ['wəːmwud] *n* assenzio; (*fig*) mortificazione.

worn-out ['wɔːn'aut] *a* logoro; (*fig*) esausto, sfinito.

worry ['wʌri] *n* inquietudine, fastidio, preoccupazione; *vt* infastidire, importunare; *vi* preoccuparsi, tormentarsi.

worse [wəːs] *a* peggiore; *n* (il) peggio; *ad* peggio.

worsen ['wəːsn] *vti* peggiorare, aggravare, aggravarsi.

worship ['wəːʃip] *n* adorazione, culto; *vt* adorare, venerare; *vi* prestare culto.

worshipper ['wəːʃipə] *n* adoratore; *pl* i fedeli *pl*.

worst [wəːst] *a* (il) peggiore; *ad* (il) peggio; *vt* sopraffare.

worsted ['wəːstid] *n* pettinato di lana; *a* di lana pettinata.

worth [wəːθ] *a* degno di, meritevole di; del valore di; *n* valore, merito; **to be w.** valere; **to be worthwhile** valere la pena.

worthiness ['wəːðinis] *n* merito, rispettabilità.

worthless ['wəːθlis] *a* senza valore, indegno.

worthlessness ['wəːθlisnis] *n* mancanza di valore, indegnità.

worthy ['wəːði] *a* meritevole, degno; *n* persona illustre, personaggio.

would-be ['wudbiː] *a* sedicente; aspirante.

wound [wuːnd] *n* ferita; *vt* ferire.

wraith [reiθ] *n* fantasma, spettro.

wrangle ['ræŋgl] *n* alterco, rissa; *vi* altercare, azzuffarsi.

wrangler ['ræŋglə] *n* attaccabrighe; (*Cambridge*) studente che ha ottenuto la laurea con lode in matematica; (*US*) guardiano di cavalli.

wrap [ræp] *n* scialle; *vt* avvolgere; **w. up** *vi* avvolgersi, imbaccuccarsi.

wrapper ['ræpə] *n* accappatoio; fascia, copertina di libro; carta da imballo.

wrath [rɔːθ] *n* collera, ira.

wrathful ['rɔːθful] *a* furioso, irato.

wreak [riːk] *vt* sfogare, soddisfare il desiderio di.

wreath [riːθ] *n* ghirlanda, corona (funeraria).

wreathe [riːð] *vti* inghirlandare, intrecciare, attorcigliarsi.

wreck [rek] *n* naufragio, rovina, relitti *pl*; persona che ha ricevuto gravi colpi; *vt* far naufragare, rovinare, distruggere; *vi* naufragare, andare in pezzi.

wreckage ['rekidʒ] *n* naufragio, relitti, rottami *pl*.

wren [ren] *n* scricciolo.

wrench [rentʃ] *n* violento strappo, slogatura, storta; (*fig*) dolore, strazio; (*mech*) chiave inglese; *vt* strappare violentemente, (con)torcere, slogare; (*fig*) svisare.

wrest [rest] *vt* strappare.

wrestle ['resl] *vi* lottare, fare la lotta.

wrestling ['resliŋ] *n* lotta, (*sport*) lotta libera.

wrestler ['reslə] *n* lottatore.

wretch [retʃ] *n* miserabile, sciagurato.

wretched ['retʃid] *a* miserabile, misero, spregevole.

wretchedness ['retʃidnis] *n* infelicità, miseria, squallore.

wriggle ['rigl] *vi* contorcersi, dimenarsi.

wring [riŋ] *vti* torcere, torcersi, stringere, strizzare, spremere; estorcere.

wringer ['riŋə] *n* asciugatrice meccanica.

wrinkle ['riŋkl] *n* ruga, grinza; *vti* corrugare, increspare.

wrist [rist] *n* polso.

wristband ['ristbænd] *n* polsino.

writ [rit] *n* citazione, mandato, ordine.

write [rait] *vti* scrivere.

writer ['raitə] *n* scrivente, scrittore.

writhe [raið] *vi* contorcersi.

writing ['raitiŋ] *n* scrittura, calligrafia, lo scrivere; *pl* scritti *pl*; **w. paper** carta da lettera, carta da scrivere.

wrong [rɔŋ] *a* sbagliato, erroneo, inesatto, scorretto; ingiusto; *n* torto, danno, male; *vt* far torto a, giudicare erroneamente; **be w.** aver torto; *ad* male, erroneamente;

w.-doer peccatore, trasgressore, offensore.
wrongful ['rɔɲful] *a* ingiusto.
wrought [rɔːt] *a (di ferro)* battuto, lavorato; **w.-up** nervoso, agitato.
wry [rai] *a* contorto, storto; ironico.

X

Xanthippe [zæn'θipi] *n pr* Santippe; moglie bisbetica.
Xmas ['krisməs] *see* **Christmas**.
X-ray ['eks'rei] *a* di raggi X; **X-ray photograph** radiografia; *vt* sottoporre a raggi X.
X-rays ['eks'reiz] *n pl* raggi X *pl*.
xylography [zai'lɔgrəfi] *n* xilografia.
xylophone ['zailəfoun] *n (mus)* xilofono.

Y

yacht [jɔt] *n* panfilo, yacht.
yankee ['jæŋki] *a n (fam)* americano.
yap [jæp] *vi* guaire, uggiolare, abbaiare.
yard [jɑːd] *n* iarda *(misura di lunghezza=cm 91 circa)*; cortile, recinto.
yarn [jɑːn] *n* filato; *(tale)* racconto, storia; *vi (fam)* raccontare storie.
yawn [jɔːn] *n* sbadiglio; *vi* sbadigliare.
ye [jiː] *pron (poet)* voi; *def art (arc)* il *etc.*
year [jəː] *n* anno, annata; età.
yearling ['jəːliŋ] *n* animale di un anno.
yearly ['jəːli] *a* annuale, annuo; *ad* annualmente.
yearn [jəːn] *vi* **y. for** agognare, struggersi di.
yearning ['jəːniŋ] *n* desiderio ardente, struggimento.
yeast [jiːst] *n* lievito.
yell [jel] *n* urlo; *vi* urlare.
yellow ['jelou] *a n* giallo.
yellowish ['jelouiʃ] *a* giallastro, giallognolo.
yellowness ['jelounis] *n* color giallastro.
yelp [jelp] *n* guaito; *vi* guaire.
yeoman ['joumən] *n* piccolo proprietario terriero.
yeomanry ['joumənri] *n* classe dei piccoli proprietari terrieri; corpo di cavalleria volontaria.
yes [jes] *ad* sì.
yesterday ['jestədi] *n ad* ieri.
yet [jet] *ad* ancora, finora, tuttora; eppure, ciononondimeno; *cj* tuttavia.

yew (tree) ['juː(triː)] *n* tasso.
yield [jiːld] *n* raccolto, produzione; *vt* produrre, rendere; *vi* arrendersi, cedere.
yoghurt ['jɔgə(ː)t] *n* yogurt.
yoke [jouk] *n* giogo; coppia, paio; *vt* aggiogare, soggiogare.
yolk [jouk] *n* rosso d'uovo, tuorlo.
yonder ['jɔndə] *a* quello là; *ad* laggiù, lassù.
yore [jɔː] *n (poet)* tempo passato; **of y.** *ad* anticamente.
you [juː] *pron* tu, voi, ti, te, vi, ve, Lei, Loro.
young [jʌŋ] *a* giovane; *n* piccolo, piccoli, *(of animals)* prole.
youngster ['jʌŋstə] *n* ragazzo, giovane.
your [jɔː] *a* (il) tuo *etc*, (il) vostro *etc*; **yours** *pron* (il) tuo *etc*, (il) vostro *etc*; **yourself** *pron* tu stesso, te stesso, ti; **yourselves** *pl pron* voi stessi, vi *etc pl*.
youth [juːθ] *n* giovane, gioventù, giovinezza.
youthful ['juːθful] *a* giovanile.
youthfulness ['juːθfulnis] *n* aspetto, spirito giovanile.
Yugoslavia ['jugou'slɑːviə] *n* Jugoslavia.
Yule [juːl] *n* Natale, feste natalizie; **y. log** ceppo di Natale.

Z

Zagreb ['zɑːgreb] *n* Zagabria.
zany ['zeini] *n* buffone, zanni.
zeal [ziːl] *n* zelo.
zealot ['zelət] *n* fanatico, zelatore.
zealous ['zeləs] *a* zelante.
zebra ['ziːbrə] *n* zebra.
zenith ['zeniθ] *n* zenit; *(fig)* culmine, apice.
zephyr ['zefə] *n* zeffiro, brezza.
zero ['ziərou] *n* zero.
zest [zest] *n* sapore piccante; *(fig)* gusto, interesse.
zigzag ['zigzæg] *n* zig-zag; *a ad* a zig-zag; *vi* andare a zig-zag, zigzagare.
zinc [ziŋk] *n* zinco.
zip [zip] *n* chiusura lampo.
zither ['ziðə] *pl* **zithern** *n (mus)* cetra tirolese.
zodiac ['zoudiæk] *n* zodiaco.
zodiacal [zou'daiəkəl] *a* zodiacale.
zone [zoun] *n* zona.
zoo [zuː] *n* giardino zoologico, zoo.
zoologist [zou'ɔlɔdʒist] *n* zoologo.
zoology [zou'ɔlɔdʒi] *n* zoologia.
Zulu ['zuːluː] *a n* Zulù.
Zurich ['zjuərik] *n* Zurigo.

Italian Grammar—Grammatica italiana

GENDER OF NOUNS

In Italian there are two genders: masculine and feminine.

Masculine
- nouns ending in **o** (exceptions: **la màno** etc.)
- nouns ending in **i** (exceptions: nouns of Greek origin, like **la crísi, la diòcesi, la tèsi** etc.)

Feminine
- nouns ending in **a** (exceptions: some words ending in **ta** and **ma** of Greek origin, like **il telegràmma, il dràmma, il poèma** etc.)

Nouns ending in **e** are sometimes masculine, sometimes feminine.

The following are masculine: nouns referring to male human beings and animals, names of fruit trees (whose corresponding fruit is feminine) names of months, days, mountains, lakes.

The following are feminine: nouns referring to female human beings and animals; names of fruits (whose corresponding tree is masculine); names of islands, abstract nouns indicating quality.

PLURAL OF NOUNS AND ADJECTIVES

The plural of masculine nouns and adjectives is **i**: **artísta, artísti; càne, càni; pòrto, pòrti.**

The plural of feminine nouns and adjectives is **e** if the word in the singular ends in **a**: **pàtria, pàtrie.** It is **i** if the singular ends in **e**: **nàve, nàvi.** Exceptions: **àla** (wing), **àli.** The word **màno** (hand) is feminine and its plural is **màni.**

Note:—

1. Nouns and adjectives ending in the singular in **ca** and **ga** end in the plural in **che** and **ghe** if they are feminine; in **chi** and **ghi** if they are masculine: **amíca** (lady friend), **amíche; dúca** (duke), **dúchi; stréga** (witch), **stréghe; collèga** (colleague), **collèghi.** Exception: **bèlga** (Belgian), **bèlgi** (m.)

2. Nouns and adjectives ending in the singular in **cia** and **gia** end in the plural in **e** keeping the **i** if it is stressed, omitting it if it is not: **bugía** (lie), **bugíe; fàccia** (face) **fàcce.** Sometimes—to avoid ambiguity—the unaccented **i** is kept, as in the noun **audàcia** (daring), **audàcie,** to distinguish it from the adjective **audàce** (bold).

3. Nouns and adjectives ending in the singular in **io** end in the plural in **ii** if the **i** of **io** is stressed; if it is unstressed the plural is simply **i**: **zío** (uncle), **zíi**; **fàggio** (beech tree), **fàggi**. Again, to avoid ambiguity the **i**, even if unstressed, is sometimes retained: **òdio** (hatred), **òdii**, to distinguish it from **òde** (ode), **òdi**.

4. Nouns and adjectives consisting of two syllables and ending in the singular in **co** and **go** end in the plural in **chi** and **ghi**: **biànco** (white) **biànchi**; **làgo** (lake) **làghi**. Exceptions: **pòrco** (pig), **pòrci**; **grèco** (Greek), **grèci**.

5. Nouns and adjectives of more than two syllables, ending in the singular in **co** and **go** end in the plural in **chi** and **ghi** if **co** and **go** are preceded by a consonant: **almanàcco** (almanac) **almanàcchi**; **albèrgo** (hotel), **albèrghi**. They end in **ci** and **gi** if **co** and **go** are preceded by a vowel: **amíco** (friend), **amíci** etc. This category, however, presents a considerable number of exceptions. To help the student we have indicated in the Dictionary all the exceptions concerning (2) and (3) and the plural of all the words—regular or exceptions —concerning (4) and (5).

6. Some nouns change their gender in the plural: singular **uòvo** (egg), **uòva**; **díti** (finger), **díta** etc. There are nouns which have two plurals with different meanings: **úrlo** (shout), **úrli** (cries of animals), **úrla** (shouts of human beings). Such irregularities and peculiarities have been indicated in the Dictionary.

7. Some nouns are used only in the singular (**pròle, sàngue, mièle, fàme**); some only in the plural (**esèquie, fòrbici, occhiàli, nòzze**, etc.)

8. Some nouns have the same form both for the singular and for the plural. They are: words accented on the last syllable; *e.g.* la **città**, le **città** (city, cities); monosyllables, *e.g.* il **re**, i **re** (king, kings); surnames; words ending in a consonant, *e.g.* il **gas**, i **gas** (gas, gasses); compounds made of a verb and of a plural noun, *e.g.* il **portalèttere**, i **portalèttere** (postman, postmen); nouns ending in **ie**, *e.g.* **progènie** (progeny). Exceptions to this are **superfície** (surface) and **móglie** (wife) which, in the plural become **superfíci** and **mógli**.

9. Compounds, other than those mentioned in (8), form their plural as follows: some change into plural only the second part of the word, *e.g.* **cartapècora** (parchment) **cartapècore**. Some have both parts in plural form *e.g.* **mezzanòtte** (midnight) **mezzenòtti**.

Compounds of **càpo** either change both parts *e.g.*
capocuòco (chef), **capicuòchi**, or use the plural only
in the first part, *e.g.* **caposquàdra** (foreman, group-
leader), **capisquàdra**, or only in the second, *e.g.*
capolavóro (masterpiece), **capolavóri**. These plurals
are duly indicated in their place in the Dictionary.

10. Some words have an entirely irregular plural: **uòmo**
(man), **uòmini**; **dío** (god), **dèi**; **búe** (ox), **buoi**;
mílle (one thousand), **míla**.

FEMININE OF NOUNS AND ADJECTIVES

When the masculine noun or adjective ends in **o** the
feminine ends in **a**: **il maéstro, la maéstra**.

When the masculine noun or adjective ends in **e** the
feminine ends in **e**: **il nipóte, la nipóte**.

When the masculine noun or adjective ends in **a** the
feminine ends in **a**: **un artísta, un' artísta**.

When the masculine noun or adjective ends in **ière** the
feminine ends in **ièra**: **il consiglière, la consiglièra**.

When the masculine noun or adjective ends in **tóre** the
feminine ends in **tríce**: **il pittóre, la pittríce**. Exception:
il fattóre (the land agent), **la fattóra**, or **la fattoréssa**.

There are some exceptions like: **studènte, studentéssa**
(student); **avvocàto, avvocatéssa** (lawyer, lady lawyer)
etc. These are indicated in the Dictionary. Names of animals
ending in **e** and **u** are common: *e.g.* **il lèpre, la lèpre** (the
hare); **il gru, la gru** (the crane). Some have no feminine:
e.g. **il tòpo** (the mouse), **il coníglio** (the rabbit). Some have
no masculine: *e.g.* **la vòlpe** (the fox), **l'àquila** (the eagle).
In these cases the word **fémmina** (female) or the word
màschio (male) is added as explicatory: *e.g.* **il tòpo
fémmina** (or **la fémmina del tòpo**), **la vòlpe màschio**
etc.

Italian Verbs—Verbi Italiani

PROGRESSIVE FORM

In Italian there are three progressive tenses: the present, the past and the future, formed respectively by the Present Indicative, the Imperfect and the Future of **stàre** and less frequently **andàre**; *e.g.* he is sleeping, **sta dormèndo**; he was sleeping, **stava dormèndo**; he will be sleeping, **starà dormèndo**. These tenses can be rendered in Italian by the simple tense; *e.g.* he is sleeping, **dorme**.

ORTHOGRAPHIC CHANGES OF SOME VERBS IN–ÀRE

1. Verbs ending in **càre** and **gàre**, as **pagàre**, **cercàre**, when the **c** or **g** is followed by **e** or **i**, take in **h** in order to preserve the hard sound of the consonant; *e.g.* **paghiàmo**, **cercherò**.
2. Verbs in **ciàre** and **giàre**, as **cominciàre**, **mangiàre**, drop the **i** before **e** or **i**; *e.g.* **màngi**, **mangerò**.
3. Verbs in **iàre** having a sounded **i**, as **spiàre**, **inviàre**, retain the **i** except before **iàmo** and **iàte**; *e.g.* **invìi**, **spierémo**, **inviàmo**, **spiàte**.
4. Verbs in **iàre** where the **i** is not sounded, as **pigliàre**, **invecchiàre**, **annoiàre**, drop the **i** when followed by another **i**; *e.g.* **pìgli**, **pìglio**, **invècchi**.

NOTE ON THE VERBS IN–ÍRE

Verbs in –**íre** take the terminations **ísco**, **ísci**, **ísce**, **íscono** in the 1st, 2nd, and 3rd singular, and in the 3rd plural of the Indicative. Similarly in the Present Subjunctive and in the Imperative.

Regular Verbs

Conjugation 1	Conjugation 2	Conjugation 3
	INFINITIVE	
Parlàre. to speak	**Temére,** to fear	**Sentíre,** to hear
	PRESENT INDICATIVE	
I speak	*I fear*	*I hear*
io pàrl-o	tém-o	sènt-o
tu pàrl-i	tém-i	sènt-i
egli pàrl-a	tém-e	sènt-e
noi parl-iàmo	tem-iàmo	sent-iàmo
voi parl-àte	tem-éte	sent-íte
essi pàrl-ano	tém-ono	sènt-ono

399

I used to speak	*I used to fear*	*I used to hear*
io parl-àvo	tem-évo	sent-ívo
tu parl-àvi	tem-évi	sent-ívi
egli parl-àva	tem-éva	sent-íva
noi parl-avàmo	tem-evàmo	sent-ivàmo
voi parl-avàte	tem-evàte	sent-ivàte
essi parl-àvano	tem-évano	sent-ívano

GERUND

parl-àndo, *speaking*	tem-èndo, *fearing*	sent-èndo, *hearing*

PAST PARTICIPLE

parl-àto, *spoken*	tem-úto, *feared*	sent-íto, *heard*

Subjunctive

PRESENT

that I speak	*that I fear*	*that I hear*
ch'io-pàrl-i	ch'io tém-a	ch'io sènt-a
che tu pàrl-i	che tu tém-a	che tu sènt-a
ch'egli pàrl-i	ch'egli tém-a	ch'egli sènt-a
che noi parl-iàmo	che noi tem-iàmo	che noi sent-iàmo
che voi parl-iàte	che voi tem-iàte	che voi sent-iàte
ch'essi pàrl-ino	che essi tém-ano	ch'essi sènt-ano

IMPERFECT

If I spoke	*if I feared*	*if I heard*
se io parl-àssi	tem-éssi	sent-íssi
se tu parl-àssi	tem-éssi	sent-íssi
se egli parl-àsse	tem-ésse	sent-ísse
se noi parl-àssimo	tem-éssimo	sent-íssimo
se voi parl-àste	tem-éste	sente-íste
se essi parl-àssero	tem-éssero	sent-íssero

Compound Tenses

Perfect	io ho	⎫ parlàto	*I have*	⎫ *spoken,*
Pluperfect	io avévo		*I had*	
2nd Pluperf.	io èbbi		*I had*	
2nd Future	io avrò	or	*I shall have*	or
2nd Condit.	io avrèi		*I should have*	
		⎫ temúto,		⎫ *feared,*
Subj. Perfect.	ch'io àbbia		*that I have*	
Subj. Pluperf.	se io avéssi	or	*if I had*	or
Past Infin.	avér(e)		*to have*	
Past Gerund	avèndo	⎭ sentíto	*having*	⎭ *heard*

PAST DEFINITE

I spoke	*I feared*	*I heard*
io parl-ài	tem-éi or -étti	sent-íi
tu parl-àsti	tem-ésti	sent-ísti
egli parl-ò	tem-è or -ètte	sent-í
noi parl-àmmo	tem-émmo	sent-ímmo
voi parl-àste	tem-éste	sent-íste
essi parl-àrono	tem-érono or -èttero	sent-írono

I shall speak	*I shall fear*	*I shall hear*
io parl-erò	tem-erò	sent-irò
tu parl-eràí	tem-eràí	sent-iràí
egli parl-erà	tem-erà	sent-irà
noi parl-erémo	tem-erémo	sent-irémo
voi parl-eréte	tem-eréte	sent-iréte
essi parl-erànno	tem-erànno	sent-irànno

CONDITIONAL

I should speak	*I should fear*	*I should hear*
io parl-erèi	tem-erèi	sent-irèi
tu parl-erésti	tem-erésti	sent-irésti
egli parl-erèbbe	tem-erèbbe	sent-irèbbe
noi parl-erèmmo	tem-erèmmo	sent-irèmmo
voi parl-eréste	tem-eréste	sent-iréste
essi parl-erèbbero	tem-erèbbero	sent-irèbbero

IMPERATIVE

speak	*fear*	*hear*
pàrl-a	tém-i	sènt-i
pàrl-i	tém-a	sènt-a
parl-iàmo	tem-iàmo	sent-iàmo
parl-àte	tem-éte	sent-íte
pàrl-ino	tém-ano	sént-ano

PRESENT INFINITIVE

parl-àre, *to speak*   tem-ére, *to fear*   sent-íre, *to hear*

PRESENT PARTICIPLE

parl-ànte, *speaking*   tem-ènte, *fearing*   sent-ènte, *hearing*

Auxiliary Verbs

NOTE: **Veníre** and **andàre** may be used as auxiliaries instead of **èssere** with a past participle or with a gerund.

Èssere, to be   **Avére**, to have

PRESENT INDICATIVE

I am	*I have*
io sóno	io ho
tu sèi	tu hai
egli ⎱ è	egli ⎱ ha
essa ⎰	essa ⎰
noi siàmo	noi abbiàmo
voi siète	voi avéte
essi ⎱ sóno	essi ⎱ hànno
esse ⎰	esse ⎰

I was	*I had*
io èro	io avévo
tu èri	tu avévi
egli èra	egli avéva
noi eravàmo	noi avevàmo
voi eravàte	voi avevàte
essi èrano	essi avévano

PAST DEFINITE

I was	*I had*
io fúi	io èbbi
tu fósti	tu avésti
egli fu	egli èbbe
noi fúmmo	noi avémmo
voi fóste	voi avéste
essi fúrono	essi èbbero

FUTURE

I shall be	*I shall have*
io sarò	io avrò
tu sarài	tu avrài
egli sarà	egli avrà
noi sarémo	noi avrémo
voi saréte	voi avréte
essi sarànno	essi avrànno

CONDITIONAL

I should be	*I should have*
io sarèi	io avrèi
tu sarésti	tu avrésti
egli sarèbbe	egli avrèbbe
noi sarèmmo	noi avrémmo
voi saréste	voi avréste
essi sarèbbero	essi avrèbbero

IMPERATIVE

be	*have*
síi	àbbi
sía	àbbia
siàmo	abbiàmo
siàte	abbiàte
síano	àbbiano

INFINITIVE

èssere, *to be*	avére, *to have*

GERUND

essèndo, *being*	avèndo, *having*

PAST PARTICIPLE

stàto, stàta }been	avúto, avúta }had
stàti, stàte	avúti, avúte

402

Compound Tenses

I have been
io sóno stàto
tu sèi stàto
egli è stàto }
essa è stàta }
noi siàmo stàti
voi siète stàti
essi sóno stàti }
esse sóno stàte }

I have had
io ho avúto
tu hai avúto
egli } ha avúto
essa }
noi abbiàmo avúto
voi avéte avúto
essi } hànno avúto
esse }

PLUPERFECT

I had been
io èro stàto
tu èri stàto
egli èra stàto }
essa èra stàta }
noi eravàmo stàti
voi eravàte stàti
essi èrano stàti }
esse èrano stàte }

I had had
io avévo avúto
tu avévi avúto
egli } avéva avúto
essa }
noi avevàmo avúto
voi avevàte avúto
essi } avévano avúto
esse }

SECOND PLUPERFECT

I had been
io fúi stàto
tu fósti stàto
egli fu stàto }
essa fu stàta }
noi fúmmo stàti
voi fóste stàti
essi fúrono stàti }
esse fúrono stàte }

I had had
io èbbi avúto
tu avésti avúto
egli } èbbe avúto
essa }
noi avémmo avúto
voi avéste avúto
essi } èbbero avúto
esse }

FUTURE PERFECT

I shall have been
io sarò stàto
tu sarài stàto
egli sarà stàto }
essa sarà stàta }
noi sarémo stàti
voi saréte stàti
essi sarànno stàti }
esse sarànno stàte }

I shall have had
io avrò avúto
tu avrài avúto
egli } avrà avúto
essa }
noi avrémo avúto
voi avréte avúto
essi } avrànno avúto
esse }

PERFECT CONDITIONAL

I should have been
io sarèi stàto
tu sarésti stàto
egli sarèbbe stàto }
essa sarèbbe stàta }

I should have had
io avrèi avúto
tu avrésti avúto
egli } avrèbbe avúto
essa }

noi sarémmo stàti   noi avrémmo avúto
voi saréste stàti   voi avréste avúto

essi sarèbbero stàti }
esse sarèbbero stàte }

essi }
esse } avrèbbero avúto

to have been   *to have had*
èssere stàto   avére avúto
èssere stàta   avére avúta

having been   *having had*
essèndo stàto   avèndo avúto
essèndo stàta   avèndo avúta

that I be   *that I have*
ch'io sía   ch'io àbbia
che tu sía   che tu àbbia
che egli sía   che egli àbbia
che noi siàmo   che noi abbiàmo
che voi siàte   che voi abbiàte
che essi síano   che essi àbbiano

if I were   *if I had*
se io fóssi   se io avéssi
se tu fóssi   se tu avéssi
se egli fósse   se egli avésse
se noi fóssimo   se noi avéssimo
se voi fóste   se voi avéste
se essi fóssero   se essi avéssero

that I have been   *that I have had*
ch'io sía stàto   ch'io àbbia avúto
che tu sía stàto   che tu àbbia avúto

che egli sía stàto }
che essa sía stàta }

che egli }
che essa } àbbia avúto

che noi siàmo stàti   che noi abbiàmo avúto
che voi siàte stàti   che voi abbiàte avúto

che essi síano stàti }
che esse síano stàte }

che essi }
che esse } àbbiano avúto

if I had been   *if I had had*
se io fóssi stàto   se io avéssi avúto
se tu fóssi stàto   se tu avéssi avúto

se egli fósse stàto }
se essa fósse stàta }

se egli avésse avúto }
se essa avésse avúto }

se noi fóssimo stàti   se noi avéssimo avúto
se voi fóste stàti   se voi avéste avúto

se essi fóssero stàti }
se esse fóssero stàte }

se essi avéssero avúto }
se esse avéssero avúto }

The following regular verbs in –íre do not insert **ìsc**:

apríre	to open	**àpro**	**dormíre**	to sleep	**dòrmo**	
copríre	to cover	**còpro**	**fuggíre**	to escape	**fúggo**	
cucíre	to sew	**cúcio**	**partíre**	to depart	**pàrto**	
pentírsi	to repent	**mi pènto**	**servíre**	to serve	**sèrvo**	
seguíre	to follow	**séguo**	**vestíre**	to dress	**vèsto**	
sentíre	to hear, feel	**sènto**				

Bollíre (to boil) when used intransitively prefers not to
insert **ìsc**.

Nutríre (to nourish) uses either form.

Irregular Verbs

Accèndere *to light*
past accesi, accendesti, accese, accendemmo, ac-
cendeste, accésero
past part. acceso

Acclúdere *to enclose*
past acclusi, accludesti, accluse, accludemmo, ac-
cludeste, acclúsero
past part. accluso

Addúrre *to adduce*
past addussi, adducesti, addusse, adducemmo, ad-
duceste, addússero
fut. addurrò
cond. addurrei
past part. addotto

Adémpiere, Adempíre *to accomplish*
pres. ind. adempio, adempi, adempie, adempiamo, adempite, adémpiono
pres. sub. adempia
imper. adempi, adempia, adempite, adémpiano
past adempii, adempisti, adempí, adempimmo,
adempiste, adempirono
past part. adempito *or* adempiuto

Afflíggere *to afflict*
past afflissi, affliggesti, afflisse, affliggemmo, afflig-
geste, afflíssero
past part. afflitto

Allúdere *to allude*
past allusi, alludesti, alluse, alludemmo, alludeste,
allúsero
past part. alluso

Andàre   *to go*
pres. ind.   vado, vai, va, andiamo, andate, vanno
pres. sub.   vada, vada, vada, andiamo, andiate, vàdano
imp.   vai *or* va', vada, andiamo, andate, vàdano
fut.   andrò
cond.   andrei

Annèttere   *to annex*
past   annessi, annettesti, annesse, annettemmo, annetteste, annèssero
past part.   annesso

Apparíre   *to appear*
pres. ind.   apparisco *or* appaio, apparisci *or* appari, apparisce *or* appare, appariamo, apparite, apparíscono *or* appàiono
past   apparvi *or* apparii, apparisti, apparve *or* apparí *or* apparse, apparimmo, appariste, appàrvero *or* apparírono *or* appàrsero
pres. sub.   apparisca *or* appaia, apparisca *or* appaia, apparisca *or* appaia, appariamo, appariate, apparíscano *or* appàiano
imper.   apparisci *or* appari, apparisca *or* appaia, apparite, apparíscano *or* appàiano
past. part.   apparso

Appèndere   *to hang*
past   appesi, appendesti, appese, appendemmo, appendeste, appésero
past. part.   appeso

Apríre   *to open*
pres. ind.   apro, apri, apre, apriamo, aprite, àprono
past   aprii, *or* apersi, apristi, aprí *or* aperse, aprimmo, apriste, aprírono *or* apèrsero
past. part.   aperto

Àrdere   *to burn*
past   arsi, ardesti, arse, ardemmo, ardeste, àrsero
past. part.   arso

Aspèrgere   *to sprinkle*
past   aspersi, aspergesti, asperse, aspergemmo, aspergeste, aspèrsero
past. part.   asperso

Assalíre   *to assail*
pres. ind.   assalgo *or* assalisco, assali *or* assalisci, assale *or* assalisce, assaliamo, assalite, assàlgono *or* assalíscono

past	assalii *or* assalsi, assalisti, assalì *or* assalse, assalimmo, assaliste, assalírono *or* assàlsero
pres. sub.	assalga *or* assalisca, assalga *or* assalisca, assalga *or* assalisca, assaliamo, assaliate, assàlgano *or* assalíscano

Assídersi   *to take one's seat*

past	mi assisi, ti assidesti, si assise, ci assidemmo, vi assideste, si assísero
past part.	assiso

Assístere   *to assist*

past	assistei *or* assistetti, assistesti, assistè *or* assistette, assistemmo, assisteste, assistérono or assistèttero
past part.	assistito

Assòlvere   *to absolve*

past	assolsi *or* assolvei *or* assolvetti, assolvesti, assolse *or* assolvette, assolvemmo, assolveste, assòlsero *or* assolvèttero
past part.	assolto *or* assoluto

Assorbíre   *to absorb*

pres.	assorbo *or* assorbisco, assorbi *or* assorbisci, assorbe *or* assorbisce, assorbiamo, assorbite, assòrbono *or* assorbíscono
past part.	assorbito *or* assorto

Assúmere   *to assume*

past	assunsi, assumesti, assunse, assumemmo, assumeste, assúnsero
past part.	assunto

Assúrgere   *to rise*

past	assursi, assurgesti, assurse, assurgemmo, assurgeste, assursero
past part.	assurto

Bére   *to drink*

pres. ind.	bevo, bevi, beve, beviamo, bevete, bévono
imp. ind.	bevevo, bevevi, beveva, bevevamo, bevevate, bevévano
past	bevvi *or* bevei, bevesti, bevve *or* bevè *or* bevette, bevemmo, beveste, bèvvero *or* bevérono *or* bevèttero
fut.	berrò
cond.	berrei
pres. sub.	beva
imp. sub.	bevessi
imper.	bevi, beva, bevete, bévano
past part.	bevuto

Cadére   *to fall*
past   caddi, cadesti, cadde, cademmo, cadeste, càddero
fut.   cadrò
cond.   cadrei

Cèdere   *to give*
past   cedei *or* cedetti, cedesti, cedè *or* cedette, cedemmo, cedeste, cedérono *or* cedèttero

Chiédere   *to ask*
past   chiesi, chiedesti, chiese, chiedemmo, chiedeste, chiésero
past part. chiesto

Chiúdere   *to close*
past   chiusi, chiudesti, chiuse, chiudemmo, chiudeste, chiúsero
past part. chiuso

Cíngere   *to gird*
past   cinsi, cingesti, cinse, cingemmo, cingeste, cínsero
past part. cinto

Cògliere   *to gather*
pres. ind. colgo, cogli, coglie, cogliamo, cogliete, còlgono
past   colsi, cogliesti, colse, cogliemmo, coglieste, còlsero
pres. sub. colga, colga, colga, cogliamo, cogliate, còlgano
past part. colto

Còmpiere, Compíre   *to complete*
pres. ind. cómpio, compi, cómpie, compiamo, compite, cómpiono
past   compii, compisti, compí, compimmo, compiste, compírono
pres. sub. compia
imper.   compi, cómpia, compite, cómpiano
past part. complto *or* compiúto

Comprímere   *to compress*
past   compressi, comprimesti, compresse, comprimemmo, comprimeste, comprèssero
past part. compresso

Conóscere   *to know*
past   conobbi, conoscesti, conobbe, conoscemmo, conosceste, conòbbero

Contúndere   *to bruise*
past   contusi, contundesti, contuse, contundemmo, contundeste, contúsero
past part. contuso

Convèrgere *to converge*
past	conversi *or* convergei, convergesti, converse *or* convergè, convergemmo, convergeste, convèrsero *or* convergèrono
past part.	converso

Copríre *to cover*
pres. ind.	copro, copri, copre, copriamo, coprite, còprono
past	coprii *or* copersi, copristi, coprí *or* coperse, coprimmo, copriste, coprírono *or* copèrsero
past part.	coperto

Córrere *to run*
past	corsi, corresti, corse, corremmo, correste, córsero
past part.	corso

Créscere *to grow*
past	crebbi, crescesti, crebbe, crescemmo, cresceste, crébbero

Cuòcere *to cook*
pres. ind.	cuocio, cuoci, cuoce, cociamo, cocete, cuòciono
past	cossi, cocesti, cosse, cocemmo, coceste, còssero
past part.	cotto

Dàre *to give*
pres. ind.	do, dài, dà, diamo, date, dànno
imp. ind.	davo
past	diedi, desti, diede, demmo, deste, dièdero
fut.	darò
pres. sub.	dia
imp. sub.	dessi
cond.	darei
imper.	da, dia, date, díano
pres. part.	dando
past part.	dato

Decídere *to decide*
past	decisi, decidesti, decise, decidemmo, decideste, decísero
past part.	deciso

Devòlvere *to devolve*
past	devolvei *or* devolvetti, devolvesti, devolvè *or* devolvette, devolvemmo, devolveste, devolvérono *or* devolvèttero
past part.	devoluto

Difèndere *to defend*
past	difesi, difendesti, difese, difendemmo, difendeste, difésero
past part.	difeso

Díre *to say*
pres. ind.	dico, dici, dice, diciamo, dite, dícono
imp. ind.	dicevo
past	dissi, dicesti, disse, dicemmo, diceste, díssero
fut.	dirò
pres. sub.	dica
imp. subj.	dicesse
cond.	direi
imper.	di', dica, dite, dìcano
pres. part.	dicendo
past part.	detto

Dirígere *to direct*
past	diressi, dirigesti, diresse, dirigemmo, dirigeste, dirèssero
past part.	diretto

Discútere *to discuss*
past	discussi *or* discutei, discutesti, discusse *or* discutè, discutemmo, discuteste, discússero *or* discutérono
past part.	discusso

Distínguere *to distinguish*
past	distinsi, distinguesti, distinse, distinguemmo, distingueste, distínsero
past part.	distinto

Divídere *to divide*
past	divisi, dividesti, divise, dividemmo, divideste, divísero
past part.	diviso

Dolérsi *to regret*
pres. ind.	mi dolgo, ti duoli, si duole, ci doliamo *or* dogliamo, vi dolete, si dólgono
past	mi dolsi, ti dolesti, si dolse, ci dolemmo, vi doleste, si dólsero
fut.	mi dorrò
pres. sub.	mi dolga, ti dolga, si dolga, ci doliamo, vi doliate, si dólgano
imp. sub.	mi dolessi
cond.	mi dorrei
imper.	duoliti, si dolga, doletevi, si dólgano
pres. part.	dolente
past part.	dolutosi

Dovére *to have to*

pres. ind.	devo *or* debbo, devi, deve, dobbiamo, dovete, dévono *or* dèbbono
past	dovei *or* dovetti, dovesti, dovè *or* dovette, dovemmo, doveste, dovérono *or* dovèttero
fut.	— dovrò
pres. sub.	deva *or* debba, deva *or* debba, deva *or* debba, dobbiamo, dobbiate, dévano *or* dèbbono
imper.	devi, deve, dovete, dévono
past part.	dovuto

Emèrgere *to emerge*

past	emersi, emergesti, emerse, emergemmo, emergeste, emèrsero
past part.	emerso

Émpiere *to fill: conjugate like* **empíre**

Empíre *to fill*

pres. ind.	empio, empi, empie, empiamo, empite, émpiono
pres. sub.	empia, empia, empia, empiamo, empiate, émpiano
imper.	empi, empia, empite, émpiano
pres. part.	empiente

Èrgere *to raise*

past	ersi, ergesti, erse, ergemmo, ergeste, èrsero
past part.	erto

Esauríre *to exhaust*

past part.	esaurito *or* esàusto

Esígere *to exact*

past	esigei *or* esigetti, esigesti, esigè *or* esigette, esigemmo, esigeste, esigérono *or* esigèttero
past part.	esatto

Esímere *to exempt*

past	esimei *or* esimetti, esimesti, esimè *or* esimette, esimemmo, esimeste, esimérono *or* esimèttero
past part.	Not used. Use esente or esentato

Espèllere *to expel*

past	espulsi, espellesti, espulse, espellemmo, espelleste, espúlsero
past part.	espulso

Esplòdere *to explode*

past	esplosi, esplodesti, esplose, esplodemmo, esplodeste, esplòsero
past part.	esploso

Evàdere *to escape*

past	evasi, evadesti, evase, evademmo, evadeste, evàsero
past part.	evaso

Fàre *to do, make*

pres. ind.	faccio *or* fo, fai, fa, facciamo, fate, fanno
imp. ind.	facevo
past	feci, facesti, fece, facemmo, faceste, fécero
fut.	farò
cond.	farei
pres. sub.	faccia
imp. sub.	facessi
imper.	fai *or* fa', faccia, fate, fàcciano
pres. part.	facente
past part.	fatto

Fèndere *to split*

past	fendei *or* fendetti, fendesti, fendè *or* fendette, fendemmo, fendeste, fendérono *or* fendèttero
past part.	fesso *or* fenduto

Fìggere *to fix*

past	fissi, figgesti, fisse, figgemmo, figgeste, fìssero
past part.	fitto

Flèttere *to bend*

past	flettei *or* flessi, flettesti, flettè *or* flesse, flettemmo, fletteste, flettérono *or* flèssero
past part.	flesso

Fóndere *to melt*

past	fusi, fondesti, fuse, fondemmo, fondeste, fúsero
past part.	fuso

Fràngere *to break*

past	fransi, frangesti, franse, frangemmo, frangeste, frànsero
past part.	franto

Frìggere *to fry*

past	frissi, friggesti, frisse, friggemmo, friggeste, frìssero
past part.	fritto

Giacére *to lie*

pres. ind.	giaccio, giaci, giace, giacciamo *or* giaciamo, giacete, giàcciono
past	giacqui, giacesti, giacque, giacemmo, giaceste, giàcquero
pres. sub.	giaccia
past part.	giaciuto

Indúlgere   *to indulge*
past   indulsi, indulgesti, indulse, indulgemmo, indulgeste, indúlsero
past part.   indulto

Inferíre   *to infer*
past   inferii *or* infersi, inferisti, inferí *or* inferse, inferimmo, inferiste, inferírono *or* infèrsero
past part.   inferito *or* inferto

Inseríre   *to insert*
past part.   inserito *or* (*rare*) inserto

Intrúdere   *to intrude*
past   intrusi, intrudesti, intruse, intrudemmo, intrudeste, intrúsero
past part.   intruso

Lèdere   *to offend*
past   lesi, ledesti, lese, ledemmo, ledeste, lèsero
past part.   leso

Lèggere   *to read*
past   lessi, leggesti, lesse, leggemmo, leggeste, lèssero
past part.   letto

Méscere   *to pour*
pres. ind.   mesco, mesci, mesce, mesciamo, mescete, méscono
pres. sub.   mesca, mesca, mesca, mesciamo, mesciate, méscano
past part.   mesciuto *or* misto

Méttere   *to place*
past   misi, mettesti, mise, mettemmo, metteste, mísero
past part.   messo

Mòrdere   *to bite*
past   morsi, mordesti, morse, mordemmo, mordeste, mòrsero
past part.   morso

Moríre   *to die*
pres. ind.   muoio, muori, muore, moriàmo, morite, muòiono
fut.   morirò *or* morrò, morirai *or* morrai, morirà *or* morrà, moriremo *or* morremo, morirete *or* morrete, morirànno *or* morrànno
cond.   morirei *or* morrei, moriresti *or* morresti, morirebbe *or* morrebbe, moriremmo *or* morremmo, morireste *or* morreste, morirèbbero *or* morrèbbero

pres. sub.	muoia, muoia, muoia, moriamo, moriate, muòiano
imper.	muori, muoia, morite, muòiano
past part.	morto

Múngere *to milk*

past	munsi, mungesti, munse, mungemmo, mungeste, múnsero
past part.	munto

Muòvere *to move*

past	mossi, movesti, mosse, movemmo, moveste, mòssero
past part.	mosso

Nàscere *to be born*

past	nacqui, nascesti, nacque, nascemmo, nasceste, nàcquero
past part.	nato

Nascóndere *to hide*

past	nascosi, nascondesti, nascose, nascondemmo, nascondeste, nascósero
past part.	nascosto

Nuòcere *to harm*

pres. ind.	nuoccio *or* noccio, nuoci, nuoce, nociamo, nocete, nuòcciono *or* nòcciono
past	nocqui, nocesti, nocque, nocemmo, noceste, nòcquero
pres. subj.	noccia, noccia, noccia, nociamo, nociate, nòcciano
imper.	nuoci, noccia, nocete, nocciano
past part.	nociuto

Offríre *to offer*

past	offrii *or* offersi, offristi, offrí *or* offerse, offrimmo, offriste, offrírono *or* offèrsero
past part.	offerto

Parére *to seem*

pres. ind.	paio, pari, pare, paiamo, parete, pàiono
past	parvi, paresti, parve, paremmo, pareste, pàrvero
fut.	parrò
pres. sub.	paia, paia, paia, pariamo, pariate *or* paiate, pàiano
cond.	parrei
imper.	*lacking*
pres. part.	parvente
past part.	parso

Pèrdere *to lose*
past   persi *or* perdetti, perdesti, perse *or* perdette, perdemmo, perdeste, pèrsero *or* perdèttero
past part.   perso *or* perduto

Persuadére *to persuade*
past   persuasi, persuadesti, persuase, persuademmo, persuadeste, persuàsero
past part.   persuaso

Piacére *to please*
pres. ind.   piaccio, piaci, piace, piacciamo, piacete, piàcciono
past   piacqui, piacesti, piacque, piacemmo, piaceste, piàcquero
pres. sub.   piaccia
past part.   piaciuto

Piàngere *to weep*
past   piansi, piangesti, pianse, piangemmo, piangeste, piànsero
past part.   pianto

Piòvere *to rain*
past   piovvi, piovesti, piovve, piovemmo, pioveste, piòvvero

Pòrgere *to offer*
past   porsi, porgesti, porse, porgemmo, porgeste, pòrsero
past part.   porto

Pórre *to place*
pres. ind.   pongo, poni, pone, poniamo, ponete, póngono
imp. ind.   ponevo
past   posi, ponesti, pose, ponemmo, poneste, pósero
fut.   porrò
cond.   porrei
pres. sub.   ponga, ponga, ponga, poniamo, poniate, póngano
imp. sub.   ponessi
imper.   poni, ponga, ponete, póngano
pres. part.   ponente
past part.   posto

Potére *to be able*
pres. ind.   posso, puoi, può, possiamo, potete, pòssono
fut.   potrò
cond.   potrei
pres. sub.   possa
past part.   potuto

Predilígere   *to prefer*
past   predilessi, prediligesti, predilesse, predili-
              gemmo, prediligeste, predilessero
past part.   prediletto

Prèndere   *to take*
past   presi, prendesti, prese, prendemmo, prendeste,
              présero
past part.   preso

Prescíndere   *to leave out of consideration*
past   prescindei *or* prescissi, prescindesti, pres-
              cindè *or* prescisse, prescindemmo, prescindeste,
              prescindérono *or* prescíssero
past part.   prescisso

Prevedére   *to foresee*
              see **vedere**

Proferíre   *to utter*
past   proferii, proferisti, proferí, proferimmo, pro-
              feriste, proferírono
past part.   proferito

Profferíre   *to proffer*
past   proffersi, profferisti, profferse, profferimmo,
              profferiste, profferśero
past part.   profferto

Protèggere   *to protest*
past   protessi, proteggesti, protesse, proteggemmo,
              proteggeste, protèssero
past part.   protetto

Púngere   *to prick*
past   punsi, pungesti, punse, pungemmo, pungeste,
              púnsero
past part.   punto

Ràdere   *to shave*
past   rasi, radesti, rase, rademmo, radeste, ràsero
past part.   raso

Redígere   *to draw up*
past   redassi, redigesti, redasse, redigemmo, re-
              digeste, redàssero
past part.   redatto

Redímere   *to redeem*
past   redensi, redimesti, redense, redimemmo, re-
              dimeste, redénsero
past part.   redento

Règgere   *to support*
past   ressi, reggesti, resse, reggemmo, reggeste, rèssero
past part.   retto

Rèndere   *to give back*
past   resi, rendesti, rese, rendemmo, rendeste, résero
past part.   reso

Restríngere   *to restrict*
past part.   ristretto

Rídere   *to laugh*
past   risi, ridesti, rise, ridemmo, rideste, rísero
past part.   riso

Riflèttere   *to reflect*
past   riflettei *or* riflessi, riflettesti, riflettè *or* riflesse, riflettemmo, rifletteste, riflettérono *or* riflèssero
past part.   riflettuto *or* riflesso

Rifúlgere   *to shine*
past   rifulsi, rifulgesti, rifulse, rifulgemmo, rifulgeste, rifúlsero
past part.   rifulso

Rilúcere   *to shine*
past   rilucei, rilucesti, rilucè, rilucemmo, riluceste, rilucérono
past part.   *lacking*

Rimanére   *to remain*
pres. ind.   rimango, rimani, rimane, rimaniamo, rimanete, rimàngono
past   rimasi, rimanesti, rimase, rimanemmo, rimaneste, rimàsero
fut.   rimarrò
cond.   rimarrei
pres. sub.   rimanga, rimanga, rimanga, rimaniamo, rimaniate, rimàngano
imper.   rimani, rimanga, rimanete, rimàngano
past part.   rimasto

Rispóndere   *to reply*
past   risposi, rispondesti, rispose, rispondemmo, rispondeste, rispósero
past part.   risposto

Ródere   *to gnaw*
past   rosi, rodesti, rose, rodemmo, rodeste, rósero
past part.   roso

E.I.D.

P

Rómpere   *to break*
past   ruppi, rompesti, ruppe, rompemmo, rompeste, rúppero
past part.   rotto

Salíre   *to climb*
pres. ind.   salgo, sali, sale, saliamo, salite, sàlgono
pres. sub.   salga, salga, salga, saliamo, saliate, sàlgano
imper.   sali, salga, salite, sàlgano

Sapére   *to know*
pres. ind.   so, sai, sa, sappiamo, sapete, sanno
past   seppi, sapesti, seppe, sapemmo, sapeste, sèppero
fut.   saprò
cond.   saprei
pres. sub.   sappia
imper.   sappi, sappia, sappiate, sàppiano
pres. part.   sapiente

Scégliere   *to choose*
pres. ind.   scelgo, scegli, sceglie, scegliamo, scegliete, scélgono
past   scelsi, scegliesti, scelse, scegliemmo, sceglieste scélsero
pres. sub.   scelga, scelga, scelga, scegliamo, scegliate, scélgano
imper.   scegli, scelga, scegliete, scélgano
past part.   scelto

Scéndere   *to descend*
past   scesi, scendesti, scese, scendemmo, scendeste, scésero
past part.   sceso

Scèrnere   *to choose*
past   scernei or scernetti, scernesti, scernè or scernette, scernemmo, scernérono or scernèttero
past part.   *lacking*

Scíndere   *to cut*
past   scissi, scindesti, scisse, scindemmo, scindeste, scíssero
past part.   scisso

Sciògliere   *to melt*
past   sciolsi, sciogliesti, sciolse, sciogliemmo, scioglieste, sciòlsero
past part.   sciolto

Scolpíre   *to carve*
past part.   scolpii, scolpisti, scolpì, scolpimmo, scolpiste,

scolpírono; *poet.* sculsi, scolpisti, sculse, scolpimmo, scolpiste, scúlsero
past part.   scolpito; *poet.* sculto

Scòrgere   *to perceive*
past   scorsi, scorgesti, scorse, scorgemmo, scor-
geste, scòrsero
past part.   scorto

Scrívere   *to write*
past   scrissi, scrivesti, scrisse, scrivemmo, scriveste,
scríssero
past part.   scritto

Scuòtere   *to shake*
past   scossi, scotesti, scosse, scotemmo, scoteste,
scòssero
past part.   scosso

Sedére   *to sit*
pres. ind.   siedo *or* seggo, siedi, siede, sediamo, sedete,
sièdono *or* sèggono
past   sedei *or* sedetti, sedesti, sedè *or* sedette, sedem-
mo, sedeste, sedérono *or* sedèttero
pres. sub.   sieda *or* segga, sieda *or* segga, sieda *or* segga,
sediamo, sediate, sièdano *or* sèggano
imper.   siedi, sieda *or* segga, sedete, sièdano *or* sèggano

Seppellíre   *to bury*
past part.   seppellito *or* sepolto

Soddisfàre   *to satisfy*
pres. ind.   soddisfo *or* soddisfaccio, soddisfi *or* soddisfai,
soddìsfa,   soddisfiamo   *or*   soddisfacciamo,
soddisfate, soddísfano *or* soddisfànno
pres. sub.   soddisfi *or* soddisfaccia, soddisfi *or* soddisfaccia, soddisfi *or* soddisfaccia, soddisfacciamo,
soddisfacciate, soddísfino *or* soddisfàcciano
imper.   soddisfa, soddisfi *or* soddisfaccia, soddisfate,
soddísfino *or* soddisfàcciano
past part.   soddisfatto

Solére   *to be used to*
pres. ind.   soglio, suoli, suole, sogliamo, solete, sògliono;
or sono sòlito, sei sòlito è sòlito, siamo sòliti,
siete sòliti, sono sòliti
fut.   *lacking*
cond.   *lacking*
pres. sub.   soglia
imp. sub.   solessi

past   solei, solesti, solè, solemmo, soleste, solérono (*rare*); *now most commonly*: fui sòlito, fosti sòlito, fu sòlito, fummo sòliti, foste sòliti, fúrono sòliti

imper.   *lacking*

pres. part. *lacking*

past. part. sòlito

Sórgere *to rise*

past   sorsi, sorgesti, sórse, sorgemmo, sorgeste, sórsero

past part. sorto

Spàndere *to spread*

past   spandei *or* spansi, spandesti, spandè *or* spanse, spandemmo, spandeste, spandérono *or* spànsero

past part. *Not used. Use* Sparso (pp. of spargere)

Spàrgere *to scatter*

past   sparsi, spargesti, sparse, spargemmo, spargeste, spàrsero

past part. sparso

Sparíre *to disappear*

past   sparii *or* sparvi, sparisti, sparí *or* sparve, sparimmo, spariste, sparírono *or* spàrvero

Spégnere *or* **Spéngere** *to extinguish*

pres. ind. spengo, spegni *or* spengi, spegne *or* spenge, spegniamo *or* spengiamo, spegnete *or* spengete, spéngono

past   spensi, spegnesti *or* spengesti, spense, spegnemmo *or* spengemmo, spegneste *or* spengeste, spénsero

pres. sub. spenga, spenga, spenga, spegniamo *or* spengiamo, spegniate *or* spengiate, spéngano

imper.   spegni *or* spengi, spenga, spegnete *or* spengete, spéngano

past part. spento

Stàre *to stay*

pres. ind. sto, stai, sta, stiamo, state, stanno

past   stetti, stesti, stette, stemmo, steste, stéttero

fut.   starò

cond.   starei

pres. sub. stia

imp. sub.   stessi

imper.   stai *or* sta', stia, state, stíano

past part. stato

Stríngere   *to press*
past   strinsi, stringesti, strinse, stringemmo, strin-
                geste, st`rí`nsero
past part.   stretto

Strúggere   *to melt*
past   strussi, struggesti, strusse, struggemmo, strug-
                geste, strússero
past part.   strutto

Svèllere   *to eradicate*
pres. ind.   svelgo *or* svello, svelli, svelle, svelliamo,
                svellete, svèlgono *or* svèllono
past   svelsi, svellesti, svelse, svellemmo, svelleste,
                svèlsero
past part.   svelto

Tacére   *to be silent*
pres. ind.   taccio, taci, tace, taciamo, tacete, tàcciono
past.   tacqui, tacesti, tacque, tacemmo, taceste,
                tàcquero
pres. sub.   taccia
imper.   taci, taccia, tacete, tacciano

Tèndere   *to stretch out*
past   tesi, tendesti, tese, tendemmo, tendeste, tésero
past part.   teso

Tenére   *to hold*
pres. ind.   tengo, tieni, tiene, teniamo, tenete, tèngono
past   tenni, tenesti, tenne, tenemmo, teneste, tènnero
fut.   terrò
cond.   terrei
pres. sub.   tenga, tenga, tenga, teniamo, teniate, tèngano
imper.   tieni, tenga, tenete, tèngano

Tèrgere   *to dry*
past   tersi, tergesti, terse, tergemmo, tergeste, tèrsero
past part.   terso

Tíngere   *to dye*
past   tinsi, tingesti, tinse, tingemmo, tingeste, tínsero
past part   tinto

Tògliere   *to take away*
pres. ind.   tolgo, togli, toglie, togliamo, togliete, tòlgono
past   tolsi, togliesti, tolse, togliemmo, toglieste,
                tòlsero
pres. sub.   tolga, tolga, tolga, togliamo, togliate, tòlgano
imper.   togli, tolga, togliete, tòlgano
cond.   toglierei *or* torrei, toglieresti *or* torresti, toglie-
                rebbe *or* torrebbe, toglieremmo *or* torremmo,

421

	togliereste *or* torreste, toglierèbbero *or* torrèbbero
fut.	toglierò *or* torrò, toglierai *or* torrai, toglierà *or* torrà, toglieremo *or* torremo, toglierete *or* torrete, toglieranno *or* torranno
past part.	tolto

Tòrcere   *to twist*

| *past* | torsi, torcesti, torse, torcemmo, torceste, tòrsero |
| *past part.* | torto |

Tràrre   *to draw*

pres. ind.	traggo, trai, trae, traiamo, traete, tràggono
imp. ind.	traevo
fut.	trarrò
past	trassi, traesti, trasse, traemmo, traeste, tràssero
cond.	trarrei
pres. sub.	tragga, tragga, tragga, traiamo, traiate, tràggano
imp. sub.	traessi
imper.	trai, tragga, traete, tràggano
pres. part.	traente
past part.	tratto

Uccídere   *to kill*

| *past* | uccisi, uccidesti, uccise, uccidemmo, uccideste, uccísero |
| *past part* | ucciso |

Udíre   *to hear*

pres. ind.	odo, odi, ode, udiamo, udite, òdono
fut.	udirò *or* udrò, udirai *or* udrai, udirà *or* udrà, udiremo *or* udremo, udirete *or* udrete, udiranno *or* udranno
pres. sub.	oda, oda, oda, udiamo, udiate, òdano
imper.	odi, oda, udite, òdano
pres. part.	udente *or* udiente

Uscíre   *to go out*

pres. ind.	esco, esci, esce, usciamo, uscite, éscono
pres. sub.	esca, esca, esca, usciamo, usciate, éscano
imper.	esci, esca, uscite, éscano

Valére   *to be worth*

pres. ind.	valgo, vali, vale, valiamo, valete, vàlgono
past	valsi, valesti, valse, valemmo, valeste, vàlsero
fut.	varrò
cond.	varrei
pres. sub.	valga, valga, valga, valiamo, valiate, vàlgano
imper.	vali, valga, valete, vàlgano
past part.	valso

Vedére *to see*
past   vidi, vedesti, vide, vedemmo, vedeste, vídero
fut.   vedrò
cond.   vedrei
pres. part. vedente *or* veggente
past part. visto *or* veduto

Veníre *to come*
pres. ind. vengo, vieni, viene, veniamo, venite, vèngono
past   venni, venisti, venne, venimmo, veniste, vènnero
fut.   verrò
cond.   verrei
pres. sub. venga, venga, venga, veniamo, veníate, vèngano
imper.   vieni, venga, venite, vèngano
pres. part. veniente
past part. venuto

Víncere *to win*
past   vinsi, vincesti, vinse, vincemmo, vinceste, vínsero
past part. vinto

Vívere *to live*
past   vissi, vivesti, visse, vivemmo, viveste, víssero
fut.   vivrò
cond.   vivrei
past part. vissuto

Volére *to want*
pres. ind. voglio, vuoi, vuole, vogliamo, volete, vògliono
past   volli, volesti, volle, volemmo, voleste, vòllero
fut.   vorrò
cond.   vorrei
pres. sub. voglia
past part. voluto

Vòlgere *to turn*
past   volsi, volgesti, volse, volgemmo, volgeste, vòlsero
past part. volto

IL PLURALE DEI SOSTANTIVI

1. Normalmente il plurale si forma aggiungendo –s: **chair** (sedia), **chairs**; **table** (tavolo), **tables**.

2. –ch, –s, –sh, –x, –z. I sostantivi terminanti in questo modo aggiungono –es, che costituisce una sillaba extra: **arch** (arco), **arches**; **kiss** (bacio), **kisses**; **dish** (piatto), **dishes**; **box** (scatola), **boxes**; **buzz** (ronzio), **buzzes**.

3. –y. Se la –y è preceduta da vocale, il plurale si forma normalmente: **boy** (ragazzo), **boys**. Se la –y è precuduto da consonante, il plurale si forma in –ies: **lady** (signora), **ladies**.

4. –fe, –f. I sostantivi in –fe, e molti in –f, formano il plurale in –ves: **wife** (moglie), **wives**; **leaf** (foglia), **leaves**.

5. –o. Alcuni sostantivi formano il plurale in –oes: **hero** (eroe), **heroes**; altri in –os: **piano** (pianoforte), **pianos**.

6. Molti sostantivi di origine latina o greca fanno il plurale come in latino o in greco, specialmente nel caso di termini scientifici: **radius** (raggio), **radii**; **thesis** (tesi), **theses**; **medium** (mezzo), **media**.

7. Alcuni nomi di animali non cambiano nel plurale: **sheep** (pecora); **deer** (cervo).

8. Alcuni sostantivi hanno il plurale irregolare: **man** (uomo), **men**; **woman** (donna), **women**; **child** (bambino), **children**; **foot** (piede), **feet**; **tooth** (dente), **teeth**; **goose** (oca), **geese**; **mouse** (sorcio), **mice**; **louse** (pidocchio), **lice**; **ox** (bue), **oxen**.

Nel dizionario il plurale è indicato dei sostantivi che entrano nelle categorie trattate nelle note 4-8.

Verbi Inglesi—English Verbs

Verbi Ausiliari

To be, *essere*   **To have,** *avere*

INDICATIVO PRESENTE

Sono, ecc   *Ho, ecc*

I am   I have
You are (thou art)   You have (thou hast)
He ⎫   He ⎫
She ⎬ is   She ⎬ has
It ⎭   It ⎭
We are   We have
You are   You have
They are   They have

INDICATIVO PASSATO

Ero, fui, ecc   *Avevo, ebbi, ecc*

I was   I had
You were (thou wert)   You had (thou hadst)
He ⎫   He ⎫
She ⎬ was   She ⎬ had
It ⎭   It ⎭
We were   We had
You were   You had
They were   They had

FUTURO

sarò, ecc   *Avrò, ecc*

I shall be   I shall have
You will (thou wilt) be   You will (thou wilt) have
He ⎫   He ⎫
She ⎬ will be   She ⎬ will have
It ⎭   It ⎭
We shall be   We shall have
You will be   You will have
They will be   They will have

CONDIZIONALE

Sarei, ecc   *Avrei, ecc*

I should be   I should have
You would (thou wouldst) be   You would (thou wouldst)
                                          have

He ⎫   He ⎫
She ⎬ would be   She ⎬ would have
It ⎭   It ⎭
We should be   We should have
You would be   You would have
They would be   They would have

[*Ch'io sia*], *sii*   [*Ch'io abbia*], *abbi*

Let me be   Let me have
Be   Have
Let him ⎫   Let him ⎫
    her ⎬ be   her ⎬ have
    it ⎭   it ⎭
Let us be   Let us have
Be   Have
Let them be   Let them have

INFINITO

To be, *essere*   To have, *avere*

GERUNDIO E PARTICIPIO PRESENTE

Being, *essendo*   Having, *avendo, avente*

PARTICIPIO PASSATO

Been, *stato*   Had, *avuto*

Tempi Composti

PERFETTO

  Sono stato, ecc   *Ho avuto, ecc*

I have been   I have had
You have been   You have had
He ⎫   He ⎫
She ⎬ has been   She ⎬ has had
It ⎭   It ⎭
We have been   We have had
You have been   You have had
They have been   They have had

PIUCCHEPERFETTO

  Ero, fui stato, ecc   *Avevo, ebbi avuto, ecc*

I had been   I had had
You had been   You had had
He ⎫   He ⎫
She ⎬ had been   She ⎬ had had
It ⎭   It ⎭
We had been   We had had
You had been   You had had
They had been   They had had

FUTURO PERFETTO

  Sarò stato, ecc   *Avrò avuto, ecc*

I shall have been   I shall have had
You will have been   You will have had
He ⎫   He ⎫
She ⎬ will have been   She ⎬ will have had
It ⎭   It ⎭
We shall have been   We shall have had
You will have been   You will have had
They will have been   They will have had

Sarei stato, ecc

I should have been
You would have been
He ⎫
She ⎬ would have been
It ⎭
We should have been
You would have been
They would have been

Avrei avuto, ecc

I should have had
You would have had
He ⎫
She ⎬ would have had
It ⎭
We should have had
You would have had
They would have had

INFINITO PASSATO

Essere stato
To have been

Avere avuto
To have had

GERUNDIO PASSATO

Essendo stato
Having been

Avendo avuto
Having had

CONGIUNTIVO PRESENTE

Ch'io sia, ecc

That I be
That you be
That he ⎫
    she ⎬ be
    it ⎭
That we be
That you be
That they be

Ch'io abbia, ecc

That I have
That you have
That he ⎫
    she ⎬ have
    it ⎭
That we have
That you have
That they have

N.B.—Il congiuntivo presente non si usa ormai più in inglese se non in qualche frase idiomatica

CONGIUNTIVO PASSATO

Se io fossi, ecc

If I were
If you were
If he ⎫
    she ⎬ were
    it ⎭
If we were
If you were
If they were

Se io avessi, ecc

If I had
If you had
If he ⎫
    she ⎬ had
    it ⎭
If we had
If you had
If they had

Verbi Irregolari Inglesi
English Irregular Verbs

Infinito		*Passato*	*Part. passato*
abide	dimorare	abode	abode
arise	alzarsi	arose	arisen
awake	svegliare, svegliarsi	awoke	awaked*
bear	portare	bore	borne
beat	battere	beat	beaten

Infinito		Passato	Part. passato
begin	cominciare	began	begun
bend	piegare	bent	bent
bereave	orbare	bereft	bereft*
beseech	implorare	besought	besought
bid	ordinare	bade (bid)	bidden (bid)
bind	legare	bound	bound
bite	mordere	bit	bitten
bleed	sanguinare	bled	bled
blow	soffiare	blew	blown
break	rompere	broke	broken
breed	generare, allevare	bred	bred
bring	portare	brought	brought
build	costruire	built	built
burn	bruciare	burnt	burnt*
burst	scoppiare	burst	burst
buy	comperare	bought	bought
cast	gettare	cast	cast
catch	afferrare	caught	caught
chide	sgridare	chid	chidden, chid*
choose	scegliere	chose	chosen
cleave	fendere	cleft, clove	cleft, cloven*
cling	aggrapparsi	clung	clung
come	venire	came	come
cost	costare	cost	cost
creep	strisciare	crept	crept
crow	cantare (del gallo)	crew	crowed
cut	tagliare	cut	cut
dare	osare	(durst)	dared*
deal	trattare	dealt	dealt
dig	scavare	dug	dug
do	fare	did	done
draw	disegnare, trarre	drew	drawn
dream	sognare	dreamt	dreamt*
drink	bere	drank	drunk
drive	guidare	drove	driven
dwell	abitare	dwelt	dwelt
eat	mangiare	ate	eaten
fall	cadere	fell	fallen
feed	nutrire	fed	fed
feel	sentire	felt	felt
fight	combattere	fought	fought
find	trovare	found	found
flee	fuggire	fled	fled
fling	lanciare	flung	flung
fly	volare	flew	flown
forsake	abbandonare	forsook	forsaken
freeze	gelare	froze	frozen
get	acquisire	got	got, (US) gotten
gild	dorare	gilt	gilt*
gird	cingere	girt	girt*
give	dare	gave	given
go	andare	went	gone

grind	macinare	ground	ground
grow	crescere	grew	grown
hang	appendere	hung	hung (=impiccare)*
hear	udire	heard	heard
hew	spaccare	hewed	hewn
hide	nascondere	hid	hidden, hid
hit	colpire	hit	hit
hold	tenere	held	held
hurt	dolere	hurt	hurt
keep	conservare	kept	kept
kneel	inginocchiarsi	knelt	knelt
know	conoscere, sapere	knew	known
lay	deporre	laid	laid
lead	guidare	led	led
leave	lasciare	left	left
lend	prestare	lent	lent
let	lasciare, affittare	let	let
lie	giacere	lay	lain (=mentire*)
light	accendere, illuminare	lit	lit*
lose	perdere	lost	lost
make	fare	made	made
mean	significare	meant	meant
meet	incontrare	met	met
mow	mietere	mowed	mown
pay	pagare	paid	paid
put	mettere	put	put
read	leggere	read	read
rend	strappare	rent	rent
rid	liberare	rid	rid
ride	cavalcare	rode	ridden
ring	suonare	rang, rung	rung
rise	alzarsi, sorgere	rose	risen
rive	spaccare	rived	riven
run	correre	ran	run
say	dire	said	said
see	vedere	saw	seen
seek	cercare	sought	sought
sell	vendere	sold	sold
send	mandare	sent	sent
set	mettere	set	set
shake	scuotere	shook	shaken
shear	tosare	sheared, (shore)	shorn
shed	versare	shed	shed
shine	brillare	shone	shone
shoe	calzare, ferrare	shod	shod
shoot	sparare	shot	shot
show	mostrare	showed	shown
shrink	ritirarsi	shrank	shrunk
shut	chiudere	shut	shut
sing	cantare	sang	sung
sink	affondare	sank	sunk

Infinito		Passato	Part. passato
sit	sedere	sat	sat
slay	uccidere	slew	slain
sleep	dormire	slept	slept
slide	slittare	slid	slid
sling	lanciare, appendere	slung	slung
slink	sgattaiolare	slunk	slunk
slit	fendere	slit	slit
smell	fiutare	smelt	smelt
smite	colpire	smote	smitten
sow	seminare	sowed	sown*
speak	parlare	spoke	spoken
spend	spendere	spent	spent
spill	versare	spilt	spilt
spin	filare	span, spun	spun
spit	sputare	spat, spit	spit
split	spaccare, dividere	split	split
spread	spandere	spread	spread
spring	balzare, scaturire	sprang	sprung
stand	stare in piedi	stood	stood
steal	rubare	stole	stolen
stick	attaccare	stuck	stuck
sting	pungere	stung	stung
stink	puzzare	stank, stunk	stunk
stride	camminare a grandi passi	strode	stridden
strike	colpire	struck	struck
string	infilare	strung	strung
strive	sforzarsi	strove	striven
swear	giurare, imprecare	swore	sworn
sweep	scopare	swept	swept
swell	gonfiarsi	swelled	swollen
swim	nuotare	swam	swum
swing	dondolare	swung	swung
take	prendere	took	taken
teach	insegnare	taught	taught
tear	stracciare	tore	torn
tell	dire, raccontare	told	told
think	pensare	thought	thought
thrive	prosperare	throve	thriven*
throw	gettare	threw	thrown
thrust	spingere	thrust	thrust
tread	camminare, calpestare	trod	trod, trodden
wear	indossare	wore	worn
weave	tessere	wove	woven
weep	piangere	wept	wept
win	vincere	won	won
wind	attorcigliare	wound	wound
work	lavorare	(wrought)	(wrought)*
wring	torcere	wrung	wrung
write	scrivere	wrote	written

NOTE: I verbi contrassegnati da asterisco si coniugano anche regolarmente.

Numerals - Numerali

NUMERI CARDINALI		CARDINAL NUMBERS
uno	1	one
due	2	two
tre	3	three
quattro	4	four
cinque	5	five
sei	6	six
sette	7	seven
otto	8	eight
nove	9	nine
dieci	10	ten
undici	11	eleven
dodici	12	twelve
tredici	13	thirteen
quattordici	14	fourteen
quindici	15	fifteen
sedici	16	sixteen
diciassette	17	seventeen
diciotto	18	eighteen
diciannove	19	nineteen
venti	20	twenty
ventuno	21	twenty-one
ventidue	22	twenty-two
ventitre etc.	23	twenty-three etc.
trenta	30	thirty
trentuno	31	thirty-one
trentadue	32	thirty-two
quaranta	40	forty
cinquanta	50	fifty
sessanta	60	sixty
settanta	70	seventy
ottanta	80	eighty
novanta	90	ninety
cento	100	one hundred
centouno	101	one hundred and one
centodue	102	one hundred and two
duecento	200	two hundred
trecento	300	three hundred
quattrocento	400	four hundred
cinquecento	500	five hundred
mille	1,000	one thousand
mille e cento	1,100	one thousand one hundred
mille e duecento	1,200	one thousand two hundred
duemila	2,000	two thousand
tremila	3,000	three thousand

diecimila	10,000	ten thousand
centomila	100,000	one hundred thousand
un milione	1,000,000	one million
due milioni	2,000,000	two million

NUMERI ORDINALI		ORDINAL NUMBERS
primo	1st	the first
secondo	2nd	the second
terzo	3rd	the third
quarto	4th	the fourth
quinto	5th	the fifth
sesto	6th	the sixth
settimo	7th	the seventh
ottavo	8th	the eighth
nono	9th	the ninth
decimo	10th	the tenth
undicesimo	11th	the eleventh
dodicesimo	12th	the twelfth
tredicesimo	13th	the thirteenth
quattordicesimo	14th	the fourteenth
quindicesimo	15th	the fifteenth
sedicesimo	16th	the sixteenth
diciasettesimo	17th	the seventeenth
diciottesimo	18th	the eighteenth
dicianovesimo	19th	the nineteenth
ventesimo	20th	the twentieth
ventesimoprimo	21st	the twenty-first
ventesimosecondo etc.	22nd	the twenty-second etc.
trentesimo	30th	the thirtieth
quarantesimo	40th	the fortieth
cinquantesimo	50th	the fiftieth
sessantesimo	60th	the sixtieth
settantesimo	70th	the seventieth
ottantesimo	80th	the eightieth
novantesimo	90th	the ninetieth
centesimo	100th	the hundredth
centesimoprimo	101st	the hundred and first
centocinquantesimo	150th	the hundred and fiftieth
centonovantesimo	190th	the hundred and ninetieth
ducentesimo	200th	the two hundredth
millesimo	1,000th	the thousandth
duemillesimo	2,000th	the two thousandth
diecimillesimo	10,000th	the ten thousandth
centomillesimo	100,000th	the hundred thousandth
milionesimo	1,000,000th	the millionth

Italian Measures and Weights
Misure e Pesi Italiani

LUNGHEZZA—LENGTH

1 Millimetro	= ·001 Metro	= ·0394 inch
1 Centimetro	= ·01 Metro	= ·394 inch
1 Metro	= 39·4 inches	= *1 yard
1 Chilometro	= 1000 Metri	= *1094 yards or ⅝ mile
8 Chilometri	= 5 miles	

SUPERFICIE—AREA

1 Ettaro	= 11960·11 square yards
1 Quadrachilometro	= 247·11 acres

CAPACITÀ—CAPACITY

1 Centilitro	= ·01 Litro	= ·0176 pint	
1 Litro	= *1¾ pints	= ·2201 gallon	
1 Ettolitro	= 100 Litri	= *22 gallons	= 2¾ bushels
1 Chilolitro	= 1000 Litri	= *220 gallons	= 27½ bushels

PESI—WEIGHTS

1 Milligrammo	= ·001 Grammo	= ·0154 grain
1 Centigrammo	= ·01 Grammo	= ·1543 grain
1 Grammo		= 15·43 grains
1 Ettogrammo	= 1000 Grammi	= *3½ oz
1 Tonnellata	= 1000 Chilogrammi	= *1 ton

IL TERMOMETRO—THE THERMOMETER

Punto di Congelamento	= Centigrade 0°
Freezing Point	= Fahrenheit 32°
Punto d'Ebollizione	= Centigrade 100°
Boiling Point	= Fahrenheit 212°

*roughly

Sistema Monetario Inglese, Misure e Pesi
English Weights, Measures and Money

LENGTH—LUNGHEZZA

Inch (in)	=25 Millimetri
Foot (ft) (12 in)	=304 Millimetri
Yard (yd) (3 ft)	=913 Millimetri (quasi 1 Metro)
Fathom (fthm) (2 yards)	=1 Metro 828 Millimetri
Mile (8 furlongs, 1760 yards)	=1609 Metri
Nautical mile, knot	=1853 Metri
5 miles	=8 Chilometri

AREA—SUPERFICIE

Square inch	=6,45 Centimetri quadrati (cm²)
Square foot	=929 cm²
Square yard	=0,8360 Metri quadrati (m²)
Acre	=4047 m²

CAPACITY—CAPACITÀ

Pint	=0,567 Litro
Quart (2 pints)	=1,136 Litri
Gallon (4 quarts)	=4,53 Litri
Peck (2 gallons)	=9,086 Litri
Bushel (8 gallons)	=36,348 Litri
Quarter (8 bushels)	=290,8 Litri

WEIGHTS (AVOIRDUPOIS)—PESI

Ounce (oz)	=28,35 Grammi
Pound (lb) (16 oz)	=453,59 Grammi
Stone (st) (14 lb)	=6,35 Chili
Quarter (qr) (28 lb)	=12,7 Chili
Hundredweight (cwt) (112 lb)	=50,8 Chili
Ton (T) (20 cwts)	=1016 Chili

THE THERMOMETER—IL TERMOMETRO

Freezing Point	=Fahrenheit 32°
Punto di Congelamento	=Centigrade 0°
Boiling Point	=Fahrenheit 212°
Punto d'Ebollizione	=Centigrade 100°

SISTEMA MONETARIO INGLESE

1 pound (£1)	=20 shillings
1 shilling (1s)	=12 pence (pennies)
1 penny (1d)	=2 halfpennies

Dal 1971:

1 pound (£1)	=100 pence

Italian Abbreviations—Abbreviazioni Italiane

AA	Accademia Aeronautica (*Air Force Academy*); Assistenza Automobilistica (*organization for assisting motorists*)
aC	avanti Cristo (*before Christ*)
ACDG	Associazione Cristiana dei Giovani (*Young Men's Christian Association*)
ACI	Automobile Club d'Italia (*Italian Automobile Association*); Azione Cattolica Italiana (*Italian Catholic Action*)
ACIS	Alto Commissariato per l'Igiene e la Sanità (*Public Health Board*)
AGIP	Azienda Generale Italiana Petroli (*National Italian Oil Company*)
ago	agosto (*August*)
AI	Aeronautica Italiana (*Italian Air Force*)
ALITALIA	Aerolinee Italiane Internazionali (*Italian International Airlines*)
all	allegato (*enclosure*)
alt	altezza (*height*); altitudine (*altitude*)
ANAS	Azienda Nazionale Autonoma della Strada (*National Road Board*)
ANSA	Agenzia Nazionale Stampa Associata (*Associated Press*)
apr	aprile (*April*)
AR	Altezza Reale (*Royal Highness*); andata e ritorno (*return ticket*)
ASC	Associazione Scoutistica Cattolica (*Catholic Scout Movement*)
ATM	Azienda Tranviaria Municipale (*Municipal Tram Company*)
AVIS	Associazione Volontari Italiani del Sangue (*Association of Italian Blood Donors*)
avv	avverbio (*adverb*); avvocato (*lawyer*)
BI	Banca d'Italia (*Bank of Italy*)
brev	brevetto (*patent*)
c	capitolo (*chapter*); circa (*about*); codice ((*leg*) code); corpo (*type-size*)
cabl	cablogramma (*cable*)
cad	cadauno (*each*)
CAI	Club Alpino Italiano (*Italian Alpine Club*)
Cap	Capitano (*Captain*); capitolo (*chapter*)
Cav	Cavaliere (*Knight*)
cc	conto corrente (*current account*)
CC	Corpo Carabinieri (*Carabiniere Corps*); Corte di Cassazione (*Supreme Court of Appeal*)
CCI	Camera di Commercio Internazionale (*International Chamber of Commerce*)
ccp	conto corrente postale (*current postal account*)
Cd'A	Corte d'Assise (*Court of Assizes*)
CdL	Camera del Lavoro (*Trade Union*)
CdS	Circolo della Stampa (*Press Club*); Codice della Strada (*Highway Code*); Consiglio di Sicurezza (*Security Council*)
CECA	Comunità Europea per il Carbone e l'Acciaio (*European Coal and Steel Community*)
CERN	Consiglio Europeo per le Ricerche Nucleari (*European Council for Nuclear Research*)

CGIL	Confederazione Generale Italiana del Lavoro (*Federation of Italian Trade Unions*)
CIT	Compagnia Italiana Turismo (*Italian Travel Agency*)
CLN	Comitato di Liberazione Nazionale (*Resistance Movement Committee* (*World War II*))
cm	corrente mese (*present month*)
CONFINDUSTRIA	Confederazione Generale dell'Industria Italiana (*General Confederation of Italian Industry*)
CONI	Comitato Olimpico Nazionale Italiano (*Italian Olympic Games Committee*)
CP	Casella Postale (*Post Office Box*)
CRI	Croce Rossa Internazionale (*International Red Cross*); Croce Rossa Italiana (*Italian Red Cross*)
c. to	conto (*account*)
CV	cavallo vapore (*horse power*)
dC	dopo Cristo (*Anno Domini, in the year of the Lord*)
DC	Democrazia Cristiana (*Christian Democrat Party*)
devmo	devotissimo ((*in letters*) *yours truly*)
dic	dicembre (*December*)
dott	Dottore (*Doctor*)
dr	Dottore (*Doctor*)
dr.ssa	Dottoressa (*Doctor*)
ecc	eccetera (*et cetera*)
Ecc	Eccellenza (*Excellency*)
Egr.Sig.	Egregio Signore ((*in addresses*) *Mr.*; (*in letters*) Dear Sir)
ENAL	Ente Nazionale Assistenza Lavoratori (*National Association for Assistance to Workers*)
ENIC	Ente Nazionale Industrie Cinematografiche (*National Association of the Cinema Industry*)
ENIT	Ente Nazionale Industrie Turistiche (*National Tourist Office*)
feb	febbraio (*February*)
ferr	ferrovia (*railway*)
FFSS	Ferrovie dello Stato (*State Railways*)
FIAT	Fabbrica Italiana Automobili Torino (*Italian Automobile Works Torino*)
FIGC	Federazione Italiana Giuoco Calcio (*Italian Football Association*)
FIT	Federazione Italiana Tennis (*Italian Lawn Tennis Association*)
Flli	Fratelli ((*com*) *Brothers*)
FPI	Federazione Pugilistica Italiana (*Italian Boxing Association*)
Fr b	franco belga (*Belgian franc*)
Fr f	franco francese (*French franc*)
Fr s	franco svizzero (*Swiss franc*)
GB	Gran Bretagna (*Great Britain*)
GdF	Guardia di Finanza (*Revenue Guard*)
GEI	Giovani Esploratori Italiani (*Italian Boy Scouts*)
gen	genitivo (*genitive*); gennaio (*January*)
GU	Gazzetta Ufficiale (*Official Gazette*)
h	ora (*hour*)
HF	alta frequenza (*high frequency*)
IGE	Imposta Generale sull'Entrata (*Income Tax*)
INA	Istituto Nazionale Assicurazioni (*National Insurance*)
INAM	Istituto Nazionale per l'Assicurazione contro le malattie (*National Health Insurance*)

436

INCOM	Industria Cortometraggi (*Short-Film Industry*)
INPI	Istituto Nazionale per la Prevenzione degli Infortuni (*National Institute for the Prevention of Accidents*)
INPS	Istituto Nazionale Previdenza Sociale (*National Institute of Social Security*)
IPS	Istituto Poligrafico dello Stato (*Stationery Office*)
Italcable	Compagnia Italiana dei Cavi Telegrafici e Telefonici Sottomarini (*Italian Cable Company*)
kg	chilogrammo (*kilogram(me)*)
lett.	letterario (*literary*); letteratura (*literature*)
LF	bassa frequenza (*low frequency*)
Lit	Lire italiane (*Italian lire*)
LLPP	Lavori Pubblici (*Public Works*)
lm	livello del mare (*sea level*)
Lsr	lira sterlina (*£ pound (sterling)*)
lug	luglio (*July*)
M	Monte (*Mount*)
mag	maggio (*May*)
mar	marzo (*March*)
MAS	motoscafo antisommergibile (*motor torpedo-boat*)
MCD	massimo comun divisore (*highest common factor*)
mcm	minimo comune multiplo (*lowest common multiple*)
ME	Medio Evo (*Middle Ages*)
MEC	Mercato Europeo Comune ((*European*) *Common Market*)
MM	Marina Militare (*Royal Navy*)
M/N	motonave (*motorship*)
Mo	Maestro ((*mus*) *maestro*)
MPPTT	Ministero delle Poste e delle Telecomunicazioni (*Post Office*)
Msa	Marchesa (*Marchioness*)
Mse	Marchese (*Marquis*)
MSI	Movimento Sociale Italiano (*neo-Fascist Party*)
n	nato (*born*); neutro (*neuter*)
ND	Nobil Donna (*lady of a noble family*)
NdA	Nota dell'Autore (*author's note*)
NdE	Nota dell'Editore (*publisher's note*)
NdT	Nota del Traduttore (*translator's note*)
NH	Nobil Uomo (*member of a noble family*)
NN	(L. *Nescio nomen*) di paternità ignota (*name of father unknown*)
nov	novembre (*November*)
NU	Nazioni Unite (*United Nations*)
OdG	ordine del giorno (*agenda*)
OECE	Organizzazione Economica per la Cooperazione Europea (*Organization for European Economic Co-operation*)
OIL	Organizzazione Internazionale del Lavoro (*International Labour Organization*)
OMR	Ordine al Merito della Repubblica (*Order of Merit of the Republic*)
ONMI	Opera Nazionale per il Mezzogiorno d'Italia (*National Board for the South of Italy*); Opera Nazionale per la Protezione della Maternità e dell'Infanzia (*National Board for Maternity and Child Welfare*)
ONU	Organizzazione delle Nazioni Unite (*United Nations Organization*)

437

OSSSA	Ordine Supremo della Santissima Annunziata (*Supreme Order of the Holy Annunciation*)
ott	ottobre (*October*)
OVRA	Opera Volontaria per la Repressione dell'Antifascismo (*Fascist Secret Police*)
P	Padre (*eccl*) *Father*)
pag	pagina (*page*)
pcc	per copia conforme (*certified copy*)
PCI	Partito Comunista Italiano (*Italian Communist Party*)
PdA	Partito d'Azione (*Action Party*)
PDC	Partito Democratico Cristiano (*Christian Democrat Party*)
PDI	Partito Democratico Italiano (*Italian Democratic Party*)
pes	per esempio (*for example*)
pf	per favore (*please*)
PG	Procuratore Generale (*Attorney General*)
PI	Pubblica Istruzione (*Public Education*)
PLI	Partito Liberale Italiano (*Italian Liberal Party*)
PM	Polizia Militare (*Military Police*); Pubblico Ministero (*Public Prosecutor*)
PNF	Partito Nazionale Fascista (*National Fascist Party*)
pp	pacco postale (*parcel post*)
pr	per ringraziamento (*with thanks*)
PRI	Partito Repubblicano Italiano (*Italian Republican Party*)
Proc Gen	Procuratore Generale (*Attorney General*)
profsta	professionista (*professional man*)
PSDI	Partito Socialista Democratico Italiano (*Italian Socialist Democratic Party*)
PSI	Partito Socialista Italiano (*Italian Socialist Party*)
PT	Poste e Telegrafi (*Post and Telegraph Service*)
PTP	Posto Telefonico Pubblico (*public telephone*)
pza	piazza (*square*)
q	quadrato (*square*)
qb	quanto basta (*a sufficient quantity*)
QG	Quartier Generale (*Headquarters*)
R	raccomandata (*registered letter*)
racc	raccomandata (*registered letter*)
rag	ragioniere (*certified accountant*)
RAI	Radio Audizioni Italiane (*Italian Broadcasting Corporation*)
RAU	Repubblica Araba Unita (*United Arab Republic*)
RI	Repubblica Italiana (*Italian Republic*)
RU	Regno Unito (*United Kingdom*)
S	Santo (*Saint*); Sud (*South*)
SA	Sua Altezza (*His, Her Highness*)
SAR	Sua Altezza Reale (*His, Her Royal Highness*)
sbf	salvo buon fine ((*com*) *under usual reserve*)
SCV	Stato della Città del Vaticano (*Vatican City*)
SEDI	Società Editrice Documentari Italiani (*Italian Newsreel Company*)
SEO	salvo errori ed omissioni (*com*) (*errors and omissions excepted*)
serg	sergente (*sergeant*)
sett	settembre (*September*)
sfr	sotto fascia raccomandata (*registered printed matter*)
sfs	sotto fascia semplice (*unregistered printed matter*)
Sig	Signore (*Mr, Mister*)
Siga	Signora (*Mrs, Mistress*)
Sigg	Signori (*Messrs, Messieurs*)

438

Signa	Signorina (*Miss*)
SISAL	Società Italiana Sistemi a Lotto (*Italian Society of State Lottery Systems*)
SMG	Stato Maggiore Generale (*General Staff*)
SMOM	Sovrano Militare Ordine di Malta (*Sovereign Military Order of Malta*)
SNDA	Società Nazionale Dante Alighieri (*National Dante Alighieri Society*)
SO	Sud-Ovest (*South-West*)
Soc	Società (*Society*)
Sottte	Sottotenente (*Sub-Lieutenant*)
SpA	Società per Azioni (*joint-stock company or limited liability company*)
SPA	Società Protettrice degli Animali (*Society for the Prevention of Cruelty to Animals*)
Spett	Spettabile
SPM	sue proprie mani (*personal* (*for addressee*))
SRC	Santa Romana Chiesa (*Holy Roman Church*)
Srl	Società a responsabilità limitata (*Limited Company*)
SSPP	Santi Padri (*Holy Fathers*)
STIPEL	Società Telefonica Interregionale Piemonte e Lombardia (*Telephone Company* (*Piedmont and Lombardy*))
SU	Stati Uniti (*United States*)
SUA	Stati Uniti d'America (*United States of America*)
SVP	(*German* Südtiroler Volkspartei) Partito Popolare Sudtirolese (*People's Party of South Tyrol*)
tbc, TBC	tubercolosi (*tuberculosis*)
TCI	Touring Club Italiano (*Italian Touring Club*)
tel	telefono (*telephone*)
Ten	Tenente (*Lieutenant*)
TOTIP	Totalizzatore Ippico (*horse-race pools*)
TOTOCALCIO	Totalizzatore Calcistico (*Football Pools*)
tr	tratta (*draft*)
UCDG	Unione Cristiana delle Giovani (*Young Women's Christian Association*)
UCI	Unione Ciclistica Internazionale (*International Cycling Union*)
UDE	Unione Doganale Europea (*European Customs Union*)
UDI	Unione Donne Italiane (*Association of Italian Women*)
urg	urgente (*urgent*)
URSS	Unione Repubbliche Socialiste Sovietiche (*Union of Soviet Socialist Republics*)
US	Ufficio Stampa (*Press Agency*); Uscita di Sicurezza (*Emergency Exit*)
V	Via (*Street*)
Vat	Vaticano (*Vatican*)
VE	Vostra Eccellenza (*Your Excellency*)
VEm	Vostra Eminenza (*Your Eminence*)
Vle	Viale (*avenue*)
VM	Vostra Maestà (*Your Majesty*)
vr	vedi retro (*please turn over*)
vs	vostro (*your, yours*)
W	viva! (*long live*); watt (*watt*)
WL	carrozza-letto (*sleeping car*)
YCI	Yacht Club Italia (*Italian Yacht Club*)

Abbreviazioni inglesi—English Abbreviations

A	adults (*adulti*)
AA	Automobile Association (*Automobile Club*); Alcoholics Anonymous (*Alcoolizzati Anonimi*)
AAA	American Automobile Association (*Automobile Club d'America*)
a/c	account (current) *conto* (*corrente*)
AEA	Atomic Energy Authority (*Commissione per l'Energia Atomica*)
A1	first class (*Prima Categoria*)
AID	Artificial Insemination by Donor (*Fecondazione Artificiale da parte di Donatore*)
anon	anonymous (*anonimo*)
approx	approximate(ly) (*approssimato, approssimativamente*)
ARA	Associate of the Royal Academy (*Membro dell'Accademia Reale*)
ARIBA	Associate of the Royal Institute of British Architects (*Membro del Reale Istituto degli Architetti Britannici*)
arr	arrives (*arrivo*)
assn, assoc,	association (*associazione*)
asst	assistant (*assistente*)
av	average (*medio*)
Ave	Avenue (*viale*)
b	born (*nato*)
BA	Bachelor of Arts (*Diplomato in Lettere*); British Academy (*Accadèmia Britannica*); British Association (For the Advancement of Sciences) (*Associazione Britannica (per il Progresso della Scienza*))
Bart	Baronet (*Baronetto*)
BBC	British Broadcasting Corporation (*Ente Radiofonico Britannico*)
BC	before Christ (*avanti Cristo*); British Columbia (*Colombia Britannica*)
BD	Bachelor of Divinity (*Diplomato in Teologia*)
Bd	Board (*Commissione, Consiglio, Ministero*)
BDS	Bachelor of Dental Surgery (*Diplomato in Odontoiatria*); bomb disposal squad (*gruppo addetto al disinnestamento delle bombe*)
be, B/E	bill of exchange (*cambiale*)
BEA	British European Airways (*Compagnia Britannica delle Linee Europee*)
BEM	British Empire Medal (*Medaglia dell'Impero Britannico*)
BIF	British Industries Fair (*Fiera dell'Industria Britannica*)
B Litt	Bachelor of Letters (*Diplomato in Lettere*)
BM	British Museum (*Museo Britannico*); Bachelor of Medicine (*Diplomato in Medicina*)
BMA	British Medical Association (*Ordine Britannico dei Medici*)
B. Mus	Bachelor of Music (*Diplomato in Musica*)
BOAC	British Overseas Airways Corporation (*Compagnia Britannica delle Linee Transoceaniche*)
B of A	Bank of America (*Banca d'America*)
B of E	Bank of England (*Banca d'Inghilterra*); Board of Education (*Ministero della Pubblica Istruzione*)
B of T	Board of Trade (*Ministero del Commercio e dell'Industria*)

BR	British Rail (*Ferrovie Britanniche*)
Brit	Britain ((*Gran*) *Bretagna*); British (*Britannico*)
Bros	Brothers (*com*) (*Fratelli*)
B/S	Bill of Sale (*nota di vendita, fattura*)
BSc	Bachelor of Science (*Diplomato in Scienze*)
Bt	Baronet (*Baronetto*)
B. Th.U	British Thermal Unit (*unità* (*inglese*) *de misura de calore*)
BUP	British United Press (*Stampa Unita Britannica*)
C	Cape (*Capo*); centigrade (*centigrado*); Central (*Centrale*); Conservative (*Conservatore*)
c	cent (*centesimo*); century (*secolo*); about (*L. circa*) (*circa*); chapter (*capitolo*)
Cantab	Cambridge (*cantabrigense*)
cap	capital letter (*lettera maiuscola*); chapter (*capitolo*)
Capt	Captain (*Capitano*)
CBE	Commander of the Order of the British Empire (*Comandante dell'Ordine dell'Impero Britannico*)
CD	Civil Defence (*Difesa Civile*)
cf	compare (*confronta*)
CIA	(*US*) Central Intelligence Agency (*Agenzia Centrale Informazioni* (*Servizio Segreto*))
CID	Criminal Investigation Department (*Polizia Giudiziaria*)
cif	cost, insurance, freight (*costo compreso il nolo e l'assicurazione*)
CND	Campaign for Nuclear Disarmament (*Campagna per il Disarmo Nucleare*)
CO	Commanding Officer (*Ufficiale Comandante*); conscientious objector (*obiettore di coscienza*)
Co	Company (*Compagnia*)
c/o	care of (*presso*)
COD	cash on delivery (*pagamento alla consegna*)
C of E	Church of England (*Chiesa d'Inghilterra*)
C of S	Church of Scotland (*Chiesa di Scozia*)
Col	Colonel (*Colonnello*)
cont	continued (*continuazione*)
Co-op	Co-operative (*Cooperativa*)
Cpl	Corporal (*caporale*)
CUP	Cambridge University Press (*Edizioni dell'Università di Cambridge*)
CWS	Co-operative Wholesale Society (*Società Cooperativa all' ingrosso*)
cwt	hundredweight(s)
d	died (*morta*); date (*data*); daughter (*figlia*); penny
DBE	Dame Commander of the Order of the British Empire (*Dama Comandante dell'Ordine dell'Impero Britannico*)
DC	District of Columbia (*Distretto di Colombia*); (*mus*) (*da capo*); Direct Current (*corrente continua*)
DD	Doctor of Divinity (*Dottore in Teologia*)
dep	departs (*partenza*); deputy (*vice*)
dept	department (*reparto*); deponent (*deponente*)
DG	*Deo gratias, Dei gratia*, thanks to God, by the grace of God (*grazie a Dio, per grazia di Dio*)
diam	diameter (*diametro*)
dim	diminuendo (*diminuendo*); diminutive (*diminutivo*)
D. Litt.	Doctor of Letters (*Dottore in Lettere*)
DM	Doctor of Medicine (*Dottore in Medicina*)
do	ditto (the same) (*suddetto*)

doz	dozen (*dozzina*)
Dr.	Doctor (*dottore, dottoressa*)
DSC	Distinguished Service Cross (*Croce per Meriti Speciali*)
DSM	Distinguished Service Medal (*Medaglia per Meriti Speciali*)
DSO	Distinguished Service Order (*Ordine dei Meriti Speciali*)
E	East (*Est*); Eastern (*Orientale*)
EEC	European Economic Community (Common Market) (*Comunità Economica Europea*) (*Mercato Comune*)
EFTA	European Free Trade Association (*Associazione Europea di Libero Scambio*)
eg	for example (L. *exempli gratia*) (*per esempio*)
EP	Extended Play (gramophone record)
ER	Queen Elizabeth (L. *Elizabeth Regina*)
ESP	extra sensory perception (*percezione metapsìchica*)
esp	especially (*specialmente*)
Esq	Esquire (*Signore*)
est	established (*fondato*)
etc	and the rest (L. *et cetera*) (*eccetera*)
FA	Football Association (*Associazione Calcìstica*)
FAO	Food and Agriculture Organization (*Organizzazione Alimenti e Agricoltura*)
FBI	(*US*) Federal Bureau of Investigation (*Polizia Federale Statunitense*)
FC	Football Club (*Club Calcìstico*)
F'hold	Freehold (*proprietà fondiaria assoluta*)
Fid. Def.	Defender of the Faith (L. *Fidei Defensor*) (*Difensore della Fede*)
fig	figurative (*figurato*)
fin	financial (*finanziario*)
FO	Foreign Office (*Ministero degli Affari Esteri*)
fob	free on board (*franco a bordo*)
FRAM	Fellow of the Royal Academy of Music (*Membro della Reale Accadèmia di Musica*)
FRCS	Fellow of the Royal College of Surgeons (*Membro del Reale Collegio dei Chirurghi*)
FRS	Fellow of the Royal Society (*Membro della "Royal Society"*)
ft	foot (*piede*); feet (*piedi*); fort (*forte*); fortification (*fortificazione*)
gal	gallon(s) (*gallone, galloni*)
GATT	General Agreement on Tariffs and Trade (*Accordo Generale Tariffe e Commercio*)
GB	Great Britain (*Gran Bretagna*)
GC	George Cross (*Croce di San Giorgio*)
GCE	General Certificate of Education (*Certificato di Studi Superiori*)
gen	gender (*genere*); general (*generale*); genitive (*genitivo*)
GHQ	General Headquarters (*Quartier Generale*)
GI	(*US*) Government Issue (American private soldier) (*soldato semplice*)
Gib	(*fam*) Gibraltar (*Gibilterra*)
GLC	Greater London Council (*Consiglio della Contea di Londra e Dintorni*)
gm	gramme (*grammo*)
GMT	Greenwich Mean Time (*Ora di Greenwich*)
Govt	Government (*Governo*)

GP	General Practitioner (*medico generico*)
GPO	General Post Office (*Posta Centrale*)
h & c	hot and cold (water) (*acqua calda e fredda*)
HE	high-explosive (*alto esplosivo*); His Eminence (*Sua Eminenza*); His Excellency (*Sua Eccellenza*)
HH	His (Her) Highness (*Sua Altezza*); His Holiness (*Sua Santità*)
HM	His (Her) Majesty (*Sua Maestà*)
HMS	Her Majesty's Service (*Servizio di Sua Maestà*); Her Majesty's Ship (*Nave della marina Reale*)
HMSO	Her Majesty's Stationery Office (*Istituto Poligrafico dello Stato*)
Hon	Honorary (*Onorario*); Honourable (*Onorevole*)
HP	Houses of Parliament (*Palazzo del Parlamento*); House Physician (*medico interno (di ospedale)*)
hp	hire purchase (*vendita a rate*); horse-power (*potenza in cavalli vapore*)
HQ	headquarters (*Quartier Generale*)
hr	hour (*ora*)
HRH	His (Her) Royal Highness (*Sua Altezza Reale*)
I, Is	Island(s) (*Isola (Isole)*)
ib, ibid	in the same place (L. *ibidem*) (*nello stesso luogo*)
i/c	in charge (*incaricato, addetto*)
ICBM	Inter-Continental Ballistic Missile (*Missile Balistico Intercontinentale*)
Ice	Iceland (*Islanda*)
ICI	Imperial Chemical Industries (*Industrie Chimiche Imperiali*)
id	the same (L. *idem*) (*lo stesso*)
ie	that is, namely (L. *id est*) (*cioè*)
ILO	International Labour Organization (*Organizzazione Internazionale del Lavoro*)
IMF	International Monetary Fund (*Fondo Monetario Internazionale*)
in	inch (*pollice*); inches (*pollici*)
Inc, Incorp	incorporated (*incorporato*)
incl	included, including, inclusive (*incluso, compreso*)
incog	incognito (*incognito*)
INS	(*US*) International News Service (*Agenzia Stampa Internazionale*)
Inst	Institute (*Istituto*); inst, instant, the present month (*corrente mese*)
IoM	Isle of Man (*Isola di Man*)
IOU	I owe you (*com*) (*pagherò*)
IoW	Isle of Wight (*Isola di Wight*)
IQ	Intelligence Quotient (*coefficiente di intelligenza*)
IRA	Irish Republican Army (*Esercito della Repubblica Irlandese*)
IS	Island(s) (*isola, isole*)
ITA	Independent Television Authority (*Ente Televisivo Indipendente*)
ITV	Independent Television (*Televisione Indipendente*)
JP	Justice of the Peace (*Giudice di Pace*)
jr	junior
KBE	Knight Commander of the British Empire (*Cavaliere dell'Impero Britannico*)
KC	King's Counsel (*Avvocato di Corte suprema*)

443

KCB	Knight Commander of the Bath (*Cavaliere Maestro (dell'Ordine) del Bagno*))
KG	Knight of the Garter (*Cavaliere (dell'Ordine) della Giarrettiera*)
KKK	(*US*) Ku Klux Klan
KO	(*boxing*) knock out; kick off (*calcio d'inizio*)
Kt	Knight (*Cavaliere*)
kw	kilowatt (*chilowatt*)

L	Latin (*Latino*); Law (*Legge*); Learner (on motor cars); Liberal (*Liberale*)
l	lake (*lago*); left (*sinistra*); lira
£	pound (*sterlina*)
lab	laboratory (*laboratorio*); Labour (*laburista*)
Lat	Latin (*Latino*)
lb	pound (*libbra*)
LCC	London County Council (*Consiglio della Contea di Londra*)
Lib	Library (*Biblioteca*); Liberal (*Liberale*)
lit	literal (*letterale*); literally (*letteralmente*); literature (*letteratura*); litre (*litro*)
LLB	Bachelor of Laws (*Diplomato in Legge*)
log	logarithm (*logaritmo*)
LP	Labour Party (*Partito Laburista*); Long Playing (gramophone record)
LSD	lysergic acid diethylamide (*acido lisergico dietilamidico*)
£sd	Pounds Shillings Pence (*L librae, solidi, denarii*) (*sterline, scellini, pence*)
LSE	London School of Economics (*Instituto di Economia di Londra*)
Ltd (Co)	Limited (Company) (*Società a responsabilità limitata*)
LV	Luncheon Voucher (*tagliando pasti*)
Lw	Long wave (*onda lunga*)

m	metre (*metro*); married (*coniugato*); male (*sesso maschile*); masculine (*maschile*); mile (*miglio*); minute (*minuto*); month (*mese*)
MA	Master of Arts (*Dottore in Lettere*)
MB, ChB	Bachelor of Medicine; Bachelor of Surgery (*Dottore in Medicina*)
MBE	Member of the Order of the British Empire (*Membro dell'Ordine dell'Impero Britannico*)
MC	Master of Ceremonies (*Cerimoniere*); Member of Congress (*Membro del Congresso*); Military Cross (*Croce di Guerra*)
MD	Doctor of Medicine (*Dottore in Medicina*); mentally deficient (*deficiente mentale*)
memo	memorandum (*memorandum*)
Messrs	the plural of Mr. (*Signori*); (*com*) Ditta (*in indirizzi*))
Mgr	Monsignor (*Monsignore*)
MI5	Military Intelligence, Department 5 (*Ufficio Controspionaggio*)
MO	Medical Officer (*Ufficiale Medico*)
MOH	Medical Officer of Health (*Ufficiale Medico d'Igiene*)
MP	Member of Parliament (*Deputato al Parlamento*); Military Police (*Polizia Militare*); Metropolitan Police (*Polizia Metropolitana*)
mpg	miles per gallon (*miglia per gallone*)
mph	miles per hour (*miglia all'ora*)

444

Mr	Mister (*Signore*)
MRCP	Member of Royal College of Physicians (*Membro del Reale Collegio dei Medici*)
Mrs	Mistress (*Signora*)
Mt	Mount, mountain (*monte*)
Mw	medium wave (*onda media*)
N	North (*Nord*); Northern (*Settentrionale*)
n	name (*nome*); noun (*sostantivo*); neuter (*neutro*); noon (*mezzogiorno*); born (*L. natus*) (*nato*); nephew (*nipote*)
Nat	National (*nazionale*); nationalist (*nazionalista*)
NBC	(*US*) National Broadcasting Company (*Ente Radiofonico Nazionale*)
NCB	National Coal Board (*Azienda Carbonifera Nazionale*)
NCO	Non-commissioned officer (*sottufficiale*)
NE	New England (*Nuova Inghilterra*); North-East(ern) (*Nord-Est, Nord-Orientale*); new edition (*nuova edizione*)
neg	negative (*negativo*)
NHS	National Health Service (*Servizio Sanitario Statale*)
NSPCC	National Society for the Prevention of Cruelty to Children (*Società Nazionale per la Protezione dell' Infanzia*)
NW	North-West (*Nord-Ovest*); North-western (*Nord-Occidentale*)
NY	New York
NZ	New Zealand (*Nuova Zelanda*)
OAS	Organization of American States (*Organizzazione di Stati Americani*); Organisation Armée Secrète (*Organizzazione Armata segreta*)
OBE	Order of the British Empire (*Ordine dell' Impero Britannico*)
OECD	Organization for Economic Co-operation and Development (*Organizzazione per la Cooperazione e lo Sviluppo Economici*)
OEEC	Organization for European Economic Co-operation (*Organizzazione Economica per la Cooperazione Europea*)
OED	Oxford English Dictionary (*Dizionario Inglese di Oxford*)
OHMS	On His (Her) Majesty's Service (*al servizio di Sua Maestà*)
OM	Order of Merit (*ordine di merito*)
op	out of print (*esaurito*)
OT	Old Testament (*Antico Testamento*)
OUP	Oxford University Press (*Edizioni dell' Università di Oxford*)
OXFAM	Oxford Committee for Famine Relief
Oxon	Oxford, of Oxford (*L. Oxoniensis*) (*di Oxford, Ossoniano*)
oz	ounce(s) (*oncia, once*)
p	page (*pagina*); participle (*participio*)
pa	per annum, by the year (*all'anno*)
PAA	(*US*) Pan American Airways (*Linee Aeree Pan Americane*)
P & O	Peninsular and Oriental (Steam Navigation Company) (*Compagnia di Navigazione Peninsulare-Orientale*)
PAYE	Pay as you earn (Income Tax) (*trattenuta imposte su paghe da parte del datore di lavoro*)
PC	police constable (*agente di polizia*); Privy Council (*Consiglio Privato*); Privy Councillor (*Consigliere Privato*); postcard (*cartolina postale*)
pd	paid (*pagato*)

PhD	Doctor of Philosophy (*Dottore in Filosofia*)
PM	Prime Minister (*Primo Ministro*)
PMG	Postmaster-General (*Direttore Generale delle Poste*)
PO	Petty Officer (*naut*) (*sottufficiale*); Pilot Officer (*Ufficiale Pilota*); Post Office (*Ufficio postale*); Postal Order (*Vaglia Postale*)
POB	post office box (*cassetta postale*)
POW	Prisoner of War (*Prigioniero di Guerra*)
p.p.	on behalf of (L. *per procurationem*) (*per procura*)
Pres	President (*Presidente*); Presbyterian (*Presbiteriano*)
PRO	Public Relations Officer (*Addetto alla Pubblicità*)
PT	Physical Training (*Educazione Fisica*)
pt	part (*parte*); pint(s) (*pinta, pinte*)
PTO	Please Turn Over (*vedi retro*)
PVC	Polyvinyl chloride (*cloruro di polivinile* (*plastica*))
QC	Queen's Counsel (*Avvocato di Corte superiore*)
QMG	Quartermaster-General (*mil*) (*capo del dipartimento amministrazione e alloggi*)
qr	Quarter(s)
qt	quart
qv	which see (L. *Quod vide*) (*vedi*)
RA	Royal Academy (*Accademia Reale*)
RAC	Royal Automobile Club (*Real Automobile Club*)
RADA	Royal Academy of Dramatic Art (*Accademia Reale d'Arte Drammatica*)
RAF	Royal Air Force (*Regia Aeronautica*)
RC	Roman Catholic (*Cattolico Apostolico Romano*); Red Cross (*Croce Rossa*)
Rd	Road (*Via, Corso*)
ref	reference (*riferimento*)
regd	registered (*raccomandato*)
rel	relative (*relativo*); related (*riferentesi*); religion (*religione*)
Rep	Representative (*Rappresentante*); Republic (*Repubblica*); Republican (*Repubblicano*); Repertory (*Repertorio*); Reporter (*cronista, corrispondente*)
Repub	Republic (*Repubblica*)
Rev	Reverend (*Reverendo*); Revelations (*Rivelazioni*); Revised (*riveduto*)
RN	Royal Navy (*Regia Marina*)
rpm	revolutions per minute (*giri al minuto*)
RSPA	Royal Society for the Prevention of Accidents (*Regia Società per la prevenzione degli infortuni*)
RSPCA	Royal Society for the Prevention of Cruelty to Animals (*Regia Società per la protezione degli animali*)
Rt. Hon	Right Honourable (*Molto Onorevole*)
S	South (*Sud*); Saint (*Santo*); Socialist (*Socialista*); Society (*Società*)
s	second (*secondo*); shilling (*scellino*); son (*figlio*); singular (*singolare*); substantive (*sostantivo*); solubility (*solubilità*)
SA	South Africa (*Sud-Africa*)
s.a.e.	stamped addressed envelope (*busta indirizzata e affrancata*)
SCE	Scottish Certificate of Education (*Certificato di Studi Superiori* (*Scozia*))
Sch	School (*scuola*)

SE	South-East (*Sud-Est*); South-Eastern (*Sud-Orientale*)
Sec, Secy	Secretary (*segretario*)
SHAPE	Supreme Headquarters Allied Powers, Europe (*Supremo Quartier Generale delle Truppe Alleate in Europa*)
SRN	State Registered Nurse (*Infermiera Diplomata*)
S/S	steamship (*piroscafo*)
St	Saint (*Santo*); Strait (*Stretto*); Street (*strada, via*)
st	stone
STD	Subscriber Trunk Dialling (*Chiamata Interurbana Automatica*)
SW	South-West (*Sud-Ovest*); South-Western (*Sud-Occidentale*)
TB	Tuberculosis
TNT	trinitrotoluene (explosive) (*trinitrotoluolo*)
TT	total abstainer (teetotal) (*astemio*); Tourist Trophy; tuberculin tested
TU	Trade Union (*Sindacato*)
TUC	Trade Union Congress (*Congresso dei Sindacati*)
TWA	(*US*) Trans World Airlines (*Linee Aeree Intercontinentali*)
UAR	United Arab Republic (*Repubblica Araba Unita*)
UDI	Unilateral Declaration of Independence (*Dichiarazione Unilaterale d'Indipendenza*)
UK	United Kingdom (*Regno Unito*)
ult	(L. *ultimo*) last (month) (*ultimo scorso*)
UN(O)	United Nations (Organization) ((*Organizzazione delle*) *Nazioni Unite*)
UNA	United Nations Association (*Associazione delle Nazioni Unite*)
UNICEF	United Nations International Children's Emergency Fund (*fondo di emergenza delle Nazioni Unite per l'Infanzia*)
UP	United Press (*Stampe Associate*)
US	United States (*Stati Uniti*)
USA	United States of America (*Stati Uniti d'America*)
USAF	United States Air Force (*Aeronautica Militare Statunitense*)
USIS	United States Information Service (*Ufficio Informazioni per gli Stati Uniti d'America*)
USN	United States Navy (*Marina Militare Statunitense*)
USSR	Union of Soviet Socialist Republics (*Unione delle Repubbliche Socialiste Sovietiche*)
v	(L. *vide*) see (*vedi*); versus (*contro*)
VC	Victoria Cross (*Croce della Regina Vittoria*)
VD	Venereal Disease (*Malattie veneree*)
Vet	Veterinary Surgeon (*veterinario*)
vg	very good (*molto bene, ottimo, lodevole*)
VIP	(*fam*) very important person (*pezzo grosso, persona molto importante*)
viz	(L. *videlicet*) namely (*vale a dire*)
W	West (*Ovest*); Western (*Occidentale*); Welsh (*gallese*)
WD	War Department (*Ministero della Guerra*)
WHO	World Health Organization (*Organizzazione Mondiale della Sanità*)
WI	Women's Institute (*Instituto Femminile*)
wk	week (*settimana*)

wp	weather permitting (*tempo permettendo*)
WRAC	Women's Royal Army Corps (*Corpo Femminile del Regio Esercito*)
WRAF	Women's Royal Air Force (*Corpo Femminile della Regia Aeronautica*)
wt	weight (*peso*)
WRVS	Women's Royal Voluntary Services (*Servizio Volontario Femminile*)
yd	yard(s) (*iarda, iarde*)
YHA	Youth Hostels Association (*Associazione degli Ostelli della Gioventù*)
YMCA	Young Men's Christian Association (*Associazione Cristiana dei Giovani*)
yr	year (*anno*); younger (*più giovane*); your (*vostro*)
YWCA	Young Women's Christian Association (*Unione Cristiana delle Giovani*)